THE AGES OF HOMER

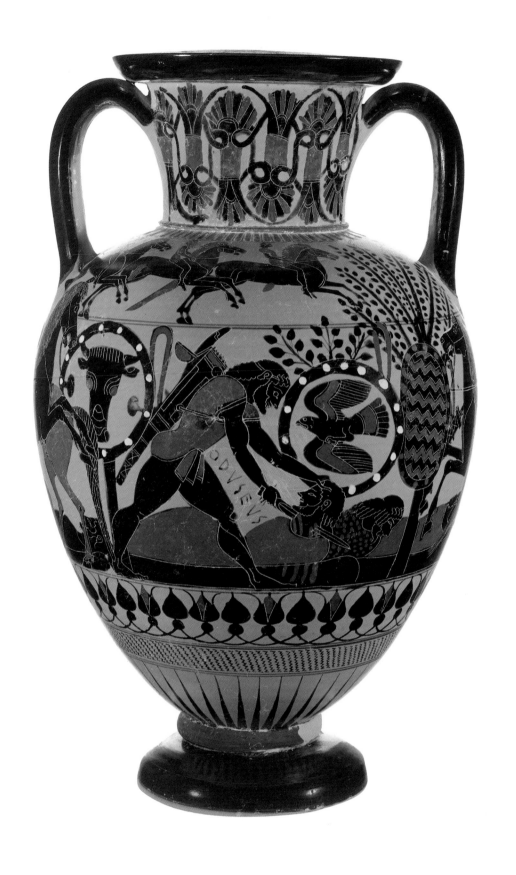

THE AGES OF
HOMER

A TRIBUTE TO EMILY TOWNSEND VERMEULE

Edited by

Jane B. Carter and Sarah P. Morris

UNIVERSITY OF TEXAS PRESS

AUSTIN

Requests for permission to reproduce material from this
work should be sent to
Permissions, University of Texas Press, Box 7819, Austin,
TX 78713-7819.

⊚ The paper used in this publication meets the minimum
requirements of American National Standard for
Information Sciences—Permanence of Paper for Printed
Library Materials, ANSI Z39.48-1984.

Library of Congress Cataloging-in-Publication Data

The Ages of Homer : a tribute to Emily Townsend
Vermeule / edited by
    Jane B. Carter and Sarah P. Morris.—1st ed.
        p.   cm.
    Includes bibliographical references and index.
    ISBN 0-292-71169-7 (cl.: alk. paper)
    ISBN 0-292-71208-1 (pbk.: alk. paper)
    1. Homer—Criticism and interpretation. 2. Epic
poetry, Greek—History and criticism. 3. Homer—
Contemporary Greece. 4. Civilization, Homeric.
I. Carter, Jane Burr, date. II. Morris, Sarah P., date.
III. Vermeule, Emily.
PA4037.A59   1995
883'.01—DC20   94-13817

Frontispiece no. 1: Chalcidian Amphora by the Inscription Painter, on loan to the J. Paul Getty Museum (L. 88. AE.56). Side B: Odysseus kills a sleeping Thracian. On the shoulder, three mounted youths gallop to the right. (Photograph courtesy of the J. Paul Getty Museum.)

Frontispiece no. 2: Side B/A of Chalcidian Amphora: team of Thracian horses. (Photograph courtesy of the J. Paul Getty Museum.)

ΑΙΜΙΛΙΑΙ

τιμῆς ἕνεκα

Ἢ οἵη ΑΙΜΙΛΙΗ ποτ᾽ ἀπ᾽ ἐσχατιῆς πτολιέθρου
(τὴν καὶ ϝερμεύλεω θνητοὶ καλέουσι δάμαρτα)
Ἑλλάδος ἀρχαίης ἥ τ᾽ ἄστεα καὶ νόον ἔγνω
Μαιονίδεω τ᾽ ἐπέων ἦν ἑρμηνεύτρια ἱρῶν,
κλεινὰ γὰρ ἐξεκάλυψε τεθαμμένα δώματα γαίης
καὶ γραφθ᾽ ἡρώων ἠπίστατο σήματ᾽ Ἀχαιῶν.
τὴν νῦν ἄειδε, θέα, σοφίην γὰρ ἐπάξιον αἰνεῖν.

UNPUBLISHED FRAGMENT
(Hesiod *Eoiae?*-vel simile)
COURTESY OF FRANK STUBBINGS

RESILIENCE

When it became apparent
to the long-wandering Ithacan,
weary and morose, far from home,
that Euryalos' snide sneer—
"you don't *look* like an athlete"—
was aimed at the very soul of his being,
his first impulse was to doubt himself,
to doubt he still possessed the
necessary strength to shine
among the curious Phaeacians.
His arm seemed too unpractised,
his will worn too thin by the consuming sea
to lift the discus, let alone attempt to throw it.
But then, remembering the rousing words of Peleus,
"To be the best and excel over others,"
he sensed the fiery old determination
coursing through his tawny limbs,
and he grabbed the biggest discus
and hurled it way beyond the rest.

JODY MAXMIN

CONTENTS

Tabula Gratulatoria   xiii

List of Abbreviations   xv

Introduction   1
Jane B. Carter and Sarah P. Morris

Emily T. Vermeule: Biography and Bibliography   11
Mary B. Comstock, Amy E. Raymond, and Florence Z. Wolsky

Toumba tou Skourou: A Brief Personal Memoir of Emily Vermeule in Cyprus   19
Michael W. Taylor

PART I

HOMER AND THE BRONZE AGE: MEMORY AND ARCHAEOLOGY

1.   The Bronze Age Context of Homer   25
Sinclair Hood

2.   Homer, Lycia, and Lukka   33
Machteld J. Mellink

3.   A Hittite Silver Vessel in the Form of a Fist   45
H. G. Güterbock and Timothy Kendall
APPENDIX: The Silver Stag "BIBRU" from Mycenae   61
Robert B. Koehl

4.   Mycenaean Pottery at Saqqara: Finds from Excavations by the Egypt Exploration Society of London
and the Rijksmuseum Van Oudheden, Leiden, 1975–1990   67
Vronwy Hankey and David Aston

5.   Cyprus and the Western Mediterranean: Some New Evidence for Interrelations   93
Vassos Karageorghis

6. Shining and Fragrant Cloth in Homeric Epic   99
Cynthia W. Shelmerdine

7.   Death and the Tanagra Larnakes   109
Sara Immerwahr

8.   Heroes Returned? Subminoan Burials from Crete   123
Hector Catling

CONTENTS

PART II
HOMER AND THE IRON AGE: HISTORY AND POETICS

9.   Lydia between East and West or How to Date the Trojan War:
A Study in Herodotus   139
Walter Burkert

10.   War Story into Wrath Story   149
Mabel L. Lang

11.   An Evolutionary Model for the Making of Homeric Poetry:
Comparative Perspectives   163
Gregory Nagy

12.   The Geometric Catalogue of Ships   181
J. K. Anderson

13.   Glaucus, the Leaves, and the Heroic Boast of *Iliad* 6.146–211   193
Eddie R. Lowry, Jr.

14.   The (Re)Marriage of Penelope and Odysseus: Architecture, Gender, Philosophy. A Homeric Dialogue   205
Ann L. T. Bergren

15.   The Sacrifice of Astyanax: Near Eastern Contributions to the Siege of Troy   221
Sarah P. Morris

16.   Homer's Phoenicians: History, Ethnography, or Literary Trope?
[A Perspective on Early Orientalism]   247
Irene J. Winter

17.   A Dancing Floor for Ariadne (*Iliad* 18.590–592):
Aspects of Ritual Movement in Homer and Minoan Religion   273
Steven H. Lonsdale

18.   Ancestor Cult and the Occasion of Homeric Performance   285
Jane B. Carter

PART III
AFTER HOMER: NARRATIVE AND REPRESENTATION

19.   Reading Pictorial Narrative: The Law Court Scene of the Shield of Achilles   315
Mark D. Stansbury-O'Donnell

20.   Human Figures, the Ajax Painter, and Narrative Scenes
in Earlier Corinthian Vase Painting   335
J. L. Benson

21.   Story Lines: Observations on Sophilan Narrative   363
Ann Blair Brownlee

22.   Some Homeric Animals on the Lion Painter's Pitcher at Harvard   373
David Gordon Mitten

23.   A Geometric Bard   389
J. Michael Padgett

CONTENTS

24. Early Images of Daidalos in Flight   407
     Erika Simon

25. The Murder of Rhesos on a Chalcidian Neck-Amphora
     by the Inscription Painter   415
     Marion True

26. Menelaos and Helen in Troy   431
     Martin Robertson

27. Stories from the Trojan Cycle in the Work of Douris   437
     Diana Buitron-Oliver

28. Priam, King of Troy   449
     Margaret C. Miller

29. Neon Ilion and Ilium Novum:
     Kings, Soldiers, Citizens, and Tourists at Classical Troy   467
     Cornelius C. Vermeule III

30. Alexander and Achilles—Macedonians and "Mycenaeans"   483
     Ada Cohen

31. An Arretine Bowl and the Revenge of Achilles   507
     John J. Herrmann, Jr.

Notes on Contributors   523
Index of Homeric Passages   529
Index of Homeric Words (Cited in Greek Script)   537
Index of Homeric Words (Cited as Transliteration)   540

xi

TABULA GRATULATORIA

This volume was made possible through the generosity of the following Special Patrons and Contributors

SPECIAL PATRONS

Ceramica-Stiftung, Basel

Landon T. Clay

Cotsen Family Foundation

Mr. and Mrs. Lawrence A. Fleischman

William P. and Diana Poteat Hobby

Sinclair F. Hood

Leon Levy and Shelby White

Harvard University, Department of the Classics
and Loeb Classical Library Foundation

James R. McCredie

Christos Mihailidis and Robin Symes

Doreen Canaday Spitzer

Maurice Tempelsman

Catherine Sayre Comstock Vermeule

The Malcolm Hewitt Wiener Foundation

Darrell Amyx

J. K. Anderson

Maxwell L. Anderson

Helen Bacon

Ernst Badian

Norman and Miriam Balmuth

Mark Beers and Steven Urice

Emmett L. Bennett, Jr.

Herbert Bloch

Alan and Julie Boegehold

Ann Blair Brownlee and David B. Brownlee

Walter Burkert

Mary B. Comstock

DeCoursey Fales, Jr.

Richard Hamilton

Mason Hammond

John Herrmann and Annewies van den Hoek

Caroline Houser

Sara A. Immerwahr

Michael and Virginia Jameson

Bernard Knox

Robert B. Koehl

Christine Kondoleon

Guenter Kopcke

Suzanne Labiner

Mabel Lang

Phyllis Williams Lehmann

William T. Loomis

Steven H. Lonsdale

Sylvia Stallings Lowe

Eddie R. Lowry, Jr.

Stella Lubsen-Admiraal

Ian McPhee and Elizabeth Pemberton

Mary Patterson McPherson

Susan Matheson and Jerry Pollitt

Thomas Martin

Jody Maxmin

Machteld Mellink

Margaret Miller

Sarah Morris and John Papadopoulos

Gregory Nagy

J. Michael and Judith B. Padgett

Martin and Louise Robertson

Thomas Rosenmeyer

L. Hugh Sackett

Charles Segal

Juliet Shelmerdine

Mark and Wendy Stansbury-O'Donnell

Zeph and Diana Stewart

Frank Stubbings

Michael W. Taylor

Homer and Dorothy Thompson

Arthur Dale Trendall

Marion True

Marie Zarwell Uihlein Endowment for

Classical Studies, Ripon College

Calvert Watkins

Elizabeth Lyding Will

Leonard and Florence Wolsky

The editors would also like to express their gratitude for logistical and moral support to the Department of Classical Art at the Museum of Fine Arts, Boston, and to the Department of Classical and Near Eastern Archaeology at Bryn Mawr College. Major financial and technical assistance in the preparation of the manuscript was provided by Tulane University and the University of California at Los Angeles. Finally, this volume would not have become a publication without the University of Texas and its press, in particular the enthusiasm and guidance of Joanna Hitchcock and the superb editorial skills of Kathleen Cox.

LIST OF ABBREVIATIONS

Additional abbreviations may be found in the notes to each chapter.

AA	Archäologischer Anzeiger
AAA	Ἀρχαιολογικὰ ἀνάλεκτα ἐξ Ἀθηνῶν
AbhGött	Abhandlungen Göttingen
AbhMainz	Abhandlungen der Geistes- und Sozialwissenschaftlichen Klasse, Akademie der Wissenschaften und der Literatur, Mainz
ABL	C. H. E. Haspels, *Attic Black-figured Lekythoi* (Paris 1936).
ABV	J. D. Beazley, *Attic Black-figure Vase-painters* (Oxford 1956).
Addenda	L. Burn and R. Glynn. *Beazley Addenda. Additional References to ABV, ARV², and Paralipomena* (Oxford 1982).
AfO	Archiv für Orientforschung
AHR	American Historical Review
AJA	American Journal of Archaeology
AJAH	American Journal of Ancient History
AJP	American Journal of Philology
AMIran	Archäologische Mitteilungen aus Iran
AnatStud	Anatolian Studies
AncW	The Ancient World
ANET	J. Pritchard, *Ancient Near Eastern Texts Relating to the Old Testament*
ANRW	*Aufstieg und Niedergang der römischen Welt* (Berlin 1972–).
AntCl	L'Antiquité classique
AntDenk	Antike Denkmäler

AntK	Antike Kunst
AntP	Antike Plastik
AntW	Antike Welt
AOAT	Alter Orient und Altes Testament
AR	Archaeological Reports
ArchCl	Archeologia classica
ArchDelt	Ἀρχαιολογικὸν Δελτίον
ArchEph	Ἀρχαιολογικὴ Ἐφημερίς
ArchHom	Archaeologia Homerica
ArchNews	Archaeological News
ArtB	Art Bulletin
ARV	J. D. Beazley, *Athenian Red-Figure Vase-painters,* 2d ed. (Oxford 1963).
ASAE	Annales du Service des Antiquités de l'Égypte
ASAtene	Annuario della Scuola Archeologica di Atene
AthMitt	Athenische Mitteilungen
AttiMGrecia	Atti e memorie della Società Magna Grecia
BA	Biblical Archaeologist
BABesch	Bulletin Antieke Beschaving
BalkSt	Balkan Studies
BaM	Baghdader Mitteilungen
BAR	Biblical Archaeology Review
BAR-IS	British Archaeological Reports, International Series
BCH	Bulletin de correspondance hellénique
BdI	Bulletino dell'Instituto di Diritto Romano

BEFAR	Bibliothèque des Écoles Françaises d'Athènes et de Rome	*GGA*	Göttingische Gelehrte Anzeigen
BibO	Bibliotheca Orientalis	*GaR*	Greece and Rome
BICS	Bulletin of the Institute of Classical Studies of the University of London	*GRBM*	Greek, Roman and Byzantine Monographs
BMFA	Bulletin of the Museum of Fine Arts, Boston	*GRBS*	Greek, Roman and Byzantine Studies
		HBA	Hamburger Beiträge zur Archäologie
BMMA	Bulletin of the Metropolitan Museum of Art, New York	*HSCP*	Harvard Studies in Classical Philology
		HThR	Harvard Theological Review
BonnJbb	Bonner Jahrbücher des Rheinischen Landesmuseums in Bonn und des Vereins von Altertumsfreunden im Rheinlande	*IEJ*	Israel Exploration Journal
		IG	Inscriptiones Graecae
		IstMitt	Istanbuler Mitteilungen
		JARCE	Journal of the American Research Center in Egypt
BSA	The Annual of the British School at Athens	*JBerlMus*	Jahrbuch der Berliner Museen
BWPr	Winckelmannsprogramm der Archäologischen Gesellschaft zu Berlin	*JdI*	Jahrbuch des Deutschen Archäologischen Instituts Athen
		JHS	The Journal of Hellenic Studies
CA	Classical Antiquity (since 1982: formerly CSCA)	*JMA*	Journal of Mediterranean Archaeology
		JMGS	Journal of Modern Greek Studies
*CAH*³	The Cambridge Ancient History 3d. ed. Cambridge: Cambridge University Press.	*JNES*	Journal of Near Eastern Studies
		JRGZM	Jahrbuch des Römisch-Germanischen Zentralmuseums, Mainz
		JSOT	Journal for the Study of the Old Testament
CJ	Classical Journal		
ClMed	Classica et mediaevalia	*JSSEA*	Journal of the Society for the Study of Egyptian Antiquities
CMS	Corpus der minoischen und mykenischen Siegel	*JWalt*	The Journal of the Walters Art Gallery
CP	Classical Philology	*JWarb*	Journal of the Warburg and Courtauld Galleries
CQ	Classical Quarterly		
CR	Classical Review	*Karo*	G. Karo, *Die Schachtgräber von Mykenai* (Munich 1930–1933).
CRAI	Comptes rendus des séances de l'Académie des Inscriptions et Belles-lettres	*KBo*	Keilschrifttexte aus Bogazköi
		KlPauly	Der kleine Pauly
CSCA	California Studies in Classical Antiquity	*KrChr*	Κρητικὰ Χρονικά
		KTU	Die Keilalphabetischen Texte aus Ugarit. AOAT 24, 1976
CVA	Corpus Vasorum Antiquorum		
CW	The Classical World	*KUB*	Keilschrifturkunden aus Boghazköi
Dar Sag	C. Daremburg and E. Saglio, *Dictionnaire des antiquités grecques et romaines* (Paris 1875).	*LEC*	Les études classiques
		LIMC	Lexicon Iconographicum Mythologiae Classicae
Deltion	Ἀρχαιολογικὸν Δελτίον	*LSJ*	H. G. Liddell and R. Scott. Rev. ed. H. Stuart Jones and R. McKenzie. *A Greek-English Lexicon* (Oxford 1968).
DHA	Dialogues d'Histoire Ancienne		
*Docs.*²	J. Chadwick and M. Ventris. *Documents in Mycenaean Greek* 2d. ed. Cambridge 1973.		
		MAAR	Memoirs of the American Academy in Rome
DOP	Dumbarton Oaks Papers		
EranJb	Eranos jahrbuch	*MDAIK*	Mittheilungen des Deutschen Archäologischen Instituts: Kairo
Ergon	Τὸ Ἔργον τῆς ἐν Ἀθήναις Ἀρχαιολογικῆς Ἑταιρείας		
		MDOG	Mittheilungen des Deutschen Orient-Gesellschaft zu Berlin
EVP	J. D. Beazley, *Etruscan Red-Figure Vase Painting.*	*Meded*	Mededeelingen van het Nederlands Historisch Instituut te Rome
FdD	Fouilles de Delphes. École Française d'Athènes		
		MeditArch	Mediterranean Archaeology
FGrHist	F. Jacoby, *Fragmente der griechischen Historiker* (Berlin 1926–1958).	*MF*	Madrider Forschungen
		MM	Madrider Mitteilungen
FR	A. Furtwängler and O. Reichhold, *Griechische Vasenmalerei* (Munich 1900–1925).	*MMAJ*	Metropolitan Museum of Art Journal
		*MMR*²	M. P. Nilsson *The Minoan-Mycenaean Religion*, 2d. ed. (Lund 1950).
GettyMusJ	The J. Paul Getty Museum Journal	*MonAnt*	Monumenti antichi

MonPiot	Monuments et mémoires. Fondation E. Piot
MP	A. Furumark, *The Mycenaean Pottery. Analysis and Classification* (Stockholm 1941).
MVAG	Mitteilungen der Vorderasiatisch-Aegyptischen Gesellschaft
NouvClio	La nouvelle Clio
OJA	Oxford Journal of Archaeology
OlBer	Berichte über die Ausgrabungen in Olympia
OlForsch	Olympische Forschungen
OpArch	Opuscula archaeologica
OpAth	Opuscula atheniensia
OpRom	Opuscula romana
PapOxy	Papyri Oxyrhynchi London
Paralipomena	J. D. Beazley, *Paralipomena* (Oxford 1971).
PBSR	Papers of the British School at Rome
PCPS	Proceedings of the Cambridge Philosophical Society
PEQ	Palestine Exploration Quarterly
PM	Arthur Evans, *The Palace of Minos at Knossos* (London 1921–1935).
PP	La parola del passato
Prakt	Πρακτικὰ τῆς ᾿Ακαδημίας ᾿Αθηνῶν
ProcBritAc	Proceedings of the British Academy
PZ	Prähistorische Zeitschrift
QUUC	Quaderni urbinati di cultura classica
RA	Revue archéologique
RAss	Reallexikon der Assyriologie
RB	Revue biblique
RDAC	Report of the Department of Antiquities, Cyprus
RE	Pauly-Wissowa-Kroll, *Real-Encyclopädie der klassischen Altertumswissenschaft*

REA	Revue des études anciennes
REG	Revue des études grecques
RendLinc	Atti dell'Accademia Nazionale dei Lincei. Rendiconti
RivIstArch	Rivisti dell'Istituto Nazionale d'Archeologia e Storia dell'Arte
RivStudAnt	Rivista di studi antici
RM	Römische Mitteilungen
RSF	Rivista di studi fenici
RVAp	A. D. Trendall and A. Cambitoglou, *The Red-figured Vases of Apulia.* (Oxford 1978–).
SAOC	Studies in Ancient Oriental Civilization
SBHeid	Sitzungsberichte der Heidelberger Akademie der Wissenschaften, Philosophisch-historischer Klasse
SCE	The Swedish Cyprus Expedition
SEG	Supplementum Epigraphicum Graecum
SIMA	Studies in Mediterranean Archaeology
SMEA	Studi micenei ed egeo-anatolici
StClass	Studii clasice
SymOslo	Symbolae osloenses
TAPA	Transactions of the American Philological Association
TAPS	Transactions of the American Philosophical Society
TLS	Times Literary Supplement
VT	Vetus Testamentum
WS	Wiener Studien
WürzJbb	Würzburger Jahrbücher
YCS	Yale Classical Studies
ZPE	Zeitschrift für Papyrologie und Epigraphik

THE AGES OF HOMER

INTRODUCTION

Greece's earliest preserved playwright, the tragic poet Aeschylus, described his plays as mere "samples from Homer's great banquets,"[1] a metaphor that applies just as aptly to manifold aspects of Greek thought and culture. This volume extends the Aeschylean metaphor to current scholarship; our aim is to present samples of the Homeric banquet in a broad range of fields including philology, history, archaeology, and art history. The essays were inspired by the unique achievements of Emily Vermeule, poet, scholar, and archaeologist, who embodies in a single career the spirit of Homer: as excavator, as interpreter of his world, and as ambassador between his many ages. Her example has encouraged us, her students, colleagues, and admirers, to bring over two millennia of ages and artifacts, from Minoan Crete to the Roman period, to the study of the Homeric epics.

In principle, the poetry of Homer is ageless, a dialogue with the past constantly revitalized by the present. In this volume we have chosen three ages and their interconnections: the Bronze Age setting of heroic adventures, the early Iron Age when epic poems assumed something like their present form, and the Classical centuries inspired by the epic tradition. All three phases of

poetic experience are central to what we mean by "Homer" today. In looking at the Homeric theme from these perspectives, the authors make use of different techniques of analysis, from comparative philology and mythology, literary theory, historical linguistics, anthropology, and iconography, in order to "read" material culture and literature relevant to epic poetry. The results display a variety of current solutions to old "Homeric questions" such as the date of the Trojan War, the historical context of the Catalogue of Ships, the development of early Greek narrative, and the relationship of Homeric culture to the rest of the Mediterranean. Collectively, the essays in this volume describe a conversation between different voices of human experience, memory, and art.

PART I. HOMER AND THE BRONZE AGE: MEMORY AND ARCHAEOLOGY

The volume opens with the connections between epic poetry and Aegean prehistory seen in specific archaeological artifacts and areas. Before the advent of modern archaeology just over a century ago, the poems of Homer were the only window onto the heroic era of the Bronze Age. Since Schliemann, excavations have pieced together a complex picture of Bronze Age cultures in Greece and other Mediterranean countries, such that readers of Homer are now informed of archaeological correspondences to the world of epic heroes, of which many are assembled in the *Archaeologia Homerica* series. These correspondences place the Homeric narratives at the end of the Late Helladic period near 1200 B.C., not long before a series of destructions ended Bronze Age empires in Greece, Asia Minor, and Syria-Palestine. Yet the poems themselves acquired their present form much later, in the eighth century B.C., and only became fixed texts in the sixth century, in a process Gregory Nagy discusses in his essay.

What relationship can be articulated between epic events and the realities revealed by archaeology? The difficulty of the question has increased as our knowledge of the Mediterranean Bronze Age has expanded and as our reading of the Homeric text has become more exacting: understanding the connections between these two eras challenges archaeologists and philologists together. The essays in Part I broach three aspects of understanding the Bronze Age past: the historical setting of the Trojan War, the foreign connections of the Mycenaean world, and the continuity of cultural forms from the Bronze Age into the world of Homer and the Greek *polis*.

Appropriately, this volume begins with the oldest of all Homeric questions and the quest of Schliemann: the date and historical authenticity of the Trojan War. Its locale—Anatolia and the Troad—has attracted recent attention with renewed excavations at the site of Troy and a new publication (*Studia Troica*). The recognition of Mycenaean sherds of the twelfth century (Late Helladic IIIC) in levels called Troy VIIa has displaced "Homeric" Troy to the citadel's phase VI (1500–1200 B.C.) in the view of many archaeologists and philologists.[2] The first essay takes a different direction: Sinclair Hood locates the sack of Troy even later—in Troy VIIb, or the eleventh century B.C.—bolstered by a similar date for the Catalogue of Ships. That naval roster from the second book of the *Iliad* continues to dominate reconstructions of Greek history. It is with equal frequency claimed or challenged as an authentic Bronze Age gaz-

etteer of Aegean geography; in this volume, J. K. Anderson reminds us of its connections with the eighth century. Such balancing acts between archaeology and poetry are drastically challenged by Walter Burkert's rejection, in Part II, of precise Greek knowledge about the Trojan War. His conclusions might undermine Homeric archaeology if they did not liberate it from the mirage of an historical moment to be certified by excavation. The history of the "Trojan War" belongs not to Homer but to Anatolian archaeology, where Hissarlik and its Mycenaean finds join other sites of coastal Asia Minor—from Knidos to Beşik Tepe—where Mycenaean, even Minoan, pottery appears in local contexts. If such finds suggest years of Mycenaean habitation in Asia Minor, how did Mycenaean presence become the heroic campaign of epic?

Some answers may lie in Anatolia. Who were the Trojans, what language did they speak, whose material culture did they share, and who were their allies? Hood's attention to non-Helladic pottery from Troy introduces the debate on foreign cultures in the Bronze Age Aegean, and the competing scenarios for "invasion" and migration. Anatolian natives emerge next in literature and art. Machteld Mellink, longtime investigator of Lycia, assembles Homeric references to these Trojan allies, Anatolian testimonia on Bronze Age "Lukka," and a tour of the land of Lycia itself. Hittite and Homeric names and places are animated by her expertise in Lycian history, geography, and archaeology, and Mellink's essay should encourage the interdisciplinary exploration of other provinces of Homeric Anatolia.

Dominating Bronze Age Anatolia are the Hittites, who loom large and near, yet remain at a distance from Homeric geography, history, and poetry. In addition to Hittite sources on Ahhiyawa and convergences with Greek literature, Hittite objects offer parallels for the Aegean world. Long before the decipherment of Hittite cuneiform records, Anatolia attracted Homeric scholars with Schliemann's discovery of a silver stag-shaped rhyton at Mycenae. This volume introduces a new silver vessel of similar type from Anatolia (figs. 3.1–3.7), this one in the shape of a human fist (now on loan to the Boston Museum of Fine Arts). Its unusual shape and decoration suggest ritual use; the proposed date would revise the chronology of monumental relief sculpture (Alaca Höyük) and of Aegean art. An Aegean archaeologist joins an eminent Hittitologist and the Boston Museum's curator of Near Eastern art in considering the name and functions of such ritual shapes in the Aegean and the Hittite homeland.

Do these connections in literature and art reflect historical relations between the Hittite kingdom of central Anatolia and the inhabitants of the Aegean? Archaeological documents for interaction are meager, both in Hittite imports to the Aegean[3] and in Mycenaean exports to central Anatolia, as illustrated by finds of Mycenaean pottery at provincial Maşat Höyük but not at the Hittite capital, Hattušas. Hittite testimonia for interaction with "Ahhiyawa" (Achaians?), limited to vassal states in western Anatolia, seem too hostile for sophisticated exchange in poetry and cult. Another scenario brings Greeks and Hittites together in southeast Anatolia and North Syria, whence literature (and the alphabet) could have traveled with Phoenicians in later centuries from East to West.

This plunges the Homeric reader into the world of the Near East, moving from Anatolian conflicts in the *Iliad* to the heroic adventures abroad of the *Odyssey*. Tall tales in that poem invoke foreign ports and trade routes familiar to Mycenaean voyagers and their descendants. Exploration of Bronze Age shipwrecks off the Lycian coast changes with each season the picture of trade and travel. From the theoretical side, radical arguments by Martin Bernal (*Black Athena: The Afro-Asiatic Roots of Classical Civilization*) and Walter Burkert (*The Orientalizing Revolution*) challenge traditional views of early "Greek" culture. The next essays span the Mediterranean from Egypt, to Cyprus and the Levant, and far to the west, tracking the prints of Homeric adventurers in recent discoveries.

In Egypt itself, Aegean tracks are still turning up, often with close connections to Cyprus and the Levant. The latest and most dramatic such discoveries are confined to a Canaanite community in the Delta, where unmistakably Minoan frescoes have appeared in a Hyksos-period settlement, Tell el-Dab'a. But the Late Bronze Age still harbors surprises and explanations, as Vronwy Hankey and David Aston show with new Mycenaean discoveries from Ramesside tombs at Saqqara. Modest in number, these sherds shed important light on the nature of contact between the Aegean and Egypt and its subtle fluctuations. Vessels formerly considered acci-

dental burials in Egyptian tombs are now seen as original grave goods, while other vases show signs of reuse long after their manufacture: both circumstances suggest the prestige value of Aegean products and/or containers among Egyptians. Evidently admiration was mutual, from Greek reports of Egypt and Greek emulation of its art and architecture. The finds from Saqqara complement Greek observation of Egyptian reliefs also carved in the Ramesside period; this prehistoric contact was necessary for the creative results in Homeric poetry and art explored by Sarah Morris in Part II.

Aegean finds in Egypt presume seafarers active in both locales but probably native to neither. A likely home for these seafarers is Cyprus, the crossroads of activity between Anatolia, the Levant, Egypt, and Greece; at the coastal Egyptian sites of Marsa Matruh, the predominance of Cypriot pottery points to the island's role in international trade. The godfather of Cypriot archaeology, Vassos Karageorghis, reminds us that this maritime commercial network extended to Sicily and Sardinia in the Bronze Age, as shown by recent discoveries and analyses of pottery and bronzes in the West. When Athena disguises herself as Mentes, king of the "Taphians," in the *Odyssey* (1.180–184), she claims to be bound for "Temese" in order to exchange iron for bronze; though a fictitious tale, it derives from actual voyages of metal merchants between Cyprus, Sicily, Sardinia, and even Spain. This makes Homer's "Phoenicians" more plausible in the Bronze Age, as increasing numbers of scholars now accept. Yet their incorporation into the Homeric world reflects later conditions: in Part II, Irene Winter shows how Bronze Age realities are filtered through Iron Age attitudes.

The fruits of foreign exploits enriched the material culture of the Mycenaean world: its artifacts, archives, and burials reveal foreign connections but also anticipate later Greek habits and beliefs. Through the poetry of Homer, aspects of vanished palatial culture were inherited and transformed in the world of ritual. An example is the industry which supplied Egyptian nobility with Aegean jars of perfumed oil like those at Saqqara. Cynthia Shelmerdine considers the afterlife of this industry in Homeric allusions to perfume. The treatment of textiles with perfumed oil was popular in Mycenaean palatial wardrobes, according to Linear B tablets, but became exclusive to the "ambrosial" outfits of the gods in Homeric poetry. This migration of customs from elite privilege to divine prerogative determined much of Greek cultural history: gift exchange among Homeric kings merged into votive offerings for the gods, with similar expectations of reciprocal benefit.[4] Funerary rites survived more faithfully, if they lost some prehistoric grandeur: Sara Immerwahr explores them through depictions on Mycenaean funerary larnakes. These clay sarcophagi from Boiotia and Crete may imitate Egyptian wooden coffins, but their decoration illustrates funeral ritual and imagery from Homer and Geometric art. The dead are laid out, women mourn, men wear priestly garb, pour libations, and bear simulacra of the dead; chariots and athletes attend funeral games as elaborate as those for Patroklos in the *Iliad*. Allusions to the soul and the afterlife anticipate the heroic attitude toward death, one of the most characteristic features of Greek culture.

This intimacy between Mycenaean and Homeric Greece, closely linked through ceremonies for the dead, is vivid in the remarkable Cretan burials interpreted by Hector Catling. His special preview of new Subminoan tombs from Knossos reveals a set of multiple cremations with weapons as obsolete as a boar's-tusk helmet and as novel as iron knives. Dead warriors were buried with women and children, whose jewelry of ivory and iron was imported from Cyprus and Italy, along with a wheeled stand like Helen's silver "work-basket" (*Odyssey* 4.125–127). These burials find striking parallels at Tiryns and Lefkandi, and on Cyprus, not only for their connections overseas and over time, but for their heroic spirit. In articulating how these burials evoke the world of Homer, Catling expresses what it means to be a hero, in an archaeological sense, in the eleventh century B.C. This returns us to Hood's century for the destruction of Troy as it brings home artifacts from distant places with heroes returned. Are these the graves of veterans of *Iliad* battles and *Odyssey* travels, or of Sea Peoples, military adventurers (like the figures on the Warrior Vase from Mycenae?) who buried themselves near deserted Mycenaean strongholds? How did post-Mycenaean activity by such opportunists confuse or create memories of a single Trojan War?

The sum of these essays suggests that poetic memory owes more to imagination than to history. Beyond new discoveries or revisions of the material record, they offer new ways of visualizing the Homeric significance of such artifacts. An incremental case emerges for the intimacy of Late Bronze Age life with early Greek civilization, a relationship diluted by the demise of palaces, frescoes, and writing but reinforced by the strands of poetry and ritual.

PART II. HOMER AND THE IRON AGE: HISTORY AND POETICS

Implicit in the rich archaeological introduction to the Homeric world are the heroic dimensions of poetic memory. But *how* poetry remembers can mirror the time of its composition at least as much as the era of its subject matter. It is extraordinary that, after four centuries or more of apparent illiteracy in Greece, the first surviving texts longer than a few words are the poems of Homer, with a total of 27,800 lines. Embedded within these massive texts lies material from various traditions passed down through long centuries of oral recitation. And yet, in their present form, the two poems have been shaped by a poetic mind (or minds) of great breadth, profound vision, and exquisite sensibility. The essays in Part II address the problems created for literary historians and critics by this combination of traditional material and individual genius. They pivot on Homer's poetry to consider sources which contributed to its composition, including prehistoric and Near Eastern narrative, local poetic traditions, and preoccupations with history, politics, and ritual.

From behind the present form of the texts emerge older forms; epic recitations incorporate local interests of Geometric listeners into earlier compositions of praise poetry, but the epics also reformulate mythic structures of gender and borrow elements of non-Greek ritual. As the process of absorption and appropriation moves the narrative from regional specificity to pan-Greek importance, the primary poetic core becomes more and more indistinct. The essays in Part II bring strategies of comparative philology and mythology, literary theory, historical linguistics, anthropology, and iconography to the interpretation of Homer. These approaches by no means exhaust the strategies available; the object is rather to illustrate the multiplicity of methodologies necessary for understanding these enormously complex texts.

In the first essay, Walter Burkert asks a fundamental

question: How did the Greeks know when the Trojan War took place? A century ago, Eduard Meyer argued that Herodotus followed Hecataeus and the Spartan king-lists to reach one of his dates (1300 B.C.) but derived another date, c. 910 B.C., from his bizarre Egyptian chronology. Meyer's work has been fundamental to ancient chronology: now Burkert rejects Hecataeus as the Greek source for Herodotus' earlier date and traces it to the Lydian king-list. The Greeks, having no tradition of their own for dating the Trojan War, depended on fictitious insertions of Greek heroes into foreign king-lists. According to Burkert, the Greeks knew no date for the Trojan War, and the thread to their heroic past was irretrievably broken; this makes modern attempts to match ancient Greek dates with archaeological remains an exercise in illusion. Thus the first essay in this section leaves Greek history no closer to past events than poetry.

The introduction of local heroes into distant traditions, patent in this Greek fabrication of history, is also a fundamental technique of Homeric composition. Mabel Lang unravels two main themes of the *Iliad*, the story of the war between the Achaians and the Trojans and the story of the wrath of Achilles. An original, chronological war story, Lang maintains, was turned inside-out to start *in medias res* with Achilles' anger; the role of Diomedes in Book 5 makes clear that this is not a simple inversion but a thorough reintegration of the two stories, with Diomedes as a prefiguration of Achilles. What historical circumstance prompted this evolution from war story to wrath story? Lang credits this evolution to the expansion of Mycenae's political power into central and northern Greece. The original Trojan War was an independent exploit undertaken by Mycenae, embellished by local poets with heroes from Boiotia and Thessaly in order to add the prestige of older, Minyan traditions. An archaeologist would find this dialogue between local traditions appropriate in light of the regional cultures into which the Mycenaean world dissolved after 1200 B.C.

The evolution from local chronicle into national epic explains how a poem in the oral tradition, recomposed at each telling, became the fixed Homeric text. In exploring models for this formation, Gregory Nagy finds the process of diffusion as important to the development of the epics as composition and performance: "the widest possible reception entails, teleologically, the strictest possible degree of adherence to a normative and unified

version." Nagy here adduces living oral traditions on the Indian subcontinent. Sanskrit epics gradually lost their regional references to places and people in making the transition from a local to a supraregional tradition, just as the pan-Hellenic Homeric epics emphasize material appropriate for any Greek audience. Another interesting parallel is that Indian epics are performed in segments, not all of which are equally popular, just as Greek rhapsodes performed favorite selections from the Homeric poems. This prevailed, according to ancient accounts, until Hipparchos established new rules for the Panathenaic competition, requiring competing singers to recite the entire narrative in proper order. The story of the "Peisistratid recension," recently set out by Nagy,[5] is the Greek equivalent of Persian, Old Irish, Old French, and Indian legends in which a whole work is reconstituted from lost or scattered pieces.

An important exception to the pan-Hellenic character of the *Iliad* is the Catalogue of Ships in Book 2, with its wealth of specific local detail. The date when the Catalogue was composed continues to preoccupy discussions not only about the age of Homer but also about the date of the Trojan War itself. J. K. Anderson offers a new hypothesis: a Boiotian rhapsode of the late eighth century B.C. compiled the Catalogue as he toured the places mentioned in heroic tradition. Along the way, he heard local accounts of heroic times from his hosts and learned about the past existence of towns and cities then in ruins. The traveling rhapsode's attempts to collect antiquarian memories and honor his hosts produced, in Anderson's view, the combination of authentic tradition and courteous compliment preserved in the Catalogue.

If Greek epic originated as praise poetry in the cults of local heroes, elements of such praise poems may survive in the heroic credentials exchanged by Diomedes and Glaucus (*Iliad* 6), a famous passage analyzed here by Eddie Lowry. Glaucus begins his speech by comparing the race of men to the generations of leaves: rather than a poetic or philosophical meditation, this passage belongs to the genre of boast and reproach. With his simile, Lowry argues, Glaucus subtly reproaches the ancestry of Diomedes as a "forest of indistinction": the simile is not just the pessimistic reflection on mortality that it became in lyric poetry. Praise and blame are more than poetic genres: they divide ordinary men from heroes, and even women from men. Ann Bergren examines how the need to win praise and escape blame structures Homeric society and, in particular, the rôles of women. Women must act within this framework to gain security and prestige, yet they can, as in the case of Penelope, manipulate social imperatives by the use of *mētis*, contriving intelligence. Bergren finds the myth of Zeus and Mētis reenacted in the *Odyssey*'s ideal construction of (re)marriage, an architecture that is the union of female weaving and male joining, in the shroud woven by Penelope and the tree carpentered by Odysseus for his bed. Yet this union of female *mētis* and male body reveals the ambiguity of woman's place in an inherently unstable system. Penelope gains praise in sustaining the house of Odysseus through her intelligence but is blamed among men for refusing the patriarchal requirement to (re)marry. In allowing her to do both, Bergren argues, the text of the *Odyssey* admits the flaw in its ideal social construction.

Seams in the social fabric of the poems can be as vivid along ethnic boundaries as in gender issues. Part II concludes with essays that introduce a dialogue concerning non-Greek traditions as formative elements in Homer. First, Sarah Morris brings into Homeric focus the Canaanite and Phoenician practice of sacrificing a firstborn child as an ultimate offering for the salvation of a besieged city. Near Eastern images and episodes closely match the fate assigned to Astyanax, son of Hektor. In Greek literature, the boy dies when he is thrown from the walls of Troy by a victorious Greek, but, in Greek art, a warrior swings the body of Astyanax by an ankle or arm in the vicinity of an altar. Traditional accounts of this iconography condemn the divergence as a "conflict" or victim of lost accounts; another way to understand its Homeric dimensions lies outside Greece. Verbal and visual accounts portray the death of Astyanax as a sacrifice in the Phoenician tradition. Greek responses to Semitic rites are one episode in the circulation of religious and artistic traditions in the eastern Mediterranean which fertilized the formation of Homeric poetry.

How does this oblique use of Near Eastern traditions coexist with an ambiguous attitude towards Levantine peoples? Irene Winter tackles discrepancies between Homer's Phoenicians and those in archaeological and historical sources. In Assyrian documents, Phoenicians traded in metal under the supervision of the state, while the *Odyssey* portrays them as "rogue-sailors"

and traders in trinkets. Unlike most scholars, Winter does not blame these disparities on chronology, but considers them in the light of how and why the Homeric text came about. The ambiguous portrayal of Phoenicians—makers of exquisite objects in the *Iliad* but greedy and duplicitous hucksters in the *Odyssey*—indicates more than different periods or poets. In a larger literary framework and cultural context, Homer's Phoenicians are foils for individual and collective Greeks, the "other" against which Greek identity is defined. Living Greeks of the eighth and seventh centuries resembled and competed with historical Phoenicians but displaced them by creating a remote, heroic past in poetry and a new, national, ethos. Winter's understanding of the Homeric text illuminates the role of ethnic stereotypes in the process of state-formation. Thus the formation of the Homeric corpus celebrates becoming Greek in an era when foreigners were long familiar in the Aegean but only newly defined as different. It is this context which made the poems of Homer the cultural manifesto of Greek civilization.

More difficult to trace than the Near Eastern influences are prehistoric poetic traditions in the Aegean. The existence of Mycenaean poetry has long been defended by Emily Vermeule herself, but she and others have claimed older antecedents in the form of Minoan poetry. One of the *Iliad*'s most intriguing retrospectives occurs in the elaborate description of the shield made by Hephaistos for Achilles, where the poet compares a dancing floor depicted on the shield to the dancing floor at Knossos made by Daidalos for Ariadne (*Iliad* 18.590–592). Steven Lonsdale finds in this simile a fragment of Bronze Age poetry, where "Ariadne's dancing floor" alludes to ecstatic dances in Minoan ritual, meant to attract the presence of the deity, sometimes in conjunction with an act of sacrifice. The Homeric allusion, Lonsdale argues, uses myth to evoke its ritual analogue and so prefigures the "dance" of Achilles and Hektor around the walls of Troy, and the death of Hektor in Book 22. This is intertextuality at its richest and densest, and it prepares the reader of Homer for the ritual background of Homeric performance itself. Jane Carter demonstrates the ancestry of sympotic performances of poetry in ritual banquets for the dead, traditional in the Near East (as the *marzeaḥ* feast attended by the *rephaim*) and already integral in Mycenaean palaces, as the frescoes of the Pylos throne room make clear. Thus Homeric performance, as well as its heroes, spans the Bronze and Iron Ages: epic songs began as celebrations of royal ancestors and became praise poems for aristocrats, as social groups changed but the need for social bonding remained. The second group of essays demonstrates that the subject of Homeric poetry is not exclusively the Mycenaean past, and that its medium is not exclusively an archaic aristocracy: form and content partake of both ages.

PART III. AFTER HOMER: NARRATIVE AND REPRESENTATION

The Homeric poems were not only the first works of Greek literature, they remained preeminent literary texts until the end of classical antiquity, a reputation highly visible in art. To an extent that we are unable to measure, this vitality in later Greek and Roman art has molded our understanding of Homer. The essays in Part III follow Homer in the visual arts from the Geometric period (when the poems were composed), through Greek and Macedonian art and into Roman, analyzing the process by which textual narrative becomes visual narrative, and how the visual arts reinterpret the heroic texts.

Since antiquity, readers of Homer—scholars, travelers, and artists—have envisioned episodes and personalities from epic poetry in art of their time. In the Roman period, Pausanias believed that a marble relief at Knossos represented the *choros* or "dancing floor" which Daidalos made for Ariadne (9.4.2; compare *Iliad* 18.590–592 and the essay by Lonsdale); in the past century, archaeologists have sought to correlate epic realia with ancient artifacts and styles. One goal of this exercise, to affix epic composition or redaction to a particular moment in Greek culture, has led scholarship in a circle: Homeric poetry is linked with works of art themselves identified from epic passages. The effective reduction of images to "illustrations," or of epic verses to captions for art, implies that one subject need reflect another in order to be understood, and such simplified equations serve neither art nor literature. Since Carl Robert's *Bild und Lied*, scholars have sought to move away from these assumptions and to develop a concept of narrative useful for understanding visual representa-

tion and the significance of visual allusion. Homeric themes in surviving Greek and Roman art are more than illustrations for known texts, just as they are more than testimonia for missing artistic masterpieces; their functions demonstrate independence from literary purposes and reflect contemporary concerns in public and private life. The insights of individuals, from ancient painters to modern scholars, in this finale show what keeps Homer personal in appeal, as well as enduring and universal.

The first essays in Part III concern art contemporary with Nagy's Homer, from the "formation" of the Homeric corpus in the later eighth century to their "fixation" in the Archaic period (sixth-century Athens). Will an artist imagine differently a scene heard in many versions of a poem cycle and one fixed in a canonized text? These questions should inform a new understanding of famous passages such as the description of the Shield of Achilles in *Iliad* Book 18. Analyzing an epic passage in which the poet imagines a work of art, Mark Stansbury-O'Donnell reveals patterns of narrative whose principles, rather than contents, are relevant to pictorial composition. In helping to liberate early Greek art from its confining classification into "Sagenbilder" and "Lebensbilder," he opens up "narrative" to conditions essential to storytelling in text as well as art—time sequence, setting, actions.

His theoretical considerations serve the reader well in the next two essays in this section, which turn to non-Attic narrative traditions in early Greek art. Much as Boardman has expanded the conventional emphasis on Attic Geometric art to include Argive Geometric,[6] J. L. Benson offers narrative reflections from the province of Corinthian pottery. His focus is the Ajax Painter, creator of the "first identifiable epic theme in Corinthian vase painting," the suicide of Ajax from the Epic Cycle poem, the *Aithiopis*. Benson identifies subtle principles within this artist's oeuvre: polarity, the juxtaposition of the deeds of a hero with those of a lion (the visual equivalent of an epic simile), and dramatic devices such as elevating the status of an enemy to increase the measure of heroic worth. Benson's essay is a timely reminder that the seventh century was one of Peloponnesian achievements in mythological narrative, neglected in Athens after its creative debut in Geometric art.

The first generation of Attic black-figure painters who sponsored an explosion of mythological narrative does not appear until the 560s B.C., a watershed recently and fruitfully explored by Alan Shapiro.[7] Ann Brownlee considers the period before this Attic moment in vases by Sophilos. In his mythological subjects, he tells "the picture of a story" by assembling "those elements which best represent" rather than "illustrate the story." She also explores his use of "synoptic narrative" and compares his "denial of time" to that of other Archaic vase painters. Her explanation for many of these features, including the use of inscriptions as "the visual creation of a sound" rather than a word, emphasizes keener ears than eyes in a society still attuned to oral poetry in the decades near the fixation of these poems as texts.

Sophilos was also the first Athenian artist to name himself and claim credit for his work, something "Homer" never did. David Mitten's subject, the Lion Painter, is an artist whose repertoire never included human figures, a challenge and contrast to the figural narrative explored by Stansbury-O'Donnell and Benson. The Lion Painter's devotion to felines and florals teaches a modern eye that dramatic action in Homeric similes, alive with flora and fauna, may have been just as entertaining, even more vivid, to the ancient ear than the deeds of heroes they accompany.

Such an expansion of what "Homeric iconography" means is echoed by Michael Padgett, who reminds us that it is not only specific epic characters or episodes in art which reveal "an awareness and appreciation of Homer by his contemporaries." He offers an imaginative identification of the bard himself in the bronze group of a lyre-player and his young escort in the J. Paul Getty Museum. This charming pair finds its closest stylistic and iconographic partner in a bronze lyre-player from Crete and may have been produced there in the eighth century B.C. A Cretan-looking portrait of Homer is appropriate to an island which also boasted the earliest Homeric artist, Daidalos: the discussion of a Cretan bard is followed by Erika Simon's tribute to Greek literature's earliest master craftsman. Daidalos' adventures in Greek art of the "Daedalic" seventh century B.C. appear in western Greece, home to his earliest inscribed portrait, and the Corinthian world explored by Benson. Figures called Daidalos are compared to other "winged craftsmen" and lead Simon to eliminate identities proposed for "Aristaios." In comparing her portrait of the

artist with Padgett's portrait of the poet, it is appropriate to recall that similar divine powers—wings for rapid and magic travel—were bestowed alike on gifted craftsmen and on the words of the poet, *epea pteroenta.*

These six essays celebrate personalities and principles of early Greek art intimate with Homeric poetry in its age of redaction; they are accompanied by essays which focus on specific epic subjects and their evolution in Greek and Roman art. Marion True gives us the debut of a magnificent Chalcidian amphora (see frontispiece). It celebrates one of the *Iliad*'s most poignant episodes, the murder of the sleeping Thracians and their horses by Odysseus and Diomedes (the so-called Doloneia of *Iliad* Book 10). This first Archaic representation of the Homeric story also demonstrates subtle variations on the Iliadic version, reflecting alternate traditions beyond the debated "uniqueness" of Homer. Martin Robertson uses familiar vases to rescue lost epic episodes with his examination of the Boston skyphos painted by Makron with the life and loves of Helen of Troy. His careful attention to her confrontation with her estranged husband, Menelaos, recasts a scene to the beginning of the Trojan War rather than to its *denouement.* A number of related scenes in Greek vase painting are implicated in Robertson's astute reinterpretation of this "recovery" of Helen as an early embassy requesting her return, moments separated by many poems in the Epic Cycle.

What is more difficult in the Archaic period than in Classical and later times is discerning the forces in history and politics which informed re-visions of Homer. Yet this inspiration accounts for the most remarkable aspect of Homer's agelessness: that cultures no longer heroic, and sometimes not even Greek, continued to identify so strongly with the sentiments and situations in the epic tradition. The final four essays address these intriguing connections between Homer and history. Diana Buitron-Oliver, leading authority on the vase painter Douris, compares two sets of Homeric compositions by this fifth-century painter to contemporary social and political values. Two white-ground lekythoi by Douris are unusual for their provenance—one comes from a chthonic sanctuary of Demeter in Sicily—and their mythological, rather than funerary, subject matter. Epic heroines like Atalante and Iphigenia may have been portrayed not for their dramatic biographies but as paradigms for the fate of Greek women. In Classical art, as in Classical literature, epic figures represented emblematic characters and values to contemporary Greeks: this is part of the way "Homer" became the basis of a classical education. Another vase by Douris introduces a subject critical to current iconographic studies, the play of political allusions in art. On this cup, votes cast by the Achaians to award the arms of Achilles take on special meaning for post-Kleisthenic Athenians newly empowered with civic duties. This re-vision of the Homeric community in the Classical *polis* exemplifies the political factor keeping Homer alive in later ages, just as his words served public debate and philosophical discourse for centuries.

In this spirit, Margaret Miller continues her extended study of Greek attitudes towards Persia with a look at how representations of Priam change in response to shifting perceptions of Eastern imagery. Her essay demonstrates subtle variations in the orientalization of non-Greek figures in Homer and detects historical fluctuations behind the commonplace that Greeks patterned epic enemies on contemporary ones after the Persian Wars.

It was a Persian king, Xerxes, whose pilgrimage to Troy and homage to its cults were the first recorded in antiquity, followed by centuries of Hellenistic and Roman rulers. Cornelius Vermeule assembles the first gazetteer of visitors to Troy in the Greek and Roman period, their rebuilding of its monuments and revival of its cults, commemorated in coinage, historical anecdotes, and literary maintenance of Trojan connections. Why did Troy mean so much to those who destroyed it (the Greeks) as well as to those descended from its defenders (the Romans), and even to Persians, Macedonians, and Turks (self-styled "Teukroi") uninvolved in Homer's Troy?

It was Alexander the Great who made the most famous pilgrimage to Troy, and who initiated these sentimental journeys and pious building donations to the city made famous by Homer. If encounters with Persians altered Greek visions of their epic past, Macedonians changed the geographical and cultural parameters of the Greek world forever, and they did so with the help of Homer. Beyond the traditional confrontation of Alexander the Great with his Homeric idol Achilles, Ada Cohen focuses on Hellenistic Macedonia and its Mycenaean past to explore why Macedonians needed Homeric heroes and traditions and even fabricated a Homeric Bronze Age. Figures like Achilles survive not

only as Macedonian heroes but, among the descendants of Trojans, as Roman ones. In the age when Rome found its own national epic voice devoted to a Homeric hero, Aeneas, the influence of Homeric prototypes reached the humbler workshops of potters. An Arretine bowl which receives its first scholarly publication here by John Herrmann displays two Homeric moments: the dragging of Hektor and the funeral of Patroklos, both demonstrations of unflattering, even brutal, behavior by Achilles. Details unique to the Arretine corpus of stamps suggest deliberate fidelity to the text of Homer, while the same artist lifts figures from contemporary Augustan triumphal monuments, making the bowl more Greek but also more Roman. A figure representing Asia, for example, has a Roman historical pedigree commemorating the recovery of the standards from the Parthians, but here she stands for an enemy defeated by Greeks. Thus Roman sensibilities, however sympathetic to Rome's ancestors, the Trojans, recruited contemporary motifs to celebrate the triumph of epic enemies, the Greeks: such configurations adumbrate complexity in the afterlife of Homeric traditions.

These cross-cultural defections of Homeric values close a volume which is only a beginning. The ages of Homer continued to inspire Late Antique mosaicists, and medieval poets and artists, long before manuscripts of Homer reached the West and Greek art was rediscovered. The spirit of Homer breathed its influence over a generation of romantics and revolutionaries, and helped make Hellas "free once more" from the Turks, successors and avengers of the Trojans. Modern Greek literature remembers Homer in a new *Odyssey* (by Nikos Kazantzakis) and in the name of a Nobel laureate (Odysseus Elytis); the same prize has now been awarded to a Caribbean poet (Derek Walcot) for a new Homeric epic (*Omeros*) set in an archipelago of the New World. New ages of Homer lie ahead.

NOTES

1. Fr. 112 Radt, from Ath. 8.347d.
2. G. S. Kirk, *The Iliad: A Commentary* II (Cambridge 1990) 40–50.
3. E. Cline, "A Possible Hittite Embargo against the My-

cenaeans," *Historia* 40 (1991) 1–9; "Hittite Objects in the Bronze Age Aegean," *AnatStud* 41 (1991) 133–143.

4. S. Langdon, "Gift Exchange in the Geometric Sanctuaries," in T. Linders and G. C. Nordquist, eds., *Gifts to the Gods* (Uppsala 1987) 107–113.

5. G. Nagy, "Homeric Questions," *TAPA* 122 (1992) 17–60.

6. J. Boardman, "Symbol and Story in Greek Art," in W. G. Moon, ed., *Ancient Greek Art and Iconography* (Madison 1983) 15–36.

7. A. Shapiro, "Old and New Heroes: Narrative, Composition and Subject in Attic Black-Figure," *CA* 9 (1990) 114–148.

BIOGRAPHY AND BIBLIOGRAPHY

✦

EMILY T. VERMEULE

Personal:

Born August 11, 1928, New York City, to Clinton Blake Townsend and Eleanor Mary Meneely.

Married February 2, 1957, to Cornelius Clarkson Vermeule III.

Children: Emily Dickinson Blake Vermeule, July 14, 1966.
    Cornelius Adrian Comstock Vermeule, May 2, 1968.

Education:

The Brearley School, New York City, 1934–1946.

Bryn Mawr College 1946–1950, B.A. summa cum laude in Greek and Philosophy.

American School of Classical Studies, Athens, 1950–1951 (Fulbright).

St. Anne's College, Oxford University, 1953–1954 (Catherwood).

Radcliffe College, M.A. 1954, Classical Archaeology.

Bryn Mawr College, Ph.D. 1956; diss. "Bacchylides and Lyric Style."

Positions:

Instructor in Greek, Bryn Mawr College, 1956–1957.

Instructor in Greek, Wellesley College, 1957–1958.

Assistant Professor of Classics, Boston University, 1958–1961.

Associate Professor of Classics, Boston University, 1961–1964.

Professor of Art and Greek, Wellesley College, 1965–1970.

Fellow for Research, Classical Art, Museum of Fine Arts, Boston, 1965–present.

James Loeb Visiting Professor of Classical Philology, Harvard University, 1969.

Samuel E. Zemurray, Jr., and Doris Zemurray Stone-Radcliffe Professor, Harvard University, 1970–present.

Sather Professor of Classical Literature, University of California, Berkeley, 1975.

Geddes-Harrower Chair of Greek Art and Archaeology, University of Aberdeen, 1980–1981.

A. Bernhard Visiting Professor of the History of Art, Williams College, 1986.

John and Penelope Biggs Visiting Professor, Washington University, St. Louis, 1990.

Honors:

Guggenheim Fellow, Athens, 1964–1965.
Radcliffe Graduate Society Gold Medal, 1968.
Litt.D., Douglass College, Rutgers University, 1968.
D.F.A., University of Massachusetts, Amherst, 1970.
LL.D., Regis College, 1970.
Litt.D., Smith College, 1972.
Litt.D., Wheaton College, 1973.
L.H.D., Trinity College, Hartford, 1974.
L.H.D., Emmanuel College, 1980.
Litt.D., Tufts University, 1980.
Charles J. Goodwin Award of Merit, American Philological Association, 1980.
Jefferson Lecturer in the Humanities, National Endowment for the Humanities, 1982.
Frances Riker Davis Award, The Brearley School, 1983.
L.H.D., University of Pittsburgh, 1983.
Litt.D., Bates College, 1983.
L.H.D., Miami University (Oxford, Ohio), 1986.
L.H.D., Princeton University, 1989.
L.H.D., Bard College, 1993.

Other:

Bryn Mawr College, Alumnae Director, 1968–1972.
Radcliffe College, Board of Trustees, 1974–1981.
Harvard University Press, Board of Syndics, 1981–1986.
Library of Congress, Board of Scholars, 1982–1987.
University of California Humanities Research Institute, Board of Governors, 1988–1991.
Isabella Stewart Gardner Museum, Board of Trustees, 1989–present.

Societies:

American Academy of Arts and Sciences, 1971–present.
American Philosophical Society, 1972–present; vice-president (Humanities) 1978–1982.
American Philological Association; president-elect 1994.
American School of Classical Studies (Managing Committee, Committee on Committees).
Archaeological Institute of America.
British Academy, Corresponding Fellow, 1981–present.
German Archaeological Institute, Corresponding Fellow, 1970–present.
Dumbarton Oaks, Senior Fellow, 1976–1979.
Smithsonian Institution, Member of the Council, 1984–present.
Society of Antiquaries, London (Fellow), 1978–present.
Society for the Promotion of Hellenic Studies.
The Cosmopolitan Club, New York.
The Signet Society.

Excavations:

Athenian Agora (for the American School of Classical Studies), 1951, 1965.
Gordion, Turkey (for the University Museum, University of Pennsylvania), 1955–1957.
Kephallenia and Messenia (Archaeological Society of Athens), 1960–1961.
Coastal East Libya (for the University Museum, University of Pennsylvania), 1962.
Müşkebi (Halikarnassos), Turkey (for the University Museum, University of Pennsylvania), 1963.
Thera-Santorini (Archaeological Society of Athens), 1967–1968.
Toumba tou Skourou, Cyprus, Director (for the Department of Antiquities of the Republic of Cyprus, Harvard University, and the Museum of Fine Arts, Boston), 1971–1973.

BIBLIOGRAPHY

1955
"A Mycenaean Chamber Tomb Under the Temple of Ares," *Hesperia* 24 (1955) 187–219.

1956
Review of E. L. Bennett, Jr., *The Pylos Tablets: Text of the Inscriptions Found, 1939–1954*, in *AJA* 60 (1956) 291–294.
Review of R. Browning, *The Linear "B" Texts from Knossos*, in *AJA* 60 (1956) 453.
Review of A. Parrot, *Discovering Buried Worlds*, in *AJA* 60 (1956) 453.

1957
Review of J. H. Finley, Jr., *Pindar and Aeschylus*, in *CJ* 53 (1957) 95–96.
Review of R. Hampe, *Die homerische Welt im Lichte der neuesten Ausgrabungen*, in *AJA* 61 (1957) 295–296.
Review of M. Ventris and J. Chadwick, *Documents in Mycenaean Greek*, in *AJA* 61 (1957) 196–201.

1958
"The Mycenaeans in Achaia," *AJA* 62 (1958) 227.
"Mythology in Mycenaean Art," *CJ* 54 (1958) 97–108.
Review of A. Garzya, ed. and trans., *Alcmane: I frammenti*, in *CP* 53 (1958) 135–137.
Review of B. E. Moon, *Mycenaean Civilization: Publications since 1935*, in *AJA* 62 (1958) 441–443.
Review of G. E. Mylonas, *Ancient Mycenae: The Capital City of Agamemnon*, in *AJA* 62 (1958) 115–118.

1959

"Fish," *The New Yorker*, February 21, 1959, 103.

"A Gold Minoan Double Axe," *BMFA* 57 (1959) 4–16.

"Introduction to Electra," and "Electra" in D. Grene and R. Lattimore, eds., *The Complete Greek Tragedies: Euripides* 4 (Chicago 1959) 390–394, 396–454.

Review of C. W. Blegen, C. G. Boulter, J. L. Caskey, and M. Rawson, *Troy*, IV: *Settlements VIIa, VIIb and VIII*, in *AJA* 63 (1959) 203–206.

Review of F. Cassola, *La Ionia nel mondo miceneo*, in *AJP* 80 (1959) 450–451.

Review of J. Chadwick, *The Decipherment of Linear B*, in *AHR* 64 (1959) 340–341.

Review of C. Zervos, *L'Art des Cyclades: Du début à la fin de l'age de bronze, 2500–1100 avant notre ère*, in *AJA* 63 (1959) 398.

1960

"The Fall of Mycenaean Empire," *Archaeology* 13 (1960) 66–75.

"The Mycenaeans in Achaia," *AJA* 64 (1960) 1–21.

Review of B. Gentili, *Anacreon*, in *CP* 55 (1960) 264–265.

Review of M. Lejeune, *Mémoires de philologie mycénienne: Première série*, in *AJA* 64 (1960) 87–88.

1961

"Dactylo-Epitrites for Dudley Fitts, or, Thoughts of an Inveterate Smoker," *Poetry* 98 (1961) 157.

"New Excavations in Western Greece," *Boston University Graduate Journal* 9 (1961) 73–84, 119–127.

"New Mycenaean Discoveries in Western Greece," *AJA* 65 (1961) 193.

Review of T. Burton-Brown, *Early Mediterranean Migrations: An Essay in Archaeological Interpretation*, in *AJA* 65 (1961) 317–318.

Review of V. E. G. Kenna, *Cretan Seals, With a Catalogue of the Minoan Gems in the Ashmolean Collection*, in *ArtB* 43 (1961) 241–245.

1962

"Fish," *Poetry Pilot*, July 1962, 15.

Review of B. A. von Groningen, *Pindare au banquet: Les fragments des scolies édités avec un commentaire critique et explicatif*, in *CP* 57 (1962) 184–187.

Review of L. R. Palmer, *Mycenaeans and Minoans: Aegean Prehistory in the Light of the Linear B Tablets*, in *CW* 55 (1962) 255–256.

1963

"Apollo and Euphronios at the Banquet," *The Classical Association of New England, Annual Bulletin* 58 (1963) 9–10.

"Excavation of the Mycenaean citadel and royal tomb at Peristeria and study of Mycenaean pottery from Pylos," *The American Philosophical Society Year Book 1962* (Philadelphia 1963) 639–641.

"The Fall of Knossos and the Palace Style," *AJA* 67 (1963) 195–199.

"Three New Illustrations of the Trojan War," *AJA* 67 (1963) 218–219.

Review of W. C. Brice, ed., *Inscriptions in the Minoan Linear Script of Class A*, in *AJA* 67 (1963) 305–306.

Review of V. Desborough and N. G. L. Hammond, *The End of the Mycenaean Civilization and the Dark Age. D.: The archaeological background. H.: The literary tradition* (*CAH*, rev. ed.), in *Gnomon* 35 (1963) 495–499.

Review of R. Fagles, *Bacchylides, Complete Poems*, in *AJP* 84 (1963) 441–443.

Review of J. W. Graham, *The Palaces of Crete*, in *AHR* 68 (1963) 705–707.

Review of B. E. Moon, *Mycenaean Civilization, Publications 1956–1960*, in *AJA* 67 (1963) 89.

Review of R. F. Willetts, *Cretan Cults and Festivals*, in *AHR* 68 (1963) 705–707.

Review of L. Woolley, *History Unearthed*, in *Archaeology* 16 (1963) 72.

1964

Greece in the Bronze Age. Chicago 1964.

"Aesthetics and Religion in the Late Mycenaean World," *Fourth International Congress of Classical Studies*, Philadelphia.

"The Early Bronze Age in Caria," *Archaeology* 17 (1964) 244–249.

"Hymn to Pan," *Arion* 3:1 (1964) 61–62.

Review of C. W. Blegen, *Troy and the Trojans*, in *CW* 57 (1964) 187–188.

Review of J. Chadwick, ed., with contributions from E. Bennett, E. French, W. Taylour, N. Verdelis, and C. Williams, *The Mycenae Tablets III*, in *AJA* 68 (1964) 310–311.

Review of L. Cottrell, *Realms of Gold: A Journey in Search of the Mycenaeans*, in *Archaeology* 17 (1964) 294, 296.

1965

The Trojan War in Greek Art: An Engagement Calendar for 1965. With M. Comstock, A. Graves, and C. Vermeule. Museum of Fine Arts, Boston 1965. (Reprinted as picture book, Boston 1965.)

"Fragments of a Symposium by Euphronios," *AntK* 8 (1965) 34–39.

"Painted Mycenaean Larnakes," *JHS* 85 (1965) 123–148.

"The Vengeance of Achilles: The Dragging of Hektor at Troy," *BMFA* 63 1965) 34–52.

Review of V. Karageorghis, *CVA* Cyprus I, in *AJA* 69 (1965) 188–189.

1966

Greece in the Bronze Age. 2nd printing. Chicago 1966.

"The Boston Oresteia Krater," *AJA* 70 (1966) 1–22.

"Classics are Superb," *The Brearley Bulletin*, Spring 1966, 15–18.

"The Mycenaean Age in Crete," summary report, *Second International Cretan Congress*, Chania.

"A Mycenaean Dipinto and Graffito," *Kadmos* 5 (1966) 142–146.

"Mycenaean Tomb beneath the Middle Stoa," with J. Travlos, *Hesperia* 35 (1966) 55–78.

Review of L. R. Palmer, *Mycenaeans and Minoans: Aegean Prehistory in the Light of the Linear B Tablets*, 2nd rev. ed., in *CW* 59 (1966) 192.

Review of A. Sakellariou, *Die minoischen und mykenischen Siegel des Nationalmuseums in Athen*, in *AJA* 70 (1966) 201–202.

1967

Greece in the Bronze Age. 3rd printing. Chicago 1967.

"A Love Scene by the Panaitios Painter," *AJA* 71 (1967) 311–314.

"A Mycenaean Jeweler's Mold," *BMFA* 65 (1967) 19–31.

"Myth, Shapes and Colours," *Apollo*, December 1967, 418–427.

"The Promise of Thera: A Bronze Age Pompeii," *The Atlantic Monthly*, December 1967, 83–94.

Review of A. E. Samuel, *The Mycenaeans in History*, in *Archaeology* 20 (1967) 313.

1968

"The Decline and End of Minoan and Mycenaean Culture," in *A Land Called Crete: A Symposium in Memory of Harriet Boyd Hawes, 1871–1945* (Northampton, Mass. 1967) 81–98.

"The World of Odysseus," in *Greece and Rome: Builders of Our World* (The National Geographic Society 1968) 43–73.

Review of R. J. Forbes, *Bergbau, Steinbruchtätigkeit und Hüttenwesen*, ArchHom 2.K (Göttingen 1967), in *CW* 62 (1968) 143.

Review of W. A. McDonald, *Progress into the Past: The Rediscovery of Mycenaean Civilization*, in *CW* 61 (1968) 353–354.

Review of S. Marinatos, *Kleidung, Haar- und Barttracht*, ArchHom 1.A/B (Göttingen 1967), in *CW* 62 (1968) 143.

1969

Greece in the Bronze Age. 4th printing. Chicago 1969.

"A Culture Beneath the Ashes," *Science Year* 1969, 140–151.

"Some Erotica in Boston," *AntK* 12 (1969) 9–15.

Review of W. C. Brice, ed., *Europa: Studien zur Geschichte und Epigraphik der frühen Aegaeis. Festschrift für Ernest Grumach*, in *AHR* 74 (1969) 1252–1253.

Review of A. Galanopoulos and E. Bacon, *Atlantis: The Truth Behind the Legend*, in *Sunday Herald Traveler* (Boston), October 12, 1969, 3 (Book Guide).

Review of G. M. A. Richter, *The Engraved Gems of the Greeks, Etruscans and Romans-Part One: Engraved Gems of the Greeks and the Etruscans: A History of Greek Art in Miniature*, in *CW* 63 (1969) 54.

1970

"Aegean Gold Hoard and the Court of Egypt," with C. Vermeule, *Curator* 13 (1970) 32–42.

"An Aegean Gold Hoard and the Court of Egypt," with C. Vermeule, *ILN*, March 21, 1970, 23–25.

"An Aegean Gold Treasure and the Court of Egypt," *AJA* 74 (1970) 204–205.

"Excavations on Thera," *The American Philosophical Society Year Book 1969* (Philadelphia 1970) 679–680.

"Five Vases from the Grave Precinct of Dexileos," *JdI* 85 (1970) 94–111.

"The Pennsylvania Declaration," *Antiquity* 44 (1970) 314–316.

In Tribute to Suzanne E. Chapman, W. M. Whitehill, ed. (Boston 1970) unnumbered 9–10.

Review of J. Boardman, *Archaic Greek Gems: Schools and Artists in the Sixth and Early Fifth Centuries B.C.*, in *CJ* 65 (1970) 237.

Review of J. N. Coldstream, *Greek Geometric Pottery: A Survey of ten local styles and their chronology*, in *CJ* 66 (1970) 83–84.

Review of N.-G. Gejvall, *Lerna, a Preclassical Site in the Argolid: Results of Excavations Conducted by the American School of Classical Studies at Athens*, I: *The Fauna*, in *CW* 63 (1970) 304.

Review of V. E. G. Kenna, *The Cretan Talismanic Stone in the Late Minoan Age*, SIMA 24, in *CW* 64 (1970) 128.

Review of A. D. Lacy, *Greek Pottery in the Bronze Age*, in *Archaeology* 23 (1970) 271–272.

Review of M. L. Lang, *The Palace of Nestor at Pylos in Western Messenia*, II: *The Frescoes*, in *ArtB* 52 (1970) 428–430.

Review of K. E. Meyer, *The Pleasures of Archaeology*, in *Washington Post*, November 15, 1970, 10.

Review of P. Throckmorton, *Shipwrecks and Archaeology*, in *Sunday Herald Traveler* (Boston), February 22, 1970, 3 (Book Guide).

Review (with C. Vermeule) of C. Doumas, *The N. P. Goulandris Collection of Early Cycladic Art*, in *CW* 63 (1970) 239–240.

1971

Grecia en la Edad del Bronce. C. Villegas, trans. Mexico City 1971.

"Golden Links to the Bronze Age," *Horizon* 13:1 (1971) 50–53.

"Kadmos and the Dragon," in D. G. Mitten, J. G. Pedley, and J. A. Scott, eds., *Studies Presented to George M. A. Hanfmann* (Mainz 1971) 177–188.

"A Protoattic Human Sacrifice?" with S. Chapman, *AJA* 75 (1971) 285–293.

"A Tiger's Heart Wrapped in a Woman's Hide," 1971 Commencement Address, *Bryn Mawr Alumnae Bulletin* (Summer 1971) 2–4.

"The Santorini Volcano: A Review Article," review of D. L. Page, *The Santorini Volcano and the Destruction (Desolation) of Minoan Crete*, in *Archaeology* 24 (1971) 130–135.

Review of H. Hoffmann et al., *Dädalische Kunst auf Kreta im 7. Jahrhundert v. Chr.*, in *American Classical Review* 1 (1971) 241.

1972

Greece in the Bronze Age. 2nd rev. ed., 5th printing. Chicago 1972.

A New Introduction and Bibliography for reissue of M. P. Nilsson, *The Mycenaean Origin of Greek Mythology* (Berkeley 1972) vii–xv.

"Antiquities at Wellesley," with C. Vermeule, *Archaeology* 25 (1972) 276–282.

"Rally Day," *Smith Alumnae Quarterly*, April 1972, 18.

"Toumba tou Skourou, Cyprus," *AJA* 76 (1972) 223–224.

Review of J. L. Angel, *Lerna, a Preclassical Site in the Argolid*, II: *The People*, in *American Classical Review* 2 (1972) 175.

Review of C. Doumas, trans. by P. G. Preziosi, *The N. P. Goulandris Collection of Early Cycladic Art*, in *CJ* 67 (1972) 287–288.

Review of S. Iakovides, *Perati: To Nekrotapheion*.

Review of S. A. Immerwahr, *The Athenian Agora: Results of Excavations Conducted by The American School of Classical Studies at Athens*, XIII: *The Neolithic and Bronze Ages*, in *American Classical Review* 2 (1972) 255–256.

Review of N. Platon, *Zakros: The Discovery of a Lost Palace of Ancient Crete*, in *Sunday Herald Traveler* (Boston), January 2, 1972, section seven, 11 (Book Guide).

1973

"Excavations at Toumba tou Skourou, Morphou, 1971," in V. Karageorghis, ed., *Acts of the International Archaeological Symposium, "The Mycenaeans in the Eastern Mediterranean"* (Nicosia 1973) 25–33.

"Toumba tou Skourou, Cyprus," *AJA* 77 (1973) 230.

Review of M. I. Finley, *Early Greece: The Bronze and Archaic Ages*, in *CP* 68 (1973) 145–46.

Review of S. Hood, *The Minoans: The Story of Bronze Age Crete*, in *Archaeology* 26 (1973) 151–152.

Review of T. B. L. Webster, *Potter and Patron in Classical Athens*, in *AHR* 78 (1973) 1432.

1974

Götterkult, ArchHom 3.V Göttingen 1974.

Greece in the Bronze Age. 2nd rev. ed., 6th printing. Chicago 1974.

Toumba tou Skourou, The Mound of Darkness. A Bronze Age Town on Morphou Bay in Cyprus. Harvard University, Museum of Fine Arts, Boston, Cyprus Expedition 1974.

Inauguration speech for Sister Theresa Higgins, seventh president of Regis College, in *The Town Crier* (Weston, Mass.), October 10, 1974, 11, 25.

"Market Alert: Cypriote Antiquities Missing," *JFA* 1 (1974) 390–391.

"The Press and Cyprus," *Nieman Reports*, Winter 1974, 46–48.

Review of H.-G. Buchholz and V. Karageorghis, *Altägäis und Altkypros*, in *Gnomon* 46 (1974) 497–500.

Review of P. Dikaios, *Enkomi, Excavations, 1948–1958*, vols. I–III, in *AJA* 78 (1974) 86–88.

Review of W. A. McDonald and G. R. Rapp, Jr., eds., *The Minnesota Messenia Expedition: Reconstructing a Bronze Age Regional Environment*, in *Journal of Interdisciplinary History* 5 (1974) 150–151.

Review of P. Warren, *Minoan Stone Vases*, in *CJ* 69 (1974) 177–180.

1975

The Art of the Shaft Graves of Mycenae, Lectures in Memory of Louise Taft Semple, University of Cincinnati, April 30–May 1, 1973. Norman, Okla. 1975.

"Cyprus: Politics and Antiquities," *Archaeology* 28 (1975) 273–274.

"A Note on Cypriote Antiquities in Turkish-(Occupied) Cyprus," *Archaeology* 28 (1975) 58.

Review of *Die kretisch-mykenische Glyptik und ihre gegenwärtigen Probleme. Das Corpus der minoischen und mykenischen Siegel*, in *AJA* 79 (1975) 291–292.

Review of M. Ventris and J. Chadwick, *Documents in Mycenaean Greek*, 2nd ed. by J. Chadwick, in *AHR* 80 (1975) 943–944.

1976

"Pot-Marks and Graffiti from Toumba tou Skourou, Cyprus," with F. Wolsky, *Kadmos* 15 (1976) 61–76.

"Toumba tou Skourou, Northwest Cyprus," *AJA* 80 (1976) 78.

Review of Boulton-Hawker Films, *Journey into the Past* (1962), R. Garner, *Greece: The Golden Age* (1963) and J. Winter, *Egypt: Land of Antiquity* (1968), in *American Anthropologist* 78 (1976) 128.

Review of M. Lindgren, *The People of Pylos: Prosopographical and Methodological Studies in the Pylos Archives*, Boreas, 3), in *AJP* 97 (1976) 191–194.

1977

"The Bone and Ivory of Toumba tou Skourou," with F. Z. Wolsky, *RDAC* 1977, 80–96.

"Herakles Brings a Tribute," in U. Höckmann and A. Krug, eds., *Festschrift für Frank Brommer* (Mainz 1977) 295–301.

"The Parthenon is Shrinking," *The Atlantic Monthly*, May 1977, 82–85.

"The World of Odysseus," in *Greece and Rome: Builders of Our World*, 2nd edition (The National Geographic Society 1977) 43–73.

Review of J. Chadwick, *The Mycenaean World*, in *AHR* 82 (1977) 338–339.

Review of G. Walberg, *Kamares, A Study of the Character of Palatial Middle Minoan Pottery*, in *CW* 70 (1977) 472.

1978

"It's not a myth—they're immortal; Gallant Red Sox didn't really fail," *The Boston Globe*, October 5, 1978, 17.

"It's Not a Myth—They're Immortal," *Nieman Reports*, Winter 1978, 30.

"New Aegean Relations with Cyprus: The Minoan and Mycenaean Pottery from Toumba tou Skourou, Morphou," with F. Wolsky, *PCPS* 122 (1978) 294–317.

"A Tribute to Millicent Carey McIntosh," *The Bryn Mawr College Alumnae Bulletin*, and *The Annual Report of the President of Bryn Mawr College*.

"Tribute to Millicent Carey McIntosh," reprinted in *The Brearley Bulletin*, Fall 1978, 8ff. (from *Bryn Mawr College Calendar*, December 1977, 31–34).

Contributing author to M. True et al., *CVA*, Museum of Fine Arts, Boston: Attic Black-figured Pelike, Kraters, Dinoi, Hydriai, and Kylikes. Boston 1978.

Review of N. G. L. Hammond, *Migrations and Invasions in Greece and Adjacent Areas*, in *CW* 72 (1978) 45–46.

Review of S. Hiller, *Alt-Ägina*, IV.I: *Mykenische Keramik*, in *AJA* (1978) 118–119.

Review of *Scripta minora 1977–1978 in honorem Einari Gjerstad*, in *ArchNews* 7.3 (1978) 70–71.

1979

Aspects of Death in Early Greek Art and Poetry, Sather Classical Lectures, vol. 46. Berkeley and Los Angeles 1979.

"More Sleeping Furies," in G. Kopcke and M. B. Moore, eds., *Studies in Classical Art and Archaeology: A Tribute to Peter Heinrich von Blanckenhagen* (Locust Valley, N.Y. 1979) 185–188.

"A Painted Mycenaean Coffin," in E. Berger and R. Lullies, eds., *Antike Kunstwerke aus der Sammlung Ludwig*, I: *Frühe Tonsarkophage und Vasen* (Basel 1979) 201–205.

"Small Terracotta Sculptures from Toumba tou Skourou," with F. Z. Wolsky in V. Karageorghis et al., eds., *Studies Presented in Memory of Porphyrios Dikaios* (Nicosia 1979) 53–59.

Review of R.E. Wycherley, *The Stones of Athens*, in *JSAH* 38 (1979) 177.

1980

"The Care and Feeding of the Child in Antiquity," *The Brearley Bulletin*, Fall 1980, 8–17.

Entry (with S. A. Immerwahr) for Mary Hamilton Swindler, in B. Sicherman, C. H. Green, I. Kantrov, and H. Walker, eds., *Notable American Women, The Modern Period: A Biographical Dictionary* (Cambridge, Mass. 1980) 667–669.

"Minoan Relations with Cyprus: The Late Minoan I Pottery from Toumba tou Skourou, Morphou," *Temple University Aegean Symposium* 5 (1980) 22–24.

Review of S. Hood, *The Arts in Prehistoric Greece*, in *JSAH* 39 (1980) 61.

Review of J. Thimme, P. Getz-Preziosi, B. Otto, et al., *Art and Culture of the Cyclades*, in *ArtB* 62 (1980) 483–484.

1981

"Mycenaean Drawing, Amarna, and Egyptian Ostraka," in W. K. Simpson and W. M. Davis, eds., *Studies in Ancient Egypt, the Aegean, and the Sudan, essays in honor of Dows Dunham on the occasion of his 90th birthday, June 1, 1980* (Boston 1981) 193–199.

Review of C. Doumas, ed., *Thera und the Aegean World*, I: *Papers presented at the Second International Scientific Congress, Santorini, Greece, August 1979*, in *AJA* 85 (1981) 93–94.

Review of D. Levi, *Festòs e la civiltà minoica*, I, in *Gnomon* 53 (1981) 41–46.

Review of R. Willetts, *The Civilization of Ancient Crete*, in *AJP* 102 (1981) 109–110.

1982

Mycenaean Pictorial Vase Painting, with V. Karageorghis. Cambridge, Mass. 1982.

"Egyptian Imitations of Aegean Vases," in E. Brovarski, S. K. Doll, and R. E. Freed, eds., *Egypt's Golden Age: The Art of Living in the New Kingdom, 1558–1085 B.C.* (Boston 1982), 152–158.

"Odysseus at Fenway," *The New York Times Sunday Magazine*, September 26, 1982, 48–49, 111–113.

1983

ΕΛΛΑΣ ΕΠΟΧΗ ΤΟΥ ΧΑΛΚΟΥ. T. Zenos, trans. Athens 1983.

"Response to Hans Güterbock" (to "The Hittites and the Aegean World, Part 1: The Ahhiyawa Problem Reconsidered"), *AJA* 87 (1983) 141–143.

Review of J.-C. Courtois, *Alasia 2, Les tombes d'Enkomi: Le mobilier funéraire*, in *AJA* 87 (1983) 110.

1984

"Tyres the Lecher?" in *Studies Presented by Sterling Dow on his Eightieth Birthday* 10 (Durham, N.C. 1984) 301–304.

"The Homeric Brearley," *The Brearley Bulletin*, Spring 1984, 45–48.

1985

ΕΛΛΑΣ ΕΠΟΧΗ ΤΟΥ ΧΑΛΚΟΥ. 2nd printing. Athens 1985.

Review of V. Karageorghis and M. Demas, *Pyla-Kokkinokremos: A Late 13th Century B.C. Fortified Settlement in Cyprus*, in *AJA* 89 (1985) 359–360.

1986

"The Corinth Chariot Krater and Some Relatives," in M. A. Del Chiaro and W. R. Biers, eds., *Corinthiaca: Studies in Honor of Darrell A. Amyx* (Columbia, Mo. 1986) 81–87.

"'Priam's Castle Blazing': A Thousand Years of Trojan Memories," in M. J. Mellink, ed., *Troy and the Trojan War: A Symposium held at Bryn Mawr College, October 1984* (Bryn Mawr 1986) 77–92.

"Richmond Alexander Lattimore (1906–1984)," *The American Philosophical Society Year Book 1985* (Philadelphia 1986) 154–159.

Review of *Aux origines de l'hellénisme. La Crète et la Grèce. Hommage à Henri Van Effenterre*, in *AJA* 90 (1986) 354–355.

Review of B. J. Kemp and R. S. Merrillees, *Minoan Pottery in Second Millennium Egypt*, in *BibO* 43 (1986) cols. 85–87.

Review of F. Canciani, *Bildkunst (Arch Hom, Kap. N, Teil 2.)*, in *Gnomon* 58 (1986) 668–669.

1987

"Baby Aigisthos and the Bronze Age," *PCPS* 33 (1987) 122–152.

"The Key to the Fields: The Classics at Bryn Mawr," in P. H. Labalme, ed., *A Century Recalled: Essays in Honor of Bryn Mawr College* (Bryn Mawr 1987) 163–172.

Review of R. Garland, *The Greek Way of Death*, in *The Classical Outlook* 65 (1987–1988) 34.

1988

"The Afterlife: Greece," in M. Grant and R. Kitzinger, eds., *Civilization of the Ancient Mediterranean: Greece and Rome* vol. II (New York 1988) 987–996.

"A Mycenaean Dead Head?" *RDAC* 1988 (part 1), 299–300.

Contributing author to C. C. Vermeule III, M. B. Comstock, et al., *Sculpture in Stone and Bronze: Additions to the Collections of Greek, Etruscan, and Roman Art 1971–1988*, Boston 1988.

Review of C. Renfrew, et al., *The Archaeology of Cult: The Sanctuary at Phylakopi*, in *AJA* 92 (1988) 293–294.

1989

"Carved Bones from Corinth," in A. Leonard and B. B. Williams, eds., *Essays in Ancient Civilization Presented to Helene J. Kantor*, SAOC 47 (Chicago 1989) 271–286.

1990

Toumba tou Skourou: A Bronze Age Potters' Quarter on Morphou Bay in Cyprus, with F. Z. Wolsky. Boston 1990.

"Why Boston Still Hates the Yankees," Review of D. Shaughnessy, *The Curse of the Bambino*, in *The Boston Globe*, June 14, 1990, 103.

Review of W. Burkert, *Ancient Mystery Cults*, in *AHR* 95 (1990) 140–141.

Review of I. Morris, *Burial and Ancient Society: The Rise of the Greek City-State*, in *AHR* 95 (1990) 793.

1991

"Myth and Tradition from Mycenae to Homer," in D. Buitron-Oliver, ed., *New Perspectives in Early Greek Art* (Symposium Papers 16, National Gallery of Art) (Washington, D.C. 1991) 99–121.

1992

Review of M. Bernal, *Black Athena*, vol. 2, in *The New York Review of Books* 39, no. 6 (March 26, 1992) 40–43; ibid., no. 9 (May 14, 1992) 52–53.

"Aegean Civilizations," with S. Hood in the *Encyclopaedia Britannica*, 1992 printing, vol. 20, 205–218.

1993

"Jefferson and Homer," *PCPS* 137 (1993) 689–703.

Reviews of T. W. Gallant, *Risk and Survival in Ancient Greece. Reconstructing the Rural Domestic Economy*, and of J. Whitley, *Style and Society in Dark Age Greece. The Changing Face of a Pre-literate Society 1100–700 B.C.*, in *CJ* 89 (1993) 215–217.

"Toumba tou Skourou and Its Relationships with Other Sites," in *Abstracts, Archaeological Institute of America* 17 (Washington, D.C., December 27–30, 1993) 23.

Contribution to J. M. Padgett et al., eds., *Vase-Painting in Italy: Red-Figure and Related Works in the Museum of Fine Arts, Boston* (Boston 1993).

TOUMBA TOU SKOUROU:
A BRIEF PERSONAL MEMOIR
OF EMILY VERMEULE IN CYPRUS

✦

MICHAEL W. TAYLOR

In early September the cranes fly south across Cyprus toward Africa. At night comes the first hint of moderation in the fierce heat of the Cypriot summer. On some days, the mountains are starkly clear as the hot weather haze begins to dissipate. It is a time for inward reflection and, on an excavation (still tied—like the armies of old—to summer campaigning), a time for storing and cataloguing, for instructions to winter pot-menders, and for journeys home. As we closed up the excavation at Toumba tou Skourou in September 1973, we had few forebodings that war was about to come to the peaceful environs of Morphou.

However, war did come. I have never returned to Toumba tou Skourou, and I have a deep feeling of nostalgia for that time and place, to which I was brought by Professor Emily Vermeule and the Bronze Age.

From the balcony of the Emporiki Scholi, we had a sense, which still lingers, of being able to see the whole panorama of Cyprus across both space and time. From Paphos to Cape St. Andrew, over the mountains and across the Mesaoria, the peoples of Cyprus came into view: the indigenous Cypriots with their various and fascinating ceramic and metal objects, the emissaries of

Minos, the ostrich egg salesmen, the Mycenaeans, the Near Easterners, the Classical Greeks, the Romans, the Byzantines, the Arabs, the English, the Lusignans, the Venetians, and the Turks. It was a lot to see from the modest second-floor balcony of a cement-block secondary school. The actual physical landscape was imposing enough: to the west, a smudge of sea on the horizon; to the south, the range rising to Mount Olympus; to the northeast, the magnificent Pentadaktuli; and to the east, the Mesaoria across which lay Nicosia. This vision of the people of Cypriot history was provided by Professor Vermeule and, of course, her husband, Cornelius Vermeule. What a rare and great opportunity to sit and talk and walk and work with scholars of their erudition and to learn about Cyprus from the Swedish Expedition to the Cyprus Railway.

And yet, it was the Bronze Age remains in the orange groves north of Morphou which brought us there. It was to these remains, primarily, that the Vermeules applied their erudition; and it was through my participation in these efforts that I came to appreciate Professor Vermeule's scholarly greatness.

Lytton Strachey, in an essay on Macaulay (in *The*

Nation and the Atheneum, 42, January 21, 1928), said that a historian must have three qualities: the capacity for absorbing facts, the capacity for storing them, and a point of view. Archaeology, being history's handmaiden, requires essentially the same qualities in its servants. What then is Emily Vermeule's point of view? It is, I believe, a respect for and a sincere desire to understand the peoples of the Bronze Age. Emily Vermeule is a scholar gifted with the rare insight and ability to understand these peoples of the second millennium B.C., who can seem so alien to the people living in the last years of the second millennium A.C. An archaeologist must have the most profound respect for the people about whom understanding is being sought. It is a respect made up of diligent care, patience, humility, openness, and reverence. The respect with which Professor Vermeule approached Toumba Tou Skourou was more than simply scientific care. It had a spiritual quality. Humility before the ancients is required of an archaeologist. Otherwise, the signs can be missed and the trail can easily be lost. In Cyprus, Professor Vermeule constantly exhibited a profound respect for the peoples of the Bronze Age, coupled with a deep and unique insight into that past, an insight based on learning of an extent seldom seen.

An archaeologist works in modern surroundings with the help of the modern people who live nearby. Again, it was a great education to observe Professor Vermeule's excellent relations with our Cypriot friends and helpers. She showed great respect and affection, especially for the septuagenarians who worked all day in sun and heat which could strike down strong young Americans (but not Mrs. Vermeule).

Some account of the lighter side of the Harvard University–Museum of Fine Arts, Boston, Cyprus Expedition should be given. A partridge in a large cage was obtained for an alarm clock, but it tended to call in the middle of the night. The Vermeule children, Blakey and Adrian, were underfoot and about to our constant entertainment. Marvelous beef steak, found at great effort and cost and meant for the grille to alleviate a surfeit of olive oil was . . . deep-fried in olive oil. We snorkeled in view of the Neolithic Petra tou Liminiti and walked upon Vouni.

Our best times were those spent with Cypriot friends. Our Maronite coworkers provided us with many afternoons of wonderful hospitality at Karphashia, as did the people from many of the surrounding villages who worked with us. I remember Morphou's dear postman decrying the extravagance of a village wedding at Kyra where we were all roundly enjoying ourselves amidst boards on trestles groaning with food and drink and crowds dancing to the music. "In England, they have a little champagne and cake," he sniffed. Kyria Polyxene received great respect from Mrs. Vermeule and provided spiritual guidance at tomb openings. One tiny woman delighted in telling about derailing a British train single-handedly during the Cypriot revolt against the British. Old Mr. Kostas, far into his seventies, continued to dig in the 110° heat, stopping only to recount his experiences as a British artillery mule-driver on the Salonika front in World War I. An afternoon's visit to Mr. Stephanou's front porch in Loutros made us understand something about his spirit of calm, as we looked from that mountain height far out across the Mediterranean Sea. With each Cypriot, Professor Vermeule had a deep and sympathetic relationship from which the whole technical staff of the excavation benefited.

I have to say also that my memories of Cyprus arouse deep anger in me. I am grateful that Emily Vermeule had the courage to speak out and voice the outrage which many should have felt and expressed. How my heart was pained by her letter published in the *New York Times* on October 8, 1974:

> The State Department has informed us that the Harvard University Cyprus Expedition's antiquities in Morphou, toward the western end of the Turkish front in Cyprus, have been totally plundered and the works of art and scientific records irretrievably scattered. While the looting at Morphou was not, apparently, accompanied by murder of the custodians, as at other licensed excavation headquarters, the Turkish Army has occupied the premises, and the sixty-odd employees of the Harvard excavations are under village arrest. . . .

I believe that God is just, and I am sure that the people of ancient Cyprus, could they speak, would warn that impiety before ancient altars, such as the carnage wrought in 1974, brings a certain harvest of ruin. And so, it was given to me to understand, more fully than I wished, why Cyprus is called the Island of Bitter Lemons:

Better leave the rest unsaid,
Beauty, darkness, vehemence
Let the old sea nurses keep
Their memorials of sleep
And the Greek sea's curly head
Keep its calms like tears unshed
Keep its calms like tears unshed.
(from "Bitter Lemons," Lawrence Durrell)

PART I

HOMER AND THE BRONZE AGE: MEMORY AND ARCHAEOLOGY

I

THE BRONZE AGE CONTEXT OF HOMER

✦

SINCLAIR HOOD

The aim of this paper is to suggest that the core of Homer, and the Trojan War, if there was one, are best placed in LH IIIC. On this view the Troy of an Achaian sack must be Troy VII, and perhaps Troy VIIb 2 rather than Troy VIIa. The end of Troy VIIb 2 was set by Blegen in the region of c. 1100 B.C. A sack of Troy then on this estimate would fall towards the middle of the scatter of ancient "guesses" for its date which, as Walter Burkert shows (pp. 139ff.), range over a period of more than 400 years from 1334 B.C. to 910 B.C. Whether or not there was an Achaian sack of Troy cannot be proved one way or the other on existing evidence.[1] But the question remains: if there was no basis in fact for the story of the Trojan War, why select Troy as the scene for it?

Assuming an Achaian sack of Troy, when did this occur? Troy II, originally favored by Schliemann, is no longer acceptable. Troy VIIa, which Blegen urged as a candidate, is now widely rejected. Blegen claimed that Troy VIIa was destroyed in LH IIIB, but it seems agreed that the latest Mycenaean pottery from levels of Troy VIIa belongs to the following period, LH IIIC, if not to an advanced phase of it.[2] The Bronze Age palace at Pylos, which Blegen assumed to be that of Nestor,

was destroyed in LH IIIB before the end of Troy VIIIa. Popham has indeed argued that the destruction took place back in the early phase of LH IIIB, LH IIIB 1.[3] I am not convinced of this, but the LH IIIC and later, Early Iron Age, pottery found in the area of the palace at Pylos must surely be assigned to a subsequent reoccupation of the site as Popham claims.

Troy VI, which was Dörpfeld's city of the Achaian sack, is coming back into favor as a candidate.[4] But there is strong evidence that Troy VI ended with a destruction by earthquake as Blegen supposed.[5] It is always possible, however, that an earthquake which shook the defenses facilitated a sack by enemies. But there are other difficulties in the way of making the last stage of Troy VI, Troy VIh, the city of the Homeric sack.

One major difficulty is the picture which is beginning to emerge from Hittite records of events in western Anatolia between the fifteenth and thirteenth centuries B.C. in LH IIIA–B. In particular there is the light that is being thrown on relations during this period from the fifteenth century onwards between the Hittites themselves and Ahhiya or Ahhiyawa, which it seems increasingly difficult to avoid identifying with a Mycenaean state or states, the territory of the Achaioi.[6] Possible Hittite-Mycenaean connections are also reflected in the archaeological record. There is the picture of a warrior, armed like a Mycenaean, incised on the inside of a shallow bowl found at the Hittite capital, Boğazköy, to which Emily Vermeule has drawn attention.[7] The bowl is of local Hittite ware, but Bittel has emphasized the probability that the engraving was by a foreign hand, which might of course have been Mycenaean. There is little evidence, however, for commercial links between Hittites and Mycenaeans. A good deal of Mycenaean pottery has been found in Anatolia, but little if any of it is from the heartland of the Hittite empire,[8] and relatively few Hittite objects seem to have reached Greece.[9] Nevertheless the scenario in Anatolia during this part of the Late Bronze Age, when the Hittite empire flourished, does not appear to be one into which it is easy to fit an Achaian sack of Troy.[10] Nor does Homer seem to reflect the world of the literate bureaucracies of Mycenaean Greece in LH IIIB.

There are two ways of dealing with this problem. One is to assume that the Trojan War and the core of Homer belong to a period before the rise of the literate bureaucracies in Greece in LH IIIA–B, and before the time of the Hittite records which refer to dealings with Ahhiyawa. The alternative, which I am advocating, is to place them in LH IIIC, after the fall of the Mycenaean bureaucracies and after the disappearance of the Hittites from the scene in Anatolia.

There are certainly strong arguments for thinking that substantial elements in Homer date from as early as the time of the Mycenae Shaft Graves. This view also has the merit of being in accordance with the ideas of Schliemann, who believed that in the Shaft Graves he had gazed upon the face of Agamemnon and found treasures of the king described in Homer. A date in the time of the Shaft Graves or in the period immediately following for the earliest elements in Homer is now being advocated by many of those who are sensitive to the difficulty of reconciling Homer with the age of the literate bureaucracies on the Greek mainland.[11] Emily Vermeule has suggested the possibility that a destruction at Troy c. 1400 B.C., early in the Late Phase of Troy VI, when LH II–IIIA I pottery was being imported there, might be that which lies behind the story of the Trojan War.[12]

The difficulty it seems to me with assigning important elements of Homer, including the tradition of a Trojan War, to a period as early as that of the Shaft Graves and their immediate aftermath, is the long gap in time between then and the date of composition of the *Iliad* in the eighth or, if Oliver Taplin is right, early in the seventh century B.C.[13] It is hard to see how traditions about a Trojan War as early as this could have survived through the centuries of the literate bureaucracies without being "contaminated" by them and retaining some distinct memories of them. I would therefore like to urge the merits of the alternative: that the core of Homer dates from LH IIIC, after the fall of the Mycenaean bureaucracies, and that, if there was an Achaian sack of Troy, it must have taken place during this period.

The *Iliad* is set in an age of bronze weapons before the appearance of Dorian Argos and Sparta. The only possible hint of the existence of literate bureaucracies in Greece is in the story of Bellerophon, and that is set in the past. In Anatolia there are Phrygians, but no Hittites, unless the Amazons, against whom Priam fought in his youth as an ally of the Phrygians, are a garbled memory of them.[14]

There has been a tendency to dismiss the idea of an Achaian sack of Troy in LH IIIC as impossible or even inconceivable.[15] The reasons for this are not altogether clear, although one seems to have been the apparent material poverty of LH IIIC Greece. But this appearance of poverty may be deceptive. A degree of austerity in the material sphere was in any case often linked with prowess in war in early times. There are hints of an improvement in the weaponry in use in the Aegean in LH IIIC. I can see nothing in the material background of the LH IIIC period in Greece incompatible with the existence of a loose federation of Achaians for some martial enterprise of the kind described in the *Iliad*. The formation of local pottery styles in LH IIIC, contrasting with the relative uniformity which prevailed in LH IIIB, is not in itself an argument against the possible existence of such a federation. It is hardly necessary to emphasize that warlike operations on such a scale would not require literate bureaucracies to initiate them.

A more serious reason for rejecting the idea of a Trojan War then is the widely held belief that the destruction of the Mycenaean palaces at the end of LH IIIB, with the consequent disappearance of the bureaucracies and their writing systems, must have been the work of the Dorians. The changes in Greece at this time were certainly dramatic and radical. There was evidently a complete overthrow of the previous social order. But it is not necessary to invoke Dorians to account for the changes. Other explanations for them are to hand, in various combinations: non-Dorian invaders, ephemeral raiders, self-destructive warfare between the Mycenaean states, civil uprisings, earthquakes, famine, systems collapse.[16] The Dorian hypothesis is difficult to reconcile with later Greek traditions about them, such as they are, and the chronology which they suggest; it also seems hard to make the archaeological evidence fit with it.

The picture of a feeble and impoverished Greek world in LH IIIC stands in need of some revision.[17] Kilian has drawn attention to the dramatic increase in size of the settlement at Tiryns during this period. Admittedly, however, this was balanced by a marked drop in the number of occupied sites in the rest of the Argolid.[18] No important palaces, and no rich burials of the time, have been identified. The royal or princely burials, and those with luxurious imports connected with them, at Lefkandi in Euboea date from the following Protogeometric period. But the comparable royal burials in the more or less contemporary Greek cemetery at Kourion in Cyprus show that they were not unique.[19] The discovery of royal burials of a similar character dating from LH IIIC somewhere in Greece remains a possibility for the future.

James Muhly has stressed the vigor and enterprise which led to the creation of a new world order during this period on the eve of the Early Iron Age in the eastern Mediterranean. One visible sign of this in Greece is the emergence in the Argolid of the remarkable Close Style of vase decoration. The quality of this has always been appreciated by discriminating judges like Arne Furumark, Fritz Schachermeyr, and Emily Vermeule.[20] Furumark indeed named it "the Palace Style of Agamemnon."[21]

I am suggesting that the core of the Homeric poems, and more especially that of the *Iliad,* may reflect the situation in Greece in LH IIIC.[22] Some elements in the poems could hardly be later: the use of bronze weapons, the boar's-tusk helmet described in the Doloneia, and perhaps the corslet which Kinyras of Cyprus gave to

Agamemnon and which Catling has suggested may have been of scale armor.[23] But many elements in the poems clearly date from periods after LH IIIC, while some may well be earlier. There is evidently a degree of stratification in the objects and also in the customs described.[24]

The best candidates in the poems for objects which may have been obsolete by LH IIIC appear to be the boar's-tusk helmet of the Doloneia, large body-covering shields, and silver-studded swords. The silver-studded swords may refer to bronze weapons with silver-capped rivets as found in earlier Mycenaean times. But ancient weapons decorated with gold or silver might well have been treasured and preserved into LH IIIC; in any case the technique of making silver-capped rivets is found in later times and may have survived through the Dark Age.[25]

Large body-covering shields are widely documented in the *Iliad.*[26] The use of smaller round shields is attested in the Aegean in LH IIIC and well back in LH IIIB or earlier.[27] Such shields combined with body armor may have been considered suitable for chariot warfare. But the existence of round shields does not preclude the continued use of the earlier body-covering shields.[28] There is likely to have been some degree of overlap, and older fashions of armament may have survived in some areas or among certain groups of warriors. Differences in armament described in the *Iliad* might even to some extent at least reflect the realities of warfare in the Aegean in LH IIIC.

In the case of the Doloneia helmet there is no doubt that what is described is one adorned with boar's tusks like those found in Greece during the Bronze Age from the time of the Mycenae Shaft Graves or earlier.[29] It has been claimed that such helmets went out of use before the end of LH IIIB, and none of the representations of them, in wall-paintings or carved in ivory, can certainly be dated later. But the actual remains of a boar's-tusk helmet were found with the burial of a warrior assignable to LH IIIC in a chamber tomb at Kallithea in Achaia.[30] Such helmets may have been obsolescent, however, by LH IIIC, and it is perhaps no accident that only one is mentioned in the *Iliad,* and that it has a long and curious pedigree attached to it, beginning with a break-in in Boiotia: Autolycus, who stole it there, gave it to Amphidamas of Kythera, and he presented it to the father of Meriones, who had it at Troy. This helmet was therefore already old when Meriones offered it to Odysseus.

It can be argued that descriptions of palaces in Homer indicate a knowledge or memory of Mycenaean ones destroyed at the end of LH IIIB. When buildings of a size and character that might qualify them to be called palaces or rulers' houses are recognizable again in Greece they are of a different type, basically long halls which may have an apse at one end opposite the entrance. The long Megaron Hall inside the acropolis above the early Greek town at Emporio in Chios appears to have been the home of the local ruler.[31] The magnificent apsidal building with royal or princely burials below the floor at Lefkandi, even if it was not the actual house of a ruler, seems likely to represent what such a house in that area at the time was like.[32]

The plans of palaces suggested by the accounts in Homer are not similar to these, and they are in some ways reminiscent of the Mycenaean palaces of LH IIIA–B. But certain key elements of these Mycenaean palaces are lacking from the Homeric accounts. There is no hint of the paintings which adorned their walls, and nothing to suggest the existence of literate bureaucracies. Indeed the whole way of life in Homeric palaces, so vividly described in the *Odyssey,* seems alien to what it is reasonable to imagine it was like in the LH IIIA–B palaces of Mycenae, Tiryns, and Pylos.[33]

There is some evidence that buildings of earlier Mycenaean types continued in existence together with long houses in Greece after the destruction of the palaces at the end of LH IIIB. While the Megaron Hall at Emporio was a long house, buildings which seem to reflect both the earlier Mycenaean and the new long house traditions coexisted in the town below it.[34] It is always possible that in some areas of Greece existing Mycenaean houses and even small palaces survived the destructions at the end of LH IIIB and were adapted by new owners for their use.

While there are elements in the Homeric poems, such as the boar's-tusk helmet, which can hardly be regarded as later than LH IIIC, only vague and garbled memories of LH IIIA–B appear to survive in them. Among such memories may be the description of massed chariot warfare contrasting with the taxilike use of chariots standard in the *Iliad.*[35] This is appropriately being organized and praised by Nestor as something from the past. There

are also a few genealogies and legends which appear to refer back to earlier times.

Troy VI, or even the rather bedraggled Troy VIIa, may seem at first sight worthier of an Achaian sack than Troy VIIb. Troy VIIb has indeed had a thoroughly bad press. This is partly at any rate the fault of the barbaric-looking Coarse Ware and Knobbed Ware (Buckelkeramik) used by some of the inhabitants. The descriptions of what has been revealed of Troy VIIb by excavation, however, suggest that it was in fact no mean city. The area of houses within the citadel defense walls appears to have been if anything marginally greater than it was in the time of Troy VI or Troy VIIa. But it seems doubtful whether the settlement of Troy VIIb extended beyond the citadel as that of Troy VI did.

Dörpfeld regarded the settlement of Troy VIIb (his VII.2) as merely a large unwalled "Dorf"; but his own plans contradict the idea that it was unwalled, and Blegen had no doubt that it was fortified.[36] It is worth noting that Dörpfeld observed, and Blegen agreed, that some of the buildings of Troy VIIb were larger and more complex than any of those of previous Trojan settlements: with many rooms linked by doors, and perhaps with open courts.[37] There is even some evidence for the use of gold and ivory in Troy VIIb, in the shape of a scrap of gold leaf and a piece of ivory, perhaps an inlay, from House 768.[38] In this respect, for what it is worth, Troy VIIb can hold its own. No gold, and only two bits of ivory, were recovered from Troy VIIa; while a mere speck of gold, a solitary pin of silver or electrum, but some ten or more objects of ivory, are certainly attributable to the later levels of Troy VI.[39]

Dörpfeld and Blegen both emphasized that Troy VIIb did not end with a general conflagration. On the other hand, Blegen identified many traces of a great conflagration responsible for the destruction of Troy VIIa. Dörpfeld does not appear to comment on a conflagration which brought Troy VIIa to an end, but he refers to sporadic traces of destruction by fire in levels of Troy VIIb.[40] Blegen's admirably detailed accounts of his excavations also describe some buildings of Troy VIIb with evidence of fire destruction in them.[41] In House 768 for instance Blegen noted a destruction by fire during his final phase of Troy VIIb, VIIb 2, followed by a reoccupation within the same VIIb 2 period.[42]

The core of Homer and an Achaian sack of Troy, if

there was one, can hardly be later than LH IIIC. A date for them in LH IIIC, however, seems to have many advantages. The span of time until the composition of the *Iliad* in the eighth or early seventh century is narrowed to three or four centuries. Various elements in the Homeric poems are drawn closer together. Hope Simpson and Lazenby have argued that the Catalogue of Ships reflects the state of settlement in Greece in LH IIIC.[43] Their methods have been criticized, and the archaeological evidence on which they rely is often ambiguous, but I feel that they may be right in their main conclusion. The Catalogue of Ships and the Trojan Catalogue offer maps of Greece and of the area round Troy that seem more credible in LH IIIC than earlier or later.

The Trojans of Homer are said by Kirk to appear as "a prosperous horse-breeding people surprisingly like the Achaeans in most of their customs."[44] This is not surprising, however, in the context of Troy VIIb 2. The makers of the Knobbed Ware, who formed a large and perhaps dominant section of the population of Troy VIIb 2, are now widely thought to have been Thracians, or people of some other nation bordering on the Greeks like the Illyrians.[45] Both the Thracians and the Illyrians were much involved with the Greeks during the Dark Age, and were evidently close to them in manners and customs. The closest relatives for Knobbed Ware lie in the area of the Balkans immediately west of Troy, and Troy itself appears to have been a solitary bastion of this distinctive style of pottery beyond the Dardanelles.

There are ambiguities about Troy VIIb, and I am not entirely certain that Blegen was right in claiming that Knobbed Ware was confined to Troy VIIb 2.[46] In any case, the Coarse Ware of Troy VIIb 1 seems to be related to Knobbed Ware, and was found in Troy VIIb 2 along with it. Coarse Ware, like Knobbed Ware, appears to me at least to be intrusive, reflecting the presence of a new, and perhaps dominant, element in the Trojan population in the time of Troy VIIb 1.

The date estimated by Blegen for the end of Troy VIIb 2, c. 1100 B.C., falls in the middle of Mycenaean IIIC 1c on the system of Furumark. But the dates for Troy VIIa and Troy VIIb are now being drastically lowered, and that for the end of Troy VIIb 2 is altogether in the melting pot. The dating for different phases of Troy VII depends at present upon an assessment of im-

ported Mycenaean pottery and local imitations of it. Bloedow has made a careful survey of this based upon the expert opinion of Elizabeth French.[47] He places the whole of Troy VIIa in the early part of LH IIIC, making Troy VIIb 1 coeval with the later part of that period. In the opinion of Elizabeth French only one sherd recovered by Blegen from Troy VIIa was a possible Mycenaean import of contemporary manufacture, and no contemporary Mycenaean imports came from levels of Troy VIIb. Contemporary Mycenaean-style sherds from Troy VIIb were all local imitations. Such local imitations, as Bloedow stresses, may well reflect earlier fashions.

From the Mycenaean-style pottery so far recovered it therefore seems hardly possible to assign dates for the various phases of Troy VII except within very wide limits. Hertel and Podzuweit argue that Troy VIIb actually lasted until the time of the foundation of the Greek colony (Troy VIII) as Schliemann believed.[48] Podzuweit in fact places the last phase of Troy VI well inside LH IIIC between c. 1150 and 1100 B.C., with Troy VIIa covering the latest part of LH IIIC and lasting through Submycenaean into Protogeometric, making the whole of Troy VIIb parallel with Protogeometric. The Protogeometric sherd to which he draws attention, however, appears to have been out of context in a level of Troy VIIb 1 along with other sherds attributable to Troy VIII.[49] The rest of the Early Iron Age pottery to which he refers came from deposits of Troy VIIb 1 and 2 and was Middle and Late Geometric, according to Blegen.[50] It seems reasonable to make allowances for unrecognized disturbances and to regard these sherds as intrusive.

The Greek colony, however, appears to have been founded considerably earlier than Blegen assumed. Hertel suggests a date for its foundation c. 950 B.C. on the basis of sherds from the old excavations which he has identified as Protogeometric. Like Podzuweit he argues that Troy VIIb lasted until the time of the foundation of the Greek colony without any gap in time between them. But he emphasizes that there is no safe evidence for Protogeometric imports in levels of Troy VIIb.

Hertel's arguments are impressive, and he may well be right. If he is right, it would give the whole of Troy VII a span of 200 years or more, allowing some sixty or seventy years for each of the three phases. This seems not impossible, although in such a turbulent period as the Dark Age the phases might be expected to be rather shorter in duration. Blegen only identified three building levels, one in each phase of Troy VII, with very few instances of successive floors or surfaces within them. In two houses of Troy VIIa he noted two successive floors, and in one as many as three. He considered that Troy VIIa had "a relatively short existence" with a span "within a century or less, possibly within a generation of men." [51] Blegen allowed Troy VIIa a life of only thirty-five years, from 1275–1240 B.C.; but this short life was partly dictated by the need to end Troy VIIa, Homer's Troy for him, before the destruction of the "Palace of Nestor" at Pylos at the end of LH IIIB dated by Furumark c. 1230 B.C.

Blegen estimated that Troy VIIb 1 covered "at least one generation." Only one occupation level seems to have been observed in deposits of Troy VIIb 1. Troy VIIb 2 similarly appears to have consisted of a single occupation level, apart from two successive floors in Square J-K 5. Blegen thought that "as a pure guess a duration of at least two or three generations might perhaps safely be postulated" for Troy VIIb 2.[52] It is not altogether clear, however, why Troy VIIb 2 should be allotted a longer span than Troy VIIa or Troy VIIb 1.

Blegen considered that Troy VIIa began c. 1275 B.C., and that Troy VIIb 2 might have come to an end around 1100 B.C. This gave the whole of Troy VII a span of about 175 years, of which the two phases of Troy VIIb accounted for some 140 years between them. The more recent estimate by Bloedow assigns about forty years to each of the three phases of Troy VII, a span of 120 years in all from c. 1170–1050 B.C.[53] This more or less coincides with the period of time c. 1185/1180–1065 B.C. allotted by Warren and Hankey to LH IIIC.[54]

Bloedow places all of Troy VIIa within the earlier part of LH IIIC. This may well prove to be right. For the moment, however, I am tempted to opt for the view originally proposed by Furumark, that Troy VIIa began within LH IIIB and came to an end early in LH IIIC.[55] On this view, allowing a span of 120 years for the whole of Troy VII as Bloedow does, the end of Troy VIIb 2 might fall some time during the latter part of LH IIIC. But all this is extremely speculative pending the results of further research into the evidence from the old excavations and new discoveries from those which Korfmann is now directing at Troy itself and in its environs.[56]

It seems to me that the core of Homer, including the story of the Trojan War, is likely to go back to LH IIIC and not earlier. I can see no reason why a major Greek expedition against Troy, like that described in the *Iliad,* should not have taken place then. If there was an Achaian sack of Troy, I would provisionally opt for Troy VIIb 2 as the best candidate for it.

SUMMARY

The core of the Homeric poems, and more especially that of the *Iliad,* appears to reflect the Mycenaean world as it was in the final stage of the Late Bronze Age in LH IIIC. Only vague and garbled memories of the literate bureaucracies of Greece and of the Hittite empire in Anatolia survive in them. This makes it hard to accept that elements in the poems go back to LH II–IIIA or earlier. None of the material objects described by Homer need be dated before the end of LH IIIB. Boar's-tusk helmets seem to have been still in use, even if obsolescent, in LH IIIC. The Catalogue of Ships and the Trojan Catalogue may date from that time. There seems no reason why an allied Greek expedition against Troy might not have been organized in LH IIIC. If there was an Achaian sack, the best candidate for the moment seems to be Troy VIIb 2. The makers of Knobbed Ware dominant in Troy VIIb 2 were apparently Thracians or some other people close to the Greeks in manners and customs. But there are great uncertainties about the dating of the phases of Troy VII, and Troy VIIb 2 may have lasted until the foundation of the Greek colony (Troy VIII) in the tenth century B.C.

I am deeply grateful to Professor Sarah Morris for many valuable references.

NOTES

1. M. I. Finley, "Schliemann's Troy: One Hundred Years After," *ProcBritAc* 60 (1974) 393–412. But ten years earlier Finley himself had speculated about the possibility of Achaian

participation in a sack of Troy VIIa (M. I. Finley, "The Trojan War," *JHS* 84 [1964] 6). Cf. M. J. Mellink, "Postscript," in M. J. Mellink, ed., *Troy and the Trojan War* (Bryn Mawr 1986) 100, for a similar suggestion, but adding a major attack before that early in LH IIIB.

2. A. Furumark was the first to draw attention to the presence of LH IIIC sherds in Troy VIIa, as recorded by C. Nylander, "The Fall of Troy," *Antiquity* 37 (1963) 6–11. Cf. C. B. Mee, "The Mycenaeans and Troy," in L. Foxhall and J. K. Davies, eds., *The Trojan War: Its Historicity and Context*, Papers of the First Greenbank Colloquium, Liverpool, 1981 (Bristol 1984) 45–56; M. Wood, *In Search of the Trojan War* (London 1985) 224; E. F. Bloedow, "The Trojan War and Late Helladic IIIC," *PZ* 63 (1988) 23–52, with comments on the pottery by Elizabeth French.

3. M. R. Popham, "Pylos: Reflections on the Date of its Destruction and on its Iron Age Reoccupation," *OJA* 10 (1991) 315–324.

4. Nylander (supra n. 2) citing Schachermeyr had urged this in 1963.

5. G. Rapp, "Earthquakes in the Troad," in G. Rapp and J. A. Gifford, eds., *Troy Supplementary Monograph 4. The Archaeological Geology* (Princeton 1982) 43–58.

6. See H. G. Güterbock, "The Hittites and the Aegean World: 1. The Ahhiyawa Problem Reconsidered," and comments by M. J. Mellink, *AJA* 87 (1983) 133–141.

7. K. Bittel, "Tonschale mit Ritzzeichnung von Boğazköy," *RA* 1976, 9–14.

8. C. B. Mee, "Aegean Trade and Settlement in Anatolia in the Second Millennium BC," *AnatStud* 28 (1978) 121–155. Mycenaean pottery from Maşat northeast of Boğazköy is discussed by Bloedow (supra n. 2) 40–41, fig. 2.

9. E. Cline, "Hittite Objects in the Bronze Age Aegean," *AnatStud* 41 (1991) 133–143.

10. Cf. J. D. Muhly, "The Crisis Years in the Mediterranean World: Transition or Cultural Disintegration?", in W. A. Ward and M. S. Joukowsky, *The Crisis Years: the 12th Century B.C. From Beyond the Danube to the Tigris* (Dubuque, Iowa 1992) 10–26.

11. E. T. Vermeule, "Response to Hans Güterbock," *AJA* 87 (1983) 141–143. S. P. Morris, "A Tale of Two Cities: the Miniature Frescoes from Thera and the Origins of Greek Poetry," *AJA* 93 (1989) 511–535.

12. E. T. Vermeule, " 'Priams's Castle Blazing': A Thousand Years of Trojan Memories," in Mellink, ed. (supra n. 1) 77–92, esp. 90–91.

13. O. Taplin, *Homeric Soundings: The Shaping of the Iliad* (Oxford 1992) 33–35. At the other end of the scale, B. B. Powell, *Homer and the Origin of the Greek Alphabet* (Cam-

bridge 1991), has argued a date for the composition of the *Iliad* and the *Odyssey* at the beginning of the eighth century on the attractive but unlikely assumption that writing was developed in Greece for the purpose of recording the poems.

14. *Iliad* 3.184–190.

15. E.g., V. Desborough, *The Last Mycenaeans and their Successors* (Oxford 1964) 164, accepts Blegen's arguments for Troy VIIa. Cf. S. Hiller, "Two Trojan Wars? On the Destructions of Troy VIh and VIIa," *Studia Troica* 1 (1991) 152.

16. My own views are outlined in S. Hood, "Mycenaean Settlement in Cyprus and the Coming of the Greeks," in V. Karageorghis, ed., *Acts of the International Archaeological Symposium, "The Mycenaeans in the Eastern Mediterranean"* (Nicosia 1973) 40–50.

17. As forcefully urged by Muhly (supra n. 10).

18. K. Kilian, "Zum Ende der mykenischen Epoche in der Argolis," *JRGZM* 27 (1980) 166–195, esp. 171–172, fig. 2. Cf. K. Kilian, "Neue historische Aspekte des Spätmykenischen. Ergebnisse der Grabungen in Tiryns," *Jahrbuch der Heidelberger Akademie der Wissenschaften* 1981, 76–83.

19. *AR* 1988–1989, 117–129 for Lefkandi. G. H. McFadden, "A Late Cypriote III Tomb from Kourion, Kaloriziki No. 40," *AJA* 58 (1954) 131–142, where both burials appear to have been cremated.

20. E. Vermeule, *Greece in the Bronze Age* (Chicago and London 1964) 206–210.

21. *MP* 573. Cf. A. Furumark, "The Mycenaean IIIC pottery and its relation to Cypriote fabrics," *OpArch* 3 (1944) 263.

22. Cf. O. T. P. K. Dickinson, "Homer, the Poet of the Dark Age," *GaR* 33 (1986) 20–37, for a wide-ranging discussion which reaches similar conclusions.

23. H. W. Catling, "A Bronze Plate from a Scale-Corslet found at Mycenae," *AA* 1970, 441–449, esp. 448. It is interesting that the piece found at Mycenae came from a good LH IIIC context.

24. E. S. Sherratt, " 'Reading the texts': archaeology and the Homeric question," *Antiquity* 64 (1990) 807–824, in a comprehensive study has emphasized this stratigraphy in every aspect of the Homeric poems, suggesting that the earliest elements may go back to the sixteenth century B.C.

25. Dickinson (supra n. 22) 27–28. Vermeule (supra n. 20) 225–227 reasonably suggests that the magnificent gold sceptre from the Protogeometric royal tomb at Kourion in Cyprus (see McFadden [supra n. 19]) must have been treasured above ground for a good many generations before it was placed with the burials.

26. H. L. Lorimer, *Homer and the Monuments* (London 1950) 132–188, 245. D. L. Page, *History and the Homeric Iliad* (Berkeley and Los Angeles 1959) 232–235. H. Borch-

hardt, *Kriegswesen, ArchHom I.E* (Göttingen 1977) 1–56, with an exhaustive treatment of shields of all kinds.

27. Lorimer (supra n. 26) 153 thought that after 1300 or even 1350 B.C. body-covering shields no longer figured in any serious fighting even in the Aegean. But the Delos ivory (Borchhardt [supra n. 26] E 11, E 8, fig. 2) showing a warrior with boar's-tusk helmet and large figure-of-eight body-covering shield appears to date from LH IIIB, and, if of Cypriot origin as has been suggested, might be even later. Assuming, however, that the warrior is a god, he might well retain obsolete fashions in armament.

28. Cf. Dickinson (supra n. 22) 28.

29. *Iliad* 10.261–271. Lorimer (supra n. 26) 212–219. Page (supra n. 26) 218–219. J. Borchhardt, *ArchHom* I.E, E 62 and distribution map on E 64.

30. N. Yalouris, "Mykenische Bronzeschutzwaffen," *Ath-Mitt* 75 (1960) 42–48, esp. 44–45, 48. Cf. Sherratt (supra n. 24) 818, and Catling, below, p. 129.

31. J. Boardman, *Greek Emporio* (London 1967) 5, 31–34, fig. 16.

32. *AR* 1988–1989, 129, fig. 28. See also M. R. Popham, P. G. Calligas, and L. H. Sackett, *Lefkandi* II.2: *The Protogeometric Building at Toumba* (London 1992).

33. Cf. Dickinson (supra n. 22) 29–30.

34. Boardman (supra n. 31) 34–37.

35. *Iliad* 4.292–309. Lorimer (supra n. 26) 324–325.

36. W. Dörpfeld, *Troja und Ilion* I (Athens 1902) 198; but the plan (p. 195, fig. 75) shows what appears to be a stretch of defense wall assignable to his Troy VII.2. C. W. Blegen, *Troy* IV (Princeton 1958) 140–141; cf. p. 182 for repair of the old defense wall of Troy VI.

37. Blegen (supra n. 36) 140–142. Dörpfeld (supra n. 36) 194.

38. Blegen (supra n. 36) 205.

39. C. W. Blegen, *Troy* III (Princeton 1953) 22, table 2, 297, fig. 297: no. 34–380 (pin); no. 29–30: table 5 (ivory).

40. Dörpfeld (supra n. 36) 199. Hertel (infra n. 48) 140 states that Troy VIIb2 ended with a burnt destruction, but it is not entirely clear whether this is based on new evidence or not.

41. Blegen (supra n. 36) 192 (House 771), 204 (House 768).

42. Blegen (supra n. 36) 204–205.

43. R. Hope Simpson and J. F. Lazenby, *The Catalogue of Ships in Homer's Iliad* (Oxford, 1970).

44. G. S. Kirk, *CAH*³ II.2, 834.

45. G. S. Kirk, *The Iliad: A Commentary* II (Cambridge 1990) 45 for Thracians. M. L. West, "The Rise of the Greek Epic," *JHS* 108 (1988) 151–172, suggests that the people responsible for the "much derided Knobbed Ware" were an Illyrian group known as Dardanoi. He notes that Homer constantly speaks of Dardanoi and Troes, indicating a mixed population, and that Priam is called Dardanid.

46. S. Hood, "Buckelkeramik at Mycenae?" in W. C. Brice, ed., *Europa: Studien zur Geschichte und Epigraphik der frühen Aegaeis. Festschrift für Ernst Grumach* (Berlin 1967) 124.

47. Bloedow (supra n. 2).

48. D. Hertel, "Schliemanns These vom Fortleben Troias in den 'Dark Ages' im Lichte neuer Forschungsergebnisse," *Studia Troica* I (1991) 131–144. C. Podzuweit, "Die mykenische Welt und Troja," in B. Hänsel, ed., *Südosteuropa zwischen 1600 und 1000 v. Chr.*, Prähistorische Archäologie in Südosteuropa I (Berlin 1982) 65–88.

49. Blegen (supra n. 36) 233, fig. 278 no. 26. Podzuweit (supra n. 48) 81.

50. Blegen (supra n. 36) 181, 228, fig. 277 nos. 14, 15; 233, 235, fig. 279 nos. 19–23.

51. Blegen (supra n. 36) 8.

52. Blegen (supra n. 36) 142.

53. Bloedow (supra n. 2). Cf. E. F. Bloedow, "Handmade Burnished Ware or 'Barbarian' pottery and Troy VIIB," *PP* 40 (1985) 187.

54. P. Warren and V. Hankey, *Aegean Bronze Age Chronology* (Bristol 1989) 169.

55. Nylander (supra n. 2).

56. The excavations in the area of Beşik bay have a special interest. This is likely to have been the scene of an Achaian camp as Korfmann claims. But the cemetery of the period of Troy VI identified here seems to belong to an ordinary settlement of that time. Korfmann has found evidence for occupation by the natural harbor which existed at Beşik bay during other periods of the Bronze Age and earlier.

2

HOMER, LYCIA, AND LUKKA

◆

MACHTELD J. MELLINK

Homer, if we may with Emily Vermeule's blessing refer to the creator of the *Iliad* by this name, has a somewhat remote but confident knowledge of Lycia and Lycians. The Lycians are the leading allies of the Trojans. In battle Hektor shouts loud encouragement to the Trojans, Lycians, and Dardanians, in metrical order but with equal emphasis; in a crisis Helenos refers to the toil of Trojans and Lycians (*Iliad* 6.78). The Lycians came from faraway Lycia, from the banks of the eddying Xanthos, led by Sarpedon and Glaukos, who enjoyed wealth, rank, and godlike respect, and owned domains with orchards and fields in the Xanthos valley (*Iliad* 12.310–314). As a ruler, Sarpedon protected Lycia by his judgment and strength (*Iliad* 16.542).

The Lycian dynasty, according to the *Iliad,* had Achaian affiliations. The story of Glaukos (*Iliad* 6.150–211) traces the male line directly back to Sisyphos, king of Ephyra, whose grandson Bellerophon incurred the wrath of Proitos of Argos and his wife, a daughter of the Lycian king. Proitos sent Bellerophon to his father-in-law with a long written message (*Iliad* 6.168–169) intended as a death sentence, but Bellerophon survives his Lycian ordeals and finally marries another one of the Lycian king's daughters, sharing the kingdom and receiving his separate domain. The elegant story in the *Iliad* tells us about the grand style of Lycian hospitality: Bellerophon was entertained with feasts for nine days before he was asked for his credentials. Hospitality was mutual between Achaians and Lycians. Bellerophon once was the guest of Oineus for twenty days, as Diomedes remembers, confirming the *xeinos*-relationship with Glaukos explicitly (*Iliad* 6.224–225).

Lycian cult and beliefs are sketchily indicated in the *Iliad*. Apollo is the god of the Lycians, as he is of the Trojans. Whatever his epithet λυκηγενής (*Iliad* 4.101, 119) means, Apollo is the god to whom Glaukos prays for strength (*Iliad* 16.514–515), and it is Apollo who ultimately rescues Sarpedon's body, cleanses, anoints, and dresses it, and entrusts it to the twins Hypnos and Thanatos for speedy conveyance to Lycia for burial in a mound with a stele (*Iliad* 16.676–683).

The Lycians, who came to help the Trojans in large numbers (*Iliad* 16.550–551), speak Greek in Homer, as do the Trojans. In this respect both of these peoples differ from the Carians, who are explicitly designated as βαρβαρόφωνοι (*Iliad* 2.867) and barely enter the context of the *Iliad*. Homer does not make a distinction between the kings of the Lycians and the Lycian warriors whom they led to Troy. The Achaian affiliation of the dynasty is a matter of two generations ago; by the time of the Trojan War the leaders Sarpedon and Glaukos are Lycians.

Our first question concerns the position of the Lycians as the principal allies of the Trojans. Why does Homer give the Lycians such a prominent position? Did the Lycians indeed form part of the Bronze Age story of the Trojan War as transmitted in the Greek tradition, true allies who came from far away but proved themselves valiant in the battles around Troy?

We have no access to Lycian traditions of the same Dark Age vintage, but the Bronze Age Anatolian records concerning the Lukka are relevant. The oddity of the nomenclature of the Lycians is exposed by Herodotus (1.173) and confirmed by Lycian inscriptions of the Classical era. The Classical Lycians called themselves Termilai (Trm̃mili). On the trilingual stele from Xanthos the equivalent of Λυκία of the Greek text is Lycian Trm̃mis.[1] The Greek custom of calling the Classical Termilai Lycians must be due to the persistence of Bronze Age and Homeric usage, when Greeks began to hellenize the name Lukka into Greek Λύκιοι. The identity of Lukka and Λύκιοι is no longer disputed,[2] although the geographical habitat of the Bronze Age Lukka in western Anatolia is still being debated. The language of the Lycians is a late form of Luwian, confirming the Bronze Age ancestry of the Lycians in western Anatolia, where Luwian was the dominant linguistic family of the second millennium B.C.[3]

The role of the Lukka in the Late Bronze Age is emerging from Hittite, Egyptian, and Ugaritic texts. Our aim here is to explore three aspects: (1) Lukka contacts with Troy, (2) Lukka contacts with Greeks, and (3) the principal habitat of the Lukka in the Late Bronze Age, in order to compare Homer's tradition with written testimony of venerable Bronze Age origin. In the end, we must check the archaeological aspect of Lukka and Lycians. With Emily Vermeule, we proceed on the assumptions that Ahhiyawa in the Hittite texts stands for Achaians, and that Wilusiya-Wilusa and Taruisa are the names of Ilion and Troy-Troia.[4] All interpretations will therefore be subject to skepticism on the part of nonbe-

lievers, but the testing of the identifications may continue here to explore new configurations and warning signals.

LUKKA AND TROY

The earliest Hittite reference to Lukka owes its likelihood to the restoration of the initial sign of the name of Lukka. The chronicle of the late fifteenth-century B.C. king Tudhaliya II starts the list of his West Anatolian enemies forming the Assuwa coalition with -*ukka* and ends with the names of Wilusiya and Taruisa.[5] The list of names is difficult to put in geographical order, but the possibility exists that the Assuwa coalition against Tudhaliya extends from the south to the north of West Anatolia. In any case, if Lukka is the correct reading, we have here a reference to a late fifteenth-century anti-Hittite alliance of which Trojans as well as Lukka-Lycians formed a part.

In the treaty concluded by Alaksandus of Wilusa with the Hittite king Muwatalli,[6] Wilusa-Troy is praised in historical context for its loyalty to the Hittites, and is obliged to lend military assistance (chariotry and infantry) to the Hittite king and his generals both in case of West Anatolian wars, including potential troubles with the Lukka, and in larger international conflicts with Egypt, Mitanni, or Assyria. Indeed, at the battle of Kadesh, as we learn from Egyptian records, in year 5 of Ramses II, the Dardanoi-Drdny-Trojans were among the auxiliaries of Muwatalli, and the Lukka fought as fellow auxiliaries, as did several other West Anatolian peoples.[7] The Luwian West Anatolian contingent can be presumed to have been mutually acquainted as warriors on such far-flung foreign campaigns.

We do not know if these allies all came overland to join Muwatalli in the Lower Lands. From what we know of the Lukka, they were notorious and enterprising sailors. In the era of the Sea Peoples, the Lukka conspired with the Libyans against Merneptah (year 5); the allies of the Libyans also included the Ekwesh-Achaians, the Teresh, the Shardana, and Shekelesh—with the Lukka and possibly the Teresh representing the West Anatolian contingent. The Teresh are problematic, but a Trojan connection (Taruisa) can be considered.[8] If Teresh indeed stands for Trojans, the Libyan conspiracy would have brought Trojans and Lycians as well as Achaians into an ambitious alliance with Sicilians and Sardinians to plot an assault on Egypt from Libyan harbors.

LUKKA AND ACHAIANS

The activities of the Ahhiyawa-Achaians often overlap with those of the Lukka on sea and on land. Madduwatta, who had yielded ground to his Achaian rival Attarissiya, is blamed by the Hittite king Arnuwanda, son of Tudhaliya II, for making raids on Alashiya-Cyprus. Madduwatta explains that such raids had also been made by others, such as Attarissiya.[9] We note that the Lukka made such raids in the Amarna period.[10]

In the Tawagalawa letter (Hattusili III), the Lukka are said to have approached Tawagalawa, the brother of the Ahhiyawa king, for help (I.1–5), and he came into their lands. This is a clear attempt at joint anti-Hittite action by Achaians and Lukka. The Tawagalawa letter also refers to actions by the Ahhiyawa king and the Hittite king concerning Wilusa, which may have led to a peaceful solution. In the Milawata letter, a Hittite king (Tudhaliya IV, probably) is trying to reinstate Walmus on the throne of Wilusa. In both the Tawagalawa and Milawata letters,[11] Wilusa-Troy is in some trouble between Hittites and Ahhiyawa and/or Milawata-Miletus. The Lukka appreciate the power of the Achaian prince Tawagalawa.

LUKKA GEOGRAPHY

The geography of the various encounters so far suggests: a general West Anatolian coastal and inland interaction among Ahhiyawa and coalitions of West Anatolian rulers, including Lukka; overseas raids in the fourteenth century by Ahhiyawa (Attarissiya), his southwest Anatolian rival Madduwatta, and by the Lukka; international concern over these naval activities by the Hittite king, the ruler of Alashiya, and to some extent by Egypt (Amenhotep III). The Lukka in the later thirteenth century are trying to conspire with the Libyans and Achaians for an attack on Merneptah from the

west, an enterprise surely based on previous acquaintance with the Libyan coast and its harbors.[12] In the Sea Peoples' Wars during the later rule of Suppiluliuma II, the king of Ugarit had to send his ships to the Lukka region to battle the attackers.[13] The Lukka coast had become the crucial place for the attempt to stop the naval invasion of the Hittite Lower Land, Cyprus, and Syria. The Lukka themselves must have been on the side of the attackers, as they were in the days of Merneptah. The West Anatolian participants in the raids still included the Teresh.

The main problem here is the relationship of Homeric Lycia, the Xanthos valley principally, to the Bronze Age abodes of the Lukka. There have been many suggestions placing the Lukka in the southwest or elsewhere in the west of Anatolia, and there is some reason to assume that they extended over an area larger than the Classical Lycia of the Termilai and the Lycian League.[14]

In the Hittite records cited above for Achaian-Lukka interaction, we find geographical hints concerning territory in the Xanthos valley (fig. 2.1). Madduwatta was chased from his original land by Attarissiya and settled by the Hittite king in the mountainous land of Zippašla. Among his military intrigues is a plot with the people of Dalawa to lure the Hittite general Kišnapili into a trap on the road to Hinduwa. After the Hittite defeat, Dalawa, formerly Hittite, becomes a vassal of Madduwatta (obv. 66–74). The identity of Dalawa-Talawa = Lycian Tlawa-Tlos is generally accepted.[15] Tlos is in the Xanthos valley, some forty kilometers from the coast, overlooking the left bank of the river. Kandyba-Gendeve, which may be Hinduwa, where the Hittite general had tried to go, lies some forty kilometers southeast of Tlos as the crow flies, part of central Lycia and west of the Kasaba valley. The Dalawa forces intercepted the Hittite troops on their way south or east.

In a later part of the Madduwatta text the Hittite king explicitly states that he had given Madduwatta the land of the river Siyanta to live in (rev. 11–19) where he had to guard the Hittite frontier. Madduwatta trespassed extensively and took Arzawa. The Siyanta River is also referred to in the treaty of Mursili II with the king of Mira-Kuwaliya as one of the borders of Mira, not to be crossed by Kupanta-ᵈKAL (C 33–38) for the founda-

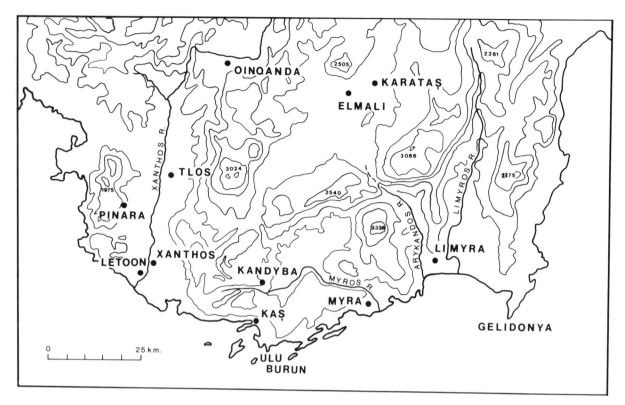

FIGURE 2.1 Map of Lycia with sites mentioned in text.

tion of cities, with the exception of the sanctuary of Mašhuiluwa which lay across the river.[16]

The identification of the Siyanta River is disputed. Garstang once opted for the Xanthos River but later thought that the Siyanta was one of the tributaries of the Maeander.[17] There is more than the assonance of Siyanta-Xanthos to keep the possibility of a geographic connection open. Madduwatta is assigned the Siyanta River land after his takeover of Dalawa-Tlos. In the treaty with Kupanta-dKAL, one of the borders of Mira-Kuwaliya is designated as the dKASKAL.KUR of the town of Wiyanawanda (C 30); this Wiyanawanda could be the site of Oinoanda in the upper reaches of the Xanthos valley.

The Milawata letter, which deals with repercussions of Wilusa troubles in Hittite and Ahhiyawa context, refers to hostages from the towns of Awarna and Pina.[18] These towns, as well as Wiyanawanda, also appear in hieroglyphic Luwian inscriptions; at Emirgazi V, as Pi-na-L416, and Awarna, period of Tudhaliya IV;[19] at Yalburt near Ilgın, in the hieroglyphic inscription on the rim of a basin excavated by Raci Temizer, the Lukka land, Wiyanawanda, and the towns Pina and Awarna are part of the southwest attacked by Tudhaliya IV.[20] The topography of the Lukka land goes well beyond the names listed here and will be studied in detail when the Yalburt inscriptions are fully published. Here the possibility is raised that the Xanthos valley known to us from the Homeric record as the fief of the Lycian kings may indeed have been a prominent part of the Bronze Age Lukka lands.

The geographical names which suggest the connection are: Talawa-Tlos; Pina, which may be the short name for Pinara, a Lycian town west of the Xanthos River, some twenty-nine kilometers inland from the Mediterranean; Awarna, referred to in the Milawata letter, which also occurs in a statement of the people of Talawa and Kuwalapasa. The name for the Iron Age Lycian citadel of Xanthos is Arñna-Arina.[21] The identification with Awarna is also probable. The Siyanta River, if identifiable with the Xanthos River, would tie the sites together as the principal artery of western Lycia. The

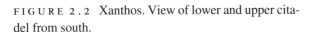

FIGURE 2.2 Xanthos. View of lower and upper citadel from south.

FIGURE 2.3 Xanthos River. View to north from lower citadel.

sanctuary on the other bank of the river could then be a proto-Letoon. In the upper valley of the Xanthos, Oinoanda offers itself as the option for Wiyanawanda.

The time frame of these references, whether correctly identified or not, is from the era of Madduwatta (c. 1400 B.C., or earlier) to the rule of Tudhaliya IV. It is to be expected that the newly discovered hieroglyphic inscriptions in the vaulted chamber of Suppiluliuma II at the south citadel in Boğazköy will give us more geographical enlightenment about the southwest and Lukka.[22]

ARCHAEOLOGY

All these speculations call for an archaeological examination of Bronze Age facts. The Xanthos valley is not only the most famous part of Lycia for Homer, but it is also the largest river valley in Lycia, with a harbor site at the river mouth, which is sanded and silted over so that geomorphologists will have to extricate the Bronze Age configuration of coast and harbor at Patara.[23] The

river plain is fertile and major citadels watched its approaches in the Lycian period.

XANTHOS

Xanthos itself, inland from its harbor, was located on a lower and an upper citadel (figs. 2.2–2.3). The lower citadel, a rocky plateau overlooking the river, is thoroughly eroded so far as Bronze Age remains are concerned.[24] The excavators themselves pointed out that no probings had taken place in the plain around the acropolis and near the river. The upper citadel has only been partly investigated, principally in the necropolis area. The sanctuary of the Lycians is across the river at the Letoon, where soundings below ground-water level have reached seventh- and eighth-century remains but no Bronze Age.

PINARA

Pinara, one of the major Lycian cities of the later period, has its citadel set in a spectacular location west of the Xanthos River on one of the spurs of the Antikragos

FIGURE 2.4 Pinara. Upper citadel seen from east.

FIGURE 2.5 Pinara. Lower city and citadel view, from theater area.

(figs. 2.4–2.5). As Spratt and Forbes wrote after their visit in 1842: "A stupendous tower of rock, faced by a perpendicular precipice, perforated with a thousand tombs, and crowned by ruined fortifications, rose out of a deep ravine which was thronged with ruins and sarcophagi, and intersected by ridges bearing the more important edifices." [25] The surface remains belong to the Lycian and Roman periods, and nobody has made any regular excavations or soundings at the site. The core of Pinara is the natural citadel formed by the steep rock formation from the top of which one has a strategic view of the upper Xanthos valley.

TLOS

A similar dominant position is characteristic of the citadel of Tlos (figs. 2.6–2.7). Spratt and Forbes remained here for three days: "It is a most delightful place. Few ancient sites can vie with it. Built on the summit of a hill of great height, bounded by perpendicular precipices and deep ravines, commanding a view of the entire length of the valley of the Xanthos—the snow-capped Taurus in one distance, the sea in another,

the whole mass of Cragus and its towering peaks and the citadel of Pinara in front, itself immediately overhung by the snowy summits of the Massicytus—a grander site for a great city could scarcely have been selected in all Lycia." [26]

This splendid citadel was still inhabited by Turkish Ağas in the last century; Spratt and Forbes were guests in the residence on top. They describe the scenery with appreciation of the natural beauty of the site as well as its eminent position. Tlos dominates the northern Xanthos valley, with a clear view to the second great fortress of Pinara. As one visits this site, and walks on unexcavated ground and bare rock cuttings, the Bronze Age role of such fortresses becomes a vivid reality. The Lycian warriors of the Iron Age dwelled on these citadels and carved their tombs in the cliffs, but Tlawa as a predecessor suited the warlike Lukka who put their garrisons on fortified acropoleis, not on open sites in the valley.

Tlos has never been excavated, and it will require long and careful work of digging through Ottoman, Byzantine, Roman, and Lycian levels to yield any traces of Bronze Age occupation. There is Bronze Age mate-

FIGURE 2.6 Tlos. Citadel from northeast. (Lithograph from T. A. B. Spratt and E. Forbes, *Travels in Lycia* I [London 1847] p. 8.)

rial from Tlos in the form of three tin-bronze objects collected by Ormerod, now in the Ashmolean Museum in Oxford. The pieces are a flat adze, half of a double axe, and a flat dagger blade. All three have a high tin content and are dated by Moorey to the Late Bronze II–III periods.[27] The association with Tlos is not considered certain by Moorey, but there would seem little reason to confuse provenances in this part of Lycia.

The Xanthos River must have been the lifeline into western Lycia, with ships coming up the river to Patara and Xanthos, if not beyond. The existence of Late Bronze Age local strongholds along this river, and the knowledge of these Lukka fortresses that Hittites seem to display, fit the fourteenth- and thirteenth-century situation well.

For an analogy we can look at the situation in Pamphylia, which belonged to Tarhuntassa in the period in question. The recently found bronze copy of the treaty of Tudhaliya IV with Kurunta describes the western border of Tarhuntassa as the river Kastaraya in the territory of the city Parha.[28] Here we have a clear Hittite record of Perge as a city of strategic importance in the thirteenth century B.C., and the river Kastaraya-Kestros as a boundary of Hittite territory. The topography of Perge is similar to that of Pinara and Tlos: at the north side of the Hellenistic-Roman lower city rises a natural acropolis of limestone, forming a terrace of some 750 by 330 m on a plateau about sixty meters above the plain and the lower city. This would have been the original citadel of the Late Bronze Age Perge-Parha, easily defended and offering a lookout station in all directions, including the approach from the sea via the Kestros River, which was navigable as late as Strabo's time.[29]

The land of the city of Parha occurs twice in other Hittite texts, once in a context with all hostile Lukka lands, and once in a context of cult provisions.[30] The Lukka reference suits the military vicissitudes in the Tarhuntassa border area; the cult of Parha deserves special notice since the local goddess Artemis Pergaia—Wanassa Preiia evidently has Bronze Age roots.[31]

Excavations have been in progress at Perge from 1946 (with an interval in 1957–1967) under the direction of Arif Müfid Mansel, Jale Inan, and now Haluk Abbassoğlu, and have revealed a wealth of architecture,

FIGURE 2.7 Tlos. Citadel from northeast.

sculpture, epigraphy, and history. The acropolis has not been extensively investigated. Soundings were made in search of the temple of Artemis Pergaia.[32] The surface was found much disturbed by cultivation and the Byzantine level had suffered. Yet, in earlier context, the acropolis can be considered unexplored.

A second prominent citadel, in full view from the acropolis of Perge, is Sillyon, northeast from Perge across the Kestros; third is the river city of Aspendos with its citadel on the Eurymedon. Neither of these has been excavated or explored with modern techniques and geomorphological considerations in mind such as would be required to test the Bronze Age archaeological residue. The mythological and linguistic stratification has been explored.[33]

The Tarhuntassa tablet from Boğazköy now presents a great challenge to the archaeologists to match the historical reality of Parha in the days of Tudhaliya IV with archaeological substance on the acropolis and to geomorphologists to explore the history of naval access to the Kestros and the location of the coastal harbor.

The old theories of an archaeological vacuum in Lycia and Pamphylia in the second millennium B.C. were based on the exclusive belief that mounds have to

be present to prove the existence of ancient settlements. The traveler in Lycia and Pamphylia knows that the local building materials were not mud brick and plaster, but timber and stone. The Classical Lycians were the first to make this amply visible in their rock-cut copies of houses and storage sheds. These media leave no residue in stratified settlement form except if builders partially relied on clay and mud, e.g., by use of the wattle-and-daub technique. In Lycia, the results of the Elmalı plain excavations at Karataş and Bağbaşı have shown that slow mound formation can result and can preserve traces of burnt wooden buildings if there is enough cover by decayed mud and timber of subsequent levels. At Bağbaşı, in an open settlement area dating from the Late Chalcolithic to the Iron Age, remnants of second-millennium habitation came to light in the form of pits and fragmentary floors with pottery scatter, but no walls were preserved. Burials contained in banded pithoi were the clearest sign of settlement.[34] These traces of settlement date to the end of the Middle Bronze Age and the early Late Bronze Age; they prove that settlements did exist in the upland plains of Lycia at this time, although the architecture eludes the excavator.

The other major factor obscuring the second-millennium residue of the Lukka and their Pamphylian neighbors in Tarhuntassa is the geomorphological change of the coastal and river plains, with the enormous silting up of areas near river mouths, problems equally serious at the Late Bronze Age sites of Ephesus and Miletus and in southwest Anatolia. Emily Vermeule demonstrated the situation in Caria with her survey and publication of Early Bronze Age domestic pottery that came from wells dug in orchards south of Müskebi on the coast of the Halicarnassus peninsula.[35] These pots came from a depth of eight to ten meters below the modern surface and some five meters below the water table. In Lycian Myra-Demre, the church of St. Nicholas was buried under a similar mass of alluvium, making one wonder about the accessibility of Classical and Preclassical remains under additional overburdens.

If land excavation has not yet coped with the challenge to bring the Lukka to light in Classical Lycian cities, the underwater excavators have contributed greatly to the perspective of Bronze Age trade and contacts along the Lycian coasts in the fourteenth and thirteenth centuries B.C. The excavation of the shipwreck near Uluburun east of Kaş has now been in progress for a decade under the direction of George Bass and Cemal Pulak. The work here and at the wreck off Cape Gelidonya reveals that large ships, with cargoes of metal ingots (copper and tin) and other raw materials, sailed from the Levant and Cyprus along the southern coast of Anatolia, and were heavily loaded as they arrived at the Lycian shores, where some of them foundered on the rocks before reaching the safe harbors of Limyra, Myra, Kaş-Habessos, or Xanthos. Even if the principal cargo was destined for the Aegean, the Lukka coast must have been visited by such ships for trade, shelter, and supplies. The bronze implements from Tlos show that Lukka metallurgy was up-to-date and had access to tin.

The most tantalizing object retrieved from the Uluburun wreck is the wooden folding tablet with panels prepared for writing on wax and with ivory hinges for neat closing.[36] We do not know if this was a tablet used by a member of the crew for administrative purposes, or a message carried folded and sealed to be delivered somewhere in the Lukka lands or Ahhiyawa. The first tablet of this kind excavated in Anatolia, ironically or poignantly, came to the surface in Lycian waters, near the shore where Bellerophon landed, according to *Iliad* 6.168–69, carrying ominous signs on a folding tablet to the king of Lycia.

WRITING

The coincidence reinforces the suspicion that the epic tradition had a lingering memory of letter-writing to Lycia. From Hittite texts, we know that West Anatolian rulers in Arzawa, Wilusa, and Mira, including the rebel Madduwatta, did correspond among themselves, with the Hittite king, and on occasion even with the king of Egypt, witness the Arzawa letters in Amarna. The Uluburun ship carried a gold scarab of Nefertiti that may have been part of an official message rather than loot, and that in any case helps to date the wreck after year 5 of Akhenaten.[37] The ceramic date is LH IIIA 2.

Madduwatta, probably in the pre-Amarna era, keeps up a lively correspondence with the Hittite king, with Arzawa, and Attarissiya. He prepares his intrigues

against the Hittite general by writing letters to the general Kišnapili himself as well as to the people of Dalawa (obv. 66–69); thus a letter is addressed to the people of a Lukka-Lycian city in the upper Xanthos valley. We do not know whether all this correspondence was in Hittite rather than Luwian, or whether the tablets were of clay or of wood. The Arzawa letters to Amarna are in Hittite and on clay, and the Luwian king Tarhundaradu is explicit in wanting the answers in clear Hittite. Kupanta-[d]KAL of Mira wrote to Ramses II (in Akkadian?); the seal of the Mira king Tarkasna/Targašnamuwa has a cuneiform and hieroglyphic legend.[38]

Given the proclivity of the Lycians to use timber for their architecture rather than mud and clay, and the fact that a large part of the record-keeping and correspondence in the Hittite world was written on wood, we may have lost the majority of the West Anatolian Late Bronze Age archives, including those of Wilusa-Troy, Millawanda-Miletus, Talawa-Tlos, and Madduwatta's residence in the Siyanta River land. But the conscientious record-keeping of the Hittites in the archives of their capital has rescued a good part of the history and geography of West Anatolia, enough in the case of the Lukka, of their exploits on land and on sea, and their citadels once disputed by Madduwatta and captured by Tudhaliya IV, to suggest that the Xanthos valley has to be counted in when we reconstruct the Lukka territory of the fourteenth and thirteenth centuries B.C. Homer's bias in favor of the kings of this river valley may be based on historical realities in this period, and it is up to the land archaeologists to match the underwater discoveries of the Uluburun team for a proper rehabilitation of the historical reality behind the world of Sarpedon and Glaukos, and Bellerophon and his father-in-law. This calls for a Xanthos valley project of Bronze Age focus and interdisciplinary scope, working in modern alliance with the team that has now begun a new investigation of Wilusa-Troy.

NOTES

1. E. Laroche, "Lyciens et Termiles," *RA* 1976, 15–19, and "L'inscription lycienne," in H. Metzger, E. Laroche,

et al., *Fouilles de Xanthos* VI, *La stèle trilingue du Létoon* (Paris 1979) 44–197.

2. Ph. Houwink ten Cate, *The Luwian Population Groups of Lycia and Cilicia* (Leiden 1961) 195–196. T. R. Bryce, *The Lycians in Literary and Epigraphic Sources* (Copenhagen 1986) 3–23. G. Neumann, *RAss* 7 (1988) 189–191, s.v. Lykien.

3. E. Laroche, "Luwier, Luwisch, Lu(w)iya," *RAss* 7 (1988) 181–184.

4. H. G. Güterbock, M. J. Mellink, and E. T. Vermeule, "The Hittites and the Aegean World," *AJA* 87 (1983) 133–143. H. G. Güterbock, "Troy in Hittite Texts? Wilusa, Ahhiyawa, and Hittite History," in M. J. Mellink, ed., *Troy and the Trojan War* (Bryn Mawr 1986) 33–44.

5. J. Garstang and O. R. Gurney, *The Geography of the Hittite Empire* (London 1959) 105–107; Güterbock 1986 (supra n. 4) 34–37. The historicity of the Assuwa war is confirmed by the discovery of a sword captured by Tudhaliya in the Assuwa war and dedicated (as part of a group of swords) to the storm-god in the Hittite capital; see A. Ünal, A. Ertekin, and I. Ediz, "The Hittite Sword from Boğazköy-Hattuša, found 1991 and its Akkadian Inscription," *Müze-Museum* 4 (1990–1991) 50–52. The same authors offer comments on the sword in M. J. Mellink, E. Porada, and T. Özgüç, eds., *Studies in Honor of Nimet Özgüç* (Ankara 1993) 719–730.

6. Garstang and Gurney (supra n. 5) 102; Güterbock 1986 (supra n. 4) 34–37.

7. A. Goetze in *CAH*³ II.2, 253; N. K. Sandars, *The Sea Peoples,* rev. ed. (London 1985) 36–37.

8. Sandars (supra n. 7) 111–12.

9. A. Götze, *Madduwattaš,* MVAG 32.1 (Leipzig 1928) 36–39.

10. Amarna letter 38:10. Cord Kühne, *Die Chronologie der internationalen Korrespondenz von El-Amarna,* AOAT 17 (Neukirchen-Vluyn 1973) 87–88, n. 438.

11. Güterbock 1986 (supra n. 4) 37–39; H. Hoffner, "The Milawata Letter Augmented and Reinterpreted," *AfO-BH* 19 (1982) 130–137.

12. Relevant evidence has come to light in recent excavations: D. White, "1985 Excavations on Bates's Island, Marsa Matruh," *JARCE* 23 (1986) 51–84.

13. C. F. A. Schaeffer et al., eds., *Ugaritica* V (Paris 1968) 87–89, R.S. 20.238. Sandars (supra n. 7) 143.

14. T. R. Bryce, "The Lukka Problem," *JNES* 33 (1974) 395–404; idem, "Lukka Revisited," *JNES* 51 (1992) 121–130.

15. Garstang and Gurney (supra n. 5) 80; Bryce 1974 (supra n. 14) 399; G. F. Del Monte and J. Tischler, *Die Orts- und Gewässernamen der hethitischen Texte* (Wiesbaden 1978) 389, s.v. Talawa. For the text, see Götze (supra n. 9).

16. J. Friedrich, *Staatsverträge des Hatti-Reiches in hethitischer Sprache* I, MVAG 31 (Leipzig 1926) 116–117.

17. Garstang and Gurney (supra n. 5) 91; Del Monte and Tischler (supra n. 15) 548–549.

18. Hoffner (supra n. 11); I. Singer, "Western Anatolia in the Thirteenth Century B.C.," *AnatStud* 33 (1983) 216; T. R. Bryce, "A Reinterpretation of the Milawata Letter," *AnatStud* 35 (1985) 13–23.

19. Bryce (supra n. 18) 18, 20; Singer (supra n. 18) 216; K. Kohlmeyer, "Felsbilder der hethitischen Grossreichszeit," *Acta Praehistorica et Archaeologica* 15 (1983) 41.

20. T. Özgüç and R. Temizer, *İnandıktepe* (Ankara 1988) XXV-XXVII, pls. 85–95, figs. 60–63. J. D. Hawkins, "The new inscription from the Südburg of Boğazköy-Hattuša," *AA* 1990, 306 and 313, n. 60; idem, "The inscriptions of the Kızıldağ and the Karadağ in the light of the Yalburt inscription," in H. Otten, E. Akurgal, H. Ertem, and A. Süel, eds., *Hittite and Other Anatolian and Near Eastern Studies in Honour of Sedat Alp* (Ankara 1992) 259–275, especially 264.

21. Del Monte and Tischler (supra n. 15) 32, Arina I = Arñna; p. 58, Awarna. Hoffner (supra n. 11) 135; Bryce (supra n. 18) 13. Laroche (supra n. 1) 7, 53, 62, 86. For Awarna, see the Aramaic 'WRN, H. Metzger et al. (supra n. 1) 139, and a forthcoming study of the Yalburt inscription by M. Poetto, as J. D. Hawkins kindly informs me.

22. P. Neve and H. Otten, "Die Ausgrabungen in Boğazköy-Hattuša 1988," *AA* 1989, 316–337. Suppiluliuma II claims his conquest of Wiyanawanda and Lukka: see Hawkins 1990 (supra n. 20) 312–313 and n. 60, and *Studien zu den Boğazköy-Texten,* Beiheft 2 (forthcoming). A general discussion of the Lukka in the historical context of Hatti, Ahhiyawa, and Sea Peoples is now given by G. Steiner, "Die historische Rolle der Lukka," in J. Borchhardt and G. Dobesch, eds., *Akten des II. Internationalen Lykien-Symposions, Wien 6–12 Mai 1990* I (Vienna 1993) 123–127.

23. S. Buluç, "Patara Yüzey Araştırması," in *I. Araştırma Sonuçları Toplantısı* (Istanbul 1983) 139–144, 287–291.

24. H. Metzger, *Fouilles de Xanthos* II, *L'acropole lycienne* (Paris 1963); P. Demargne and H. Metzger, "Xanthos," in *RE* IX.A.2 (1967) 1381–1382.

25. T. A. B. Spratt and E. Forbes, *Travels in Lycia, Milyas and the Cibyratis* (London 1847) 8. O. Benndorf and G. Niemann, *Reisen in Lykien und Karien* (Vienna 1884) 45–56.

26. Spratt and Forbes (supra n. 25) 33–38; Benndorf and Niemann (supra n. 25) 138–140; W. Wurster, "Antike Siedlungen in Lykien," *AA* 1976, 27–44.

27. P. R. S. Moorey and F. Schweizer, "Copper and Copper Alloys in Ancient Turkey: Some New Analyses," *Archaeo-*

metry 16 (1974) 112–115; S. Przeworski, *Die Metallindustrie anatoliens in der Zeit von 1500–700 vor Chr.* (Leiden 1939) 30, 40, 49, pl. IX.8–10.

28. H. Otten, *Die Bronzetafel von Boğazköy. Ein Staatsvertrag Tuthaliyas IV* (Wiesbaden 1988) 12–13, line 61, comment pp. 37–38.

29. A. Pekman, *Perge Tarihi — History of Perge* (Ankara 1973) 53–56.

30. Otten (supra n. 28) 37–38.

31. Pekman (supra n. 29) 58, 91; S. Onurkan, "Artemis Pergaia," *IstMitt* 19–20 (1969–1970) 289–298; C. Brixhe, *Le dialecte grec de Pamphylie* (Paris 1976) 159–161.

32. A. M. Mansel and A. Akarca, *Excavations and Researches at Perge* (Ankara 1949) 66–67, figs. 78–90.

33. Brixhe (supra n. 31) 163–190 (Sillyon), 191–286 (Aspendos).

34. M. J. Mellink, "The Remains of Second Millennium B.C. Habitation at Karataş-Semayük," in *VII. Kazı Sonuçları Toplantısı* (Ankara 1985) 287–291. C. Eslick, *Elmalı-Karataş I. The Neolithic and Chalcolithic Periods: Bağbaşi and Other Sites* (Bryn Mawr 1992) 1–5.

35. E. Vermeule, "The Early Bronze Age in Caria," *Archaeology* 17 (1964) 244–249.

36. G. F. Bass, C. Pulak, et al., "The Bronze Age Shipwreck at Ulu Burun, Turkey: 1986 Campaign," *AJA* 93 (1989) 10, fig. 19; G. F. Bass, "Oldest Known Shipwreck Reveals Bronze Age Splendors," *National Geographic* 172 (1987) 731. R. Payton, "The Ulu Burun writing-board set," *AnatStud* 41 (1991) 99–110; D. Symington, "Late Bronze Age writing-boards and their uses: textual evidence from Anatolia and Syria," *AnatStud* 41 (1991) 111–123.

37. J. Weinstein, "The Gold Scarab of Nefertiti from Ulu Burun," *AJA* 93 (1989) 12–29.

38. I. Singer (supra n. 18) 206–207; H. G. Güterbock, "The Hittite Seals in the Walters Art Gallery," *JWalt* 36 (1977) 11–16; R. M. Boehmer and H. G. Güterbock, *Glyptik aus dem Stadtgebiet von Boğazköy,* Boğazköy-Hattuša XIV.2 (Berlin 1987) 83.

3

A HITTITE SILVER VESSEL IN THE
FORM OF A FIST

♦

H. G. GÜTERBOCK AND

TIMOTHY KENDALL

In 1977 a remarkable object was deposited on loan in the Museum of Fine Arts, Boston. This was a much-corroded silver cup, pieced together from many fragments, in the form of a clenched fist, replicating almost exactly the natural size and form of an average male hand (fig. 3.1).[1] At the time of its appearance in the Museum there was no immediate indication of its origin. The present owner, who wishes to remain anonymous, acquired it from a London-based art dealer, who sold the piece claiming it to be "Assyrian." It might at once have been recognized as Hittite had not the surface, with its frieze of distinctive miniature figures, been so thickly encrusted with corrosion. At the time of its purchase, little attempt had been made to clean the vessel's fragile metal surface, probably because the previous owner feared the risk of further damaging the object. The thirteen fragments had merely been reassembled and secured with epoxy resin and fiberglass, thus recreating the form of the vessel as it was when originally found. In this condition, its rim was pressed inward, suggesting that during or shortly after burial it had been crushed—either accidentally or on purpose. Probably as a result of careless handling during recovery, the fragile

vessel had fractured into pieces. Three lacunae on the surface indicate the places of pieces either lost or not recovered by those who found the object.

When the vessel was first brought into the Museum, Kendall, who examined it, realized at once that it was not Assyrian. The fist shape was not a particularly Assyrian form nor did the small figures, partly visible in the frieze around the rim, look Assyrian. The key to identifying the object obviously lay in the details of the relief figures, but these were largely obscured by the surface corrosion. Close examination revealed that "intaglios" of some of the hidden repoussé images remained exposed on the inside of the pinched rim and that, where they were not covered by strips of fiberglass, impressions of them could be made with small pieces of plasticene. Parts of the relief scene obscured on the surface could be recovered in this way. One impression revealed an archetypal figure of a Hittite king, holding the crooked lituus in one hand, and pouring out a libation from a vessel held in the other. To the left of his head could be seen clearly the hieroglyphs of a familiar royal name: "Tudhaliya, Great King."[2] It was at once obvious that this object was a third addition to the very small

45

FIGURE 3.1 The Hittite fist-shaped cup on loan to the Museum of Fine Arts, Boston (RL 1977.144): before cleaning (verso).

done to return the vessel to its original form. However, in 1988 a successful pilot cleaning study was undertaken by the Museum's Research Laboratory to see if more surface details could be revealed through local electrolytic reduction. Using this technique, during the winter and spring of 1990, Senior Conservator Merville Nichols effected the cleaning of the vessel's surface with miraculous results, revealing all its previously hidden details (figs. 3.2–3.4).[5]

From the moment the fist entered the museum, we were urged repeatedly by Dr. Emily Vermeule to publish it. Between 1977 and 1980 we jointly examined the piece, and Kendall prepared a tentative reconstruction drawing of the relief scene together with photographs of the object so that Güterbock could present it before the XXVI⁰ Rencontre Assyriologique in Paris in 1980, and again in a lecture at the University of Iowa in 1984. However neither of us, either singly or jointly, undertook a preliminary publication of the piece. This task was in a sense performed by Sarah M. Carrig, a student of Professor Irene Winter at Harvard, who wrote a particularly fine term paper about the object in 1983, which, though never published, was privately distributed.[6] With the completion of the cleaning process in June 1990, and with our invitation to contribute papers to this volume, we realized that no more fitting tribute could be offered to Emily Vermeule than the publication of this important object, in which she has taken so much delight over the years and which even she has not yet seen in its newly revealed state. It is thus with extreme pleasure that we present it here at last in her honor.

PHYSICAL DESCRIPTION OF THE VESSEL

The fist was wrought from a single sheet of metal, to which was attached a handle, now lost. As Carrig first noted, this had been soldered at the lip on the side above the curled little finger, where a tear in the metal can be seen. The lower end of the handle joined the cup at the ball of the palm; before cleaning there was a hemispherical lump of epoxy here, but afterwards a torn solder joint appeared. The form of this missing handle was probably similar to that still remaining on the Schimmel

corpus of Hittite vessels in precious metal, which then consisted only of the famous silver stag and bull "rhyta" (properly protome cups) in the Norbert Schimmel collection, now in the Metropolitan Museum of Art.[3] Of these, only the stag cup possessed its rim intact as well as a similar band of relief (fig. 3.8 below); but the fist was the only one of the three that bore an identifiable royal name and hence a possible clue to its date.

Once the owner of the fist had generously deposited it on long-term loan in the museum, studies were undertaken on the exact condition of the vessel, its composition,[4] and how it might be more fully restored. Because of the extent of corrosion and the limitations imposed by the former treatment, it was felt that little could be stag cup;[7] a hypothetical restoration drawing of the fist with its handle appears in fig. 3.5.

The cup itself duplicates faithfully the features of the human hand, and great attention has been paid to detail. The back of the hand is rippled, as if to suggest the taut tendons of a clenched fist. V-shaped ridges behind the four knuckles also simulate the ribs of the metacarpals and the natural pattern of the veins, although the regularity of the pattern is artificially stylized. The thumb of the hand has been modeled correctly with creases of skin at the joints, and the exterior base of the thumb is framed by a narrow splaying ridge imitating a forked vein. The nails of the thumb and fingers are accentuated by elongated crescentic cuticles.

The fingers themselves are clasped tightly around an unidentifiable object, the rounded ends of which slightly protrude on either side of the bent fingers. This is perhaps not a real implement but rather a decorative device employed by the smith to avoid having to recreate in silver the deep concavities that form at the axes of the curling fingers when the hand is clenched into a fist. It is possible that the Hittite craftsman was influenced by the identical device employed in Egyptian statuary, where male images are customarily shown with hands tightly closed around a barlike object.[8] In the Hittite version the rounded ends have been delicately chased with a design composed of two concentric rings of petals radiating from a tiny central umbo (fig. 3.4).

The bottom of the cup is formed by the flat plane between the first and second joints of the four folded fingers. The vessel, however, does not rest flat on this surface but wobbles on the tip of the thumb, which projects beyond this plane by one centimeter. Like both of the Schimmel vessels, the cup was clearly not designed to rest stably in any attitude but on its side, suggesting that during whatever ritual it was used for, its contents were to be entirely drunk or drained before it was set down. On the thumb side the existing height of the vessel is 16.3 cm; on that of the small finger, 12.5 cm.

The sides of the vessel flared slightly, somewhat like a glove.[9] The circumference of the wrist is about 20 cm, while that of the mouth is about 28 cm. Originally the sides of the vessel were about 6.5 cm high and formed an elliptical mouth, which, before it was crushed, probably measured about 7.5 by 11 cm.

Once the body of the cup had been wrought, the smith formed the lip by uniformly folding back upon itself, one centimeter all around, the raw top edge of the silver sheet, clamping and soldering the two layers together and providing a smooth, rounded rim for drinking. On the sides of the vessel, above the wrist, he formed a delicate band of relief, 2.8 cm wide, which gave the effect of a bracelet. This relief scene was modeled on a groundline consisting of three narrow bands. The upper and lower bands are decorated with periodic hatched sections; the middle is composed of raised lunettes in a continuous row.[10]

DESCRIPTION AND INTERPRETATION OF THE FRIEZE

The subject of the frieze is a cult scene (figs. 3.6 and 3.7). Its focal point appears on the back of the hand (fig. 3.3), where we see a king pouring out a libation in front of an offering table, behind which stands the figure of a god holding a bull's reins. Following the king, around the reverse of the cup (fig. 3.2), is a row of cult personnel. The last figure in the row is a divine being also, who stands in front of a masonry structure. This last element, which would have been directly under the lost handle, marks the beginning and/or the end of the scene. Since the two of us hold differing opinions on the interpretation of the last two items and hence on the scene itself, we will present these opinions following a description of all the details.

The first of the primary figures in the scene is the god, who appears immediately to the right of the masonry structure. He is bearded and faces right toward an offering table. While his beard is short, his hair sweeps behind his shoulder in a tress that, were it to fall vertically, would hang below his waist.[11] On his head he wears the tall conical crown of divinity, which is brimmed with an upturning hatched element that can only be one of a pair of horns, the familiar attribute of gods. He wears a tunic with short sleeves that bunch just below the elbow in several folds or layers, indicated by hatched bands. He also wears a short kilt with a fringed hem that ties in the front. The crescentic hilt of a sword appears at his waist, hung from his left side. His legs

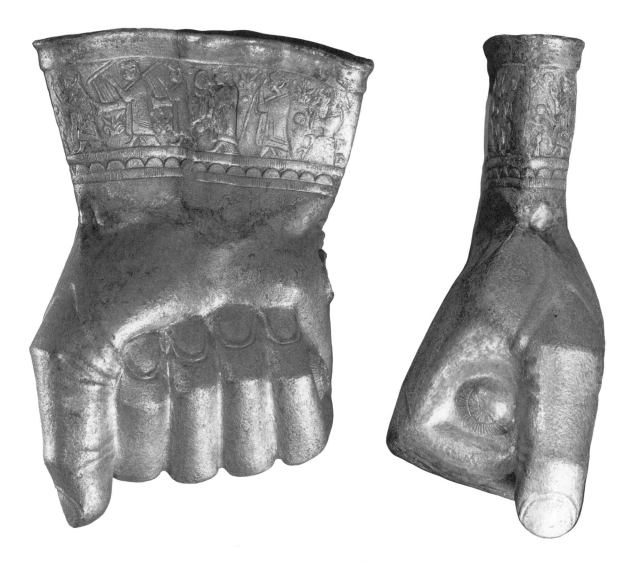

FIGURE 3.2 The Boston fist-shaped cup (verso) after cleaning. Photograph © Justin Kerr.

FIGURE 3.4A. The Boston fist-shaped cup from the side, after cleaning. Photograph © Justin Kerr.

seem bare, displaying well-delineated kneecaps. Although no details of his footwear have been preserved, the position of his toes indicates that he must have been wearing typical Hittite shoes with upturned toes. Bracelets can be seen around his wrists.

The god brandishes in his upraised hand a weapon tipped with a round head. Cracks or striations in the surface of the metal, radiating from the ball of the weapon, at first suggested an axe blade held backward, but this seems an illusion. The object is apparently a round-headed mace.[12] In his left hand he grasps two ropes that extended to the head of a bull. Unfortunately, with the exception of the possible tip of the bull's horns, only the hindquarters of the animal survive, since the piece of silver bearing the bull's foreparts has been lost. The upward direction of the ropes at first suggested that the bull may have been in a rampant position, but the presumed horn tip that appeared in cleaning suggests that the ani-

48

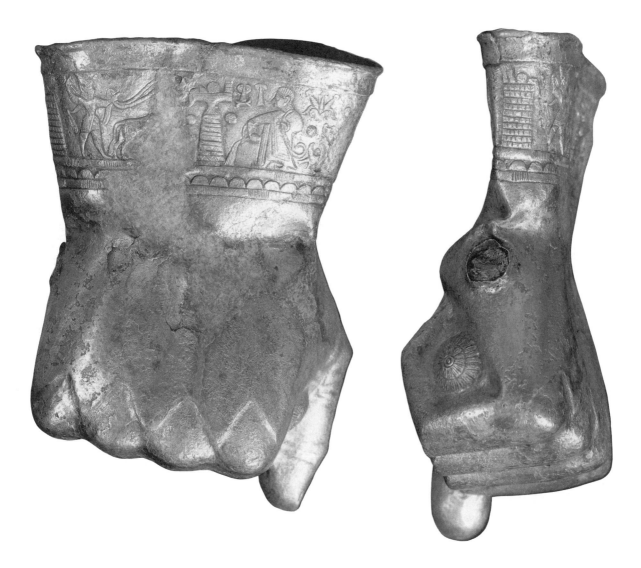

FIGURES 3.3 AND 3.4B The Boston fist-shaped cup (recto and side) after cleaning. Photographs © Justin Kerr.

mal was in a statant pose. How the ropes were attached to the head, therefore, remains unclear.[13]

The mace-wielding god accompanied by a bull is generally known as the Weather-God, although in Hittite he bore the name Tarhuna.[14] The cult scene depicted here shows the king worshipping this deity, and it is probable that the vessel itself was employed in this god's service.

To the right of the god and the bull is an offering table. Its base is conical and marked with eleven horizontal bands. The lowest is hatched; above this five bands marked with zigzags alternate with plain bands. Several such objects are shown on the relief vase from Inandıktepe, where some of them are being carried, indicating that they were made of a lightweight material.[15] The stripes or hatched texture shown on this and most of the other examples would indicate that they were probably of wickerwork construction, either wrapped with colored bands of cloth or woven with multicolored geometric patterns. Wickerwork tables are and drapes over the edge of the table. A similar cloth hangs from the table like a napkin and extends to the knees of the seated goddess on the relief of Puduhepa at Fraktin.[17] Judging by the reliefs on the Inandık vase this type of table was used both for ritual offerings and for secular meals.[18]

Standing on the opposite side of the table, facing the god, is the figure of the king, who, like other Hittite dignitaries, is beardless. He grasps a pitcher in his extended right hand, with thumb pointing, and pours out the liquid contents at the foot of the table. In his left hand, which emerges from a sleeve hole in his robe, he holds the crook-shaped lituus or *kalmuš,* symbol of Hittite royalty. His robe is ankle-length and adorned with decorative bands, presumably indicating embroidered or woven designs or fringes. From his extended right arm a long, fringed hem falls to his feet, suggesting that the robe was open at one side. This apparel is known from many other representations.[19] Like the god's, the king's shoes have upturned toes.

Normally in stone relief sculpture the king wears what appears to be a round skullcap. Here, however, where the silver has permitted more detailing, the artisan has added chased vertical lines to the crown of the head, intending perhaps to suggest wavy hair encircled by a fillet. Just above and to the left of the king's head are the hieroglyphs reading "Tudhaliya, Great King." [20]

On the groundline immediately behind the king is a small figure of a bird—possibly an eagle—with its wings upraised, standing on a small mound or base of indeterminate form. The body of the bird faces right, away from the king, but its head is turned backward to face him. A bird in the same position sits on an offering table at Fraktin.[21] It is not immediately clear whether this is a bird-shaped vessel [22] or a real bird that was to be sacrificed and used in the ritual. Texts sometimes mention birds or their wings as being part of the divine offerings,[23] and evidence of bird sacrifices has been discovered at Yazılıkaya.[24]

The king is followed by a procession of seven figures moving or facing left. Most of the figure directly behind the king is lost in a break, but surviving traces reveal that here was a kneeling man very much like the one appearing on the Schimmel stag (see fig. 3.8). On the left side of the lacuna, at the waist level of the other figures, can be seen an outstretched hand grasping an

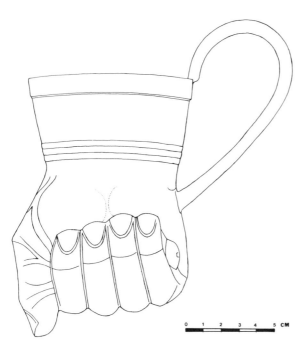

FIGURE 3.5 The Boston fist-shaped cup as it may have looked with handle.

mentioned in the texts, written with the Sumerogram GIŠ.BANŠUR.AD.KID. The tops of some of these tables, which are shown as if they had some depth, may actually have been more like open baskets than flat tabletops. A stone altar from Emirgazi of a similar shape, bearing an inscription of Tudhaliya IV, is in the Istanbul Museum.[16]

The upper part of the table has been given a lightly hatched and textured surface with a perimeter outlined in a row of dots. Lying on the center of the tabletop is a circular object, which appears to be a round loaf, much like pita bread. The bread surface is speckled and bisected by a vertical chased line. The dotting is probably an attempt on the part of the artisan to represent the blisters that form on this type of bread during baking. The line may suggest a ridge sliced in the dough surface before baking, along which the bread could later be broken into halves for offering. To the right of the bread is a rectangular form marked with two deep horizontal lines and chased with shallow vertical lines, possibly suggesting a stack of three objects. On the left is a triangular form, from which a clothlike object emerges amphora and another upraised at the same level, closed in a fist. At ground level is the upturned toe of a shoe. The back of the figure is indicated by a slim, raised ridge descending at a diagonal, slightly curled at the end, which doubtless represents a long tress of hair of the sort also worn by figures in the Alaca reliefs.[25] The bottom of the rear shoe appears at the right edge of the break in a vertical position, just as would the rear shoe of a kneeling person. Directly behind this figure is a short conical stand supporting a handleless jar.

The next five figures are beardless males and all seem to be dressed and coiffed similarly. The delicate chased patterns on their heads suggest that the artisan has tried to depict hair rather than any kind of cap. The same chasing pattern continues on what is clearly the hair that falls down their backs and disappears into their cloaks behind their shoulders. On each of these figures the hair on the top of the head is surrounded not by a flat band, like the one encircling the king's head, but rather by something which looks like a padded roll, somewhat resembling an Arab *agal*. This object even peaks or curls in front just as does the horn on the god's crown. Whether this roll represents part of the hairdo or something else is not clear. In any case there is no difference between the way the artisan has depicted it and the horn on the god's crown.

Although only four of these five figures have well-preserved heads, all seem to have been wearing a large loop earring. Each is also clad in a long, open robe with long, draping sleeves hemmed by decorative bands of embroidery. Beneath this, each also wears an undergarment with closely fitting sleeves, probably once all crosshatched, that extends beyond the shorter sleeves of the outer robe. A long skirt, also banded with embroidery, falls below the hem of the robe, partly concealing the rear foot and trailing on the ground as the figure walks.

The first of the five standing attendants in the relief holds a round object in his upraised right hand and makes a fist with his similarly raised left hand. That he holds a round loaf of bread is suggested by the frieze on the Schimmel stag cup where a figure holds an identical object (fig. 3.8), which is rendered similarly to the round loaf appearing on the offering table of our frieze. Identical, too, is the Hittite hieroglyph meaning "bread."[26] Unfortunately, in the case of the loaf held by this first standing attendant, the surface of the metal is so damaged by corrosion that its chased details have disappeared.

The second and third figures hold lyres of identical type. Each instrument has a rectangular sound box with a concave top. The strings are attached to a slanting crossbar by two upright arms set at divergent angles. The shorter (higher) strings are farthest from the players' bodies. Each player is shown with his left hand on the strings; the right is not shown. In this they differ from the representation of the harpist on a fragment of a relief vase from Boğazköy where both hands are represented on the strings.[27] Very likely these instruments were suspended from the players' necks by means of straps.[28]

Behind these two musicians follows a man holding a pair of disklike objects, which appear to be cymbals. The artisan shows the one in the man's right hand as lower than that in his left, perhaps to suggest that he has just sounded the instrument. A long, looping cloth or strap hangs from the farther disk, indicating something either by which these objects can be carried or by which their clangs can be muted. The fifth figure in the row merely holds a long staff decorated with horizontal hatchings; he grasps it with both hands near its tip.

The scene described thus far closely corresponds to textual descriptions of the offering ceremonies that form the most important part of the rituals performed by the king during cult festivals.[29] In these the king first drinks—an act not shown in our relief; he then pours a libation. According to the texts, the "cupbearer of squatting" (i.e., a kneeling attendant) comes prior to the act of libation, presumably in order to bring the king a necessary beverage (wine or beer). In the present representation this figure had, of course, to be shown behind, in deference to the king. On the Schimmel vessel he is even the last in the row (fig. 3.8). Next in the relief there stands a figure holding the loaf of bread, while in the ritual an attendant is said to hand a loaf of bread to the king, who breaks it. The attendant then takes it back and puts it on the table. The bread on the offering stand in our relief probably appears in anticipation of this act, but of course it could represent an earlier offering.

The texts, like the frieze itself, reveal that these acts were accompanied by music. The instrument most frequently mentioned in the texts is called the "instrument

FIGURE 3.7 Drawing of the relief scene about the rim of the Boston fist-shaped cup. (Drawing by T. Kendall.)

of Inanna (i.e., Ishtar)." It is sometimes called *zinar* with a Hattic word, and comes in a large and small variety: Hattic *hunzinar* and *ippizinar,* respectively. The old Hittite relief vase from Inandıktepe shows two lyre sizes, a large one played by two standing men and a small one carried on the arm.[30] It is certainly no coincidence that the Inandık vase shows two instrument sizes, just like those mentioned in the texts. We can therefore suggest that the lyres in our relief probably represent the "small Inanna instrument."

The texts mention other musical instruments as well,

FIGURE 3.6 Photomosaic of the relief scene about the rim of the Boston fist-shaped cup. Photograph © Justin Kerr.

but these are harder to identify.[31] The name of one, *galgalturi,* seems onomatopoetic and may possibly have been the word for cymbals.[32]

The man with the long stick could be the "man of the staff" mentioned in the texts. This official is said to walk in front of the worshippers and to lead them to their places. He seems out of place here at the end of the line, but it is apparent that the artisan had to compress into one scene individual activities that may not have occurred simultaneously.

Before cleaning nothing was visible on the fist behind these figures. It was a surprise when the removal of the corrosion revealed here a figure somewhat resembling the well-known Hittite mountain gods[33] but possessing several unique features. This is a bearded deity with a waist-length tress of hair, who rises from a moundlike "skirt" decorated with imbrications. While Hittite mountain gods normally have imbrications on their skirts that suggest rising outcrops or overlapping hills, the ones on this figure would appear to be overlapping rows of veined leaves. Similarly, the rows of projecting points normally appearing on the sides of the skirts of mountain gods depict rocky crags, but these suggest outwardly curling foliage. The question arises whether these details represent merely vegetation, or trees on a hillside.

The transition between the god's earthlike and fleshlike halves is marked by a belt. Above this he wears a short-sleeved tunic, with sleeves bunched at the elbow. On his arm, upraised before his face, he wears an armlet and a bracelet, and his hand clasps what appears to be a

piece of cloth. His headdress differs markedly from those of other mountain gods, for while the latter wear tall conical crowns with tiers of horns, this figure wears a crown composed of curling leaves emerging from a horned brim.

Behind this figure, also largely invisible before cleaning, is the masonry structure mentioned above, which marks the beginning and/or the end of the frieze. It has ten courses of masonry, lacks crenellations, and, like the offering stand, displays what can be interpreted as several objects on its top. Since the finely chased details that would have made the identification of these objects absolutely certain have been destroyed by corrosion, we, the joint authors, have found ourselves in some disagreement over the interpretation of this structure and the features on its top, and hence over the interpretation of the scene itself.

Güterbock proposes that the figure resembling the mountain god, with its leafy skirt and crown, may represent a "vegetation god" or perhaps a tree god. He notes that on the Schimmel stag cup and on a stamp seal in Adana a tree marks both the beginning and the end of the scene.[34] That the tree in these cases is more than a mere divider is shown by the fact that on the Schimmel vessel and probably on the unfinished relief from Alaca Höyük a dead stag is deposited at its foot.[35] The leafy figure here thus may be a deified form of this tree.

Also suggestive of vegetative powers in the scene are the small floral elements that fill all the open spaces between the figures. A flowering plant motif much like a *fleur de lis* appears behind the head of the king, again

below the lyres of each of the musicians, and again in front of the faces of both the "vegetation god" and the man with the staff. Except for the flower behind the king's head, which has five petals emerging from its pair of curling sepals, all the others have three; and with one exception, each of these flowers has petals tipped with small circles. In each, the leaves or blossoms have been chased with fine hatching. One other flower appears behind the figure of the Weather-God, but this, it will be seen, is a blossom that has not yet opened. One must wonder whether this detail had some significance originally. Elsewhere in the frieze the vacant space has been filled with small raised circles, chased with fine lines radiating from tiny central spots—not unlike the faces of daisies. At first glance all these patterns seem to have no function beyond being space fillers, but, as Güterbock proposes, they may suggest that this procession was walking through a flowering landscape, and that the ceremony took place in the spring, perhaps outside the city where parts of the Spring Festival are known to have been celebrated.[36]

Behind the "vegetation god" is the brickwork structure over which rose the handle. It marks the beginning and the end of the composition and could be connected either to the scene on the left or on the right or both. The two of us have questioned what it represents. The solution, of course, depends upon the correct understanding of the objects visible on top of the structure, but we each view them differently. Their nature is not absolutely certain due to the blurring of detail in the corrosion damage. The brickwork structure does not show any open-

53

FIGURE 3.8 Drawing of the relief scene about the rim of the Schimmel stag cup, now in the Metropolitan Museum of Art, New York. (Drawing by Ms. C. Coken.)

ing, and we cannot be sure whether the procession and the "vegetation god" on one side or the Weather-God on the other emanated from it. No gate is visible on either face.

Güterbock feels that the elements shown on top of the structure make it doubtful that this was a gate at all. He suggests that it might be yet another altar or stand for cultic objects behind the god, since some of the things on its top have virtually the same appearance as those atop the offering stand: a round object, which looks like bread, and a draped cloth. He thinks that the cloth hanging down on the right forms a link with the Weather-God in a way similar to the cloth on the offering table, and to that seen in front of the goddess at Fraktin.[37] Responding to Kendall (see below), he doubts that the perfectly round breadlike object could depict a human head, and speculates that the two objects that look like hands with extended arms might perhaps be cult objects or vessels fashioned in that shape.

Kendall, for his part, interprets the masonry structure not as an altar but as the tower of a city. He sees the "objects" on its top as the parts of a single, necessarily compressed human form rising above the walls with hands upraised. The round "bread" is the figure's head, although the facial details have been lost. The "cloth" is either the figure's hair or a kind of scarf or cape.[38] Since the figure's upraised arms are directed *toward* the leafy figure and the procession beyond, the tower and figure emerging from it would seem to mark the begin-

ning of the scene, all of which, with the exception of the Weather-God, rotates leftward.

The so-called "vegetation god" Kendall would identify as a mountain god covered with trees, which, he believes, would have symbolized the hill on or beside which the city stood and over which the procession has passed.[39] Like the figure on the tower, this god, too, gazes in the direction of the procession and thus seems merely an ancillary figure without important cultic significance. This god seems, in other words, merely an element of landscape.

Kendall, fully supporting Güterbock's opinion that the relief depicts a ceremony that took place during springtime, interprets it as a pictorial narrative of an event that began inside a city and concluded in the countryside. A procession, led by the king, has departed a town and has passed over a mountain covered with trees, across a field or through a wood to a suburban sanctuary of the Weather-God. The ceremony would have been observed by the city's multitudes who, represented by the single figure emerging from the tower, would have lined the city walls to watch and give praise or to vent their joy.

Looking for an interpretation for these simple motifs, it is impossible to avoid the suspicion that the "tower" actually symbolizes the Hittite capital itself—Hattuša—and that the suburban sanctuary of the Weather-God, reached by walking over a hill, is in fact Yazılıkaya, the famous rock shrine.[40]

Despite our differing opinions, each of us will admit the possibility that the masonry structure placed beneath the handle may have served a dual function. As city, it represents the beginning of the scene and the origination of the procession. As stone altar or masonry backdrop for the god, it represents the end of the procession: the inside of a temple.

THE FORM OF THE VESSEL AND POSSIBLE TEXTUAL REFERENCES TO ITS TYPE

The shape of this vessel raises the question of whether the fist form had a special meaning and whether a cup in this shape had a particular ritual significance. It seems evident that the gesture of clenching one or both hands in a fist and holding them either over the chest or before one was a kind of reverential salute. The gesture appears to have been assumed by votaries as they approached the sanctuary of a god and perhaps also the presence of the king. The gods, too, are shown with their hands displayed thus. It cannot have been simply an artistic convention, for the gesture seems too unusual and too specific.

Male figures in relief, when they are not holding implements, typically have both hands clenched in a fist as they walk. When the figures move left, it is the left fist which is held over the breast and the right which is extended. When they move right, the right fist is placed over the chest and the left extended. Females, on the other hand, are shown with one hand clenched in a fist and the other raised slightly and open, with the thumb and forefinger parted and directed toward the mouth. The meaning of the gesture is not at all clear, but the fist is so characteristic of figures in Hittite art that it does not really come as a surprise to find a vessel in this shape, although the piece is quite without parallel.

A cult vessel in the shape of a fist is something new. The question arises whether there is mention of such an object in the texts. There is no known Hittite word for "fist." As far as logograms are concerned, Akkadian UPNU ("balled hand, clenched fist") is used in Hittite only as a measure of capacity, meaning "handful." [41] A more intriguing candidate is the Sumerogram GEŠPÚ, although in Sumerian and Akkadian it has the meaning 'force' rather than 'fist.' A Hittite verb derived from the still unknown reading of GEŠPÚ is written GEŠPÚ-ahh- 'to force.' In Hittite, however, GEŠPÚ also describes a body part and is occasionally prefixed by the body-part determinative UZU. Since it is written with the combination of the signs ŠU ('hand') + DIM$_4$ ('bent'), Sommer tentatively proposed the meaning 'arm' or 'fist.' [42]

The Babylonian lexical texts offer two readings for GEŠPÚ. One equation of the logogram is with Akkadian emāqu, the meanings of which include 'force.' [43] Another is with umāšu, a noun derived from the verb amāšu which seems to mean 'to be bent, cramped' (said of fingers and toes). [44] Von Soden defines umāšu as 'the hold' in which a wrestler holds his adversary by his arm. [45] M. Civil rather thinks of the bent fingers of a wrestler grasping his adversary. [46] The "man of umāšu" is believed to be a wrestler, [47] and at some Hittite festivals the young men were said to engage in GEŠPÚ, [48] where either wrestling or boxing may be meant. One Hittite text mentions two iron GEŠPÚ's of a hunting bag (kurša), [49] and presumably these were the bent hooks by which the shoulder strap was fastened to the bag. Thus it seems possible that, as a body part, the Hittites interpreted this composite logogram as 'bent hand,' hence 'fist.'

Difficulties in the interpretation of GEŠPÚ as 'fist' arise from a text partly communicated by Otten, [50] which mentions offerings to various parts of the body of the Weather-God. These body parts are listed in the following order: UZU.ZAG.LU 'shoulder,' UZU.GAB 'chest,' and UTUL.HIA 'nipples,' 2 išhunau (?), 2 GEŠPÚ, followed by ŠU.MEŠ 'hands' and ŠU.SI.HIA humandaš 'to all fingers.' Because 'hands' are listed, Otten thought of 'upper arm' and 'forearm' respectively for išhunau and GEŠPÚ. [51] The mention of GEŠPÚ's and hands side by side would seem to suggest that the former could not signify the hands. Conversely, it is possible that the author of the text may have wanted offerings made to the god's hands in both their manifestations as powerful fists and protective hands.

Another text provides a list of objects mentioning side by side a silver GEŠPÚ and a silver 'hand' (akkadographically rittu) among metal objects including vessels. [52] That one would have had the shape of a fist and the other that of an open hand would be understandable.

In the prayer of Muwattali the god is asked to "walk by my right GEŠPÚ." [53] Here one would hardly expect 'fist,' but rather something like 'arm' or 'wrist.' Bittel reminds us of the fact that in the Yazılıkaya relief,[54] the god Sharruma holds Tudhaliya IV by the forearm, while the same is true of the Weather-God on the seals of Muwattali.[55] In each case, however, the hand of the king is shown as a fist.

Possibly the hand or fist joined together with the wrist or forearm was considered a unit just as the hieroglyphs depicting hands or fists include a part of the forearm.[56]

The texts frequently mention objects called GEŠPÚ. Once, with determinative GIŠ, which designates wooden objects, a GEŠPÚ is said to have been made of cedar.[57] More often GEŠPÚ's are made of precious metal. Hattusili I of the Old Kingdom, for example, donated one GEŠPÚ of silver and one bull of silver to the temple of the Weather-God (although GEŠPÚ is omitted in the Akkadian version),[58] and a later text notes that the Weather-God had a gold GEŠPÚ.[59] According to a description of cult images it seems that the divine image (šiuniyatar) of Zababa was a silver GEŠPÚ of 20 shekels.[60] This would explain why GEŠPÚ's are among deities and deified objects worshipped. Most probably there were vessels in the shape of GEŠPÚ containing a beverage, since a passage in one text can hardly be restored other than ištu [bi-ib-ri] GEŠPÚ . . . akuwanzi ("from the vessel in the shape of a GEŠPÚ . . . they drink").[61] The word bibru is the term used by the Hittites to designate vessels in animal or other fancy shapes.[62]

In light of this evidence it is tempting to propose that our silver fist was the type of object described in the texts as a bibru GEŠPÚ or simply a GEŠPÚ of silver, regardless of whether the logogram GEŠPÚ actually meant 'fist' or simply 'hand and wrist' as a unit.

THE DATE OF THE VESSEL

It is safe to assume that our fist-shaped cup was made for a "Great King Tudhaliya," because his name and title are inscribed on it. The question is, which Tudhaliya? There were three known kings of that name, Tudhaliya II (c. 1460–1440 B.C.), Tudhaliya III (c. 1400–1380 B.C.), and Tudhaliya IV (c. 1250–1220 B.C.). A Tudhaliya I, though once suspected, seems never to have existed.

On monuments and seals royal names are usually framed by the so-called aedicula, which consists of a winged sun-disk canopy supported at either end by the combination of the hieroglyphs GREAT and KING, which border the king's name in the middle. In some cases an additional group of two signs, probably representing the royal title Tabarna, is inserted on both sides between the name and the epithet GREAT KING.[63] It has been observed by Otten that the latter additions were only used by the last two kings of the thirteenth century, Tudhaliya IV and Suppiluliuma II.[64] The names of their earlier namesakes never have this addition. Since the short form of the royal name appears on the fist, one would thus suspect that the Tudhaliya represented here was one of the earlier kings of that name. On the other hand, since we cannot be absolutely certain that Tudhaliya IV never used the short form of his name, the attribution to Tudhaliya II or III must remain in doubt, judging from a purely textual basis. Adding to the problem are the inscriptions of Suppiluliuma II recently found on the "Südburg" in Boğazköy, which do indeed employ the short writing of the royal name.[65]

From here on the dating criteria must depend entirely on stylistic comparisons with other works of art. The most obvious parallels to the frieze on the fist are provided by the reliefs at Alaca Höyük. The Alaca reliefs bear certain details and stylistic features which are also represented on the fist but which do not appear in other reliefs, or on the relief vases, or on the Schimmel stag cup. We note, for example, the very close relationship of the dress of the cult attendants at both Alaca and on the fist, who wear robes with long, hanging sleeves and long underskirts which trail on the ground as they walk.[66] Figures dressed thus do not appear elsewhere. Similarly, both the figures on the fist and those at Alaca wear large loop earrings.[67] At Yazılıkaya, however, those worn by the only human figure depicted—the king—are much reduced in size, and on the Schimmel cup the figures do not wear them at all. Another more particular detail is the stylized leaflike design applied to the thighs of the stags and bulls in the Alaca reliefs to indicate muscles.[68] The very same pattern, it will be noted, appears on the preserved hindquarter of the bull on the fist. At Alaca this design has been added rather slavishly and naively to the animals, giving them an artificial look. The artisan who created the Schimmel vessels, however, has used the motif much more subtly and naturalistically on the forelegs of the bull cup but has disdained its use altogether in the standing stag appearing in the frieze of the stag cup.[69] Since the Schimmel vessels appear artistically and technically more sophisticated than the fist, one would assume that they are both products of a later period. The similarities between the fist and the Alaca reliefs suggest that they must be more closely related in time. Since the Alaca reliefs are themselves far less accomplished—and presumably much earlier—than the reliefs at Yazılıkaya, which are dated to Tudhaliya IV, it would appear that the king on the fist is one of the earlier monarchs of this name. It must, however, be admitted that the same trilobate rendering of the muscles is found in the representation of a bull on a seal of Muwattali II, son of Mursili, who reigned after 1300 B.C.[70]

Perhaps a more decisive clue to the date of the fist is provided by the peculiar flowers and raised circles that adorn the vacant space of the frieze. While such elements do not appear in the relief of the stag cup, similar floral motifs can be seen in the Alaca reliefs, where they appear in the landscape with animals. One such blossoming plant appears beside a standing stag, while a second stag nibbles another.[71] The same plant motifs, again together with raised circles or rosettes, also appear on a Hittite ivory plaque from Megiddo, which the excavators assigned to the latter half of the fourteenth century.[72] The same filler motifs may also be seen on the gold bowl from Ugarit, which is dated stratigraphically to the period just prior to the destruction of the city in an earthquake reported by Abi-milki of Tyre to Akhenaten in the Amarna letters—an event which must have occurred about 1365 B.C.[73] Related floral and filler motifs also occur in certain objects from the tomb of Tutankhamun but soon thereafter go out of style.[74]

The conclusion we reach is that the fist cannot have belonged to Tudhaliya IV, since he is identified with the Yazılıkaya reliefs, which, with the Schimmel pieces, obviously belong to the latest, most developed phase of Hittite art. Because of its affinities with the Ras Shamra gold bowl, the Megiddo plaque, and imitative Egyptian pieces, all of which belong to the early or mid-fourteenth century B.C., it seems most likely that the fist belonged to Tudhaliya III, although an identification with Tudhaliya II cannot be absolutely ruled out. The fist, then, would lend further support to the long-held view that the Sphinx Gate of Alaca Höyük should be dated to the late fifteenth or early fourteenth century B.C.[75]

NOTES

1. The object bears the MFA loan number RL 144.1977.

2. See infra n. 20.

3. O. W. Muscarella, *Ancient Art: The Norbert Schimmel Collection* (Mainz 1974) nos. 123–124 (stag: MMA 1989.281.10; bull: 1989.281.11). Cf. also K. Tuchelt, *Tiergefässe in Kopf- und Protomengestalt* (Berlin 1962); O. Carruba, "Rhyta in den Hethitischen Texten," *Kadmos* 6 (1968) 88–97; and especially R. B. Koehl, "The Silver Stag 'Bibru' from Mycenae," in this volume. These vessels, long called "rhyta" after their similarity to later horn-shaped vessels with animal protomes used for pouring and aerating wine, are technically not rhyta since they lack drain holes in their bottoms. They are merely fancy drinking cups of a peculiar type that were known in Hittite/Akkadian as *bibru*. The authors would like to thank Dr. Koehl for emending our paper and suggesting that we cease using the traditional, if inaccurate, term "rhyton" to describe these objects.

4. Richard Newman, Research Scientist at the Museum of Fine Arts, prepared the following metallographic analysis of the fist on December 28, 1988: "A fragment of silver, taken during an earlier examination of the fist in 1980 from the edge of the large circular loss on the back of the hand, was repolished and analyzed in an electron beam microprobe. In overall appearance, the metal in the section is highly fractured and shows considerable corrosion. The thickness of the metal is about 0.4 mm. The inner surface, which is next to the old epoxy fill, shows a well-crystallized layer of silver sulfide (up to about 0.04 mm thick). The outer surface of the section shows no distinct corrosion layer, but the metal has been partially corroded well into the interior: corrosion can be seen extending through nearly half the thickness of the metal (about 0.2 mm). Lenses of corrosion have developed roughly parallel to the surface; heavily cold-worked metal typically corrodes in this way. Qualitative energy-dispersive X-ray fluorescence analyses in the microprobe suggest that both silver chloride and silver sulfide are present in the corroded areas.

The alloy composition was determined by wavelength-dispersive X-ray fluorescence in the microprobe. Pure element standards were used, and matrix corrections were carried out by the ZAF method. The metal composition is an average of four spot analyses (with standard deviations in parentheses);

two partially corroded areas close to the outer surface were also analyzed.

	Uncorroded metal	Partially corroded area (about 0.1 mm from surface)	Partially corroded area (at outer surface)
Silver	97.8% ($\pm$0.7)	78.1%	67.1%
Gold	0.4% ($\pm$0.1)	0.8%	1.6%
Copper	0.2% ($\pm$0.03)	ND	ND
Total	98.4%	78.9%	68.7%

The analytical totals for the surface analyses are low due to the presence of corrosion. Lead was not detected in any of the areas analyzed (the minimum detection level for this element under the analytical conditions employed was about 0.1%). Copper, with a minimum detection limit of 0.09%, was not detected in two partially corroded areas which were analyzed.

A number of energy-dispersive X-ray fluorescence analyses of the surface of the fist were carried out on electrolytically cleaned areas and uncleaned (but only slightly corroded) areas. Alloy compositions were calculated on the basis of a silver standard. Two cleaned areas showed a composition of about 98.6% silver and 1.4% gold; copper was detected at trace level, and lead was not detected. The four uncleaned areas showed a slightly different composition: about 98.9% silver, 0.9% gold, 0.2% lead, and a trace of copper. Microprobe analysis of the metallographic section shows that the outer surface of the metal is depleted in silver and copper and enriched in gold with respect to the uncorroded interior metal . . ."

5. On June 6, 1990, two weeks after completing his restoration of the fist, Merville Nichols, conservator at the Museum of Fine Arts since 1948, died suddenly at his home of heart failure. He was a master conservator, with a specialty in metalwork, whose dedication, infinite patience, talent, and sense of humor are missed by all (TK).

6. Sarah M. Carrig, "The Hittite Fist Rhyton at the Museum of Fine Arts in Boston" (Harvard University: Fine Arts 131, Professor Irene Winter; May 17, 1983).

7. The handle on the Schimmel stag cup is attached to the rim directly over the tree in its relief scene and joins the protome of the stag just above the thigh of the folded leg. (See Muscarella [supra n. 3] no. 123, third fig.) The handle arches outward, above and away from the rim, in a near perfect half-circle and returns to the stag's thigh as a straight diagonal. The handle is hollow, being flat on the outside and curved on the inside, and is 1.45 cm in width. Running the length of the curved edge is a solder seam. The lost handle of the fist must

have been nearly identical. The torn solder joint on the rim is 1.6 cm in width, while that on the ball of the palm is 1.45 cm. I would like to express my profound thanks to Dr. Prudence O. Harper for inviting me to make a close visual examination of the Schimmel vessel in the Metropolitan Museum (TK).

8. H. G. Fischer, "An Elusive Shape Within the Fisted Hands of Egyptian Statues," *MMAJ* 10 (1975) 9–21.

9. When the fist was first viewed by Dr. Jeanny V. Canby in 1977, she suggested that the object might have been intended to represent a glove rather than a hand—possibly a falconer's glove—since Hittite divinities are often shown holding birds of prey on their hands (see, for example, H. Th. Bossert, *Altanatolien* [Berlin 1942], figs. 570, 699–700, 816, and Muscarella [supra n. 3], no. 123, second fig.). Following the cleaning of the fist, however, it became apparent, particularly in the detailing of the thumb surface, that the object indeed represents a closed hand. The curious row of v-shaped ridges behind the knuckles, which we take to be a highly stylized vein pattern, could possibly be interpreted as the zigzag edge of a half-glove, but since the line disappears before rounding either side of the hand and does not appear on the thumb, this seems most unlikely.

10. The lip of the stag cup exhibits a far more sophisticated treatment. Here the craftsman has folded the original raw edge of the rim over upon itself in the same manner as on the fist but has created a thicker, more rounded lip by applying a second metal roll to the edge of the first. This piece was adorned with intermittent niello sections, while the metal directly below was patterned with niello lunettes. Because the stag cup exhibits more advanced style and technique, it would seem to be later in date.

11. This hairstyle is represented in the round, for example, on a small bronze statuette of a beardless Hittite god in the Louvre, which appears photographed from behind in E. Akurgal and M. Hirmer, *The Art of the Hittites* (New York 1962), monochrome pl. 50. The waist-length hair has been gathered behind the ears and appears to have been loosely braided in a single strand or bound with a kind of net.

12. See H. G. Güterbock, "Hethitische Götterbilder und Kultobjekte," in R. M. Boehmer and H. Hauptmann, eds., *Beiträge zur Altertumskunde Kleinasiens: Festschrift für Kurt Bittel* (Mainz 1983) 203–217, esp. 216.

13. Presumably the bull was rendered in much the same manner here as in the cult figure of the bull appearing in the reliefs at Alaca (see K. Bittel, *Die Hethiter* [Munich 1976] = *Les Hittites* [Paris 1976], fig. 214). For further discussion of the motif, cf. M. Wäfler, "Zum Felsrelief von Imamkulu," *MDOG* 107 (1975) 17–26.

14. E. Laroche, *Les noms des Hittites* (Paris 1966) 176 and 289.

15. T. Özgüç and R. Temizer, *Inandıktepe* (Ankara 1988). See fig. 64 for an overall drawing of the reliefs.

16. Bossert (supra n. 9), fig. 549.

17. Bittel (supra n. 13), fig. 198.

18. See Özgüç (supra n. 15).

19. Bittel (supra n. 13), figs. 195, 214, 221, 234, 249, 253. One of the most detailed representations is in the so-called seal of "Tarkondemos" in Baltimore: Bittel (supra n. 13), fig. 185. Cf. H. G. Güterbock, "The Hittite Seals in the Walters Art Gallery," *JWalt* 34 (1977) 11–16.

20. E. Laroche, *Les hieroglyphs hittites* I (Paris 1960) nos. 207 over 88 and no. 18. We read the inscription from left to right because it accompanies the figure looking to the left and because the title normally follows the name, although the sign *tu* is in the opposite direction. Cf. P. Neve, "Die Ausgrabungen in Boğazköy-Hattuša, 1985," *AA* 1986, 395–396, fig. 29a, where the king and sign look in the same direction.

21. Bittel (supra n. 13), fig. 198.

22. Bittel (supra n. 13), figs. 160 and 165.

23. See, for example, *ANET* 352.

24. K. Bittel et al., *Das hethitische Felsheiligtum Yazılıkaya* (Berlin 1975) 12; and K. Bittel, *Hattusha, The Capital of the Hittites* (New York 1970) 109.

25. Cf. Bittel (supra n. 13), fig. 218.

26. Laroche (supra n. 20) 181.

27. Bittel (supra n. 13), fig. 139.

28. For a discussion of nearly identical contemporary instruments from Egypt, see *Egypt's Golden Age: The Art of Living in the New Kingdom, 1558–1085 B.C.* (Boston 1982) 255–260.

29. Cf. *ANET* 358–361.

30. See Özgüç (supra n. 15).

31. See, for example, *ANET* 358, 361.

32. Cymbals of Bronze Age date are actually known from the so-called Vulchitrun Treasure from northern Bulgaria. This is a ritual service consisting of a large two-handled kantharos, a smaller single-handled dipper, three smaller single-handled cups, and a triple vessel used for filling the latter simultaneously; these were accompanied by one large pair of cymbals and two and a half pairs of smaller cymbals, all of solid gold. Cf. *Thracian Treasures from Bulgaria* (New York 1977) 13–14, pl. I; and A. Fol and I. Marazov, *Thrace and the Thracians* (New York 1977) 60, 64 (fig.). Cymbals are known to have been used commonly in Anatolian cults in the first millennium. Cf. M. J. Vermaseren, *Cybele and Attis: The Myth and the Cult* (London 1977) 118–119, and G. Showerman, *The Great Mother of the Gods* (Chicago 1969) 17–19.

33. Bittel et al. (supra n. 24) 129.

34. H. G. Güterbock, "Hittite *kurša* 'Hunting Bag,'" in

A. Leonard and B. B. Williams, eds., *Essays in Ancient Civilization Presented to Helene J. Kantor,* SAOC 47 (Chicago 1989) 113, n. 4, pl. 18a.

35. Güterbock (supra n. 34) 119, pl. 19. S. Alp, *Beiträge zur Erforschung des hethitischen Tempels* (Ankara 1983) 98, proposes to equate this tree with the Hittite *eya*-tree. This is possible but not provable.

36. H. G. Güterbock, "An Outline of the Hittite *AN. TAH.ŠUM* Festival," *JNES* 19 (1960) 80–89, esp. the fourteenth and fifteenth days mentioning the worship of the stele of the Weather-God, near the boxwood trees adjacent to the *tarnu* house.

37. See supra n. 21.

38. Note the similarity between these details and the features of the upper part of the "sword-swallower" in the relief from Alaca (Bittel [supra n. 13], fig. 218).

39. Note highly relevant comments on the ancient forestation of the environs of Boğazköy in Bittel (supra n. 24) 12–14.

40. See Bittel et al. (supra n. 24) and Bittel (supra n. 24) 91–112.

41. W. von Soden, *Akkadisches Handwörterbuch* (*AH*) (Wiesbaden 1965–1981) s.v. *upnu*.

42. F. Sommer, *Die Ahhiyawa-Urkunden* (München 1932; reprint Hildesheim 1975) 180–181.

43. *Chicago Assyrian Dictionary* (*CAD*) 4, "E" (Chicago 1958) 157–161.

44. *AH* (supra n. 41) s.v. *umāšu, amāšu,* and *CAD* 1, "A" pt. 2, 28.

45. *AH* (supra n. 41) s.v. *umāšu.*

46. M. Civil in F. Rochberg-Halton, ed., *Language, Literature and History: Philological and Historical Studies Presented to Erica Reiner,* American Oriental Series 67 (New Haven 1987) 52, n. 24, kindly shown to HGG by the author.

47. B. Landsberger, *WZKM* (1960) 115–117.

48. *KUB* 25.23 i 22; *KUB* 44.42 obv. 16; cf. *KUB* 44.20 11–12.

49. *KUB* 5.7 rev. 24, and cf. Sommer (supra n. 42) 181.

50. H. Otten, "Die Textfunde der Campagnen 1958 und 1959," *MDOG* 93 (1962) 76; H. G. Güterbock, "A new look at one Ahhiyawa text," in H. Otten, E. Akurgal, H. Ertem, and A. Süel, eds., *Hittite and Other Anatolian and Near Eastern Studies in Honour of Sedat Alp* (Ankara 1992) 238.

51. The evidence does not support the meaning 'sinew, bowstring' proposed for *išhunau,* as demonstrated by Güterbock (supra n. 50) 239ff.

52. *KUB* 32.129 i 14. I thank Harry Hoffner for this reference (HGG).

53. *KUB* 6.45 iii 71. *ANET* 398b.

54. Bittel (supra n. 13), fig. 253.

55. H. G. Güterbock, *Siegel aus Boğazköy* I, AfO-BH 5,

nos. 38, 39; T. Beran, *Die hethitische Glyptik von Boğazköy* (Berlin 1967) no. 250, 251. Cf. Bittel (supra n. 13), fig. 191.

56. Laroche, *Les hieroglyphs hittites,* nos. 28–41.

57. *KUB* 23.27 i 23.

58. Ph. Houwink ten Cate, *Anatolica* 11 (1983) 47.

59. *KBo* 21.34 ii 45–49.

60. *KUB* 38.1 i 4.

61. *KUB* 10.89 ii 2–3.

62. See supra n. 3.

63. Laroche (supra n. 20) no. 277. J. D. Hawkins, "The New Inscription from the Südburg of Boğazköy-Hattuša," *AA* 1990, 303–314. P. Neve, "Ausgrabungen in Boğazköy-Hattuša 1988," *AA* 1989, 271–332, esp. 327, fig. 58.

64. H. Otten, "Ausgrabungen in Boğazköy-Hattuša 1988: Die Hieroglyphisch-Luwische Inschrift," in Neve (supra n. 63) 333–337.

65. Otten (supra n. 64).

66. Bittel (supra n. 13), fig. 212.

67. Bittel (supra n. 13), figs. 218, 220–222.

68. Bittel (supra n. 13), figs. 224, 225, 228. For a discussion of this motif see H. L. Kantor, "Oriental Institute Museum Notes, No. 9: A 'Syro-Hittite' Treasure in the Oriental Institute Museum," *JNES* 16 (1957) 151–153.

69. Muscarella (supra n. 3) no. 124.

70. H. G. Güterbock, *Siegel aus Boğazköy* II, AfO=BH 7, no. 1.

71. Bittel (supra n. 13), figs. 224, 225.

72. G. Loud, *The Megiddo Ivories* (Chicago 1939) 10, pl. 11.a–h. The same rosettes and similar plant motifs occur on a gold disk in the Oriental Institute Museum (A 29188): Kantor (supra n. 68), pls. 20, 21.

73. C. F. A. Schaeffer, *Ugaritica* II (Paris 1949) 5, pls. 2–5, 8. We wish to thank Dr. Irene Winter for bringing this parallel to our attention.

74. Schaeffer (supra n. 73) 29, fig. 8, and pls. 9, 11, and G. M. Crowfoot and N. de G. Davies, "The Tunic of Tutankhamun," *JEA* 27 (1941) 113–130, pls. 14–22.

75. Bittel (supra n. 13) 200–201 had dated the Alaca reliefs to the fourteenth century B.C., while M. J. Mellink, "Observations on the Sculptures of Alaca Hüyük," *Anadolu* 14 (1970) [1972] 15–27, considers an even higher date possible.

THE SILVER STAG "BIBRU" FROM MYCENAE

◆

ROBERT B. KOEHL

The publication of this silver Hittite fist-shaped cup calls to mind not only the stag and bull protome cups from the Schimmel collection, but also the silver stag-shaped vessel from Shaft Grave IV at Mycenae (Athens National Museum no. 388) (fig. 3.9).[1] Schliemann found the vessel in the grave's southeast corner, placed inside a copper vessel, and he compared it to zoomorphic vessels that he had found at Troy. It was von Bissing who first recognized the object's similarity to ceramic zoomorphic vessels from central Anatolia, citing as a parallel a deer-shaped vessel in Berlin reportedly from Kültepe.[2] Not only did both vessels demonstrate an attempt at a somewhat naturalistic rendering of their animal subjects, but each also had a spout emerging from the center of the animal's back.

Von Bissing's note was written to supplement an article by Karo on Aegean rhyta, in which Karo left open the question of the silver stag's origin, although doubting that it was Minoan.[3] Both scholars' contributions are significant: Karo published the first general classification of rhyta; von Bissing pointed out the vessel's likely Anatolian origin—although their designation of it as a "rhyton" is misleading. Karo had correctly adopted the term "rhyton," from the Greek *rheo,* meaning 'to flow,' for Aegean vessels furnished with two openings; their location was dependent on the particular shape of the object. Karo, however, mistakenly took the hole which pierces the stag's right nostril as a second opening or outlet, beside the spout, on its back—an observation which he subsequently corrected in his publication of the Shaft Grave material (fig. 3.10).[4] Nevertheless, the term "rhyton" still attaches itself to the silver stag, even in some of the most recent discussions of it.[5] Unlike many, however, Professor Vermeule, in her famous Semple Lectures on the Shaft Graves, called the vase a "drinking-cup," a term which indicates her sensitivity to the subject and awareness of these terminological difficulties.[6] In tribute to Professor Vermeule, I would like to explore some of the questions which linger about the vessel's ultimate origin and its position within the context of the Aegean.

Many scholars after von Bissing, including Professor Vermeule, have felt that the object is exotic to the Aegean and find Anatolia as its most likely source.[7] The closest parallels are certainly the stag-, lion-, and bull-shaped vessels from Kültepe, which date to the

FIGURE 3.9 Silver Stag *BIBRU*, Athens, National Archaeological Museum no. 388. (Photo by R. B. Koehl.)

FIGURE 3.10 Detail of Silver Stag *BIBRU* (Photo by R. B. Koehl.)

nineteenth–eighteenth centuries B.C.[8] Like these, the silver stag has a prominent spout on its back through which the vessel was filled. The spout's interior diameter of 4.1 cm is quite capacious, considering that the piece's length, including the head, is only 25.3 cm.[9] Unlike the silver vessel, its Anatolian ceramic counterparts have holes in the nostrils which communicate with the interior. Perhaps these were functional, and thus the ceramic vessels might be classified as rhyta. Yet the ceramic vessels in the form of an animal's head have unpierced nostrils; these were apparently used as cups.[10] I think it likely that the animal vessels with the spouts on their back were also used for drinking and that the holes are "firing holes" (discussed further below). This same type of zoomorphic vessel continued in the Hittite world at least into the late fifteenth or early fourteenth century B.C., as witnessed by the discovery of a pair of ninety-centimeter-high terracotta bull-shaped vessels from the Büyükkale at Boğazköy.[11] Thus a rather continuous series of Anatolian zoomorphic vases emerges, with the stag vessel from Shaft Grave IV falling in the middle. Its LH I context provides a *terminus ante quem* of c. 1500, or c. 1625 B.C., according to the most recently proposed chronology.[12]

Indeed, it is the spout which primarily distinguishes

Anatolian zoomorphic vessels from their Aegean counterparts, a feature which will be considered further, in regard to the different functions of these containers. Instead of a spout, the Aegean zoomorphic vessels, all of which are ceramic, have a small opening behind the animal's head, no more than 1.3 cm in diameter.[13] A second, smaller, hole, .4–.5 cm in diameter, pierces the muzzle or, more rarely, the chest. The size and placement of these openings correspond to the openings on Aegean zoomorphic head rhyta of the "perpendicular" type.[14]

The Hittite origin of the silver stag vessel seems likely, not only on typological but also on metallurgical grounds. Schliemann published the results of an analysis which found that the vessel was 67% silver and 33% lead.[15] This finding has been cited by some scholars as evidence for the vessel's Anatolian origin,[16] and by others for a possible Cycladic origin.[17] However, a recent analysis of the vessel's metallurgical contents has yielded surprisingly different results. It appears that the vessel is composed of 99% silver, about 0.5% gold, and no more than 0.2% lead, proportions which match almost exactly those of the Hittite fist-shaped vessel, according to the results reported above.[18] That these two vessels should be made almost entirely of pure silver is consistent with their purpose as cult equipment and royal gifts (discussed below). The purity of these vessels also corresponds to the Hittite and other Near Eastern texts which list zoomorphic vessels by material, usually silver or gold, and weight.[19] *BIBRI* were apparently made in various stones and also silver- or gold-plated wood, although silver *BIBRI* are mentioned most often.[20]

The terms for Hittite zoomorphic vessels have been examined by several scholars, most notably Professor Güterbock, and, in many cases, have been successfully compared with actual known specimens.[21] *BIBRU* seems to be the generic term for specially shaped vessels which are usually zoomorphic. In its original Akkadian context the word designated a bird. Besides material and weight, the Hittite inventories of cult equipment list various types of *BIBRI*, and, in the case of zoomorphic *BIBRI*, their species.[22] As we have just learned, the *BIBRU GEŠPÚ*, or simply *GEŠPÚ*, may refer to a fist-shaped cup. Another type of *BIBRU* is the *BIBRU GU* or 'neck.' This "neck *BIBRU*" is always accompanied by a species of animal, which is also described as "kneeling" or "standing forward."[23] As Professor Güterbock has proposed, this type corresponds well with the silver stag and bull protome cups now in the Metropolitan Museum, which indeed depict the animal resting on its knees.[24] The silver stag-shaped vessel from Shaft Grave IV undoubtedly belongs to a third category of zoomorphic vessel, designated in the inventory lists simply as a *BIBRU*, followed by the animal's species, its material(s), and sometimes the added descriptive formula, "standing on all fours."[25] It may well be to this type of *BIBRU* that the Hittite king Suppiluliuma I refers in a letter to the pharaoh of Egypt in which he states, "I am sending you a present of one silver *BIBRU*, stag-shaped, five minas in weight."[26]

While never specified in the texts, the zoomorphic *BIBRI* described as "standing on all fours" would surely have had spouts in the middle of their backs, a feature which is common to many zoomorphic vessels in the Near East, from the fourth millennium onward.[27] When the spout is considered in light of the textual evidence, the manner in which this type of *BIBRU* was used becomes clear. In addition to inventories of cult vessels, *BIBRI* are mentioned in Hittite texts relating to cult practices.[28] In these we learn that the king or the royal couple would drink from a *BIBRU* and after-

wards offer a drink to the deity.[29] In some cases the type of *BIBRU* must be the complete animal type, like the silver stag from Mycenae, since the royal couple is described as seated and drinking from an animal-shaped *BIBRU* "standing on all fours."[30] While the two other types of *BIBRI*, the *GU* and *GEŠPÚ*, are provided with rims and handles to facilitate drinking, the only opening on the *BIBRU* "standing on all fours" is its spout. Since it is unlikely that large vessels, such as the clay bulls from Boğazköy, were lifted and tilted back for drinking directly from the spout, we should imagine that drinking tubes were inserted into the spout. Indeed, the use of drinking tubes is attested on seals of Middle Bronze Age date from Acemhüyük and Kültepe, and on a late fifteenth–early fourteenth-century relief vessel from Boğazköy.[31]

This custom seems peculiarly Anatolian and Near Eastern and is nowhere attested in the Aegean. Indeed, we cannot know how the silver stag *BIBRU* was used by its Mycenaean owner, although its discovery inside a copper vessel may establish a positive association with liquids. Aegean zoomorphic rhyta were probably not drunk from directly—their openings are rather small and unobtrusive—but rather used to pour libations and to fill drinking vessels, in the manner described above. The confusion which may have confronted the Mycenean who came into possession of the silver stag *BIBRU* may explain the hole which was drilled through the stag's right nostril (fig. 3.10). The drilling apparently caused this nostril to extend much further than the left nostril. I suspect that the hole and the distorted right nostril were the results of an unsuccessful attempt by an Aegean metalsmith to transform the Hittite cult vessel into a more familiar Aegean rhyton. After all, it comes from the grave "with all of the best rhyta": the gold lion's head, silver bull's head, and silver "Siege Rhyton."[32] Since its head, up to the snout, as well as the legs and body, is hollow, an Aegean craftsman might have thought it a relatively simple task to bore an opening through its muzzle. Originally, this nostril may have had a small indentation, like that preserved on the left, which merely gives the appearance of an opening. Yet, as mentioned above, the ceramic Anatolian zoomorphic vessels in the form of a complete animal do have perforations through both nostrils. While these may have served for pouring libations, the *BIBRI* from which "drinks to the gods" are poured are metal or stone, according to the texts cited above. And, as none of these have perforations, perhaps the nostril holes on the ceramic *BIBRI* are "firing holes," placed in an anatomically correct and inconspicuous manner. On closed vessels such as these, whose only other opening was the spout, firing holes may well have been necessary to prevent their cracking or exploding in the kiln.[33]

Not only might its original function have been unknown to its Mycenaean owner, but the religious and iconographic significance of the silver stag *BIBRU* may also have been obscure. Hittite zoomorphic *BIBRI* take the form of the animal with which a particular divinity is associated and may even be considered the "property" of that divinity.[34] Thus, the silver stag *BIBRU.GU* in the Metropolitan Museum and the silver stag *BIBRU* "standing on all fours" were probably *BIBRI* of the "Protective Deity," who is often depicted in Hittite art standing on the back of a stag (see here Güterbock, fig. 3.8).[35] Whether or not its Mycenaean owner was aware of its religious worth may have been of secondary importance: its principal worth may have been entirely its weight. We recall the Amarna letter mentioned earlier, in which Suppiluliuma I complains of having not received the gifts which he expected but nonetheless sends the pharaoh a silver stag *BIBRU,* weighing 5 minas.[36] By contrast, Hittite texts, such as the cult inventories, mention specific types of vessels by name, appearance, and material, but not by weight.[37] It is therefore likely that the silver stag *BIBRU* would have come to Mycenae through royal gift-giving or exchange.[38] At Mari, texts that refer to the manufacture of silver and gold zoomorphic head cups, which were subsequently sent as royal gifts, always record their weight.[39]

If, indeed, royal gift-giving explains the presence of the silver stag *BIBRU* at Mycenae, it would push back the evidence for ties between the Aegean and central Anatolia at least a century prior to the earliest textual evidence. As it now stands, the Madduwatta text, dated c. 1450–1430 B.C., documents the earliest contact between Mycenaeans and Hittites.[40] Mycenaean interest in this area, however, was preceded by Minoan settlements on the western shores, which date at least to MM III, c. 1600 B.C., i.e., contemporary with the Shaft Graves.[41] This is the same date assigned to the only other known Anatolian import which may have arrived in the Aegean through royal gift exchange: the stone leopard-protome scepter-axe from Mallia.[42] Thus, while it is possible that the silver *BIBRU* came to Mycenae directly from a Hittite prince, it may originally have been a gift to a Minoan chieftain, who subsequently passed it on to a Mycenaean *wanax,* along with many more of the items found in the Shaft Graves.[43]

The possibility that royal gifts were exchanged between Anatolian and Aegean dynasts in the early years of the Late Bronze Age is exciting to ponder, especially in view of the apparent deterioration in relations between these areas in the following years. Recently, Eric Cline suggested that the scarcity of Mycenaean pottery from Hittite contexts of the fourteenth and thirteenth centuries and the dearth of textual references to trade between these regions may be explained as the result of a Hittite trade embargo against the Mycenaeans.[44] This situation stands in marked contrast to the evidence for Mycenaean trade with Cyprus and the Levant, where the finding of Mycenaean pottery is a common occurrence.[45] The silver *BIBRU* and stone scepter-axe, however, may reflect a period of more cordial ties, when Minoan coastal settlements were established, apparently without any use of force. The tenor of these initial contacts was upset, however, during the fifteenth century, as the Madduwatta letter implies. Mycenaeans replace Minoans at these sites and the contacts, at least as reflected in the texts, are often hostile and always volatile. It is these post-sixteenth-century B.C. contacts with Mycenaeans that provide the historical background out of which Homer's vision of a Trojan War must have grown, one in which the exchange of Aegeo-Anatolian diplomatic gifts, such as the silver *BIBRU,* would have seemed a distant memory.

NOTES

1. H. Schliemann, *Mycenae: A Narrative of Researches and Discoveries at Mycenae and Tiryns* (1880; reprint New York 1976) 257–260.

2. F. W. von Bissing, "Zur Geschichte der antiken Rhyta," *AA* 1923–1924, 106–108.

3. G. Karo, "Minoische Rhyta," *JdI* 26 (1911) 249–270.

4. G. Karo, *Die Schachtgräber von Mykenai* (Munich 1930–1933) no. 388, pls. 115–116.

5. W. Orthmann, *Propyläen Kunstgeschichte 14. Der Alte Orient* (Berlin 1975) no. 367b; Z. A. Stos-Gale and C. F. Mac-Donald, "Sources of Metals and Trade in the Bronze Age Aegean," in N. H. Gale, ed., *Bronze Age Trade in the Mediterranean* (Jonsered 1990) 249–288, esp. 271–273 and 285; E. Cline, "Hittite Objects in the Bronze Age Aegean," *AnatStud* 41 (1991) 134–135.

6. E. T. Vermeule, *The Art of the Shaft Graves at Mycenae* (Norman, Okla. 1975) 15.

7. T. Özgüç and N. Özgüç, *Kültepe Raporu 1949* (Ankara 1953) 224, pl. 39; E. Akurgal and M. Hirmer, *The Art of the Hittites* (New York 1962) 40; K. Tuchelt, *Tiergefässe in Kopf- und Protomengestalt* (Berlin 1962) 28, 32; H.-G. Buchholz, "Das Blei in der mykenischen Kultur und in der bronzezeit-lichen Metallurgie Zyperns," *JdI* 87 (1972) 22; Orthmann (supra n. 5); Vermeule (supra n. 6); E. N. Davis, *The Vapheio Cups and Aegean Gold and Silver Ware* (New York 1977) 233–234.

8. H. Th. Bossert, *Altanatolien* (Berlin 1942), figs. 397, 398, 402, 403; Akurgal and Hirmer (supra n. 7), pls. XII, 34. See, also, discussions by Özgüç and Özgüç (supra n. 7) 224, pl. 39, and Tuchelt (supra n. 7) 28–33.

9. I would like to express my thanks to Professor C. Doumas for permission to examine the vessel in the Athens National Museum during the winter of 1981.

10. Zoomorphic head cups are illustrated in Akurgal and Hirmer (supra n. 7), pls. 31 (above), 32 (above).

11. P. Neve, "Die Grabungen auf Büyükkale 1963," *MDOG* 95 (1965) 47–53; K. Bittel, *Hattusha, The Capital of the Hittites* (New York 1970) 72–73, pls. 15–16.

12. P. P. Betancourt, "Dating the Aegean Late Bronze Age with radiocarbon," *Archaeometry* 29 (1987) 45–49; H. N. Michael and P. P. Betancourt, "Further arguments for an early date" and "Addendum," *Archaeometry* 30 (1988) 169–175, 180–181. See also Hardy, ed. (1990) infra n. 14.

13. These and all types of Aegean rhyta are the subject of a monograph in preparation by the present author. For all types of Aegean zoomorphic vessels, including rhyta, see E. B. Miller, "Zoomorphic Vases in the Bronze Age Aegean" (Ph.D. diss., N.Y.U., 1984). For convenient illustrations, see S. Marinatos and M. Hirmer, *Kreta, Thera, und mykenische Hellas* (Munich 1976), pl. 90.

14. On the classifications of Aegean rhyta, see now R. B. Koehl, "The Functions of Aegean Bronze Age Rhyta," in R. Hägg and N. Marinatos, eds., *Sanctuaries and Cults in the Aegean Bronze Age* (Stockholm 1981) 179–188; R. B. Koehl, "The Rhyta from Akrotiri and Some Preliminary Observations on their Functions in Selected Contexts," in D. A. Hardy, ed., *Thera and the Aegean World* III (London 1990) I.350–359.

15. Schliemann (supra n. 1) 257.

16. Davis (supra n. 7) 233–234; Buchholz (supra n. 7) 22.

17. Vermeule (supra n. 6) 15.

18. Stos-Gale and MacDonald (supra n. 5) The authors state that the lead isotope composition of the silver stag "looks reasonably consistent" with lead and silver ore deposits from the Taurus. The proportions are quoted from Cline (supra n. 5).

19. See, e.g., O. Carruba, "Rhyta in den Hethitischen Texten," *Kadmos* 6 (1968) 88–97, esp. 92; O. W. Muscarella, *Ancient Art: The Norbert Schimmel Collection* (Mainz 1974) no. 123; K. Deller, "SAG.DU UR.MAH, 'Löwenkopfsitula und Löwenkopfbecher,'" *BaM* 16 (1985) 327–345, esp. 335ff.; S. Dunham, "Metal animal-headed cups at Mari," in O. M. C. Haex, H. H. Curvers, and P. M. M. G. Akkermans, eds., *To the Euphrates and Beyond: Archaeological Studies in honour of Maurits N. van Loon* (Brookfield 1989) 213–220.

20. The tendency of scholars to see the wooden *BIBRI* as statues, and not as vessels, seems overly cautious; e.g., Tuchelt (supra n. 7) 51; H. G. Güterbock, "Hethitische Götterbilder und Kultobjekte," in R. M. Boehmer and H. Hauptmann, eds., *Beiträge zur Altertumskunde Kleinasiens: Festschrift für Kurt Bittel* (Mainz 1983) 203–217, esp. 213. Wooden vessels are certainly capable of retaining fluids, especially as these are invariably described as covered with silver or gold plating.

21. The following comments are based on Tuchelt (supra n. 7) 49–54; Carruba (supra n. 19); Güterbock (supra n. 20); Deller (supra n. 19). For an excellent recent discussion of the archaeological evidence for the various types of animal-head vessels in the Near East and Aegean, see U. Zevulun, "A Canaanite Ram-Headed Cup," *IEJ* 37 (1987) 88–104.

22. See especially Carruba (supra n. 19) 91–93.

23. See especially Carruba (supra n. 19) 93; Güterbock (supra n. 20) 212–213.

24. Güterbock (supra n. 20) 213.

25. Carruba (supra n. 19) 93; Güterbock (supra n. 20) 212–213.

26. W. L. Moran, *The Amarna Letters* (Baltimore 1992) 114–115.

27. Tuchelt (supra n. 7) 17–23.

28. A. Kammenhuber, *Materialien zu einem hethitischen Thesaurus*, Lieferung 7–8 (Heidelberg 1978) 328–329.

29. Güterbock (supra n. 20) 212.

30. Güterbock (supra n. 20) 212–213.

31. N. Özgüç, "Seals of the Old Assyrian Colony Period and Some Observations on the Seal Impressions," in J. V. Canby, E. Porada, B. S. Ridgway, and T. Stech, eds., *Ancient Anatolia: Aspects of Change and Cultural Development. Essays in Honor of Machteld J. Mellink* (Wisconsin 1986) 52, ill. 4–3, figs. 4.10 and 4.11; N. Özgüç, *The Anatolian Group of Cylinder Seal Impressions from Kültepe* (Ankara 1965)

nos. 23, 25, 39, 40, 41, 46, 49b, 71, 80, and 84. I am grateful to Barbara Porter for these references. For the relief vessel, see R. M. Boehmer, *Die Reliefkeramik von Bogazköy,* Bogazköy-Hattusa XIII (Berlin 1983) 55–59 (no. 97). For further discussion, see Tuchelt (supra n. 7) 51–52.

32. Vermeule (supra n. 6) 15. For convenient illustrations, see Marinatos and Hirmer (supra n. 13), pls. 196–198 and LIII.

33. Cf. E. French, "The Figures and Figurines," in C. Renfrew, *The Archaeology of Cult, BSA* Suppl. 18 (London 1985) 240.

34. Carruba (supra n. 19) 96–97; Tuchelt (supra n. 7) 53; Muscarella (supra n. 19); Kammenhuber (supra n. 28); Güterbock (supra n. 20) 208, 212.

35. Akurgal and Hirmer (supra n. 7), pl. 47 (below).

36. Moran (supra n. 26); discussed also in Tuchelt (supra n. 7) 54–55.

37. C. W. Carter, "Hittite Cult Inventories" (Ph.D. diss., Univ. of Chicago, 1962).

38. For a recent treatment of the subject see M. Liverani, *Prestige and Interest: International Relations in the Near East c. 1600–1100 B.C.* (Padua 1990).

39. Dunham (supra n. 19) 214.

40. For a current assessment of the evidence for Aegean-Anatolian relations, see H. G. Güterbock, "The Hittites and the Aegean World: 1. The Ahhiyawa Problem Reconsidered," *AJA* 87 (1983) 133–138; M. J. Mellink, "The Hittites and the Aegean World: 2. Archaeological Comments on Ahhiyawa-Achaians in Western Anatolia," *AJA* 87 (1983) 138–141; E. T. Vermeule, "Response to Hans Güterbock," *AJA* 87 (1983) 141–143.

41. M. J. Mellink (supra n. 40) 139. C. Laviosa, "The Minoan thalassocracy, Iasos and the Carian coast," in R. Hägg and N. Marinatos, eds., *The Minoan Thalassocracy. Myth and Reality* (Stockholm 1984) 183; W. Schiering, "The Connections between the Oldest Settlement at Miletus and Crete," in R. Hägg and N. Marinatos, ibid., 187–188.

42. On the possible Anatolian provenience of this stone scepter-axe head, see Davis (supra n. 7) 85. See Marinatos and Hirmer (supra n. 13), pl. 68, for an illustration. For a recent assessment of Hittite objects in the Aegean and their meaning, see Cline (supra n. 5).

43. On the Minoan items in the Shaft Graves, see Vermeule (supra n. 6) 27–51.

44. E. Cline, "A Possible Hittite Embargo Against the Mycenaeans," *Historia* 40 (1991) 1–9.

45. The bibliography on this topic is exhaustive. The standard work is F. H. Stubbings, *Mycenaean Pottery in the Levant* (Cambridge 1951). For recent discussion and bibliography, see R. B. Koehl, *Sarepta III. The Imported Bronze and Iron Age Wares from Area II,X* (Beirut 1985) 25, 37–45.

4

MYCENAEAN POTTERY AT SAQQARA: FINDS FROM EXCAVATIONS BY THE EGYPT EXPLORATION SOCIETY OF LONDON AND THE RIJKSMUSEUM VAN OUDHEDEN, LEIDEN, 1975 – 1990*

◆

VRONWY HANKEY AND DAVID ASTON

This paper is offered to Emily Vermeule in recognition both of her perceptive interpretation of the Aegeans and their neighbors and of her ability to communicate her scholarship and enthusiasm to others. In her many works Emily has helped to achieve a wider understanding of international contacts within an intelligible chronological framework, without which "the few stable Late Bronze Age scenes which we can recognize now in the procession of archaeological events would dissolve in artistic anarchy." [1]

ABSTRACT

Mycenaean pottery found in prestigious contexts during recent excavations at Saqqara provides new information about Mycenaean relations with Pharaonic Egypt. The introduction describes the discovery of the connections which provided Aegean prehistory with an approximate place in Egyptian history. It also discusses Homer's references to Egypt and their relevance to reality. The initial aim of the excavations was to relocate the tomb of Maya, the treasurer of Tutankhamun, found by Lepsius in the 1840s, and subsequently buried by

sand. This was eventually found in 1987, after the discovery, in close proximity, of the tombs of Horemheb (prepared before he became pharaoh), of close relatives of Ramesses II, and of high officials of the late Eighteenth and early Nineteenth Dynasties. Among pottery of Late Helladic IIIA 2 and early IIIB found between 1975 and 1990, six pieces from Shaft i in the tomb of Horemheb had an unusually long life, or were reused as symbols of luxuries no longer readily available when trade with the Aegean began to be inhibited by Hittite pressure.

INTRODUCTION

1. THE EGYPTIAN CONNECTION

William Matthew Flinders Petrie, 1853–1942, proved that Pharaonic Egypt and the Aegean had been in contact long before the foundation of Naukratis in the Nile Delta in the seventh century B.C.[2] In his childhood it was accepted that Greek history began with the first Olympiad in 776 B.C. Earlier events were wrapped in clouds of idealized Homeric traditions. In 1870 these illusions were shaken at Hissarlik, near the Hellespont and the Aegean sea. Heinrich Schliemann repopulated the plains of windy Troy with Homer's heroes, certain as he was that his second city, in which he found the great treasure, was the city of Priam destroyed by the Achaians in the twelfth century B.C. At Mycenae in November 1876 he announced that he had found the tomb of Agamemnon in the location described by Pausanias. We now know that Schliemann's Troy II was not the city of Priam, and that the Grave Circle inside the walls at Mycenae belonged, not to Agamemnon, but to an earlier Mycenaean dynasty, living between about 1600 and the mid-fifteenth century B.C. In 1877 Charles Newton suggested a connection between Mycenae and Egypt in the Eighteenth Dynasty,[3] but, when Petrie went to Egypt in 1880 to test the pyramidal theories of Piazzi Smyth, few thought that this was possible.

In January 1882, Petrie visited El-Amarna, on the east bank of the Nile above Minya, collected sherds, and saw the ruined tombs. This journey was the prelude to years of excavation in Egypt. At Hawara in 1889 he was visited by Schliemann, and we may imagine their enthusiasm over the papyrus fragment of *Iliad* Book 2, which Petrie had found placed as a safe conduct to the next world under the head of a woman buried in the second century A.C. They agreed on the importance of pottery for dating, but Schliemann's death later that year ended their friendship.

At Kahun, Petrie uncovered the administrative town attached to the pyramid of Sesostris II (Twelfth Dynasty, 1884–1878 B.C.). Among the domestic rubbish he found twenty-eight sherds which were not Egyptian. With "prescient instinct," as Arthur Evans put it, he called them "Aegean" (the first use of this word to describe pre-Hellenic objects). At Gurob, nearby, he found pottery like Schliemann's "Mykenaean" and published this with the Aegean sherds and a Mycenaean juglet from the Tomb of Maket at Kahun, claiming that "Mykenaean" pottery was pre-Dorian, dating to between 1400 and 1100 B.C., and that Mycenaeans had traveled to Egypt about 1500 B.C.[4]

The Egyptian connection proved

Meanwhile in 1893, in the museum at Candia in Crete, John Myres and the Italian scholar L. Mariani independently recognized Cretan parallels for Petrie's

"Aegean" sherds among pottery found in 1886 by shepherds in a cave on the southern flank of Mt. Ida. The Kamares cave, we now know, was a mountain sanctuary visible from the Minoan palace at Phaistos.[5] This meant that, before systematic excavation in Crete began, a phase of Minoan prehistory had its place in Egyptian history.[6] Further evidence for connections between the first Minoan palaces and Egypt comes from Middle Minoan pottery found: at Tell el-Dab'a in the eastern Delta; at Lisht, Haraga near Kahun, Abydos; at Tod, Aswan; at points on the return route via the Levant coast; and in Egyptian objects and influences traceable in Crete itself.[7]

In April 1890 Petrie stayed with the Gardners at the British School at Athens, saw Schliemann's finds, and visited Mycenae and Tiryns. He persuaded his hosts that he had done more in a week than the Germans in ten years to clear up Mycenaean chronology. Now he needed proof that Aegean pottery in Egypt *was* datable by its context.

El-Amarna, the perfect site

Between 1883 and 1890 a French expedition had cleared and recorded rock-cut tombs, including the recently looted royal tomb. In 1887 clay tablets (the Amarna letters) were found, and the hunt was on for more tablets and movable antiquities. Petrie excavated in the central city from October 1891 to late April 1892, hoping to find tablets and to elucidate the city custom-built for Akhenaten, the pharaoh condemned to oblivion by his successors. Mycenaean pottery appeared immediately. In one season, in the royal palace and rubbish heaps, Petrie found 1,329 Mycenaean sherds and over eighty Late Cypriot sherds. On the evidence of labels of wine jars stating the regnal year of vintage, and of finds from a glass factory active in the reign of Tutankhamun (nine years), he concluded that El-Amarna had been the capital and administrative center of Egypt for not more than twenty years. The Mycenaean pottery could be dated by the life span of the city. "There are few facts in all archaeology determined with a more overwhelming amount of evidence than the dating of this earlier stage of Aegean pottery."[8] His claims were immediately challenged, and still stimulate discussion.

Petrie's distribution of pottery to favored institutions disseminated the good news but complicated study. No distribution list exists, so Petrie's sherds cannot be studied with the finds which his successors presented to institutions in Britain, the Republic of Ireland, Cairo, New Zealand, and the United States.[9]

2. EL-AMARNA AND CHRONOLOGY

The Mycenaean pottery from El-Amarna consists mainly of small containers, particularly flasks (FS 189), of LH IIIA 2.[10] A few pieces belong to the style of early IIIB. Their interest for chronology depends partly on the status of Akhetaten (El-Amarna) after the return to orthodoxy. Recent excavations have shown that the Workmen's Village was set up in year 4 of Amenophis IV (Akhenaten), who moved to Akhetaten in year 5.[11] Very few Mycenaean sherds came from the village, which was abandoned, like the city, early in the reign of Tutankhamun. Later in the *same* reign it was reoccupied by a pig-keeping community and finally deserted by the reign of Horemheb, about four years after the death of Tutankhamun. It is unlikely that anyone of social standing would have returned (pigs and presumably swineherds were never highly regarded in Egypt, certainly not by the upper classes), and there is no evidence that pig-keepers bought foreign luxuries. The few pieces of LH IIIB 1 pottery should have arrived at El-Amarna before year 3 of Tutankhamun.[12]

Mycenaean pottery ranging from LH IIA to within LH IIIB has been found at over fifty sites in the Nile valley from the Delta to Argo Island, above the Third Cataract.[13] Mycenaean pottery at Saqqara illustrates trade at a time when Mycenaeans were becoming economic as well as military leaders in the Aegean. Its presence in contexts involving the funerary rites of known officials or royal persons during and after the religious and political upheaval of the Amarna period helps to bring Mycenaeans and Egyptians together in the same scenes. The tomb of Aper-El at Saqqara is a particular instance.

In 1976, in the cliff facing the Nile below the rest house of La Mission Française de Saqqarah, Alain Zivie found a rock-cut room with carved inscriptions, titles, and the name Aperia, which was traced by Dr. Jaromir Malek, at the Griffith Institute in Oxford, to unpublished notes made by Petrie in 1881. He had recorded the same room and inscription, plus a second version, Aper-El,

and a reference to the Aten. Excavation began in 1980.[14] From the room found by Petrie, with damaged sculptures in the Amarna style, steps lead down to a second room, then follows a vertical drop of seven meters to a third room. A shaft over six meters deep leads to steps to the burial chamber, containing the skeletal remains and inner coffins of Aper-El's wife Ouria and a son Houy. Among Aper-El's possessions were objects inscribed with cartouches of Amenophis III and of his Great Wife Tiy, a clay sealing with the throne name of Amenophis IV *before* he changed his name to Akhenaten in year 6, and a wine label of year 10 of Akhenaten (wine of year 10 of Amenophis III could not have lasted into the reign of Akhenaten). Pottery included Egyptian, "syro-chypriote," and two Mycenaean pots—a piriform jar FS 45, and stirrup jar FS 166 (as in Shaft i of Horemheb's tomb)—both of LH IIIA 2 and identical with pottery from El-Amarna. More Aegean pottery is being studied (information from Dr. Zivie). Aper-El lay under his possessions. He died late in the reign of Amenophis III. Houy completed the tomb, and added the inscription "First Prophet of the Aten," in Room I to give his father the protection of the divinity worshipped by Akhenaten, Houy's master. This find places the use of the LH IIIA 2 pots within the last years of Amenophis III to at latest year 10 of Akhenaten, or between about 1360 and 1342 B.C.

Chronology, high or low?

The "traditional" chronology of the Aegean Bronze Age is essentially dependent on Egyptian and Near Eastern correlations. A high date for the beginning of the Aegean Late Bronze Age and a drastic lowering of its end are very hard to accommodate. The debate is lively but inconclusive, and will continue so until the opposing parties agree upon bases for discussion. In practice it is more important to establish in relative terms what people and which events were contemporary. In this paper, we follow Kitchen's dates B.C., as follows:

Amenophis III, 1390–1352;
Amenophis IV (Akhenaten), 1352–1336;
Smenkhkare, 1338–1336;
Tutankhamun, 1336–1327;
Ay, 1327–1323;

Horemheb, 1323–1295;
Ramesses I, 1295–1294;
Sethos I, 1294–1279;
Ramesses II, 1279–1213;
Merneptah, 1213–1210;
Ramesses III, 1184–1153.[15]

3. HOMER'S REFERENCES AND REALITY

The following references concern Egypt:

The wealth of Egyptian Thebes: *Iliad* 9.382.
Egypt, the country: *Odyssey* 3.300; 4.351; 14.246, 275;
    17.426, 448.
Egypt, the river: *Odyssey* 4.477, 483, 581; 14.257, 258;
    17.427.
Egyptian: *Odyssey* 4.83, 127, 229, 385; 14.263, 286;
    17.432.

Conditions for contact by sea in the Bronze Age

At the Strait of Gibraltar the inflow of water from the Atlantic creates a counterclockwise circulation of surface water, accelerated in the summer by the Etesian winds blowing from northwest to northeast.[16] Evidence from EM Crete pinpoints the Minoans as pioneers in the contact, arriving at the Delta by accident or intent, and returning counterclockwise via the Levantine coast and Cyprus. A direct but hazardous northward return route to Crete and the Aegean may have been attempted.[17]

Menelaos and Odysseus   Odyssey 3.300

Menelaos set out from Troy, but was blown off course, to Egypt, with five ships. In *Odyssey* 4.355–359, he says he wanted to go to Egypt, but his ships were held up for twenty days by contrary winds on an island called Pharos, a day's sail with a following wind from Egypt. It had a good anchorage and water supply. After the episode with the Old Man of the Sea, Menelaos rowed and sailed a long weary way over the misty deep to Egypt, moored his ships, offered a hecatomb, and made a memorial mound to Agamemnon. Then he sailed home via Sidon.

Comment

There is no island a day's sail north of the Nile Delta. Since, however, *ai-ku-pi-ti-jo* ('Aiguptios') occurs in

Linear B at Knossos, as well as an Ithacan named "Aiguptios" in *Odyssey* 2.15, a nonexpert may suggest that *pharos*, first found in Homer, was also known to the Mycenaeans.[18] Is *pharos* a version of *pr-'ah*, the 'great house'? In the time of Amenophis IV (Akhenaten), *pr-'ah* meant 'king' rather than his palace.[19] Perhaps the first landfall in the Delta was known to sailors as *phara* or *pharo* long before the famous *pharos* was built in the Ptolemaic period.

Homeric voyages   Odyssey 14.246–304

Odysseus pretends to be a Cretan who had led nine seaborne raids on foreign lands before joining the expedition against Troy (14.229). After a short postwar stay in Crete, he sailed with nine ships, running before the north wind as if sailing downstream. Without disease, accident, or hard work, the helmsman and wind steered the ships. On the fifth day they came to fair-flowing Aigyptos and moored in the river. Odysseus stayed in Egypt for seven years and became rich. Then he was tricked into going to Phoenicia by a Phoenician, who a year later sent him on a false business trip to Libya. He sailed across the north wind, along the north coast of Crete, but was wrecked by a storm. In *Odyssey* 17.426–444 the story is changed. Odysseus was sent by Zeus on a practical expedition to Egypt. After a disastrous shore battle he was given to a friend of the defenders to take to Dmetor, son of Iasus, ruler of Cyprus, and returned to Ithaca from Cyprus.

Comment

Bradford's voyage confirmed the Homeric account.[20] Menelaos and Odysseus both returned via Phoenicia, following the counterclockwise route to the Aegean. The trading pattern of exported Mycenaean pottery in Cyprus, the Levant, and Egypt at the end of the line (particularly in LH IIIA 2 and early IIIB) shows that it was practicable to sail clockwise to Egypt via Cyprus and Ugarit, and south along the Levantine coast.[21] Egypt imported timber from Lebanon from at least the Fourth Dynasty, presumably by sea, and maintained some control over Levantine coastal waters up to north Syria until the southward move of the Hittites late in the Eighteenth Dynasty. The Sea Peoples reached the Nile Delta from the north by ship and land in year eight of Ramesses III. Euboea made maritime contact with north Syria (Al

Mina) in the ninth century, and Ionian exploration southwards led to the foundation of Naukratis. Homer's account matches patterns of navigation in Mycenaean times and after the Bronze Age.

Action in Egypt   Odyssey 17.421−444

Odysseus' landing party laid waste the fields, carried off women and children, and killed their men. In the battle many of his crew were killed or taken prisoner into slavery. Odysseus was rescued by the king, who took him home in his chariot. Or, as he told the suitors later, he was given to a friend of the defenders to take to Dmetor, ruler of Cyprus, and had subsequently come to Ithaca from Cyprus.

Comment

Is this yarn a folk memory of piracy on prosperous Late Bronze Age trade routes? Or of the battle between Ramesses III and the Sea Peoples at the Nile? Or is it about Ionian and Carian adventurers, expirates serving Psammetichus I, or Ionians prospecting in the Delta? Herodotus placed the foundation of Naukratis in the reign of Amasis (570−526 B.C.), but, since pottery there points to an earlier settlement, he may refer to confirmation of the Ionian settlement rather than permission to land.[22]

Piracy

In the Eighteenth and Nineteenth Dynasties piracy and privateering along the trade routes was a fact, as was the recruitment of healthy prisoners of war into the Egyptian army. The rescue of an outstanding foreigner and his subsequent removal to Cyprus would not be inconsistent with this practice. Homer's "Sackers of Cities" would be at home in the international scene of the late Eighteenth Dynasty. Movements of people at the end of the thirteenth century B.C. perhaps reduced the recruitment of mercenaries.[23]

Comment

At the colloquium "Egypt, the Aegean and the Levant" at the British Museum (July 9, 1991), Drs. R. Parkinson and L. Schofield gave an account of a miniature papyrus from El-Amarna, excavated by Pendlebury in 1936, and recently acquired by the British Museum.[24] This shows foreign soldiers fighting alongside Egyptians against Libyans. If the foreigners, wearing what may be boar's-tusk helmets and oxhide tunics, *are* Mycenaeans, they neatly fit the scenario of a diplomatic mission to the Aegean, in particular to Mycenae, late in the reign of Amenophis III.[25] Officials on the mission took home perfumed oil whose empties (FS 189) are the major type at El-Amarna. The Egyptians, moreover, were aware of and perhaps alarmed by Hittite aggression (a later embargo by Tudhaliya IV on Ahhiyawa shipping was identified by Houwink ten Cate).[26] Amenophis' defense advisers may have gladly recruited well-trained Mycenaean toughs who were bored with the *pax Mycenaeca* established following the downfall of Knossos about 1360 B.C. Did they, like the Egyptian visitors, take their favorite perfumes with them, or were they glad to leave a home which had abandoned the arts of war in favor of the manufacture of cosmetics?

Residence in Egypt   Odyssey 3.300

In Egypt Menelaos earned a good living and much gold, wandering with his ships among foreign-speaking people (*Odyssey* 14.286). Odysseus, too, stayed in Egypt on good terms for seven years, and became rich.

Comment

Unless "Egypt" includes the coastal area of Palestine under Egyptian control in the Eighteenth Dynasty, the Homeric accounts suggest that foreigners were free to sail upriver for trade or employment. Tombs of the Eighteenth Dynasty at western Thebes show scenes of apparently foreign seagoing ships unloading at riverside quays. Amenophis III employed foreigners, particularly from Retenu and Djahi, but there is no evidence for independent foreign enterprise.

Wealth and exchange of gifts

At *Iliad* 9.380−384 Achilles rejects Agamemnon's offer of vast wealth as enticement back to the fighting force, saying he would not rejoin the war, not even if Agamemnon were to add the wealth of Orchomenos or Egyptian Thebes, where the greatest treasures were stored in houses—Thebes, the city of a hundred gates, through each of which two hundred soldiers drove out with their chariots and horses.

Odyssey 4.124−130 lists gifts from Polybus and Alcandre of Egyptian Thebes to Helen as a silver basket (*talaron*), a gold distaff (*elakaten*), and a silver basket with gold or gilded rim, on wheels. Menelaos was given two silver baths (*asaminthous*), two tripods, and ten gold talents.

Comment

The most elaborate travelers' tales about Egypt must relate to the period of Theban opulence from the Eighteenth to early in the Twentieth Dynasty. The Greek name "Thebes," a corruption of "Ipet-esut," is likely to have been invented during the Eighteenth or Nineteenth Dynasty, rather than in the period before the foundation of Naukratis, when the main center of Egypt had shifted from Thebes to the Delta.

After the end of the Bronze Age, Egyptian and Egyptianizing goods in Protogeometric and Geometric tombs, particularly in Euboea and Crete, appear to have arrived via Phoenician traders, also remembered by Homer.[27] None of the gifts to Menalaos and Helen can be said specifically to recall Mycenaean objects, except possibly her basket on wheels, which could be a recollection of bronze-wheeled stands that are not found later than LH IIIC.[28] Homer's account, retold and embroidered by Ionians, may well have originated in the late Eighteenth Dynasty.

Egyptian Medicine   Odyssey 4.220–234

Helen's panacea for all ills is a drug given her by the Egyptian Polydamna, wife of Thon, for in Egypt, where the earth produces the greatest variety of drugs, good and bad, everyone is a doctor, because Egyptians are of Paëon's race.

Comment

Pa-ja-wo in Linear B at Knossos may refer to a healing deity.[29] For Homer the word was an attribute of Apollo, but this does not prove an Egyptian connection. In the eastern Mediterranean the common analgesic or anaesthetic seems to have been opium, produced and processed in Cyprus, and widely exported to the Levant and Egypt in small Base-Ring ware containers imitating seed pods slashed to release the latex.[30] These juglets are rare among Cypriot pottery in the Aegean.[31] The production of opium has not been traced through succeeding centuries, so it is not possible to say whether Homer reflects contemporary Ionian admiration for Egyptian medicine and knowledge of the human body acquired through the process of mummification, or a transmitted knowledge of skills observed in Mycenaean times.

THE EXCAVATIONS, 1975 – 1990

In 1975 the Egypt Exploration Society of London and the Rijksmuseum van Oudheden, Leiden, with permission from the Department of Antiquities of Egypt, began a joint excavation in the New Kingdom necropolis south of the causeway of the Pyramid of Unas at Saqqara, an area long known to be rich in tombs of the late Eighteenth and early Nineteenth Dynasties. In 1843 Lepsius uncovered parts of superstructures, the most famous of which came from the tomb of the Treasurer of Tutankhamun, Maya, and his wife Meryt. Some of the sculptures found then are preserved in several museums, including the Rijksmuseum, Leiden, which has three charming statues of Maya and Meryt. The main aim of the joint mission was to relocate Maya's tomb, then buried under the sand, and excavation began where the account of Lepsius suggested that Maya's tomb was sited. Unfortunately this was not so, but the excavators were not too disappointed since it quickly became clear that the large tomb they were excavating was that of Maya's contemporary, the Army commander Horemheb. This monument had been known for a long time through the reliefs preserved in several museums.[32]

The tomb of Horemheb consists of a forecourt and entrance pylon, an outer (first) court with colonnaded portico, a statue room flanked by two magazines, an inner (second) court, and three cult chapels (pl. 4.1). The main burial shaft (Shaft iv), cut from the inner court, descended to a complex substructure which eventually led to the main burial chamber. The tomb was presumably constructed during the reign of Tutankhamun, but when Horemheb became pharaoh his tomb was prepared in the Valley of the Kings, Thebes. The remains of a rich burial were found in the main complex of Shaft iv, and it is possible that Horemheb's wife, Queen Mutnodjmet, was buried there.[33] No Mycenaean pots were found here. Sometime during the Ramesside period the upper level of Shaft i, cut from the first court, was used for the burial of at least four people, one a princess, possibly Bnt-'nt, the eldest daughter of

Ramesses II.[34] Two stirrup jars and a vertical flask (infra, Cat. nos. 1–3) were associated with these burials. Sherds from stirrup jars (Cat. nos. 13, 14, 19) and a closed vessel (Cat. no. 22) were found in surface débris.

Immediately west of the tomb of Horemheb two smaller tombs were found, of Paser, the Royal Scribe and Overseer of the Builders of Pharaoh, and Ra'ia, the Chief Singer of Ptah-Lord-of-Truth.[35] Sherds from a stirrup jar (Cat. no. 11) and an alabastron (Cat. no. 21) were found in the surface débris, but cannot be unequivocally associated with these tombs, which are datable to the reign of Ramesses II.

North of the tomb of Horemheb is the tomb of Tia, Overseer of the Treasury of the Temple of Ramesses II in the Domain of Amun, and his wife, also named Tia, elder sister of Ramesses II (pl. 4.2).[36] This is the first large tomb of the Ramesside period in the Memphite necropolis to have been completely cleared and planned. It consists of a paved forecourt, a pylon with a small porch in front, an outer (first) court, a colonnaded inner (second) court, an antechapel, side chapels, cult room, and a small pyramid. There was no Mycenaean pottery in the main burial chambers, but parts of two stirrup jars (Cat. nos. 4, 5) came from a tomb cut below the southwest corner of the first court, and backing on to the north wall of the tomb of Horemheb. This is the small tomb of Iurudef, Scribe of the Treasury, named in reliefs and inscriptions in the Tias' tomb, and therefore contemporary with them.[37] Presumably he died sometime during the long reign of Ramesses II (c. 1279–1213). His burial chambers were on two levels. The upper level, rooms A–D, had been reused during the late New Kingdom and early Third Intermediate Period. The lower level, rooms E–G, had been used only during the Nineteenth Dynasty. Despite the later reuse of this tomb, much of the original funeral furniture remained. The two stirrup jars (Cat. nos. 4, 5) evidently belonged to Iurudef or his immediate family.

Directly opposite the tomb of Iurudef was another tomb (Shaft C), which had been destroyed in antiquity. The superstructure had not survived, and the name of the owner was not recovered. Its burial chambers were in imminent danger of collapse and so were not fully excavated. Part of a Mycenaean stirrup jar was found (Cat. no. 6). In view of its location, Shaft C was presumably the tomb of another favored servant of the crown,

like Iurudef, and can probably be dated to the reign of Ramesses II.

To the west of the Tias' tomb, and partly overlaid by it, was the tomb of Ramose, the Chief of the Bowmen of the Army, probably dating to the late Eighteenth Dynasty.[38] The tomb was a simple one, with two courts, the inner one having three cult chapels and the main burial shaft. The ceramic material has not yet been studied, but a sherd from a stirrup jar (Cat. no. 7) found in the burial chamber joined one from the surface.

In 1987, immediately north of the tombs of Ramose and the Tias, and twelve years after their search had begun, the team found the tomb of the Overseer of the Treasury, Maya, and his wife Meryt (pl. 4.3).[39] Maya, who held his official position under Tutankhamun, Ay, and Horemheb, probably died in or shortly after year 9 of Horemheb (c. 1314), since a docket of that year was found. In plan the tomb resembles that of Horemheb, the only difference being that the outer (first) court had a portico with columns at the west (innermost) end only, and not on all four sides. The main shaft descended, as in Horemheb's tomb, from the second (inner) court. The burial chambers are on two levels. Sherds from two stirrup jars (Cat. nos. 8, 9) were found in the lower level, joining sherds from the surface débris. Warren and Hankey suggested that the pieces found underground had fallen in with débris when the tomb was closed.[40] Further study of the Egyptian material, however, shows that funerary detritus found overlying the central chapel at the west end of the tomb had been taken out from the underground rooms at a later date. We can therefore be certain that pots 8 and 9 were part of Maya and Meryt's original grave goods and not accidentally mixed in at the final closing of the tomb.

Directly in front of the entrance pylon, at the eastern end of Maya's tomb, some later shafts were also cleared. One (Shaft xv) contained New Kingdom pottery, including a wine amphora with a hieratic docket of year 40 of Ramesses II (c. 1239 B.C.). The base of a closed vessel (Cat. no. 10), probably a stirrup jar, comes from this dated deposit.

Other sherds (Cat. nos. 11–25) were found in the surface débris, mixed in with a vast quantity of material from Old Kingdom to Coptic times, and cannot be allocated to any specific New Kingdom tomb. They could originally have come from any one tomb, or even from

PLATE 4.1 The Memphite tomb of Horemheb, Saqqara, from west. From foreground to background: first (outer) court, entrance pylon. Shaft i is located adjacent to the column at bottom left. Photo by G. T. Martin.

tombs not yet found. They are presented here to round off the account of Mycenaean pottery found so far by the joint expedition.

THE MYCENAEAN POTTERY

The clay, which has not been analyzed, is fine, fired buff to pink, with a shiny slip of the same color or lighter than the body. Particles of mica and dark and white grits may be present. Decoration ranges from orange to light red, brown, and black. The variation in color, often in the same pot, is due to its position in a vertical up-draught kiln. The pottery is classified according to Furumark, with modifications by Mountjoy.[41] The following shapes are represented: straight-sided alabastron (pyxis) FS 94 (cat. no. 21); stirrup jar (cat. nos. 1, 2, 4–9, 11–20); globular vertical flask FS 189 (cat. no. 3); shallow cup FS 220 (cat. no. 24); kylix FS 264 (cat. no. 25). Among the stirrup jars FS 166 (piriform); 171 (globular, H. = D.); 178, 180 (squat); and 182 (conical) are present. It is difficult to be precise about types of stirrup jar whose profile is not complete or definite. Cat. nos. 10, 22, 23 are from closed vessels of unidentified type. The fine distinctions between stirrup jars of LH IIIA 2 late, of the transition to IIIB, and of early IIIB are elusive, particularly in the case of sherds.[42] The stylistic dates suggested are referred to as "Late Helladic" (LH) rather than "Mycenaean" (Myc), the term frequently used in the Eastern Mediterranean. These are imprecise where the pieces have details common to the late stage of LH IIIA 2 and the beginning of LHIIIB. "LH IIIA 2 – IIIB 1" indicates the transition between the

two phases. Inv. no. 87–208, a badly damaged sherd from a stirrup jar, is not catalogued. Only one sherd from a Mycenaean shape in local clay was identified, and no imitations of the stirrup jar in faience or calcite were reported.

Measurements (H. = height, D. = maximum diameter) are in centimeters.

PLATE 4.2 Tomb of Tia and Tia, Saqqara, from east. From foreground to background: first (outer) court, colonnaded second (inner) court. Stirrup jars (cat. nos. 4–5) came from the Tomb of Iurudef, visible on the left side of the outer court. Another stirrup jar (cat. no. 6) came from the tomb on the right side of the outer court. Photo by G. T. Martin.

CATALOGUE
(Catalogue numbers also refer to the line drawings)

1 – 10. POTTERY FOUND INSIDE TOMB SHAFTS OR ROOMS, LISTED IN ORDER OF EXCAVATION.

1. P298 + 914 and unmarked sherds. Stirrup jar, piriform FS 166, with hollow torus base, hollow false neck, flat disk added separately, flattened handle, concave spout with sloping rim. Poor condition. Part of body missing. H. 14.5, D. 10.7, base 4.6. Fine dirty buff clay, pinker on the surface, white and dark grits, the body splitting into two layers where buff and pink meet. Shiny buff slip, almost worn off. Decoration in shiny orange to red and brown, worn. Zone of bands and fine lines above painted foot. Multiple Stem FM 19.21 on shoulder. Broad bands round base of false neck and base of spout. Large solid circle in reserve on disk, badly placed reserved triangle on handle, broad band round rim of spout. Tomb of Horemheb, Shaft i, level 9, at entrance to corridor to rooms A to H, in rooms F, G, H,

PLATE 4.3 Tomb of Maya, Saqqara, from east. From foreground to background: column bases at west side of first (outer) court, statue room flanked by side chapels, colonnaded second (inner) court. The shaft to the main burial chamber descends from the second (inner) court.

pit in F, and surface débris. LH IIIA 2.[43] (Fig. 4.1 and pl. 4.4.)

2. P1185. Stirrup jar, globular FS 171. Drawn-up false neck, concave spout with sloping rim. Poor condition. Base, handle, and false neck missing. H. (extant) 8.0, D. 10.4. Fine yellow to buff clay, greenish inside, splitting into two layers. Yellow buff slip, once shiny, decoration in orange to red. Zones of bands and medium fine lines on body. Foliate Band FM 64.20 on shoulder, band round base of spout. Tomb of Horemheb, Shaft i, level 12, rooms B, E, F, H. LH IIIA 2.[44] (Fig. 4.2 and pl. 4.5.)

3. P1184. Globular flask FS 189, complete except for two small body sherds. Thrown from the small ring base upwards, small sloping rim, unevenly laid-on handles, slight ridge at base of neck. H. 13.9, D. 10.4, base 3.7. Fine deep pink to buff clay, surface redder than core, large dark red inclusions. Slighty shiny buff slip, decoration in shiny orange to red. Groups of Foliate Band FS 64, variant of 22 in handle panel. On side (a) twenty-four, (b) eighteen evenly spaced medium to fine concentric circles, within a narrow border (a broad border is more usual on FS 189 at El-Amarna and elsewhere). Tomb of Horemheb, Shaft i, level 9, rooms A, E, H. LH IIIA 2, late.[45] (Fig. 4.3 and pl. 4.6.)

4. 85–214. Part of upper body of stirrup jar FS 171, 178, or 180. D. 12.0. Fine buff clay with pink interior, shiny buff slip. Decoration in black, almost worn off. Circles with central dot on shoulder, a variant on FM 27, Sea Anemone (?), single loop round base of false neck and spout, very sloppy triangle in reserve on handle. Tomb of Iurudef, shaft and room E. LH IIIA 2–IIIB 1.[46] (Fig. 4.4 and pl. 4.7.)

76

5. 85–216. Short concave false neck, flat disk, and part of handle of a stirrup jar. D. 2.7. Loop at base of false neck, concentric circles on disk. Tomb of Iurudef, chamber B among burnt material of the Nineteenth Dynasty. LH IIIA 2–LH IIIB 1. (Fig. 4.5 and pl. 4.8.)

6. 83–222. Body sherd from squat stirrup jar, FS 178, or 180. D. 13.2. Pink clay, shiny buff slip, decoration in shiny red. Two zones of broad and fine bands. Tomb of Tia and Tia, shaft C, burial chamber. The tomb was not excavated owing to the danger of imminent collapse. Time of Ramesses II or later. LH IIIA 2–IIIB 1.[47] (Fig. 4.6.)

7. 88–207. Upper part of squat stirrup jar, FS 178 or 180. Thin false neck and slightly domed disk made in one piece. Rather tall spout with sloping rim. D. 13.5. Buff clay and slip, decoration in red to brown. Body zone of band and fine lines, two bands below. No pattern on shoulder area, loop round base of false neck and spout. Disk has two concentric circles round central "U." Tomb of Ramose, burial chamber and surface. LH IIIB 1. (Fig. 4.7 and pl. 4.9.)

8. 87–207 A+B. Sherds from globular to squat stirrup jar, FS 178 rather than 171. Thick slightly concave base. H. extant 8.3, D. 10.4, base 3.4. Fine dark buff clay, dark grits, shiny buff slip, decoration in shiny red brown. Isolated Semi-circles FM 43, or Concentric Arcs FM 44, or widely spaced Multiple Stem FM 19, on shoulder. Tomb of Maya. Shoulder from surface, base and two body sherds from rooms Q and R, nonjoining sherds from room Q and surface. LH IIIA 2–IIIB 1.[48] (Fig. 4.8 and pl. 4.10.)

9. 87–206 + 88–554. Small globular to squat stirrup jar, FS 171, with narrow hollow false neck and flattened disk made in one piece, ring base. Spout and most of shoulder missing. H. 11.0, D. 11.8. Fine buff clay and shiny slip, decoration in red. Three body zones of bands and fine lines, and one of fine lines, no pattern on shoulder, large solid circle in reserve on disk, small reserved triangles on handle. Tomb of Maya, rooms I, Q, R, and surface. LH IIIB 1 rather than IIIA 2.[49] (Fig. 4.9 and pl. 4.11.)

10. 90–258. Torus base of closed vessel, perhaps stirrup jar, FS 182. Bands in shiny black above base. H. extant 1.7, D. base 7.6. Tomb of Maya, Shaft XV, Chamber B. Date of deposit not earlier than year 40 of Ramesses II (c. 1239). LH IIIB 1.[50] (Fig. 4.10.)

I I – 2 6. SHERDS FROM SURFACE DEBRIS, THE MIXTURE OF WIND-BLOWN SAND AND MATERIAL THROWN OUT OF THE UNDERGROUND TOMBS BY TOMB ROBBERS.

I I – 2 0. STIRRUP JARS (APPROXIMATELY IN ORDER OF FURUMARK'S CLASSIFICATION).

11. 87–238. Part of disk and handle. Concentric circles on spiral round solid center. LH IIIA 2 or IIIB 1. (Fig. 4.11.)

12. 88–596. Part of shoulder and spout, globular or squat. H. extant 4.6. Incomplete loop round base of false neck and spout. Mycenaean Flower FM 18 on shoulder. LH IIIB 1. (Fig. 4.12 and pl. 4.12.)

13. P166. Body sherd from FS 180. D. 13.5. Two zones of bands and fine lines on body, Multiple Stem FM 19.28 on shoulder. LH IIIA 2–IIIB 1. Listed with surface finds from the tomb of Horemheb. (Fig. 4.13 and pl. 4.13.)

14. P158. Body sherd from of FS 178–180. D. 12.0. Two zones of bands and fine lines, plain shoulder. LH IIIA 2-IIIB 1. Listed with surface finds from the tomb of Horemheb. (Fig. 4.14 and pl. 4.14.)

15. 87–260. Lower body of FS 178–180. H. extant 4.7, D. 11.8, D. base 6.0. Zone of bands and fine lines at greatest diameter. LH IIIA 2–IIIB 1. (Fig. 4.15 and pl. 4.15.)

16. 88–553. Lower body of FS 178–180. Zones of bands and fine lines. Three concentric circles on slightly concave base. LH IIIB 1.[51] (Fig. 4.16 and pl. 4.16.)

17. 88–349. Body sherd of FS 180. D. 12.0. Two zones of bands and fine lines on body. LH IIIB 1. (Fig. 4.17.)

18. 82–234 + 83–224 + 86–212 + 87–210. Profile of angular FS 180 (spout missing) with small domed disk. Two body zones of broad and fine bands, shoulder plain, loop round base of false neck. LH IIIB.[52] (Fig. 4.18 and pl. 4.17.)

19. P267. Body sherd, FS 182. Max. D. 14.0. Two zones of bands and fine lines, plain shoulder. LH IIIB 1.[53] Listed with surface finds from the tomb of Horemheb. (Fig. 4.19 and pl. 4.18.)

20. 86–213 + 86–221 + 86–346 + 90–201. Joined sherds from upper part of FS 182. Narrow false neck made separately, disk missing, concave spout. Zone of bands and fine lines below shoulder, Mycenaean Flower FM 18.128 on shoulder, loop enclosing base of false neck and spout, small reserved triangle on handle. The decoration suggests a date late in LH IIIB 1 or even in IIIB 2. This could be the latest Mycenaean import found. LH IIIB. (Fig. 4.20 and pl. 4.19.)

21 – 23. OTHER CLOSED VESSELS

21. 81–275. Straight-sided alabastron (pyxis), FS 94, profile almost complete. H. 7.3, D. 10.5. LH IIIA 2 or IIIB 1.[54] (Fig. 4.21.)

22. P1116. Sherd from upper body of medium to large piriform jar, FS 35, or jug, or large fine ware stirrup jar. H. extant 4.0, D. more than 27.0. Zones of bands and fine lines. LH IIIA 2 or IIIB 1. Listed with surface finds from the tomb of Horemheb.[55] (Fig. 4.22.)

23. 88–597. Body sherd from ovoid vessel. Buff micaceous clay, inner surface eroded, two bands above base. LH IIIA 2 or IIIB 1. (Fig. 4.23.)

24 – 25. OPEN VESSELS

24. 83–212. Rim sherd from cup, FS 220, very worn. H. extant 2.7, D. of rim 11.2. V pattern FM 59. LH IIIA 2 or IIIB 1. A few of this shape reached El-Amarna.[56] (Fig. 4.24 and pl. 4.20.)

25. 82–206 + 82–260. Two joining sherds from a kylix, FS 264. Fine buff clay, light red shiny monochrome in and out. LH IIIA 2. A few sherds from a kylix are among the El-Amarna deposit. So far as we know, this is the only recorded example of a monochrome kylix from Egypt, here shown in a reconstruction of somewhat bizarre appearance.[57] (Fig. 4.25 and pl. 4.21.)

DISCUSSION

Of the pots found in the closed deposits, **1–3** would be at home in the El-Amarna deposit.[58] In particular **3**, FS 189, thrown from the base up, is the most numerous shape found there. It was apparently made only in LH IIIA 2.[59] In their Ramesside context, **1–3** are survivals from the Amarna period. **4–5**, with features found in late IIIA 2 and early IIIB, came from a tomb used within the sixty-six years of Ramesses II's reign. **6**, of similar stylistic date, may have been deposited later in the Nineteenth Dynasty. **7**, however, of LH IIIB 1 rather than IIIA 2, may come from a burial of the late Eighteenth Dynasty. The context of **8** (LH IIIA 2–IIIB 1) and **9** (LH IIIB 1 rather than IIIA 2) added weight to evidence for placing the end of LH IIIA 2 *before* the reign of Ramesses II (c. 1279–1213 in the Nineteenth Dynasty).[60] The context of **10**, apparently IIIB 1 in type, is placed in or after year 40 of Ramesses II.

Assuming that their stylistic dates are acceptable, six of the ten fragments in these dated contexts were not new, filled with fresh contents, when used. None of the containers could have preserved the original contents, presumably refined and perfumed olive oil, in good condition for very long in Egyptian heat. So, like old perfume jars or vintage wine bottles, the jars may have been kept in use by the good and the great of Memphis long after the original contents had gone, and after production of containers in the Aegean had evolved.[61] In Egypt the domestic life of imported pottery before deposition in a tomb is obscured because most areas of ancient occupation in Egypt now lie under the silt deposited by the annual rise and fall of the Nile (El-Amarna is a notable exception). At Memphis, however, sherds of similar pots of LH IIIA 2 are being found in current excavations by the Egypt Exploration Society.[62] Reuse of old vessels is fairly common. A Tell El-Yahudiyeh juglet of the Second Intermediate Period was found in one of the cache burials of the Late New Kingdom within the tomb of Iurudef. A Red Lustrous spindle bottle was also found in surface débris.[63]

Except for **20**, the pieces from surface débris also belong to the ceramic range of LH IIIA 2 and IIIB 1, the period when the main trade route to the east was by way of Cyprus, Ugarit, and Tell Abu Hawam.[64] At even these major destinations Mycenaean wares were a minor accompaniment to bulk shipments of White Slip and Base-Ring wares. This is illustrated in the Uluburun wreck, which carried a few Mycenaean pieces, and large storage jars packed with Cypriot pottery.[65] At present we do not know the extent of Aegean trade with Egypt in the Nineteenth Dynasty, or what route was followed. Since Cypriots and/or Ugarites were involved in the Aegean trade with Egypt, Mycenaean pottery should have decreased or even disappeared from Egypt, as Cypriot wares did, when Cypriot traders began to feel the pressure of Hittite influence at Ugarit at the end of the Eighteenth Dynasty. This was before the decline of Aegean trade with Cyprus and the Levant sometime in LH IIIB.[66] Recent excavations at Bates' Island, Marsah Matruh, where Cypriot pottery formed eighty percent of the Late Bronze Age sherds found, will help to trace at least one of the possible trade routes.[67]

NOTES

* We are very grateful to the Egypt Exploration Society of London, to Professor G. T. Martin of the Department of Egyptology, University College London, and to Professor H. D. Schneider of the Rijksmuseum van Oudheden for permission to publish this material and for help in its study. We also thank Will Schenk, who drew pots **1–3, 13, 14, 19, 22,** and Henry Hankey for help with other drawings; the staff of Promotion House, Edenbridge, Kent, for patience over copying; Swan Hellenic of London, for Hankey's many visits to Saqqara in the course of Nile Cruises, and the Egyptian staff at Saqqara who helped to uncover these tombs.

1. E. Vermeule, *Greece in the Bronze Age* (Chicago 1964) 139.

2. M. S. Drower, *Flinders Petrie: A Life in Archaeology* (London 1985) 136–138.

3. R. A. Higgins, *Minoan and Mycenaean Art* (London 1967) 10.

4. W. M. F. Petrie, "The Egyptian Bases of Greek History," *JHS* 11 (1890) 271–277; idem, *Illahun, Kahun and Gurob* (London 1891); idem, "Notes on the Antiquities of Mykenae," *JHS* 12 (1891) 199–205; V. Hankey and O. Tufnell, "The Tomb of Maket and its Mycenaean Import," *BSA* 68 (1973) 103–113.

5. A. Brown, " 'I propose to begin at Gnossos,' " *BSA* 81 (1986) 37–44, especially 41, n. 19.

6. P. M. Warren and V. Hankey, *Aegean Bronze Age Chronology* (Bristol 1989) 125–135; V. Hankey, "From Chronos to Chronology: Egyptian Evidence for dating the Aegean Bronze Age," Isis Fellowship Lecture 1991, *Journal of Ancient Chronology Forum* 5 (1991/1992) 7–29.

7. Warren and Hankey (supra n. 6) 125–131, 135–137; V. Hankey, "Pottery as Evidence for Trade: 1. The Levant from the mouth of the river Orontes to the Egyptian border; 2. Egypt and Nubia," in E. French and C. Zerner, eds., *Wace and Blegen. Pottery as Evidence for Trade in the Aegean Bronze Age: 1939–1989,* Proceedings of the Conference sponsored by the American School of Classical Studies and the British School at Athens, December 2–3, 1989 (Amsterdam 1993) 101–116.

8. W. M. F. Petrie, *Tell El Amarna* (London 1894) 15–17. On chronology see below and n. 15.

9. Howard Carter, a seventeen-year-old art student collecting for a wealthy patron, worked at El-Amarna with Petrie and found about twenty sherds, which were eventually bought by the Allard Pierson Museum of Amsterdam (displayed in the exhibition *Howard Carter: Before Tutankhamun,* which opened on November 18, 1992, at the British Museum).

10. Furumark, *MP,* Catalogue of Shapes 583–643 (= FS), of Motifs 236–429 (= FM); P. A. Mountjoy, *Mycenaean Decorated Pottery: A Guide to Identification* (Göteborg 1986).

11. B. J. Kemp, "The Amarna workmen's village in retrospect," *JEA* 73 (1987) 21–50.

12. Warren and Hankey (supra n. 6) 148–152.

13. V. Hankey and A. Leonard, *Ägypte und die Levante: Ägäische Importe des 2. Jahrtausends v. Chr.* Tübingen Atlas des Vorderen Orients der Universität, B III 4/5 (Tübingen 1992); Hankey (supra n. 7).

14. A. Zivie, *Découverte à Saqqarah: Le vizir oublié* (Paris 1990), beautifully illustrated (Mycenaean pots on pls. 89, 90).

15. K. A. Kitchen, "The Basics of Egyptian Chronology in Relation to the Bronze Age," in P. Åström, ed., *High, Middle or Low? Acts of an International Colloquium on Absolute Chronology held at the University of Gothenburg 20th–22nd August 1987,* Part 1 (Gothenburg 1987) 37–55, and idem, "Supplementary Notes on the Basics of Egyptian Chronology in Relation to the Bronze Age," ibid., Part 3 (1989) 152–159. On the convergence of radiocarbon and Egyptian dates, see F. A. Hassan and S. W. Robinson, "Radiocarbon chronometry of Egypt," *Antiquity* 61 (1987) 119–135. For a recent assessment see S. W. Manning and B. Weninger, "A light in the dark: archaeological wiggle-matching and the absolute chronology of the close of the Aegean Late Bronze Age," *Antiquity* 66 (1992) 636–663. Discoveries in 1990–1993 by Professor M. Bietak at Tell el-Dab'a in the eastern Nile Delta may modify the high date proposed for the beginning of the Aegean Late Bronze Age at the Third International Thera Congress in 1989: D. A. Hardy, ed., *Thera and the Aegean World* III (London 1990). Lowering the end of the Aegean Late Bronze Age by up to 350 years is proposed by P. James et al., *Centuries of Darkness* (London 1991) and by many studies in *Journal of the Ancient Chronology Forum* 1–5 (1987–1992) of the Institute for the Study of Interdisciplinary Sciences. For the conventional view see Warren and Hankey (supra n. 6) 119–120, 127–128, 137–138; P. M. Warren, "The Minoan Civilization of Crete and the Volcano of Thera,"

Isis Fellowship Lecture 1990, *Journal of the Ancient Chronology Forum* 4 (1990/1991) 29–39; Hankey (supra n. 6).

16. C. Lambrou-Phillipson, "Sea-faring in the Bronze Age Mediterranean: The Parameters Involved in Maritime Travel," in R. Laffineur and L. Basch, eds., *Thalassa: L'Égée préhistorique et la mer,* Aegaeum 7 (Liège 1991) 11–19. B. J. Kemp and R. S. Merrillees, *Minoan Pottery in Second Millennium Egypt* (Mainz 1980) 268–286.

17. L. V. Watrous, *Kommos III: The Late Bronze Age Pottery* (Princeton 1992) 177–178.

18. *Docs.*² 136.

19. A. Gardiner, *Egyptian Grammar* (Oxford 1957) 75.

20. E. Bradford, *Ulysses Found* (London 1963) 40–43, 49.

21. Kemp and Merrillees (supra n. 16) 268–271; H. W. Catling, *Cyprus and the West,* Ian Sanders' Memorial Lecture (University of Sheffield 1980).

22. J. Boardman, *The Greeks Overseas* (Harmondsworth 1964) ch. 4.

23. N. Sandars, *The Sea Peoples* (London 1978) 49–50, 186–187.

24. A. Spawforth, "History re-written on a scrap of paper," *Daily Telegraph* (August 10, 1992) 15.

25. V. Hankey, "The Aegean Interest at El Amarna," *Journal of Mediterranean Anthropology and Archaeology* 1 (1981) 38–49; E. Cline, "Amenhotep and the Aegean: A Reassessment of Egypto-Aegean Relations in the 14th Century BC," *Orientalia* 56 (1987) 1–36; idem, "An Unpublished Amenhotep III Faience Plaque from Mycenae," *JAOS* 110 (1990) 200–212.

26. Watrous (supra n. 17) 178–179, with references; E. Cline, "A Possible Hittite Embargo against the Mycenaeans," *Historia* 40 (1991) 1–9.

27. Boardman (supra n. 22) passim; J. N. Coldstream, "Early Greek Visitors to the Levant," Isis Fellowship Lecture 1992 (in press).

28. H. W. Catling, *Cypriot Bronzework in the Mycenaean World* (Oxford 1964) 207–210.

29. *Docs*² 46, 126, 312.

30. R. S. Merrillees, *The Cypriote Bronze Age Pottery found in Egypt* (Lund 1968) 154–158.

31. Watrous (supra n. 17) 174–175.

32. G. T. Martin's *The Hidden Tombs of Memphis* (London 1991) is fully illustrated. See 208–209 for bibliography and references to preliminary reports, general plan on fig. 5. For the Tomb of Horemheb see 35–98 with figs. 9 and 11.

33. Martin (supra n. 32) 91–93; R. Hari, *Haremhab et la Reine Moutnodjmet* (Geneva 1965) 69–128.

34. Martin (supra n. 32) 83, 89–91; on Bnt-'nt/Bint-Anath, see K. A. Kitchen, *Pharaoh Triumphant: The Life and Times of Ramesses II* (Warminster 1982) 40, 99–100, 110.

35. Martin (supra n. 32) 120–123, 124–130, fig. 79.

36. Kitchen (supra n. 34) 28, 98; Martin (supra n. 32) ch. 4, 101–115, with fig. 64. G. T. Martin, "The Tomb of Tia and Tia: Preliminary Report on the Saqqara Excavations, 1982," *JEA* 69 (1983) 25–29, and "The Tomb of Tia and Tia: Preliminary Report on the Saqqara Excavations, 1983," *JEA* 70 (1984) 5–12; G. T Martin, M. J. Raven, and D. A. Aston, "The Tomb Chambers of Iurudef: Preliminary Report on the Saqqara Excavations, 1985," *JEA* 72 (1986) 15–22.

37. Martin (supra n. 32) 134–139.

38. Martin (supra n. 32) 118–120, fig. 78. G. T. Martin, "The Saqqara New Kingdom Necropolis Excavations, 1986," *JEA* 73 (1987) 1–10.

39. Martin (supra n. 32) ch. 6, 147–188, with figs. 100, 101, and 112.

40. Warren and Hankey (supra n. 6) 151–152.

41. *MP* and Mountjoy (supra n. 10).

42. Mountjoy (supra n. 10) 108.

43. Mountjoy (supra n. 10) 77.

44. Mountjoy (supra n. 10) 77–78.

45. Mountjoy (supra n. 10) 81, fig. 95.2.

46. Aston in Martin, Raven, and Aston (supra n. 36) 15–22.

47. Aston in Martin 1984 (supra n. 36) 8–9.

48. Warren and Hankey (supra n. 6) 151–152; Mountjoy (supra n. 10) 79, 95–96.

49. Warren and Hankey (supra n. 6) 151–152.

50. Mountjoy (supra n. 10) 106–107.

51. Mountjoy (supra n. 10) 107–108.

52. Mountjoy (supra n. 10) 107.

53. Mountjoy (supra n. 10) 107–108.

54. Mountjoy (supra n. 10) 73–74, 100.

55. Mountjoy (supra n. 10) 70–71.

56. V. Hankey, "The Aegean Deposit at El Amarna," in V. Karageorghis, ed., *Acts of the International Archaeological Symposium, "The Mycenaeans in the Eastern Mediterranean"* (Nicosia 1973) 128–136.

57. Mountjoy (supra n. 10) 90 notes that this shape was very popular in the Aegean mainland in LH IIIA 2.

58. Hankey (supra n. 56).

59. Mountjoy (supra n. 10) 81; Martin (supra n. 32) 90–91.

60. Warren and Hankey (supra n. 6) 117–18, 148–154 place LH IIIB between the late Eighteenth and early Twentieth Dynasties (1340/1330–c. 1190 B.C.).

61. On contents see M. R. Bell, "Preliminary Report on the Mycenaean Pottery from Deir El-Medina," *ASAE* 68 (1982) 143–163. At the conference on Bronze Age Trade in the Mediterranean (Oxford, December 1989), Dr. J. Evans of East London Polytechnic described gas chromatography, a non-destructive method of identifying substances trapped in the

MYCENAEAN POTTERY AT SAQQARA

body of a clay vessel. This application, which is not costly, is particularly valuable in Egypt where pots rarely need washing before study. In Mediterranean lands the shelf life of olive oil for culinary purposes is about one year.

62. We thank Drs. J. Bourriau and D. G. Jeffreys for this information.

63. We thank Professor M. Bietak for dating the Yahudiyeh juglet, c. 1630-1590/1570 B.C.; Aston in Martin, Raven, and Aston (supra n. 36) 21.

64. Reexamination of old material and new excavation here by Dr. J. Balensi of the Centre nationale de recherches scientifiques, Maison de l'Orient, Lyon, has shown that Tell Abu Hawam, near Haifa, was a major point of entry for Cypriot and Mycenaean pottery. We thank Dr. Balensi for information on her work, now in process of publication. Catling (supra n. 21) suggests that the Mycenaean exports went di-rectly to Ugarit, from where they were reshipped to Cyprus, the Levantine coast, and Egypt.

65. G. F. Bass, "A Bronze Age shipwreck at Ulu Burun (Kaş): 1984 Campaign," *AJA* 90 (1986) 269–296; C. Pulak, "The Bronze Age shipwreck at Ulu Burun, Turkey: 1985 Campaign," *AJA* 92 (1988) 1–37. G. F. Bass, C. Pulak, et al., "The Bronze Age Shipwreck at Ulu Burun, Turkey: 1986 Campaign," *AJA* 93 (1989) 1–29.

66. M. Drower, *CAH*[3] II.2, 137–141; Merrillees (supra n. 30) 202; on White-Slip sherds at Saqqara, see Aston in Martin, Raven, and Aston (supra n. 36) 9; P. Åström, "Comments on the Corpus of Mycenaean Pottery in Cyprus," in V. Karageorghis, ed. (supra n. 56) 123–127.

67. D. White, "1985 Excavations on Bates' Island, Marsa Matruh," *JARCE* 23 (1986) 51–84.

81

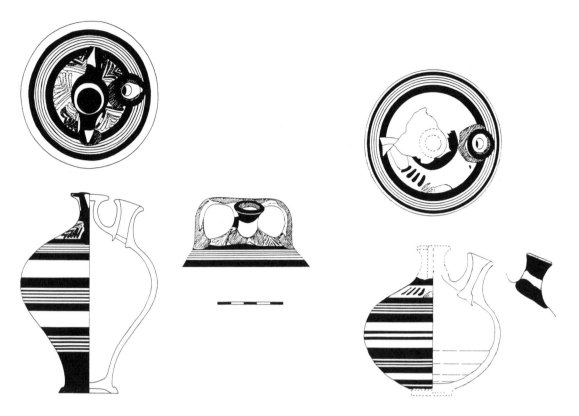

FIGURE 4.1 Cat. no. 1, stirrup jar, LH IIIA 2. Tomb of Horemheb, Shaft i. (see plate 4.4)

FIGURE 4.2 Cat. no. 2, stirrup jar, LH IIIA 2. Tomb of Horemheb, Shaft i. (see plate 4.5)

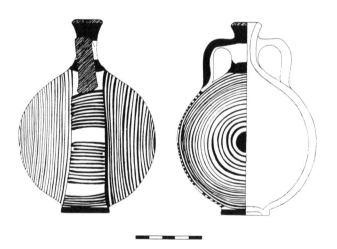

FIGURE 4.3 Cat. no. 3, globular flask, LH IIIA 2, late. Tomb of Horemheb, Shaft i. (see plate 4.6)

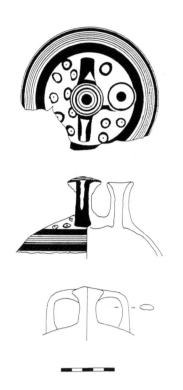

FIGURE 4.4 Cat. no. 4, stirrup jar, LH IIIA 2–IIIB 1. Tomb of Iurudef. (see plate 4.7)

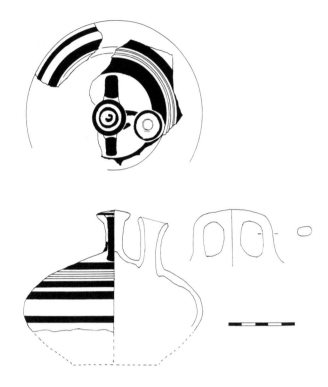

FIGURE 4.7 Cat. no. 7, stirrup jar, LH IIIB 1. Tomb of Ramose. (see plate 4.9.)

FIGURE 4.5 Cat. no. 5, stirrup jar, LH IIIA 2–IIIB 1. Tomb of Iurudef. (see plate 4.8)

FIGURE 4.6 Cat. no. 6, stirrup jar, LH IIIA 2–IIIB 1. Tomb of Tia and Tia, Shaft C.

FIGURE 4.8 Cat. no. 8, stirrup jar, LH IIIA 2–IIIB 1. Tomb of Maya. (see plate 4.10)

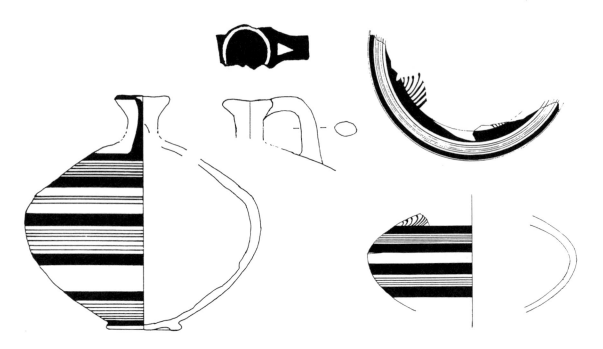

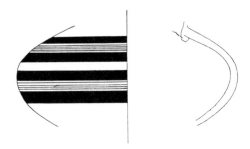

FIGURE 4.9 Cat. no. 9, stirrup jar, LH IIIB 1 rather than III A2. Tomb of Maya. (see plate 4.11)

FIGURE 4.13 Cat. no. 13, stirrup jar, LH IIIA 2–IIIB 1. (see plate 4.13)

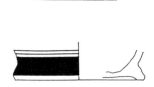

FIGURE 4.10 Cat. no. 10, stirrup jar (?), LH IIIB 1. Tomb of Maya.

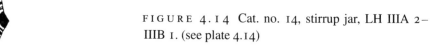

FIGURE 4.11 Cat. no. 11, stirrup jar, LH IIIA 2 or IIIB 1.

FIGURE 4.14 Cat. no. 14, stirrup jar, LH IIIA 2–IIIB 1. (see plate 4.14)

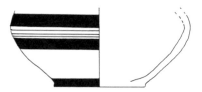

FIGURE 4.12 Cat. no. 12, stirrup jar, LH IIIB 1. (see plate 4.12)

FIGURE 4.15 Cat. no. 15, stirrup jar, LH IIIA 2–IIIB 1. (see plate 4.15)

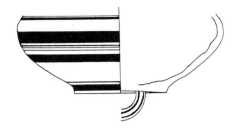

FIGURE 4.16 Cat. no. 16, stirrup jar, LH IIIB 1. (see plate 4.16)

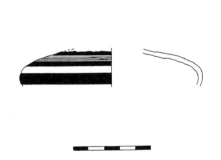

FIGURE 4.17 Cat. no. 17, stirrup jar, LH IIIB 1.

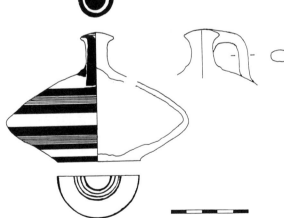

FIGURE 4.18 Cat. no. 18, stirrup jar, LH IIIB. (see plate 4.17)

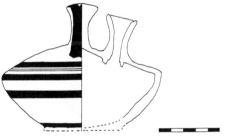

FIGURE 4.19 Cat. no. 19, stirrup jar, LH IIIB 1. (see plate 4.18)

FIGURE 4.20 Cat. no. 20, stirrup jar, LH IIIB. (see plate 4.19)

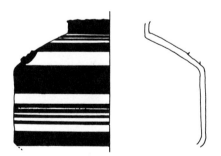

FIGURE 4.21 Cat. no. 21, alabastron, LH IIIA 2 or IIIB 1.

FIGURE 4.22   Cat. no. 22, closed vessel, LH IIIA 2 or IIIB 1.

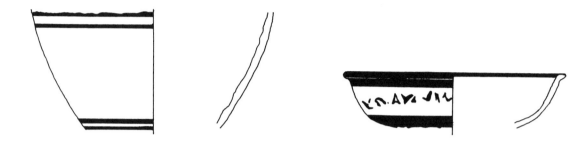

FIGURE 4.23   Cat. no. 23, closed vessel, LH IIIA 2
or IIIB 1.

FIGURE 4.24   Cat. no. 24, cup, LH IIIA 2 or IIIB 1.
(see plate 4.20)

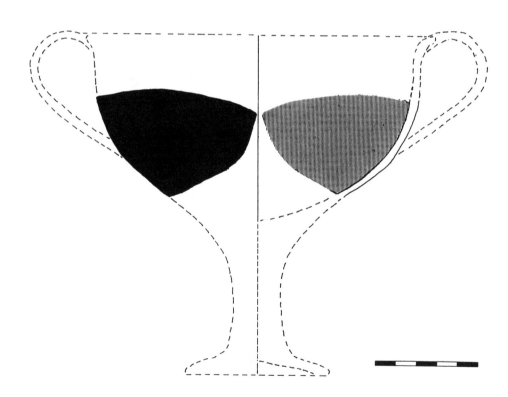

FIGURE 4.25   Cat. no. 25, kylix, LH IIIA 2. (see plate 4.21)

PLATE 4.4 Cat. no. 1, stirrup jar, LH IIIA 2. Tomb of Horemheb, Shaft i. (see figure 4.1)

PLATE 4.6 Cat. no. 3, globular flask, LH IIIA 2, late. Tomb of Horemheb, Shaft i. (see figure 4.3)

PLATE 4.5 Cat. no. 2, stirrup jar, LH IIIA 2. Tomb of Horemheb, Shaft i. (see figure 4.2)

PLATE 4.7 Cat. no. 4, stirrup jar, LH IIIA 2–IIIB 1. Tomb of Iurudef. (see figure 4.4)

PLATE 4.8 Cat. no. 5, stirrup jar, LH IIIA 2–IIIB 1. Tomb of Iurudef. (see figure 4.5)

PLATE 4.9 Cat. no. 7, stirrup jar, LH IIIB 1. Tomb of Ramose. (see figure 4.7)

PLATE 4.10 Cat. no. 8, stirrup jar, LH IIIA 2–IIIB 1. Tomb of Maya. (see figure 4.8)

PLATE 4.11 Cat. no. 9, stirrup jar, LH IIIB 1 rather than III A2. Tomb of Maya. (see figure 4.9)

PLATE 4.12 Cat. no. 12, stirrup jar, LH IIIB 1. (see figure 4.12)

PLATE 4.13 Cat. no. 13, stirrup jar, LH IIIA 2–IIIB 1. (see figure 4.13)

PLATE 4.14 Cat. no. 14, stirrup jar, LH IIIA 2–IIIB 1. (see figure 4.14)

PLATE 4.15 Cat. no. 15, stirrup jar, LH IIIA 2–
IIIB 1. (see figure 4.15)

PLATE 4.18 Cat. no. 19, stirrup jar, LH IIIB 1. (see
figure 4.19)

PLATE 4.16 Cat. no. 16, stirrup jar, LH IIIB 1. (see
figure 4.16)

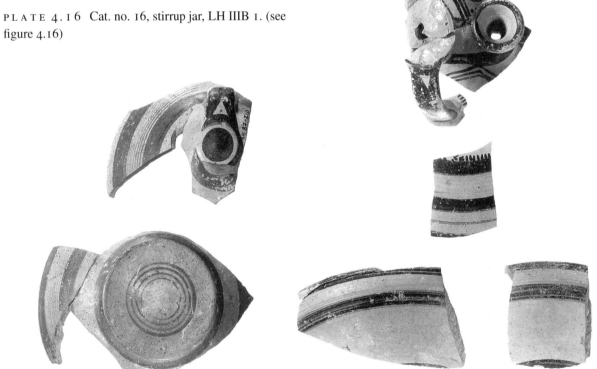

PLATE 4.17 Cat. no. 18, stirrup jar, LH IIIB. (see
figure 4.18)

PLATE 4.19 Cat. no. 20, stirrup jar, LH IIIB. (see
figure 4.20)

PLATE 4.20 Cat. no. 24, cup, LH IIIA 2 or IIIB 1. (see figure 4.24)

PLATE 4.21 Cat. no. 25, kylix, LH IIIA 2. (see figure 4.25)

5

CYPRUS AND THE WESTERN MEDITERRANEAN: SOME NEW EVIDENCE FOR INTERRELATIONS

◆

VASSOS KARAGEORGHIS

Emily Vermeule started her scholarly career in Aegean studies by concentrating on the Aegean area and particularly on the site of Mycenae. She soon discovered that Aegean culture had much broader borders, and she included Cyprus in her areas of interest, excavating the important Late Bronze Age site of Toumba tou Skourou in the north of the island. I hope that this short note, which will deal with one small aspect of the broader Aegean world, will serve as a temoignage of a long friendship and collaboration.

Having studied Cypriot archaeology for nearly forty years, I have reached a similar conclusion: the study of ancient Cypriot cultures is impossible without reference to the Levant and the Aegean. Indeed, the borders of Cypriot archaeology have broadened considerably and now include the entire Mediterranean region. I am convinced that this is also the case for the Aegean. Recent developments urge us to consider that the study of Aegean civilization should include the whole of the Mediterranean, from the Levantine coast to the Iberian peninsula. In this regard the increasing evidence for contacts between all the regions of the Mediterranean is relevant here. This evidence is particularly compelling

for the eighth–seventh centuries B.C. when the Phoenicians dominated Mediterranean trade; it is now clearer that similar conditions, though to a lesser degree, must have existed in the Mediterranean during the Late Bronze Age, when the Mycenaeans conducted such trade.

In this note I shall not examine in detail the present state of evidence of Late Bronze Age interrelations in the Mediterranean, as several scholars have already discussed this, each dealing with a specific regional or chronological aspect. Here I will underline the necessity that scholars keep an open mind when considering new evidence which has emerged almost every year during the last decade or so, and should reassess it continuously; I also wish to draw attention to some fresh evidence.

At this point I should stress the danger of considering imported goods as evidence for the presence of foreign peoples. The discovery of Mycenaean pottery in Spain, for example, should not be interpreted as attesting to the settlement of Mycenaeans in that region. Much more material is needed before proposing such a phenomenon, including other imported goods of daily use such

FIGURE 5.1 Bowl imitating a Cypriot shape, from Thapsos, Tomb 10.15 (inv. 14679).

FIGURE 5.2 Bowl imitating a Cypriot shape, from Thapsos, Tomb 19.19 (inv. 14703).

as personal ornaments and weapons, as well as a greater knowledge of architectural styles, burial customs, etc. The problem is not easily solved and for some time has caused considerable controversy among scholars. An interesting phenomenon, which might help ascertain the presence of people of foreign origin, is the occurrence of imitations of foreign pottery shapes in local clay, not for their particular beauty, but for their function. In recent years the discovery in Greece and Cyprus of "Handmade Burnished ware" (known as "Barbarian" ware), a particularly ugly fabric, has opened new horizons in the study of the movement of peoples from other regions to the Aegean and the eastern Mediterranean.[1]

The theme here therefore is the connection between Cyprus and the central Mediterranean area during the Late Bronze Age. This has already been the subject of various studies. In 1968 Lucia Vagnetti pointed out the relations between Cyprus and the central Mediterranean when she suggested that some bronze bowls from Caldare are of Cypriot origin.[2] In 1973 G. Voza published a short account on the foreign material from tombs excavated on the small promontory of Thapsos, on the east coast of Sicily, where LH IIIA and B vases were found, as well as a juglet of White Shaved ware and two juglets which he considered to be Cypriot Base-Ring II. He dated this material to the end of the fifteenth-fourteenth centuries B.C.[3] I was able to handle this "Cypriot" material in 1976 through the kindness of G. Voza, during

my first visit to Sicily It was immediately obvious that the two "Cypriot" Base-Ring II ware juglets were not in fact of Cypriot fabric. Only their form imitated Cypriot prototypes. Their clay is buff-pinkish and they are covered with a buff slip (not unlike Plain White wares which appear in other lands during various periods).[4] The White Shaved ware juglet is genuinely Cypriot.

R. Ross Holloway repeated this information in his book *Italy and the Aegean 3000–700 B.C.*, published in 1981.[5] Lucia Vagnetti, in her 1985 article on Late Cypriot ceramic imports to Italy,[6] expresses the opinion that their fabric is not Cypriot but Levantine. In a more recent article, she states that they "are apparently not of Cypriot fabric."[7]

A third "Base-Ring jug" was found in 1987 in a tomb in the center of Syracuse, together with an LH IIIA 2 angular alabastron and local pottery.[8] I examined this jug in the Syracuse Museum in April 1989: it is exactly like the two juglets mentioned above, i.e., it is an *imitation* Base-Ring vessel, of buff-pinkish fabric.

During the same visit I saw three bowls exhibited in the Syracuse Museum which were found at Thapsos in the 1890s. All three bowls were illustrated in Orsi's report in 1895[9] but have since remained unnoticed, as far as I can tell. One of the bowls is deep and conical (fig. 5.1: Tomb 10.15, inv. 14679); the other two are slightly shallow, with convex sides (fig. 5.2: Tomb 19.19, inv. 14703; fig. 5.3: Tomb 22.20, inv. 14712). All

FIGURE 5.3 Bowl imitating a Cypriot shape, from Thapsos, Tomb 22.20 (inv. 14712).

three have a wishbone handle below the rim which is sharply out-turned; the base is ring-shaped. They are handmade, of a local dark gray fabric, and bear a striking resemblance to Cypriot Base-Ring ware bowls, with regard both to their shape and appearance.

If this "diagnosis" is correct, it means there are six vases, five from Thapsos and one from Syracuse, which are imitation Base-Ring. Their fabric is certainly not Cypriot, but only chemical analysis will establish their local manufacture. There is no reason *prima facie* why they should have been made outside Sicily (e.g., somewhere in the Levant, as Vagnetti suggests) and imported to the island, since it was easy to import genuine Base-Ring wares which were plentiful on the Levantine market. The simplest explanation is that these six vases were made locally, in imitation of Cypriot Base-Ring shapes which would have been well known in Sicily, where they were appreciated for one reason or another. Real Base-Ring ware required a special kind of clay which occurs in Cyprus in the Troodos mountain range.[10] I am not aware of any genuine Base-Ring ware vases which have been found in Sicily, but there are two fragments from Sardinia,[11] and, if one looks carefully, there may be more.

More pottery of Cypriot origin has been found in Italy in recent years, namely a fragment from a large pithos from Sardinia and a fragment from a Pastoral-style crater from Eboli in southern Campania.[12] Vagnetti

rightly compares the discovery of the large pithos from Sardinia with the large pithoi from the Kaş shipwreck, which were used as containers for the transport of smaller goods and particularly of Cypriot pottery.[13] There is also some "Cypro-Mycenaean" pottery, though the Cypriot provenance of these pieces is not definite.[14]

As already mentioned, I do not intend to give here a corpus of Cypriot objects found in the central Mediterranean as this task has been masterly undertaken by Lucia Vagnetti, Fulvia Lo Schiavo, and Ellen Macnamara, who look out for new evidence. I have merely reiterated the importance of the connections between Cyprus and the central Mediterranean by underlining the significance of some recently discovered local (?) imitations of Cypriot Base-Ring shapes. Imitations can be far more important than actual imports, since they testify that those who imitated certain shapes were very familiar with the prototypes and that there must have been a special reason for making such imitations. The juglets may have been used for opium,[15] but what about the bowls? Are we to propose that they are the work of Cypriot potters working in Sicily side by side with Mycenaean potters and using local clay (see n. 14), in the same way as Cypriot bronzeworkers who settled in Sardinia may have been responsible for Cypriot bronzes found on the island?[16]

Another question worthy of consideration is whether the Cypriot objects found in the central Mediterranean were directly imported from Cyprus or indirectly from Rhodes or Egypt. The evidence from the Kaş shipwreck and the cosmopolitan character of its cargo may give us a clue. To be able to bring "exotic" goods to the West, Mycenaean ships must have sailed regularly to the eastern Mediterranean, perhaps along the northern coast of Africa, up the Levantine coast, and then to Cyprus. Some of these goods could be taken further west to the central Mediterranean, where there were small groups of Mycenaean settlers, who even produced Mycenaean-type pottery.[17]

How far west did the Mycenaeans and the Cypriots (or at least their goods) go? In the eighth-seventh centuries B.C. Cypriot and Phoenicians goods reached the Atlantic coast of Spain.[18] Something similar may have happened during the Late Bronze Age, perhaps in the thirteenth century B.C. Already one Mycenaean sherd has been found in Spain.[19]

At Thapsos, which is almost an "island" (in reality a peninsula connected to the mainland by a very narrow strip of land), the majority of imitation Base-Ring-type vases were found side by side with Mycenaean pottery. The "island" has abrupt sides and could thus be easily defended. The architectural remains uncovered so far at Thapsos are of a type and size that led several scholars to argue that they were built by foreigners who settled on the "island." [20] They are courtyard buildings and have been compared with buildings in Late Bronze Age Enkomi in Cyprus. We may now compare them with buildings of c. 1200 B.C. brought to light at Pyla-*Kokkinokremos* in Cyprus. [21] Ross Holloway is quite explicit: ". . . Cyprus must figure among the possible centres from which the builders of the Thapsos structures came. In this context, the Cypriote pottery from tombs D and A1 takes on further significance. . . . The buildings at Thapsos, which needed knowledgeable architects from abroad for their construction and suggest a veritable foreign colony on the site, are the most important elements in this cumulative picture of Cypriot activity. It required men and ideas to transform a Sicilian village into an emporium with some urban configuration, and this appears to have been the work of Cypriot residents in the 14th and 13th centuries." [22] I tend to support this interesting theory, though with considerable caution. Before the final results of the excavations at Thapsos are published it is not possible to determine whether the material from the tombs corresponds chronologically to the new town plan or whether it is earlier. It is of crucial importance to establish the date of the ceramic material found on the floors of the new houses. If it is of LH IIIC I type, then one would assume that trade relations may have preceded the establishment of settlers, or that the process of "settlement" covered a long period of time and culminated in the establishment of a new town plan.

Groups of people, whether merchants or refugees, who were planning to settle in a foreign land would often choose remote, easily defendable sites, preferably promontories. Aegean refugees did the same when they first settled at Maa-*Palaeokastro:* [23] the Phoenicians also chose promontories and offshore islands to establish their commercial colonies in the central Mediterranean. [24]

Research on the relations between Cyprus and the Levant on the one hand and the central Mediterranean on the other is only in its initial stages, but all indications point to a promising new field of scholarship. Scholars in both regions should become more alert, and watch for evidence for further interconnections. A bronze obelos, of a type common in Spain but also known in Sardinia (from where it may have come to Cyprus), was recently found in Cyprus in an eleventh-century B.C. tomb. [25]

Though this is the only central Mediterranean import known in Cyprus so far, archaeologists should be watchful for further evidence, for example among pottery sherds from their excavations. The movements of populations, even as early as the Late Bronze Age, and the possible establishment of small commercial "colonies" in several Mediterranean islands, should be carefully considered. There are ample modern models for this phenomenon. Cyprus, lying between the Levant and the rest of the Mediterranean, no doubt played a crucial role in interrelations, especially when one bears in mind her wealth in copper which was exported to both East and West.

It is with this in mind that these few lines have been written [26] and dedicated with much affection to a good scholar and friend, who has always been alert in her Aegean investigations.

POSTSCRIPT

The above note deals mainly with ceramic evidence. I should like to make a cautious suggestion for a possible Cypriot influence on a type of bronze object found in Sardinia, namely the small "rattles" of which several specimens are known and are dated to the ninth-eighth centuries B.C. [27] The Cypriot prototypes date to the Late Bronze Age (c. 1200 B.C.) and have been identified as rattles or standards, perhaps for ceremonial use. [28] If this suggestion is correct, then this is another metallurgical connection between Cyprus and Sardinia.

NOTES

1. D. Pilides, "Handmade Burnished Wares of the Late Bronze Age. Toward a Clearer Classification System," in J. A.

Barlow, D. L. Bolger, and B. Kling, eds., *Cypriot Ceramics: Reading the Prehistoric Record* (Philadelphia 1991) 139–148; D. Pilides, "Handmade Burnished Ware in Prehistoric Cyprus" (Ph.D. diss., University of London, 1991).

2. L. Vagnetti, "I bacili di bronzo di Caldare sono Ciprioti?" *SMEA* 7 (1968) 129–138.

3. See G. Voza, "Thapsos," in P. Pelagatti and G. Voza, eds., *Archeologia nella Sicilia sudorientale* (Napoli 1973) 31, 36, nos. 85–87, pl. 7.

4. See Voza (supra n. 3) 36, where the clay is described as "argilla di colore rosa."

5. R. Ross Holloway, *Italy and the Aegean 3000–700 B.C.* (Louvain-la- Neuve and Providence 1981) 83, figs. 47–48.

6. F. Lo Schiavo, E. Macnamara, and L. Vagnetti, "Late Cypriot imports to Italy and their influence on local bronzework," *BSR* 53 (1985) 5, fig. 2.1–3.

7. L. Vagnetti and F. Lo Schiavo, "Late Bronze Age long-distance trade in the Mediterranean: The role of the Cypriots," in E. Peltenburg, ed., *Early Society in Cyprus* (Edinburgh 1989) 219.

8. Vagnetti and Lo Schiavo (supra n. 7) 237, 11.4A. I report on this jug with the kind permission of Giuseppe Voza, Archaeological Superintendent of eastern Sicily, who excavated it.

9. P. Orsi, "Thapsos," *MonAnt* 6 (1895) 24–25, sep. 10, no. 15; 28, sep. 10, no. 19; 28–30, sep. 22, no. 20.

10. R. E. Jones, *Greek and Cypriot Pottery. A Review of Scientific Studies* (Athens 1986) 340–341, 528–529.

11. Vagnetti in Lo Schiavo, Macnamara, and Vagnetti (supra n. 6) 5, fig. 2.4, 5; see, however, Vagnetti in Vagnetti and Lo Schiavo (supra n. 7) 220–221, where it is stated that "the original hypothesis that they could be ascribed to Base-Ring fabric has not been confirmed by chemical analysis. The same analysis, however, seems to rule out an Aegean or local origin at least for one of the sherds."

12. Vagnetti and Lo Schiavo (supra n. 7) 219–220, fig. 28.

13. Vagnetti and Lo Schiavo (supra n. 7) 224.

14. Lo Schiavo, Macnamara, and Vagnetti (supra n. 6) 5–7, fig. 2:6–7.

15. For references see V. Karageorghis and M. Demas, *Excavations at Kition. V. The Pre-Phoenician Levels,* Part I (Nicosia 1985) 259.

16. Lo Schiavo, Macnamara, and Vagnetti (supra n. 6) 63. For a more recent bibliography, see M. S. Balmuth, ed., *Studies in Sardinian Archaeology 3: Nuragic Sardinia and the Mycenaean World,* BAR-IS 387 (Oxford 1987), and A. B. Knapp, "Ethnicity, entrepreneurship and exchange: Mediterranean inter-island relations in the Late Bronze Age," *BSA* 85 (1990) 116–153.

17. See recently R. E. Jones, "Chemical analysis of Aegean-type Late Bronze Age pottery found in Italy," in M. Marazzi, S. Tusa, and L. Vagnetti, eds., *Traffici micenei nel Mediterraneo. Problemi storici e documentazione archeologica, Atti del Convegno di Palermo, maggio e dicembre 1984* (Taranto 1986). For other possible Cypriot objects (other than pottery) which reached the central Mediterranean in the Late Bronze Age see Lo Schiavo, Macnamara, and Vagnetti (supra n. 6).

18. J. M. Blazquez, *Tartessos y los origines de la colonización fenicie en Occidente* (Salamanca 1968).

19. J. C. M. de la Cruz, "Mykenische Keramik aus Bronzezeitlichen Siedlungsschichten von Montoro am Guadalquivir," *MM* 29 (1988) 77–92, pl. 9.b–d. (I owe this reference to Lucia Vagnetti, who also read a draft of this paper and made valuable suggestions.)

20. Holloway (supra n. 5) 85; for further references, see Knapp (supra n. 16) 125–126.

21. V. Karageorghis and M. Demas, *Pyla-Kokkinokremos, a Late 13th Century B.C. Fortified Settlement in Cyprus* (Nicosia 1984) 24–28.

22. Karageorghis and Demas (supra n. 21) 85–87.

23. V. Karageorghis and M. Demas, *Excavations at Maa-Palaeokastro 1979–1986* (Nicosia 1988) 261–264.

24. Karageorghis and Demas (supra n. 23) 263 and n. 16; to these one may also add the site of Tharros in Sardinia.

25. V. Karageorghis and F. Lo Schiavo, "A West Mediterranean obelos from Amathus," *Rivista di studi fenici* 17 (1989) 15–29. For relations between Cyprus and Sardinia in later periods see H. Matthäus, "Cypern und Sardinien im frühen 1. Jahrtausend v. Chr.," in Peltenburg, ed. (supra n. 7) 244–255.

26. Since this article was written (1989), several studies have appeared, dealing with the problem of the relations between Cyprus, the Aegean, and the central Mediterranean area. See in particular F.-W. von Hase, "Ägäische Importe im Zentralen Mittelmeergebiet im Späthelladischer Zeit (SH I–SH IIIC)," in *Orientalisch-Ägäische Einflüsse in der Europäischen Bronzezeit* (Bonn 1990) 80–108; important new evidence was also presented at the Second International Congress of Mycenology held in Rome and Naples in October 1991.

27. E.g., E. Macnamara, D. Ridgway, and F. Ridgway, *The Bronze Hoard from S. Maria in Paulis, Sardinia,* British Museum Occasional Paper no. 45 (London 1984) 14–15, nos. 136, 137; *Kunst und Kultur Sardiniens vom Neolithicum bis zum Ende der Nuragherzeit* (Ausstellung Badisches Landesmuseums Karlsruhe im Karlsruher Schloss vom 18 April-13 Juli 1980) 410, no. 203.

28. Karageorghis and Demas (supra n. 23) 112, 224, pls. LIV, CLXXVII, no. 270.

97

6

SHINING AND FRAGRANT CLOTH
IN HOMERIC EPIC

♦

CYNTHIA W. SHELMERDINE

I first learned of the Aegean Bronze Age and Linear B some twenty-five years ago from Emily Vermeule. She has taught me a great deal, but perhaps her most important lesson has been the value of an interdisciplinary approach to the study of this earliest stage of Greek history. I am glad to have this chance to thank her in print, with an essay bringing together two of her favorite topics, Homer and the Mycenaeans.

The Homeric epics are not a reliable guide to the culture and habits of Mycenaean Greeks, but it is sometimes possible to work the other way, and to show from Late Bronze Age data that an object or practice in the *Iliad* or the *Odyssey* does accurately reflect that period. This is the case with Homeric references to shining and fragrant cloth, which current knowledge about Mycenaean perfumes and textiles can illuminate.[1] A number of adjectives in Homeric epic describe cloth as 'shiny' or 'gleaming,' and several specify that a textile is 'fragrant' (see tables 6.1 and 6.2).[2] However, only one garment is described as both shining and fragrant: Helen's robe, at *Iliad* 3.141, 385, 419. In Table 6.2 I include the adjectives ἀμβρόσιος ('sweet-smelling,' 'fragrant') and νεκτάρεος ('fragrant'). The nouns from which

these words come are ambrosia and nectar, the food and drink of the gods. The terms themselves are relevant here because, though their general sense is 'immortal,' they actually mean 'fragrant,' and the substances are often synonymous with perfume. Oil is both ambrosial and perfumed in the *Homeric Hymn to Aphrodite* 63–64, as are clothes in the *Homeric Hymn to Apollo* 184. Ambrosia is used, like oil, as a cleanser at *Iliad* 14.170–171 and *Odyssey* 18.192–193; and in Vergil's *Georgics* 4.415–416 it is a perfume.[3] Scholiasts regularly gloss the words as 'fragrant.' Thus at *Iliad* 19.38, where Thetis embalms Patroklos' corpse with red nectar and ambrosia, a scholiast explains ambrosia as τὸ θεῖον καὶ εὐῶδες ἔλαιον ('the divine and fragrant oil'); we may compare *Iliad* 23.186–187, where the job is done with ῥοδόεντι . . . ἐλαίῳ / ἀμβροσίῳ ('fragrant rose-scented oil').

Adjectives of shining and fragrance are applied to both linen and wool. ῥήγεα ('bedclothes') are generally assumed to be woolen; they are mentioned with linen at *Iliad* 9.661 and *Odyssey* 13.73, 118, and with wool at *Odyssey* 11.189, 19.318, 337. A τάπης ('rug,' 'blanket') is made of wool at *Iliad* 16.224 and *Odyssey*

Table 6.1. *Shining Cloth*
(Underlined book numbers refer to the *Iliad,* those not underlined refer to the *Odyssey*. Abbreviations for the Epic Cycle and the Homeric Hymns are conventional, as follows: H. = Homeric Hymn; Ap. = Apollo; Cer. = Demeter (Ceres); Merc. = Hermes (Mercury); Ven. = Aphrodite (Venus); Kyp. = Kypria.)

	σιγαλόεις	φαεινός/ (-ότερος)	ἀργύφεος/ (ἄργυφος)	στίλβων	other
ἑανός		3.419			3.419 ἀργής
εἷμα	22.154 6.26 H. Ven. 85 H. Ven. 164		(H. Merc. 250)	3.392	
ἐσθής/ ἔσθος		6.74			H. 31.13 λάμπεται
ὀθόνη					3.141 ἀργεννῇσι
πέπλος		5.315 (H. Ven. 86, πυρὸς αὐγῆς)			6.295 ἀπέλαμπεν
φᾶρος			5.230 10.543		24.148 like sun or moon
χιτών	15.60 19.232			18.596	19.234 λαμπρός
καλύπτρη					22.406 λιπαρήν
κρήδεμνον					14.185 sun-white 18.382 λιπαρό- 1.334 λιπαρά 13.388 λιπαρά 16.416 λιπαρά 18.210 λιπαρά 21.65 λιπαρά H. Cer. 25 λιπαρο- H. Cer. 438 λιπαρο- H. Cer. 459 λιπαρο-
ῥῆγος	6.38 11.189 13.118 19.318 19.337 23.180				
τάπης		10.156			

Table 6.2. *Fragrant Cloth*

	θυώδης	κηώδης	τεθυωμένος	θυήεις	ἀμβρόσιος/ (ἄμβροτος)	νεκτάρεος
ἑανός					<u>14</u>.178 <u>21</u>.507	<u>3</u>.385
εἷμα	5.264 21.52		H. Ap. 184 Kyp. fr. 4.7		(16.670) (7.260) (7.265) (24.59) (H. Ap. 184)	
πέπλος				H. Cer. 277	<u>5</u>.338	
χιτών						<u>18</u>.25
κόλπος	H. Cer. 231	<u>6</u>.483				
κρήδεμνον					(5.347)	
σπάργανον				H. Merc. 237		

4.124. ὀθόναι ('cloths,' 'garments') are probably of linen in Homer, as they are later, though this is not certain.[4] Several Homeric passages show that fabrics get their sheen from treatment with oil or fat: the word σιγαλόεις ('glossy,' 'fatty') is related to σίαλος ('fat pig'), and the root of λιπαρός means 'fat' or 'grease.' The chitons of the youths on Achilles' shield (*Iliad* 18.595–596) are στίλβοντας ἐλαίῳ ('gleaming with oil'). Epic hyperbole, for a nonexistent society in which all the women are strong, all the men good-looking, and all the clothing above average? Rather, oil treatment is thought by some to reflect a real practice, since, as Lorimer notes, "up to modern times oil . . . has been used in many regions to give a glossy finish to linen."[5] It has been confirmed by experiment that, in addition to cleaning and softening linen, soaking in oil does make the fabric gleam.[6]

But was this an ancient practice? And did wool ever receive similar treatment? Lorimer states categorically that it did not, while conversely Gow (having consulted, among others, the Directors of the British Launderers'

Association) reports that oil will restore suppleness to wool after washing, but that it " 'is not used for treating linen fabrics.' "[7] This is a problem, since both wool and linen are called 'shining' in epic. There is also an explicit reference to oil treatment in *Odyssey* 7.105–107:

αἱ δ' ἱστοὺς ὑφόωσι καὶ ἠλάκατα στρωφῶσιν
ἥμεναι, οἷά τε φύλλα μακεδνῆς αἰγείροιο·
καιροσέων δ' ὀθονέων ἀπολείβεται ὑγρὸν ἔλαιον.[8]

Plutarch and the scholiasts misinterpret this passage as meaning that the cloth was so closely woven that oil could not penetrate it but ran off the surface, or that the cloth was shiny or soft *like* oil.[9] They have been followed by a number of translators, including Chapman and T. E. Shaw. Lattimore translated 107: "and from the cloths where it is sieved oozes the limpid olive oil," as though the line referred to oil processing and not to textile treatment at all. But as others have recognized, it is much more likely that we have here a reference to the sort of fabric treatment mentioned above.[10] However, there is no ancient post-Homeric confirmation of the passage, and epic allusions to 'fragrant' cloth remain even more obscure.

The fact that ancient commentators misunderstood *Odyssey* 7.105–107 suggests that it was not common practice to treat cloth in this way, during or after weaving, and this inference is borne out by the silence of Classical and later authors on the topic. The epic adjectives in tables 6.1 and 6.2 are not applied to clothing elsewhere.[11] Allusions to shining or fragrant cloth, or to the association of oil with textiles, are quite rare from the fifth century B.C. on, and the information that is available may therefore be summarized briefly.

(1) The third century B.C. comic poet Machon (fragment XVIII; Athenaeus 13.582e) mentions oil required by a fuller, presumably for cleaning.[12]

(2) Oil combines with sodium carbonate as a detergent in late alchemical texts.[13]

(3) Athenaeus (15.691e–f) describes an extravagant banquet at which pigeons dipped in perfume sprinkle the guests' cloaks while flying around the room. This is clearly an exotic and isolated case, and not an instance of oil treatment.

(4) Plutarch (*Life of Alexander* 36, 686c) says that because white oil is used in white dye, cloths colored with it retain their clear and shining brilliance even after 190 years: [ἔχουσι] τὴν λαμπρότητα καθαρὰν καὶ στίλβουσαν ὁρᾶσθαι.[14] This passage has been cited as showing that textiles were treated with oil.[15] However, strictly it refers to oil used in a dye, and this is not a likely parallel for the Homeric references to shining cloth.

(5) Marinatos wrongly cites Varro (*De Re Rustica* II.11.7) as saying that oil was used in antiquity in connection with wool-working.[16] In fact the passage refers to the treatment of lambs after shearing. They should be rubbed in an oil mixture, and if covered with a skin, this should be treated on the *inside* with the same mixture.

(6) The Hippocratic corpus (*De Diaeta Salubri* 3) recommends wearing καθαρά ('clean') himations in winter, but ἐλαιοπινέα ('oil-soaked') clothing in summer, to prevent dryness.

(7) A fragment attributed to Aristophanes' *Thesmophoriazusae* (fragment 319, Kock i.474; Athenaeus 15.690c) mentions the scent of perfumes rising from a clothes bag. The fragment does not form part of the play as we know it, and the context is unclear. This is the only post-Homeric reference I know of to scented clothing, and passage (6) is the only instance of textiles soaked in oil for a purpose other than laundering. Such passages have received little attention, and scholars of ancient technology do not mention oil treatment in connection with ancient weaving, fulling, and the like.[17]

(8) Finally, a squat oinochoe in New York by the Meidias Painter has been interpreted as showing women perfuming clothing.[18] However the process used is fumigation, not the direct application of oil to textiles. The clothes are suspended above a fire, on which a woman is sprinkling the contents of a lekythos, a standard oil container.

Thus according to Classical and later sources, oil is used with detergents to clean cloth, and with coloring agents to make some dyes. However, clothing is only once described as fragrant, indirectly and in an uncertain context, and once as shining, in reference to the color achieved with a white dye. We must rely, then, almost entirely on the Homeric epics for information on this subject, when it is precisely the Homeric references we wish to understand.[19]

Some help is available from Greek Bronze Age documents, which confirm and supplement the Homeric references to oil treatment of cloth. Indeed, though the adjective 'shining' is missing, Homeric and Mycenaean textile vocabularies are quite similar. Both attest the ἑανός (Myc. *we-a₂-no*, /wehanos/, 'robe'), χιτών (Myc. *ki-to*, /khiton/, 'chiton,' 'man's garment') and φᾶρος (Myc. *pa-wo*, /pharwos/, 'cloak,' 'piece of cloth'). They share the color words for textiles λευκός (Myc. *re-u-ko*, /leukos/, 'white'), ποίκιλος (Myc. *po-ki-ro-*, /poikilo/, 'parti-colored,' in compounds; perhaps complete on KN Ld 5845), πόλιος (Myc. *po-ri-wo*, /poliwos/, 'grey'), πορφύρεος (Myc. *po-pu-ro₂*, *po-pu-re-ja*, *po-pu-re-jọ[*, /porphurios/, /porphureia/, /porphurios/, 'blood-red'), and φοινικόεις (Myc. *po-ni-ke-ja*, /phoinikeia/, 'purple-red'). Clothes are described as having tassels (τερμιόεις, *Odyssey* 19.242; Myc. *o-nu-ke*, /onukhes/).[20] As for the material, in Homer there is no indication for the chiton, the φᾶρος, or the ἑανός.[21] Mycenaean chitons are of *linon lepton* on KN L 693, and this is not surprising; the Semitic root of the word means flax and linen. The *pharwos* is described in several tablets as made of linen (KN L 594, etc.), but on others it is woolen (KN L 173 *we-we-e-a*, /*wer-w[h]e[h]a/*). The *wehanos* is represented by the cloth ideogram **146*, at both Pylos and Knossos,[22] and the word itself appears in two very interesting Pylos texts:

PY Un 1322.5

we-a₂-no[ri]-no , re-po-to   **146*   GRA   5

wehano[li]non lepton WEHANOS WHEAT 480 liters

cloth   li]nen fine   CLOTH   WHEAT 480 liters

PY Fr 1225.1   e-ra₃-wo , u-po-jo , po-ti-ni-ja

.2   we-a₂-no-i , a-ro-pa   OLE+A S 1

.1   elaiwon hupoio potniai

.2   wehanoihi aloipha   OIL 9.6 liters

.1   Oil for Potnia of *Hup–*

.2   for cloths as ointment   OIL+A 9.6 liters

Un 1322 is confidently restored to define the *wehanos* as 'fine linen,' with the wheat perhaps fixing its price; and Fr 1225 gives us an explicit reference to the use of olive oil 'as an ointment for *wehanoihi*.' This confirms a very ancient use of oil with linen. A good parallel is available in the Bronze Age Mari texts, where references to "(sesame)-oil to make cloth shine"[23] have puzzled the editors of those texts. Fr 1225 thus provides direct evidence that oil was applied to finished cloths, and the Mari references specify that the purpose of such applications was to produce a shine. Further, the Pylos oil has been treated by perfumers, though the exact meaning of the ligatured oil ideogram is not known.[24] The Pylians scented their oil with rose, sage, and other herbs; this was Homeric and Classical practice as well.[25] Experiment has confirmed that textiles treated with these perfumes become fragrant, as well as shiny.[26]

Mycenaean documents, therefore, seem to provide the explanation for both shining and fragrant clothing in Homer, at least when the material is linen. There is also evidence that wool was treated the same way. On Mycenae tablet Oe 127, wool is allocated for *pharwea* which are to be 'well boiled':

pa-we-a₂ ,   e-we-pe-se-so-me-na ,   LANA 20

pharweha   eu hepsesomena   WOOL 1920 liters

cloths   to be well boiled[27]   WOOL 1920 liters

Boiling thus figures in the Mycenaean treatment of wool; an interesting partial parallel is found in Tebtunis Papyrus 703.100ff.,[28] where the makers of ὀθόνια use a detergent of oil and sodium carbonate in the boiling of linen. More indicative, though, are several Knossos tablets recording the allocation of oil to several places known to be centers of wool production and textile manufacture, and to a tailor. The quantities range from 1.6 liters to 126.4 liters. The purpose is not stated, but the number of references, the size of the allocations, and the exclusively business nature of the Linear B tablets all make it reasonable to assume the recipients will use the oil in connection with their work.[29]

Since much of the textile industry at Knossos deals with wool, we have here evidence for a probable association between wool and oil, in particular scented oil, to complement the linen evidence from Pylos. This inference receives further support from KN Xe 7711, where *Etawoneus*—a man known through John Killen's work to be a 'finisher' of textiles—who takes woven cloth and supervises its final decoration and treatment, receives something from a perfumer. The tablet is broken, and I used to think the perfumer was giving some of his oil. Now, however, "traces to the right," in the conservative words of the editors, "are not inconsistent with" the ideogram WOOL.[30] Thus a perfumer has apparently treated wool with oil, and is now transferring it not to a weaver but to a man in charge of its final decoration.[31]

This Bronze Age information, then, provides a real-life analogy to explain Homeric references to fragrant and shining cloth, just as oil tannage, accurately described at *Iliad* 17.389–393, is reflected in the Mycenaean allocation of oil to tanners (Fh 5428, 5435) and for hides (Fh 353, 5432) at Knossos.[32] But the topic of fragrance requires further discussion, for scented clothing, like nectar and ambrosia, is mostly divine. Of the thirteen Homeric references to fragrant cloth (see table 6.2), nine refer to the gods (fifteen of nineteen including the Homeric Hymns and the Epic Cycle). The four exceptions are the following: adjectives of fragrance describe Helen's ἑανός ('robe,' *Iliad* 3.385), Achilles' chiton (*Iliad* 18.25), Andromache's κόλπος ('bosom of the robe,' *Iliad* 6.483), and Odysseus' εἵματα ('clothing,' *Odyssey* 21.52). The last instance should perhaps not be counted as an exception: Odysseus' clothing is usually assumed to be redolent of cedar, from the chests in which it lies.[33] In any case, the great majority of references to fragrant clothing involve deities. Perfumed oil is likewise used as a body ointment in Homer only by the gods.[34] Indeed, fragrance has long been recognized as an attribute of divinity, in ancient Greece as elsewhere.[35] Scented cloth is thus appropriately associated with the gods in Homeric epic, where it clearly has a more special status than it does in Mycenaean reality. Though radiance is also a feature of divine epiphanies in post-Homeric literature,[36] shining clothing is not so exclusively the gods' prerogative in Homer (see table 6.1): only six of thirty-one references apply to divinities (fourteen of thirty-nine including the Homeric Hymns, none in the Epic Cycle).

There are two possible explanations, not mutually exclusive, for the close link between gods and fragrant cloth. The clothing on the PY Fr 1225 is for the goddess Potnia, so one could postulate a divine association with perfumed oil even in Bronze Age Greece. But at least one perfume allocation at Pylos is secular,[37] and we have seen Mycenaean evidence for oil treatment of textiles at Knossos which have no religious connection. We may therefore suggest a second reason for the Homeric tendency to ascribe fragrant clothing to divinities. It is, after all, typical of epic to romanticize the Mycenaean past. This is true not just of the larger themes of the story—if the Trojan War ever took place, I doubt it was fought for the most beautiful woman in the world—but also of the details. From this mythologizing process come the σήματα λυγρά ('baneful signs') which are all that epic memory retains of writing; the special but curious tower shield and boar's-tooth helmet; the demotion of war chariots to taxicabs; the elevation to heroic simile of lion and boar hunts, which are retold by successive generations of bards in ever later language, but preserve the generic preoccupations of Mycenaean art.

In my view it is quite consistent with other features of Homeric epic that it should preserve a regular Mycenaean practice—the treatment of textiles with oil to make them fragrant and/or shining—not in its original state but in a more limited and elevated form. In particular the near but not total restriction of fragrant textiles to gods suggests a progression during which the association became more and more exclusive. The process reached the point we see in the Homeric poems, and perhaps continued thereafter, given the rarity and ambiguity of later references to mortals with scented clothing. It thus seems very likely that this is yet another case where a Bronze Age practice is discontinued, but plays a distorted and specialized role in Homer.

As Emily Vermeule once wrote, "the desire to endow Homer with roots and ancestors to whom he is faithful is deeply felt by many, as though it were all we could do to repay him for his poetry."[38] It is satisfying to find, in incidental adjectives describing textiles, some justification for this impulse.

NOTES

1. On Mycenaean perfumery see E. D. Foster, "An Administrative Department at Knossos Dealing with Perfumery and Offerings," *Minos* 16 (1975) 19–51; J. L. Melena, "Olive Oil and Other Sorts of Oil," *Minos* 18 (1983) 89–123; C. W. Shelmerdine, *The Perfume Industry of Mycenaean Pylos* (Göteburg 1985); M. Wylock, "La fabrication des parfums à l'époque mycénienne," *SMEA* 11 (1970) 116–133.

On textiles, E. J. W. Barber has now provided a comprehensive study of the Neolithic period and the Bronze Age: *Prehistoric Textiles* (Princeton 1991). On Linear B evidence for textiles see especially a series of articles by J. T. Killen, including: "The Wool Industry of Crete in the Late Bronze Age," *BSA* 59 (1964) 1–15; "The Knossos Lc (Cloth) Tablets," *BICS* 13 (1966) 105–109; "The Knossos o-pi Tablets," in *Atti e memorie del I° Congresso Internazionale di Micenologia* (Rome 1968) II.636–643; "Two Notes on the Knossos Ak Tablets," in M. S. Ruipérez, ed., *Acta Mycenaea*, Minos 11–12 (Salamanca 1970–1971 [1972]) II.425–440; "Mycenaean a-ko-ra-ja/-jo," in A. M. Davies and W. Meid, eds., *Studies in Greek, Italic and Indo-European Linguistics Offered to Leonard R. Palmer*, Innsbrucker Beiträge zur Sprachwissenschaft 16 (Innsbruck 1976) 117–125; "The Knossos Ld(1) Tablets," in E. Risch and H. Mühlestein, eds., *Colloquium Mycenaeum* (Neuchâtel-Geneva 1979) 151–181; "The Textile Industries at Pylos and Knossos," in C. W. Shelmerdine and T. G. Palaima, eds., *Pylos Comes Alive* (New York 1984) 49–63; "Linear B Sign *115 on KN Ws 1703: Commodity or Weight?" *Kadmos* 24 (1985) 149–152; "Epigraphy and Interpretation in the Knossos WOMAN and CLOTH Records," in J.-P. Olivier and T. G. Palaima, eds., *Texts, Tablets and Scribes. Studies in Mycenaean Epigraphy and Economy Offered to Emmett L. Bennett, Jr.*, Suplementos a Minos 10 (Salamanca 1988) 167–183; See also J. L. Melena, *Studies on Some Mycenaean Inscriptions from Knossos Dealing with Textiles*, Suplementos a Minos 5 (Salamanca 1975).

2. The picture in the Homeric Hymns and the Epic Cycle is similar; those references are included in tables 6.1 and 6.2 for convenience.

3. References are collected by N. J. Richardson, *The Homeric Hymn to Demeter* (Oxford 1974) 238–239 ad 237. Also useful is F. R. Adrados, "Sobre el aceite perfumado: Esquilo, Agam. 96, las tablillas Fr y la ambrosia," *Kadmos* 3 (1965) 122–148.

4. S. Marinatos, *Kleidung*, ArchHom I.A/B (Göttingen 1967) 5, 6, n. 19. E. Pernice, "Die Tracht," in A. Gercke et al., *Einleitung in die Altertumswissenschaft* II, 3rd ed. (Leipzig-Berlin 1922) 35, takes the ὀθόναι at *Odyssey* 7.107 (discussed supra 101) as linen. For ὀθόναι as linen see P. Chantraine, *Dictionnaire étymologique de la langue grecque* (Paris 1974) 778, s.v. ὀθόνη with references; O. Schrader, "Aus griechischer Frühzeit," in T. Siebs, ed., *Festschrift zur Jahrhundertfeier der Universität zu Breslau, im Namen der Schlesischen Gesellschaft für Volkskunde,* Mitteilungen der Schlesischen Gesellschaft für Volkskunde 13–14 (Breslau 1911) 470; references to post-Homeric ὀθόναι in LSJ.

5. H. L. Lorimer, *Homer and the Monuments* (London 1950) 371–372.

6. A. L. H. Robkin, "The Endogram WE on Mycenaean Textiles *146 and *166+WE: A Proposed Identification," *AJA* 85 (1981) 213. Barber (supra n. 1) 14 notes that linen thread and fabric are naturally "lustrous, smooth, even slippery," but her point is the way the fabric feels, not the way it looks.

7. A. F. S. Gow, *Machon. The Fragments* (Cambridge 1965) 130 ad XVIII.416 f. ἐλαδίου, quoting Mr. Derrett-Smith of the Linen Industry Research Association.

8. "And the women weave webs and keep turning the carded wool, seated, like leaves of the tall black poplar; and from the close-woven cloths drips the moist oil."

9. As an argument that a thing can be both λεπτόν ('fine,' 'thin') and πυκνόν ('dense'), Plutarch (*Moralia* 396B–C) cites *Odyssey* 7.107; Homer, he says, shows: τὴν ἀκρίβειαν καὶ λεπτότητα τοῦ ὕφους τῷ μὴ προσμένειν τὸ ἔλαιον, ἀλλ' ἀπορρεῖν καὶ ἀπολισθάνειν, τῆς λεπτότητος καὶ πυκνότητος οὐ διιείσης ("[indicating] the precision and fineness of the cloth by the oil not adhering to it but flowing off and slipping off, because the denseness does not let it pass

through"). Schol. *Odyssey* 7.107: τὸ δέ, ἀπολείβεται ὑγρὸν ἔλαιον, ἤτοι οὕτως ἦσαν πυκναὶ ὡς μηδὲ ἔλαιον δι' αὐτῶν ἐλθεῖν, ἢ ἔξωθεν ὡς ἔλαιον ἔστιλβον διὰ τὴν λευκότητα, ἢ τρυφεραὶ ἦσαν ὡς δοκεῖν ἔλαιον ἀπορρεῖν· ἢ ἀποστίλβειν ὡς τὸν μίτον, ὡς δοκεῖν ἔλαιον ἐκχεῖν ("the phrase 'drips the moist oil' means either that [the cloths] were so close woven that not even oil could go through them, or that they were gleaming like oil from the outside because of their whiteness, or that they were soft so that oil seemed to flow off them; or that they seemed to gleam like the web, so that oil seemed to pour out of them").

10. So W. B. Stanford, *Homer, Odyssey* (London 1964) 324 ad 107. A. Heubeck et al., *A Commentary on Homer's Odyssey*, vol. I (Oxford 1988) 328–329 ad 107 have a different explanation than the one adopted here. They cite Marinatos' explanation (supra n. 4) 4 with n. 14 that "in the preparation of woollen cloth a bath of oil and other substances (called ἀμόργη) might be used as a bleach." In fact, as Marinatos notes, the bath is used to dye rather than bleach: "weich oder zugleich dunkel gefärbt." A scholion to Ar. *Lys.* 150 gives χρώματος εἶδος ('type of color') as a definition, as do the *Suda* A 1623 s.v. Ἀμόργεια, Stephanus of Byzantium s.v. Ἄμοργος, and Herodian the grammarian (A. Lentz, *Grammatici Graeci* [Leipzig 1867–1868] III.I 184 line 14, III.II 888 line 26). See J. van Leeuwen, *Aristophanis Lysistrata* (Leiden 1903) 26 ad 150 ff., J. Henderson, *Aristophanes Lysistrata* (Oxford 1987) 85 ad 150. Aristotle, *De Coloribus* 796a27, says that the ἀμόργης (here 'lees'?) of the olive turn from light to dark. Stephanus of Byzantium s.v. and the *Etymologicum Magnum* 129.15 specify the color purple. Further discussion by G. M. A. Richter, "Silk in Greece," *AJA* 33 (1929) 27–33; her identification of the material as silk has not been accepted.

11. An apparent exception is Hes. *Theog.* 574, where Pandora's dress is ἀργυφέη ('silver-shining'); however, this passage is still within the early epic tradition. At the other end of the ancient spectrum, in the Gospel according to St. Mark 9.3, Christ is transfigured before his apostles. His clothing becomes στίλβοντα λευκά ('shining white'), "so as no fuller on earth can white them" (King James version). In this case, however, the adjective describes a color, not a gleaming quality in the cloth itself such as oil treatment would produce.

12. Gow (supra n. 7) 129–130 ad 416 ff.; H. Blümner, *Technologie und Terminologie der Gewerbe und Künste bei Griechen und Römern* (Leipzig 1875–1887) I.184–185 n. 10.

13. M. Berthelot, *Collection des anciens alchimistes grecs* (Paris 1887) 38, 91, 123, 134, 147. Gow (supra n. 7) 130 is unaware of earlier references to such a detergent, but a few exist; for example B. Grenfell et al., *Tebtunis Papyri* III.1 (London 1933) no. 703, lines 99–103 (cited supra, p. 103).

14. '[they have] their brilliance clear and gleaming to be seen.'

15. For example, *Dar Sag* vol. 5, 166 s.v. TEXTRINUM.

16. (Supra n. 4) 5, n. 14.

17. Barber (supra n. 1). R. J. Forbes, *Studies in Ancient Technology* IV (Leiden 1964) and A. Neuberger, *The Technical Arts and Sciences of the Ancients*, trans. H. L. Brose (New York 1930) omit any mention of oil in this connection. Blümner (supra n. 12) I.184 suggests oil was used in the process of weaving linen, but the only evidence he cites is *Odyssey* 7.105–107.

18. New York 75.2.11 (GR 1243); *ARV*² II.1313.11. In addition to the references cited by Beazley, H. Immerwahr, "Choes and Chytroi," *TAPA* 77 (1946) 256–257. M.-C. Amouretti, *Le pain et l'huile dans la Grèce antique*, Annales littéraires de l'Université de Besançon 328 (Paris 1986) 191 n. 50, wrongly states that the women are sprinkling the clothes with oil.

19. *Dar Sag* vol. 5, 166 s.v. TEXTRINUM observe that oiling threads during weaving would help to separate the strands, and make them "plus lisses, plus souples et plus brillants." (The point is also made at vol. 4.1, 169 s.v. OLEA, OLEUM, where the reference to *Iliad* 19.595 is presumably an error for 18.596.) The context is a discussion of *Odyssey* 7.105–107, and the only other ancient references they give are *Iliad* 18.596 and Plut. *Alex.* 36. The latter passage is not strictly relevant, as we have seen, so their evidence for the practice is effectively restricted to the Homeric epics themselves.

20. For the Mycenaean terms see *Docs.*², Glossary; Marinatos (supra n. 4) 19–20. For tassels or fringes see Killen 1979 (supra n. 1) 157–167. The Mycenaean word *te-pa* (MY Oe 107), a woolen cloth, may be related to the Homeric τάπης. Linear B tablets are designated by site (KN = Knossos, MY = Mycenae, PY = Pylos) and series. The following editions are used: J. T. Killen and J.-P. Olivier, eds., *The Knossos Tablets* 5 (Salamanca 1990); J.-P. Olivier, ed., *The Mycenae Tablets* IV; E. L. Bennett, Jr., and J.-P. Olivier, eds., *The Pylos Tablets Transcribed* (Rome 1973, 1976).

21. Marinatos (supra n. 4) 7–8, 10–11. Lorimer (supra n. 5) 371–372 assumes that chitons described as 'shining' were linen, but as noted above this is not necessarily the case. Similarly she doubts (pp. 373–374) that the purple-red φάρεα at *Iliad* 8.221, *Odyssey* 8.84, 13.108 can be linen, since she thinks that linen could not be dyed. Barber (supra n. 1) passim notes that linen is difficult, though not impossible, to dye; see her index s.v. linen.

22. J. Chadwick, "Pylos Tablet Un 1322," in E. L. Bennett, Jr., ed., *Mycenaean Studies* (Madison 1966) 23–24; Marinatos (supra n. 4) 19–20.

23. J.-M. Durand, *Archives royales de Mari* XXI (Paris 1983) 146–147 no. 131, and n. 12, with further references.

24. J. L. Melena 1983 (supra n. 1) 119 suggests the oil on Fr 1225 may be for cleaning rather than perfuming. I follow Bennett in thinking that the ligature *A* may stand for *aloipha* ('unguent') rather than for a fragrance: E. L. Bennett, Jr., *The Olive Oil Tablets of Pylos*, Suplementos a Minos 2 (Salamanca 1958) 16, 32; Shelmerdine (supra n. 1) 34–35. Nevertheless it is clear from the context of the Fr tablets that the oil has received some sort of treatment by perfumers.

25. *Iliad* 23.186 refers to rose oil. Many Classical perfumes are oil-based; information comes chiefly from Theophrastus, *De Odoribus*, and Dioscorides, *De Materia Medica* I.42–63. Pliny discusses both aromatic plants (*HN* 12.41–135) and perfumes (13.1–25). R. J. Forbes, *Studies in Ancient Technology* III (Leiden 1965) 1–50, provides a good account of ancient perfumery; further references are available in Shelmerdine (supra n. 1) 12.

26. Robkin (supra n. 6).

27. The form is actually future middle, where a passive is expected. This translation gives the sense generally accepted.

28. Supra n. 13.

29. Oil to textile centers: Fh 357 (126.4 liters total), Fh 373 (amount not preserved), possibly Fh 5443 (amount not preserved), Fh 9067 (amount not preserved); to a man from a textile center: Fh 1059 (1.6 liters); to a tailor: Fh 1056 (4.8 liters), the plural possibly on Fh 5432 (9.6 liters), with 'for hides' (57.6 liters) on the *verso*.

30. Killen and Olivier (supra n. 20) 384.

31. Melena 1975 (supra n. 1) 92–93 tentatively connects this tablet and the Fh oil allocations with the textile industry, though his interpretation of the man's name as a title is not persuasive.

32. The word ἀλοιφή in the Homeric passage is elsewhere thought to mean pork lard or some other fat; but in the Mycenaean texts *a-ro-pa*, /aloipha/ is a liquid, and appears with the OIL ideogram. The Knossos allocations suggest that the scholiast is right at *Iliad* 17.389–393 to interpret the word as ἔλαιον, 'oil.'

33. Stanford (supra n. 10) 359 ad 52.

34. For example, Hera anoints herself with perfumed oil while preparing to seduce Zeus, *Iliad* 14.171–174. Aphrodite anoints Hektor's corpse with rose perfume to prevent decay, *Iliad* 23.186–187 (compare *Iliad* 19.38, where ambrosia is similarly employed). These are divine variants, as it were, on the normal practices of anointing oneself after a bath (*Iliad* 10.577, *Odyssey* 3.466, etc.) and washing a corpse in water and (plain) oil (*Iliad* 18.349–351, *Odyssey* 24.44–45).

35. The classic work is E. Lohmeyer, *Vom göttlichen*

Wohlgeruch, SBHeid. 1919, Philol.-hist. Klasse, Abh. 9. Some references to Classical literature are assembled by Adrados (supra n. 3) 144. A curious modern instance of this 'odor of sanctity' is reported in John Aubrey's *Life of Nicholas Towes*: an apparition in 1670 near Cirencester, which, "being demanded, whether a good Spirit or a bad? returned no answer, but disappeared with a curious Perfume and most melodious Twang"; see O. L. Dick, ed., *Aubrey's Brief Lives* (London 1949) 297.

36. See Richardson (supra n. 3) 208–209 ad 188–190.

37. Fr 1205 records an allocation to *amphiqʷoloihi* ('attendants'); an allocation to the *wanax* ('king'), on Fr 1215, may also be secular. See Shelmerdine (supra n. 1) 178, 197–198, with references for the opposite view that these allocations are religious.

38. E. Vermeule, *Greece in the Bronze Age* (Chicago 1964: reprint 1972) 311.

7

DEATH AND THE TANAGRA LARNAKES*

◆

SARA IMMERWAHR

Emily Vermeule in a brilliant article in the *Journal of Hellenic Studies* for 1965 called the attention of the scholarly world to an important new class of objects appearing on the art market.[1] Although dealing with little more than a dozen examples, some of them fragmentary, and provided with a certain amount of rumor, she anticipated in a remarkably prescient way what was to be discovered at Tanagra when Theodore Spyropoulos opened his excavation of a Mycenaean cemetery there in 1968.[2] Continuing these excavations annually until he moved to the ephorate at Sparta, he tantalized Aegean archaeologists with his reports, and generously illustrated a number of the larnakes and some of the pottery and terracottas that were being unearthed in the chamber tombs of a vast cemetery that seems to have been in use from LH IIIA to the end of LH IIIB, and probably beyond.[3]

Fortunately for the general public, as well as for the scholar, there is a fine display of sixteen larnakes, as well as some of the pottery and other artifacts from the cemetery, in Room D of the Thebes Museum, and four have been illustrated in color in Demakopoulou's *Guide*.[4] However, we all await the full publication of

this important find, which has done much to enlarge our picture of Mycenaean funeral practices and the ideas on death of this early Greek people.[5]

The Tanagra larnakes have far-reaching importance from both the archaeological and the iconographic sides. The prevalence of larnax burials in this cemetery, with as many as sixteen in one tomb,[6] is strongly suggestive of some close contact with Crete, yet the pottery from the tombs that has been illustrated as well as that on display in the museum seems purely Mycenaean. Furthermore, the choice of subject matter and the style of drawing are so different from the contemporary Cretan larnakes that it is difficult to establish a direct link.[7]

One can only speculate. Does the palace at Thebes, the Kadmeia, with its storeroom filled with coarse-ware stirrup jars with place-names in Linear B which have been attributed to Cretan centers, and with our earliest mainland processional fresco, the Knossian-inspired "Frauenfries," suggest the means of transmission of the larnax burial custom from Crete to Boiotia?[8] Without more chronological guidance, it is difficult to say, and also impossible to know whether the procession of mourning women on such larnakes as No. 7 and its sisters (figs. 7.1a-c)[9] can be seen as deriving from that frieze, which seems not to have been visible after the end of the fourteenth century B.C.

A full publication of the cemetery is necessary before we can know who was buried in the larnakes. Some of them are very small, less than half a meter in length, and could only have accommodated the bones of a small child.[10] Even the largest of those on display (Nos. 7, 12, and 15) barely exceed a meter in length, indicating that the skeleton must have been buried in a contracted position. Possibly some had been used as ossuaries.[11]

Obviously it is useless to speculate on these archaeological or anthropological matters without more evidence, such as properly belongs to the excavator. Nonetheless, even the casual visitor to the museum cannot help being struck by the power of some of the representations, however crude the drawing may seem, and the Aegean art historian or iconographer will have his curiosity piqued. To what extent is this art the end product of the Minoan-Mycenaean legacy and to what extent does it form a bridge to the powerful funerary images of Geometric art, particularly on the Attic Dipylon vases? It is from this aspect that I would like to consider some of the Tanagra larnakes.

Clearly the most conspicuous feature of the majority of the larnakes is the processions of mourning women. While there are two predominant styles, as Vermeule has shown—the fresco-inspired type wearing a derivative of the Minoan flounced skirt, but with a bodice that modestly covers the breast (figs. 7.1a–c), and the linear, cruder, yet more powerful type that seems to have been a creation of the larnax painters (figs. 7.1e–f)—others have come to light, for example the dark-silhouetted curvilinear women of Thebes Museum No. 1 (fig. 7.1d) who remind one of the dark-robed woman bidding farewell to the departing warriors on the Warrior Vase from Mycenae[12] and in a remarkable way anticipate the troupes of dark-robed mourners on Geometric and Early Attic funerary vases, where some also seem to show a ritualistic funerary dance.[13]

In later Greek times it was the role of women to perform the lament for the dead, the family members assisted by other women, while the body, which had been prepared by the older women of the immediate family, lay in state on the day after death. This, the so-called *prothesis,* corresponding to our contemporary "view-ing," had the function of ascertaining that death had occurred, as well as allowing final farewells to be made.[14] The Greek way of expressing mourning was for the women to tear their hair and scratch their faces, while uttering the funeral lament.[15]

The mourners on the larnakes conform to later Greek tradition in a striking fashion. With few exceptions— fig. 7.1f and one or two others[16]—only women are shown with both arms raised to the head and only women handle the body. In a few cases (fig. 7.1e)[17] drops of red paint fall from the face of a mourning woman, and must represent either tears or, more likely, blood from scarification.

In two cases—Thebes Museum No. 1 and No. 4 (here fig. 7.2)—the mourning women are associated with a representation of the *prothesis,* in which the deceased is shown being lowered into a larnax. These are in quite different styles, that from Tomb 22 (fig. 7.2a) in expressive silhouette, the other from Tomb 3 (fig. 7.2b) in the linear "stringy" style. On the first the scene occurs twice in the lower end-panels of perhaps the most ambitious larnax of those yet published, an example in true bichrome technique using both black and red matte paint and having double registers on all four sides.[18] Here we are concerned only with the *prothesis* and mourning scenes, although we shall return briefly to the two long sides, one of which has a troupe of thirteen swaying, mourning women (as if in a funeral dance) alternately in red and black silhouette above a register of chariot and boxer scenes, while the other has a scene with a hunter and wild goats above one with bull-vaulting, these perhaps more loosely connected with the dead (see infra n. 29).

The *prothesis* on Thebes No. 1 (fig. 7.2a) is in my opinion the most remarkable and moving representation in Mycenaean art, far removed from any adaptation of a Minoan model and reflecting observation of real-life experience. Two women in black silhouette, with the exception of their heads, bend forward with curved backs, lowering a small form tenderly into a larnax which is shown in X-ray fashion, its frame decorated with rows of white circles. The larnax, rectangular with legs, would seem a fair facsimile of those in the Tanagra cemetery, and judging by the size of the corpse within, it must have been that of a small child. Our larnax was 0.73 m in length, and it would be interesting to know something

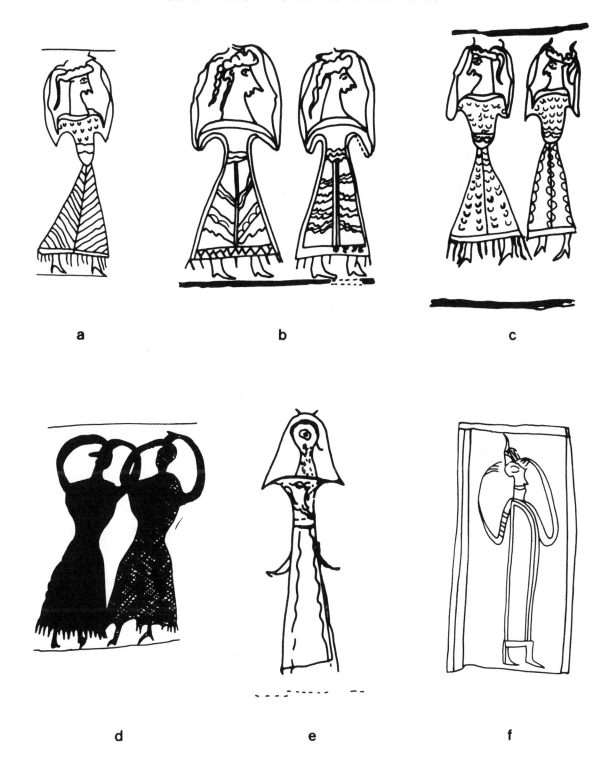

FIGURE 7.1 Mourners: (a) *Guide* No. 7 (after *BCH* 94 [1970], fig. 321); (b) *Guide* No. 15 (after *AAA* 3 [1970], fig. 12); (c) *Guide* No. 7 (after *AAA* 3 [1970], fig. 10); (d) *Guide* No. 1 (after *Prakt* 1969, pl. 14b); (e) Ludwig Larnax, Kassel (after Vermeule 1965, pl. XXVa); (f) Larnax, Tomb 115 (after *Prakt* 1979, pl. 21b).

a

b

FIGURE 7.2 Two Scenes of *Prothesis:* (a) *Guide* No. 1 (after *Prakt* 1969, pl. 14b); (b) *Guide* No. 4 (after Vermeule 1979, 64, fig. 20).

of the bones found within, and any funeral offerings that might suggest the interment of a child. On the other hand, one should perhaps interpret the scene generically, even if it has the poignancy of real-life experience.

The generic is certainly the interpretation I would make for the scene on the larnax from Tomb 3 (fig. 7.2b), which is highly abstract.[19] Here the *prothesis* occurs in the middle of one of the long sides and is flanked by two additional mourners, frontal sticklike figures with elongated necks and angular arms raised to their heads. They are drawn in outline and their board-like garments are decorated with linear patterns. In the figures standing by the larnax a slight concession is made to reality in the inclined head of the figure on the left and the bent stance of the right-hand figure. The larnax, however, floats in air, and the corpse is a barely recognizable tangle of lines suspended above. The style of drawing is allied to that on the Kassel Larnax[20] and even closer to the figures of a larnax from Tomb 115[21] which has single mourners on its end panels (fig. 7.1f) and a pair flanking a panel decorated with careless spirals on one of its long sides, while the other has a sphinx and solitary mourner. I suppose (from their postures) these mourners are intended to be women, but they are of the generic type of Vermeule's "discouraged Mycenaean."

The fresco-inspired mourners (figs. 7.1a–c) represent apparently the most numerous class and ought to be earlier. No *prothesis* is found in this group, which had its origin in the Minoan-Mycenaean tradition of wall-painting, the mourners being a free adaptation of the processions of women at Thebes, Mycenae, Tiryns, and Pylos.[22] Here, instead of offerings of nosegays or vases, jewelry, statuettes, etc., to the goddess, they raise their arms to their heads in the mourning gesture, but otherwise display no emotion. Although more elegant in their drawing, they lack the power of the other two types. Their costume is based on the Minoan festal garment, the flounced skirt, but here with a blouse that covers the breast. The large larnax from Tomb 6 on display in the Thebes Museum (No. 7) is perhaps the best example of this type, where four or five figures move to the right on one long side, and to the left on the other, with a single figure in somewhat more frontal pose on the short ends.[23] The standard decoration on this typical form of larnax uses a checkerboard or checkered grid frame on the posts and legs, which gives a kind of architectural setting and suggests an interior. That this was the intention is borne out by the small larnax, Thebes Museum No. 16, which is decorated with the heads of three women in windows on one long side and with a single head on one of the short sides.[24] This motif was also of fresco derivation.[25] That all our examples of this type come from illicit excavation or from Tomb No. 6 is perhaps indicative of one or two artists working in close collaboration, perhaps at the beginning of the series of Tanagra larnakes.[26]

Men also were involved in the ritual of death as depicted on the Tanagra larnakes, but their role was less intimate, a fact which agrees with the Greek tradition.[27] From Geometric times on they are shown in connection with the *ekphora,* or the bearing of the body to the grave or funeral pyre.[28] Our larnakes have no representation of the *ekphora,*[29] and indeed one cannot expect an exact duplication of burial rites in a period which practiced inhumation in chamber tombs with multiple burials as opposed to cremation and single burials.[30]

Male figures occur in two basically different schemes, in a processional or panel arrangement corresponding to that of the female mourners of the fresco-inspired type, and in scenes involving some kind of ritual activity connected with burial. With the exception of a single larnax that does not fit into the group, and where the two male figures are clad in the short tunics and greaves of warriors,[31] all other male figures on the larnakes are dressed in fairly long robes that come almost to the ankle and often have a vertical or diagonal border.[32] Such robes are characteristic of priests or others engaged in ceremonial activities, and have a time-honored tradition going back to Minoan and earlier Mycenaean times, for example in the Theran miniature "The Meeting on the Hill," and on early pictorial vases.[33]

That the figures in long tunics on our larnakes are most probably male is shown by those on a larnax from Tomb 6,[34] where two pairs of figures face each other on either side of a gridwork panel, those on the left having a short beard (fig. 7.3b), those on the right wearing a cap with plume, while the single figure in the end panel has a conical helmet (fig. 7.3c). The robes all have borders at the bottom and either a diagonal or vertical band, and several of the men carry a short stick. Is this a reminis-

cence of the sword and diagonal sword strap on some of the earlier ceremonial processions? Such an interpretation fits the figures on the larnax Thebes No. 2,[35] which has a file of four figures to the left on one side (fig. 7.3d), five to the right on the other, and a single figure in each end panel. All wear the bordered robe with diagonal band (but have no weapons), and there seems to be a desire to suggest some interior setting in the rectangular apertures (?) between several figures. Could the variation in color, with some heads painted dark, others reserved, be intended as a sex distinction?[36] At any rate I would interpret these larnakes as showing a ceremonial procession of priestly figures corresponding to the processions of female mourners, with both types showing the influence of the Minoan-Mycenaean pictorial tradition.

For this reason I would interpret the figures on the interesting and unusual larnax, Thebes Museum No. 14,[37] as priests, rather than priestesses, engaged in some funeral ritual of blessing the house of the deceased, perhaps exorcising death.[38] A column with cushion capital, but tapering upward in un-Minoan fashion, is the focal point of both sides, with two pairs of figures in long robes approaching it on one side, the leaders touching the shaft, whereas on the other (the obverse) a single figure in a more elaborate bordered robe approaches from the right and is met by a large sphinx coming from the left (fig. 7.3a). The sphinx is wingless, and equipped with human arms (as well as four legs!); both figures touch the column, and both wear the flat cap characteristic of sphinxes, the sphinx's with the usual floating plume.[39]

The association of the sphinx with death in the iconography of the larnakes is not limited to this example, which is, however, the most compelling in its suggestion of the sphinx as guardian of the house and tomb, a role it was destined to play in Archaic Greece.[40] In another example it is used more decoratively, but perhaps has a symbolic function. A larnax from Tomb 15 that has not been displayed depicts on each long side a winged sphinx (male and bearded on one side, female on the other) between two Mycenaean palms and other filling ornaments in a rich, allover composition more akin to that on Late Minoan larnakes (figs. 7.4a–b).[41] Male sphinxes are practically unknown in Aegean art, but occur in Orientalizing, and there is a generally Near East-

a

b

c

d

FIGURE 7.3 Male Figures: (a) *Guide* No. 14 (after *BCH* 96 [1972], fig. 265); (b) Larnax, Tomb 6 (after *Prakt* 1969, pl. 4b); (c) Larnax, Tomb 6 (after *Prakt* 1969, pl. 5a); (d) *Guide* No. 2 (after *BCH* 96 [1972], fig. 268).

a   b

FIGURE 7.4 Sphinxes on Larnax from Tomb 15:
(a) male sphinx (after *Prakt* 1974, pl. 10b); (b) female sphinx (after *BCH* 99 [1975], fig. 119).

a   b

FIGURE 7.5 Other Funeral Rites: (a) figure preparing for libation (after *Prakt* 1973, pl. 10b); (b) priest with statuette (after *BCH* 99 [1975] fig. 118).

FIGURE 7.6 Winged Figure (*psyche* or *eidolon*) from Ludwig Larnax, Kassel (after Vermeule [1979] 65, fig. 23).

FIGURE 7.7 Ship in Underworld (?): Larnax from Tomb 47 (after *ArchDelt* 28 B′ [1973], pl. 2210).

ern look to this figure, with which the type of palm accords.[42] Another larnax on display comes from Tomb 32 and shows in a rather debased curvilinear, outline style a winged sphinx with a rope around its neck and being led in by three mourning women.[43] And the larnax from Tomb 115 with the linear dejected mourners referred to above has on one long side a winged sphinx.[44] Apparently the sphinx was an important funerary symbol running through several styles, and probably several generations of larnax painters on the mainland, although not used on the Minoan larnakes.

In addition to the ubiquitous processions of mourning women and priests and the occasional *prothesis* scenes, other ritual activities connected with burial are depicted on only a few larnakes. One from Tomb 36 shows two figures separated by a checkerboard panel, the left a female mourner, while the right, who may also be female, holds aloft in her left hand a dark stemmed kylix (fig. 7.5a), doubtless a reference to the pouring of a funeral libation at the entrance to the tomb.[45] A still more interesting scene is depicted on a larnax from Tomb 15 where a procession of mourners (three females with the foremost likely male) approaches a priest holding aloft on his outstretched arm what clearly appears to be a large figurine with raised arms (fig. 7.5b).[46] While we know of the existence of such large statuettes in the late temples at Mycenae, Phylakopi, and Tiryns, we have until now no evidence for their use in funerary cult.

For other burial practices described in Homer and known in later Greek times we have no representations on the larnakes unless the chariot and boxer scenes on one of the long sides of larnax No. 1 are thought to represent funeral games.[47] There are no scenes of animal sacrifice or the bringing of offerings to the tomb, although the archaeological evidence in Mycenaean chamber tombs confirms such practices.[48]

What beliefs about death had the people who used the Tanagra cemetery? Here we are on more speculative ground, having no literary tradition to back up the few iconographic clues. Vermeule has already pointed to the existence of a winged figure on the end panel of the Kassel Larnax (fig. 7.6), which she suggested may be a representation of the *psyche* or *eidolon* (the soul or likeness of the deceased) presumably leaving the body on its way to the hereafter.[49] This figure floats above the groundline (but so do many of the mourners); however, the wings are unmistakable and batlike. They are quite different from the winglike attachments to the skirts of the mourners on this same larnax which are more like the streamers worn by the priestesses and other officiants on the Ayia Triadha sarcophagus.[50] They are stiff, flangelike excrescences from wrist to armpit, and from the top of the head sprouts a feathery plume. Clearly this is no human figure, but a *psyche* or, more properly, an *eidolon* of the deceased. There are apparently other instances of such winged figures on the Tanagra larnakes, but they have been less fully published.[51] One must conclude that these winged apparitions, along with the curious figurines or "soul-birds" which decorated the lid of larnax No. 13 and perhaps others,[52] while some may have been hung, show that the Mycenaean Greeks made a distinction between the corporeal body that perished at death and the spirit or *psyche* which left the body and continued some kind of existence.[53]

Where did the *psyche* or *eidolon* go? Later Greek literature and iconography (especially on the white-ground lekythoi) are full of depictions of the Underworld, the plants and "shades" that inhabited it, as well as its rivers with Charon the ferryman, who conducted new souls there. Is it possible that the larnax from Tomb 47, with its curiously unorganized composition (fig. 7.7), depicts a Mycenaean conception of such a journey?[54] Because of the flaking slip and its poor preservation, the amorphous forms are rather hard to interpret with the exception of an oared ship in the lower right corner. The rest of the field is full of plantlike forms, or more likely "shades," which resemble Mycenaean phi and psi figurines. Did the larnax painter endeavor to depict an Underworld scene?[55]

If Watrous is correct that the iconography of the Minoan larnakes is far more complex than mere decoration and deals primarily with the soul's pilgrimage to the afterlife, this is expressed in quite a different way from the Tanagra example. Whereas the Minoan larnakes stress the idyllic nature of the destination in terms of a Nilotic landscape, the mainland scene is stark and amorphous. Likewise where human figures appear (as a rarity) in the Cretan examples they are more apt to be engaged in hunting or sport, and only exceptionally does a mourner appear. On the Tanagra larnakes, however, the emphasis

is much more on the grim reality of death with its accompanying funerary rites—the procession of mourning women, the *prothesis,* the male priests—that are needed to insure a safe passage to the other world. Although there was some interaction between Crete and the mainland, the iconography of the Minoan larnakes developed primarily from their Minoan background, whereas that of the Tanagra larnakes was groping toward a new realism. They are thus far closer to the Homeric conception of death than to the Egyptian, with an iconography that anticipates the scenes on Geometric vases.

NOTES

* The following abbreviations are used for frequently cited works:

Guide = K. Demakopoulou and D. Konsola, *Archaeological Museum of Thebes* (Athens 1981).
Totenkult = M. Andronikos, *Totenkult,* ArchHom 3. W (Göttingen 1968).
Vermeule (1964) = E. Vermeule, *Greece in the Bronze Age* (Chicago 1964).
Vermeule (1965) = E. Vermeule, "Painted Mycenaean Larnakes," *JHS* 85 (1965) 123–148.
Vermeule (1979) = E. Vermeule, *Aspects of Death in Early Greek Art and Poetry* (Berkeley and Los Angeles 1979).
Watrous (1991) = L. V. Watrous, "The Origin and Iconography of the Late Minoan Painted Larnax," *Hesperia* 60 (1991) 285–307, which came out after this paper had been submitted.

The illustrations were drawn by Margaret M. Reid after published photographs, sources for which are given in the captions.

1. Vermeule (1965) 123–148; see also Vermeule (1964) 210–214, fig. 37, pls. XXXIV–XXXV, and eadem, "A Painted Mycenaean Coffin," in E. Berger and R. Lullies, eds., *Antike Kunstwerke aus der Sammlung Ludwig* (Basel 1979) 201–205.
2. See reports by Th. Spyropoulos in *Prakt* 1969–1976 and articles: "The Mycenaean Cemetery at Tanagra," *AAA* 2 (1969) 20–25, and "Excavations in the Mycenaean Cemetery at Tanagra," *AAA* 3 (1970) 184–197 (both in Greek with En-

glish summary); "Funebre mais sensationelle decouverte à Tanagra," *Connaisance des Arts* (April 1971) 72–77; "Mycenaean Tanagra: Terracotta Sarcophagi," *Archaeology* 25 (1972) 206–209.

3. Until the cemetery is published in full, with the pottery and artifacts from each tomb, it is impossible to judge the dates of the individual larnakes, but some certainly suggest an LH IIIC date through stylistic comparisons with the pictorial pottery of that period. K. Demakopoulou, *Guide* 82, says, "The pottery finds demonstrate that the cemetery was in use for about two centuries, i.e., from the late 15th to the mid-13th century B.C. (LH IIIA1 to LH IIIB1)" with the larnakes not appearing at the beginning, "but later, around the middle or towards the end of the 14th century B.C., and their use is continued into the first half of the 13th century B.C."

4. *Guide,* pls. 42–44 (larnax No. 1 from Tomb 22; larnax No. 7 from Tomb 6; larnax No. 14 from Tomb 51; and larnax No. 13 from Tomb 6).

5. With the realization that the picture can be far from complete, I hope that this article will serve as a tribute to my long-time friend, the excavator of two important Mycenaean tombs in the Athenian Agora (Tombs VII and XL: see S. A. Immerwahr, *The Athenian Agora* XIII [Princeton 1971] 183–190 and 242–247). Her book *Aspects of Death in Early Greek Art and Poetry* (Berkeley 1979) is an inspiration for anyone attempting to interpret the meaning behind the scenes on the Tanagra larnakes.

6. *Guide* 82.

7. See now the study by Vance Watrous of the Minoan larnakes (Watrous [1991] 285–306), in which he stresses the derivation of the larnax form from the Egyptian wooden funerary chest (not, however, used as a coffin), and sees the influence of Egyptian ideas about the afterlife on the iconography of the Cretan examples, especially pertaining to the journey of the deceased across the sea to the Land of the Blessed. On this second point, I feel he has gone too far in interpretating motifs (spirals, fish, octopodes, lilies, palms, birds, bulls, as well as Minoan religious symbols) as specifically funereal, since many of the same are found in juxtaposition on Palace-style jars which are not funereal. Watrous hardly touches upon the relationship of the Cretan to the Tanagrean larnakes, and indeed in most respects the two series seem to be quite distinct. While the inspiration must have come from Crete to Boiotia, there may have been counterinfluences from the mainland to Crete in some of the Armenoi larnakes with hunt scenes (Watrous [1991], pl. 87e, f) and in the Hierapetra larnax with the chariot procession and hunt (Watrous [1991], pl. 93a–d). The small larnax Thebes No. 11 (*Guide* 84), with its gabled roof and early birds, looks more

like the Cretan examples, and could perhaps have been an import, but can hardly have been the inspiration for the main series of Tanagra larnakes with their processions of mourners and scenes typical of mainland funerary practices. If there is a *prothesis* represented on an unpublished larnax from Pigi (Watrous [1991] 292, n. 42) which has been compared to the Tanagra examples, this need not mean (with Watrous [1991] 292) that "the Minoan funeral scenes then can be taken as antecedents for similar representations on the *later* (sic) Mainland larnakes." Without a complete corpus of the Minoan and mainland larnakes, which only our Greek colleagues can provide, articles like this one and Watrous' can only raise suggestions.

8. For Thebes see S. Symeonoglou, *Kadmeia* I, SIMA 35 (Göteborg 1973) which deals with the new excavations, and summarizes their relation to the House of Kadmos (72–76); also idem, "The Palaces of the Kadmeia," in *The Topography of Thebes from the Bronze Age to Modern Times* (Princeton 1985) 40–50 and Site 1, 213–225, with full bibliography. For the stirrup jars see especially J. Raison, *Les vases à inscriptions peintes de l'âge mycénien et leur contexte archéologique,* Incunabula Graeca 19 (Rome 1968). For the "Frauenfries" see H. Reusch, *Die zeichnerische Rekonstruktion des Frauenfrieses im böotischen Theben* (Berlin 1955).

9. Closely related processions of mourning women wearing Minoan-inspired flounced skirts occur on Thebes Museum Nos. 7 and 15 plus several whole or fragmentary examples in private collections acquired before the cemetery was excavated (see infra n. 23).

10. Thebes Museum No. 8, 0.62 m in length, is exhibited with its contents, the bones of a small child, and some of the funerary offerings: "two feeding bottles, a small jug, and two figurines, one of a woman, the other of a bird" (*Guide* 84). Larnax No. 9 is still smaller, only 0.43 m in length.

11. *Guide* 82. The dimensions of the sixteen examples there published range from 1.13 m down to 0.43 m in length, with only four approaching or exceeding a meter, the majority being in the 0.60 to 0.80 m range. The Minoan clay larnakes average about 1.0 m in length, 0.60 m in height, and 0.45 m in width. See Watrous (1991) 287, n. 8, and C. Long, *The Ayia Triadha Sarcophagus,* SIMA 41 (Göteborg 1974) 75–77. The Ayia Triadha sarcophagus is 1.37 m in length.

12. S. Marinatos and M. Hirmer, *Crete and Mycenae* (New York 1959), pl. 232. Because of the break by the handle it is impossible to decide whether the left arm was also raised to her head, in which case she ought to be interpreted as showing the mourning gesture, perhaps anticipating the foredoomed death of her warrior, as Vermeule has suggested. She is, however, in a more complete profile position than the mourners on

the larnax, where only the heads and feet are in profile to the left.

13. B. Schweitzer, *Greek Geometric Art* (London 1971), pls. 47, 49–50, for mourners tearing their hair; pls. 52–55 and 66 for dancing women (mourners?).

14. See *Totenkult* 43–51; D. Kurtz and J. Boardman, *Greek Burial Customs* (London 1971) 143–144; Vermeule (1979) 12–17, 63; C. Sourvinou-Inwood, "Death in Greece: Homer, Before and After," in J. Whaley, ed., *Mirrors of Mortality: Studies in the Social History of Death* (New York 1981) 15–39, especially 25–31; M. Alexiou, *The Ritual Lament in Greek Tradition* (Cambridge 1974), considers the literary tradition, as do Sourvinou-Inwood, Andronikos, and Vermeule for the epic period.

15. Cf. Briseis' lament and mourning for Patroklos (*Iliad* 19.276–300) and Hekabe's and Andromache's lament for Hektor (*Iliad* 22. 405ff.).

16. Vermeule (1965) 132, fig. 3b, considers a similar figure male and describes it as "the most discouraged Mycenaean to last beyond the Bronze Age." Occurring on a confiscated larnax in Athens collected by Threpsiades in 1962, it was surely from illicit digging at Tanagra. The mourners in panels on a larnax from Tomb 32 might possibly be male (*Prakt* 1971, pl. 19b, and *BCH* 96 [1972] 702, fig. 270).

17. Notably on the Kassel Larnax (Vermeule [1965], pl. XXVa, right figure) but possibly on others.

18. *Prakt* 1969, pls. 13a and 14; *Ergon* 1969, 10–11, figs. 6–7; *AAA* 3 (1970) 195, figs. 15–17; *BCH* 94 (1970) 1040, figs. 323–324; *Guide* 83, pl. 42 (in color).

19. *Prakt* 1970, pl. 48a; *Ergon* 1970, 19, fig. 17; *BCH* 95 (1971) 929, fig. 290; Vermeule (1979) 64, fig. 20.

20. Vermeule (1965), pls. XXV–XXVIa; Vermeule (1964), pl. XXXIV. See also the color plates in Berger and Lullies (supra n. 1).

21. *Prakt* 1979, 34–35, pls. 20–21. One might also speculate that this figure is not a conventional mourner, but rather the *eidolon* of the deceased, because of the curious feathery excrescence that sprouts from his head (compare fig. 7.6).

22. See S. A. Immerwahr, *Aegean Painting in the Bronze Age* (University Park, Penn. 1990) 114–121.

23. Several of the larnakes and fragments that appeared on the art market in the late 1950s and early 1960s were of this type: see Vermeule (1965) pls. XXVIb and XXVII, and Lorandou-Papantoniou, *AAA* 6 (1973) 169–176, figs. 1–2. From excavated tombs at Tanagra, in addition to Thebes Museum No. 7 from Tomb 6 (*AAA* 3 [1970] 191–193, figs. 9–11); *Ergon* 1969, 8, fig. 4; *BCH* 94 [1970] 1039, fig. 321; *BCH* 95 [1971] 931, fig. 293; *Guide* 84, pl. 43a; here figs. 7.1a and 7.1c) I count the following:

Thebes Museum No. 15, also from Tomb No. 6: *Prakt* 1969, pl. 5a; *BCH* 95 (1971) 931, fig. 292; *AAA* 3 (1970) 193, fig. 12: *Guide* 85; here fig. 7.1b.

Thebes Museum No. 5, also from Tomb No. 6: *Prakt* 1969, pl. 5b.

24. Also from Tomb 6: see *Prakt* 1969, pl. 13b; *Ergon* 1969, 9, fig. 5; *BCH* 94 (1970) 1039, fig. 322; *AAA* 3 (1970) 194, fig. 13; *Guide* 85. One of the smaller larnakes, only 0.60 m in length, it contained the bones of a child.

25. See Immerwahr (supra n. 22) 173 (**Kn No. 17b**); 190 (**My No. 1a**); 192 (**My No. 11a**); 240 ("women in windows").

26. This conclusion, however, is based only on the published examples.

27. See Sourvinou-Inwood, and Kurtz and Boardman (supra n. 14).

28. As on the Attic Geometric krater (Athens, N.M. 990: P. E. Arias, M. Hirmer, and B. B. Shefton, *A History of Greek Vase Painting* [London 1962] 267–268, pl. 5) and the Dipylon amphora (Athens, N.M. 803: Schweitzer [supra n. 13] pl. 35). However, on the Dipylon amphora (Athens, N.M. 804: P. E. Arias, M. Hirmer, and B. B. Shefton, 267, pl. 4), while the figures seated below the bier in the *prothesis* scene are clearly distinguished as women by their long skirts, the balanced groups of mourners on either side are shown without clothing (male, or perhaps generic mourners?).

29. Unless one connects the chariot scenes on the lower register of Thebes Museum No. 1 (*Guide,* pl. 42a) with such a procession, as Vermeule was wont to do in the case of the chariot scenes on Pictorial-style kraters from Cypriot tombs (Vermeule [1964] 205–206). But surely a wagon would have been used for an *ekphora* of the Geometric type with the deceased lying on his bier? If this register has a funeral connotation, I would prefer to associate it with some funerary games, because of the presence of boxers in the middle. Watrous, however, (Watrous [1991] 301) would connect the chariots that appear on the Hierapetra (pl. 93a) and Kavrochori (pl. 89c) larnakes as "a Cretan version of the Mycenaean funerary concept, in which the deceased rides in his chariot to the Afterworld" (i.e., symbolically). The goat hunt and the acrobatic bull sports that appear in the two registers on the other side of the larnax Thebes No. 1 would then also be illustrative of the sports the deceased would enjoy in the afterlife.

30. See the cogent remarks of Andronikos, *Totenkult* 132–135. Although he takes account of the runnels at the entrance to some Mycenaean chamber tombs as perhaps wheel-marks from wagons, he thinks them more likely from skidpoles of biers (45). I wonder whether our larnakes were not merely carried (or slid?) into the tomb by pall-bearers, who would have been men.

31. Swiss Market: Vermeule (1965), pl. XXVIII and (1964) 212–213, pl. XXXVb.

32. See Thebes Museum No. 14 from Tomb 51: *Prakt* 1971, pls. 18b, 19a; *Ergon* 1971, 15, figs. 12–13; *BCH* 96 (1972) 700, figs. 265–266; Demakopoulou, *Guide* 84, pl. 43b, considers the figures female. This larnax (here fig. 7.3a) will be discussed below.

33. See L. Morgan, *The Miniature Wall Paintings of Thera* (Cambridge 1988) 93–96, pls. 1 and 122. For the occurrence of this type of long tunic or robe in a ceremonial use on early pictorial vases, note the examples in E. Vermeule and V. Karageorghis, *Mycenaean Pictorial Vase Painting* (Cambridge, Mass. 1982) 21 and 23–24, III.19–21, III.29, where the figures are clearly male and are sometimes equipped with long swords.

34. *Prakt* 1969, pls. 4b and 6a (probably from the same larnax).

35. From Tomb 60: *Prakt* 1971, pls. 17–18a; *BCH* 96 (1972) 701, figs. 267–269; *Guide* 83.

36. See the ceremonial processions on the Ayia Triadha sarcophagus where both sexes wear the bordered robe (Marinatos and Hirmer [supra n. 12] pls. XXVIII–XXIXA), as was also apparently the case with the figures at the beginning of the Corridor of the Procession at Knossos (*PM* II.2, 704ff., fig. 428 and suppl. pl. XXV). For the theory that the color code may not be exclusively a means of sex determination see N. Marinatos, "The Bull as an Adversary: Some Observations on Bull-Hunting and Bull-Leaping," *Ariadne* 5 (1989) 23–32, esp. 29–32.

37. From Tomb 51: see n. 32.

38. In this case the bones found within were those of a child (*Guide* 84) and the size of the larnax was smallish (0.69 m long). I suppose, however, that one can hardly expect the iconography of each larnax to reflect a specific use, since it would have to be ready by at least the second day after death. One meets a similar problem in connection with the Attic grave stelai.

39. The only reason I see to consider these figures female (with Demakopoulou, *Guide* 84) is the type of cap which is worn by certain female priestesses in bordered robes on the Ayia Triadha sarcophagus (supra n. 36). N. Kourou, "Aegean Orientalizing versus Oriental Art," in *Civilizations of the Aegean* (Nicosia 1989) 114 n. 28, considers the "sphinx" on the Tanagra larnax "a first attempt at the creation of a new type" and calls it a proto-Centaur, following M. R. Belgiorno, "Centauressa o Sfinge su una Larnax Micenea da Tanagra," *SMEA* 68 (1978) 205–228, pl. 1. Kourou calls attention to the curious bird talons and bovine body, as well as the human arms.

40. See Vermeule (1979) 69 and 171.

41. *Prakt* 1974, pls. 10b, 11a; *ArchDelt* 28 B′ (1973) pl.

221b; *BCH* 99 (1975) 644, fig. 119. For the Late Minoan larnakes, see Mavriyannaki, *Recherches sur larnakes minoennes occidentales de la Crète occidentale*, Incunabula Graeca 54 (Rome 1972). See now Watrous on the use of palms to create a Nilotic landscape and to suggest the Afterworld (Watrous [1991] 298). Sphinxes, however, do not occur on the Minoan larnakes.

42. Two male sphinxes (unbearded) confront a more carelessly drawn palm on a Rude or "Pastoral" krater from Enkomi (BM C417: Vermeule and Karageorghis [supra n. 33] 64, VI.16) which was surely made in the East. For the type of palm on our larnax, see *MP*, FM 15 (Palm II) which he believes of glyptic or ivory derivation.

43. I have not been able to find an illustration of the sphinx side of this larnax which I have seen in the Thebes Museum (*Guide* 83–84, No. 6). For other views see *Ergon* 1970, figs. 18–19.

44. *Prakt* 1979, pl. 20b.

45. *Prakt* 1973, pl. 10b. For the practice of pouring a libation to the dead, see *Totenkult* 93 with reference to the archaeological evidence from Mycenaean cemeteries. The Hierapetra larnax (Watrous [1991] 301, pl. 93a) is the only Minoan example to suggest the farewell toast, presumably under Mycenaean influence.

46. *Prakt* 1974, pl. 10a; *Ergon* 1974, 15, fig. 10; *BCH* 99 (1975) 644, fig. 118. The drawing is vigorous, but crude, and I assume that the statuette was of the large psi-type like those from Tiryns which measure 0.33 m in height (see *The Mycenaean World: Five Centuries of Early Greek Culture* [Athens 1988], nos. 25, 168; also K. Kilian, *AA* 1978, 464, figs. 20–21).

47. See supra n. 29.

48. *Totenkult* 84–93 and 97–102. As Andronikos points out, there were significant distinctions between the world of the epic and the Mycenaean, particularly in the manner of burial, cremation versus inhumation, single graves versus family tombs, etc. However, while Homer was describing the customs of Geometric Greece, the mourning customs, including the *prothesis* and the assigned roles of men and women at the funeral, had apparently changed little from Late Mycenaean times. See also Vermeule (1979) 12 and 63 on the unbroken continuity of funerary imagery between the Bronze Age and the Classical period.

49. Vermeule (1965) 146ff., pl. XXVIa; Vermeule (1979) 65, fig. 23 and 7–9, 23, 35 for discussion of *psyche;* 31–33 for discussion of *eidolon.*

50. See supra n. 36. The streamers must have been separate attachments used in the funerary ritual; they have never been fully explained, but clearly the people on the sarcophagus are corporeal beings with the exception of the armless figure of

the deceased standing in front of his tomb on Side A (Marinatos and Hirmer [supra n. 11] pl. XXIXA) and the goddesses in the chariots of the end panels. See especially C. R. Long, *The Ayia Triadha Sarcophagus*, SIMA 41 (Göteborg 1974) for a study of the iconography, especially 38–39 for a discussion of the streamers and their possible funeral significance.

51. See the larnax from an unspecified tomb found in 1977: *Prakt* 1977, 31, pl. 12; *Ergon* 1977, 17–18, figs. 9–10.

52. *Guide* 84, pl. 44; Spyropoulos, *AAA* 3 (1970) 190, fig. 8; Vermeule (1979) 75–76 for Greek soul-bird and mythological offshoots, the Siren and Harpy.

53. In the Shaft Graves at Mycenae in the Early Mycenaean period, there occur objects that suggest a notion of the separation of body and soul at the time of death, e.g., the symbolic gold-leaf scale pans and discs with butterflies (Karo, pls. XXXIV, nos. 81–82, and XXVIII, no. 2). See also

the article by R. Laffineur, "Iconographie minoenne et iconographie mycénienne à l'époque des tombes à fosse," *L'Iconographie minoenne,* BCH suppl. 11 (1985) 245–265, esp. 250ff. See also the gold "bees" from Tholos 2 at Peristeria (S. Marinatos, *SMEA* 57 [1967] 12, fig. 20), which are strikingly similar to the Tanagrean "soul-birds" yet are two or more centuries earlier.

54. *Prakt* 1973, 10ff., pl. 10a; *ArchDelt* 28 B' (1973), pl. 221c; *Ergon* 1973, 14.

55. I note that Spyropoulos also comments on the symbolic and metaphoric character of the scene which he thinks is related to the afterlife fate of the dead. See also Watrous' discussion of the ship as the conveyance of the soul to the Afterworld and its appearance on a Minoan larnax from Gazi (Watrous [1991] 298, pl. 90e).

8

HEROES RETURNED?
SUBMINOAN BURIALS FROM CRETE

✦

HECTOR CATLING

It is a great compliment to have been invited to contribute to this volume of essays to be presented to Emily Vermeule. She has, throughout her distinguished career, championed a particular style of archaeological exegesis that has provided a rock of humanity amid the contemporary turbulent sea of trends and processes, systems and models. She has played a prominent role in unraveling the Sibylline archaeology enshrined in the text of Homer. I hope that the following account of discoveries made in Crete in 1978, and the explanation that I offer, may be of interest to her and, perhaps, stimulate her to propound one of the many alternative explanations which, certainly, there must be.

I gave a brief account of two small tombs of the type called "Pit-Caves" by Sir Arthur Evans when he described a number excavated by him in the Zapher Papoura cemetery at Knossos.[1] Both tombs, as we shall see, date c. 1050 B.C., in the Subminoan period; both had been used for the interment of cremations. They were found within eight meters of each other during the joint Greek-British excavation of 1978 one kilometer north of the Knossos palace, on the site now occupied by the buildings of the University of Crete. It is likely they were the earliest graves in a cemetery whose use was, with certain interruptions, to continue until Early Christian times, culminating in the construction of a large mortuary church, associated with numerous osteothekes. The church was surrounded by a substantial enclosure wall.[2] During the many centuries this burial ground was in use, a majority of the graves suffered disturbance of one kind or another. The Dark Age chamber tombs, for instance, had repeatedly been reopened for the committal of additional cremation urns; later tombs had cut into earlier ones, chamber tombs had been virtually destroyed by close-packed Hellenistic inhumations, other tombs had been all but obliterated when the enclosure wall was built for the mortuary church. Against this background of disturbance it was a remarkable bonus that the tombs that concern us, nos. 186 and 200–202, were found to all intents and purposes intact. Both tombs had probably suffered some loss in the upper parts of their pits, but the lower fillings of these pits were found undisturbed, and the little "caves" which contained the cremations and accompanying grave offerings, sealed by small stone slabs, were untouched.

Relatively clean *kouskouras* (soft white marl bedrock) filled the pit of Tomb 186. This may be interpreted as redeposited upcast from the digging of the grave. The "cave," with its sealing slab, was set at the bottom of the pit, cut into the east face. On opening, this little chamber was found partly filled with *kouskouras,* with which were mixed 743 g of cremated bone, doubtless originally wrapped in a container of perishable materials. Study of the cremation by Dr. J. H. Musgrave shows it represented a not very old adult. That it was male seems certain from the accompanying objects. These included (fig. 8.1) a Subminoan stirrup jar, a large bronze spearhead with unusually long socket, an iron dirk, an iron knife, a badly crushed bronze *phalaron* with prominent central spike (or shield boss?),[3] and two whetstones.

Tombs 200–202 had a rather large pit, the fill of which was not as clean as the Tomb 186 pit-fill. It was heavily stained with black matter, and contained many fire-blackened fragments of what proved to be a Subminoan neck-handled amphora, the handles twisted (fig. 8.2). Low down, in three out of the four cut faces of the pit, little chambers ("caves") had been cut, the openings sealed again by stone slabs. Two large decorated Subminoan stirrup jars had been placed on the pit floor, in the northeast and southeast corners respectively (fig. 8.3).

To facilitate recording, each of the three "caves" was given its own tomb-number—nos. 200, 201, and 202. Tomb 202 proved empty, apart from fallen *kouskouras* and an indeterminate fragment of cremated bone. As well as a cremation, Tomb 200 contained a decorated Subminoan stirrup jar (fig. 8.4) and a selection of ornaments that suggests this was a woman's tomb. There were: the bronze, wheel-shaped head of a pin, whose antecedents may be Italian;[4] a gold finger-ring; two damaged gold disks with impressed stylized rosette pattern; a necklace of over eighty small spherical gold beads; other beads of serpentine, glass, and faience; and a much-damaged ivory comb. Dr. Musgrave suggests the cremation was that of a not very old adult, perhaps female. The grave offerings support such an identification.

There was no pottery in Tomb 201. There was an exceptionally large amount of cremated bone—2.388 kg—which Dr. Musgrave's examination suggests be-

longed to two adults, probably male and female, with the possibility that a child's remains were also included. The series of grave offerings was rich (figs. 8.5 and 8.6). The most readily recognizable were bronze weapons, including a Type II sword,[5] a large spearhead, and several large arrowheads, or projectiles.[6] A bronze *phalaron* (circular disk with central boss, usually hemispherical) was represented solely by the diminutive centerpiece, more knob than spike. A scrap of iron was probably the tip of a knife. Nearly ninety bronze fragments, many of them much-distorted by fire, could be attributed to a four-sided stand, or vessel-support, the sides decorated *à jour* with figured ornament: birds, animals, fantastic creatures, and (probably) draped human figures.[7] There were the shafts of two large iron dress-pins. Not immediately recognized at the time of excavation were several items of bone, ivory, and boar's tusk, taken up with the cremated bone and subsequently separated from it when the cremations were studied. It has been possible to deduce from this material the former existence of an ivory hilt, or handle, decorated with incised concentric circles, an ivory object (perhaps a comb), and something to which slices of boar's tusk had been attached.

The full account of these exceptional Subminoan graves is reserved for the final published report, shortly to go to press. In the meantime, we may be permitted to speculate on the kind of people with whom we are dealing, and to ask whether these are unique assemblages, or whether they can be matched anywhere in the contemporary Eastern Mediterranean world.

It should be emphasized that the burial ground in which their remains were laid was a very new one at the time of their deaths, so new, in fact, that they could have been the first people to be buried there. At this date at Knossos, there was no uniformity of funerary custom, for some of their contemporaries were inhumed in chamber tombs, with more than one companion, while others were inhumed singly in very small slab-covered shaft graves. The proposition that this was an old Minoan burial ground, and that its chamber tombs had been cut and used by the Minoans, subsequently to be cleared out and reused from Subminoan times onwards, will not stand scrutiny.

No other contemporary North Cemetery assemblages are as informative about the individuals that they commemorate. Tomb 186 suggests a man-at-arms, equipped with bronze spear and iron dirk, iron knife, and two stones for honing his blades for the most effective performance of the roles for which they were designed. The bronze *phalaron* could have been the centerpiece of a shield otherwise made of organic materials. Rather less plausibly, it might have been a belt decoration.[8] Tomb 201 was even more emphatically for a man-at-arms who was equipped with a sturdy bronze sword, a large bronze spearhead, and a set of bronze projectile heads perhaps best identified as arrowheads. He probably also had an iron knife. He, too, had a shield boss, or belt attachment (*phalaron*) and, I suggest, the fragments of boar's tusk mean he had a helmet of felt or leather to the outer surface of which slices of boar's tusk were stitched as added protection—a boar's-tusk helmet, in fact. If I suggest that the bone inlays had once decorated a quiver for his projectiles, that is merely to give an example of the kind of object that could have been involved.

Can we explain the complex of cremations in Tombs 200–202? By combining the evidence of the cremated remains, studied by J. H. Musgrave, and the grave offerings, we have a population comprising a man whose remains were intermingled with a woman and, perhaps, a child in Tomb 201, and a second woman in Tomb 200. Thus, remains of two, perhaps three individuals were simultaneously committed to Tomb 201, remains of one individual to Tomb 200. But it is probable that Tombs 200–202 were a single complex, used only once (for what it is worth, the larger Minoan "pit-caves" were used only once, with the difference, however, that they were for inhumations), so that it can be argued (but not proved) that all these cremated remains were buried on the same occasion. By extension, it could be argued that the respective cremations took place on the same occasion, something which is highly likely in the case of Tomb 201. We may suppose, further, that the primary death was the male and that in the course of the ceremonial that followed his death and culminated in the burning of his body and subsequent committal of his ashes to the tomb, two women and, perhaps, a child died and their bodies were burnt simultaneously. I would, further, argue that the body of one of the women, and the child if it really existed, were burnt on the same pyre as the male, their ashes subsequently taken up and com-

mitted together, without any attempt at separation. I suppose the body of the second woman was burnt on a different pyre, her ashes taken up and committed at the same time as the others, but in a separate receptacle. I explain the empty "cave," Tomb 202, by suggesting that the complex was prepared before the cremation rite was performed, when it was known that three adults would be burned, but not that the ashes of two of them would be inextricably confused.

The woman represented by the ashes of Tomb 200 was equipped more richly than any contemporary Subminoan or Submycenaean burial known to me. Her ornaments and jewelery are somewhat ambivalent concerning their place of origin, but there are elements which could have come from Cyprus,[9] the bronze pin-head might well be Italian, while other pieces could well be local to Crete.

For obvious reasons, it is more difficult to attribute items in Tomb 201 to the female element in the multiple cremation. Perhaps the iron dress-pins (if such indeed they are) could have been hers; if an ivory comb has been correctly identified, that is likely to be a female possession. More tendentious would be to ascribe the bronze four-sided stand to her. This would be on grounds that there is a connection between this class of metalwork (which includes[10] several stands mounted on wheels) and the silver work-basket that ran on "castors" given to Helen by Alcandre, wife of Polybus, of Egyptian Thebes (*Odyssey* 4.125–127). To whichever of them it belonged, and by whatever means it came into their possession, it was almost certainly made in Cyprus.

There are other signs that point to Cyprus, either as a possible place of origin for some of the material I have mentioned or, at the very least, as a location where very similar equipment was in circulation. Let us start with Tomb 186, where the iron dirk and iron knife (the latter an example of bimetallism because of its bronze rivet) recall the early prominence of Cyprus in iron technology, a topic which has stimulated much recent discussion and debate. The dirk may be the earliest weapon of this type yet reported from Crete. Surprisingly, the best parallels for the two honing stones are also to be found in Cyprus, where in the Early Iron Age and later cemetery at Skales, Kouklia, in southwest Cyprus, twelve stones were found, mostly singly, but in pairs in two cases.[11] There is also some evidence to show that whetstones in graves are regularly associated with weapons (unsurprising), and in several cases come from the graves of grandees.[12]

Tomb 201 also has its links with Cyprus, as we have already seen is the case with the bronze stand. In addition, the use of heavy projectiles finds a good parallel in Cyprus, where not only have they been found in large numbers, particularly at Enkomi,[13] but the find of a multiple mould for them at Hala Sultan Tekke shows they were almost certainly manufactured there.[14] Bone inlays were reported in Tombs 50 and 76 at Kouklia, Skales,[15] dated Cypro-Geometric I. Others, though, this time with stitch-holes, were found in Perati Tomb 1, in a context dated by the excavator 1190/85–1165/60 B.C.[16]

I should like for the moment to style our two men-at-arms as "grandees," justifying that word by the extent to which the circumstances of burial and their relative degree of wealth cause them to stand out from their contemporaries, and that not only at Knossos, but further afield, too. Now, can we identify the burials of comparable grandees of reasonably similar date? I believe there are at least three contexts, one on Cyprus, one at Tiryns, one on Euboea which, though by no means identical, seem to belong to a very similar milieu. They are well enough known. On Cyprus, to take that first, is the exceptional Late Cypriot IIIB grave at Episkopi, Kaloriziki, Tomb 40,[17] of which only part was scientifically excavated. This complex seems originally to have contained the cremations of a man and a woman, the latter certainly committed to a bronze krater, the former probably committed to a second and more elaborate krater. With them were found two bronze tripod stands decorated with animal protomes, three bronze *phalara* and items of trim which may between them have composed the facings of a shield,[18] a bronze spearhead, a gold toggle, other bronze vessels, decorated pottery and, most remarkable of all, the gold and cloisonné-enamel scepter-head, known as the Curium scepter. The conventional date for this group is mid-eleventh century B.C. The Tiryns complex is an inhumation grave. This is Tomb XXVIII in the series of Dark Age graves excavated and published by Nikolaos Verdelis.[19] The tomb contained the skeletons of a man and a woman, of which

the latter lacked offerings. With the man was a Submycenaean stirrup jar, two iron dirks, a bronze spearhead, a bronze *phalaron* with elaborate spike, and the remains of bronze facings of what has been identified as a helmet, with separate cheek-pieces. The date may be approximately fixed in the mid-eleventh century B.C. There is a close correspondence between this group of objects and our Tomb 186, described above.

A good fifty years later than these burials is the remarkable "hero-burial" (as it has been styled by the excavators[20]) at Toumba, Lefkandi, between Chalkis and Eretria, on Euboea. For our purpose, it does not matter whether the great building in which the burials were found was constructed specially for funerary use, or whether it started life as a Dark Age palace, and was subsequently converted into a vast tomb. There were two grave pits below the floor of the main room, or hall. In one were the skeletons of four horses. In the other was a cremation in a bronze amphora, of the same class as the Kaloriziki amphorae, associated with a large iron sword, an iron spear, knife, and whetstone. The ashes had been wrapped in a remarkable textile. Beside the cremation urn lay the extended inhumation of a woman, decked in jewelry, including decorated sheet-gold ornaments for the breasts, gold and iron dress-pins, and a remarkable gold pendant. Beside her head was a long iron knife with bone or ivory handgrip. A possible explanation for this combination of male cremation and female inhumation is that the woman died in the course of the man's funeral ceremonies, that, indeed, she may have been killed by someone using the knife that was buried with her, and that her splendidly decked body was placed beside the cremation urn in the grave pit as a fitting accompaniment for the grandee beside whose ashes she lay. Such circumstances would recall the description written in the tenth century A.C. by an Arab traveler, Ahmad bin Fudhlan, of the funeral of a Scandinavian chieftain on the banks of the Volga, at whose funeral pyre a girl was slain and her body burnt with the chieftain's. An English translation of the text was published a good many years ago by Miss Lorimer.[21] *Mutatis mutandis*, I believe we may have another example of the same custom in our Tomb 201.

There are several cross-links between these four sets of burials which suggest some common factor that links them. Some of the links, doubtless, are more apparent than significant, but the parallels are strong enough to require us to take their conjunction seriously. I list the most obvious:

(1) They are all associated with major sites, all of which had both an important past and an important future.
(2) They are the earliest, or nearly the earliest, graves in new burial grounds.
(3) None of the graves was reused.
(4) All were a focus for long subsequent use of the burial grounds.
(5) They are warrior burials.
(6) Knossos Tomb 186 aside, women were buried simultaneously with men.
(7) Tiryns XVIII excepted, the warriors were cremated.
(8) Knossos, Tiryns, and Lefkandi have iron weapons.
(9) Tiryns and Kaloriziki have bronze armor with pointillé decoration.
(10) Knossos (twice), Tiryns, and Kaloriziki have *phalara*.
(11) Knossos (twice) and Tiryns have stirrup jars immediately associated with the burials.
(12) Knossos (twice), Tiryns, and Kaloriziki have bronze spearheads.

Though I have drawn attention to features that these burials have in common, I am not suggesting that they have a common source in the narrow sense, nor am I arguing that any of their varied possessions were necessarily made in one and the same place. That *might* be the case, but it would not be central to what I think can be said about them.

I see as a most powerful clue to the way in which I suggest we look at these graves those remains in Knossos Tomb 201 which I believe once formed part of a boar's-tusk helmet. Such helmets, it is well known, had a long currency in use, and in representational art in the Aegean Bronze Age, from Middle Helladic times until a previously accepted latest appearance in an early twelfth century tomb at Kallithea, in Achaia.[22] In the Tomb 201 find, I believe we are dealing with a most striking archaeological instance of an heirloom helmet surviving long after the helmet-type had become obsolete. It serves as a perfect illustration of that passage rightly so dear to Homeric archaeologists in *Iliad*

10.261–271, where is described the arming of Odysseus by Meriones, and an explanation offered for the extraordinary helmet Odysseus was given to wear (I quote from E. V. Rieu's Penguin translation):

> . . . this helmet originally came from Eleon, where Autolykos stole it from Amyntor, son of Ormenus, by breaking into his well-built home. Autolykos gave it to Amphidamas of Kythera to take to Skandaea, and Amphidamas gave it to his son Meriones to wear, and now it was Odysseus' head it served to cover.

The train of thought induced by the boar's-tusk helmet leads one to look for other reminiscences of Homer in the evidence I have described. By "reminiscences of Homer" I mean no more than the *kind* of people who appear in the *Iliad* and the *Odyssey*, the material objects with which they were associated, and their behavior. I do not mean I am looking for congruence between these sets of archaeological evidence and Homeric *events*. If I am right about the reason for women being buried simultaneously with my "grandees," this would recall both the chattel-like status of Chryseis as a hero's booty, described in *Iliad* 1, and the fate of Polyxena, slain, according to the *Ilioupersis,* at Achilles' tomb following the sack of Troy. The slaughter of human victims and the cremations of their bodies with the hero's on his pyre is, of course, clearly documented in *Iliad* Book 23, at the funeral of Patroklos. The slaughter and burning of four horses on the same occasion makes a link with the four horses *buried* at Toumba, Lefkandi. The rite of cremation as the normal means of dealing with a hero's body is, of course, standard practice in the Homeric poems. *Odyssey* Book 24 gives interesting details concerning the committal of heroic ashes, where we learn that Achilles' ashes were mingled with Patroklos' ashes, and consigned to a golden vessel, and that in a separate group, but under the same mound, were also interred the ashes of Antilochus. This recalls the multiple cremations of Tombs 200 and Tomb 201 at Knossos, though the circumstances giving rise to the multiple committal differ from those I have suggested for the Knossos complex, introducing in particular the practice of retaining a group of ashes unburied until circumstances arose when they could be buried in the most appropriate fashion. The use of a metal container as receptacle for Achilles' and Patroklos' ashes recalls both Kaloriziki and Toumba.

These have been links with the *Iliad*. There are links, too, with the world of the *Odyssey*. By this I refer to the exotic elements among the grave offerings, especially the four-sided stand of Tomb 201, the wheel-shaped pin-head of Tomb 200, and some of its gold jewelry, glass, and faience beads. These put me in mind of the evocation by Menelaos in *Odyssey* 4 of the life-style—and prizes—of a wandering hero, related for the benefit of Telemachos when he visits Sparta in search of news of his father's whereabouts. Menelaos gives a thumbnail sketch of his wanderings (4.83–85):

> My travels took me to Cyprus, to Phoenicia,
> and to Egypt. Ethiopians, Sidonians, Erembi,
> I visited them all; and I saw Libya. . . .

We have already noted the remarkable silver work-basket which Helen had received as a gift from the wife of Polybus, Alcandre, in Egypt. Another guest-gift was chronicled by Menelaos as he makes a gift to Telemachos (4.615–619):

> I'll give you a mixing bowl of wrought metal.
> It is solid silver with a rim of gold round the top,
> and was made by Hephaestus himself. I had it from
> my royal friend the King of Sidon, when I put up
> under his roof on my journey home.

Among our burials, this flavor is most apparent at Knossos and Lefkandi. At the latter site the hero's ashes, as we have seen, were placed in a bronze vessel, the only other known examples of which have been found in Cyprus. Among the gold ornaments that decked the woman's body was a gold pendant, perhaps an heirloom that originated in Mesopotamia.

The title of my paper is "Heroes Returned?" I have, I hope, explained why I consider my "grandees," buried at Knossos in the middle of the eleventh century B.C., should be styled "heroes," in the sense that Homer's *dramatis personae* are heroes. That they are "heroes returned" seems a reasonable inference drawn from a combination of circumstances, none decisive on its own, but quite persuasive cumulatively.

There is evidence of regular contact between Crete and Cyprus at the end of the Bronze Age. While Minoan goods, chiefly pottery, had made not infrequent appearances at Late Cypriot sites from LC I onwards,[23] there is evidence at Pyla-*Kokkinokremos* at the end of the thirteenth–beginning of the twelfth centuries B.C.[24] of an unusually strong Minoan element at the site, of which the giant LM IIIB amphoroid kraters are the most prominent, but not the only, symptom.[25] Less tangible, but probably of greater significance, is the relationship between LC IIIB decorated pottery ("Proto-White Painted Ware") and LM IIIC and Subminoan decorated pottery.[26] This is not the occasion to elaborate this matter, the detail of which is not agreed among ceramic experts; suffice it to say that the relationship exists. It might even mean that some Cretans spent extended periods in Cyprus in the first half of the eleventh century B.C. I suggest that the grandees/heroes of North Cemetery Tombs 186 and 201 could have spent part of their lives in Cyprus, where they might have been children of ethnic Cretans, born and bred in Cyprus, or they might have started their lives in Crete and returned there after a prolonged absence, of which part at least was spent in Cyprus.

I believe additional support comes for the view they are "returned" from the fact that they were interred in a completely new burial ground, according to the exotic funerary rite of cremation. That they made use of an old Minoan grave type—the "pit-cave"—for interring the ashes points to some degree of kinship with their environment, and for this reason in particular I suggest they were "heroes returned."

Professor Peter Warren, in the light of his recent excavations in the town of Knossos,[27] has called attention to the sharp contrast between the Subminoan community of Knossos, which continued to occupy a prime location of settlement—albeit the center had shifted sensibly, apparently without particular concern for security—and the contemporary mountain refuge-settlements, epitomized by Karphi.[28] The underlying causes of that dichotomy of settlement pattern might include the consequences of our "heroes returned" arrival on the scene which could, indeed, provide another echo, from Homer's insight into the consequences of the Nostoi.

NOTES

*The rescue excavation which led to the discovery of the two graves described in this paper was carried out at Knossos in 1978 and 1979 with the joint resources of the Greek Ministry of Culture, the University of Crete, and the British School at Athens. Dr. Angeliki Lembessis, at that time Ephor of Prehistoric and Classical Antiquities at Herakleion, gave all help and assistance. Dr. Jill Carington Smith, at that time the School's Knossos Fellow, was responsible for the day-to-day direction in the field, jointly with myself, during May and June 1978, when these graves were dug. A preliminary account of the excavation was published in *AR* 1978–1979, 43–58. The site survey and final site and tomb drawings were undertaken by Mr. David Smyth, the British School's Honorary Surveyor. These two tombs were actually excavated by the late Mr. Antonis Zidianakis, the School's Foreman at Knossos. The notebook was kept by Mrs. Anne Thomas, Student of the School. The vases were repaired by the late Mr. Petros Petrakis, Hon. MBE, the School's Vase Mender. The cremations were studied by Dr. J. H. Musgrave. The boar's-tusk fragments were identified by Miss Sheilagh Wall (Mrs. Charles Crowther). The drawings reproduced here were made by Mrs. Elizabeth Catling and Miss Emma Faull. I am most grateful to all those persons named for their roles in the North Cemetery excavation. I am also grateful to the Managing Committee for agreeing to the publication of this material in advance of the final report.

1. A. Evans, "The Prehistoric Tombs of Knossos," *Archaeologia* 59 (1905) 405–411. These are I. Pini's *Schachtnischengräber* (I. Pini, *Beiträge zur minoischen Gräberkunde* [Wiesbaden 1969] 46).

2. A. H. S. Megaw's plan of this building is published in *AR* 1978–1979, 56, fig. 48.

3. See the considerable literature, now centered on B. Fellmann, *Frühe Gürtelschmuckscheiben aus Bronze*, OlForsch 16 (Berlin 1983). For another view, see A. M. Snodgrass, "Bronze 'Phalara'—a review," *HBA* 3 (1973) 41–50.

4. See H. Matthäus, "Italien und Griechenland in der ausgehenden Bronzezeit," *JdI* 95 (1980) 109–139. Also J. Bouzek, *The Aegean, Anatolia and Egypt: Cultural Interrelations in the Second Millennium B.C.* (Prague 1986) 166, 171–172. K. Kilian, "Civiltà micenea in Grecia: Nuovi aspetti storici ed interculturali," in *Atti del 22. Convegno dei Studi sulla Magna Grecia, Taranto 1982* (Taranto 1983–1985) 53–96, esp. 83–84. A. Hochstetter, *Kastanas: Die Kleinfunde*, Prähistorische Archäologie in Südosteuropa 6 (Berlin 1987).

5. There is an extensive literature on these weapons, their origins, and developments now in need of revision to take account of new material and fuller publication of already known examples. Among recent accounts note should be taken of Bouzek (supra n. 4) 119–132 and references. The Knossos T. 201 sword may belong to his Group V, of which the Bitola sword, now in Istanbul, is the type-weapon. A fragment from the Heraion on Samos may also belong.

6. Four of Buchholz Type VIIa, one of Type VIIc—H.-G. Buchholz, "Die Pfeilglätter aus dem VI. Schachtgrab von Mykenai und die helladischen Pfeilspitzen," *JdI* 77 (1962) 1–58, esp. 11, fig. 7 and 22–23, figs. 13–14.

7. Illustrated in *RDAC* 1984, pl. XV, nos. 1–3, 5, and 6.

8. For discussion, see Fellmann (supra n. 3).

9. The gold rosettes have been found in very early Cypro-Geometric I contexts at Lapithos—*SCE* I, pl. 44 (Tomb 403) and pl. 57 (Tomb 428)—and Salamis, Tomb 1: M. Yon, *Salamine de Chypre* II (Lyon 1971) 12–13 and pl. 14, nos. 5–24. Seed-shaped faience beads have been found at Kition, Floor IV, in Area II–V. Karageorghis, *Kition* II, 90 and pl. 186, no. 2510; Hala Sultan Tekke: P. Åström, *Hala Sultan Tekke 8. Excavations 1971–1979*, SIMA 45:8 (Göteborg 1983) 94, fig. 268, and at Kouklia, *Asproyi* (unpublished).

10. See H. Matthäus, *Metallgefässe und Gefässuntersätze der Bronzezeit, der geometrischen und archaischen Periode auf Zypern*, Prähistorische Bronzefunde II.8 (Munich 1985).

11. V. Karageorghis, *Palaepaphos-Skales: An Iron Age cemetery in Cyprus* (Konstanz 1983) appendix IX, 426–432.

12. For instance, they have been found in Grave Circle A at Mycenae: Karo 149, nos. 860, 861; 163, fig. 79, no. 930 and pl. CII, 512. They occurred at the LH I–II grave circle at Epano Englianos—C. W. Blegen et al., *The Palace of Nestor at Pylos* III (Princeton 1973) 161, fig. 232.2 (found in the bronze cauldron in Pit 2); 167, fig. 232.3—and were found with the LH I–II warrior burial from Dendra (Tomb 8: A. Persson, *New Tombs at Dendra near Midea* [1942] 49, no. 15 and fig. 9).

13. E.g., J.-Cl. Courtois, *Alasia* III (Paris 1984) 1316 and fig. 3.

14. G. Hult and D. McCaslin, *Hala Sultan Tekke* 4, SIMA 45:4 (Göteborg 1978) 83, figs. 67 and 183, no. 1055.

15. Karageorghis (supra n. 11) T. 50.11, pl. 68, fig. 94; T. 76.119, pl. 144, fig. 143.

16. S. Iakovides, *Perati* (Athens 1969) I. 160, 165; vol. II, 381 and pl. 49a.

17. G. H. McFadden, "A Late Cypriote III tomb from Kourion: Kaloriziki No. 40," *AJA* 58 (1954) 131–142.

18. H. W. and E. A. Catling in J. L. Benson, *The Necropolis of Kaloriziki*, SIMA 36 (Göteborg 1973) 130–132, appendix B. For another view see J. Bouzek, *RDAC* 1988, 319–320; also Fellmann (supra n. 3) 104–107.

19. N. Verdelis, "Neue geometrische Gräber in Tiryns," *AM* 78 (1963) 1–62, esp. 10–24.

20. M. R. Popham et al., "The Hero of Lefkandi," *Antiquity* 56 (1982) 169–174.

21. H. L. Lorimer, "A Scandinavian Cremation-Ceremony," *Antiquity* 8 (1934) 58–62.

22. N. Yalouris, "Mykenische Bronzeschutzwappen," *AM* 75 (1960) 44, 54–56, Beil. 31.4. Cf. Hood, supra, p. 27.

23. Notably at Toumba tou Skourou, Morphou Bay: E. Vermeule and F. Wolsky, "New Aegean Relations with Cyprus: The Minoan and Mycenaean Pottery from Toumba tou Skourou, Morphou," *ProcPhilSoc* 122 (1978) 294–317; eaedem, *Toumba tou Skourou. A Bronze Age Potters' Quarter on Morphou Bay in Cyprus* (Cambridge 1990) 381–385. The general account by H. Catling and V. Karageorghis, "Minoika in Cyprus," *BSA* 55 (1960) 109–127 is now very much out of date. A completer account is due to be published in the forthcoming *History of Cyprus,* in preparation by the Archbishop Makarios III foundation. For the later part of the period, see in particular M. R. Popham, "Connections between Crete and Cyprus between 1300–1100 B.C.," in *Acts of the International Archaeological Symposium, "The Relations between Cyprus and Crete. c. 2000–500 B.C.,"* (Nicosia 1979) 178–191.

24. V. Karageorghis and M. Demas, *Pyla-Kokkinokremos, a Late 13th Century B.C. Fortified Settlement in Cyprus* (Nicosia 1984) 51.

25. Catling and Karageorghis (supra n. 23) nos. 17–20.

26. On this, see, for instance, V. Desborough, *The Greek Dark Ages* (London 1972) 49–63. Maria Iakovou has stressed, however, that the direction and significance of the relationship is far from clear: *The Pictorial Pottery of Eleventh Century B.C. Cyprus,* SIMA 79 (Göteborg 1988) 80.

27. *AR* 1982–1983, 83.

28. H. W. Pendlebury, J. D. S. Pendlebury, and M. B. Money-Coutts, "Excavations in the Plain of Lasithi III. Karphi: A City of Refuge in the Early Iron Age in Crete," *BSA* 38 (1937–1938) 57–145; cf. Desborough (supra n. 26) 120–139.

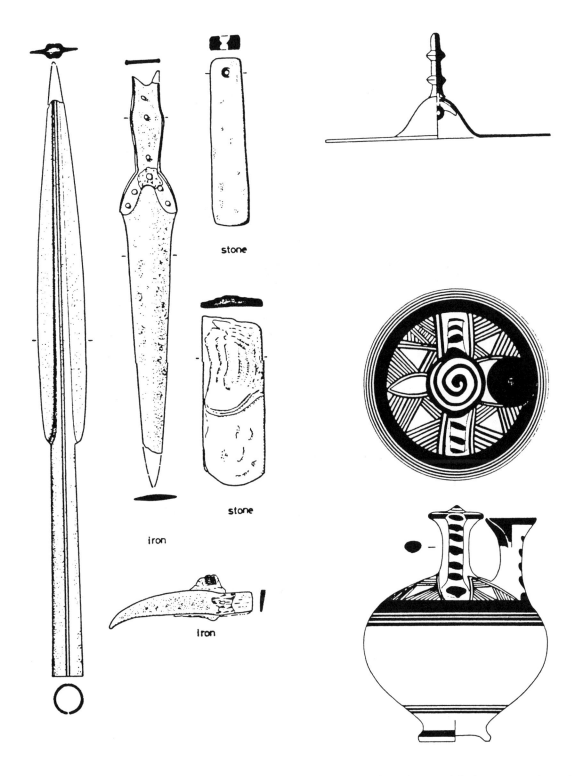

stone

stone

iron

iron

FIGURE 8.1 Knossos, North Cemetery, 1978. Contents of Tomb 186 (scale: metal finds, c. 1:2; stirrup jar, 1:3).

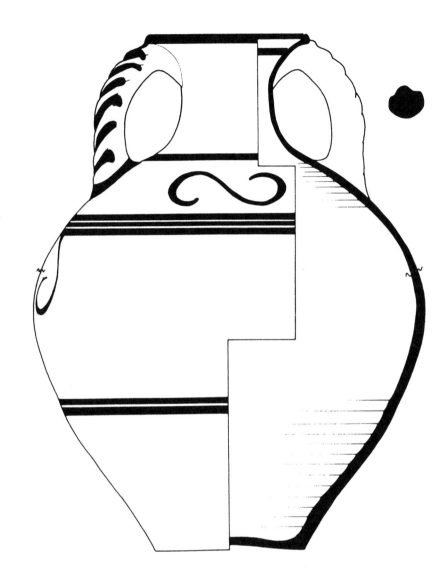

FIGURE 8.2 Knossos, North Cemetery, 1978. Subminoan neck-handled amphora from pit of Tombs 200–202 (scale: c. 1:5).

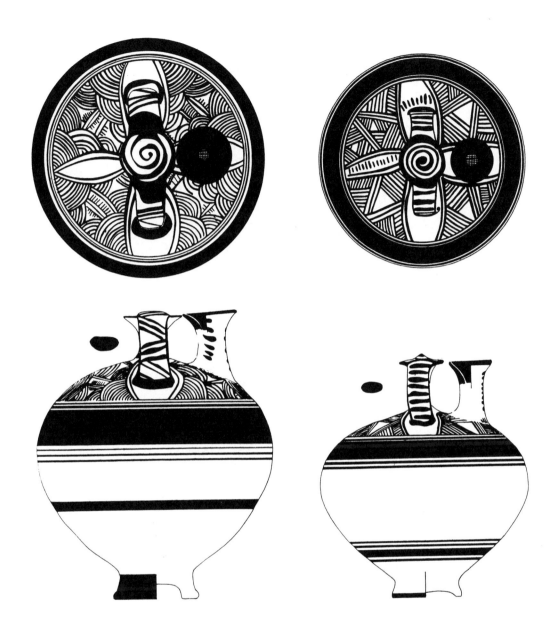

FIGURE 8.3 Knossos, North Cemetery, 1978. Subminoan stirrup jars from pit floor Tombs 200–202 (scale: c.
1:3).

FIGURE 8.4 Knossos, North Cemetery, 1978. Subminoan stirrup jar from Tomb 200 (scale: c. 1:3).

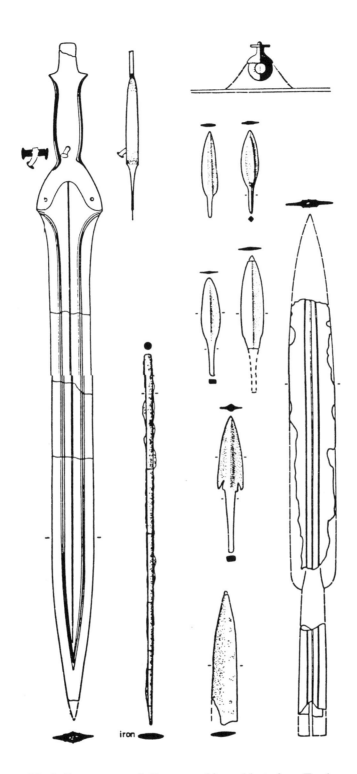

iron

FIGURE 8.5 Knossos, North Cemetery, 1978. Bronze and iron objects from Tomb 201 (scale: c. 1:3).

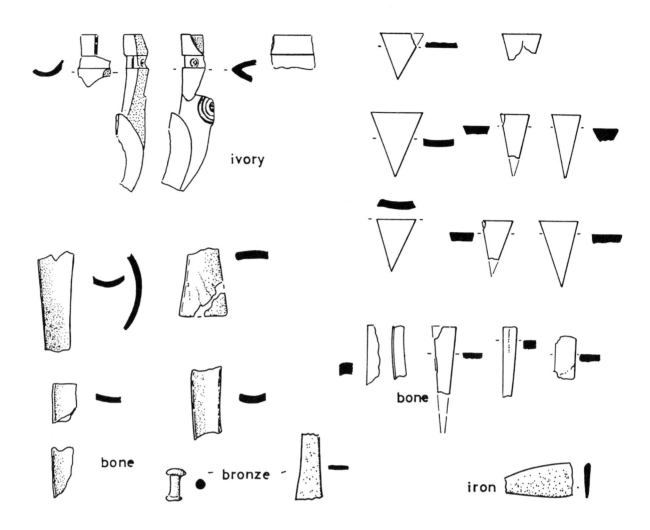

FIGURE 8.6 Knossos, North Cemetery, 1978. Ivory, bone, boar's tusk, bronze, and iron objects from Tomb 201 (scale c. 2:3).

PART II

HOMER AND THE IRON AGE: HISTORY AND POETICS

9

LYDIA BETWEEN EAST AND WEST OR HOW TO DATE THE TROJAN WAR: A STUDY IN HERODOTUS *

◆

WALTER BURKERT

It is with the Greeks that our historical consciousness usually begins. Yet compared to the Near Eastern evidence, Greek literature and Greek history must be considered "late." The earliest, and most decisive, historical work preserved is that of Herodotus, published about 430 B.C. Herodotus is well informed about the history of the fifth century and still knows much about the sixth, but he becomes less and less precise about earlier events or persons; practically nothing in his narrative seems to antedate the epoch of the Cimmerian invasion and Gyges, roughly 700 B.C. This is exactly what modern research on "oral history" leads us to expect:[1] oral history covers a maximum of about 200 years—up to grandfather's grandfather, as it were—but nothing earlier. In fact, Greeks were able to reconstruct some events before what Herodotus tells us, including the history of the Messenian Wars, using Tyrtaeus, and the Lelantine War, referred to by Archilochus; before this lies *terra incognita.*

There was no historical tradition in Greece to penetrate the dark. Some families maintained memories about ancestors and their migrations; later these were combined to make up the "Dorian migration" and the

"Ionian migration," movements that somehow evolved into what we call the period of colonization from the eighth century onwards. Traditions of this kind would contain names, genealogies, localities, and indications of kinship, friendship, and enmities. "We came from Pindus, we conquered Amyklai"[2]—this was told and remembered at Sparta. One private genealogy is extant from Chios, that of Heropythos.[3] Genealogies can give an idea of distance in time, as names are counted; but they do not preserve historical facts to make up "pragmatic" history. Mythical stereotypes enter to fill the gaps. The dearth of Greek tradition about the tenth, ninth, eighth centuries is depressing indeed. We shall never know the name of that remarkable prince who received a splendid burial in the so-called Heroon of Lefkandi in the tenth century B.C.[4]

Yet beyond all this, about 1200 B.C. in our chronology, appears the Trojan War in all its splendor and detail. We get pragmatic history with persons, nay characters: Mycenaean Agamemnon and Pylian Nestor, Trojans and allies, Dardanoi, Achaioi, Danaoi; bright light is shed on the preceding generation, too, that of the Seven against Thebes, the Argonauts, and Herakles. We find conflicts, decisions, motivations, and especially that favorite object of traditional historiography, war—great wars that have made their way right into the *Cambridge Ancient History*: the Theban War, the Trojan War.[5] And what is most surprising: the date for these wars as given by Greek tradition agrees with the dates suggested by archaeology, within a margin of just a few decades. According to Eratosthenes' calculation, Troy fell in 1183, while Herodotus' account points to about 1300. Blegen, excavator of Troy, thought he had established "1250 or somewhat earlier" for the destruction of Troy VIIa and hence for the Trojan War. This is practically within one century, the correct century, as it seems, of the Late Bronze Age. The conclusion seems to be inevitable: this is historical fact, and the Greeks knew about it. How they could have known, beyond that vacuum of five centuries, remains a mystery. Fritz Schachermeyr, who tried to solve it, came to postulate that written records must have existed after all, possibly through the Teucrids on Cyprus[6]—an almost desperate hypothesis.

Yet Blegen's date, which has dominated our ideas about a Trojan War for some time, has come under serious attack recently. Bloedow's reexamination of the archaeological evidence in 1988 leaves no doubt that the destruction of Troy VIIa, associated since Blegen with Homeric Troy and the Trojan War, must be dated well into the LH IIIC period, later than 1180, about 1140, Bloedow thinks—that is, to an epoch when no palace stood at Mycenae, no powerful *wanax* was left to lead an expedition to the Dardanelles.[7] Thus the foundations for any "historical" Trojan War of Homeric type, for the attack, siege, and conquest of that citadel at Hissarlik by Mycenaean warriors, have crumbled again. The Trojan War as sung by Homer did not take place.[8] And yet the new date is still closer to that of Eratosthenes', 1183—how strange a precision concerning a nonevent!

The paradox may prompt us to ask once more how the Greeks ever arrived at a date for the fall of Troy. This means investigating the foundations of Greek chronological constructions, to attempt another happy "marriage of genealogy and arithmetic,"[9] with dim prospects of success. Nevertheless it seems worthwhile to question the widely accepted results of a famous study by Eduard Meyer published in 1892, while paying more attention to Near Eastern history and sources than is usual.

In the following, dates will be given with reference to the Christian era and the Julian calendar. It is more convenient for us to write, and to understand, "1200 B.C." than "424 years before the first Olympiad" or "720 years before the battle of Salamis." This is not, of course, to imply that Herodotus, Eratosthenes, or any Greek chronographer was aware of such an era. As a reminder that we are dealing with an abbreviated construct, such dates will always appear in quotation marks.

The fundamental text remains Herodotus. There have been widely divergent judgments about Herodotus' chronology.[10] It need not be stressed how important his work is for all we know about early Greek history, and for a most lively and picturesque view of the whole of the ancient world. It is no less clear that his chronological statements lead to gross contradictions, about which he does not seem to care.

The basic facts are simple. Herodotus is making use of king-lists of Near Eastern type. This includes the Twenty-sixth Dynasty of Egypt since the time of Psammetichus, the Lydian lists from Gyges to Croesus, the Persians from Cyrus to Xerxes, and also the Medes from Deioces to Astyages. King-lists had been current in the ancient Near East for a long time; they are known from Egypt, Mesopotamia, and Israel. Their function is to provide legitimation for the ruling dynasty; thus they tend to start with mythical epochs—as the "Sumerian king-list" already does[11]—but eventually reach the time of reliable records. They become most valuable as historical documents if the years each king reigned are included, as is the case with Egypt, Mesopotamia, and Israel, providing a continuous chart of chronology. Manetho's lists of Egyptian dynasties form the basis for all early chronology. The list of kings of Israel and Judaea from Saul to the conquest of Jerusalem in 586 is basically trustworthy, too. The Assyrians had a king-list comprising more than 100 kings.[12]

It may be useful to give an example of how "historical consciousness" could take its origin from such a list. There is an inscription for the mother of King Nabunaid, last king of Babylon (555–539), in which the old lady is made to say: "From the 20th year of Assurbanipal, King of Assyria, that I was born—until the 42nd year of Assurbanipal, the 3rd year of Assur-Etukku-Ili, the 21st year of Nabopolassar, the 43rd year of Nebuchadrezzar, the 2nd year of Awel-Marduk, the 4th year of Neriglissar: in 95 years . . . ," i.e., when I was ninety-five years old, Sin the Moon God had mercy, and "(my) only son, Nabuna'id, . . . to the kingship he was called." [13] This was in 555 B.C.; born in 650, she still recalled the reign of Assurbanipal, and assured herself of the interval in time, and her own age, through the official list of kings.

Turning to Herodotus, the three types of information contained in Near Eastern king-lists—the name, the number of years, and the sequence—are given in systematic fashion in his text with relation to the kings of Egypt, Lydia, Media, and Persia; the lists have long been reconstructed by commentators. [14] Only one of these lists can be controlled in detail, that of the Twenty-sixth Dynasty of Egypt. It contains one serious mistake, the reign of Apries as given by Herodotus is too long by six years; Herodotus' list would put the beginning of Psammetichus' reign in 670, instead of 664, as accepted by modern historians. The other figures are correct, as are the names and the sequence. [15] So there is no question here about Herodotus elaborating, inventing, or lying: [16] he was simply copying, or memorizing, a list.

As for the list of Persian kings, there is independent information in cuneiform documents dated to a special year of Achaemenid kings and in the Babylonian records used by Ptolemy in his *Syntaxis.* [17] Herodotus here proves to be correct; discrepancies are limited to one or two years. The list of Median kings presents special problems within the cuneiform evidence as well as in terms of conflicts with Herodotus; these need not be discussed here. For the Lydian king-list, the problems are more serious. There is no authentic Lydian tradition for independent control. Eusebius has somewhat shorter regnal dates, and since the annals of Assurbanipal (668–627) indicate that Gyges was his contemporary, Herodotus is proved false: his list would place Gyges about twenty-five years too early. We cannot be sure where to locate the error. One usually accepts Herodotus' date for Croesus' reign and shortens those of his predecessors. [18]

With the epoch of Psammetichus and Gyges, Herodotus' knowledge seems to come to an end; he did not use any source such as Manetho. As to Greek history, he still makes a few remarks that point much farther back in time. There are three groups of them:

(1) In his excursus on Egypt, Herodotus tells how Hecataeus arrived at Thebes and recited his own genealogy, tracing his family back to a god in the sixteenth generation (ἀναδήσαντι τὴν πατριὴν ἐς ἑκκαιδεκα-

τον θεόν, 2.143). Then the priests showed him 345 statues in a row, explaining that these had all been priests, son succeeding father, without any god intervening in the series. Egyptian history thus comprises 345 generations before Hecataeus. [19] Herodotus goes on to calculate: 341 generations until Psammetichus, with three generations making up one century, would yield 11, 340 years down to "670 B.C." [20] Herodotus had been working with this series of generations, and of Egyptian kings, from Book 2.99 onwards: Egyptian history, he says, begins with King Menes; then there were 330 kings "of whom nothing memorable is told" (2.101.1), then ten kings about whom there are stories to tell. These total 341 before Psammetichus. Among those ten memorable kings are the builders of the pyramids, Cheops, Chephren, and Mykerinos, numbers 336 to 338, if we do the counting—Herodotus does not; they lived, accordingly, four to six generations before Psammetichus, "870–770 B.C." Their names are correct, their date is wrong by nearly 2,000 years. Two generations before Cheops, number 334, we find Proteus, "936/903." This Proteus is the king who was host of Helen during the Trojan War. Thus he is dated to the very era of the Trojan War—even if Herodotus does not make explicit calculations here. We know that Proteus comes right out of the fourth book of the *Odyssey;* the mythical master of animals, master of seals had already been changed into an "historical" king of Egypt prior to Herodotus. [21] Still his name cannot come from any Egyptian king-list. Why he was inserted into the sequence of kings at this spot is a question that cannot be answered from what Herodotus tells us. A pre-Herodotean but still Greek tradition must be in the background. Some Greek "source" of Herodotus thought that the Trojan War had occurred seven generations before Psammetichus, or twelve generations before the Ionian revolt, say, "910 B.C."

(2) Again within his Egyptian excursus, Herodotus gives a few absolute dates (2.145): Dionysus the grandchild of Kadmos lived 1,000 years ago, Herakles about 900 years (εἰς ἐμέ: 2.145.4 *bis*), Pan son of Penelope somewhat after the Trojan War, i.e., about 800 years ago. [22] At first glance it seems troubling that the Trojan War should be separated from Herakles by nearly 100 years, whereas Greek tradition, starting from the *Iliad,* leaves no doubt that Herakles lived about one generation before the *Troika,* being a contemporary both

of Laomedon and of the Argonaut expedition. But the problem disappears upon closer inspection. Pan's birth should have occurred about twenty years after the beginning of the Trojan War; this, in turn, would be separated by more than thirty years from Herakles' *akmé,* by more than sixty years from Herakles' birth; thus the difference in age between Herakles and Pan exceeds eighty years, and as Herodotus in this passage is giving rough estimates ($\mu\acute{\alpha}\lambda\iota\sigma\tau\alpha$), indicating whole centuries, the dates for Herakles ("900") and Pan ("800") in fact agree with each other and with the general tradition. Now if we are prepared to accept Apollodorus' date for Herodotus—444 B.C.—we arrive at "1344" for the epoch of Herakles, and something like "1310/1300" for the Trojan War, with the birth of Pan about "1290." If we chose the putative birth date of Herodotus, 484, or the probable publication date of his work, about 430, figures would change accordingly, without making much difference. In any case the Trojan era implied here is about 400 years distant from the epoch of Proteus and the Trojan era presupposed in the other passage of the same book of Herodotus.

(3) At the beginning of his treatment of Lydian history (1.7), Herodotus tells us that, prior to Gyges, Heraklids had been ruling the Lydians for 505 years, passing on kingship from father to son for twenty-two generations altogether; the first was Agron, the last one Kandaules, murdered by Gyges. The two figures, twenty-two generations and 505 years, do not agree; one generation would amount to c. 22.95 years. One must conclude that the two kinds of information—the sum of years and the number of kings—are independent of each other; in other words, Herodotus, or his source, is not using a simple count of generations here, but a king-list with variable lengths of reigns, which Herodotus did not copy in this case. As Herodotus has a king-list for the Medes before Cyrus, a similar list for Lydia before Gyges would have to be postulated anyhow. The sum of reigns for a specific dynasty is explicitly given by Herodotus in the case of the Medes.[23]

But Herodotus has more to say about the Lydians before Gyges: Agron, first Lydian king, was the son of Ninos, son of Belos, son of Alcaeus, son of Herakles. With an astonishing zigzag leap, this genealogy leads first to Nineveh and then back to Greece. But calculations first:

Gyges, in Herodotus' list, would have become king in "716 B.C.," hence Agron in "1221"; the epoch of Herakles, four generations back, would thus be "1354 B.C." Herodotus does not perform this arithmetic, but anybody could have done in at his time. The remarkable result is that this Lydian calculation, with Herakles' epoch in "1354," is practically identical with the date for Herakles given by Herodotus in his own name: "900 years before my time." There remains the same discrepancy with the Trojan era implied in the insertion of Proteus and Helen into the Egyptian king-list.

A brief survey of other dates for the Trojan era: Pindar, in his fourth *Pythian,* performed 462 B.C., counts "seventeen generations" from the Argonauts to King Battos of Kyrene, then "8 generations of kings" from Battos to his day.[24] Starting from 631 as the foundation date of Kyrene, we arrive at "1164" for the expedition of the Argonauts, including Herakles, hence at "1131" for the Trojan War.

Democritus chose to date his great work *Mikros Diakosmos* "730 years after the Fall of Troy," $\sigma\upsilon\nu\tau\epsilon\tau\acute{\alpha}\chi$-$\theta\alpha\iota$ $\tau\grave{o}\nu$ $\mathrm{M}\iota\kappa\rho\grave{o}\nu$ $\Delta\iota\acute{\alpha}\kappa\sigma\mu\sigma\nu$ $\check{\epsilon}\tau\epsilon\sigma\iota\nu$ $\tilde{\upsilon}\sigma\tau\epsilon\rho\sigma\nu$ $\tau\tilde{\eta}\varsigma$ $\mathrm{^{\prime}I}\eta\lambda\acute{\iota}\sigma\upsilon$ $\mathring{\alpha}\lambda\acute{\omega}\sigma\epsilon\omega\varsigma$ $\tau\rho\iota\acute{\alpha}\kappa\sigma\nu\tau\alpha$ $\kappa\alpha\grave{\iota}$ $\mathring{\epsilon}\pi\tau\alpha\kappa\sigma\sigma\acute{\iota}\sigma\iota\varsigma$ (D.L. 9.41 = VS 68 B 5). Democritus thus presupposes an established era for the Trojan War. He will have relied on some influential chronographer; it is tempting to think of Hellanicus,[25] but this cannot be verified. Following Apollodorus[26] we put the *akmé* of Democritus in 420, which leads to a Trojan War of "1160–1150" —about the mean of the two conflicting Herodotean dates.

Thucydides, too, has a Trojan era: it was sixty years after the *halosis* (the capture of Troy), he says, that the Boiotians came to Boiotia (1.12.3), and twenty years later, eighty years after the *halosis,* the Dorians conquered the Peloponnese under the leadership of the Heraklids. After this the Ionians migrated to Asia Minor, via Athens. It is remarkable that the *halosis* has become connected with the "Dorian migration." There is no simple count of generations, those "eighty years" are difficult to reconcile with generations of Heraklids— Eurysthenes and Prokles, the first kings of Sparta, are located five generations after Herakles (Hdt. 8.131).[27] In another passage (5.112), Thucydides remarks that Melos was colonized by Dorians "700 years" before the catastrophe of 416, hence about "1116." This seems to agree with the archaeological evidence[28]—but still leaves us in doubt as to Thucydides' date for the "Return of the Heraklids" and the fall of Troy.[29]

Great discrepancies as to the Trojan era still mark the constructs or guesses of historians throughout the fourth and third centuries B.C.:

Ephorus dated the "Return of the Heraklids," which he considered to be the beginning of real "history" of Greece, 735 years before Alexander's expedition to Asia (*FGrHist* 70 F 223), i.e., "1069"; this date did not acquire any authority.[30] Adding the eighty-year interval of Thucydides, the fall of Troy would have happened in "1149."

Dicaearchus, in his *Bios Hellados* (Fr. 58 Wehrli), put the *halosis* 306 years before the first Olympiad, "1082." It is remarkable that here, for the first time, the Olympic era comes into play; Olympia seems to have loomed large in Aristotle's historical studies.[31]

Duris has the fall of Troy take place just 1,000 years before Alexander's expedition to Asia (*FGrHist* 76 F 41), i.e., "1334"—"chiliastic" speculation no doubt. The tribute of the Locrian maidens to Ilion, too, was thought to have been ordained for 1,000 years—but there was (and is) controversy as to when this period came to an end.[32]

The Marmor Parium places the Trojan War in "1218–1208" (*FGrHist* 239 ep. 23/24; written in 264/3). There are various inconclusive explanations for this date.[33]

Finally, Eratosthenes and Apollodorus established the era of 1184/3, 407 years before the first Olympiad (*FGrHist* 241 F 1, 244 F 61). This became the official date, accepted also by Porphyry and Eusebius.[34] There was no doubt about its foundation: "from the Spartan king-list," ἀπὸ τῶν ἐν Λακεδαίμονι βασιλευσάντων, as Diodorus (1.5.1) explicitly says, following Apollodorus.[35] In the meantime, following Herodotus, the genealogy of Agiad and Eurypontid kings had developed into a "real" king-list, with individual lengths of reigns; the first Olympiad was placed in the 9th year of Alkamenes; before him, genealogy produced eight kings up to the "Return" or Dorian migration, which in turn was placed eighty years after the fall of Troy, following Thucydides.

The striking fact is that in the Spartan king-list, one generation is estimated at forty years; the lengths of individual reigns are variable, but their sum, divided through the number of kings, clearly gives "40." This was demonstrated by Eduard Meyer, in his study of 1892, and it was from this observation that he developed the hypotheses that have dominated studies of Greek chronography ever since. He claimed that the use of the Spartan king-list, calculating one generation at forty years, goes back to Hecataeus (170), and that Herodotus' date for Herakles, "900 years before my time," is derived from this very source. In fact, Herodotus gives both the genealogies of Agiad and Eurypontid kings (7.204; 8.131); for him Leonidas is the twentieth descendant of Heracles. In Meyer's calculation, if Leonidas was born about "530," Herakles would have been 20 × 40 = 800 years earlier, i.e., "1330," and this indeed is about "900 years" before Herodotus published his work. Eduard Meyer's theory has been widely accepted by later scholars, including Wade-Gery and Schachermeyr, even if some have raised general doubts.[36]

There is no question of Eduard Meyer's rank as a scholar, but on this point his authority must be radically challenged. First, his arithmetic is wrong: the date for Herakles, "1330," corresponding to Leonidas' supposed birth in 530, would be Herakles' birth date, but Herodotus in all probability was thinking of Herakles' *akmé;* thus one generation would be missing. Some later scholars saw this flaw, but did not succeed in correcting it.[37]

More importantly, the foundation of his thesis on the authority of Hecataeus is impossible: it is ruled out by the story of how Hecataeus "genealogized" himself up to a god "in the sixteenth generation." No self-respecting Greek family ever claimed a divine ancestor more recent than the Trojan War. In the catalogues of Hesiod, one of the main models for Hecataeus' genealogies, the Trojan War is made the great divide: no mingling of divine and human afterwards (Fr. 204, 101–103). This means that Hecataeus could place the Trojan War at a maximum distance of fourteen generations; he did not take into account the nineteen generations of Heraklids already remembered at Sparta in his time. If the Milesian was thinking in terms of Milesian Neileids, their genealogy *Poseidon—Neleus—Nestor—?—Neileos* would push the Trojan era at least one generation later. This means that in Hecataeus' view the Trojan War must have happened in "966" at the earliest, or somewhat later. This, however, is very close to or even identical with the date for Proteus implied in Herodotus, "936/903." The reconstruction of Egyptian history we meet in Herodotus refers to Hecataeus more than once; the very backbone of those "345 generations" is related to Hecataeus' adventure in Thebes. If we dare to attribute any date for *Troika* to Hecataeus, it should be this.[38]

For confirmation, we may point to the genealogy of the Athenian Philaids, as given by Pherekydes of Athens (*FGrHist* 3 F 2):[39] they count thirteen generations from Ajax to Hippokleides, archon of the first Great Panathenaia in 566. Assuming, with Herodotus, three generations per century, the interval of twelve generations would locate Ajax, and the Trojan War, 400 years earlier, i.e., "966." Herodotus knew about the family traditions of Philaids (6.35.1). This doubly confirms that the place of Proteus and Helen in the list of pharaohs before Psammetichus is indeed based on Greek tradition, though it becomes problematical to assign it to a single "source," be it Hecataeus or the Philaids' genealogy. The conflict with Herodotus' other date, the location of Herakles "900 years before my time," remains all the more startling.

To come back to Eduard Meyer's theses: to make one generation forty years is empirical nonsense, and no such an interval appears in any Greek text on the ages of life.[40] Hellanicus counts thirty or thirty-three years for one generation (*FGrHist* 4 F 38ff., F 125), as does Herodotus. If the interval of forty years ever entered Greek chronography—and there is no doubt that Eratosthenes and Apollodorus adopted it—this must have been due to the conflict between different traditions: generations had to be stretched artificially in order to meet some other date. In other words, there was an authoritative early dating of Herakles and/or *Troika* which forced chronographers to extend genealogies to an average of forty years. Note that a more normal calculation of thirty years per generation would place Agias and Eurypon at the end of the eleventh century, instead of the twelfth, and that such a later date seems much more plausible today for the establishment of Dorian Sparta.[41]

Contrary to Eduard Meyer's thesis, then, the absolute dates given by Herodotus for Herakles and Pan, i.e., *Troika*, do not go back to Hecataeus and have nothing to do with Greek estimates of generations, either Spartan or Athenian. All Greek genealogies would lead to much lower dates. Yet the later elaborations on chronology presuppose an early date of Herakles and/or *Troika*, first met in Herodotus, and they unnaturally stretch Greek traditions to make them meet the point. What then was the basis for the disturbingly early date?

There remains the third group of Herodotean references, in the context of Lydian history. Eduard Meyer of course did not overlook this evidence, but thought he could dismiss it easily. These are reconstructions from a Greek point of view, he wrote (166)—of course the myth of Omphale is implied in the story of Lydian Heraklids[42]—and if Herodotus is wrong about the date for Gyges, how could his dates for Lydian Heraklids be historical? What Eduard Meyer the historian overlooked was that the question is not about historical fact, but about traditions Herodotus could use, and the message implied in these. Herodotus refers to a Lydian king-list,[43] which is not surprising; what is startling is that this king-list is made dependent on Ninos and Belos, that is, on Nineveh and the god of Nineveh, called by his title *Belu*, "Lord," in Assyrian. No doubt with such a god the genealogy would have reached its end, or rather its divine starting point.

If there is any sense in this—and reconstructed genealogies do make sense—it resides in the interrelations of Lydia and Assyria. Now these relations are directly attested in the annals of Assurbanipal: "Guggu king of Luddi, a province on the other side of the sea, a distant region, whose name the kings who went before me, my fathers, had not heard mentioned, Assur the god who created me, revealed the honored name of my majesty to him in a dream, saying: 'Lay hold of the feet of his highness, Assurbanipal' . . . On the (same) day that he saw this dream, he sent his couriers to me to ask my peace . . ."[44] To phrase things differently: Gyges, the new king, murderer of his predecessor, is anxious to achieve recognition by the Eastern superpower, using the diplomatic forms expected at Nineveh, including the tale of the king's dream.[45] Evidently it was in this situation that a genealogy made sense that traced Lydian kingship back to the earliest times of Nineveh: Lydian kingship is derived from Nineveh, even if this had been forgotten in preceding generations; the new king is renewing this dependency, he comes "to the feet of Assurbanipal"—and thus obtains legitimation of his usurpation.

As has often been noted, the statement of Herodotus as to 505 years of Heraklid kings in Lydia fits his other statement that the Assyrian empire lasted for 520 years (1.95).[46] The Assyrians were ousted by the Medes, these in turn by the Persians. Starting from "558" for the beginning of Cyrus' reign, the Median empire would have begun in "708," that of Ninos son of Bel in "1228." Lydian "history," starting from Gyges, resulted in a date "1221" for Agron son of Ninos; both dates evidently belong to the same construct.[47] This confirms the thesis that the reconstruction of pre-Gyges kingship in Lydia has been cast in terms of Assyrian Nineveh. We can hardly guess what prompted the epoch for the beginning of the Assyrian empire; the Assyrian king-list was much longer.[48] At any rate this is not an idea of Herodotus, and it made sense only in the seventh century, up to the destruction of Nineveh in 612. Of course the construct may well have been made in the Greek language, and by a Greek from the start; but the reference is not to Homer and Hesiod in this case, but to "Ninos."

A comparable genealogical construct seems to come to the surface right in Homer's *Iliad*.[49] Among Trojan allies the Lycians are prominent, led by Sarpedon and Glaukos. In a well-known passage (6.145ff.), this royal house is provided with a Greek origin: it is descended from Bellerophontes, hence from Ephyra and Argos. But Ephyra is also the home of Tlepolemos the Heraklid, the *oikistes* of Rhodes, who meets with Sarpedon and is killed in battle (5.632ff.; cf. 2.659ff.). This seems to reflect conflicts between Rhodes and the Lycians, when the Rhodians tried to appropriate their *Peraia* or territory on the mainland. The genealogies are fictitious, no doubt, but they make sense, linking to each other difficult partners who still had to come to terms. The invented Lycian genealogy may nearly be contemporary with the Lydian constructs of Gyges' epoch. Still such methods are not restricted to a single historical period. In the epoch of the Maccabees, Jews tried to reinforce their diplomatic relations with Sparta by producing a genealogy that made the Spartans descendants of Abraham.[50]

The genealogy of Lydian kings as presented by Herodotus still shows a second step of elaboration, an unforeseen extension: Belos, changing from god to human, is made a son of Alcaeus, grandson of Herakles. "Alcaeus" is one of the most obvious names for a son of Herakles, whose children were Alkaidai at Thebes, and who was said to have been called Alkeides himself.[51] If this reelaboration is again presumed to make sense, the reference is easy to find: derived from Herakles, Lydian kingship gains equal status with other Heraklid dynasties, the most prominent of which was that of Sparta. In fact it was Croesus, king of Lydia, who sought relations with the West—with Greece—and made a pact with Sparta (Hdt. 1.56ff., 1.70).[52] Once more we find an invented tradition that clearly antedates Herodotus and that makes sense only before the fall of Sardis. The Heraklid tradition still was not accepted throughout Lydian tradition;[53] it could also be turned against the house of Croesus (Hdt. 1.91; cf. 1.13.2).

To sum up: the information about kings of Lydia before Gyges as given by Herodotus must go back to Lydian, or Greco-Lydian, traditions of the seventh and sixth centuries. A king-list had been constructed in order to establish relations and equality of rank first with Assyria, then Sparta. The role of Greece is secondary; the first construction of the Lydian king-list should be associated with Gyges who turned to Assyria, while its expansion to include Greek ancestors only began with Croesus, who chose the West and met with catastrophe from the East.

Still it was this Lydian tradition, Lydian pseudo-history, that led to a date for Herakles accepted by Herodotus, "900 years before my time." This, not calculations about Spartan kings with impossible forty-year generations, gave rise to the presupposition of a very early date for Herakles, and for *Troika* in consequence. None of the Greek genealogies went back that far. "No authentic pedigree reached the Trojan War."[54] But those interested in chronography—Herodotus was not—probably were guided by the presumption that families may easily have "forgotten" some of their ancestors, hence the longest list was the most trustworthy one, and the earliest date all the more likely to be correct. Thus the longest of Greek genealogies, that of the Spartan kings, was chosen, then stretched beyond probability. If "40 years" was held to be the maximum possible, and if the Olympian era had been established in correlation to a Spartan king, the date of Eratosthenes would emerge as the most satisfactory conclusion.

The result is not surprising, but sobering: the Greeks knew nothing about the dates for either Herakles or *Troika*. The earliest indications, in Herodotus, show the widest divergence. Serious genealogies led back to the epoch of migrations, to the eleventh/tenth centuries. Beyond this there was a blank, in which the "heroes" as delineated in Homeric poetry could dwell at ease. This would overlap somehow with what we call the end of the Bronze Age. The precision of calculations should not disguise the fact that they were nothing but guesses: "910," "966," "1082," "1150," "1184," "1208," "1296," "1300," "1334"—that one or the other figure should agree with the actual destruction of Troy VI or VIIa is not "Rückerinnerung" but inescapable coincidence.

[Editor's note: See now P. James et al., *Centuries of Darkness* (London 1991) 326–334, and J. Vanschoonwinkel, *L'Égee et la Mediterranée Orientale à la fin du IIe millénaire* (Louvain 1991) 33–39.]

NOTES

* The following abbreviations have been used in this chapter:

Asheri = D. Asheri, "Il millennio di Troia," in *Saggi di Letteratura e Storiografia Antiche,* Biblioteca di Athenaeum 2 (Como 1983) 53–98.

How-Wells = W. W. How and J. Wells, *A Commentary on Herodotus* (Oxford 1928²).

Jacoby, *Apollodor* = F. Jacoby, *Apollodors Chronik* (Berlin 1902).

Lloyd = A. B. Lloyd, *Herodotus Book II,* vols. I, II, III (Leiden 1975, 1976, 1988).

Meyer = Eduard Meyer, "Herodots Chronologie der griechischen Sagengeschichte," in *Forschungen zur Alten Geschichte* I (1892) 151–209.

Mosshammer = A. A. Mosshammer, *The Chronicle of Eusebius and Greek Chronographic Tradition* (Lewisburg 1979).

Piérart = M. Piérart, "Les dates de la chute de Troie et de la fondation de Rome: Comput par génération ou compte à rebours?" in *Historia Testis. Mélanges d' épigraphie, d' histoire ancienne et de philologie offerts à T. Zawadzki* (Fribourg 1989) 1–20.

Schachermeyr = F. Schachermeyr, *Die griechische Rückerinnerung im Lichte neuer Forschungen* (*SBWien* 404, 1983).

Wade-Gery = H. T. Wade-Gery, *The Poet of the Iliad* (Cambridge 1952).

1. D. P. Henige, *The Chronology of Oral Tradition* (Oxford 1974); J. Vansina, *Oral Tradition as History* (London 1985); O. Murray, "Herodotus and Oral History," in H. Sancisi-Weerdenburg and A. Kuhrt, eds., *Achaemenid History II: The Greek Sources* (Leiden 1987) 93–115.

2. Cf. Pind. *Pyth.* 1.66.

3. Wade-Gery 8ff.; Schachermeyr 72ff.

4. *AR* 1982–1983, 12–15; M. R. Popham, "The Hero of Lefkandi," *Antiquity* 56 (1982) 169–176; P. Blome, "Lefkandi und Homer," *WürzJbb* 10 (1984) 9–22. See now: M. R. Popham, P. G. Calligas, and L. H. Sackett, *Lefkandi II: The Protogeometric Building at Toumba* Parts I and II (Oxford 1990, 1993).

5. F. H. Stubbings, "The Eclipse of Thebes," *CAH*³ II.2, 165–169: 169, "The Sack of Thebes may be regarded as one of the certain events of Mycenaean history." "The Trojan War," 342–350: 350 on the destruction of Troy VIIa, "there can be no reasonable doubt that this was the event which has echoed through the world's literature ever since."

6. Schachermeyr 78–81, refering to the Marmor Parium, which mentions the Trojan War and Teucrus in immediate succession.

7. E. F. Bloedow, "The Trojan War and Late Helladic IIIC," *PZ* 63 (1988) 23–52. In order to salvage the Trojan War he suggests that fighting happened outside the walls, without ensuing destruction of the city, whereas G. S. Kirk, *The Iliad: A Commentary* II (Cambridge 1990) 41–50, comes back to the idea that Troy VI should be the "Homeric" city: the earthquake that destroyed it "opened up the city to attack," a happy coincidence for the Achaians.

8. Doubts against an historical "Trojan War" had been raised especially by M. I. Finley, "The Trojan War," *JHS* 84 (1964) 1–9; "Schliemann's Troy: One Hundred Years After," *ProcBritAc* 60 (1974) 393–412, see also J. Cobet, "Gab es einen Troianischen Krieg?" *AntW* 14:4 (1983) 39–58.

9. The bon mot is due to M. Miller, "Herodotus as a chronographer," *Klio* 46 (1965) 109, quoted by Mosshammer 107. One pitfall in calculating generations is the ambiguity of inclusive versus exclusive reckoning: normally the interval between two generations will be just one generation, and "thirteen generations" are twelve generations apart.

10. Basic was the 1892 study of Eduard Meyer (see Meyer); cf. How-Wells 437–442; H. Strasburger, "Herodots Zeitrechnung," *Historia* 5 (1956) 126–161, and idem, "Berichtigte und erweiterte Fassung" in W. Marg, ed., *Herodot. Eine Auswahl aus der neueren Forschung* (Darmstadt 1982³) 688–736, crediting Herodotus with "eine Gründertat hohen Ranges," was too benevolent; see further W. den Boer, "Herodot und die Systeme der Chronologie," *Mnemosyne* 20 (1967) 30–60; K. v. Fritz, *Die griechische Geschichtsschreibung* I (Berlin 1967) 364–406; R. Drews, "The Fall of Astyages and Herodotus' Chronology of the Early Kingdoms," *Historia* 18 (1969) 1–11; Lloyd I 171–194.

11. Th. Jacobsen, *The Sumerian King List* (Chicago 1939); ANET 265–266.

12. See *RAss* 6, s.v. Königslisten; *ANET* 271ff.; E. Reiner, *Neues Handbuch der Literaturgeschichte 1: Altorientalische Literaturen* (Wiesbaden 1978) 158; *ANET* 271–272.

13. Edited and translated by C. J. Gadd, "The Harran inscriptions of Nabonidus," *AnatStud* 8 (1958) 46–56.

14. How-Wells I 375 (Lydians), 383 (Medes), 424 (Egyptians); Persian kings: Hdt. 1.214.3, 3.66.2, 3.67.2, 7.4, 7.7, 7.20.1.

15. Lloyd I 189–194; cf. F. K. Kienitz, *Die politische Geschichte Ägyptens vom 7. bis zum 4. Jh.* (Berlin 1953).

16. For a very critical approach to Herodotus' reliability, see D. Fehling, *Herodotus and his "Sources"* (Leeds 1989; German ed. Berlin 1971).

17. For some important cuneiform sources see How-Wells I 385ff.; dating by years of Kambyses and Darius: Ptol., *Synt.* 4.9, 5.14.

18. Infra n. 44; H. Kaletsch, "Zur lydischen Chronologie," *Historia* 7 (1958) 1–41; C. Talamo, *La Lidia arcaica* (Bologna 1979).

19. Hdt. 2.143–145, printed by Jacoby as Hecataeus *FGrHist* 1 F 300; I would rather think the text belonged to the *Genealogiai*. See Lloyd III 107–110; H. Diels, "Herodot und Hekataios," *Hermes* 22 (1887) 411–444 = *Kleine Schriften zur Geschichte der antiken Philosophie* (Darmstadt 1969) 93–126.

20. On the apparent miscalculation see Mosshammer 108.

21. See H. Herter *RE* XXIII.951–955.

22. The date for Dionysus is conjectural, the manuscripts have (with variants) "1600 years." Pan son of Penelope can hardly be separated from the tradition that Penelope copulated with "all" the suitors to produce a monster ("neoteroi," i.e., cyclic epic in schol. Opp.*Hal.* 3.15); Herodotus nevertheless makes Hermes the father of Pan, cf. Pind. *Fr.* 100. For mythological connections of Penelope and Arcadia see E. Wüst, *RE* XIX 463–465, 479.

23. 1.130.1 (with an error in calculation, cf. D. Asheri, *Erodoto, Le Storie* I [Milano 1988] ad loc.).

24. Pind. *Pyth.* 4.10 ff., 65; cf. Hdt. 4.154ff.; *RE* XII 160ff. See also Synesius *Catast.* 303 A (p. 291 Terzaghi), about Cyrenian genealogies: "The public records contain the sequence of generations from Herakles down to my time," αἱ δημόσιαι κύρβεις μέχρις ἐμοῦ κατάγουσι τὰς ἀφ' Ἡρακλέους διαδοχάς.

25. His date for the fall of Troy is unknown, see Jacoby on *FGrHist* 4 F 152.

26. Jacoby, *Apollodor* 290–295, who thinks Apollodorus did not know which era Democritus meant.

27. The "eighty years" in Thucydides were taken by Meyer to confirm the forty-years principle; but they primarily refer to Boeotian, not to Spartan, tradition. See also G. L. Huxley, "Thucydides and the date of the Trojan War," *PP* 12 (1957) 209–212. According to the tradition of Tegea (Hdt. 9.26.4ff.), the conquest of the Peloponnese occurred 100 years after the death of Hyllos. Still other intervals between *Troika* and *Kathodos*—120 or 180 years—in Clem. *Strom.* 1.139.3.

28. Zietschmann *RE* XV 581.

29. According to Konon, *FGrHist* 26 F 1.36.2, Melos was colonized three generations after the Return of the Heraklids; hence "return" "1216," *halosis* "1296"? See also Plut. *Mul. Virt.* 8. 247d, who combines the settlements at Melos and at Lyktos. Isokrates 6.12 (cf. 8.95) refers to "700 years" of Sparta's glory down to the battle at Leuktra in 371; hence "return" in "1071"?

30. Other calculations: "Return" "715 years" before Alexander, i.e., "1049": Phainias Fr.19 Wehrli; "820 years," i.e., "1154": Kleitarchos, *FGrHist* 137 F 7; Timaeus, *FGrHist* 566 F 126, is quoted for the same opinion, but according to F 125 Timaeus made the *Troika* precede the first Olympiad by 417 years, i.e., "1193," whereas F 80 puts the colonization of Kerkyra 600 years after the *Troika*, which would thus be shifted to "1334"; the text is considered corrupt by Jacoby; cf. Asheri 56–60, and 60–62 on Ephorus.

31. Disk of Iphitos, Arist. *Fr.* 533, Rose = 541 Gigon. *Troika* and Olympiads are also correlated in Timaeus *FGrHist* 566 F 125.

32. See Asheri 67–77; see now D. Hughes, *Human Sacrifice in Ancient Greece* (London and New York 1991) 166–184. An inscription from Dodona, end of fourth cent.?, has "1000 years after Kassandra," Asheri 77. Pliny, *HN* 30.3 dates Zoroaster 6,000 years before Plato's death, and Zoroaster's teacher 5,000 years before the *Troika,* which would make the distance between *Troika* and Plato 1,000 years (*Troika* "1377"?).

33. On Schachermeyr see n. 6; Jacoby thinks the author

reckoned thirteen generations before Pind. *Ol.*1; cf. Piérart 1–11.

34. There is a difference of one year, see Jacoby, *Apollodor* 76–79.

35. See also Plut. *Lyc.* 1.3; Tzetz. *Exeg. in Iliadem* p.18.14 Hermann (from Diodorus). On the Spartan king-lists see also E. Schwartz, "Die Königslisten des Eratosthenes und Kastor," *AbhGött* 40 (1894) 60–72; J. Beloch, *Griechische Geschichte* I.2² (Strassburg 1913) 171–191; P. Carlier, *La royauté en Grèce avant Alexandre* (Strasbourg 1984) 316–317; D. Musti, *Storia greca* (Bari 1989) 143.

36. Wade-Gery 90ff.: "I have no doubt," cf. 28; Schachermeyr 71; Asheri 58; but see How-Wells I 440: "It is possible, however, that the '900 years' for Heracles is based on calculations from Oriental and not from Greek families." Mosshammer 109: ". . . may have been quite independent from the Heraclid genealogy."

37. Wade-Gery 88 starts from an epoch "500" for Leonidas and correctly arrives at "1300" for Heracles; Schachermeyr 76 counts twenty-one generations, thus arriving from "500" (Leonidas) at "1330" (Herakles)—but the distance from first to twenty-first generation is twenty, not twenty-one.

38. One should consider the possibility that the original version of Hecataeus F 300 served as a conversion story: the prophet is confuted only to arrive at a new truth; the Egyptian experience proved "the *logoi* of the Hellenes" wrong, and Hecataeus was to tell them what had really happened. But this would not eliminate Helen nor Proteus, although it could make the latter a king instead of a *daimon* (cf. F 27).

39. Cf. J. Toepffer, *Attische Genealogie* (Berlin 1889) 278ff.; Wade-Gery 88. Heropythos (fifth century) lists fourteen ancestors (up to the Ionian migration?).

40. F. Boll, "Die Lebensalter," in *Kleine Schriften zur Sternkunde des Altertums* (Leipzig 1950) 156–224. For the "forty years" genealogies, nothing better has been adduced than Hdt. 1.163.2; cf. 3.23.1: fantastic cases of men living up to 120 years in contrast to eighty, as normal men do.

41. On the problem of the "Dorian Migration," see D. Musti, ed., *Le origini dei greci: Dori e mondo egeo* (Rome 1985). Foundation of Sparta about 950: W. G. Forrest, *A History of Sparta* (1968; 2nd ed. 1980); by calculating generations of thirty years, he puts Agias and Eurypon about 900 (1968, 20ff.); cf. P. Cartledge, *Sparta and Laconia. A Regional History 1300–362* (London 1979) 92–93; "before 1000": O. Murray, *Early Greece* (Stanford 1980) 155.

42. Iardanos: Hdt. 1.7.4, cf. L. Preller and C. Robert, *Griechische Heldensage* II.2 (Berlin 1920) 589–594; Pherekydes,

FGrHist 3 F 82; Soph. *Trach.* 69ff., 248–257; U. v. Wilamowitz-Moellendorff, *Euripides Herakles* I (Berlin 1895², vol. II; reprint Darmstadt 1959) 71–78, in order to get rid of the "orientalisierende Tendenz" (71), made Omphale a Greek and attributed the Lydian localization to Kreophylos' *Oichalias Halosis*—an old source indeed. Preller and Robert 594, following Wilamowitz and E. Meyer, *Geschichte des Altertums* I.2 (Stuttgart 1913³) 730, think the effeminate role of Heracles in relation to Queen Omphale was invented only in the Hellenistic age; but the stereotype of "effeminate" Oriental kings appears earlier, with Sardanapallos and Midas (Klearchos Fr. 43 Wehrli).

43. The position of Meles in this list is not clear, Hdt. 1.84.3, cf. K. v. Fritz *RE* Suppl. IX s.v. Meles appears as a son of Herakles (schol. T *Iliad* 18.219), but in Euseb. *Chron.* he is the immediate predecessor of Kandaules.

44. D. D. Luckenbill, *Ancient Records of Assyria* (Chicago 1927) II 352 #909ff., cf. 326 #849; M. Streck, *Assurbanipal* (Leipzig 1916) 21, *Annalen* II 95ff. On the varying subsequent redactions of Assurbanipal's *Annals*, see M. Cogan and H. Tadmor, "Gyges and Ashurbanipal," *Orientalia* 46 (1977) 65–85. Lydians and "Babylon" also have relations in Nikolaos of Damascus, *FGrHist* 90 F 45.

45. Cf. A. L. Oppenheim, *The Interpretation of Dreams in the Ancient Near East,* TAPS 46:3 (Philadelphia 1956) 202, 249.

46. See Asheri in his commentary (supra n. 23) ad loc.

47. The calculation cannot be made with Herodotean dates alone, since Herodotus does not say in which year of his reign Cyrus conquered Sardis, which would give the correlation of Assyrian/Persian and Lydian dates; "546" has been used here.

48. The Assyrian empire begins with Tukulti-Ninurta I (1243–1221), but Tukulti-Ninurta II (889–884) made Nineveh the capital (see *RAss* I 268; 274).

49. This was pointed out to me by Peter Frei; on Tleptolemos cf. Hes. Fr. 232, Pind. *Ol.* 7.20, Pherekydes, *FGrHist* 3 F 2.

50. *I Makk.*12, 1–23, followed by Joseph. *Ant.*12.4, 10 #226; 13.5, 8 #167.

51. Schol. Pind. *Isthm.* 4.104g, 110a; Apollod. *Bibl.* 2.73; Diod. 1.24.4, etc.

52. The Macedonian Argeadai too were made Heraklids before Herodotus: Hdt. 8.137.1; Thuc. 2.99.3; 5.80.2.

53. Jacoby, following Meyer, thinks that Xanthos did not have Heraklid kings of Lydia; in Nikolaos of Damascus, Heraklids are introduced in an obviously secondary way.

54. Wade-Gery 88.

10

WAR STORY INTO WRATH STORY*

◆

MABEL L. LANG

It is obvious that the *Iliad*, despite its concentration on Achilles' wrath and its consequences, does in various ways cover most aspects of the whole Trojan War. Everything from the expedition's launching at Aulis to the death of Achilles and the destruction of Troy is included in what purports to be the narrative of some forty days in the war's tenth year. And in between, many other situations and events, more relevant to the first and middle years of the war than to the tale of Achilles' wrath, are included in the *Iliad*'s narrative. Some of these even seem incongruous, countering as they do Zeus' stated promise to give power to the Trojans until the Achaians pay honor to Achilles: throughout Books 3–7 (and to a large extent in Books 10–14) not only are the Trojans clear underdogs with a far greater number of casualties than the Achaians but also the Achaians enjoy far more effective divine help than do the Trojans.

Any attempt to explain this inconcinnity necessarily involves speculation about varying traditions known and used by bards up to and including Homer as they orally created and recreated in varying combinations and recombinations their repertory of songs. Of course one chief source of those traditions will be the various

incongruities in the *Iliad* itself, which also provides at least three facts about its own poetic prehistory.

(1) The pre-Homeric story of the Trojan War was so familiar to Homer's audience that he could in his first book assume knowledge not only of its object (unnamed except as "the city of Priam") but also of all the chief heroes (only Kalchas and Nestor are formally introduced, the former in order to give authority to his prophecy, the latter as generationally out-of-place).

(2) At least one early and highly influential account of the Trojan War began at the beginning and included at the outset of the Achaian expedition a Catalogue of Ships which was so respected that, when the *Ur-Iliad* bards incorporated it in their account of events in the tenth year of the war, they brought it up to date, as it were, not by omitting leaders of contingents not currently active in the fighting, but by leaving them in place and adding notes about their substitutes, if any. It almost goes without saying that any account of the war which began at the beginning with the sailing of the expeditionary force would have gone on in chronicle form and ended with the war's end. Moreover, such a simple linear narrative of the war's events seems to provide the

most likely raw material out of which the admittedly complex and organic structure of the wrath story could have been fashioned.

(3) And that such a preexisting chronicle ended with an Achaian victory is made clear in the *Iliad* not only by Zeus' prediction (15.69–71) of that victory and the sack of Troy but also by the comparative casualty figures of Achaians and Trojans: in that part of the poem which purportedly concerns Achaian defeat (Books 3– 17) only fifty-two Achaians are killed to 162 Trojans (Achilles later kills twenty-four more Trojans).

In addition, the Trojan War has always seemed to be the last great event of the heroic age because many of the chief Achaians in the *Iliad* are sons or grandsons of heroes active in what must therefore have been earlier endeavors (Voyage of the Argo, Kalydonian Boar Hunt, Battle of Lapiths and Centaurs, Seven against Thebes, Herakles cycle). But there is a very real distinction between such sons or grandsons (like Achilles or Diomedes) and the Atreidai, without whom the war would quite literally not have taken place, but whose forbears have no part in those myth-cycles of northern and central Greece. That is, there is a good chance: (1) that there was in the Peloponnese a tradition about a Mycenaean-sponsored Trojan War which involved only the Atreidai and other heroes who, like them, had no such other connections; (2) that when the Mycenaeans took over political power and influence from northern and central Greece they took over as well the heroes and "history" that gave authority to that power; (3) that it was thus that later bards and poets had available those "Minyan" heroes' sons and grandsons to recruit and add luster to Mycenae's own great endeavor.

Whether this particular speculation has any basis or not,[1] the possibility that some of the *Iliad*'s Achaian heroes may have been borrowed from other circumstances is suggested not only by the *Iliad*-attested victory of Diomedes and Sthenelos at Thebes (4.406) but also by the particular role of Achilles in the *Iliad*. For it seems fair to say that the Achilles of the *Iliad* is unique and could never, as such, have played any other role in the Trojan War story; his superiority as a warrior would not only have cast everyone else in the shade but also have meant immediate Achaian victory unless he spent all of his time raiding the neighborhood (as Homer has had to make him do to explain how, with such a champion, the

war has reached its tenth year). But his presence in the Trojan War chronicle's unannotated Catalogue of Ships suggests that an Achilles of some sort along with other Thessalian heroes had already been recruited for the Achaian force. At first his part in the war must have been little more than such as the present *Iliad* gives to Eumelos, another Thessalian hero, whose only appearance outside the Catalogue of Ships is in the funeral games for Patroklos. For Achilles' absence from all of the general fighting combined with the complete absence of other Achaians fighting alongside Achilles when he is on the battlefield makes it likely that the tradition provided nothing for Achilles comparable to the interaction and cooperation among Achaian heroes like Odysseus, Diomedes, Idomeneus, Meriones, and the Aiante.

It looks, therefore, as if it was only sometime after Achilles had been brought into the Troy story that as a man of wrath he assumed his *Iliad* role of withdrawal and return. It may be that he had already played that part in other circumstances and in local lays. Or it may be that his local reputation of outstanding prowess unfitted him for any merely cooperative role, in which case the only way so outstanding a hero could be used without taking over the war completely was as a champion who was more absent than present on the battlefield and whose great achievement entailed his death before the final victory, since always, even in the *Aithiopis*, he was absent from the general fighting.

The question then arises whether such a role could have been fitted into the chronicle-type version of the Trojan War that is presumed to have preceded the *Ur-Iliad*. Would not any insertion of that sort have involved such unusual concentration not only on the hero and his motivation for withdrawal but also on the Achaian defeat following his withdrawal that as a result the "episode" would overbalance the narrative and force the inversion of chronicle into epic? This must be so, and it must have been the effort to bring Achilles' wrath story into the Trojan War chronicle that resulted first in experimentation, then in the discovery of the tail-wagging-the-dog phenomenon, and finally in the inspiration to turn the whole thing inside out and enclose the Trojan War in the wrath story, with the *Ur-Iliad* as the result.

It was during this process of transmutation that the bards (or bard?) were faced with the challenge of how to preserve the best of both tales and how to use all the material that contributed to an Achaian victory in a story which required Achaian suffering and defeat. It seems that one solution, which may have been attempted earlier but certainly culminated in the *Iliad*, was to intermingle the tales by means of various kinds of reverberation, echo, and reflection. So, just as the war tale may always have been launched by introducing the cause of conflict between two peoples, so the wrath tale could take its beginnings from a cause of conflict between two men. And if the carrying-off of a woman had served the one purpose, why should it not serve the other? So if the Achaians' expedition against Troy had been motivated by the Trojans' rape of their woman, why should not Achilles' withdrawal from battle be motivated by the "rape" of his woman by someone who would have to suffer from his withdrawal as the Trojans were to suffer from the Achaian expedition? A very neat reversal, with the raping enemy suffering from invasion and the raping ally suffering from desertion. All that was then necessary was a motive for Agamemnon to take Achilles' woman. And here again the Trojan War story could be useful: if a divinity caused Paris to carry off Helen, why should it not be a divinity who caused Agamemnon to carry off Briseis? So Homer starts his tale with "What god was it then set them together in bitter collision?" And the answer is that it was Apollo, whose plague caused the confrontation; but it was Achilles' assumption of authority that provoked Agamemnon's demand for recompense against him and the taking of Briseis. Thus the human responsibility that contributed to Achilles' fate in the wrath story is counterpointed against the divinely directed defeat of the Trojans in the war story.[2]

In Book 1 of the *Iliad*[3] the beginning of the wrath story echoes the beginning of the war story with a reverberation of causes for the conflict to come. The rest of Book 1 completes the launching of the wrath story in three ways: first, by characterizing the two quarreling heroes as the two opposing armies will be characterized for the war story in the Catalogues of Book 2; second, by describing Achilles' withdrawal and his request of Thetis that Zeus assure its effectiveness, the one resonating with the Achaians' (abortive) withdrawal in Book 2 and the other with assurance from Zeus of the expedition's tenth-year success (2.319–325); and third, by mirroring the human conflict in a divine contest of wills between Zeus and Hera, who will continue to play

important roles in the ongoing course of both the war and the wrath.

On the assumption that the war story was being enclosed and framed by the wrath story, it was necessary in what was to become Book 2 of the *Iliad* to start the face-off between Achaians and Trojans in a way that would serve both as the first beginning of the war and as its renewal after the plague and withdrawal of Achilles. How was that done? In the first place, it should be noted that the false dream in no way fulfills Zeus' promise to Thetis but simply motivates the beginning of battle between Achaians and Trojans. Furthermore, as a dream promising victory, it is simply a renewal of the promise that had been made at the beginning of the war which is now remembered in three different ways: (1) Agamemnon finds the early promise proven false as he acts on the present dream as false (2.111–115); (2) Kalchas interprets the omen foretelling a tenth-year victory (2.326–329); (3) Nestor remembers lightning on the right as a sign of Zeus' favor (2.350–353). It is only in its function as a renewal of this prewar promise that the dream's promise has to be called false and used as such by Agamemnon to test the troops. That is, only if the poet was trying to review the war's beginning was it necessary for the dream to be acted on as false. And it is the testing of the troops on the grounds of the assumed falseness of both the original promise and the dream that evokes the move to go home, thereby making possible the new beginning that will echo and repeat the first beginning.

As an action in and of itself the testing of the troops is troublesome, but if it is seen both as an echo of Agamemnon's "testing" Achilles, resulting in his refusal to fight, and as a way to present the renewal of the war as an echo of its beginning, it not only makes sense but makes possible a reverberation with the wrath story and a partial reenactment of the war's beginning. By allowing the troops to give up the war and return home Agamemnon prepares the way, as it were, for a new mobilization and a new beginning. Thersites is made to give voice to the popular discontent that motivated the rush to the ships; at the same time his ranting against Agamemnon and demand for withdrawal echo more blatantly Achilles' charges and wrathful refusal to continue fighting. So exaggerated, however, is Thersites' expression of the general dissatisfaction that, unlike Achilles, he can be discredited, and the troops can be persuaded to disown him and regain their eagerness to see the war to a victorious conclusion. Odysseus accomplishes this both by ridicule as brutal as Thersites' own attack on Agamemnon and by a detailed reminder and replay of the expedition's mobilization at Aulis, complete with initiatory sacrifice and nine-bird omen. That reenactment of the expedition's beginnings is then supplemented and substantiated by the listing of the complete Catalogue of Ships, which is introduced as if to remarshal the troops after their withdrawal and return.[4]

So far, then, Book 2 combines both the first- and tenth-year beginnings by recounting the renewal in terms of the original beginning, and so allowing the war story here both to encompass and echo the wrath story. Or, to put it differently, just as in Book 1 there is resonance in the carrying-off of women as the cause of both the war and the wrath, so here in Book 2 the renewed beginning of the war involves not only an echo and replay of the original beginning but also a thwarted withdrawal counterpointing the wrath story's actual withdrawal in Book 1.

In Books 3–7 there are occasional reminders of Achilles and his absence from the fighting (4.512; 5.788; 6.99, 414, 423; 7.113, 228), but both on the battlefield and in Troy the Achaians are seen to be carrying all before them, and the *Dios boule* by which they are to suffer defeat in Achilles' absence is definitely in abeyance. The narrative in these books might therefore seem to have been taken without any change from some Trojan War story in chronicle form. But closer examination suggests that the events in these books were designed to provide for the wrath story a war context that would be both frame and portending parallel. Thus although the wrath story acts as vehicle to frame and intensify the war story, it is itself framed by the war story. This frame-within-a-frame arrangement emphasizes the two stories' interconnections.

We look first to Book 3 to determine the nature of this context that both frames and brings into focus the wrath story. The action in Book 3 goes backward and forward at the same time: with the introduction of Paris it both goes backward from the gathering of the ships in Book 2 to Paris as the cause of the war and goes forward to the duel of Paris and Menelaos as the appropriate

opening of hostilities. The book begins with Paris' bold challenge to the Achaians, replaying implicitly the challenge of the rape that had brought the Achaians against Troy. Then when he falters at the approach of Menelaos, who had not been there when he carried Helen off, Hektor reproaches him, with explicit reference to the rape. The duel is thus motivated as a personal conflict imaging the war that was brought about by the rape. Forward action thus seems to arise directly from the past, which is further echoed later in the book when Aphrodite carries Paris off the battlefield just as she had piloted him to Greece and again delivers Helen to his bed.

At the same time, because the war story has been embedded in the wrath story, Paris' rape as the cause of the war is seen to be parallel to Agamemnon's "rape" of Briseis and the cause of the wrath. That is, the actual duel of Paris and Menelaos in Book 3 is a mirror image of the verbal conflict between Agamemnon and Achilles in Book 1: Paris' rape led to the physical conflict; verbal conflict led to Agamemnon's "rape." In both cases the aggressor is saved from death by a goddess, again in counterpoint: Aphrodite's bodily removal of Paris reflects the physical and straightforward nature of the war story; Athena's restraint of Achilles points up the wrath story's psychological complications of character and custom. And in both cases a fatal personal confrontation is short-circuited by divine intervention and escalated into public strife.

Despite its apparent concern with beginnings, Book 3 also emphasizes the extent of the long war's toils and sufferings (98–100, 125–128, 156–157, 164–165). This may, of course, be simply war-story rhetoric, but in view of the way in which Book 3's evocation of the war's cause and beginning looks back to Book 1's beginning and cause of the wrath, it may be that these effects of the war serve to foreshadow the dire effects of the wrath. Whether such unremitting reverberation between wrath story and war story is to be expected will only become clear as our examination progresses.

The *Teichoskopia* may well be a traditional war-story episode but its introduction here in Book 3 provides necessary background for the role of Troy and the Trojans in the wrath story. Zeus must use the Trojans to grant Achilles' plea; and the resolution of the wrath will come only through the death of their champion. Achilles will choose his own fate, and that choice, seen in the context of the god-contrived doom of Hektor and of Troy, needs such Trojan background as the *Teichoskopia* introduces and Books 4–7 will continue.

In Book 4, after the duel of Paris and Menelaos has been interrupted, there still has to be a beginning of general fighting, whether as of the war's first year or as of the renewal in the tenth year. Here again, as in the rape, it is by divine direction that, as both Hera and Zeus say, "the Trojans are first-offenders" (4.66). And because effects are immanent in causes and ends in beginnings, this renewal of Trojan guilt brings with it the certainty of eventual Trojan defeat. Agamemnon speaks (4.164–168):

> There will come a day when sacred Ilion shall perish,
> and Priam, and the people of Priam of the strong ash
> spear,
> and Zeus son of Kronos who sits on high, the sky-
> dwelling,
> himself shall shake the gloom of his aegis over all of them
> in anger for this deception.

And so the gods arrange that the beginning of fighting, like the cause of the war itself, should hold the seeds of the war's end and the Trojan defeat. Book 4 ties this beginning back to Book 3 and the cause of the war with a divinely directed Trojan act of hostility against the Achaian Menelaos (once again!), thereby breaking the truce, putting the Trojans in the wrong, and justifying the fall of Troy.

This adding of injury to insult to Menelaos is necessary to start up the general fighting, but the substitution of Pandaros for Paris as the agent needs closer examination. Note in particular its similarity to the substitution of Patroklos for Achilles. In both these very different situations the heroes, Paris and Achilles, are out of action, and yet something must be done: in the one case the truce must be broken so that fighting can begin; in the other the Trojans must be pushed back to give the Achaians relief. Both substitutes are urged to act: Pandaros by Laodokos (Athena); Patroklos by Nestor. Both are appropriate stand-ins: Pandaros is a bowman like Paris; Patroklos is Achilles' *alter ego* and wears his armor. Both fight gallantly with an important enemy:

Pandaros only wounds Diomedes while Patroklos kills Sarpedon, but that is to be expected in a war where the Trojan casualty rate is more than thrice that of the Achaians. Both substitutes are killed only with the aid of a divinity: in Pandaros' case, "Pallas Athena guided the weapon / to the nose next to the eye, and it cut through the white teeth" (5.290–292); Apollo disarmed Patroklos before Euphorbos and Hektor finished him off (16.791–804).

Surely Paris himself, as the cause of Troy's troubles, was the appropriate breaker of the truce, but if the traitor had to die to herald the defeat of the Trojans while Paris must survive to oppose the return of Helen (7.355–362),[5] Pandaros' role as substitute must all along have belonged to the war story. Its continued use here in the wrath story's buildup of the war might be thought merely to parallel and presage Patroklos' substitute role. But it may rather be that this substitution actually inspired the use of Patroklos as a substitute for Achilles, so that his death might turn Achilles' wrath against a legitimate object and make possible his entry into battle without loss of face. But whether or not there was any connection of this sort between the Trojan and Achaian substitutes, their parallelism shows once again how the war story supports and anticipates the wrath story which frames it.

The characterization of Agamemnon in the war scene of Book 4 echoes and confirms that of the wrath story in Book 1. His fear for his brother's life, that Menelaos, like Chryseis, might be taken from him, leads him to bluster and find fault with the various heroes he seeks out. Their responses serve not only to characterize both him and themselves but as commentary, by parallel and contrast, on Achilles' reaction to Agamemnon's bullying in Book 1. Where Achilles took offense and withdrew in high dudgeon, these responses to their leader's challenge suggest how differently other heroes might have managed to defuse that Book 1 confrontation: Odysseus tells him not to be silly; Sthenelos reminds him of the record; and Diomedes kindly makes allowances for him. Wrath story and war story complement each other.

After Book 4 the enforced absence of the indispensable hero required by the wrath story provides a logical opportunity for the inclusion of much war-story material which may at the same time prepare in various ways for the hero's return. Least immediately important, apparently, if we may judge from the narrative in Books 5–7, is any desperate need for that return. More important, again apparently, is a buildup to that return through a kind of prefiguration of the indispensable hero and the magnification of his eventual opponent. That the prefiguration takes the form of Diomedes, an established hero of an earlier generation, is perhaps not unexpected. For if in the forward progression of Books 2–4 there is a reaching backward to the war's causes so that the present is endorsed by the past, Book 5's full-scale fighting properly harks back even before the war's beginning to its "historical" context, the saga of Thebes, to find an appropriate substitute for the absent hero. Perhaps this was triggered, after a fashion, by Agamemnon's reproach to Diomedes in Book 4 that he was not the man his father was as one of the Seven against Thebes.

What is obvious is the extent to which Diomedes is different from the other chief Achaian heroes before Troy: he alone has a previous war record; he alone fights with divinities and wounds them; he alone fits awkwardly in the Catalogue's Argolid, and he is both most like Achilles in various ways and least associated with him. It is possible therefore to make a case for his having been brought into the wrath story from some tradition of his exploits at Thebes not only to serve as chief champion (a role only rarely granted to Menelaos and Agamemnon), particularly in Book 5, but also to preview Achilles' prowess and ascendancy on his return.[6]

How is Diomedes most like Achilles? Other men pray to Athena, but only Diomedes (5.815) and Achilles (1.201; 22.224) acknowledge the goddess' presence and speak directly to her. Other men are helped by her in more or less routine fashion,[7] but for Achilles and Diomedes she takes action in person and is liberal with help and encouragement, in fairy-godmother style. To both she gives advice: to Achilles not to kill Agamemnon (1.197–221); to Diomedes not to fight with divinities other than Aphrodite (5.129–132), and to leave off killing Thracians and return to the ships (10.507–512). To both she gives physical support: she feeds Achilles "intrastethosly" when he is too impatient to eat (19.349–354) and gives him great strength (21.304); she answers Diomedes' prayer for help when

he is wounded (5.115–126) and gives him speed to run down Dolon (10.366). She encourages both and helps both in the fighting: she turns Hektor's spear back from Achilles (20.438–440), urges him to catch his breath while she goes to impersonate Deiphobos and persuade Hektor to fight (22.215–227), and returns his spear to him (22.276); she encourages Diomedes, teasing him about not being a fighter like his father and, when he answers rather pertly that he was just following her orders, she allows him to go even against Ares and joins him as his charioteer to help in wounding the god (5.799–859). Both heroes are confident of her help: Achilles knows that she will deliver Hektor to his spear (22.270–271); Diomedes knows that she will not let him flee before Pandaros and Aeneas (5.256).

Diomedes is like Achilles in his independence and lack of reverence for authority. Achilles' readiness (1.54–171; 9.314–426; 19.199–208) to hold Agamemnon's leadership of little account and take command himself finds echoes in Diomedes' strenuous objections (9.32–49; 14.110–132) when Agamemnon again proposes abandoning the war. When the Trojan herald Idaios proposes to Agamemnon the only terms that Paris is willing to grant, it is Diomedes who takes the lead in voicing the rejection that Agamemnon then tamely reports to Idaios (7.381–411). And again after the failure of the embassy to Achilles it is Diomedes who both finds fault with Agamemnon's supplication as only adding fuel to the wrath and urges a better course of action (9.696–709).

Not only in their relations with Athena and Agamemnon are Achilles and Diomedes alike, but the roles they play in the fighting are often more significantly similar than is the case in ordinary thematic repetition. Both have important contests with Aeneas, the Trojan hero second in importance;[8] and these seem to serve as dress rehearsals for their later meetings with Hektor. Although different in circumstance and buildup, the two contests (5.166–317; 20.70–339) do involve, in different combinations, terrible yelling, throwing a huge stone, and Aeneas being saved by a divinity, with the implication that both Diomedes and Achilles are humanly invincible.

Aside from Ajax, who is allotted to accept Hektor's challenge to a duel in Book 7 and who leads the defense at the wall against Hektor in Books 13–16, Diomedes and Achilles alone among the Achaians take serious offensive action against Hektor (11.338–367; 20.419–454) before the final duel to the death. To be sure, Teukros twice (8.300–302; 15.458–465) aims an arrow at Hektor but misses, and Idomeneus throws an ineffective spear at him (17.605–607). But generally Achaian heroes retreat before Hektor: Odysseus, when summoned to help Nestor against Hektor, rushes past to the ships (8.92–98); Antilochos runs away (15.582–590); Menelaos backs off reluctantly (17.87–112); Patroklos only tussles with Hektor over the body of Kebriones (16.759–764). Although Diomedes may urge retreat (5.590–606) when Ares is seen to accompany Hektor, in Book 8 (87–136) as he goes alone to the help of Nestor against Hektor he can be stopped only by a thunderbolt from Zeus.

In Book 11 (338–367) Diomedes' encounter with Hektor closely parallels that of Achilles in Book 20 (419–454): in both cases Hektor, seeing a fellow Trojan slain by the Achaian hero, turns to attack him. That Achilles, whose aim is to avenge Patroklos' death, welcomes the meeting is natural:

> Here is the man who beyond all others has troubled my
> anger,
> who slaughtered my beloved companion. Let us no longer
> shrink away from each other along the edgeworks of
> battle.
>
> 20.425–427

With less reason Diomedes makes a similar comment:

> Here is this curse, Hektor the huge, wheeling down
> upon us.
> Let us stand, and hold our ground against him, and beat
> him off from us.
>
> 11.347–348

Diomedes attacks immediately, but an exchange of insults appropriately marks the more significant meeting of Achilles and Hektor. Only the helmet given him by Apollo saves Hektor from the spear cast by Diomedes; Apollo himself rescues Hektor from Achilles' furious charge, wrapping him in a mist. And in their frustration both Achilles and Diomedes make the same speech:

> Once again now you escaped death, dog. And yet the evil
> came near you, but now once more Phoibos Apollo has
> saved you,
> he to whom you must pray when you go into the thunder
> of spears thrown.
> Yet I may win you, if I encounter you hereafter,
> if beside me also there is some god who will help me.
> Now I must chase whomever I can overtake of the others.
>
> 11.362–367 (repeated at 20.449–454)

This is properly prophetic in Achilles' case, but for Diomedes, whose imminent wound will effectively remove him from combat, the speech serves chiefly to point up his role as Achilles' precursor and forerunner.

The very introduction of this speech provides a further parallel for Diomedes with Patroklos as well as with Achilles:[9]

> τρὶς μὲν ἔπειτ' ἐπόρουσε ποδάρκης δῖος Ἀχιλλεὺς
> ἔγχεϊ χαλκείῳ, τρὶς δ' ἠέρα τύψε βαθεῖαν.
> ἀλλ' ὅτε δὴ τὸ τέταρτον ἐπέσσυτο δαίμονι ἶσος,
> δεινὰ δ' ὁμοκλήσας ἔπεα πτερόεντα προσηύδα·
>
> (20.445–448)

(Diomedes)

> τρὶς μὲν ἔπειτ' ἐπόρουσε κατακτάμεναι μενεαίνων
> τρὶς δέ οἱ ἐστυφέλιξε φαεινὴν ἀσπίδ' Ἀπόλλων·
> ἀλλ' ὅτε δὴ τὸ τέταρτον ἐπέσσυτο δαίμονι ἶσος,
> δεινὰ δ' ὁμοκλήσας προσέφη ἑκάεργος Ἀπόλλων·
>
> (5.436–439)

(Patroklos)

> τρὶς μὲν ἔπειτ' ἐπόρουσε θοῷ ἀτάλαντος Ἄρηϊ,
> σμερδαλέα ἰάχων, τρὶς δ' ἐννέα φῶτας ἔπεφνεν,
> ἀλλ' ὅτε δὴ τὸ τέταρτον ἐπέσσυτο δαίμονι ἶσος,
> ἔνθ' ἄρα τοι, Πάτροκλε, φάνη βιότοιο τελευτή·
>
> (16.784–787)[10]

Just as Diomedes shares with Achilles the care and attendance of Athena, so he has the enmity of Apollo, chief protector of Hektor and Troy, in common not only with Achilles but also with Achilles' stand-in Patroklos.

Diomedes and Patroklos are described with the same two lines, respectively, by Aeneas (5.175–176) and by Sarpedon (16.424–425). They are seen as dangerous unknowns, apparently in relation to, and in the place of, Achilles as the acknowledged but absent peril:

ὅς τις ὅδε κρατέει καὶ δὴ κακὰ πολλὰ ἔοργε
Τρῶας, ἐπεὶ πολλῶν τε καὶ ἐσθλῶν γούνατ᾽ ἔλυσεν·

Both Diomedes and Patroklos as substitutes for and forerunners of Achilles take on something of that hero's character and coloration, so that the coming hero, as it were, casts his shadow before. Their own roles are, however, very different. Diomedes is in many ways an outsider from another sphere of action, completely unrelated to Achilles, and serving as chief warrior in Achilles' absence, excellent in both deed and word (9.53–54) like Achilles and unlike other more specialized heroes. As soon as Achilles once again plays a part in the war, either through Patroklos or in his own person, Diomedes fades out of the picture completely, as if he had never been there at all.

Patroklos, on the other hand, is Achilles' dear friend and *alter ego* whose death motivates and signals not only the hero's return to battle but also his death. Patroklos seems quite literally to be more an emanation of Achilles than a person in his own right. Thus he has almost no formulaic epithets as an active subject in the nominative case but only in the oblique cases as a corpse;[11] dying is his purpose and function.

The contrast and parallel between these two Achilles-precursors are important in the reverberation between the war story and the wrath story. In addition to their parallel actions, Diomedes in his wounding and Patroklos in his death prefigure the wounding and death of Achilles. Not only is Achilles' death assured when he avenges the death of his friend, but his death will come, like that of Patroklos, at the hands of both a god and a man (19.416–417), of Apollo and Paris (22.359–360). Less divinely authorized, perhaps because it serves merely to render Diomedes *hors de combat*, is the wounding of Diomedes by Paris alone (11.369–390). But that the wound is on Diomedes' foot (*tarsos*) suggests again his parallelism with Achilles, whether the "Achilles' heel" was already known to Homer[12]—

although not appearing in the *Iliad*—or was patterned on Diomedes' wound.

Book 5 and consideration of Diomedes generally have perhaps entangled us too soon in the seamless web of war story and wrath story. It will be better now to turn back to the orderly progression through Books 6 and 7 to continue the examination of how the preeminently war-story material there prefigures various aspects of the wrath story. For only with Book 8 is the wrath story proper taken up again from Book 1 to show the effects of Achilles' withdrawal leading to the appeal and offer of restitution of Book 9.

In Book 6 Hektor visits Troy to ask for divine protection against Diomedes, who is appropriately bracketed with Achilles by Helenos (6.97–101). The following description of Hektor in Troy then serves the double purpose of prefiguring the Troy that will suffer at the hands of a returned and vengeful Achilles and of providing a picture of Hektor and what he is fighting for to set against Achilles' motivation as it will be revealed in Books 9, 16, and 19. That is, when Achilles, having acquired a stake in the war, returns to take revenge on Hektor for his friend's death and acquiesces in his own death, the contest must be a significant one, between mighty heroes who stand for something, not simply a punitive action. For Achilles that something is the moving force of the wrath story, the personal honor that not only involved him in conflict with Agamemnon and kept him out of the war but also required him to take vengeance:

> since the spirit within does not drive me
> to go on living and be among men except on condition
> that Hektor first be beaten down under my spear, lose his
> life
> and pay the price for stripping Patroklos, the son of
> Menoitios.
>
> (16.90–93)

But what Hektor stands for can come clear only through material from the war story, where the concern was necessarily more equally divided between Achaians and Trojans than in the Achaian-centered wrath story. The introduction into the wrath story of that Trojan material to give substance to Hektor's position and cause is neatly engineered by using the damage done to Troy by Achilles' first substitute and forerunner to motivate Hektor's visit. But whether or not Andromache played any part in the original war story, certainly her present role symbolizing what Hektor is fighting for resonates with that of Briseis motivating Achilles' wrath. It may even be that the part played by a woman in Achilles' wrath and withdrawal was instrumental in adjusting traditional Trojan material to the wrath story so that Andromache plays an equivalent but contrasting role in Hektor's motivation.

In Book 7 a second inconclusive duel, that between Hektor and Ajax, seems, like the first, to have as its chief object the introduction of war-story material into the wrath story. That is, any inconclusive duel between Paris and Menelaos which preceded general hostilities in the Trojan War chronicle would have logically been followed by negotiations for the return of Helen. When these were unsuccessful and war was inevitable, the Achaians would reasonably have built a wall to protect their camp and ships. Thus both negotiations and wall-building were essential parts of the story which any bard would feel in duty bound to cover: negotiations, because audiences could be only too ready to ask why the Trojans did not simply give Helen up; the wall, because much of the fighting in the tradition did center on the wall which therefore had to be in place. But in the wrath story the duel between Paris and Menelaos, which was used to introduce the cause of the war, was followed and confirmed by an updated replay of Trojan provocation in the form of Pandaros' attack on Menelaos, thus excluding both the possibility of negotiations and the pertinence of wall-building.

The easy answer for the story-combining bard was another duel; again a Trojan warrior would issue a challenge to all Greeks, and again Menelaos would accept, but because this duel must start from hostilities and end with a truce (as the first had started with a truce and ended with hostilities) it had to be both depersonalized and formalized, so a neutral champion had to be allotted. Its mutually agreed upon and peaceful conclusion then made possible both the introduction of negotiations about the return of Helen and a truce, ostensibly for the burial of the dead (to fix firmly the timing of this duel in the midst of hostilities) but equally useful for the build-ing of the wall, for which the continuous burial mound could provide the substructure. Thus the wall that would be necessary for later fighting was hastily cobbled up in a rather jerry-built narrative not only to include essential war-story material but also to give the impression, notwithstanding casualty statistics to the contrary, that the Greeks were very much on the defensive. And it does give Achilles in Book 9 the opportunity to cite the wall as one of the measures made necessary by his absence to hold back the Trojan advance (9.349–354).

The duel of Hektor and Ajax seems also to serve another important function: it represents the norm of heroic confrontation, as the duel of Paris and Menelaos with its personal overtones cannot, and thereby serves in prospect as a standard against which the no-holds-barred, god-driven fights between Hektor and Patroklos and between Achilles and Hektor should be viewed. Here in Book 7 there is a minuetlike movement from politely boastful speeches through spearcasts taken in dignified turn, to the hurling of boulders, with a final resort to swordplay cut off by the herald at the coming of night. Contrast the savagery of Achilles' refusal to agree about corpse disposal, of his attack aided and abetted by Athena, and of his threats to the dying Hektor (22.260–354). Hektor too is savage in his slaughter of Patroklos but seems less so, following as he does on the headlong brashness of Patroklos' assault on the Trojan wall, Apollo's rough disarming, and Euphorbos' stab in the back (16.702–821). Without the comparatively civilized contest between Hektor and Ajax as an example of heroic manners the violence and rage exhibited by the heroes later would not so conspicuously mark them out as agents of their own fate.

In Book 8 the serious fulfillment of Zeus' promise to Thetis begins, marked first by his sudden ban on divine help to either side in the war (5–26) and second by the weighting of the scales against the Achaians (69–74). Hereafter it is the wrath story that predominates, albeit often padded out with war-story material, either unadulterated or appropriately edited for wrath-story purposes, like the wounding of chief heroes in Book 11. The wrath story, largely carried by Books 9, 11.598–847, 16, and following, does also include remnants from the war-story's end: the various predictions of Achilles' death (18.95–96; 19.408–410; 20.337–339; 21.276–

278; 22.358–359; 23.80–81; 24.84–86, 131–132); the anticipated fall of Troy (12.12–33 with destruction of the Achaian wall; 15.69–71; 16.707–709); survival of Aeneas and the end of Priam's line (20.302–308).

So much for this trial-balloon attempt to suggest some of the ways in which presumed war-chronicle material was adapted to a wrath story. Only by using both the inconcinnities and the reverberating themes of the *Iliad* itself did it seem possible to search out what may have been originally separate strands. Given these, one begins to contemplate the successive and/or competing bardic combinations that culminated in the *Iliad*'s tightly woven fabric. Surely it is only by this kind of trial-and-error speculation and extrapolation backward in time that we can arrive at possibilities which might be useful in defining the genesis of the *Iliad*.

ACHAIAN HEROES IN THE TROJAN
WAR—ORIGINAL AND IMPORTED

✦

Of the Achaian heroes in the *Iliad* only twenty-three are important and active enough to have killed at least one Trojan. These twenty-three seem to fall into roughly three groups: (1) those whose participation in the Trojan War represents their families' first Panhellenic activity; (2) those who are younger relatives of heroes active in various Panhellenic exploits (Voyage of the Argo, Kalydonian Boar Hunt, Battle of Lapiths and Centaurs, Herakles cycle, Theban Wars);[13] and (3) those whose position is uncertain or completely unknown. A look at individual heroes in the three groups may suggest something about their place in and relation to the development of the Trojan War story.

Agamemnon (13)[14] and Menelaos (7), sons of Atreus, are indispensable to that story, providing as they do both cause and command. It is their war, and without it and its aftermath they have little claim to pan-Hellenic mythical fame. Neither their father Atreus nor their uncle Thyestes participated in other than scandalous domestic or narrowly Peloponnesian activities. And their grandfather Pelops was so far out of even the Peloponnesian mythical picture that he was known as a foreigner.

If the Atreidai's importance in the Trojan War combines with the absence of them and their forebears from earlier mythical activity to suggest an original isolation of both family and war from a mythical mainstream, by the same token other Achaian heroes whose only *raison d'être* is the Trojan War and its aftermath may also owe their reputation, if not their existence, to their participation in that war. Idomeneus (5), son of Deukalion, and Meriones (7), son of Molos, are like the Atreidai not only in having their nondomestic activity limited to the Trojan War but also in having no forebears involved in any of the older myth-cycles.[15] Furthermore, the guest-friendship (*Iliad* 3.230–232) between Menelaos and Idomeneus, at least, suggests the possibilty of a Mycenaean-Cretan alliance.

Odysseus (18) too is a first-generation hero solidly based in the Trojan War story. The occasional mention of his father, Laertes, in the exploits of an earlier generation seems to be merely a perfunctory mark of respect for the famous son: in only one of six Argonautic lists (Apollodoros 1.9.16); in one of three Kalydonian Boar Hunt lists (Hyginus *Fab.* 173).

Nestor's sons, Antilochos (9) and Thrasymedes (1),

are themselves limited to Trojan War activity,[16] and even their father's connection with pan-Hellenic exploits is somewhat questionable. His inclusion in only one (Ovid *Metam.* 8.380) of three Kalydonian Boar Hunt lists and in only one (Val. Flac. *Arg.* 1.380) of six Argonaut lists is not impressive; more convincing is the appearance on all six lists of Periklymenos, his older brother, who died while Nestor was still a boy (*Iliad* 11.683–684, 692–693, 717–719). As for those youthful feats of Nestor, on which he bases his reputation and advice in the *Iliad*, all but one are limited to the Peloponnese and involve heroes out of the mainstream (killing the Arcadian Ereuthalion 4.319–321 and 7.132–156; fighting in Elis and Pylos 11.669–760; winning in Elean funeral games 23.629). Only in his boast of association with the Lapiths against the Centaurs (1.260–274) does he seem to justify his father's Thessalian origins. For the most part Nestor seems to be an old Peloponnesian hero rather oddly linked to a northern family and given a fringe connection with a northern myth so that his advice will have, as it were, the Lapith seal of approval. Nestor merits closer study, but for the moment only so much is needed to show that he and his sons are closer to the Atreidai in their activities than they are to the likes of Peleus and Tydeus and their sons.

It is possible and even probable that all of these fighting heroes (Idomeneus, Meriones, Odysseus, Antilochos, Thrasymedes) were borrowed for the Trojan War from local wars; for example, Idomeneus, whose slaughter of Phaistos (5.43) suggests a Cretan contest. Such heroes may have gained so much national *kudos* from their Trojan exploits that their other more local activities paled into nothingness by comparison. Indeed, Odysseus is a somewhat skewed example of this since his probable elevation to epic esteem from resourceful folk-hero status would have meant the loss of all his former adventures if the *Odyssey*-poet had not seen his way to combining those adventures with an epic *nostos*.

The second group of Achaian heroes in the *Iliad*, those with forebears prominent in earlier exploits, includes Achilles (26), Ajax (15) and Teukros (15) (sons of Telamon), Diomedes (20), Polypoites (4), Leonteus (5), and possibly Patroklos (27) and Ajax Oiliades (2). These are the sons or grandsons of men who played roles in one or more of the myth-cycles, as we learn not only from later sources,[17] but even from the *Iliad*:

both Peleus and Achilles are closely associated with the centaur Cheiron (11.832; 16.143; 19.390); Peirithoos, father of Polypoites, and Kaineus, grandfather of Leonteus, were Lapiths fighting against the Centaurs (1.263–268; 2.740–746); both Diomedes and his father Tydeus were involved in the wars against Thebes (4.370–410; 5.800–813). The *Iliad* does not refer to any activities of Telamon, father of Ajax and Teukros, but in a variety of later sources his close association with Peleus in the Argo, the Kalydonian Boar Hunt, and Herakles' expeditions against the Amazons and Troy confirms the brotherhood attested by the later story of their joint exile for the murder of a brother (Apollodoros 3.12.6).

Only Ajax Oiliades and his father have no extra-Trojan activities attested in the *Iliad*, although Oileus appears in three later lists of Argonauts (Ap. Rh. 1.74–76; Val. Flac. 1.371; *Orph. Arg.* 193). It seems possible that it was the somewhat indeterminate dual Aiante, originally[18] an appropriate term for Ajax and his brother Teukros, that attracted this second mostly unknown Ajax into the Trojan War story. Patroklos too is perhaps on the fringes of this group, both because of and despite the *Iliad*'s strong assertion of his relation to Achilles, which is more that of an *alter ego* than of one who is a hero in his own right. The combination of Menoitios' appearance in five later lists of Argonauts (where a penteconter needs fifty men) with no mention of him in other exploits (where Peleus and Telamon are active) suggests that his only real importance is as a father.

With two possible exceptions, then, these Achaian heroes have family traditions of mythical activity which may have made them attractive recruits to a war not otherwise in the mainstream of northern and central (or Minyan) myth. That is, not only do they not owe their existence to their participation in the Trojan War, but it is even likely that they were brought into it to connect this originally Mycenaean exploit with the northern cycles.

In the third group of the *Iliad*'s heroes are three who are only somewhat distantly connected with pan-Hellenic figures and exploits: Phyleus, the father of Meges (3), is listed by Ovid (*Metam.* 8.308) as a Kalydonian Boar hunter and gave Herakles help in cleansing the stables of his father Augeias (Paus. 5.3.2, 4); Andraimon, the father of Thoas (1), married Oineus' daughter Gorge (Paus. 10.38.5) and later succeeded to the kingship of Aitolia (*Iliad* 2.638–643); Mekisteus, father of Euryalos (4), attended Oidipodes' funeral games (*Iliad* 23.677–679) and, although only Apollodoros (3.6.3) lists him among the Seven against Thebes, Herodotus reports that he was killed by Melanippos, one of the seven defenders of Thebes (5.67).

The two Boiotians in this group, Peneleos (2) and Leitos (1), stand apart because they alone of the Trojan War generation (including Achaians merely named in the Catalogue of Ships) appear in a list of Argonauts (Apollod. 1.9.16). It may be that their presence there, like their presence in the Trojan War, represents an effort to include some of the late-coming Boiotians in heroic saga (Thuc. 1.12.3). Finally, about the last three heroes in this group nothing can be said about their background since their fathers' names appear in no other connection at all: Eurypylos (3) son of Euaimon; Automedon (1) son of Diores; Lykomedes (1) son of Kreion.

The Peloponnese, Crete, and Ithaca in northwest Greece as the geographical provenience of the first recruits to the Trojan War story (Nestor and his sons, Idomeneus, Meriones, Odysseus) may reflect the earliest spread of Mycenaean power. It certainly represents the middle part or core of the Catalogue of Ships (from Mycenae through Crete) which draws in also Meges and Thoas from the third, less well-known group. The contingents from central Greece which make up the first part of the Catalogue[19] would represent the next group of recruits to the expedition against Troy, presumably to be dated to a time when the mythically undistinguished Boiotians came into Boiotia sixty years after the fall of Troy (Thuc. 1.12). The Catalogue's oddly separate Thessalian contingents would then represent the last group of recruits—the sons and grandsons of Minyan myth adding both luster and the weight of tradition to this latest heroic exploit.

The Catalogue of Ships may then be seen as a composite document which was added to not only as Mycenaean influence spread outside the Peloponnese and Crete first to the northwest, then to central Greece, and finally to Thessaly in the north but also as the Mycenaean expedition against Troy attracted as recruits the heroes of those lands. That the central Greek contingents were attached at the beginning (along with the rendezvous at Aulis) and the Thessalian at the end may reflect the strong feeling that the Atreidai and their Peloponnesian allies were the heart of the enterprise, and that their support came from all sides.

Speculative in the extreme? Yes, but sensible if one sees the Catalogue of Ships not as a survey of actual political geography, but as a poetic attempt to list as many famous heroes as might possibly have fought in the Trojan War, although in the *Iliad*, at least, several have little or no part. These heroes must have been known to the bards, complete with epithets and epitheted place-names, from their local exploits. But that there was not always complete certainty as to the heroes' relative chronology is suggested by the awkward way in which the Argolid is carved up to allow Diomedes to maintain his Theban War connections with Argos in the midst of a later generation.

NOTES

*This collection of tributes to Emily Vermeule cannot be complete without a contribution from Richmond Lattimore, poetic mentor and director of her dissertation. It therefore seems right and proper that his Homeric translations be used here.

1. See Appendix for possible supporting material.

2. Compare the divinely directed Paris as cause of the war and the divinely directed Pandaros as justification of Trojan defeat.

3. Since the *Iliad* is our only source for any possible *Ur-Iliad*, we must continue to use it for evidence of any earlier version of the combined wrath story and war story.

4. This replay, as it were, of the gathering at Aulis seems to make use of two somewhat different versions inherited by Homer. That is, the omen concerning the war's length recounted by Odysseus (2.299–330) is completely ignored by Nestor in his closely following speech of encouragement to the troops. Nestor bases his assurance of victory on Zeus' flash of lightning on the right as they boarded the ships (2.350–353). Thus one version contained a prediction of victory without any consideration of the war's length; the other, perhaps composed later, after the ten-year length had come into the tradition, prefigured that length by a much more specific omen.

5. In the wrath story too Paris must survive to kill Achilles.

Achilles' death could not, for his reputation's sake, come in hand-to-hand combat but only at the hands of a bowman attacking from a place of safety and, even so, needing the aid of the "far-shooting" god (22.358–360).

6. Again, see further in Appendix.

7. In an earlier time only Nestor (7.154; 11.714, 721), Herakles (8.362–363), and Tydeus (4.490; 5.808); the battle against Troy only Odysseus (2.171; 5.676; 10.553; 23.771–774) and Menelaos (3.439; 4.128–133; 17.567–569).

8. Aeneas kills six Achaians, second after Hektor's twenty-six; Poulydamas and Paris each kill only three; Sarpedon, Glaukos, and Agenor only two. Aeneas appears in twelve books, as does Paris, who is active less often in the fighting. Poulydamas and Agenor appear in only nine books; and Sarpedon and Glaukos in only seven. As far as actual action on the battlefield is concerned, the differences are even more impressive.

9. The use of τρίς is less generally formulaic and more closely connected to these three heroes than might be expected: of the thirty *Iliad* examples twenty-one are connected to Achilles, Diomedes, or Patroklos; that is, eight appear in the passages quoted here; eight others involve action by Achilles (18.228, 229; 21.176, 177; 22.165, 251; 23.13; 24.16); three more concern Diomedes (5.136; 8.169, 170); two relate to Patroklos' corpse (18.155, 157). The other nine occur as follows: three of gifts or ransom (1.213; 21.80; 24.686); two of Odysseus shouting and Menelaos hearing (11.462–463); one each of Troy being attacked (6.435), Poseidon striding (13.20), contestants charging (23.817), and harness being fastened (24.273). The sequence τρὶς μὲν ... τρὶς δέ ... ἀλλ' ὅτε δὴ τὸ τέταρτον is limited to these four passages, with a truncated use (τρὶς ... ἀλλ' ὅτε δὴ τὸ τέταρτον) in Achilles' pursuit of Hektor (22.165, 208).

10. In each of the three cases Apollo is the opponent, as is stressed in two nearby passages which again envisage Diomedes and Patroklos in similar roles (16.702–711; 5.439–444).

11. Only two nominative epithets, used once each: *Menoitiades* (16.760) and *theophi mestor atalantos* (spoken of him when he is dead 17.477). Four epithets are used a total of thirteen times in the vocative case when the metrical form of the name allows line-placement more conducive to epithets; this might make up for the dearth of epithets in the nominative case, but the three epithets of the dead Patroklos in the genitive case (*deiloio, pesontos, thanontos*) used fifteen times make that condition most emphatic.

12. Certainly known by the first half of the sixth century B.C.: see E. Pfuhl, *Masterpieces of Greek Drawing* (New York 1926) 19, fig. 13, for the Chalcidian amphora depicting Achilles with an arrow piercing ankle or heel. The earliest literary source for Thetis dipping the infant Achilles in the Styx is Stat. *Achill.* 1.133, 269 (no mention of foot, heel, or ankle). See also Quintus Smyrnaeus, *Posthomerica* 3.62 (*sphuron*); Hyg. *Fab.* 107 (*talus*); Apollod. *Epit.* 5.3 (*sphuron*); Fulg. *Myth.* 3.7 (*talus*); Servius in Verg. *Aen.* 6.57 ("part which she held").

13. It is obvious that the later sources on whom we largely depend for the personnel of these episodes may have added heroes indiscriminately (for example, to man the Argo as a penteconter), but such lack of discrimination makes the omission of our first group's relatives even more notable.

14. The number of the hero's victims appears in parentheses.

15. Hyginus' list of the heroes taking part in the Kalydonian Boar Hunt (*Fab.* 173) does include a Deukalion, but in view of the Cretan Deukalion's absence from other Hunt lists and the presence of a Deukalion from Pella in Valerius Flaccus' list of Argonauts (365–366) the connection is unlikely.

16. Apollodoros' inclusion of Antilochos among the suitors of Helen (3.10.8) is surely a simple deduction from his part in the war. And Xenophon's listing of Antilochos as one of some twenty-one pupils of Cheiron (*Cyn.* 1.2) seems to be equally hypothetical.

17. The universal attestation there to the activity of these men's relatives contrasts significantly with the rare notice of such activity on the part of the previous group's forebears, made apparently on the assumption that all *Iliad* heroes' relatives might have been part of the "heroic gang." Thus Peleus, Menoitios, and Telamon (fathers of Achilles, Patroklos, Ajax, and Teukros) and Meleagros (uncle of Diomedes) appear on all Argonaut lists, while Laertes and Deukalion (fathers of Odysseus and Idomeneus) appear on only one.

18. D. L. Page, *History and the Homeric Iliad* (Berkeley 1959) 235–238.

19. Included herewith should be Diomedes and his Epigone colleagues, as men without a country because they were quite literally living after their time and so were rather awkwardly inserted in a gerrymandered Argolid.

I I

AN EVOLUTIONARY MODEL FOR THE MAKING OF HOMERIC POETRY: COMPARATIVE PERSPECTIVES*

◆

GREGORY NAGY

The massive accumulation of new or newly appreciated comparative evidence about the nature of epic in oral poetry demands application to the ongoing study of individual epic traditions. I propose here to apply some of this evidence, as collected over recent years by a broad range of experts investigating a broad variety of societies in Eastern Europe, Central Asia, the Indian subcontinent, and Africa, to the study of Homer in general and the Homeric *Iliad* and *Odyssey* in particular.

In earlier work, my starting point has been the central comparative insight of Milman Parry and Albert Lord, gleaned from their fieldwork in South Slavic oral epic traditions, that *composition* and *performance* are aspects of the same process in the making of Homeric poetry.[1] Let us for the moment call this process composition-in-performance. Starting with the comparative evidence about composition-in-performance, I added the internal Greek evidence about the early diffusion of the *Iliad* and *Odyssey* in the Archaic period of Greece, positing a model for the development of Homeric poetry that requires not two but three interacting aspects of production: *composition, performance,* and *diffusion*.[2] In the present work, I move on to apply holis-

tic comparative evidence about the interaction of *composition, performance,* and *diffusion* in attested living oral epic traditions.

My original reasons for concentrating on the role of diffusion in the development of Homeric poetry had to do with the need to reconcile the comparative insight of Parry and Lord about composition-in-performance with the historical reality of an integral and unified Homeric *text* inherited from the ancient world. How the concept of diffusion helps to account for Homeric textuality is a question that will be taken up in the discussion that follows. But first, let us consider some implications of the historical "given," the survival of the Homeric text.

For some classicists, the very nature of this written text has been a source of extreme skepticism concerning the validity of applying comparative insights about oral poetics. It is the opinion of not a few of these skeptics that the artistry, cohesiveness, and sheer monumentality of the *Iliad* and *Odyssey* rule out the role of oral poetics—and supposedly prove that such marvels of artistic achievement must have required the technology of writing.[3] For other skeptics, the levels of literacy that resulted from this technology were not fundamentally incompatible with the inherited art of oral poetry, so that there is supposedly no need to treat Homeric poetry differently from any early Greek poetry ostensibly produced by a literate author.[4] Either way, whether or not oral poetry is supposed to be compatible with literacy, both these lines of reasoning reject the comparative insight of Parry and Lord about composition-in-performance, and they require either explicitly or implicitly that the technology of writing was the key to the actual composition of the Homeric text.[5]

Given that the poetry of the *Iliad* and *Odyssey* has indeed survived as a fixed text, Albert Lord offered a solution for retaining the model of composition-in-performance by postulating that these poems had been dictated.[6] There have been recent attempts to extend this dictation theory,[7] but they run into problems when it comes to explaining the early diffusion of the *Iliad* and the *Odyssey* in Archaic Greece on both sides of the Aegean—a process that was already under way as early as the fourth quarter of the seventh century before our era.[8] Any pattern of diffusion, if indeed it is to be put at so early a date, can hardly be ascribed to any hypothetical proliferation of a plethora of manuscripts, in view of the existing physical limitations on materials available for writing down, let alone circulating, a text of such monumental size as the *Iliad* or the *Odyssey*. One solution that has been proposed is to imagine a situation where a hypothetical dictated text becomes the prized possession of a special group of performers.[9] Although this modified dictation theory offers some advantages in retaining the factor of performance, there are major difficulties with it. For one thing, it leaves unexplained a basic question: How exactly is such a text supposed to be the key to the process of performance? How could a dictated text automatically become a script, a prompt, for the performer who dictated it, let alone for any other performer? In fact, such a solution does not even mesh with Albert Lord's actual experience with the phenomenon of dictation in the context of genuine living oral traditions, where the writing down of any given composition-in-performance in effect *eliminates* the performability of that particular composition. In terms of such a modified dictation theory, moreover, the technology of writing has to be invoked not only for the performance of the *Iliad* and *Odyssey* but even for the ultimate composition of these poems, to the extent that the text is imagined to achieve its status as text at the very moment that dictation transforms a composition-in-performance into a script, as it were.

I maintain that there is no internal Greek evidence to prove that the technology of writing, as it existed in the Greek Archaic period, was necessary for the process of *performance* any more than it was necessary for *composition*.[10] But there is indeed internal Greek evidence for *diffusion*, and it is in this light that I offered, in my earlier work, a different solution—combining the comparative evidence about *composition* and *performance* with the internal Greek evidence for the *diffusion* of Homeric poetry in the Archaic period of Greece. The comparative evidence from living oral epic traditions, as we are about to see, helps corroborate the Greek evidence about the factor of diffusion.

Before we proceed with comparing other epic traditions to those of ancient Greece, however, a few words of background are in order about the internal Greek evidence itself. I offer here a minimalist formulation of two basic concepts, "epic" and "Homer." For experts in the study of ancient Greek civilization, the idea of "epic" is clear in its application, if not in its definition. Following the usage of authorities like Aristotle, Hellenists can easily distinguish the poetic art form of *epopoiia* 'making of epic' (as at the beginning of Aristotle, *Poetics* 1.1447a13) from such other poetic art forms as *tragōidias poiēsis*, 'making of tragedy' (ibid.). The application of Homer's name to the authorship of the *Iliad* and the *Odyssey*, the prime examples of Greek epic, is also clear. True, the earliest attested references to *Homēros* attribute to him not only the *Iliad* and the *Odyssey* but also the epics of the so-called Cycle, such as the *Cypria* and the *Little Iliad*.[11] In fact, the very concept of *kuklos,* meaning 'circle' or 'Cycle,' stems from the ancient pre-Aristotelian tradition of applying the metaphor of cycle to the sum total of epic poetry, as if all of it were composed by Homer.[12] By the time of Aristotle, however, the epics of the Cycle are conventionally assigned to distinct authors (*Poetics* 23.1459b1–7), and it has been said about Aristotle that "his differentiation between Homer, the poet of the *Iliad* and *Odyssey*, and the rest of the early epic poets, of whom he displays intimate knowledge in chapter 23 of the *Poetics*, seems to have been final." [13]

What made decisive the differentiating of these two poems from all others was the influence exerted by the scholars at the Library of Alexandria, particularly by the first head of the Library, Zenodotus of Ephesus: "it was of the utmost importance for the whole future that the first of the great scholars . . . accepted the differentiation between these two poems as Homeric and the rest of epic narrative poetry as non-Homeric." [14] Though there were attempts to narrow down the Homeric corpus even further, as when scholars known as the "separators" or *khōrizontes* tried to separate the authorship of the *Odyssey* from that of the *Iliad* (Proclus p. 102.2–3 Allen), the Alexandrian verdict on Homer as the author of the *Iliad* and the *Odyssey* held firm in the ancient world. The "Homeric Question," as reformulated in the Renaissance and thereafter, must be viewed against this background; so also the comparative insights pioneered by Parry and Lord.

The progressive restriction of what exactly in Greek epic is to be attributed to Homer can be connected with the historical process that I have just highlighted, to wit, the relatively early diffusion of the *Iliad* and the *Odyssey* throughout the Greek-speaking world. In my earlier work, I adduced archaeological evidence, as assembled by Anthony Snodgrass, pointing towards a trend of *pan-Hellenism* that becomes especially pronounced in Archaic Greece in the eighth century before our era and thereafter.[15] The epic tradition of Homer, as Snodgrass inferred from the early proliferation of the *Iliad* and the *Odyssey,* was a reflex of this trend of pan-Hellenism.[16] I extended Snodgrass' concept of pan-Hellenism "as a hermeneutic model to help explain the nature of Homeric poetry, in that one can envisage as aspects of a single process the ongoing recomposition and diffusion of the *Iliad* and the *Odyssey*." [17] I called this model for the text-fixation of Homeric tradition "evolutionary," [18] in that the process of composition-in-performance, which is a matter of *recomposition* in each performance, can be expected to be directly affected by the degree of *diffusion*, that is, the extent to which a given tradition of composition has a chance to be performed in a varying spectrum of narrower or broader social frameworks.[19] The wider the diffusion, I argued, the fewer opportunities for recomposition, so that the widest possible reception entails, teleologically, the

strictest possible degree of adherence to a normative and unified version.[20]

I continue to describe as *text-fixation* the process whereby each composition-in-performance becomes progressively less changeable in the course of diffusion—with the proviso that we understand *text* here in a metaphorical sense. The fixity of such a "text," of course, does not necessarily mean that the process of composition-in-performance—let us continue to call it recomposition—has been stopped altogether. So long as the oral tradition is alive, some degree of ongoing recomposition is still possible in each performance, even if the tradition itself proclaims its own absolute fixity. A case in point is the so-called Invocation of the Bagre, a "hymn" sung among the LoDagaa of Northern Ghana.[21] It is clear that the expectation of both the audience and the reciters of the Bagre is that each performance be exactly like every other performance, but empirical observation shows that it is not. Reaching a size of up to 12,000 lines, the Bagre in fact exists in a variety of versions, and the differences among the versions can be considerable.[22] In sum, the rate of retardation or acceleration of change in the process of composition-in-performance depends on the stage of evolution in which we happen to find any given living oral tradition.[23]

In arguing for the notion of a single pan-Hellenic tradition of epic—let us call it Homer—as opposed to a plethora of local traditions, I stressed the relativity of the term *pan-Hellenic* from an empirical point of view:

> It should be clear that this notion of *pan-Hellenic* is absolute only from the standpoint of insiders to the tradition at a given time and place, and that it is relative from the standpoint of outsiders, such as ourselves, who are merely looking in on the tradition. Each new performance can claim to be the definitive pan-Hellenic tradition. Moreover, the degree of pan-Hellenic synthesis in the content of a composition corresponds to the degree of diffusion in the performance of this composition. Because we are dealing with a relative concept, we may speak of the poetry of the *Iliad* and *Odyssey*, for example, as more pan-Hellenic than the poetry of the Epic Cycle.[24]

In other words, I am arguing that the concept of pan-Hellenism is not at all incompatible with the factor of change. I therefore disagree with the implications of the following assessment:

> . . . although a few poems may be designed to be infinitely repeatable and as non-local and non-occasional as possible (pan[-]Hellenic, even literary?)—i.e., they may aspire to say the "last word" on their subject, and to render all previous and future attempts futile[25]—the more usual impulse is to leave loopholes for possible exceptions, pegs on which to hang possible additions, open ends to accommodate codas or modifications desired by particular audiences in the light of other existing songs or cult traditions.[26]

To repeat, the evolutionary model of pan-hellenism is not rigid, not even for Homer.

A context for the final phase of an evolutionary model is a pan-Hellenic festival like the Panathenaia at Athens, which served as the formal setting, established by law, of seasonally recurring performances of the Homeric *Iliad* and *Odyssey* (cf. Lycurgus, *Against Leokrates* 102).[27] I argue in what follows that the Feast of the Panathenaia is a clear example of a distinct pattern of diffusion in oral traditions. I hope to show from the comparative evidence of various oral epic traditions that there is more than one way to visualize the actual process of diffusion. Besides the pattern of an ever-widening radius of proliferation, with no clearly defined center of diffusion, there is also a more specialized pattern that can be predicated on a functional center point, bringing into play both centripetal and centrifugal forces. Such a center point, which I will compare to the seasonally recurring festival of the Panathenaia at Athens, can take the form of a centralized context for both the coming together of diverse audiences and the spreading outward of more unified traditions.[28]

In general as also in details, an evolutionary model for the text-fixation or textualization of the Homeric tradition is corroborated by the comparative evidence of living oral epic traditions. I cite in particular the results of recent fieldwork in the oral epic traditions of the Indian subcontinent.[29] In what follows, I quote extensively from descriptions of the Indian evidence that were formulated by observers who were at the time not at all concerned with the ancient Greek evidence to which I am now applying them. The degrees of similarity between the empirical observations of the Indian evidence, as I cite them verbatim, and some of my constructs derived from the Greek evidence are to my mind so striking that a casual reading could leave the mistaken impression that the wording of the Indologists was influenced by these constructs.

For example, researchers like Stuart Blackburn who specialize in the oral folk epic traditions of latter-day India have developed, independently of their counterparts who specialize in ancient Greece, the descriptive term *pan-Indian*, which they correlate with observable patterns of what they call geographical *diffusion* in epic traditions.[30] Matching the Greek model, the descriptive term "pan-" is used in a relative sense, as we can see from the following explicit restatement of Blackburn's position in the introduction to the book that he coedited: "Tracing a narrative pattern that moves from a local hero toward a wider, more pan-Indian identity for the hero/god, [Blackburn] concludes that this change is a response to the differing social groups and contexts encountered as an epic spreads geographically."[31] In effect, then, Blackburn is positing an ongoing process of recomposition in the making of Indian epic that is analogous to an evolutionary model for the making of ancient Greek epic.

An evolutionary model is applicable also to the two great canonical Sanskrit epics of the Indian subcontinent.[32] These are the *Mahābhārata*, an epic of truly monumental dimensions which, in its ultimate form, is roughly eight times the size of the Homeric *Iliad* and *Odyssey* combined, and the relatively smaller *Rāmāyaṇa*. The performance traditions that culminated in these two Sanskrit "primary epics" extended well into the second half of the first millennium of our era.[33] It took "several centuries" for both "to reach their final forms,"[34] with the "formative period" of the *Mahābhārata* estimated at around 400 B.C. to A.D. 400 and of the *Rāmāyaṇa*, at around 200 B.C. to A.D. 200.[35]

The relative lateness of text-fixation in the case of these two canonical Sanskrit epics is illustrated by the fact that even the earlier of the two, the *Mahābhārata*, "began to take shape" at a time when the Vedas, the "priestly literature" of the Brahmin caste which had already formalized the technology of writing, had reached an advanced stage of development.[36] "Viewed against this background the *Mahābhārata* represents, as it were, a return to the beginning. It was an oral composition; it was purely heroic in character; and it dealt with people and events of which the earlier [Brahmin] literature had taken practically no notice." [37]

This dichotomy between Vedic and epic can be explained to some degree in terms of caste distinctions: "as the Vedas and their supporting literature were the 'property' of the Brahmins, so the epic was the 'property' of the Kṣatriya-s, the caste of warriors and princes." [38] Although the Kṣatriya-s "owned" the epic, it was not composed/performed by them but by a specialized caste called the Sūta-s, performing to the accompaniment of an early form of a string instrument known as the vīṇā. [39] The relationship of these Sūta-s and the Kṣatriya-s is analogous to that of the medieval Cāraṇ court poets and their Rājpūt patrons. [40]

The Kṣatriya background of the Sanskrit epic tradition becomes accretively displaced and covered over, in the course of time, by a Brahmin superstructure, and the very process of this displacement can be interpreted as a sign of fluidity in an oral epic tradition. The pattern of displacement is so pervasive that the very authorship of the Mahābhārata is traditionally attributed to one Kṛṣṇa Dvaipāyana, a Brahmin seer who is also a major character in the plot of the Mahābhārata. [41] Similarly with the Rāmāyaṇa, where the Kṣatriya hero Rāma becomes accretively identified with the Brahmin god Viṣṇu.

Granted, experts have not yet determined to what extent such accretive patterns of displacement took place on the level of oral transmission in the two primary Sanskrit epics. [42] But, more importantly, the fact is that the living oral epic traditions in India today, affording as they do a wealth of evidence for various patterns of diffusion, provide comparative evidence for an evolutionary model that helps explain the actual process of accretion. [43]

As we proceed to consider in some detail the evidence of living oral epic traditions in contemporary India, it is important to stress the explicit role of religion in the very function of epic. For purposes of this presentation, a minimalist working definition of religion will suffice: let us consider it for the moment as simply the interaction of myth and ritual. [44] With this understanding, I propose to specify "religion" in terms of cult, which I define for the moment as a set of practices combining elements of ritual as well as myth. [45] As one

of the most powerful illustrations of the role of religion in the performance of Indian epic, I point to those situations where the performer presupposes the presence of an audience of gods "watching out for errors in performance." [46]

As the first specific example of the sort of empirical evidence that has been collected by contemporary researchers concerning the role of cult in the living traditions of epic in India, I cite the wording of a scholar specializing in Rajasthani epic, who offers the following formulation for the role of epic in the Rajasthani cultural ethos: "concern for propitiating the powerful spirits of those who died untimely deaths continually feeds the epic traditions of the area." [47] In quoting this description of heroes in the Rajasthani epic traditions, I highlight the word untimely because of its relevance for comparison with the concept of the hero in ancient Greek epic traditions. In the case of the Herakles myth, as adduced by Greek epic itself in the retelling of Iliad 19.95–133, the theme of Herakles' untimeliness goes to the very core of the hero's essence and extends to the essential untimeliness of the main hero of the Iliad, Achilles, who in the end describes himself as the 'untimeliest of them all,' pan-a-ōrios (Iliad 24.540). [48] This theme of untimeliness in ancient Greek traditions is not restricted to epic: it extends to the concept of heroes in the specific context of their being worshiped in cult, as I have argued extensively elsewhere. [49] As I have also argued, the cult of heroes is a subtext, as it were, for the development of epic traditions about heroes in ancient Greece. [50] Moreover, the relationship between the cult of heroes on a local level and the epic of heroes on a pan-Hellenic level is crucial for coming to terms with the factor of diffusion in the Homeric tradition. [51] As we shall see, there are striking analogies in the living traditions of India.

The ancient Greek hero's untimeliness in myth is to be contrasted with his or her timeliness in ritual, in that the cult of heroes is predicated on the central fact of seasonal recurrence, controlled by the goddess of timeliness herself, Hera. [52] The cults of heroes/ancestors in India too seem to operate on a cyclical principle. Although "the yearly cycle of folk epic performances has yet to be conclusively outlined for different regions and different groups within these regions," [53] there are isolated cases where we do have specific information: a notable example is the festival of Caitrī, where the performances of epic seem to be connected with the remembrance of ancestors.[54]

Pursuing the question of the relationship between epic traditions and the cult of ancestors or heroes, let us consider in some detail the evidence from Rajasthan. I cite the following summary: "The two major Rajasthani historical epics, *Pābūjī* and *Devnārāyaṇ*, appear to have developed out of a tradition of honoring powerful spirits of the dead. A continuing concern about powerful spirits provides the framework in which these epics retain their meaning and vitality."[55] In the case of the *Pābūjī* regional epic tradition, it has been argued that it developed out of a local *bhomiyā* cult.[56] The *bhomiyā* have been described as "local heroes who died while defending against cattle raids, were commemorated with a carved pillar (showing a rider on a horse), and eventually became gods at the center of a cult."[57] *Pābūjī* himself is generally worshiped as a god.[58]

As we shall see, the semantic shift from hero to god is a peculiarly Indian phenomenon, characteristic of those stages of epic tradition that have undergone the broadest patterns of diffusion and have thus attained the most normative possible levels of the "Hindu" world view. For purposes of comparison with the ancient Greek evidence, where the distinction between *hero* and *god* is for the most part clearly maintained, it is preferable to start with Indian patterns of cult on the most local levels, where we find the most straightforward evidence for the cult of *heroes* as distinct from *gods*. Before we begin, however, it is important to note that the ancient Greek distinction between *ancestor* and *hero*, unlike the distinction between *hero* and *god*, becomes increasingly blurred as we move further and further back in time.[59]

With this caution in place, let us consider further the folk culture of Rajasthan, which has been singled out for its striking differences from the upper-caste Hindu "norm."[60] I propose to pursue our consideration of the Rajasthani *bhomiyā*, who are literally the spirits of dead warriors.[61] At the shrine of the *bhomiyā*,

> the spirit manifests himself through a medium, usually a *bhopā*. The shrine [marking where the *bhomiyā* had died] becomes active through this medium and the spirit begins to solve problems of the local people. Effective and truthful

disposition by the possessed medium of the *bhomiyā* will draw people from a large area and the shrine may become an important ritual site where the hero's story is sung.[62]

As for the actual performance of the epic, "the central belief is that singing the hero's story summons him as a god, whose power is then present to protect the community."[63] What gives the hero his ultimate power is the actual fact of his death: "the death event operates as the 'generative point' for stories in local traditions. It leads to deification, to worship, to a cult, and eventually to a narrative which is ritually performed to invoke the spirits of the dead."[64]

It can be said in general about the epic traditions of India that their function is a matter of explicit ritual as well as myth: "epic performances ritually protect and cure, while epic narratives express local ideologies and form pathways between regional and pan-Indian mythologies."[65] For the moment I simply note, for the second time now, the use of the term *pan-Indian* in this description—a subject to which we shall return presently. I also note a point that may not be obvious to those unfamiliar with the perspectives of social anthropology, which is that the element of ritual in such descriptions should not be understood so narrowly as to exclude what we may ordinarily think of as entertainment: "Indian oral epics tend to have performance contexts that are either ritualistic or entertainment-oriented. These two performance contexts exist on a continuum because ritual and entertainment are not mutually exclusive."[66]

The relation of the local epic to the community is all-important in the Indian traditions: "oral epics in India have that special ability to tell a community's own story and thus help to create and maintain that community's self-identity."[67] Once the local story extends beyond the community, however, there is change in context as well as form. Let us consider the following description of what happens to the theme of the death and deification of local heroes in the context of diffusion:

> . . . when a story spreads beyond its local base by attracting new patronage outside the small group that originally worshiped the dead hero, the predominance of the death motif (but not deification) weakens. In its place, new elements are added at each of the next two successively larger geographical ranges: a supernatural birth at the sub-regional

level and an identification with a *pan-Indian* figure at the regional level. The overall effect of this development is to obscure the human origins of the hero/god with a prior divine existence, a process that is complete when the hero/god is identified with a *pan-Indian* figure. (highlighting mine)[68]

For the third time now, we note the use of the word *pan-Indian* in describing the ultimate stages of epic diffusion in India. We may note as well that the application of this term is reserved for the *regional* level of diffusion and beyond. The categories of *regional* and *subregional* are part of an overall taxonomy developed by Stuart Blackburn for the purpose of classifying the relative ranges of diffusion for fifteen samples of living epic traditions in India. The ranges of diffusion for these fifteen selected epic traditions, preceded by categories of description for these ranges, are as follows:

1) local	=	10–100 mile range
2) subregional	=	100–200 mile range
3) regional	=	200–300 mile range
4) supraregional	=	400+ mile range.[69]

I note in particular the observation that the breakthrough of an epic from local to subregional status is promoted by a cult where a large festival is held annually at a single temple.[70]

An ancient Greek analogy that immediately comes to mind is a pan-Hellenic festival like the Panathenaia at Athens, which, as I have already noted, served as the formal setting for seasonally recurring performances of the Homeric *Iliad* and *Odyssey*.[71] As the comparative evidence of oral epic traditions in contemporary India shows, the institution of Homeric performances at the Panathenaia can be visualized as a process of diffusion. In other words, diffusion is not restricted to the pattern of an ever-widening radius of proliferation, with no clearly defined center of diffusion. As the Indic comparative evidence shows, there is also a more specialized pattern that can be predicated on a functional center point, bringing into play both centripetal and centrifugal forces. Such a center point, to repeat, can take the form of a centralized context for both the coming together of diverse audiences and the spreading outward of more unified traditions.

For purposes of further comparison, we may observe that the more pan-Indian the epic, the more divergent it seems from the ancient Greek evidence. The actual phenomena of pan-Indianism and pan-Hellenism are comparable, less so the results of the respective phenomena of synthesis and diffusion. The most divergent point of comparison is the tendency of the hero's being elevated to the status of divinity in pan-Indian traditions. I have in mind such phenomena in the Indian evidence as the appropriation of epics having a ritual context by such pan-Indian trends as Vaiṣṇava veneration.[72] True, even where the hero is divinized, there can survive traces of hero-god distinctions: in the Tulu traditions, for example, there is a distinction made between the *bhūta* or deified dead and the *dēvaṟ̣u*, that is, deities of divine origins.[73] Clearly, the deified dead represent the new and augmented phase of the hero, just one step removed from the status of deities proper. Just as clearly, there are attestations of the next logical step: "new social groups accept the hero as a god and not simply as the deified dead because they have no close link to him by blood or locale."[74]

All this is not to say that the hero's elevation to the status of divinity cannot happen on the most local level.[75] Conversely, in the case of the Lorik-Candā epic, which fits Blackburn's category of supraregional epic,[76] its hero and heroine, Lorik and Candā, "are not deified and thus [this epic's] spread is not associated with that of a religious cult."[77] There are even more important exceptions: "the *Mahābhārata* heroes, like the heroes of the *Ālhā*, do not die in battle, are not deified, and are not widely worshiped. They, too, lack both the conditions and the need for deification."[78] Still, the general trend of pan-Indian oral epic traditions is the highlighting of the hero's immortalization and the shading over of his mortality: "as these stories *diffuse* (even to a limited extent within the local range), they *change* [highlighting mine]. The hero's death remains the central narrative event, evoking emotional responses in listeners and explaining the hero's new status as a god, but it becomes less local history and more narrative convention."[79] There is even a tendency in Indian traditions to avoid describing the actual death of the hero.[80] In the pan-Hellenic traditions of the *Iliad* and *Odyssey*, conversely, the topic of a hero's immortalization tends to be shaded over, while his mortality and the circumstances of his death are highlighted as the centerpiece of Homeric humanism.[81]

Either way, whatever the direction of shifts in emphasis may be, both the Greek and the Indian traditions seem to become progressively less occasional or *ad hoc* in the process of diffusion. To discover the occasional or *ad hoc* applications of ancient Greek epic, of course, is largely a matter of reconstruction or at least of inference from the surviving texts. In the case of Indian epic, on the other hand, there is a great deal of direct evidence about occasionality in the living traditions, and such testimony as we shall see affords valuable comparative insights that help us better understand the available testimony of the Greek traditions.

Let us begin with Indian evidence about the circumstances of performance and of performer-audience interaction. There are two basic performance-types: *song-recitation* and *dance-drama*;[82] "dance-drama is a secondary form in that it only exists where song-recitation also exists."[83] Performers of epic—singers, musical accompanists, dancers, and ritual specialists— are predominantly from the middle- and low-level castes; by contrast, Classical performance traditions of the Sanskrit epics "are controlled by high-level castes, often Brahmins."[84] The possibility of a performer's traveling through different districts seems to be linked with the degree of his professionalism.[85] This phenomenon of professionalization, which is key to the factor of diffusion, is analogous to the status of the ancient Greek *aoidos*, 'singer,' as a *dēmiourgos*, that is, an itinerant artisan (*Odyssey* 17.381–385).[86]

In the Indian traditions, the notion of *audience* is actually more appropriate in the case of professional singers' performances, whereas some more neutral term like *group* suits the sort of situation where "non-professional general caste groups sing for the group itself."[87] For purposes of comparison, the ongoing distinction between *audience* and *group* in these descriptions of Indian traditions is pertinent to the scenes of person-to-person or person-to-group interaction in Homeric narrative that seem to mirror the conventions of performer-audience interaction in the "real world" that frames the performance of the narrative.[88] It is also pertinent to the issues raised by Wolfgang Rösler's *Dichter und Gruppe*, a work that investigates the reception of Archaic Greek lyric in the specific social context of Archaic Lesbos.[89] We may ask, for example, on the basis of the comparative evidence, whether the interaction of Alcaeus with his group on one level simply mirrors the performance of the Alcaeus-persona to the audience on another level.[90]

In the case of the general caste-group's "non-professional" performing of epic in the Indian traditions, even this broad category for the aspect of *performers* has its own structure. There has to be a leader, who generally has had more background in performance than the others, including the mastery of a musical instrument.[91] Potential leaders, who are specialists in a sense, have to compete with one another, and I infer that increasing specialization in the performance of epic is a functional correlate of increasing formalized competition among performers.[92]

In the course of this survey of occasionality in the living epic traditions of India, we may note in passing that epic, as a public performance genre in India, is performed almost exclusively by male singers.[93] The rarely found exceptions, however, are particularly revealing. For background to the case that I am about to cite, I note that the Ahir caste of Uttar Pradesh appropriates an epic known as the Lorik-Candā;[94] this epic "helps to maintain the Ahirs' image of themselves as a warrior caste."[95] "It is primarily Ahirs who sponsor performances at occasions such as weddings and the birth of a child. The Lorik-Candā epic is also sung at various festivals, during the harvest season, and at village or town fairs."[96] In Chhattisgarh, the corresponding epic is called Candainī, and it is with reference to this tradition that we turn to an exceptional case of performance by women. The researcher reports as follows: "One night as I was recording an elderly Gond (tribal) woman singing a variety of narrative songs, she began singing about the wedding of the epic heroine and her first husband. But the woman did not consider this to be Candainī singing."[97] The narrative content in fact corresponds to Candainī, but the form is different: a distinct *rāg*, 'tune,' and style.[98] In this case, I note a striking ancient Greek parallel in Sappho *fragment* 44, the so-called Wedding of Hektor and Andromache: this song, composed in a meter that is cognate with but distinct from the epic dactylic hexameter, deals in a nonepic manner with themes that are otherwise characteristic of epic.[99] We have here a particularly striking example of the effects of a given occasion on the very nature of epic composition. Just as the song of Sappho about the wedding of Hektor and Andromache is exceptional in the history of Greek literature, so also the song of the elderly Gond woman proved to be exceptional in one particular researcher's survey of living Indian oral epic traditions. It may well be worth asking whether this discovery about women's traditions in India would have been possible if the researcher in this case, Joyce Flueckiger, did not happen to be a woman. The question is whether a woman researcher would be deemed by her women informants to be more suitable for the reception of distinctly women's traditions. I asked John Smith, an expert in this field, for his opinion (May 11, 1993, at the University of Cambridge), and his answer was "yes."

The occasion of epic performance may have a variety of effects on the content of the composition. In the many epic traditions of India, there are striking examples of selectivity in choosing not only which topics to highlight or shade over in a given sequence but also which *variant* of a given topic to use within that sequence. Such choices are tuned to the narrowness or breadth of audience reception. Let us consider two situations, one where the local aspects of an epic tradition have to be highlighted and another where the same aspects are shaded over. We begin with the Kordabbu epic tradition of the Tulu-speaking area of Karnataka, a tradition where parts of the narrative are recited by the possessed priest "in a voice characteristic of the spirits"; this stretch of narrative is marked by a switch from the third to the first person, and is known as the Words of the Hero.[100] "In his performance the possessed priest must not only recite Kordabbu's story, but also assume his character and dramatically portray his exploits for several hours on end."[101] This description applies to the Mundala caste. But there is also another performance tradition, called the *kōla*, maintained by the Nalke caste, which is "a professional bardic caste."[102] It has been reported about these performers:

> Together with their recitation, they perform a costumed dance-drama, acting out the major incidents of the spirit's life while in a state of possession. Nalkes perform *kōlas* for many other deities besides Kordabbu and thus know a sizable repertoire of different *pāḍḍanas* [a generic term for multistory tradition]. The Nalke have no greater ties to the

Mundala or Kordabbu than they do to any other caste or any other caste's heroes.[103]

I save the most important detail for last: the Nalke "are not likely to elaborate specific details that might offend the sensibilities of a particular group in a village and give rise to a dispute. The Nalke leave the details of the hero's life and his relationship to other castes to the villagers concerned."[104] An analogy that immediately comes to mind is the screening out of local traditions from the repertoire of *aoidoi* 'singers' as itinerant artisans in Archaic Greece, with the result that the subject matter controlled by such performers becomes a sort of least common denominator appropriate to the most generalized kinds of audience.[105]

In contrast to the distinct nonoccasionality of ancient Greek epic, we have by now seen a great deal of comparative evidence for occasionality on the level of local performance in the living oral epic traditions of India. There is ample evidence also from the epic traditions of Central Asia.[106] This kind of testimony is also pertinent to the existing comparative information about praise poetry. From the traditions collected in Africa, it appears that praise poetry, in the process of diffusion from local towards more regional contexts of performance, progressively takes on the characteristics of what we might otherwise call epic. This trend is markedly noticeable, for example, in the traditions of praise poetry in Xhosa society.[107] Here we may adduce the internal evidence of Greek civilization concerning the relationship of epic with praise poetry. Following the formulation of Aristotle (*Poetics* 4.1448b27, 32–34), who derives epic from praise poetry, I have argued elsewhere that the form and content of a Greek poetic tradition that calls itself *ainos* or 'praise,' as represented by the victory odes of Pindar, can be reconstructed as the basis for the development of what we know as epic.[108] In line with my avoidance of monogenetic theories for the origins of epic, I stress that praise poetry can be reconstructed as *a* basis, not *the* basis, for the development of epic. Still, the internal testimony of ancient Greek epic itself implies the outright derivation of epic from praise. We may note references made by Greek epic itself to primal scenes of praise and blame poetry, as we see in the brief retelling of the Judgment of Paris scene in *Iliad* 24.29–30, where the Homeric tradition represents the genesis of epic itself in terms of a primal opposition of praise poetry to blame poetry.[109]

As we look more closely at the comparative evidence concerning the relationship of praise poetry and epic, it seems to confirm the derivation of Greek epic from praise poetry. The *ad hoc* orientation of the ancient Greek praise poem or *ainos* can be compared with the occasionality of epic, especially on the more local levels, in the oral traditions of India. There are clear instances where plot variation is radically conditioned by the nature of the audience.[110] Such conditioning reveals the dependence of the performers on their audiences. Let us take as an example of such performers the Nayaks, a caste of hereditary singers of the Pābūjī epic tradition found primarily in central and south Rajasthan, who "circulate from village to village on a yearly beat seeking patrons."[111] The musical instruments of the professional performers tend to be chordophonic, requiring rigorous training.[112] In the commissioning of a Nayak performance of the Pābūjī epic, "the patron's devotion is the most important measure of the performance."[113] The patronage can occur on the level of festivals, but most often on the level of the village; "patrons may sponsor a performance for one night or a series of nights."[114] One motivation for a sponsor's undertaking of a sponsorship is to fulfill a vow.[115] Such a relationship between patron and poet offers a wide spectrum of comparative insights into the sociology, as it were, of praise poetry in ancient Greece.

The *ad hoc* orientation of the ancient Greek praise poem or *ainos*, with its persistent internal references to the occasion of its performance and to the expectations of its audience, stands in marked contrast to the stance taken in the Homeric tradition of epic, which programmatically shades over any reference to any specific occasion of performance and thus implies that it is worthy of universal acceptance, that is, of unconditional reception.[116] It is as if the epic of Homer had outgrown the need for occasionality of performance. Similarly in the praise poetry of the Xhosa, the phenomenon of diffusion entails the widening of perspective in the content of praise:

> The elliptical Xhosa *isibongo* [praise songs] consist of shorthand allusions that are normally understood by the poet's local audience, familiar as they are with the subjects

of the poetry and the context of historical narrative and anecdote current in the community. But if the poet is conscious that his audience is suddenly wider, expanded beyond the local limits of his usual performances, then he might wish to gloss the potentially puzzling allusions, to incorporate the footnotes into his text, as it were.[117]

The wording here, with emphasis on *text* as a metaphor for *composition* in oral poetics, is apt, in the sense that the authoritativeness of such a composition is made analogous to the potential authoritativeness of a written text. And so we come back full circle to our point of departure, which is the historical reality of the Homeric text.

It can be said in general about the earliest attested stages of ancient Greek literature that the actual writing down of any given text was in the earliest phases tantamount to the production of yet another performance, to the extent that the technology of writing could produce a text that conferred a level of authority parallel to that conferred by an actual performance.[118] While I maintain that there is no evidence for arguing that the *Iliad* and the *Odyssey*, as compositions, resulted from the production of such texts, it is clear from the later evidence of the fifth century that there are instances where the *writing down* of a composition could become equivalent to its *performance*, so that a *written copy* could become tantamount to a *speech-act*.[119]

The point, however, is that the writing down of a composition as text does not mean that writing is a prerequisite for the text's composition—*so long as the oral tradition that produced it continues to stay alive.* So long as the oral tradition retains its performative authority, any text produced by and within such a tradition will continue to enjoy the privileged status of a composition-in-performance. And the idea of *text* will continue to serve as a primary metaphor for the very authority of composition-in-performance.

The intrinsic applicability of *text* as metaphor for *recomposition* helps explain a type of myth, attested in a wide variety of cultural contexts, where the evolution of a poetic tradition, moving slowly ahead in time until it reaches a relatively static phase, is reinterpreted by the myth as if it resulted from a single incident, pictured as the instantaneous recovery or even regeneration of a lost text, an archetype. In other words, there is a type of myth that offers a "big bang" theory of the origins of epic.

A particularly striking example is the myth about the making of the Book of Kings in the Classical Persian epic tradition:

> According to Ferdowsi's *Shāhnāma* I 21.126–136, a noble vizier assembles *mōbad*-s, wise men who are experts in the Law of Zoroaster, from all over the Empire, and each of these *mōbad*-s brings with him a "fragment" of a long-lost Book of Kings that had been scattered to the winds; each of the experts is called upon to recite, in turn, his respective "fragment," and the vizier composes a book out of these recitations. . . . The vizier reassembles the old book that had been disassembled, which in turn becomes the model for the *Shāhnāma* "Book of Kings" of Ferdowsi (*Shāhnāma* I 21.156–161). We see here paradoxically a myth about the synthesis of oral traditions that is articulated in terms of written traditions.[120]

Other examples abound. I cite just one from the living oral traditions of India. In Telugu society, there is an aetiological myth explaining why the Palnāḍu epic in now sung by untouchable Malas: "the epic, it is claimed, was first written by a Brahmin poet, torn into shreds, discarded, and then picked up by the present performers."[121]

There are also two examples from ancient Greece. The first is a myth from Sparta, centering on the theme of a disassembled book, scattered here and there throughout the Greek-speaking world, and then reassembled in a single incident, at one particular time and place, by a wise man credited with the juridical framework of his society, Lycurgus the Lawgiver. According to this myth, as reported by Plutarch, *Life of Lycurgus* 4.4, Lycurgus brought to Sparta the Homeric poems, which he acquired from a lineage of *rhapsōidoi*, 'rhapsodes,' called the Kreophyleioi, descended from Kreophylos of Samos. In Archaic Sparta, it appears that the Kreophyleioi of Samos were more authoritative than the rhapsodes elsewhere credited with the transmission of Homeric poetry, the Homeridai of Chios: as Aristotle reports (fr. 611.10 Rose), the introduction of the Homeric poems took place in Sparta by way of the Kreophyleioi of Samos.[122] With reference to the Homeric poems, Plutarch reports that Lycurgus, having received

them from the Kreophyleioi, 'had them written down,' ἐγράψατο (*Life of Lycurgus* 4.4), and that he then 'assembled' them (ibid.). What follows in Plutarch's account is worth citing verbatim: ἦν γάρ τις ἤδη δόξα τῶν ἐπῶν ἀμαυρὰ παρὰ τοῖς Ἕλλησιν, **ἐκέκτηντο** δὲ οὐ πολλοὶ μέρη τινά, σποράδην τῆς ποιήσεως, ὡς ἔτυχε, διαφερομένης· γνωρίμην δὲ αὐτὴν καὶ μάλιστα πρῶτος ἐποίησε Λυκοῦργος, 'for there was already a not-too-bright fame attached to these epics among the Greeks, and some of them *were in possession* [verb *kektēmai*] of some portions, since the poetry had been *scattered*, carried here and there by chance, and it was Lycurgus who was the first to make it [= the poetry] well-known' (*Life of Lycurgus* 4.4). In this passage, I have highlighted the word *kektēmai* 'possess,' with reference to the "ownership" of Homeric poetry. The same word is used by Herodotus in referring to the "ownership" of oracular poetry on the part of the Peisistratidai, the dynasty of tyrants at Athens (5.90.2).[123] Elsewhere, Herodotus refers to the manipulation, by the Peisistratidai, of oracular poetry with the help of one Onomakritos, described in this context as *diathetēs* 'arranger' of this poetry (7.6.3).[124]

This detail about a *diathetēs* 'arranger' of poetry brings us to the second of the two ancient Greek examples of the myth that we are presently considering. This second story is from Athens. Even more than the first story, it seems at first to be not a myth but a straightforward account of an historical *event*. I shall argue, however, that it can be explained as a myth that happens to account for a historical *process*. This myth, like others we have already examined, accounts for the evolution of a poetic tradition which, moving slowly ahead in time until it reaches a relatively static phase, is reinterpreted by the myth as if it resulted from a single incident, pictured as the instantaneous recovery or even regeneration of a lost text, an archetype. Again, myth is offering a "big bang" theory for the origins of epic. What makes the Athenian version of this type of myth more distinct than other versions is that we know more about the historical circumstances of its ultimate political appropriation.

According to this myth, or quasi-myth, a certain Onomakritos, the same person whom we have just seen described by Herodotus as a *diathetēs* 'arranger' of oracular poetry (7.6.3), was the member of a group of four

men commissioned in the reign of Peisistratos to super-
vise the 'arranging' of the Homeric poems, which
were before then 'scattered about' (διέθηκαν οὑτωσὶ
σποράδην οὔσας τὸ πρίν: Anecdota Graeca 1.6 ed.
Cramer).[125] There is a convergent report in Aelian,
Varia Historia 13.14, where the introduction of Homeric poetry to Sparta by Lycurgus is explicitly compared to a subsequent introduction of the Iliad and Odyssey to Athens by Peisistratos. In these accounts of the
supposedly original Athenian reception of Homeric poetry, reinforced by such celebrated passages as "Plato,"
Hipparchus 228b, and Cicero, De oratore 3.137, we
confront the germ of the construct that we have come to
know as the "Peisistratean Recension."

My purpose here is not to review the case for positing
a "Peisistratean Recension." [126] Rather, I simply point
out that the details of reports that have led to the positing
of this construct happen to match the details of myths
that explain the composition, performance, and diffusion of epic. The emphasis of these myths on the ultimate unity or integrity of any given epic, as we see
most dramatically illustrated in the Classical Persian example, corresponds to the reality of a unified and integrated text, such as the Homeric Iliad and Odyssey. It
also corresponds to the reality of the customary law in
effect at the Athenian festival of the Panathenaia, where
it was ordained that the performance of the Iliad and the
Odyssey by rhapsōidoi, 'rhapsodes,' had to follow the
sequence of composition, and that the entire composition had to be performed by one rhapsode after another,
likewise in their own sequence. Our two clear references
to this customary law, "Plato" Hipparchus 228b and
Diogenes Laertius 1.57, disagree about the identity of
the initiator of this practice, the first source indicating
the Peisistratidai and the second, Solon the Lawgiver.
For our purposes, the question of determining the originator of this custom is irrelevant to the more basic question of the significance of the custom itself.[127] The reality of this customary law, I submit, is a clear proof that
unity or integrity of composition is itself a tradition, and
is venerated as such.

It is in this context that I am finally ready to ask the
question: When was it that the Iliad and Odyssey were
definitively recorded as written texts? On the basis of
linguistic criteria, Richard Janko has proposed 750–
725 B.C. and 743–713 B.C. as absolute dates for the text-

fixation of the Iliad and the Odyssey respectively.[128] On
the basis of historical and archaeological considerations,
Ian Morris agrees, to the extent that the contents of the
Homeric poems seem clearly to reflect a social context
datable to the eighth century before our era.[129] Both
these assessments require the "dictation theory" for establishing such an early date. I would propose, however,
given the strong parallelisms between a written text and
certain patterns of evolution in oral poetic traditions,
that the dating of text-fixation can be much more fluid.
It can be argued at length that the Homeric tradition of
epic, in the process of evolution in composition, performance, and diffusion, became increasingly less fluid and
more stable in its patterns of recomposition, moving
slowly ahead in time until it reached a relatively static
phase.[130]

The static phase could easily have lasted two centuries or so. If we were to make cross sections at either
end of this static phase, I would picture at one end a
relatively more formative status starting with the later
part of the eighth century and, at the other end, an increasingly definitive status towards the middle of the
sixth century, by which time I can imagine the achievement of a near-textual status of the Homeric poems in
the context of performance by rhapsodes at the Panathenaia.[131] This length of time is not implausible when we
consider the case of the poetry attributed to Theognis of
Megara, where the external dating criteria applied to the
contents suggest a span of evolution exceeding a century and a half.[132]

The comparative evidence of living oral epic traditions that we have considered here goes a long way to
show that unity or integrity results from the dynamic
interaction of composition, performance, and diffusion
in the making of epic. I therefore continue to propose an
evolutionary model for the making of Homeric poetry.

NOTES

*The following abbreviations are used in the notes which
follow:

Nagy (1979) = G. Nagy, The Best of Achaeans: Concepts of
the Hero in Archaic Greek Poetry (Baltimore 1979).
Nagy (1981) = G. Nagy, "An Evolutionary Model for the

Text Fixation of Homeric Epos," in J. M. Foley, ed., *Oral Traditional Literature: A Festschrift for Albert Bates Lord* (Columbus, Ohio 1981) 390–393.

Nagy (1990) = G. Nagy, *Pindar's Homer: The Lyric Possession of an Epic Past* (Baltimore 1990).

Nagy, "Homer/Mythology" = "Homer and Comparative Mythology," in G. Nagy, *Greek Mythology and Poetics* (Ithaca 1990) 8–13.

Nagy, "Mythical Foundations" = "Mythical Foundations of Greek Society," in G. Nagy, *Greek Mythology and Poetics* (Ithaca 1990) 276–293.

Nagy (1992) = G. Nagy, "Homeric Questions," *TAPA* 122 (1992) 17–60.

OEI = S. H. Blackburn, P. J. Claus, J. B. Flueckiger, and S. S. Wadley, eds., *Oral Epics in India* (Berkeley and Los Angeles 1979).

Smith = J. D. Smith, "Old Indian: The Two Sanskrit Epics," in A. T. Hatto, ed., *Traditions of Heroic and Epic Poetry* (London 1980) 48–78.

1. See in general A. B. Lord, *The Singer of Tales* (Cambridge, Mass. 1960), whose formulations represent the legacy of his own fieldwork and the earlier work of his teacher, Milman Parry. Parry's writings were eventually reedited by his son, Adam: A. Parry, ed., *The Making of Homeric Verse: The Collected Papers of Milman Parry* (Oxford 1971).

2. Nagy (1981) 390–393. Further argumentation in two of my books, Nagy (1979) 5–9, and Nagy (1990) 8–9, 53–55, 79–80. My use of the term *performance* is not intended to convey any connotations of a stage-presence, as it were, on the part of the performer. I have in mind rather the *performative* dimension of an utterance, as analyzed from an anthropological perspective. For a pragmatic application of the word *performative*, I cite for example S. J. Tambiah, *Culture, Thought, and Social Action: An Anthropological Perspective* (Cambridge, Mass. 1985) 123–166.

3. A notable example is the son of Milman Parry: A. M. Parry, "Have we Homer's *Iliad*?" *YCS* 20 (1966)·175–216. Reprinted in A. M. Parry, *The Language of Achilles and Other Papers* (Oxford 1989) 104–140.

4. J. Griffin, *Homer on Life and Death* (Oxford 1980) xii-xiv.

5. This paragraph and the following four paragraphs are recast at Nagy (1992) 31–33.

6. The premier formulation of the "dictation theory": A. B. Lord, "Homer's Originality: Oral Dictated Texts," *TAPA* 74 (1953) 124–134. Reprinted in A. B. Lord, *Epic Singers and Oral Tradition* (Ithaca 1991) 38–47, with a 1990 addendum at 47–48.

7. See especially M. L. West, "Archaïsche Helden-dichtung: Singen und Schreiben," in W. Kullmann and M. Reichl, eds., *Der Übergang von der Mündlichkeit zur Literatur bei den Griechen* (Tübingen 1990) 33–50.

8. For a formulation of such an extent of diffusion, see West (supra n. 7) 33.

9. So West (supra n. 7) 34.

10. Further argumentation in Nagy (1990) 8–9, 53–55, 79–80.

11. References and further discussion in Nagy (1990) 72–79, especially 78 (following p. 19 n. 10).

12. For a survey, see R. Pfeiffer, *The History of Classical Scholarship: From the Beginnings to the End of the Hellenistic Age* (Oxford 1968) 73. I suggest that the metaphor of *kuklos* as the sum total of epic poetry goes back to the Homeric meaning of *kuklos* as 'chariot wheel' (*Iliad* 23.340, plural *kukla* at 5.722). For an extensive discussion of the Indo-European poetic tradition of comparing a well-crafted chariot wheel to a well-composed song (as in *Rig-Veda* 1.130.6), thereby setting up as parallels the craft of the master carpenter or "joiner" and the art of the poet (as in Pind., *Pyth.* 3.112–114), see R. Schmitt, *Dichtung und Dichtersprache in indogermanischer Zeit* (Wiesbaden 1967) 296–298. Further discussion in Nagy (1979) 297–300. In this same discussion, I stress that the root *ar-* as in *arariskō*, 'join, fit together' (the verb refers to the activity of the carpenter in the expression *ērare tektōn* at *Iliad* 4.110, 23.712), is shared by the word that means 'chariot wheel' in the Linear B texts, *harmo* (Knossos tablets Sg 1811, So 0437, etc.), and by the name of Homer, *Homēros*, the etymology of which is explained as 'he who joins together' (*homo-* plus *ar-*). Thus the making of the *kuklos* by the master poet Homer seems to be a global metaphor that pictures the crafting of the ultimate chariot wheel by the ultimate carpenter or, better, 'joiner.' I note the classification of both the *aoidos* 'singer' and the *tektōn* 'carpenter, joiner' under the category of *dēmiourgos* or 'itinerant artisan' at *Odyssey* 17.381–385. See also n. 86 below.

13. Pfeiffer (supra n. 12) 73–74. This paragraph and the four that follow are recast in Nagy (1992) 36–39.

14. Pfeiffer (supra n. 12) 117. I omit Pfeiffer's phrasing ". . . followed the lead of Aristotle and . . ."

15. Nagy (1979) 7, following A. M. Snodgrass, *The Dark Age of Greece: An Archaeological Survey of the Eleventh to the Eighth Centuries* (Edinburgh 1971) 421, 435; also 352, 376, 416–417, 421, 431.

16. Updated formulation in A. M. Snodgrass, *An Archaeology of Greece: The Present State and Future Scope of a Discipline* (Berkeley and Los Angeles 1987) 160, 165; also p. 123 of I. Morris, "The Use and Abuse of Homer," *CA* 5 (1986) 81–136. Eds. note: cf. I. Winter in this volume.

17. Nagy (1990) 53. The recessive accent of Ἕλληνες

'Hellenes,' an innovation that evidently superseded the expected *Ἕλληνες, indicates that the simplex form Ἕλληνες is predicated on the compound form Πανέλληνες 'pan-Hellenes,' as attested in *Iliad* 2.530 and Hes. *Op.* 528: see P. Chantraine, *Dictionnaire étymologique de la langue grecque* (Paris 1968–1980) 341. Thus the accentual history of the word for "Hellene" shows that the very concept of "Hellene" is predicated on the concept of "pan-Hellene."

18. Nagy (1981). This model is an alternative to the "dictation theory" (cited supra n. 6).

19. Cf. Nagy (1979) 7–9; cf. also Nagy (1990) 53–55. For a favorable assessment of this hermeneutic construct, see Snodgrass (supra n. 16) 160, 165.

20. Nagy (1990) 53–55.

21. J. R. Goody, *The Myth of the Bagre* (Oxford 1972).

22. See also J. R. Goody, *The Domestication of the Savage Mind* (Cambridge 1977) 119. This comparative evidence is applied to the question of Homeric poetry in Morris (supra n. 16) 84–85; see also p. 87 concerning the application of comparative evidence from the traditions of the Tiv in Nigeria.

23. Further discussion in Nagy (1990) 53, 55, 60, 72, 73, 171.

24. Nagy (1990) 70–71.

25. The quoted passage at this point introduces a note, which I criticize in n. 26 immediately below.

26. See pp. 194–195 of M. Griffith, "Contest and Contradiction in Early Greek Poetry," in M. Griffith and D. J. Mastronarde, eds., *Cabinet of the Muses: Essays on Classical and Comparative Literature in Honor of Thomas R. Rosenmeyer* (Atlanta 1990) 185–207. At a point that I mark with n. 25 in the quoted text, Griffith (p. 205 n. 40) adds the following observation: "This is argued, e.g., by G. Nagy (forthcoming), with reference to C. Lévi-Strauss, *The Way of the Masks*, trans. S. Modelski (Seattle 1982); but it will be clear from what follows that I think few poems apart from the *Iliad* and the *Odyssey* laid much claim to pan[-]Hellenic status at the time of their composition." Here he cross-refers to his p. 204 n. 34, where he refers to his article, M. Griffith, "Personality in Hesiod," in T. D'Evelyn, P. Psoinos, and T. R. Walsh, eds., *Studies in Classical Lyric: A Homage to Elroy Bundy, CA* 2 (1983) 37–65, especially his remarks at 46–47. For a response to those remarks, see Nagy (1990) 57–65. The forthcoming work to which Griffith referred can now be cited as pp. 57–65 in the same (Nagy [1990]), with special reference to the *Works and Days* of Hesiod.

27. Detailed discussion in Nagy (1990) 21–25.

28. See also the remarks on the Panathenaia in Nagy (1990) 21–23, 28, 54, 73, 75, 160, 174, 192; not cited by H. A. Shapiro, "*Mousikoi Agones:* Music and Poetry at the Panathenaia," in J. Neils, ed., *Goddess and Polis: The Panathen-*

aic Festival in Ancient Athens (Princeton 1992) 53–75. As Shapiro can see from my remarks, I agree with his inference (p. 73) that the Panathenaia, as reorganized by the Peisistratidai of Athens, played a major role in the privileging of the *Iliad* and the *Odyssey* as the definitive poems of Homer. For more on pan-Hellenic festivals as a context for the performance of epic, cf. O. Taplin, *Homeric Soundings: The Shaping of the Iliad* (Oxford 1992) 39.

29. A key work is OEI. Crucial articles in the volume: S. H. Blackburn and J. B. Flueckiger, "Introduction," OEI 1–11; S. H. Blackburn, "Patterns of Development for Indian Oral Epics," OEI 15–32; J. B. Flueckiger, "Caste and Regional Variants in an Oral Epic Tradition," OEI 33–54; P. J. Claus, "Behind the Text: Performance and Ideology in a Tulu Oral Tradition," OEI 55–74; S. S. Wadley, "Choosing a Path: Performance Strategies in a North Indian Epic," OEI 75–101; K. Kothari, "Performers, Gods, and Heroes in the Oral Epics of Rajasthan," OEI 102–117; K. Schomer, "Paradigms for the Kali Yuga: The Heroes of the Ālhā Epic and their Fate," OEI 140–154; J. D. Smith, "Scapegoats of the Gods: The Ideology of the Indian Epics," OEI 176–194.

30. I draw attention to the specific use of the terms "pan-Indian" and "geographical diffusion" by Blackburn (supra n. 29) 27.

31. Blackburn and Flueckiger (supra n. 29) 6.

32. In what follows, I rely especially on the work of J. D. Smith, cited here as Smith.

33. Smith 48. I may add that the variations attested in the textual tradition of these two monumental epics can be cited as indirect evidence for the relative lateness of text-fixation.

34. Smith 49.

35. Smith 73 notes that "the *Rāmāyaṇa* had been composed in the manner of an epic, rather than having evolved as an epic"; I suggest a parallel in the Homeric *Odyssey*.

36. Smith 49.

37. Smith 49.

38. Smith 49. On analogies to the Brahmin/Kṣatriya distinction in the context of the Greek city-state, see Nagy, "Mythical Foundations."

39. The essence of the Sūta class is traditionally formulated in terms of genealogy: viewed as sons of a union between a female of the Brahmin class and a male of the Kṣatriya class, they are assigned the social roles of tending horses, driving chariots, and serving as court poets (cf. Nagy, "Mythical Foundations" 291–292 n. 82).

40. Smith 50.

41. Smith 75 n. 4. It is fair to say that Kṛṣṇa becomes the god of the *Mahābhārata*, to the degree that "the epic is his theophany" (Smith 72).

42. Smith's overview of accretive patterns in Sanskrit epic

is not explicit in this regard. The work of another expert, M. C. Smith, *The Warrior Code of India's Sacred Song* (New York 1992; revised version of her Ph.D. thesis, "The Core of India's Great Epic," Harvard, 1972), is pertinent to the question of accretion in the process of oral tradition, though I do not necessarily agree with her ultimate formulation. She posits a "nucleus" of 3,000 verses (distinguished by the epic "irregular" *triṣṭubh* meter) as opposed to the 75,000 verses in the Poona critical edition of the *Mahābhārata*.

43. I should stress that, besides whatever similarities we may observe between the living oral traditions of contemporary India on the one hand and the two classical Sanskrit epics on the other, we should also expect a host of differences. One particular point of interest is the special role played by the Brahmin class in the perpetuation of the Sanskrit epics. There is also a related question: To what degree was the technology of writing an actual factor in the mnemonic traditions associated with the *Mahābhārata* and *Rāmāyaṇa*?

44. For minimalist working definitions of "myth" and "ritual," see e.g. Nagy, "Homer/Mythology" 8–10, summarizing the formulations of W. Burkert, "Mythisches Denken," in H. Poser, ed., *Philosophie und Mythos* (Berlin and New York 1979) 16–39, and *Greek Religion*, translated by J. Raffan (Cambridge, Mass. 1985) 8.

45. So Nagy, "Homer/Mythology" 10.

46. Wadley (supra n. 29) 79.

47. Kothari (supra n. 29) 102.

48. See O. M. Davidson, "Indo-European Dimensions of Herakles in *Iliad* 19.95–133," *Arethusa* 13 (1980) 197–202, especially 199–200; also D. S. Sinos, *Achilles, Patroklos, and the Meaning of* Philos, Innsbrucker Beiträge zur Sprachwissenschaft 29 (Innsbruck 1980) 14, and L. M. Slatkin, "The Wrath of Thetis," *TAPA* 116 (1986) 1–24. Further comments on the thematic connections between the heroes Herakles and Achilles in R. P. Martin, *The Language of Heroes: Speech and Performance in the Iliad* (Ithaca 1989) 228–230, and Nagy, "Homer/Mythology" 12–15. On Achilles as *pan-a-ōrios* 'the untimeliest of them all' see G. Nagy, "Theognis and Megara: A Poet's Vision of his City," in T. J. Figueira and G. Nagy, eds., *Theognis of Megara: Poetry and the* Polis (Baltimore 1985) 22–81, in particular p. 62. See now also J. V. O'Brien, *The Transformation of Hera: A Study of Ritual, Hero, and the Goddess in the Iliad* (Lanham, Md. 1993) 115–119, esp. 116 n. 9.

49. Nagy (1979) 182–184 (with reference to *Iliad* 18.54–60, *Homeric Hymn to Demeter*, and Adonis rituals); cf. also 114–121, 152–153, 174, 190–193.

50. Nagy (1979), especially p. 9. For a brief overview, with further bibliography, see Nagy, "Homer/Mythology," 10–13.

51. Nagy (1979) 7–10.

52. Cf. Nagy (1990) 400; also 136–142.

53. Kothari (supra n. 29) 105.

54. Kothari (supra n. 29) 105–106.

55. Kothari (supra n. 29) 102.

56. Blackburn (supra n. 29) 25; cf. also Kothari (supra n. 29) 110.

57. Blackburn (supra n. 29) 25.

58. Blackburn (supra n. 29) 26. "Indologists have often speculated that the cults of Rāma and Kṛṣṇa underwent a similar process of development" (ibid.).

59. See Nagy, "Homer/Mythology" 11; cf. Morris (supra n.16) 129. See also I. Morris, "Tomb Cult and the 'Greek Renaissance': The Past in the Present in the 8th Century B.C.," *Antiquity* 62 (1988) 750–761.

60. See the overview at OEI 240–241.

61. Kothari (supra n. 29) 110.

62. Kothari (supra n. 29) 110.

63. Blackburn and Flueckiger (supra n. 29) 10.

64. Blackburn (supra n. 29) 22.

65. Blackburn and Flueckiger (supra n. 29) 11.

66. Blackburn (supra n. 29) 20. For an example of a stance that treats the aspect of entertainment in ancient Greek poetics exclusively, see M. Heath, "The Ancient Grasp," *TLS*, June 15–21, 1990, 645–646.

67. Blackburn and Flueckiger (supra n. 29) 11.

68. Blackburn (supra n. 29) 21–22. The last point is illustrated by Blackburn (supra n. 29) 24–25 with two examples. In the Pābūjī narrative, which counts as a regional epic in his taxonomy, the Pābūjī figure turns out to be a reincarnation of the pan-Indian figure Lakṣmaṇa, the younger brother of Rāma. In the Devnārāyaṇ narrative, another regional epic, the hero Devnārāyaṇ turns out to be none other than the god Viṣṇu himself.

69. Blackburn (supra n. 29) 17–18. We may note the gap between the maximum assigned to the regional category, 300 miles, and the minimum assigned to the supraregional, 400. This gap reflects the fact that the data gathering is still at an early stage. The map that reflects the evidence available so far, as presented by Blackburn on p. 19, "is intended to present only the approximate spread of the traditions" (p. 17). Moreover, this map represents only the positive evidence of attestations, and the negative evidence indicating where certain epic traditions are *not* being performed is so far limited to the local and subregional traditions (p. 17). Thus the accuracy of the mapping "decreases as geographical spread increases" (ibid.).

70. Smith (supra n. 29) 178.

71. Detailed discussion in Nagy (1990) 21–25.

72. On which see Blackburn (supra n. 29) 27.

73. Blackburn (supra n. 29) 23.

74. Blackburn (supra n. 29) 23.

75. As in the bow song tradition of the Tampimār (on which see Blackburn [supra n. 29] 22).

76. Blackburn (supra n. 29) 18.

77. Flueckiger (supra n. 29) 33.

78. Blackburn (supra n. 29) 30. Cf. Schomer (supra n. 29) 142–143. In general, the Ālhā epic defies the typologies established by Blackburn, as he concedes at (supra n. 29) 29. As for Blackburn's concession about the heroes of the *Mahābhārata*, there are exceptions to the exception: folk traditions can deify heroes of Sanskrit epic, as in the case of the Draupadī cults of central Tamil Nadu, on which see Blackburn (supra n. 29) 30 n. 23.

79. Blackburn (supra n. 29) 23.

80. Smith (supra n. 29) 185.

81. See, e.g., Nagy, "The Death of Sarpedon and the Question of Homeric Uniqueness," in G. Nagy, *Greek Mythology and Poetics* (Ithaca 1990) 122–142. For more on the universalization of mortality and death in Homeric poetry, see Nagy (1990) 143 n. 40.

82. Blackburn and Flueckiger (supra n. 29) 9.

83. Blackburn and Flueckiger (supra n. 29) 9. In this context, I note the following important observation: "Each north Indian folk song genre usually has a distinctive textural and melodic pattern and many genres are melody-specific" (Wadley [supra n. 29] 93).

84. Blackburn and Flueckiger (supra n. 29) 9.

85. Wadley (supra n. 29) 80.

86. Details in Nagy (1990) 56–67. Cf. supra n. 12. W. Burkert, *The Orientalizing Revolution: Near Eastern Influence on Greek Culture in the Early Archaic Age*, trans. by M. E. Pinder and W. Burkert (Cambridge, Mass. 1992), organizes his chapters along the lines of categories of *dēmiourgos* as catalogued in *Odyssey* 17.381–385.

87. Kothari (supra n. 29) 103.

88. For a far-reaching investigation of such mirroring, see Martin (supra n. 48).

89. W. Rösler, *Dichter und Gruppe: Eine Untersuchung zu den Bedingungen und zur historischen Funktion früher Lyrik am Beispiel Alkaios* (Munich 1980).

90. For an illustration of the "catholic/epichoric" dichotomy in the application of lyric compositions, see, e.g., the commentary on Theognis 367–370 in Nagy (1990) 374–375.

91. Kothari (supra n. 29) 103.

92. Cf. Kothari (supra n. 29) 103. For the attestation of competition events in Ḍholā epic performance in western Uttar Pradesh, see Wadley (supra n. 29) 98.

93. Blackburn and Flueckiger (supra n. 29) 9.

94. Flueckiger (supra n. 29) 36.

95. Flueckiger (supra n. 29) 41.

96. Flueckiger (supra n. 29) 37.

97. Flueckiger (supra n. 29) 40.

98. Flueckiger (supra n. 29) 40.

99. See Nagy, "The Wedding of Hektor and Andromache: Epic Contacts in Sappho 44LP," *Comparative Studies in Greek and Indic Meter* (Cambridge, Mass. 1974) 118–139.

100. Claus (supra n. 29) 60.

101. Claus (supra n. 29) 60. Instances of switch from third to second to first person: Claus (supra n. 29) 74.

102. Claus (supra n. 29) 72.

103. Claus (supra n. 29) 60.

104. Claus (supra n. 29) 72.

105. Further discussion in Nagy (1990) 56–57.

106. See, e.g., A. T. Hatto, "Kirghiz: Mid-Nineteenth Century," in A. T. Hatto, ed., *Traditions of Heroic and Epic Poetry* (London 1980) 307; cited, with further analogies, by Martin, (supra n. 48) 6–7.

107. A key work is J. Opland, "Xhosa: The Structure of Xhosa Eulogy and the Relation of Eulogy to Epic," in J. B. Hainsworth and A. T. Hatto, eds., *Traditions of Heroic and Epic Poetry* II: *Characteristics and Techniques*, Modern Humanities Research Association (London 1989) 121–143. Cf. also J. Opland, "Lord of the Singers," *Oral Tradition* 3 (1988) 353–367.

108. Nagy (1990), especially 146–198, an expanded version of G. Nagy, "Ancient Greek Praise and Epic Poetry," in J. M. Foley, ed., *Oral Tradition in Literature: Interpretation in Context* (Columbia, Mo. 1986) 89–102.

109. See Nagy, "Homer/Mythology," 16–17.

110. E.g., Flueckiger (supra n. 29) 50 n. 17.

111. Kothari (supra n. 29) 103.

112. Kothari (supra n. 29) 103.

113. Kothari (supra n. 29) 104.

114. Kothari (supra n. 29) 104.

115. Kothari (supra n. 29) 104.

116. Extensive discussion, with examples, in Nagy (1990) 146–214. Opland, "Xhosa" (supra n. 107) 139, offers an interesting application of comparative Xhosa evidence as a parallel to my model of pan-Hellenization.

117. Opland, "Xhosa" (supra n. 107) 139.

118. A longer version of the argumentation from here on is to be found in Nagy (1992) 43–52.

119. Further discussion in Nagy (1990) 169, 217, 219.

120. Nagy (1990) 74 n. 110, following pp. 111–127 in O. M. Davidson, "The Crown-Bestower in the Iranian Book of Kings," *Acta Iranica, Hommages et Opera Minora* 10: *Papers in Honour of Professor Mary Boyce* (Leiden 1985) 61–148.

121. Blackburn (supra n. 29) 32 n. 25.

122. More on the Kreophyleioi of Samos, as rivals of the Homeridai of Chios, in Nagy (1990) 23, 74. For a review of my diachronic approach to the concept of *rhapsōidoi* 'rhapsodes,' I refer to the detailed discussion in the same work, pp. 21–28; also in my *Greek Mythology and Poetics* (Ithaca, N.Y. 1990) 42, where I conclude: "it is simplistic and even misleading to contrast, as many have done, the 'creative' *aoidos* ['singer'] with the 'reduplicating' *rhapsōidos*." This conclusion is corroborated by A. Ford, "The Classical Definition of ΡΑΨΩΙΔΙΑ," *CP* 83 (1988) 300–307. Given that the metaphor of carpentry as songmaking in Indo-European languages is parallel to the metaphor of weaving (see Schmitt [supra n. 12] 298–301), I propose the following proportionality of metaphors: the *carpenter* of song is to the *joiner* of song as the *weaver* of song is to the *stitcher* of song, that is, to the *rhapsōidos*. In other words, just as a joiner is a specialized carpenter, capable of special feats of craftsmanship like the making of a chariot wheel (see n. 12 above), so also a stitcher is a specialized weaver. By extension, the metaphor of a joiner or a stitcher, as distinct from a carpenter or a weaver, conveys the idea of a specialized poet. Just as *Homēros* is the ultimate 'joiner,' so also the poetry of Homer is the work of the *rhapsōidos*, the one who stitches the song together. The esthetics of the rhapsode are in fact built into Homeric poetry: when Achilles is paradigmatically singing the *klea* or epics of heroes at *Iliad* 9.189, Patroklos is waiting for his turn, in order to take up the song where Achilles left off (9.190–191), much as

rhapsodes sing in sequence, one taking his turn after another ("Plato," *Hipparchus* 228b, and Diogenes Laertius 1.57). On the sequential singing of rhapsodes, see Nagy (1990) 23; see also p. 202 on the symbolism of Patroklos' listening to Achilles as equivalent to the audience's listening to Homer.

123. Further details in Nagy (1990) 159, 168–169, 220.

124. Further details in Nagy (1990) 174.

125. Nagy (1990) 174.

126. For a brief restatement and survey of primary sources, see T. W. Allen, *Homer: The Origins and the Transmission* (Oxford 1924) 225–238.

127. Further comments in Nagy (1990) 21, 23. See also the references at n. 28 above.

128. R. Janko, *Homer, Hesiod and the Hymns* (Cambridge 1982) 228–231.

129. Morris (supra n. 16), especially 93, 104.

130. See Nagy (1990) 52–81.

131. See especially Nagy (1990) 80; cf. also n. 28 above. This model differs from that of G. S. Kirk, *The Songs of Homer* (Cambridge 1962) 88–98, who posits a sequence of oral transmission starting with a monumental composer, who is to be defined as an individual Homer, and proceeding from there into the historical period of sixth-century Athens. For a critique, see M. S. Jensen, *The Homeric Question and the Oral-Formulaic Theory* (Copenhagen 1980) 113–114. For another critique, from a different angle, see West (supra n. 7) 36–37.

132. See Nagy, "Theognis and Megara" (supra n. 48) 33–34.

12

THE GEOMETRIC CATALOGUE OF SHIPS

◆

J. K. ANDERSON

On the east side of the lower course of the River Fonissa, which emerges from the mountains of the northern Peloponnese to enter the Gulf of Corinth between the modern Kato Loutron and Kamari, there stood in classical times a substantial village, now attested by broken pottery and roof tiles. On the west side of the river there is evidence for Bronze Age occupation of a small but naturally defensible foothill. These slight remains, described elsewhere by the present writer and another,[1] may serve as a starting point for a tribute to Professor Vermeule, among whose far greater contributions to Homeric studies the Sather Lectures delivered at Berkeley in 1975 hold a distinguished place.

A name for the classical site is perhaps provided by Pausanias[2]—Donussa, a township which no longer existed in the Antonine period but was remembered, puzzlingly, as having belonged to, and been destroyed by, the people of Sikyon. Pausanias was also told that Donussa had played a part, though a humble one, in world history, and that "lofty Donoessa" had been listed in the *Iliad* among the cities of Agamemnon's kingdom,[3] until Peisistratus, or his editors, changed the name, hith-

erto transmitted by word of mouth, to the "Gonoessa" that is printed in our modern texts. Pausanias does not dismiss these local pretensions out of hand, as the moderns do—rightly, if the name Donussa belongs to our site, whose elevation above the coastal plain hardly qualifies it to be called "lofty."[4] His own estimate of a city's place in history seems often to be based on the part it played in the great pan-Hellenic struggles—the Trojan War, the defeat of the Mede, and the last conflict with Rome. His Donussan informants may have shared his historiographical outlook, and found in the Catalogue of Ships the best opportunity to immortalize an otherwise forgotten corner of an obscure district.

They were not the only ones. At Chaeronea, which has no place of its own in Homer, Pausanias heard that the city was the Arne of the Catalogue of Ships.[5] This claim cannot be traced before Pausanias' time, and one might fancy that it was made up for his benefit; but it is surely connected with ties between Boiotia and a Thessalian Arne mentioned by Thucydides and Strabo. Strabo reports that the Boiotians took Coroneia when they returned from "Thessalian Arne" after the Trojan

War, and that Acraephium was called Arne by "the poet," who gave it the same name as the Thessalian Arne. But he adds that some people say that Arne was swallowed up by the lake (Copais), so there was no certainty in his time. Strabo's remark on Coroneia is consistent with the tradition recorded by Thucydides that the Boiotian expulsion from Thessalian Arne and settlement in "Boiotia" dated from sixty years after the Trojan War—a tradition reconciled with the position of the Boiotians in the Catalogue by the claim that a portion of them had settled in Boiotia previously.[6]

If there was no possible place for a city in the story of the Trojan War, a connection might be found through the scattering of the Greek fleet on its homeward voyage. Pallene in the Chalcidice provides an example at least as early as the fifth century B.C.; the postwar settlement of Diomedes in Italy is another case in point.[7] If their patrons had traditions of Trojan glory surely the poets found room for them in their recitals; if no tradition existed the Muses who know everything could supply one.

The possibility that the poets' tales were ultimately based on historic fact is of course not contradicted by this. Though the "reality" of the Trojan War remains unproved, nothing in the archaeological or other discoveries of the past century forbids us to believe that at some time during the Bronze Age a king of Mycenae led a host of Greek allies to sack and burn a stronghold in the Troad. That this stronghold stood where it was placed by the traditions of later antiquity there is every reason to believe. The present inquiry does not require us to decide which of the successive fortresses uncovered by the excavations of Schliemann and Blegen was "Priam's Troy," and whether the "Trojan War" was one incident in the turmoil that marked the end of the Bronze Age, or was, as Professor Vermeule has argued,[8] an achievement of the Shaft Grave kings of Mycenae three centuries earlier. Let us assume no more than the coalition led by the king of Mycenae, and it will follow that descendants of the members of that coalition remembered their ancestors' achievements, though how many generations back became increasingly doubtful as the centuries passed.

Dr. Morris, in a tribute more worthy of Professor Vermeule than is this, has reminded us that artists, as well as poets, could have kept alive the memory, not merely of warlike expeditions, but of individual participants.[9] One can imagine Theran children being shown the paintings in the West House and told that this was grandfather's ship, decorated, as the family's ships always were, with flying birds; that the other vessels belonged to such and such captains; that the warriors in their boars'-tusk helmets were our allies, or our mercenaries, led by such and such a king; and that the painted cities represented named seaport towns whose rulers had been numbered among world leaders a generation or two earlier. Again, the civilized warriors and their savage opponents, whose combats were represented on the walls of the palace of Messenian Pylos, and the river at whose ford the fight took place,[10] were probably names rather than abstractions to the feasters in the Great Hall.

Such monuments, if known to be complete records, will while they endure have served not merely as reminders of who did participate in the events commemorated, but as controls, forbidding poets to introduce new names to please new patrons—"No! The Naxians had no part in the Great Expedition! There is no Naxian ship in the painting." The pictures will thus have fixed, for a time, the details of the verbal catalogues that must have come first, whether these were simply instructions to the painters or had already been formalized by poets.

Nor was narrative art the only control on verbal tradition. Every Mycenaean child must have been able to attach a king's name to each tombstone in the Grave Circles, and many rare objects must have had pedigrees like those given by the poet to Agamemnon's scepter or the boars'-tusk helmet of the Doloneia.[11] But the further control, to us the most reliable and important, of the written word does not enter into the question. No names in linear script explain the subject matter of Bronze Age wall-paintings or rescue from anonymity the kings lying under their gold masks. No Delphic serpent-column recorded the states that sent their contingents to gratify the sons of Atreus. The scribes of Knossos and Pylos were perfectly capable of drawing up lists of ships and men; but they wrote for the purposes of year-by-year administration, not for posterity.[12]

We may certainly suppose that the first poet who sang of the Trojan War while the event was still fresh in people's memories included a "catalogue" of the participants, or two catalogues, one for each side. Such catalogues seem to be part of the stuff of ballad poetry:

> He chose the Gordons and the Graemes,
> With them the Lindsays light and gay,
> But the Jardines would not with him ride,
> And they rue it to this day.

It would be a tactless minstrel who told a representative of the Jardines as much to his face, and some versions substitute an innocuous reference to the Earl of Fife's raid "over Solway," marginally relevant to the poet's proper theme—the Battle of Otterburn.[13] Additions to, rather than subtractions from, the Homeric Catalogue of Ships have been suspected;[14] at all events, the possibility of tactful editing remains open. Of more concern is the general question whether the Catalogue as a whole is substantially a Bronze Age document, composed while events were fresh in everyone's mind, or a later invention.

Here it seems necessary to guard against wishful thinking. One would like to believe in the thousand (or 1,186) ships, and in the face that launched them. If the Catalogues contain no fantasies, like squadrons of Amazons on the Trojan side,[15] we note the fact with regret, while at the same time we admit it as an argument in favor of their historicity.

But, if not fantastic, the numbers recorded are wholly disproportionate to their objective. The small fortress that has been revealed by excavation (and once more it is irrelevant to this discussion whether "Priam's Troy" was Troy VI or Troy VIIa) would have been no match for an expeditionary force of perhaps a hundred thousand men.[16] Even if the Greek forces were dispersed in search of provisions, as Thucydides imagined[17] (and he probably also imagined a Troy of wide ways, temples, and palaces like the city described by the poet), there should have been more than enough available at the seat of war for a complete investment. Nor does the Bronze Age evidence suggest that fleets and armies on this scale were characteristic of the time. "The thousands of vessels which sailed from Aulis far exceed the modest number on this" [Theran] "fresco."[18] Nine ships in all—four Egyptian and five enemy—appear on the vic-

tory monument of Rameses III,[19] though no doubt his artists were restricted by the space available to them and did not attempt to show the actual numbers engaged. The forces deployed under the "Counts" of Pylos to guard the Messenian coast against the invasion that proved fatal to their kingdom are numbered by fifties and hundreds, or even tens and twenties, not by thousands. (It has however been maintained that the small number of "watchers" "does not suggest that any great peril impended in this quarter" and that the main force of the kingdom was concentrated elsewhere. The separate lists of "rowers" may provide evidence for such a concentration—but still not on a Homeric scale.[20])

It has, however, been argued that the Greek Catalogue in particular contains geographical information that is demonstrably true of the Late Bronze Age and of no other period. One of the greatest of Professor Vermeule's predecessors in the Sather Chair devoted one lecture to "The Homeric Description of Greece," and to the claim to have "vindicated the Catalogue" and "established that the Catalogue is substantially an inheritance from the Mycenaean era; that it has survived independently of that version of the story which culminates in the *Iliad;* and that it has been rather carelessly inserted into the *Iliad* after the composition of the *Iliad* in something like its present form."[21] My respect for Sir Denys Page, to say nothing of my gratitude for innumerable acts of kindness, almost forbids me to put forward my own very different opinions.

Page's conclusions are based on the fact that many places throughout the area of Greece covered by the Catalogue ceased to be inhabited at the end of the Bronze Age. There is a strong probability that some of these are to be identified with places named in the Catalogue which later Greek geographers were unable to identify.[22] Since Page wrote, the evidence for sites abandoned at the end of the Bronze Age has been multiplied by Hope Simpson and Lazenby,[23] and it is notable that the additional evidence that they have provided does not lead them to agree with Page that the Catalogue "is a list of contingents assembling for an expedition overseas; and it is so close in time to the historical event with which it is connected that it seems improbable—to me, inconceivable—that that connexion should be fictitious."[24] Their view is that the numbers of ships and men are implausible; "nor is it really any easier to believe that the Catalogue even preserves, without much exaggeration, the *extent* of the confederacy . . . it is still difficult to believe in cooperation, on the scale indicated by the Catalogue, in an overseas military expedition."[25]

But the Catalogue contains more than one sort of information.[26] What it has to tell about the names of Bronze Age kingdoms and of their rulers is not necessarily compromised by exaggerations in the military resources of each. In other words, one can believe that the kingdoms, and even the kings, named in the Catalogue existed, without necessarily believing that they furnished for the expedition against Troy the numbers of ships assigned to each, or even that they all took part in the Trojan War.[27]

For the names of kings we have no confirmation. Names famous in Greek legend have been recognized in Hittite records, but not with complete certainty and not necessarily from the right places or at the right times. Other equally famous names have been found, borne sometimes by very humble people, in the Pylos documents, but the texts that refer to the *wanax* do not name him.[28] At least we cannot say, "We have complete contemporary records of the kings of Pylos for ten generations before its final destruction, and there is no Nestor among them." The documents neither prove nor disprove that Nestor was an historic figure.

What the tablets do suggest, however, is that the places that mattered in the administration of the Bronze Age kingdom of Pylos were not those that mattered to the poet who compiled the Catalogue.[29] That the kingdom existed, and that its capital was indeed named Pylos, the records do most triumphantly prove. But that the poets—to whom we owe the stories told by Nestor in the *Iliad,* and the accounts of his kingdom in the *Odyssey,* and the entry in the Catalogue—placed Nestor's Pylos in Messenia, where Blegen's excavations have shown that the great Bronze Age Pylos actually stood, remains questionable today, as it was in antiquity.[30] And the supposed proof that the Catalogue must have been composed before the end of the Bronze Age because it contains accurate geographical information that is applicable to no other period is flawed, as A. Giovannini has pointed out.[31] In the first place, the claim that it is "inconceivable"[32] that any place-name that was known after the end of the Bronze Age could have been forgotten

during "the historic period" is ill founded. It is not a Classical writer but Strabo, relying on Apollodorus, who tells us of so many lost Boiotian cities,[33] and it is at least conceivable that the depopulation of Greece during the Hellenistic period is responsible for the disappearance of these townships, whose names were either lost or left floating like ghosts with no firm abode. We certainly do not know every name of every inhabited locality in Archaic and Classical Greece;[34] and Strabo's testimony (though not necessarily that of his source) is made doubtful by his statement that of Mycenae itself nothing was to be seen in his time; it had been completely rased by the Argives.[35]

While it is an established fact that many sites ceased to be inhabited at the end of the Bronze Age, it is often no more than conjecture that they bore in the Bronze Age the ancient names assigned to them by modern scholars. It is quite certain that an important Bronze Age site occupied a position commanding the road from Delphi to the Bay of Itea (as it is known at present).[36] Since this site was abandoned at the end of the Bronze Age, it is quite certain (for other reasons also) that this site is not the Kirrha that was destroyed early in the sixth century B.C. by the confederacy that fought the First Sacred War. But even if Kirrha is to be distinguished from Krisa it is not certain that the name "Krisa" originally belonged to the Bronze Age site and that the Catalogue's use of "Krisa" rather than "Kirrha" is proof that it transmits information originating in the Bronze Age. The modern consensus seems to distinguish Krisa from Kirrha; but "Kirrhaian" in Aeschines and Demosthenes seems to be much the same as "Krisaian" in Herodotus.[37] Again, in the *Homeric Hymn to Apollo*, the "Krisa" where Apollo builds his temple is surely Delphi itself, not, as Hope Simpson and Lazenby maintain, the Bronze Age site below it.[38] That the name is far more ancient than either the Catalogue[39] or the *Hymn* seems probable enough, but that a poet's use of it proves that he composed his lines during the Bronze Age does not follow.[40]

Again, convincing arguments are advanced for supposing that the "Dorion" of the poets is the major prehistoric settlement revealed by excavation at Malthi in Messenia.[41] Malthi was abandoned at the end of the Bronze Age, and cannot be the "Doureon" in Messenia that entertained Delphic envoys in the Hellenistic period.[42] And it may well seem that if either the inhabitants of this otherwise unknown Doureon or their Delphic guests had believed that the place had anything to do with the Dorion of the poets they would have spelled it accordingly. But the similarity is at least sufficient to raise the possibility that the name had an independent local existence which had nothing to do with the poetic tradition.[43]

Indeed at this point one might ask whether the tradition that Pylos itself stood in Messenia—a tradition that we now know was based on the facts of Bronze Age political geography—was not maintained by obstinate local memory rather than by the poets, whose accounts, as has been seen already,[44] suggest a location fifty miles to the north, closer to the Alpheios fords. For the destruction of a settlement did not necessarily mean that it disappeared without trace. At Dorion, where according to Strabo there was nothing to be seen, Pausanias found ruins, and a spring,[45] though we cannot, I suppose, be certain that the ruins were those of the Bronze Age settlement abandoned more than a thousand years earlier. Nine centuries before Pausanias, while Greece was still scantily populated and the destruction of antiquities that must have accompanied urbanization had scarcely begun, the countryside probably was full of ruins. The people of that time must often have admired the shattered remains of castles and mansions where the modern archaeologist finds only a handful of Bronze Age sherds. These buildings and their possessors may have been named either in the tales told by village grandparents round the winter fire or in the stories brought from the outer world by minstrels. The poet who fitted the homecoming of Odysseus into the topography of Ithaca[46] may have been told by the islanders that the ruins of the col of Stavros were those of their legendary king's palace. Or he may have told them. The information, whoever supplied it, might have been correct. In any case, some considerable building stood there in the Bronze Age, of which only the last miserable scraps survived to be recorded and classified in modern times.[47]

The Catalogue omits several important places which archaeological evidence shows to have been inhabited in the Mycenaean period.[48] On the other hand, it cannot be proved that any of the places named in the Catalogue was not inhabited until after the Bronze Age.[49] But if the Catalogue was compiled, at least in part, out of stories attached to Bronze Age ruins, it is possible at the same time both to accept that the places to which it refers are "real" and to deny that it itself is an authentic historical document of the Late Bronze Age. This would seem to remove at least some of the difficulties raised by the boundaries of some of the principal kingdoms. Nestor's kingdom has already been discussed, and we have seen that some of the most distinguished recent scholars accept that the poets seem to place Pylos well to the north of the actual Messenian palace, the location of which, however, was not wholly lost to tradition.[50] It has been very persuasively suggested that the poets' tales, and the Catalogue entry, reflect a time when the Triphylians were still maintaining their independence between Messenia (perhaps already a Spartan province) and Elis. At the same time they, like the Pisans beyond the Alpheios, may well have claimed to be the descendants of the original and rightful possessors of the land.[51]

The territories assigned to Agamemnon by the Catalogue might be explained in similar fashion. The present writer has been taken to task for asserting more than a third of the century ago the belief (which he still holds) that "the boundaries of the Kingdom of Mycenae in the Catalogue are too strange to be accepted."[52] He is therefore pleased that it has been more recently, and more ably, maintained that "le Cataloguiste avait fabriqué à Diomède et Agamemnon des états qui eux n'existaient pas."[53] The trouble lies not with the northern extension of Agamemnon's frontiers; the Corinthia and Argolis form a single administrative unit in modern Greece, and the network of Mycenaean roads through the passes shows that they were closely linked in the Bronze Age. Nor is there any difficulty in supposing a further extension westward along the shore of the Corinthian gulf. What is hard to suppose is that the Mycenae of the Shaft Graves, or of the Lion Gate, or even of the Warrior Vase, did not command the fertile plain that it overlooks, and was not the heart of the Mycenaean state but merely a frontier fortress. It is notable that scholars who maintain that the Catalogue is an accurate description of an actual Bronze Age kingdom do not agree on how its frontiers are to be explained, or on the date to which they are to be assigned. To Page, the solution lies in the relationship of Mycenae and Tiryns—". . . one place was subordinate to the other; and that is what the Catalogue asserts, and the *Iliad* confirms."[54] Hope Simpson and Lazenby argue that "it is difficult to think of" poets "inventing anything quite so strange as . . . the kingdom of Agamemnon" and that "the very strangeness of the kingdom, however, far from indicating that it never really existed, in fact provides the best ground for believing that it does correspond to reality." But they acknowledge that this "reality" is "hardly conceivable in LH IIIB"—the period to which they assign the Trojan War—and conclude that "we appear to find a reflection not so much of the great days of LH IIIB, as of the succeeding period when, as Desborough has shown, the cultural unity of LH IIIB had disintegrated, but the Mycenaean way of life still went on." [55]

But if we are to conclude that "the Catalogue suggests a time when a much larger state . . . had split into two, leaving the great fortress of Mycenae as the back-door to a realm in Corinthia and Achaea" [56] we may wonder why it was this realm, and not its great predecessor, that was commemorated by the poets. Another explanation of the Catalogue entry seems possible, and perhaps preferable—that the poet wished to reconcile with the facts of his own day the inescapable, and one would like to think true, tradition that the king of Mycenae led the expedition to Troy. Let us suppose that in his time the people of several districts along the south shore of the Corinthian gulf (including, perhaps, our Donussa) claimed that their ancestors had been settled in their present abodes by kings of the House of Agamemnon;[57] that he had to make allowance for the pride of contemporary Argos—the seat of kings much more capable of rewarding poetic talent than whoever then lived in Mycenae. Might not he have produced something like the Mycenaean kingdom of the Catalogue?

Ithaca, too, or rather the kingdom of Odysseus,[58] is surrounded by problems which have led to speculation on "the probability . . . that Odysseus was a folk-hero of western Greece who was drawn into the Ionian heroic tradition . . ." [59] This does not, I take it, exclude the possibility that behind the "folk-hero" there is an historic figure; but perhaps we may not take for granted that this figure did take part in the historic Trojan War, or was named by the ballad-singers who (perhaps) recorded the actual participants in their briefer catalogues. In any case it would seem to me that the Catalogue is to be faulted not for giving him a "wretched realm" [60] but for

giving him too much—at least in land, though not in ships. If Odysseus and his great opponent Salaminian Ajax (also suspected of belonging to a tradition older than that of the Trojan War)[61] muster only twelve ships apiece, surely the point is that their contribution to the Greek host is a personal one? One is the brains of the Greeks, the other the brawn. As kings, they have to have a following, but the size of that following is unimportant. If Odysseus had ruled no more than Ithaca, that would have given him a kingdom to match Salamis. And if Salamis could provide twelve ships, surely Ithaca—joined with a large part of rich Cephallenia (the most probable explanation of "Samos" of the Catalogue[62]) and the whole of Zacynthus, "pearl of the Levant," and possessions, if rather doubtful ones, on the mainland—could have done more? Did the poet of the Catalogue scrape together a kingdom for Odysseus out of whatever he could detach from the realm of Meges, because "*in the original Catalogue*" (that is, the Bronze Age document in which Meges supposedly was recorded as the ruler of the western isles) "*there was no Odysseus at all*"?[63] Or did the poet give Odysseus more than his original poor island, in order to gratify contemporaries who claimed that their ancestors had gone to Troy led by the "folk-hero of western Greece"?

If the Catalogue refers, at least sometimes, to ruins dating from the Bronze Age, it can mention "real places that were not inhabited at any later period" without being itself a Bronze Age document. Page laid great emphasis on the epithets with which places named in the Catalogue are described. "How could an Ionian poet living in the 10th or 9th or 8th century B.C. . . . know that there were many doves at Messe . . . and vineyards at Arne . . . that Aegilips was rugged, Oloosson white, Enispe windy, Pteleon a meadowland, Helos on the coast?" [64] Scholars have concerned themselves with the question of how far the epithets may in fact be regarded as conventional.[65] In this connection, Giovannini's observation that some which are not found elsewhere in the Homeric epic were used by the Delphic oracle may have a bearing on the Catalogue's date and origin.[66] But we may allow that, conventional or not, the epithets could have been chosen as appropriate, without conceding that they ceased to be appropriate after the time of the Trojan War.

The interests of the supposed contemporaries of the Catalogue poet in Bronze Age ruins manifested themselves in ways that have left traces in the archaeological record. Nearly forty years ago, J. M. Cook investigated a sanctuary of Agamemnon outside the walls of Mycenae, founded "about the end of the eighth century." He concluded that the establishment of this and other hero-cults originating at about the same time was "directly caused by the arrival of an epic on the mainland of Greece, which was powerful enough to alter people's habits."[67] Developing this suggestion elsewhere,[68] he noted, amongst other evidence, offerings laid in Late Geometric times outside Mycenaean tombs in Attica and the Argolid, the foundation of the sanctuary of Menelaos and Helen near Sparta upon the ruins of a Bronze Age mansion,[69] and the bronze tripods from the cave at Polis in Ithaca, where somebody many centuries later, in the Hellenistic period, made a humble dedication to Odysseus.[70] Whatever caused the Greeks of the Late Geometric period to take an interest in the past, whose traces were all about them, it is a fact that they did so, and in this connection particular attention may be paid to the foundation of major sanctuaries, after a gap of centuries upon sites inhabited but not necessarily sacred in the Bronze Age. A member of the University of California may excuse himself for passing over the perhaps less clear-cut cases of Olympia and Delphi and drawing attention to the history of Nemea, as revealed by Professor Stephen G. Miller.[71]

I am not, however, suggesting that the Catalogue was a cause of this revived interest in the past, but that it was a product of it. Here it will be as well to remember it is generally agreed that the Catalogue is neither an integral part of the *Iliad* nor a digest of information extracted from the rest of the poem.[72] How then did the poet of the Catalogue learn his facts—or what he reports as facts? Here one may begin by agreeing wholeheartedly with Kirk that "a detailed survey . . . suggests different dates of origin for various pieces of information."[73] The preeminence of Mycenae (though not necessarily the boundaries of its dominions); the name of Pylos (though not necessarily its geographical position)—here certainly we have tradition rooted in the Bronze Age and, one would like to think, in memories of the actual expedition to Troy. Again, Page has argued that we may

accept the antiquity of the Athenian entry in the Catalogue, though for a different reason.[74] "Menestheus the son of Peteos"[75] was not too illustrious to be forgotten, but too obscure to be invented.[76] But did his neighbor Ajax actually sail to Troy with twelve or any other number of ships, and beach them beside the Athenians? And did the Boiotians do anything in the historic Trojan War to deserve their position at the head of the Catalogue, with the largest ships and the most elaborately detailed contingent?

That the fleet mustered at Aulis is agreed by the poets almost unanimously; only Shakespeare will have it that

The princes orgulous, their high blood chaf'd
Have to the port of Athens sent their ships.[77]

One would not suggest that on the historical question of the base from which the expedition really sailed his authority is as good as Homer's. If it was not from Aulis, we do not know from where, and never will, any more than we will ever know for certain the names of the cities in the Theran wall-painting. But Aulis is not the most convenient base for a king from the Peloponnese planning to invade Anatolia. The unlucky detour of Agesilaus, in order to sacrifice where Agamemnon had sacrificed, only serves to prove as much.[78] Of course it also serves to prove, if proof were needed, that classical Greece regarded Agamemnon's muster at Aulis as historical fact and not as an invention of the poets. And if the poets did invent it, at least the tradition that Aulis was a seaport town in the late Bronze Age is based on fact.[79]

Whatever the starting point of the actual expedition against Troy, it is from Boiotia that the Catalogue starts. And Boiotia is also the starting point of an imagined itinerary, or rather sequence of itineraries, through which the different areas named in the Catalogue can be visited one after another in the same sequence as that recorded by the poet. Giovannini has noted that this sequence corresponds to that observed in an inscription which lists the various cities and towns where Delphic envoys received hospitality at some time in the Hellenistic age, and concludes that the poet of the Catalogue had a similar list in front of him.[80] This last suggestion has not won general acceptance,[81] and would indeed seem to be unnecessary. If there was an itinerary, somebody (or conceivably more than one person) had actually made the journey; it certainly was not plotted on a map. And why should not that person have been the poet himself? Those modern scholars who have even entertained the possibility have vehemently rejected it, but they have given no proofs that it cannot have been so.[82] "Nobody," says Page, "supposes that a Boeotian, or an Ionian from Asia Minor, travelled in the Dark Ages round the mainland, blazing a trail for Pausanias and Baedeker; indeed it is doubtful whether the most tactful tourist would have got far in the Dorian Peloponnese at that time."[83] But there is no question of the Dark Ages—ages illuminated in any case, as Anthony Snodgrass has shown, with twilight at their beginning and the first flush of dawn well before their end.[84] We are in the late eighth century B.C., the age of the Olympic Games (still, admittedly, something of a local festival, but beginning to assume a genuinely pan-Hellenic character); the age of reviving international commerce, of colonization, of literacy. A poet might have found a better welcome in the Sparta of the time—Sparta about to entertain, in succeeding generations, Tyrtaeus and Alcman—than in the reformed Sparta that rejected Anacreon and his musical innovations. Less than a century after the time that we are considering, the death of Archilochus "in plain shock and even play of battle" was punished by the anger of the gods.[85] Might not an eighth-century "servant of the Muses," traveling unarmed and peaceably, have wandered the length and breadth of Hellas under the divine protection?

I propose, then, that the Catalogue is the work of a Boiotian poet living in the late eighth century B.C. In his day Hellas, however divided politically, enjoyed, and was becoming aware of, a common culture almost as unified as that of the period that we know, by archaeological shorthand, as "LH IIIB." Our poet knew the *Iliad*, and was inspired by it to undertake a series of pilgrimages to the homelands of the heroes of the Trojan War—to Mycenae and Sparta, Pylos and Ithaca, Knossos and Phthia. The Greece through which he passed shared his excitement. Everybody wanted to be connected with the great war against Troy—especially perhaps those, like his own Boiotian countrymen, who felt that their ancestors had not been given their proper due

in the story of the wrath of Achilles. Wherever our poet went, ruins which had once been assigned to the Cyclopes or the Pelasgians, in the spirit of Edie Ochiltree attributing the prehistoric remains of Scotland to "the Pechts lang syne," were now being pointed out as homes of heroes of the Trojan War. If the people of some backward district had no attribution of their own, our poet, singing for his supper, was glad to supply one. If they had already claims to advance (not all of these claims need have been consistent with the *Iliad,* and some may have rested on more ancient tradition) the poet was prepared to insert his hosts' version into the list of heroes whose compilation must from the first have been a principal object of his travels. That he originally conceived this list as a muster roll of the fleet at Aulis, and thereby justified himself in giving pride of place to his own countrymen, seems to me self-evident. That he did not insert his Catalogue into its present place in the *Iliad,* for which he did not intend it, seems probable; and that whoever did insert it made some attempt to edit it to make it fit in is obvious, especially in the cases of Protesilaus and Philoctetes.[86] That the editing did not go far enough to make the Catalogue wholly consistent with the *Iliad* appears on closer inspection.

I suggested that our poet "sang for his supper." We may suppose that in his selection of places to immortalize he was in some degree moved by the quality of his entertainment. To return to the corner of the Peloponnese from which we started, are we to imagine him trudging

Still onwards, where the rude *Donussan* boor
Against the homeless stranger shuts the door?
("Pannonian")

And did he receive a warm welcome a couple of nights later at "Gonoessa above Sicyon"? More probably he bypassed "Donussa," as he must have bypassed other hamlets, without being aware of its existence, leaving its people to complain for ever more that *they* were the true heroes of the Trojan War, as the ruins on the left bank proved.

Finally, we may imagine a morning long before the poet's time when, amid the outcry of women complaining against "the orders/ That marched my man away," a file of spearmen was led down to the river mouth, where one of the King of Men's longships was waiting for them, her stern beached on the shingle.[87]

NOTES

1. J. G. T. Anderson and J. K. Anderson, "A Lost City Discovered?" *CSCA* 8 (1975) 1–6.

2. Paus. 7.26.13.

3. *Iliad* 2.573.

4. There is no trace of ancient occupation on the summit "Koryfi" where Leake placed "the ancient Gonoessa, or Donoessa, or Donussa"; W. M. Leake, *Travels in the Morea* 3 (London 1830) 385; compare Anderson and Anderson (supra n. 1) 3.

5. Paus. 9.40.5–6: *Iliad* 2.507. R. Hope Simpson and J. F. Lazenby, *The Catalogue of the Ships in Homer's Iliad* (Oxford 1970) 31–33.

6. Strabo 9.2.29; 9.2.34–35; Thuc. 1.12.6; Hope Simpson and Lazenby (supra n. 5) 28, 164.

7. Thuc. 4.120.1.

8. E. T. Vermeule, " 'Priam's Castle Blazing': a Thousand Years of Trojan Memories," in M. J. Mellink, ed., *Troy and the Trojan War* (Bryn Mawr 1986) 77–92.

9. S. P. Morris, "A Tale of Two Cities: The Miniature Frescoes from Thera and the Origins of Greek Poetry," *AJA* 93 (1989) 517.

10. Mabel Lang, *The Palace of Nestor in Western Messenia* II: *The Frescoes* (Princeton 1969) 42–49, 71–74, pl. M; N. Yalouris, "Ein Schlachtengemälde im Palast des Nestor," *AM* 104 (1988) 41–48, argues that the subject of the painting is the victory of the Pylians over the Arcadians on the river Iardanos (*Iliad* 7.133–136). I owe the reference to the volume editors. The question of the survival into the historic period of traditions concerning actual events and personages dating from the Bronze Age must be reexamined in the light of W. Burkert, "Lydia between East and West or How to Date the Trojan War: A Study in Herodotus" (supra pp. 139–148). It seems to me that the unreliability of heroic pedigrees and of chronologies based on them does not exclude the possibility of the transmission of genuine information, including proper names.

11. *Iliad* 2.102–108; 10.266–271; Paus. 9.40.6.

12. V. Burr, *NEON KATALOGOS; Untersuchungen zum homerischen Schiffskatalog*, Klio Beiheft 49 (1944) 119ff., argues that the details of the great muster at Aulis were indeed set forth in writing, and formed part of an archive whose contents were eventually memorized and versified for oral transmission. But see D. L. Page, *History and the Homeric Iliad* (Berkeley and Los Angeles 1959) 158 n. 21; Hope Simpson and Lazenby (supra n. 5) 160.

13. Different versions of the ballad are conveniently accessible in R. L. Mackie, ed., *A Book of Scottish Verse* (Oxford 1934) 103–108 and A. Quiller-Couch, ed., *The Oxford Book of Ballads* (Oxford 1910) 651–663.

14. For example, disagreements ancient and modern about the entries for Athens and Salamis: Page (supra n. 12) 145–147; Hope Simpson and Lazenby (supra n. 5) 56–60. My own position is, I hope, not wholly inconsistent with that of Mabel Lang, "War Story into Wrath Story" (supra pp. 149–162), who visualizes "a composite document which was added to not only as Mycenaean influence spread first to the northwest, then to central Greece, and finally to Thessaly in the north but also as the Mycenaean expedition against Troy attracted as recruits the heroes of those lands." To me our chief disagreement seems to be over chronology; I imagine a single "Catalogue poet" drawing everything together in one lifetime; and she separate accretions over a long period round a Mycenaean core.

15. An argument for historicity offered by W. Leaf, *Troy: A Study in Homeric Geography* (London 1912) 292.

16. Hope Simpson and Lazenby (supra n. 5) 161.

17. Thuc. 1.11.

18. Morris (supra n. 9) 517.

19. A. Nibbi, *The Sea Peoples and Egypt* (Park Ridge, N.J. 1975) 77 and pls. 37–39. For the weakness of Egyptian sea power, see pp. 124–138.

20. *Docs.*[2] 183–194. But see Page (supra n. 12) 193–194, and, on the rowers, L. R. Palmer, *Mycenaeans and Minoans* (New York 1962) 133–136.

21. Page (supra n. 12) 132, 134.

22. Burr (supra n. 12).

23. Hope Simpson and Lazenby (supra n. 5): R. Hope Simpson, *A Gazetteer and Atlas of Mycenaean Sites*, BICS Suppl. 16 (1965).

24. Page (supra n. 12) 137.

25. Hope Simpson and Lazenby (supra n. 5) 161.

26. Page (supra n. 12) 134 rightly insists that it is "not simply a list of places and persons: *it is a list of participants in a military campaign*" (his italics).

27. Page (supra n. 12) 152–153 accepts that the actual numbers of ships are "reckless exaggerations" and maintains on linguistic grounds that "about a third of the ship entries are of purely Ionian composition." This last argument is countered by G. L. Huxley, "Numbers in the Homeric Cata-

logue of Ships," *GRBS* 7 (1966) 313–318; but some of Huxley's reasons for accepting the numbers in the Catalogue seem to be mistaken. That there were at the battle of Lade "about 75,000 men from Ionia and the Aeolis alone" (Huxley p. 316) is no more evidence for the resources of these districts in the Bronze Age than the numbers of the British Expeditionary Force of 1914 are evidence for the size of English armies in the Hundred Years' War. Arguments on whether 1,186 ships could or could not have been beached together anywhere in the Troad must be reconsidered in the light of M. Korfmann, "Troy: Topography and Navigation," in M. J. Mellink, ed., (supra n. 8) 1–16, esp. 9–13.

28. *Docs.*² 103–105.

29. Hope Simpson and Lazenby (supra n. 5) 86–87 admit that "neither the names of the places in nor the boundaries of Nestor's kingdom in the Catalogue appear to coincide very well with those of the tablets," but take refuge in the thought that the tablets "are only a part of the administrative records of Ano Englianos for a single year." The greatest authority upon the tablets dismisses the Catalogue as a "poetic invention": J. Chadwick, "The Mycenaean documents," in W. A. McDonald and G. R. Rapp, eds., *The Minnesota Messenia Expedition* (Minneapolis 1972) 113–114.

30. Hope Simpson and Lazenby (supra n. 5) 87 urge caution upon those who "follow Strabo's pedantic arguments for believing that the Pylos of Nestor's tale cannot be the Messenian Pylos." But (p. 82) they allow that "perhaps the most plausible solution . . . is that although the real Pylos which lay behind the legends was the Messenian, later poets thought of it as being much nearer the Alpheios." G. S. Kirk, *The Iliad: A Commentary* I (Cambridge 1985) 295 suggests that the Homeric account of Nestor's kingdom "probably reflects a state of affairs later than" the tablets when "Pulos might well have pushed up into Triphylia to compensate" for the loss of the lower Pamisos valley. (But "later than the tablets" means later than the sack and abandonment of Messenian Pylos.)

31. A. Giovannini, *Étude historique sur les origines du Catalogue des Vaisseaux* (Berne 1969).

32. Page (supra n. 12) 122.

33. Listed by Page, with references (supra n. 12) 121–122.

34. Giovannini (supra n. 31) 11–17 cites L. Robert, "Villes de Carie et d'Ionie dans la liste des Théorodoques," *BCH* 70 (1946) 506, on the preservation in a single document of otherwise forgotten place-names. Compare A. Plassart, "Inscriptions de Delphes; la liste des Théodoroques," *BCH* 45 (1921) 1–85.

35. Strabo 8.6.10.

36. Hope Simpson and Lazenby (supra n. 5) 41.

37. Aesch. 3.107; Dem. 18.149; Hdt. 8.32. Pindar seems to use Kirrha and Krisa interchangeably with reference to the Pythian games, *Pyth.* 3.74, 5.37, 6.18, 7.16, etc.; and there is the possibility that the names were originally identical: Kirk (supra n. 30) 200 admits the possibility of "confusion between Krisa and Kirrha."

38. *HHAph* 269–285; Hope Simpson and Lazenby (supra n. 5) 41.

39. *Iliad* 2.520.

40. Giovannini (supra n. 31) 20.

41. N. Valmin, *The Swedish Messenia Expedition* (Lund 1938) 12; followed by Page (supra n. 12) 121; Hope Simpson and Lazenby (supra n. 5) 85.

42. Plassart (supra n. 34) 12 II 84 and 49–50.

43. Hope Simpson and Lazenby (supra n. 5) 85 follow Valmin (supra n. 41) 106 n. 25 in suggesting that the district of Doris, epigraphically attested, may be "the Soulima Plain, in which Malthi is the dominating centre." This also might be taken as evidence that the name survived independently of the poetical tradition.

44. Supra n. 30.

45. Paus. 4.33.6–7; Strabo 8.3.25—but he knew of an "Olouris or Oloura" that some people said was Dorion.

46. Nobody who had been walked on successive Sundays round different parts of the island by the late Miss Sylvia Benton could possibly doubt this.

47. H. L. Lorimer, *Homer and the Monuments* (London 1950) 499 accepts "the site of the 'great house' of the Bronze Age," but adds "the habitation not of Odysseus" (whose home she, as a disciple of Wilhelm Dörpfeld, placed on Leukas) "but of one of the contingent who accompanied him to Troy." But see Hope Simpson and Lazenby (supra n. 5) 103.

48. Kirk (supra n. 30) 194–195.

49. On Corinth see now S. Weinberg, "Investigations at Corinth, 1947–1948," *Hesperia* 18 (1949) 156–157; idem, "Investigations at Corinth, 1950," *Hesperia* 20 (1951) 293; Hope Simpson and Lazenby (supra n. 5) 65.

50. Supra n. 29–30.

51. Giovannini (supra n. 31) 28–29.

52. J. K. Anderson, "A Historical and Topographical study of Achaia," *BSA* 49 (1954) 72; denied by Page (supra n. 12) 165 n. 36; Hope Simpson and Lazenby (supra n. 5) 172 n. 15.

53. Giovannini (supra n. 31) 27. Compare Lang (supra n. 14) n. 20: "a gerrymandered Argolid."

54. Page (supra n. 12) 131.

55. Hope Simpson and Lazenby (supra n. 5) 70–72, 156, citing V. Desborough, *The Last Mycenaeans and their Successors* (Oxford 1964) 225–230. Kirk (supra n. 30) 180–181 reaches a similar conclusion.

56. Hope Simpson and Lazenby (supra n. 5) 163.

57. Paus. 7.1.6–8; but the tradition is much older, e.g., Hdt. 1.145.

58. Hope Simpson and Lazenby (supra n. 5) 103–105.

59. Kirk (supra n. 30) 183; cf. Page (supra n. 12) 162–163 n. 32.

60. Page (supra n. 12) 163.

61. Page (supra n. 12) 147.

62. *Iliad* 2.634; Hope Simpson and Lazenby (supra n. 5) 104.

63. Page (supra n. 12) 163 (his italics).

64. Page (supra n. 12) 123.

65. E.g., Kirk (supra n. 30) 173–175.

66. Giovannini (supra n. 31) 63.

67. J. M. Cook, "Mycenae 1939–1952: Part III; the Agamemneion," *BSA* 48 (1953) 33.

68. J. M. Cook, "The Cult of Agamemnon at Mycenae," in Γέρας Ἀντ. Κεραμοπούλου (Athens 1953) 112–118, with further references.

69. H. W. Catling, "Archaeology in Greece 1988–1989" in *AR* 1988–1989, 36, with reference to earlier work.

70. S. Benton, "Excavations in Ithaca III: the Cave at Polis I," *BSA* 35 (1934–1935) 44–73, esp., for the "prayer to Odysseus," 55 fig. 7.

71. Preliminary report in S. G. Miller, ed., *Nemea: a guide to the Site and Museum* (Berkeley and Los Angeles 1990) 51.

72. Hope Simpson and Lazenby (supra n. 5) 158–159; Page (supra n. 12) 154. Kirk (supra n. 30) 169 minimizes the discrepancies between the Catalogue and the rest of the poem to support his case that "it might be felt that the Catalogue . . . could only be accommodated in such a monumental epic" and that "it is extremely unlikely to have been composed ex nihilo for its present place." But compare his pp. 180–183 on difficulties raised by the "areas ruled by Agamemnon, Odysseus and Akhilleus."

73. Kirk (supra n. 30) 238.

74. Page (supra n. 12) 145–147; cf. Hope Simpson and Lazenby (supra n. 5) 56.

75. *Iliad* 2.546.

76. References in Page (supra n. 12) 172 n. 75.

77. Shakespeare, *Troilus and Cressida,* Prologue 2–3.

78. Xen. *Hell.* 3.4.3–4.

79. Hope Simpson and Lazenby (supra n. 5) 20 (with references also to the carvings of ships from nearby Hyrie).

80. Giovannini (supra n. 31) 51–52.

81. E.g., Kirk (supra n. 30) 183–185, who acknowledges the "conspicuous geographical sequence" of the Catalogue entries, but "finds it hard to accept" that the Catalogue is "based on a seventh-century B.C. predecessor of the surviving Delphic text."

82. Giovannini (supra n. 31) 51: "tout porte à croire que le Cataloguiste n'a pas réuni ses données géographiques lui-même . . ."—but without specifying what is covered by "tout."

83. Page (supra n. 12) 123.

84. A. M. Snodgrass, *The Dark Age of Greece* (Edinburgh 1971) passim. On eighth-century pan-Hellenism see also G. Nagy, "An Evolutionary Model for the Making of Homeric Poetry: Comparative Perspectives" (supra pp. 139–148).

85. For Archilochus, Plut. *Mor.* 560E; Aelian Fr. 80 (Hercher).

86. *Iliad* 2.699–709, 719–728; Page (supra n. 12) 149.

87. I am indebted to Miss Elizabeth Sutherland for her skill and care in preparing the typescript.

I3

GLAUCUS, THE LEAVES, AND THE HEROIC BOAST OF *ILIAD* 6.146 – 211 *

◆

E D D I E   R.   L O W R Y,   J R.

Τυδεΐδη μεγάθυμε, τίη γενεὴν ἐρεείνεις;
οἵη περ φύλλων γενεή, τοίη δὲ καὶ ἀνδρῶν.
φύλλα τὰ μέν τ' ἄνεμος χαμάδις χέει, ἄλλα δέ θ' ὕλη
τηλεθόωσα φύει, ἔαρος δ' ἐπιγίγνεται ὥρη·
ὣς ἀνδρῶν γενεὴ ἡ μὲν φύει ἡ δ' ἀπολήγει.
εἰ δ' ἐθέλεις καὶ ταῦτα δαήμεναι, ὄφρ' ἐῢ εἰδῇς
ἡμετέρην γενεήν, πολλοὶ δέ μιν ἄνδρες ἴσασιν·

Great-souled son of Tydeus, why do you ask about lineage? As is the generation of leaves, so too is the generation
of men. As for leaves, some the wind pours on the ground,
but others the burgeoning wood puts forth, and the season
of spring comes again; so of men the one generation comes
forth and the other lets go. But if you wish, learn even these
facts, that well you may know our lineage, and many men
do know it.[1]   (*Iliad* 6.145–151)

οἵη περ φύλλων γενεή, τοίη δὲ καὶ ἀνδρῶν. "As is
the generation of leaves, so too is the generation of
men." This simile expressed by Homer's Glaucus in *Iliad* 6.146 was judged the "most admirable" in Homer
(ἔν δὲ τὸ κάλλιστον Χῖος ἔειπεν ἀνήρ) by Simonides
(19W.1[2]) who quoted it in his second line and then gave

elegiacs on the vain hopefulness of youth.[2] A number of
other poets also appreciated the clarity, simplicity, and
many potential ramifications of the Homeric image, and
among them Mimnermus and Bacchylides are attractive examples of elegiac and lyric developments of the
image.[3]

Beginning with a comparison of humanity to leaves,
Mimnermus' elegiacs lead to the conclusion that after
the flourishing prime of one's life, death is preferable to
living (2.1–8W[2]):

ἡμεῖς δ', οἷά τε φύλλα φύει πολυάνθεμος ὥρη
    ἔαρος, ὅτ' αἶψ' αὐγῇς αὔξεται ἠελίου,
τοῖς ἴκελοι πήχυιον ἐπὶ χρόνον ἄνθεσιν ἥβης
    τερπόμεθα, πρὸς θεῶν εἰδότες οὔτε κακὸν
οὔτ' ἀγαθόν· Κῆρες δὲ παρεστήκασι μέλαιναι,
    ἡ μὲν ἔχουσα τέλος γήραος ἀργαλέου,
ἡ δ' ἑτέρη θανάτοιο· μίνυνθα δὲ γίνεται ἥβης
    καρπός, ὅσον τ' ἐπὶ γῆν κίδναται ἠέλιος.

And like leaves which the many-flowered season of spring
brings forth, when they increase suddenly in the rays of the
sun, we, resembling them, enjoy the flowers of youth for a

measure's time, learning from the gods neither evil nor good; but black Fates of Death stand by, the one holding the end of grievous old age, the other of death; and brief is the fruit of youth, as lasting as the sun spreading light upon the earth.

The remaining eight lines of the text cite poverty, childlessness, and sickness to justify the appeal of dying forthwith.

In Mimnermus, as Griffith has pointed out, the temporality of the leaves, which is emphasized by the spring season, by the harvest fruit, and by the periodicity of daylight, is applied to a single life whose ill-favored end is stressed.[4] The focus of the image borrowed from Homer has been directed at spring's single season of leaves, not at the leaves' successive annual generations. Since the text portrays a man without children, the final impression of the elegiacs is the end both of life and of lineage.

In a lyric development of the image of the Homeric leaves, Bacchylides' *Ode* 5 takes us beyond the boundaries of life and explores feelings of pessimism, sadness, and mortality as Heracles descends to the underworld and has his famous dialogue with Meleager. Heracles sees souls like wind-swept leaves on Mount Ida (5.63–67):

> ἔνθα δυστάνων βροτῶν
> ψυχὰς ἐδάη παρὰ Κωκυτοῦ ῥεέθροις,
> οἷά τε φύλλ' ἄνεμος
> Ἴδας ἀνὰ μηλοβότους
> πρῶνας ἀργηστὰς δονεῖ.

There beside the streams of Cocytus he learned of
the souls of miserable mortals
like the leaves the wind twirls
on Ida's sheep-nurturing
gleaming headlands.

As in Mimnermus 2, there is an elegiac attraction for the easy relief of death in preference to the evils of life. One of the souls, Meleager, summarizes his sad life's story to Heracles, who sheds a tear and exclaims (160–162):

> . . . θνατοῖσι μὴ φῦναι φέριστον
> μηδ' ἀελίου προσιδεῖν
> φέγγος· . . .

For mortals it is best not to be born
nor to look upon the light of the sun . . .

Still, having been born and anticipating his return to earth, Heracles thinks of generation and asks Meleager about a sister back home whom he might marry (165–168). That union will of course be no more productive than Meleager's, who had been likened by Heracles to a tree shoot (ἔρνος 88) when the hero first saw him and whose vital firebrand is here called a φιτρός (142), 'branch,' not a δαλός, 'torch,' as in other versions. Thus in this ode the more general mortality of the season's leaves has, as Lefkowitz has pointed out, been reformed into a particular fatality in the case of Meleager.[5]

Such pleasant, successful lyric and elegiac developments of the Homeric simile are highly memorable and impressive. In combination with the singular simplicity of Simonides' superlative judgment on the image (19.2W[2]), they form perhaps a ready lens through which to view the encounter of Glaucus and Diomedes and especially the character of Glaucus. Thus Glaucus has been seen by critics as pensive and sorrowful, in relation to both Diomedes' immediate threat and life in general. For example, Edwards sees the opening lines of Glaucus' speech as a "meditation on death" and as marking "the poet's own consciousness of the mortality of human greatness and of the consolation of the continuance of the human race . . .";[6] Redfield interprets them as expressions of nature's carelessness and human insignificance when apart from the order of culture;[7] Griffin finds humility changing to pride in awareness of inevitable death;[8] and Vivante hears an interpretation of individual existence in both glory and transience.[9]

But if there is possibly an initial elegiac predilection among these interpreters, there is definitely profit in the guidance and direction that most of them give toward other relevant Homeric passages. Thus Edwards refers to the words of Apollo containing a leaf simile in *Iliad* 21.462–467;[10] Willcock compares Glaucus' genealogical boast with that of Aeneas to Achilles in *Iliad* 20.199–258, which contains several exact verbal parallels to Glaucus' speech;[11] and Edwards and Adkins invite attention to Glaucus' nonreflective nature elsewhere in the *Iliad*.[12] These references are important, for from the images and diction of such passages an interpretation of Glaucus' speech can be attempted on the terms of Homer rather than on those of elegy or lyric. Such an interpretation will posit that Glaucus' image of the leaves is *not* primarily a spontaneous overflow of powerful pessimism engendered by human mortality or the brevity of youth, but is rather a thoughtful device entirely worthy of the great-great-grandson of Sisyphus, "the craftiest of men" (ὃ κέρδιστος γένετ' ἀνδρῶν, *Iliad* 6.153) and of a hero sent to Troy by his father under the charge not to cast shame on the race of his fathers (6.206–210).

That Glaucus is not a meditative or reflective man elsewhere in the poem can be clearly shown. While such a demonstration cannot rule out some nervousness or fear before Diomedes that might lead to a temporizing simile, it should urge caution towards this approach and bespeak the need to try to interpret Glaucus' words as those of an intrepid warrior. Indeed, such he seems to be when in *Iliad* 7.13 he joins Paris and Hector, who is returning to battle after a visit with his people in Troy (for which the Glaucus-Diomedes interview provided the poetic interval). So impressive are the deadly exploits of this threesome that Athena wants to intervene (7.17–20), though Apollo effects a temporary delay of any help for the Argives (7.24).

Sarpedon on three occasions documents the bravery of Glaucus. In 12.102 he names Glaucus and Asteropaeus as the bravest of the allies after himself. In his great speech of 12.310–328, Sarpedon states that the two of them receive the greatest honor in Lycia (310) and that they are looked upon as gods (312). Therefore, in view of the inevitability of death (ὦ πέπον, εἰ μὲν γὰρ πόλεμον περὶ τόνδε φυγόντε / αἰεὶ δὴ μέλλοιμεν ἀγήρω τ' ἀθανάτω τε / ἔσσεσθ', . . . 322–324), Sarpedon praises the gloriousness of combat, whether for himself and Glaucus or for their victors. The tone of the speech suggests well-known fact, not the motivational fancy of self-improvement, and the prowess of the Lycians and of their leaders in the immediately following combat clearly illustrates this point.

Later, when Sarpedon meets his inevitable death at the hands of Patroclus, he calls upon Glaucus to lead the fight to safeguard his armor (16.492). Expecting his faithful companion to be an audacious warrior (θαρσαλέον πολεμιστήν, 493), he reflects Diomedes' characterization of Glaucus in 6.125–126: "In your audaciousness (σῷ θάρσει) you have come forth far in advance of all. . . ." However, despite Glaucus' courageous exhortations (16.538–547) and preeminent fighting (593), Sarpedon's armor is lost (662–663). After the death of Patroclus, Hector obtained that warrior's armor but not the corpse, and he gives back before Ajax who protects it (17.125–138). For this Glaucus rebukes Hector with reference to the earlier loss of Sarpedon's armor and corpse (17.142–168). By his threat to withdraw from the battle, Glaucus urges Hector to obtain Patroclus' corpse that it may be a ransom for Sarpedon's corpse and armor.[13] He concludes with the taunt that Hector is clearly inferior to Ajax (17.168). Glaucus' wits (φρένες, which Zeus took away in the armor exchange [6.234]) figure straightaway in Hector's rejoinder (17.171). Although Hector acknowledges that Glaucus' wits are reputed to be the best in Lycia, he now holds them in scorn (17.171–173) for Glaucus' misrepresentation of the circumstances. Later, Hector makes the last reference to Glaucus in the *Iliad*, when he incites Glaucus and other allies to further battle (17.216).[14]

Therefore, if Glaucus is consistently portrayed as a valorous warrior held in high regard for his daring and intelligence, some consistency of general heroic pattern might well be discerned in his reply to Diomedes which begins with the singular image of the leaves. In other words, as the battlefield actions of Glaucus conform to expectations, does his speech conform as well? For a tentative answer to this question a survey can be made of other heroic boasts that recite genealogies in the presence of adversaries.

The encounter of Achilles and Aeneas in 20.156–258 provides a premier example. There the actual encounter of the adversaries, "the best two by far" (δύο δ' ἀνέρες ἔξοχ' ἄριστοι, 20.158), is announced by the same line which earlier introduced Glaucus and Diomedes: ἐς μέσον ἀμφοτέρων συνίτην μεμαῶτε μάχεσθαι (20.159=6.120). Though Aeneas is the first to move forth threateningly (ἀπειλήσας, 161), Achilles is the first to speak. He taunts Aeneas with specific reference to the latter's flight from him on Mount Ida to Lyrnessus, which Achilles later captured, while Aeneas was saved by the gods (20.188–194; Aeneas had given the disguised Apollo his account of the rout in 20.89–98).

Diomedes, since he claims he never encountered Glaucus previously, has no such demeaning incident to throw in his opponent's face. He is however able to adduce the story of Lycurgus' persecution of Dionysus in which the formulaic κρατερὸς Λυκόοργος (6.130) is modeled upon the formula κρατερὸς Διομήδης (4.401, 411; 5.143, 151, 251, etc.), and it suggests that Diomedes handles his opponents as efficiently as Lycurgus put to flight the young Dionysus and his nurses out of terror at their opponent's threats (6.132–137). Diomedes' exemplum also casts Glaucus in the role of a frightened child in the support of women.[15] Furthermore there is a final implication that Diomedes is even superior to Lycurgus in that he is more circumspect about encountering an opponent who might be divine (6.141).[16]

Taunted by Achilles, Aeneas like Glaucus answers the reference to flight or persecution with genealogy (20.200–214):

Πηλεΐδη, μὴ δὴ ἐπέεσσί με νηπύτιον ὣς
ἔλπεο δειδίξεσθαι, ἐπεὶ σάφα οἶδα καὶ αὐτὸς
ἠμὲν κερτομίας ἠδ' αἴσυλα μυθήσασθαι.
ἴδμεν δ' ἀλλήλων γενεήν, ἴδμεν δὲ τοκῆας,
πρόκλυτ' ἀκούοντες ἔπεα θνητῶν ἀνθρώπων·
ὄψει δ' οὔτ' ἄρ πω σὺ ἐμοὺς ἴδες οὔτ' ἄρ' ἐγὼ σούς.
φασὶ σὲ μὲν Πηλῆος ἀμύμονος ἔκγονον εἶναι,
μητρὸς δ' ἐκ Θέτιδος καλλιπλοκάμου ἁλοσύδνης·
αὐτὰρ ἐγὼν υἱὸς μεγαλήτορος Ἀγχίσαο
εὔχομαι ἐκγεγάμεν, μήτηρ δέ μοί ἐστ' Ἀφροδίτη·
τῶν δὴ νῦν ἕτεροί γε φίλον παῖδα κλαύσονται
σήμερον· οὐ γάρ φημ' ἐπέεσσί γε νηπυτίοισιν
ὧδε διακρινθέντε μάχης ἐξ ἀπονέεσθαι.
εἰ δ' ἐθέλεις καὶ ταῦτα δαήμεναι, ὄφρ' ἐὺ εἰδῇς
ἡμετέρην γενεήν, πολλοὶ δέ μιν ἄνδρες ἴσασι·[17]

Son of Peleus, do not expect by your words to frighten me, as if I were a child, since I myself also know clearly how to speak reproaches and unseemly words. We know each other's lineage, and we know each other's parents, for we have heard the famed words of mortal men; but by sight neither have you ever seen mine nor I yours. They say you are the progeny of blameless Peleus and of fair-tressed Thetis your mother, a daughter of the sea. But for my part I boast that I was born of great-hearted Anchises, and my mother is Aphrodite; of these now the ones or the others will mourn their own son today; for I say that not with childish words shall we thus separate and go away from the battle. But if you wish, learn these facts, so that well you may know our lineage, and many men know it. . . .

In this response to Achilles' overbearing challenge, Aeneas affirms his ability to throw reproaches at his adversary. He asserts a difference between hearing the words of lineage (πρόκλυτ' ἀκούοντες ἔπεα, 204) and seeing the actual persons (ὄψει . . . ἴδες, 205). By implication he casts suspicion on the veracity of Achilles' lineage, as if the Muses' claim that they can speak both the truth and the false like the true (Hes. *Theog.* 27–28) were applicable to Achilles' words. While Aeneas acknowledges Achilles' parents in an indirect report based on φασί and containing the weak copulative εἶναι (20.206–207), he names his own father in a boast and with a more vigorous infinitive (αὐτὰρ ἐγὼν υἱὸς μεγαλήτορος Ἀγχίσαο / εὔχομαι ἐκγεγάμεν, 208–209), and he cites his goddess-mother in a statement of fact: μήτηρ δέ μοί ἐστ' Ἀφροδίτη (209).[18] After enumerating his direct ancestors (Zeus, Dardanus, Erichthonius, Tros, Assaracus, Capys, Anchises) and some of their relatives and feats (20.215–241), he concludes his speech to Achilles with a variation of the theme in his introductory words about the potential for the false among the true (20.244–257):

ἀλλ' ἄγε μηκέτι ταῦτα λεγώμεθα νηπύτιοι ὥς,
ἑσταότ' ἐν μέσσῃ ὑσμίνῃ δηϊοτῆτος.
ἔστι γὰρ ἀμφοτέροισιν ὀνείδεα μυθήσασθαι
πολλὰ μάλ', οὐδ' ἂν νηῦς ἑκατόζυγος ἄχθος ἄροιτο.
στρεπτὴ δὲ γλῶσσ' ἐστὶ βροτῶν, πολέες δ' ἔνι μῦθοι
παντοῖοι, ἐπέων δὲ πολὺς νομὸς ἔνθα καὶ ἔνθα.
ὁπποῖόν κ' εἴπῃσθα ἔπος, τοῖόν κ' ἐπακούσαις.
ἀλλὰ τίη ἔριδας καὶ νείκεα νῶϊν ἀνάγκη
νεικεῖν ἀλλήλοισιν ἐναντίον, ὥς τε γυναῖκας,
αἵ τε χολωσάμεναι ἔριδος πέρι θυμοβόροιο
νεικεῦσ' ἀλλήλῃσι μέσην ἐς ἄγυιαν ἰοῦσαι,
πόλλ' ἐτεά τε καὶ οὐκί· χόλος δέ τε καὶ τὰ κελεύει.
ἀλκῆς δ' οὔ μ' ἐπέεσσιν ἀποτρέψεις μεμαῶτα
πρὶν χαλκῷ μαχέσασθαι ἐναντίον· . . .

But come, let us no longer speak these things like children, standing in the midst of the battle of death. For it is possible for each of us to speak very many reproaches, and a hundred-benched ship would not bear the burden. And twisted is the tongue of men, and many are the words of all sorts on it, and wide is the range of words from this side to that. Whatever kind of word you speak is the kind you would hear. But why must we engage in strife and reproach, like women who, angered in soul-devouring strife, reproach each other as they go into the middle of the street, speaking many things both true and false; and anger bids these things. But by your words you will not turn me, eager for battle, from my strength, before we fight with the bronze man to man. . . .

Aeneas acknowledges the vast potential for reproach, and in view of the twisted human tongue, he states that truth and falsehood can infect the discourse. But again, Aeneas has cast suspicion on Achilles' veracity by playing the self-assumed role of a critic of reproachful language that contains falsehood. He will not himself be engaging in self-criticism, so his objections are naturally directed at Achilles. Since he cannot label as false Achilles' account of the unimpressive rout from Lyrnessus (20.178–198)—for he had admitted it earlier himself (20.87–98)—he can only imply that Achilles' genealogy is suspect.

In sum, Aeneas is trying to undercut the stance of his opponent both by demeaning the latter's lineage and by enhancing his own. His facility with words of praise and of blame has been set forth in detail by Nagy with specific reference to an etymology of Αἰνείας that makes it kin to αἶνος, an ambivalent form of narrative that has the potential for both praise and blame.[19] The root of his name would be reflected in the skill and length of his genealogical boast, creating praise for him but diminution for Achilles.

Two other episodes can help clarify reproachfulness that may be inherent in genealogical recitation. One is the encounter of Achilles and Asteropaeus (21.139–202), the other that of Tlepolemus and Sarpedon (5.627–663).

The meeting of Achilles and Asteropaeus is described as follows (21.148–153):

οἱ δ' ὅτε δὴ σχεδὸν ἦσαν ἐπ' ἀλλήλοισιν ἰόντες,
τὸν πρότερος προσέειπε ποδάρκης δῖος Ἀχιλλεύς·

"τίς πόθεν εἰς ἀνδρῶν, ὅ μευ ἔτλης ἀντίος ἐλθεῖν;
δυστήνων δέ τε παῖδες ἐμῷ μένει ἀντιόωσι."
Τὸν δ' αὖ Πηλεγόνος προσεφώνεε φαίδιμος υἱός·
"Πηλεΐδη μεγάθυμε, τίη γενεὴν ἐρεείνεις;"

And when they were near, advancing on one another, godlike Achilles swift of foot first addressed him [Asteropaeus]: "Who are you among men, and from whence, that dared to come against me? Of unfortunate parents are the children who oppose my might."

The glorious son of Pelegon then addressed him: "Great-souled son of Peleus, why do you ask of my lineage?"

In this encounter, which leads into seven lines of genealogy from Asteropaeus, there is diction identical to elements found both in the Glaucus-Diomedes encounter and in the Aeneas-Achilles encounter. The description of the approach is the same (21.148 = 20.176 = 6.121, with a discrepancy in the reading ἰόντε), and the speech introduction is the same except for the name of the speaker (21.149a = 20.177a = 6.122a). However, the initial interrogation is dissimilar: Diomedes uses the phrase καταθνητῶν ἀνθρώπων (6.123), which is unique in the *Iliad* (and on which see further discussion below), whereas Achilles asks for more information from Asteropaeus with τίς πόθεν (21.150). He also refers to the daring of his adversary (ἔτλης, 21.150), as does Diomedes by reference to σῷ θάρσει in 6.126. In both episodes the interrogation ends with the reference to the unfortunate parents whose sons face the challenger (21.151 = 6.127).

When Asteropaeus responds as adversary, the beginning of his retort is the same except for the introductory vocative: . . . τί ἦ γενεὴν ἐρεείνεις; (21.153b = 6.145b). Following his seven lines of genealogical recitation, Asteropaeus proposes combat: μαχώμεθα . . . (21.160). Since the narrative then resumes, with "So he spoke threateningly . . . ("Ὣς φάτ' ἀπειλήσας . . . , 161)," Homer the narrator is defining the genealogical recitation as a threatening speech in much the same way his character Aeneas did earlier (20.200–214, 244–257, as discussed above). But to these threats Achilles responds first with violence and then with genealogy: he attacks Asteropaeus, and over the dying man he boasts (21.183, 187) of his own genealogy.

The encounter of Tlepolemus and Sarpedon (5.627–654) provides another illustration of genealogy in the employ of reproach or threat. Here a genealogy of which Sarpedon might make a praiseworthy boast is turned into a reproach by Tlepolemus. The latter first terms false the report that Sarpedon's father is Zeus, and then goes on to recount the exploits of his own father Heracles against Laomedon of Troy (5.633–639):

Σαρπῆδον, Λυκίων βουληφόρε, τίς τοι ἀνάγκη
πτώσσειν ἐνθάδ' ἐόντι μάχης ἀδαήμονι φωτί;
ψευδόμενοι δέ σέ φασι Διὸς γόνον αἰγιόχοιο
εἶναι, ἐπεὶ πολλὸν κείνων ἐπιδεύεαι ἀνδρῶν
οἳ Διὸς ἐξεγένοντο ἐπὶ προτέρων ἀνθρώπων·
ἀλλ' οἷόν τινά φασι βίην Ἡρακληείην
εἶναι, ἐμὸν πατέρα θρασυμέμνονα θυμολέοντα·

Sarpedon, counselor of the Lycians, why must you crouch there and be a man ignorant of battle? They lie when they say that you are the offspring of aegis-bearing Zeus, since you are much inferior to those who were born of Zeus in the days of men of old; yet what sort of man do they say was mighty Heracles, my father of daring mind and lion's heart . . .

Since the genealogy used by Aeneas, Asteropaeus, and Tlepolemus can be reproachful or threatening, it may be worthwhile to examine Glaucus' speech to see if he intends to employ it as a threat to Diomedes rather than as a means of temporizing his own defense.[20] Since those three genealogies are contained in episodes that have diction in common with the Glaucus-Diomedes episode, the similar diction might well accompany a similar theme.

In the episodes just reviewed the adversary begins his verbal offense as he begins to speak. If Glaucus were following this pattern, his simile of the leaves would serve to discredit Diomedes and probably to enhance himself. Yet this figure is often interpreted as Glaucus' personal expression of regret, even fear, and as a reflection more at home with the inner self than appropriate to cast at the adversary. If the leaves symbolize only mortality or transience, they necessarily refer to both Glaucus and Diomedes, and can be no reproach to the latter. The question thus arises as to whether or not in Homeric epic leaves may symbolize other qualities or

conditions. A review of other leaf similes in Homer indicates that they do: they often refer to large or indeterminate quantities.

Thus in the great list of similes introducing the Catalog of Ships in *Iliad* Book 2 a reference to innumerable leaves is found amid images of the many tribes of winged birds (ὀρνίθων πετεηνῶν ἔθνεα πολλά, 2.459) and of swarming flies (μυιάων ἀδινάων ἔθνεα πολλά, 2.469):

ἔσταν δ' ἐν λειμῶνι Σκαμανδρίῳ ἀνθεμόεντι
μυρίοι, ὅσσα τε φύλλα καὶ ἄνθεα γίγνεται ὥρῃ.

They stood in the flowery meadow of Scamander, countless, as many as the leaves and flowers that arise in the spring. (2.467–468)

Likewise, the vast Trojan forces are compared by Iris to leaves and to grains of sand (2.798–801):

ἦ μὲν δὴ μάλα πολλὰ μάχας εἰσήλυθον ἀνδρῶν,
ἀλλ' οὔ πω τοιόνδε τοσόνδε τε λαὸν ὄπωπα·
λίην γὰρ φύλλοισιν ἐοικότες ἢ ψαμάθοισιν
ἔρχονται πεδίοιο μαχησόμενοι προτὶ ἄστυ.

Indeed very many times have I come into the battles of men but not yet have I seen a host of such quality or such number; for very much like leaves or grains of sand do they come in the plain to fight against the city.[21]

In the *Odyssey* the Cicones come against Odysseus and his men in numbers like the leaves and flowers of spring (*Odyssey* 9.51):

ἦλθον ἔπειθ' ὅσα φύλλα καὶ ἄνθεα γίγνεται ὥρῃ.

And Phaeacian women weave webs and spin yarn like the leaves of a tall poplar tree (7.105–106):

αἱ δ' ἱστοὺς ὑφόωσι καὶ ἠλάκατα στρωφῶσιν
ἥμεναι, οἷά τε φύλλα μακεδνῆς αἰγείροιο·

While the simile is usually interpreted with reference to the movement of the spinning and twisting (so Mount Neriton in *Odyssey* 9.22 is εἰνοσίφυλλον, 'with shaking leaves'), the notion of moving leaves indistinguishable in their quantity cannot be ruled out as the elements of wool blend into the finished or unfinished product.

There is one leaf simile in the *Iliad* used to depict mortals. They are in fact specifically named in the speech, and several characteristics differentiating them from the immortals are identified—their food and their wasting away. Apollo proposes that he and Poseidon not fight on behalf of such "wretched mortals" (21.462–467):

"ἐννοσίγαι᾿, οὐκ ἄν με σαόφρονα μυθήσαιο
ἔμμεναι, εἰ δὴ σοί γε βροτῶν ἕνεκα πτολεμίξω
δειλῶν, οἳ φύλλοισιν ἐοικότες ἄλλοτε μέν τε
ζαφλεγέες τελέθουσιν, ἀρούρης καρπὸν ἔδοντες,
ἄλλοτε δὲ φθινύθουσιν ἀκήριοι. ἀλλὰ τάχιστα
παυώμεσθα μάχης· οἱ δ᾿ αὐτοὶ δηριαάσθων."

"Earth-shaker, you would say that I was not of sound mind, if I should fight with you on account of wretched mortals, who like leaves at one time come into being full of fire and eat the fruit of the field, but at another time wither away lifeless. But with all speed let us stop our battle, and let them fight on their own."

Thus for Homer's similes outside Glaucus' speech, leaves are clearly less a symbol of mortality or of transience than of vast number or general movement. When they are used to emphasize mortality in Apollo's words, other characteristics of mortality seem explicitly and deliberately included. Therefore if we come to Glaucus' speech without the expectation engendered by lyric of reflective pessimism or regret of human mortality, but rather from the context of Homer, we quite easily discern vast numbers and an associated indistinct movement: the wind is scattering anonymous leaves on the ground of the forest, and the process seems repeated through the infinite turn of the seasons. Such is the generic condition of humankind, and precisely at the point where Glaucus distinguishes himself from such anonymity by reciting his ancestry, he leaves Diomedes in a forest of indistinction and thereby makes his simile into a rebuke of his adversary.[22]

If Glaucus begins his reply to the dangerous Diomedes with confident control, does he maintain control in the continuation of his speech? The answer should be derived from the entire episode, beginning with Ho-

mer's introductory narrative in 6.119, continuing through the words of Diomedes' threat into Glaucus' retort, and concluding with the notorious exchange of armor.[23]

In 6.120–122 Homer brings the two warriors together in lines used elsewhere in similar circumstances (Achilles and Aeneas, Achilles and Asteropaeus, as described above). But since the names of the characters and their fathers' names fill Homer's entire introductory line (119), he seems to be casting the episode in a genealogical or generational light. Diomedes' first line (123) collocates an interrogatory formula addressed elsewhere to gods with the words "mortal men," as though suggesting a dilemma or conflict in the mind of Diomedes: τίς δὲ σύ ἐσσι, φέριστε, καταθνητῶν ἀνθρώπων. The other two occurrences in the *Iliad* of the interrogation and vocative are applied to gods. In 15.247 Hector so addresses an unknown god who comes to his aid (τίς δὲ σύ ἐσσι φέριστε θεῶν, ὅς μ᾿ εἴρεαι ἄντην), and in 24.387 Priam addresses the unknown Hermes as such (τίς δὲ σύ ἐσσι, φέριστε, τέων δ᾿ ἐξ ἐσσι τοκήων;). Yet from a reverent beginning Diomedes ends by classing his opponent among the καταθνητῶν ἀνθρώπων. The phrase with the compound καταθνητῶν is used only here in the *Iliad* and is taken to intensify human mortality.[24] In any event there seems to be a compliment in the further observation that Glaucus has come forward in advance of all in his bravery (πολὺ προβέβηκας ἁπάντων / σῷ θάρσει, 125–126), and again, after a suggestion of respect, there is a threat in the statement that unhappy are the parents of those who oppose the might of Diomedes (6.127 = 21.151).

Having suggested by his first interrogation that divinities were on his mind, Diomedes now asserts that if the stranger is a god, he will not fight with him (128–129).[25] Among the gods, Dionysus comes to mind, sometimes given to flight but always prone both to persecution and to vengeance—these are surely themes instilled in Diomedes' thoughts by his own actions and by divine admonitions made to him in the previous book (5.440–442). Additionally, Dionysus is a god whose identity is constantly in question. While it must be satisfying for κρατερός Diomedes to imagine himself in the momentarily triumphant role of κρατερός Lycurgus (130), he does not disregard the role of Zeus in his story, who intercedes on behalf of his son, in much the same way as Apollo interceded for Aphrodite's Aeneas in Book 5.[26] Now if these epithets and characters provide a connection to preceding episodes, other epithets and characters anticipate or foreshadow future events. Thus when Lycurgus' opponent Dionysus is called μαινό-μενος (132), an epithet more properly associated with his maenad attendants, the audience will understand the affront to the analogous Glaucus, and a knowledgeable audience will anticipate the ultimate exchange of armor, when Zeus will take away Glaucus' wits (234). And the assault on the nurses τιθήνας (132) foreshadows the fate of Astyanax, carried by his τιθήνη (6.389) while his mother rushes like a maenad.[27] Thus the paradigm of Lycurgus is integrated by its narrator Diomedes to its immediate context and by Homer to his larger epic plot.

Having been subjected to a tale in which he was compared to a juvenile god still attended by nurses and taking refuge with the mother goddess Thetis (136), yet ultimately identified and justified by his father Zeus, Glaucus responds to Diomedes with words and a tone initially hinting of divinity: men and leaves, items collocated by Apollo (21.463), who had just earlier put Diomedes in his place (5.440–442). Surely Diomedes with some trepidation asks himself if his interlocutor is within or without the classes of men or leaves he has just named. Then by imputing the anonymity of leaves to Diomedes, Glaucus sets himself apart and proceeds to enumerate the ancestry which he considers distinguished.

He begins with Sisyphus "the craftiest of men," mentioned only here in the *Iliad* and in *Odyssey* 11.593–600, where his punishment in the underworld is described in the company of Tityus and Tantalus. Guilt by association would suggest an attempt to gain immortality, which Tityus attempted by a rape of Leto, and Tantalus by various means according to the sources. Since Homer is concerned with the immortality gained through heroic song (e.g., *Iliad* 22.304–305, *Odyssey* 24.93–94), he omits the details of attempts at immortality through craft or trickery. Other Greek poets do, however, direct their praise at crafty heroes like Sisyphus. Alcaeus 38A L-P (= 73D) describes Sisyphus as ἄνδρων πλεῖστα νοησάμενος (6) and as πολύιδρις ἔων (7). Theognis 702–712 relates that Sisyphus returned from the underworld by his great wisdom

(πολυιδρίῃσιν, 703), by wily words directed at Persephone (αἱμυλίοισι λόγοις, 704), and by abundant wits (πολυφροσύναις, 712). When Pindar sings of Sisyphus, Bellerophon and Pegasus, and Glaucus in *Ol.* 13, he describes the first as "wisest in skill like a god" (πυκνότατον παλάμαις ὡς θεόν, 52). The scholiast on *Iliad* 6.153 tells how Sisyphus chained Death and prevented all mortals from dying until Ares intervened and gave Sisyphus to Death. When by prior arrangement his wife did not perform the necessary burial rites, Sisyphus was allowed to return to earth to set matters right, but once back in Corinth, he stayed until he died of old age. All such instances of craft might be assumed from the name of his father Αἴολος, inasmuch as αἰόλος means 'quick-moving, nimble' and 'shifty, slippery.'[28]

Of Glaucus father of Bellerophon nothing is known, and of the adventures of Bellerophon much is abbreviated in Glaucus' account.[29] He killed the Chimera of divine stock (6.179–180), but Pegasus and the voyage to Olympus are not mentioned in Homer. The hatred of the gods referred to in 200 may be attributed to that flight, accomplished by a golden bridle offered by Athena (Pind. *Ol.* 13.65), but resulting in Bellerophon's fall and Pegasus' acceptance into Olympus (*Ol.* 13.91–92; *Isth.* 7.44–47).[30]

Thus an excess of wit and cleverness in the effort to combat death and to obtain immortality seems to characterize Glaucus' ancestors, and his speech combines the reverent and the mortal, much like Diomedes' opening line (6.123). Furthermore, such heroic attempts at obtaining immortality might well be addressed specifically to the son of Tydeus, who in traditions outside Homer lost an opportunity for immortality simply offered him by Athena without condition of any superhuman exploit.[31] It cannot be ruled out that Diomedes is forced by Glaucus' narrative to recall the embarrassing loss, for Diomedes strangely elects not to remember Tydeus (6.222–223):

Τυδέα δ' οὐ μέμνημαι, ἐπεί μ' ἔτι τυτθὸν ἐόντα
κάλλιφ', ὅτ' ἐν Θήβῃσιν ἀπώλετο λαὸς Ἀχαιῶν.

His excuse of childhood seems feeble, for others in fact do recall certain exploits of Tydeus with considerable admiration. Agamemnon in his Epipolesis upbraids Diomedes with a favorable story of Tydeus (*Iliad*

4.370–400). Diomedes remains silent, while Sthenelus retorts that the men of the present generation are better than their fathers. The former took Thebes "trusting the signs of the gods" (πειθόμενοι τεράεσσι θεῶν, 4.407a = 6.183b describing Bellerophon), but the latter "perished by their own follies" (σφετέρῃσιν ἀτασθαλίῃσιν ὄλοντο, 4.409). That general description of their end can at least accommodate Tydeus' specific folly, a clear reference to which would not suit Homer's overriding concern with poetic immortality.

In any event, Glaucus remains true to the excesses of his lineage, and he goes too far in his genealogical boast, for his mention of Bellerophon makes Diomedes recall the guest-friendship between Bellerophon and his grandfather Oineus and hence propose the famous exchange of armor. The result is a loss of value if not of immortality, for if, as Piccaluga has argued, the gold armor is an emblem of immortality, then deathlessness once again slips through the grasp of a descendant of Aeolus, and it is transferred by Homer, at least symbolically, to the son of the hero from whom in his folly it had been withdrawn.[32] In Pindar *Nem.* 10.7 the gift of immortality is explicitly made to Diomedes by Athena.

Thus the themes of our episode are given in the first lines of the speeches of the two principals and in the emphasis in φρένες, which Zeus took from Glaucus at the conclusion. Glaucus is, in Diomedes' words, φέριστος καταθνητῶν ἀνθρώπων (123), a member of a brave family put down by the gods for attempting to overcome death by their wit and craft. Diomedes is, as Glaucus calls him straightaway, "son of Tydeus," the hero who outside of Homer bestially offended Athena by drinking his adversary's brains and thus lost the immortality offered him. In the exchange of armor, Glaucus was relieved of his innate wit—with which he so effectively met the challenge of Diomedes—as well as of the value of gold and possibly the deathlessness represented by the precious metal and eagerly sought by his forebears.[33]

NOTES

*The following works are referred to in the notes by the author's last name and year of publication: A. W. H. Adkins,

"ΕΥΧΟΜΑΙ, ΕΥΧΩΛΗ, and ΕΥΧΟΣ in Homer," *CQ* 19 (1969) 20–33; and *Poetic Craft in the Early Greek Elegists* (Chicago 1985); Øivind Andersen, *Die Diomedesgestalt in der Ilias* (Oslo 1978); D. Babut, "Sémonide et Mimnerme," *REG* 84 (1971) 17–43; G. Broccia, *Struttura e Spirito del Libro VI dell'Iliade* (Sapri 1963); J. D. Craig, "ΧΡΥΣΕΑ ΧΑΛΚΕΙΩΝ," *CR* 17 (1967) 243–245; P. E. Easterling and B. M. W. Knox, eds., *The Cambridge History of Classical Literature I, Greek Literature* (Cambridge 1985); M. W. Edwards, *Homer, Poet of the* Iliad (Baltimore 1987); J. H. Gaisser, "Adaptation of Traditional Material in the Glaucus-Diomedes Episode," *HSCP* 100 (1969) 165–176; J. Griffin, *Homer on Life and Death* (Oxford 1980); M. Griffith, "Man and the Leaves: A Study of Mimnermos fr. 2," *CSCA* 8 (1976) 73–88; G. S. Kirk, *The Iliad: A Commentary* I (Cambridge 1985) and II (Cambridge 1990); W. Leaf, *The Iliad I–II*[2] (London 1900–1902); R. Martin, *The Language of Heroes: Speech and Performance in the Iliad* (Ithaca 1989); G. Nagy, *The Best of the Achaeans* (Baltimore 1979); G. Piccaluga, "Il Dialogo tra Diomede e Glaukos," *Studi Storico Religiosi* 4 (1980) 237–258; G. Aurelio Privitera, *Dioniso in Omero e nella poesia greca arcaica* (Rome 1970); R. Scodel, "The Wits of Glaucus," *TAPA* 122 (1992) 73–84; E. Vermeule, *Aspects of Death in Early Greek Art and Poetry* (Berkeley and Los Angeles 1979); P. Vivante, *Homer* (New Haven 1985); M. Willcock, *A Companion to the Iliad* (Chicago 1976).

1. Unless otherwise indicated, English translations are the author's. In this passage two English words have been chosen, according to the context, to render the one Greek word γενεή that may be used in instances where English usually distinguishes 'generation' from 'descent' or 'ancestry.' R. Lattimore, *The Iliad of Homer* (Chicago 1951), does however maintain consistency by translating 6.145 "... why ask of my generation?" Problems of consistent English translations of γενεή and φύει are addressed in commentaries (e.g., Leaf [1900] I 268; Kirk [1990] 176) and by critics (e.g., Griffith [1976] 76–77, 85 nn. 20, 23; Griffin [1980] 72; Edwards [1987] 203–204).

2. Stobaeus' attribution (*Fl.* 4.34.29) of these elegiacs to Simonides has been confirmed by P.Oxy.3965; see M. L. West, "Simonides Redivivus," *ZPE* 98 (1993) 1–14. Previously some serious challenges had been raised against Stobaeus' attribution. (19W[2] = 8W[1] [Simonides "dubium"] = 85B[4] = 29D[3] [Semonides]). For earlier bibliography and discussion of authorship see Adkins (1985) 161–173; H. Lloyd-Jones, *Females of the Species* (London 1975) 97; M. L. West, *Studies in Greek Elegy and Iambus* (Berlin 1974) 179–180; Babut (1971) 23, with extensive bibliography in n. 36; and J. A. Davison, *From Archilochus to Pindar* (London 1968)

70–77. Appreciation of the poem is varied; see, for example, P. E. Easterling, "Semonides," in Easterling and Knox, eds. (1985) 157; Adkins (1985) 169, 172–173; Craig (1967) 243; A. Lesky, *A History of Greek Literature* (New York 1966) 114.

3. The long list of texts employing the leaf image extends through and beyond Greek literature. R. Garner, *From Homer to Tragedy: The Art of Allusion in Greek Poetry* (London 1990) lists ten texts after Homer's (pp. v–vi) and also discusses Mimnermus' leaf image (pp. 3–8). For other closely related leaf images, see Edwards (1987) 203–204; O. Vox, "La Prima Discendenza delle Foglie di Omero," *Belfagor* 34 (1979) 442–447; E. Norden, *P. Vergilius Maro Aeneis Buch VI*[5] (Stuttgart 1970) ad 309–312; Broccia (1963) 88 n. 48; A. Morpurgo, "ΟΙΗ ΠΕΡ ΦΥΛΛΩΝ . . . (*Iliade*, VI)," *Atene e Roma* 8 (1927) 81.

4. Griffith (1976) 77. For bibliography on the interpretation of these elegiacs see Griffith (1976) 85 n. 13; Babut (1971) 30–40; Broccia (1963) 88 n. 48.

5. M. R. Lefkowitz, "Bacchylides' *Ode* 5: Imitation and Originality," *HSCP* 73 (1969) 81. (Lefkowitz [46 n. 2] refers to E. D. Townsend, "Bacchylides and Lyric Style" [Ph.D. diss., Bryn Mawr, 1956] Appendix II, on Bacchylides' imitation.)

6. Edwards (1987) 204–205, who also very aptly points out that "Glaucus is not a meditative man elsewhere in the poem." So Adkins (1969) 32 notes that Glaucus "momentarily repines . . . but this is uncharacteristic."

7. Redfield, *Nature and Culture in the Iliad* (Chicago 1975) 102.

8. Griffin (1980) 72, who offers the speech as an example of the complexity of Homeric psychology.

9. Vivante (1985) 77.

10. Edwards (1987) 203.

11. Willcock (1976) 68–69, who detects nervousness in both Glaucus and Aeneas.

12. See n. 6 supra.

13. Martin (1989) 214–215 applies the term "rhetoric of desertion" to Glaucus' speech and compares the lack of χάρις of 17.147 to 9.316, where it is stressed by the withdrawn Achilles.

14. According to Quintus Smyrnaeus (3.212–285) Glaucus is killed in the battle for Achilles' body by Telamonian Ajax (who notes [3.258–260] that family friendships and exchange of gifts will not prevail on him as they did on Diomedes). As if giving an interpretation of the famous Iliadic simile, Quintus writes that Glaucus fell backwards on Achilles as a bush falls around a solid oak: ὁ δ᾽ ὕπτιος ἀμφ᾽ Ἀχιλῆα / κάππεσεν, εὖτ᾽ ἐν ὄρεσσι περὶ στερεὴν δρύα θάμνος (3.279–280).

15. The parallels and analogies are discussed by Privitera

(1970) 56–57 and by Martin (1989) 127–128. Dionysus need no longer be considered an interpolation in the *Iliad* and an intruder to the Greek world; see W. Burkert, *Greek Religion* (Cambridge, Mass. 1985) 161–167.

16. For a different treatment of Diomedes' confidence, see Scodel (1992) 77–81.

17. 20.213–214 = 6.150–151. Vox (supra n. 3) compares the asyndeton of the next line of the narration in each case to Hes., *Op.* 106–108, which introduces the myth of the races with a polite conditional (εἰ ἐθέλεις, 106) and continues asyndetically.

18. See the detailed discussion of εὔχομαι in secular contexts by L. C. Muellner, *The Meaning of Homeric εὔχομαι Through its Formulas* (Innsbruck 1976) 68–99, esp. 76–78, where he terms φάναι an unmarked word for speech and εὔχεσθαι its "polar contrast." The latter is an "egocentric word, since its subject and that of its infinitive are always specific and always the same." He sees it as a functionally marked word for 'say,' not correctly defined as 'boast.' It conveys superiority, contentiousness, and accuracy.

19. Nagy (1979) 274 states that "the war of words between Aeneas and Achilles . . . reveals Aeneas himself as a master of poetic skills in the language of praise and blame." He adduces Meister's proposed etymology of the name Aineias from αἴνη, which has the by-form αἶνος, 'an allusive tale containing an ulterior purpose' (238). Thus he sees a "bivalence of praise and blame" both in αἶνος and in the figure of Aeneas (275). Martin (1989) 16–18 also discusses the diction in Aeneas' speech.

20. In telling the story of Glaucus' family, Pind., *Ol.* 13.60–61, says the Danaäns trembled (τρόμεον) before Glaucus when he boasted (ἐξεύχετ᾽) of Bellerophon.

21. Cf. Pind. *Pyth.* 9.46–47 for leaves and sand indicating vast quantities.

22. Cf. Simonides 5B.37–38: τῶν γὰρ ἀλιθίων / ἀπείρων γενέθλα ("endless is the generation of the foolish").

23. Critical opinion of the episode has not been favorable. Leaf (1900) on 6.130 epitomizes older commentators in his objections to the Lycurgus story on the grounds that Dionysus was a stranger to the Homeric pantheon. He furthermore found Diomedes' words in 6.123–143 "perhaps the most patent" contradiction in the *Iliad* since they disregarded the words of Athena in 5.123–143, on which see n. 24 below. More recently Kirk (1990) 171 terms the episode (6.119–236) "inorganic"; and in Easterling and Knox, eds. (1985) 61 he says of Diomedes' *aristeia* that it "peters out on a recurring note of mild levity" and that the tale has "parody of heroic boast and counter-boast." For extensive critical bibliography on the episode see the bibliographic footnotes in Broccia (1963) 74–105 and Andersen (1978) 107–110. For analyses of the

Lycurgus story see Privitera (1970) 53–75 with bibliographic notes.

24. Kirk (1990) on 6.123.

25. The "contradiction" which Leaf (1900) 256 saw here rigidly assumes that a special vision given Diomedes by Athena continues despite the goddess's absence from her protégé. For under the special patronage of Athena who at the opening of Book 5 kindles in Diomedes a fire like the Dog Star (4–6), Diomedes is also granted the ability to discern gods from men (128) when the goddess lifts a mist (ἀχλύν, 127) from his eyes; but she instructs him to fight with Aphrodite only (131). When Aphrodite, wounded by Diomedes (330–351), flees to Dione her mother, the latter asserts that mortals who fight immortals are short-lived (406–409). If these words of Dione did not reach the ears of Diomedes, those of Apollo did, who as he rescues Aeneas admonishes Diomedes (441–443) that the races of immortal gods and earth-walking men are in no way the same. (The god of measure makes a similar observation in the *Theomachy* [21.462–467] with his comparison of mortals to leaves, as discussed above.) Diomedes yields to Ares (596–606), but accompanied by Athena, he wounds him later (846–864). But once Athena has left the fray (907), Diomedes is left with his own resources. See also Gaisser (1969) 166–167 on Diomedes' awareness of his limitations as a mortal.

26. The point is made by Andersen (1978) 99, who notes that in other accounts Dionysus makes himself the agent of vengeance (e.g., Soph. *Ant.* 955).

27. See further on τιθήνη in Privitera (1970) 61.

28. See Vermeule (1979) 26, 127 on Sisyphus and kindred characters.

29. See the discussions of Gaisser (1969) 167–174 on Glaucus' ancestry in other traditions; Kirk (1990) 178–186.

30. Vermeule (1979) 128 writes: "Ascent to Olympos is, statistically, the least successful method of escaping death. To provide an immortal future for the mortal in partnership with a long-term inhabitant, as for Ganymede and Tithonos, demands sexual cooperation from the gods. Those who went alone fueled by ambition and a sense of competence, like Bellerophon, were shunted back to earth; as Pegasos, with that famous moral wriggle, threw his human master in exchange for a divine one in the stalls of Zeus."

31. Athena withheld the gift of immortality after she saw Tydeus consume the brains of Melanippus; Apollodorus gives a summary in 3.6.8. Other references may be found in the important study of J. D. Beazley, "The Rosi Krater," *JHS* 67 (1947) 1–9. See also Vermeule (1979) 133.

32. Piccaluga (1980) 244. If divine motivation mirrors the character of mortals, then wits must be important to Glaucus before Zeus takes them away. Scodel (1992) discusses this issue, though with different emphases and conclusions. For other attempts to understand the exchange of armor see Kirk (1990) 190–191; W. Donlan, "The Unequal Exchange between Glaucus and Diomedes in the Light of the Homeric Gift-Economy," *Phoenix* 43 (1989) 1–15; D. Traill, "Gold Armor for Bronze and Homer's Use of Compensatory TIMH," *CP* 84 (1989) 301–305; W. Calder III, "Gold for Bronze: *Iliad* 6.232–36" in *Studies Presented to Sterling Dow* (Durham, N.C. 1984) 31–35.

33. An earlier version of this paper was presented at the 1989 annual meeting of the Classical Association of the Middle West and South. It has been improved by the questions and comments of that original audience, by the several relevant studies published in the meantime, and by the anonymous readers and volume editors.

14

THE (RE)MARRIAGE OF PENELOPE AND ODYSSEUS: ARCHITECTURE GENDER PHILOSOPHY. A HOMERIC DIALOGUE

✦

ANN L.T. BERGREN

In the (re)marriage of Odysseus and Penelope, the *Odyssey* initiates a dialogue with the Western traditions of architecture, gender, and philosophy.[1] Although defined conceptually by discourses "invented" as different from mythology,[2] these three modes function actively in Archaic Greek culture and thought. As there was architecture before Vitruvius, gender before Freud or Lévi-Strauss, and philosophy before Plato, so in the *Odyssey* "para-theoretical" forms of architecture, gender, and philosophy mirror one another, creating what might be called an "Odyssean architectural theory."

In the *Odyssey,* architecture is the fabrication of material meaning, the transformation of nature into a material, mortal *sēma* 'sign, tomb.' The tree supporting Odysseus' bed is dead in the ground and Penelope weaves a shroud. Gender is a political instance of such architecture, insofar as it constructs the social significations—the powers and the powerlessness—of sexual difference and of difference as sexual. Odyssean gender makes difference a *kiōn*, 'column' with roots of stone. Its agent is philosophy, the knowing *nous* 'mind' constructing and recognizing the *sēmata* of truth as unique identity.[3] Each of these three modes operates by means of *mētis*, the working and work of "transformative intelligence" common to every *technē*.[4] In a continuous relay of reciprocal production, each can imitate the other's shape (or make the other imitate its shape) to win at the other's game. But as Zeus swallows the goddess Metis so that she "will devise evil and good in his interest alone," so Odyssean architectural theory confines this capacity within an ultimately uncertain "house arrest."

What do Penelope and Odysseus have to do with architecture?

In the Western tradition, they are among its founding figures. By virtue of their *mētis*, Odysseus and Penelope become each a myth of architectural mind and hand.

Mētis means both the working and the work of "transformative intelligence." It embraces both mental and manual prowess, both language and material. *Mētis* works by continual shape-shifting, turning the *morphē* of defeat into victory's tool.[5] Its methods include the *dolos* ('trick, trap'), the *kerdos* ('profit-gaining scheme'), and the ability to seize the *kairos* ('opportunity'). Each of these exploits the essential form of *mētis*, the *tropos,* 'turning,' that binds opposites, manifest in the reversal and the circle,[6] in weaving, twisting, and knotting, and in every joint. The mistress or master of *mētis* knows how to manipulate "the circular reciprocity between what is bound and what is binding."[7] Etymologically, *mētis* is derived from a verbal root meaning "to measure" with its implication of calculation and exact knowledge, preserved also in *metron* ('measurement').[8] A traditional connection between *mētis* and the builder's skills is seen in the figure of Athena, daughter of the goddess Metis, who teaches *tektonas andras*, "builder men," to make (*poiēsai*) elaborate war chariots and *parthenikas* "maidens" to weave (*Homeric Hymn to Aphrodite* 12–15),[9] and in the mythological architect, Trophonius.[10] *Mētis* is the object of the verb of building itself in the phrase *mētin tektēnaito*, 'build a *mētis*' (*Iliad* 10.19).

The Greek myth of *mētis* dramatizes the mutual construction of architecture, gender, and philosophy under the sign of "father-ruled" marriage. Fashioned by Greek men and expressing their point of view, the myth casts *mētis* as an undying female power that must be (re)appropriated through marriage by the political and philosophical power of the male. After her husband, the king Cronus, swallows her previous children to keep them from usurping his sovereignty, Rhea plots to protect her last-born, Zeus. To Cronus, she (or her mother Gaia) presents not the baby himself, but a *mētis*.[11] Formally imitating his desire for another "swallowed" child, she gives him a stone wrapped in swaddling (that is, "swallowing") clothes.[12] Cronus "swallows the trick." So Zeus can grow up to avenge himself by forcing his father to vomit the stone, which he then "fastened down into the earth . . . to be a *sēma* ('sign') and *thauma* ('marvel') to mortals" (*Theog.* 498–500). Now a political monument, the stone signifies Zeus' regime as the containment of *mētis*, immobilized (like the petrified post of Odysseus' bed) in the ground.[13] To maintain this external, political fixation, Zeus matches it with an internal, domestic "incorporation" of *mētis* in his marriage and ultimate "swallowing" of the goddess Metis herself (*Theog.* 886–900).

The marriage of Zeus and Metis is an "architectural contest" with her embodiment as the prize.[14] In the myth, the ultimate winner is never in doubt. In their struggle over entrance into her body, although Metis "turned into many forms to avoid being joined with him,"[15] Zeus "mixes" with her in sexual intercourse (his instrument, it would appear, is the same *anagkē* that will compel the women in the *Odyssey*). Next they compete in body-making, matching their respective capacities for material and verbal transformation. Metis becomes pregnant and a prophecy reveals that she will bear a child who will usurp his father's rule. To bind the goddess within himself and thereby reverse the power of the pregnancy, Zeus "seduces her wits by a trick of wily words" and swallows her, "so that the goddess will devise evil and good in his interest alone" and he can give birth to the child himself from his own head. The proof of his victory is the goddess Athena, mistress of *mētis* as swallowed by Zeus, who presides over the (re)-marriage of Penelope and Odysseus.

In the (re)marriage of Penelope and Odysseus, the *Odyssey* tells a myth of architectural origins that prefigures and exceeds Vitruvius' aboriginal architects who build shelters by imitating the weaving and daubing of swallows' nests.[16] At a schematic level, the weaving of Penelope and the (re)marriage bed of Odysseus are emblems of the two basic elements of building: vertical space-enclosure and columns supporting a horizontal load.[17] Their collaboration constructs an ideal of architecture, gender, and philosophy in and as immovable (re)marriage. The partners in this collaboration, while mutually dependent, are not equal. Penelope is the "partner in charge" of the (re)union. It is by virtue of her *mētis*—her *kerdos* of secret, false speech, her *dolos* of weaving and her trick to test for their secret *sēmata*—that Odysseus' *mētis* of the bed can function as architect of his identity and hers. But Penelope's design serves a "program"—a system of social requirements and the power to enforce them—that she did not write. Itself an architecture, the program of Odyssean "father-rule" attempts ever to reconstruct its model of the female gender through the philosophic force of the *Odyssey* itself. The *Odyssey* divides the ambiguity (it posits as) essential to the female into an almost complete dichotomy of praise and blame.[18] It eulogizes the mind of the blameless wife, the best "Pandora" you can get.

IN PRAISE OF THE MIND OF PENELOPE

Odyssey 24.191–202

O blessed child of Laertes, Odysseus of many devices, surely you possessed a wife with great excellence (*megalēi aretēi*). How good were the wits in blameless Penelope daughter of Icarius. How well she remembered Odysseus, her wedded husband. Therefore his/her (*hōi*) fame in epic (*kleos*) for her/his (*hēs*) excellence (*aretēi*) will never perish, and the immortals will fashion for those upon the earth a song full of grace (*aoidēn chariessan*) for Penelope who possesses mind, not as the daughter of Tyndareus devised (*mēsato*) evil works, when she murdered her wedded husband, and a hateful song forever will exist among men, and will forever bestow a harsh word upon female women, even if there is one who does good.

Penelope is blameless because her wits are good. The text captures the virtue of her mind's devices in its own ambiguous expression of Penelope's *aretē* ('excellence'), a quality attributed to no other female in Homeric epic: "therefore his/her (*hōi*) fame in epic (*kleos*) for her/his (*hēs*) excellence (*aretē*) will never perish." Whether these pronouns refer to Odysseus or Penelope cannot be certainly decided.[19] For it is precisely the *aretē* of Penelope's mind—an exemplary *mētis* in its tricky circularity of active and passive stances—to win *kleos* for herself (2.125–126) by designing (re)marriage to the one in whom she locates all her *aretē* and her *meizon kai kallion kleos*, "greater and more beautiful epic fame" (18.251–255, 19.124–128). It is Penelope's *mētis* to make her excellence and praise ultimately take the shape of her husband's, the shape of her husband as "her-self." She uses the mobility built into her gender to locate herself in and as his stable *oikos*, his unmoving, immovable place and space.

As foil for its praise of Penelope, the *Odyssey* blames Clytemnestra for using her *mētis* (*mēsato*) to "dus-locate" the place of her husband.[20] But in its drive to divide female *mētis* into exclusive praise and blame, the text itself "dus-locates" the division. For it claims that the blame of Clytemnestra "will forever bestow a harsh word upon female women, even if there is one who does good"—even, that is, upon Penelope herself. With this censure of Clytemnestra, the *Odyssey* confesses the vulnerability of its architectural ideal to an independent female practice whose tropomorphic *mētis* is forever reconstructed by the drive to contain it.

THE METIS OF THE WEB

PRAISE, BLAME, AND THE AMBIGUITY OF A "WOMAN'S PLACE"

Odyssey 2.85–88

High-speaking Telemachus, unrestrained in might, what sort of thing have you said to shame us! You would like to fasten blame. But the suitors are not the cause or worthy of your blame (*aitioi*), but your mother, who beyond all others knows profit-gaining schemes (*kerdea*).

Casting the situation in the terms of praise and blame, the suitor Antinous defends himself to Telemachus. Penelope has superior knowledge of *kerdea* "profit-gaining schemes." She can make the other person look blameworthy, when it is actually she who is the *aition*, 'cause,' and thus deserves the blame. The charge introduces the ambiguity of her situation.

Architecturally, Penelope's place as an *aition*, locus of blame and origin, is co-occupied by opposite but interdependent forces. For she does not change her position either in action, by returning to her father, or in word, by choosing one of the suitors or refusing to do so. In the terms of philosophical logic, A (force *toward* marriage as change of place) and *not-A* (force *against* marriage as change of place) occupy the same *place* at the same time. Here, as in buildings, the opposition of interdependent forces produces stability, but one that would arrest the Odyssean social system.

In receiving, but deflecting the suitors' petitions, Penelope would bring to a standstill the change of place that founds society. While she collects suitors, but does not move, Penelope "gains the profit" of praise in the medium of *kleos*.[21] Even the suitor Alcinous' censure—by the "circular reciprocity" of praise and blame—functions here as indirect praise.[22] But if Penelope were *never* to move, what then? She would be *forced* to, as later "she finished the shroud, even though she was unwilling, compelled by force of necessity (*hup' anagkēs,* 110)." For the world of the *Odyssey* shares the system of father-rule charted by Lévi-Strauss in which men must exchange women in order to communicate with one another in networks of legitimate kinship and symbolic thought.[23] Men must move women from one *oikos* to another in order weave their social structure. A woman is moved from the *oikos* of her father and the status of an "Artemis" to the *oikos* of her husband and the sexual life of an "Aphrodite." From there she can be moved back to the father's house, if her husband dies, to be exchanged by her father again. Or, as in the case of Helen, she can be abducted from her husband's house by his rival. Such is the paradoxical architecture of marriage and of the female placement in it, a location built upon the necessity of dislocation.

But for now, Penelope maintains her position unmoved. By imitating the desires of her suitors in the twin strategies of secret, false messages and the treacherous (un)weaving of Laertes' shroud, she turns her adversaries into co-constructors of her ambiguous place.

THE KERDOS OF SECRET, FALSE SPEECH

Odyssey 2.89–92

> For it is now the third year, and quickly will be the fourth,
> that she has cheated the heart in the breasts of the
> Achaeans. To all she gives hope and promises each man,
> sending forth messages (*angelias*). But her mind (*noos*)
> designs other things.

Here is one of the *kerdea* that Penelope knows beyond all others. She knows how to effect the emotions of others without moving herself. She is an "unmoved mover." This is her "gain." The mechanism of her unmoved movement is secret, false speech: *secret speech,* a message to each man individually, breaking up the many into several "one"s;[24] *false speech,* a false exterior, for her interior mind designs other things.[25] This speech is not simply semiotic. It reflects and requires the operation of two architectural elements, *scale*: she analyzes a compound problem (the many suitors) into its consitutent module (the individual suitor) and designs a solution at that level, and *space*: she constructs a divi-

sion between outside and inside. This "profit-gaining scheme" of unmoved movement is an architecture of signs.

With their capacity to move bodies and minds, Penelope's secret messages illustrate the mistake in opposing speech to matter, an exclusion belied by writing, the "scandal of the talking body."[26] Like walls, signs divide and enclose. Their manipulation of scale and space is itself reproduced spatially in the "written" order of line 91: "to all she gives hope and promises each man," in which *elpei* ('gives hope') and *hupischetai* ('promises') divide *pantas* ('all') at line-beginning into *andri hekasōi* ('each man') at line-end.

If they followed regular Homeric practice, however, Penelope's *angeliai* ('messages') would not be conventional writings, but rather oral communications delivered by someone else.[27] For secret, false speech, such intangible messages would seem best. An "angelic" surrogate would allow Penelope the virtue of writing, the capacity to speak although absent. And as "winged words," the messages would leave no material trace of themselves. They would seem to escape the writing's vice of indiscriminate repetition. But the fact that Antinous can now recount Penelope's *kerdos* shows either that the messenger (or someone else) eventually revealed the message to all the suitors, telling the many what was meant for just one, or that the suitors told one another.[28] Once "written" on the mind, the message can be repeated. Intangible traces are no guarantee against iterability. Subdivision by architectural semiosis—as Penelope's scheme divides the suitors—entails its own instability.

Penelope's *kerdos* works only so long as the suitors do not speak the secret, false signs to one another. This collective silence depends upon moving each individual suitor to adopt an image of himself that matches the structure of the *kerdos*. This is the *mētis* of the *kerdos*. Each suitor must construe himself as a module divided between inside knowledge (what he knows from Penelope's message to him) and outside speech (what he says to the others). Penelope's *mētis* of "unmoved movement" plays upon the pride of each man, upon the desire of each for unique identity as the only "chosen one"—and upon the force of that desire to displace and defer his even conceiving the possibility of another treated like himself.[29] Her design "makes a profit" as long as it is supported by the client's philosophical desire.

THE DOLOS OF THE SHROUD

Odyssey 2.93–103

> And this is another trick (*dolos*) she devised in her mind. She set up a great loom in the halls and was weaving a web both delicate and symmetrical. And then she said to us: "Young men, my suitors, since shining Odysseus has died, wait, although pressing for my marriage, until I complete this mantle, lest my spinning be wasted and in vain, a shroud for the hero Laertes, for whenever the common doom of destructive death brings him down, lest someone of the Achaian women in the community blame me, if he lies without a sheet to wind him, he who acquired much." So she spoke, and the proud heart in us was persuaded.

Why is Penelope's dolos *persuasive? How does it make her worth waiting for?*

In displaying devotion to Odysseus' aged father, Penelope shows each suitor how she would act as his wife. She would not let either him or his father die without a shroud woven by the woman of his *oikos*.[30] This service to the father, enforced by the blame of other women, defers the suitors' sexual and social drive by tapping their fear of an ignominious death.

In the Homeric world death is a "common doom," erasing individual distinction. As a victor strips his victim's armor, so Plutus leaves only a bare corpse, despoiling even him who "acquired much." If the body is that of an old man like Laertes, it is *kakon*, ('degraded, ugly, blameworthy') and *aischron* ('ugly, shameful').[31] Funeral rites cover the loss. Provided as a *geras* ('gift of honor in compensation') for death (*Iliad.* 16.457, 675), burial and tombstone keep the corpse from becoming a forgotten "feast for dogs and birds." (*Iliad.* 1.4–5). Inside this outermost shield of the dead is another, ambiguous and architecturally more ambitious, materially distinct yet moulded to the body. Giving shape by screening, the shroud is the material surface of death itself.

Men depend on women for this covering. For in the Greek world only women weave shrouds. Penelope's *dolos*-speech persuades the suitors by promising to deploy this definitive mark of the female gender on behalf of the male over and against his mortality.

Why is it only women who weave shrouds?

In Greek thought weaving is a mark of gender and race. Herodotus presents the men of Egypt as "virtual females" who "reverse the customs and laws of men" by weaving in the *oikos*, while their women trade in the *agora*.[32] The aetiological myth of the female explains why weaving is her native art.

Weaving enters the human world with the woman and her *mētis*, each as the *aition* of the other. It is Athena, daughter of the goddess Metis, who teaches weaving to Pandora, the first woman and model of all females, including the goddesses (like Athena and Metis) who preceded her.[33] Weaving and *mētis*, too, are mutually originating. As Metis teaches weaving, so one is said to "weave a *mētis*." [34] In the logic of aetiological myth, such chronological contradictions and reciprocal origins represent the working of a system of jointly reinforcing constructions. Weaving, *mētis,* and Pandora: each is a tricky covering, an attractive outside that belies what is inside. Pandora is a work of plastic art, the ceramic likeness of a modest maiden, moulded by Hephaistos, the artisanal god.[35] Her modesty is a jar, an external verisimilitude. She is, like Penelope's web, a *dolos* ('trick, trap') against which men have no *mechanē*,[36] and, like the *kerdos* of secret falsehoods, a partition of outside from inside. For, as Athena teaches her weaving, Aphrodite and Hermes constitute Pandora as a treacherous division between external, sexual power—"graceful beauty" that causes "painful yearning" and "limb-devouring sorrows" [37]—and internal, mental power—the "mind of a bitch," the "character of a thief," "falsehoods," and that tool of *mētis* wielded by Zeus against the goddess Metis, "wily words" (*Op.* 67–68, 78). Pandora is an ornamental screen. Her entire skin is covered by the *kosmos* that Athena as goddess of craft has "fastened together upon" (*ephērmose: epi,* 'upon,' + *harmozō,* 'join, fit') it (*Op.* 75). In weaving, Pandora makes what she is, a covering of her (*mētis*) inside.[38]

But why women alone are assigned the particular form of *mētis* that is weaving, the myth of Pandora does not directly state. Its silence is understandable psycho-analytically. For, lacking the inhibitions of Hesiodic theology, but ultimately derivative from its formulation of the female, it is a Freudian text that locates the reason this tradition sees weaving as women's invention—and in an area of maximum male anxiety:

Freud, "Femininity"

The effect of penis-envy has a share, further, in the physical vanity of women, since they are bound to value their charms more highly as a late compensation for their original sexual inferiority. Shame, which is considered to be a feminine characteristic *par excellence* but is far more a matter of convention than might be supposed, has as its purpose, we believe, concealment [*verdecken: Decke,* 'cover, ceiling, roof, skin, envelope, coat, pretence, screen'] of genital deficiency. We are not forgetting that at a later time, shame takes on other functions. It seems that women have made few contributions to the discoveries [*Entdeckungen*] and inventions in the history of civilization; there is, however, one technique which they may have invented—that of plaiting and weaving. If that is so, we should be tempted to guess the unconscious motive for the achievement. Nature herself would seem to have given the model which this achievement imitates by causing the growth at maturity of the pubic hair that conceals the genitals. *The step that remained to be taken lay in making the threads adhere to one another,* while on the body they stick into the skin and are only matted together. If you reject this idea as fantastic and regard my belief in the influence of a lack of a penis on the configuration of femininity as an *idée fixe,* I am of course defenceless.[39]

Women invented weaving to conceal their genitals, the locus of their lack and envy of the male's (pro-)creative capacity and the place—indeed the *aition*—of the castration, the "female" condition he fears for himself. From the Greek perspective, the covering of this place is praiseworthy, for all genitals are *ta aidoia,* 'the shameful parts.' Veiling them, like wrapping a corpse, displays *aidōs,* 'shame,' that "feminine characteristic *par excellence.*"

Although based overtly upon women's "original sexual inferiority," Freud's aetiology of weaving repeats the Greek pattern of casting the male's creative capacity

as originally female. For against its assumption of their lack and envy, Freud's text attributes to women an originary *mētis,* whereby they invent "the step that remained to be taken . . . making the threads adhere to one another." This amounts to claiming that women use their inventiveness to cover their (lack of) genitals understood as their (lack of) inventiveness. And it is this very invention, weaving, that Greek men emulate in modes of creativity from which women in Greece are barred and thus might be thought to envy. For as Zeus appropriates the original Metis, so Greek men call their poetry, prophecy, and in Plato, even the art of the statesman himself, a "weaving."[40] But with weaving as figurative speech, and poetry, prophecy, and political philosophy as figurative web, each is the "non-original origin" and the "literal figure" of the other.[41] It is to overrule such reciprocal formation that Zeus fixes his *mētis* stone in the ground, the *sēma* of the philosophical and political power to erect and enforce the hierarchy of figurative over literal, "figurative" weaving for men and "literal" weaving for women.

The same arrested relay of emulative *mētis* underlies Odyssean architectural theory. For in the female invention "of making the threads adhere to one another" is also the beginning of architecture. The Vitruvian myth of aboriginal architects "imitating" the weaving and daubing of birds' nests continues a widespread aetiology. The tradition reaches to the etymology of *teīchos/ toīchos,* 'wall,' derived from a root with cognates in several Indo-European languages meaning "to mould a wall of mud"[42] and to the woven constructions that comparative architectural historian and theoretician, Gottfried Semper, adduces as the origin of vertical division between inner and outer space.

Semper, "The Textile Art"

. . . *the beginning of building coincides with the beginning of textiles.*

The wall is that architectural element that formally represents and makes visible *the enclosed space as such,* absolutely, as it were, without reference to secondary concepts.

We might recognize the *pen,* bound together from sticks and branches, and the interwoven *fence* as the earliest vertical spatial enclosure that man *invented.* . . .

Whether these inventions gradually developed in this order or another matters little to us here, for it remains certain that the use of the crude weaving that started with the pen—as a means to make the "home," the *inner life* separated from the *outer life*, and as the formal creation of the idea of space—undoubtedly preceded the wall, even the most primitive one constructed out of stone or any other material.

The structure that served to support, to secure, to carry this spatial enclosure was a requirement that had nothing directly to do with *space* and the *division of space....*

In this connection, it is of the greatest importance to note that wherever these secondary motives are not present, woven fabrics almost everywhere and especially in the southern and warm countries carry out their ancient, original function as conspicuous spatial dividers; even where solid walls become necessary they remain only the inner and unseen structure for the true and legitimate representatives of the spatial idea: namely, the more or less artificially woven and seamed-together, textile walls....

In all Germanic languages the word *Wand* (of the same root and same basic meaning as *Gewand*) directly recalls the old origin and type of the *visible* spatial enclosure. Likewise, *Decke, Bekleidung, Schranke, Zaun* (similar to *Saum*), and many other technical expressions are not somewhat late linguistic symbols applied to the building trade, but reliable indications of the textile origin of these building parts.[43]

Given Semper's account of the "beginning of building," in marking weaving as exclusively female, early Greek thought attributes to women the founding form of architectural art. But the Odyssean system of praise and blame confines the woman's architectural power to weaving its walls. A praiseworthy "Pandora" weaves to cover (herself as) shame—and blames women who do not.

Why do women enforce this confinement of their weaving?

A "woman's place" in the *Odyssey* is subject to male force—the *anagkē* that ultimately compels Penelope to finish the shroud (2.110). In this position, women have neither security nor prestige unless they weave the protection of the father-rule. It is the *mētis* of the Odyssean architecture of gender—*mētis* as "swallowed" by the *anagkē* of Zeus' regime—to elicit from women its double. Women restrict their architecture in return for protection and praise.

Penelope's *dolos* of the shroud is persuasive because it promises conformation with this ideal of female architecture. It is treacherous (an exemplary *mētis*) because it both keeps and contravenes—indeed it keeps by contravening—its promise.

How does Penelope maintain by resisting and resist by maintaining the Odyssean architectural ideal?

For as long as it operates, Penelope's *dolos* maintains the ambiguity of her position as *aition*, a movement without (re)location, toward the *oikos* of her husband's rival as she weaves by day, toward her husband's *oikos* as she unweaves at night. This is not a static stand-off here, for equal spending and saving add up to a *kerdos* of praise. This scheme of rotating reversal is Penelope's solution to the problem posed by the program of Odyssean architecture, gender, and philosophy: how to construct a praise-winning female place, when you do not know whether your husband is alive or dead? If alive, keep his place alive (unweave his father's shroud by night). If dead, make a new place for yourself (weave his father's shroud by day). Thereby make your place simultaneously that of both men and no man. Her strategy tropes the riddle of her situation with another: When is the most blameworthy female action, refusing marriage exchange or marrying husband's rival, the most praiseworthy? When they are done at the same time, just as Penelope is said to enter the room *Artemidi ikelē ēe chruseēi Aphroditēi*, "like to Artemis or golden Aphrodite" (*Odyssey* 17.37, 19.54). Hers is a *mētis* of doing both, while doing neither, a "circular reciprocity" that binds the suitors and the system they represent.

But it binds Penelope, too. Time does not stand still. With repetition, ambiguity becomes architectural. Resisting the question of whose place she is weaving allows and even courts its occupation by the suitors. Their prolonged presence attracts the allegiance of women trained to exercise their *mētis* on behalf of the man who occupies their *oikos*. Penelope's dislocating architecture provokes its "dus-location" in the figure of the servant woman who betrays her.

A treacherous double of Penelope's movement without changing place, the servant woman, like Clytemnestra, changes her place without movement. And like the ambiguity of Penelope's position, the servant's unmoved self-movement exploits the female role in marriage exchange. Although they are the passive *sēmata* of this system, exchanged so men can speak with each other, women are also, as Lévi-Strauss observes, active *"signes parlantes"* who can speak for themselves.[44] Women are thus like "linguistic shifters" (the pronouns "I" and "you," for example) whose meaning changes according to their "place" of usage. But a woman can also—as in the case of Clytemnestra with Aegisthus or that of Odysseus' disloyal maidservants with the suitors—use her place or herself as place by designating its owner.

As Penelope's *kerdos* of secret speech works only so long as the many suitors are silent, so the *dolos* of her shroud succeeds only so long as the many women in the *oikos* speak with a single voice. Such is the vulnerability of her "vertical space enclosures" to the perforation of speech. Now, with the breaking of the women's univocality, comes the *telos* of her weaving by *anagkē* (*Odyssey* 2.110) and the order to return to her father (113–114)—and the arrival of a stranger in the *oikos*.[45] Henceforth Penelope's *mētis* is devoted to the architectural philosophy of his identification.

THE MĒTIS OF THE (RE)MARRIAGE BED

THE TEST FOR ARCHITECTURAL SIGNS

The *mētis* of the (re)marriage bed begins with Penelope sleeping upon it, while Odysseus slaughters the suitors, sleeping more sweetly than ever before, since Odysseus left for Troy, so sweetly that she berates the nurse Eurycleia for awakening her with the news of Odysseus's return (*Odyssey* 23.16–19). Penelope refuses to believe the nurse. Eurycleia replies that Odysseus has returned "really" (*etumon* 26). Overjoyed, Penelope asks to hear "unerringly" (*nēmertes* 35), if he "really" (*eteon* 36) has returned, how he "although being only one," slaughtered the many (38). After listening to Eurycleia's account, she denies that it is a "true

story" (*mūthos etētumos* 62) and initiates a test for the real identity of this "stranger" (28).

Earlier in the day she set up a contest to see who could string Odysseus' bow and hit a target through a row of twelve axes, promising to marry whoever succeeded.[46] The winner had to be at least a good copy, someone *eikelos* 'like,' or *homoios*, 'same as, equal to,' Odysseus—not false pretenders to his place like the suitors, but not necessarily the original man.[47] Now, in order to determine Odysseus' unique identity, Penelope designs *peira* 'penetration to the boundary, test' that is at once a work of architectural philosophy and of philosophic architecture.[48] Penelope's *peira* will define Odysseus by penetrating the space up to the *peirata* ('boundaries') that enclose an individual, an inside distinct from all that is outside. These "boundaries" of Odysseus are architectural signs: the *sēma* of the scar engraved on his body and the *sēmata* of the bed he built. Qualified by Penelope as sēmata "which we two only know hidden from others" (*Odyssey* 23.110), the signs of the bed circumscribe an interior location, an exclusive mental place occupied by the two alone, another *kerdos* of secret, but this time not false, signification. In defining himself, Odysseus' architecture of the (re)-marriage bed defines Penelope in and as the same place. And by the circular reciprocity of *mētis*, Penelope's *peira* of Odysseus will prove her own identity as well. "Penelope" is just she who moves (herself as) the target so that it becomes something immovable and "Formal"—again, an "unmoved mover"—something only Odysseus in his "Formal" uniqueness can hit.

THE SĒMA OF THE SCAR

In keeping with the proper procedure in early Greek tradition of testing the identity of a "stranger," Penelope claims first that he is a god.[49] This alternative possibility elicits from Eurycleia the *sēma ariphrades*, 'very clear sign' (*Odyssey* 23.73), of Odysseus' scar, the one she had recognized as she bathed him the previous night. Her moment of recognition occasioned the text's own extended reconstruction of the mark: it is the sign of the wound Odysseus received from a boar's tusk, while hunting on Parnassus with the sons of his mother's father Autolycus. It was Autolycus who gave him his name as an infant and promised to give him many possessions when he grew up. It was to collect this patrimony that Odysseus came to Parnassus and during the hunt that he received this initiatory sign of naming and manhood (*Odyssey* 19.386–475).

The *sēma* in Homer is most often a three-dimensional object entailing recognition, interpretation, and knowledge, in particular the grave marker.[50] Embedded in the body, a scar is a sort of grave marker in relief, a trace of mortality in the living organism. It marks identity as born at the writing on the body of the body's death. It is the sign of name as incision.

After listening to Eurycleia's description of her discovery of the scar, a sign Penelope will have recognized as well as anyone, she leaves the bedchamber and goes down to see "these men, suitors, dead, and him who slew them" (*Odyssey* 23.84–85).

THE SĒMATA OF THE BED

The ultimate conversation of Penelope and Odysseus begins with the woman's uncertainty. She debates whether to question or to kiss him (23.85–88). The two sit apart, beside the architectural form associated with each, she by the wall, reminiscent of her weaving, and he beside the column, looking down and waiting (89–90). "At one time she looks him in the face and at another, she does not recognize (*agnōsaske*) him, wearing foul cloths on his skin" (94–95). When her son berates his mother for holding back, she avers:

Odyssey 23.107–109

If really (*eteon*) indeed he is Odysseus and has come home, indeed we two especially shall know (*gnōsometh'*) each other even better. For we have signs (*semat'*) which we two only know hidden from others.

Apparently recognizing in these words an *ainos*, an elicitation to test his knowledge of the secret signs,[51] Odysseus smiles and bids his son, "allow your mother to test me" (*peirazein emethen*). "And quickly she will point things out to herself better" (111, 113–114).

With this invitation to his wife, Odysseus sets the scene for a (re)marriage of the two. He directs the men and women to dress handsomely and the bard to sing the "wedding song" (expected after the contest of the axes to decide the bridegroom) so as to put off any rumor of

the suitors' slaughter (130–151). Alleging his ragged clothes to be the reason his wife denies him, the bridegroom himself is bathed and beautified (115, 153–163).[52] Now "like (*homoios*) to the immortals in build," he sits down again "opposite his wife" (163–165).

Accusing Penelope of a heart more stubborn than any woman's and answering her test of their private *sēmata* with an *ainos* of his own, Odysseus bids the nurse make him up a bed (166–172). His counter-*ainos* elicits from Penelope the final move of her *peira*. By way of "testing her husband" (*posios peirēmenē* 181), she orders Eurycleia to "make up a firm bed for him *outside* (*ektos*) of the well-stabilized bedchamber he made himself.[53] Put his firm bed *out there* (*entha ektheisai*)" (177–179). Odysseus responds with the self-identifying sign of the bed he built so long ago.

He first stresses the unique resistance of the bed to the instability of both the *oikos* and the female, lateral displacement. He demands to know who put his bed "in another place" (*allose* 184). Not a god himself could easily put it "in another place" (*allēi eni chorēi* 186). No mortal could "move it to the other side" (*metochlisseien* 188), "since a great sign (*mega sēma*) has been built into the skillfully-wrought bed" (*tetuktai en lechei askētōi* 188–189). Metonymic of such fixity, Odysseus emphasizes his unique architectural authorship, "I myself wrought it with toil and no one else" (*to egō kamon oude tis allos* 189). Finally, he declares the details of his building, first of the bedchamber and its entrance, and then of the bed inside:

Odyssey 23.190–201

A long-leafed trunk of an olive tree grew inside the enclosure, blooming to the topmost. Its thickness was like that of a column (*kiōn*). Surrounding this, I built the bedchamber until I finished it, with close-set stones, and I roofed it down from above well. I put upon it compacted doors, jointed closely. And then I cut off the foliage of the long-leafed olive, and trimming the trunk from the root up, I planed it around with the bronze well and with knowledge (*epistamenōs*), and I made it straight to a chalkline, thereby constructing a bed-post. I bored through it all over with an auger. Beginning from this I kept carving my bed, until I finished it, and decorating[54] it with gold and silver and ivory. And I stretched inside the thong of an ox, shining with purple. So I have articulated for you this sign (*sēma*).

But I do not know whether the bed is still in place (*empe-don*), woman, or whether now some other man put it else-where (*allose*), by cutting under the stump of the tree.

This architecture is the secret *sēma* that Odysseus and Penelope know apart from others.

What is it a sign of?

The bed is a sign of the Odyssean ideal of architecture, gender, and philosophy in and as immovable (re)marriage.

The bed is a sign of support made immovable by transmuting organism and structure, model and copy. By planing off the bark, Odysseus removes the only part of the tree that is alive, its only source of growth either lateral or vertical. Now the tree will petrify, turning into the material of monumental building. Now surpassing even the stability of its model, a *kiōn*, the tree is a copy with roots of stone. It embodies the "formal" ideal that all columnar forms imperfectly emulate.[55]

By its fixity, the bedpost signifies the ideal immovability of (re)marriage and, *a fortiori,* of the woman, once she is moved to weave the place of the bed. It is the *sēma* of female mobility limited to the movement of (re), of "again" within parentheses, of "again" within the walls of the *oikos*. Built by and for the man himself, the stationary bed betokens (re)marriage as his swallowing of the female's pharmacological movement, that *tropos* whose *logos* shares the structure of the *pharma-kon*, 'cure, poison.' A woman must be movable, so that men can communicate. She must enclose, so that he can support. But if the female can move, then her placement is unreliable. If she can weave, she can unweave space and place. What makes marriage possible makes its stability uncertain. So this constraint of the female architectural capacity is both health and harm, requiring its own architectural antidote, the immovable (re)marriage bed.

How can the bed guarantee the immovability of (re)marriage?

Built into its petrified roots is the *mega sēma* of secret knowledge. Apparatus of gender and truth as exclusive difference, the secret sign divides inside from outside. By its secret structure and its structure as a secret, the bed frames the unity of a shared knowledge that cannot be replaced with a representative, an equivalent, or an imitation.[56] Designed so that disclosure and displacement coincide, the knowledge and the location of the bed operate as *symbola*, twin tokens of unique identity as unique relationship.[57] If he knows the bed, he is (her) Odysseus. Unless he has told the secret or she has, no one other than the actual man, not a pseudo-Odysseus but only the one "like to himself" (*eikelos autōi*)[58] can speak its "hidden signs." If she has not moved the bed, she remains (his) Penelope and their (re)marriage unmoved. But if it has been moved, then Penelope has castrated the marriage and, with it, her *kleos* as female paragon.[59]

But the bed has not been moved. And Odysseus has spoken its "hidden signs." The text reiterates their architectural function:

Odyssey 23. 205–206

So he spoke, and right there her knees and her own heart were released as she recognized (*anagnousēi*) the fixed signs (*sēmata empeda*) that Odysseus spoke to her.

The *sēmata* of the bed are *empeda* "footed in" the ground, firmly standing, exclusively separating inside from out, the *telos* of Penelope's architectural and philosophic quest. Recognizing them brings ecstasy.

THE MĒTIS OF THE ODYSSEAN ARCHITECTURAL IDEAL

In acknowledging her recognition, within the security of her immovable (re)marriage, Penelope inserts a parenthesis:

Odyssey 23.225–230.

But now, since you have now spoken signs easy to recognize (*sēmata ariphradea*) of our bed, that no other mortal man has seen, but only you and I—and only one hand-maiden, Actoris, whom my father gave to me when I came here, who guarded the door of our firm chamber—you indeed persuade my spirit, though it is very unfeeling.

Here—in the "parenthetical" person of the maid Actoris—is a potential gap in the *sēmata ariphradea* of Odyssean architecture, gender, and philosophy. Stationed in the liminal position of the female, mistress of passages, Actoris, "she who leads," could have told what she knew about the bed to others, just as Penelope's disloyal handmaids earlier revealed the *mētis* of the web.

But what did Actoris know? In Greek "to know" is "to have seen." Did the sight of the bed reveal its foundation? And if Actoris did know and tell, who would be compromised? Only Penelope, since it would mean that someone other than Odysseus could speak the secret signs now or in the past. "We" know that either the present speaker is the true Odysseus or the *Odyssey* itself is a "Cretan lie." Penelope cannot. As for the past, if anyone has spoken these signs before, Penelope cannot take the present speaker for the unique Odysseus, unless she is hiding a past deception. Did a stranger melt her heart, as did Odysseus himself, with *pseudea homoia etumoisin* (19.203–212)?[60] Did he speak signs with the same uncertain footing as the *sēmata empeda* "recognized" by Penelope in Odysseus' description of his mantle and brooch?[61] Again, the authority of the *Odyssey* vouches for Penelope's fidelity. Odysseus cannot. If Actoris has told its secret, the bed fails as a construction of gender and philosophy, for it cannot maintain (re)marriage immovable nor identity unique.

Such a subversion of the system is a possibility that Odysseus overlooks. He weeps and holds the wife who is "jointed to his heart" (*thumarea* 23.232). Against all its detractors—such as the Hesiodic account of Pandora that concludes: "Any man who marries and has a praiseworthy (*kednēn*) wife, one who is jointed to his mind (*arēruīan prapidessi*), for him evil matches itself against (*antipherizei*) good forever"—with this consummate image of its ideal "joint," Odyssean architecture would close the door.[62]

NOTES

* The first version of this paper was written for the UCLA Homeric Dialogues I, May 1989. It poses a "dialogue" between the *Odyssey* and Western architectural theory. I was inspired to compare poetry and philosophy with plastic art as a student in Emily Vermeule's Harvard seminar, "The Art and Poetry of the Homeric Age." She enabled me to pursue this interest by supporting an eleventh-hour fellowship for study in Greece. At the UCLA Homeric Dialogues II, February 1991, she inspired me again by lecturing on the subject of "Minoan Poetry?" and expressing interest in the current version of this paper, the destination of which she did not then know.

It is a pleasure to thank Jane Carter and Sarah Morris for helpful reading of this paper.

A modified version of this paper appears in *Assemblage. A Critical Journal of Architecture and Design Culture* 21 (1993).

1. The term "(re)marriage" is used to designate the renewal of an existing relationship, rather than a "remarriage" proper following either divorce or death. The distinction between the two is not exclusive.

2. For the foundation of history and philosophy via the "invention" of mythology as their differentiating "other," see, e.g., M. Detienne, *The Invention of Mythology*, trans. M. Cook (Chicago and London 1986). For a psychoanalytic and an anthropological account of the relation between gender and what is understood as biological sex, see, e.g., J. Mitchell and J. Rose, eds., *Feminine Sexuality. Jacques Lacan and the école freudienne* (New York 1982), and C. MacCormack and M. Strathern, eds., *Nature, Culture and Gender* (Cambridge 1980). For a recent review of the research on gender, see T. Laqueur, *Making Sex. Body and Gender from the Greeks to Freud* (Cambridge, Mass. 1990) 1–24.

3. For *nous* as the mental faculty of recognition and knowledge of the *sēma*, see G. Nagy, "Sēma and Noēsis: Some Illustrations," *Arethusa* 16 (1983) 35–55.

4. For the essential work on *mētis*, see M. Detienne and J.-P. Vernant, *Cunning Intelligence in Greek Culture and Society*, trans. J. Lloyd (Atlantic Highlands, N.J. 1978). For the work and the intelligence of the artisan as *mētis*, see P. Vidal-Naquet, "A Study in Ambiguity: Artisans in the Platonic City," *The Black Hunter. Forms of Thought and Forms of Society in the Greek World*, trans. A. Szegedy-Maszac (Baltimore and London 1986) 224–245.

5. For classic examples, see Vernant and Detienne, (supra n. 4) 34, 37: The hunted fox reverses its direction and plays dead, lying in wait as a trap for the hunter. When caught, the fox-fish turns its body inside out, so that its interior becomes its exterior and the hook falls out.

6. See Detienne and Vernant (supra n. 4) 46: "The ultimate expression of these qualities is the circle, the bond that is perfect because it completely turns back on itself, is closed in on

itself, with neither beginning nor end, front nor rear, and which in rotation becomes both mobile and immobile, moving in both directions at once. . . . The circle unites within it several opposites, each one giving birth to its opposite, it appears as the strangest, most baffling thing in the world, *thaumasiotaton*, possessing a power which is beyond ordinary logic."

7. See Detienne and Vernant (supra n. 4) 305.

8. See P. Chantraine, *Dictionnaire étymologique de la langue grecque* (Paris 1977) 699, s.v. *mētis*. Chantraine cites the cognate verbs *medomai*, and *mēdomai*, 'devise, contrive' and the nouns, Sanskrit *māti*, 'measure, exact knowledge,' Anglo-Saxon *mǣd* 'measure.' See below on Clytemnestra's use of *mētis* to "devise" (*mēsato*) evil for her husband.

9. For the building of war machines as a part of the ancient architectural repertoire, see Vitr., *De arch.* 10.10–16, the climax of his treatise. For the connection between weaving and architecture, see also Callim., *Ap.* 55–57: "Men follow Phoebus when they measure out cities. For Phoebus always delights in founding cities, and he himself weaves (*hyphainei*) their foundations (*themeilia*)."

10. See Z. Petrie, "Trophonius ou l'architecte. À propos du statut des techniciens dans la cité grecque," *StClass* 18 (1979) 23–37. For the ancient sources of the myth of Trophonius and its many variants in other cultures, see J. G. Frazer's note on Paus. 9.37 in *Pausanias's Description of Greece. Translated with a Commentary* (London 1913) 176–179. The activities of Trophonius and his brother Agamedes exemplify architectural *mētis*. After building many monuments, including the temple of Apollo at Delphi, the pair design the treasury of a king who, like his divine counterpart, requires the products of *mētis* to preserve his political "property." But rather than securing the king's gold, the architects build a secret passage through which to steal it gradually. Thus reversing the "proper" architectural function, the architects construct a means for exposure instead of enclosure and dispossess their client of the economic talisman of his political identity. Once he discovers the *dolos,* the king sets a trap of his own in which Agamedes is caught. The contest then continues as the brothers imitate the enemy to beat him at his own game. In an ironic assimilation of the king's loss of recognition, the two prevent the king from recognizing them by depriving themselves of identifiable form: Agamedes asks Trophonius to cut off his head, and after obliging his brother, Trophonius is swallowed up by the earth and becomes an oracular hero.

11. The trick of the stone is termed a *mētis* at Hes. *Theog.* 471, when Rhea begs Gaia and Ouranus to "devise together with her (*sumphrassasthai*) a *mētis* by which she could make him forget that she bore her dear child." It is Gaia who takes the newborn Zeus to be raised secretly in the Cretan cave (479–484) and she could be the subject of the phrase "having

swaddled a great stone, she handed it to the son of Ouranos" (485), unless a change of subject back to Rhea is to be understood. M. L. West, *Hesiod. Works and Days* (Oxford 1978) ad 485, adduces the Arcadian parallel in which it is Rhea who gives Cronus a foal to swallow instead of Poseidon.

12. With the substitution of the swaddled stone for the real child, compare the Muses' capacity to substitute *pseudea homoia etumoisin* and *alēthea* "whenever we wish" (Hes., *Theog.* 27–28). See A. Bergren, "Language and the Female in Early Greek Thought," *Arethusa* 16 (1983) 69–95. For the architectural significance of such swaddling, compare the *Bekleidung,* 'dressing, cladding,' of a building in the theory of nineteenth-century comparative architectural historian and theoretician Gottfried Semper in *The Four Elements of Architecture and Other Writings,* trans. H. Mallgrave and W. Herrmann (Cambridge 1989) 24, 34, 36–40, 103–110, 240–243. On the relations between Semper's work and Karl Bötticher's *Die Tektonik der Hellenen,* see ch. 3, "Semper and the Archeologist Bötticher," in W. Herrmann, *Gottfried Semper. In Search of Architecture* (Cambridge, Mass. 1984).

13. This monolith would count among the examples of what Hegel calls "symbolic" architecture, the first stage in the progressive development toward the Classical and finally the Romantic/Gothic types. In contrast to the Classical, in which the elements must "display" (*zeigen*) their definitively architectural function, as a column, to take Hegel's prime example, demonstrates its load-bearing, the purpose of symbolic architecture is "the erection of something which is a unifying point for a nation." Its elements are often imitative of natural, organic forms and emphasize the unroofed enclosure of space rather than load-bearing support. See G. F. W. Hegel, *Aesthetics. Lectures on Fine Art,* trans. T. Knox (Oxford 1975) 2.630–700. See also D. Payot, *Le philosophe et l'architecte* (Paris 1982) 29–50.

14. Aristotle's *Gen. An.* presents a similar "battle of the sexes" as the sperm, a dynamic *tektōn*, attempts to master (*kratein*) the passive material of the menstrual fluid with the instrument of his "informing" soul (730b, 736a, 737a, 765b, 766b, 767b).

15. Apollod., *Bibl.* I.3.6.

16. See Vitr. *De Arch.* 2.2–7: "Therefore, since because of the invention of fire there was born at the beginning coming together among men and reasoning together and living together, and many came together into one place, by having from nature an advantage over other animals, so that they walked not with their head down but upright and gazed upon the magnificence of the world and the stars, and likewise with their hands and fingers they handled easily whatever they wished, they began in that joining together some to make shelters (*tecta*) from a branch, others to dig caves under moun-

tains, several by imitating (*imitantes*) the nests of swallows and their modes of constructing (*aedificationes*) to make places (*loca*) from mud and wattles which they might go under." For the view of Renaissance architect Leon Battista Alberti that it was "roof and walls" that first brought humans together in community, see *On the Art of Building*, trans. J. Rykwert, N. Leach, and R. Tavernor (Cambridge, Mass. 1988) 3. On the Western tradition of myths of original architecture deriving from both Vitruvian and Biblical exemplars, see J. Rykwert, *On Adam's House in Paradise. The Idea of the Primitive Hut in Architectural History* (New York 1972).

17. See G. Semper, "Structural Elements of Assyrian-Chaldean Architecture," ch. 10 of "Comparative Building Theory" (*Vergleichende Baulehre* 1850) in Hermann (supra n. 12) 204 for these "two basic elements of building—the roof with the supporting columns, and the vertical enclosure later to become the wall of the living room." For these two elements as exemplary functions of the "Classical" and "Symbolic" stages respectively in Hegel's philosophy of architecture, see Hegel (supra n. 13) 630–676.

18. For this ambiguity of the female, see Bergren (supra n. 12).

19. On this passage, see G. Nagy, *The Best of the Achaeans: Concepts of the Hero in Archaic Greek Poetry* (Baltimore 1979) 36–38, 255–256. Nagy interprets *aretē* here as belonging to Odysseus, taking *sun megalēi aretēi* in 193 as instrumental with *ektēsō* ("it is truly with great merit that you got a wife") and *kleos hēs aretēs* in 196–197 as "the *kleos* of his *aretē*," with the merit consisting in having won such a wife as Penelope. The *aoidē chariessa* for Penelope in 197–198, clearly a gloss upon *kleos hēs aretēs*, is "part of the overall *kleos* of Odysseus."

20. For the relationship between *medomai* and *mētis*, see Chantraine (supra n. 8).

21. See below on *Odyssey* 2.125.

22. Compare Pind. Fr. 181SM: ὁ γὰρ ἐξ οἴκου ποτὶ μῶμον ἔπαινος κίρναται "for by virtue of common origin (literally, "from the household") praise is mixed with blame."

23. See C. Lévi-Strauss, *The Elementary Structures of Kinship,* trans. J. Bell, J. von Sturmer, and R. Needham (Boston 1969) 478–497 = *Les Structures elementaires de la parenté* (Paris 1967) 548–570.

24. Compare Odysseus' ability to work as one versus the many suitors.

25. Compare Achilles' condemnation of such a dichotomy at *Iliad* 9.312–313.

26. Compare S. Felman, *Le scandal du corps parlant* (Paris 1980).

27. Compare the case of Bellerophon, *Iliad* 6.155–202.

28. Was it the woman mentioned in *Odyssey* 2.108 who revealed the *mētis* of the web to the Suitors? It could also be a herald (Medon) or the domestic Dolion (*Odyssey* 4.735).

29. Compare the clouding of logical division by the epistemological blindness of *eros* in the *Homeric Hymn to Aphrod*. See A. Bergren, "The *Homeric Hymn to Aphrodite*: Tradition and Rhetoric, Praise and Blame," *CA* 8 (1989) 1–41.

30. Antigone is a witness to the preeminent importance of proper death rites. For the role of women as leaders of funeral ritual, compare the mourning for Hektor at the end of the *Iliad* and M. Alexiou, *The Ritual Lament in Greek Tradition* (Cambridge 1974). For an analysis of the Homeric treatment of the corpse in terms of a cross-cultural account of the role of women in funerary rituals, see M. Bloch, "Death, women, and power," in M. Bloch and J. Parry, eds., *Death and the Regeneration of Life* (Cambridge 1982) 211–230.

31. Compare Priam's contrast between the corpse of a young man which retains its "beauty" (*kala*) even in death and that of an old man, when "dogs disgrace (*aischunōsi*) the gray head and the gray beard and the genitals (*aidō* 'shame')" (*Iliad* 22.71–76) and the analysis of J.-P. Vernant, "A 'Beautiful Death' and the Disfigured Corpse in Homeric Epic," in F. Zeitlin ed., *Mortals and Immortals* (Princeton 1991) 50–74.

32. See Hdt. 2.35. See also *Dissoi Logoi* 2.17.

33. See Bergren (supra n. 12) with bibliography.

34. For 'weave a *mētis*,' see *Iliad* 7.324, 9.93, *Odyssey* 4. 678, 739, Hes., *Sc.* 28. For 'weave a *dolos*', see *Iliad* 6.187, *Odyssey* 9.422.

35. Hes. *Op.* 70–71 and *Theog.* 571–572: "Immediately from earth renowned Hephaistos moulded (*plasse*) a likeness to a modest maiden."

36. Hes. *Theog.* 589–590: "Marvel held both the immortal gods and mortal men, when they saw the sheer trap (*dolon aipun*), irresistible (*amechanon*) to men."

37. Hes., *Op.* 65–66. For *guioborous* vs. *guiokorous* at 66, see West (supra n. 11) ad loc.

38. As a construction enclosing her *mētis*, Pandora is analogous to her jar containing hope. This jar is described as both a body and a house: "There in the unbreakable halls (*domoisin*) hope alone was remaining inside under the lips of the jar, and it did not fly out from the door (*thuraze*)" (Hes. *Op.* 96–97). See J.-P. Vernant, "At Man's Table: Hesiod's Foundation Myth of Sacrifice," in *The Cuisine of Sacrifice among the Greeks*, trans. P. Wissing (Chicago 1989) 77. As both body and house, the jar parallels Pandora with the *oikos*. The relation between the two is, however, hierarchical rather than equal. For the *oikos* is designed to work like the "swallowing" body of Zeus: to keep the female inside, able to use her *mētis* for "weaving" only the walls of the *oikos* as an image and extension of the ideal wife.

39. S. Freud, "Femininity," *Standard Edition*, vol. 22, 132 (my emphasis).

40. See Bergren (supra n. 12) and M. Durante, "Ricerche sulla prehistoria della lingua poetica greca. La terminologia relativa alla creazione poetica," *Atti della Academia Nazionale dei Lincei* 15 (1960) 231–249. For the stateman's art as "weaving," see Plato *Politicus* 278e4–279c3. In the *Politicus*, weaving is appropriated as the paradigm of the statesman's *epistēmē* 'knowledge,' while the weaving *technē* itself is degraded as a small, material, visible *eidolon*, 'image,' of one of "the most honorable, bodiless, most beautiful, and greatest things" (285d4–286b1). On the figure of weaving in Platonic thought, see J. Frère, "La liaison et le tissu," *Revue internationale de philosophie* 156–157 (1986) 157–181.

41. For the philosophy in Plato and Aristotle as opposed to, while founded upon, metaphor, see J. Derrida, "White Mythology: Metaphor in the Text of Philosophy," in *Margins of Philosophy*, trans. A. Bass (Chicago 1982) 207–271.

42. See Chantraine (supra n. 8) 1098, s.v. *teĩchos*. Cognates include Avestan *pairi-daēza*, 'enclosure, garden,' and its Greek derivative *paradeisos*, 'garden, Paradise.' Compare also the architectural element of the "frieze" derived via French *frise*, 'border, fringe, ornament,' from Latin *Phrygium* (cf. *Phrygiae vestes*, 'embroidered garments') and cognate with the verb "frieze" meaning 'to cover with a nap' or 'to embroider with gold.' It is a pleasure to thank my colleagues Richard Janko and Sarah Morris for suggesting these two etymological reflections of the processes of daubing and weaving respectively.

43. "The Textile Art," in Semper (supra n. 12) 254–255; see also "The Four Elements of Architecture," 102–103. Compare "Structural Elements of Assyrian-Chaldean Architecture," ch. 10 of "Comparative Building Theory" (*Vergleichende Baulehre* 1850) in Herrmann (supra n. 12) 205.

It is well known that any wild tribe is familiar with the fence or a primitive hurdle as a means of enclosing space. Weaving the fence led to weaving movable walls of bast, reed or willow twigs and later to weaving carpets of thinner animal or vegetable fiber. . . . Using wickerwork for setting apart one's property and for floor mats and protection against heat and cold far preceded making even the roughest masonry. Wickerwork was the original motif of the wall. It retained this primary significance, actually or ideally, when the light hurdles and mattings were later transformed into brick or stone walls. The essence of the wall was wickerwork.

44. See Lévi-Strauss (supra n. 23).

45. See *Odyssey* 24.146ff., where the ghost of the suitor Amphimedon indicates that the finishing of the shroud directly precedes or is contemporaneous with the return of Odysseus.

46. Penelope uses the same instrument to construct her husband's identity as Clytemnestra uses to murder Agamemnon, the axe. The basic architectural function of incising material can either edify or destroy. I thank Sarah Morris for bringing this contrasting use of the axe to my attention.

47. For the relation between Odysseus and the suitors as *simulacra* or "false pretenders" to his unique identity, compare G. Deleuze, "Plato and the Simulacrum," in *The Logic of Sense,* trans. M. Lester (New York 1990) 253–259 (this translation is quoted below with some alterations), in particular, "Platonism is the philosophical *Odyssey* and the Platonic dialectic is neither a dialectic of contradiction nor of contrariety, but a dialectic of rivalry (*amphisbetesis*), a dialectic of rivals and suitors" (254). "Copies are secondary possessors. They are well-founded pretenders, guaranteed by resemblance; simulacra are like false pretenders, built upon a dissimilarity, implying an essential perversion or a deviation. It is in this sense that Plato divides in two the domain of images-idols: on one hand there are *copies-icons*, on the other there are *simulacra-phantasms*" (256).

48. For the root *per*, 'go to the end point,' in *peirō*, 'penetrate, pierce,' *peira*, 'penetration to the end, test,' and *peirar*, 'boundary line, determinant,' see A. Bergren, *The Etymology and Usage of PEIRAR in Early Greek Poetry. A Study in the Interrelationship of Metrics, Linguistics and Poetics,* American Classical Studies, no. 2 (New York 1975).

49. Compare the procedure of Anchises in Bergren (supra n. 29).

50. For the verbs of recognition, interpretation, and knowledge of the *sēma, anagignōskō, noeō*, and *gignōskō*, see Nagy (supra n. 4). Apropos of the *sēma* as a gravestone, see E. Vermeule, *Aspects of Death in Early Greek Art and Poetry* (Berkeley and Los Angeles 1979) 45: "The classical *sēma* can be both the external sign of the invisible dead in the grave, and the substitute person, especially kept alive in memory when written upon." On the tomb as a signal instance of "symbolic architecture" in Hegelian philosophy, see Hegel (supra n. 13) esp. 650–654 on the pyramids and the Mausoleum.

51. For the *ainos*, see *Odyssey* 14.462–506 and Nagy (supra n. 19) 234–241. Compare the use of an *ainos*-mode of eliciting and testing knowledge in Bergren (supra n. 29).

52. After his bath, Athena is said to pour "great beauty" (*polu kallos*) upon Odysseus so that his body looks bigger and thicker and lets down his hair in curls that are "like (*homoias*) to hyacinths" (23.156–158), a description that recalls the girth and locks of archaic *kouroi*. See, e.g., A. Stewart, *Greek Sculpture. An Exploration* (New Haven and London 1990)

vol. 2, pls. 44–54, 57, 60, 132–135. The text then practices its own capacity to "liken" by comparing Athena's divine art to the work of a human sculptor: "And as when a man with knowledge (*anēr idris*) pours gold around silver, one whom Hephaistos and Athena have taught every sort of art (*technēn pantoiēn*) and he produces works of grace (*charienta de erga teleiei*), so did the goddess pour grace (*charin*) around his head and shoulders" (23.159–161). From Athena's sculpting (as assimilated to human art that imitates her own) Odysseus emerges "like (*homoios*) to the immortals in build" (23.163). In this context of poetic and sculptural "likening," the simile suggests a chiastic parallel between poet and sculptor made possible by (if it does not itself promote) anthropomorphic theology: as the poet fashions anthropomorphic divinities who imitate human sculptors, so the sculptor fashions humans who look like gods.

53. See W. B. Stanford, ed., *The Odyssey of Homer* (New York 1973) on line 178, citing van Leeuwen's collection of examples of the imperfect *epoiei* in artist's signatures on works of sixth-century B.C. art.

54. On the significance of the use of *daidallōn* here, see S. P. Morris, *Daidalos and the Origins of Greek Art* (Princeton 1992) 29–30.

55. For the column as derived from the tree, being already rectilinear in its truck and branches, and as exemplary of the beauty of Classical architecture, that is, the pure display of architectural purpose, see Hegel (supra n. 13) 665–669.

56. Compare the relation of truth in the Platonic system as that of the *homoion*, the 'like, same, equal to itself.' For the Platonic idiom, "to be *homoios* = true to yourself," see *Symp.* 173d4, *Resp.* 549e2. For the collocation of "like" and "true" as synonymous, see *Soph.* 252d1 and *Phlb.* 65d2–3, as reciprocal, *Phdr.* 273d1–6. The basis of this relation is the "likeness" or "sameness" of the sensible particular and the intelligible form or paradigm; see, e.g., *Tim.* 28b–29d, *Resp.* 472c9–d1, *Prm.* 132d1–4 (where the participation of the particular in the paradigm is precisely the relation of likeness), and *Soph.* 264c–268d. The vulnerability of this mimetic conception of truth is registered in the Muses' speech, when they claim they can "say many falsehoods (*pseudea*) like (*homoia* 'like, equal') to real things." See Bergren (supra n. 12).

57. On the early Greek *symbolon*, see A. Bergren, "Allegorizing Winged Words: Simile and Symbolization in *Odyssey* V," *CW* 74 (1980) 109–113. Used as a means of identification, especially to secure contracts and treaties, the *symbolon* designates an incomplete object, such as one half of a knucklebone, that must be brought together (*symballein*) with its other half to prove the identity of the bearer. The term is also used of a single object related to individuals by their exclusive knowledge of it. In the case of the objects that identify

Creusa and Ion as mother and son, for example, Creusa's description of the contents of Ion's cradle, before seeing them, works as her "half of the knucklebone" (Eur. *Ion* 1386–1442). In the same category belong the purple mantle and golden pin that the disguised Odysseus describes in response to Penelope's *peira* of his claim to have been Odysseus' host in Crete (19.215–250). Penelope "recognizes" (*anagnousēi*) them as "fixed signs" (*sēmata empeda*) of their speaker's identity, when in fact they can signify either Odysseus, his host, or any other guest present at the time.

58. The phrase is used at 20.88 in a figuration of their recognition: Penelope wakes weeping from a dream in which Odysseus appeared "like to himself, such as he was when he went with the army. And my heart was rejoicing, since I said it was not a dream, but a waking vision," and Odysseus, perceiving her cry, "imagined she had already recognized him" (*dokēse de hoi ēdē gignōskousa*).

59. See 19.109–114, where Odysseus appropriately likens Penelope's *kleos* to that of the model male, a "blameless" king.

60. See 14.124–130 where Eumaeus, although insisting that Penelope cannot be persuaded by the report of a wanderer, describes needy vagabonds who "tell lies (*pseudont'*) and are unwilling to say true things (*alēthea*)" and admits that Penelope used to receive any wanderer who came to Ithaca, entertain him, question him, and mourn, "since this is the right conduct (*themis*) of a wife, whenever her husband has perished elsewhere."

61. See discussion (supra n. 57).

62. The argument of this paper finds a confirming supplement in the analysis offered *per litteris* by Deirdre von Dornum: "The story of Aphrodite and Hephaistos at *Odyssey* 8.266–366 is the thematic and architectural counterpart to the (re)marriage of Penelope and Odysseus." In contrast to "restrained" Penelope (*echephrōn* 4.111), Aphrodite is "unrestrained" (*ouk echethumos*, 320), unstable, does move, and so endangers her marriage, leading to blame (8.309, 319). As Odysseus builds his bed as a *sēma* to keep his marriage immovable, Hephaistos constructs a *dolos* in the form of a bed (8.276, cf. 281–282) in order to stop Aphrodite's shifting (at 8.275 he makes her *empedon*, cf. Odysseus' bed as *empedon* and his *sēmata empeda* 23.203, 206). While Odysseus' bed permits mutual recognition of unique identity, Hephaistos' bed-trick forces Ares' and Aphrodite's recognition (*gignōskon*) that they cannot shift (*ouketi phukta pelonto* 299). By changing the symbol of his betrayal into the sign of his control, shifting the shape of the bed to keep Aphrodite from shifting (in) bed, Hephaistos "turns the *morphē* of defeat into victory's tool." His triumph is qualified, however, as Aphrodite receives mixed praise and blame (in contrast to Clytemnestra)

and is able to shift again (337, 342), thanks to the mediation of Poseidon. Although a master builder, Hephaistos is outwitted by Aphrodite with the complicity of her society. Their bed scene represents the construction of failed marriage through impermanent, public architecture versus successful (re)-marriage through permanent, private architecture.

15

THE SACRIFICE OF ASTYANAX: NEAR EASTERN CONTRIBUTIONS TO THE SIEGE OF TROY *

◆

SARAH P. MORRIS

To destroy the city, to destroy the temple,
  To destroy the cattle pen, to level the sheep fold,
That the cattle not stand in the pen,
  That the sheep not multiply in the fold,
That its watercourses carry brackish water,
  That weeds grow in the fertile fields
That "mourning" plants grow in the steppe,
  That the mother does not seek out her child,
That the father not say, "Oh, my (dear) wife!"
  That the junior wife not take joy in (his) embrace,
That the young child not grow vigorous on (her) knee,
  That the wet nurse not sing lullabies,
To change the location of kingship,
  To defile the rights and decrees,
To take away kingship from the land,
  To cast the eye (of the storm) on all the land, . . .

Lamentation over the Destruction of
Sumer and Ur, lines 5–20
Trans. P. Michalowski

Unlike Tolstoy's families, ancient cities enjoyed happiness in similar ways less frequently than they shared misfortune in formulas forged in grief. The capture of a city branded such formulas on Greek memory, from the defeat of Miletus and Athens by Persia to the Turkish capture of Constantinople and burning of Smyrna in modern times. The enemy's advance and ambush, their assault on the walls, the clamor of women from towers and rooftops, the city's fall to betrayal and violence, its destruction by fire, the separation and slaughter of families—all these form the earliest images in Greek art and poetry, originating in the Bronze Age.[1] But in the Near East, mourning the fall of cities in song began a thousand years earlier at Sumer and Ur, and endures in Israelite hymns of exile from Jerusalem (*Psalm* 137).[2] The fate of Assyrian Nineveh was remembered in Greek poetry and prose (Phocylides fr. 5; Aristotle, *HA* 8.18.3 = Ps. Hesiod fr. 364, Merkelbach-West; Herodotus 1.106.2); Greeks helped the Babylonians capture Ashkelon (Alcaeus fr. 48, 10–11 Voigt) and patterned their own tales of besieged cities on Near Eastern traditions.[3] Levantine inspirations form a fitting tribute to a Hellenist whose love and knowledge of Greek art and literature equal her experience and enjoyment of the Eastern Mediterranean.

The greatest city-siege in epic—the fall of Troy,

FIGURE 15.1 Bronze relief from Olympia (B 3600), 625–600 B.C. Warrior marching young boy up steps of altar (?). (Photo by author, from drawing in *OlBer* VII, pl. 80.)

FIGURE 15.2 Bronze relief from Olympia (B 987, B 1912), 590–580 B.C. Warrior attacking young boy at altar: Achilles and Troilos? (Photo by author, after *OlForsch* II, pl. 42: XV.b.)

FIGURE 15.3 Bronze relief from Olympia, c. 575 B.C. Warrior attacking old man on altar: Neoptolemos and Priam? (Photo by author, after *OlForsch* II, pl. 31: X.d.)

or *Ilioupersis*—was a story which became, in art and poetry, an encyclopedia of human experience refracted through Greek values. One episode distinctive for its poignancy and its particularity to the *Ilioupersis* was the death of the youngest son of Priam, Astyanax. In the final book of the *Iliad*, the young child's tragic fate is imagined by his mother, Andromache, now widow of Hektor (24.732–735):

... σὺ δ' αὖ, τέκος, ἢ ἐμοὶ αὐτῇ
ἕψεαι, ἔνθα κεν ἔργα ἀεικέα ἐργάζοιο
ἀθλεύων πρὸ ἄνακτος ἀμειλίχου, ἤ τις Ἀχαιῶν
ῥίψει χειρὸς ἑλὼν ἀπὸ πύργου, λυγρὸν ὄλεθρον

... But you, my child, either will follow me [into slavery]
and there will perform unsuitable tasks
laboring for a pitiless master; or one of the Achaians
will hurl you, seizing you by your limb, from the wall, a
   grim end.

Her fears are fulfilled in lost epic poems and tragedies on the fall of Troy. Euripides paraphrases Homer, as so often, in describing the death of Astyanax in his *Trojan Women* (720–785, 1120–1250, especially 725: ῥίψαι δὲ πύργων δεῖν σφε Τρωικῶν ἄπο) and in the opening of the *Andromache* (8–11):

ἥτις πόσιν μὲν Ἕκτορ' ἐξ Ἀχιλλέως
θανόντ' ἐσεῖδον, παῖδά θ' ὃν τίκτω πόσει
ῥιφθέντα πύργων Ἀστυάνακτ' ἀπ' ὀρθίων,
ἐπεὶ τὸ Τροίας εἷλον Ἕλληνες πέδον

I who saw first my husband, Hektor, by Achilles
killed, then the child whom I bore my husband,
Astyanax, thrown from the high walls,
when the Greeks captured the plain of Troy.

Scholiasts on Euripides report that Stesichorus told the story of the boy's death in his *Ilioupersis* (fr. 25, Page), and specify that the author of the epic cycle *Ilioupersis* (fr. 5, Bernabé) described how the child was thrown from the walls, the version followed by Euripides. In Arctinus' story of the fall of Troy, as summarized by Proclus, it is Odysseus who puts Astyanax to death, as he decides the boy's fate in Euripides (*Tro.* 721). Another cyclic poet, Lesches, has Neoptolemos throw the

child by the foot, in the *Little Iliad* (Bernabé fr. 21.3–5, from a scholion to Lykophron *Alexandra* 1268):

παῖδα δ' ἑλὼν ἐκ κόλπου εὐπλοκάμοιο τιθήνης
ῥῖψε ποδὸς τεταγὼν ἀπὸ πύργου. τὸν δὲ πεσόντα
ἔλλαβε πορφύρεος θάνατος καὶ μοῖρα κραταιή.

And seizing the child from the lap of his well-tressed
   nurse
he threw him, holding him by the foot, from the wall. And
crimson death and powerful fate took the falling boy.

Without exception—unless Stesichorus told a different story—the boy meets his end in poetry in a fall from the walls of Troy. But a different fate, absent from literature, claimed an exclusive popularity in the visual arts. With remarkable consistency, the death of Astyanax is never represented as a fall from the heights of a city, but takes place at the hands of a warrior with a weapon, usually at an altar (figs. 15.1–15.10a), even on those rare occasions where the walls of Troy are represented (fig. 15.8).[4] Only the gesture of Neoptolemos (or some other nameless executioner) betrays the tradition of a precipitous end: the child, dead or about to die, is held aloft by ankle, leg, or arm, as if suspended from a height (figs. 15.2, 15.4, 15.8–15.9). In its departure from poetry, the infant's death is also incorporated into the fate of his grandfather, Priam, king of Troy, who likewise in early Greek art meets death at an altar (figs. 15.3, 15.6–15.10). Most learned discussions of these scenes focus on a presumed discrepancy or creative dialogue between art and literature.[5] Instead, I have come to believe that foreign traditions may have helped shape this story, reflected in multiple versions of the fate of the youngest Trojan.

Early Archaic visions of the fall of Troy show a warrior seizing or slaying a young boy, sometimes near a brick or ashlar structure. Since the late seventh century, bronze shield-strap panels and tripod legs made in the Peloponnese illustrate this theme in vertical series of mythological "metopes" (figs. 15.1–15.2).[6] Some scenes evoke the story of Troilos, son of Priam, ambushed either at a fountain-house outside of the walls of Troy or at a sanctuary, first identified by Apollodorus (*Epitome* 3.32) as the altar of Apollo Thymbraios. Ambiguities of Archaic art make the death of Troilos too

FIGURE 15.4 Early black-figure pyxis lid by the C Painter, 570–560 B.C. Priam and Hekabe at altar; warrior and child: Neoptolemos and Astyanax, or Achilles and Troilos?; advancing army. Naples Museum, from Cumae. ABV 58, 119. (Photograph courtesy Soprintendenza Archaeologica delle Province di Napoli e Caserta—Napoli, courtesy of M. Harari.)

similar to its trope, the death of Astyanax, for consistent identification.[7] In the absence of identifying inscriptions, the warrior wielding a sword could be Achilles with Troilos, or Neoptolemos with Astyanax. If the masonry structure in these scenes is a fountain-house, it points to Troilos; as the stepped courses of a city wall, it carries young Astyanax up the ramparts to his death (fig. 15.1). An altar (fig. 15.2) would accommodate the massacre of either young Trojan.

These motifs may have been familiar without named warriors or victims in Early Archaic iconography prior to the François Vase.[8] What characterizes these early scenes of children attacked by warriors is a setting implying sacrifice, not just sacrilege, by the presence of an altar and of weapons brandished more like knives than swords (see figs. 15.1–15.2, 15.4–15.5, 15.10). These episodes are sharply distinguished from the ordinary slaughter of enemy offspring below (figs. 15.11, 15.12c–d), a cruel but accepted practice in ancient warfare. Thus the slaughter of young Trojans at the tomb of Patroklos was justified as vengeance for the Greek hero's death (*Iliad* 23.174–176; fig. 15.11), and did not qualify as a sacrifice of one's own. Members of the royal family represented the threat of the city's revival (Stasinus' *Cypria*, fr. 22 = Clement *Stromateis* VII.2.19; Eur. *Tro.* 1160–1161), and Astyanax was one young Trojan who survived in legend to refound Troy.[9] To put him to death with his grandfather was to extinguish at once the present and future kings of Troy—father and son of Hektor—and all hopes of Troy reborn.

Although no literary source specifies this scenario, the death of Priam alone belongs on his throne, in the tradition of the assassination of royalty.[10] Early Archaic art shows the king on a square box in front of the city wall. Priam appears thus on the pediment of the Artemis temple on Corcyra, and on the seat (θᾶκος) which he occupies in front of his palace on the François Vase; this is distinct in shape from the elaborate throne of Zeus on the same vase.[11] How did an altar become the seat of the king and locale of his death?

One reason may be the lack of Greek acquaintance with a "throne," in the absence of native monarchs between Mycenae and Macedon. As on the François Vase, it was the gods, not rulers, who occupied thrones in the Greek imagination, until exposure to Eastern royalty (Lydia and Persia) shaped Greek images of legendary

FIGURE 15.5 Chalcidian amphora, Louvre E 799. Warrior at altar with head of decapitated infant: Astyanax? Musée du Louvre, Département des Antiquités Grecques et Romaines. (Photo Réunion des Musées Nationaux.)

kings, a topic Meg Miller explores in this volume. Confusion between what Greeks imagined as a throne and what they knew as an altar may have substituted one for the other.[12] Compromise may have inspired unusual seats on which Priam faces Neoptolemos, not quite throne or altar (figs. 15.3, 15.6–15.7). In the most graphic attempt to integrate the two, one painter placed Priam upon a δίφρος ὀκλαδίας (the folding stool of ancient royalty) literally *on top* of an altar.[13]

Beyond visual confusion, Greek mythology introduced an altar into these scenes to suggest sacrilege, the violation of sacred laws by Achilles, Ajax, Neoptolemos, and other Greeks who paid for their impieties later in life or death. The earliest and most numerous scenes of Achilles and Troilos, for example, involve the pursuit

FIGURE 15.6 Black-figure lekythos. National Museum 11050, Athens. (Neoptolemos?) hurling head of infant (Astyanax?) at Priam. (Photograph courtesy of National Museum, Athens and T.A.P.)

or ambush of the young Trojan near a fountain-house, not his death at an altar.[14] But if Achilles overcomes Troilos in a sanctuary of Apollo, this justifies the god's role in the hero's death, perhaps even at the same altar (Tzetzes on Lykophron 269). Neoptolemos kills Priam in a sacred setting, at the very altar of Zeus Herkeios, protector of suppliants (a locale current since Arctinus' *Ilioupersis*). His violation of the laws of supplication earns the son of Achilles a death with ritual overtones, at the hands of a god with a μάχαιρα, in the sanctuary at Delphi (Pind. *Paean* 6.75–120; *Nem.* 7.42–77; Paus. 10.7.1). Ajax, son of Oileus, rapes Kassandra at Athena's statue, for which he meets a watery death from the gods on the way home from Troy (*Odyssey* 4.499–510); his Lokrian descendants still paid female tribute for his outrage, centuries later (IG IX. I², 3, no. 706). In all three violations, the presence of an altar adds impiety to Greek atrocities and justifies subsequent vengeance by the gods. The tragic consequences of these war crimes were publicized in classical paintings: Polygnotos juxtaposed, in facing tableaux, Greek acts of impiety at Troy with their expiation in the afterlife.[15]

If death near an altar incorporates the tragic view of human action and its consequences, Astyanax met an end in art which added sentiments of piety to the pity aroused by his fate. But impressions of his death under different circumstances—hurled from his helpless limbs, by an enemy warrior—must have survived. This would explain the posture of Neoptolemos hurling

the infant's body, or its parts, at Priam (fig. 15.6), like the δίσκημα πικρόν envisioned in tragedy (Eur. *Tro.* 1121) and its epic prototype, Ajax hurling the head of a hapless Trojan σφαιρηδόν (*Iliad* 13.204). The body of the dead child often exhibits bleeding wounds, as if bruised in a fall, not killed with a weapon (fig. 15.10a).

The death of Astyanax belongs to a widespread tradition: the pitiless slaughter of children which accompanies the destruction of a city. The proliferation of this cruel theme may have preceded the depiction of carefully staged events at altars, deliberately linked to retributions in future dramas of the Trojan cycle. Its earliest and most unsparing view appears in the seventh century on the famous relief pithos from Mykonos (figs. 15.12c–d).[16] Two moments in the capture of the city are depicted: on the neck of the vessel, the entry of the wooden horse into the walls of the city, with warriors lowering themselves and their weapons from its deadly carapace (figs. 15.12a–b). Across three rows of panels on the shoulder and belly of the vessel, future generations of Trojans are eliminated in scenes of warriors attacking women and children (figs. 15.12c–d). This massacre—children seized from their mothers' arms by warriors wielding weapons or already piercing flesh, those infants already slaughtered dripping blood—transcends the particular fate of the house of Priam to illustrate the widespread calamity which befell an entire city in the hands of a victorious enemy, especially its women and children (*Iliad* 6.276). Individual Trojan women and children are difficult to identify among the thirty-odd metopes on the relief vase: one child held upside down by an assailant without weapon (fig. 15.12d) has been called Astyanax, the child killed by a fall in literature. But specific identities would dilute the horror of universal calamity in the anonymity of warriors and victims. This scenario of carnage agrees with Priam's dire vision of the fate of his city (*Iliad* 22.59–76), although the enslavement of women and children was more common in ancient warfare, as feared in epic poetry (*Iliad* 9.594) and as experienced in Greek tragedy. But in this early and brutal scenario on the Mykonos vase, women and children meet death at enemy hands like their male relatives.

Visions of the fall of Troy evoke Near Eastern patterns of warfare beyond Greek experience. Impaling captured enemy heads, for example, is one Assyrian

FIGURE 15.7 Black-figure hydria, Leagros Group. Würzburg 311. Neoptolemos slays Priam on altar. (Photograph courtesy of Martin von Wagner-Museum, Würzburg.)

custom of celebrating and depicting victory (as in Tiglath-Pileser's capture of Upa: fig. 15.13) only imagined in Homer, when Iris warns Achilles that Hektor is eager to impale the head of slain Patroklos (*Iliad* 18.177). Near Eastern martial scenes offer other convergences with the city-siege on the Mykonos vessel, illustrated in the same Assyrian depiction of the capture of an enemy city (fig. 15.13). As in other reliefs from Nimrud (e.g., the siege of Gezer, fig. 15.14), the enemy city is attacked by wheeled devices, elaborate structures of leather and wood, shielding battering rams manned by warriors within their stout sides. These machines,

praised as "the most formidable weapon of the period," are variously described as "battering rams, siege machines, or mobile assault towers."[17] Made of inflammable materials, lightweight for rapid assembly by mobile armies, they were widely used in Neo-Assyrian campaigns of the ninth through seventh centuries, but first appeared in Greek warfare in the late fifth century.[18] As with new warships, Athenians and other Greeks may have learned such devices from Near Eastern enemies during the Persian Wars, only to use them against each other in the ensuing civil war.[19]

A slim reference in the *Iliad* (15.71), the Wooden Horse is the subject of a song requested by its master designer, Odysseus himself (*Odyssey* 8.492ff.; cf. 4.272–278), and appeared in lost poems like the *Little Iliad* (according to Proclus' summary) and the *Ilioupersis* of epic and lyric poets (e.g., by Stesichorus: POxy 2803). Since antiquity, the Trojan "Horse" has been

FIGURE 15.8A Black-figure hydria, Leagros Group from Vulci. Munich 1700. (belly) *Ilioupersis:* chariot entering gate near tree, statue of Athena, mourning Priam, Neoptolemos, and Astyanax at altar.

FIGURE 15.8B (shoulder) *Ilioupersis:* walls of Troy with figures of archer, warriors, women. (Photographs courtesy Munich, Staatliche Antikensammlung und Glyptothek.)

FIGURE 15.9 Attic red-figure cup (Type C) by Onesimos (Malibu 83.AE.362), c. 500–490 B.C. Tondo: Death of Priam with Polyxena, Neoptolemos, Astyanax, and dead warrior (D]aiphonos: Daiphobos?). (Photograph courtesy of the J. Paul Getty Museum, Malibu.)

recognized as an early version of a battering ram: *equum qui nunc aries appellabatur in muralibus machinis Epium ad Troiam [invenisse dicunt]* (Pliny *HN* 7.202; Paus. 1.23.10). The resemblance of Assyrian examples in art to the shape of a horse suggests that such a device was known, through art or hearsay, in Homeric times and became the story of a "horse" which entered the walls of the city, disgorged men, and brought about the city's downfall.[20] The Near Eastern connection deserves periodic reinforcement, especially after a discovery like the Mykonos pithos, whose horse agrees in specific details with Assyrian representations of the eighth century. For example, Greek and Near Eastern machines share a general equine or at least quadruped shape and details such as wheels and "windows" (figs. 15.12a–b, 15.13–15.14). Assyrian warriors, armed with helmet, shield, and spear, "float" in midair or step off the "head" of a machine to scale the walls of Gezer (fig. 15.14) the way Greek heroes disembark from their

Horse onto the walls of Troy (fig. 15.12b; in the sparse Greek literature on the Wooden Horse of Troy, after the sortie of Echion, οἱ δὲ λοιπὸν σειρᾷ ἐξάψαντες ἑαυτοὺς ἐπὶ τὰ τείχη παρεγένοντο).[21] The Horse was popular in ancient art, from Classical monuments (Paus. 1.23.8; 10.9.12, 10.26.1) through Hellenistic relief vases, Roman gems, and Late Antique illustrations like the *Tabula Iliaca* and the Vatican Vergil.[22]

The earliest manifestations of the Wooden Horse in Greek art, on the Mykonos pithos and related fragments from Tenos and in Athens (Kanellopoulos Museum), could all derive from a single prototype; perhaps one artist or poet turned a Near Eastern military machine into a Greek "invention."[23] More remote Oriental motifs were transformed into Greek narrative in the era of the Mykonos pithos. On a related vase from Tenos, an exotic Zeus, in a short dress and an Egyptian hairdo, gives birth to an Athena, in a scene so unlike Greek images that it has been called the birth of Zeus from Rhea

FIGURE 15.10A, B. Red-figure hydria by the Kleophrades Painter (Vivenzio Hydria, Naples 2422), c. 470 B.C. Scenes from the *Ilioupersis:* Neoptolemos slays Priam, Astyanax. (Photographs courtesy of Hirmer Verlag, Munich: negs. 57i-0505.)

or of Athena from Metis.[24] What may have made this scene un-Greek is a misunderstanding of an Egyptian motif, as seen on a seal buried at Byblos in the second millennium.[25] Other stories borrowed by Greek artists and poets from the Near East include legends of Egyptian pharaohs powerful enough to drive arrows through bronze; perhaps an image visible on cylinder seals from Levantine locales frequented by Greeks inspired Odysseus' contest with bow and axes.[26] A long-lived and busy network of traffic exposed Greeks over the centuries, in art, word, and deed, to images and stories in the Near East. If Assyrian siege machines did not inspire the story of an artificial wooden beast which gains entry to an enemy city, Greeks might have seen or heard of such monsters in the Bronze Age, not in seventh-century Mesopotamia. Siege devices, even zoomorphic ones, were an Old Assyrian industry at Mari, a center of production for "tower" machines (mobile protection for battering rams?) in the Near East, just as the Hittite record describes "bridges of war" known to Homer.[27]

A Bronze Age origin for the Trojan Horse is encouraged by parallels for the other scenes on the Mykonos pithos with the slaughter of children, especially in a new source I propose for their mythological paradigm, the death of Astyanax. Images of enemy cities under attack begin in the Bronze Age, and reveal other sources of Greek city-siege imagery. The triumphs of Egyptian kings over Syrian and Canaanite cities were celebrated in reliefs at Karnak, Luxor, Medinet Habu, and Abu Simbel. Merenptah's campaign in Canaan is depicted in four temple reliefs at Karnak (Thebes) in Egypt, including the siege of Ashkelon (fig. 15.15). Next to men defending the walls and women atop the towers, last rites of despair are practiced by the besieged citizens, a sign of the imminent fall of their city.[28] The ramparts of Ashkelon are crowned by figures with hands lifted skywards; on towers at the edge of the city walls, one figure raises an incense-burner, next to others who lean over the parapets, suspending the limp bodies of small children as if about to drop them. In some interpretations, these inhabitants of Ashkelon and other Levantine cities (fig. 15.16) have resorted to a traditional Canaanite practice—the offering of children to appease the gods and save the city, a sacrifice alluded to in Ugaritic religious texts and prohibited under Yahwism in the Hebrew Bible.[29] A prayer from Ras Shamra, rare among

FIGURE 15.11 Apulian krater by the Darius Painter (Naples 3422). Sacrifice of young Trojans on the pyre of Patroklos (*Iliad* 23.175). (Photograph after FR *Griechische Vasenmalerei.*)

texts chiefly devoted to hymns and epic poems, may prescribe this procedure (RS 24.266, V, 9–19; KTU 1.119):[30]

> If a strong one attacks your gate,
>> a warrior your walls;
> Raise your eyes to Baal [and pray]:
> "O Baal, drive away the strong one from our gate,
>> The warrior from our walls!
> The bull, O Baal, We shall sacrifice [to thee],
>> the vow, O Baal. we shall fulfill,
> A [(*?kr*) male or firstborn?], Baal, we shall sacrifice,
>> A (*ḥtp*) or [*ḥtk:* offspring] we shall fulfill [as vow],
> A 'tenth' [of all our wealth] we shall tithe [thee]:
> we shall ascend the sanctuary of Baal,
>> In the footpaths of the House of Baal we shall walk."
> Thus Baal will hear your prayer,
>> He will drive the strong one from your gate,
>>> the warrior from your walls.

The prayer describes how to save a city under siege—with two critical words uncertain. According to one possible reading, the chief god (at Ugarit, Baal) shall receive the ultimate appeal—not only a traditional animal offering and a percentage of wealth, but the sacrifice of a firstborn (or male) offspring: animal or infant?

FIGURE I 5 . I 2 A . Relief pithos from Mykonos with scenes of Trojan War, Mykonos Museum. (Photograph courtesy of DAI Athen, Mykonos 69.)

FIGURE 15.12B Neck scene of Mykonos pithos: Trojan Horse. (DAI, Mykonos 70).

FIGURE 15.12C Body panel: warrior attacks child with sword. (DAI, Mykonos 87.)

FIGURE 15.12D Body panel: warrior seizes woman's wrist; holds child upside down: Astyanax? (DAI, Mykonos 90.)

FIGURE 15.13 Reliefs 19 and 20, from Southwest Palace, Nimrud. London, British Museum, Western Asiatic Antiquities 115634+118903. Assyrian assault on Upa by Tiglath-Pileser III (745–727 B.C.). (Photograph courtesy of the Trustees of the British Museum.)

Semitic religion required infant sacrifice for specific occasions and rituals: in two historical episodes of the Hebrew Bible, fathers vow and offer children in exchange for military victory. When the capital of Moab, Kir-Hareseth, was besieged by an alliance of Israel, Judah, and Edom in the ninth century (II *Kings* 3:26–27), the city's ruler, Mesha, sacrificed his eldest son (*bkr*) to the god Chemosh, an act performed *as a burnt offering on the city walls*, in full view of the enemy. In eleventh-century Gilead (*Judges* 11.30–40, composed centuries later), Jephtha vowed in thanks for victory the first crea-

ture to emerge from his house (expecting an animal): when his virgin daughter appeared, she became the offering, in a passage which compares closely to Greek stories of sacrificed maidens.[31] Even the consecration of firstborn animals and children to Yahweh implies sacrifice (*Exodus* 13.2, 22.28–29); the animals are offered in sacrifice, while human infants are "redeemed" for shekels (generating income for priests [13.11–15, 34.19–20; cf. 30.13, *Num.* 3.44–51]. The celebrated sacrifice of Isaac is forestalled by the substitution of an animal (*Genesis* 22.2.13), a procedure better attested in archaeology.

These Biblical passages could be dismissed as Yahwist propaganda against Canaanite religion—infant sacrifice is one of many heretical practises ascribed to evil kings like Ahaz and Manassah (2 *Kings* 16.3, 21.2–16)—were it not for archaeology. Several Punic sites in the western Mediterranean (in North Africa,

234

FIGURE 15.14 Siege of Gezer, western campaign of Esarhaddon (681–669 B.C.). Henry Layard's drawing of slab 5a (lost) from Southwest Palace, Nimrud. (Photograph courtesy of the Trustees of the British Museum.)

FIGURE 15.15 Siege of Ashkelon by Merenptah (1221–1202 B.C.). Temple relief at Karnak, west wall of "Cour de la Cachette." (After Spalinger *JSSEA* 8 [1978], pl. VI.)

Sicily, and Sardinia) had special cemetery-enclosures where infants were sacrificed, according to inscribed stelai, and their cremated remains buried in urns.[32] Commonly called a *top(h)et(h)* today, after the Biblical cemetery in Jerusalem, these cemeteries seem to confirm the rite of *mōlek* or regular infant sacrifice attested in Phoenician and Punic inscriptions and in Semitic literature.[33] The Tunisian remains are still under study and reliable data are unavailable; fuller publication and new excavations of *topheth* sites (e.g., on Sardinia) promise more accurate information. In one *topheth* at Carthage, infant burials between 400 and 200 B.C. have been estimated at 20,000; two sample groups have been analyzed. In an Archaic group of eighty burials, twenty-four urns held the bones of a lamb or kid goat alone, while fifty-six contained a stillborn or newborn infant, six buried with remains of an animal. In a fourth-century group, only five burials contained an animal substituted for a child; the remaining forty-five urns contained human bones belonging to older children (one to three

years old), not infants. Stelai and inscriptions certify these burials as sacrifices performed to fulfill a vow to the goddess Tanit or the god Baal-Hammon, not losses to infant mortality or other natural causes. One scholar has attempted to correlate the two age-groups with different kinds of sacrifice: the regular vow of a future firstborn, and the sacrifice of an older child for a specific favor or in desperate circumstances.[34] Circumvention of such grim vows by substituting an animal for a child did not eliminate this rite over time. The proportion of infants buried actually increased between the seventh and fourth centuries—whether for social or religious reasons is disputed.

Greek, Roman, and Christian sources report sensationally on such practices among Phoenicians and Carthaginians, primarily on historical occasions for special propitiation of the gods.[35] Philo of Byblos, citing Sanchuniathon, claims that Canaanites "in times of great misfortune, either wars or droughts, used to sacrifice some one of their nearest and dearest to Kronos" (ἐν ταῖς μεγάλαις συμφοραῖς ἢ πολέμων ἢ αὐχμῶν ἔθυον φιλτάτων τινά, quoted by Eusebius in his *Praeparatio Evangelica* 4.16.6; Porphyr. *De Abst.* 2.56). Kronos was a common Greek equivalent of El and inaugurated infant sacrifice by offering his own "only begotten" (μονογενής) son to his father, Ouranos, in a "wholly burnt offering" (ὁλοκαυτοῖ, or ὁλοκαρποῖ: Philo, in the same text of Eusebius, 1.10.33). When Alexander attacked Tyre, resort to the time-honored practice of offering a worthy infant (*ingenuus puer*) was recommended, but ultimately discouraged by the elders of the city, to the relief of Roman chroniclers (Q. Curtius Rufus, *Alexander* 4.3.23). When Carthage was besieged by Agathokles of Sicily in 310 B.C., Punic citizens tried "every form of divine supplication" (Diodorus 20.14: νομίσαντες ἐκ θεῶν αὐτοῖς γεγονέναι τὴν συμφοράν, ἐτράπησαν πρὸς παντοίαν ἱκεσίαν τοῦ δαιμονίου). Their response included sending to Melqart, chief god of their mother city, Tyre, a tenth of their revenues, a tithe whose neglect they blamed for their current misfortunes (compare the possible reading of "tithe" in the Ugaritic tablet: did it survive a thousand years into Punic practice?). Then they remembered Kronos (El), to whom they used to offer their finest sons (τῶν υἱῶν τοὺς κρατίστους) until they began substituting children purchased from less-wealthy families.

When the Roman advance on their walls inspired anxiety for rites neglected, they compensated with the selection and public sacrifice of two hundred "outstanding children" (τῶν ἐπιφανεστάτων παίδων), amplified by three hundred volunteers. These reports fed Christian propaganda against pagans and Jews, but why not early Greek stories of Kronos eating his own children, or the Christian idea of a god who offers the world his only begotten son, who agrees to the supreme self-sacrifice?[36]

The rite of human sacrifice is best understood as one of many tenets of Semitic religion which influenced Aegean culture, like animal sacrifice itself. While European scholarship since Meuli has mistakenly pursued connections to Paleolithic hunting, animal sacrifice belongs to the sphere of cultural practices which entered Greek religion from the Near East, and the Hebrew Bible remains the best source for Greek as well as Jewish practices.[37] Greek sensibilities rejected infant (and all human) sacrifice, but Greek imagination often transformed alien cult into native myth, as the epic siege of Thebes was inspired by a Near Eastern purification ritual (above, n. 3). Hence Greek *mythology* is full of human sacrifice, in stories of prohibition and punishment by the gods, especially in Greek tragedy.[38] Euripides, in particular, explored human sacrifice with an almost unhealthy appetite.[39] In Athens, the daughters of Erechtheus are victims in an early war with Eleusis (Eur. *Ion* 278; *Erechtheus*), and Makaria offers herself in order to save Athens from the enemy (Eur. *Heracl.* 406–629). In the most famous Greek case (Eur. *IA*), a king, Agamemnon, is forced to offer his daughter, Iphigeneia, to propitiate the gods for a favorable wind and ultimately for military success. The Greek tale buries the offending rite in a cycle of offenses and atonements: the sacred deer of the goddess Artemis is shot, she retaliates by refusing a favorable wind, until an augur discloses the dreadful vow required to appease her anger.[40] The sacrifice of the king's child satisfies the goddess but perpetuates violence and misfortune in the House of Atreus. Yet even the *Iliad*, in its deliberate avoidance of this tale, betrays its ritual dimensions: Iphigenia's name and fate are deftly avoided, but the telltale substitution of the name "Iphianassa" for the daughter Agamemnon offers Achilles (9.287; cf. ἶφι ἀνάσσειν at 1.38) cannot disguise her true name or her fate.

Closest to the Trojan death of Astyanax is the story

FIGURE 15.16 Siege of Syrian city by Ramses II (1290–1223 B.C.). Painted relief from rock-cut temple at Beit el-Weli, Nubia. British Museum: Department of Egyptian Antiquities. (Photograph courtesy of the Trustees of the British Museum.)

invented by Euripides of the self-sacrifice of Menoikeus in the siege of Thebes (*Phoen.* 896–1017).[41] The "salvation" (σωτηρία) prescribed for the city requires the sacrifice of Menoikeus, which his father seeks to avert by advising his son to flee to Dodona. Although the son pretends to follow this advice, he decides to offer himself to the war god, Ares, for the sake of his city. He prepares to die "standing on the tallest heights" (1009: στὰς ἐξ ἐπάλξεων ἄκρων); the messenger describes the deed as death by sword, in this locale (1091: πύργων ἐπ' ἄκρων στὰς μελάνδετον ξίφος || λαιμῶν διῆκε τῆδε γῇ σωτήριον). Like Makaria and Iphigeneia in the same playwright's dramas of royal children who must die for their city, the victim here offers himself willingly, which clears the city of the taboo of human sacrifice, enobling and Hellenizing a Semitic rite. Even Astyanax throws himself from the walls of Troy in versions where he is old enough for a mature and noble act worthy of a Roman hero (Seneca *Troades* 1063–1119). What the story of Astyanax could reveal is how the tragic view of death as a sacrifice is not a creative Greek metaphor, but a transformation of a specific (and rejected) alien rite into a narrative device.

Mythology frequently blames these practices on non-Greeks. Only a barbarian like Medea would put her own children to death; her neighbors, the Taurians, sacrifice guests and strangers; an Ethiopian like Andromeda's father would offer a daughter to a sea monster, just as Egyptians perform human sacrifice in the myth about Herakles and Busiris.[42] Some Greek tales of human sacrifice point to Semitic sources. The Minotaur of Crete, a bull-headed monster who "ate" children, must derive from a Near Eastern god in the shape of a bull who expected occasional infant sacrifice. Aristotle provides a ritual link for this story: in his *Constitution of the Bottiaeans* (fr. 485, at Plutarch's *Theseus* 16), he reports that Cretans sent their firstborn sons to Delphi "in fulfillment of an ancient vow." According to Aristotle and Plutarch, this offering included descendants of Athenians enslaved, not exacted as tribute for the monster. This substitution of other (purchased) children for one's own, as practiced by the Carthaginians (Diodorus 20.14.4), helps affiliate the Cretan rite with Semitic ones.

Excavation has confirmed the presence of Phoenicians on Crete in the Early Iron Age, in the cemeteries of Knossos but also at the sanctuary of Kommos.[43] Archaeology's best case for ritual consumption—if not killing—of children is a recent discovery from Knossos; yet the myth of the Minotaur never enters published discussions.[44] In Lakonia, bizarre rites for Artemis Ortheia performed since the time of Lykourgos involved whipping young boys to draw blood, shed at an altar (Paus. 3.16.9–11). These rites have been called a substitution for human sacrifice (demanded in an oracle) and traced to offerings of children for Ortheia's Phoenician ancestor, Asherah.[45] It is no coincidence that Greek reports of human sacrifice implicate Sparta, Crete, and Carthage (e.g., Soph. *Andromeda* fr. 126.2–3), all locales where Phoenicians settled. Thus archaeology confirms what Greeks observed when comparing human sacrifice in the tragedies of Euripides, or Arkadian human sacrifice for Lykaian Zeus, to equivalent rites in Carthage (Diodorus 20.14.6; Theophrastus in Porphy., *De Abst.* II.27). Even Medea's widely publicized murder of her own children is a late version of the story by Euripides: in older legends, she poisons her rival, while her children are put to death by the Corinthians, a deed expiated in

local cult (Pausanias 2.3.5–7; Eur. *Med.* 1378). Ubiquitous in local legend, Greek myths of human sacrifice are not mere metaphors for violent experience: their locales claim ritual connections with the Near East (as the Corinthia does in its Melikertes/Melqart and Aphrodite traditions) and a milieu of intellectual migration.

Let us return to the Late Bronze Age to consider the transmission of such ideas. In art, Canaanite cities humiliated by Egypt appear to enact a ritual still active among their Phoenician and Punic descendants centuries later. Some form of this Near Eastern custom may have inspired, in art, rite, or tale, the story of Astyanax, the child who is thrown off the walls of the city in a siege by the enemy, but "sacrificed" in art. His story suggests early awareness (or misunderstanding) of a Semitic rite, through autopsy of Canaanite rites or Bronze Age art, or through more intimate contact in the Levant, Greece, or the West. The findspot of the suggestive Ugaritic prayer tablet offers one agency of transmission. It was not found in the city's main temple area but in a private house, among the property of a "priest" named Agaptari. His religious equipment included anatomical models in clay for divination; Aegean rhyta (ritual pouring vessels) and local imitations, one dedicated to Reshep the protector; a mug with a banqueting scene related to the Baal cycle in Canaanite myth; gold libation bowls, and other paraphernalia useful to practitioners of cult in the Eastern Mediterranean.[46] It may have been learned men like Agaptari who belonged to Homer's δημιοεργοί (*Odyssey* 17.383–385), magicians and medicine men who knew and practiced a variety of rites, had access to international equipment, and probably commanded more than one language and script. Such informal mixtures of Aegean and Levantine traditions in the East are also implied at newly discovered shrines at Mycenae, Phylakopi, and Tiryns, suggesting how religious traditions circulated in the Eastern Mediterranean.[47]

This allows more than visual motifs to express this grisly rite, as if ritual terminology and practices were familiar to early Greek poets. If the context of the Ugaritic tablet suggests a path to Greek ears, its contents evoke Homeric comparanda. For its language and occasion are most closely matched in epic poetry not in episodes surrounding the fate of Astyanax, but in the special rites ordered by Hektor from the women of

Troy, in *Iliad* 6 (297–310). Following instructions from Helenos, the bird-seeing son of Priam, Hektor bids his mother call other women of the city and go to the temple of Athena on the heights of the city (ἐν πόλει ἄκρῃ: 88). They are to offer her a special gift, a πέπλος, and promise her a sacrifice of twelve oxen if she will take pity on "the city and the wives of the Trojans and their innocent children" (6.276, a caption for the Mykonos pithos) and restrain the might of Diomedes. Hekabe obeys, assembles the women, chooses an appropriate πέπλος—ironically a Phoenician garment, the work of Sidonian women (290–292). They ascend to the temple with another royal family member, Theano, wife of Antenor, who begins the actual prayer (305):

πότνι' Ἀθηναίη, ῥυσίπτολι, δῖα θεάων

The goddess is invoked by a title, "Lady Athena," unique to the *Iliad* or *Odyssey*, on one of the few epic occasions for a prayer in direct speech. Her title may be ancient: Mycenaean Greek texts indicate an *a-ta-na po-ti-ni-ja* at Knossos in the Late Bronze Age (Kn V52). Ῥυσίπτολι makes explicit her protection of the city, a familiar function for a goddess widely worshiped as Πόλιας, city goddess (*Homeric Hymns to Athena* 11.1; 28.3). This epithet, unique here in epic poetry, is all the more poignant for Athena's failure to heed the Trojan prayer, as admitted by the poet (311).

This appeal might be predictable in any city under siege, its elements traditional to many Greek city-cults. But what might an epic poet have absorbed from Near Eastern traditions, selecting and adapting Ugaritic elements into ones more appropriate to Greek religious practice? Hektor prays "with hands uplifted, on the heights of the city" in his mother's vision (ἐξ ἄκρης πόλιος Διὶ χεῖρας ἀνασχεῖν, 6.257), just as the leaders of Ashkelon lift their hands to heaven in supplication for their city (fig. 15.15). The ritual which Hektor recommends involves the royal family: in times of crisis, rulers were responsible for the safety and welfare of their cities, but their direct intervention in ritual is more suggestive of Near Eastern patterns than of Greek ones. In a Canaanite city, the royal family might sacrifice its own children: for a Greek audience, this formula of despair was cleansed of its unacceptable cruelty—infant sacrifice—and transformed into a rite for the chief

city-cult of Greek Ilion, that of Athena. Even the goddess' refusal to respond, expressed by shaking her head (6.311: ἀνένευε δὲ) complements the "divine abandonment" of cities in Mesopotamian literature, as in the Lamentation for Sumer and Ur (n. 2: l. 68).

Oriental inspiration also seems plausible if it explains the name(s) of Astyanax as a clue to the process of transmission. In the *Iliad*, the son of Hektor has two names: known to his father as "Skamandrios" after the chief river of Troy (like other local heroes: *Iliad* 5.49), to other Trojans he is "Astyanax" (6.402–403):[48]

τὸν ῥ' Ἕκτωρ καλέεσκε Σκαμάνδριον, αὐτὰρ οἱ ἄλλοι
Ἀστυάνακτ'· οἶος γὰρ ἐρύετο Ἴλιον Ἕκτωρ.

He whom Hektor used to call "Skamandrios," but the others [called him]
"Astyanax" ['Lord of the City']; for Hektor alone used to protect Ilion.

The second line implies that Hektor, not his son, holds the title "Astyanax," or "Lord of the City." His heroic defense of the city was still praised in historical times; long after he failed to protect Troy and died in the attempt, his statue is praised as τὸν ἄριστον ἀμύντορα Τρῳάδος αἴης (*Inschriften von Ilion* 142). A similar dimorphism colors his son's final appearance in the *Iliad*: Andromache mourns her husband, now dead, while addressing her son (22.506):

Ἀστυάναξ, ὃν Τρῶες ἐπίκλησιν καλέουσιν,
οἶος γάρ σφιν ἔρυσο πύλας καὶ τείχεα μακρά.

Astyanax, whom the Trojans call in title,
for you alone used to protect for them the gates and the long walls.

Although Andromache has just applied the name to her child (in 22.500), in this lament she explains "Astyanax" as an honorific epithet appropriate to Hektor, not his son. Confusion raised by this doubling of names and by the existence of Hektor's other children (not by Andromache: Eur. *Andr.* 224) gave rise to post-Homeric legends of the "survival" of another son of Hektor, Skamandrios, who grew up to refound Troy.[49] If

"Astyanax" is a title meaning "Lord of the City," its Phoenician equivalent would be "Melqart," chief god of Tyre and patron of Phoenicians abroad, including on Greek Thasos (Herodotus 2.144). Melqart was never worshipped at Troy, nor offered infant sacrifices in any Semitic context.[50] But a Greek version of his name suits propitiation of the chief god of a city, culminating in the sacrifice of an infant member of the royal family. Did some such title become "Astyanax" (the way "Adoni" became a Greek god, Adonis), with a human sacrifice his fate, instead of death from the walls of the city? The emphasis on a "burnt offering" or "sacrifice" in Near Eastern sources of his fate (II *Kings* 3:27) could have assisted the migration of his death from the walls of the city to an altar. In other words, competing Greek scenarios for the death of Astyanax reflect Near Eastern sources, where the royal son singled out for sacrifice is, in some accounts, first slaughtered (with a sacrificial knife), then brought to the walls of the city for a full display of his death (by holocaust sacrifice) to the enemy. In the Greek transformation, Astyanax meets a wartime death at the hands of the enemy at an altar as if "sacrificed;" a knife, not a sword (fig. 15.10b), and a severed head (fig. 15.5) imply slaughter before burnt sacrifice, proper procedure in both Greek and Near Eastern ritual. In legend, the locale of the walls survives, but in art only the flying limbs betray a fall. In some Greek accounts, the infant's death retains its ritual elements: "Sacrificing to all the gods, the Greeks threw Astyanax from the height of the ramparts" (before slaughtering Polyxena on the tomb of Achilles) (Apollodorus *Epitome* 5.23). As late as Seneca, the (self-)sacrifice of Astyanax is performed as a ritual, with Ulixes speaking prayers prescribed by Calchas and invoking "cruel gods" (*Troades* 1088–1103). If the memory of a sacrificed royal son persists in classical mythology, it remains to examine it in art.

Our point of departure for this journey to the East was a series of scenes in early Greek art, to which we return with newly "oriented" eyes. The Mykonos vessel transforms, on both of its decorative zones, motifs traditional to the siege of a city in the Levant (figs. 15.12a–d): breaking and entering the walls with a "Horse" (machine), and the sacrifice of royal children, now become slaughter by the enemy (cf. fig. 15.1, of the later seventh century). A few decades later, an early black-figure pyxis lid from Cumae by the C Painter shows a scene still suggestive of infant sacrifice (fig. 15.4). Priam and Hekabe stand left of an altar, arms upraised as if in supplication. From the right a warrior rushes towards the altar, carrying a child upside down by the ankle. He is closely followed by a pair of horsemen with spears raised, then a long line of running hoplites who encircle the rest of the lid, broken by three pairs of horsemen. If one suspends Greek expectations, are a king and queen overseeing the sacrifice of their child, before an enemy host advancing on their city? In eccentric versions of the death of Troilos, the child is held upside down over the altar of Apollo like a sacrificial victim (as on Louvre E 638 bis, an Early Corinthian krater), not a boy ambushed by the enemy. Before an audience of advancing hoplites, is this a victor's vengeance on the kingdom he has conquered, or the last desperate act of its defenders? Do scenes where a warrior puts a child to death with sword or knife (fig. 15.5) imply deliberate sacrifice to save the city, rather than enemy slaughter?

Even the most ambitious of Archaic city-sieges allows a new vista of the fall of Troy. A black-figure hydria by an imaginative, if illiterate, painter of the Leagros Group combines shoulder and belly scenes into a panorama of the *Ilioupersis* (figs. 15.8a, b). On the shoulder (fig. 15.8b) is a rare representation of the battlements of Troy. From the left, a Scythian-dressed archer (Pandaros?) aims his bow below, perhaps at the team of horses storming through the city gate. Near him, two armed warriors defend the city; then a warrior with helmet pushed back pours from a rhyton into his mouth—in celebration after the Trojans admitted the Wooden Horse? (Apollodorus 5.18), or performing rites in despair? This τειχομαχία closes on the right with women clutching their hair and gesturing to the enemy, most traditional of all motifs in the fall of a city. Across the vase below them (fig. 15.8a) unfolds the moment of capture: a team of horses bursts through the gate of the city, marked by a tree, perhaps one of those which mark gates in the *Iliad* (6.433; cf. 5.693). Defending the city against intrusion stands (a statue of?) the goddess Athena, larger in scale than the human figures in the same scene, as befits her epic proportions (*Iliad* 18.519). Behind her crouches an elderly man, presumably Priam, with hand extended down to the altar which borders the scene on the right. Three unequal steps are crowned by a tripod with huge handles. It is the focus of action for the warrior and chief agent: in full armor, he brandishes with upraised right arm the body of a child, hanging upside down by the leg. Beyond the death of Astyanax in Athena's sanctuary, or Troilos with Achilles, this vase invokes a Near Eastern fall of a city, a companion to the Karnak relief with the siege of Ashkelon (fig. 15.15). In both scenes, the enemy storms the walls while men defend the city, women wail and gesture, and others performs last rites of appeal to the gods, pouring from a rhyton (equivalent to the Canaanite incense-burners?) and offering a last sacrifice, the son of the ruling family, to the protector deity of the city.

Greek art infrequently reveals its sources; in episodes like this we can imagine a tradition which enriched Greek visions of the fall of Troy. Before the Persian sack, Athenians had not witnessed the defeat and destruction of a city, unless they came from Lydia and Ionia; we would expect their imagination to be informed by voices with a longer experience of siege warfare. Beyond the fate of Troilos or Astyanax, these scenes suggest multiple sacrifices as in Phoenician cities; dismemberment of royal children could have preserved images of warriors hurling parts of a child's body in Trojan War scenes (fig. 15.6). Ritual repetition of sacrifice might explain the presence of more than one young boy in scenes of slaughter at an altar, whether in art (e.g., on Greek vases: Athens 1046; Bonn AK 39; Louvre G 152) or its *ekphrasis* (Polygnotus' paintings at Delphi: Paus. 10.26.1).

The Greek capacity for compassion and curiosity made the Trojans, not the Greeks, victims and heroes of the Trojan War; even Euripides did not turn the death of Astyanax back into a barbarian rite. Instead, it is Greeks who are accused by their Asian enemies of barbarian practices in war, with the death of Astyanax, in particular, bewailed by Hekabe, queen of Troy (*Tro.* 764–65; cf. Sen. *Troades* 1104–1109):

ὦ βάρβαρ' ἐξευρόντες Ἕλληνες κακά,
τί τόνδε παῖδα κτείνετ' οὐδὲν αἴτιον;

The same tragic poet salvaged the notion of infant sacrifice in a besieged city for the sacrifice of Menoikeus in the siege of Thebes, whose "Phoenician" context alludes to an Oriental background (see n. 41). In the long-lived exchange between Greece and the Levant, it is important to examine what and how Greeks rejected as well as what they borrowed; the special circumstances surrounding the death of Astyanax suggest one creative result of rejection. This exchange was alive as early as Homer, and still inspired new arrangements of traditional stories in tragedy. Sacrifice itself, long courted as a uniquely Greek view of misfortune, must be understood as a practice borrowed in specific ways from the Orient, even when the two cultures disagreed over offering human victims. It is the voice of the victim as well as of those who mourn which is silent in the Orient; in Greece, it is more often the victim whom poets imagine and artists portray.

NOTES

*The following abbreviations have been used:

Brown, *Child Sacrifice* = S. Brown, *Late Carthaginian Child Sacrifice and Sacrificial Monuments in their Mediterranean Contexts* (Sheffield 1991).

Dugas (1937) = Ch. Dugas, "Tradition littéraire et tradition graphique dans l'antiquité grecque," *AntCl* 6 (1937) 5–26.

Garlan = Y. Garlan, *Recherches de poliorcétique grecque* (Paris 1974).

Henrichs, "Human Sacrifice" = A. Henrichs, "Human Sacrifice in Greek Religion: Three Case Studies," in *Le sacrifice dans l'antiquité* 195–235.

Heydemann (1888) = H. Heydemann, "Osservazioni sulla morte di Priamo e di Astianatte," *RM* 3 (1888) 101–112.

Hughes = D. Hughes, *Human Sacrifice in Ancient Greece* (London and New York 1991).

Kossatz-Deissmann = A. Kossatz-Deissmann, *LIMC* I, "Achilles VII: Das Troilos-Abenteuer," 72–95.

Margalit = B. Margalit, "Why King Mesha of Moab Sacrificed his Oldest Son," *BAR* 1986, 62–63, 76.

Morris, *Daidalos* = S. P. Morris, *Daidalos and the Origins of Greek Art* (Princeton 1992).

Mota (1957) = C. Mota, "Sur les représentations figurées de la mort de Troilos et de la mort d'Astyanax," *RA* 49 (1957) 25–44.

Le sacrifice dans l'antiquité. J. Rudhart and O. Renerdin, eds. Fondation Hardt, Entretiens 27 (Geneva 1980).

Smith (1981) = P. Smith, "Aineiadai as Patrons of *Iliad* XX and the Homeric *Hymn to Aphrodite*," *HSCP* 85 (1981) 17–58.

Touchefeu *LIMC* = O. Touchefeu, *LIMC* I, "Astyanax" (1974) 929–937.

——— (1983) = "Lecture des images mythologiques. Un example d'images sans texte, la mort d'Astyanax," in F. Lissarrague and F. Thelamon, eds., *Image et céramique grecque* (Rouen 1983) 21–27.

Wiencke (1954) = M. Wiencke, "An Epic Theme in Greek Art," *AJA* 58 (1954) 285–306.

Williams (1991) = D. Williams, "Onesimos and the Getty *Iliupersis*," *Greek Vases in the J. Paul Getty Museum* 5, Occasional Papers 7 (1991) 41–64.

Yadin, *Art of Warfare* = Y. Yadin, *The Art of Warfare in Biblical Lands* (London 1967).

1. S. P. Morris, "A Tale of Two Cities: The Miniature Frescoes from Thera and the Origins of Greek Poetry," *AJA* 93 (1989) 511–535. In modern Greece, see M. Alexiou, *The Ritual Lament in Greek Tradition* (Cambridge 1974) ch. 5, "The Historical Lament for the Fall or Destruction of Cities"; R. Beaton, *Folk Poetry of Modern Greece* (Cambridge 1980) 95–102.

2. S. N. Kramer, *Lamentation over the Destruction of Ur* (Chicago 1940); P. Michalowski, *The Lamentation over the Destruction of Sumer and Ur* (Winona Lake 1989); M. Coogan, *Stories from Ancient Canaan* (Philadelphia 1978) 60 for the siege of Udm (Keret epic).

3. See G. L. Huxley, "A Fragment of the Ἀσσύριοι λόγοι of Herodotos," *GRBS* 6 (1965) 207–212, on Herodotus' (lost) account of the fall of Nineveh; R. Drews, *The Greek Accounts of Eastern History* (Cambridge 1971) 92–95. W. Burkert, "Seven against Thebes: an oral tradition between Babylonian magic and Greek literature," in C. Brilliante, M. Cantilena, and C. O. Pavese, eds., *I Poemi epici rapsodici non omerici e la tradizione orale* (Padua 1981) 29–48, esp. 40–46, 49. S. Scully, *Homer and the Sacred City* (Cornell 1990) explores the imagery of the city in Greek epic and the Near East.

4. Touchefeu, *LIMC*, and (1983).

5. Heydemann (1888) 101–112; Dugas (1937) 5–26; Wiencke (1954) 285–306; Touchefeu (1983); J. Boardman, "The Kleophrades Painter at Troy," *AntK* 19 (1976) 3–18, esp. 7–9; M. Hart, "Athens and Troy: The Narrative Treatment of the *Iliupersis* in Archaic Attic Vase-painting" (Ph.D. diss., UCLA, 1992).

6. F. Willemsen, "Ein frühgarchaisches Dreifussbein," *OlBer* VII (Berlin 1961) 181–195; Kossatz-Deissmann 89–90.

7. Mota (1957) 25–44; Touchefeu (1983).

8. H. A. Shapiro, "Old and new heroes: narrative, composition, and subject in Attic black-figure," *CA* 9 (1990) 114–148 on new myth in Attic vase painting around 560 B.C., including the story of Troilos.

9. Smith (1981) 17–58 on the refounding of Troy by Ascanius and Astyanax/Skamandrios, whose double name allowed one to survive in legend (infra, nn. 48–49). I thank Richard Janko for this reference and for valuable criticism of this work.

10. The best discussion of this theme is by G. Siebert: *Recherches sur les ateliers de bols à reliefs du Péloponnèse à l'époque hellénistique*, BEFAR 223 (Paris 1978) 250–252, and "Thèmes troyens dans la céramique grecque à reliefs hellénistiques de l'Argolide," in L. Kahil, C. Augé, and P. Linant de Bellefords, eds., *L'Iconographie classique et identitiés regionales*, BCH Suppl. 14 (1986) 61–63.

11. Compare pl. 25.3 and 4 in J. D. Beazley, *The Development of Attic Black-Figure*, rev. ed. D. von Bothmer and Mary B. Moore (Berkeley and Los Angeles 1986).

12. H. Cassimatis, "A propos de l'utilisation du motif iconographique: autel-trône? Une bizarrerie de l'image," in J. Christiansen and T. Melander, eds., *Ancient Greek and Related Pottery* (Copenhagen 1988) 117–127. Confusion begins in the Orient, where a conflation of visual forms for temple and seat involves a Semitic pun, as I learned from I. Winter: see her "The King and the Cup," in M. Kelly-Buccellati, ed., *Insight through Images. Studies in Honor of Edith Porada*, Bibliotheca Mesopotamica 21 (Malibu 1986) 254–255, n. 1.

13. Heydemann (1888) 105–106 for this scene on a hydria by the Haimon Painter (now lost). Morris, *Daidalos* 264–266, and references for this type of royal stool.

14. A romance made this episode popular, like the one which paired Achilles with Polyxena: Lykoph. *Alex.* 307–313; E. Kunze, *Archaische Schildbänder*, OlForsch 2 (Berlin 1950) 142; Kossatz-Deissmann 73; M. Robertson, "Troilos and Polyxene: Notes on a Changing Legend," in J.-P. Descoeudres, ed., *Eumousia. Ceramic and Iconographical Studies in Honour of Alexander Cambitoglou*, MeditArch Suppl. 1 (Sydney 1990) 63–70.

15. M. Stansbury-O'Donnell, "Polygnotos' *Iliupersis*: A New Reconstruction," *AJA* 93 (1989) 203–215; idem, "Polygnotos' *Nekyia*: A Reconstruction and Analysis," *AJA* 94 (1990) 213–235; idem, "Narrative Structure in the Lesche Paintings of Polygnotus and its Relationship to the Tragedy of Aeschylus," *AJA* 96 (1992) 369–370. Atrocities like the rape of Kassandra and the deaths of Priam and Astyanax are moderated to promote Greek virtue at the expense of Asia: D. Castriota, *Myth, Ethos and Actuality: Official Art in Fifth-Century B.C. Athens* (Madison 1992) ch. 3. Hence Astyanax still lives

in his mother's arms in the painting at Delphi (10.25.2, but a small boy clutches an altar near Neoptolemos: 10.26.1); the corpse of Priam appears alone (10.27.2), separated from the death of his grandson.

16. First published by M. Ervin, "A Relief Pithos from Mykonos," *Deltion* 18:A (1963) 37–75.

17. By D. Ussishkin, *The Conquest of Lachish by Sennacherib* (Tel Aviv 1982) 101; cf. Yadin, *Art of Warfare* 314–316; E. Bleibtreu, "Five Ways to Conquer a City," *BAR* May/June 1990, 37–44, esp. 41–43.

18. Garlan 136–143. Thucydides dates their use to the siege of Plataea in 429/428 B.C. (2.76.4), although Diodorus (28.3) and Plutarch (27.3–4), citing Ephorus, claim that the Athenians invented them to attack Samos in 441/440 B.C. Thucydides' elaborate description of their manufacture and use, and the countermeasures at Plataea, agrees remarkably with Assyrian reliefs: Garlan 139 n. 7 compares a ninth-century siege from the throne room at Nimrud (British Museum, W.A. A. 124554) to Thuc. 2.75–78.

19. Garlan 139–140 suggests that Greeks could have learned of siege machines in the West (Carthage) as easily as in the Levant; thus Phoenician and Punic engineers invented the ramp and ram, later perfected by Geras of Chalcedon, at the siege of Gadiz (Vitr., *De arch.* 10.131–132): P. Bosch-Gimpera, "Phéniciens et Grecs dans l'Extrême-Occident," *NClio* 3 (1951) 287. On Greek and Phoenician triremes, see Morris, *Daidalos* 376.

20. J. K. Anderson, "The Trojan Horse Again," *CJ* 66 (1970–1971) 21–25; J. C. Rouman and W. H. Held, "More Still on the Trojan Horse," *CJ* 67 (1972) 327–330; R. Gallucci, "Bronze Age Siege Machines and the Trojan Horse," delivered at the American Philological Association, December 1989. I thank Ralph Gallucci for a copy of this paper.

21. A. Bernabé, *Poetae Epicae Graeci* (Leipzig 1987) fr. 2; Ervin (supra n. 16) 56; "Echion on the Mykonos pithos: The fulfillment of prophecy," in ΣΤΗΛΗ. Τόμος εἰς μνήμην Νικολάου Κοντολέοντος (Athens 1980) 33–36.

22. Ervin (supra n. 16) 52–56; B. Sparkes, "The Trojan Horse in Classical Art," *GaR* 18 (1971) 54–70; M. Robertson, "Epeios," 798–799 and A. Sadurska, "Equus," 813–817 in *LIMC* III.1.

23. Assyrian themes in Greek art: A. Gunter, "Models of the Orient in the Art History of the Orientalizing Period," in H. Sancisi-Weerdenburg and J.W. Drijvers, eds., *Achaemenid History V. The Roots of the European Tradition* (Leiden 1990) 137–141.

24. N. Kondoleon, "Ἡ Γέννησις τοῦ Διός," *KrChr* 15–16 (1961–1962) 282–293; E. Simon, "Die Geburt der Athena auf der Reliefamphora in Tenos," *AntK* 25 (1982) 35–38; E.

Condoléon-Bondonacchi, "À propos de l' 'Amphore de la Naissance' de Xobourgo (Ténos)," *AK* 27 (1984) 21–24; Morris, *Daidalos* 91–92, figs. 13–15.

25. P. Montet, *Byblos et l'Egypte* (Paris 1923) 62–68, fig. 20, pl. XXXIX: 42; discussed in Morris, *Daidalos* 91–92.

26. W. Burkert, "Von Amenophis II zur Bogenprobe des Odysseus, " *GrazBeitr* 1 (1973) 69–78; P. Walcot, "Odysseus and the Contest of the Bow: The Comparative Evidence," *SMEA* 84 (1984) 357–369. A Hittite parallel is the story of Gurparanzakhus. E. Forrer in *Mélanges Franz Cumont* (Brussels 1936) 712.

27. J. Sasson, *The Military Establishment at Mari* (Rome 1969) 33–34, on "towers" ordered by Shamshi-Adad: one sports the name of Ḫaradan or "wild donkey"; cf. Yadin, *Art of Warfare* I, 69–71; idem, "Hyksos Fortifications and the Battering-Ram," *BASOR* 137 (1955) 23–32. The earliest battering ram in action appears in a tomb painting at Beni Hasan, Egypt, c. 1900 B.C. (Yadin, *Art of Warfare* I, 159). I am grateful to Ralph Gallucci (n. 20) for enlightenment on Bronze Age siege machines, and to Jaan Puhvel for reminding me of his "Πολέμοιο γέφυραι," *IGForsch* 81 (1976) 60–66.

28. Yadin, *Art of Warfare* I, 228–233; F. Yurco, "Merenptah's Canaanite Campaign," *JARCE* 23 (1986) 189–215; cf. his "3,200-Year-Old Pictures of Israelites Found in Egypt," *BAR* Sept./Oct. 1990, 20–38.

29. A. Spalinger, "A Canaanite Ritual Found in Egyptian Military Reliefs," *JSSEA* 8 (1978) 47–60; Margalit 62–63, 76; M. Artzy, "Pomegranate Scepters and Incense Stand with Pomegranates Found in Priest's Grave," *BAR* Jan/Feb 1990, 48–51. The same rite appears in other Syrian cities under siege, at Luxor, in Nubia (fig. 15.16, from Beit el-Wali), and at Medinet Habu: Spalinger 50–52; Yadin, *Art of Warfare* I, 232; Yurco (supra n. 28 [1990]) 29–31. Some see live children being offered as tribute or hostages, not sacrifice: O. Keel, "Kanaanäische Sühnenriten auf ägyptischen Tempelreliefs," *VT* 25 (1975) 413–469, esp. 437–442; cf. E. Weidner, "Die älteste Nachricht über das persische Königshaus. Kyros I. Ein Zeitgenosse Assurbanipals," *AfO* 7 (1931/1932) 1–14, a reference I owe to Elizabeth Carter.

30. A. Herdner, "Une prière à Baal des Ugaritains en danger," *CRAI* 1972 (1973) 693–703 and in *Ugaritica* VII (Paris 1978) 31–38; J. C. de Moor, *An Anthology of Religious Texts from Ugarit* (Leiden 1987) 172–173. The incomplete word **[?]kr** could be **[b]kr** = bᵉkor, 'firstborn,' or **[d]kr**, 'male' [animal]; **ḥtp** is emended to **ḥtk**, 'offspring': C. Schaeffer, *Ugaritica* IV, 77–83; P. Xella, "Un Testo Ugaritico Recente (RS 24.266, *verso*, 9–19) e il 'Sacrifico dei Primo Nati'," *RStF* 6 (1978) 127–136; Margalit 76, nn. 2–3. I was

saved from misunderstanding and misusing these passages by Ron Hendel.

31. M. Alexiou and P. Dronke, "The Lament for Jephtha's Daughter: Themes, Traditions and Originality," *Studi Medievali* 12 (1971) 819–863. Cf. Eur. *IT* 20–21.

32. Brown, *Child Sacrifice* 37–75, for a summary of previous studies (L. Stager, "The Rite of Child Sacrifice at Carthage," in J. G. Pedley, ed., *New Light on Ancient Carthage* [Ann Arbor 1980] 1–11; idem, "Carthage: A View from the Tophet," in H.-G. Niemeyer, ed., *Phönizier im Westen*, MM Beih. 8 [Mainz 1982] 155–166; L. Stager and S. Wolff, "Child Sacrifice at Carthage: Religious Rite or Population Control?" *BAR* Jan/Feb 1984, 31–51). I am grateful for Shelby Brown's advice and her critique of this article.

33. T. Heider, *The Cult of Molek: A Reassessment* (JSOTS 1985); Brown, *Child Sacrifice* 28–35. See now J. Day, *Molech: a God of Human Sacrifice in the Old Testament* (Cambridge 1989), a reference I owe to Mark Smith, along with thanks for his criticism.

34. E. Lipiński, "Sacrifices d'enfants à Carthage et dans le monde sémitique Oriental," in E. Lipiński, ed., *Studia Phoenicia VI. Carthago*, Orientalia Lovaniensis Analecta 26 (Leuven 1988) 151–162.

35. Classical and patristic references to Semitic human sacrifice in Day (supra n. 33) 86–91. For this essay, it suffices that Greeks and Romans *believed* the rite was practiced; some Punic specialists remain unconvinced it was: S. Moscati, *Il sacrificio punico dei fanciulli: Realtà o invenzione* (Rome 1987); S. Moscati and S. Ribichini, *Il sacrifico dei bambini: Un aggiornamento* (Rome 1991).

36. Henrichs, "Human Sacrifice" 195–242, esp. Part III, "Cannibalism and the Christian Eucharist," 224–232; J. Levenson, *The Death and Resurrection of the Beloved Son: The Transformation of Child Sacrifice in Judaism and Christianity* (Yale 1994).

37. Burkert's appreciation of this has gone unnoticed: "Greek Tragedy and Sacrificial Ritual," *GRBS* 7 (1966) 103, n. 34: "It seems to be well established that . . . Semitic (Phoenician and Hebrew) sacrificial rites offer the closest parallel to Greek ritual. . . . It is one of the paradoxes of our profession that neither Nilsson nor Meuli, in their expositions of Greek sacrificial ritual, refer to the Old Testament, which contains the largest extant collection of ancient sacrificial rites." Revisions of the Meuli-Burkert-Girard approach: M. Alexiou, "Reappropriating Greek Sacrifice: *homo necans* or ἄνθρωπος θυσιάζων?" *JMGS* 8 (1990) 97–123; S. Peirce, "Death, Revelry, and *Thysia*," *CA* 12 (1993) 219–266.

38. Henrichs, "Human Sacrifice"; Brown, *Child Sacrifice* 159–162; Hughes disputes archaeological claims for human sacrifice. E. Kearns, *The Heroes of Attica* (London 1989) 56–63.

39. H. P. Foley *Ritual Irony. Poetry and Sacrifice in Euripides* (Cornell 1985); E. O'Connor-Visser, *Aspects of Human Sacrifice in the Tragedies of Euripides* (Amsterdam 1987) 211–230, "The Evidence for Greek Human Sacrifice"; J. Wilkins, "The State and the Individual: Euripides' Plays of Voluntary Self-Sacrifice," in A. Powell, ed., *Euripides, Women, and Sexuality* (London 1990) 177ff. J. Connelly, "The Parthenon Frieze and the Sacrifice of the Erechtheids: Reinterpreting the Peplos Scene," *AJA* 97 (1993) 309–310.

40. Henrichs, "Human Sacrifice" 198–208, on Iphigenia and ritual; cf. Hughes 71–81.

41. R. Rebuffat, "Le sacrifice du fils de Créon dans les *Phéniciennes* d'Euripide," *REA* 74 (1972) 14–31, connects Menoikeus and the "Phoenician" chorus with Carthage, enemy of Greeks in Sicily; W. Burkert, "Glauben und Verhalten: Zeichengehalt und Wirkungsmacht von Opferritualen," in *Le sacrifice dans l'antiquité*, 119–121; O'Connor-Visser (supra n. 39) 73–98, "The Sacrifice of Menoeceus"; E. Kearns, "Saving the City," in O. Murray and S. Price, eds., *The Greek City. From Homer to Alexander* (Oxford 1990) 322–344.

42. E. Hall, *Inventing the Barbarian: Greek Self-Definition through Tragedy* (Oxford 1989) 146–148; C. Segal, "Violence and the Other: Greek, Female and Barbarian in Euripides' *Hecuba*," *TAPA* 120 (1990) 109–131.

43. J. N. Coldstream, "Greeks and Phoenicians in the Aegean," in H.-G. Niemeyer, ed. (supra n. 32) 261–275; J. Shaw, "Phoenicians in Southern Crete," *AJA* 93 (1989) 165–183.

44. P. Warren, "Minoan Crete and Ecstatic Religion," in R. Hägg and N. Marinatos, eds., *Sanctuaries and Cults in the Aegean Bronze Age* (Stockholm 1981); S. M. Wall, J. H. Musgrave, and P. M. Warren, "Human Bones from a Late Minoan Ib house at Knossos," *BSA* 81 (1986) 333–388. Morris, *Daidalos* 113–115.

45. J. Carter, "The Masks of Ortheia," *AJA* 91 (1987) 355–383.

46. Herdner (supra n. 30) 697; J.-Cl. Courtois, "La Maison du Prêtre aux modèles de poumon et de foies d'Ugarit," *Ugaritica* VI (1969) 91–119; C. F. A. Schaeffer, "Contexte archéologique de date du Rhyton Léontocéphale de la Maison d'Agaptari," *Ugaritica* VII (1978) 149ff. Morris, *Daidalos* 107–108.

47. O. Negbi, "Levantine Elements in the Sacred Architecture of the Aegean," *BSA* 83 (1988) 339–357 (*contra*, G. Gilmour, "Aegean Sanctuaries and the Levant in the Late Bronze Age," *BSA* 88 [1993] 125–134); W. Burkert, *The Orientalizing Revolution* (Harvard 1992) on δημιοεργοί, whose travels

can be traced in Late Bronze Age shipwrecks (Morris, *Daidalos* 107–115).

48. P. Roussel, "Astyanax," *REG* 32 (1919) 482–489; not in J. Redfield's *Nature and Culture in the Iliad. The Tragedy of Hektor* (Chicago 1975); G. Nagy, *The Best of the Achaeans* (Baltimore 1979) 145–147.

49. Smith (1981), "Appendix: Skamandrios as Survivor," 53–58.

50. C. Bonnet, *Melqart. Cultes et mythes de l'Héraclès tyrien en Mediterranée*, Studia Phoenicia VIII (Leuven and Na-mur 1988) supersedes earlier studies. Unhelpful but intriguing is L. Benloew's *Les Sémites à Ilion. La vérité sur la guerre de Troie* (Paris 1863). Richard Thomas reminded me that the Trojan child who meets death in the *Aeneid* is Polites rather than Astyanax (2.526–544): a variant name for the hope of the city? But Walter Burkert believes that Astyanax was invented for the family episode in *Iliad* 6, his death separately developed in the *Ilioupersis*, with no possible connection between his name and his fate (personal communication).

16

HOMER'S PHOENICIANS:
HISTORY, ETHNOGRAPHY, OR LITERARY TROPE?
[A PERSPECTIVE ON EARLY ORIENTALISM] *

◆

IRENE J. WINTER

In what I like to call the serendipity of scholarship, it sometimes happens that responding to a framework set for a conference or volume brings one to the unexpected: a new perspective on one's own material occasioned by an unusual lens, or, more rarely, by an unanticipated view of the lens itself.

It had been my intention to proceed from the evocative accounts of Phoenician merchant-seamen in the *Odyssey* to the *realia* of evidence for Phoenician trade—an interest that stems from work done on ivories from Spain and the westward expansion of the Phoenicians in the eighth–seventh centuries B.C.[1]—and, by so doing, to pay tribute to the inspiring work of Emily Vermeule, who has done so much to bring the world(s) of "Homer"—that putative individual to whom we attribute the *Iliad* and the *Odyssey*—alive. As research for the present article proceeded, however, I became more and more interested in the texts themselves: specifically, in how to account for anomalies between the historical evidence and the way Phoenicians are represented.

Seductive though it may be to move from eloquence in a given text to mental image to historical reconstruction, recent work in literary and cultural studies has shown that one can no longer read the Homeric poems, or indeed any literary work, with an innocent assumption of transparency between "the world" and "the word"; archaeological data and other textual studies are necessary as corroboration or corrective. With respect to the Phoenicians, at issue is whether and to what degree one can distinguish historical and ethnographic description from literary construct—"fact" from fiction—in the epics. I hope my classical colleagues will permit me this foray into their territory, and see in it a response to Professor Vermeule's passionate commitment throughout her career to the enduring life in those texts.

PHOENICIANS IN HOMER

The generic Phoenicians (*Phoinikes*) and the specific Sidonians (*Sidones*) are synonymous in the *Iliad* and the *Odyssey*, with the city standing for the people as a whole.[2] References in the *Iliad* are but two, both associated with luxury production. In the first case, embroidered garments described as the handiwork of Sidonian women (*Iliad* 6.288ff.) are said to have been brought from Sidon by Paris himself on the same sea voyage in which he brought Helen to Troy. They were kept in the treasure chamber of Priam's palace, and were clearly highly valued, the most beautiful of them selected by Hekabe, queen of Troy, as an offering to Athena. The second passage recounts the large, "richly wrought" silver bowl (*krater*) of surpassing beauty that was set by Achilles as a prize in the funeral games of Patroklos (*Iliad* 23.740ff.). We are told that it was made cunningly by Sidonians well skilled in deft handiwork (*Sidones poludaidaloi*) and brought over the sea by Phoenicians as a gift—presumably a royal gift—to Thoas, whose grandson gave it to Patroklos as ransom for a son of Priam. In other words, the bowl is not only described as being of superb craftsmanship; it has also had a complex history of elite ownership.

Inclusion of the *krater*'s previous owners both attests to and establishes the bowl's quality and value; it also provides us with an example of the circuit of royal gifting well known in the Levant in both the Late Bronze and Early Iron Ages.[3] The reference to Hekabe's garments, by contrast, attests to the acquisition of luxury goods through purchase in foreign ports during the course of sea voyages. Taken together, the two set up an interesting opposition: apart from setting the stage for the luxurious appointments of the Trojan court, mention of the Sidonian garments suggests a relationship between women and luxury, women and commodity, even, as both Helen and the garments are carried in the same ship; while the Sidonian silver vessel with its royal associations is owned and transmitted in a male universe of fellowship and gifting.

The same elite male universe is reproduced in the first reference to Phoenician work in the *Odyssey*, when Menelaos of Sparta gives Telemachos a silver mixing bowl that had been a gift from the king of Sidon (*Odyssey* 4.614–619). By referring to the king of Sidon as a warrior (*hērōs*) and by acknowledging his gift within the frame of appropriate Greek standards of hospitality, the two rulers are established as equals, Menelaos having been received in Sidon as Telemachos was now received in Sparta. Both the vessel given Telemachos and the prize set by Achilles in the *Iliad* are kraters, both are well wrought; this one, with gilded rim, is called the best and costliest (*kalliston kai timēestaton*). As yet another royal gift passed on in high social circles, it does not

significantly add to our picture, except that the gilding suggests even greater luxury than the bowl given to Patroklos.

The other references in the *Odyssey* deal with Phoenician sailing practice, not products, and reflect a significant shift in tone. In Odysseus' meeting with a disguised Athena upon his return to Ithaca, for example (*Odyssey* 13.256–286), a Phoenician ship moored off the coast of Crete is described as the means by which the hero escapes the island, buying his passage with a portion of the booty from Troy. Odysseus claims to have been put ashore on Ithaca with the rest of his goods after the ship had been blown off course in a storm. This tale was invented by Odysseus to explain his hoard of booty without having to divulge his true identity to a presumed stranger. In fact, he had been quite purposively carried to Ithaca by Phaeacian sailors after having been nobly received and laden with gifts by their rulers (*Odyssey* 8.387ff.). Significant here is that, as noted by Carpenter,[4] the pointed references to seagoing Phoenicians who kept to their bargain and did not rob him of his personal goods effectively underscore expectations to the contrary.

The second negative reference also comes in a fabricated tale, as Odysseus presents himself in disguise to Eumaeus upon returning to Ithaca (*Odyssey* 14. 287–315). In yet another fabricated scenario, Odysseus describes himself as a highborn Cretan who, on his return voyage from the Trojan War, landed in Egypt, where he stayed for seven years. Then, in the eighth year, a Phoenician ship arrived, its captain described as one 'well versed in guile' (*apatēlia eidōs*), a greedy knave (*trōktēs*; literally, 'gobbler') who had already 'wrought much evil among men' (14.288–289), who tricks Odysseus with cunning persuasion (*parpepithōn hēisi phresin*, 14.290), and who gives false counsel (*pseudea bouleusas*, 14.296). This description introduces epithets and attributes that will be repeated in the more familiar story of the abduction of the faithful swineherd Eumaeus that follows. Here, the fictive Phoenician captain prevailed upon the veteran to accompany him home to Phoenicia, where he had a house and possessions. After a year, the two were to set out again, ostensibly in a joint venture with a cargo for Libya, but in fact the Phoenician's intention was to sell the "Cretan" as well. Punishment comes when the ship is destroyed en route by a Zeus-inspired storm, from which only the speaker-hero is said to have been saved.

This passage tends to be omitted by scholars seeking information about or perspective on the Phoenicians, but in fact it introduces some important elements. The story contains what seems to be a most realistic pattern of foreign movement related to the shipping ventures of the Phoenician shipmaster: he is first encountered on an expedition to Egypt; he returns home to a situation of means, spends a long period between voyages, provisions his ship, and then sets out again on a lengthy voyage, this time to Libya. At the same time, we are presented with an array of negative character traits attributed to the Phoenician. These traits go beyond mere description to serve a moralizing subtext, the underlying message of which is that hunger for commercial profit leads to the breaking of higher laws of social honor, punishable by divine retribution.

Many of these elements are repeated in the better-known story of Eumaeus' abduction as a child from his native island (*Odyssey* 15.403–484), which follows almost immediately upon Odysseus' account of himself as a Cretan. Indeed, the two should really be seen as a paired exchange of personal histories, the common thread of which is the deceitfulness of Phoenicians. Initially, the description of the Phoenician nursemaid of the young Eumaeus is a sympathetic one: her homeland, Sidon, is described as rich in bronze (*polukhalkou, Odyssey* 15.425), another echo of the *Iliad*'s reference to fine metalwork; she is skilled, as women should be, "in glorious handiwork" (i.e., embroidery); and she has suffered, having been abducted by Taphian pirates and sold into service. As we progress through the narrative, however, she is described more negatively, as is the crew of the Phoenician ship that subsequently lands at the island. The Phoenician sailors are 'famed for their ships' (*nausiklutoi, Odyssey* 15.415); but, like the Phoenician captain of Odysseus' tale, they are also 'greedy' (*trōktai, Odyssey* 15.416), their ships filled with goods for which the term used, *athurmata* (*Odyssey* 15.416), suggests trinkets, baubles, items of minor value. In their planned seduction of Eumaeus' nursemaid, they are described as *polupaipaloi*—often translated as 'wily,' but a very different term from that applied to the clever, 'wily' Odysseus (*polumētis*, cf. below). The Phoenicians are more "tricky" or "crafty" than cunning; and

as Carpenter pointed out, the *polupaipaloi* of the *Odyssey* is likely a conscious wordplay on the *poludaidaloi* of the *Iliad*.

As the Sidonian woman and the sailors plan her escape from the island, a picture so detailed and realistic is drawn of their activities that it is tempting for the modern historian to read it as standard Phoenician trading practice. The sailors proceed in the bartering of their wares and the filling up of their black ship with new goods, a process that takes a full year. When finally loaded and ready to sail, a farewell visit is made to the palace to offer one last item of value. The particular amber and gold necklace brought for scrutiny by the noble women (which in the narrative serves as the departure signal to the faithless nurse) seems to represent those very *athurmata*, or trinkets, described earlier as cargo and found on occasion as orientalizing objects in archaeological contexts. In sum, then, what is represented is a consistent picture of able but greedy and duplicitous seamen, carrying goods of minor consequence to be exchanged through barter for replacement goods, and who are not above trafficking in humans as well (i.e., the abduction of the child Eumaeus—*Odyssey* 15.452–453), in their trading circuit of over a year's duration.

HISTORY AND ETHNOGRAPHY

In the absence of contemporary Phoenician historical texts, hungry scholars of the Near East have mined Homer's pictures for generations, emphasizing their historical value when compared with archaeological evidence. Over the past twenty years, however, renewed scholarly interest in the Phoenicians has yielded considerable information and perspective. A great deal of progress has been made toward understanding the nature and role of the Phoenicians in their homeland.[5] The relationship between the designation "Phoenician" as used in Greek sources and the population of the Levantine coast to whom it refers has been discussed, including continuities with the second millennium Canaanites and Syrians of the same geographical region.[6] The coastal strip of the Eastern Mediterranean inhabited by "Phoenicians" in the first millennium B.C. can be generally defined, and is known to have been organized not as a unified polity but as a series of only sometimes confederated city-states.[7] At the same time, since the Phoenicians as a whole are often glossed in terms of the two dominant cities, Tyre and Sidon (e.g., men of Tyre, Sidonian bowl), studies like Katzenstein's *History of Tyre* are in essence reviews of all Phoenician sources.[8] At the same time, series of recent excavations have added significantly to our understanding, by providing better ceramic typologies of local materials and better synchronisms with Greek and Cypriote wares.[9] Greater precision in defining and describing Phoenician art has further helped in the evaluation of materials found throughout the Mediterranean,[10] while specific topics, such as Phoenician religion, have been the subject of scholarly meetings, resulting in valuable studies of various aspects of social and cultic life.[11] And finally, considerable attention has been paid to the role of the Phoenicians in seafaring and colonization of the Mediterranean in the same period.[12] Consequently, we are in a much better position to assess the accuracy of the "fit" between data and the picture drawn of Phoenicians in both the *Iliad* and the *Odyssey*.

Homer's references to well-wrought silver kraters of high quality and great value parallel closely the language used by the biblical chronicler in describing the cunning and skill "to grave all manner of graving" of the Phoenician craftsman sent to build David's palace and temple (II Chron. 2:14). Similar vessels recorded as tribute from Phoenician rulers by the Assyrian king Assurnasirpal II in the ninth century B.C. further attest to quality production, as well as to the practice of elite gifting of metalwork.[13] The texts are corroborated by archaeological finds of vessels attributed to Phoenician workshops in the Assyrian capital of Nimrud; that some were also reaching Cyprus and Etruria in the West has been known for many years.[14] Most important of the recent finds is a bronze bowl found at the site of Lefkandi in Euboea along with Late Protogeometric/Early Geometric pottery of c. 900 B.C.[15] This represents the earliest context known to date for decorated Phoenician materials in mainland Greece; and, as we shall see below, with the special role claimed for Euboea in both early Greek mercantile ventures and the fixation of the text of the *Odyssey*, the importance of this vessel at Lefkandi takes on major historical proportions.

No fragments of textiles have been recovered analogous to the embroidered garments mentioned as having been brought to Troy from Sidon; however, tribute from various Phoenician kings to Assyrian rulers regularly included multicolored garments of sufficient value to be mentioned along with bulk silver and gold and the metal vessels.[16] In addition, the later (probably sixth century) account of the trade of Tyre in the Hebrew Bible lists multicolored textiles and garments as Tyre's own merchandise traded abroad (Exekiel 27:23). These sources support the view that the region was likely to have been among those producing and distributing luxury garments in the Early Iron Age, and that rulers of equal status to the queen of Troy would have been acquiring such garments.[17]

Homeric references to Phoenician seafaring certainly are corroborated by other textual references. Among these are the more or less contemporary treaty of Esarhaddon of Assyria with Tyre (dated 676 B.C.) and the biblical citations that bracket the period in question.[18] That seafaring in the Eastern Mediterranean was a well-developed tradition going back at least into the Late Bronze Age has been supported by two excavated shipwrecks—Cape Gelidonya and Ulu Burun.[19] In both cases, extremely varied cargoes, including bulk metals, ceramic containers, and small luxury items from a variety of home ports, were gathered on vessels that foundered off the southern coast of Turkey. The Solomonic reference to naval expeditions lasting three years further supports both Odysseus' and Eumaeus' accounts of lengthy voyages and sojourns away from home.

Unfortunately, when Phoenician objects are found in Greek or other contexts, it is virtually impossible to establish whether or not the goods were carried by Phoenician sailors, except in those cases where additional evidence may be adduced to suggest the ethnic makeup of segments of the local population and/or the patterns of access thereto.[20] As we continue to accumulate archaeological evidence and find new correlations between textual references to Phoenicians as seafarers and material culture distributed across the Mediterranean,[21] it is hoped that we will be able to expand the picture of maritime activity in this period. It has certainly become clear that the process of Phoenician expansion into the Mediterranean is more complex than had been thought merely on the basis of later classical sources. Carpenter was among the first to argue for the down-dating of the establishment of Phoenician colonies in the West, based upon then-known archaeological data. While he was not wrong to question the traditional dates of eleventh century for Utica and Cádiz, ninth century for Carthage, it would seem that his revised estimates were too low, and the pendulum is swinging back up again. Two primary issues have emerged: first, that we should distinguish Phoenician activity in the Eastern Mediterranean from activity in the West, as it would seem the former preceded the latter by several centuries; and second, that Phoenician expansion into the West must be understood as occurring in several phases.

As far as the first issue is concerned, with recent excavations on Cyprus, particularly at Kition, historians have come to agree with the original formulation of Emil Forrer that Classical sources may have inadvertently erred in attributing early foundation dates to Carthage (*karthadasht*, literally, 'new city' in Phoenician) by confusing it with an installation of the same name on Cyprus.[22] Indeed, an entire colloquium devoted to aspects of Phoenician activity in the Eastern Mediterranean has underscored this issue.[23] With evidence now for not only an inscribed Phoenician bowl on Crete, but an actual installation and shrine near Kommos on the southeastern coast dated to the tenth century, we can certainly speak of a presence very early in the first millennium B.C.[24] Shaw has wondered whether the coastal installation might not have served as a staging platform for trips into the interior;[25] however, in a world of coastal sailing, where port anchorage is frequent, it is equally important to see such installations as possible links in a chain of landfalls. What is particularly satisfying about the new Cretan finds is how well they fit with the Homeric image in the story invented by Odysseus (*Odyssey* 13.256ff., cited above) of a Phoenician ship sitting off the coast of Crete that agreed to take him to Pylos, but got blown off course to Ithaca; or the later reference (*Odyssey* 14.300) to a course between the Phoenician coast and Libya passing to the windward (i.e., along the north shore) of Crete, where the ship foundered in a storm.

Such stories illustrate the hazards of Mediterranean sailing, although we still have a lot to learn about the limits and possibilities of oar-driven sailing ships. While

Crete could well have been a staging point en route to North Africa or other Western locations, no systematic study of trade winds, sailing patterns, or intervals between landfalls has yet been undertaken of the sort incorporated into popular reenactments of ancient voyages[26] that would permit archaeologists to reconstruct likely itineraries with any assurance. The relatively few inquiries into sailing conditions by archaeologists and ancient historians add elements of the picture, and attest to generally counterclockwise currents and prevailing wind patterns, hence circuits, in both the Western and the Eastern Mediterranean.[27] Nevertheless, what does seem evident is that Phoenician activity may have been contained within the Eastern Mediterranean for some time before moving westward toward Spain, Italy, and even Carthage, since archaeological evidence to date cannot support a presence in the West before the early eighth century B.C.[28]—an historical situation which becomes relevant when discussing the degree to which second or first millennium conditions govern context in the Homeric epics.

On the second issue, Niemeyer has distinguished three developmental phases of Phoenician expansion to the West: an early, "seafaring" phase, in which sources of metal and markets were identified and began to be exploited; a middle, "settlement" phase, in which permanent Phoenician installations were established in proximity to sources and markets; and a third, "impact" phase, in which Phoenician/Oriental "influence" was absorbed and became evident in the material produce and cultural patterns of local populations in contact with Phoenician goods and settlers.[29] These distinctions are useful for an understanding of the dynamics of Phoenician penetration of the West, and a number of recent studies have presented archaeological data in support of one or another of the phases.[30]

Although all of the references to Phoenicians in the *Iliad* or the *Odyssey* seem to be confined to the first phase of simple, itinerant "seafaring," this in itself constitutes neither historical evidence *per se* nor evidence for the date of the texts. For, despite the apparent "fit" between Homeric references to the Phoenicians and extratextual data—largely in the realm of individual details—there are a number of missing dimensions that speak to the lack of historical transparency between phenomenon and textual representation. The larger picture resulting from additional textual and archaeological data is not touched upon in either the *Iliad* or the *Odyssey*, and must be accounted for before we can hope to understand Homer's Phoenicians.

References to Sidon as a developed port city into which Paris sailed en route to Troy (*Iliad* 6.290–291)—where Menelaos was given hospitality en route home after the war (*Odyssey* 15.118–119), and whose king was an equal, integrated into the elite gifting network of his times (ibid.)—imply a highly developed urban polity with complex sociopolitical organization. This is corroborated by other attributes associated with urbanization and the state, such as the keeping of annals and historical records—a practice that is well known for the contemporary Assyrians and Babylonians. It is attested for the Phoenicians as well, preserved in both Pseudo-Aristotle (*De Mirabilibus* 134) and Josephus, who wrote: "For years, the people of Tyre have kept public records . . . of memorable events in their internal history and relations with foreign nations" (*Contra Apionem* i.106; also *Antiquitates Iudaicae* viii.146). Yet this picture is at variance with the rogue sailor-traders of Odysseus' invented and Eumaeus' autobiographical tales, who seem to operate entirely independently, within no sociopolitical hierarchy and answerable to no official oversight. Nevertheless, it is clear from Assyrian sources that trade was supervised by and under the control of the state, since it was with the ruler that Assyrians set terms of trade in the course of Assyrian political expansion. In a letter of the reign of Tiglath-Pileser III (745–724 B.C.), for example, Phoenician trade with Philistia and Egypt is ordered curtailed, the benefits to be channeled to Assyria; and in the treaty written by Esarhaddon with the ruler of Tyre, there is a lengthy elaboration of each king's rights to shipwrecks and access to ports along the Levantine coast.[31] In addition, there was an established system of weights maintained,[32] which equally speaks to a complex state organization. And finally, the complex balance of independent and official trading operations implied in the account of Ezekiel for the sixth century suggests a well-established system of long duration.[33]

We know little of how the production of luxury materials was organized, given the limited exposure of Phoenician sites and the lack of contemporary economic texts.[34] Objects attributed to Phoenician work are largely known from findspots outside of the homeland and assigned on the basis of stylistic arguments.[35] The two classes of works best preserved are metalwork and ivory carving, luxury goods of which the vast majority have been found as part of the treasuries of royal palaces like Nimrud and Khorsabad in Assyria, and Samaria in Israel. Various scenarios for their manufacture may be envisioned: i.e., made expressly for a ruler of a foreign state, as part of the tradition of royal gift-giving in the ancient Near East; made for a Phoenician ruler and presented as a gift from royal stores to a foreign court; or taken as booty from royal contexts during some military campaign. Unfortunately, however, it is rarely possible to demonstrate the agency of one or another of these mechanisms.

Due to the elite nature of the findspots, compounded by the lack of attention to excavation in nonelite quarters at most sites, the sample we have consists mainly of works of the very highest quality—comparable therefore to the silver mixing bowls described in the Homeric texts. This has given rise to some unfortunate chronologies—particularly concerning ivories—based upon assumptions that pieces of lesser quality found elsewhere must represent degenerate, provincial, and/or later work. Nevertheless, if one looks at the major collections (Samaria, for example, or Nimrud), it is very often the case that fairly crude, often incised works have been found along with pieces of superb craftsmanship, although they are frequently buried in publications and not fully studied in analyses.[36] This is important, for such pieces call for the reevaluation of Phoenician objects found in so-called provincial contexts. For example, the ivory objects known from various grave sites in the Guadalquivir River region of southwest Spain fall into the class of works of generally lesser quality, and so have often been assigned relatively late dates and considered as provincial products—either manufactured in Spain itself or coming from the colonies of Cádiz or Carthage.[37] If, however, it is possible to establish close parallels in technique, style, and iconography with works attributed to the Phoenician homeland,[38] then a very different picture emerges: one which suggests differential quality products aimed at specific markets and audiences. In the Spanish case, for example, the ivories can be seen as the coin of small luxury trade for a less-elite or less-discriminating populace than the rulers of Near Eastern states, more along the lines of the *athurmata* being carried by the traders of Eumaeus' tale.[39] It also leads to a far more complex picture of the Phoenician economy: one in which production was not monolithic, but rather complex and differentially geared to the different socioeconomic levels of consumers.[40]

With this more calibrated view of Phoenician goods, one begins to see the Homeric references as extremes in what was probably a graded continuum of production appropriate to targeted consumers. Thus, neither Eumaeus' *athurmata* nor Patroklos' bowl alone, nor indeed the two together as reductive exemplars, would do justice to the range of Phoenician production.

The Homeric references to Phoenician shipping also require some commentary. Clearly, some goods of high quality were moving by Phoenician carriers, as for example the bowl eventually acquired by Patroklos. When it was initially given to Thoas, we are told, "men of the Phoenicians brought it over the murky deep, and landed it in harbor . . ." (*Iliad* 23.744ff.). By contrast, the goods carried by the Phoenician ship in Eumaeus' tale are implied to have been of minor consequence. In no case is mention made of metals or other raw materials being carried as part of large-scale trade. Yet, even if we cannot assume the application to the eighth/seventh century of the later, sixth-century biblical account of the complex, multileveled trade of Tyre,[41] we can bracket the period by reference to the two Late Bronze Age shipwrecks—Cape Gelidonya and Ulu Burun—that also included metal ingots and other raw materials along with finished goods of a range of quality and value.[42] Now, the author/narrator of the *Odyssey* is not ignorant of the seagoing traffic in metals in the period, since Athena presents herself in disguise to Telemachus (*Odyssey* 1.156ff.) as an "oar-loving" Taphian merchant en route to "Temesse," carrying "shining iron" to exchange for copper (*Odyssey* 1.184).[43] It is well established from other sources that the primary basis for Phoenician maritime activity was the acquisition of metals.[44] In addition, we now have good archaeological corroboration that Phoenicians were exploiting the silver sources of the Riotinto mines in Spain by the period in which the *Odyssey* would have been written down.[45]

There are at least two ways to view the absence of any reference to the metals trade in Homeric references to the seafaring Phoenicians. First, there may have been more than one class of Phoenician trading vessel plying the Mediterranean: ships with extensive inventories including raw materials touching at major ports, while others, with more limited inventories, doing the rounds of smaller, less resource-rich ports like Syriē, the home island of Eumaeus, and Ithaca, to which he was brought. Second, however, it is possible that the Homeric picture is a reductive one. Since we are told nothing of the prospective cargoes of either Odysseus' fictive Phoenicians anchored off Crete or his fictive Phoenician trader setting off for Libya, I am inclined to the opinion that information has been provided (and/or omitted) as and when it suits narrative purposes, rather than in an attempt to be historically accurate and comprehensive, and therefore the shipload of *athurmata* should not be taken as documentary evidence for the general nature of Phoenician cargoes in the period.

The variety of type and range of value of Phoenician goods that turn up in the votive deposits of Greek sanctuaries like Samos, Ephesus, and Olympia further supports the existence of varied cargoes.[46] While it is impossible to know for certain who was carrying and depositing these objects, Gunther Kopcke has suggested that it is not accidental that most of these sanctuaries were on the coast and had access from the sea, their deposits probably representing some sort of ritualized propitiation of the gods with a portion of one's cargo and/or selected objects acquired en route.[47] Further evidence that religious preoccupations were merged with early practices of navigation can be seen in the various coastal sanctuaries attributed to the Phoenicians—on the coast of Crete, in Carthage prior to the formation of the colony (as argued by Frézouls), on Kythera according to Herodotus (1.105), and on the Moroccan coast near Lixus before the founding of Cádiz according to Pliny (*NH* 19.63).[48] Such practice seems only too necessary when one thinks of the risks attendant upon seafaring and the agency ascribed to the gods with respect to natural phenomena in the texts we have been considering. Both risk and divine agency are vividly described by Odysseus for his fictive voyage with the Phoenician captain past Crete. They are also reflected in Phoenician invocations against destruction at sea, and in the curses at the end of the Esarhaddon treaty with Tyre, where the Assyrian king declares that if the terms of the treaty are broken, "may [the Phoenician gods] . . . raise an evil wind against your ships . . . may a strong wave sink them in the sea and a violent tide [rise up] against you."⁴⁹

Striking by its absence is any reference in either the *Iliad* or the *Odyssey* to Niemeyer's second phase of Phoenician penetration into the Western Mediterranean: the establishment of permanent colonies. Yet the current evidence for the founding of Carthage suggests that, however the traditional date of 814 B.C. may be challenged, an installation was in place by at least the second half of the eighth century B.C.—that is, by the time the Homeric poems were beginning to be fixed as texts.⁵⁰ The duplicitous Phoenician captain's intended expedition to Libya cannot be used to imply an awareness of the Greek colony at Naukratis, and thereby a mid-seventh century *terminus post quem* for the text (consistent with the recorded foundation date), since recent excavations on Bates Island off the Egyptian/Libyan coast suggest that individuals from the more eastern Mediterranean—Cypriotes and possibly Cretans and Mycenaeans—were touching there already in the Late Bronze Age.⁵¹ However, the locations traditionally associated with the stories of Calypso, the Land of the Lotus Eaters, Scylla and Charybdis, etc., put Odysseus in his wanderings on the coast of North Africa and in the area of Sicily immediately east and north of the Carthage colony.⁵² Whether the lack of mention is a case of the Homeric author recognizing that Carthage was a relatively new installation and so anachronistic in his tale of Mycenaean Greeks, or whether he simply chose to ignore it as it did not pertain to his narrative needs, we cannot say. Nevertheless, the omission of any Phoenician, or indeed Greek, colonial activity is striking, and can only be explained as driven by literary ends.

One final component in this picture of the purposeful reduction of Phoenician activities is the evidence from other sources for commercial and maritime competition between Phoenicians and others in the period. Archaeological evidence, while circumstantial, is suggestive. For both metalwork and ivory carving, distribution patterns of Phoenician and North Syrian goods of the ninth–seventh centuries B.C.—when not found mixed in elite contexts as the result of high-level, eclectic acquisition, as in the Assyrian palaces—can be shown to be quite distinct, reflecting separate spheres of influence

and activity.⁵³ A possible conclusion to be drawn from this pattern is that Phoenician and North Syrian city-states guarded access to resources and to markets. Such a conclusion is further supported by evidence of a Phoenician presence in Cilicia, which can be argued to represent an alternate route to the metal (particularly iron) resources of eastern Anatolia, the inland routes being controlled by North Syrian states.⁵⁴

Of relevance here is whether or not one can posit Phoenician competition with Greece in the same period. Aubet-Semmler has argued that such competition was not operative in the eighth century.⁵⁵ In part, her argument is based upon the presence of relatively large numbers of Phoenician goods found in the Greek colony of Pithekoussai along with "non-Greek" type burials (suggesting a mixed population of resident Phoenicians and Greeks) and of Greek ceramics in Phoenician sites, particularly in Spain.⁵⁶ She suggests that only after the Phoenician establishment of the colony at Gades (Cádiz) in the seventh century were there attempts to close access to the Atlantic route and maintain a monopoly on Spanish metals.

Later Classical sources do refer to a climate of competition existing between Phoenicians and Greeks in the Mediterranean. In Strabo, for example, mention is made of the closeness with which Phoenician sources of metal were guarded—one captain actually running his ship aground rather than allow it to be followed to Cádiz (3.5.11). While one could argue that this state of competitive relations is typical only of later periods, I think one must first challenge Aubet's premise that the presence of goods of mixed origin necessarily reflects co-operation and precludes competition. Humphreys, for example, speaks of competitors meeting in "open" ports of trade.⁵⁷ Important to examine would be whether the very fact of seafaring under Mediterranean conditions of frequent landfalls and windward circuits predisposes ship cargoes to reflect finished goods from multiple places of origin, collected sequentially en route, as described in the account of Eumaeus and as actually reflected in the materials found on both the Cape Gelidonya and Ulu Burun wrecks, at the same time as special contracts and exclusive access to raw materials would be maintained when possible. If so, then the mixture of goods at sites like Pithekoussai would not necessarily reflect cooperative ventures. Studies of the distribution of subtypes of Late Geometric pottery have led to the proposition of intense competition between regions within Greece in Mediterranean trade and the establishment of colonies in the same period, resulting in alliances that ultimately divided and cut across regions.[58] There is every logical reason to believe therefore that access to important markets and resources would have been jealously guarded wherever possible, and that a dynamic of commercial competition would have been operative between Greeks and Phoenicians in the period as well.[59]

Yet there is no overt reference to such competition in the Homeric texts; rather, Phoenician and Greek sailors seem to operate in parallel fashion, often with similar epithets and descriptions of vessels applied to both (on which, see below). It is here that questions of the date of "Homer," and particularly of the *Odyssey* as a written text, intrude upon the discussion. It *could* be that the text was written prior to active competition between the two groups, thus reflecting accurately the current historical conditions of contemporary Mediterranean maritime life. But, since I would question Aubet's and Coldstream's constructs in any case, and find it difficult to believe that there would *not* have been some degree of competition operative in the Mediterranean sea trade, it could just as well be that the text—whether attributed to the eighth, the seventh, or even the sixth century— simply omits an important aspect of contemporary life for its own purposes.

In sum, then, the picture of Phoenician shipping in the Mediterranean reconstructable from archaeological and historical evidence is one that includes complex urban organization and production in the homeland, a high degree of state control, varied cargoes and sophisticated targeting of differing socioeconomic markets, extensive coastal installations along routes, the establishment of permanent settlements as "daughter"-colonies, and a strong likelihood of competitive interactions with neighboring communities. Yet, substantial parts of this picture were not incorporated into the various Homeric references to Phoenician goods and sailors. "Historical accuracy" is therefore partial at best, and seems to parallel closely what Baslez has found for the later fourth and third centuries: that Phoenician activity in economic

and social spheres is far more varied and nuanced than is suggested by Greek sources.[60]

As for "ethnographic accuracy," if we distinguish the events and sociopolitical structures of history from cultural and personal details related to experience, then nowhere do we find evidence of direct informants serving as spokespersons for the culture (as *is* the case for Herodotus 2.113–120).[61] Observations of behavior and activities that might be appropriate to ethnography are reduced to stereotyped character traits—greed, craft, duplicitousness, etc.—and made to stand for national or cultural practice. As a result, both individual references to Phoenicians in the *Iliad* and the *Odyssey*, as well as the overall picture of Phoenicians in the two texts, seem flattened and one-dimensional, thereby supporting the argument that the references serve a narrative rather than a documentary purpose. As Auerbach observed of the *Odyssey* years ago, what is foregrounded is what we need to know to meet the requirements of the text.[62]

If we conclude that the Phoenicians of the *Iliad* and the *Odyssey* do not represent three-dimensional historic or ethnographic entities, the question arises of how to account for the picture(s) drawn. In the following portion of this paper, I would like to consider two aspects of that question: first, a double-pronged inquiry into the role the Phoenicians can be seen to play within the texts, along with an analysis of the narrative goals of those portions of the text in which Phoenicians appear, that would account for the way they were represented; and second, a consideration of the role the Homeric texts themselves may be said to have played within the larger context of eighth/seventh-century Greece, the presumed time of their writing.

LITERARY TROPE

Once it is established that our picture of the Phoenicians as historical and cultural entities does not map perfectly over their representation in the *Iliad* and the *Odyssey*, one may begin to examine the degree to which those traits that are represented are consistent and functional in terms of textual strategy. At the same time, it is important to note that the Phoenicians *were* in fact an historically attested, "real" people, as opposed to the invented Taphians and Phaeacians who also appear in various episodes, and therefore it is important also to keep in mind that the partial verisimilitude of the Phoenicans' associated traits and practices may be relevant in understanding their role in the narrative.

The combination of reduced roles and repetitive portrayals lends itself well to the distinction made in the analysis of literary texts between a "trope" and general terms of description. The trope is generally reliant upon traditional associations, and is manifest in repeated and formulaic usage for purposes of definition or characterization;[63] the particular attribute or element may well be apt, but it also has been selected to stand for a larger bundle of meaning. Tropes easily become equated with stock phrases, therefore, and are often applied as repeated adjectival modifiers of substantives. At the same time, the substantive itself can serve as a trope for some quality or collection of qualities with respect to the overall narrative. It is my point here that both the epithets applied to Phoenicians and the Phoenicians themselves can best be understood as tropes in the Homeric poems.

Perhaps the best etymology for the term is reflected in one of the epithets applied to Odysseus, *polutropos* (*Odyssey* 10.331), literally, 'he of much turning'—i.e., wily, 'he of many *devices*.' The epithet underscores the consciously applied nature of the literary "trope": a device deployed in the text in the service of strategic ends. A discussion of the use of *tropoi* in the *Odyssey* as a whole is undertaken by Pucci, who sees the use of the word *polutropos* in the opening line of the poem, although not explicitly associated with Odysseus at that point, as anticipating the hero who will be not only a man of many devices, but of many *turns* of language.[64] Indeed, this first line sets the stage for the very argument I would make—that troping as a device is being consciously applied by the poet, and fully acknowledged to his audience from the outset.

A number of qualities are repeatedly ascribed to Phoenicians in the *Iliad* and the *Odyssey*: masters of craft production, particularly in metalwork and textiles; possessed of black (dark) ships; sea-loving; avaricious; deceitful. What is striking is that virtually all of the neutral or positive descriptive terms associated with them are also found applied to others. Thus, Hephaistos (*Iliad* 19.367–383) or any (Greek) craftsman taught by him (*Odyssey* 6.232–234) is equally "skilled in

metalwork." Telemachos' ship as he travels to Pylos and Sparta is also 'black/dark' (*nēa melainan*; *Odyssey* 2.430), as were the ships of the Phaeacians who carry Odysseus to Ithaca and Odysseus' own ship in his recounting of his adventures (*Odyssey* 8.34, 445; 10.332)—suggesting that the designation is generic, not typologically specific to Phoenician vessels (and could reflect either a class of vessel or a standard term of description related to features such as the weathered color of the timbers, or pitch caulking on the exterior).

Parallels with the Phaeacians are especially significant in establishing the literary construction of the Phoenicians. The two groups share a number of attributes in addition to their black ships. Phaeacians, too, are 'famed for their ships' (*nausiklutoi*; *Odyssey* 7.39; 8.191, 369); and, as their men are skilled in seafaring, so their women, like the Sidonian nurse of Eumaeus, are skilled in fair handiwork (7.108–111).

But here the similarities cease. The Phaeacians are called heroes (7.44); their women are virtuous; they observe all of the proper customs of honoring guests with banqueting and gifts (8.61, 387ff.); their poets sing, as presumably Homer sang, of glorious deeds (8.73); some of their sailors may be crude of speech (6.273–275), but they are neither greedy (*trōktai*) nor devious (*polupaipaloi*); and they do not give false counsel. In brief, they manifest all of the social values that the Phoenicians negate by their actions.[65]

Nowhere is the contrast more clear, albeit subtly drawn, than between the Phoenicians and Odysseus himself. While Odysseus has long been identified as a sort of trickster throughout the *Iliad* and the *Odyssey*,[66] his artifice and his various stratagems do not cross the line into dishonorable deceit, as do the acts of Phoenicians. Many English translations blur the distinctions by using the same words for both ("greedy," "wily," "crafty"); but in the Greek texts, even when playing upon similar characteristics, a careful separation of terms and epithets is maintained.

Odysseus eats and drinks greedily, but the term used is *harpaleōs* (*Odyssey* 14.110), not *trōktēs*. When he is being cunning, he is *polumētis*, 'of many wiles' (8.412, 474; 13.382, etc.), a quality in fact shared with the goddess Athena (13.299); but he is never *polupaipalos*, 'crafty' in the sense of duplicitous. When he practices guile, as in the episode of the Trojan Horse (8.492–495) or the tricking of Polyphemus (9.408), or as he is described by Athena (13.292f.), the word applied to him is *dolos*, not the *apatēlia eidōs* of Odysseus' treacherous Phoenician (14.288). And in the end, in sharp contrast with the false counseling (*pseudea bouleusas*) of that same Phoenician, Odysseus is 'best of all men in counsel,' *aristos hapantōn boulēi* (13.297–298). So, while Odysseus may play the role of a trickster, the subtlety of the text is that while some apparent characteristics of guile and artifice are shared with Phoenicians described in the *Odyssey*, Odysseus himself never stoops to behavior that violates Greek social codes. A variation on this situation is discussed by Pucci, where the same epithet is applied to both Achilles and Odysseus, *ptoliporthos*, 'sacker of cities,' but where "the sameness of the signifier masks a difference of the signified." [67] Between Odysseus and the Phoenicians, by contrast, social value is coded by a separation in descriptive terms, in order to underscore the nuanced differences in some of what could otherwise be understood as overlapping behavioral characteristics.

The line observed by Odysseus in his trickery is very important, for I believe we cannot fully understand the role played by the Phoenicians in the Homeric epics, particularly the *Odyssey*, unless we factor into it the character and role of Odysseus himself. As Nagy has shown,[68] if the contrasting heroes of the *Iliad* and the *Odyssey* are Achilles, possessed of *biē* ('heroic strength or force'), and Odysseus, possessed of *mētis* ('craft, artifice'), respectively, then the task of the later poem is to validate Odysseus' qualities as equally, if not more, heroic. It is a testimony to the careful construction of the text that this theme is played out in a number of places. When Odysseus recounts his successful escape from Polyphemus, for example, he has the monster assert through direct speech that he is being slain by 'guile' (a major attribute of Odysseus') 'and not by force' (*dolōi oude biēphin*, *Odyssey* 9.408–409). And when Odysseus meets Achilles in Hades (*Odyssey* 11.489–491), the hero of the *Iliad* asserts that he would relinquish his glory, achieved by *biē*, to be alive. In the discussion of this passage by Nagy,[69] it is made clear that only Odysseus' *mētis* will permit both glory *and* a safe return home.

Olson has pursued this distinction in his discussion of Odysseus' cleverness and guile pitted against the violence of other heroes, emphasizing the consistent binary play in the Homeric text.[70] I would suggest that the Phoenicians also play a part in this structure. Rather than seeing it only in terms of a single binary opposition, it is possible to see Odysseus as centered between extremes: he is clever, and thereby victorious, with respect to the too-violent; at the same time, he is noble, and thereby heroic, with respect to the too-wily and deceitful.

While the character of Odysseus can be contrasted to that of the Phoenicians, it is possible to observe deep structural similarities between the descriptions of Phoenicians and those of the Trojans. At the simplest level, both Troy and Sidon are rich in bronze, *polukhalkos* (*Iliad* 18.289). Trojans are also consumers of Phoenician luxury goods (6.290). The breaking of acceptable social codes by Paris in abducting Helen (as reproached by Hector, *Iliad* 6.281ff., 326ff.) is comparable to the various abductions attributed to Phoenicians. And the two areas are directly linked by the fact that Paris stopped in Sidon on the same journey that brought Helen to Troy (*Iliad* 6.290–292).

In this linkage of the luxury goods of the Phoenicians with the wealth of the Trojans, Wathelet sees also a deeper level of shared identification with the riches of Asia, riches that are ultimately corrupting.[71] What is more, the pairing of Trojans and Phoenicians helps to establish the opposition of both to Odysseus and the Greeks. In this respect, it is part of a well-attested pattern in later Greek literature, with respect not only to Phoenicians, but to Egyptians, Persians, Phrygians, and others as well: one of the ways in which "otherness" is established is through distinctions of barbarian from civilized.[72]

In the present case, the Phoenicians stand as foils against the positive character traits of the Phaeacians, the Greeks, and especially Odysseus. The Phaeacians, although similarly sea-loving, remain honorable in all dealings, while the Phoenicians break the social code by piracy and abduction. The Phoenicians are also foils for the character traits of Odysseus, representing the "evil" side of guile as opposed to the righteous and socially constructive. And they are linked with the other major "other," the Trojans, in shared qualities like the association with luxury goods, viewed with ambivalence by the Greeks. These carefully drawn traits, seen in the light of the equally carefully constructed parallelism of the two tales in which these traits are developed (the one invented by Odysseus in *Odyssey* 14 and that of Eumaeus in *Odyssey* 15), leave little doubt that what we are faced with is a highly selective and masterfully constructed system of representation woven into the text with clear narrative aims.

As Vernant has noted for the language of myth,[73] so also the language of epic draws upon concrete images. Thus, the historical identity of the Phoenicians adds weight and substance to their imagery. But these images are put in the service of a particular historical reality: in this case, a Greek reality. As such, despite the aptness of any particular detail, the Phoenicians of the *Iliad* and the *Odyssey* must be seen as neither historical nor ethnographic entities, but rather as well-crafted literary tropes.

Once the *facts* of troping and the narrative strategies served by the particular tropes are established, we can move to the second aspect of the question posed above: how to account for the way in which the Phoenicians are represented—particularly in view of how interwoven the whole Eastern Mediterranean was from at least the second millennium B.C. on, and how "oriental" we know Greece to have been, how great their cultural debts, in the first millennium.[74] Clearly, any attempt to "recover and understand the process of troping in another language"[75] calls for some inquiry into the role the text(s) might have played in the larger context of their originating culture.

A recent analysis of the *Odyssey* argues that the text served to socialize the ancient reader/listener to a series of institutions and values, including a political organization grounded in peace, prosperity, friendship with one's own people, and war with the enemy.[76] The problem as I see it, however, is the same for the classicist as for the Near Eastern archaeologist mining Homer for an understanding of the Phoenicians: to what extent are the values expressed in and by the text to be taken as transparent windows into the world of its times? It was evident fairly early on that the picture of the "towns" drawn by Homer is based upon incipient notions at least of the *polis*, and hence postdates developments of the Iron Age.[77] In the early days of matching Homeric description with archaeological evidence, the two worlds

of Homer were seen as interwoven throughout the text, and scholars tended to play elaborate games with which details were historically "accurate" for the Mycenaeans of the Late Bronze Age (the boars'-tusk helmet or the tower shield of Ajax) and which details were to be seen as relevant to his own period (i.e., the towns).[78] As Snodgrass has noted, however, it has become increasingly clear that the two phases are not as clearly divided as had been thought; there are some details that are neither Late Bronze Age nor specifically eighth century, but rather represent an "artificial amalgam of widely separated historical stages."[79] These last must be seen as the stuff of which literature is made: inventions that, while not implausible, essentially serve narrative, rather than historical, ends. Establishing which details or elements actually do have a place in history, and where, is obviously easier with respect to items of material culture, more difficult with respect to social attitudes and organization. For the early first millennium B.C. which concerns us here, we are working in the absence of contemporary historical documentation.[80] Nevertheless, significant progress has been made in the past decade, principally through methodological advances in the analysis of archaeological data, which will help us to come closer to a reconstruction of the period, and at the same time to avoid circularity by leaving the Homeric texts aside and basing a reconstruction upon independent evidence.

However the current debates concerning the dates of the Homeric texts and whether they represent a gradual process of taking shape or one-time dictation may ultimately be resolved,[81] it seems evident that the range of possibilities keeps us within the mid-eighth through the late seventh/early sixth centuries, corresponding archaeologically to the Middle/Late Geometric through the Orientalizing periods. Throughout this period, the most salient social and political feature is the rise and consolidation of the city-state, the *polis*, with all it entailed of social stratification, economic development, and cultural change.[82]

Stimulated by studies of state-formation and urbanization in the ancient Near East and elsewhere, a number of scholars have turned their attention to comparable processes in Greece.[83] These studies document the powerful forces of change operating in Greek society from the ninth through the seventh centuries—leading to greater bureaucratization of an increasingly centralized government, more rigid demarcation between strata in social hierarchies within towns, dominance of larger towns over smaller ones, the breaking up of old kinship bonds as the basis for power, and complex economic development.[84] This economic development includes the broadening of trade networks and the establishment of colonies, for which archaeological evidence has demonstrated a considerable degree of activity.[85] Concomitant with these social, political, and economic developments is the shift in organized warfare from an emphasis on individual combat to greater dependence on the strategic deployment of the phalanx, as well as significant developments in the religious sphere, including a new emphasis on pan-Hellenic sanctuaries.[86]

The eighth century B.C. is thought to mark an important watershed in the institutionalization of all of the above, with different regions of Greece following different paths toward complexity and statehood.[87] By the end of the seventh century, not only was the process of local state-formation relatively complete, but also there emerge complicated patterns of economic competition between city-states and ensuing regional alliances.[88] It is remarkable how *little* of this process is reflected in the Homeric epics. Indeed, Runciman's analysis of the period describes the world depicted in the epics as more like transitional "semi-states" with their preservation of leadership based to a greater extent on heroic prowess, personal bonds, and eloquence;[89] one cannot even call them "proto-states," in that the inevitable seeds of change leading to state-formation are not evident. In short, the epics are not at all a mirror of their time of composition.

Now, there are at least two ways to understand this: one, that our dates for the texts are wrong and the epics were fixed in an historical period before these social and political developments, reflecting the world *as it was*; or two, that the epics were contemporary with the new sociopolitical developments, but were consciously archaizing. I think we may dismiss the former, since all present evidence suggests that the Homeric texts did indeed come into being at the time of or subsequent to the developments enumerated above. If, then, we may assume purposive selection and conscious archaisms, I believe

it is important to focus not only on questions of verisimilitude, whether for past or present, but also on what ends such representative strategies may have served in the "present" of these texts.

An illuminating parallel to the situation of Homer with respect to the rise of the Greek city-state may be found in the comparable situation of the literature of Chrétien de Troyes with respect to the reorganization of social patterns that took place in northern France in the twelfth century A.C. In a most remarkable analysis by Eugene Vance,[90] it is argued that the elevation of the medieval knight to chivalric hero in romantic poetry in fact coincided with a period in which, in practical terms, the political, social, and military independence of these knights was being neutralized by urban forces within an increasingly centralized state. In literature, as in newly established public festivals like jousts, heroic action was acclaimed; but it was also confined and controlled—the shift from political action to romantic championship resulting in the *detachment* of the knight from immediate social and political involvement.

Many of the same factors we have observed in the development of the Greek state can be seen in twelfth-century France: greater social stratification; an increase in economic activity and commerce; changes in military tactics, including greater stress on infantry and less on individual combat; and the rise of an urban aristocracy that sought to authenticate its claims of nobility by locating its origins in the high deeds of a past heroic age.[91]

On the surface, Chrétien (like Homer) seems to ignore the social developments congruent with the trends of his own times toward urbanization. However, at the level of underlying code, he is in fact reinforcing those developments by a complex rhetorical strategy: transforming the aggressions of a former warrior elite into vicarious nostalgia, and in fact disempowering the "hero" while simultaneously elevating him rhetorically.[92]

Indeed, Vance suggests that there are strong parallels between the conditions underlying twelfth century France and those of the seventh-century B.C. Greek *polis* as reflected in Hesiod. I would suggest that the parallels are already visible in Homer, and already begin to be relevant in the eighth century. The jousts of which Vance speaks find a direct parallel in the establishment of the Olympic games, traditionally put in the first quarter of the eighth century (776 B.C.). Hoplite military organization, while somewhat later, is still well attested within the period of the likely formation of the Homeric texts that continue to glorify individual combat and the individual hero; and there is a marked absence of reference to what we know to have been contemporary economic developments and activities, which require collective, state-organized enterprises as opposed to individual actions.

Seen in this light, we must wonder whether the Homeric poems, rather than representing a justification of aristocratic powers in the face of the rising *polis*,[93] do not, like the lays of Chrétien de Troyes, actually represent a displacement, or at least a replacement of the hero, and heroic deeds, to a more golden (or silver!) age.

Such a perspective might well affect how we view the complex phenomenon of the establishment of "hero-cults" in Greece, which appear to have shown a significant increase in cultural investment during the period that concerns us here. These hero-cults, marked by worship at Bronze Age tomb sites or the inauguration of new shrines to Bronze Age/Homeric heroes, have been the subject of a good deal of recent discussion. The dominant view, held through the mid-1970s, was that interest in the hero-cults was the direct result of the dissemination of the Homeric poems. This has been challenged by Hadzisteliou-Price and especially by Snodgrass, who argues on artistic, archaeological, and philological grounds that the development of the cult both preceded and was independent of the epics.[94] The earlier dates seem to have been generally accepted, although the explanation of Snodgrass that the cults served the interests of a free peasantry has been seriously challenged. Instead, evidence seems to support a picture of regional differentiation, with multiple paths to state development and diverse roles for the hero-cults in different regions of Greece.[95] For Whitley, Attic hero-cults were supported in the outlying areas by Greeks opposed to the increasingly central power of Athens, while in the Argolid the same cults were an extension of central ideology; he nevertheless argues that support for the cult activities was politically motivated in both cases.[96] If we factor Vance's construct into the equation, however, and see such heroization as a conscious or unconscious strategy of displacement, then even the Attic

phenomenon could well be in the service of the "center"—providing rhetorical value and focus for behavior no longer socially useful while leaving the new social system focused on the urban core free to go about its business. Morris similarly distinguishes between Ionian and Dorian cult practice.[97] He suggests that the hero-cults could have been a way the old aristocracy, antagonistic to *polis* ideals, worked to maintain their traditional legitimacy. But again, I believe we must leave open, with the model of Chrétien in mind, the equally plausible scenario that, both hero-elevating texts and hero-cults in fact served the *polis*. I would certainly agree with Morris' plea for a plurality in the readings of text and cultic practices. At the same time, to his opposition of *either* "justify(ing) aristocratic powers in the face of the rising *polis*" in one place *or* helping to legitimate a new urban elite by asserting links with the past in another,[98] I would add that by displacing the former heroic tradition of independent action into the literary and ritual domain, such texts and cult practices would in fact serve the interests of the *polis* in *both* of his cases, and indeed fulfill both of his functions simultaneously, in some cases.

This perspective allows for a more nuanced reading of the early hero-cults, as well as of the Homeric texts. Once the primary concerns of the early state are established, we are forced, on additional grounds to those delineated by Snodgrass, to abandon the early hypothesis that the Homeric texts *caused* the cults, or that either texts or Olympic games served as major catalysts for the spread of the cults.[99] Rather, all of these phenomena—games, cults, and texts—would have sprung from the same social and cultural needs, and served the same social and cultural ends: the displacement of a former code of values and behavior into particular, rhetorical channels subject to containment, thereby permitting the development of a new code of values and behavior more appropriate to contemporary social and political developments.

In many respects, what I am suggesting echoes the analysis of Bérard, which linked "heroization" to the formation of the city (i.e., the city-state).[100] I am also suggesting, while at no time denying the powerful aesthetic and emotional impact of the poetic experience, that the codification of the Homeric poems may have been a fundamental part of this social process.[101]

This view fits especially well with the provocative conclusions arrived at by West in his recent study of the rise of the Greek epic. In a series of essentially linguistic and philological arguments, West concludes that the *Odyssey* in particular represents not an "eastern Ionian" composition, as has generally been thought, but rather a "central" (Euboean) or "western Ionian" (Attic) work.[102] Of these options, West and others tend to incline toward Euboea, which, with its high coefficient of social stratification and extensive commercial and colonial enterprises, best matches the profile of a region that *should* be producing the *Odyssey*.[103] This is particularly compelling if we see the epic, along with hero-cults and games, as the product of cultural processes congruent with early state-formation, in which heroic action and archaizing values are at once glorified and displaced onto a rhetorical plane, in order to make way for institutions and values more appropriate to new forms of sociocultural organization.

It is within this frame, I believe, that we can best account for the way in which Phoenicians are represented in the Homeric texts, especially the more negative characterizations of the *Odyssey*.

The complex social and commercial organization of the Phoenicians reconstructable historically for the period in which the epics would have been consolidated has been discussed at length above, and contrasted with the reductive picture contained in the texts. At the same time, it can be argued that the reality of the Phoenicians would have been well known to the Greeks of the period, with Phoenician cities possibly providing an external model to shape the internal developments leading to the Greek *polis*.[104] The borrowing and assimilation of artifact types, and the general impact of Phoenician and general Levantine art forms during this period, a phenomenon already occurring in the "Geometric" and clearly acknowledged in the naming of the "Orientalizing" period in Greece, can also be amply demonstrated.[105] It has even been suggested that not only Phoenician goods but Phoenicians themselves were resident in Euboea and Crete, as well as in the colony of Pithekoussai.[106] Certainly, the bronze-working implied in the very name of Chalkis in Euboea is reminiscent of the *polukhalkos* Phoenician, while the colonial and commercial activity of the newly formed Greek states paralleled closely that of the Phoenicians. Indeed, based on

demonstrable Near Eastern literary parallels, West has gone so far as to propose that the *Odyssey* itself should be seen in the context of a time when Greek culture as a whole received important new stimuli from the Levant.[107]

Yet, in the *Odyssey*, the commercial activies of the Phoenicians are either corrupting or corrupt; Phoenicians are described as willing to break codes of honor for profit, much as Levantine merchants have been stereotyped throughout history in the West; and their behavior is set up as the antithesis of the heroic values of the Greeks. In short, in the epic Odysseus is what "man" should be—successful warrior, survivor, obedient to the gods and the king he serves, wily, but faithful to the social code;[108] the Phoenician sailors are the "other"—makers and merchants as opposed to warriors, associated with no gods or family ties, deceitful, disrespectful of accepted codes of hospitality and friendship, unbound by social constraints. In contemporary social life, by contrast, the Phoenicians may well have been models for newly emerging Greek social roles; at the very least, they constituted significant parallels in mercantile activities and important sources for desirable goods.

I believe this analysis moves us a step closer to understanding the complex double role played by Homer's Phoenicians. On the one hand, they represent the "different and foreign" of the traditional enemy, and we must read them in terms of alterity;[109] on the other hand, they represent a projection of the social and economic present, the becoming "self," and we must read them with all of the ambivalence and discomfort, denial even, that contemporary Greeks must have felt about the changes their society was presently undergoing.

Two competing scenarios offer themselves as possible social contexts for the foregoing. If, with West, one sees the *Odyssey* as a Euboean product, the complexity described above makes perfectly good sense. Phoenicians were clearly known, as we see from the archaeological evidence at Lefkandi and at Pithekoussai, which was an early Euboean installation; yet at the same time, if Boardman is correct in seeing Euboeans with special interest at Al Mina, and I am correct in seeing Al Mina as outside of Phoenician control and a competing port for Near Eastern goods going into the Mediterranean,[110] then the picture of parallel and negative attributes, fraught with ambivalence, with which the Phoenicians have been represented would fit the historical situation quite well indeed. It would work best with a date for the text in the eighth century B.C., and in fact, it would be entirely consistent with West's argument for Euboean composition.

If, however, we leave open West's own possibility that the text could also have Attic ties, then the competition between Athens and Aigina in early trade becomes an equally interesting context for the poem. Sarah Morris has documented the seafaring skills of the islanders and their mercantile activities, along with the considerable number of Phoenician goods (including "lyre-player" seals) that turn up on the island, as well as the negative connotation of goods known as *aiginē-tika*—i.e., small trinkets circulated by island merchants.[111] These last bear a striking resemblance to the Phoenicians' *athurmata*, while the Aiginetan connection to Naukratis, in the direction of which Odysseus' fictive Phoenician sea captain was heading, is also notable. Indeed, Morris actually suggests that the qualities ascribed to the Aiginetans made them the Phoenicians of the Greek world.[112] The question then arises whether the qualities ascribed to "Phoenicians" might not actually represent a veiled reference to Aigina in an Attic composition. Such a construct would probably work best with a date for the text in the seventh century.

I must say that for the moment, I am more inclined toward the many consistencies evident in the "Euboean" scenario, not least of which is West's observation that hints of Euboeo-centricity are to be found in the reference to Euboea as the seafaring Phaeacians' furthest horizon (*Odyssey* 7.321–326); however, given the way in which later Athens claimed the poem, one could argue that Athens' investment goes back to the very fixing of the text.[113] Perhaps the next round of analysis must come from the philological side, toward a more precise dating and location of the final version of the text, before we can attempt to determine the best historical "fit" for its contents (see Nagy's essay in this volume).

In any case, wherever and over however long a period the *Odyssey* as poetic enterprise is to be located, good historical circumstances exist that would help account for the particular roles in which Phoenicians are cast. And the more limited and descriptive roles attributed to the Phoenicians in the *Iliad* also make sense if

that text continues to be seen as an essentially eastern Ionian product, consolidated sometime earlier than the *Odyssey*—when Anatolian Greeks could well have viewed the luxury-producing Phoenicians of the Eastern Mediterranean as a contemporary analogue for the earlier but equally eastern Trojans, yet without the added social charge of being in direct competition or identity conflct with them.[114] The differences in construction of the Phoenicians in the two texts thus falls into place as well.

In the end, it is the degree of constructedness that it so striking in the texts. At first, moved by the apparent verisimilitude of description, it is indeed tempting to read "The Phoenicians" from the poems, since there are "true" details presented. Then, as one gathers data, one begins to notice the absences: what is *not* being said also becomes revealing, and makes apparent those traits that have been reduced to formulaic stereotype in what *is* represented. Next, as one sees through comparison what elements and attributes are being set in opposition to the Phoenicians, their role as "other" emerges vis-à-vis a purported Greek ideal. But it is only when the sociocultural context is explored as well, that an even subtler role of ambivalent "self" is manifest in Greek attitudes toward the Phoenicians.

How the "self" is culturally constituted with respect to the identification of, *with*, and against an "other" is currently a topic of widespread intellectual attention. Representing the other as opposite—and particularly, as exoticized, sensualized, savage, irrational opposite—is the better understood of these strategies.[115] Ribichini applied the principle directly to the representation of Phoenicians in Classical sources, observing a general pattern, from Homer to Herodotus, of characterizing in the negative all surrounding populations, which was itself part of a larger cultural design of recuperation and control of the social environment.[116] Tamara Green has suggested that the creation of the "other" in texts like the Homeric epics was a way for Greeks to assert their own view of cultural norms.[117] This is also the theme of the recent book of François Hartog, *The Mirror of Herodotus*, the subtitle of which, *The Representation of the Other in the Writing of History*, implies his agenda of cultural constitution.[118] And yet, the ambiguities inherent in the issue should not be obscured. Perhaps the clearest exposition is to be found in Todorov's study of the conquest of America, in which he first defines "the other" as ". . . exterior to interior . . . female to male . . . poor to rich . . . crazy to normal . . . or another society to one's own . . . near or far . . . on the cultural, moral or historical level" and then argues that, in fact, to identify the "exterior" is to discover the "other" in oneself.[119] It is useful to consider, therefore, whether in the Homeric texts as well it is in relation to the "other" that the ideal "self" is both defined and integrated. In such a view, the Phoenicians would represent what the Greeks need to socialize, what they fear most to be in the new social order, and what they are most mindful of becoming.

A long-standing enmity between Greece and the peoples of Asia is observed by Ribichini in Herodotus and Thucydides as well as in Homer. In this perpetuation of a traditional "other" we see the seeds of an early "orientalism," so powerfully raised with regard to classical scholarship by Bernal,[120] and responded to in the recent publications of Sarah Morris. One of Morris' principal points is that it is not only classical scholarship in the recent West, but the Classical Greeks themselves, who evinced discomfort in acknowledging, and so often obscured, their enormous debts to the Levant, at the same time as they absorbed, and even admired, so many of its goods and traditions.[121]

I would stress that this pattern can be seen already in the Homeric treatment of the Phoenicians. It should probably come as no surprise that an "Orientalizing" period should be one most prone to "orientalism." From Said's important study of 1979 to its myriad offshoots,[122] it is clear that a powerful component of orientalism is the attribution of the exotic, of luxury, and even of transgression to a putative "East"—an East constituted in an amalgam of both knowledge and prejudice, in which exoticism and xenophobia, constraint and desire, consumption and denial combine to tell us a great deal more about the "constructing" culture than about the constructed.

Such a pattern is all the more to be expected at critical junctures of nation- or, in this case, *state*-building. It should also not be lost sight of that for the Greeks, the period of state-building happened to coincide with a period of intensive mercantile development and colonization. In addition to all of the issues discussed thus far, the very fact of the Phoenicians' status in that mercantile

world, as well as their already established colonies and mobility as seafarers, needs to be kept in focus. The composite picture presented in the *Odyssey* of the Phoenician king of Sidon acting according to proper rules of behavior, but his people on the seas clearly not observing the rules, leads one to wonder whether this is not an expression of the trepidation the Greeks must have felt anticipating the dispersal of their own population into the colonies and onto the seas of commerce. Seen through the lens of a nostalgia not only for the past but for the integrity of the "homeland," the particular state of Greek social (colonial) and economic, not just political, development becomes a significant factor in the representation of Phoenicians in the Homeric epics.[123]

Those texts most associated with national "identity" at a time of state-building, such as national myths of origin or epics, often contain highly developed expressions of the constitutive signs conveying "belonging" and "collective values."[124] In such texts, as in the construction of a national or civic identity itself, the oppositions of civilized vs. barbaric, law-based vs. lawless, fair vs. treacherous come to stand for the choices the socialized "citizen" must make in order to belong, and in order for the society to function.[125] This perspective helps us to read the Homeric construct of honor (and its opposites, shame and dishonor) at the explicit level within the text, and to see the representation of the Phoenicians with respect to Odysseus in particular, and Greeks in general, as a way of articulating Greek values. At the same time, if we understand nationalism, or state-ism, as a social process maintained at least in part by *not* articulating all of its political ideologies, but rather through allying itself with (an often fabricated) "tradition" that preceded it,[126] then the casting of a national text into a heroic past can be seen as part of the very process of state-formation.

Vance's understanding of the texts of Chrétien de Troyes helps to make clear that much can be happening at the nonexplicit level in providing channels or detours for collective energies. By his account, the "really vital problems that arise as the poetic mind reacts to change are expressed *beneath the narrative or thematic surface of a work*."[127] For this reason, at the most general level, any work that we call "literary" is by definition "suspect as a document of history."[128] And in particular, as noted by Runciman, "the *Odyssey* as a work of fiction is a poor guide to the sociological realities of contemporary Greece."[129]

That the *Iliad* and the *Odyssey* are indeed "literary" constructs will come as no surprise to literary historians and classicists; but the point must be underscored for those who have optimistically sought to read "history" therein. To come to grips with the full complexity of the representational strategies involved in Phoenicians-astrope in both the *Odyssey* and the *Iliad*, it is necessary to pursue not only an internal analysis of how they function structurally within the texts, but also an external analysis of how the texts themselves functioned in their contemporary world. Only with such an external analysis do the issues of purposeful selectivity, alterity, and "orientalism" take on a full complement of meaning.

Less a mirror of their time than a deflector, the Homeric texts elevate an ideal of the warrior-hero at the very moment that Greeks were embarking upon mercantile ventures not unlike those of the very Phoenicians whom the texts disparage. If we see the heroic ideal—of Odysseus no less than of Achilles—as a displacement, a detour around current social realities, and see the Phoenicians in terms at once of grudging respect for quality in manufacture, contempt with regard to social values, powerful ambivalence in commercial practice, and suspicion regarding the consequences of dispersal and mobility, then virtually all aspects of the way in which the Phoenicians are represented in the *Iliad* and the *Odyssey* can be accounted for. "Homer's Phoenicians," then, do not represent the world of the Phoenicians; rather, they present a masterful literary construct, at once produced by and working *to* produce the broader social, political, economic, and symbolic fabric of the early state in Archaic Greece.

NOTES

*My debts to the editors of this volume, Jane Carter and Sarah Morris, are enormous, as they are to Jülide Aker, Henry Immerwahr, Greg Nagy, and Frederick Winter—all of whom have worked hard to keep my zeal in check and my errors of transliteration from the Greek under control. Emily Vermeule helped on a number of occasions as well; I trust she now understands why she did not get the whole manuscript to read! I am grateful to all of the above for the richness of our exchanges; they are absolutely not responsible for any howlers that may have managed to intrude in the text. The Loeb Classical Library bilingual editions of the *Iliad* and the *Odyssey* have been used for all text citations (trans. by A. T. Murray [Cambridge, Mass., 1924–1925 and 1919, resp.]).

1. I. J. Winter, "The Carmona Ivories and the Phoenicians in Spain," (M.A. thesis, Univ. of Chicago, 1966)—presented as a talk at the annual meetings of the AIA, December 1970, an abstract of which was published in *AJA* 75 (1971) 217.

2. See on this the general discussions in J. D. Muhly, "Homer and the Phoenicians: The Relations between Greece and the Near East in the Late Bronze and Early Iron Age," *Berytus* 19 (1970) 19–64, and P. Wathelet, "Les phéniciens et la tradition homerique," in E. Gubel et al., eds., *Studia Phoenicia* I/II: *Sauvons Tyr/Histoire phénicienne* (Leuven 1983) 235–243.

3. C. Zaccagnini, *Lo scambio dei doni nel Vicino Oriente* . . . (Rome 1973). See also, T. O. Beidelman, "Agonistic Exchange: Homeric Reciprocity and the Heritage of Simmel and Mauss," *Cultural Anthropology* 4 (1989) 227–259, esp. 231, 244, 250, for the importance of exchange in Greek tradition specifically. Beidelman's point is that exchange is a central mechanism by which social relationships, and thereby the social self, are established, so that with *whom* gifts are exchanged is important.

4. R. Carpenter, "Phoenicians in the West," *AJA* 62 (1958) 35–54, esp. 35.

5. See especially W. Röllig, "Die Phönizier des Mutterlandes zur Zeit der Kolonisierung," in H.-G. Niemeyer, ed., *Phönizier im Westen*, (MM Beih. 8) (Mainz 1982) 15–30. See also the various essays in the catalogue of the major exhibition on the Phoenicians that took place at the Palazzo Grassi, Venice: S. Moscati, ed., *The Phoenicians* (New York 1988).

6. See on this Muhly (supra n. 2); C. Baurain, "Portées chronologiques et géographiques du terme 'Phénicien'," in C. Bonnet et al., eds., *Studia Phoenicia* IV: *Religio-Phoenicia* (Namur 1986) 7–28; and now M. Kochavi, "Some Connections between the Aegean and the Levant in the Second Millennium B.C.: A View from the East," in G. Kopcke and I. Tokumaru, eds., *Greece between East and West: 10th–8th Centuries B.C.*, (Mainz 1992) 7–15. For relatively recently excavated material that bridges the second and first millennia, see the catalogue of an exhibition in Saarbrücken: R. Hachmann, ed., *Frühe Phöniker im Libanon: 20 Jahre deutsche Ausgrabungen in Kāmid el-Lōz* (Mainz am Rhein 1983).

7. The collective term "Kings of the Seacoast" is used extensively in Neo-Assyrian texts, see for example A. K. Grayson, *Assyrian Royal Inscriptions* II (Toronto 1976) para. 586. The sources are reviewed in G. Kestemont, "Tyr et les Assyriens," in E. Gubel et al., eds. (supra n. 2) 53–78. Attempts have been made to define the southern and northern limits of this area. Essential for our purposes is that the area seems to extend only as far as Arwad in the north, and distinctly not as far as the mouth of the Orontes, thus leaving the port of Al-Mina out of Phoenician territory (contra A. J. Graham, "The Historical Interpretation of Al-Mina," *DHA* 12 [1986] 51–65).

8. H. J. Katzenstein, *The History of Tyre from the Beginning of the 2nd Millennium BCE until the Fall of the Neo-Babylonian Empire in 538 BCE* (Jerusalem 1973).

9. See in particular P. Bikai, *The Pottery of Tyre* (Warminster 1978); J.-P. Thalmann, "Tell 'Arqa (Liban Nord): Campagnes I–III (1972–1974)," *Syria* 55 (1978) 1–152; R. Saidah, "Archaeology in the Lebanon, 1968–9," *Berytus* 18 (1969) 122, for a small site near Sidon; J. LaGarce, "Rapports de Ras Ibn Hani avec la Phénicie et la Mediterranée orientale à L'Age du Fer," in P. Bartolini and S. F. Bondi, eds., *Atti del I. Congresso Internazionale di studi fenici e punici* (Rome 1983) 223–226; and M. W. Prausnitz, "Die Nekropolen von Akhziv und die Entwicklung der Keramik von 10. bis zur 7. Jahr. v. Chr. in Akhziv, Samarra und Ashdod," in Niemeyer, ed. (supra n. 5) 31–44.

We now know that the Greek Geometric pottery chronology is in need of revision, and that synchronisms are fraught with difficulty (see E. D. Francis and M. Vickers, "Greek Geometric Pottery at Hama and its Implications for Near Eastern Chronology," *Levant* 17 [1984] 131–138, for example). Nevertheless, the mixed contexts at least give us established points of co-occurrence. Two dissertations are presently under way on materials from Near Eastern sites of the Early Iron Age that should help to clarify matters: one by Karen Bradley at the University of Chicago on pottery found at the Amuq sites in northern Syria; the other by Amelie Beyhum at Harvard University on pottery from the site of Tell es-Saidiyeh in Lebanon. In both cases, red-slip wares traditionally thought of as "Phoenician," but which may well be simply generic Levantine, are found mixed with both Cypriot and Greek imports. The stratigraphic control of these materials should serve to increase our knowledge of the development of red-slip ware itself and also of the synchronisms with other pottery types.

10. Cf. I. J. Winter, "Phoenician and North Syrian Ivory Carving in Historical Context: Questions of style and distribution," *Iraq* 38 (1976) 1–22; E. Gubel, "Art in Tyre during the First and Second Iron Age: A preliminary survey," in Gubel et al., eds. (supra n. 2) 25–45; S. Brown, "Perspectives on Phoenician Art," *BA* 55 (1992) 6–24.

11. Cf. E. Gubel and E. Lipiński, eds., *Studia Phoenicia III: Phoenicia and its Neighbors* (Leuven 1985); and Bonnet et al., eds. (supra n. 6).

12. See colloquia, studies, and volumes of F. Barecca et al., *L'espansione fenicia nel Mediterraneo*, Studi Semitici 38 (Rome 1971); G. Bunnens, *L'expansion phénicienne en Mediterranée* (Bruxelles-Rome 1979); S. Frankenstein, "The Impact of Phoenician and Greek Expansion on the Early Iron Age Societies of Southern Iberia and Southwestern Germany" (Ph.D. diss., London 1977); E. Lipiński, ed., *Studia Phoenicia V: Phoenicia and the East Mediterranean in the First Millennium* B.C. (Leuven 1987); Niemeyer, ed. (supra n. 5); and H. G. Niemeyer, "Die Phönizier und die Mittelmeerwelt im Zeitalter Homers," *JRGZM* 31 (1984) 1–94.

13. Grayson (supra n. 7).

14. See catalogue and bibliography in G. Markoe, *Phoenician Bronze and Silver Bowls from Cyprus and the Mediterranean* (Berkeley 1985).

15. Found in Tomb 55; see M. R. Popham et al., "Further Excavation of the Toumba Cemetery at Lefkandi, 1984 and 1986," *AR* 35, 1988–1989, 117–129.

16. For example Grayson (supra n. 7); see also Röllig (supra n. 5) 28.

17. Sarah Morris also reminds me that textile fragments and the remains of a garment have been found in Lefkandi (M. R. Popham et al., "The hero of Lefkandi," *Antiquity* 56 [1983] 169–174), though of course there is no evidence that any were of Phoenician manufacture.

18. For Esarhaddon, see S. Parpola and K. Watanabe, *Neo-Assyrian Treaties and Loyalty Oaths* (Helsinki 1988) Treaty III. The biblical accounts include the joint sea ventures of Solomon of Israel and Hiram of Tyre in the tenth century B.C. (I. Kings 9:26–28 and 10:11, 22; II. Chron. 9:21) and the long description of the port and trade of Tyre in the sixth century (Ezekiel 27). Recent discussions include G. Bunnens, "Tyr et la mer," in Gubel et al., eds. (supra n. 2); M. Elat, "Phoenician Overland Trade within the Mesopotamian Empires," in M. Cogan and I. Ephal, eds., *Ah, Assyria . . . Studies in Assyrian History . . . presented to H. Tadmor* (Jerusalem 1991) 21–35; M. Liverani, "The Trade Network of Tyre according to Ezek. 27," in Cogan and Ephal, eds. (supra this note) 65–79; and I. M. Diakonoff, "The Naval Power and Trade of Tyre," *IEJ* 42/3–4 (1992) 168–193.

19. Cf. G. F. Bass, *Cape Gelidonya: A Bronze Age Shipwreck* (Philadephia, 1967), and "A Bronze-Age Shipwreck at Ulu Burun (Kaş): 1984 campaign," *AJA* 90 (1986) 269–296.

20. For example, at Pithekoussai or at Lefkandi: G. Buchner, "Die Beziehungen zwischen der euboischen Kolonie Pithekoussai auf der Insel Ischia und dem nordwestsemitischen Mittelmeerraum in der zweiten Halfte des 8. Jhs. v. Chr," in Niemeyer, ed. (supra n. 5) 277–297; Popham et al. (supra n. 15). See also on this issue J. N. Coldstream, "Greeks and Phoenicians in the Aegean," in Niemeyer, ed. (supra n. 5) 261–272, and Diakonoff (supra n. 18) 193 re goods imported to Tyre for *re*-export elsewhere, which suggests that, at least in the sixth century, Phoenicians were carrying materials not necessarily Phoenician in manufacture.

21. For example, at Thasos, cf. A. J. Graham, "The Foundation of Thasos," *BSA* 63 (1978) 86–97.

22. See E. Forrer, "Karthago wurde erst 673/663 vor Christ gegründet," in H. Kusch, ed., *Festschrift Franz Dornseiff* (Leipzig 1953) 85–93, and subsequently E. Lipiński, "La Carthage de Chypre," in Gubel et al., eds. (supra n. 2) 209–234, and D. Neiman, "Carchedon = 'New City'," *JNES* 25 (1966) 42–47.

23. Lipiński, ed. (supra n. 12).

24. M. Sznycer, "L'inscription phénicienne de Tekke près de Cnossos," *Kadmos* 18 (1979) 89–93; J. W. Shaw, "Phoenicians in Southern Crete," *AJA* 93 (1989) 165–184; O. Negbi, "Evidence for Early Phoenician Communities on the Eastern Mediterranean Islands," *Levant* 14 (1982) 179–182.

25. Shaw (supra n. 24) 182.

26. For example, T. Severin, *The Ulysses Voyage: Sea Search for the Odyssey* (London 1987).

27. For the western Mediterranean, see C. Picard, "Les navigateurs de Carthage vers l'ouest, Carthage et le pays de Tarsis aux VIIIᵉ–VIᵉ siècles," in Niemeyer, ed. (supra n. 5) 167–173, especially Map, p. 170. Aspects of the eastern Mediterranean circuit are discussed in D. Conwell, "On Ostrich Eggs and Libyans: Traces of a Bronze Age People from Bates' Island, Egypt," *Expedition* 29 (1987) 25–37; Bass 1986 (supra n. 19), and M. Korfmann, "Troy: Topography and Navigation," in M. J. Mellink, ed., *Troy and the Trojan War*, (Bryn Mawr 1986) 1–16.

28. Cf. H. G. Niemeyer, "Los comienzos de Cartago y la expansión fenicia en el area mediterranea," *Gerion* 7 (1989) 11–40.

29. Niemeyer (supra n. 12).

30. With regard to Spain alone, see M. E. Aubet, "Los fenicios en España: estado de la cuestión y perspectivas," *Aula Orientalis* 3 (1985) 9–38; M. E. Aubet-Semmler, "Aspectos de la colonización fenicia en Andalucía durante el siglo VIII A.C.," in Bartolini and Bondi, eds. (supra n. 9) 815–824; and J. M. Blazquez, "Panorama general de la presencia fenicia y punica en España," in Bartolini and Bondi, eds. (supra n. 9);

for overviews, see J. Ferron, "À propos de la civilisation phénicienne d'occident," *Latomus* 29 (1970) 1026–1037; J. P. Garrido-Roiz, "Presencia fenicia en el area átlantica andaluza: La necropólis orientalizante de Huelva (la Joya)," in Bartolini and Bondi, eds. (supra n. 9) 857–864; M. Koch, *Tarschisch und Hispanien. Historische, geographische und namenkundliche Untersuchungen zur Phönizische Kolonisation der Iberischen Halbinsel*, Madrider Forschungen 14 (Berlin 1984); G. Maass-Kindemann, "Vasos fenicios de los siglos VIII-VI en España: Su procedencia y su posición dentro del mundo fenicio occidental," *Aula Orientalis* 3 (1985) 227–239; F. Molina Fajardo, "Almuñecar a la luz de los nuevos hallazgos fenicios," *Aula Orientalis* 3 (1985) 193–216; Niemeyer (supra n. 12); P. Rufete Tomico, "Die phönizische Rote Ware aus Huelva," *MM* 30 (1989) 118–134; and H. Schubart, "Phönizische Niederlassungen an der iberischen Südküste," in Niemeyer, ed. (supra n. 5) 207–230.

31. See discussion in Winter (supra n. 10) 20; the text in Parpola and Watanabe (supra n. 18).

32. F. Bron and A. Lemaire, "Poids inscrits phénicio-araméens du VIIIᵉ siècle av. J.C.," in Bartolini and Bondi, eds. (supra n. 9) 763–770.

33. Diakonoff (supra n. 18) 182.

34. M. Heltzer, "A recently discovered Phoenician Inscription and the Problem of the Guild of Metal-Casters," in Bartolini and Bondi, eds. (supra n. 9) 119–123, has suggested the existence of guilds, at least of metalworkers, on the basis of an inscribed Phoenician silver bowl found in Italy on which the owner was described as *bn nsk*, lit. 'son of the caster,' but which he would read 'son—i.e., member—of the (guild of) casters.' If true, this, too, speaks to a degree of urban organization; however I am not fully persuaded, since it is unclear that individuals identified themselves by profession, rather than by patronym. The reference in II. Chron. 13–14 to the Phoenician craftsman sent by Hiram of Tyre to David in Jerusalem tells us that his father, too, was a man of Tyre, but it is not clear whether the following clause, "skillful to work in gold and in silver," refers directly to the son or to the father. In any case, there is no mention of membership in any work group, even if craft specialization was passed on from generation to generation.

35. Cf. Winter (supra n. 10).

36. For example, R. D. Barnett, *Catalogue of the Nimrud Ivories* (London 1957), fig. 79.

37. B. Freyer-Schauenberg, *Elfenbeine aus dem sämischen Heraion* (Hamburg 1966[a]) and "Kolaios und die westphönizischen Elfenbeine," *MM* 7 (1966[b]) 89–108; M. E. Aubet, *Marfiles fenicios del Bajo Guadalquivir II: Acebuchal y Alcantarilla* (Valladolid 1980); Aubet (supra n. 30); Picard (su-

pra n. 27); and mention in R. Harrison, *Spain at the Dawn of History* (London 1988) 57 and 64.

38. This is not the place to present all of the evidence for such an assessment of the Carmona ivories; however a few comparisons may help to establish the point that it is not necessary to view these pieces as either provincial or late, however the local archaeological assemblage may be dated. Several pieces are of extremely high quality in carving, and would rank with fine pieces from elsewhere (e.g., Hispanic Society of America, *Catalogue of Early Engraved Ivories* [New York 1928] Ac/C.I). Close parallels are apparent in type between a trapezoidal plaque-handle for a cosmetic palette from the site of Acebuchal with pieces from Beth Zur in Palestine and Nimrud, its incised decoration of horned animal with head turned back equally comparable to carved plaques from Fort Shalmaneser in Nimrud (Hispanic Society of America, Ac/B.V and Barnett [supra n. 36] S.125). For incised plaques decorated with griffins from Bencarron, both technique and stylistic details are closely paralleled in a piece of uncertain function found at Nimrud (see Hispanic Society of America, B.I-IV, and Barnett [supra n. 36] fig. 79), while the variant on a common "sacred tree" motif that shows multiple volute-branches depicted on a plaque from Cruz del Negro is not necessarily a late debasement of the standard Near Eastern tree, as similar multiple volutes are shown on pieces from both Cyprus and Nimrud (Hispanic Society of America, C.XIII and XIV; V. Karageorghis, *Excavations in the Necropolis of Salamis*, III [Nicosia 1973] Pl. 241; and G. Herrmann, *Ivories from Room SW37, Fort Shalmaneser* [Ivories from Nimrud IV, 2] [London 1986] nos. 767 and 768).

39. Directly relevant are the so-called "Lyre-Player" seals found distributed across the Central and Eastern Mediterranean, from Pithekoussai to Rhodes and Tarsus and along the Eastern Mediterranean littoral. Often found in private graves and nonelite contexts, they represent fairly crude, incised work. Initially studied by Porada, who suggested they might have originated in Rhodes, they were restudied once the Ischia finds were known, and suggested to be of Cilician origin (G. Buchner and J. Boardman, "Seals from Ischia and the Lyre-Player Group," *JdI* 81 [1966] 1–62). The group has recently been reexamined by J. Boardman, "The Lyre-Player Group of Seals: An Encore," *AA* (1990) 1–17, who now suggests that they may be Aramaean. However, this has not been generally accepted (see discussion in M. G. Amadasi Guzzo, "Fenici o Aramei in Occidente nell'VIII sec. a.c.?" in Lipiński, ed. [supra n. 12]). Their iconographic repertoire is most closely allied to Phoenician egyptianizing products. Indeed, the parallels between some of the incised ivories from the Carmona group and these seals are striking, including elements

such as birds sitting on the backs of couchant lions, and details of rendering lions' tongues, paws, and manes. I find myself unpersuaded by Boardman's new hypothesis for their Aramaean origin—particularly as examples have been found at Phoenician sites, such as Byblos. The lack of numerous examples from Phoenician sites must be understood as a product of the scarcity of excavation at the major centers. New finds from Francavilla Marittima in Italy, and in Eretria, parallel the distribution of other Phoenician goods throughout the Mediterranean. This distribution pattern in combination with iconographic and stylistic parallels to Phoenician works would privilege the hypothesis of a Phoenician origin for the group based upon current evidence; and if so, then we have another class of relatively crude, incised objects of homeland manufacture that could serve as comparanda for our hypothesis of mainland production of incised, lesser-quality ivories.

40. Here, I would also differ from the conclusions reached by S. Lancel ("Ivoires phénico-puniques de la peuple archaique de Byrsa, à Carthage," in Bartolini and Bondi, eds. [supra n. 9] 687–692), who published the wonderful new ivories found in a seventh-century tomb of the Byrsa Hill at Carthage in 1978. Her argument that the ivories, including *à-jour* fragments of a sacred tree with multiple volutes and of rampant cervids grazing among the branches of a sacred tree, represent "a certain hieratisation of the motifs" and hence Carthaginian work (pp. 691–692) seems undemonstrated, given the parallels she herself draws to works from Cyprus and Nimrud. To me, by contrast, their virtual identity to Levantine work, along with the fact that these pieces were carefully stowed inside an amphora, suggests that fine-quality pieces of homeland manufacture could have been moving west along with those of lesser quality. The issue of production at Carthage must remain an open question; but until we know a lot more about the order of establishments (whether or not exploitation of the Spanish ore sources preceded the Carthage colony, for example), and the relationships maintained with the parent culture in Tyre in the early years, I do not think we can argue on any but visual criteria for provincial vs. central production. In the case of the Byrsa ivories, I do not think there is evidence to argue for stylistic features outside of the range of mainland Phoenician production (as, for example one *can* demonstrate for some "orientalizing" ivories found in Etrurian contexts).

41. Exekiel 27; on which, see the recent cautions of both Elat and Liverani (supra n. 18).

42. See on this also the discussion in S. P. Morris, "Daidalos and Kadmos: Classicism and 'Orientalism'," in *Arethusa, Special issue* (1989) 39–54.

43. S. P. Morris discusses this passage in *Daidalos and the*

Origins of Greek Art (Princeton 1992) 119 and n. 79, where she notes that the etymology behind "Temesse"—*t'mss*—means 'forge' or 'foundry.' At the same time, it is tempting to identify Athena's Temesse with Tamassos on Cyprus, to which it would make great sense to be going for copper. The place-name "Tamesu" is included in Esarhaddon of Assyria's list of ten Cypriot kingdoms on which he imposed contributions for his new palace (D. D. Luckenbill, *Ancient Records of Assyria and Babylonia*, II [Chicago 1928] para. 690, just before "Kartihadasti," which must be the Cypriot Carthage, on which see supra n. 22). Therefore, by the early seventh century, a place on the island was known by a cognate name. In addition, the present site known as Tamassos has produced material (cited in J. B. Carter, *The Beginning of Greek Sculpture* [New Haven forthcoming] ch. 4) associated with Phoenician remains. Since Athena's "Taphians" represent invented peoples anyway, it is not at all impossible that they reflect a portmanteau toponym created as a conflation of two Cypriot sites, Tamassos and Paphos (suggested by Fred Winter), or that the people themselves were modeled after (Cypriot) Phoenicians—an association that goes back as far as Late Classical texts (S. P. Morris, personal communication). It is also interesting to note that in the catalogue of trade goods coming in to Tyre of the sixth century B.C., preserved in Ezekiel 27:19, the term "bright iron" is used and associated with Javan, or Greece! Could we have in the *Odyssey* story an invented synthesis of several elements related to first millennium trade in the Mediterranean: an acknowledgment of the importance of Cyprus in Mediterranean commerce, Greek wealth in iron being traded for Cypriot wealth in copper (by the fictional persona adopted by Athena, herself a Greek goddess), and a Cypro-Phoenician or Phoenician model for her "Taphians?"

44. See discussion in Frankenstein (supra n. 12); I. J. Winter, "On the Problems of Karatepe: The reliefs and their context," *AnatStud* 29 (1979) 115–151.

45. A. Blanco and J. M. Luzon, "Pre-Roman Silver Miners at Riotinto," *Antiquity* 43 (1969) 124–131; B. Rothenberg and A. Blanco Freijeiro, *Studies in Ancient Mining and Metallurgy in Southwest Spain: Explorations and Excavations in the Province of Huelva* (London 1981); and G. W. Cariveau, "Dating of 'Phoenician' slag from Iberia using Thermoluminescence Techniques," *MASCA Newsletter* 10 (1974) 1–2. See also the general reviews of this issue in Harrison (supra n. 37) ch. 4, "The Orientalizing Period," pp. 51–68; and B. Treumann-Watkins, "Phoenicians in Spain," *BA* 55 (1992) 29–35.

46. Cf. G. Kopcke, "Heraion von Samos: Die Kampagnen 1961/1965 im Südtemenos," *AthMitt* 83 (1968) 250–314; A. Bammer, "Spuren der Phöniker im Artemision von Ephesos," *Anat.Stud.* 35 (1985) 103–108; and the exciting work of I.

Kilian-Dirlmeier, "Fremde Weihungen in griechischen Heiligtümern vom 8. bis zum Beginn des 7. Jahrhundert vor Christ," *JRGZM* 32 (1985) 215–254.

47. G. Kopcke, personal communication, 1980; also mentioned in Kochavi (supra n. 6).

48. See on this, Shaw (supra n. 24); E. Frézouls, "Une nouvelle hypothèse sur la fondation de Carthage," *BCH* 79 (1955) 153–176.

49. G. Bunnens, "Aspects religieux de l'expansion phénicienne," in Bonnet et al., eds. (supra n. 6) 119–125; Parpola and Watanabe (supra n. 18) III.10.

50. Cf. S. Benichou-Safar, *Les Tombes puniques de Carthage. Topographie, structures, inscriptions et rites funeraires* (Paris 1982) and H.-G. Niemeyer, "Karthago, Stadt der Phönizier am Mittelmeer," *Antike Welt* 21 (1990) 80–105 for the Carthage dates; G. Nagy, "Homeric Questions," *TAPA* 122 (1992) 37–38, for the period over which the texts are likely to have been formed. This is also the period in which the first Phoenician materials are found in Spain (see references supra n. 30), so that it is impossible at present to determine whether the founding of the colony preceded or followed the beginning of commerce with the Iberian peninsula.

51. Conwell (supra n. 27) 33.

52. Cf. map in Severin (supra n. 26) 20–21.

53. Cf. Winter (supra n. 10) maps, figs. 1 and 2, and discussion p. 21.

54. Cf. argument in Winter (supra n. 44).

55. In Bartolini and Bondi, eds. (supra n. 30).

56. See also for mixed residence Coldstream (supra n. 20) and Morris (supra n. 42) 43.

57. S. C. Humphreys, *Anthropology and the Greeks* (London 1978) 119.

58. J. Boardman, *The Greeks Overseas*, 3rd ed. (London 1980); W. G. Forrest, "Colonisation and the Rise of Delphi," *Historia* 6 (1957) 160–175; W. G. Runciman, "Origins of States: The case of Archaic Greece," *Journal of Comparative Study of Society and History* 24 (1982) 351–377.

59. See on this topic G. Markoe, "In Pursuit of Metal: Phoenicians and Greeks in Italy," in Kopcke and Tokumaru, eds. (supra n. 6) 61–84.

60. M. F. Baslez, "Le rôle et la place des Phéniciens dans la vie économique des ports de l'Egée," in Lipiński, ed. (supra n. 12) 267–269, 284.

61. See discussion by E. Bickerman, "*Origines Gentium*," *CP* 47 (1952) 72.

62. E. Auerbach, *Mimesis: The representation of reality in Western literature*, trans. W. R. Trask (Princeton 1953) 23.

63. This is not the place to enter into discussions of the difference between written and oral "texts"; however, it is useful to note how close Nagy's working definition for "formula"

in oral composition is to the definition for "trope" presented here (see *Greek Mythology and Poetics* [Ithaca 1990] 29 and also Nagy [supra n. 50] 17–60: "the formula is a fixed phrase conditioned by the traditional themes of oral poetry"). What may be necessary to consider in future is how the phenomenon of the trope may merge with the need for repetitive formulae as an artifact of performance in oral traditions—on which, see I. de Jong, "Narratology and Oral Poetry: The Case of Homer," *Poetics Today* 12 (1991) 405–424.

64. P. Pucci, "The Proem of the Odyssey," *Arethusa* 15 (1982) 53–54.

65. A blurring of the clear boundaries between those who act in accord with the social code and those who contravene the code seems to occur in references to piracy and the traffic in humans, attributed to both the Phoenicians and the Taphians—the fictitious people with whom Athena associates herself when she appears in disguise to Telemachos at the beginning of the *Odyssey* (1.156ff.). These Taphians, like the Phaeacians and Phoenicians, are "oar-loving," able sailors and traders; but they were also responsible for the initial abduction of Eumaeus' Sidonian nurse, parallel to his own later abduction by the Sidonian conspirators and the intended abduction of Odysseus' invented persona by his Phoenician host. It is possible that such traits could be attributed to the Taphians precisely because they were invented and not identified as Greek or related to the Greeks, as were the Phaeacians. (Indeed, if the invented Taphians were modeled after Cypriot Phoenicians, as per supra n. 43, this is all the more reason for them to be engaged in abduction and the traffic in humans, and the apparent ambiguity disappears.) The further irony is that, if Eumaeus was abducted by Phoenicians, he was bought by Greeks (by Odysseus' own father, in fact); hence his presence on Ithaca. That slavery was very much a part of Greek society in the eighth/seventh centuries B.C. is clear (see I. Morris, *Burial and Ancient Society: The rise of the Greek city-state* [Cambridge and New York 1987] 174–177); but it is glossed over rapidly in the texts, and may well have been a source of some discomfort.

66. See G. Nagy, *The Best of the Achaeans* (Baltimore 1979) 51ff.

67. Pucci (supra n. 64) 48.

68. Nagy (supra n. 66).

69. Nagy (supra n. 66) 35–39.

70. S. D. Olson, "Odyssey 8: Guile, Force and the Subversive Poetics of Desire," *Arethusa* 22 (1989) 135–145.

71. Wathelet (supra n. 2) 242–243.

72. A second way is by ascribing "female" characteristics to a national group, distinct from the "male" ideal of the Greeks. Thus, later texts contrast the gynecocracy of Dido at Carthage to the democracy of male rule in Greece, or distin-guish customs, such as the use of perfumes by the Persians rather than oils, as inherently feminine (see, for example, S. Ribichini, "Mito e storia: L'imagine dei fenici nelle fonte classiche," in Bartolini and Bondi, eds. [supra n. 9] 443–448; K. De Vries, "Attic Pottery and the Achaemenid Empire," *AJA* 81 [1977] 544–548).

73. J.-P. Vernant, *Myth and Society in Ancient Greece*, trans. J. Lloyd (New York 1988) 244.

74. Cf. Morris (supra n. 42); Carter (supra n. 43).

75. P. Michalowski, "Presence at the Creation," in T. Abusch et al., eds., *Lingering Over Words, Studies . . . in Honor of William L. Moran* (Atlanta 1990) 383.

76. G. Dietz, "Der Weg des Odysseus," *Symbolon NF* 9 (1988) 104.

77. A. M. Snodgrass, "Poet and Painter in 8th century Greece," *PCPS* 205 (1979) 435.

78. M. L. West, "The Rise of the Greek Epic," *JHS* 108 (1988) 156; see also the overview of E. S. Sherratt, " 'Reading the texts': Archaeology and the Homeric Question," *Antiquity* 64 (1990) 807–824, on how the reading of the texts has fluctuated over time.

79. A. M. Snodgrass, *The Dark Age of Greece: An archaeological survey of the 11th to the 8th centuries* B.C. (Edinburgh 1971) 389; discussed also by Sherratt (supra n. 78) 808.

80. As noted by A. M. Snodgrass, *Archaic Greece: The Age of Experiment* (London 1980) 123.

81. See on this, G. Nagy, "An Evolutionary Model for the Text Fixation of Homeric Epos," in J. M. Foley, ed., *Oral Traditional Literature: A Festschrift for Albert Bates Lord* (Columbus, Ohio 1981) 390–393 and supra n. 66, pp. 5–9; R. Janko, *Homer, Hesiod and the Hymns: A diachronic development in epic dictation* (Cambridge and New York 1982); M. L. West, "Archäische Heldendichtung: Singen und Schreiben," in W. Kullmann and M. Reichl, eds., *Der Übergang von der Mündlichkeit zur Literatur bei den Griechen* (Tübingen 1990) 33–50.

82. See on this now S. Scully, *Homer and the Sacred City* (Ithaca 1992).

83. For example, C. G. Starr, *The Economic and Social Growth of Early Greece, 800–500 B.C.* (1977); Humphreys (supra n. 57) 130ff.; Snodgrass (supra n. 79) 87ff.; Runciman (supra n. 58); I. Morris (supra n. 65) 171–210; and the entire symposium on Greece in the eighth century, the papers of which were published by R. Hägg, ed., *The Greek Renaissance of the 8th century B.C.: Tradition and Innovation* (Stockholm 1983).

84. The issue of kingship vs. citizen-rule in the *polis* is too complex for treatment in the present context, and indeed Jane Carter reminds me that there is little solid evidence in any

case. It has been suggested that different city-states in early Greece were organized according to different principles, with some, like those of Euboea, showing greater social differentiation and a longer attachment to the institution of kingship (cf. I. Morris, "Tomb Cult and the 'Greek renaissance': The past in the present in the 8th century BC," *Antiquity* 62 [1988] 752). Even if in some cases the *polis* was organized around power dispersed through the citizenry, the fact remains that the status of citizen was a restricted one, and there still was a significant degree of hierarchical stratification evident between citizens and noncitizens. It is also clear from the persistence of Alcmeonid dominance in Classical Athens that these traditional hierarchies continued to function even in the "democratized" state, an observation I owe to Fred Winter.

85. Cf. Boardman (supra n. 58) for a general overview; O.-H. Frey, "Zur Seefahrt im Mittelmeer während der Früheisenzeit," in H. Müller-Karpe, ed., *Zur geschichtlichen Bedeutung der frühen Seefahrt* (Munich 1982) on maritime activity from the tenth–eighth centuries; B. B. Shefton, "Greeks and Greek Imports in the South of the Iberian Peninsula. The archaeological evidence," in Niemeyer, ed. (supra n. 5) 337–370, on the distribution of Greek SOS amphorae in the western Mediterranean from the late eighth century through the seventh.

86. See on this Forrest (supra n. 58) and C. Rolley, "Les grands sanctuaires panhelléniques," in Hägg, ed. (supra n. 83) for sanctuaries; P. Vidal-Naquet, *Le chasseur noir: Formes de pensée et formes de société dans le monde grec* (Paris 1981), Vernant (supra n. 73) 29–53, and Runciman (supra n. 58) for warfare.

87. Runciman (supra n. 58) 373; J. Whitley, "Early States and Hero Cults: A reappraisal," *JHS* 108 (1988) 173–182.

88. As between Aigina and Athens, see S. P. Morris, *The Black and White Style: Athens and Aegina in the Orientalizing Period* (New York and London, 1984); or between Chalcis and Eretria in Euboea, see Runciman (supra n. 58) 368.

89. Runciman (supra n. 58) 354, 358.

90. E. Vance, "Signs of the City: Medieval Poetry as Detour," *New Literary History* 4 (1973) 557–574.

91. Vance (supra n. 90) 562–563, 572.

92. Vance (supra n. 90) 573.

93. I. Morris (supra n. 65) 757.

94. Compare, for example, J. N. Coldstream, *Geometric Greece* (London 1977) 15 with T. Hadzisteliou-Price, "Hero Cult and Homer," *Historia* 22 (1973) 129–142, and Snodgrass (supra n. 77). See also the discussion in Popham et al. (supra n. 17), where the materials from Lefkandi are used to suggest a well-established hero-cult tradition by at least the tenth century.

95. See S. Hiller, "Possible Historical Reasons for the Rediscovery of the Mycenaean Past in the Age of Homer," in Hägg, ed. (supra n. 83) 9–15; Whitley (supra n. 87); I. Morris (supra n. 84).

96. Whitley (supra n. 87) 178–179, 181.

97. I. Morris (supra n. 84) 756–757.

98. Ibid., 757, 758.

99. As per Hiller (supra n. 95) 13.

100. C. Bérard, "Récuperer la mort du prince: heroisation et formation de la cité," in G. Gnoli and J.-P. Vernant, eds., *La mort, les morts, dans les sociétés anciennes* (Cambridge 1982) 89–105.

101. Supported as well in Nagy, *Greek Poetics* (supra n. 63) 10–11; see also, Sherratt (supra n. 78) 808, who reviews those archaeologists and historians who have stressed the "role of epic in the establishment and enhancement of social and political structures."

102. West (supra n. 78) 166.

103. For the particular nature of the Euboean city-states, see Forrest (supra n. 58); Boardman (supra n. 58); P. Carlier, *La royauté en Grèce avant Alexandre* (Strasbourg 1984); Runciman (supra n. 58) 368ff. Circumstantial support of this profile may be found in Hesiod's reference (*Op.* 654–659, cited by Whitley [supra n. 87] 175) to the elaborate and "heroic" funeral games of Amphidamas of Chalcis in Euboea. Further discussion of this event may be found in Runciman (supra n. 58) 369, where his description of the games suggests very close parallels to those described in Homer.

104. Snodgrass (supra n. 79) 32; Runciman (supra n. 58) 369.

105. G. Kopcke, "What Role for Phoenicians?" in Kopcke and Tokumaru, eds. (supra n. 6) 103–113; W. Burkert, *The Orientalizing Revolution: Near Eastern Influence on Greek Culture in the Early Archaic Age*, trans. M. E. Pinder and W. Burkert (Cambridge, Mass. 1992) 14–24; Morris (supra n. 43) passim; Carter (supra n. 43).

106. For Euboea and Crete, see Popham et al. (supra n. 15), J. N. Coldstream, "Greeks and Phoenicians in the Aegean," in Niemeyer, ed. (supra n. 5), Shaw (supra n. 24), West (supra n. 78). For Pithekoussai, see Niemeyer (supra n. 12), Buchner (supra n. 20).

107. West (supra n. 78) 170. See also Burkert (supra n. 105) 114ff.

108. All of the things at which Herakles fails, in Dumézil's early study of the function of the "warrior" in Indo-European tradition: G. Dumézil, *Aspects de la fonction guerrière chez les Indo-européens* (Paris 1956) 93–98.

109. Vernant (supra n. 73) 30; Ribichini (supra n. 72).

110. With J. Boardman, "Al Mina and History," *OJA* 9 (2) (1990) 169–190 and Kestemont (supra n. 7). See discussion above (n. 7) and also in Winter (supra n. 10) 21.

111. Morris (supra n. 88) 92–96.

112. Morris, ibid., 103.

113. For Euboea, see M. L. West (supra n. 78) 172. But see also P. V. Jones, *Homer's Odyssey* (Bristol 1988) 66, re alternate views that the mention of Euboea is if anything pejorative—either suggesting that it is set at the ends of the earth or implying the provincialism of the Phaeacians in their lack of knowledge of the further north and east. Indeed, one could read the references to Euboea as an indication that we are on the fulcrum of the shift from Euboean to Athenian dominance in trade, which might in turn support the argument for Athens! (I am indebted to Fred Winter for this perspective.)

114. West (supra n. 78).

115. E. Shohat, "Imaging Terra Incognita," *Public Culture* 3 (1991) 59. In this respect, the "ethnic" otherness of the Phoenicians in the Homeric poems plays the same role as racial otherness does in later Western literature—see K. A. Appiah, "Race," in F. Lentricchia and T. McLaughlin, eds., *Critical Terms for Literary Studies*, (Chicago and London 1990) 274–287, esp. 281.

116. Ribichini (supra n. 72) 446, 448.

117. T. M. Green, "*Black Athena* and Classical Historiography: Other approaches, other views," in *Arethusa, Special issue* (1989) 55–65.

118. Translated by J. Lloyd (The New Historicism: Studies in Cultural Poetics 5) (Berkeley 1988).

119. T. Todorov, *La conquête de l'Amérique, la question de l'autre* (Paris 1982) 11, 252.

120. M. Bernal, *Black Athena: The Afroasiatic Roots of Classical Civilization I: The Fabrication of Ancient Greece* (New Brunswick 1987).

121. Morris (supra n. 42) 40–41; eadem (supra n. 43) passim. As a gloss on this, see Sherratt (supra n. 78), who notes that ostentation—and particularly the consumption of high-value goods like those proferred by the Phoenicians—is frequently characteristic of periods of social and political fluidity, when new groups and individuals jostle for power and so engage in display.

122. E. Said, *Orientalism* (New York 1979); T. Brennan, "The National Longing for Form," in H. Bhabha, ed., *Nation and Narration* (London 1990) 47.

123. N. Purcell, "Mobility and the *Polis*," in O. Murray and S. Price, eds., *The Greek City from Homer to Alexander*, (Oxford 1990) 29–58.

124. Brennan (supra n. 122) 44–70.

125. Cf. J. Friedman, "Culture, identity and world process," in D. Miller et al., eds, *Domination & Resistance* (London 1989) 252.

126. H. Bhabha, "Introduction," in Bhabha, ed. (supra n. 122) 1–7.

127. Vance (supra n. 90) 557, emphasis added.

128. Vance, ibid.

129. Runciman (supra n. 58) 362.

17

A DANCING FLOOR FOR ARIADNE
(*ILIAD* 18.590–592):
ASPECTS OF RITUAL MOVEMENT IN
HOMER AND MINOAN RELIGION

✦

STEVEN H. LONSDALE

'Εν δὲ χορὸν ποίκιλλε περικλυτὸς ἀμφιγυήεις,
τῷ ἴκελον οἷόν ποτ' ἐνὶ Κνωσῷ εὐρείῃ
Δαίδαλος ἤσκησεν καλλιπλοκάμῳ 'Αριάδνῃ.

And upon the shield the illustrious smith, lame in both
legs, hammered out a dance, similar to [what took place
on] the dancing floor Daidalos once made in broad
Knossos for Ariadne with intricately plaited locks.

Iliad 18.590–592

I

The final vignette on the Shield of Achilles (*Iliad*
18. 590–606)[1] describes how the renowned smith,
though himself lame in both legs, hammered out a dance
of young men and women with two acrobats in their
midst. As is fitting for the polished surface on which the
dance is imagined to be taking place, the *ekphrasis* sin-
gles out the brilliant adornments of the dancers and
traces the patterns of their movements. In the manner of
a *khorēgos* outfitting his choir, Hephaistos clothes the
women in light robes and crowns their heads with fair
diadems that shine like Ariadne's tresses;[2] he dresses the
men in chitons glistening with oil and hangs gold daggers from their silver baldrics. Next, to parade their finery to best advantage, he sets them in motion: now they
course lightly, their feet wound round in circular motion, now they advance and retreat in opposing rows.
Finally, he interjects two tumblers, who titillate the
crowd of onlookers as they puckishly promote the erotic
undercurrents of the mixed dance.

Like the acrobats which the smith weaves into his
rows of dancers, the poet inserts in his lines two short
similes—the one lending a geographical and chronological dimension, the other indicating, among other
things, the tempo of the dance. Appearing as an upbeat
to the actual description, the first simile situates the
dance in the context of Minoan Crete. The poet salutes
Ariadne and Daidalos, that Bronze Age *poiētēs* famed
for his labyrinth and *khoros*, whose exact nature has
been disputed since antiquity.[3] The context of the heroic
age is reinforced by reversing the normal practice of
similes, which is to take a heroic action and compare it

273

to a scene from everyday life.[4] The short Ariadne simile compares what is presumably a mixed dance familiar to epic audiences with a folk memory of dancing from Minoan Crete. The second simile of a potter testing his wheel helps shift the mixed dance back to the contemporary and the commonplace. The technological simile further animates the scene by indicating the rapid tempo and circular shape of the dance.[5] If the potter's simile, then, is meant to reinforce the circular aspect of their movements, the allusion to Daidalos points to a linear, perhaps labyrinthine, configuration. The description suggests a conjunction of the reel and the ring dance, a wedding of the linear dances that may have been thought characteristically Cretan, and the ring dances known best to contemporary audiences.

Although the poet portrays scenes from contemporary life, he makes a special effort to link his age with the heroic past by equating himself with divine and legendary creators, Hephaistos and Daidalos, and with technical skills known from the Bronze Age—metallurgy and pottery, and especially musical skills, including his own profession and the related art of dancing.[6] The skill of the smith is intimately connected with dance rituals through the manufacture of bronze cymbals; and the craftsmanlike skill required to order the steps of the dance is preserved in Homer in the name of the famed dancers at the Phaeacian court, the *bētarmones*, a compound of *bainein* ('to step') and *arariskein* ('to join'), a verb appropriate to all manner of technical endeavor. In this very Shield vignette *armenon* occurs in the potter simile to describe the craftsman testing his wheel by cupping it in his hands (*Iliad* 18.601–602). The *khorēgos'* talent of joining steps is moreover linked to the skill required of the *stratēgos* to marshal soldiers' bodies on the battlefield, and of the soldier "to tread the measures on the grim floor of the war god," as Hektor says to Ajax (*Iliad* 7.241). The overlap of strategic and choreographic activities is summed up in the weapon dance of the Archaic and Classical periods, and the idea that the best dancers made the best warriors became a literary *topos*.[7] The agonistic element, of course, is not absent from the arena of love, and a reading of the Shield vignette in the larger context of the *Iliad* suggests that what took place on Ariadne's dancing floor was competitive in nature.

Whatever reminiscences the earliest surviving mention of Daidalos' creation may have stirred up for listeners in the Archaic period, its very brevity suggests that audiences had an automatic familiarity with the legendary dances of Crete and their role in Ariadne's tale; otherwise the brief simile would have been intrusive and obscure. The technical context suggests a renewed interest in the dance, a traditional skill involving ordered steps which, like epic poetry, was passed down from generation to generation by people with special knowledge. But does the passage, in fact, point to information about a continuous choreographic tradition stretching back to the Bronze Age, or is it only part of a vague collective memory that Cretans like Meriones (*Iliad* 16.617) were (as they are today in the Eastern Mediterranean) the best dancers?[8] A simple answer to the relationship between the dancing floor of Ariadne and the dance of youths and maidens of course might be found in the mazelike dance in Theseus' myth as we have it. But even assuming that the dance of the youths and maidens somehow recalls the mixed dance which Theseus was said to have invented when he taught it to his companions (either upon emerging from the labyrinth or upon landing at Delos[9]), such an interpretation tells us little about any Bronze Age customs that may be convergent with the myth.[10] Moreover, this explanation imposes an overly restricted meaning on the mixed dance which, like other Shield vignettes, is generic. It is better to take the mixed dance for what it is—an ornate description of a courtship ritual (sc. *alphesiboiai*, 593)—and not as an allusion to any specific dance in Theseus' repertoire. The question needs to be rephrased to ask what an analysis of the dance in its larger context can reveal about the elliptical Ariadne simile. Then it is feasible to examine possible thematic and structural links between Bronze Age rituals and the Iron Age custom as presented in the *Iliad*.

Reading supposed Bronze Age traditions through Greek, especially Homeric, lenses is a perilous and often misguided activity. Recently, however, Emily Vermeule has again reminded us of the potential rewards of using evidence from the historical period to interpret the prehistoric world.[11] That the Greeks had a distinct impression of the Bronze Age nurtured by the vision of Archaic and Classical poets and artists is clear. But did they invent their version of the Bronze Age virtually *ex nihilo*, or did they have access to knowledge now available to archaeologists? Certainly these same artists and poets had information all but irretrievable to us in the form of Bronze Age poetry, most of it now lost, though some of it embedded in surviving epic. With this body of poetry as part of their cultural legacy, they thought of the Bronze Age as an "inherited world that could be activated by skill, *technē*." [12] The *technai* alluded to on the Shield—dance, architecture, metalwork, decorated pottery—had all reached very high levels in the Bronze Age, and the poet is celebrating the renewed surge in technical ability in the Iron Age, as seen elsewhere in the technological similes in the *Odyssey*. Unlike writing, which had to be reinvented, there was a more or less continuous tradition of poetry, metalwork, wheel-made pottery, and, by implication, dance. In the epic poets' repertoire *ekphrasis* and simile are among the most virtuosic poetic techniques—what more obvious opportunity for a poet to display his special vision of the Bronze Age and his link to its craftsmen than in the culmination of his ekphrastic tour de force? With the Ariadne-Daidalos simile the poet gives the final vignette a special rub that activates a memory of Bronze Age dancing rituals.

In order to evaluate the likelihood of this assertion we can rely on philology and an understanding of the dynamics of dance in art, myth, and ritual, especially the habit dance has of facilitating unions and separations, and its coordination with the communal rite of sacrifice. Dance is one area of ritual that has, until recently, received little attention from anthropologists. In less than a decade, however, the anthropology of dance has demonstrated its usefulness in correlating the ritual language of bodily movement with other forms of communication, including visual and mythical narratives. [13] The usefulness of dance anthropology as an interpretive tool in traditional cultures is, ironically, enhanced by avoiding a strict definition of dance as a separate entity; it is more productive to see dance as it interacts with other playful forms of ritual movement. [14]

One appropriate methodological procedure is to ask how dance, broadly defined, relates to the characteristic feature of religious experience with the divinity. In Minoan religion dance *is* the mode of expressing the char-

acteristic feature of divine religious experience which occurs in the epiphany of the goddess. According to the prevalent interpretation of a Late Minoan gold signet ring from Knossos (which Hooker calls the *locus classicus* for the "descending divinity" type [15]) and related examples of Matz's "ferne Götter," the divinity appears from above in the dance. The supposed supernatural movement is mirrored by the adorants, who invoke the deity by gestures and dancing. An epiphany of another sort is effected from the lower realms, as a plate and a fragment of a second from Phaistos suggest. [16] Again dance is the vehicle for manipulating the appearance of a goddess. (In the Classical period, chthonic ascents find an analogy in the so-called *anodoi* of females, such as Persephone, effected by dancing Pans and satyrs. [17]) How the two types of epiphany are to be related is unclear; however, the appearance of a goddess is not an isolated event but part of a repeated cycle that is circumscribed by ritual actions.

In Greek religion, dance is coordinate with the preparatory and reparatory phases of sacrifice. In the preparatory stage of sacrifice the joyous anticipation of the event is expressed through group dances, sometimes lasting through the night (*pannychides*). In the Classical period choral competitions such as the pyrrhic, for which the prize was an ox, were followed by sacrifices. [18] The meanings of sacrifice are expressed in symbolic form in hero myths, initiation structures, and in mystery cults. [19] In the myth of Theseus there are several symbolic dances, related directly or indirectly to the hero's encounter with death. These include Theseus' contest with the Minotaur in the labyrinth, legible as a maze-dance with analogues in initiation rites, and the Crane dance on the island of Delos after Ariadne's disappearance; the related abduction (and abandonment) of Ariadne recalls Theseus' attempt to spirit Helen away from the sanctuary of Artemis Ortheia and his role in assisting Perithous to abscond with Persephone. [20]

The story of Theseus, in short, *is* itself a dance which has become a myth, as Gerardus van der Leeuw once observed, though this is not the place to pursue the choreographic significance of the threads of his legend. [21] This essay concentrates on exploring the links between the dancing floor of Ariadne as a locus (which I take to be the correct reading of *khoros* [22]) and the religious dynamics of dance in myth and in Minoan art. Recent archaeological discoveries on Crete, including three circular platforms and associated finds at Knossos in the vicinity of the Stratigraphical Museum,[23] as well as advances in the understanding of ritual action in Minoan ecstatic religion (including Carter's article in this volume), now make it possible to interpret dance rituals in relation to a locus and to various ecstatic phenomena, such as epiphanies, robe, flower, and baetylic rituals, and the sacrifice of animals, and perhaps humans.[24] In keeping with the nonverbal nature of dance, choreographic activity in literature, myth, and ritual is a versatile, sometimes elusive, metaphor. Dance and other forms of movement constitute a ritual language useful for communicating with the divinity and for describing that experience in ways inaccessible to and forbidden by the spoken word. Dance has playful (and deceitful) aspects, well suited, for example, for (re)enacting hunting and the mute act of sacrifice. The overlapping activities of hunting and dancing are expressed through the ambiguous meanings of the verb *paizō*, 'to play/dance,' as in the Nausikaa episode where the ball-dance is compared in a simile to Artemis at the hunt (*Odyssey* 6.100, 106).[25]

II

Why did Daidalos build the dancing floor for Ariadne? As recent scholarship has shown, the courtship dance on the Shield is mawkishly mirrored by the whirling motion of Achilles and Hektor about the eddying streams of Skamandros prior to Hektor's death.[26] The mixed dance is preparatory to the act of marital union, much as the dance of death is a grim prelude to Achilles' clash with Hektor, whose death forms a link in the chain of sacrifices beginning with Zeus' own son Sarpedon. This parallelism has significance beyond the purely literary, since dancing and circumambulation rituals in Greek religion accompany sacrifice.

What has most struck critics about the final Shield vignette is its description of males and females holding hands at the wrist, the type of row dance best known in the Archaic period as a primarily female activity. This apparent anomaly has led some scholars to unsub-

stantiated conclusions about the poem's apparent ignorance of the gender-specific nature of Minoan dance, and encouraged others to see in any representation of mixed dances in Archaic art an automatic reference to the dances of Theseus and Ariadne.[27] If mixed dances are rare in Aegean and in Greek art of the Iron Age, it is in part because artists were prompted to record cult dances, and not courtship, wedding, and other socially circumscribed dances of the sort the Homeric passage clearly describes.

An analogy for the mixed dance is the *hormos*, a courtship dance described by Lucian (*Salt.* 12–13) in which males and females alternate in a chain. A young man leads, displaying his knowledge of the postures that will later be useful to him in war, while a young woman follows, demonstrating that she knows how to move with feminine decorum. It is also a mimetic dance in imitation of a string of beads, and as Lucian says, the collier is plaited with modesty and manliness. After describing the *hormos*, Lucian goes on to mention Ariadne and the *khoros* Daidalos built for her. But, assuming that the reader knows the passage, he passes it over. The context in which he mentions the *Iliad* passage, however, is telling. Prior to describing the *hormos* Lucian touches on contemporary dances in Sparta. Spartan men, he says, practice dancing as much as warfare, and they perform not only war dances but choral dances, including those dear to Aphrodite. While they dance they sing an invocation to Aphrodite and the Erotes, that they may join in their dances. The Spartan dances, like the *hormos* and the Shield vignette, blend the martial and the amorous; Lucian is implying that what took place on the dancing floor Daidalos fashioned for Ariadne was suitable for a young maiden and a hero like Theseus.

The interpretation of the mixed dance as a courtship dance is supported by the women's epithet, *alphesiboiai* 'bringing many oxen' (as dowry) (*Iliad* 18.593). The position of the final vignette on the Shield, an *ekphrasis* clearly composed according to the principles of ring composition, corroborates the interpretation. The first vignette (*Iliad* 18.491–496) describes a bridal procession; in their train follow young men performing what must be acrobatic dances. Together the two vignettes form a frame for the scenes of everyday life. The courtship dance is in a sense preparatory to the wedding procession, and the presence of multiple couples perhaps reflects the custom of marrying off more than one pair at once, as in the weddings at the Spartan court.[28]

In the *Odyssey*, dance always occurs in the context of a wedding, real or imagined. When Telemachos arrives at the court of Menelaos and Helen (*Odyssey* 4.17–19), the palace is jointly celebrating the weddings of Megapenthes and Hermione, and as in the Shield vignette "twin acrobats led the measures of song and dance, revolving among them." In the Nausikaa episode the princess explains to Alkinoos the constant need for clean linen for her bachelor brothers when they attend the dance, presumably as a means of one day attracting a wife (*Odyssey* 6.63–65). What the princess does not yet realize is that she herself is about to enter into a romantic interlude facilitated by dance. When Odysseus first catches sight of the princess she is playing the ball-dance with her handmaidens. The Artemis simile (*Odyssey* 6.102–109) provides a clear context for the playful dances of Nausikaa and her companions. They are analogous to the type of behavior instilled in marriageable girls in cults of goddesses of the Artemis-type.[29] But it is important that a young girl not be violated before she reaches her term, as the myth of Theseus' attempted abduction of prepubescent Helen from the sanctuary of Artemis illustrates. In the structure of hero myth, Nausikaa's willingness to assist Odysseus corresponds to the conflict encountered by the king's daughter when she falls in love with a foreign hero: she is willing to betray her father in order to help out the hero. Before that time she has been content to dance for her father, and the unconflicted affection of the young daughter for the father is expressed by the motif of "dancing for daddy," as in the story of Jephthah's daughter, or in the dances of the virgin Artemis (and Apollo) which delight Zeus (and Leto) (*Hymn. Hom. Ap.* 197–206). In the *Odyssey* the shift of loyalties from father to hero is divinely orchestrated by Athena through the ball game that leads to her encounter with Odysseus. Courtship and wedding dances have a similar role in transferring affections outside the immediate family and effecting the union of young lovers (cf. Plato, *Laws* 771e–772a). The situation between Nausikaa and Odysseus and that between Theseus and Ariadne are parallel. Although the Ariadne simile does not yield

any details, Daidalos, in constructing the dancing floor, plays an ancillary role similar to that of Athena in the Nausikaa episode.

The automatic association between dance and weddings is evident in the subterfuge perpetrated by Odysseus after the slaying of the suitors. Odysseus orders Telemachos and the oxherd and swineherd to wash, dress, and put on their tunics, and has the women dress up as well. The bard is to play music for a festive dance so that passersby will think "we are having a wedding" (*Odyssey* 23.130–136). What Odysseus tries to conceal from passersby through this charade is that a slaughter (*phonos*, *Odyssey* 23.137) has taken place. He tells his people to wait until they can go out safely to their orchards where Zeus will indicate to them a plan. Odysseus has turned the tables on the suitors, who in his absence have consumed his livelihood. In punishing them, he slaughters them like animals.

Analysis of the role of dance elsewhere in Homer indicates that it is an activity suitable for encouraging and effecting the union of young lovers; but it may lead to unions which are temporary or illusory. It is an activity that can lead to vulnerability; it can also be put to duplicitous use by a divinity (Athena) or a hero (Odysseus). The general idea of courtship leading to union can now be read back into the Ariadne simile: Daidalos built the *khoros* for Ariadne so that she might attract a suitable lover (such as Theseus). A reading of the larger context of the Shield vignette can now provide an answer to the question of what took place on the dancing floor.

A simile may interact with its context in several ways, linguistic, thematic, aesthetic. The highly condensed Ariadne simile shares with the ensuing mixed dance the romantic theme of the pairing of young lovers, who are referred to in the first line of the dance description by the phrase *ēitheoi kai parthenoi* (*Iliad* 18.593). A variation of this formula, *parthenoi ēitheoi t'*, occurs twice in successive lines in Hektor's soliloquy (*Iliad* 22.127–128), but nowhere else in the poem. In itself the repeated phraseology is perhaps not significant. But it is clear from the ensuing description of the chase around the walls of Troy (*Iliad* 22.145–166) that the image of the courtship dance is revived by repeated language, by the circular and linear movement of Hektor and Achilles, and by the presence of an audience.[30] Whereas before the audience was mortal, now it is divine. All the gods are looking on (*Iliad* 22.166). The sight of Hektor being pursued around the wall prompts Zeus to speak, and as he debates the fate of Hektor he recalls the many sacrificial victims offered to him on Mt. Ida. A sacrifice has been alluded to earlier in the poet's ironic comment that Achilles and Hektor "ran not for a sacred ox or hide such as are given as prizes to winners in running contests" (*Iliad* 22.159–160). A racehorse simile follows (*Iliad* 22.162–166).

These poetic interjections foreshadow aspects of Patroklos' funerary ritual, including the footrace and chariot race at his games, as well as the circumambulation of the Myrmidons and their horses three times around his corpse (*Iliad* 23.13–14). The ritual is preparatory to the mixed offering of animals and humans (*Iliad* 23.21–23), followed by a sacrifice of various animals and a communal feast (*Iliad* 23.30–34). Encircling motion around an altar or other significant object is a preparatory rite for ritual killing of both animals and men. In Greek scapegoat rituals the victim was paraded around the city walls before being symbolically put to death.[31]

The agonistic context of the chase scene repays attention because it provides a clue to the context of the highly condensed Ariadne simile. In Book 22 the poet introduces the idea of a contest in his ironic comment about the footrace and in the horseracing simile. In both cases mention is made of the prizes. The presence of a divine audience reinforces the analogy between races involving running men and horses and the running of Hektor and Achilles. The emphasis on feet and running is explicit in the use of the verb to 'run' *trekhō* (and its derivatives: 22.157, 161, 163), and the words for feet and horses' hooves (*podessi*, 160, 166; *monukhes*, 162).

In the final Shield vignette there is also an audience and contests. The idea of prizes is implied by the epithet *alphesiboiai* ('bringing in many oxen'), referring to the eventual rewards a girl will earn her family in the form of a dowry. Cattle as a prize are mentioned in the honors awarded the victor in a footrace (*Iliad* 22.159), and the underlying idea that the bride herself is a prize finds a parallel in the mention of *gunē* ([slave] 'woman,' *Iliad* 22.164) in the list of prizes for the chariot race. The idea of a reward is perhaps also contained in the potter's simile: the earliest Greek alphabetic inscription recalls that jugs were awarded as prizes in dance contests.[32] Finally, in the Shield vignette again the verb for running, *trekhō* (*Iliad* 18.599, 601), and the word for foot (*podessi*, 599) occur.

Can the idea of a competition through fancy footwork be read into the Ariadne simile? One thinks of the vulgar dancing of Hippokleides, one of the suitors for the daughter of Kleisthenes of Sikyon who staged musical contests (Hdt. 6.128.2–130.1). The myths of Atalanta and Pelops recall the related idea of races on horse or foot among suitors. Hippodameia gave thanks to Hera for her marriage to Pelops by celebrating games with sixteen women, and according to Pausanias sixteen women chosen from Pisaian cities arrange dances they call Hippodameia's.[33] In the case of the Pelops myth the ritual killing of the failed suitors dominates the background of Pelops' successful attempt. In the Herodotus passage the musical contest is immediately preceded by the sacrifice of one hundred cows, followed by a feast. A vignette on the Shield occurring a few lines before our simile describes the scene common in the marauding lion similes of predators feasting on cattle (*Iliad* 18.583–587).[34]

When the soliloquy of Hektor and the subsequent portion of the chase scene and the mixed dance are refracted back onto the final Shield vignette, the meaning of the laconic Ariadne simile can be spun out to imply that what took place on Ariadne's dancing floor was a competitive display of behavior appropriate to a suitable husband through dancing, much as the men do in the courtship dance. Of course, such normal behavior does not make for a very gripping story. Assuming that the Ariadne simile is a fragment cut loose from a narrative that explained what actually took place on Ariadne's dancing floor, we would expect some risqué inversion on the theme, such as that contained in the story of the geriatric Theseus' illicit attempt to woo seven-year-old Helen when she was dancing in the sanctuary of Artemis; and perhaps something of this nature lies behind the abduction of Ariadne in a version now lost. The conjunction of weddings and sacrifice and the related institution of bride-price would make such a narrative appropriate for epic, in which bride- and cattle-raids are alternating themes.[35] As we have seen, the interweaving of an inverted dance motif and the theme of sacrifice is preserved in *Odyssey* Book 23, which is set against the backdrop of the gradual theft of Odysseus' livestock by the suitors.

III

Memory of the role of dance in expressing the union of Ariadne and a male consort in the Classical period is not confined to the simile in the Shield vignette. Ariadne's marriage to Dionysos, a favorite theme in Classical vase painting, was celebrated in dance at the conclusion of Xenophon's *Symposium* (9.2–6) as a validation of heterosexual union. The facts that the dance was thought an appropriate medium for expressing the sacred marriage, and that the pantomime was performed at a symposium, the fourth-century version of a *kōmos*, are consistent with the overlapping of dance with unions and communions in the *Iliad*.[36] Clearly some cumulative image of Ariadne and the ritual dance gripped the imagination of poets and artists throughout the Classical period and beyond.

Does the context of Ariadne's dancing floor in the *Iliad* provide a basis for making a leap back to Bronze Age antecedents? The reading of the Ariadne simile as a fragment of Bronze Age poetry embedded in the *Iliad* would encourage a reconstruction of a ritual that had as its dynamic the attraction (or entrapment) of a female divinity to a locus manipulated by human activity of a competitive nature (bull-leaping[37] or acrobatic dancing, cf. the tumblers on the Shield), and the union of worshipper with divinity through sacrifice.

The alliance of Ariadne with Dionysos in Classical cult and myth would encourage an ecstatic context for antecedents. The similarity of the myths about Theseus' abduction of Helen and Ariadne, the apotheosis of Ariadne, and the divine status of Helen in cult led Nilsson to argue convincingly that Ariadne was originally a Minoan goddess who competed with Dionysos and who either, "on the one hand, was pushed out by him, or on the other hand, became associated with his cult."[38] Is this mythological transformation of Ariadne into a goddess anticipated by the dynamics of epiphany as seen in Minoan art?

Among the difficulties in understanding the Aegean Bronze Age is the lack of textual evidence and the elusive nature of much of its art. The candidates for mythological narratives in Aegean art are few and disappointing, especially in art from Minoan Crete, which is the setting for some of the most vibrant tales, as the Ariadne-Daidalos simile recalls. There are, for example, no convincing representations of Theseus and the Minotaur, an episode from the hero's tale with clear prehistoric origins in Crete. But what of art with a ritual context? Gisela Walberg, in the introduction to her recent essays on Minoan art,[39] challenges the views of scholars from Poulsen to Hood who have seen Minoan art as expressive of a spontaneous *joie de vivre*. One of the reasons for this opinion, she argues, is the interpretation of the movement of figures as dancing or playing. A study of the movements that have been called "playful," she asserts, shows that they have distant origins in Minoan motifs that have "little to do with dance or play."[40] She draws attention to the fact that dancers are represented lifting their arms, but not actually dancing.[41] At the other extreme is Elfriede Brandt's study of ritual gesture in Minoan and Mycenaean art, a development of Matz's theory that the upraised arms and animated gestures of the participants in cult scenes represented in Minoan and Mycenaean art indicate dances that had as their magical goal inducing the epiphany of the goddess. Brandt goes as far as to see the large LM III idols and almost all votive statuettes of the Petsopha-type from MM I to the second palace phase, as well as the bronze and terracottas from Tylissos, Piskokephalo, etc., as representations of dancing figures.[42]

A middle position is offered by H. A. Groenewegen-Frankfort in her chapter on Minoan art entitled *Homo Ludens*.[43] As the title (borrowed from Huizinga's classic study on play in culture[44]) implies, she is referring both to the subjects of Minoan art, including ritual games, contests, and dances, and the freedom of movement suggested by the playful use of space that, for example, violated a sense of a fixed groundline and allowed a figure to appear suspended in mid-air or to float into view. As examples she cites dancers, precisely the type of figure whose interpretation Walberg questions.[45] Is it not reasonable to suppose that Aegean artists, perceiving dance and related activities as playful behavior, themselves indulged in playfulness in representing the activity? In the same way that an artist of the Archaic period did not seek to illustrate the shipwreck of Odysseus, but came up with his own artistic version of a shipwreck, the Minoan artist is not illustrating cult dances but rather his own version of a ritual dance.[46] In so doing he is capturing the essential playfulness of the activity. The Isopata ring is not a snapshot of an epiphany; but the activity depicted on it and related examples can be interpreted in relation to objects that are focalized and magically activated by ritual movement.

Two linguistic clues of possible relevance to Ariadne's dancing floor occur in Linear B tablets from Knossos: the *daidaleon* and "Mistress of the Labyrinth."[47] They suggest places and share in common with Ariadne's dancing floor an emphasis on the *khoros* as a loosely defined locus—places endowed with what Evans called the "magic of the spot."[48] In Minoan religion caves, cleared spaces, or hewn platforms were all places that could be activated by dancing votaries to effect divine epiphanies, and the recently discovered circular platforms at Knossos presumably had a similar function. In Mycenaean and Minoan glyptic art the magic of the spot is suggested by the presence of significant objects, including poppies, lion's heads, horns, altars, and so on.

Many of these same objects are found on the heads of the idols with arms upraised in gestures that double as epiphany and mourning.[49] A typical example is the LM III Gazi idol in clay with horns of consecration and doves on her head.[50] The ring base shows that it was made on a wheel. The base allows it to be set up temporarily in the open, perhaps to define a dancing space. The circular shape may also indicate circumambulation about the figurine. Of special interest are the horns which appear early on in Minoan art. On a bronze votive table from the Psykhro cave three horns appear along with birds and other symbols next to a dancing (?) man.[51] Bronze gifts at Arkalokhori are a reminder of the intimate relationship between dance rituals and the smith who makes the bronze cymbals and other percussion instruments. An Early Bronze Age sistrum, a grave find from Horoztepe in the Ankara Museum of Anatolian Culture,[52] has modeled figures around the upper three sides of its frame. They depict two felines pursuing eight horned animals, one of which is twice as large as the other seven. How this ritual object was manipulated in funerary cult is unclear, but the meaning of this hunting scene can be related to Neolithic Çatal Hüyük, where in a wall-painting c. 6,000 leopard men surround bull and

boar in a kind of hunting dance.[53] Horns display the power to overcome the horned animal, to appropriate it for sacrifice in order to enjoy most palpably a divine presence. They also present a partial restitution of the slain animal, a reparation that can be promoted by the dance.

The bull is a unifying theme in the various strands of the Theseus narratives, and it appears significantly in the horned altar (*keraton*) Ariadne gives to Theseus along with the cult statue of Aphrodite. These two cult objects become the focus of the dance on Delos reported by Plutarch (*Thes.* 21); they indicate that a *khoros*, both as a ritual dance and as a locus, is transportable. Together they provide a link to the ritual origin of the dance on Crete. But the most important details for present purposes concern the context of the dance. Before performing the dance Theseus sacrifices and before leaving Delos he institutes games. The account suggests continuity with a Minoan source in terms of ritual, locale, and context. The horned altar in Plutarch's account, the focal point of the dance, is perhaps anticipated by the use of horned altars as significant objects in Minoan ecstatic dance rituals. As R. Hägg has shown, epiphanies, accompanied by ecstatic dances, occur in architecturally specific places and culminate in the raising up of the horns of a bull previously sacrificed by the priestess to the goddess to confirm that the staged spectacle had won the desired attention.[54] Presumably a successful epiphany was not automatically insured, and prompted at times different approaches or dire expedients.

Recent discoveries on Crete suggest that bull sacrifice in Minoan religion may have overlapped with human, even child, sacrifice.[55] Moreover, there is evidence to suggest that the flesh of children may have been ritually consumed or offered to the divinity. A ring from Khania depicts a girl in a skirt before an enthroned goddess in a shrine structure.[56] A knife, reminiscent of the sacrificial axes above the sacrifice on the Ayia Triadha sarcophagus, is poised above her head, indicating she is about to be killed. The unsavory scene brings to mind the child tributes offered to the Minotaur, who embodies bull and man, and who in turn is slain by Theseus. Something of a tauromorphic *daimōn* finds its way into the myth about Zagreus, whose name and presence in Crete before Dionysos suggest a Minoan heritage. As a child under the guard of the Kouretes, Zagreus was lured away by toys dangled by the Titans. Proteus-like, he attempts to avoid his aggressors by taking on various shapes, including the bull, but in this form is captured, torn apart, and devoured.[57] In the myth of Dionysos, god of epiphany, the motif of child sacrifice reappears in the tale of the Proetides, who are punished and driven mad by dance. However distantly removed the myths are from Minoan religious practices, the convergence of sacrifice and violently playful activity offers an analogy to ecstatic phenomena visible in Minoan art.

The connection between sacrifice and ritual contest occurs strikingly in the narratives surrounding the Minotaur, an aspect of Theseus' legend clearly embellished in the Classical period but generally agreed to preserve allusions to Minoan Crete. But the pretext for the killing of Minos' son Androgeos (because he was too successful in athletic competitions) that led to the demand for sacrificial victims may be as old as the *Iliad*. The funeral games established by Minos in honor of Androgeos and the related spectacle implied by the offering of the sacrificial victims have an analogy in the poetic treatment of the chase scene and death of Hektor as a spectacular contest for divine consumption followed by sacrifice analyzed earlier.[58] Knowledge about the shared background of the two legends would explain the otherwise curious equation between Ariadne and Theseus, and Hektor and Achilles as ironic lovers.

The difficulty of evaluating the possible thematic and structural links between Bronze Age rituals and the Iron Age custom as presented in the *Iliad*, of course, lies in the nature of the prehistoric sources. To a large extent we must trust that the poet of the *Iliad* had paths of access to preceding ages and that hints about information are embedded in the structure of the poem. A reading of the text in conjunction with an awareness of the role of dance in Minoan ecstatic ritual and related myths suggests that, as the innocent courtship dance on the Shield is poetically parallel with a darker reality, so behind the dancing floor of Ariadne lies a ritual with a deadlier *opus*. As the innocent union of males and females in the courtship dance on the Shield is linked with the chase of Achilles and Hektor preparatory to the death of the latter, so Ariadne's union with Theseus, facilitated by Daidalos' dancing floor, may be read as a mythological analogue for the ecstatic dances that attract the divinity in concert with the act of ritual killing. Such dramas can be acted out on or about a dancing ground, which is a movable locus with the magnetic power to attract a divinity or lover, to experience union, to dismember, to reconstitute, in short a *theatron* for recreating and manipulating the natural and supernatural worlds.

NOTES

1. Nineteenth-century philologists rejected these lines as spurious largely on linguistic grounds (e.g., the unparalleled use of *poikille* as a verb), and they are bracketed in the 1908 Teubner edition of Ameis and Hentze. Assessments of Minoan allusions in this passage include G. Glotz, *The Aegean Civilization* (New York 1925) 290–291; F. Chamoux, "Un souvenir minoen dans les poèmes homériques," *L'information littéraire* (1949) 69–71; J. V. Ooteghem, "La danse minoenne dans l' *Iliad* 18, 590–606," *LEC* 18 (1950) 323–333; S. P. Morris, *Daidalos and the Origins of Greek Art* (Princeton 1992) 14.

2. The emphasis on the hair of Ariadne and the crowns of the dancers may be an allusion to the ritual importance of what is on the head of the dancer; loose hair (as opposed to hair bound in a mitre) connotes an unmarried woman, cf. C. Calame, *Les chœurs des jeunes filles en Grèce archaïque* (Rome 1977) II 112. In Minoan art attention is drawn to the hair and headdresses of dancers. One thinks immediately of the flying tresses of the woman in the Queen's Megaron Fresco, cf. *PM* III 70–71 and pl. XXV.

3. P. Warren, "Circular Platforms at Minoan Knossos," *BSA* 79 (1984) 323, sees in *khoros* a reminiscence of an architectural structure akin to the dancing platforms at Knossos; cf. *PM* III 28, and A. Evans, "Knossos Excavations 1903," *BSA* 9 (1902–1903) 111, who inferred an allusion to the theatral areas near Minoan palaces. In antiquity Daidalos' creation was widely understood to be a marble relief. Pausanias (9.40.2) mentions in his catalogue of Daidalos' surviving works a white marble relief at Knossos of Ariadne's dancing floor. The scholiast in Venetus A (H. Erbse, ed., *Scholia Graeca in Homeri Iliadem* [Berlin 1969–1988] IV 561) interpreted *khoros* as an actual dance. The local meaning is the generally accepted interpretation, first proposed by E. Petersen, "Zur ältest. Gsch. d. griech. Kunst," *Gymn. Progr. von Ploen* (1871) 20, cf. P. Faure, *La fonction des cavernes crétoises* (Paris 1964) 168 n. 3, and K. Fittchen, *Der Schild des Achilleus*, ArchHom 2.N (Göttingen 1973) 15, nn. 70 and 71; so M. Edwards, *The Iliad. A Commentary*, vol. 5 (Cambridge 1991) ad loc., and W. Marg, *Homer über die Dichtung. Der Schild des*

Achilleus[2] (Münster Westfalen 1971) 37, n. 50. Contra: W. Schadewalt, *Von Homers Welt und Werk*[3] (Stuttgart 1965) 484, n. 1; E. Kunze, *Kretische Bronzereliefs* (Stuttgart 1931) 213 and n. 45, believes the word designates the band of dancers portrayed on the shield. The other ancient debate about the passage centered around whether it was blasphemous to compare the work of a god to that of a mortal.

4. M. Edwards (supra n. 3) ad loc.

5. M. Edwards, *Homer, Poet of the Iliad* (Baltimore 1987) 283, comments that the dance is a popular subject on pottery in Homer's time, "and perhaps this is subtly hinted at in the simile of the potter at his wheel."

6. For a comprehensive account of the complex relationships between legendary craftsmen and poetry, ritual, and technical productions in the Bronze and Iron Ages in the Eastern Mediterranean, see Morris (supra n. 1) passim, esp. 4–15.

7. The martial aspect of the mixed dance on the Shield vignette is hinted at in the phrase *epi stikhas* (*Iliad* 18.602), in the gold swords, and by virtue of its appearance on armor. On weapon dances, see S. H. Lonsdale, *Dance and Ritual Play in Greek Religion* (Baltimore 1993) ch. 5 passim.

8. A. Hopkins, *Crete. Its Past, Present and People* (London 1977) 219, describes a modern Cretan dance performed by a line of dancers with hands joined. On ancient Cretan dance, see Ath. 181a–b; *PM* III.6, 69–80; L. Lawler, "The Dance in Ancient Crete," in G. Mylonas, ed., *Studies Presented to D. M. Robinson* (1951) I.23–51; T. B. L. Webster, *The Greek Chorus* (1970) 4–5; P. Warren (supra n. 3) 319–323.

9. K. Friis Johansen, *Thésée et la danse à Délos* (1946) 14–18, convincingly argues that the François Vase depicts Theseus performing the dance not on Delos but on Crete in honor of Ariadne. Cf. the reading by H. A. Shapiro, "Theseus: Aspects of the Hero in Archaic Greece," in D. Buitron-Oliver, ed., *New Perspectives in Early Greek Art* (Washington 1991) 124–126.

10. A. Burns, "The Chorus of Ariadne," *CJ* 70 (1974–1975) 1–13, argues that the Homeric passage describes a dance that perpetuates a Minoan ritual dance; K. J. Gutzwiller, "Homer and Ariadne," *CJ* 73 (1977) 32–36, believes that the version of the Theseus-Ariadne myth known to the *Iliad* poet encoded a specific dance of males and females performing in labyrinthine motions.

11. The challenges of using Homer and evidence from the historic period to interpret the Bronze Age are discussed by E. Vermeule, *Greece in the Bronze Age*, 2nd ed. (Chicago and London 1972) xi, and "Baby Aigisthos and the Bronze Age," *PCPS* 33 (1987) 122–124.

12. Vermeule (1987) (supra n. 11) 124.

13. See P. Spencer, ed., *Society and The Dance* (Cambridge 1985), a collection of essays by seven social anthropologists.

14. Lawler (supra n. 8) 41 notes many rhythmic activities which would not pass for dance that were so considered in antiquity.

15. J. T. Hooker, *Mycenaean Greece* (London 1977) 199; *PM* I 159–160 and fig. 115.

16. S. A. Immerwahr, *Aegean Painting in the Bronze Age* (University Park, Penn. 1990), pls. II and III.

17. Boston, MFA 01.8032, cf. C. Bérard, *Anodoi* (Rome 1974), pl. 12, fig. 42.

18. *SIG*[3] 1055, 72–74.

19. For a recent view of the range of meanings of sacrifice to the participants, see M. Alexiou, "Reappropriating Greek Sacrifice: *Homo necans* or ἄνθρωπος θυσιάζων?" *JMGS* 8 (1990) 97–123.

20. On dance and initiation, see J. W. Fitton, "Greek Dance," *CQ* 23 (1973) 256. The rape of Helen from the sanctuary of Artemis Ortheia at Sparta is reported by Plut. *Thes.* 31 = Hellan., *FGrHist.* 4 F 134 and 168a; cf. L. B. Ghali-Kahil, *Les enlèvements et le retour d'Hélène dans les textes et les documents figurés* (Paris 1955) 305–313; Calame (supra n. 2) 281–284. On young women being abducted while dancing in a sanctuary in general, see J. B. Carter, "Masks and Poetry in Early Sparta," in R. Hägg, N. Marinatos, and G. C. Nordquist, eds., *Early Greek Cult Practice* (Stockholm 1988) 94–95, n. 46; Lonsdale (supra n. 7), chs. 6 and 7 passim.

21. G. van der Leeuw, *Sacred and Profane Beauty. The Holy in Art*, trans. D. Green (London 1963) 46–47.

22. *Khoros* as a locus (and symbol of a city's political stability) appears elsewhere in the *Iliad* in an epithet for Mykalessos in the Catalogue of Ships (*Iliad* 2.498) in compound with the adjective *euru-*, the same epithet for Knossos in the Shield passage.

23. P. Warren (supra n. 3) 319–323.

24. E.g., Carter's article in this volume (285–312); P. Warren, *Minoan Religion as Ritual Action* (Göteborg 1988); R. Hägg, "Die göttliche Epiphanie im minoischen Ritual," *MDAI (A)* 101 (1986) 41–62.

25. Cf. *Odyssey* 8.251, 23.147; *Homeric Hymn to Apollo* 206; Pind. *Ol.* 13.86; Ar., *Ran.* 407b (Dover), etc. I must leave to others such tantalizing questions as the significance of the dangling feet in *Gliederpuppen*, as seen in one of the Karphi idols, cf. E. Vermeule, *Götterkult*, ArchHom 3.V (Göttingen 1974) 24. Nor do I hazard to enter into the labyrinth implied by deciphering the language of ritual gestures in Minoan iconography, except as they relate to epiphany; cf. E. Brandt, *Gruss und Gebet. Eine Studie zu Gebärden in der minoisch-mykenischen und frühgriechischen Kunst* (Waldsassen Bayern 1965) and the review by St. Alexiou, *Gnomon* 39 (1967)

609–613. Such an examination would entail a classification of artifacts by material and an analysis of movements by parts of the body, in relation to significant and focalized objects.

26. R. J. Rabel, "The Shield of Achilles and the Death of Hector," *Eranos* 87 (1989) 81–90.

27. Eustathius and certain modern scholars equate the *khoros* of males and females holding hands at the wrist with the celebratory dance of the youths led by Theseus, the so-called Crane Dance on Delos reported by Plutarch (*Thes.* 21) and possibly depicted in Greek art. Proponents of this identification argue that the mixed dance on the Shield and in Greek art must be the dance led by Theseus, who allegedly invented the arrangement of dancers *anamix*. Contra: L. Lawler, *The Dance in Ancient Greece* (Seattle and London 1964) 46. It is questionable that any artistic portrayal of men and women dancing, such as that on the Analatos loutrophoros, is a representation of the Crane Dance. While single-sex dancing is more common in the Eastern Mediterranean, it is not anomalous, and the lack of evidence for mixed dance in Aegean art may be purely accidental, cf. F. Stoessl, *Die Vorgeschichte des griechischen Theaters* (Darmstadt 1987) 15. The juxtaposition of male and female in Minoan dance is not forbidden. The dancers in the model of the ring dance from Kamilari have characteristics of both sexes: Warren (supra n. 24) 14; D. Levi, *ASAtene* 39–40 (1961–1962) 139, identifies them as male and discusses the curious exaggerated breasts on one of the figures (cf. "La tomba a tholos di Kamilari," *Annuario* 23–24 [1963], figs. 125–126). The female dancers in the model from Palaikastro, if the reconstruction is correct, surround a female lyre-player; cf. R. M. Dawkins, "Excavations at Palaikastro, III," *BSA* 10 (1903–1904) 217–220 and R. Bosanquet, "The Unpublished Objects from the Palaikastro Excavations (1902–1906)," *BSA* Supp. 1 (1923) 88, fig. 71. See also the article by Carter in this volume, p. 291 and fig. 18.4.

28. On group weddings see L. Gernet, "Ancient Feasts," in *The Anthropology of Ancient Greece*, trans. J. Hamilton and B. Nagy (Baltimore and London 1981) 23.

29. On choral song and dance in cults of goddesses of the Artemis-type, see Calame (supra n. 2) passim.

30. Rabel (supra n. 26) notes in addition to these parallels the use of the dual followed by the verb *dineō* (*Iliad* 22.165) to describe the whirling motion of Hektor and Achilles around the city, cf. the use of the dual and the verb *dineō* for the movement of the acrobats in the Shield vignette.

31. S. Eitrem, "Der Rundgang," in *Opferritus und Voropfer der Griechen und Römer* (Kristiania 1915) 6–29. J. Bremmer, "Scapegoat Rituals in Ancient Greece," *HSCP* 87 (1983) 314, and n. 84.

32. L. H. Jeffrey, *The Local Scripts of Archaic Greece* (Oxford 1961; rev. ed. 1990) 68.

33. Paus. 5.16.4–6.

34. The description of the pasture in the three immediately preceding lines (*Iliad* 18.587–589) seems to be an afterthought modeled on the opening of the dance vignette; note the repetition of the smith's full honorific epithets, *periklutos amphiguēeis* (*Iliad* 18.587, 590), which are appropriate for the finale, but not for the lackluster description of the pasture.

35. Hesiod (*Op.* 161–165) attributed the perdition of the race of heroes to two underlying causes: the Trojan War precipitated by the theft of Helen, and the fight over the cattle of Oedipus in Thebes.

36. The wedding of Ariadne and Dionysos was also acted out at the Anthesteria in Athens where the wife of the king-archon was surrendered to the god as wife; cf. W. Burkert, *Greek Religion* (Cambridge 1985) 109.

37. Bull-leaping has been the subject of several studies: J. Pinset, "Bull-leaping," in O. Krzyszkowska and L. Nixon, eds., *Minoan Society* (Bristol 1983) 259–272; J. Younger, "Bronze Age Representations of Aegean Bull-Leaping," *AJA* 80 (1976) 125–137; A. Ward, "The Cretan Bull Sports," *Antiquity* 42 (1968) 117–122; A. Evans, "On a Minoan Bronze Group of a Galloping Bull and Acrobatic Figure from Crete," *JHS* 41 (1921) 247–259.

38. M. P. Nilsson, *Griechische Feste* (1906; rep. Stuttgart 1957) 382–384, cf. *GGR*² I 314–315, and *The Mycenaean Origin of Greek Mythology, with a New Introduction and Bibliography by Emily Vermeule* (Berkeley, Los Angeles, London 1972) 171–173.

39. G. Walberg, *Tradition and Innovation* (Mainz 1986) 1–5.

40. Ibid. 3, cf. ch. 5.

41. Ibid. 90.

42. Brandt (supra n. 25) passim, cf. F. Matz, "Göttererscheinung und Kultbild im minoischen Kreta," *AbhMainz* (1958) 383–449.

43. *Arrest and Movement. An Essay on Space and Time in the Representational Art of the Ancient Near East* (1951; reprint Cambridge, Mass. 1987).

44. J. Huizinga, *Homo Ludens* (1950; reprint Boston 1955).

45. Groenewegen-Frankfort (supra n. 43) 198; cf. Walberg (supra n. 39) 89.

46. R. Kannicht, "Poetry and Art. Homer and the Monuments Afresh," *CA* 1 (1982) 70–86 and pls. 1–6.

47. The word *Dadarejode* is found twice on inventories of oil at Knossos and was perhaps a sacred place. See Vermeule (supra n. 25) 60–61; cf. M. Gérard-Rousseau, *Les mentions religieuses dans les tablettes mycéniennes* (Rome 1968) 51, and Morris (supra n. 1) 75–77. K. Kerényi, "Möglicher Sinn von *di-wo-no-so-jo* und *da-da-re-jo-de*," *Atti e memorie*

del 1° congresso internazionale di micenologia 1967 (Rome 1968) II.101–105, speculates that *da-da-re-jo-de* (as a neuter adjective turned substantive) may refer to an edifice constructed by Daidalos, the dancing floor of Ariadne. On the Mistress of the Labyrinth, see Burkert (supra n. 36) 23 and n. 24.

48. *PM* III 80.

49. Cf. V. Karageorghis, *The Goddess With Uplifted Arms in Cyprus* (Lund 1977).

50. S. Marinatos, *ArchEph* 8 (1937) I.278–291; St. Alexiou, *KrChr* 12 (1958) 179–294.

51. *PM* I 632, fig. 470.

52. Bronze sistrum from Horoztepe. Ankara Museum of Anatolian Culture. Inv. no. 18519.

53. J. Mellaart, *The Neolithic of the Near East* (London 1975) 110, fig. 60.

54. Hägg (supra n. 24) 41–62.

55. See P. M. Warren, "Minoan Crete and Ecstatic Religion," in R. Hägg and N. Marinatos, eds., *Sanctuaries and Cults in the Aegean Bronze Age* (Stockholm 1981) 155–166; for a critical view of human sacrifice in Crete, see D. Hughes, *Human Sacrifice in Ancient Greece* (London and New York 1991) 13–25.

56. Warren (supra n. 24) fig. 17.

57. *Orphicorum fragmenta* 31, 210–214 Kern. Ael., *NA* 12.23, reports that a child or a newborn calf was sacrificed to Dionysos Anthroporrhaistes.

58. Plut. *Thes.* 15.

18

ANCESTOR CULT AND THE OCCASION OF HOMERIC PERFORMANCE*

✦

JANE B. CARTER

A passage in the first book of the *Odyssey* describes a performance of oral poetry. The setting is inside the lofty house of Odysseus (ἔντοσθεν . . . δόμου ὑψη-λοῖο, *Odyssey* 1.126); in addition to chairs and tables, the room contains a stand (δουροδόκη, *Odyssey* 1.128) filled with the spears of the absent warrior Odysseus.

> Ἐς δ᾽ ἦλθον μνηστῆρες ἀγήνορες. οἱ μὲν ἔπειτα
> ἑξείης ἕζοντο κατὰ κλισμούς τε θρόνους τε.
> τοῖσι δὲ κήρυκες μὲν ὕδωρ ἐπὶ χεῖρας ἔχευαν,
> σῖτον δὲ δμῳαὶ παρενήνεον ἐν κανέοισι,
> κοῦροι δὲ κρητῆρας ἐπεστέψαντο ποτοῖο.
> οἱ δ᾽ ἐπ᾽ ὀνείαθ᾽ ἑτοῖμα προκείμενα χεῖρας ἴαλλον.
> αὐτὰρ ἐπεὶ πόσιος καὶ ἐδητύος ἐξ ἔρον ἕντο
> μνηστῆρες, τοῖσιν μὲν ἐνὶ φρεσὶν ἄλλα μεμήλει,
> μολπῇ τ᾽ ὀρχηστύς τε· τὰ γάρ τ᾽ ἀναθήματα δαιτός.
> κῆρυξ δ᾽ ἐν χερσὶν κίθαριν περικαλλέα θῆκε
> Φημίῳ, ὅς ῥ᾽ ἤειδε παρὰ μνηστῆρσιν ἀνάγκῃ.

The arrogant suitors came in and sat one after another on the couches and chairs. Heralds poured water on their hands, slave women piled up bread in baskets, and young men topped off kraters with wine. They put forth their hands upon the provisions lying ready before them. Then, freed from the desire of drink and food, the hearts of the suitors cared for other things, for singing and dance, the delights of a feast. And the herald placed a most beautiful lyre in the hands of Phemios, who was compelled to sing beside the suitors. *Odyssey* 1.144–155

The suitors are the elite (ἄριστοι, *Odyssey* 16.247–253) of Ithaca and neighboring islands. Phemios sings about the woeful return from Troy that Athena has caused for the Achaians. Penelope, hearing the song from upstairs, descends and asks Phemios to sing some other of the many things enchanting to mortals, the deeds of men and gods, which singers make famous (*Odyssey* 1.325–338).

All the important elements are here: the chieftain's house, the warriors' gear, the piled food, the kraters full of wine, the slave women and attendant youths, the singer and his lyre, the song about heroic events, and a recognition of the immortalizing power of song. This scene is replayed in the house of Menelaos at Sparta, at the court of the Phaeacians, and in the halls of Zeus on Olympos.[1]

This is what happens in the epics, but can this description simply be transposed from the epic narrative into the lives of Late Geometric aristocrats? Homeric scholars carefully avoid confusing the methods of warfare employed in the *Iliad* with the manner of fighting practiced in eighth-century B.C. Greece. Nor do they suppose that the lofty house of Odysseus corresponds to real Late Geometric architecture. Yet most make little distinction between the occasions of bardic entertainment within the epics and actual performances in Late Geometric life. Compare M. L. West, for example: "There is little doubt that they [the performers described in Homer] are a reflection (perhaps a little idealized as regards the honour in which they are held) of the Homeric poets themselves."[2] Or Charles Segal: "The Demodocus scene [at the Phaeacian court] probably reflects the ideal rather than the actual. . . . Nevertheless, the basic situation may not be beyond the possibilities of an eighth-century aristocrat."[3] The court of the Phaeacians certainly does represent an idealized society, but that ideal is not necessarily an idealized version of eighth-century Greece.

The occasions of epic recitation in the early historical period may have been quite different from the fictional recitations in the narrative. With equal, or better, justification, one might look to the earliest known occasions of actual epic recitation for the model of epic recitation in the eighth century. The first recorded occasion is Hesiod's victory at Chalkis:

ἔνθα δ' ἐγὼν ἐπ' ἄεθλα δαΐφρονος Ἀμφιδάμαντος
Χαλκίδα [τ'] εἰσεπέρησα· τὰ δὲ προπεφραδμένα
    πολλὰ
ἄεθλ' ἔθεσαν παῖδες μεγαλήτορες· ἔνθα μέ φημι
ὕμνῳ νικήσαντα φέρειν τρίποδ' ὠτώεντα.

Then, for the games of battle-minded Amphidamas, I passed over to Chalkis; and his great-hearted sons set out the many prizes that had been announced beforehand. There, I say, I was victorious with my song and carried away a handled tripod.   Hesiod, *Op.* 654–657

Hesiod does not say so explicitly, but no one doubts that battle-minded Amphidamas is dead and that the contests attended by Hesiod belong to the funerary rituals celebrated for the great man. In the early sixth century, rhap-

sodes competed in Homeric recitations at Sikyon until the tyrant Kleisthenes put a stop to them because the poetry praised the Argives (Hdt. 5.67.1). Kleisthenes' action might seem a little petulant, but Herodotus mentions it in the context of ancestor cult, and it seems clear that the recitations had some association with ancestor cult in Herodotus' mind.[4] The tradition of the "Peisistratean recension" attests to recitations of Homeric poetry during the Panathenaic festival of Athena in mid-sixth-century Athens.[5] The common element in these instances is a ritual context, and Oliver Taplin has recently proposed that the entire *Iliad* was performed during three successive nights at large panegyric festivals in important sanctuaries.[6]

I shall offer here another possibility for the occasion of epic performances. Taplin argues that such long epics as the *Iliad* and the *Odyssey* are an innovation responding to the needs of the great new festivals, which are themselves reflections of the new internationalism and panhellenism of the first half of the seventh century B.C. I do agree with Taplin that the occasion of epic performance was basically religious in nature, but I think that the nature of the occasion was of an antiquity similar to the poetic tradition from which the Homeric epics descend. If epic recitals in the eighth century took place in a religious context, in connection with ancestor cult for example, then recitations may have been part of such religious observances for a long time. My effort to envision the performance of Homeric poetry in a context of epic performance dating from the Mycenaean period is dedicated to Emily Vermeule, who of all scholars has thought most deeply on Homer and the Mycenaeans.

The topic of epic performance, we begin to see, is one with many avenues of approach, and I ask the reader's patience if I have not chosen the most obvious. Singers in Homer accompany themselves on lyres. There exist many visual representations of lyre-players from the Bronze Age and after, and some of these scenes must show occasions of epic recitation. By trying to define the occasions of lyre-playing in Mycenaean and Submycenaean depictions, we may be able to suggest occasions of epic recitation in the Mycenaean period and later. Of course, the visual arts employ as many conventions, and may be as far removed from lived experience, as literary texts. We cannot be sure that a Mycenaean picture is closer to real life than Homeric poetry. Nevertheless, it is by understanding how both poetic and visual conventions function that we may understand something of their relation to actual practice.

The Late Bronze Age representations that include lyre-players differ in many regards, but one fixture in all of them is the presence of a bird or birds. In the Homeric poems, birds have very special associations with deities. It is worth asking whether the conventional presence of birds in the visual arts has anything in common with the birds in poetry, and it is thus with birds that I begin.

GODS IN BIRD FORM IN THE HOMERIC EPICS

It has long been a matter of debate whether or not deities in Homeric poetry change themselves at times into birds. In a phrase such as ὄρνισιν ἐοικότες αἰγυπιοῖσι ("like birds, vultures," *Iliad* 7.59), that is, does the poet merely suggest a comparison, or does he mean to indicate an actual transformation?

The recent history of the debate began in 1967 with Franz Dirlmeier, who examined in detail six passages that he deemed central to the issue of *Vergleich oder Verwandlung*.[7] These passages, which continue to dominate the discussion, are the following.

(1) *Iliad* 7.58–61. Apollo and Athena agree to spare the hosts of Greeks and Trojans one day of battle by causing Hektor to fight against one of the Greeks in single combat. They transmit the idea to the Trojan seer (οἰωνο-πόλος) Helenos, and Helenos so proposes to Hektor. Hektor puts a stop to the battle, and both sides sit down on the battlefield. The gods responsible for this turn of events are also present:

κὰδ δ' ἄρ' Ἀθηναίη τε καὶ ἀργυρότοξος Ἀπόλλων
ἑζέσθην ὄρνισιν ἐοικότες αἰγυπιοῖσι
φηγῷ ἐφ' ὑψηλῇ πατρὸς Διὸς αἰγιόχοιο,
ἀνδράσι τερπόμενοι.

Then Athena and Apollo of the silver bow sat down like birds, vultures, upon the high oak of father Zeus the aegis-bearer, taking pleasure in the men.

(2) *Iliad* 14.286–291. As the Trojans advance relentlessly on the Greek ships, Hera persuades Hypnos (Sleep) to help her distract Zeus, who favors the Trojans. Hypnos lets himself be bribed, and the two make their way to Mount Ida, where Zeus sits watching the battle on the plain below. Hera approaches Zeus, but Hypnos wishes to escape notice.

ἔνθ' Ὕπνος μὲν ἔμεινε πάρος Διὸς ὄσσε ἰδέσθαι,
εἰς ἐλάτην ἀναβὰς περιμήκετον, ἣ τότ' ἐν Ἴδῃ
μακροτάτη πεφυυῖα δι' ἠέρος αἰθέρ' ἵκανεν·
ἔνθ' ἧστ' ὄζοισιν πεπυκασμένος εἰλατίνοισιν,
ὄρνιθι λιγυρῇ ἐναλίγκιος, ἥν τ' ἐν ὄρεσσι
χαλκίδα κικλήσκουσι θεοί, ἄνδρες δὲ κύμινδιν.

Then, before the eyes of Zeus saw him, Hypnos stayed back and ascended a very tall pine tree, the one that then on Ida, having grown highest, reached aether through the air. There he sat, hidden by the pine branches, like the clear-voiced bird in the mountains that the gods call the chalkis, but men the kymindis.

(3) *Odyssey* 1.319–320. Athena comes to the house of Odysseus in the guise of Mentes, leader of the Taphians. She encourages Telemachos to drive the suitors away and to go abroad in search of news about Odysseus. Mentes-Athena then takes an abrupt leave.

Ἡ μὲν ἄρ' ὣς εἰποῦσ' ἀπέβη γλαυκῶπις Ἀθήνη,
ὄρνις δ' ὣς ἀνοπαῖα διέπτατο . . .

Thus having spoken, gray-eyed Athena departed, and as a bird she flew away, upwards (*or*, through the openings, ὀπαί, of the roof).

(4) *Odyssey* 3.371–372. Athena, taking the appearance of Mentor, accompanies Telemachos to Pylos. The Ithacans arrive as Nestor and his people sacrifice beside the sea to Poseidon. Nestor has no news of Odysseus and advises Telemachos to go on to Sparta. When night falls, Nestor invites Telemachos and Mentor to sleep in his house rather than at the ship. Mentor-Athena refuses, saying that he will take the ship in the morning to collect a debt from the Kaukonians, while Telemachos proceeds to Sparta by chariot.

Ὣς ἄρα φωνήσασ᾽ ἀπέβη γλαυκῶπις Ἀθήνη
φήνῃ εἰδομένη . . .

Thus, then, having spoken, gray-eyed Athena departed seeming like an osprey . . .

(5) *Odyssey* 5.337–338 and 351–353. Poseidon, returning from his stay among the Ethiopians, sees Odysseus sailing in his raft from the island of Kalypso towards the land of the Phaeacians. Angry that Odysseus has again attempted to return homewards, Poseidon sends a terrific storm. The goddess Leukothea pities Odysseus and comes to his aid.

αἰθυίη δ᾽ ἐϊκυῖα ποτῇ ἀνεδύσετο λίμνης,
ἷζε δ᾽ ἐπὶ σχεδίης καί μιν πρὸς μῦθον ἔειπε.

Like a sea gull she emerged from the water in flight, and she sat upon the raft and spoke to him a word.

Leukothea gives Odysseus an immortal veil (*krēdemnon*) and tells him to spread it beneath his chest and swim to land.

Ὣς ἄρα φωνήσασα θεὰ κρήδεμνον ἔδωκεν,
αὐτὴ δ᾽ ἂψ ἐς πόντον ἐδύσετο κυμαίνοντα
αἰθυίη ἐϊκυῖα· μέλαν δέ ἑ κῦμα κάλυψεν.

Thus having spoken, the goddess gave him the veil, and she herself at once entered into the stormy sea like a sea gull, and a black wave covered her.

(6) *Odyssey* 22.239–240. Odysseus and Telemachos, with Eumaios the swineherd and the cattle-herder, stand on the threshold of the megaron and engage the suitors in battle. Athena, again in the form of Mentor, approaches them, apparently coming from the rooms within the house behind them. Odysseus knows that this is Athena but speaks as if to Mentor. The suitors, of course, take the goddess for Mentor, and Agelaos shouts a contemptuous warning. His insolence angers Mentor-Athena, who exhorts Odysseus to show himself the fighter he was at Troy.

αὐτὴ δ᾽ αἰθαλόεντος ἀνὰ μεγάροιο μέλαθρον
ἕζετ᾽ ἀναΐξασα, χελιδόνι εἰκέλη ἄντην.

Then she herself, darting up to the roof beam of the smoky megaron, sat, like a swallow to look on.

As the battle turns in favor of Odysseus, Athena lends her aid.

δὴ τότ᾽ Ἀθηναίη φθισίμβροτον αἰγίδ᾽ ἀνέσχεν
ὑψόθεν ἐξ ὀροφῆς· τῶν δὲ φρένες ἐπτοίηθεν.

Then, indeed, Athena held up the mortal-destroying aegis aloft from the roof, and their wits were dismayed.

Odyssey 22.297–298

Dirlmeier concludes that in each case, and in all other Homeric passages in which a deity is said to be like a bird, the poetic intent is metaphoric. In every instance, Dirlmeier believes, the poet *compares* the deity to a bird, usually to the swiftness of a bird; never does the poet mean to say that a deity assumed the physical form of a bird. Such primitive theriomorphism, holds Dirlmeier, cannot be found in Homer.

Dirlmeier's view met some resistance, a feeling that he had removed a certain numinous dimension from the epics. Wolfgang Fauth missed "the effect of a suddenly suspected recognition, and the moment of ambivalence resulting from this possibility—the uncertainty as to whether the person startled by the appearance saw only a bird or a divine being concealed in the bird—as symptom of an impenetrable secret."[8] Still, many accepted Dirlmeier's explanation until Herbert Bannert challenged it on the grounds that it exercised too strong a rationalizing control over the text.[9] The point of Mentor-Athena's disappearance from the seashore at Pylos (no. 4 above), Bannert argues, is neither a simple comparison nor a literal transformation. Rather, Bannert suggests, the poet describes an amazing occurrence, witnessed by all present: the stranger next to Nestor is suddenly gone, and an osprey appears in the sky. Nestor realizes that a deity is present, just as Telemachos had earlier recognized the presence of a god with the sudden departure of Mentes-Athena (no. 3 above).[10]

Bannert believes that it is again the suddenness of Mentor-Athena's appearance beside Odysseus on the megaron threshold that causes Odysseus to recognize the presence of Athena as he prepares to fight the suitors (*Odyssey* 22.205–210, see no. 6 above). The goddess then flies rapidly upwards (ἀναΐξασα) like a swallow (χελιδόνι εἰκέλη ἄντην). But how absurd it would be to picture a little swallow shaking the terrible aegis, as Athena does in the following lines, and Bannert is surely right to plead that such passages not be read too literally. The singer Medon later tells the assembly of Ithacans that Odysseus acted with divine aid.

> I myself saw an immortal god who stood near Odysseus and was altogether like (πάντα ἐῴκει) Mentor. The deathless god at one time appeared (φαίνετο) before Odysseus, encouraging him, and at another time, routing the suitors, the god raged down the megaron, and the suitors fell close together. (Odyssey 24.445–449)

Medon's account flatly contradicts the earlier description of Athena shaking her aegis from the roof beam, but it is the perception of divine presence, not its specific form, that matters.

Some of the passages, Bannert agrees, should be understood as comparisons (for example, nos. 3 and 5 above, and Iliad 13.62: Poseidon ὥς τ' ἴρηξ ὠκύπτερος ὦρτο πέτεσθαι), and he sees the main motivation for such comparisons in the suddenness of the god's appearance and disappearance. For the rest, Bannert is sympathetic, as Dirlmeier is not, to Martin Nilsson's conception of divine epiphanies in Vogelgestalt in Bronze Age and later religious imagery.

Hartmut Erbse also rejected the rationalizing approach of Dirlmeier.[11] For Erbse, it is not a question of divine metamorphoses but of human perceptions. He uses another passage as illustration. After Aphrodite has foiled Menelaos' victory over Paris by bodily removing Paris from the battlefield, Hera and Zeus argue about whether Menelaos should now be entitled to take back Helen or whether the battle must resume. Hera prevails, and Athena causes the fighting to continue.

> And as the son of crooked-counseling Kronos sends a star, an omen either to sailors or to a wide army of hosts, a bright star from which many sparks go forth, like this (οἷον δ' ἀστέρα) Pallas Athena darted to earth, and leapt down into their midst, and amazement held them as they looked on, both the horse-taming Trojans and the well-greaved Achaeans. So might someone say, looking at another next

to him, "Indeed, again there will be evil war and the dread battle-noise, or Zeus will set friendship on both sides, he who is paymaster of war for men." (Iliad 4.75–84)

Dirlmeier comments on this passage that the poet does not worry about a falling star appearing in daylight; the point is the swiftness of Athena's movement. Erbse objects: this cannot be simply a metaphor because the Trojans and Greeks react with amazement to what they actually see, and, if they see a bright falling star, then Athena has masked herself as a falling star. Erbse would extend this interpretation to the appearances of gods as birds. When the poet says that a god is like a bird, this is not what the god actually is but how the god appears to mortal eyes; the appearance of a god in bird form is not different from the epiphany of a god in human form.

B. C. Dietrich, in a subsequent discussion of divine epiphanies in Homer,[12] argues that gods appear to mortals in the epics as a vivid poetic technique for describing divine inspiration and intervention. The gods, Dietrich points out, do not *need* to assume physical form in order to communicate with humankind. Helenos, in Iliad 7.44, understood in his heart (σύνθετο θυμῷ) the plan of Apollo and Athena to stop the fighting for a day (see no. 1 above). In the first book of the Odyssey, although Telemachos has just witnessed the sudden disappearance of Athena in the guise of Mentes (see no. 3 above), he becomes aware of her inspiration inwardly (φρεσὶν ᾗσι νοήσας, Odyssey 1.322) and not through sensory perception. Dietrich remarks that Homeric epiphanies are "redundant to the process of comprehending divine presence."[13] Thus, for Dietrich, when Apollo and Athena settle down in a tree like vultures to watch Hektor's single combat (no. 1 above), their apparent metamorphosis occurs for the purpose of neither epiphany nor disguise but rather simply as the poetic device for locating divine presences within the immediate sphere of human activity.

Dietrich's discussion has reformulated the question in a useful way. Rather than asking whether the gods are merely compared to birds or indeed become birds, Dietrich asks whether such apparent transformations belong to the realm of poetic convention or to the actual religious beliefs of Homer and his audience. He decides in favor of poetic convention, and he is inclined moreover to think that his interpretation should be retroactively applied to the Bronze Age: "doubt must surely fall on the many scenes in Minoan/Mycenaean art which appear to depict the physical epiphany of a deity in human, bird or animal form."[14]

Dietrich's arguments, I think, insist on too much inner logic in the poems. If the gods can implant their wishes directly into the minds of mortals, that is no reason they should not also appear to mortals or visit the mortal world in disguise. The redundancy that sometimes results need not mean that one element of the gods' behavior represents real beliefs while the other is merely poetic decoration. In any event, even if one agrees with Dietrich that bird epiphanies in Homer are a poetic convention, it would be very dubious methodology to conclude that divine epiphanies are therefore not to be found in Bronze Age art. As I hope to show, the conventions in Homeric poetry and in Aegean visual arts operated in rather different spheres.

BIRD EPIPHANIES IN MINOAN AND MYCENAEAN ART

Since the beginning of this century, many scholars have viewed certain Minoan and Mycenaean representations of flying creatures—birds and butterflies—as divine epiphanies.[15] Whether the bird is to be understood as the actual presence of the goddess in bird form or as a sign that symbolizes the goddess' (invisible) presence, the very close link between the bird and the goddess in many Minoan representations is obvious, and perhaps the distinction is not very important. Bird vases and bird figurines occur in forms and contexts that indicate their religious significance in the Pre-Palatial and Old Palace periods.[16] A good example from the Old Palace period is the set of miniature columns with birds perched on top (fig. 18.1) from the Loomweight Basement Deposit at Knossos.[17] In the New Palace period, birds are found with female figurines, possibly goddesses, in cult deposits.[18] The winged, eagle-headed female figure (fig. 18.2) on many of the sealings from Zakro suggests the virtual identification of the goddess with a bird.[19] In the Post-Palace period, birds are affixed to the headdresses of goddesses with upraised hands from the Shrine of the Double Axes at Knossos and from Gazi, Kannia, and

FIGURE 18.1 Terracotta group of miniature columns with birds on top. From the Loomweight Basement Deposit at Knossos. Old Palace Period. Herakleion, Archaeological Museum. (Photograph courtesy of Alison Frantz [negative Cr 122].)

Karphi.[20] A bird appears in some form in every known sanctuary of the Post-Palatial goddess with upraised hands.[21]

The Mycenaeans also associated birds and goddesses. Birds appear with tripartite shrines and nude female figures among the gold ornaments from the Shaft Graves.[22] These particular examples may copy Minoan images without reflecting indigenous Mycenaean beliefs, but later Mycenaean art shows a close alliance between bird and goddess in representations that are more distinctly Mycenaean than Minoan. The Homage Krater from Aradippo, Cyprus (fig. 18.3), has two scenes of warriors in procession to an enthroned figure usually identified as a goddess; in one case, a plump, spotted bird perches on the back of the throne. Karageorghis compares the enthroned figure to the Dove Goddess mentioned twice in Linear B tablets.[23] On the great gold ring from Tiryns, an enthroned goddess with an august

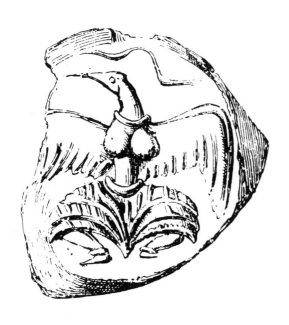

FIGURE 18.2 Terracotta sealing from Zakro with eagle-headed female figure. New Palace Period. (After D. G. Hogarth, *JHS* 22 [1902] 79, fig. 8, no. 20.)

bird behind her chair receives a procession of four genii with pitchers of liquid offerings.[24]

In Minoan depictions of a more narrative character, certain ritual actions appear to invoke the presence of a deity. On an Old Palace bowl from Phaistos, two women, both raising one arm and lowering the other, dance around a strange, armless figure outlined with snaky loops (the Snake Goddess?).[25] A similar dancer lifts one arm and lowers the other before a female figure (goddess?) with upraised hands on the famous ring, of the New Palace Period, from Isopata Tomb I.[26] Instead of dancing, the worshipper may kneel and embrace a baetylic stone.[27] In some representations, the deity appears as a tiny form suspended in the air.[28] Elsewhere, a bird (or sometimes a butterfly) responds to the same kind of summons and reveals a divine presence.[29] In the Post-Palatial terracotta group from Palaikastro, three women dance around a central female lyre-player (fig. 18.4), and, as if in response, a bird alights on the circular base in front of the lyre-player.[30]

Recent archaeological discoveries have dramatically clarified the relation between these visual representations and actual ritual performances. In 1978–1982, Peter Warren excavated three circular platforms just west of the Knossos Stratigraphical Museum.[31] On the basis of the Palaikastro group of dancers (fig. 18.4) and similar evidence, Warren has identified these imposing ashlar structures as dancing platforms, perhaps used in rituals meant to invite a divine epiphany. The ceramics associated with the circular platforms at Knossos indicate that they were built in LM II and went out of use in LM III A2 (c. 1425/1400–1375/1350 B.C.); they therefore belong to the period of possible Mycenaean occupation at Knossos. If there were Mycenaeans at Knossos, they may have adopted the Minoan dancing ritual or brought to Crete one of their own. In either case, as Warren observed, a famous vignette of Cretan dances survives in the *Iliad*. On the shield Hephaistos made for Achilles, the smith-god depicted a χορός (dance-[-place]), which, the poet says, is like the one that Daidalos once fashioned at Knossos for Ariadne (*Iliad* 18.590–592).

With the dancing platforms at Knossos and the χορός of Daidalos in the *Iliad*, we again confront the relation between Bronze Age evidence and Homer. What kind of tenuous link with the past, which Emily Vermeule might call "spiritual archaeology," has the poetry here preserved?[32] In an essay in this volume, Steven Lonsdale explores the connections between the dancing platforms at Knossos and the χορός on Achilles' shield. He finds that Homer's picture of innocent, marriageable young people has sinister echoes both within the *Iliad* and in the archaeological record. The circular dance on the shield, Lonsdale believes, foreshadows the grim dance of Achilles and Hektor around the walls of Troy in Book 22. Likewise, Ariadne's dancing-place, which in the *Iliad* seems made by the master craftsman for the pleasure of the young princess, is a distant echo of the monumental stone platforms for actual ecstatic dances, perhaps, as Lonsdale suggests, accompanied by human sacrifice. The Homeric dance on Achilles's shield occurs in apparently secular festivities, perhaps weddings. The Minoan-Mycenaean prototype, by contrast, belongs to an intensely sacred context.[33]

FIGURE 18.3 The Homage Krater, from Aradippo, Cyprus. LH III A1 (early fourteenth century B.C.). Louvre, Département des Antiquités Orientales, AM 676. (Photo Réunion des Musées Nationaux.)

The kind of interplay Lonsdale finds between Bronze Age life and Homeric text provides a helpful paradigm for describing the relation between divine epiphanies in Minoan-Mycenaean art and in Homer. The Bronze Age depictions refer to performed rituals, but divine epiphanies (as birds or humans) in Homer occur outside any ritual context, as events in the narrative of heroic action. In the Minoan and Mycenaean images, the deity appears in response to ritual summons; in Homer, the gods interfere, usually without invitation, in human affairs. The difference is that between religious ideas in the performance of organized religious rites and the same ideas played out in a fictional narrative. In representing the rituals, Bronze Age art uses certain conventions, among them the appearance of birds, to indicate divine presence. Homeric poetry draws on the same basic iconography to give the gods active parts in the epic

stories. The way in which gods become birds in Homeric poetry is both a poetic convention and a reflection of Bronze Age (and later) religious beliefs.

BIRDS AND LYRE-PLAYERS

In the Bronze Age, then, the appearance of a bird or birds among cult objects and in depictions of cult scenes refers to a divinity. In some cases, such representations of cult scenes include a lyre-player.

In a chamber tomb excavated near Chania, Crete, there was found a pyxis dating to early Late Minoan IIIB, c. 1300–1250 B.C. (fig. 18.5).[34] On the pyxis stands a figure, thought to be male, who wears a long chiton and supports with his right hand a seven-stringed lyre taller than himself. To the left of the lyre are two horns of consecration, one above the other, each with a double axe standing in its center. Two birds descend above the lyre-player. In the adjacent panel to the right are three ascending birds and three bird-heads (presumably the bodies are meant to be outside the picture frame or behind another bird). We may surmise that the horns

FIGURE 18.4 Terracotta group of dancing women around a female lyre-player. From Palaikastro, Crete, Post-Palace Period. (After *PM* III, 72, fig. 41.)

FIGURE 18.5 Pyxis from the cemetery at Kalami Apokoronou (Tomb 1), near Chania. Chania Archaeological Museum 2308. Late Minoan IIIB (first half of the thirteenth century B.C.). (Photograph courtesy of the Archaeological Museum, Chania, Crete.)

of consecration and the double axes signal a religious context. The birds that answer the lyre-player's call indicate the arrival of divine beings.

A long-robed musician with a monumental lyre appears again on a fragmentary vase (fig. 18.6), of approximately the same date as the Chania pyxis, found in 1974 during salvage excavations of chamber tombs in Nafplion.[35] The Nafplion musician and his instrument appear alone, without the cult symbols and birds of the Chania pyxis, but the Nafplion vase may add an element not present in the pyxis. The fragments are part of a krater, an open-mouthed jar for serving wine; it is possible that the lyre-player is painted on the krater because an actual lyre-player performed at occasions on which this vase was used. The lyre-players on the Chania and Nafplion vases are similar, both vases were found in tombs, and the two vases are virtual contemporaries. The significance of the Chania scene and the abbreviated Argolid version may be similar as well.

The Chania pyxis in turn seems to be an abbreviated version of the much fuller scenes on the limestone sarcophagus from Ayia Triadha (figs. 18.7a–c).[36] In the pouring scene on the left half of the front side (fig. 18.7a), a long-robed male musician plays a seven-stringed lyre while a priestess pours liquid offerings into

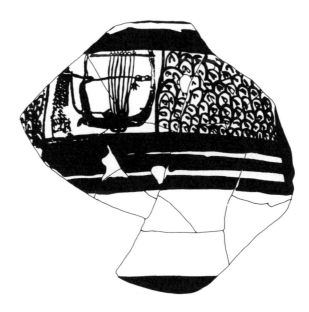

FIGURE 18.6 Fragmentary krater from Tomb IV in the Lagoumia necropolis in Nafplion. Nafplion Archaeological Museum 23536. Late Helladic IIIA 2 (c. 1375–1350 B.C.). (Drawing by Devra Goldstein after *ArchEph* 1977, pl. 20.)

FIGURE 18.7A Limestone sarcophagus from Ayia Triadha, front. Pouring of libations and offering procession. LM IIIA (early fourteenth century B.C.). (Photograph courtesy of Alison Frantz [negative Cr 8].)

a large jar. The jar stands between two tall double axes, each with a bird on top. On the right half of the front side, three male figures carry calves and a boat towards an armless male figure in a long robe who stands facing them before an imposing structure covered with running spiral friezes. A bull has been sacrificed on the back of the sarcophagus (fig. 18.7b); to the right of the bull, a woman in a shaggy skirt stretches her hands over an altar and faces a tall double axe, this one also with a bird on top. On one end of the sarcophagus (fig. 18.7c), two goddesses arrive in a chariot drawn by griffins; a bird accompanies them overhead.

The music-making and the rituals depicted on the Ayia Triadha sarcophagus are presumably funerary in nature. The lyre-playing on the Chania pyxis and on the Nafplion krater, both from tombs, may have been part of funerary ritual as well. On the sarcophagus, the ritual included the sacrifice of a bull. Likewise, the double axes and horns of consecration on the Chania pyxis probably imply a sacrifice,[37] and the lone lyre-player on the Nafplion krater, a vessel designed to hold wine at a feast, may allude to the whole complex of images fully depicted on the sarcophagus and to the feast that followed the sacrifice as well. The lyre-players' task is to summon divine attendance at the sacrifice, and the divine presence is signified by the birds.[38] The pyxis, the krater, and the sarcophagus all belong to the period after the fall of the Minoan palaces, but the iconography on both Cretan pieces has a strong Minoan flavor.

The combination of lyres, birds, and sacrifice does not occur only in funereal circumstances. Among the wall-paintings from Room 6 (the "Throne Room") of the palace at Mycenaean Pylos is a composition that includes a bull, a lyre-player, and a conspicuous bird (fig. 18.8). Also part of this composition, but painted on a smaller scale, are male banqueters seated in pairs at small tables. Mabel Lang believed that the bull was standing.[39] Lucinda McCallum, whose reconstruction is reproduced here, has restudied the Pylos frescoes and found an unpublished fragment that seems to show a

FIGURE 18.7B Limestone sarcophagus from Ayia Triadha, back. Bull sacrifice and sacred enclosure. LM IIIA (early fourteenth century B.C.). (Photograph courtesy of Alison Frantz [negative Cr 9].)

horizontal platform below the bull; she therefore concludes that the bull lay on a sacrificial table as on the Ayia Triadha sarcophagus.[40] This composition occupied the right half of the wall against which the "throne" stood; a large, emblematic griffin and lion flanked the "throne" on the left side.

Decorating as they do the megaron hall, the very sort of setting in which one envisions Demodokos singing at the Phaeacian court, the painted lyre-player and banqueters would seem to mirror the "equal feasts" that living Pylians shared in this room. This interpretation, however, does not account for the relative sizes of the different elements of the wall-painting. McCallum reduces the size of the bull in her restoration, but the bull, the lyre-player, and the bird still dominate the composition; the seated banqueters are clearly subsidiary. McCallum connects the sacrificial bull in Room 6 (the

FIGURE 18.7C Limestone sarcophagus from Ayia Triadha, east end. Two goddesses in griffin-drawn chariot with bird overhead. LM IIIA (early fourteenth century B.C.). (Photograph courtesy of Alison Frantz [negative Cr 10].)

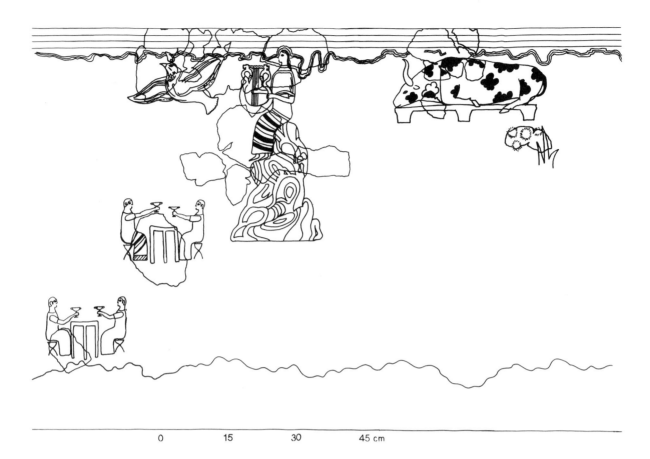

0   15   30   45 cm

FIGURE 18.8 Fresco from Room 6 (the "Throne Room") at Pylos. Restored drawing by Lucinda R. McCallum. (By permission of Lucinda R. McCallum.)

"Throne Room") with the large bull walking in a procession in Room 5, the vestibule that leads immediately into Room 6.[41] Citing Linear B tablets from Pylos that record offertory processions and the offering of a bull, McCallum argues that the frescoes in the megaron complex represent a major religious festival held at Pylos.[42] McCallum's reconstruction is a convincing hypothesis. In the "formulaic" manner of Mycenaean wall-painting (the word is Lang's[43]), the bull indicates a sacrifice, the lyre-player and the banqueters represent the rituals that accompanied the sacrifice, and the bird signifies the attendance of the deity.

Around the same time that a Mycenaean artist painted the lyre-player in the "Throne Room" at Pylos,

an artist at the east end of the Mediterranean incised a scene with some of the same elements on an ivory plaque (fig. 18.9) found at the Canaanite city of Megiddo.[44] On the right-hand side of the plaque, a victorious king drives two naked captives in front of his chariot. On the left-hand side, at a subsequent moment, the same king sits in his sphinx-guarded throne and raises a cup to his lips. A standing female, queen or priestess, faces the king, and immediately behind this personage is a female figure playing a nine-stringed lyre. A bird with outstretched wings flies just below the lyre, another stands on the floor beneath the king's throne, and two more (one partly lost) flutter in the air behind the throne. Two servants have drawn wine from a large jar at the far left and carry full cups towards the king and queen. Above the wine jar, resting on a flat shelf, are two animal-head vessels, one an ibex and the other a lion. This ivory plaque was attached to a piece of wooden furniture; six round dowel holes for its attachment are

FIGURE 18.9 Ivory plaque from Megiddo. From the thirteenth or first half of the twelfth century B.C. IDAM 38.780. (After Gordon Loud, *The Megiddo Ivories* [Chicago 1939], pl. 4.)

drilled through the plaque without particular regard for the incised composition. Perhaps the piece decorated a throne or footstool similar to those depicted on it.

In its elegant Canaanite idiom, the incised ivory includes more details and places its figures more conventionally than the Pylos fresco, but both compositions show banqueting, lyre-player, and bird(s); moreover, the location of the wall-painting, like the setting of the left-hand scene on the ivory, is a room with a ceremonial seat. Missing on the ivory is the sacrificial bull, but the animal-head vessels convey the ritual nature of the Canaanite drinking scene and, at the same time, may provide a link to the animal-head vessels of Aegean rituals.[45] Excavations at Megiddo brought to light Mycenaean and Cypriot pottery, and, among the ivory-carvings found at Megiddo, there are possible Mycenaean and Cypriot imports.[46] The Mycenaean wall-painting and the Canaanite ivory share several important elements, and the archaeological record shows clearly that there was interchange between the two cultures; this is at least circumstantial evidence that the rituals they depict may have elements in common.

An important link between the Aegean and the Levant has always been the island of Cyprus, and, if the connection between the Pylos wall-painting and the Megiddo ivory seems tenuous, Cyprus offers mediating evidence. The British Museum has a four-sided, wheeled, bronze stand that once belonged to the Duke of Buccleuch (figs. 18.10a–e).[47] The stand belongs to a type of which about sixteen examples are known; roughly half of these were found on Cyprus and can be dated by their find-contexts (when known) to the twelfth century B.C.[48] Most of the others have no known provenance. There is little doubt that the stand once owned by the Duke of Buccleuch was made in Cyprus in the twelfth century B.C. Some of the figures that decorate this stand, such as the sphinx with the low, flat-topped hat, come unequivocally from Aegean sources. On the other hand, one four-sided bronze stand that has a documented provenance other than Cyprus was excavated at Megiddo.[49] Literary traditions in both the Levant and Greece remember these objects; Hiram of Tyre made wheeled stands for King Solomon's temple in Jerusalem (I Kings 7:27–37),[50] and Homer says that Hephaistos made wheeled tripods for the banquets of the gods (*Iliad* 18.373–377, and cf. Helen's wheeled basket, *Odyssey* 4.130–132).

The Buccleuch stand is the most elaborate known of this type. Each side has a main panel with a subsidiary register, and the round ring on top has a frieze of predatory lions and a grazing deer. On one side, a lion moves to the right, holding a water bird in its jaws (fig. 18.10a). In front of the lion, on the adjacent side to the right, a two-horse chariot driven by a charioteer and carrying a warrior proceeds rightward (fig. 18.10b). On the next panel to the right, the winged sphinx with the Aegean flat-topped cap also advances to the right (figs. 18.10c and 18.10e). In the last panel, two standing figures advance to the right toward a seated figure facing left (figs. 18.10d and 18.10e). The standing figure on the far left, wearing only a kilt, brings an oinochoe and cup. Before him stands a harp- or lyre-player. The seated figure, wearing a long robe, plays an identical instrument. Read as a formulaic composition, the lion, emblematic

FIGURE 18.10A Bronze, four-sided, wheeled stand. Probably Cypriot, twelfth century B.C. Side with lion. British Museum no. 1946/10–17/1. (Photograph courtesy of the Trustees of the British Museum.)

FIGURE 18.10B Bronze, four-sided, wheeled stand. Probably Cypriot, twelfth century B.C. Side with chariot. British Museum no. 1946/10–17/1. (Photograph courtesy of the Trustees of the British Museum.)

FIGURE 18.10C Bronze, four-sided, wheeled stand. Probably Cypriot, twelfth century B.C. Side with sphinx. British Museum no. 1946/10–17/1. (Photograph courtesy of the Trustees of the British Museum.)

FIGURE 18.10D Bronze, four-sided, wheeled stand. Probably Cypriot, twelfth century B.C. Side with seated lyre-player and two attendants. British Museum no. 1946/10–17/1. (Photograph courtesy of the Trustees of the British Museum.)

FIGURE 18.10E Bronze, four-sided, wheeled stand. Probably Cypriot, twelfth century B.C. Corner view. British Museum no. 1946/10–17/1. (Photograph courtesy of the Trustees of the British Museum.)

of the king in battle, presages the royal warrior in his battle chariot, while the sphinx, emblematic of the king at home (cf. fig. 18.9, the sphinx-guarded throne on the Megiddo ivory), introduces the king sitting in his palace and celebrating his deeds with wine and song.

The stand itself, moreover, is much too exquisite for utilitarian use; it probably held a wine jar on occasions like that depicted on its fourth side. The divine presence at these occasions is marked by the figures of birds, modeled in the round, that perch on each corner of the stand. Powerful men, one in Megiddo and one in Cyprus, chose the same two scenes as distinctive of their prominent status; the king of Pylos may have drawn on the same images for the same purposes.

A century later on Cyprus conditions had changed for the worse, but an eleventh-century clay kalathos continues basic iconographic elements from better days. The kalathos was looted from a chamber tomb in the region of Palaepaphos and subsequently recovered by the Cyprus Museum.[51] In the interior (fig. 18.11a), a male lyre-player wearing a long sword faces a tethered goat across a metope of lozenges. In front of the goat is a palm tree, surely meant here as a sacred tree in the Near Eastern and Minoan tradition. The goat seems to be presented for sacrifice to a deity represented by the tree, while the lyre-player in the next metope provides the music. In the metope behind the lyre-player are four squares, two (or three?) of which contain birds. The shape of this vase is Aegean; at a later period, miniature kalathiskoi were characteristic votives at the Sanctuary of Demeter on Acrocorinth and at the Perachora Heraion.[52] On the exterior of the vase (fig. 18.11b) are three metopes with stylized bucrania, allusions to sacrifice.[53]

LYRE-PLAYERS AND BANQUETERS

The funerary significance of the scenes on the Ayia Triadha sarcophagus seems indisputable, and the funerary significance of the Chania pyxis and the Nafplion krater possible, but what kind of ritual occasion is attended by lyre-players in the Pylos wall-painting (fig. 18.8), the ivory plaque from Megiddo (fig. 18.9), and the bronze stand in the British Museum

(figs. 18.10a–e)? Of these three examples, the Megiddo plaque (fig. 18.9) offers the fullest representation, and R. D. Barnett has offered an interpretation for it that may provide help with the Mycenaean and Cypriot scenes. The occasion at which the king on the ivory plaque raises his cup, according to Barnett, is the *marzeah*.[54]

The *marzeah* was one of the longest-lived institutions of ancient Syria-Palestine, attested at various places and times from Ugarit in the fourteenth century B.C. to the sixth-century A.C. mosaic map at Madeba. References to the *marzeah* occur in Ugaritic, Phoenician, Biblical, Elephantine, Nabatean, Palmyrene, and rabbinical texts.[55]

Four Akkadian texts and four alphabetic Ugaritic texts from Ugarit mention the *marzeah*. Of these, six are legal in nature and two are mythological. The legal texts transmit some idea of what the *marzeah* was and its place in the social structure; for the meaning of the *marzeah*, we are dependent on the much more ambiguous mythological texts.

The Ugaritic *marzeah* was an association of prominent men who owned or leased a house for their gatherings. In addition to the *bêt marzeah* (house of the *marzeah*), the *marzeah* possessed vineyards, fields, and probably storerooms. The king of Ugarit and kings of smaller towns authorized and confirmed the *marzeah's* ownership of such property; this royal attention attests to the high social rank of the "men of the *marzeah*."[56] There is no indication that the membership of the *marzeah* was defined by kinship relations, but membership was hereditary, passed from father to son. The organization is spoken of as belonging to a particular deity; the Ugaritic texts mention the *marzeah* of Shatrana, that of Hurrian Ishtar, and probably that of Anat.

One of the two mythological texts (KTU 1.114) describes the extreme inebriation of El, the chief god of the Ugaritic pantheon, who becomes so drunken while sitting with his *marzeah* that he falls into his own excrement.[57] To judge from this scurrilous account, the chief activity of the *marzeah* is drinking. The other mythological text (KTU 1.21) probably belongs to the epic of Aqhat. The young hero Aqhat, son of Danel, has been killed. Most Ugaritic scholars believe that the group of texts known as the "*rp'um* texts," of which KTU 1.21 is one, relates Danel's efforts to bring Aqhat back to the

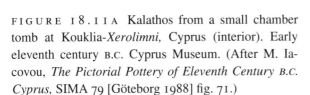

FIGURE 18.11B Kalathos from a small chamber tomb at Kouklia-*Xerolimni*, Cyprus (exterior). Early eleventh century B.C. Cyprus Museum. (After M. Ia-covou, *The Pictorial Pottery of Eleventh Century B.C. Cyprus*, SIMA 79 [Göteborg 1988] fig. 65.)

FIGURE 18.11A Kalathos from a small chamber tomb at Kouklia-*Xerolimni*, Cyprus (interior). Early eleventh century B.C. Cyprus Museum. (After M. Ia-covou, *The Pictorial Pottery of Eleventh Century B.C. Cyprus*, SIMA 79 [Göteborg 1988] fig. 71.)

world of the living.[58] Danel makes his request to Baal, and Baal gives Danel instructions:

> [Then Danel should say:]
> ["Come into the house of] my *marzeaḥ,*
>   go into my house [for the *rp'um*].
> I invite you [into] my [hou]se,
>   I call [you into] my [pa]lace.
> May the *rp'um* flutter to the holy place,
>   may the ghosts flutter [to] the [holy place,]
>   [may they come into the house of my] *marzeaḥ.*
> Then he will he[al you],
>   the Shepherd will [give you life again]." . . .[59]

Baal tells Danel to summon the *rp'um* into his (Danel's) *marzeaḥ;* Danel does so, and KTU 1.22 describes the gathering of the *rp'um:*

> There, shoulder to shoulder were the brothers,
>   whom El made to stand up in haste.

There the name of El revivified the dead,
  the blessings of the name of El revivified the heroes.
There rose up Baal Rapiu,
  the warriors of Baal and the warriors of Anat.
There rustled the host of the filth,
  the highness, the king, the unrelated,
as when Anat chases the game,
  and causes to fly up the birds of heaven.
He [Danel] slaughtered oxen,
  also small stock.
He slew bulls
  and the fattest of rams,
yearling calves,
  sheep, a multitude of lambkins.
To those who came over the olives were like silver,
  to those who came over the gourds were like gold,
among the fruit on the table in the hall,
  in the hall of kings.
Lo, one day he poured the wine of Thamuka,
  must of wine fit for rulers,
wine without aftereffect,
  wine of happiness,
the purple necklace of the Lebanon,
  dew of must grown by a god.
Lo, one day and a second they ate,

the *rp'um* drank
a third, a fourth day,
a fifth, a sixth day they ate,
the *rp'um* drank
in the dining room on the summit,
on the crest, on the flank of the Lebanon.[60]

The *rp'um* are the heroic ancestors, dead warriors of elite status, who dwell in the netherworld among the lower ranks of the gods and who can be summoned to partake of food and drink with the living. Another text shows that the spirits of the dead were summoned on real as well as mythological occasions. This text (KTU 1.161) appears to be the actual, contemporary record of the ritual performed at the accession of Ammurapi, last king of Ugarit. Someone, perhaps the presiding priest, invokes all the deceased kings of Ugarit along with the ancestral Amorite tribe of the Ugarit dynasty and the *rp'um*. These ghosts receive sacrifices seven times over, and the ceremony ends by blessing the new king and queen and the city of Ugarit. The communion with the dead ancestors insures the authority of their living successors and the well-being of the city.

Despite the disputations that continue concerning these Ugaritic texts, the invitation of the *rp'um* to a *marzeah* is clear in the mythological text KTU 1.21 and the invitation of the *rp'um* to receive sacrifices at Ammurapi's accession is clear in the archival text KTU 1.161. If Danel's banquet is a mythological *marzeah*, then Ammurapi's accession may have been an historical *marzeah*. The scenes depicted on the Megiddo plaque (fig. 18.9) show us how the *marzeah* was visualized in a contemporary Canaanite city, and the birds in that representation may be the Rephaim fluttering (cf. KTU 1.21) about the wine.[61] One purpose of the *marzeah*, then, seems to have been the performance of rituals for the cult of the dead. If this interpretation is tentative for Ugarit, it becomes surer with later evidence for the *marzeah*.

In the Hebrew Bible, the eighth-century B.C. prophet Amos denounces the luxurious *marzeah* in Samaria, the participants of which are oblivious to the disaster impending for the Kingdom of Israel:

Lying on ivory beds
and sprawling on their divans,

they dine on lambs from the flock,
and stall-fattened veal;
they bawl to the sound of the lyre
and, like David, they invent musical instruments;
they drink wine by the bowlful,
and lard themselves with the finest oils,
but for the ruin of Joseph they care nothing.
That is why they will now go into captivity,
heading the column of captives.
The sprawlers' revelry [*marzeah*] is over.

(Amos 6:4–7)[62]

Amos ironically implies that the "sprawlers" observe rituals for the dead yet do not mourn the death of Israel.[63] The connection of the *marzeah* with lamentation for the dead is made explicit in the words of Yahweh to Jeremiah in the late seventh century B.C. Yahweh prohibits Jeremiah from taking part in the established patterns of life that will disappear with the coming devastation of Judah. Jeremiah is not to marry or have children or enter the *marzeah* for the dead.

Yes, Yahweh says this, "Go into no house [*bêt marzeah*] where there is mourning, do not go and lament or grieve with them; for I have withdrawn my peace from this people," Yahweh declares, and faithful love and pity too. High or low, they will die in this country, without burial or lament; there will be no gashing, no shaving of the head for them. No bread will be broken for the mourner to comfort him for the dead; no cup of consolation will be offered him for his father or his mother. (Jeremiah 16:5–7)[64]

In the early sixth century B.C., Ezekiel in his Babylonian exile had a vision of the apostasies practiced in Jerusalem. Yahweh, visible as fire below and glittering amber above, leads the prophet from a gate in the city wall of Jerusalem to the inner court of the temple, showing him four progressively more abhorrent forms of desecration.[65] First he sees the "image of jealousy," perhaps the cult object of the goddess Asherah. His divine guide then takes Ezekiel to the gate of the wall that surrounds the temple and the palace.

And he [Yahweh] brought me to the entrance of the courtyard, and I looked, and there was a hole in the wall. And he said to me, "Son of man, dig into the wall." And I dug into the wall, and there was an opening. And he said to me, "Enter, and see the abominations which they are doing there." And there was every kind of unclean food and all the idols of the house of Israel engraved on the wall round about. And seventy men from among the elders of the house of Israel (including Jaazaniah son of Shaphan) were worshiping before them, and each held his censer in his hand, and the scent of incense rose. And he said to me, "Son of man, do you see what the leaders of the house of Israel are doing, each in his room of reliefs, for they say, 'Yahweh does not see; Yahweh has forsaken the land.'" And he said to me, "But you will see still greater abominations which they do."   (Ezekiel 8:7–13)[66]

Ezekiel then sees women weeping for Tammuz and finally men in the inner court of the Temple of Yahweh prostrating themselves to the sun.

As Susan Ackerman has convincingly explained, with the second abomination Ezekiel penetrates the casement wall that encloses the temple and palace and enters a house built against the inside of the wall.[67] He cannot enter by the door of the house because the group inside is exclusive. What he sees, according to Ackerman, is a *marzeah* in progress, celebrated by the most important men in Jerusalem. Significantly, the place inside the casement wall is near the centers of religious and secular authority. The *marzeah* seen by Ezekiel seems to be a feast in commemoration of dead ancestors but not directly connected to funeral or burial.

The Canaanite tradition of Ugarit, condemned by Amos and Ezekiel, survived among the Phoenicians, who carried the ritual with them into the western Mediterranean. A Phoenician inscription of the fourth or third century B.C. was found in 1844 in the area of the old harbor at Marseilles; the stone seems to be Carthaginian and may have come to Marseilles reused as a ship's ballast.[68] The inscription speaks of the *marzeah* of the god, probably Baal Saphon. A bilingual Phoenician and Greek inscription found in 1871 in the Piraeus, dated to the third or first century B.C., records that the Sidonians there celebrated a *marzeah* that lasted at least four days and honored the head of the community.[69] A bronze phiale of the fourth century B.C., perhaps itself a wine cup used in a *marzeah*, carries this Phoenician inscription: "2 cups we offer to the *marzeah* of Shamash."[70] Aramaic-speaking communities likewise continued the

practice. From the Jewish settlement at Elephantine in Egypt is an Aramaic ostracon that concerns "money for the *marzeah*."[71] An inscription from Petra, in the Nabataean dialect of Aramaic, echoes the Canaanite cult of the dead with its reference to the *marzeah* of [dedicated to?] the deified Nabataean king Ododas I.[72]

Some aspects of the *marzeah* remained remarkably constant over long periods of time. At Nabataean 'Avdat and at Palmyra, the head of the *marzeah* was called the *rb mrzh*, the same title used 1,500 years earlier at Ugarit.[73] The *marzeah* continued to have an important role in both the social and religious life of communities. Membership was a prerogative of the upper levels of society, and the *marzeah* probably exercised considerable influence in local affairs. The *marzeah* was dedicated to a certain deity. Ritual feasting, at a house owned or leased by the group, was a regular activity of the organization. Fields and vineyards owned by the *marzeah*, or dues paid by members, supplied food and drink for the feasts. The feasts could include music, particularly lyre-playing (Amos 6:5). Mourning and memorials for the recent dead and for ancestors was at least one purpose of the *marzeah*.

There exists, then, a fairly substantial amount of textual and visual documentation for the *marzeah* in the Late Bronze Age and the Iron Age in the Levant.[74] In the Aegean, it is possible that Linear B tablets from Pylos preserve some traces of a *marzeah*-like institution. Tablets Er 312 and Un 718 both refer to four divisions of Pylian society: (1) *Ekhelâwôn* (the "king" or his representative), (2) the *lawagetas* (military leader), (3) the *telestai* ("fief-holders") in Er 312, who may or may not amount to the same as the *damos* (town) in Un 718, and (4) the *worgiones*.[75] The *worgiones*, who are inferred from the adjectival form *wo-ro-ki-jo-ne-jo*, may be ὀρ-γεῶνες, "members of a religious organization."[76] Tablet Er 312 appears to specify the amount of seed-corn distributed to the land-holdings of each of these four individuals or groups. The second tablet, Un 718, again refers to land-holdings of four individuals or groups; the holdings are apparently located in a place called the Sarapeda. From another tablet (Er 880), we learn that the temenos (estate) of Ekhelâwôn in the Sarapeda was planted with fruit trees.[77] Tablet Un 718 lists the offerings that each holding in the Sarapeda will make to Poseidon. Ekhelâwôn will give a bull as well as wheat, wine, cheeses, a sheepskin, and honey; the other estates will contribute similarly but in lesser amounts.

The *worgiones* at Pylos, if this interpretation of the tablets is correct, offer a most interesting Mycenaean parallel for the *marzeaḥ* of Ugarit. Like the aristocratic men of the Ugaritic *marzeaḥ*, the Pylian *worgiones* seem to be ranked closely with the wanax Ekhelâwôn, the lawagetas, and the "fief-holders." At Ugarit and at Pylos, the associations held land that was planted with corn and produced wine. And both the Ugaritic *marzeaḥ* and the Pylian *worgiones* were connected to organized rituals.

To supplement this rather meagre textual evidence, we have the evidence of such Aegean artifacts as the four-sided bronze stand in the British Museum (figs. 18.10a–e), which may have been used for something like a *marzeaḥ* feast on Cyprus, and the megaron of the palace at Pylos (fig. 18.8), perhaps the Mycenaean equivalent of the *bêt marzeaḥ*. Here, under the patronage of a deity invoked by the lyre-player, the Pylos aristocracy may have feasted in a ceremony meant to nourish the bonds among living and dead, part of a mutually reinforcing complex of religious, political, and social systems. The presiding figure, corresponding to the Ugaritic *rb mrzḥ*, must have occupied the "throne" for which there is evidence in the Pylos megaron. The two small basins and connecting channel in the plaster floor beside the "throne" at Pylos may have been used for libations poured during a drinking ritual like that depicted in the frescoes from this room.[78]

On a larger scale, those who held power in Mycenaean society expressed their proprietary interest in the elite dead through monumental architecture. The enclosure of Grave Circle A at Mycenae is only the most obvious example. James Wright has pointed out a similar linkage between the seat of power and the illustrious dead in the alignment of the impressive northeast entrance (Entrance Porch 41) to the palace at Pylos with the gateway in the circuit wall and the tholos tomb beyond.[79]

I do not mean to suggest simply that the Mycenaeans borrowed this ceremony from the Canaanites or other Levantine peoples. Some such institution had probably existed in the Aegean from the Early Bronze Age, if not before.[80] It is more likely to be the case that, in the meta-culture of the Eastern Mediterranean, certain religious,

social, and political structures occurred with similar forms in different regional cultures. Elite feasting associated with a cult of the dead appears in various forms among the Hittites, Canaanites, Phoenicians, Israelites, Aramaeans, and Egyptians. In these circumstances, it would be odd if a similar institution did not exist in the Aegean world. When correspondences exist between the Near Eastern and Aegean iconographies, then the Near Eastern ritual, for which there is textual as well as visual evidence, may illuminate practices behind the Mycenaean images.

In the Levant, the *marzeaḥ* survived the end of the Bronze Age and continued to be an important social and religious institution for at least 1,500 years longer. The Mycenaean version, I would argue, also survived and became the institution known to us as the *symposion* (and its variants, the *syssition*, *phiditia*, or *eranoi*). As in the Oriental world, the elite status of the participants and the recognition of their heroic and eminent forebears were important aspects of the *symposion*. In both East and West, a natural linkage was assumed between one's ancestors and one's privileged place in the social hierarchy; the *marzeaḥ/symposion* was the visible and institutionalized expression of this belief.[81]

When Mediterranean cultures had close and mutually beneficial ties, resemblances between their respective institutions seem to have become stronger. A heightened similarity between the Eastern *marzeaḥ* and its Greek counterpart may have developed in the Late Mycenaean period, and this was certainly a phenomenon of the orientalizing phase of Greek culture that became strong in the eighth century and lasted until c. 500 B.C. It is a famous fact that Greeks changed their dining posture, at least for some occasions, from a seated position to a reclining position around the end of the seventh century B.C. A reclining position for banqueting was also relatively new in the Near East. The custom may have its origins among nomads, perhaps the nomadic Aramaeans; it would have become more elaborate after the nomads became sedentary, perhaps when the Aramaeans settled in North Syria in the early Iron Age (eleventh or tenth century B.C.). Assyrians adopted the custom probably during the reign of Assurbanipal (668–627 B.C.), who is shown reclining at a banquet in a famous relief from Nineveh.[82] Since reclining diners appear in the Near East (for example, in the passage from Amos quoted above) before they appear in Greece, it is clear that the Greeks adopted the reclining position from the Near East. Along with the practice of reclining, the Greeks adopted the high-legged, Oriental type of couch (*klinē*) and dippers and strainers of Eastern derivation.[83] Like the beds of the Samarians in Amos, Greek couches were decorated with ivory, examples of which survive.[84]

The ivory hoards from Arslan-Tash, Samaria, Nimrud, and Khorsabad provide plentiful evidence for furniture inlaid with ivory in Syria, Israel, and Assyria in the ninth through seventh centuries B.C. Amos explicitly situates ivory couches at a *marzeah*, and Barnett has long thought that many ivory-covered couches were designed for the *marzeah*. More recently, Barnett has also argued that the Assurbanipal relief also depicts a *marzeah*.[85] Greeks may have introduced such couches into Greece specifically for use in a *marzeah*-like context.

As Boardman has pointed out, such couches are equally conspicuous as unlikely furniture for sleeping and as objects of considerable luxury. The Greeks who used these couches clearly wanted a highly visible display of wealth, and, as I will suggest below, there may be historical reasons for believing that the Greeks wanted this particular ostentation specifically for the symbolic value that emanated from the Eastern *marzeah*.

Another famous aspect of the Greek world during this period (c. 800–500 B.C.) is the continuing development of the hoplite army. Although hoplite warfare, with ranks of infantry, may have been standard by the time of the twelfth-century Warrior Vase from Mycenae (or earlier), the possession of hoplite armor before the seventh century was probably restricted to the wealthiest classes. The equipment required for such fighting seems to have become affordable to an increasing percentage of the population in the eighth and seventh centuries.[86] Previously, warfare had been the preserve of a warrior elite on whom the entire community depended for its security; the emergence of a broader-based hoplite army robbed the aristocracy of a powerful claim to privileged status in the community.

Oswyn Murray takes this line of thought further: the democratization of warfare led to more elaborate and stylized sympotic rituals. The burial of an aristocratic warrior had been an occasion for marking the exalted position of his class, but, as the warrior class expanded, "the warrior grave . . . with its public funeral and posthumous cult gave way to the iconography and furniture of the drinking party."[87] The *symposion* replaced warfare as the characteristic activity of the elite classes. In particular, I think, the awkwardly tall, ivory-incrusted dining couches of the Oriental *marzeah* were adopted by Greek symposiasts as a conspicuous marker of an exclusively aristocratic occasion. But this was not the first use to which Greeks put the Oriental couch.

It is true, as Boardman remarks, that the Oriental couch appeared in Geometric art as a funeral bier more than a hundred years before we see it used for feasting. Moreover, depictions of such couches in feasting scenes appear, often accompanied by a side table full of food, in the richest graves of Persians, Anatolians, Greeks, and Italians.[88] The reason for the adoption of the Oriental couch as funeral furniture was surely similar to the reason for its subsequent adoption as feasting furniture, because it was appropriate for aristocratic display at a warrior funeral. Its dual use in Greek society strikingly reflects the original context of the Oriental couch in a ritual feast, the *marzeah*, that sometimes (if not always) commemorated a cult of the dead. Analogously, the continued use of the *klinē* in funerary art suggests that, just as the idea of feasting had a place in the iconography of death, so a consciousness of the heroic and aristocratic dead was present in the iconography of the symposium.

LYRES AND BIRDS

To summarize: the *symposion* had its origin in a Bronze Age feast dedicated to a deity and was held, at least sometimes, with or for the dead. Lyre-players occupied an important place in depictions of Bronze Age proto-symposia (figs. 18.8, 18.9, 18.10d). This is perhaps why lyre-players appear on vases buried with the dead, such as the wine-krater from Nafplion (fig. 18.6), the pyxis from Chania (fig. 18.5), and the kalathos from Palaepaphos (fig. 18.11a), and why ivory lyres were found in the Mycenaean tholos tomb at Menidi.[89] Lyres are again prominent in Amos' complaint about the singing sprawlers of Samaria. And, of course, lyres are virtually ubiquitous in the *symposia* of Archaic and Classical vase paintings. It is, in fact, in the form of lyres that continuity between the Bronze Age and the Iron Age can be clearly seen.

The lyre held by the musician in the fresco from Pylos (fig. 18.8) has arms that curve inwards at the top and terminate in the form of birds' heads; perhaps, with their sinuous necks, they are swans.[90] Like the lyre from Pylos, the lyre on the Ayia Triadha sarcophagus (fig. 18.7a) has a rounded bottom, an arched, lower bridge to which the strings are attached, a straight upper yoke joined to pegs mounted above the in-curved tops of the arms, and, most notably, bird-heads at the ends of the arms. A third such lyre, again carried by a male musician, appears on the procession fresco from Ayia Triadha.[91] Nicolas Platon studied these representations carefully when he restored alabaster fragments from Knossos as a lyre; the preserved arm of the alabaster lyre ends in the head of a bird.[92]

Evans seems to have found the alabaster fragments during the early years of his excavations, and, as he did not record their context, the date of the alabaster lyre is not known. The sarcophagus and the procession fresco from Ayia Triadha, however, may have been painted by the same hand and probably belong in early LM IIIA, that is, during the presumed Mycenaean period on Crete. Like the lyre in the Pylos fresco, the lyres of Knossos and Ayia Triadha should perhaps be considered Mycenaean. Nevertheless, they owe their bird-heads to Minoan and Cycladic prototypes. Minoan seals of the Middle Minoan period show lyres in the shape of closed, horizontal ellipsoids, and several of these have a single stylized bird-head positioned above the strings.[93] This Minoan type, in turn, finds a precedent in the triangular harps with bird-heads held by Cycladic marble figures, and other seated Cycladic marble figures holding cups may prefigure the seated banqueters in the Pylos fresco.[94]

Geometric vases depict lyre-players in scenes of banquets and dancing,[95] and a sherd of the first half of the seventh century from Smyrna has a long-necked bird above a lyre,[96] but not until after the middle of the seventh century does a lyre with bird-heads reappear. The earliest may be an elaborate ivory group, now in Berlin, that perhaps formed the arm of a lyre. A female figure in ceremonial dress stands on a sphinx; her tall head-dress is surmounted by a large swan-head.[97] If this group did form the arm of a lyre, the attire of the priestess

FIGURE 18.12 Komast with bird-head barbitos, on a plate painted by Psiax. Black figure on white ground. Late sixth century B.C. Basel Antikenmuseum Kä 421. (Detail.) (Photograph courtesy of the Antikenmuseum und Skulpturhalle Basel.)

could place this instrument in a religious context. Like the lyres from Ayia Triadha and Pylos, a projection on top of the swan's bent neck would have supported the upper horizontal yoke. The style of the female figure is East Greek/Anatolian, and the ivory group may be iconographically related to the sculptural group from Boğaz-köy in which a goddess is flanked by two attendants, one playing the pipes and the other a bird-head lyre.[98] Ivory swan-heads excavated by Hogarth in the Sanctuary of Artemis at Ephesos lack an upper projection and may have belonged to simpler lyres like Platon's alabaster lyre from Knossos.[99]

The surest evidence for bird-head lyres in historical Greece comes from vase paintings. In most of the *symposia,* recitations, and music lessons shown on sixth- and fifth-century vases, the stringed instruments are not animated. But some are, like the barbitos carried by a symposiast on a late sixth-century plate painted by Psiax in black figure on white ground (fig. 18.12).[100] These bird-heads, too, look like swans, and swan-heads decorate barbitoi on fifth-century Athenian vases and kitharai on fourth-century Italian vases.[101] In harps on fourth-century Italian vases, the complete figure of a leggy, swanlike bird often forms the vertical post.[102]

We thus return to birds. Birds on Bronze Age and later instruments, like the birds summoned by lyre-players in Bronze Age art, are visualizations of a divine presence. The birds tell us that the lyre-playing belonged to a ritual context, and the ritual may often have been the Greek counterpart of the Oriental *marzeaḥ*. This occasion is the natural setting for the recitation of poems about heroic ancestors, and it corresponds well to early occasions of epic performance recorded by Hesiod and Herodotus.

In the Homeric poems, recitations of epic poetry take place in a secular setting in aristocratic houses and palaces. The occasion of epic performance proposed here requires that we accept instead a ritual context for actual performances and their visual representations in the Mycenaean period and later. So poetry differs from life, and the instances of bird epiphany in the Homeric poems and in visual representations offer an analogy. In Homer, epiphanies, like recitations, occur as an integrated part of the secular action; in visual representations, epiphanies and recitations appear in the context of enacted ritual. But poetry and life come together when the performance of epic is set in the larger frame of enacted ancestor cult.

NOTES

* The abbreviation *TPHC* will be used for G. C. Gesell, *Town, Palace, and House Cult in Minoan Crete*, SIMA 67 (Göteborg 1985). Ancestor cult in this paper means the rituals and beliefs associated with the illustrious dead, that is to say, with heroes. Heroes may be distinguished from ancestors in that heroes are not always tied to their worshippers by (supposed) blood lines (W. Burkert, *Greek Religion* [Cambridge, Mass. 1985] 204). But heroes without surviving lineages tend to be thought of as tribal ancestors, and I suspect that it is not possible to draw accurate distinctions between ancestor cult and hero cult. I would like to thank Robert Koehl, Sarah Morris, Paul Rehak, and Barbette Spaeth for their help with this paper.

1. Sparta: *Odyssey* 4.15–19; Phaeacians: *Odyssey* 8.40–45, 8.57–82, 8.469–491, 13.24–28; Olympos: *Iliad* 1.601–604. All translations by the author.

2. M. L. West, "The Singing of Homer and the Modes of Early Greek Music," *JHS* 101 (1981) 113–129 (see 113).

3. C. Segal, "Bard and Audience in Homer," in R. Lamberton, ed., *Homer's Ancient Readers* (Princeton 1992) 3–29 (see 6).

4. The passage begins with an account of how Kleisthenes of Athens increased the number of Athenian tribes and named the new ones after native Athenian heroes (and Ajax). Here, says Herodotus, he was probably following the example of his grandfather Kleisthenes of Sikyon, who had stopped the Homeric recitations, had tried to displace the cult of Argive Adrastos in Sikyon by installing a cult of the Theban hero Melanippos, and had changed the names of the Dorian tribes at Sikyon. The eponymous heroes at Athens had cults, and the eponymous ancestors of the Dorian tribes probably had cults as well. The reference to Homeric recitations thus occurs within a discussion of ancestors and their cults. This placement implies that the rhapsodic competitions had some connection to cults for Argive heroes.

5. G. Nagy, "Homeric Questions," *TAPA* 122 (1992) 17–60 (see 47–51). See also H. A. Shapiro, "Hipparchos and the Rhapsodes," in C. Dougherty and L. Kurke, eds., *Cultural Poetics in Archaic Greece: Cult, Performance, Politics* (Cambridge 1993) 92–107.

6. O. Taplin, *Homeric Soundings: The Shaping of the Iliad* (Oxford 1992) 39–41.

7. F. Dirlmeier, "Die Vogelgestalt homerischer Götter," *SBHeid* 2 (1967) 5–36.

8. W. Fauth, "Zur Typologie mythischer Metamorphosen in der Homerischen Dichtung," *Poetica* 7 (1975) 235–268 (249).

9. H. Bannert, "Zur Vogelgestalt der Götter bei Homer," *WS* 91 N.S. 12 (1978) 29–42. See also A. Heubeck, "Zur Neueren Homerforschung (VII)," *Gymnasium* 89 (1982) 385, 439–440.

10. Bannert argues that the phrasing of *Odyssey* 1.320 (ὄρνις δ᾽ ὣς ἀνοπαῖα διέπτατο) must signify a comparison, because ὡς could not indicate an actual change of form. He thinks, however, that εἰδομένος (as in φήνη εἰδομένη, *Odyssey* 3.372) always signifies change of form. Thus, on the beach at Pylos, Athena changes from the form of Mentor into the form of an osprey.

11. H. Erbse, "Homerische Götter in Vogelgestalt," *Hermes* 108 (1980) 259–274.

12. B. C. Dietrich, "Divine Epiphanies in Homer," *Numen* 30 (1983) 53–79.

13. Dietrich (supra n. 12) 66.

14. Dietrich (supra n. 12) 70.

15. A. Evans, "Mycenaean Tree and Pillar Cult and Its Mediterranean Relations," *JHS* 21 (1901) 99–204 (see 105). Nilsson's chapter on "Bird Epiphanies of the Gods" (*MMR*[2] 330–340) remains the standard argument in favor of interpreting many birds in Aegean representations as divine epiphanies. See also: F. Matz, "Göttererscheinung und Kultbild im minoischen Kreta," *AbhMainz* 7 (1958) 1–69 (see 17–18); P. Warren, "Of Baetyls," *OpAth* 18 (1990) 193–206 (see 196).

16. Examples from Pre-Palace and Old Palace periods: the Early Minoan bird rhyton from a tholos tomb at Koumasa: K. Branigan, *Pre-Palatial. The Foundations of Palatial Crete, A Survey of Crete in the Early Bronze Age,* 2nd ed. (Amsterdam 1988) 111, pl. 12b; *PM* I, 116, fig. 85; the Middle Minoan I bird vase from the pillar crypt of the House of the Monolithic Pillars at Knossos: *PM* I, 146, fig. 107; the bird incised (with an animal) on a stone bowl from the Lower West Court Sanctuary Complex at Phaistos: *TPHC* 124–125; the bird vase from the pillar crypt of House Theta at Mallia: *TPHC* 110–112, cat. 84, pl. 101; the terracotta bird figurines from the ash altar of the Old Palace period at the peak sanctuary on Mount Juktas: A. Karetsou, "The peak sanctuary of Mt. Juktas," in R. Hägg and N. Marinatos, eds., *Sanctuaries and Cults in the Aegean Bronze Age* (Stockholm 1981) 137–153 (see 146).

17. *TPHC* 92, cat. 40, pl. 102. This deposit also included miniature structures decorated with horns of consecration. Evans believed that the objects fell from a shrine in an upper room during the destruction of the Old Palace: *PM* I, 248–253. In a recent reinterpretation of the stratigraphy here, Rebecca Mersereau suggests that much of the material from the Loomweight Basement represents leveling fill brought in by the builders of the New Palace: "A Reevaluation of the Loomweight Basement Deposit at Knossos with Special Reference to its Architectural Models," *AJA* 96 (1992) 334 (abstract).

18. For example, the deposit from the rooms west of Room 9 at Ayia Triadha: *TPHC* 74, cat. 13.

19. D. G. Hogarth, "The Zakro Sealings," *JHS* 22 (1902) 76–93; see nos. 20–33. S. Hood, *The Arts in Prehistoric Greece* (New York 1978) 221, fig. 223 D. and E. J. Weingarten, *The Zakro Master and His Place in Prehistory,* SIMA Pocket-book 26 (Göteborg 1983) 60–63 and 110–113 (with examples of Bird-Ladies and Bird-Men from elsewhere), and pl. 20.

20. Shrine of Double Axes: S. Marinatos and M. Hirmer, *Crete and Mycenae* (London 1960) pl. 132 (bottom); *TPHC* cat. 37, pl. 46a. Kannia: *TPHC* cat. 21, pl. 43. Gazi: Marinatos and Hirmer (supra this note), pls. 128–131; *TPHC* cat. 5, pls. 44–45. Karphi: Marinatos and Hirmer (supra this note), pls. 135–137; *TPHC* cat. 22, pls. 48a–b, 49a–b.

21. *TPHC* 62. In addition, bird figurines were found associated with goddess figures at Gournia (*TPHC* cat. 10, pl. 119), and a small bird is attached to the offering stand found at Kommos (*TPHC* 69, pl. 144).

22. *MMR*[2] 173, fig. 77, 331, 333, fig. 154. Hood (supra n. 19) 203, fig. 203 G and H. E. Vermeule, *Greece in the Bronze Age* (Chicago and London 1972) 96–97, fig. 19. Marinatos and Hirmer (supra n. 20), pl. 205.

23. Louvre, AM 676. V. Karageorghis, "Myth and Epic in Mycenaean Vase Painting," *AJA* 62 (1958) 383–387 (see 386, no. 4). E. Vermeule and V. Karageorghis, *Mycenaean Pictorial Vase Painting* (Cambridge, Mass. 1982) no. III.29, pp. 23–24, 197, pl. III.29. LM III A1, early fourteenth century B.C.

24. *CMS* I.179. *MMR*[2] 147, fig. 55. Marinatos and Hirmer (supra n. 20), pl. 207.

25. *TPHC* 124–127, cat. 103, pl. 40.

26. *CMS* II.3.51. Marinatos and Hirmer (supra n. 20), pl. 111, upper left. C. Zervos, *L'Art de la Crète: Néolithique et minoenne* (Paris 1956), pl. 632. *MMR*[2] 279–280, fig. 139.

27. Warren (supra n. 15).

28. The sex of the miniature deity varies. Female: the Isopata ring, Marinatos and Hirmer (supra n. 20), pl. 111 (upper left). Male: gold ring in the Ashmolean, perhaps from Vapheio, Warren (supra n. 15) 200, fig. 15; gold ring from Knossos, Evans (supra n. 15) 170, fig. 48. Indeterminate sex behind its figure-eight shield on the gold ring from the Akropolis Treasure, Mycenae, Evans (supra n. 15) 108, fig. 4; Marinatos and Hirmer (supra n. 20), pl. 207 (bottom).

29. For example, birds on gold rings from Kalyvia and from Sellopoulo at Knossos: Warren (supra n. 15) 194, figs. 4 and 5.

30. Herakleion Museum no. 3903. For full references: Warren (infra n. 31) 318–319 n. 29; *TPHC* 119, cat. 97, pl. 66. The dancing figures and the lyre-player were found in a deposit that also includes a fragmentary female figure with her hands on her breasts, three small birds, three larger birds, the fragmentary circular base, and several kernoi. Doubt has been expressed about whether the circular base, on which one of the small birds seems to fit, belongs with the dancing group. Warren thinks that it does. In any case, the dancers, lyre-player, and birds all come from a single deposit in a storeroom. An earlier circle of dancers, all male and without a musician, was found at Kamilari: Warren (infra n. 31) 318 n. 28, pl. 34d; *TPHC*, pl. 117.

31. P. Warren, "Circular Platforms at Minoan Knossos," *BSA* 79 (1984) 307–323.

32. E. T. Vermeule, "Baby Aigisthos and the Bronze Age," *PCPS* 33 (1987) 122–152 (see 131–134).

33. The last three lines in this section of the shield's de-

scription recur in identical form in the marriage of Menelaos' daughter and son: *Iliad* 18.604–606 = *Odyssey* 4.17–19.

34. The pyxis is from Tomb 1 at Kalami Apokoronou, Chania, Crete. J. Tzedakis, "Μινωϊκὸς Κιθαρῳδός," *AAA* 3 (1970) 111–112. K. Demakopoulou, ed., *The Mycenaean World: Five Centuries of Early Greek Culture, 1600–1100 B.C.* (Athens 1988) no. 105. N. Marinatos, *Minoan Religion: Ritual, Image, and Symbol* (Columbia, S.C. 1993) 138–139.

35. A. Dragona-Latsoude, "Μυκηναϊκὸς κιθαρῳδὸς ἀπὸ τῆ Ναυπλία," *ArchEph* 1977, 86–98; the krater is dated to the end of LH IIIA or the beginning of LH IIIB. See also Vermeule and Karageorghis (supra n. 23) no. IX.14.1, pp. 92 and 212, pl. IX.14.1, where the krater is dated LH IIIB.

36. Matz (supra n. 15) 398–407. C. Long, *The Ayia Triadha Sarcophagus*, SIMA 41 (Göteborg 1974). S. A. Immerwahr, *Aegean Painting in the Bronze Age* (University Park, Penn. 1990) 100–102 (A.T. No. 2), 180–181, pls. 50–53. Marinatos (supra n. 35) 31–36.

37. Cf. *MMR*² 229–235.

38. Long (supra n. 36) 73.

39. M. L. Lang, *The Palace of Nestor at Pylos in Western Messenia*, II: *The Frescoes* (Princeton 1969) 79–81, 109–110, 194–196 (fragments 43 H 6, 44 H 6, and 19 C 6), pls. 27, 28, 53, 125, 126, and color pl. A. See also Immerwahr (supra n. 36) 133–134, pls. XVIII and 78.

40. L. R. McCallum, "The Decorative Program in the Mycenaean Palace of Pylos: The Megaron Frescoes" (Ph.D. diss., Univ. of Pennsylvania, 1987) 95, fragment 6NE(Q3?):C:9, see 155–156, pls. 24 and 39. In addition to the visual comparanda cited by McCallum for bull sacrifices, one might add the bull on a gold ring found in a Mycenaean tomb near Thebes: *MMR*² 179 and fig. 82.

41. McCallum (supra n. 40) 77–87, pls. 8a–c.

42. McCallum (supra n. 40) 108–113. The "Campstool Fresco" from Knossos, which shows pairs of seated men wearing long robes and holding drinking vessels in their hands, could be a prototype of the Pylos fresco. See Lang (supra n. 39) 81 and Immerwahr (supra n. 36) Kn No. 26, pp. 95, 176. The fresco dates from the period when Mycenaeans may have controlled Knossos. James C. Wright has recently identified the two preserved vessels among the "Campstool" fragments as a Mycenaean goblet and a Minoan chalice, and he has suggested that the occasion was a ceremonial "protohistorical *symposion*" in which elite Mycenaean and Minoan men honored each other; see "Empty cups and empty jugs: The social role of wine in Minoan and Mycenaean societies," in P. McGovern, S. Fleming, and S. Katz, eds., *The Origins and Ancient History of Wine* (New York, in press).

43. Lang (supra n. 39) 59, 195, 221–222.

44. Israel Museum (IDAM) 38.780. G. Loud, *The Megiddo Ivories* (Chicago 1939) 13 no. 2, pl. 4. H. Frankfort, *The Art and Architecture of the Ancient Orient* (New York 1970) 270–271. *The Phoenicians* (Milan 1988) 36–37. U. Avida et al., *Treasures from the Holy Land. Ancient Art from the Israel Museum* (New York 1986) 148–149, no. 69 (where the plaque is dated thirteenth to mid-twelfth century).

45. U. Zevulun, "A Canaanite Ram-Headed Cup," *IEJ* 37 (1987) 88–104 (see 100), summarizes evidence that animal-head cups in Syria-Palestine had a ritual function. The two animal-head vessels on the Megiddo plaque are Zevulun's bent-necked type, with faces set at a right angle to the necks; this type, unlike the straight-necked Canaanite animal-head cups, has links with the Aegean. See also, in this volume, R. Koehl's remarks on "The Silver Stag 'Bibru' from Mycenae."

46. Loud (supra n. 44) 9. H. J. Kantor, "Syro-Palestinian Ivories," *JNES* 15 (1956) 153–174, see 166–171; R. D. Barnett, *Ancient Ivories in the Middle East and Adjacent Countries* (Jerusalem 1982) 24–28; O. H. Krzyszkowska, "The Enkomi Head Reconsidered," *BSA* 86 (1991) 107–120, esp. 109 and n. 10. The Mycenaeans also possessed elaborate furniture with ivory inlays and perhaps used it for occasions like that shown in the Megiddo plaque; of particular interest are the Linear B tablets from Pylos that describe such furniture. See *Docs.*² 333, 339–346. For the general picture of Aegean-Near Eastern connections in the Late Bronze Age, see J. D. Muhly, "The Role of the Sea Peoples in Cyprus during the LC III Period," in V. Karageorghis and J. D. Muhly, eds., *Cyprus at the Close of the Late Bronze Age* (Nicosia 1984) 39–56.

47. British Museum 1946/10–17/1. H. W. Catling, *Cypriot Bronzework in the Mycenaean World* (Oxford 1964) 208–210, no. 36, pl. 35 and "Workshop and Heirloom: Prehistoric Bronze Stands in the East Mediterranean," *RDAC* 1984, 69–91 (see 82–83).

48. In addition to the examples listed in Catling 1964 (supra n. 47), there are four additional fragmentary four-sided stands now known: one without provenance, one in Nicosia, one from Knossos North Cemetery Tomb 201, and the wheels, which apparently belonged to a large example, from Lefkandi Toumba Tomb 39. See Catling 1984 (supra n. 47) 83–87. For the Lefkandi wheels: M. R. Popham, E. Touloupa, and H. Sackett, "Further Excavation of the Toumba Cemetery at Lefkandi, 1981," *BSA* 77 (1982) 213–248, esp. 219 (no. 30 in Tomb 39), 239–240. The diameter of these wheels (25 cm) is twice the diameter of the wheels of Cypriot stands (c. 12 cm).

49. Megiddo stand: Catling 1964 (supra n. 47) 205, no. 33, pl. 33d.

50. The text reads:

He [Hiram] made the ten bronze stands; each stand was four cubits long, four cubits wide, and three high. They were designed as follows; they had an undercarriage and crosspieces to the undercarriage. On the crosspieces of the undercarriage were lions and bulls and winged creatures, and on top of the undercarriage was a support. . . . Each stand had four bronze wheels with bronze axles. . . . Its mouth was round like a stand for a vessel, and on the mouth there were engravings too; the crosspieces, however, were rectangular and not round. (I Kings 7:27–32, *New Jerusalem Bible* [London 1985])

The basic design, a square stand with wheels on the bottom and a round support on top, is identical to the Cypriot stands. Hiram's stands, however, were much larger—1.83 m square and 1.37 m tall (using 45.7 cm or 18 inches per cubit); the stand in the British Museum (1946/10–17/1) is .31 m high and has panels that are .15 m square.

51. V. Karageorghis, "An Early XIth Century B.C. Tomb from Palaepaphos," *RDAC* 1967, 1–24 (see 17–18, no. 7). M. Iacovou, *The Pictorial Pottery of Eleventh Century B.C. Cyprus,* SIMA 79 (Göteborg 1988) 26, no. 29, figs. 64–71. The continuation of this iconography on Cyprus in the tenth century B.C. and later can be seen in the Kaloriziki amphora, found in a cemetery near Kourion, and the Hubbard amphora, probably from a cemetery at Vartivounas. See P. Dikaios, "An Iron Age Amphora in the Cyprus Museum," *BSA* 37 (1936–1937) 56–72.

52. A. Steiner, "Pottery and Cult in Corinth: Oil and Water at the Sacred Spring," *Hesperia* 61 (1992) 385–408 (see 387). I am grateful to Professor Steiner for pointing this out to me.

53. The bucrania have been described as frogmen, monsters, and unidentifiable creatures. On the side of the vase illustrated here (fig. 18.11b), the left-hand bucranium is fairly clear. The snout of the bull is a star pattern in a circle, the eyes are large, black lozenges, and the ears are placed low, between the snout and the eyes. The other two bucrania do resemble diving frogs, but their basic character can be recognized by reference to the first.

54. R. D. Barnett, "Assurbanipal's Feast," *Eretz-Israel* 18 (1985) *1–*6. For the *marzeah* see: S. Ackerman, "A Marzeah in Ezekiel 8:7–13?," *HThR* (1989) 267–281; N. Avigad and J. C. Greenfield, "A Bronze Phialê with a Phoenician Dedicatory Inscription," *IEJ* 32 (1982) 118–128; E. F. Beach, "The Samaria Ivories, Marzeah and Biblical Texts," *BA* 55 (1992) 130–139; D. B. Bryan, "Texts Relating to the Marzeah: A Study of an Ancient Semitic Institution" (Ph.D. diss., The Johns Hopkins Univ., 1973); M. Dahood, "Additional Notes on the Mrzh Text," in L. R. Fisher, ed., *The Claremont Ras Shamra Tablets* (Rome 1971) 51–54; O. Eissfeldt, "Kultvereine in Ugarit," in J.-C. Courtois, ed., *Ugaritica* VI (Paris 1969) 187–195; J. C. Greenfield, "Un rite religieux araméen

et ses parallèles," *Revue Biblique* 70 (1973) 46–52 and "The Marzeah as a Social Institution," *Acta Antiqua* 22 (1974) 451–455; P. J. King, *Amos, Hosea, Micah: An Archaeological Commentary* (Philadelphia 1988) 137–161 and "The Marzeah: Textual and Archaeological Evidence," *Eretz-Israel* 20 (1989) *98–*106; T. J. Lewis, *Cults of the Dead in Ancient Israel and Ugarit* (Atlanta 1989) 80–98; P. D. Miller, "The Mrzh Text," in *The Claremont Ras Shamra Tablets* (supra this note) 37–49 and "Aspects of the Religion of Ugarit," in P. D. Hanson and P. D. Miller, Jr., eds., *Ancient Israelite Religion: Essays in Honor of Frank Moore Cross* (Philadelphia 1987) 53–66; M. H. Pope, "A Divine Banquet at Ugarit," in J. M. Efird, ed., *The Use of the Old Testament in the New and Other Essays: Studies in Honor of William Franklin Stinespring* (Durham, N.C. 1972) 170–203; B. Porten, *Archives from Elephantine: The Life of an Ancient Jewish Military Colony* (Berkeley 1968); J. M. Roberts, "Amos 6.1–7," in J. T. Butler, E. W. Conrad, and B. C. Ollenburger, eds., *Understanding the Word: Essays in Honor of Bernhard W. Anderson* (Sheffield 1985) 155–166; K. Spronk, *Beatific Afterlife in Ancient Israel and in the Ancient Near East* (Neukirchen-Vluyn 1986) 196–202; J. Teixidor, *The Pagan God: Popular Religion in the Greco-Roman Near East* (Princeton 1977) 44–45.

55. For rabbinical references: M. Jastrow, *A Dictionary of the Targumim, the Talmud Babli and Yerushalmi, and the Midrashic Literature,* vol. I (New York and Berlin 1926) 840.

56. RS (Ras Shamra tablets) 14.16, 15.88.

57. *KTU,* vol. I, no. 1.114. Text and translation: Spronk (supra n. 54) 198–200.

58. The texts of the Aqhat epic are *KTU* 1.17–19. The so-called "*rp'um* texts" are *KTU* 1.20–22. The same hand seems to have written *KTU* 1.17–19 and *KTU* 1.21–22; *KTU* 1.20 may be a copy by a different hand of *KTU* 1.22. See Spronk (supra n. 54) 160–161.

59. *KTU* 1.21. Text and translation: Spronk (supra n. 54) 169. It has been argued that the *marzeah* in *KTU* 1.21 is El's rather than Danel's. For those who favor a *marzeah* held by Danel, see Lewis (supra n. 54) 86 n. 33 and add Spronk (supra n. 54) 169–171. For those who favor a *marzeah* held by El: see Lewis (supra n. 54) 87 no. 34 and add Eissfeldt (supra n. 54). I find those who support a *marzeah* of Danel more convincing (and more numerous).

60. *KTU* 1.22. Text and translation: Spronk (supra n. 54) 171–172.

61. R. D. Barnett, "Sirens and Rephaim," in J. Vorys Canby, E. Porada, B. S. Ridgway, and T. Stech, eds., *Ancient Anatolia: Aspects of Change and Cultural Development. Essays in Honor of Machteld J. Mellink* (Madison 1986) 112–120, thinks that the winged, human-headed attachments of Oriental and Greek bronze cauldrons of the eighth and sev-

enth centuries B.C. represent Rephaim fluttering to drink from the cauldron at a *marzeaḥ*.

62. Translation: *The New Jerusalem Bible* (supra n. 50) 1532. I would like to thank Professor Alan Avery-Peck for help with the Hebrew texts.

63. Beach (supra n. 54) 136.

64. Translation: *The New Jerusalem Bible* (supra n. 50) 1324.

65. This is the interpretation of Ackerman (supra n. 54).

66. Translation from Ackerman (supra n. 54).

67. Ackerman (supra n. 54).

68. The "Marsielles Tariff": H. Donner and W. Röllig, *Kanaanäische und Aramäische Inschriften* (Wiesbaden 1966–1969) vol. I, 15 (no. 69); vol. II, 83–87, line 16; vol. III, pl. VI. Avigad and Greenfield (supra n. 54) 125. *ANET* 656–657. The inscription is variously dated from the fourth century to the early second century B.C.

69. Donner and Röllig (supra n. 68) I, 13 (no. 60); II, 73–74. Greenfield 1974 (supra n. 54) 454, n. 17.

70. Avigad and Greenfield (supra n. 54).

71. Porten (supra n. 54) 179 and n. 117. Miller 1971 (supra n. 54) 47–48.

72. Porten (supra n. 54) 181 and n. 125. Lewis (supra n. 54) 90–91 and nn. 44–47. For Nabataean practices, see also N. Glueck, *Deities and Dolphins* (New York 1965) 164–165.

73. Lewis (supra n. 54) 91.

74. For *marzeaḥ* iconography in Iron Age Syria-Palestine, see Beach (supra n. 54). For possible *marzeaḥ* iconography in eighth- and seventh-century B.C. Greece, see J. B. Carter, "Thiasos and Marzeaḥ: The Iconography of Ancestor Cult in the Age of Homer," in S. Langdon, ed., *From Pasture to Polis: Art in the Age of Homer* (Columbia, forthcoming).

75. *Docs.*² 264–267, 280–284, 453–454, 458. McCallum (supra n. 40) discusses Un 718 as evidence for offertory processions at Pylos.

76. *Docs.*² 265. Chadwick (254) notes that there are difficulties with this interpretation of *wo-ro-ki-jo-ne-jo* but does not recommend a better solution.

77. *Docs.*² 267–268, 454.

78. The personage who occupied the "throne" may have been a priestess, as argued by P. Rehak, "Enthroned Figures in Aegean Art and the Function of the Mycenaean Megaron," *AJA* 97 (1993) 322 (abstract), or the *wanax,* as maintained by T. G. Palaima, "Wanax, Basileus, and Mycenaean Kings," *AJA* 97 (1993) 322 (abstract). For the libation basins and channel: C. W. Blegen and M. Rawson, *The Palace of Nestor at Pylos in Western Messenia, Vol. 1: The Buildings and Their Contents* (Princeton 1966) 88; R. Hägg, "The Role of Libations in Mycenaean Ceremony and Cult," in R. Hägg and G. C. Nordquist, eds., *Celebrations of Death and Divinity in the Bronze Age Argolid. Proceedings of the Sixth International Symposium at the Swedish Institute at Athens, 11–13 June, 1988* (Stockholm 1990) 177–184 (see 178, 183, and figs. 3 and 9); Wright, "Empty cups and empty jugs" (supra n. 42).

79. J. C. Wright, "Changes in Form and Function of the Palace at Pylos," in C. W. Shelmerdine and T. G. Palaima, eds., *Pylos Comes Alive* (New York 1984) 19–29, see 26–27. See also C. Gates, "Rethinking the Building History of Grave Circle A at Mycenae," *AJA* 89 (1985) 263–274; J. C. Wright, "Death and Power at Mycenae," in Robert Laffineur, ed., *Thanatos. Les coutumes funéraires en Egée à l'âge du bronze,* Aegaeum 1 (Liège 1987) 171–184; M. Dabney and J. C. Wright, "Mortuary Customs, Palatial Society and State Formation in the Aegean Area: A Comparative Study," in Hägg and Nordquist, eds. (supra n. 78) 45–53; J. C. Wright, "Religion and the Role of Ideology in Mycenaean Society," *AJA* 95 (1991) 316 (abstract); S. P. Morris, "Prehistoric Iconography and Historical Sources: Hindsight through Texts?" in R. Laffineur and J. L. Crowley, eds., EIKΩN. *Aegean Bronze Age Iconography: Shaping a Methodology,* Aegaeum 8 (Liège 1992) 205–212 (see 209).

80. Marinatos (supra n. 34) 13–37.

81. James C. Wright has stressed the importance of lineage in Helladic culture and has argued that Mycenaean religious beliefs shaped the power structures in Mycenaean society and not, at least initially, the reverse. See J. C. Wright, "The Spatial Configuration of Belief: The Archaeology of Mycenaean Religion," in R. Osborne and S. Alcock, eds., *Placing the Gods: Greek Sanctuaries in Space* (Oxford, forthcoming); J. C. Wright, "From Chief to King in Mycenaean Society," in P. Rehak, ed., *The Role of the Ruler in the Prehistoric Aegean,* Aegaeum 10 (Liège, forthcoming 1994).

82. J.-M. Dentzer, *Le motif du banquet couché dans le Proche-Orient et le monde grec du VIIe au IVe siècle avant J.-C.* (Rome 1982) 51–58. Dentzer favors an origin of the reclining banquet in Syria, perhaps introduced by the Aramaeans. B. Fehr, cited by Dentzer, argues that the Assyrians borrowed the custom from their nomadic neighbors in Iran. Assurbanipal relief: R. D. Barnett, *Sculptures from the North Palace of Ashurbanipal at Nineveh (668–627)* (London 1976) pls. XLIII–XLIV; Frankfort (supra n. 54) 192–194, fig. 217.

83. J. Boardman, "Symposion Furniture," in O. Murray, ed., *Sympotica: A Symposium on the Symposion* (Oxford 1990) 122–131 (see 122, 125, 129).

84. For ivory inlay from a kline found in a sixth-century burial in the Kerameikos at Athens: U. Knigge, *Der Südhügel* (Berlin 1976) 60–83. Cf. Hdt. 1.50.1.

85. Barnett 1985 (supra n. 54) 3*. See now also King 1988 and Beach (both supra n. 54).

86. I take here a moderate position between the orthodox idea of a radical hoplite reform that changed the nature of Greek society and the revisionist argument that no such hoplite reform occurred. For the latter position, see A. M. Snodgrass, "The Hoplite Reform and History," *JHS* 85 (1965) 110–122. J. Latacz, *Kampfparänese, Kampfdarstellung und Kampfwirklichkeit in der Ilias, bei Kallinos und Tyrtaios* (Munich 1977); W. K. Pritchett, *The Greek State at War*, Part IV (Berkeley 1985) 7–44; I. Morris, *Burial and Ancient Society: The Rise of the Greek City-State* (Cambridge, Eng. 1987) 196–201.

87. O. Murray, "The Greek Symposion in History," in E. Gabba, ed., *Tria Corda. Scritti in Onore Di Arnaldo Momigliano* (Como 1983) I. 257–272 (see 263). I am not sure that Murray is correct when he argues that the *symposion* became a more elaborate affair as a result of the changing nature of warfare; it may simply have been that the rich became richer and could afford more lavish entertainments.

88. Boardman (supra n. 83) 122–125.

89. N. Platon, "Μινωϊκὴ Λύρα," in Χαριστήριον εἰς Ἀναστάσιον Κ. Ὀρλάνδον (Athens 1966) 3.208–232 (see 222–223, fig. 11, pls. 70–71a). J.-C. Poursat, *Catalogue des ivoires mycéniens du Musée National d'Athènes* (Athens 1977) no. 431/1972, pl. 45. Barnett (supra n. 46) 37 and pl. 32d. Platon mentions another ivory lyre fragment found in a chamber tomb at Mycenae.

90. Platon (supra n. 89) 212–214.

91. Immerwahr (supra n. 36) 181 (A.T. No. 3, not illustrated). Illustrations: *MMR*² 436, fig. 198 A; Long (supra n. 36), fig. 43; Platon (supra n. 88), pl. 69.

92. Platon (supra n. 89).

93. Platon (supra n. 89) 217, figs. 7, 8.2, 9.1. See also L. Vorreiter, "The Swan-Neck Lyres of Minoan-Mycenean Culture," *The Galpin Society Journal* 28 (1975) 93–97. Ancient Egypt had lyres decorated with bird-heads and horseheads: see B. Lawergren, "Lyres in the West (Italy, Greece) and East (Egypt, the Near East), ca. 2000–400 B.C.," *OpRom* 19 (1993) 55–76.

94. Platon (supra n. 89) 217–218, fig. 10. P. Getz-Preziosi, *Early Cycladic Art in North American Collections* (Richmond 1987) 261–262 (continuity of bird ornament on harp), 262–269 (harp-players). J. Thimme, *Art and Culture of the Cyclades in the Third Millennium B.C.*, trans. and ed. P. Getz-Preziosi (Chicago 1977) 494–496, nos. 253–255. The importance of lyres in Late Cycladic ritual is shown by the blue monkey who plays a lyre in the wall-paintings from Xeste 3 at Akrotiri: C. Doumas, *The Wall Paintings of Thera* (Athens 1992) 134, fig. 95. Actual tortoise shells were found in the East and West shrines at Phylakopi on Melos; several of the tortoiseshell fragments found here had drilled holes, apparently for the attachment of arms to form a lyre. See C. Renfrew, *The Archaeology of Cult, BSA* Suppl. 18 (London 1985) 325–326, 384.

95. M. Maas and J. McIntosh Snyder, *Stringed Instruments of Ancient Greece* (New Haven 1989) 11–14; M. Wegner, *Musik und Tanz* (Göttingen 1968) U2–U18.

96. Maas and Snyder (supra n. 95) 27–28, 42 fig. 1; J. Boardman, *The Greeks Overseas,* 3rd ed. (London 1980) 97–98, fig. 111.

97. Berlin Staatliche Museen 1964.36. J. B. Carter, *Greek Ivory-Carving in the Orientalizing and Archaic Periods* (New York 1985) 243–248, figs. 85a–b; A. Greifenhagen, "Ein Ostgriechisches Elfenbein," *JBerlMus* 7 (1965) 125–156 and "Schmuck und Gerät eines lydischen Mädchens," *AntK* 8 (1965) 13–19.

98. K. Bittel, "Phrygisches Kultbild aus Bogazköy," *AntP* 2 (1963) 7–21, esp. pl. 8.

99. D. G. Hogarth et al., *Excavations at Ephesus. The Archaic Artemisia* (London 1908) 165–166, nos. 30–32, pl. 25.7, 10, 11.

100. I would like to thank Pat Getz-Preziosi, who gave me a slide of this vase after a discussion in 1987 about bird-head lyres and who recently helped me find references for it. The plate is Basel, Antikenmuseum Kä 421, *ABV* 294.21; *Paralipomena* 128.21; *Beazley Addenda* 77 (294.21). For illustrations: G. M. A. Richter, *Attic Red-Figured Vases: A Survey* (New Haven 1946) 47, 176 n. 61, fig. 36; I. Rácz, *Antikes Erbe: Meisterwerke aus Schweizer Sammlungen* (Zürich 1965) pl. 50; D. Paquette, *L'Instrument de musique dans la céramique de la Grèce antique: Études d'organologie* (Lyon 1984; Diffusion de Boccard, Paris) 179, B5; Maas and Snyder (supra n. 95) 138, fig. 21. See also the kithara on a lekythos by the Meidias Painter: Paquette (supra this note) 168, L41.

101. Maas and Snyder (supra n. 95) 124–125 (barbitoi), 173 (kitharai), 242 n. 55 (other swan-head instruments).

102. Maas and Snyder (supra n. 95) 183, 195 fig. 14, 197 fig. 17, 243–244 nn. 108 and 110. See also M. Wegner, *Musikgeschichte in Bildern. Band II: Musik Des Altertums. Lieferung 4: Griechenland* (Leipzig n.d., c. 1965) 110–111, fig. 70; *RVA* pl. 172.1. Paquette (supra n. 100) 198, H9.

PART III

AFTER HOMER: NARRATIVE AND REPRESENTATION

19

READING PICTORIAL NARRATIVE:
THE LAW COURT SCENE
OF THE SHIELD OF ACHILLES

✦

MARK D. STANSBURY-O'DONNELL

When Hephaistos set his bellows working and took up his hammer and tongs to make new armor for Thetis' son Achilles, he was undoubtedly aware that his handiwork would be the last that Achilles would bear, and probably could have guessed that it would become the cause of strife between Ajax and Odysseus. Little, however, would he or the poet of the *Iliad* have realized that the shield would generate dispute among scholars over two and a half millennia later.[1]

Heinrich Schliemann's discovery of the treasures from the Shaft Graves of Mycenae brought to light bronze daggers inlaid with figural scenes of more precious metals, and consequently spurred some students of the *Iliad* to argue that the long and detailed account of the Shield of Achilles in Book 18 was in fact the description of a real object of Mycenaean manufacture.[2] Reconstructions were proposed, using a variety of shield types, arrangement of scenes, and visual sources. Countering these efforts, others claimed that the works of Hephaistos were complete fabrications of the poetic imagination, and even that the shield description did not belong to the original core of the poem, a position going back to Xenodotos.[3] This debate has given way today,

for the most part, to a compromise position. W. Schadewaldt proposed that the passage is both free fantasy and description of existing work. The poet drew some of the images depicted on the shield and the plastic, almost palpable quality of the description from the eighth-century B.C. world of art objects, but also made the shield a godly production that was far greater than and unlike any mortal work.[4] The poet's choice of scenes transforms the shield into a microcosm of the world of the *Iliad*, providing its listeners and readers with both a retrospective and prospective picture of the course of the poem and making them think about the price of the war by its contrast with scenes of peace.[5]

The graphic, almost tangible qualities of the shield described by the poet of the *Iliad* still tempt one to try to imagine the appearance of this marvelous, godly handiwork. The materials of the shield—bronze, gold, silver, tin—and the characteristics of the settings and figures of its scenes receive careful attention in the poem, almost as if they were real beings or places. In terms of the organization of the shield's decoration, it is clear that the poet begins the description at its center and works outward through its different zones. The overall shape of the shield is generally thought to be round, although tower, figure-of-eight, and Boiotian shield forms, as well as a different ordering of the scenes, have also been proposed.[6] One may understand the appeal behind these early efforts to recreate it in an actual physical form. Nevertheless, it is not likely that the poet had a clear and precise picture of the shield in mind.[7] Despite the very plastic quality of the shield's description, there is too much imprecision in the location of the various scenes and their visual continuity or division to allow a reconstruction. As W. Marg pointed out, the scenes are enumerated in the form of a catalogue, and though placed into distinct groups corresponding to the bands of the shield, the most populated scenes would appear to inhabit the smallest zones of the shield.[8] Nor is the way scenes are separated from one another or the way in which the figures stand within the picture space or on the picture surface always clear, to name only the broadest pictorial problems. In summary, it is clear that the poet was not describing a specific, real object, but rather a literary, imaginary, and divinely created vision. Any reconstruction of the shield would, therefore, be built without foundation.

The passage remains, nevertheless, the oldest description in Greek of a work of art, real or imaginary, and the prominence of Achilles and of the *Iliad* insured that the shield would be remembered and recalled throughout antiquity.[9] Later writers reiterate its magnificence, and it became the model for other heroic shields in later poems, such as the pseudo-Hesiodic *Shield of Herakles* and Vergil's shield for Aeneas.[10] These later shields do, however, deviate from the Homeric model, reflecting the artwork of their own time. In the *Shield of Herakles*, for example, some of the scenes are less generic or prototypical than in *Iliad* 18 and are drawn more clearly from myth and legend.[11] Individual figures are more often named and the action is usually taken from a very precise moment of the depicted story. In this, the scenes of the *Shield of Herakles* resemble more those that survive from a sixth-century B.C. vase painting such as the François Vase, and indeed some who dismiss the reality of Achilles' shield leave open the possibility for the shield of Herakles.[12]

The divinely wrought armor of Achilles is a subject of vase and mural painting in Greek and Roman art, although detailed depictions of the shield are rarer.[13] The shield and other weapons made by Hephaistos are depicted in fifth-century B.C. Attic vase painting as part of the later scene in *Iliad* 19 where Thetis presents the new arms to her son. Here, however, the shield is shown as a round or Boiotian shield with a simple device, bearing little resemblance to the *Iliad*'s description. The presence of Nereids in many of these depictions points less to the *Iliad* as a source for these vase depictions than to a lost play of Aeschylus that dealt with the story of Achilles.[14] According to K. Fittschen, only in Hellenistic times did pictures based on the poem itself originate. In Pompeii, the shield is often shown still in the forge of Hephaistos, where it bears only cosmological signs. There were a few efforts to make more detailed depictions of the shield, including two Iliac tablets. One of these in the Capitoline Museum is a fragmentary circular shield of stone inscribed on a central band as the Shield of Achilles.[15] There are only two scenes set in registers above one another, the upper showing the city at peace and the lower showing the agricultural scenes and the dancers in a circle. Another depiction of the shield occurs in the middle of the missing Sarti fragment.[16] This is again a round shield, now held on the one surviving side by a female figure and divided into four registers with an encircling band of zodiacal signs around the perimeter. The scenes are not identifiable but one would seem to have included a city. In both cases the ancient artist has abandoned the circular arrangement of scenes described in the *Iliad* in favor of a simplified, abridged, and friezelike composition, which may improve legibility on this scale but hardly does justice to the original description. More modern attempts to reconstruct the shield have been perhaps more meticulous in following the details provided by the poet, but their diversity points ultimately to the problems of "reconstructing" an object that never truly existed except in the mind of the poet.

The appeal of the Shield of Achilles has, therefore, been varied and enduring. Despite its fictional nature, the shield description is not without potential value for the present study of Greek art. Although the poet did not describe a real object or even a fully and pictorially conceived one, it would appear that he had in his mind's eye real examples of artwork that supplied some of the minute physical details of the poetic shield. For example, the technique of placing inlaid figural scenes on bronze was not practiced when the poem came to take its form in the eighth century B.C., so that some memory of art like that found in the Shaft Graves must have been preserved, either in poetry or through a few surviving artifacts, to provide the poet with this information.[17] As has been pointed out by D. H. F. Gray, the description of the shield's metals and manufacture also include features more typical of iron than of bronze work, such as the use of tin and κύανος as an inlaying material or the employment of hard, hot hammering, and bellows and tongs.[18] Such modifications to Bronze Age metalworking techniques argue for the poet's awareness of contemporary art and its manufacture in composing the description, as does the general resemblance between the organization of the shield's pictorial field and contemporary Phoenician bowls and other objects of the eighth century B.C.[19] Furthermore, the meticulous attention to details of costume and setting, of gesture and pose in most of the individual scenes of the shield clearly suggests that the poet had a vivid picture of each separate scene in mind, even if it was blurred at its edges or if its size and position on the shield were uncertain.

The *Iliad* forms our only source of literary evidence for the reception of art during the Geometric period. The very pictorial quality of the shield description raises the question of whether it is possible to use these verses to further our understanding of the way in which contemporary art of the Geometric period would have been perceived or "read" by its viewers. More specifically, can the poet's method of describing a fictional picture be applied to figural scenes on Geometric vases? Do such scenes function as pictorial narratives and how would a Geometric viewer have constructed a story from their elements? Although a work of poetic imagination, I would argue that the Shield of Achilles can provide a model for understanding the ways in which an eighth-century B.C. viewer might have understood a contemporary painting or relief, and more specifically, how they may have perceived a narrative within these compositions. This hypothesis raises some issues that must first be addressed before delving into the shield in more detail. First, does pictorial narrative exist in eighth-century B.C. art and if so, what are its characteristics? Second, is an *ekphrasis* such as the Shield of Achilles related closely enough to works of contemporary art that its use as a model can be justified?

The existence of pictorial narrative in eighth-century B.C. art is a subject of some controversy. In an effort to differentiate mythological narrative from nonnarrative, several German scholars have divided the scenes on early Greek vases into two categories: *Sagenbild*, showing scenes with identifiable individuals and situations drawn from myth and legend, and *Lebensbild*, representing more ordinary situations and able to be understood without reference to a story.[20] This distinction is useful, and it is certainly the case that most of the figural scenes on Geometric vases appear to fall into the latter category, but there have been conflicting opinions as to the mythological content of a relatively small number of scenes on Geometric vases.[21] Such is the case with the funeral depicted on a Late Geometric krater in New York (fig. 19.1). For every effort to identify its subject as the funeral of King Amarynkeus recounted in *Iliad* 23.638–642, there are an equal if not greater number of skeptics who see it as a mostly typical *prothesis* and procession. Pictorial narrative, it is often thought, developed in the seventh and sixth centuries B.C. and these scenes of Geometric art are at best prenarrative since they lack any specific content. There have been attempts to find a compromise position, that Geometric pictures begin to explore fundamental situations of human life and that their themes parallel those of epic poetry, but this is still a minority position.[22] Clearly, the ability of scholars to take a specific scene such as the funeral on the New York krater and call it a *Sagenbild* on the one hand and a *Lebensbild* on the other points out the ambiguous nature of the depiction and its rather complicated composition and set of actions. There could well have been numerous tales unknown to us, whether in the form of crafted poems or of more ephemerally shaped folk stories and traditions, that would decide the question of category and yet would not change the potential for a specific scene to function as a pictorial narrative. To divide scenes into either *Sagenbild* or *Lebensbild* may, therefore, artificially preclude the existence of narrative in so-called generic scenes.

A full consideration of the existence of narrative in Geometric art is beyond the scope of the present essay, but will be considered more fully in a future monograph. Here, I would argue that the dependence of many proponents and opponents of Geometric narrative upon mythology and epic for their arguments serves to restrict

FIGURE 19.1. Obverse of a Late Geometric funerary krater, third quarter of eighth century B.C. New York, The Metropolitan Museum of Art, Rogers Fund, 1914 (14.130.15). (Photograph courtesy of the Metropolitan Museum.)

and obscure our understanding of the existence, nature, and structure of pictorial narrative in early Greek art. The potential for hearing or reading in a story or seeing in a picture a sequence of time, a series of actions or oppositions, a setting, and references to related stories, characters, or ideas fulfills the basic requirements of narration, regardless of whether a picture can be related to a specific mythological story and set of characters or not.[23] If such conditions can be fulfilled in some Geometric vase scenes, then one should consider that pictorial narrative did exist even if now we are not always sure how to understand the story. There could exist, therefore, both mythological narratives and generic narratives in addition to pictures without narrative content.

The need to separate at least partially the potential mythological content of a scene from its narrative structure has been recognized recently by A. M. Snodgrass and J. N. Coldstream.[24] Snodgrass, for example, has proposed the category of "generalized heroic" scenes in Geometric art, which attempts to bridge the gap between *Lebensbild* and *Sagenbild*. Generalized heroic consists of battle or other scenes of heroic nature where a specific action and story cannot be identified, but where narrative exists.[25] More recently Snodgrass has refined this position further, stating, "What I am suggesting is not that the context of these scenes need necessarily therefore be heroic; but that they are likely to have a narrative content of some kind." Since the existence of narrative does not depend upon a specific or general heroic content, perhaps a term such as "generic narrative" would be more useful. This proposal has not received universal acceptance. J. Boardman, for example, rejects the "generalized heroic" and insists that narrative demands a mythic or heroic setting. The stumbling block to the existence of narrative is, for Boardman, the "lack of both specific actions and recognizable attributes." Without an external source of evidence, the existence of pictorial narrative in Geometric vase painting, generalized or mythological, remains an open question. Here, I would suggest, is where the Shield of Achilles may provide another perspective on Geometric painting. An examination of the pictorial structure of a scene from the Shield may help to shed some light on the problem by examining the description of poetic creation as a model for the way in which an eighth-century

B.C. viewer might have approached a real work of art.

Comparisons of the *Iliad* with contemporary Geometric vase painting have already revealed parallels in their overall composition and basic construction. B. Andreae and H. Flashar have pointed out, for example, that the *Iliad* uses an elaborate triadic principle of composition, both in terms of the overall organization of the poem and in the pattern of its individual episodes.[26] This triadic principle applies as well to the pattern of digressions into past and future and to the levels of the events, or, to paraphrase, the realm of the individual, the group, and the gods. These different levels are unified by "action-hinges," such as the argument of Achilles and Agamemnon. Within this architectural framework the poet uses the traditional aids of the oral poet—iterata, formulas, typical or generic scenes as well as compositions—and gives them a new monumentality and power. There is also the use of repeated units to create longer sequences that again are fitted within the triadic structure of the whole. When these authors turn to Geometric pottery, they find the same triadic principle at work in the structure of the bands and patterns that decorate an Attic vase such as Athens 804. Further, they point to the rhythmic, repetitive, and additive nature of the decorative forms such as the meander, similar to the hexameter meter and the formulae of the *Iliad*. Similarities also occur in the use of typical scenes and compositions. These parallels in composition, rhythm, and structure that Andreae and Flasher illuminate suggest that the principles of organization in poetry and art are similar, so that an *ekphrasis* such as the Shield of Achilles may well share a common intellectual and aesthetic foundation with contemporary art, opening the possibility of using it as a model for understanding the pictorial structure of works of art.

The parallels that Andreae and Flasher find for the eighth century B.C. indicate that the popular linkage of the literary and visual arts in later ancient literature may be extended back to the Geometric period.[27] Roman writers such as Cicero, Quintilian, and Horace compare limited aspects of the characteristics and history of the visual arts and poetry. Earlier Plato and Aristotle had made analogous comparisons, and Plutarch (*Moralia* 346F) records the still earlier remark of Simonides that painting is mute poetry and poetry is a speaking picture.

Although this attitude cannot be traced back before the Late Archaic period, it may be glimpsed in the power of an *ekphrasis* like the Shield of Achilles.

Just how closely may one take an *ekphrasis* such as the Shield of Achilles as reflecting works of contemporary art? Beginning with the *Iliad*, the *ekphrasis* is a popular literary device in ancient literature, including several other heroic shields mentioned earlier.[28] *Ekphrasis* was also a rhetorical and didactic device during the Roman Empire, as the works of Philostratus the Elder demonstrate.[29] In the later literature of Western Europe, *ekphrasis* continued to be a popular literary device and its relationship to a known visual model is often demonstrable. This is not the case for ancient *ekphrasis*, despite the claims of Philostratus to be describing works that he had seen. Still, the comparability of many ancient *ekphrases* such as those of Philostratus to contemporary art has at least demonstrated the often close connection between literature and art. In the much older Shield of Achilles, however, there is clearly no work of contemporary art that could be mistaken for the poetic description. Is, though, the relationship of *ekphrasis* and picture close enough to permit the use of the Shield of Achilles as a model for understanding a real image? Or is the shield so much a product of the poetic imagination that it has no real links with the actual art historical and archaeological context of the *Iliad*?

I would suggest that there are links between the two, that although the shield as a whole did not exist as a real object, the details of its composition, style, and materials closely parallel characteristics of contemporary works of art, making comparison of the two possible. A detailed theoretical exposition of this position must await a larger-scale forum, but I would here outline several points demonstrating the links between visual models and poetic description in the *Iliad*. To begin, one might point to the physical nature of the shield. The poet's concentration upon the process of manufacturing as well as upon the materials and tools used shows an awareness of contemporary metalworking techniques, as we have seen in some detail above.[30] The types and colors of the materials are described in graphic detail, further demonstrating an awareness of the appearance of art objects. Beyond this there are several other factors that link the worlds of artistic form and poetic description.

First, one can look at the compositional principles of the shield. It is divided into long, continuous friezes that circle back upon themselves. This is a type of articulation of surface, common both to Geometric vases (fig. 19.1) and to Phoenician bowls, that may well have stimulated the poet.[31] Within each frieze the individual scenes are often arranged in three parts, with a central group or object flanked by two other, similar groupings. Such is the case in the law court scene, where crowds appear to flank both sides of the dispute in the center (*Iliad* 18.497–505), and in the besieged city that is flanked by two armies (*Iliad* 18.509–510). Another variation of this triadic principle is in the series of scenes, where scenes of farming (ploughing and harvesting) and husbandry (cattle and sheep) flank a central vineyard (*Iliad* 18.541–589). These kinds of tripartite compositions coexist in the shield with unidirectional, processional scenes, such as the wedding dance (*Iliad* 18.492–496), the dancing floor of Daidalos (*Iliad* 18.590–605), and the Ocean river running around the rim (*Iliad* 18.606–607).[32] One can see this type of composition used as well on the New York krater and in numerous other examples of Geometric art. The use of both types of composition within the continuous friezes or bands that divide the entire object, therefore, is common both to the Shield of Achilles and to contemporary Geometric art.

A second parallel between *ekphrasis* in the *Iliad* and eighth-century B.C. art lies in stylistic qualities, or the more detailed way in which an individual scene is constructed. Throughout the shield description there are many groups that consist of repetitive units with just a few distinctive, more individualized figures. In the besieged city, for example, there are two armies, defenders, women, and old men, groups that appear to be collections of mostly undifferentiated units. The figures would appear to be roughly equal in size, except for Ares and Athena who are huge while the people around them are smaller (*Iliad* 18.516–519). The gods are the only figures out of hundreds who are singled out in this way. This pattern holds true in other scenes, such as the harvest where there are groups of reapers, sheaf-binders, and children along with the solitary king who is distinguished from the others by the staff that he holds (*Iliad* 18.550–557). The poet usually describes only the actions or deportment of the group figures, and occasionally their type of costume, including the presence of armor. Throughout the poet provides virtually no details as to the appearance of these figures or to specific parts of their anatomy or costume. In other words, despite the vivid nature of the scenes on the shield, there is little emphasis upon differentiation among the figures or to their detailed and specific description. Glancing once more at the New York krater these are qualities that also apply to Geometric painted figures: the lack of details inside the silhouetted figure; the lack of anatomical features beyond limbs, hair, and beak; concentration upon a series of standardized gestures relating to the actions of the ceremony; and the limitation of armor to shields and swords or knives, without belts or greaves. Only a few individual figures are distinguished, such as the Siamese twins that will be discussed in more detail later and the rightmost seated figure under the bier. Therefore, the style of the compositions for both shield and pot is similar, with their emphasis upon groups composed of mostly undifferentiated and broadly described repetitive units.

A third parallel between shield and art is the generic nature of the scenes and of their actions and figures. In all of the shield only a few figures are named: Athena, Ares, and the group of Hate, Confusion, and Death (Iliad 18.535–540). The vast majority are nameless and are distinguished only by their function: dancers, warriors, reapers, shepherds, elders, etc. Their actions might also be described as ritualistic and oft-repeated. This anonymity is clearly found in most of Geometric art, where only a few figures occur in circumstances, such as a shipwreck, that permit even a tentative identification. Further, the scenes themselves are taken out of the fabric of daily life in both shield and vase painting. The shield is meant, after all, to be a summary of Achilles' world, and all of the scenes belong to the normal rhythms of that world and not to the realm of mythology or history. The predominance of *Lebensbilder* among Geometric vases and the paucity of examples that might be related to a specific tale demonstrate a strong parallel in the mind of both poet and painter. Pictures were clearly intended to be visions of the contemporary world and therefore generic in their nature. This is even true of their narrative, which often stops short of completion, as S. Morris has pointed out.[33]

There are, then, several important parallels between the poetic description of the Shield of Achilles and contemporary Geometric art. Clearly the poet imagines scenes far richer in color, materials, and craft than would have been possible in the real world, but the scenes on the shield share with vase painting some of the same basic pictorial structure. In principle it is not that hard to imagine that the figures of Geometric art were signs that represented a real type of person or thing and that these functioned in an analogous way to words themselves, abstract significations of the world. When looking at a vase it is, I would argue, likely that an eighth-century B.C. viewer thought less in terms of the component shapes making up a form, than of their pattern that suggested a warrior, a woman, a goat, a funeral bier, or some other form of the visible world like that imagined by the poet of the *Iliad*.[34] One additional argument in favor of *ekphrasis* as a potential model for understanding the reception of a real visual image is the changes in *ekphrasis* itself in the following centuries. As mentioned above, the *Shield of Herakles*, dating perhaps two centuries later than the *Iliad* and based in good measure upon the Shield of Achilles, has a number of clear differences in terms of its pictorial description. Many more individual figures are named; more details of clothing, armor, and especially of anatomy—such as teeth, eyes, brow, jaws—are provided. Some of the subjects are certainly mythological; ornamental bands include animal friezes. All of these reflect the developments in style, subject, and composition of Archaic Greek art and show that the poets of both shields shaped their descriptions in forms similar to the art around them.

We may then cautiously turn to a more detailed consideration of a scene from the Shield of Achilles to examine how it works as a model for pictorial reception, and whether or not it is possible to find the elements of narrative in Geometric vase painting. For this purpose I have chosen the second of two scenes from the city of peace, which describes in twelve lines (*Iliad* 18.497–508) a law court dispute.

λαοὶ δ᾿ εἰν ἀγορῇ ἔσαν ἀθρόοι· ἔνθα δὲ νεῖκος
ὠρώρει, δύο δ᾿ ἄνδρες ἐνείκεον εἵνεκα ποινῆς
ἀνδρὸς ἀποφθιμένου· ὁ μὲν εὔχετο πάντ᾿ ἀποδοῦναι
δήμῳ πιφαύσκων, ὁ δ᾿ ἀναίνετο μηδὲν ἑλέσθαι·
ἄμφω δ᾿ ἱέσθην ἐπὶ ἴστορι πεῖραρ ἑλέσθαι.

λαοὶ δ'ἀμφοτέροισιν ἐπήπυον, ἀμφὶς ἀρωγοί.
κήρυκες δ'ἄρα λαὸν ἐρήτυον· οἱ δὲ γέροντες
ἥατ' ἐπὶ ξεστοῖσι λίθοις ἱερῷ ἐνὶ κύκλῳ,
σκῆπτρα δὲ κηρύκων ἐν χέρσ' ἔχον ἠεροφώνων·
τοῖσιν ἔπειτ' ἤισσον, ἀμοιβηδὶς δὲ δίκαζον.
κεῖτο δ'ἄρ'ἐν μέσσοισι δύω χρυσοῖο τάλαντα,
τῷ δόμεν, ὃς μετὰ τοῖσι δίκην ἰθύντατα εἴποι.

But the people were crowded together in the agora. And there a quarrel had arisen, for two men were arguing on account of the penalty of slaying a man. The first had been swearing to have made full atonement [by] making declaration to the people; the other had declined to accept. But both then had sent forth the issue to an arbitrator to decide.

But the people were shouting for both sides [and] helping on both sides. The heralds then kept back the people. But the elders were sitting in the sacred circle upon [the bench] of polished stone, and were holding in their hands the staves of the heralds who lift up their voices. With them thereupon they leapt to their feet, in turn they were passing judgment. Then in the middle were sitting two talents of gold, to be given to him among them who should speak most justly.

No similar scene has been found in Greek art, which led Lorimer to view the passage as completely the work of the eighth-century B.C. Homer.[35] One may imagine the setting of the scene, the agora, as an open area of assembly without a definite architectural form such as a stoa or colonnade.[36] The cast of characters includes the two litigants, the crowd, the heralds, and the elders. In addition, two talents of gold lay on the ground. A corpse is not mentioned in the scene, and considering the already lengthy nature of the legal proceedings it is difficult to imagine the corpse still being around. It is possible that the arrangement of the proceedings and participants or the two talents of gold could serve as a signal for the nature of the dispute in the mind of the poet. The dispute itself has been the subject of much scholarly debate, but recent opinion favors the interpretation that the "trial concerns the question whether blood price for the slain man should be accepted or not."[37] Thus the facts are not in dispute, but the nature and extent of the punishment are the subject of arbitration. The two talents are generally thought to be court fees given jointly by the two litigants and to be paid to the elder who makes the most righteous decision, since the sum would not be a sufficient price for the crime of manslaughter or murder.[38] The determination of which pronouncement is most just is probably achieved by a consensus of litigants, elders, and the crowd.[39]

The relative simplicity of the scene when one breaks it down into its components provides little hint of the complex sequence of events that the poet packs into these twelve lines, and this has stirred disagreement as to the actual number of scenes or episodes depicted on the shield. W. Leaf thought that there were two separate scenes or panels, one showing the argument of the litigants and the other the pronouncement of the elders. The transition between the scenes was marked by the action of the heralds thrusting back the crowd.[40] K. Fittschen sees, at least in the adjoining war scenes, that the several phases of the action were shown each as a separate picture, although he does not comment specifically on the number of pictures for the law court scene.[41] Others, such as A. Lesky, see a single scene, with the two men standing in the middle gesturing against each other.[42] On one side is the crowd, and on the other the elders, one of whom is standing up to give judgment. This disagreement over the passage of time in the poetic narrative and its pictorial reconstruction is what makes the scene interesting in terms of the reading of pictorial narrative in the eighth century B.C..

A closer examination of the passage shows that the poet used various elements of his imaginary picture as signals to read several different moments of time into the picture. The poet begins by saying that the people were assembled in the agora, using the imperfect ἔσαν to describe the scene. Although this is the only past tense of εἰμί, the poet's use of the imperfect sets the basic key for passages describing the scene. As we shall see in a moment, it is used consistently throughout this passage and for the shield as a whole to indicate what actually appears on the shield and in the present time of the world of the *Iliad*.[43] In the next sentence describing the quarrel between the two men the poet shifts to the pluperfect of ὄρνυμι, ὠρώρει. This shift places the events described in the following lines into a time before the scene depicted on the shield, the assembly of the people. While the poet uses a mixture of verbs in the following lines (499–501), the elaboration of both the cause of the quarrel and the decision to take the issue to an arbitrator falls readily within this past time and serves to explain the events that led to the actions actually described on the shield. In line 502 the poet repeats the beginning of line 497, λαοὶ δέ, and combined with a return to the imperfect ἐπήπυον signals a return to the present moment of the picture on the shield. The next lines (502–507), that paint vividly the shouting and support of the crowd, the restraint of the crowd by the heralds, the sitting of the judges, and their individual pronouncement of judgment, are again described in the imperfect, as is the fact that there are two talents of gold lying on the ground. In the last line (508) the poet uses a clause with indefinite antecedent and the aorist optative to indicate that the gold should be given to the judge who would pronounce most justly. This creates a future within the overall time of the description, and hence a time after the events depicted on the shield. In summary, the poet describes three different moments, past, present, and future, while "reading" the pictorial narrative on the shield.

From this analysis, it would appear that the poet probably imagined only a single composition for this scene and that it is unnecessary to view the digression into the actual quarrel and its cause as a separate scene. The attitude of the two litigants is not described, but since their argument is placed into the past, since the heralds are attempting to quiet the crowd's shouting, and since the elders are rendering their judgments, it is unlikely that they themselves are still in the process of arguing. Instead, they are probably standing still.[44] Around the two men are the crowd and the elders, and it is likely that these were on opposite sides of the men in the center. The heralds stood between the men and the crowd, and it is probable that the two talents of gold lay on the ground on the other side of the two men, toward the elders. The elders were seated together, perhaps in a row, with one of them standing up with his stave in hand to speak. It is entirely possible, then, to conceive of the scene as having a friezelike composition, with lines of repeated figures at either end and a fewer figures in different attitudes at the center, as well as objects like staves and gold.

Such a compositional scheme could easily be imagined on a Late Geometric vase, with the men, gold, heralds, and speaking elder toward the center and the crowd and other elders stretching out around to the sides of the vessel. This is, in fact, a common compositional scheme used for a variety of scenes in the Geometric period, such as the funeral seen on the krater from New York mentioned earlier (fig.19.1). The key to the poet's reading of time lies in the contrast between figures or objects at rest and those in motion. The crowd, the heralds, and the speaking elder are in some state of activity— variously shouting and gesticulating, pushing, standing, speaking with arm outstretched. All of these actions are described vividly and in the imperfect tense, showing that they belong to the figures seen in the picture. In contrast, only the substance of the argument between the litigants is described, and this in the past, so that one may assume that these two figures were still, especially compared to the crowd next to them. The poet uses the antagonists' inactivity as a signal to digress into the past. In addition, the two talents of gold are inert, and the other elders are presumably sitting without making distinctive gestures like the one standing, speaking elder. It is this group of seated, inanimate elders and gold that the poet links to the outcome of the story. This conjunction of inanimate object and figure with narrative time is probably not random, for the two talents of gold are given, in the future, to one of the elders. Thus, one could argue that the contrast between motion and rest was the key for reading a sequence of moments, a story, into a picture. This process of discovering multiple episodes within a single scene that does not repeat any individual character has long been recognized as a type of pictorial narration, under the various headings of simultaneous, complementary, or synoptic narrative. The antiquity of this method, as Snodgrass has argued from pictorial evidence, would seem to find a parallel here in the poetic description.[45]

The general poetic use of contrast in the shield's subject matter has long been noted by scholars and has been used to reconstruct an Archaic Greek mindset that viewed the world as a series of oppositions.[46] The use of motion has also received attention. Marg commented that movement is integral to the structure of the scenes on the shield:

Each of the figural scenes is carried through and borne by verbs of motion; the sitting, standing, or lying, as a contrast, confirm this. . . . The movements are not chaotic; it is graceful to follow their change. The joyful processions through the city; the two boisterous parties, with the quiet elders, who now rise and sit down, the restraining heralds, the prize lying there . . .

While this contrast between motion and rest has a definite pictorial value in varying and enlivening the composition, it has a further use in the reading of pictorial narrative by the viewer. The fact that the poet of the Iliad could imagine a chronological sequence of events within a single composition indicates that such a scheme of "reading" pictures was not foreign to the contemporary viewer of eighth-century B.C. art, and was based upon the contrast between animation and inanimation in the elements of the composition.

With this in mind, I would like to turn to a few examples of Geometric vase painting, to see if a similar contrast can be found in pictures generally contemporary with the poem and whether a similar sequence of moments could be interpreted for them. To reiterate, this is not to say that there is a direct connection between the Iliad and vase painting or that the latter ever illustrates the former. Indeed, it is likely, as Boardman objects to such comparisons, that "Homer probably never saw an Attic Geometric vase in his life" and that "no Attic Geometric artist had ever read or heard recited a single line of Homer." [47] This sentiment is welcomed by Snodgrass, and I would agree that the development of representation on Geometric vases is not a response to epic poetry, but runs parallel to it. The reading scheme proposed here, however, does not seek to link poetry and art directly, but considers the approach that the poet, and thereby a general Geometric viewer, uses to describe and understand a figural scene. Such a scheme could have been applied by a Geometric viewer to a local Geometric vase or to any scene that he or she did not know well, whether a Phoenician bowl or an Attic pot. The connections between Athens and East Greece, even if they do not include the direct linkage of Homer and Attic vase painters, at least make the exercise not entirely futile. A survey of East Greek Geometric pottery reveals far fewer figural scenes than in contemporary Attic ware, but Attic pottery would seem not to have been entirely unknown and some figures exist in East Greek pottery.[48]

As mentioned earlier, the Late Geometric krater in New York transitional to the workshop of the Hirschfeld Painter has long generated debate as to whether its figured scenes depict a mythological story, and hence constitute pictorial narrative (fig. 19.1).[49] The surface of the large vase contains three figured friezes. Uppermost is the figure of a warrior lying on a bier; highly unusual among funerary scenes, the figure wears a helmet. To the left are eleven women who place both hands on top of their heads in gestures of mourning; to the right are seven warriors plus a pair of Siamese twins at the end of the frieze near the handle. The warriors bear offerings of fish, flesh, and fowl in one hand and touch the sword of the preceding figure with their other hand.[50] Six seated figures are placed below the bier and two on top of it. On the other side of the vase set between four large circular emblems are two warriors bearing the so-called Dipylon shield and in the center a tripod being grasped by a single warrior and another set of Siamese twins (fig. 19.2).[51] Immediately below the main frieze is a second of chariots with single nude warriors driving pairs of horses; as Boardman has pointed out, the central chariot under the bier contains two figures, an adult and a smaller figure, possibly a child.[52] Separated by a meander and a dotted diamond band is a lower frieze of chariots; here Dipylon warriors drive single horses, except for two chariots on the right that contain nude Siamese twins driving pairs of horses.

The presence of four pairs of Siamese twins on the krater has generated a considerable controversy over its subject matter. A number of scholars have identified the figures as the Aktorione/Molione twins and the general subject as the funeral games of King Amarynkeus that Nestor describes in Iliad 23.638–642.[53] Furthermore, their presence at the funeral bier, in a chariot procession or race, and with the tripod has led to the conclusion that the scenes follow a temporal order and constitute a prototypical continuous narrative.[54] Another group of scholars has seen in the Siamese twins only a pictorial convention for showing two figures overlapping one another, using the same type of scheme as that employed for the pairs of horses drawing the chariots.[55] The scenes, therefore, present only a picture of contemporary life. The question of the twins' identity has been central to the arguments of both sides, and to their conclusions regarding the existence of true pictorial narrative on the krater. It is, perhaps, impossible to resolve the problem as it has been formulated, and there is no

FIGURE 19.2. Reverse of a Late Geometric funerary krater, third quarter of eighth century B.C. New York, The Metropolitan Museum of Art, Rogers Fund, 1914 (14.130.15). (Photograph courtesy of the Metropolitan Museum.)

FIGURE 19.3. Middle Geometric skyphos, third quarter of eighth century B.C. Eleusis 741. (Photograph courtesy of the Archaeological Receipts Fund [TAP Service], Greek Ministry of Culture.)

guarantee that there was not some other legend now lost to us that could have explained the scenes on the vase better. Further, if one accepts the idea that figures in the same frieze, even if separated by ornamental panels or on the other side of the vase, share the same space, then there is not one but actually two duplications of the twins on the krater.[56] It is possible that there are two different pairs of Siamese twins, as Hampe suggests, and that the occasion is one not preserved in our literary sources.[57] Whether or not the krater depicts a specific mythological story, it is sufficiently complicated to bear such an attempt at narrative interpretation. By looking at its funeral scene once more with the law court scene of the shield of Achilles in mind, it is at least possible to consider whether one can view it as possessing a functional narrative in the mind of an eighth-century B.C. viewer.

The focal point of the main frieze is the bier where the dead warrior lies. This figure is obviously not in motion, nor apparently are the women beneath and to the left of the bier. These women are performing an act, but

the effect of their two-handed mourning gesture is to create a very static area of the composition. One should also view them as already being present in the same space as the bier itself.[58] The small figure on top of the right side of the bier, however, is performing a different act over the corpse's head, an action that Boardman and Ahlberg agree in describing as someone feeding the corpse, although they disagree over the identity of the figure as either a woman or child.[59] To the right the warriors are linked hand to sword; this and the leftward projection of their limbs gives a sense of slow movement to this side of the frieze. The first warrior, like the figure on top of the bier, performs an action different from the others, and reaches out his hand to touch the bier. One could see the moving warriors as just having arrived at the scene with offerings they will present to the corpse one by one, not unlike the manner in which the judges on the shield of Achilles present their verdicts. The arrangement of moving and static figures within the composition indeed shares a number of similarities with the composition of the imaginary law court scene of the *Iliad*. In the center is a static figure, like the two litigants and the gold on the shield. Immediately next to them are figures performing very distinct acts, feeding the corpse and touching the bier, that are not shared by the figures further to the sides. Clearly these figures belong to the immediate present of the scene, just as the heralds and

326

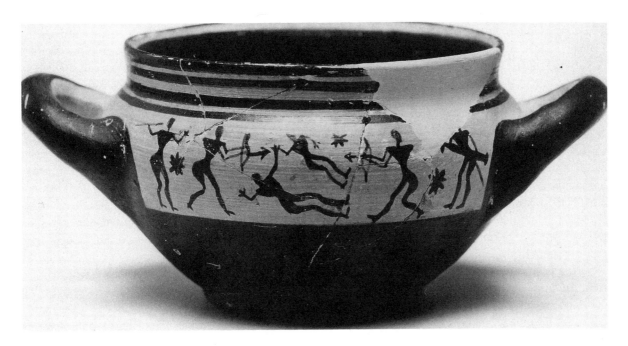

FIGURE 19.4. Middle Geometric skyphos, third quarter of eighth century B.C. Eleusis 741. (Photograph courtesy of the Archaeological Receipts Fund [TAP Service], Greek Ministry of Culture.)

single, pronouncing judge did on the shield. To the sides are additional figures who can signify the present as well as the past or future, especially the warriors. The bier provides some indication of the setting, but the couple of live birds scattered among the warriors might also indicate a setting slightly different from the left side of the frieze where the women mourn. Choosing among these possibilities and deciding the details of setting and scene would presumably have been easier for the eighth-century B.C. viewer than for us, but the possiblity of such elaboration appears to exist within the picture.

It is possible, then, to reconstruct from this picture a past, present, and future set of events, as the poet did in the law court scene. Although we cannot be as specific as the poet in our interpretation, there clearly seems to be some kind of narrative at work, and incidents or objects can call forth a story to explain themselves. The present time seems to be the transition from the *threnos* performed by the mourners to the presentation of the offerings, a change in actions and group performing them not unlike the boisterous arguments of the crowd

in the law court scene giving way to the pronouncements of the elders. The next stages of the story on the krater are probably indicated by the warriors, who will present their offerings before the final disposition of the corpse. Here, the processions of chariots underneath the frieze with the bier and the disposition of the tripod, perhaps as part of the grave goods as Boardman proposes, provide further depictions of the future events implied by the main scene. In any case, the episode will conclude at the end of the ritual acts, as did the law court scene. The immediate past of the story consists of the *prothesis*, but it is entirely possible that the Geometric viewer would have noted the plumed helmet, the type of bier, and the specific offerings as indicative of the deeds or some other biographical aspect of the deceased, not unlike the way in which the poet portrays the quarrel of the two men in the agora. There appear, therefore, to be sufficient pictorial elements on the krater to suggest a setting, a plausible sequence of time, contrasts in action, and an interpretive potential for the scene. These factors arguably confirm it as a pictorial narrative regardless of its potential mythological content.

One can similarly read a simpler figured scene on a Middle Geometric skyphos from Eleusis (figs. 19.3 and 19.4).[60] In the center on one side of the cup is a ship with a bird on its prow and a helmsman steering it. Over the deck runs a figure with bow and drawn arrow. On either side of the ship are Dipylon warriors, each bearing two spears at an upward angle and a third spear leveled at the ship. Behind the right warrior is a seven-pointed star. On the other side of the cup is a combat scene, with two reclining figures clasping hands in the center. To either side of these are pairs of figures; each group consists of an archer closest to the center and a spearman at the ends of the composition. The two groups confront each other, but do not engage in direct combat. Three more seven- or eight-pointed stars are interspersed among the figures. The composition of the scenes is much freer than ornamental decoration in contemporary vase painting, and there is no observation of a groundline as there is in figured scenes of the Late Geometric period.[61] A wide variety of dates have been proposed for the cup, ranging from the second half of the ninth century B.C. to almost 700 B.C., but the cup probably belongs to the second quarter of the eighth century B.C. and stands at the beginning of the appearance of figured scenes in Geometric painting.[62]

Like the New York krater, disagreements surround the interpretation of the scenes on the Eleusis skyphos. The way in which the figures float on the picture surface has been seen as an attempt to suggest spatial depth, just as the reduced size of the upper reclining body in the battle scene is thought to represent a recession in space.[63] This is probably not the case and the differences in the sizes of the figures on both sides of the vase most likely are the results of the artist's efforts to fill the picture surface with the figures. Ahlberg has proposed that the two reclining figures who hold hands in the battle scene are in fact alive and floating in the water; she points to the stars as indicating the presence of water.[64] The placement of a star behind one of the Dipylon warriors on the other side of the vase, who clearly stands on land, would suggest that if the stars have a symbolic or iconographical value, they signify land and not water. There is also some disagreement as to whether the ship is leaving or departing, and whether the land-battle and sea-battle are part of the same story. Carter, for example, names this cup as among the earliest manifestations of artistic interest in action, but argues that its Homeric-type battle is arranged symbolically rather than narratively and that there is not necessarily any spatial or temporal connection among the objects.[65]

In the scenes on the skyphos there are no Siamese twins or other unusual elements to suggest that a specific mythological episode is being depicted. This does not reduce them, however, to being emblematic battles and not pictorial narrative. The scenes consist of relatively simple units that recall the many formulaic descriptions of battles and death in the *Iliad*. In combination, these pictorial units create vivid scenes of action that have the same potential for narrative interpretation as the scenes described on the Shield of Achilles or found on the New York krater. As in these real and imaginary artworks, one finds on the skyphos a contrast between figures in motion and figures at rest. Clearly the motion of the ship and the figures on it, whether it is landing or departing, belongs to the present moment. Countering the ship, the two Dipylon warriors are motionless. Whether one should interpret them as awaiting the landing of the ship and battle or as bidding a guarded farewell to the intruders is uncertain, but they clearly signify either past or future events in relationship to the ship. Although the actions of the shipboard figures are quite vigorous, the presence of the Dipylon warriors indicates that the raid or invasion was not a complete surprise, and that the course of events has reached at least a temporary stasis between intruder and defender not unlike that described in the city at war on the Shield of Achilles (*Iliad* 18.509–519). On the other side of the cup, the two inanimate warriors clearly represent the course of the prior moments of the story, while the more active warriors continue the fight and probably attempt to retrieve or despoil the bodies. The way in which the archers seem to be covered by the spearmen is reminiscent of tactics used by Ajax and Teukros in *Iliad* 8.266–272 and elsewhere, although there are no shields here to provide a hiding place for the bowmen. The large object held by the warrior on the left of the land-battle could point to some superweapon or advantage for that side, much like the mighty spear of Achilles could be viewed as portending an ultimate advantage for the Greeks in the Trojan War. Again, there appears to be a stasis, but this in itself is typical of the scenes described on the Shield of Achilles and of Homeric similes in general and is not an impediment to the narrative potential of the scene. Just as it is not necessary to know which of the two litigants will emerge successful from the agora in order to understand that scene as pictorial narrative, since there will be a victor, it is also not required for there to be a specific outcome to the battles on the Eleusis skyphos. It is sufficient that there be some hint of an eventual resolution.

It is uncertain whether the land-battle and sea-battle should be viewed as successive moments in a single saga and, if so, which should come first. It is entirely possible that a Geometric viewer would have made some connection between them, in much the same way that an ambush and raid on the livestock on the Shield of Achilles follow the description of the siege itself (*Iliad* 18.520–540). If one connects the two sides of the cup into a single story, a more complex series of events can be plausibly reconstructed that includes an invasion for some unknown cause that is followed by a pitched battle (or alternatively a battle followed by the retreat of one side). In addition to their being ornamental fillers, the repetition of stars on both sides of the cup could serve to signify such a connection of the two scenes.

Like the New York krater, these simple scenes present sufficient contrasts in time and action, indications of setting, and the potential for a complex interpretation that should qualify them as a narrative. Turning to one last vase, an Argive Geometric krater fragment showing a horse-leader taming a horse, one can also argue that it is possible to construct a course of events that gives the scene a narrative structure (fig. 19.5).[66] The fragment is one of the earliest figured scenes in Argive Geometric art and dates to c. 750–735 B.C. It has not attracted as much attention as the previous two vases, but its composition and variety of components make as complex a picture as the others. The central elements of the composition are a horse and a male figure with a tall headdress who controls the horse with reins in one hand and a prod in the other. Fish in a vertical position appear to either side of the horse, who stands amid a dotted field and over a series of four herringbone lines. These signify water, as does the waterfowl next to them, while the dots are a pebbled shore. In the upper portion of the picture is a procession of four nude figures who gesticulate and carry palms in their hands. Boardman proposes that this and other Argive scenes are realistic in their depiction of motifs and settings of paramount importance in the Argolid, and that no element of this or other Argive compositions "demands a heroic or mythical setting," a position advocated in general by P. Courbin.[67] S. Langdon sees the inclusion of the dancers, fish, and waterbird

FIGURE 19.5. Late Geometric Argive krater fragment, third quarter of eighth century B.C. Argos, C240. (Photograph courtesy of the École Française d'Archéologie, Athens.)

as giving a specifically religious content to the vase that recalls later sacrifices of horses to Poseidon in Argos.[68]

There is, indeed, no need to read a specific mythological or heroic tale in the work, but this fact does not reduce the scene to being an emblem of contemporary Argive life without narrative potential. Just as on the Shield of Achilles, one could point to the actions of the horse-leader as comprising the essence of the present moment. The tether of the horse and the angle of the prod suggest a vibrant activity reminiscent of the Eleusis skyphos. The dancers have accompanied the central figures to the shore, but now appear to stand to the side as observers. This shift in action from one part of the ritual to another is similar to that signaled by the arriving warriors who bear offerings on the New York krater, while the women on the other side of the bier stand more quietly. The dancers' palms and the horse-leader's head-dress might have suggested a specific occasion or context for the scene, in the same way that the poet describes the murder and quarrel as the cause for the case in the law court scene on the Shield of Achilles. The other inanimate objects could also have provided clues to the past or present, as well as to the future course of events. Boardman has shown, for example, that the fish are symbolic of Poseidon, and their presence here might signify the impending sacrifice of the horse. If the scene does in fact depict a ritual, as Langdon suggests, then the actual sacrifice would represent the following stage and climax of the episode, as the *ekphora* and burial are the culmination of the *prothesis* on the New York krater. Indeed the possibly repetitive and religious nature of the episode on the Argive krater fragment recalls the general flavor of many of the events on the Shield of Achilles.

The examination of these three vase depictions in light of the law court scene on the Shield of Achilles indicates the potential for a complex reading of essentially simple and direct Geometric compositions. Just as the poet of the *Iliad* could imagine a rather straightforward scene drawn from contemporary life and art and read into it a succession of moments, actions, and consequences, so too could viewers of the Geometric period have potentially read a tale into many of the figured scenes on Geometric vases. Indeed, one can find in many of them most of the basic components of narrative—an indication of setting, a progression of time, a series of oppositions or contrasts in actions, a potential for interpretation. It is, therefore, too simplistic to separate the scenes of this period simply into either *Sagenbild* or *Lebensbild*, since these do not fully take into account the narrative potential of the Argive fragment or of some of the Attic Geometric funeral scenes. The fact that not much specific appears to happen in these compositions, especially when compared to later Greek art, or that the sequence of events does not progress in a linear fashion, should not be deterrents to granting them the potential for narrative, since the *Iliad* itself arguably has some of these same qualities. As a narrative, the *Iliad* is rather slow and repetitive, and it is rare that one goes along in it for any significant length before some reason for a chronological detour arises or someone like Nestor begins to reminisce yet again about the good old

days. However, we do not read the *Iliad* for a recitation of events. Too many of our definitions of what constitutes pictorial narrative are conditioned by later developments, especially of the Hellenistic period, and the poet of the Shield of Achilles suggests that the content and reception of pictures in the Geometric period was far richer than we generally think.

NOTES

1. The question of the identity of the poet of the *Iliad* and of the *Odyssey*, and of the stratigraphy of their verses, is beyond the scope of this paper, and I have decided to follow the lead of Professor Vermeule—who first introduced me to the magnificence of the *Iliad* in a seminar—by referring to the author of the *Iliad* as "the poet." I would also like to thank Susan Matheson, Edward Douglas, Alan Shapiro, Steven Lowenstam, Jane Carter, Steven Lonsdale, and the anonymous reader for the University of Texas Press for their advice and comments. The errors that remain are my own.

The following abbreviations will be used in this article:

Boardman, "Symbol and Story" = J. Boardman, "Symbol and Story in Geometric Art," in W. G. Moon, ed., *Ancient Greek Art and Iconography* (Madison 1983) 15–36.
Carter = J. Carter, "The Beginning of Narrative Art in the Greek Geometric Period," *BSA* 67 (1972) 25–58.
Coldstream, *GGP* = J. N. Coldstream, *Greek Geometric Pottery* (London 1968).
Fittschen = K. Fittschen, *Der Schild des Achilleus,* ArchHom 2.N (Göttingen 1973).
Hurwit = J. Hurwit, *The Art and Culture of Early Greece, 1100–480 B.C.* (Ithaca 1985).
Marg = W. Marg, *Homer über die Dichtung* (Münster 1957).
Snodgrass, *Archaeology* = A. M. Snodgrass, *An Archaeology of Greece. The Present and Future Scope of a Discipline,* Sather Classical Lectures, vol. 53 (Berkeley 1987).
Snodgrass, *Archaic* = A. M. Snodgrass, *Archaic Greece: The Age of Experiment* (London 1980).

2. Description of the shield: *Iliad* 18.478–607. For arguments on the reality of the shield, see A. S. Murray, *A History of Greek Sculpture*[2] (London 1890) 1, 42–57; W. Reichel, *Homerische Waffen*[2] (Vienna 1901) 147–165. For a summary and bibliography on the problem of the shield, see Fittschen.

3. See, for example, W. Helbig, *Das homerische Epos aus den Denkmälern erläutert. Archäologische Untersuchungen²* (Leipzig 1887) 400–416; C. Robert, *Studien zur Ilias* (Berlin 1901) 15. A summary of these arguments and an argument against them can be found in Marg 21–23. For a discussion of Xenodotos, as quoted by Aristonikos on l. 483, see W. Leaf, ed., *The Iliad* (London 1900–1902; rep. Amsterdam 1971) Appendix I, 607. K. Reinhardt, *Der Ilias und ihr Dichter* (Göttingen 1961) 405, also notes that the iconography of the shield has little directly to do with Achilles.

4. W. Schadewaldt, *Von Homers Welt und Werk⁴* (Stuttgart 1965) 357–360. See also A. Lesky, "Bildwerk und Deutung bei Philostrat und Homer," *Hermes* 75 (1940) 48.

5. On aspects of this position, see Marg 23–24; T. B. L. Webster, *From Mycenae to Homer* (London 1958) 214; K. J. Atchity, *Homer's Iliad. The Shield of Memory* (Carbondale, Ill. 1978) 172; O. Taplin, "The Shield of Achilles within the *Iliad*," *GR* 27 (1980) 15; Hurwit 46–47, 71–73. Taplin 12 comments that the compromise position was more accepted by German than by English scholars, but a consensus appears to have been formed in recent scholarship. Such a symbolic interpretation of the shield scenes goes back to the Hellenistic period; see P. R. Hardie, "Imago Mundi. Cosmological and Ideological Aspects of the Shield of Achilles," *JHS* 105 (1985) 15–17.

6. A sampling of the variety of shield shapes includes the tower shield (Reichel [supra n. 2] 147; Leaf [supra n. 3] 602–604 and fig. 5), Boiotian (Murray [supra n. 2] 46), round with a *telamon* (F. H. Stubbings, "Arms and Armor," *A Companion to Homer* [New York 1963] 513), and figure-of-eight (Leaf 602–604 and fig. 4).

7. Marg 25.

8. Marg 26. Such problems led to various interpretations and rearrangements of the scenes, all of them involving a re-ordering of the sequence and description of the overall structure of the shield in *Iliad*. 18. See, for example, Leaf (supra n. 3) 602–614, Murray (supra n. 2) 46–49, Reichel (supra n. 2) 149–151. Indeed, Reichel is perhaps most frequent in his emendations of the poet's account, and states bluntly (163) that the poet makes many errors in his description. Undermining the credibility of the source, however, makes any effort at reconstruction even more dubious, even if one accepts the premise that the shield was a real object. It is this sort of attitude that lay at least in part behind the more general reluctance of scholars in the twentieth century to attempt reconstructions based on literary accounts.

9. See, for example, Ov., *Met.* 13.110–111, 288–295; Philostr. *Imag.* 10.5–20; Paus. 8.16.3. For discussion of the later history and influence of the shield see Fittschen 1–5 and Hardie (supra n. 5) 15–17.

10. Shield of Herakles: Hes. *Sc.* 139–320. Shield of Aeneas: Verg. *Aen.* 8.626–731.

11. On the Shield of Herakles see Fittschen 18–23 and Hurwit 230–231.

12. P. Friedländer, *Johannes von Gaza und Paulus Silentiarius. Kunstbeschreibungen justinianischer Zeit* (Berlin 1912) 9–10. Friedländer (11) comments that the pseudo-Hesiodic formula came to dominate later descriptions.

13. On representations of the shield see Fittschen 2–3, A. Kossatz-Deissman, *LIMC* I, "Achilleus," 122–28. S. Lowenstam, "The Arming of Achilleus on Early Greek Vases," *Cl Ant* 12 (1993) 199–218, disputes the conclusion that arming scenes with Achilles are generally of the first and not the second arming with the works of Hephaistos. Hardie (supra n. 5) 11–12 notes that the star imagery of the central zone or boss of the shield finds the most frequent representation, while the figured scenes are usually left out. He notes that this astronomical portion of the shield description "comes closer to the possibilities of real shield decorations."

14. See Kossatz-Deissman (supra n. 13) 122 and 127–128, and J. Barringer, "The Form and Meaning of Nereids in Archaic and Classical Greek Art" (Ph.D. diss., Yale University, 1990) 19–57.

15. A. Sadurska, *Les tables iliaques* (Warsaw 1964) 50, no. 4N; P. Bienkowski, "Lo Scudo di Achille," *RM* 6 (1891) 183–207 and pl. IV; Hardie (supra n. 5) 21 and pl. Id.

16. Sadurska (supra n. 15) no. 6B; O. Jahn and A. Michaelis, *Griechische Bilderchroniken* (Bonn 1873) 20 and pl. II, "B"; Hardie (supra n. 5) 22 and fig. I.

17. See H. L. Lorimer, "Homer's Use of the Past," *JHS* 49 (1929) 146–147, who is reminded of Minoan work by the subject, color, and inlay technique of the shield. Lorimer (152) even proposes that such pictorial art may have led to the desire in poetry "for similes which were also pictures complete and finished."

18. D. H. F. Gray, "Metal-Working in Homer," *JHS* 74 (1954) 4, comments that the poet knew of Mycenaean decoration, but not of its technique: "Tin, so far as is known, was never used as an inlaying material, nor was κύανος, whether it means blue glass paste or lapis lazuli." The overall design is more like "incised Cretan shields or 'Phoenician' bowls than anything known from the Bronze Age." Gray (12–13) also points out that the hard, hot hammering of Hephaistos is typical of iron work, not of bronze, as are the bellows and fire tongs; see also S. P. Morris, *Daidalos and the Origins of Greek Art* (Princeton 1992) 7.

19. See Fittschen 9; Schadewaldt (supra n. 4) 358–360.

20. K. Fittschen, *Untersuchungen zum Beginn der Sagendarstellungen bei den Griechen* (Berlin 1969) 9–14, provides definitions of these categories and reviews earlier theories on

the existence of *Sagenbilder* in Geometric art. He recognizes the possibility of other categories (12), but does not explore this more fully. See also R. Kannicht, "Poetry and Art. Homer and the Monuments Afresh," *CA* 1 (1982) 73–76, for a discussion of these categories and their implications.

21. Snodgrass, *Archaeology* 147–148, summarizes the current state of affairs on this question. Another essay in this volume by J. L. Benson, "Human Figures, the Ajax Painter, and Narrative Scenes in Earlier Corinthian Vase Painting," sides with the existence of *Sagenbilder* and explores the Homeric content or atmosphere of figural scenes on some Protocorinthian vases. B. S. Ridgway, "Birds, 'Meniskoi,' and Head Attributes in Archaic Greece," *AJA* 94 (1990) 583–585, provides a cogent summary of the problems of iconography and the identification of scenes. A sample of the more recent bibliography on this debate includes H. Froning, "Anfänge der kontinuierende Bilderzählung in der griechischen Kunst," *JdI* 103 (1988) 169–199; Hurwit; Boardman, "Symbol and Story"; Kannicht (supra n. 20) 70–86; Snodgrass, *Archaic* 67–74; A. M. Snodgrass, "Towards the Interpretation of the Geometric Figure-Scenes," *AthMitt* 95 (1980) 51–58; P. G. P. Meyboom, "Some Observations on Narration in Greek Art," *Meded* 40 (n.s. 5, 1978) 55–82; Carter; G. Ahlberg, *Prothesis and Ekphora in Greek Geometric Art*, SIMA 32 (Göteborg 1971); Fittschen 1969 (supra n. 20); Coldstream, *GGP*.

22. Kannicht (supra n. 20) 76; Snodgrass, *Archaeology* 156–157.

23. On the theory of narrative see R. Barthes, "Introduction to the Structural Analysis of Narratives," in S. Sontag, ed., *A Barthes Reader* (New York 1982) 251–295. The issue obviously demands a fuller theoretical treatment than can be done here and is the subject of a monograph in preparation.

24. A. M. Snodgrass, *Narration and Allusion in Archaic Greek Art*, The Eleventh J. L. Myres Memorial Lecture (Oxford 1982); J. N. Coldstream, "The Geometric Style: Birth of the Picture," in T. Rasmussen and N. Spivey, eds., *Looking at Greek Vases* (Cambridge 1991) 49–51.

25. Snodgrass 1980 (supra n. 21) 52, and later Snodgrass, *Archaeology* 153; J. Boardman, "Symbol and Story" 25–26.

26. B. Andreae and H. Flashar, "Strukturaequivalenzen zwischen den homerischen Epen und der frühgriechischen Vasenkunst," *Poetica* 9 (1977) 217–265, esp. 218–222 and 236–237.

27. On the relationship of literature and art see the introduction in J. H. Hagstrum, *The Sister Arts. The Tradition of Literary Pictorialism and English Poetry from Dryden to Gray* (Chicago 1958) 3–36; M. Praz, *Mnemosyne. The Parallel between Literature and the Visual Arts* (Princeton 1967) 3–28.

28. On *ekphrasis*: Friedländer (supra n. 12); P. Dubois, *History, Rhetorical Description and the Epic. From Homer to*

Spenser (Cambridge 1982); M. Krieger, "The Ekphrastic Principle and the Still Movement of Poetry; or Laokoön Revisited," *The Play and Place of Criticism* (Baltimore 1967) 107–108; J. Meyers, *Painting and the Novel* (Manchester 1975).

29. On rhetoric and *ekphrasis* see S. Bartsch, *Decoding the Ancient Novel: The Reader and the Role of Description in Heliodorus and Achilles Tatius* (Princeton 1989) 3–39; A. S. Becker, "The Shield of Achilles and the Poetics of Homeric Description," *AJP* 111 (1990) 139–153; A. S. Becker, "Reading Poetry through a Distant Lens: Ecphrasis, Ancient Greek Rhetoricians, and the Pseudo-Hesiodic 'Shield of Herakles,'" *AJP* 113 (1992) 5–24.

30. See also Morris (supra n. 18) 11–12.

31. For examples of Phoenician bowls see H. G. Güterbock, "Narration in Anatolian, Syrian, and Assyrian Art," *AJA* 61 (1957), pl. 26, and Fittschen pl. VIIIb and figs. 2–5. On the relationship of these works to the shield see Fittschen 8–17.

32. See Morris (supra n. 18) 11 and S. H. Lonsdale, "A Dancing Floor for Ariadne: Aspects of Ritual Movement in Homer and Minoan Religion," in this volume.

33. Morris (supra n. 18) 12.

34. Becker (1990) (supra n. 29) 140–141 discusses this in terms of treating the referent, the thing represented, as if it were real and then constructing a story around it.

35. Fittschen 11–12 notes that "city at peace" themes are rare in Greek art. Lorimer (supra n. 17) 148 states that "one may hazard the guess that the famous trial-scene, for which no parallel has been found in the representative art of any period, is the original work of Homer himself." The Lambros oinochoe has been compared to this scene; illustration: B. Schweitzer, "Untersuchungen zur Chronologie und Geschichte der geometrischen Stile in Griechenland. II," *AthMitt* 43 (1918), pl. III. Here one finds a frieze of warriors with Dipylon shields around a scene of three unshielded figures flanking a corpse. Two hold long staves in their hands and face in the same direction, standing on either side of the corpse. While some similarities with the law court scene exist, there are too many divergences for it to be closely related.

36. See also *Odyssey* 2.10 and 9.171. On Homeric assemblies see M. I. Finley, *The World of Odysseus*, 2nd ed. (New York 1978) 78–82. My thanks to Steven Lowenstam for his suggestions. From the archaeological perspective, H. A. Thompson and R. E. Wycherley, *The Agora of Athens. The History, Shape and Uses of an Ancient City Center*, The Athenian Agora 14 (Princeton 1972) 19, state, "we can conjecture that the 'ancient Agora' was comparatively small in extent and modest in form, probably containing little except a few simple shrines; one should not imagine extensive public places or

substantial and well-developed public buildings in the early Archaic city."

37. Anderson, "Some Thoughts on the Shield of Achilles," *SymbOslo* 51 (1976) 12. For a recent review of the debate of the legal aspects of this passage see M. Gagarin, *Early Greek Law* (Berkeley 1986) 26–33. On this point of view see also L. C. Muellner, *The Meaning of Homeric εὔχομαι through its Formulas* (Innsbruck 1976) 100–106, and É. Benveniste, *Le vocabulaire des institutions indo-européennes* (Paris 1969) 2, 233–243. For earlier studies of the legal nature of this scene see W. Leaf, "The Trial Scene in *Iliad* XVIII," *JHS* 8 (1887) 126; H. H. Pflueger, "Die Gerichtsszene auf dem Schilde des Achilleus," *Hermes* 77 (1942) 140–148; H. J. Wolff, "The Origin of Judicial Litigation among the Greeks," *Traditio* 4 (1946) 34–49, esp. 36–38; H. Hommel, "Die Gerichtsszene auf dem Schild des Achilleus. Zur Pflege des Rechts in homerischer Zeit," in *Politeia und Res publica* (Wiesbaden 1969) 11–38.

38. W. Ridgeway, "The Homeric Talent, Its Origin, Value, and Affinities," *JHS* 8 (1887) 136; Leaf (supra n. 3) 612–613; M. M. Willcock, ed., *The Iliad of Homer* (New York 1984) 271. Reichel (supra n. 2) 158 views the two talents as the fine and the poet as having misunderstood their function, since the description is "gegen den natürlichen Sinn der künstlerischen Darstellung." According to Ridgeway, two talents were the equivalent of two oxen; by comparison, a slave woman was worth four oxen, or possibly more.

39. Gagarin (supra n. 37) 31.

40. Leaf (supra n. 37) 123 and 129.

41. Fittschen 12.

42. Lesky (supra n. 4) 50.

43. Atchity (supra n. 5) 174 comments that "the consistent use of the imperfect tense throughout the description serves to qualify the impression of contemporaneity. The effect of the verbs is supported by the anonymous character of the men fashioned by Hephaistos. The result of this technical combination is that time is conflated—presented in an idealized manner by which past, present, and future become indistinguishable." Hurwit 103 also comments, "Homeric reality was in fact the narrative moment—a flat, continuous present," filled with digressions. While time is not treated as a series of distinct, sequential episodes in either the *Iliad* or Geometric art, time still does exist and the poet does indicate a progression in time in the law court scene, although not in a clear, linear fashion.

44. Here I disagree with Lesky (supra n. 4) 50, who describes the two men "die sich in lebhafter Geste gegenüberstehen."

45. Snodgrass 1982 (supra n. 24); Snodgrass, *Archaeology* 135–136.

46. See Hurwit 71–73 and Marg 27–28. Fittschen 13 also uses Homer's description as proof that contemporary Greeks would connect separate scenes into a single narrative. The point is well taken, but is less applicable to the shield description than Fittschen maintains.

47. Boardman, "Symbol and Story" 29. See also Snodgrass, *Archaeology* 160, and Kannicht (supra n. 20) 72–75.

48. See Coldstream, *GGP* 263, 268–269, 271–272, 296–297.

49. New York, Metropolitan Museum 14.130.15. The bibliography on this krater is large; see Boardman, "Symbol and Story" 25–26 and n. 77, and J. Boardman, "Attic Geometric Vase Scenes, Old and New," *JHS* 86 (1966) 1–4, with previous bibliography. The best descriptions of the figured scenes are Boardman (supra) and Ahlberg (supra n. 21) 240–252. For this discussion the following additional works will be referred to: I. Froning (supra n. 21) 181–186; R. Hampe, *LIMC* I, "Aktorione," 473; Snodgrass, *Archaic* 76–77; J. N. Coldstream, *Geometric Greece* (New York 1977) 352–354; Carter 52–53; J. L. Benson, *Horse, Bird and Man. The Origins of Greek Painting* (Amherst 1970) 53–55; Fittschen (1969) (supra n. 20) 68–75; Coldstream, *GGP* 42–44 and 184.

50. This is described in the most precise detail by Boardman 1966 (supra n. 49) 1–2.

51. The meaning of the shield type is itself a subject of controversy. T. B. L. Webster, "Homer and Attic Geometric Vases," *BSA* 50 (1955) 41–43 and passim, first proposed that it was derived from Mycenaean heroic shields, especially the figure-of-eight type, and that its presence in Geometric figure scenes signifies a heroic setting. This proposal has met with stiff opposition. Boardman, "Symbol and Story" 27–28, reviews the arguments again and provides bibliography for the controversy. He suggests (31) that the shields are not fictional, but are based on a real Boiotian shield type. Webster's theory has been defended, with a few modifications, by Snodgrass, *Archaic* 73–74, and Snodgrass (1980) (supra n. 21) 54–58. Certainly there appears to be some differentiation in its use on the New York krater as well as on the Eleusis skyphos (see below), but the meaning of this is uncertain whether or not the shield type is real or fictional. One wonders, for example, why the warriors would be wearing their shields in the lowest chariot frieze (see below) if this represents a race from the funeral games of King Amarynkeus, as some maintain. The question of the meaning and use of the shield could certainly bear further examination. Ahlberg (supra n. 21) 244 suggests that the circular devices indicate a semi-outdoor setting, and that the tripod is the prize of the chariot race of the funeral games shown on the lowest figured frieze. Boardman (supra n. 49) 4 sees the tripod as related to the offerings of the warriors on the

other side of the vase and suggests that it was to be buried with the deceased.

52. Boardman (supra n. 49) 3.

53. Those who identify the twins as Aktorione/Molione include Froning (supra n. 21) 184, Hampe (supra n. 49) 473 and 476 (with extensive bibliography on the pair); Snodgrass, *Archaic* 76–77; Coldstream, *Geometric Greece* (supra n. 49) 352–354; Ahlberg (supra n. 21) 248. The twins are mentioned in *Iliad* 2.621, 11.708–709, 11.749–751, 23.638–642, and in a fragment (17a Merkelbach/West) of Hesiod. For other literary references see Hampe (supra n. 49) 472.

54. Froning (supra n. 21) 185–186 labels it as "eine Vorstufe der kontinuierenden Darstellungsweise." She follows Ahlberg (supra n. 21) 248–249 in her assessment of narrative on the krater.

55. Those who see the twins as a convention for overlapping figures include Boardman, "Symbol and Story" 25–26; Carter 52–53; Benson (supra n. 49) 54–55; Fittschen 1969 (supra n. 20) 71. Boardman (supra n. 49) initially supported the identification of the Siamese twins as Aktorione/Molione, but in his review of J. N. Coldstream's *Greek Geometric Pottery, Gnomon* 42 (1970) 501, he stated instead that the scenes provided "evidence about contemporary life and events."

56. On the connection of figures in the same frieze see Boardman, "Symbol and Story" 19, and Fittschen 13.

57. Hampe (supra n. 49) 472 and 476. Hampe cites Pherekydes, who speaks of two sets of twins that fight Herakles.

58. Ahlberg (supra n. 21) 270. Just how continuous this space is with the figures on the other side of the vase is problematic, since the handles intervene. Boardman, "Symbol and Story" 19, would not view their separation into discrete panels as indicating their belonging to distinct scenes. If one were to consider it part of the same space, as Boardman does, then the tripod being set up belongs to the same present moment as the *prothesis* but to a different space. The presence of a second set of Siamese twins there would therefore indicate that there were two sets in the main scene and two sets in the lowest frieze. Thus the often-noted duplication of Siamese twins in the lowest figured register would be paralleled in the uppermost. Would this, then, suggest that there were two different sets of weird twins present at this funeral instead of just one,

and if so, what are the implications of this in terms of its possible mythological content?

59. Boardman (supra n. 49) 2; Ahlberg (supra n. 21) 242.

60. Eleusis 741, identified in its most recent publication as Eleusis, Archaeological Museum, 910; see *The Human Figure in Early Greek Art* (Athens/Washington 1988) 62–63, Cat. no. 3. The bibliography on this vase is also considerable; see Coldstream, *Geometric Greece* (supra n. 49) 110; M. Robertson, *A History of Greek Art* (Cambridge 1975) 19; B. Schweitzer, *Greek Geometric Art* (London 1971) 35–37, 39–40; G. Ahlberg, *Fighting on Land and Sea in Greek Geometric Art* (Stockholm 1971) 10–11 and 34–37; Carter 34–35 (with bibliography from 1959 to 1971); Coldstream, *GGP* 26–28; J. Marwitz, "Kreis und Figur in der attisch-geometrischen Vasenmalerei," *JdI* 74 (1959) 69–71 and 81 (with earlier bibliography). Marwitz and several other scholars proposed dating this skyphos to near the end of the Geometric period, but their arguments were refuted by Carter 34–35.

61. Schweitzer (supra n. 60) 39; Robertson (supra n. 60) 19 comments that the artist sought to keep the figured scene "as something separate from his carefully evolved system of abstract decoration." The liveliness of the depiction more than compensates for its lack of detail and displays a real effort to treat a complicated scene with clarity. Schweitzer 37 also notes that the proportions of the figures are closer to nature than are Late Geometric figures.

62. Robertson (supra n. 60) 19 and in *Human Figure* (supra n. 60) 38; *Human Figure* (62) dates the cup to c. 770 B.C.

63. S. Brunnsåker, "The Pithecusan Shipwreck," *OpRom* 4 (1962) 203; Ahlberg (supra n. 60) 36. Schweitzer (supra n. 60) 36 rejects this suggestions.

64. Ahlberg (supra n. 60) 36.

65. Carter 35.

66. Argos, C240. Bibliography: S. Langdon, "The Return of the Horse Leader," *AJA* 93 (1989) 198; Boardman, "Symbol and Story" 19–20; Coldstream, *GGP* 126, 129–130; P. Courbin, *La céramique géométrique de l'Argolide* (Paris 1966).

67. Boardman, "Symbol and Story" 23 and 25; Courbin (supra n. 64) 495.

68. Langdon (supra n. 64) 198.

20

HUMAN FIGURES, THE AJAX PAINTER, AND NARRATIVE SCENES IN EARLIER CORINTHIAN VASE PAINTING*

♦

J. L. BENSON

In another part (of the palace of Neptune) was represented the war of the gods and Giants with Typhoeus now buried beneath towering Aetna, that sprouted crackling flames . . .
Camoens, *The Luciads*, Canto VI
(W. G. Atkinson translation)

The scholar honored in this volume has a profound knowledge of the Greek myths. The following few comments about scenes on accessible pieces that can perhaps bear reinterpretation are offered as suggestions that may be useful, even if faulty, to her overall view.

Narration *ipso facto* implies human figures; one may well feel that the converse is also true in the world of the early Greeks—without being able to prove this to the sceptics. This is a very old controversy: Did the Greek artisans who decorated pottery and other objects found in graves—both in their own cities and abroad—depict everyday objects and happenings around them or were their representations an expression of a mythic consciousness in which they lived and which impelled them to decorate the objects at all? This has been aired specifically in regard to Attic Geometric pottery in recent

decades and I have not hesitated to defend the latter alternative.[1] Corinthian pottery of the same period cannot be considered apart from the situation in Athens, since what little there is in the way of figural representations on Corinthian Geometric or even Early Protocorinthian pottery seems to follow Attic prototypes slavishly, as the list presented below (with some materials not yet very well known) shows. Corinthian artists, not having created a tradition of figures on their own, would have needed to look in the direction of the reigning masters of the figural scene. But apparently not many Corinthian artists actually did so. In fact, some of the existing scenes on Corinthian clay might—for all we know—have been painted by Attic artists who had come to Corinth. Some interaction between the two styles is evident as early as Middle Geometric and Late Geometric times in Attic bird types that turn up on Corinthian pottery.

The situation is actually quite curious for, in the eighth century, virtually no instances of human representations have been found on pottery in the city of Corinth itself (but see no. 13 below). It is among finds in Delphi that a few traces of this occur. And the inspira-

335

FIGURE 20.1b. Krater fr. Delphi Museum inv. 6401. (Photo by author.)

FIGURE 20.1a. Krater fr. Delphi Museum inv. 6402. (Adapted from *BCH* 85 [1961] fig. 15.)

FIGURE 20.1c. Krater fr. Delphi Museum inv. 6401. (Drawing by Benson.)

tion for the few fragments of this type—some of which could even perhaps have come from the same vase—is so obviously Attic that some scholars have been tempted to detach these, and particularly other closely related pottery (Thapsos Class), from Corinth and speculate about some other provenance (Aigina, Megara). I believe that all such speculations founder on the fabric and technique, which can in the end only be explained as genuinely Corinthian.

In order to throw as much light as possible on this problem I offer an updated review of the latest complete listing of Geometric Corinthian (human) figural instances, that of T. Dunbabin, in *Perachora II*, 121, note 1.

1. Krater, *Corinth* XIII, pl. 9, 47–1. This is now recognized as an Argive work: *CP* 61 (1966) 271; *GGP*, pl. 30c.
2. Louterion (?), Toronto, *GVROM* no. 113, pl. VIII. Frequently illustrated, e.g., *EAA* III, 829, fig. 1030. Ship with crew of about twenty rowers. The clay has been variously identified as Corinthian, Attic, and Megarian. The style, particularly of the rubbed animals on the back, is either Attic or heavily indebted to Attic and possibly contemporary with EPC.
3. Oinochoe, Berlin Antikenmuseum, *ECW* 17. Boat Workshop 1. Even though only a ship is represented, Dunbabin probably included it because rowers are im-

plied. On that basis two fragments from the Potters' Quarter: *Corinth* XV, 3 nos. 44–45 and a kotyle from Eleusis, *ArchEph* 1898, pl. 5.3, may be added.

4. Krater frr., Delphi, *BCH* 62 (1938) 317, pl. 36.1; *BCH* 85 (1961) 328, fig. 15. Two fragments with a chariot scene: inv. 6402 (here fig. 20.1a) show two men standing on the floor of a chariot; inv. 6401 (figs. 20.1b–c) shows head and arm of a man holding a javelin (?) in the manner of a *metabatis* (a rider who controls two horses: see below p. 339ff.). However, at the time of tracing this I thought I detected winglike appendages in the javelin—which would leave the identification of the object in doubt.
5. Krater frr., Delphi, *FdD* V, 138, fig. 536. Charioteer (fig. 20.2a).
6. Krater frr., Delphi, *FdD* V, 138, fig. 537. Warrior with plumed helmet and part of mane of horse (fig. 20.2b)? Nos. 5 and 6 are listed under the inventory number 7408, mentioned also by Johansen 10 n. 19 and in *BCH* 62 (1938) 318 n. 2. They are probably from one pot and constitute a chariot scene. Shape not entirely certain.

FIGURE 20.2a. Krater fr. Delphi Museum inv. 7408. (Photo by author.)

FIGURE 20.3. Krater fr. Delphi Museum inv. 7410. (Drawing by Benson.)

FIGURE 20.2b. Krater fr. Delphi Museum inv. 7408. (Photo by author.)

7. Krater fr. (or skyphos?), Delphi, *FdD* V, 138, fig. 538. Inv. 7410. Archer attacking man with Boiotian shield (fig. 20.3).
8. Krater fr., Delphi, *BCH* 68/69 (1944–1945) 37, fig. 2. This refers to inv. 6088 from a skyphos that has no human representation, only a degenerate swastika between the bars of the frieze and the handle. I cannot guess what piece Dunbabin really intended.
9. Small hydria, *Perachora* II no. 1297, pl. 57. Dancing women. Dunbabin apparently included this as a reflection of Geometric style in the Protocorinthian period.
10. Oinochoe (?) fr., *Corinth* XV, 3, no. 266, pls. 14, 83. Part of male head. Not Geometric; probably MPC IA. Silhouette and outline technique.

Of Dunbabin's list, no. 1 is not, and no. 2 may not be, Corinthian. No. 8 is not relevant. Nos. 9–10 are later than Corinthian Geometric and probably later than EPC. Thus five examples are left but of these nos. 5–6 probably go together, leaving only four certain instances of human representation—or the implication of it (no. 3). To these may be added two further

examples from Delphi and one each from Corinth and Ithaca.

11. Krater fr., Delphi, inventoried under the group designation 1957/9, unpublished as far as I know. Below a frieze of metopes and panels a panel with part of a shoulder and head of warrior (figs. 20.4a–b). The latter is somewhat rubbed; it extends onto the lower bar.
12. Oinochoe (?) fr., Delphi, inventoried as preceding and unpublished. Lower part of figure of woman (?) in long gown (but part of lower legs show); stick or long strands of hair at one side; reserved patterns on gown. Figure flanked by M's (figs. 20.5a–b).
13. Skyphos fr., Corinth C-66-216. One metope shows Molione; another shows male figure holding (?) snake in each hand (fig. 20.6).
14. Oinochoe handle, Ithaca, *BSA* 43 (1948) 42 no. 163. Man with club (?) and short-skirted woman with long hair and headdress (fig. 20.7). M. Robertson remarked that the skirt was surprisingly short.

The four (technically three) examples recovered from Dunbabin's list are thus augmented by four more not known to him. This means that we have only eight rigorously unexceptionable representations preserved from the Corinthian Geometric style and of these only one was found in the city of Corinth itself. That this very small number in comparison with Athens (or probably even with Argos) is not purely accidental seems confirmed by the fact that in the Early Protocorinthian period there are even fewer. These can be listed as follows.

1. Aryballos frr., Ithaca, *BSA* 43 (1948) 50 no. 235; *ECW* 25, Ephoreia Workshop no. 5. Basic description: part of

FIGURE 20.4a. Krater fr. Delphi Museum inv. 1957/9. (Drawing by author.)

FIGURE 20.5a. Oinochoe fr. Delphi Museum inv. 1957/9. (Photo by author.)

FIGURE 20.4b. Krater fr. Delphi Museum inv. 1957/9. (Drawing by author.)

FIGURE 20.5b. Oinochoe fr. Delphi Museum inv. 1957/9. (Drawing by author.)

man, R (here fig. 20.8) and head of sphinx, R, in heraldic relationship to florals. The reserved technique and other stylistic factors imply continuing dependence on Attic prototypes.

2. Aryballos, London, BM 1969, 12–15.1. *ECW* 26 no. 1 (with earlier literature); D. A. Amyx, *Corinthian Vase Painting of the Archaic Period* (Berkeley 1988) 17 no. 1. For descriptions see below: Evelyn Painter (figs. 20.9a–f).

3. Aryballos, Athens, NM (?). *ECW* 26 no. 2 (with literature); Amyx (see no. 2 above) 17 no. 2. Part of hoplite.

The Evelyn Painter (see no. 2 in the Protocorinthian list above), like his colleagues in the Ephoreia Workshop, depended heavily on Attic figural models but his syntax is purely Corinthian and original. He divided his frieze into two equal sections by means of a flower-tree under the handle (fig. 20.9f) and another opposite the handle (fig. 20.9c), although the placement is not pedantically precise. The elements in each half thus form part of an equation. On one side a horseman (figs. 20.9a–b) followed by a hoplite (R); on the other side a lion or a

hound or a jackal (fig. 20.9d) lowering at an apprehensive deer (R). The artist has filled the space behind the hoplite with a water bird (L), which is a natural accompaniment of a flower-tree, but there was no room to insert the corresponding bird on the opposite side of the ornament, so he has contented himself with a vertical cable pattern (fig. 20.9f). Some space remained also behind the hound, but not enough for a standing bird, so a flying bird (R) was inserted (fig. 20.9d), although with no possibility of an answering figure. In any case, the eagle fulfills an important dramatic function: the chase has been swift as a bird's flight and the deer (fig. 20.9e) is now trapped and must expect the attack of its pursuer. Notice that organic filling ornaments (rosettes) are used to indicate a nature setting for the deer hunt, while only a few geometricized ornaments are in the field above the warriors.

At this point there is a choice of interpretations. Brian Cook takes it for granted that the human pair is *hunting* the deer. That supposition, however, entails consequences which he has not adequately explored, although his words suggest that he is troubled by one of them.

FIGURE 20.6 Skyphos fr. Corinth Museum C-66-216. (Drawing by author; courtesy C. K. Williams.)

FIGURE 20.7. Oinochoe. Ithaca. (After *BSA* 43 [1948] 42, no. 163.)

First, why would one hunt deer in full military garb? Where are there any parallels or preconditions in the Early Archaic period? Secondly, why is the horseman alone unarmed—if he is unarmed (for Cook states that he has only a riding crop)?

It can readily be granted that this frieze brings us a relatively new horseman type and a hitherto unknown combination of figures. In regard to the first factor, until the publication by A. Alföldi[2] of a detail of a Late Geometric amphora (fig. 20.10) in Buffalo, there was no recognized documentation for *metabatai* in that early period (but see my Geometric list no. 4): on the Buffalo amphora, the artist invented a way of illustrating the concept. A rider sits astride his horse saddleless, while controlling the reins of his own mount and the side horse with his left hand. With his right he carries his spear at shoulder level (prepared to launch it). However common *metabatai* may have been in contemporary practice,[3] no more *full* representations have been preserved before the Chigi olpe, to my knowledge, and by that time and a little later, the riders may carry a riding crop or one spear or two spears but in a more comfortable forward position suitable for parading.

Nevertheless, the original Geometric pose does continue in a modified form in Attic painting, that is, the side horse is omitted. Jean Davison[4] published several Early Protoattic examples on which the object in the right hand is turned downward, beginning at the hand, so that the appearance is more of a crop than of a spear. But the context is nevertheless military. This is true even

FIGURE 20.8. Aryballos fr. Ithaca. (After *BSA* 43 [1948] 50 no. 235.)

of a variant[5] in which the rider's right arm is brought forward as if merely holding the reins.

In the Corinthian sphere, the Evelyn Painter has also adopted the pose of the Buffalo *metabatis*. Although the object in the right hand (fig. 20.9b) has drifted somewhat more from the horizontal than in the prototype (as in no. 4 of my Corinthian Geometric list), it is probably a spear and not a riding crop. If Alföldi's explanation for the practice of *metaballein* is correct—namely, that it is physically unbearable to ride a saddleless horse very long in the heat of battle because of the horse's sweat and, also, that the ability to change over became a point of athletic pride in any case—then presumably any horseman relatable by his position to the prototype can be thought of as having a side horse, whether it is shown or not. Geometric artists and their successors were quite capable of abbreviating whatever they liked; but by about the middle of the seventh century it must have seemed desirable to be more explicit about this old-fashioned aristocratic practice, as we have seen. Thus,

FIGURE 20.9a – f. Aryballos. London, British Museum, inv. 1969, 12–15.1. (Photographs courtesy of the Trustees of the British Museum).

the Evelyn Painter's knight can be thought of as having his two horses.

The combination with a hoplite (fig. 20.9a) is something else and its occurrence, as Cook saw, is the first we know of. But in the later expanded forms presented by Alföldi,[6] it means a military situation in which the cavalry play one role and hoplites another. At this earlier date we may at least postulate, along with Snodgrass,[7] a somewhat experimental situation leading up to the creation of a really formidable phalanx system. In any case, the corpus of Geometric vases tells us that a man with round shield and helmet is *always* part of a military formation, and it cannot be any different here. An excerpt on a small vase does not make any sense in its own right but only as an abbreviation of more figures. How skillful Corinthian miniaturists became in this respect is shown on the works of the Chigi Painter.

With the two scenes of the London aryballos now identified, how shall they be thought to form a unity? I believe that there is only one reasonable possibility, and it leads right into the epic mentality of the age. Beginning at the right-hand side of the handle, a force of infantry and cavalry is attacking—we shall never know exactly whom but one can speculate. Beyond the front flower-tree we are told that the attack will be swift and deadly, as when "the Trojans beset (Odysseus) like

tawny jackals . . . round a wounded horned stag, that a man hath smitten with an arrow, and the stag has fled him by speed of foot . . . (but) . . . the ravening jackals rend him in the hills" (*Iliad* 11.473–480).[8] Even if the foot soldiers were routing the cavalry—which seems to me less likely militarily—the Homeric simile would be apt.

The Evelyn Painter has embroidered on a theme like this and in so doing has laid the ground for the extraordinarily expansive spirit that came over the artists of the Corinthian Potters' Quarter in the next two decades. In this scene the two flower-trees decisively separate the military action from the epic reference.

At this point it may be advisable to introduce some thoughts about method. If the above interpretation seems to any reader too ingenious, it must first of all be understood that the idea that the Greeks did not restrict the simile practice to literary situations is not entirely new, even though up to now only rather limited use has been made of it as an analytical tool. In scattered instances other scholars have found depictions in which the use of a visual simile recognizable as pertaining to epic fairly "leaps to the eye."[9] However, a very recent study by Glenn Markoe[10] written independently of mine makes extensive use of the technique. He deals primarily with Attic art—thus complementing for a stretch my study—and actually *traces* the use of the idea of the lion attack on vases and other objects as a feature of heroic triumph throughout the entire Archaic period. He sees the rationale for this in the Homeric simile and reveals this as the departure point for a broader interest in

340

other aspects of Near Eastern lion iconography among Greeks. Obviously, this is congenial to my viewpoint; working on a less-broad scale I have found that such imagery can be understood in an almost incredibly detailed way in the works of one (admittedly extraordinary) Protocorinthian artist—the Ajax Painter—who paved the way for a slightly later colleague actually to substitute animals for the human agent in a primary scene (Berlin 3318, below). This shows that other painters in the Potters' Quarter were well aware of what the Ajax Painter had been doing. This is a totally new discovery—as is also the extent to which early painters understood the technique.

To my knowledge, no one has previously taken an approach based on similes to explain Protocorinthian narrative scenes, partly, perhaps, because the time was not ripe, and partly because the subsidiary frieze as such has never been studied in detail or accorded much significance—that is, it has usually been seen not as an integral part of the artist's conception of the whole narrative project but rather as a kind of "Orientalizing style" space-filler tacked on. My observations over many years convinced me that this explanation was not likely to be valid. The more or less usual assumption that the rich array of visual images on all parts of Middle Protocorinthian vases could only be casual and mostly unrelated representations (as one might expect from unskilled or at least humble artisans) did not seem to me to fit in with the acknowledged commercial and artistic brilliance of early Corinth (the latter especially in the realm of architecture and in the literary tradition of Corinth's preemi-

nence in painting).[11] Perhaps we are *not* dealing with just humble artisans (though there must have been some). Eventually, and only through the controversy about mythic thinking mentioned above, I found a way to unlock the meaning of these scenes—to my own satisfaction, at least—and that is what is offered here. Out of this approach I have attempted to formulate some premises (at the end of this paper) to leave no doubt about my conception of method; but over and above that I have found that the more dialectically one reasons about the Greeks' creativity, the more one discovers what they put into their works.

While on the subject of methods, I want to present a few other ideas germane to the following discussion. I have shown elsewhere that Greek vase painters had an interest in ratios from an early stage and advanced to a considerable sophistication in this respect.[12] It is, of course, immaterial whether they defined this interest to themselves consciously, since the friezes on their vases show the principle of arithmetical ratios in operation. Thus it cannot be a question of composer-reciters of epic having a prior claim on cultural creativity. For if one can see arithmetical ratios as a kind of visual trope parallel in principle to the literary simile (e.g., on a given vase, taller frieze is to shorter frieze as 4 : 2; Warrior A is to Warrior B as a lion is to a deer), then the practitioners of the visual arts in early Greece were at least as inventive as their literary colleagues, and we can by the same token understand how natural it might be for an intelligent artist to interweave the word-picture of the epic with visual illustrations on the vase. It is not even speculative

FIGURE 20.10. Amphora, Buffalo Museum of Science. (Detail). (After *Gestalt und Geschichte*, 4. Beiheft *AntK* [Bern 1967] pl. 7.1.)

to ask whether a vase painter on occasion *recited* epic stories or whether a bard happened to earn his sustenance by putting his hand to a visual illustration. We should try to imagine how a moneyless society might have functioned.

MIDDLE PROTOCORINTHIAN IA (C. 690 – 675 B.C.)

Leaving quite aside the swelling volume and sweeping curves of the Toulouse Workshop figures we can find a good example of that expansive spirit of this period in a skyphos from Aigina (Kraiker's no. 191: here fig. 20.11). Moreover, this piece is of unusual value for our pursuit of the rider theme. First of all, the dainty, rectangular horse of the Evelyn Painter (fig. 20.9b), with its straight-line triangle for the forelegs, has metamorphosed into huge, massive steeds with short, powerful forelegs and high swung-up rumps with bushy tails. The animals' sheer volume dwarfs the riders, who seem to slide forward to the base of the necks of their mounts. Apart from that peculiarity, these figures taken together allow a hypothesis. If, as seems likely, the Evelyn Painter's knight is a *metabatis* (because of his association with a hoplite and his pose, which is comparable to the Attic Geometric *metabatis*), then a procession of four very similar figures—even without the hoplites—prob-

ably constitutes a parade of *metabatai*. Of the four horsemen, three are wielding spears in the manner of the Evelyn horsemen—except that the angle of elbows is reversed. It is difficult to believe that this latter feature could make any difference to the interpretation; it is an artistic variant that afterwards remained standard for this pose (and there is no other pose to represent a *metabatis*).

The fourth rider, however, is of the greatest interest because he holds not a lance but what is clearly depicted as a riding crop with the whip ends hanging down from the handle. Such a differentiation suggests that an established convention has been modified to express a subtler content. If the frieze does indeed represent a military parade, the crop-wielder may be exercising the function of a marshal or commanding officer of a unit of cavalry (note that he has a key position: under the handle). No later than the time of the Chigi olpe a third variant occurs: a rider who uses both hands to control the reins.[13] All of this gives us a little insight into the practices of the aristocratic horse-owning class which was gradually being displaced by the new military realities so graphically depicted in other parts of the Chigi olpe.

The bold and practiced style of the painter of the Aigina kotyle makes us regret that other works by him have not come down to us—at least other figural representations that may well have taken the form of dramatic narratives like those of his colleague, the Ajax Painter, to whom we now turn.

My current view of the Ajax Painter is given by the listing of four aryballoi in *ECW*, pp. 43–44. Although no attempt was made there to deal with internal chronology (with the exception of no. 4), the time has arrived to do just that. That omission in itself implied that the oeuvre, as conceived by others and myself, is somewhat an act of faith insofar as it pertains to an era when we can hardly expect much consistency in details. For that era is one of intense innovation and experimentation, not the least of which is the new—or renewed—interest in narration. Within this framework the four aryballoi assigned to the Ajax Painter form a tight unit in regard to shape, decoration, and type of representation so that, despite recurring doubts, one is always brought back to the first impression that this is one man's way of working. The attempt to see development in this situation is, I think, salutary and makes the case stronger. I shall therefore discuss the works in what I now conceive to be the order of their creation, granted certainly that we need not assume a great lapse of time between the one and the next.

BERLIN PERGAMON MUSEUM NO. 3319
(*ECW* 44:3; figs. 20.12a–d)

Although the shape of the aryballos is already completely standard ovoid, the animals of the lower frieze retain much of the awkwardness of animals on the plumper, slightly earlier shape.[14] And the combination of a subordinate frieze at all with a narrative scene is a striking innovation which may well be owed to this master, although he did not follow it up on any of his other known works. The shoulder floral also has the loose quality of the earlier aryballoi mentioned above. It will accordingly not be surprising that the horses in their structure still echo the modest volume and sticklike legs of the Evelyn Master's type, although the hind leg reentrant is higher and the mane is shaggy, not clipped—in both features generally parallel with the structure of the Aigina kotyle horses. The practiced floral ornaments of the shoulder and the cable design on the handle guarantee some experience; this aryballos is not a beginner's effort despite awkwardness in the main frieze. In fact the very commitment to a complicated narrative scene is evidence of a pioneering quality.

Most astonishing in the latter respect is the representation under the handle: a figure that has been universally interpreted as the Suicide of Ajax (fig. 20.12a) and hence the first identifiable epic theme in Corinthian vase painting (the Geometric Molione cannot be considered here because it is obviously simply a copy of an Attic representation). K. F. Johansen[15] has described in detail the infelicities of the representation (although the dramatic impact of a great sword running through the falling body is unmistakable!), leaving us in little doubt that the painter conjured up the scene from his own prolific imagination, rather than from a direct visual prototype, on the basis of inspiration from epic poetry such as the *Aithiopis*.

The purpose of the rest of the frieze is not immediately evident, and Johansen did not attempt to interpret it, apart from seeing the figure to Ajax' left as connected with him (fig. 20.12b); rather, he claimed that "Manifes-

FIGURE 20.11. Kotyle, Aigina Museum. (After W. Kraiker, *Aigina: Die Vasen des 10. bis 7. Jahrhunderts vor Chr.* [Berlin 1951] 112 no. 191.)

tement les autres figures de la zone sont sans rapport avec ce sujet." However, if one cannot say who these figures are, one is hardly authorized to deny any connection; in fact, the logic of narration would lead us to expect it.[16] The figure turning away from Ajax in agitation must surely be his son, Eurysakes, the only witness to the suicide. On the opposite side of the handle we see a groom (R) leading a reserve horse (fig. 20.12c) behind a man of substance (judging by his hair style), who is about to mount his chariot, the team of which is preceded by a cock (fig. 20.12d)—symbol of aggressive strength.[17] Opposing the chariot is a warrior (L) menacing with a raised spear (fig. 20.12b). These are the elements—reduced to the absolute minimum—of a heroic battle, and it is hardly far-fetched to regard the scene as a retrospective celebration of an exploit of the legendary prowess of the tragic, shamefully treated hero, Ajax. Further than this we cannot go, although the artist may well have had a specific occasion in mind; we cannot even be absolutely sure which of the figures is Ajax, but the drawing of the hair and eyes of the falling figure and the mounting figure is identical, in contrast to that of the spearman, who looks younger. Moreover the cock is the attribute of the chariot rider, suggesting a victorious outcome for him. On the basis of this interpretation we can suggest that our painter already was grasping the principle of polarity—and very subtly. For a viewer of the vase from the front would immediately identify the scene as an epic battle but would have to turn the vase around to see who was involved. As a final subtle comment on this theme of the bitter reversal of Destiny, the

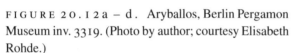

FIGURE 20.12a–d. Aryballos, Berlin Pergamon Museum inv. 3319. (Photo by author; courtesy Elisabeth Rohde.)

artist has pitted a marauding lion against a hapless goat (cf. *Iliad* 10.485) *exactly* under the Ajax scene, while the other animals are still browsing peaceably. In an era when subordinate animal friezes were unknown, or scarcely known, it cannot be an accident that the Ajax Painter introduced one organized in this way. While no assured interpretation can be given, the lion/goat combination certainly looks like a simile reinforcing the scene directly above it by suggesting the sudden collapse of Ajax' flourishing career under the enmity of Athena or recalling that Ajax in his madness turned destructively on the hapless cattle of the Achaians.

BERLIN PERGAMON MUSEUM NO. 3318
(*ECW* 43:2; figs. 20.13a–d)

Characterization

The still somewhat regular composition of the extended scene on the Ajax aryballos gives way like a burst dam to figures whose very weight forces an expansion of the frieze downward, thereby displacing the animal frieze. As if in response, the shoulder decoration is somewhat clarified, the rays at the base slightly elongated. Moreover, the excitement of the figures spills down into the ray zone in the form of pendent spiral hooks. The back of the handle drops the regularity of the cable pattern in favor of a slashing hatched pattern (fig. 20.13a). The new spirit is best understood by comparing the advancing spearman in the two friezes (figs. 20.12b and 20.13c). While the stances are quite the same—leaning forward, with the cock in the same position, the spearman on Berlin 3318 is much more massive and convincingly a threat to his opponent.

The space immediately under the handle of no. 3318 (fig. 20.13a) shows no significant representation but rather serves as dividing line between movement of figures in opposite directions. Immediately under the handle is what Johansen [18] identifies as a bird held by the tail (upside down) in the raised arm of a winged demon who moves to left in the *Knielaufschema* but looks backwards. A snake grasped by its neck is suspended from the other hand. To the right of the handle space is a *metabatis* (R) holding a riding crop (fig. 20.13d). Again, not only is the demon a heavy figure but the horse is both taller and longer than on Berlin 3319, although still retaining its exaggeratedly high reentrant; but the effect is not so misshapen as that of the horses of Aigina 191 (fig. 20.11). The rider sits (and leans) quite

far forward. Separating the rider from the main scene (what is between him and the demon) is a large starburst filling ornament (rosette) just below a cross-in-lozenge; the demon is also separated, although not so spaciously, from the main scene, by a lozenge-derived ornament. This plainly represents a premeditated *structural* use of filling ornaments—again apparently an innovation of this painter.

The main scene consists of, from left, an enormous lion (R) rearing on hind legs (fig. 20.13b) and towering over a man (R) with widely stretched out legs running to escape the beast—whose jaws are in a position to bite the man's neck. Although the victim has drawn his sword, he is not in a position to use it. There is a spotted cock immediately before him, and facing him is a much larger warrior (L), whose spear is already pressing against the lion's cranium (fig. 20.13c).

Interpretation

The artist is experimenting with the problem of composing dramatic forces. Eliminating the previous front-back contrast he now places a "main scene" directly opposite the handle and flanks it with a figure directed toward it from each side. The problem is the same, but now on a more complex level, as that grappled with by Attic Late Geometric artists: dramatic focality.[19] If the

main scene is mythical, as indicated by the lion, then the right-hand figure (the demon) represents the sphere of divine beings, and the left-hand figure (the rider) should be—if the polarity were logically enforced—the sphere of the artist's contemporary society. And the *metabatis* is that *in type*, but almost certainly not in this context, as we shall see. This illustrates the phenomenon of ambiguity, which I have found to be a characteristic of Attic Geometric narrative.[20]

The central group is dominated by the attacking lion and the opposing hero, with the smaller man between them. Thus there is a triad—a "mini-focus" at the very center of the triadic frieze itself. At first it might seem strange that this most central figure is visually small and weak. On reflection, however, it seems that he is anything but conceptually unimportant. For several reasons I believe him to be the raison d'être of the whole composition. First of all, to clear the way, I retract unconditionally my earlier, unreflective description (*ECW* 43), "duel between swordsman and spearman." The duel here is between the lion and the two human beings combined. Secondly, the cock placed in front of the smaller man is a guarantee of his bravery and, presumably, ultimate triumph. Thirdly, and most important, the spear of the taller man is aimed not at his human counterpart but specifically at the head of the lion.

345

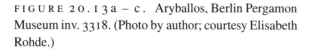

FIGURE 20.13a – c. Aryballos, Berlin Pergamon Museum inv. 3318. (Photo by author; courtesy Elisabeth Rohde.)

From these facts we are virtually compelled to identify this scene as the rescue of a brave warrior who has become isolated from his fellows and has been surrounded by the enemy. Two notable descriptions of such a predicament of Greek heroes[21] occur in the *Iliad*: the rescue of Odysseus and slightly later of Ajax, both of whom singlehandedly and under great duress held off the battering of powerful Trojan opponents until Greek reinforcements could rescue them. Homer (11.585–591) describes the latter incident as follows:

> Then Eurypylos withdrew back into the host of his comrades, avoiding fate, and with a piercing voice he shouted to the Danaans: "O friends, leaders and counselors of the Argives, turn and stand and ward off the pitiless day from Aias, that is oppressed with darts, nor methinks will he escape out of the evil din of battle. Nay, stand ye the rather at bay round great Aias, son of Telamon."

Earlier in the battle something similar had happened to Odysseus (11.480–488):

> . . . and then god ($\delta\alpha\acute{\iota}\mu\omega\nu$) leadeth a murderous lion thither, and the jackals flee before him, but he rendeth them, so then, round wise-hearted Odysseus of the crafty counsels, did the Trojans gather, many and mighty, but that hero thrusting on with the spear held off the pitiless day. Then Aias drew near, bearing his shield like a tower, and stood thereby, and the Trojans fled from him, where each man might. Then warlike Menelaos led Odysseus out of the press, holding him by the hand, till the squire drove up the horses.

In both incidents Ajax is involved, once as the rescued, once as the rescuer. Given the penchant of the Ajax Painter for the Telamonian hero and the close correspondence of the visual to the literary rendition, it is hardly conjecture that one of these rescues is the theme. Perhaps we should not press the question as to which one, even though the image of the lion actually occurs in the second passage.[22] This reminds us that the lion is ubiquitous in the *Iliad* in similes to denote the strength and fighting fury of individual heroes or of collective warriors on either side in the conflict. In the last cited passage Homer comes very close to using the lion as a metaphor, and it is exactly this leap that the Ajax Painter has taken in *his* scene: the lion here *is* the Trojan contingent. The result has an imaginative quality that does full justice to the excitement of the Homeric epic.

346

Can the military force represented by the *metabatis* be more closely characterized? That it is not a passive spectator but is affected by the sphere of the central scene seems given by the impatient eagerness with which the rider is urging his horse into action. The open mouth visible in the detail photograph (fig. 20.13e) suggests that he is shouting as well. I do not see any way to decide whether this is the Greek army rushing to the rescue or the Trojan army pressing on to finish off the lone combatant.

If physical movement toward the center is implied on the left, a distinct contrast is offered on the right by the *Knielaufschema* of the demon (fig. 20.13a). Movement forward is canceled by the reverted head. The demon then represents nothing physical but a soul-force or soul quality[23] which might appropriately be connected with the innate natural courage of the lion—especially since the demon is, or surely is connected with, the mistress or the master of the animals. But whether this quality of surging fury has to be limited to the Trojans, as the attackers, can hardly be decided. In any case, the conception is poetically brilliant, corresponding at one slight remove to the Homeric practice of letting heroes be inspired in battle by their patron deities, as for example Aeneas by Apollo (20.117–118).

A final word on "orientalizing" influences is required. The lotus-and-palmette is a relatively new orna-

FIGURE 20.13d. Aryballos, Berlin Pergamon Museum inv. 3318. (After Payne, pl. 10.6.)

ment, adapted from the East and Egypt, and here adds a touch of elegance that has not yet been assimilated into the spirit of the decorative scheme of the whole vessel—in fact, it is rather incongruous with the bristling martial energy otherwise in evidence. An idea of lion anatomy is, of course, owed to Eastern prototypes and seems here relatively advanced, yet handled in an independent way. A considerable flaking of paint in the area of the lion makes it impossible to be sure how the paws are handled and also whether the man attacked has a garment on the upper part of his body just below the raised forepaw of the beast. Yet, in any case, this scene seems to have little similarity to the most usual version of the Near Eastern lion hunt, the formal representations of lion-mastering by kings, or lion hunts from chariots, as in Assyrian art.[24] Above all, I am not convinced by Johansen's claim[25] that our lion's head " . . . se présente de face et non de profil, manière de figurer les fauves mordant qui, on le sait, a été empruntée à l'Orient." My eyes distinctly see a profile view of the head. All in all, the Ajax Painter has created a totally Homeric composition—one completely native Greek in its conception and execution.

FIGURE 20.13e. Aryballos, Berlin Pergamon Museum inv. 3318. (Photo museum; courtesy Elisabeth Rohde).

PARIS LOUVRE CA 617
(*ECW* 43; figs. 20.14a–c)

In analyzing the two latest known works of the Ajax Painter, one confronts the fact that both stem from one phase of the artist's career in terms of their dramatic power. Nevertheless, a temporal order can be established: in terms of depicting action figures plausibly and of the subtlety of subordinate decoration, the Boston aryballos is indisputably riper than the Louvre aryballos.

CA 617 stands in an easily recognized relationship to Berlin 3319; the cable pattern of the handle is virtually identical but the dotted cells of the latter's disk have been transferred to the shoulder area as the sole ornamentation (fig. 20.14a). A very great lapse of time cannot be assumed. On the other hand, the Paris aryballos

also reflects the frieze psychology of Berlin 3318—which in every way had dynamically broken through the format of Berlin 3319. CA 617 retains the wide narrative frieze and the tall base rays; moreover, even the disk pattern of Berlin 3319 is retained (see Johansen, pl. XXII, 1d); the very full elaboration of that pattern and other decorative features on the Boston aryballos (Johansen, pl. XXII, 2c) thus provides the final proof of the order of the works established in this paper.

The stylistic maturation of the artist is more apparent on the horses and riders of CA 617 than on the other figures, which still have totally unresolved structural awkwardnesses. However, the horses now have virtually horizontal trunks and normal proportions (fig. 20.14b). The heads have a plausible equine contour, while the horsemen are centered on their mounts' backs and hold the reins more naturally. To some extent this must probably be reckoned not only as an advance in draughtsmanship but also as an expression of the artist's intention to show figures that are not engaged emotionally in the action of the scene—as in the rescue depicted on Berlin 3318—but are more or less passive spectators of a happening. But links remain to Berlin 3318, particularly in the sunburst rosette that separates the horsemen from the main figure and in the prominent ornament on the other side of that figure separating it from the figures on the right. Just as in the earlier work, the rosette seems to indicate physical separation, while the right ornament points to a psychological relationship. New is an accretion of minor filling ornaments in the field, while the cock has been relegated from the dramatic part of the frieze and tucked between the hind feet of the horse farthest to the left. In this position it seems to be more a general symbol of strength and victory than an augury as before. Furthermore, it is "balanced," as it were, by a small fish between the legs of the man farthest to the right—which may provide a clue as to his identity.

The dramatic similarity of the two late scenes lies in the clarification and concentration provided by focusing on one central figure in CA 617 and by reducing the number of figures to three in the Boston aryballos. With this goes, in the Paris scene, a kind of tension in the triadic composition. Although the space immediately under the handle (fig. 20.14c) is still the dividing line between movement from either side toward the center, the cynosure of the scene is not immediately opposite that space on the front but pushed to one side by the horsemen coming from the left (fig. 20.14a), one of whom occupies the central space (fig. 20.14b). Since by no stretch of the imagination can this figure be the dramatic focus of the scene, I take it to mean that these *metabatai* represent a dominating military presence as a framework for the scene.

The first *metabatis* has the spear, while what was held by the second one is no longer discernible, but this figure is in every visible respect a copy of the other one, so that the presence of a spear in the original drawing is a reasonable assumption. In general, these horsemen seem more to be standing than advancing. Two heroes approach from the opposite direction, one in a striding position brandishing a sword and the other already standing. Holding a spear in his left hand, he is apparently seizing by the wrist an exceedingly large figure, its feet and head turned to the left—away from the attackers. Since artists of this period did not draw frontal heads, we may not read too much importance into this fact, but it would be natural for a captured person to look away in horror or even disdain. The figure wears a long, one-piece garment that flares out to sharp points just above the feet; the hair is arranged as an *Etagenperücke* rising to about the level of the ears in Payne's drawing so that the upper part of the head is bald. The figure is so massive that the head pierces through the frieze line, breaking the usual isocephaly. The face has a bold profile and prominent eye, nose and, below the mouth, a strange, squared-off area exactly in the position of a beard. Could this be a beard cut off, torn off—or even a double chin? Further, there is a long vertical line beginning with a slight hook near the eye and curving down to meet the area under the chin. Given the inventiveness and dramatic economy of this artist, I take all of these to have significance.

Starting from the methods and predilections found in the artist's previous works, I suggest that we might here expect him to be contrasting victorious Greeks and great, but defeated, Trojans. The presence of two *metabatai* instead of one conveys not only the presence but the overwhelming presence of a victorious Greek army, symbolized by the cock—so much so that they deflect the central figure away from dead center toward the right. The two *metabatai* (R) on the left side are balanced by the two unmounted warriors (L) on the right

side. In terms of polarity the latter should be Trojans but this is unlikely because they are capturing a highly important person. Rather, it seems that the Greeks are pressing from two sides towards the center, which itself provides the polar element.

This interpretation finds confirmation in the symbolic animals. The cock on the left labels the cavalry as brave. The fish at the right should not be a polar contrast to, but a reinforcement of, that quality. The only fish simile I find in the *Iliad* occurs in Book 21.20–21:

> As before a dolphin of huge maw fly other fish and fill the nooks of some fair-havened bay, in terror, for he devoureth amain whichsoever of them he may catch; so along the channels of that dread stream the Trojans crowded beneath the precipitous sides.

What is particularly significant about this simile is that it uses only one species of animal so that the adversarial effect resides solely in the advantage given by greater size and strength. Thus it constitutes a unicum in the *Iliad* occasioned by an episode occurring where fish are, namely, the River, which Achilles attacks because of its efforts to aid the Trojans. Moreover, the trope is used by Homer not only to point to the destruction of some Trojans (the fish eaten by the dolphin) but also to the capture of twelve Trojan youths who are sent back to the Greek camp to await their fate (23.174–176). The River motif of Book 21 is a vivid portent of the downfall of Troy.

All of this is so specific that its appearance here might point to the destruction of Troy and, as well, to the capture of a highly placed Trojan. Then the fish falls into place as calling up the consequences of the Greek army's bravery—thereby complementing, not contrasting with, the cock. I need hardly point out regarding the fish simile that in earlier Corinthian art fish always refer to water (for example, schools of fish shown by multiple specimens)[26] and the appearance of one here—the only instance so far of a fish in a Protocorinthian narrative frieze—cannot be a meaningless detail. In fact, I believe it has, perhaps serendipitously, an additional overtone in this scene (see below).

Who, then, is the great Trojan in the center of the scene? Surely it must be one of the members of the royal family still alive at the end of the war. Unfortunately, the sex of the figure in question is not definable with assur-

FIGURE 20.14a. Aryballos, Paris Louvre Museum inv. CA 617. (After Johansen, pl. XXII.1b.)

FIGURE 20.14c. Aryballos, Paris Louvre Museum inv. CA 617. (After Payne, pl. 10.1.)

ance[27] (by us, at least) from its characteristics. The garment could be a chiton or an ankle-length flared skirt. It could be some sort of ceremonial garment. If the figure is supposed to be male, it could be Priam; yet there are problems with that identification. The less serious is that there is no indication of an altar here—later, at least, a prop in his death scene. A more serious discrepancy is that Priam died fighting nobly, if feebly, being struck down by Pyrrhus, who perhaps returned Priam's own lance. He was not first captured and then later executed.

If the figure is female, it could be Cassandra—but she too was associated with an altar. In any case Queen Hekabe—led off by Odysseus as booty—takes precedence over her daughter as a tragic figure. Could this head not be seen as an imaginative—if perhaps not quite successful—rendering of the destitute wife of a slain king and the mother of many butchered princes: balding, or with much of her hair torn out—or both—and with a deep wrinkle (or else a violent scratch mark) on her cheek? She would appear to be stout, with a double or sagging chin, but drawn up to an impressive height. Her dignity is nevertheless such that various commentators have noted the similarity of her figure with a cult statue. In any case, with her size, which dwarfs all the other figures, the Ajax Painter uses the dramatic device of enhancing the opponent to emphasize the greatness of the victor (compare the huge lion in Berlin 3318). I

suggest that she cannot be looking at the horsemen, who are separated from her in space (and time), but is looking away in disdain from Odysseus (she later cursed him).

If the captor is Odysseus, to whose lot Hekabe fell, not because she would be a desirable concubine but because of his previous complex associations with her,[28] who is the second man shown? There is nothing specifically in the legend to tell us, but we may recall that Odysseus also had a complex relationship with Ajax Minor, son of his great friend Ajax Major. In fact, both Odysseus and Ajax Minor had unsavory aspects to their characters even though the former was the more famous recipient of the epithet "wily." To a seventh-century Homeric enthusiast, Odysseus must have been inalienably associated with fish, because of his many shipwrecks.[29] Although the Ajax Painter did not put this fish directly under the figure I am interpreting as Odysseus, one can think of reasons for that. By his action Odysseus' legs are less wide apart than those of the figure at the right. And because the cock is at the extreme left, the fish had to be at the extreme right. The principal purpose of the fish has already been described. But if the fish also by a happy coincidence refers to Odysseus, the dramatic irony beloved by later Greek playwrights would already be announced here: while Hekabe's fate is bitter, Odysseus will be condemned to wander the seas endlessly and barely escape the fate of becoming

FIGURE 20.14b. Aryballos, Paris Louvre Museum inv. CA 617. (After Johansen, pl. XXII.1a.)

food for the fish. There is scarcely an English term to characterize this kind of (conscious or unconscious) inventiveness; shall we deny it to the Ajax Painter out of a preconceived notion that it cannot be so? At the very least he has created a scene out of epic materials that looks forward to drama.[30]

Given the artistic means at his disposal, it is arguable that the Ajax Painter, in his series of Homeric studies, was as profoundly humanistic, in the sense that that word is employed in our concept of Western culture, as anything in the entire Greek repertory of dramatic invention. It is even possible that he satirized his own themes, if an aryballos once in Paros (*ECW* 44:1a), which for safety's sake I have always listed as "manner," is actually his work (fig. 20.15), as has elsewhere been assumed.[31] Be that as it may, in his latest known work he turned away from directly Homeric soul-searching situations and applied his ample talents to a mythological theme that allowed him somewhat more distance by way of its setting in divine spheres.

BOSTON MUSEUM OF FINE ARTS 95.12
(*ECW* 44:4; figs. 20.16a–e)

The Ajax Painter's ever-restless drive to experiment took him back, as he designed the Boston aryballos, to the combination of main frieze and animal frieze; yet

here he swept away the decorative shoulder design to make way for the animals (fig. 20.16a), and yet combined these with the most elaborate disk and handle ornamentation yet seen (fig. 20.16b). A lion (R) roars at a ram (L) which is back-to-back with a browsing goat (R). This orientation reflects exactly the orientation of the figures in the frieze below, with the back-to-back figures being in roughly the same vertical axis. In his previous animal frieze the Ajax Painter did not employ filling ornaments; in this one he uses a rather large double-voluted plant apparently to specify the natural floral environment of these fauna, whereas the other ornaments are not specifically floral except for one dot-rosette. It should be noted also that the prominent double volute is in the same relative position as the standed vessel that interrupts the main frieze below. The filling ornaments in the main frieze—only one of them a (spoke-)rosette—are concentrated in the area of the two combatants, providing a kind of "fireworks" of hostile energies.

In an even bolder departure from rigid symmetry of composition than that of CA 617, the Ajax Painter has here displaced the back-to-back split of movement-into-opposite-directions, which was previously centered under the handle, well to the left of that point. This feature can be appreciated in Johansen's development of the frieze (fig. 20.16d) but not in Payne's (fig. 20.16e), which, however, has other advantages, particularly in that it allows us to appreciate the physical distance between the running man and the centaur, even though the object that achieves this, the standed vessel,[32] has,

351

FIGURE 20.15. Aryballos. Once Paros. (After J. L. Benson, *Die Geschichte der Korinthischen Vasen* [Basel 1953] pl. 1a.)

in my opinion, something other than a *rallentando* significance.

The operation of a polar opposition of end parts in the other compositions of the Ajax Painter might, if applied here, indicate that the running man is contrasted with the figure opposite the centaur and is therefore his opponent, not his assistant. In this case he must be hastening to give help to the centaur against Zeus. It is hardly necessary to point out that, although Johansen declined to identify the latter figure at all, it has, since Buschor's study of the New York bronze group,[33] been customary to see it as the lightning-wielding, scepter-holding king of gods, here additionally outfitted with a formidable sword. In fact, the scepter is disputed: both Zeus and the centaur grasp it, as if wrestling for its possession. This detail helps to harden the identification as Zeus, since it is well known from the mythological tradition, for example, from Hesiod's *Theogony*, a work perhaps only slightly earlier than this aryballos, that

Zeus did indeed have to wrest his kingship away from the previous occupant of that position. That would have been Kronos; however, no such incident as the one depicted here is recorded in the existing literature. Unfortunately, our knowledge of what, for example, Hesiod drew on and what other writers earlier than or contemporary with him said, is based on scarce and late hints.[34] Thus, any suggestions we can make are purely speculative. It is *possible*, for instance, that Eumelos wrote an epic on this subject from which it would have been natural for the Ajax Painter to draw for this scene. At least, *some* literary work must have explained why Kronos—if indeed the opposing figure represents that being—has here the form of a centaur or, alternatively, if the opponent is Typhon, as some suggest, how that horrendous monster could be shown in such a relatively noble form. For indeed, if one studies Payne's drawing (fig. 20.16e) of this totally human figure to which a horse's rump is arbitrarily added, one finds a dignity and confidence quite as impressive as that of Zeus himself.

In these circumstances I confine myself simply to the dynamics and logic of the composition itself. It has already been proposed that the running figure, somewhat demonlike in its *Knielaufschema*, is opposed to Zeus and must therefore be approaching to give assistance to the centaur. This explains the purpose of the standed vessel in the composition. For, if the running man were immediately behind the centaur, we should have to understand him as another attacker of the centaur beset from two sides. But the stand, spaciously set off by the flanking birds, provides a breathing space by deliberately and decisively breaking up the action. If we were to take this object literally, it would at the very least mean that the swordsman would have to swerve in his course to avoid it. Merely to state such a proposition, when a pair of birds is hanging in the air, is to recognize the stand as an *idea*, not an object in space. To identify it, then, as a simile of Homeric type (though it could come from another source or combination of sources) is to apprehend once again how cleverly inventive the Ajax Painter is. Taken visually, the stand does, of course, interpose a vertical obstacle to the flow of the composition (and the artist *has* achieved a sense of flow, particularly in the centaur's movement). But taken as a simile, it must have *exactly* the opposite effect. Furthermore, it is a complicated and involved one, indeed a compound simile.

First of all, flying birds indicate swiftness. This pair, shown from the underside, seem to be shooting up (or down) vertically, thus conforming exactly to the vessel itself, like eagles or falcons. We recall *Iliad* 18.616:

> Then she like a falcon sprang down from snowy Olympos . . .

But what about the other pair of birds?[35] Placed back to back yet with their heads turned to each other, they express the exact opposite of movement and help us to identify the stand. Must it not be a metal cauldron inspired by the one given in the games of *Iliad* 23.740–744?

> Then straightway the son of Peleus set forth other prizes for fleetness of foot: a mixing bowl of silver, chased; six measures it held, and in beauty it was far the best in all the earth, for artificers of Sidon wrought it cunningly, and men of the Phoenicians brought it over the misty sea . . .

The complete simile is, then, something like this: "Swift as a falcon he raced to help the centaur, as fleet of foot as the one who wins the gloriously wrought bowl in the foot races at the games for Patroklos." In such a context the *Knielaufschema* must mean literal physical running (cf. the different use of it on Berlin 3318). The *two* falcons are like parentheses showing that one simile is enclosed in the other. And what better motif could have been chosen by a witty painter to represent the cunning chasing on the bowl than another *pair* of birds, this time decoratively formalized?

Without a fortunate discovery, in the sands of Egypt or in an obscure library, of a fragment describing an epic scene of this sort, we shall never be able to put names on the centaur and his comradely demon.

MIDDLE PROTOCORINTHIAN IB (675 – 660 B.C.)

My study of the Ajax Painter's repertoire has convinced me that he was incomparably more ambitious and talented as a designer of dramatic narrative than any other

FIGURE 20.16a. Aryballos, Boston Museum of Fine Arts inv. 95.12. (After Johansen, pl. XXII.2a.)

FIGURE 20.16b. Aryballos, Boston Museum of Fine Arts inv. 95.12. (After Johansen, pl. XXII.2c.)

FIGURE 20.16c. Aryballos, Boston Museum of Fine Arts inv. 95.12. (After Johansen, pl. XXII.2b.)

FIGURE 20.16d. Aryballos, Boston Museum of Fine Arts inv. 95.12. (After Johansen, pl. XXII.2d.)

FIGURE 20.16e. Aryballos, Boston Museum of Fine Arts inv. 95.12. (After Payne, pl. 11.1.)

artist of the Early Archaic period in Corinth and perhaps until the Iole Painter himself. This is, of course, a judgment *ex silentio*. I hope that we shall some day know from excavations at least one other contemporary artist of stature who competed with this master. No doubt it was the very absence of fixed canons of beautiful human and animal structure that allowed the Ajax Painter the freedom to experiment so daringly with figures and arrangement to express his feeling for epic stories. When such standards started to be recognized, starting with Middle Protocorinthian IB, they seem to have restricted artists from such experimentation, for which in any case they lacked the precocious dramatic gift of our painter. The new ideal came to be spread-out individual scenes of warfare or processions of *metabatai*, or of animals (this applies even to the Chigi Painter). This opinion is in no way intended to be a substitute for further detailed investigations. While these would go beyond the scope of this paper, I should like at least to make a few comments on the Nola-Falkenhausen Workshop, which stands in immediate succession to the Ajax Painter in the next period.

LONDON BRITISH MUSEUM WT 199
(*ECW* 50 Nola 1: here figs. 20.17a–e. N.B.: *ECW*, pl. 18, 2b also belongs to this vase)

The subsidiary decoration has a tired look in comparison with that of the Ajax Painter, and a narrow frieze below the main scene has—perhaps inaugurates—the schematic hare hunt that was to become a more or less standard feature henceforth (here the hare is being caught up in a net). Thus by this time a firm link is forged with the numerous class of aryballoi[36] decorated only with unincised versions of this theme. In all his frieze figures the artist has picked up, exaggerated, and concentrated exclusively on the quality of fluid movement which the Ajax Painter had gradually developed (but only as an expressive by-product). In this sense there is a certain forward leap from the powerful figures of the Ajax Painter's latest work, especially the centaur (fig. 20.16e), to the rubbery figures of the London aryballos (fig. 20.17a); the latter have only minimal incisions, which enhances the flowing effect. The London artist has also picked up the depiction of similes, which were a means to an end for the Ajax Painter, and appar-

ently made this depiction the whole sum and substance of his composition. He has displaced the point of division into opposite streams of movement somewhat to the right of the under-handle position (fig. 20.17d); no good reason for this occurs to me. On the other hand, in the case of the one-part theme as here, it would have made sense to center the bull, as the cynosure of the whole composition, on the front just opposite the handle; at least the artist has aligned the threatened hare with the beleaguered bull (fig. 20.17c). This fine point is distorted in the drawing published by Johansen (fig. 20.17e). However, subtle logic was not so much a factor in this artist's creative mind as smoothly flowing physical energy embodied in a rather grand and elaborate simile conceived of as an end in itself.

Interpretation

A bull (R) is attacked both front and rear by a pair of marauding lions. In itself this is a powerful motif, a forerunner of Archaic pediment designs.[37] Whether formally derived from Eastern sources or not, here it works as a fresh invention, for it is certainly part and parcel of a Homeric situation in which not "hunters" but the owners of cattle, represented by antithetic spearmen and an archer, converge to rescue their property. Haste to get to the scene is stressed not only by the outstretched legs of the men but by a flying bird (fig. 20.17d). This is a visual "unrolling" of telescoped aspects of such a simile as *Iliad* 16.751–753:

> So speaking he set on the hero Kebriones with the rush of a lion, that while wasting the cattle-pen is smitten in the breast . . .

The visual aspects of the actual attack are suggested by the following simile that occurs just a few lines further in the Homeric text (16.756–758):

> And these twain strive for Kebriones like lions, that on the mountain peaks fight, both hungering, both high of heart, for a slain hind . . .

One is reminded also of *Iliad* 17.656–664 (or the very similar 11.548–555):

> Menelaos . . . went forth as a lion from a steading when he is tired of vexing men and dogs that suffer him not to de-

FIGURE 20.17a – d. Aryballos, London, British Museum inv. WT 199. (Photos Benson and museum; courtesy Trustees of the British Museum.)

vour fat oxen and all night keep their watch; but he in hunger for flesh presseth onward yet availeth nought, for thickly fly the javelins against him from hardy hands, with blazing firebrands, wherefrom he shrinketh for all his fury . . . .

The motif of hound and hare is equally Homeric and as this particular painter, like the Ajax Painter himself, seems to have been well versed in that author, we may credit him with having in mind such a passage as *Iliad* 10.360–362:

> And as when two sharp-toothed hounds, well skilled in the chase, press ever hard on a doe or a hare through a wooded land, and it runs screaming before them, even so Tydeus' son and Odysseus . . .

In this particular case the painter has embellished the scene with a net (fig. 20.17c), implying the presence of owners of the hounds—or at least their existence; however, the painter of Nola 3 (see below), like the vast majority of those using this motif, limits himself to the bare Homeric description. The painter of WT 199 became in effect so absorbed in the manipulation of similes that he

did not bother to provide the actual heroic action that a simile reinforces. For him the simile describing that action has sufficed, except that he provided a second simile, mirroring the action of the first, in the secondary register. To put this in yet another way, he has given us a simile of a simile while eliminating the primary reference which both similes ultimately describe.

SYRACUSE MUSEO NAZIONALE 13839
(*ECW* 50, Nola 3: figs. 20.18a–c. N.B.: *ECW* pl. 18, 2b does not belong to this vase)

There is a considerable difference in the quality of drawing, as well as in the mind set, of the designer of this scene from that of the preceding vase; to claim an attribution to one hand, at least without links not known to me, is inappropriate. In place of the involved formality of the similes of the previous aryballos, this artist presents a basic Homeric situation and then some *seemingly* random figures. A boar is attacked front and rear by spearmen (figs. 20.18a–b). There are far fewer boar similes in the *Iliad* than lion similes, yet enough to inspire a vivid memory in a painter. Probably the best of these to cite, in view of the gauntness of the aryballos composition, is *Iliad* 13.471–473:

> (Idomeneus) stood at bay, like a boar in the hills that trusteth to his strength, and abides the great assailing throng of men in a lonely place . . .

FIGURE 20.17e. Aryballos, London, British Museum inv. WT 199. (After Johansen pl. XXIX.2b.)

In contradistinction to the old drawing published by Johansen (fig. 20.18c), the boar attack belongs somewhat closer to the center, though not really opposite the handle, with the stag (R) on the right-hand side and the rearing goat (R) on the left-hand side, under the handle. This leaves the griffin (L) more or less opposite the main scene. Moreover, the beleaguered hare is directly under the threatened boar. The goat and the stag can be thought to indicate or underline the sylvan setting ("in a lonely place") and this is also emphasized by the presence of two spoke- and two dot-rosettes surrounding the stag. That animal appears to be raising his head, presumably from a grazing stance, and possibly in surprise at the griffin with wide-open jaws. If that apparition is not alarming him, the commotion at his back might be, but in either case his irresolute position suggests that he will soon bound away. The goat also seems to be ready to bolt. Thus, it may be possible to see some narrative logic (if not humor) in the arrangement despite the impression at first of random figures. Even the griffin is not out of keeping with that interpretation if we assume that it is there to heighten the mythical quality of the happening (and it may have a more specific meaning not yet decipherable by us). The imaginative streak in the work of the Nola artists is given also by the curved or wavy handle of the javelin shown flying through the air (in both aryballoi discussed; in the present one, at least, it is also clearly looped in the middle). Does this indicate speed, or quivering when it hits the target?

BRINDISI, MUSEO PROVINCIALE FRANCESCO RIBEZZO INV. 1609
(*ECW* 50 Nola 2: fig. 20.19)

The artist of this piece has created an interesting problem for interpretation by placing the simile dead center in front, thus giving it the maximum prominence, and then flanking it with two scenes (fig. 20.19). To its left is a totally conventional but certainly heroic duel of two warriors (hoplites); the applicability of the simile is obvious because one of the two must in the end be destroyed by the "pitiless" iron. But does the simile also apply, in a real or a facetious sense, to the violent erotic scene on the other side? In any case the final pictorial element—sphinxes with elaborate floral headdress flanking a small bird with a cock's tail, but otherwise quite unlike a cock—may not have any direct connection with either scene and may have the same balancing and "mythicizing" function as the griffin in the Nola 1 frieze.[38] The simile consists of a flying bird (R), a lion (R) in a half-seated position seizing a rearing goat (R) by its back, forcing it to look back at the attacker. The uniform direction of all components stresses the chase which has ended badly for the goat. Goats as prey are mentioned only infrequently in the *Iliad*; perhaps the best passage to cite is Book 10.485–488:

> And like as a lion cometh on flocks without a herdsman,
> on goats and sheep, and leaps upon them with evil intent,

FIGURE 20.18a – b. Aryballos, Syracuse NM inv. 13839. (Photos by author; courtesy Syracuse NM.)

FIGURE 20.18c. Aryballos, Syracuse NM inv. 13839. (After Johansen, pl. XXIX.1b.)

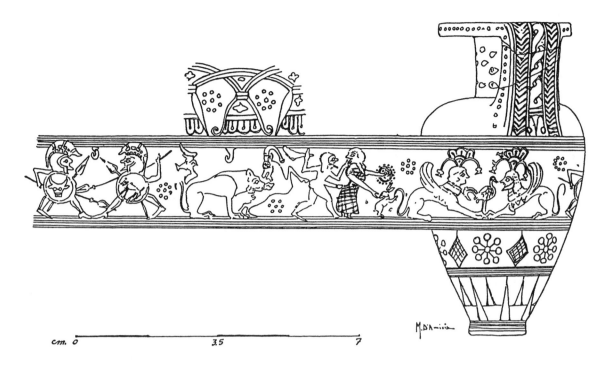

FIGURE 20.19. Aryballos, Museo Provinciale Francesco Ribazza inv. 1609. (After *AttiMGrecia* N.S.V. [Rome 1964] 121.)

so set the son of Tydeus on the men of Thrace, till he had slain twelve . . .

The artist composed the duel in a highly formal manner, but not the pendant erotic scene. There are no descriptions of violent rape in the *Iliad*, however much occurrences in the erotic sphere are powerful incentives in its plot. But it is not difficult to suppose that uncontrolled passions filled the air when Troy was finally captured and sacked. Yet the graphic spelling out of physical details is not in keeping with the heroic literature or with tragedy; rather it found its place in the sphere of comedy and satire. The Brindisi scene, therefore, surprising as it is at this early date, can hardly be otherwise interpreted than as it was by its first editor: proto-satyrical.[39] This means that the unity of the frieze conception inheres in the abrupt transition from the mythical-heroic level, where the simile is taken seriously, to the slapstick-satirical level, where the simile

is virtually parodied. This is underlined by the club in the rapist's right hand—obviously a case of excessive force—and by the fact that the victim is being interrupted in the process of playing with or feeding what looks like a pet hare, which might characterize her as quite young, little more than a child. What does the wreath (?) in her hand mean? The realm of flowers? The harvest of corn? Could this be a parody on the rape of Persephone?[40] The dignified sphinxes next door prevent us from sinking too far into the gutter in our perception of the artist's obvious satisfaction in his creation.

PERSPECTIVE

In order to facilitate further investigation along these lines I offer the following summary of the premises which, after my initial inspiration on the basis of a single vase, were developed more pragmatically than theoretically.

The first premise is that the compositional programs of Protocorinthian figural vase painters are not desultory but have intellectual content; and further, that they can be understood as unified to the extent that the individual

---

artist skillfully manipulated his chosen theme in accordance with—or even transcending—the artistic conventions of his time.

The second premise is that knowledge of the contents and poetic techniques of the Homeric and Hesiodic epics, not excluding others less well documented at this time, was so all-pervasive in Early Archaic, and probably also Late Geometric, times that these contents and techniques shaped the mentality and methods of visual artists to a degree not hitherto suspected. This means, applied to the analysis of narrative techniques, thinking in visual similes for use in dramatic composition.

The third premise is that at least one very gifted Protocorinthian artist, the Ajax Painter, had the ability and the impulse to transpose the latent dramatic stuff of the epic(s) into a kind of proto-tragic form based on contrast and juxtaposition of opposites and (sometimes) their resolution by a third component in a consciously triadic composition. This went so far as to include not only the tragic element but also a parody of it. Not discounting all this as the invention of a presumably very brilliant and precocious individual, we may still wonder what may have lain behind his achievements in terms of his social position and possible participation in recitations of epic poetry and in proto-dramatic events. This suggestion seems to me to be in keeping with the thesis of G. Nagy in this volume that "composition-in-performance" may well have been an integral part of the fixation process of the (already essentially formed) Homeric epics during the course of the earlier Archaic period. The interpretation of scenes presented in this paper rests heavily on the assumption that epic tradition was a major, if not *the* major, cultural determinant in seventh-century Greece, so that public familiarity with, and recognition of, Homeric tales was at least as great as that enjoyed by Biblical tales in medieval times.[41]

NOTES

*The following abbreviations will be used in this paper:
GGP = J. N. Coldstream, *Greek Geometric Pottery* (London 1968).
Corinth XIII = C. W. Blegen, H. Palmer, and R. S. Young, *The North Cemetery* (Princeton 1964).

Corinth XV:3 = A. N. Stillwell and J. L. Benson, *The Potters' Quarter: The Pottery* (Princeton 1984).
ECW = J. L. Benson, *Earlier Corinthian Workshops*, Allard Pierson Scripta Minora I (Amsterdam 1989).
GVROM = D. Robinson, C. Harcum, and J. Iliffe, *A Catalogue of Greek Vases in the Royal Ontario Museum of Archaeology*, Toronto (Toronto 1930).
Johansen = K. F. Johansen, *Les Vases sicyoniens* (Paris 1923).
Payne = H. Payne, *Protokorinthische Vasenmalerei* (Berlin 1933).
Perachora II = T. J. Dunbabin, *Perachora: The Sanctuaries of Hera Akraia and Limeneia*, II (Oxford 1962).

1. J. L. Benson, "Picture, Ornament and Periodicity in Attic Geometric Vase Painting," *ArtB* 64 (1982) 535–549. Some of the same ground as in my writings—and with similar tendencies in interpretation—is covered in the paper of M. D. Stansbury-O'Donnell in this volume. He underscores in new and interesting ways the compositional similarities between the *Iliad* and Geometric scenes.

2. A. Alföldi, "Die Herrschaft der Reiterei in Griechenland und Rom nach dem Sturz der Könige," in *Gestalt und Geschichte*, Festschrift Karl Schefold, 4. Beiheft *AntK* (Bern 1967) 13–47; see 20–31 and pl. 7.1.

3. Alföldi (supra n. 2) 23 and H. Jucker, "Bronzehenkel und Bronzehydria in Pesaro," *Studia Oliveriana* 12–14 (1966) 39–40, have no doubts that it was an eighth-century practice.

4. J. Davison, *Attic Geometric Workshops*, YCS 16 (1961), figs. 69–70 and apparently also fig. 119.

5. Davison (supra n. 4), fig. 58.

6. Alföldi (supra n. 2), pls. 1, 4, 5.2, and 6.2.

7. A. M. Snodgrass, *Archaic Greece* (London 1980) 102–106. See I. Morris, *Burial and Ancient Society* (New York 1987) 198–201, for a more recent—and drastic—view of the hoplite and phalanx problem in the eighth and seventh centuries. [See now Snodgrass in *DHA* 19 (1993) 47–61.]

8. *Iliad of Homer* done into English Prose by A. Lang, W. Leaf, and E. Meyers (London 1892). This is also the reference for all subsequent citations of the *Iliad*.

9. E.g., Exekias' calyx-krater, Athens, Agora A-P 1044: the main panel of the reverse shows the fight over the body of Patroklos while the subsidiary register below shows two lions fighting over the body of a bull. J. D. Beazley, *The Development of Attic Black-figure*, rev. ed. D. von Bothmer and M. B. Moore (Berkeley 1986), pl. 73.

10. G. Markoe, "The 'Lion Attack' in Archaic Greek Art: Heroic Triumph," *CA* 8 (1987) 85–115. Markoe (85–92) initially reviews the various interpretations of animal representations in Archaic Greek art. Although artifacts and written

sources document a spiritual significance of animals in the consciousness of early peoples totally different from our present attitudes, the rich complexity that this entails in such works as those treated by Markoe and myself is all too easily dismissed by some commentators who "forget" this and ignore the widespread tendency of artists to use animals as stand-ins for human beings from the ancient Near East (e.g., on Sumerian harps) right down to today's comic strips.

11. J. L. Benson, *Die Geschichte der Korinthischen Vasen* (Basel 1953) 87–94.

12. J. L. Benson, "Ratio in Attic Geometric Vase Painting," *Source: Notes on the History of Art* 6 (1987) 1–7 (see 3–6). The use of an arithmetical principle was investigated independently but with comparable results by B. Andreae, "Zum Dekorationssystem der geometrischen Amphora 804 im National Museum Athen," in *Studies in Classical Art and Archaeology, A Tribute to P. H. von Blanckenhagen* (New York 1979) 1–16.

13. See detail in Payne pl. 28 (lower).

14. Cf. Payne pl. 9.1,2,6,7.

15. Johansen 144.

16. Other commentators also make this mistake. For example, D. A. Amyx, *Corinthian Vase Painting of the Archaic Period* (Berkeley 1988) 367, claims that "unity of subject in friezes . . . is not yet a matter of much concern to Protocorinthian vase-painters."

17. Cf. J. L. Benson, "An Early Protocorinthian Workshop and the Sources of its Motifs," *BABesch* 61 (1986) 1–20; see 11. The cocks of the Ajax Painter should be added there to n. 26 on p. 9.

18. Johansen 148.

19. Cf. Benson (supra n. 1) passim.

20. J. L. Benson, "Symptom and Story in Geometric Art," *BABesch* 62 (1988) 69–76 (see 71). The presence of the lion could also be taken in this sense. Perhaps lions of some sort belonged to the fauna of Greece, but then so did deer, and in that case the presence of lions and deer on Geometric gold bands could be explained as an illustration of what a shepherd told the artist rather than as evidence that the gold-band maker was influenced by Oriental iconography. In my view, the lion figure—whether derived from Mycenaean or Eastern iconography—is inextricably involved with the heroic/mythic sphere; animals are what priests, poets, artists—and in our day, scientists—make of them. In Egypt, even the "household cat" belonged to the divine sphere.

21. Hektor is seen in a somewhat similar predicament in *Iliad* 14.412ff.

22. In the second passage cited it appears that Odysseus is equated with the lion and the Trojans with the jackals. Yet the plight of Odysseus was actually more desperate than that implies, so this imagery must be taken as quite generalized. For by the time Ajax arrived, Odysseus must have been trembling and near collapse, since Menelaos had to lead him off "holding him by the hand" to a waiting emergency vehicle. The plight of Ajax in his beleaguered state appears to have been more critical from the very beginning, but not to have lasted so long. Thus the comparison to the lion and its attackers would be fully justified.

23. J. L. Benson, "The Central Group of the Corfu Pediment," in *Gestalt und Geschichte* (supra n. 2) 48–60 (see 48–52). The association of the scheme with such monsters as the Gorgo, also winged, suggests the possibility of coalesced layers of meaning which have to be interpreted according to the circumstances of each individual occurrence. In any case, a technical question may arise here. My words imply that the *Knielauf* demon could be a visualization of the δαίμων of Homer's text (11.480)—a natural inference if the Ajax Painter knew this episode of the *Iliad* by heart, or even remembered it vividly. Why, then, did he not place the δαίμων behind the lion? For one thing, that would have destroyed the overall balance of two figures facing on either side, that is, the symmetry customarily observed at this time. Since the δαίμων is an imaginative rather than a physical entity, it could have been thought of as swirling around the action, not necessarily as pushing the lion from behind.

24. On this point see Markoe (supra n. 10) 88.

25. Johansen 150.

26. See for example *Corinth* XV:3, pl. 82.

27. The first scholar to discuss the figure was uncertain about identifying its sex: L. Couve, "Un lecythe inédit du Musée du Louvre," *RA* I (1898) 213–234, on p. 232, first of all, justly calls it "un personnage monstrueux." On p. 233 he continues, "Remarquant que cette figure peut être aussi bien féminine que virile, j'y verrais volontiers la représentation d'Eris, la déesse de la désordre."

28. On this see R. Graves, *The Greek Myths* II (Baltimore 1955) 345. For the stories about Odysseus and Ajax Minor, see p. 344.

29. It has always seemed to me that Attic Geometric scenes of shipwrecked men among fish could refer only to the mishaps of Odysseus.

30. Above all to Euripides, who in other ways found the events of Hekabe's life arresting. My discussion of CA 617 here explains why I placed a question mark after "Rape of Helen" in the entry of this aryballos in *ECW* 43.1. I had long wondered how the huge, ungainly figure who is the focus of this scene could be identified as the very young, prenubile Helen, virtually a child. The identification seems to rest on the coincidence that there are two horsemen instead of the usual one to represent the Greek army (but there are good internal

reasons for that amplification). In order to maintain the identification as the Dioskouroi, B. Schweitzer (*JdI* 44 [1929] 111ff.) had to apologize for the "Uebergewicht des gedanklicherzählenden Moments über die Schilderung des Anschaulichen-Zuständlichen" and for the "noch nicht vollkommen erreichte Einheit des Bildfeldes." What needs apology is not the painter's creation but the modern interpretation. From the mythological-technical viewpoint, L. B. Ghali-Kahil, *Les enlèvements et le retour d'Hélène* (Paris 1955) 309, had to go to much further lengths—one must say to quite devious reasoning—to maintain the identification: "L'artiste a fait un rapprochement osé dans le temps, puisque, d'après la légende, Thésée et Perithoos étaient absents quand arrivèrent les défenseurs; mais il se peut aussi que l'absence du héros athénien et de son compagnon ait fait déjà partie d'une version plus jeune, toute à la gloire de Thésée: celui-ci en effet ne peut être vaincu par les Dioscures, puisqu'il était absent au moment du rapt; mais anciennement la victoire des frères d'Hélène avait peut-être été réelle; il est possible qu'il y ait eu un combat, à la suite duquel les vainqueurs ramenèrent Hélène dans sa patrie. Dans ce cas, c'est le peintre de l'aryballe que nous devrions croire de préférence aux témoignages littéraires." Certainly, none of this constitutes "die nähere Begründung" (for the interpretation as the rape of Helen) called for by a sceptical R. Hampe, *Frühe griechische Sagenbilder* (Athens 1936) 180 n. 1. The gesture of *Brautraub*, sometimes used to justify the identification, would obviously be both inappropriate and unworthy on the part of Theseus applied to a mere child; but the same gesture on the part of Odysseus applied to Hekabe becomes real dramatic irony.

31. Cf. Amyx (supra n. 16) 24.B. The pose used is that of a *metabatis* but the rider visible in the photograph appears to be an ape—thus perhaps a takeoff on the motif.

32. This was referred to by Johansen (147) as a "hypercraterion" and by Amyx (supra n. 16) 24 as a "standed dinos." The basic forms of this vessel and that of the standed cauldron shown by Payne, pl. 9.3, are not dissimilar, given their quite schematic representation (Johansen also made this comparison). I take the round object on top of the stand to be a bird's-eye view of the bowl, so as to show the birds affixed to its sides (no other space was available for this because of the flying birds in the surroundings). The list of early seventh-century cauldrons given by H. V. Herrmann, *Die Kessel der orientalisierenden Zeit*, olForsch 6 (Berlin 1966) 2, shows that the element under the actual cauldron connecting it to the stand could be a circle, a triangle, or a flattened circle, as here.

33. E. Buschor, "Kentauren," *AJA* 38 (1934) 128–136 (see 128).

34. These problems have been thoroughly aired by J. Dörig and O. Gigon, *Der Kampf der Götter und Titanen*, Bibliotheca Helvetica Romana 4 (Olten 1961) passim and in the corresponding review by R. Hampe, *GGA* 215 (1963) 125–152.

35. Taken at face value they could be plastic additions in the manner of siren-attachments. However, it is hardly permissible to demand an exact explanation of such a schematized, condensed representation, since this could never be verified.

36. Studied extensively by C. W. Neeft, *Protocorinthian Subgeometric Aryballoi*, Allard Pierson Series 7 (Amsterdam 1987).

37. On this subject see Markoe (supra n. 10) 96–102.

38. It is possible that this is a very early example of the usage described by Markoe (supra n. 10, 112–113, sphinxes in funerary iconography). In that case the sphinxes here would have to refer to the impending death of one of the duelists.

39. F. G. Lo Porto, "Ceramica della Necropoli arcaica di 'Tor Pisano' a Brindisi," *AttiMGrecia* 5 (Rome 1964) 111–127; see 124. On the other hand I do not think it necessary to proceed so far as to identify the girl as a maenad and a dancer. She is surely intended to be very young, as Lo Porto saw, which hardly suits the idea of a maenad. Thus one is fully justified in weighing other explanations.

40. On the use of wreaths as a symbol of marriage or as a (dignified) love-gift, see J. B. Carter, "Masks and Poetry in Early Sparta," in R. Hägg, N. Marinatos, and G. C. Nordquist, eds., *Early Greek Cult Practice* (Stockholm 1988) 94–95. In the Brindisi scene the girl is holding a wreath stretched out in front of her, almost as if to keep it safe from her pursuer. The question is, is it something she happened to have in her hand (as an attribute of her youth) or is it a symbol of her nubile but still virgin state, of which—unless a rescuer appears—she will soon be despoiled? The satirical quality of the representation may also be reflected in the rabbit's playful grip on the sphinx's tail and in the differentation of the sphinxes into male and female, both with floral appurtenances and with a comical-looking bird between them (tail of a cock and water-bird head).

41. The present study, together with a sequel bringing the theme down to the Late Protocorinthian period (to be published in *Hesperia*), provides a "fleshing out" in humanistic terms of the largely technical study of stylistic groups necessary to clarify relative chronology of the Protocorinthian period provided by *ECW*.

21

STORY LINES: OBSERVATIONS ON SOPHILAN NARRATIVE

◆

ANN BLAIR BROWNLEE

The artist Sophilos, the earliest vase painter whose name is known, is an important figure in early Attic black-figure vase painting.[1] Like his contemporaries in the first quarter of the sixth century and a little later, he is primarily a painter of animal vases; even on those vases where humans intrude, animals are still very prominent. Mythological and heroic themes play a much more significant role, however, in Sophilos' work than in that of his predecessors and contemporaries, and he is a master teller of tales in visual form. Despite his hasty draftsmanship and his often imperfect spelling, he deserves our serious evaluation.

Sophilos illustrates a wide variety of mythological and heroic stories, especially on kraters and dinoi, which provide large fields for his often multifigured compositions. These narratives constitute a sizable portion of Sophilos' work; out of some forty vases attributed to him, nine are certainly decorated with mythological scenes.[2] I would like first to examine those depictions, and then to look more carefully at two of them, the dinos from Pharsalos (fig. 21.1) and the so-called Erskine dinos now in the British Museum (figs. 21.2–21.3).[3]

Prominent among Sophilos' works are depictions of subjects from the Trojan cycle, which appear on at least four vases. The dinos from Pharsalos has as its principal subject the games at the funeral of Patroklos. The procession to the wedding of Peleus and Thetis, the parents of Achilles, is shown on the Erskine dinos, and it was also the subject of the fragmentary Acropolis 587.[4] A more condensed procession, consisting only of two chariots, decorates one side of the lebes gamikos from Smyrna.[5] Several of the figures here are identified by inscriptions: Helen rides in the first chariot, probably accompanied by Menelaos, and in the second chariot are Helen's two brothers, Kastor and Polydeukes. The subject is apparently another Homeric wedding procession, at the marriage of Helen and Menelaos. The fight between Achilles and Memnon, urged on by his mother Eos, is probably the scene depicted on a small Sophilan fragment from the Acropolis.[6]

Herakles appears on several vases by Sophilos. He is shown in combat with the sea monster Nereus on one of the painter's early works, a column-krater now in Athens, and the same scene surely appears on a hydria fragment in Maidstone, which preserves Nereus' head and

FIGURE 21.1. Athens, National Museum 15499. (Photograph courtesy National Museum, Athens.)

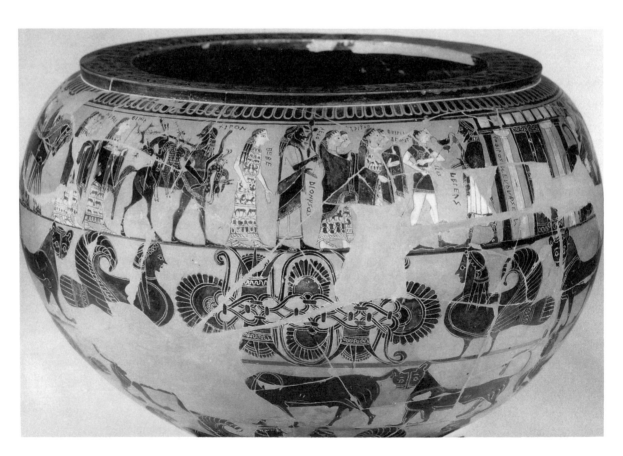

FIGURE 21.2. London, British Museum 1971. 11−1.1. (Photograph courtesy of the Trustees of the British Museum.)

arm and Hermes' caduceus.[7] In both of these pictures, the figures seem a little stiff and posed, but Herakles appears also in a big and vividly portrayed action scene: the fight with the centaurs on one side of the louterion from Menidi.[8]

On the Menidi louterion, Herakles stands in the middle, attacking with his sword. He has dropped his bow, but not before wounding the centaurs, who collapse around him. The picture has a complicated composition with some very powerful images of wounded and dying centaurs, and it compares favorably with the fight between centaurs and Lapiths on the neck of the François Vase, of perhaps a decade later.[9]

The other side of the Menidi louterion is very poorly preserved, but it was also decorated with at least one narrative scene. The spout is in the middle of the panel, and it is not certain that the figures preserved on either side are from the same scene, although it seems likely

that they are.[10] At left on the figured fragment from this side (fig. 21.4) are the heads of two horses and a snake to right. On the right side of the fragment is the foot of a woman to left. Between the foot and the snake are three lines of inscriptions. The middle line is usually restored as a signature of Sophilos as potter; the other two are very difficult to read.[11]

It is not easy to say what the scene might be. If the three elements—the horses, the snake, and the woman's foot—are part of the same scene, it might be the death of Eriphyle.[12] This story is not often illustrated, but the three elements preserved on the Menidi louterion are also included in the depiction of the death of Eriphyle on a Tyrrhenian amphora in Berlin.[13]

To this array of mythological and heroic images, we may add one more, the departure of Amphiaraos, which is probably the subject partially preserved on a fragment from the Athenian Agora, P 18567 (fig. 21.5).[14] It shows

FIGURE 21.3. London, British Museum 1971. 11–1.1. (Photograph courtesy of the Trustees of the British Museum.)

FIGURE 21.4. Athens, National Museum 15918. (Photograph courtesy National Museum, Athens.)

part of a frontal chariot, an old man who is seated or crouching and holding his hand to his face in grief or in worry, and the lower part of a female figure. Above the old man's head is part of an inscription: ΧΟΣ. This scene has been thought to be connected in some way with Antilochos and to depict his departure or his death, but I think it is more likely the departure of Amphiaraos.[15] Although Amphiaraos usually mounts his chariot shown in profile to right,[16] in the version preserved on a fragment from Naukratis attributed to the the Prometheus Painter, Amphiaraos' chariot is placed frontally, probably flanked by the cast of characters.[17] That is what we have here. The inscription is then part of the name Amphilochos, one of the sons of Amphiaraos, who is usually shown as a small child, sometimes in the arms of a woman.[18] The old man is certainly, as Bakır has observed, a seer, and he is here the seated (or crouching), worried seer who is a fixture of scenes of the departure of Amphiaraos.[19]

Sophilos decorated three vases, the Erskine dinos, Acropolis 587, and the Smyrna lebes gamikos, with processions, and there are four fragments on which the same subject seems to have been depicted. Part of a procession probably appears on two fragments, Acropolis 585a and 585b, which Bakır believes belong to the same vase, a large kotyle-krater.[20] On Acropolis 585a, there are three figures facing left. A pair of women, with mantles held out in front, walk together, and a man with

a scepter follows them. One of the women is named by an inscription as Pandrosos, so the man with the scepter is usually identified as her father, Kekrops, and the other woman is likely to be one of her sisters, Aglauros or Herse. Kekrops stands at the right edge of the picture; traces of one of the vessel's handles are preserved right behind him. At the left edge is a caduceus, held by a figure who faces right—Hermes, or perhaps Iris. On the other fragment, Acropolis 585b, there is the head of a horse to right and the heads of a man and a woman also to right. The inscription to the left probably belongs to the partly preserved man, identifying him as Poseidon.[21]

I think it likely that the two fragments show Hermes (or Iris) heading up a procession to greet Kekrops and his daughters. The composition can thus be compared to that on the Erskine dinos, where Iris leads the procession, which moves to the right, up to Peleus, facing left, who stands outside his house to greet his guests.[22] We cannot say who else was in the procession on the Acropolis fragments nor how long it was, but the collection of figures as preserved is unusual, and the particularly Athenian character of the scene is very striking.[23]

Processions may also have been depicted on two other Sophilan pieces. Peleus stands in front of his house and greets his guests on both the Erskine dinos and the very fragmentary Acropolis 587, and a similar structure, perhaps also the goal of a procession, is preserved on a fragment of a column-krater from the Athenian Agora.[24] The area around the handle is preserved: to the left, an anta, a column, and part of a door, and beneath the handle, a bird. On a fragment of a kotyle-krater from the Kerameikos assigned to Sophilos by Bakır, there are two figures in a chariot, and they are perhaps also part of a procession.[25] Although Sophilos is usually very free with his inscriptions, there are none preserved on either the Kerameikos or the Agora fragments, so we cannot be certain who is in the procession or where it is going.

Finally, we have examples of Sophilos' approach to Dionysiac subjects in several fragments of dinoi or column-kraters that preserve depictions of satyrs. On the fragment from Lindos, a shaggy ithyphallic satyr pursues a nymph who wears an elaborately decorated short chiton.[26] Three ithyphallic satyrs appear on a fragment once in the New York market. One satyr, who holds a two-handled cup, is identified by an inscription.[27]

FIGURE 21.5. Athens, Agora Museum P 18567. (Photograph courtesy of the American School of Classical Studies at Athens: Agora Excavations.)

This survey of the representations of myth in the work of Sophilos has shown the great breadth of his subject matter, and it has also shown that he sometimes depicts unusual scenes, or familiar scenes in unusual ways. But what else can we say about his particular approach to the problems of depicting narrative? On the Pharsalos dinos, I think we can say that Sophilos has painted a picture of a story—the chariot race at the funeral games of Patroklos. That is, in his picture, he has put together those elements which best *represent*, not necessarily illustrate, the story.

The Pharsalos dinos is very incomplete, but the same subject appears on a neck-amphora by the Castellani Painter, and that vase can be used to suggest what the scene on the dinos might have looked like.[28] We can see that the painter has combined—into one picture—elements which were not simultaneous, but rather spread over time. The chariot accident did not happen as the race was about to end, and the agitated figures on the grandstand had settled down by the time the chariots came in sight.

Sophilos and the Castellani Painter seem to have defied or manipulated time—and, indeed, with the Phar-

salos dinos, also space—to combine these elements into a single picture.[29] The result is an example of what Anthony Snodgrass calls the "synoptic" method of narrative, "whereby a single picture combines a series of episodes in a story as if they were simultaneous, but . . . without allowing any single figure to appear in the picture more than once." [30]

The classic illustration of the synoptic method is a Merrythought cup, the name vase of the Painter of the Boston Polyphemos, which portrays the story of the transformation of Odysseus' sailors by the enchantress Circe, a story that is recounted in Book 10 of the *Odyssey*.[31] In the center, Circe mixes the potion that will transform Odysseus' men into animals, and indeed some of the sailors have already undergone the metamorphosis, at least partially. On the right, a man runs away, apparently alarmed by what he is witnessing; he must be Eurylochos, who steals off to tell Odysseus of the strange happenings. On the left, a man runs toward the center, with sword drawn; he must be Odysseus, who, having been enlightened by Eurylochos, comes forward to threaten Circe and demand that she reverse her horrible magic. There are four distinct phases in a progression of events—the potion, the transformation, the alarm, and the threat—presented as though they were simultaneous. And, of course, they seem to be simultaneous because we can take them all in at a single glance; the one side of the cup can be perceived as a single image.

Now the notion of confining an image to what one can take in at a single glance is not alien to Sophilos—he uses it on an early work, a column-krater in Athens with Herakles and Nereus, where a rather small Herakles fights Nereus in the midst of onlookers.[32] But, with a dinos, such as our two examples, the Erskine dinos and the Pharsalos dinos, he is dealing with (and perhaps one could even say creating) problems which result from the way he decorates it: you cannot see the "sides" and the "back" at the same time as you can see the "front." Is he then sacrificing some of the dramatic power of the synoptic method? Maybe he is, but he is replacing it with another kind of power. And that is the reinforcement, quite literally, of the story line. As one moves around the Pharsalos dinos, one witnesses a kind of spatial progression from one end of the race to the other and through the grandstand to Achilles, which would seem to mimic the temporal sequence of the narrative. It reinforces the story line.

There may seem to be a contradiction here. I have already said that by employing the synoptic method, Sophilos is defying or manipulating time, which would seem to say that he is ignoring or dismantling the story line. I think we can find our way out of this dilemma by considering the fact that in sixth-century Athens, oral communication existed side by side with the written word, and, to a certain extent, overshadowed it. That is to say, although writing had existed in Greece for more than a hundred years by the time of Sophilos, literacy was not widespread. Indeed, Greek society must still have been very much an oral society, characterized, at least partly, by orality—the quality of those societies that are nonliterate, whose citizens have no knowledge of writing and communicate orally.[33]

In his study of orality, Walter J. Ong notes that narrative is a particularly important genre in primary oral cultures.[34] But an oral culture's notion of a narrative plot, or a story line, is quite different from ours. A story line is not necessarily a "strict linear presentation of events in temporal sequence."[35] It may move forward, then back in time, and forward again; what really matters is the progression, so that the "situation at the end is subsequent to what it was at the beginning."[36] If we simply modify our idea of a story line and make it less strictly linear, then the apparent contradiction between the synoptic method and the reinforcing of the story line ceases to be an issue.[37]

On the Erskine dinos, I do not know if we can really say for certain that Sophilos employed the synoptic method. I think that he has done so, and that, for example, not *all* the guests were walking simultaneously as they stood outside Peleus' house, but that Sophilos has shown them that way in order to depict a procession of worthies in the clearest way possible. But certainly we are following here a story line, as we move along in space while the catalogue of guests spreads out before us from Hephaistos at the very end to Iris at the very beginning.

It seems clear to me that while Sophilos employs the synoptic method on his dinoi, he also sees them as a potential vehicle for expressing something else that the synoptic method may sometimes seem to devalue: the story line. He has, I think, successfully dealt with the problems of representing expansive narratives on vases without sacrificing any of their drama or meaning or integrity.

In this consideration of Sophilos' approach to narrative, we have looked only at the figures on the vases. We cannot, however, ignore the fact that the inscriptions play an important part in each picture. The main frieze of the Erskine dinos is covered with inscriptions, and it is likely that there were originally a good many more on the Pharsalos dinos than are now preserved. The inscriptions are almost all names, except for signatures and for the caption on the Pharsalos dinos.

The many names may be an expression of an age-old notion in oral societies that a name—especially a name named, a name pronounced—confers power and identity.[38] And the names on the vases stay close to their characters, almost as though they were attached. A name is precious, and even a character in a narrative needs to hold on to it.

But that is not all. The air is full of words, of names. Sophilos not only names the names, he uses those words to charge, magically, the atmosphere of his narrative. It is as though he were trying to create visually the sensation that members of an oral society experience, that sound is everywhere–one is immersed in it.

Sophilos' Muses did not write, they sang, and surely they are singing on the Erskine dinos.[39] There are three alongside the chariot of Hermes and Apollo, and five, including Kalliope with her pipes, alongside the chariot of Ares and Aphrodite (fig. 21.3). Sophilos himself, however, paints and has learned how to write, and, clearly, he recognizes and exploits the particular power of the conjoined image and word.

NOTES

1. I trace my interest in Sophilos and the iconography of Attic black-figure vases to a graduate seminar I took with Emily Vermeule, and it is a great pleasure to offer this article to her in appreciation of all she has taught me. I am also grateful to A. A. Donohue, G. F. Pinney, and J. P. Small, who kindly discussed some of this material with me, and to D. Williams, J. Jordan, and the National Museum, Athens, for providing photographs.

Sophilos' style has been thoroughly examined in G. Bakır,

Sophilos. Ein Beitrag zu seinem Stil (Mainz 1981), hereafter Bakır; I will concentrate here on iconographic issues. For other recent studies of Sophilos, see D. Williams, "Sophilos in the British Museum," *Greek Vases in the J. Paul Getty Museum* 1, Occasional Papers on Antiquities 1 (Malibu 1983) 9–34; D. von Bothmer, "Observations on Proto-Volute Kraters," in M. A. Del Chiaro, ed., *Corinthiaca. Studies in Honor of Darrell A. Amyx* (Columbia, Mo. 1985) 107–116; and A. B. Brownlee, "Sophilos and Early Attic Black-figured Dinoi," in J. Christiansen and T. Melander, eds., *Ancient Greek and Related Pottery* (Copenhagen 1988) 80–87.

2. London 1971.11–1.1 (Bakır, no. A1); Acropolis 587 (Bakır, no. A2); Athens 15499 (Bakır, no. A3); Athens 12587 (Bakır, no. A15); Acropolis 585a and 585b (Bakır, no. A17); Athens 15918 and 15942 (Bakır, no. A20); Izmir 3332 (Bakır, no. A21); Istanbul 4514 (Bakır, no. A35); and Maidstone (Bakır, no. A36). Both sides of Athens 15918 and 15942 (the Menidi louterion) are decorated with mythological scenes. Two fragments, perhaps from the same vase, which preserve parts of satyrs, are not included in Bakır's monograph; they may be added to the list of mythological representations. One fragment was once in the New York market: *Greek and Etruscan Art of the Archaic Period*, Atlantis Antiquities (New York 1988) 55, no. 48, and G. M. Hedreen, *Silens in Attic Black-figure Vase-painting* (Ann Arbor 1992) 74. The other, New York 1977.193, is unpublished. All of these works are discussed below, in addition to other fragments whose attribution to Sophilos himself is not certain. For a vase (New York 1977.11.2) that is not included in Bakır's list and is decorated only with animals, see von Bothmer (supra n. 1).

3. For the Pharsalos dinos, Athens 15499, see *ABV* 39.16, p. 681; *Paralipomena* 18; *Beazley Addenda*² 10; Bakır, no. A3, pls. 6–7. For an additional fragment, not included in Bakır's illustration, see Y. Béquignon, "Un nouveau vase du peintre Sophilos," *MonPiot* 33 (1933) 47, fig. 5 (rightmost; fragment is upside down). I have argued elsewhere that the main frieze on the Pharsalos dinos showed only the chariot race from the funeral games; no other events were depicted. See Brownlee (supra n. 1). Only the principal fragment is illustrated here in fig. 21.1. Erskine dinos (London 1971.11–1.1): *Paralipomena* 19.16bis; *Beazley Addenda*² 10; Bakır, no. A1, pls. 1–2; Williams (supra n. 1), figs. 1–8, 13–34.

4. Acropolis 587: *ABV* 39.15, p. 681; *Beazley Addenda*² 10; Bakır, no. A2, pls. 3–5, 89–90.

5. Izmir 3332: *ABV* 40.20, p. 714; *Paralipomena* 18; *Beazley Addenda*² 11; Bakır, no. A21, pls. 39–45. There has been some disagreement as to whether the lebes gamikos was the work of Sophilos himself. Bakır has firmly established the piece as Sophilos' own work.

6. Acropolis 586: *ABV* 43.5; *Beazley Addenda*² 12; Bakır, no. B17, pl. 83. Beazley calls the fragment "near Sophilos," and Bakır places it in his circle. It is a tiny fragment, and one cannot be certain of the attribution. Memnon and Eos are identified by inscriptions that are only partly preserved, but the readings seem likely.

7. Athens 12587: *ABV* 40.24; *Paralipomena* 18; *Beazley Addenda*² 11; Bakır, no. A15, pls. 18–23; *A Voyage into Time and Legend Aboard the Kyrenia Ship* (Athens 1987) 42 (color ill.) and 104 no. 124. Maidstone: Bakır, no. A36, pl. 64.

8. Athens 15918 and 15942: *ABV* 40.21, and 42.36; *Paralipomena* 18; *Beazley Addenda*² 11, Bakır, no. A20, pls. 8–10; D. Calliopolitis-Feytmans, *Les "loutéria" attiques* (Athens 1965), pl. 16 (shows all seven fragments). For the shape of the vase, see Calliopolitis-Feytmans 51–56; see also Bakır, fig. 6. Only one fragment (15918) is illustrated here; see fig. 21.4.

9. For the centauromachy on the François Vase (Florence 4209: *ABV* 76.1; *Paralipomena* 29–30; *Beazley Addenda*² 21), see *Materiali per servire alla storia del Vaso François*, BdA, serie speciale 1 (Rome 1980), figs. 66–69.

10. A single scene decorates the panel on the spout side of the louterion from Vari (Athens 16385: *ABV* 40.19; *Paralipomena* 18; *Beazley Addenda*² 11; Bakır, no. C1, pls. 85–86). Beazley attributed the louterion to Sophilos; Bakır believes it is not the painter's work. The louterion from Phokaia, assigned to Sophilos by Bakır, is incomplete on the spout side, but it appears to have been decorated with only two confronted sphinxes. See Bakır, no. A19, pls. 15–17. "Prometheus freed" decorates the entire panel on the spout side of a louterion-like column-krater with spout assigned to the Tyrrhenian Group, Berlin 1722: *ABV* 104.124; *Paralipomena* 39; *Beazley Addenda*² 28; Calliopolitis-Feytmans (supra n. 8) 33–34, pl. 10a; *CVA* Berlin 7, pls. 6–7, 8.1–2. Although the Berlin vase is said in *Paralipomena* to be by the Prometheus Painter, Mommsen (*CVA* Berlin 7, p. 14) believes it is not his work and also notes that it does not appear in the list of vases by the Prometheus Painter compiled by D. von Bothmer in *CVA* New York 4, p. 3.

11. For the signature of Sophilos as potter, see Bakır's discussion, pp. 6–7. For a full discussion of the other lines, see P. Wolters, "Vasen aus Menidi," *JdI* 13 (1898) 13–28.

12. I thank Gloria Ferrari Pinney, who first suggested this interpretation to me.

13. Berlin V.I. 4841, attributed to the Tyrrhenian Group: *ABV* 97.22; *Beazley Addenda*² 26; *LIMC* I, "Alkmaion," 548, no. 3, pl. 410. See also A. J. N. W. Prag, *The Oresteia. Iconographic and Narrative Tradition* (Warminster 1985) 39, pl. 28a. For Eriphyle, see *LIMC* I, "Alkmaion," 546–552; *LIMC* III, "Eriphyle," 843–846; and J. P. Small, "The Matricide of Alcmaeon," *RM* 83 (1976) 113–144, esp. 124–126, pl. 19.3.

The first two letters of the rightmost line of the inscription are certainly EP, and the third letter might be a Φ, so the inscription could be restored to read Eriphyle. Sophilos omits letters from time to time, as in the partially preserved inscription KET on the opposite side of the louterion; the word was surely some form of the word Κένταυρος, and he left out the N. The third letter of the inscription on the spout side of the louterion, however, seems to be followed by a three-point punctuation mark, although this is no longer visible. This might have been an I, but it is now impossible to read the inscription. For the inscription, see Wolters (supra n. 11) 17–20. Whatever the inscription might have said, its very length might suggest a caption as well as a signature, as on the Pharsalos dinos.

It should be noted that there is another possible explanation for the omission of the N from the partially preserved KET in the centauromachy on the Menidi louterion. L. Threatte (*The Grammar of Attic Inscriptions*, I [Berlin and New York 1980] 485) notes that the omission of a N before a T—a nasal before a stop—is common enough to suggest that there was a tendency to drop the nasal when it was in this position. It is thus impossible to say for certain that Sophilos has made an error.

14. Beazley thought Agora P 18567 might be by Sophilos himself (*ABV* 43.4; *Beazley Addenda*[2] 12) and Moore and Philippides agree (M. B. Moore and M. Z. P. Philippides, *The Athenian Agora* XXIII, *Attic Black-figured Pottery* [Princeton 1986] 322–323, no. 1912, pl. 121). Bakır, however, places the fragment in the workshop of Sophilos (Bakır, no. B19, pl. 83).

15. I proposed this interpretation in a paper, "The Departure of Amphiaraos on a Sophilan Krater," presented at the annual meeting of the AIA in December 1992; see also *AJA* 97 (1993) 328–329 (abstract). For the connection with Antilochos, see Moore and Philippides (supra n. 14) 322–323.

16. As, e.g., on a Tyrrhenian amphora by the Castellani Painter (Florence 3773 and Berlin F 1711: *ABV* 95.8; *Paralipomena* 34, 36; *Beazley Addenda*[2] 25; I. Krauskopf, "Die Ausfahrt des Amphiaraos auf Amphoren der tyrrhenischen Gruppe," in *Tainia. Festschrift für Roland Hampe* [Mainz 1980] pl. 24:1).

For the departure of Amphiaraos, see *LIMC* I, "Amphiaraos," 691–713; Krauskopf (supra this note) 105–116; and D. A. Amyx, "Archaic Vase-Painting vis-à-vis 'Free' Painting at Corinth," in W. G. Moon ed., *Ancient Greek Art and Iconography* (Madison 1983) 38–43.

17. Oxford G 137.53: *ABV* 96.11 (Tyrrhenian Group); *Beazley Addenda*[2] 25; *CVA* New York 4, p. 3 (attributed by von Bothmer to the Prometheus Painter); Krauskopf (supra n. 16), pl. 24:3.

The scene on the Oxford fragment is identified as a departure of Amphiaraos because of the inscription (ΕΡΙΦΥΛΕ, retrograde) beside the preserved female figure.

18. Amphilochos appears in the departure of Amphiaraos depicted on the chest of Kypselos. According to Pausanias (5.17.7), in the scene of the departure, Amphiaraos' house is represented, and there is an old woman carrying the baby Amphilochos. Alkmaion, the better-known and probably elder son, is shown on the chest as a "boy." On the Agora fragment, the child Amphilochos could be in the arms of the woman behind the old man. There are two short marks above the old man's shoulder, and they could be part of an inscription (see Moore and Philippides [supra n. 14] 322) that identifies either the old man or the woman. For Amphilochos, see *LIMC* I, s.v., 713–717.

19. Bakır, p. 75. The crouching seer appears just to the right of Amphiaraos' chariot on the Castellani Painter's neck-amphora Florence 3773 and Berlin 1711 mentioned above (see n. 16) and on the neck-amphora Leipzig T 3323 by the Kyllenios Painter (*ABV* 96.9; *Beazley Addenda*[2] 25; Krauskopf [supra n. 16] 106, fig. 1). On the now lost Late Corinthian column-krater attributed to the Amphiaraos Painter, Berlin F 1655, the seer appears on the right side of the scene and is identified by an inscription as Halimedes. The name is not otherwise known in scenes of the departure. For the Amphiaraos krater, see D. A. Amyx, *Corinthian Vase-Painting of the Archaic Period* (Berkeley 1988) 263, no. A1; 390–391, 571–572.

20. Acropolis 585a and 585b: *ABV* 40.17–18; *Beazley Addenda*[2] 11; Bakır, 26–27, no. A17, pls. 35–36; *LIMC* I, "Aglauros," 286 no. 4, pl. 210; H. A. Shapiro, *Art and Cult under the Tyrants in Athens* (Mainz 1989) 104–105. For Aglauros and Pandrosos, see *LIMC* I, 283–298. For Kekrops, see U. Kron, *Die zehn attischen Phylenheroen*, AthMitt-BH 5 (1976) 84–103.

21. The man and woman on Acropolis 585b—Poseidon and Amphitrite, presumably—are probably standing in a chariot, although, as Shapiro (supra n. 20) 105 points out, there is no certain evidence that they are. Bakır (p. 27) believed that the horse could not be part of a chariot team. While one would expect to see traces of the other horses' heads on what is preserved, it is hard to say what other sort of horse is depicted here. Its head seems too close to the line at the top edge of the fragment to be a horse with a rider, and it is not easy to see the horse being led by a figure on foot. I do not think we can say for certain; Sophilos does vary the positions of the horses' heads in chariot teams, as, for example, on the Erskine dinos.

22. Kekrops and his daughters cannot be standing directly in front of their house and greeting their visitors, for there is

no room for the house between Kekrops and what is preserved of the handle. It is possible, however, that the house was below the handle.

23. For discussion of the enigmatic subject, see Shapiro (supra n. 20) 105, and Kron (supra n. 20) 90. Bakır (p. 27) believes that the scene decorated only the front of the vase, as is common on kotyle-kraters. On the Smyrna lebes gamikos, for example, Sophilos does confine Menelaos and Helen and her brothers to the front of the vase, although the two men under the handles may also belong to the main scene. The kotyle-krater, a kind of precursor of the dinos, was by now, however, a somewhat old-fashioned shape, and it is possible that Sophilos chose to decorate it in a new way—the way that he would decorate a dinos—with a single continuous frieze.

24. Agora P 13848: *ABV* 41.26; *Beazley Addenda*² 11; Bakır, no. B18, pl. 83; Moore and Philippides (supra n. 14) 154, no. 419, pl. 42. Beazley gave the fragment to Sophilos himself, and Moore and Philippides agree with that attribution. Bakır, however, assigns the fragment to Sophilos' circle.

25. Kerameikos 109: Bakır, no. A18, pl. 34.

26. Istanbul 4514: *ABV*, 42, no. 37; *Beazley Addenda*² 11; Bakır, no. A35, pl. 35. See also Hedreen (supra n. 2) 126, where the satyr is identified as a man in costume.

27. See *Greek and Etruscan Art* (supra n. 2) 55, fig. 48, and Hedreen (supra n. 2) 74. The inscription is not complete. The six letters ΤΡΑΤΟΣ are preserved, probably preceded by a Σ.

If the satyr's right arm is upright, as it appears to be, the preserved letters could be part of a fairly long name. Ἐλασίστρατος is the name of the crouching ithyphallic satyr beneath the vine on the shoulder frieze of a Tyrrhenian amphora in Cerveteri. See A. Kossatz-Deißmann, "Satyr- und Mänadennamen auf Vasenbildern . . . ," *Greek Vases in the J. Paul Getty Museum* 5, Occasional Papers on Antiquities 7 (Malibu 1991) 131–134, figs. 1a-c. The Cerveteri neck-amphora has been attributed to the Timiades Painter by D. von Bothmer; see K. Schauenburg, "Herakles und Bellerophon auf einer Randschale in Kiel," *Meded* 6 (1979) 16, n. 20, and *LIMC* III, "Elasistratos," 708. Elasistratos is not otherwise known as a satyr's name.

Two satyrs appear on an unpublished fragment (probably of a column-krater, but perhaps of a dinos) in New York (MMA 1977.193; see Moore and Philippides [supra n. 14] 78, no. 50, and p. 80), which is close to the fragment once in the New York market and may be from the same vase. I am grateful to D. von Bothmer for information about the two fragments.

28. Florence 3773 and Berlin F 1711: see supra n. 16. See also H. Thiersch, *"Tyrrhenische" Amphoren* (Leipzig 1899),

pl. 4. The vase has since been cleaned, so the drawing in Thiersch, although it shows the composition very clearly, is inaccurate in some details.

29. As I have noted elsewhere (Brownlee [supra n. 1] 81), Sophilos uses the grandstand with gesticulating spectators as a device to intensify the action and the unity of the scene. The spectators are involved in the action to the left, to the right, and even, in a sense, across the dinos.

30. A. M. Snodgrass, *An Archaeology of Greece* (Berkeley 1987) 136.

31. Boston 99.518: *ABV* 198; *Paralipomena* 80; *Beazley Addenda*² 53; A. M. Snodgrass, *Narrative and Allusion in Archaic Greek Art* (London 1982) 5–9, fig. 2; N. Himmelmann-Wildschütz, "Erzählung und Figur in der archaischen Kunst," *AbhMainz* 2 (1967) 74–75. See also Snodgrass (supra n. 30) 136–138.

32. Athens 12587; see supra n. 7.

33. A number of works dealing with literacy and orality in the Greek world have appeared recently: R. Thomas, *Oral Tradition and Written Record in Classical Athens* (Cambridge 1989) and *Literacy and Orality in Ancient Greece* (Cambridge 1992); W. V. Harris, *Ancient Literacy* (Cambridge, Mass. 1989); T. M. Lentz, *Orality and Literacy in Hellenic Greece* (Carbondale, Ill. 1989). See also the work of E. A. Havelock, e.g., *The Literate Revolution in Greece and Its Cultural Context* (Princeton 1982) esp. 185–207, and *The Muse Learns to Write* (New Haven 1986). Three articles have considered aspects of Greek art in relation to theories of orality: C. G. Thomas, "Greek Geometric Narrative Art and Orality," *Art History* 12 (1989) 257–267; and J. M. Hurwit, "Words in Images in Early Greek Art," in *The World of Early Greek Art* (Chicago 1989) 37–63, and "The Words in the Image: Orality, Literacy, and Early Greek Art," *Word and Image* 6 (1990) 180–197 (an expanded and revised version of his earlier article). J. P. Small called the first article to my attention and started me thinking about orality and Archaic Greek art, and I am very grateful to her.

We must be careful in our application of characteristics of oral or literate societies to Archaic Greece. R. Thomas (*Oral Tradition* 9–10, and *Literacy and Orality* 4–5) rightly cautions against creating an image of Preclassical Greece as an almost purely oral society. She believes that oral tradition and written records coexisted for a long period of time, and that there was a complicated interrelationship between them. It is, therefore, oversimplifying to see Greek society as either entirely oral or entirely literate.

34. W. J. Ong, *Orality and Literacy. The Technologizing of the Word* (London 1982) 140–141.

35. Ibid., 147.

36. Ibid.

37. And, of course, Book 23 of the *Iliad*, the source for the representation of the funeral games of Patroklos on the Pharsalos dinos, also cannot be said to have a strictly linear plot.

38. Ong (supra n. 34) 33. Hurwit 1990 (supra n. 33) 194

and Havelock 1982 (supra n. 33) 191 also discuss the naming of names.

39. For singing and writing Muses, see Havelock 1986 (supra n. 33) esp. 19–23.

22

SOME HOMERIC ANIMALS ON THE LION PAINTER'S PITCHER AT HARVARD *

◆

DAVID GORDON MITTEN

Among the Homeric garlands offered to Emily Vermeule, it might be appropriate to include an examination of the animals and birds on a large Attic Late Geometric vase that for four decades has conveyed the essence of Greek Geometric aesthetic sense to students, teachers, and visitors to the Harvard University Art Museums (figs. 22.1–22.4).[1] This vase is especially interesting because of the insertion of panels containing representations of these creatures into the lateral bands of ornament that encircle the body and neck of the vessel. Their presence and forms reveal an ephemeral stage in the use of such figural motifs just before the final dissolution and transformation of Late Geometric Attic vase painting under the accelerating influence of motifs from the eastern Mediterranean region during the final quarter of the eighth century B.C. As such, it constitutes an eloquent document for the meanings and roles of animals in Attic funerary vase painting during those very years in which many scholars believe that the *Iliad* received its essential form.

The vase itself is a sturdy construction, in which a concave neck sits atop a generously swelling ovoid body. The juncture between neck and shoulder is clearly marked by a sharp shift in the profile of the vessel, where the concave surface of the neck changes to the convexity of the shoulder. The body rests on a ring-foot, hollow beneath. The rim, flaring outward from the upper neck, is marked by a meander band. The vessel has a high vertical handle that rises to a point c. 3 cm above the rim, then curves straight down to join it. The handle is anchored to the back of the neck by two cylindrical struts (figs. 22.2–22.3). The vase is in excellent condition, having only sustained a single fracture extending around the lower part of the neck, within the meander band, and three breaks in the handle which have been mended. A missing piece of the rim, just to the right of the point where the handle intersects it, is infilled with plaster. With the exception of a small area on the front of the vessel, a larger area on the proper left side of the body, and part of the top of the handle, the painted decoration is also in fine condition.

Except for the black area around the foot and lowest part of the body, the pitcher is completely enveloped by an intricate network of lateral bands of painted ornament. Literally no space is unoccupied by some form of decoration. The neck and body display a program of ma-

FIGURE 22.1. Harvard 1950.64, front view. (Photographs courtesy Harvard University Art Museums, Francis H. Burr Memorial Fund.)

FIGURE 22.2. 1950.64, right profile.

FIGURE 22.3. 1950.64, left profile.

FIGURE 22.4. 1950.64, rear (handle) view.

jor and subordinate sequences of ornamental elements. The three principal zones—in the middle of the neck, on the shoulder next to its juncture with the neck, and girdling the widest part of the body—consist of alternating metopelike square panels within which there are four-petal rosettes, diamond-shaped lozenges, counterclockwise swastikas, and other geometric motifs alternating with panels that contain animals and birds. It is these figural panels that will form the principal focus of this study, because space will not allow a detailed analysis of the entire system of ornament. Below these major lateral zones are lesser bands of continuous meander: one under the chief zone on the body, one below the shoulder zone, and one on the neck below the major zone of square panels. The fourth meander band, one that encircles the flaring lip just below the rim, forms a sort of cornice for the entire vessel.

The ornamental system is further divided by thin bands of continuous lozenges: four on the body enclose the major zones and subsidiary meanders, and two on the neck lie beneath the major zone of panels and beneath the crowning meander on the lip. Other zones of ornament include, on the neck just above the juncture with the shoulder, a continuous frieze of four rows of dots disposed in alternating fashion, and a frieze of stylized birds, a "bird file," facing right, just above the main zone of panels. On the lower part of the body, below the lowest continuous band of lozenges, occur two further continuous bands of ornament: a zone of tiny crosshatched triangles, each one of which sprouts a tendril that points to the left and alternates with an intermediate dot, and a final, lowest band of separate, upright oval lozenges with central dots, not contiguous as are the diamond-shaped lozenges in the higher bands.

All these zones, major and minor, are further framed and separated by groups of three horizontal lines, with the exception of two lines at the juncture of shoulder and body, below the zone of dots, and a bottommost zone of five parallel lines just above the solid dark painted area above the foot.

The painted brushwork on this vase shows a vigorous, sure hand at work, whose successive progression around the vase can be seen, among other places, in the regular alternation of dark X-like marks within the bands of contiguous lozenges, forming adjacent sides of two lozenges where the painter replenished his brush

with paint (cf. fig. 22.5). This individual was termed the "Lion Painter" or "Lion Master" by P. Kahane;[2] his known work was expanded and revised by J. Cook,[3] J. M. Davison,[4] and J. N. Coldstream.[5] By 1968, the time of Coldstream's study, the Lion Painter's oeuvre numbered six vases: three round-mouthed pitchers (including the Harvard example), two kotylai, and a bowl with stand.[6] Coldstream has characterized him as a mannerist working at the beginning of Late Geometric IIb, perhaps c. 720–710 B.C.[7] Given the prominence of this painter in discussions of the final phases of Attic Late Geometric vase painting, and the frequency with which the Harvard pitcher is cited (without anyone being aware of its present whereabouts!), it may contribute to our understanding of this painter's style and iconography to concentrate upon the figured panels here, since they provide an unusually numerous and varied series of Late Geometric painted animals, unusual both in themselves and as a collection upon a single vase.

The figural panels are decorated as following: two with horses, one with two large-eyed grazing quadrupeds, probably deer; one containing two long-necked confronted birds; another with two confronting, kneeling goats; and three panels containing lions. These panels are disposed as follows: one lion in the center of the major zone of panels, on the front of the neck (fig. 22.5). On the shoulder frieze of panels, reading from left to right there are: confronting goats (fig. 22.7); confronting birds (fig. 22.6); a grazing deer facing right (fig. 22.8); a grazing deer, facing left (fig. 22.9). On the zone of panels around the body: lion facing right (fig. 22.12); standing horse, facing right (fig. 22.10); standing horse, facing right (fig. 22.11); lion facing right (fig. 22.13). On the shoulder and body zones, the animal panels are placed in alternating positions above and below each other, except for the right-hand lion on the body, which appears almost directly beneath the left-facing grazing deer.

Small stylized birds appear frequently in the design scheme as well. A continuous file of birds with long, curved necks, which alternate with vertical columns of minute dots, completely encircles the neck just above the principal zone of panels.[8] In addition, tiny birds appear: as elements of filling ornament within the alternating curves of the serpent that climbs the handle (fig. 22.4); perched on the backs or under the bodies of the goats, deer, and horses (but not the lions!); and within the arms of the two swastika panels that flank the central lion on the neck zone. In addition, a small, vertically disposed rectangular panel that appears between the right-hand horse and the right-hand lion on the major body zone contains several tiny birds amid a plethora of dots, almost as if it were an afterthought of the painter, still trying to fit yet more figural ornament onto the surface, although not having estimated his overall spacing accurately (best seen in fig. 22.1).

Each square panel, figural and containing geometric or floral motifs alike, is framed by a pair of upright elements, consisting of a vertical band of finely drawn zigzags enclosed between two groups of three vertical parallel lines each. Each of these groups is approximately the same width as the bands of zigzag that they enclose. Between each square panel and its pair of frames is a wider vertically disposed rectangular panel filled with six or seven horizontal zigzag lines. The vertical elements framing the major panels can thus be regarded as framing these intermediate "spacing" panels as well. The ends of the shoulder band and the neck band consist of groups of five vertical lines, and two panels of carefully drawn grid ornament, whose alternate squares are painted and provided with single central dots, where they are interrupted by the handle zone.

As seen from the rear of the vessel (fig. 22.4), the handle consists of a broad strap band, flanked by two relief fillets, which are separated from the central band by deep grooves. The central band, painted with the vertical serpent and its subsidiary birds, also contains curving files of tiny dots, similar to those that fill the spaces between the individuals in the "bird file" frieze on the neck, and delicate dot-rosettes, consisting of a central dot surrounded by a circle of smaller ones. Although the upper, curving part of the handle is badly abraded, it appears to carry a single small swastika with arms disposed in counterclockwise fashion, similar to the larger swastikas in panels on the vase proper. The flanking fillets are decorated on top with closely spaced dots and with stripes on the sides, as are the two struts that anchor the handle to the neck.

The Harvard vase itself is an unusually large example of a shape peculiar to Attic Late Geometric II pottery: the round-mouthed pitcher, or "pitcher-olpe," as Davison calls it.[9] These vases are usually provided with low

FIGURE 22.5. 1950.64, lion on neck.

conical lids, which are sometimes surmounted by elaborate knobbed handles. A smaller form of round-mouthed pitcher with flat bottom also exists within the same time range. Neither form survives into the earliest phases of Protoattic pottery manufacture at the beginning of the seventh century B.C. Vases as large as ours can hardly have been used for containing or pouring liquids; more likely, they would have served as prestige items for display and deposit in funerary ceremonies, and perhaps in some instances even as grave markers or monuments. The history and uses of the large round-mouthed Late Geometric Attic pitcher remain to be studied.

While the antecedents and origins of these pitchers are still not known, there are some close resemblances to some late Phrygian painted and monochrome one-handled round-mouthed jugs of the late eighth century B.C. from Gordion,[10] as well as to some bronze exam-

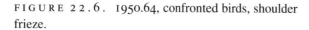

FIGURE 22.6. 1950.64, confronted birds, shoulder frieze.

FIGURE 22.7. 1950.64, confronted goats, shoulder frieze.

ples.[11] Such resemblances seem almost coincidental, made improbable by marked geographical separation, but similarities between Late Geometric Greek painted pottery and contemporary Phrygian painted pottery have been noted before.[12] While no examples of such Phrygian painted pottery have yet been found in Attica, it is possible that the shape, at least, imitates imported metal vessels, in the ways that both shape and painted motifs of Late Geometric Attic cups and bowls follow the models provided by bronze bowls with repoussé animals, especially bulls, imported from the Levant into Attica and elsewhere in Greece during the eighth century B.C. and perhaps even earlier.[13] Whatever their origins, these large pitchers provided an attractive alternative, or fashion, for a generation of Late Geometric town and country Athenians who were seeking impressive funerary pottery, but examples less expensive than the great "Dipylon" amphorae and kraters of Late Geometric I. Why they ceased being made and used must be connected with the causes for the marked decline both in quality and quantity of cultural remains in Attica during the first half of the seventh century B.C.[14]

It remains to examine the individual figured motifs and their treatment by the Lion Painter on this vase. The confronted birds in their panel on the shoulder are not quite symmetrical, the right-hand one being slightly narrower than the left (fig. 22.6). Their oval bodies are filled

with crosshatching, and their long, curving, antithetical necks end in heads with prominent eye-knobs and narrow beaks. Their short legs end in hooklike feet, two with secondary digits. In each case, the front foot directly continues the line of the neck, while the back leg projects from the middle of the body. The intervening spaces within the panel are filled with ornament. Short zigzag segments fill the gap between the birds' beaks and occupy the corners under their tails. Files of tiny dots follow the contours of the necks, ending in dot-rosettes under their beaks. A further short file of dots parallels the back of the right-hand bird's head. Rosettes occupy the space between the necks and the tops of the back of each bird. Two circles with central dots appear vertically placed in the upper left-hand corner of the panel; although the paint is too faint to be certain, they appear to be linked by diagonal lines, thus forming a pair of false spirals, on the analogy of longer segments of this motif that occur in other panels.

These birds are similar to many that appear on a variety of Late Geometric bowls and cups, as well as larger vessels, produced in Attica and other centers from the second half of the eighth century B.C. onward.[15] Confronted birds also occur on the Lion Painter's pitcher in the British Museum (1913.11–13.1).[16] As the principal figural decoration on Rhodian "bird bowls," they persist until the end of the seventh century. They are also com-

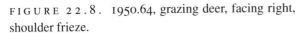

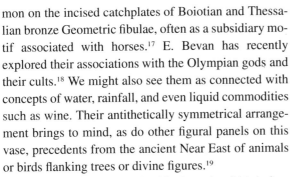

FIGURE 22.8. 1950.64, grazing deer, facing right, shoulder frieze.

FIGURE 22.9. 1950.64, grazing deer, facing left, shoulder frieze.

mon on the incised catchplates of Boiotian and Thessalian bronze Geometric fibulae, often as a subsidiary motif associated with horses.[17] E. Bevan has recently explored their associations with the Olympian gods and their cults.[18] We might also see them as connected with concepts of water, rainfall, and even liquid commodities such as wine. Their antithetically symmetrical arrangement brings to mind, as do other figural panels on this vase, precedents from the ancient Near East of animals or birds flanking trees or divine figures.[19]

To the left of the panel with the pair of birds is a longer, rectangular and containing two kneeling, confronting goats (fig. 22.7). The left-hand goat is nearly twice as long as the right-hand goat, suggesting again that the Lion Painter may have had trouble in planning his spatial allotments adequately when laying out his figural designs. The goats recline, with their front and hind legs folded inward toward each other. In both cases, what appears to be the further right leg is raised toward the belly. The heads are oval and completely reserved, with a dot for an eye in each case. It almost appears as if the heads are large eyes, as also seems to be the case in the pair of panels with grazing deer farther to the right on the shoulder. The carefully drawn horns parallel each other and the long curves of the goats' necks. Because they are smooth and unmarked by any knobs or other features, one cannot definitely call them either

ibex or agrimi. Details, however, are carefully described, like the hooves, the short, upturned tails, and even a pair of wattles under each chin executed by delicate short strokes; to the Lion Painter, these were essential features of goats.

The filling ornament in this panel is complex. Four of the small elongated-necked birds that appear in the frieze on the neck perch on the back of the left-hand goat, but face left instead of right; as above, curving files of tiny dots alternate with their necks. Single bands of zigzagging lie under the hind leg of the left-hand goat and over the head of each goat just under the top framing line; a rayed rosette lies between these two, in the interval just above the goats' heads. Stacks of chevrons extend under the chins of the goats: vertical under the left-hand one, and following the curve of the neck on the right-hand one. A third file of chevrons, very summarily painted, parallels the right-hand framing line, behind the rump of the goat on the right. What appears to be a rayed rosette fills the interval between the underbelly and the raised rear leg of the left-hand goat.

Although single kneeling goats occur fairly frequently in Late Geometric Attic vase painting,[20] pairs of antithetical goats disposed in panels are rare. A close parallel does appear on both sides of a high-rimmed bowl from a grave in Promachos Street, Athens,[21] on which the goats are more nearly equal in size than are

FIGURE 22.10. 1950.64, left-hand horse, body frieze.

FIGURE 22.11. 1950.64, right-hand horse, body frieze.

the Lion Painter's pair. More frequent are friezes of kneeling or reclining goats.[22] There, they often turn their heads backward, in the "regardant" pose. Some time ago, Amandry analyzed the Near Eastern origin of the variants in pose of reclining goats.[23] Thus, these animals, forerunners of those that populate the eastern Greek "Wild Goat" style, constitute yet another incipiently orientalizing motif used by the Lion Painter in his rich recipe of ornament on this vase.

The next two animal panels—to the right of the panel with the pair of birds—portray grazing deer, the first facing right (fig. 22.8), that beyond it facing left (fig. 22.9). These animals are clearly deer, as opposed to horses, because of their short, upcurving tails, high, spindly legs, short ears, and long necks. Both animals show short, projecting tabs above their hooves, characteristics also seen on contemporary bronze statuettes of deer, such as the group of a doe suckling a fawn in Boston.[24] Both deer have large, oval heads, rendered entirely in reserve with a prominent eye-dot, more visible in the left-facing deer than in the one facing right, because the head and the neck of the right-facing deer are abraded. These heads are identical to the heads of the goats. Both deer bend their necks and heads downward to graze in the lower right and the lower left corners of their panels, respectively. Between the right and hind legs of each deer is a long-necked bird, facing toward the tail in each

case. A file of chevrons stands behind the left-hand bird, while short files occur behind and in front of the right-hand bird. The right-hand bird faces an elaborate rosette consisting of a dotted circle surrounded by a ring of minute dots. The left-hand bird faces a solid-rayed rosette. A stack of chevrons extends the full height of each panel behind the hind legs of each deer; the left-hand stack of chevrons is connected by a vertical line, forming a kind of spine. A shorter file of chevrons fills the interval between the neck and the foreleg of each deer as well. A zigzag segment extends along the top of each panel. A large solid double axe or bow-tie motif fills the upper corner above each deer's head. There are no ornaments, however, between each deer's pair of front and hind legs.

Although physically separated from each other, these two panels in fact form yet another pair of antithetical creatures. The Lion Painter probably separated them after realizing that putting the two grazing deer nose to nose would create an elongated rectangular panel even longer than the one containing the kneeling goats farther to the left, and would cause an unbalanced and disharmonious sequence on the shoulder.

Friezes of grazing deer occur on a number of vases in Late Geometric II Attic pottery, as well as individual panels with grazing deer. Rombos notes the popularity of this motif in Late Geometric II, citing no fewer than

FIGURE 22.12. 1950.64, left-hand lion, body frieze.

FIGURE 22.13. 1950.64, right-hand lion, body frieze.

forty-three examples known to her.[25] Deer also appear as free-standing bronze statuettes throughout mainland Greece, from Thessaly south through Boiotia and into the Peloponnese.[26] They may be connected with hunting, in which they were favored prey, or perhaps with deities connected with the propagation and protection of wild creatures, like Artemis, in both native Greek and imported "Mistress of Animals" versions.

If we look at the subjects of the shoulder-band panels, we see goats, water birds, and deer, all wild creatures, hunted by human and animal predators alike. Their occurrence together and their placement on the shoulder suggest a programmatic element here in the Lion Painter's decision to associate them in this particular position on the vase.

The major band of panels on the widest part of the body of the vase contains four animal panels: two standing horses, facing right (figs. 22.10, 22.11), between two lions, also facing right (figs. 22.12, 22.13). The horses are nearly identical, with widely spaced spindly vertical legs.[27] The hind legs project from highly placed vertical haunches; the front legs project straight downward from the lower edges of the bodies in a most nonanatomical but distinctive fashion. Each leg ends in a widened, black form, the hoof, which in each case is accompanied by a short projecting spur a little further up the leg. As with the deer, no filling ornament occurs between the

pairs of front and hind legs. The penis is prominently depicted as a short line projecting diagonally downward from the hindquarters. The tail arches from the hindquarters, then falls vertically, stopping just short of the groundline. The neck and mane are formed by a triangular area of dark paint; very delicate upright lines project from the top of the head, emphasizing the mane. The horses' muzzles are V-shaped, ending in flaring tips. In all these aspects, the Lion Painter's horses follow closely the silhouette construction of many Greek Geometric bronze horses.[28]

The filling ornament of both panels is also closely similar. A stack of chevrons rises parallel to the left-hand framing line to the full height of the panel on the left of each horse. In front of (to the right) of each horse is a vertically disposed file of circles with central dots, linked by curving diagonal lines: four by the right-hand horse, perhaps five to the right of the left-hand horse (although abrasion of this area makes it difficult to count the exact number). Three small, long-necked birds, each accompanied by its "bird-seed" file of dots, perch atop the back or the right horse, facing right (fig. 22.11). Similar birds perch on the left horse's back, although the exact number (four?) cannot be determined because of the abraded surface at this point. The spaces between the pairs of front and hind legs of these horses are occupied by large diamond-shaped lozenges, surrounded by a ring of dots. The left-hand lozenge is crosshatched (fig. 22.10); the right-hand one (fig. 22.11) has alternate squares of the crosshatched grid painted in, in a manner similar to that employed on the rectangular grid panels at either end of the main frieze on the neck of the vase.

The three lions, one on the neck frieze[29] (fig. 22.5), the other two on the main frieze of the body of the vase (figs. 22.12, 22.13), are virtually identical. Their idiosyncratic modeling, with enormous front- and hindquarters, tiny constricted waists, elongated curving grasshopperlike legs, open tooth-filled jaws and tiny dot-filled eyes placed gogglelike atop their heads, have given the Lion Painter both his name and his trademark. In each lion, the tail bends forward, parallel with the top of the body, with its tip bending backwards again, ending with a crinkled zigzag tip. The tongue projects horizontally forward from the middle of a huge open maw; to either side, both jaws sprout tiny, closely placed, comblike teeth. There are traces of even tinier lines under the jaws of the neck lion and the right-hand one on the body frieze, representing bristles. The eyes are placed side by side on the top of the head, giving a comic, froglike appearance; at least one scholar interprets them as ears.[30] Being a master of precision in placing tiny dots, the Lion Painter had no trouble in providing each eye with its distinct pupil. Evidently showing both eyes seemed to him to be essential for proclaiming the lion's essential nature. Their arrangement side by side seems analogous to the side-by-side placement of both chariot wheels on some Late Geometric I chariot processions.[31]

In view of such explicit description, it is all the more remarkable that the painter did not choose to represent all four legs of each lion, preferring instead to rely upon the overall effect of the massive, powerful haunches and shoulders and the two curving, branchlike legs. As a result, the predominantly black silhouettes of the lions, when seen in the overall context of each vessel, as one first regards it from a distance, immediately and forcefully catch the eye with their unmistakable "lionness."

The filling ornament of the lion panels seems like a deliberate extension of their fur and manes, as well as their essential ferociousness. Zigzag remnants fill the spaces above the lions' backs, and a single zigzag segment fits beneath the lions' elongated curving hind legs,

thus perhaps "reading" as a further set of bristles as well. On the neck lion, a fourth short zigzag segment underlies the foreleg. In all three lions, stacks of chevrons fill the vertical spaces between lower jaws and front legs, and a curving stack of chevrons extends from the waist downward, paralleling the curve of the back side of the forequarters. In the neck lion (fig. 22.5), rayed rosettes occur to the right of the curve before the tip of the tail and in the angle between the hindquarters and the right leg. This scheme repeats itself on the left-hand lion panel on the body frieze, with the addition of a third rayed rosettes under its foreleg; there are not certainly discernable rayed rosettes in the third lion's filling ornament. The neck lion has a clearly drawn vertical segment of linked dotted circles, or false spiral, which "reads" like a vine tendril; in the other two lions, this is replaced by a vertical stack of chevrons extending the entire height of the panel.

In considering all three lions, the clearer drawing of the neck lion, as well as the presence of the false spiral segment, suggests that this was meant to be the principal lion, with the other two serving as subordinate repetitions in their positions as parentheses for the horses on the frieze of panels around the body of the vessel. Three is indeed a large number of lions on any Attic Late Geometric painted vase, and one may well ask why this painter should choose to show three here. The ravening, irresistible ferocity of lions, already prominent in the *Iliad*, becomes increasingly explicit in Greek vase painting and sculpture during the seventh and early sixth centuries B.C. The lion combat, in which a lion or lions attack and devour a bull or other animal, was placed on many different kinds of objects during the Archaic period,[32] becoming both an apotropaic device and a symbol of the all-devouring ravages of death. Could not the lions on this impressive pitcher, therefore, have served both as watchful, savage guardians of the dead and as signs of the triumph of death, the inevitable, universal fate of mortals? We might suspect that such significance, as well as other connotations that must elude us, would have been in the minds and visions of both the Geometric Athenians for whose use this vase was intended, as well as in the intentions of the Lion Painter himself, who lavished such detailed, yet expressive, brush strokes in executing his lions.

It is unlikely that eighth-century Athenians would have seen and hunted living lions on the slopes of Mts. Pentelikon or Parnes. The consensus remains that such Late Geometric and Protoattic lions are derived from artistic influences and objects imported from the Near East.[33] It is not impossible that Protocorinthian lions might have been among the models in the mind's eye of the Lion Painter when he sat down to organize the decoration of this vase.[34] Such lions remain the most distinctive single feature of the vases (between five and six) thus far attributed to the Lion Painter. They also remain distinctive among the other lions known on Late Geometric Attic vases (sixteen by the time Rombos wrote).[35] Other lions appear singly, in files, as on the early Protoattic krater by the Analatos Painter in Munich,[36] or fighting over a human corpse, as on the kantharos in Copenhagen,[37] perhaps both as illustration of Homeric metaphors and as a visual surrogate for the motif of two warriors fighting over the body of a third, which was to become a *Leitmotif* of Archaic vase painting. Lions are also present, if sparingly, among Greek Geometric bronze statuettes, both freestanding and surmounting the ring-handles of tripod-cauldrons.[38] It is clear that lions were attracting the fascinated and fearful attention of eighth-century Greeks and were acquiring a complex set of symbolic meanings as well.

Coldstream has characterized the Lion Painter as a principal figure in the disintegration of linear ornament in the vase painting of Late Geometric II times, with easily recognizable mannerisms such as his massive, narrow-waisted, two-legged lions, his use of the double axe motif, and his treatment of square metopelike panels.[39] On the Harvard pitcher, his double axes seem to be limited to the two in the grazing deer panels. On the other hand, his friezes with metopelike panels contain the impressive animals and birds that we have examined, alternating with carefully drawn four-petal rosettes, elaborate lozenges, and counterclockwise swastikas whose arms are filled with dot-rosettes or tiny birds.[40] Coldstream comments: "His dotted bird files are based on the Birdseed Painter's, but their necks are absurdly elongated." Similarly, he terms the Lion Painter's meanders "thin" and "fragile."[41] Coldstream considers the Harvard pitcher to be early in his work, before his drawing and his systems of ornament fell apart seriously, "yet the drawing never falls below a certain standard of mannered neatness."[42] Close examination of the figured panels on the Harvard pitcher suggests a revision of this judgment, revealing an artist who not only filled every available space with painted ornament but who also, on this vase at least, combined everything into a harmonious, even stately, whole.

Much more could be learned by detailed comparison and analysis of individual figurative and decorative elements within the oeuvre of the Lion Painter, in particular those on the London pitcher, British Museum 1913.11–13.1, which still remains inadequately illustrated and examined.[43] Interesting insights into his working methods could be obtained by close study of the sequence in which he drew his basic structural elements and his detailed figural ornamental sequences. We may hope that more of the Lion Painter's works will come to light in securely datable contexts, and that, together with vases already known like the Harvard pitcher, they may help to enhance the reputation of one of the most individual painters of animals active in Attica during the late eighth century B.C. It is fascinating to try to imagine what kind of human figures the Lion Painter would have drawn. It is tempting, too, to suppose that the Lion Painter was familiar with the *Iliad* in its early, substantially complete form, and that the hearing of it is strongly influenced his choice of animal subjects, as well as even perhaps the structure of the overall ornamental program on his vases.[44] Even more likely, however, is that he embraced the increasingly diverse flood of motifs and ornaments arriving in Attica from sources farther east, and that in so doing, he anticipated the more overt incorporation of orientalizing subjects and ornamental motifs that we see so clearly in the Analatos Painter's work. Probably illiterate himself, his "signatures" are nevertheless unmistakable: the massive, two-legged lions, the tiny birds that pop up everywhere, his idiosyncratic use of dot-rosettes, false spirals, zigzag segments, and chevron stacks, and of course his hilarious parades of "flamingoes" and their accompanying "bird-seed" files. The Harvard pitcher, then, reveals the Lion Painter at his best: an eclectic, unconventional, and whimsically inventive artistic personality experimenting on the verge of far-reaching changes in composition and imagery that were shortly to transform

Attic Late Geometric vase painting into a monumental vehicle of mythological narrative: the early Protoattic style.

NOTES

*In writing this essay, I have received valuable help from Amy Brauer and Aaron Paul, respectively Assistant Curator and Curatorial Associate in the Department of Ancient Art, Harvard University Art Museums, who provided me with information about the vessel from departmental files. Much of this information consisted of notes collected by the late Professor George M. A. Hanfmann, longtime Curator of Ancient Art, who purchased the vase for Harvard in 1950. I am deeply grateful to the staff of the Photographic Department of the Harvard University Art Museums: Michael Nedzweski and Rick Stafford for their care in making new photographs of the individual figured panels on this vase, and Elizabeth Gombosi for her help in making arrangements for the photography and for sending prints to me. Keith Dickey and Sarah P. Morris suggested valuable parallels for the lions and provided helpful bibliographical references. Kimberley C. Patton typed the footnotes on the Macintosh word processor at the American School and provided much additional help. Publication of the vase is by permission of the Harvard University Art Museums.

The following abbreviations will be used throughout:

Borell = B. Borell, *Attisch geometrische Schalen* (Mainz 1978).

Coldstream = J. N. Coldstream, *Greek Geometric Pottery* (London 1968).

Davison = J. M. Davidson, *Attic Geometric Workshops,* YCS 16 (New Haven 1961).

Kübler = K. Kübler, *Kerameikos VI.2. Ergebnisse der Ausgrabungen. Die Nekropole des späten 8. bis frühen 6. Jhr.* (Berlin 1970).

Rombos = T. Rombos, *The Iconography of Attic Late Geometric II Pottery* (Jonsered 1988).

1. Harvard University Art Museums, 1950.64. H: 52.2 cm. Diameter of mouth: 26 cm. Diameter of body: 35.2 cm. Francis H. Burr Fund. Formerly on the Athens market. Purchased from Walter Ephron, New York City. P. Kahane, "Die Entwicklungsphasen der attisch-geometrischen Keramik," *AJA* 44 (1940) 479–480; 482; pl. XXVII:3. (Attribution credited to E. Kunze.) J. M. Cook, "Athenian Workshops around 700,"

BSA 42 (1947) 143–144. Davison 143, no. 1, fig. 30; C. Brokaw, "Concurrent Styles in Late Geometric and Early Protoattic Vase Painting," *AthMitt* 78 (1963) 65, n. 5, 66; Beil. 29, 1. Coldstream 73 (XV.1), 74. Kübler 581, no. 82; 10, 11, 12, 13, 14, 17–19, 20, 45, 56, 63 n. 189, 80; D. G. Mitten and A. Brauer, *Dialogue with Antiquity* (Cambridge, Mass. 1982) no. 4. Rombos, cat. no. 264, 485. D. G. Mitten, in S. Langdon, ed., *From Pasture to Polis: Art in the Age of Homer* (Columbia 1993) no. 79, pp. 202–205.

2. Kahane (supra n. 1) 479–480, 482.

3. Cook (supra n. 1) 143–144.

4. Davison 143, figs. 30–32a–b.

5. Coldstream 73–74.

6. Coldstream 74.

7. Coldstream 331, chart.

8. Kübler 17 notes the exceptionally elongated necks in the "bird file" on the Harvard vase.

9. Davison 10, fig. A, 12.

10. R. S. Young et al., *Three Great Early Tumuli*, Gordion I. (Philadelphia, University Museum 1981) 34–35 (general remarks); Tumulus P. 54; Black on red round-mouthed jug; 35, pl. 16, D; Tumulus P. 55:35, Pl. 16, E–F, Pl. 17, A–B (detail, C); Tumulus P. 56:35, pl. 17, D, E; Tumulus P. 57:30, pl. 17 F. Also Tumulus P. 66:39, pl. 18, G (black-polished round-mouthed jug with ring-foot).

11. Young (supra n. 10) Tumulus W 6. Bronze round-mouthed jug with pedestal foot: 202, pl. 88, E. Two Near Eastern (Phoenician?) bronze round-mouthed jugs from Lefkandi (*BSA* 77 [1982] 239; Sub-PG III (T 33, 15) and LPG [T 39,31], fig. 8; pl. 20, 31).

12. Cf. Kübler 56–57, n. 144, with rich bibliography, on this possibility.

13. Borell 74–83, 87–94 (connections in archaeological evidence); G. Markoe, *Phoenician Bronze and Silver Bowls from Cyprus and the Mediterranean*, University of California Publications, Classical Studies, vol. 26 (Berkeley and Los Angeles 1985) esp. 117–127.

14. R. Osborne, "A Crisis in Archaeological History? The Seventh Century B.C. in Attica," *BSA* 84 (1989) 297–322.

15. Kübler 17.

16. Cf. Davison, fig. 31; Coldstream, pl. 14a.

17. K. Kilian, *Fibeln in Thessalien von der mykenischen bis zur archaischen Zeit*, Prähistorische Bronzefunde, XIV.2 (Munich 1975), e.g., no. 1371, Taf. 49; 1882, Taf. 61; 1884, Taf. 62 (top). Also D. G. Mitten in A. P. Kozloff, ed., *Animals in Ancient Art from the Leo Mildenberg Collection* (Cleveland 1981), no. 72, 90–91. Rombos 75, n. 37.

18. E. Bevan, "Waterbirds and the Olympian Gods," *BSA* 84 (1989) 163–169.

19. See exhaustive discussion of birds on late eighth- and

early seventh-century Athenian painted pottery: Kübler 232–236.

20. Rombos 43–45, chart on 36, theme 43.

21. Rombos 420, cat. no. 66; *AD* 23 (1968), pl. 50; *AAA* 3 (1970) 115, figs. 1–2. For the theme of two kneeling goats flanking a tree and its Near Eastern connections, cf. Rombos 41–43.

22. Rombos 46–51.

23. P. Amandry, "Un motif scythe en Iran et en Grèce," *JNES* 24 (1965) 149–160.

24. M. Comstock and C. C. Vermeule III, *Greek, Etruscan, and Roman Bronzes in the Museum of Fine Arts, Boston* (Greenwich 1971) 5, no. 3; inv. no. 98.750.

25. Kübler 49–58; Rombos, chart on 36, theme 43; cf. her extensive discussion of grazing deer, 56–64, and Table 6 (57) and 7 (62).

26. W.-D. Heilmeyer, *Frühe olympische Bronzefiguren. Die Tiervotive,* OlForsch 12 (Berlin 1979) 148–151, nos. 721, 722, 723, Taf. 87; "Olympische Hirschgruppen," 253–254, 151, n. 197.

27. Cf. nearly identical horse in panel on body frieze of the Lion Painter's pitcher in London, British Museum 1913.11–13.1, Davison, fig. 31. On standing horses in panels, cf. Rombos 65–77, table 8 (66), table 9 (68–69).

28. J.-L. Zimmerman, *Les chevaux de bronze dans l'art géométrique grec* (Mainz 1989) esp. general remarks, 1–15.

29. A similar lion panel is also placed on the center of the neck frieze on British Museum 1913.11–13; Davison, fig. 31.

30. E. T. H. Brann, *The Athenian Agora VIII: Late Geometric and Protoattic Pottery,* (Princeton 1962) 9, 16. In contrast to the two legs of our lions, note the four legs clearly shown on the lion in the central tondo of the Late Geometric II cup from the workshop of the Hirschfeld Painter in the Charles Politis Collection, Goulandris Museum, Athens: X. Παπαδοπουλου-Κανελλοπουλου, ΣΥΛΛΟΓΗ ΚΑΡΟΛΟΥ ΠΟΛΙΤΗ (Athens 1989) no. 23 (ΣΠ 4): 48–49, fig. 37.

31. E.g., on LG I kraters Paris A 517, Paris A 552, and Athens 990 (Coldstream, pls. 7a, 8a, and 8b respectively).

32. F. Hölscher, *Die Bedeutung archaischer Tierkampf-bilder* (Würzburg 1972); see now G. Markoe, "The 'Lion Attack' in Archaic Greek Art: Heroic Triumph," *CA* 8 (1989) 86–115 (this reference thanks to S. P. Morris).

33. Cf. Kübler 69–88, for full discussion of the problems connected with late Geometric and Early Orientalizing lions. Also G. Ahlberg-Cornell, "Games, Play and Performance in Greek Geometric Art: The Kantharos Copenhagen NM 727 Reconsidered," *Acta Archaeologica* 58 (1987) 55–86 (on "tame" lions and Greek "circuses"; this reference thanks to S. P. Morris).

34. Cf. Coldstream's discussion of the appearance of double axes in the Lion Painter's repertoire of ornament as caused by Protocorinthian influence, 74.

35. Rombos, table 1, theme 50 (36); discussion of single lions and lions attacking animals or men, 185–208; the Lion Painter's lions, 189 (table 28), 190.

36. Munich 6077; R. M. Cook, *Greek Painted Pottery,* 2nd edition (London, 1972) 67, pl. 14B. Rombos 191, table 29.

37. Copenhagen, National Museum 727, from the Burly Workshop. Rombos, cat. no. 305, 499–500, pl. 37c. (I am grateful to Keith Dickey for citing this example to me.)

38. Heilmeyer (supra n. 26) 196, n. 262; D. G. Mitten (supra n. 17) 86–87, no. 70; Rombos 186.

39. Coldstream 73–74.

40. Kübler 63, n. 189, on the birds in the arms of swastikas on the Harvard vase.

41. Coldstream 74.

42. Coldstream 74.

43. Davison 41, fig. 31; Coldstream 73, pl. 14a; Rombos, cat. no. 263, 484–485, pl. 36b.

44. For an early attempt at correlation of the structure of Attic Geometric vase ornament with thematic and metric structure in the Iliad, cf. J. L. Myres, "The Last Book of the 'Iliad,'" *JHS* 52 (1932) 264–296, esp. 271ff. and 273, fig. 4 (neck frieze of the Lion Painter's pitcher British Museum 1913.11–13.1); refinement of these parallels: C. Whitman, *Homer and the Heroic Tradition* (Cambridge, Mass. 1958) 52–54; ch. 5, "Homer and Geometric Art," 87–101; ch. 11, "The Geometric Structure of the Iliad," 249–284.

23

A GEOMETRIC BARD*

◆

J. MICHAEL PADGETT

The study of Homeric iconography is not limited to representations of specific characters or episodes from the *Iliad* or the *Odyssey,* nor is the small amount of narrative art from the Geometric period the only possible testimony to an awareness and appreciation of Homer by his contemporaries. It is a pleasure to offer this study of a Geometric bronze lyre-player and boy to Emily Vermeule, whose devotion to the bard is unsurpassed, and whose understanding of "Homeric" art is informed by the soul of a poet.

The bronze statuette of a man playing a lyre in the presence of a small boy is in the J. Paul Getty Museum, Malibu (figs. 23.1–23.7).[1] The provenance is unknown, but there is reason to believe that it originated on Crete, the home and locale of many of the heroes and tales of which Homer sang. The two solid-cast figures stand side by side on a common base, which consists of a thin, narrow strip 0.075 m in length and roughly rectangular in shape. In the center of the front and back edges of the base are shallow, vertical notches, two in front and four in back; their purpose is unknown, but it is clear they were added by hammering after the casting was complete.

The plate is pierced by two holes, one at the far right, by the left foot of the lyre-player, the other in the center, between the two figures. The holes were obviously made to allow the pair to be attached to something else, but it is not clear what this was. The composition strongly suggests that the group was conceived as an independent sculpture and not as a structural component, such as the ring-holders on the rims of bronze cauldrons.[2] The shape of the base and the very fact that it supports a group rather than an individual figure also argue against attachment to a vessel.[3] If the sculpture was a votive offering, it may have been attached to a small block of wood, stone, or bronze.

Both the lyre-player and the boy stand frontally, their feet firmly on the ground. The heads of both figures are turned slightly to the left, and the boy, who stands at the musician's right, extends his left hand to rest on the right hip of his larger companion. The stance of the nude musician is somewhat unstable; in fact, he seems not only knock-kneed, but pigeon-toed as well. His legs are rubbery, with thick thighs, and there is pronounced swelling around the knees. The kneecaps are represented by small circular incisions; similar circles also represent

FIGURE 23.1 Bronze lyre-player and boy, frontal view. Collection of the J. Paul Getty Museum, Malibu, California (inv. 90.AB.6). (Photographs courtesy J. Paul Getty Museum.)

FIGURE 23.2. Bronze lyre-player and boy, Malibu (fig. 23.1); detail of frontal view.

the nipples and navel. The slender waist flares up to a roughly triangular upper body. The man holds the lyre at an angle in his left arm, away from the body. The right arm is raised rather high, so that by bending it to strike the lyre-strings with a plektron, the elbow sticks out at a sharp angle. The plektron is represented as a flaccid rectangle with no resemblance to the standard form of later years; one forgives its nondescript appearance when one considers that it may be the earliest known example in Greek sculpture.[4]

The musician's head is broad and massive, sitting directly upon the shoulders, with no trace of a neck. The mouth is a short horizontal line, devoid of expression. The nose is broad and flat, without nostrils. The eyes are almond-shaped and slightly asymmetrical, and are surrounded by raised rings marked with parallel incisions representing eyelashes.[5] The low, ring-shaped ears have shallow indentions in the center.[6] The man's nudity is emphasized by his somewhat oversized genitals; the penis is represented perpendicular but can hardly be called erect. The pubic hair is represented by a well-defined

triangle with a slightly roughened surface; strangely, the apex of the triangle is at the top, rather than the bottom.

The man's hair is shaped like a cap or bowl, without sideburns or pendant locks, and rows of braids marked with parallel lines radiate from the crown.[7] The hair of the smaller figure is rendered in the same manner; he too, therefore, should be male, and because of his size, a boy. Unlike the nude musician, he wears a cylindrical belt and a triangular codpiece or loincloth; the latter apparently hangs freely, not extending behind to cover the buttocks. The vertical incision in the center of the loincloth might be taken for an indication of female sex, but in addition to the "male" hairstyle, other factors argue against this: the slit is too high, stopping well short of the crotch; bronze statuettes of females are uncommon in this period, and only rarely is a nude woman represented wearing a belt;[8] and the pubic area is rendered differently on the man, with the apex of the triangle at the top. Moreover, one may wonder if a little girl would have her genitals thus represented, even in Dorian Crete.[9] The pelletlike breasts are too small to be considered female; plastic breasts are not the rule on Cretan male figurines, but they do occur, both in bronze and terracotta.[10]

Although clearly present in a supporting role, the boy is the more beguiling figure, with a slight but definite smile that animates his features. His torso is slender and nearly cylindrical. The knees are more tubular than the man's, but the kneecaps are marked by the same circular incisions, the right one with a short tangent line. The buttocks are more prominent than the lyre-player's, and the face, though narrower, projects more in profile. The nose is grotesquely broad, almost bestial, its parameters defined by the raised rings with incised lashes which surround the almond-shaped eyes. Because the child's face is smaller than the man's, the rings of the eyes abut the cruder rings representing the ears. With his left arm, the boy reaches out to touch the hip of the lyre-player; his boneless right arm curves down like a fishhook. On both figures, the toes and fingers are roughly indicated by incisions.

Although various details of the figures in Malibu can also be found among Geometric bronzes and terracottas from mainland Greece, the massive heads and relatively squat proportions do not find good parallels

FIGURE 23.3. Bronze lyre-player and boy, Malibu (fig. 23.1); three-quarter view from right.

FIGURE 23.4. Bronze lyre-player and boy, Malibu (fig. 23.1); three-quarter view from left.

FIGURE 23.5. Bronze lyre-player and boy, Malibu (fig. 23.1); right profile.

FIGURE 23.6. Bronze lyre-player and boy, Malibu (fig. 23.1); left profile.

FIGURE 23.7. Bronze lyre-player and boy, Malibu (fig. 23.1); rear view.

there; eighth-century bronzes from Olympia, Delphi, and the Athenian Acropolis tend to be more slender and elongated. Although the lyre-player and the boy have the narrow waists and rubbery limbs associated with mainland Geometric figures, and the lyre-player has the triangular chest of a typical *Lanzenschwinger,* there are elements that suggest a different origin and a somewhat later date. The concern for detail and the softness and rotundity of the modeling are uncharacteristic of eighth-century bronzes. The pubic hair of the lyre-player is a feature usually not encountered before the early seventh century,[11] and the slight smile and touching gesture of the boy introduce a note of humanity usually lacking in earlier sculptures. Taken together, and independent of iconographic considerations, these elements suggest a date of about 700–680 B.C.[12]

Group compositions are rare in Geometric bronze sculpture. Most consist either entirely of animals, such as the deer suckling a fawn in Boston, or of an animal and a human, like the man holding a ram at Harvard.[13] In some examples an element of narrative is added, such as the hunter and dog attacking a lion, from the Samian Heraion, or the Centauromachy in New York.[14] Groups of two or more human figures are even rarer, and very few employ the basic composition of the Malibu bronze, with the figures standing side by side. Some Syrian and Levantine bronzes of the early first millennium have two or more figures in this arrangement, and paired males with linked arms are found in Etruria and Southern Italy in the eighth and early seventh centuries.[15] Greek examples are few and date mostly to the eighth century: for example, a warrior and chariot driver from Olympia, or the so-called Zeus and Hera in Boston.[16] A late eighth-century bronze from Kato Syme, in Crete, offers perhaps the best parallel, with two nude males—one tall, one short—standing with joined hands on a narrow rectangular base (fig. 23.8).[17] Although crudely modeled, with small, pinched heads, the figures from Syme may be considered predecessors of the pair in Malibu, which additional evidence suggests originated in a Cretan workshop.

Belts and loincloths were among the most distinctive elements of Cretan male dress from Minoan times to the end of the seventh century. Minoan male votaries normally wear a belt and either a narrow codpiece, a triangular loincloth, or a fuller kiltlike loincloth that covers the hips and buttocks as well as the genitals.[18] Loincloths continued on some bronze Subminoan and Protogeometric male figurines,[19] but from the Protogeometric on, many figures wear only a belt and are otherwise nude.[20] Loincloths, however, continued to appear down through the seventh century, and are particularly common on figurines in the Daedalic style, like the well-known ram-bearer in Berlin.[21] A few bronze statuettes demonstrate the continuity of the fashion in the eighth and early seventh centuries, notably the well-known *sphyrelaton* Apollo from Dreros,[22] and a smaller, solid-cast statuette found in a late eighth-century deposit at Afrati.[23] Not only do these youths wear belts and loincloths, but their bowl haircuts are quite similar to those of the Getty figures, with the addition of a long queue hanging down the back. Variations of this coiffure, with and without the queue, are found on a number of bronze male figures from Crete, from the Protogeometric to the

FIGURE 23.8. Pair of bronze males from Kato Syme, Crete. Herakleion Museum, inv. 3137. (After A. Lebessi, *Expedition* 18.3 [Spring 1976] 4, fig. 4.)

early seventh century.[24] It is the combination of bowl-shaped hair and belted loincloth, as well as the compositional precedent of the group from Kato Syme, which argues most convincingly for a Cretan origin for the figures in Malibu.[25]

A further Cretan note is struck by the subject of the group, as the best-known figure of a lyre-player from this period is the seated bronze bard in Herakleion (fig. 23.9).[26] Of unknown provenance, but generally considered Cretan in origin, the figure has been variously dated, most convincingly to the early seventh century.[27] A small bronze lyre-player in a private collection in New York is very similar to the Herakleion musician and has been attributed to the same Cretan workshop.[28] Unlike the Getty musician, both the Herakleion and the New York lyre-players are seated on a low stool, with the lyre resting on the knees. The posture is reminiscent of mainland statuettes of seated figures who hold an object to their mouth, sometimes interpreted as a flute.[29] Unlike the lyre-players, these figures are affixed to a base-plate or sit on top of a "bottle-stopper" pendant.[30] In style, they are simpler and less detailed than the lyre-players in Malibu and Herakleion (the one in New York is perhaps closer akin), nor is it completely certain that they are making music.[31]

The subjects alone call for a comparison between the Getty lyre-player and those in Herakleion and New York, and there are in fact some stylistic similarities as well, particularly the oversized heads, fluid limbs, and thin, tapering trunks. The Herakleion musician is distinguished by his bold features: long nose, protruding ears, button eyes, beetling brows, and wide mouth, the latter clearly open in song. The features of the New York lyre-player, being smaller, are less distinct and more simian in nature. The lyres of the two seated players rest on their knees so that they may use both hands, plucking the strings with the right hand and stopping them with the left. The musician in Malibu, on the other hand, uses his left hand to support the lyre and strikes the strings with the plektron in his right hand. This may not be a completely realistic representation, as the fingerwork of the left hand would probably have been indispensable. In many later depictions of lyre-players, the lyre or kithara is held by a strap looped around the wrist, freeing the left hand, an innovation which apparently postdates the introduction of the plektron.[32]

The sound boxes of the lyres played by the musicians in Herakleion and New York have the rounded base and straight upper edge of many of the lyres illustrated on Geometric vases. The latter are frequently identified with the Homeric *phorminx*;[33] a reasonable assumption, though some have doubted it, and as Jeffrey Hurwit has noted, both *kitharis* (not kithara) and *phorminx* are used to denote the same instrument in Homer.[34] Although most of the lyres on eighth-century vases have rounded bases, there is considerable variation in the shape of the sound box, the extension of the crossbar, and the height and curvature of the vertical arms.[35] Most share the same basic shape, however, and we are probably justified in using Homer's most common name for them, *phorminx*.

The lyre of the Herakleion singer is larger than the

FIGURE 23.9. Bronze lyre-player. Herakleion Museum, inv. 2064. (Photograph courtesy DAI Athen, neg. 73/1027.)

instrument in the Getty and has four thick strings anchored below by a parabola-shaped tailpiece. The Getty lyre is similar in construction, but the sound box is squarer on the bottom and has a rounded upper edge. There are only two strings, which extend almost to the base, where they are attached to a block-shaped tailpiece that holds them away from the box. The paucity of strings is nothing more than artistic economy; most examples in Geometric vase painting have four or five strings, but these too may be abbreviations. Later lyres had seven strings, and the Homeric *Hymn to Hermes* ascribes a similar number to the first lyre, made by Hermes from a tortoise shell.[36] The arms of the Getty lyre are shorter than those of the instrument in Herakleion, and the crosspiece extends slightly beyond them, resting within notches at the tips. These differences in detail would be more significant if we were dealing with actual instruments, but when comparing two small and highly schematic sculptures, we cannot be sure they are not the result of artistic license or inexactitude. The lyre-player in New York plays an instrument very similar to the one in Herakleion, except that the sound box is convex on one side. Hurwit suggests it is made of hollowed-out or bent wood, a truly "hollowed lyre" (*phorminx glaphura*).[37]

Musicians of any kind are uncommon in Geometric sculpture, although they are frequently represented on Late Geometric vases. A bronze lyre-player in Brussels, clearly a mainland creation, is the only known example securely datable to the eighth century, while those in Malibu, Herakleion, and New York are at present the only representatives from the early seventh century.[38] Psychro, on Crete, has yielded a bronze flute-player from this period, which, although stylistically unrelated to the lyre-players, is dressed in a Cretan belt and loincloth.[39] A bronze statuette in the Ortiz collection represents a nude man in a rustic cap sitting on a stool and playing a *syrinx*, his erect posture distinguishing him from the seated lyre-players in Herakleion and New York. Although Geometric in style, this piper is modeled with greater naturalism than the seated "flute-players," mentioned above, and has been rightly dated to the early seventh century.[40]

Unlike representations on vases, where lyre-players are sometimes shown accompanying dancers or in other surroundings, most bronze statuettes lack an internal narrative context that would enable us to divine their particular meaning, though properly excavated examples may provide clues as to their use. The Dreros Apollo, for example, was found in the corner of a temple of Apollo Delphinios; frequently referred to as a cult statue, it was more likely placed there as a votive offering. The two female statuettes found with it are often identified as Artemis and Leto,[41] but if instead they are mortal votaries whose status is indicated by their much smaller size, one might ask if the figures in Malibu have a similar relationship. Apollo, of course, was the god of music and played the *phorminx* at the feast of the gods (*Iliad* 1.603) and at the wedding of Peleus and Thetis (*Iliad* 24.63). In art, the lyre is one of Apollo's attributes as early as the mid-seventh century, and it is possible that he is to be identified with some of the lyre-players on Geometric vases.[42] If the musician in Malibu is Apollo, however, and the boy a votary, we may wonder at the latter's unseemly familiarity in touching the god and the easy way he stands beside him.

Another possibility is that the boy is Hermes, precocious inventor of the lyre, who gave the instrument to Apollo to ease his anger over the theft of his cattle. In support of this interpretation is the fact that the bronze pair from Kato Syme was found among the offerings in a sanctuary of Hermes and Aphrodite. The principal objection is that the man's lyre is clearly not constructed from a tortoise shell, a crucial element of the story as related in the *Hymn to Hermes*.

If the lyre-player is not a god, he must be a mortal bard, an *aoidos*, like Homer's Demodokos, the blind singer at the court of Alkinoos in Phaiakia.[43] Demodokos, "the divine singer," moved Odysseus to tears with his song of the fall of Troy (*Odyssey* 8.499ff.) and struck his "hollowed lyre" to sing of how crafty Hephaistos caught Aphrodite in bed with Ares (*Odyssey* 8.266ff.). Phemios, the *aoidos* who was forced to entertain Penelope's unwanted suitors, was spared by Odysseus when the minstrel told him,

You will be sorry in time to come if you kill the singer of
  songs.
I sing to the gods and to human people, and I am taught
  by myself,

but the god has inspired me in the song-ways of every
    kind. I am
such a one as can sing before you as to a god.

Odyssey 22.345–349
(trans. R. Lattimore)

The respect in which Demodokos, Phemios, and other *aoidoi* were held is repeatedly emphasized by Homer, who calls them not only "divine," but "versatile," "renowned," and "prized among the people." Their utility extended beyond the banquet hall to other occasions. Demodokos set a tune for a dance of Phaiakian youth (*Odyssey* 8.262–265), and at the wedding feast given at Sparta by Menelaos, both dancers and acrobats moved to the music of the lyre (*Odyssey* 4.17–19). Several Late Geometric vase paintings show a lyre-player or flutist accompanying dancers, who leap high into the air, or, like the dancers on the shield of Achilles, move in procession with linked hands (*Iliad* 18.593).[44] Usually the musician stands apart from the procession, but in one example the lyre-player is touched on the hip by the female dancer next to him.[45] Sometimes children are present, as on a fragment from the Athenian Acropolis with a lyre-player and flutist standing on either side of a small boy. The boy stands on a low platform with his knees flexed and his hands clasped together; he may be performing an acrobatic dance, keeping his balance on a narrow beam while moving to the music.[46] This recalls not only the Spartan acrobats mentioned above, but also the two Phaiakian boys, Halios and Laodamas, who demonstrated grace and agility by playing catch with a ball (*Odyssey* 8.370ff.).[47]

It may be that the fashioner of the Getty bronze had in mind an epic bard rather than the musician at a village dance (although these could easily have been the same person). It might be thought unlikely that the bronze lyre-players from Dorian Crete would have been singing the songs of Homer, an Ionian poet, so soon after his supposed floruit in the late eighth century. However, language and nationality were no bar to Homer's later adoption by Greeks of all stripes, nor does the performance of his works in early seventh-century Crete require that their authorship be moved back in time to allow for a more leisurely dissemination. Homeric subjects and references appear on pottery in a variety of fabrics in the first half of the seventh century, not only in Ionian Athens, but also Dorian Argos and Aigina, colonial Campania, and even Etruria.[48] The impact of the Homeric poems on ceramic iconography was relatively rapid, and it is probably only the paucity of figural vase paintings in Crete which accounts for the dearth of unequivocally Homeric subjects in Cretan art of this period. Crete in the late eighth and early seventh centuries was open to artistic influence and perhaps even settlement from the barbarian East, and it would not be surprising if welcome was also extended to Greek bards from Ionia, or their disciples. The *Iliad*, which celebrates heroes from many Greek lands, including Crete, and the *Odyssey*, with its broad Mediterranean stage, were as much at home in Crete as anywhere else. When spinning tales to deceive those who questioned him on his return to Ithaka, Odysseus identified himself as a Cretan, a vagabond warrior whose travels, often in Phoenician ships, took him everywhere from Troy and Egypt to Phoenicia and Libya (*Odyssey* 13.256–286; 14.199–359; 19.172–202). The fact that all of the bronze lyre-players known from this period are Cretan may be fortuitous, and in one sense they are but further manifestations of the impetus given to sculptural bronze-casting by the arrival of immigrant or itinerant artisans from the East. What is lost is the nature of the songs themselves and any meaningful clue as to their origin or inspiration. The lyre-players from Crete are a reminder that not all of the cultural imports from Asia and Ionia were of a kind to be preserved in the archaeological record.

Although the individual figures in Malibu can be placed within a wider cultural and artistic context, the meaning of the sculpture remains elusive. The reason, of course, is that the man and boy are presented as a pair, and to understand them one must try to discern the nature of their relationship to each other. To suggest the song of a bard or the divine music of Apollo, the musician alone would suffice. If it was a ceremonial dance that was to be perpetuated by a votive offering, an adult dancer, or at least a more animated child, might be expected. The principal enigma is the boy. An interpretation as Hermes has been rejected because of the nature of the lyre, but this might remain a possibility if the artistic license said to explain the paucity of strings can be extended to the shape of the sound box. The identification remains improbable, nor is there any obvious reason why the Cretan-born Zeus should be associated with an *aoidos*; the shield-banging of the Curetes who watched over the infant god scarcely qualifies as music.

Like the bard beside him, the boy is probably mortal, and there is in fact something touchingly human in his aspect and behavior. If viewed in a Homeric vein, certain associations inevitably arise, and one recalls the "boy with a clear-toned lyre," who sings the Linos-song on the shield of Achilles (*Iliad* 18.569). Unlike the self-taught Phemios, most singers must have learned their art as boys at the knees of venerable masters. It may be that this boy is an apprentice, still too young to be represented with the sacred instrument, his duties limited to caring for his master's lyre by oiling the wood and twisting gut for new strings. Whether so humble a beginner would rate portrayal in bronze is questionable, but his touching of the musician calls up further Homeric associations.

Recalling that Homer was said to be blind, and that the sightless Demodokos was helped to his seat by a herald, who later assisted him to the athletic events (*Odyssey* 8.62–70 and 104–108), one could imagine that the singer in Malibu may also be glad of a steadying hand.[49] Blindness could have been more clearly represented with greater detailing of the eyes, perhaps showing them closed, but such subtlety is exactly what is lacking in the fledgling sculpture of the period; some other means of suggesting sightlessness would be necessary. Without Homer, one might not think of interpreting the boy's gesture this way, but it is during this very period, when the poet's fame was spread across the seas, that he *would* have come to mind. Cretan aristocrats, tracing their lineage to heroic ancestors whose deeds were celebrated in songs, would naturally have embraced the Homeric epics, which exalt the breeding and manly *aretē* of the Greeks who sailed to Troy, among whom was the Cretan king Idomeneus. In this context, the little boy evokes also the pederasty so notoriously practiced in Dorian Crete, where a man might abduct a boy with the acquiescence of his family, carrying him off to the hills for a few months before returning him laden with presents.[50] Any depiction of a man and boy together from Dorian Crete must have at least some undercurrent of this practice. It may be only co-

incidence that during this relationship, the boy—the *eromenos*—was referred to as a *parastatheis*, "one posted beside" the older man.[51]

NOTES

*I would like thank Marion True, Curator of Antiquities at the J. Paul Getty Museum, for permitting me to publish the bronze lyre-player and his companion. David Mitten and Jane Carter read an early draft of this article and offered many helpful suggestions; the conclusions are my own, as are any mistakes. Among other individuals who have helped with advice, photographs, or other forms of assistance are Jean-Charles Balty, Michael Bennett, Diane Broderick, K.-V. von Eickstedt, Susan Langdon, Betsy Lewis, Karen Manchester, Sarah Morris, George Ortiz, Judith Nugée, Judith Padgett, and Cornelius Vermeule.

Abbreviations used in this article are the following:

American Private = *Ancient Art in American Private Collections,* exhib. cat., Fogg Art Museum (Cambridge, Mass. 1954).

Blome (1982) = P. Blome, *Die figürliche Bildwelt Kretas in der geometrischen und fr001harchaischen Periode* (Mainz 1982).

Boardman (1978) = J. Boardman, *Greek Sculpture: The Archaic Period* (London 1978).

Boardman (1961) = J. Boardman, *The Cretan Collection at Oxford* (Oxford 1961).

De Ridder (1896) = A. De Ridder, *Catalogue des bronzes trouvés sur l'acropole d'Athènes* (Paris 1896).

Herrmann (1964) = H.-V. Herrmann, "Werkstätten geometrischer Bronzeplastik," *JdI* 79 (1964) 17–71.

Heilmeyer (1972) = W.-D. Heilmeyer, *Frühe olympische Tonfiguren,* OlForsch 7 (Berlin 1972).

Hurwit (1982) = Hurwit, Jeffrey M., "*Thespis Aoiodos:* A Bronze Harper from the James Coats Collection," *Yale University Art Gallery Bulletin* 38:2 (1982) 18–23.

Langdon (1991) = S. Langdon, "A Votive Figurine from Early Crete," *Muse* 25 (1991) 21–29.

Langdon (1993) = S. Langdon, ed., *From Pasture to Polis: Art in the Age of Homer,* (Columbia 1993).

Lebessi (1980) = A. Lebessi, "Chalkino geometriko eidolio apo ten Krete," in *Stele. Tomos eis mnemen Nikolaou Kontoleontos* (Athens 1980) 87–95.

Maas and Snyder (1989) = M. Maas and J. M. Snyder,

Stringed Instruments of Ancient Greece (New Haven and London 1989).

Naumann (1976) = U. Naumann, *Subminoische und protogeometrische Bronzeplastik auf Kreta,* AthMitt Beiheft 6 (Berlin 1976).

Rolley (1969) = C. Rolley, *Les statuettes de Bronze,* FdD V (Paris 1969).

Schefold (1964) = K. Schefold, *Frühgriechische Sagenbilder* (Munich 1964).

Schweitzer (1971) = B. Schweitzer, *Greek Geometric Art* (London 1971).

Wegner (1968) = M. Wegner, *Musik und Tanz,* ArchHom 3.U (Göttingen 1968).

1. J. Paul Getty Museum, inv. 90.AB.6. Height: 0.115 m. Published: *The J. Paul Getty Museum Journal* 19 (1991) 136–137, no. 8; J. M. Padgett, in Langdon (1993) 239–241, no. 101.

The group is intact and undamaged, with traces of brown incrustation confined to recessed areas. The surface has a thin, lustrous patina, more black than green. According to an internal museum report of January 10, 1990, prepared by Martina Edelmann, "Microscopic examination of this surface reveals a deep corrosion layer, and the thin layer of cuprite between this layer and the uncorroded metal of the body indicates that the patina developed naturally over centuries."

2. For bronze figurines acting as ring-holders on Geometric tripods, see S. Papaspyridi-Karouzou, "Chalkinon agalmation ek tes Akropoleos," *ArchEph* (1952) 137–149; Schweitzer (1971) 140–143; and Herrmann (1964) 56–62, figs. 49–57.

3. At Olympia, an early eighth-century bronze of a man and a horse was attached to the top of a tripod ring (inv. B 4567), but as with the single horses that more normally crown the rings, there is no base-plate; see Herrmann (1964) 45, fig. 30; and Schweitzer (1971) 154–155, pls. 191–192. It is likely that some of the "horse-leaders" of the second and third quarter of the century also stood on rings, but these too have bases of a different design; see Herrmann (1964) 47, figs. 31–32, and p. 54, figs. 45–48; and Schweitzer (1971) 131–133, pls. 125 and 132–139.

4. For plektrons, see K. Schneider, "Plectrum," *RE,* Series 2. vol. 21, part 1, 187–189. The canonical plektron shape is perhaps best exemplified by the ivory examples from the sanctuary of Artemis Orthia at Sparta; R. M. Dawkins, *The Sanctuary of Artemis Orthia at Sparta* (London 1929), pl. 167A. Schneider thinks the plektron was unknown in Homer's day, but Maas and Snyder believe it was known as early as the Late Bronze Age, pointing to the object held by the lyre-player on the Ayia Triadha sarcophagus, and to the article suspended from a lyre on a lost seal from Knossos; Maas and Snyder (1989), 3, 16–17, figs. 2a and 2d. In neither case is the object clearly a plektron, but there is less doubt about the object hanging from a lyre on an early Protoattic hydria fragment in Berlin (inv. 31573); Maas and Snyder (1989) 22, fig. 10.

5. Cf. the incised eyelashes on Athens NM 6620, from the Acropolis: De Ridder (1896) 241–242, fig. 211, no. 694.

6. Similar ears occur on other seventh-century bronze figures from Crete: *e.g.* University of Missouri, Museum of Art and Archaeology, inv. 69.950; and Oxford, Ashmolean inv. AE.16. For the Missouri figure, see Langdon (1991) 22, fig. 1; and Langdon (1993) 142–144. For the Oxford bronze, see Boardman (1961), pl. 44, no. 523; and Langdon (1991) 25, fig. 5.

7. The braids would seem to preclude any identification of these head coverings as hats; the caps of wool or leather worn by cowherds and other rustic characters in later representations are more peaked in form.

8. In the Delphi Museum are at least four Geometric bronze statuettes of females: (1) Inv. 3144 (wearing a peplos): Schweitzer (1971) 131, pl. 124; Rolley (1969) 28–29, pl. 4, no. 8. (2) Inv. 7730 (nude): Schweitzer (1971), 131, pls. 130–131; Herrmann (1964) 48, figs. 33–35; Rolley (1969) 17, pl. I, no. 1. (3) Inv. 3938 (nude): Rolley (1969) 49–50, pl. X, no. 33. (4) Inv. 2617 (wearing a belt with a spiral ornament): Rolley (1969) 44–45, pl. IX, no. 26. At least one bronze nude female in Geometric style was found on the Athenian Acropolis, Athens NM 6503: Herrmann (1964) 49, figs. 36–38; De Ridder (1896) 294–295, fig. 279, no. 771. For bronze figurines of women riding sidesaddle on horseback, or dancing in circular groups, see Schweitzer (1971) 155–159, pls. 193–196. Belted females are rare; in addition to the example from Delphi, noted above, a terracotta woman from Olympia may have a painted belt, inv. Tc 2762: Heilmeyer (1972) 116, pl. 35, no. 208.

9. Later Cretan sculptures in the Daedalic style, perhaps influenced by Phoenician or Syrian models, do represent nude women, but not little girls—e.g., the reliefs on the temple of Apollo at Gortyn: Boardman (1978), fig. 31. Contrast the representation of children on a Boiotian Geometric pithos in the Thebes Museum (inv. Be469): between a lyre-player and a group of dancing women, a nude boy stands next to a little girl wearing a dress; A. Ruckert, *Frühe Keramik Böotiens* (Bern 1976) pl. 16, 3; and K. Demakopoulou and D. Konsola, *Archaeological Museum of Thebes* (Athens 1981) 57, pl. 28.

10. For Cretan Protogeometric bronze males with pellet breasts, see Naumann (1976) pl. 28, 1 and pl. 30, 3. Among Late Geometric examples, cf. a votary from Kato Syme: A. Lebessi and P. Muhly, "The Sanctuary of Hermes and Aphrodite at Syme, Crete" *National Geographic Research* 3 (1987)

109, fig. 11; and *AR* 1978–1979, 38, fig. 50. For a mainland example, cf. an early seventh-century "Zeus" from Thessaly (Volos Museum, inv. 750): H. Biesantz, *Die thessalischen Grabreliefs* (Mainz 1965) pl. 56, no. L80. For terracotta males from Olympia with pellet breasts instead of the more usual circular incisions, see Heilmeyer (1972) pl. 27, no. 168, and pl. 34, no. 203.

11. Cf. the pubic hair on an early seventh-century bronze warrior in the Delphi Museum (inv. 3232): Schweitzer (1971) 145–146, pls. 174–175; Herrmann (1964) 67, fig. 62; Rolley (1969) 35–38, pl. VI, no. 15.

12. Judging solely by style, a later date seems unlikely; compare, for example, the more naturalistic modeling of the face, breasts, and clavicles of Athens NM 6618, a pre-Daedalic, seventh-century bronze male from the Acropolis: Herrmann (1964) 67, fig. 61; De Ridder (1896) 246, fig. 216, no. 699.

13. *Deer and fawn*—Museum of Fine Arts, Boston, inv. 98.650: M. Comstock and C. Vermeule, *Greek, Etruscan & Roman Bronzes in the Museum of Fine Arts, Boston* (Boston 1971) 5, no. 3; Schweitzer [1971] pl. 189; Boardman (1978) fig. 9; D. Mitten, "The Earliest Greek Sculptures in the Museum," *BMFA* 65 (1967) 13, figs. 12–15. *Man and ram*—Harvard University Art Museums, inv. 1970.26: D. Mitten, *Fogg Museum Acquisitions* (1969–1970) 71; and Langdon (1993) 148–150, no. 51.

14. *Lion hunt*—formerly Samos Museum, inv. B 190: Schweitzer (1971) 151–152, pls. 186–187; Boardman (1978), fig. 12. A similar hunt group, described by Schweitzer (p. 152), is now in the Ortiz collection, Geneva; see C. Rolley, *Les Bronzes grecs* (Fribourg 1983) 59, fig. 35; and *The George Ortiz Collection,* exhib. cat. Hermitage Museum (St. Petersburg 1993) no. 83. *Centauromachy*—New York, Metropolitan Museum, inv. 17.190.2072: Schweitzer (1971) 150–151, pl. 185; Boardman (1978), fig. 13; J. Mertens, "Greek Bronzes in the Metropolitan Museum of Art," *BMMA* 43 : 2 (fall 1985) 18–19, no. 7.

15. For examples of Syrian and Levantine bronze groups, see *The Pomerance Collection of Ancient Art,* exhib. cat., Brooklyn Museum of Art (Brooklyn 1966) 24, no. 18, and Langdon (1993) 133–134, no. 42. For an example of paired figures from Italy, see *Wealth of the Ancient World: The Nelson Bunker Hunt and William Herbert Hunt Collections,* exhib. cat., Kimbell Art Museum (Fort Worth 1983) 94, no. 20.

16. The warrior and driver in a votive chariot from Olympia (inv. B 1671) stand side by side, but do not touch; see Schweitzer (1971) 146, pl. 178; and Palmer (infra) 67, fig. 6. For the "Zeus and Hera" in the Museum of Fine Arts, Boston (inv. 63.2755), see Comstock and Vermeule (supra n. 13) 4, no. 2; Mitten (supra n. 13, 1967) 12, fig. 11; Langdon (1993)

130–133; and H. Palmer, "A Lord and Lady from Olympia," *BMFA* 56 (1958) 64–68. A belted bronze male of eighth-century date, in the Ortiz collection, has the hand of a missing second figure on his back; it has been suggested that both were wrestlers; see D. Vanhove, ed., *Le Sport dans la Grèce antique,* exhib. cat., Palais des Beaux-Arts (Brussels 1992) 337, no. 205.

17. For the pair from Syme (Herakleion Museum, inv. 3137), see A. Lebessi, "A Sanctuary of Hermes and Aphrodite in Crete," *Expedition* vol. 18, no. 3 (spring 1976) p. 4, fig. 4; and A. Lebessi, *Prakt* 1972, pl. 188d. Another bronze male from Syme may have shared his rectangular base with a second figure, now lost; see *Ergon* 1981, 69, pl. 114.

18. *Codpiece*—e.g., New York, Metropolitan Museum of Art, inv. 1972.118.45: *American Private,* pl. 35, no. 129; and J. Mertens, in *Greek Art of the Aegean Islands,* exhib. cat. Metropolitan Museum of Art (New York 1979) 92, no. 46. For an example in terracotta, from Petsofa, see M. Andronicos, *Herakleion Museum* (Athens 1985) 58, fig. 47. *Triangular loincloth*—e.g., Andronicos (supra) 59, fig. 50. *Kilt*—e.g., Ortiz Collection (supra n. 14) nos. 60–61; Boardman (1961) pl. 1.3.

19. For a Subminoan example, cf. Vienna, Kunsthistorishes Museum, inv. 2552: Naumann (1976) pl. 1.2. For an example of Protogeometric date, cf. Herakleion Museum, inv. Br. 2308; Naumann (1976) pl. 32.

20. See Langdon (1991) figs. 1–4, for several belted, nude male votive figurines from Crete.

21. *Ram-bearer*—Berlin, Staatliche Museen inv. 7477: Boardman (1978), fig. 45; Blome (1982), pl. 22, 1; and P. Blome, *Dädalische Kunst auf Kreta im 7. Jahrhunderts v. Chr.,* exhib. cat., Museum für Kunst und Gewerbe (Hamburg 1970) 46–48, pls. 18–19 and color pl. II. A similar belt and loincloth are worn by an ivory male statuette from the Samian Heraion, which Vierneisel and Walter identified as a South Phoenician import of the seventh century; H. Walter and K. Vierneisel, "Ägyptische und orientalische Funde aus Brunnen G und dem Bothros," *AthMitt* 74 (1959) 40–41, pl. 84.3. Kyrieleis has suggested that this ivory is Mycenaean, but the figure still seems Oriental in character, despite the crown; see H. Kyrieleis, "Eine mykenische Elfenbeinfigur aus dem Heraion von Samos," *Festschrift für Nikolaus Himmelmann* (Mainz 1989) 11–21, pl. 2.

22. Apollo from Dreros: Boardman (1978) 11 and 32, fig. 16; Blome (1982), pl. 4; Lebessi (1980), pl. 26β–γ; S. Marinatos, "Ausgrabungen und Funde auf Kreta 1935–1936," *AA* (1936) 215–222, figs. 2–3; I. Beyer, *Die Tempel von Dreros und Prinias A* (Freiburg 1976) 154–156, pls. 47 and 51.4–5.

23. Statuette from Afrati: H. W. Catling, *AR* (1973–1974) 36–37, fig. 76; Boardman (1978) 11 and 33, fig. 17; Lebessi

(1980) 91, pls. 25–26α. The figures from Dreros have sometimes been dated to the seventh century; e.g., K. Schefold, in C. Davaras, *Die Statue aus Astritsi,* AntK-BH 8 (Bern 1972) 3; and G. Rizza and V. Santa Maria Scrinari, *Il Santuario sull'Acropoli di Gortina I* (Rome 1968) 224–225, 242, and 272. However, Boardman's suggestion that the figures could date much earlier, based on the resemblance between the Apollo and the gold kriophoros from Khaniale Tekke, is supported by the eighth-century context of the Afrati bronze: Boardman (1961) 137; and Boardman (1978) 11. Beyer (supra n. 22) also favors an eighth-century date for the Dreros bronzes. Coldstream dates the Dreros Apollo, the Afrati bronze, and the Tekke Kriophoros to about 700 B.C.: J. N. Coldstream, *Geometric Greece* (New York 1977) 284. According to Boardman and Coldstream, the greater naturalism and general precocity of these bronzes when compared to contemporary mainland works is due to the influence of Oriental metalworkers who emigrated to Crete in the late ninth century and produced the sophisticated gold jewelry found at Khaniale Tekke and the repoussé bronzes from Fortetsa; see Boardman (1978) 11–12; Coldstream, *Geometric Greece,* 100 and 284; and J. Boardman, "The Khaniale Tekke Tombs, II," *BSA* 62 (1967) 57–75.

24. Most of the belted males illustrated by Langdon have either bowl haircuts or skullcaps: Langdon (1991), figs. 1–3. Langdon interprets them as caps, and it is in fact difficult to be certain about the examples she discusses. The braids on the Getty figures, however, and the clearly incised hair on the Dreros and Afrati figures, are conclusive proof that hair was cut in this distinctive, bowl-shaped fashion in Crete. When braids or incision are not clearly indicated, as on the belted male in Missouri (supra n. 6), or an early seventh-century running man (nude and belted) in the Ortiz collection (*Ortiz Collection* [supra n. 14] no. 87), it may still be hair and not a cap that is represented.

25. In some cases, a loincloth or bowl haircut alone may indicate a possible Cretan origin. The garments worn by a lost wooden "Zeus" from Samos and by a bronze statuette of a male from the Athenian Acropolis suggest Cretan influence if not actual origin. For the Zeus, see Boardman (1978), fig. 50; and D. Ohly, "Holz," *AthMitt* 68 (1953) 77–83, Beil. 13–15. For the Acropolis bronze (inv. 6619), see De Ridder (1896) 243–244, fig. 213, no. 696; Blome (1982), pl. 21.1–3; and G. Kaulen, *Daidalika* (Munich 1967), pls. 1–3.

26. Herakleion Museum, inv. 2064 (H. 0.055 m.): Schweitzer (1971) 161, pl. 203, Maas and Snyder (1989) 9 and 20, fig. 6; Boardman (1978), fig. 43; D. Levi, *ASAtene* 10–12 (1927–1929) 541–542, fig. 609; Hurwit [1982] 22–23, figs. 7–8).

27. Schweitzer (1971) 161, placed it in the third quarter of

the eighth century and thought it "obviously Cretan." Maas and Snyder (1989) 9 call it "ninth- or eighth-century." Boardman (1978), fig. 43 prefers a date in the early seventh century, and finds it "hard to say whether the little lyre-player is an easterner or a Cretan" (p. 16). I would date it around 700 to 690 B.C., a little earlier than the figures in Malibu.

28. Hurwit (1982) passim; and Langdon (1993) 76–78, no. 17. The figure, formerly in the Coats collection and on loan to Yale, is now in the Leon Levy and Shelby White collection, New York. The height is 4.5 cm. Langdon dates it 750–700 B.C. and suggests a similar date for the Herakleion musician.

29. For the seated figures holding objects to their mouths, see Schweitzer (1971) 160, pls. 197 and 199; M. True, in *The Gods Delight: The Human Figure in Classical Bronze,* exhib. cat., Cleveland Museum of Art (Cleveland 1988) 48–51, no. 1; and S. Langdon, "From Monkey to Man: The Evolution of a Geometric Sculptural Type," *AJA* 94 (1990) 407–424.

30. For "bottle-stopper" pendants, see Schweitzer (1971) 160–161; Langdon (supra n. 29) 160–161; Langdon (1993) 112–114, no. 32; U. Jantzen, "Geometrische Kannenverschlüsse," *AA* (1953) 56–67; I. Kilian-Dirlmeier, *Anhänger in Griechenland von der mykenischen bis zur spätgeometrischen Zeit* (Munich 1979) 194–208, pls. 61–73; and D. Metzler, "Zum Schamanismus in Griechenland," in *Antidoron. Festschrift für Jürgen Thimme* (Karlsruhe 1983) 75–82. It is now generally accepted that these curious objects were worn as pendants; see M. Vickers, "Some Early Iron Age Bronzes from Macedonia," in *ARCHAIA MAKEDONIA* II (Thessaloniki 1977) 18–19.

31. Schweitzer (1971) 160 thinks the figures are drinking wine, and follows Buschor in suggesting they might be early satyrs; see E. Buschor, *Satyrtänze und frühes Drama* (Munich 1943) 9. True (supra n. 29) 50 agrees with Jantzen that the object is too small to be a flute and is the wrong shape. That could not be said, however, of the long, narrow object "played" by a seated man formerly in the Pomerance collection; *Pomerance Collection* (supra n. 15) 79, no. 89; Langdon (1993) 153–154, no. 54. Langdon's argument (supra n. 29) that the bronzes were inspired by Egyptian amulets of monkeys and baboons is convincing, but I am less convinced that they should be understood as an intentional mixture of human and simian elements, never becoming "purely human" in the hands of Greek artists.

32. Among numerous examples, cf. a kitharist by the Berlin Painter in the Metropolitan Museum (inv. 56.171.38); J. Boardman, *Athenian Red Figure Vases: The Archaic Period* (Oxford 1975), fig. 152.2; *ARV²* 197.3.

33. For example, by Maas and Snyder (1989) 13; Hurwit (1982) 21; and M. Wegner, *Das Musikleben der Griechen*

(Berlin 1949) 29–30. On present evidence, there is little justification for the further assumption of Maas and Snyder that because the Homeric epics reflect the traditions of the Bronze Age, *phorminx* was also the name of the lyres depicted in Mycenaean art. Cf. essay by Carter in this volume.

34. Among the doubters is D. D. Feaver, "Musical Scenes on a Greek Vase," *Muse* 2 (1968) 18 and 20, n. 18. For Homer's use of *phorminx, kitharis, phormizō,* and *kitharizō,* see Hurwit (1982) 18–20.

35. For a summary of these variations, see Maas and Snyder (1989) 12–13. The *phorminx* with rounded sound box may be ancestral to the so-called cradle-kithara; for the type, see A. Bélis, "À propos de la coupe CA 482 du Louvre," *BCH* 116 (1992) 53–59. A few vase paintings show lyres with pointed or flat bases, differences fundamental enough perhaps to warrant different classifications. The lyre on a sherd from the Argive Heraion has a flat base and a sound box that extends upward to form two wide flat arms; Maas and Snyder (1989) 23, fig. 13. Maas and Snyder may be right in seeing in this instrument the ancestor of the kithara, although it is difficult to accept their suggestion that this line of development should also include the lyres with pointed bases on Athens 18542 and Copenhagen 9367 (Maas and Snyder [1989] 13 and 21, fig. 8). The vase paintings are schematic, and we are often left in doubt as to how certain instruments should be classified. The instrument on a hydria in Cambridge (Museum of Classical Archaeology, inv. 345) has the general shape of a tortoiseshell lyre, but the sound box has a hole in the center; Wegner (1968) 76, no. 72, pl. IIb. The lyre on Basel Bs 406 has a pointed base, but differs in shape from the pointed examples mentioned above (Wegner [1968] 75, no. 61, pl. IIIb).

36. *Hymn to Hermes* 51. Boardman suggests the seven-stringed lyre was a seventh-century Lydian innovation, citing vase paintings from Smyrna and Pitane: J. Boardman, *The Greeks Overseas,* 3rd ed. (London 1980) 97–98, fig. 111. Strabo 13.2.4 quotes a song of Terpander in which he gives himself credit for increasing the number of strings from four to seven, and that too accords with a seventh-century date. Nonetheless, Geometric representations are a poor basis for assuming, as West does, that "the epic bard's established instrument was the one with four strings only"; see M. L. West, "The Singing of Homer and the Modes of Early Greek Music," *JHS* 101 (1981) 116.

37. *Odyssey* 8.257; *Hymn to Hermes* 64. See Hurwit (1982) 21.

38. For the Brussels lyre-player, see R. Tolle, *Frühgriechische Reingentanzen* (Waldsassen 1964), fig. 27b. Even in the later seventh century, bronze lyre-players are scarce; Lebessi 1976 (supra n. 17) 7 mentions an early Daedalic example from Kato Syme. Some of the small lead votive lyres and lyre-players from the sanctuary of Artemis Orthia at Sparta date to the seventh century; with one exception (pl. 189.7), the lyres are of the tortoiseshell variety; see Dawkins (supra n. 4), pls. 180.19, 183.18–20, and 189.10–11. A bronze statuette of a lyre-player formerly in the Geneva art market, described as seventh century, may not be Greek; see Christie's, Geneva, May 5, 1979, pl. 4, no. 20. The most numerous class of Geometric lyre-players is the schematic musicians on engraved sealstones of the "Lyre-Player Group," produced in North Syria or Cilicia in the second half of the eighth century and distributed throughout the Greek world by Euboean traders; see J. Boardman and G. Buchner, "Seals from Ischia and the Lyre-Player Group," *JdI* 81 (1966) 1–62; and J. Boardman, "The Lyre-Player Group of Seals: An Encore," *AA* (1990) 1–17.

39. Flute-player from Psychro: Lebessi (1980), pl. 29γ–δ. Lebessi rightly draws a parallel with the eighth-century limestone head from Amnisos (pl. 29α), but what may be hair on the Amnisos head is clearly a piloslike cap on the Psychro figure.

40. Syrinx-player in the Ortiz collection, Geneva: *American Private,* 30, pl. 57, no. 195 (where the owner suggests a Peloponnesian origin); and W. Rudolph and A. Calinescu, eds., *Ancient Art from the V. G. Simkhovich Collection* (Bloomington 1988) 82, no. 55. The pose, the well-proportioned head, the shape of the stool, and the presence of a base-plate all suggest a development from the earlier mainland "flute-players" rather than any connection with the lyre-players from Crete.

41. For example, by Coldstream (supra n. 23) 280.

42. I know of no certain depiction of Apollo as lyre-player earlier than his appearance on a polychrome krater from Melos of the third quarter of the seventh century (Athens NM 911); see Schefold (1964) pl. 10; and D. von Bothmer, in *Greek Art of the Aegean Islands* (supra n. 18) 122–124, no. 71. The identification of the damaged lyre-player on the Middle Protoattic "Oresteia Krater" (once E. Berlin, inv. A 32; *CVA* Berlin 1, pls. 18–21) is uncertain. For the difficulty of identifying gods by their attributes, see F. Brommer, "Gott oder Mensch," *JdI* 101 (1986) 37–53; and B. Ridgway, "Birds, 'meniskoi,' and head attributes in Archaic Greece," *AJA* 94 (1990) 584–585.

43. For a good summary of lyres and lyre-players in Homer, see Maas and Snyder (1989) 3–7 and 10–11. See also A. B. Lord, in A. J. B. Wace and F. H. Stubbings, *A Companion to Homer* (London 1962) 182–185.

44. For dancers and musicians in Geometric vase painting, see Wegner (1968) passim; R. Tolle (supra n. 38) passim; and Maas and Snyder (1989) 11–12.

45. Interior of a skyphos, Athens NM 874: B. Borell, *Attisch geometrische Schalen* (Mainz 1978), pl. 14, 62; and *The*

Human Figure in Early Greek Art, exhib. cat. National Gallery of Art (Washington, D.C. 1987) 80–81, no. 13.

46. Athens, Acrop. 291: Wegner (1968) 71, no. 23, pl. IVc; B. Graef and E. Langlotz, *Die antiken Vasen von der Akropolis zu Athen* I (Berlin 1925), pl. 11, no. 303. A fragment from the Athenian Agora (inv. P 10201) may be from a similar scene. Three adults stand around a boy, who is apparently clapping his hands. The adult at left seems to hold the boy aloft by his lower legs. Brann identified the subject as Neoptolemos killing Astyanax; Friis Johansen and Schefold agree. Fittschen, however, restores the two adults at right as an aulist and lyre-player, and the child as a participant in a processional dance. The aulist, whose bent elbows are preserved, is convincingly reconstructed, but the lyre-player is much more speculative. Moreover, the reconstruction shows the adult at left holding the boy at an awkward angle, with their bodies not touching. On the basis of the Acropolis fragment, I would restore a low platform below the boy's feet. See E. Brann, "A Figured Geometric Fragment from the Athenian Agora," *AntK* 2 (1959) 35–37; E. Brann, *The Athenian Agora VIII: Late Geometric and Protoattic Pottery* (Princeton 1962) 66, pl. 18, no. 311; K. Friis Johansen, *The Iliad in Early Greek Art* (Copenhagen 1967) 30–31, fig. 2b; Schefold (1964) 25, fig. 2; and K. Fittschen, *Untersuchungen zum Beginn der Sagendarstellungen bei den Griechen* (Berlin 1969) 23, no. A12, fig. 11. For another example of children at the dance, cf. those on the pithos in Thebes (supra n. 9).

47. Another challenging dance is represented on a Geometric kantharos in Copenhagen (Nat. Mus. 727), with a lyre-player accompanying two dancers balancing jugs on their heads; Wegner (1968) 79, no. 99, pl. VIb. More distant geographically, but perhaps closer in date to the Getty bronze, is an Etruscan amphora of c. 670 B.C. in the Fujita collection, with a lyre-player accompanying two tumbling acrobats; M. Martelli, ed., *La Ceramica degli Etruschi* (Novara 1987) 92, fig. 38.

48. The Blinding of Polyphemos appears not only on a Middle Protoattic neck-amphora in the Eleusis Museum, but also on a krater fragment from Argos and on the Aristonothos Krater from Caere, all of about 670–650 B.C. The same subject is depicted on a large, unpublished, red impasto pithos of a type made in Cerveteri around mid-century, now in the Fleischman collection, New York. For the vase in Eleusis, the name vase of the Polyphemos Painter, see Schefold (1964), pl. 16; and S. P. Morris, *The Black and White Style* (New Haven 1984) 44–45, pl. 6; for the fragment in the Argos Museum

(inv. C 149), see P. Courbin, "Un fragment de cratère protoargien," *BCH* 79 (1955) 1–49; O. Touchefeu-Meynier, *Thèmes odysséens dans l'art antique* (Paris 1968) 11, no. 2, pl. I.2; and *Human Figure* (supra n. 45) 96–97, no. 21; for the Aristonothos Krater, in the Palazzo dei Conservatori, see B. Schweitzer, "Zum Krater des Aristonothos," *RM* 62 (1955) 78–106; and Touchefeu-Meynier 10–11, no. 1, pl. I.1. The name vase of the Ram Jug Painter, of about 670–650 B.C., with Odysseus and companions escaping from the cave of Polyphemos, is Middle Protoattic but was apparently made on Aigina; see Morris, *Black and White Style,* 51–53, pl. 10; Schefold (1964) pl. 37; *Human Figure* (supra n. 45), 97–99, no. 22; and J. D. Beazley, *The Development of Attic Black-figure,* rev. ed. (Berkeley 1986) 8–9, pl. 9, figs. 1–2. A late eighth-century Rhodian skyphos with an incised verse inscription comparing itself to the cup of Nestor was found at Pithekoussai, the earliest Greek colony in Italy; G. Buchner and C. F. Russo, "La coppa di Nestore e un'inscrizione metrica da Pitecusa dell' VIII secolo av. Cr.," *RendLinc* (1955) 215–234; and Boardman (supra n. 36) 167, fig. 205.

49. I know of no representation of a child helping a blind bard, but on two Apulian vases by the Darius Painter, a boy assists the blind seer Teiresias: calyx-krater, Museum of Fine Arts, Boston, inv. 1989.100: *RVAp* Suppl. II, vol. 1, p. 151, no. 65b; J. M. Padgett et al., *Vase-Painting in Italy: Red-Figure and Related Works in the Museum of Fine Arts, Boston* (Boston 1993) 119–121, no. 43. Oinochoe, Antikenmuseum, Basel, inv. BS 473; *RVAp,* II 503, no. 73a; and K. Schefold and F. Jung, *Die Sagen von den Argonauten, von Theben und Troja in der klassischen und hellenistischen Kunst* (Munich 1989) 66, fig. 46.

50. Strabo 10.4.21, who quotes an earlier account by Ephoros (*FGrH* 70F 149). For pederasty and homosexuality in Crete, see K. J. Dover, *Greek Homosexuality* (Cambridge, Mass. 1978) 185–190.

51. Strabo 10.4.21. R. B. Koehl has interpreted the two youths on the so-called Chieftain Cup from Hagia Triada as participants in a similar Bronze Age rite of passage: "The Chieftain Cup and a Minoan Rite of Passage," *JHS* 106 (1986) 99–110. Koehl suggests (p. 107) that the bronze pair from Kato Syme (supra n. 17) represent a young *parastatheis* and his older lover. It is difficult to see the lyre-player in the Getty as a lusty hunter and abductor of boys, but the group may be one artist's variation of what may be called the *parastatheis* type.

24

EARLY IMAGES OF DAIDALOS IN FLIGHT *

♦

ERIKA SIMON

And on it the renowned, ambidextrous artist inlaid a
   dance,
like the one which once in broad Knossos
Daidalos crafted for Ariadne of the lovely hair.

Iliad 18.590–592

In a number of significant contributions, Emily Vermeule has woven the many threads which run between Minoan Crete and the Helladic mainland into a fascinating tapestry. One creature of legend who communicates between the two regions is Daidalos. Beyond these connections he links the Minoan-Mycenaean Aegean with the West: with Sicily, the Apennine peninsula, and with Sardinia.[1] Hence no wonder that Jacob Nyenhuis' recent treatment of the iconography of Daidalos included several Etruscan representations of him and his son, Ikaros.[2] But who would have expected the earliest inscribed image of Daidalos known thus far to appear on a bucchero olpe? It emerged in 1988 in a grave at Cerveteri and comes from a local workshop of the third quarter of the seventh century B.C. (fig. 24.1).[3] Next to other images on the olpe, a winged man moving to the left in *Knielauf* formula with upraised arms is labelled TAI-

TALE, the early Etruscan name for Daidalos. Later syncopation turns this into TAITLE, as he is called on scarabs of the Classical style.[4] On these he can appear with wings, hurrying across the sea with axe and saw,[5] or wingless, bending with an amphora to a fountain.[6] This last scene, on a scarab from the Dressel collection (now lost), has also been interpreted as the underworld punishment of Tantalos, but unnecessarily. For Daidalos is credited with various hydraulic engineering works in Sicily, such as the reservoir from the springs of the river Alabon near Megara Hyblaea and the natural hot springs within caves in the region of Selinus (Diod. 4.78). The Etruscan gem-engraver must have addressed himself to these Sicilian traditions. However, Daidalos the architect and engineer plays no role in this essay, which focuses on Daidalos as sculptor and carpenter, and as the first man who rose into the air on artificial plumage, hence provided with wings on the vases discussed here.

A few years ago Brian Cook assembled a list of Archaic representations of a winged man purported by many scholars to be Aristaios.[7] This derived from an idea of Semni Karouzou's, developed in the publication of an olpe from Vari by the Ceramicus Painter.[8] J. D.

407

Beazley had initially named the winged figure hurrying across the olpe Daidalos, but later retracted:[9] "I accept Mrs. Karouzou's interpretation of the winged figure as Aristaios . . . in preference to my own tentative conjecture, Daidalos." His earlier interpretation is here to be vindicated; it seems in every respect to be the better alternative. Moreover, after closer analysis, none of the winged creatures designated as Aristaios in the *LIMC* article can carry this name any longer.[10]

The chief argument which Semni Karouzou mustered against Beazley was the instrument held in the right hand of this winged figure, who is unfortunately never named by an inscription.[11] Beazley saw this instrument with handle as a *skeparnon*, a tool for wood-

working, which would be appropriate to the image of Daidalos as wood-carver and carpenter.[12] Karouzou explains this object as an agricultural tool, of a type still in use in modern Greece. The sharp end of the horizontal part grafted to the handle would serve as a type of pick, the blunt end for breaking up clods of earth.[13] Accordingly, Cook usually calls the attribute of his "Aristaeus" figures an "agricultural implement," even when he observes that it does not always display the asymmetrical shape of the object on the Vari olpe. Instead, it can be pointed on both ends[14] or double-bladed, a double axe (figs. 24.3–24.4). Its variation in width resembles that of the instruments of Daidalos which surround the figure of Ikaros on an early Hellenistic mirror from central It-

FIGURE 24.1. Daidalos with large wings; TAITALE inscribed to right of back. Bucchero olpe from Caere (Cerveteri), third quarter of the seventh century B.C. (Reproduced by kind permission of Marina Martelli, Rome/ Viterbo.)

aly.[15] But, to return to the Archaic world, Beazley had already invoked the instrument held by the artist carving a herm on the tondo of the cup by Epiktetos in Copenhagen. Karouzou's objection, that the crosspiece on this instrument was too short, can be easily overruled with the help of the cup tondo by the Carpenter Painter in London.[16] The herm-carver's instrument has simply been truncated by the reserved band encircling the tondo, just as the same border, on the lower left of the tondo, cuts off the back leg of the stool on which the young artist is seated. He is also using a different, unshafted instrument, presumably for smoothing the surface of the nearly completed wooden herm. One wonders whether such objects are stored in the bag carried by figures who have been identified as Aristaios (figs. 24.2–24.5). While this cannot be verified, even less likely are the hypothetical alabastra of milk, honey, and oil which Karouzou assumes to be stored in them.[17]

Thus the attributes of our winged creature cannot be certified as tools for cultivation, and with them collapses the argument for the agricultural hero Aristaios, son of Apollo and the nymph Kyrene.[18] Since wood is one of the most important materials in which Daidalos is reputed to have worked—as the first creator of *xoana*—the presence of a *skeparnon* in his hand makes sense. To this one can add the evidence of a saw, visible on an Italian black-figured amphora in Kiel (fig. 24.2) which represents Daidalos in flight with Ikaros, where the craftsman wields both *skeparnon* and saw, the latter an instrument which he invented.[19] Father and son are here shown in full flight rather than in *Knielauf* as on the black-figured sherd with an inscribed "Ikaros" from the Athenian Acropolis.[20]

Only one of the winged figures identified as Aristaios by Cook does not appear in *Knielauf*: the one on an ivory relief in London presumed to be of Lakonian manufacture (fig. 24.5). This object, like the bucchero olpe (fig. 24.1), stems from the third quarter of the seventh century B.C.[21] Since the art of flight belongs among the proverbial inventions of Daidalos, the *Knielauf* position, in which he rushes through the air like a winged daimon, may be as characteristic an attribute as the instruments he carries. Like those on "real" Archaic daimons, his wings can spring from his chest, back, or hips.[22] Actual winged shoes are sometimes shown, too.[23] They can be put on and removed like the artificial wings

FIGURE 24.2. Daidalos and Ikaros (both bearded) in flight with carpenter's utensils. Italian black-figure amphora: Kiel, Antikensammlung, Inv. B 700. (Museum photograph, with kind permission of Konrad Schauenburg.)

attached to the upper body, which appear in fact on one of the images claimed as Aristaios. This is a Boiotian alabastron in Bonn (figs. 24.3–24.4) which belongs to the successors of the Early Corinthian alabastra and must have been made around 570 B.C.[24] The young man with long hair and beard depicted here wears cross straps over his chest, to which his wings are presumably fastened.

Even genuinely supernatural beings can wear such detachable wings, like the four creatures with snakes on the well-known helmet in the Schimmel collection.[25] Because of their wings attached with leather straps these figures were once interpreted as Daidalos and Ikaros, especially since the helmet is itself a Cretan work of art.[26] However, this interpretation has since been rejected, with justification. But to call it a purely artistic convention without intrinsic meaning[27] seems questionable. Why not imagine these daimons putting on and removing their upper wings as they do their winged sandals, which they wear on the same helmet? Hermes himself provides a suitable precedent in Homer, where he puts on his wind-swift shoes for the flight to Kalypso's island (*Odyssey* 5.44ff.). If the Cretan daimons on the helmet are represented as dancing,[28] they could have put on their wings for this activity. Or perhaps the wings on their bodies and feet are a reference to the speed with which they seize and tame the snakes in their hands.

FIGURES 24.3 – 24.4. Winged Daidalos with double axe and bucket. Boiotian Corinthianizing alabastron in Bonn, c. 570 B.C. Bonn, Akademisches Kunstmuseum, Inv. 604. (Museum photographs, with kind permission of Nikolaus Himmelmann.)

And perhaps the legend of man-made wings built by Daidalos for himself and Ikaros on Crete is connected to dances customary there. The phenomenon of wings needs to be understood on a broader basis, as Sarah Morris attempts in her new book on Daidalos.

What does seem certain to me, in all of this, is that the artificially winged creature on the Boiotian alabastron in Bonn (figs. 24.3–24.4) is Daidalos, as Konrad Schauenburg has also recognized.[29] This Corinthianizing Daidalos carries a double axe in his right hand, while only the handle of the object he carries in his left is visible. The rest has worn away, but probably cannot be restored in length to resemble the bag on the olpe from Vari or on the ivory relief (fig. 24.5), since the rosette ornament in front of the left foot of the creature in motion fills the field. In the same scene on two Atticizing Boiotian tripod-cothons (*exaleiptra*) in Athens and New York, the handles of this instrument do not meet its upper rim but emerge from two holes in its "side" (fig. 24.6).[30] Semni Karouzou assumes some kind of clay vessel in the shape of an alabastron, once again as a container for honey or oil, but the object in question does not resemble a vase. It seems possible to me that a vertical line or plumb-bob (*perpendiculum*) is indicated here, an invention of Daidalos the carpenter along with saw, axe, drill, and carpenter's glue (Pliny *HN* 7.198). The attributes held by the figure purported to be Aristaios would then all be related to woodworking, no surprise if the figure represents Daidalos, renowned above all as the creator of wooden cult images (*xoana*).[31]

This eliminates all of the nine Archaic representations of "Aristaeus" on vases, terracotta, and ivory relief.[32] Also unlikely as "Aristaeus" is the winged figure on the Affecter's amphora in Kassel, which surely must be connected to the combat of Theseus and the Minotaur on the opposite side[33] (and one would therefore expect a fellow enemy of Minos, like Daidalos). The Affecter was a craftsman primarily concerned with form rather than with the content of his scenes, but meaningless juxtapositions of themes are unlikely even for him. Daidalos fits easily into Attic-Cretan experience, especially since he was connected with Athens[34] and carried out commissions for the royal house of Crete as early as in the *Iliad* (18.590–592; see opening quotation), where the god Hephaistos imitates a *choros* by Daidalos for Ariadne.[35] On the other hand, Daidalos imitates divine

FIGURE 24.5. Winged bearded Daidalos on Archaic (Lakonian?) ivory relief. London, British Museum 1954.9–10.1, third quarter of the seventh century B.C. (Museum photograph, with kind permission of Brian Cook.)

FIGURE 24.6. Daidalos in flight with carpenter's utensils. Foot of a Boiotian Atticizing tripod-cothon. New York, Metropolitan Museum of Art 60.11.10. (Museum photograph 173776A, with kind permission of Joan Mertens.)

movement by his wings. It is possible that he or his son Ikaros is linked with Theseus and the Minotaur another time in Archaic art, on the Boiotian skyphos of the mid-sixth century B.C. in the Louvre.[36] This image was hailed one hundred years ago as the earliest representation of Daidalos, until Beazley questioned the interpretation.[37] A winged figure floats horizontally, legs extended, away from the Athenian youths and maidens watching Theseus fight the Minotaur. The rider represented on the reverse of the skyphos is surely a filling motif, but the same cannot be true for the airborne figure more closely connected to the main scene. The newly discovered bucchero olpe takes the history of Daidalos a hundred years earlier than this controversial image and onto safer ground, thanks to its inscription (fig. 24.1). Greek representations now lost to us must have preceded it, and the ivory relief in London (fig. 24.5) gives us an impres-

sion of those lost images. This gives us, for the first time, images from the "Daedalic" period of its eponymous craftsman.

NOTES

*The following abbreviations will be used in this chapter:

Beazley = J. D. Beazley, "Icarus," *JHS* 47 (1927) 222–233.
Cook = B. F. Cook, *LIMC* II, "Aristaios I," 603–607.
Karouzou = S. Papaspyridi-Karouzou, "Un Πρῶτος Εὑρετής dans quelques monuments archaïques," *ASAtene* 24–26 (1946–1948) 37–46.
Morris = S. P. Morris, *Daidalos and the Origins of Greek Art* (Princeton 1992).
Nyenhuis = J. Nyenhuis, *LIMC* III, "Daidalos et Ikaros," 313–321.
Robert = C. Robert, *RE* IV 2 (1901) 1994–2007, s.v. Daidalos.
Schauenburg = K. Schauenburg, "Zwei seltene mythologische Bilder auf einer Amphora in Privatbesitz," in G. Schwarz and E. Pochmarski, eds., *Classica et Provincialia, Festschrift Erna Diez* (Graz 1978) 169–176.

1. On Daidalos' sojourn in the west: Robert 2001–2005; G. M. A. Hanfmann, "Daidalos in Etruria," *AJA* 39 (1935) 189–194; F. Frontisi-Ducroux, *Dédale* (Paris 1975) 171ff.; E. Simon, "Dedalo," *Enciclopedia Virgiliana* II (Rome 1985) 12–14; Morris 195–211.

2. Nyenhuis 314ff., nos. 1–4, 11a, 12a–d, 13, 32, 53.

3. The olpe was presented in December 1989 at the memorial celebration for P. Zancani-Montuoro in Naples. M. A. Rizzo and M. Martelli, "Un incunabolo del mito greco in Etruria," *ASAtene* 66/67 (1988–1989) 7–56. See M. Schmidt, *LIMC* VI, "Medeia," 388 no. 1 for a discussion of the other side of the olpe, which is also illustrated in *AttiMGrecia* 3. serie I (1992) 243–245, pl. 46.

4. C. de Simone, *Die griechischen Entlehnungen im Etruskischen* I (Wiesbaden 1968) 65, 112; P. Zazoff, *Etruskische Skarabäen* (Mainz 1968) no. 397, 1333.

5. Nyenhuis 315, no. 12 = Zazoff no. 397 (London BM 663).

6. Nyenhuis 320, no. 53 = Zazoff no. 1333 (once Berlin, Dressel Collection); F. D. Van Keuren, *The Frieze from the Hera I Temple at Foce del Sele*, Archaeologica 82 (Rome 1989) 144ff., pl. 43b: "I believe with Boardman that TAITLE

was inscribed in error," likewise Furtwängler and Zazoff (supra n. 4); contra Hanfmann (supra n. 1) 192 and de Simone (supra n. 4) 113, with whom I concur; cf. *Gnomon* 64 (1992) 243. The turtle at the feet of Daidalos indicates watery surroundings, not an underworld creature as Van Keuren assumes.

7. Cook 604, nos. 1–9.

8. Karouzou 29ff.

9. *ABV* 19.3.

10. None of the post-Archaic representations of Aristaios (Cook 604ff. nos. 9a–15) shows him with wings, which, as Cook explains (607), is because "the Archaic iconographic tradition had evidently been lost." As I would like to propose, we have no indication that such a tradition ever existed.

11. Karouzou 39ff.; likewise Cook 606 and earlier in *BMMA* 21 (1962–1963) 31–36; cf. infra n. 21.

12. J. D. Beazley, "Groups of Early Attic Black-Figure," *Hesperia* 12 (1944) 43. On wooden statues by Daidalos, see Frontisi-Ducroux (supra n. 1) 102ff.; A. A. Donohue, *Xoana and the Origins of Greek Sculpture* (Atlanta 1988); Morris 215–256.

13. Karouzou 39, n. 4. The instrument in the hands of the winged creature is surely too flimsy for breaking up clumps of earth: see the much heavier instruments held by the silens represented as farm workers on red figure vases: E. Simon, "Hermeneutisches zur Anodos von Göttinnen," in H.-U. Cain, H. Gabelmann, and D. Salzmann, eds., *Festschrift Nikolaus Himmelmann* (Mainz 1989) 197–203.

14. Cook 604, no. 3 = H. Mommsen, *Der Affecter* (Mainz 1975) 97, pl. 62.

15. Nyenhuis 315ff., no. 12d; illustrations in E. Gerhard, *Etruskische Spiegel* (1834–1897; reprint Berlin 1974) IV 1, pl. 330.

16. Epiktetos: Karouzou 39, n. 3; *ARV*² 75.59; E. Simon, *Die Götter der Griechen*³ (Munich 1985) 307, fig. 293. Carpenter Painter = London E 23: *ARV*² 179.1.

17. Karouzou 40ff. fig. 5 (detail restored as a proposed interpretation; does not correspond to actual state).

18. For ancient testimonia see Cook 603ff.

19. Schauenburg 171ff., with reference to Pliny *HN* 7.198 and the scarab in the British Museum cited previously (supra n. 5). Additional sources on the invention of the saw assembled by Robert 1996. According to Apollod. 3.214, the nephew and pupil of Daidalos (Kalos or Talos: see Morris 259–561) first used the jawbone of a snake as a saw.

20. Beazley 223, fig. 2; *ABV* 80.1: Painter of Acropolis 601. Nyenhuis 316, no. 14; Morris 191, fig. 9.

21. L. Marangou, "Aristaios," *AthMitt* 87 (1972) 77–83; Cook 604, no. 9. Supra n. 11.

22. Wings on chest: Cook 604, nos. 3–5 (illustrated); see also no. 9, the ivory relief (fig. 24.4).

23. As on Cook 604, no. 4. Winged shoes alone: ibidem no. 7.

24. Cook 604, no. 6: add Schauenburg 171, with nn. 17–18 for a discussion of the Aristaios-Daidalos problem.

25. H. Hoffmann, *Early Cretan Armourers* (Mainz 1972) 2ff., pls. 1ff.; Morris, pl. 33.

26. Summary of scholarship in P. Blome, *Die figürliche Bildwelt Kretas in der geometrischen und früharchaischen Periode* (Mainz 1982) 69, n. 41ff.; see now Morris 191–192, nn. 159–160.

27. Hoffmann (supra n. 25) 34ff.

28. See R. Hampe and E. Simon, *Tausend Jahre frühgriechische Kunst* (Fribourg 1980) 116ff., fig. 190, whence Blome (supra n. 26).

29. Schauenburg 171, n. 18: "möglicherweise Daidalos."

30. Karouzou 39, fig. 2 (Athens) = Cook 604, n. 4; cothon New York: Cook, no. 5 (both illustrated).

31. Robert 2002ff.; see now Donohue (supra n. 12) and Morris; E. Simon, "Euphronios und seine Zeit," *Kolloquium Berlin* (Berlin 1992) 94–95.

32. Cook 604, nos. 1–9. Uncertain remain two terracotta reliefs with winged figures holding tendrils, classified as possible representations of Aristaeus (Cook 605, nos. 17–18; also a dubious candidate in Karouzou 41ff.). In "Aristeo," *EAA* I (1958) 643, this appears as the sole representation. Since these two reliefs (mold-mates?) are votives from the Hera sanctuaries at Argos and Perachora, they could represent a creature affiliated with Argive Hera. Near the Argive Heraion there was a river and a plant beside it named Asterion (Paus. 2.17.1–2); his three daughters (Prosymna, Euboia, and Akraia) served as nurses to Hera. Asterion had sided with Hera in her dispute with Poseidon over Argos (Paus. 2.15.5). These terracotta reliefs dedicated to Hera could have represented this figure, Asterion, to those who dedicated them. The tendrils in his hands would fit in with the name.

33. Cook 604, no. 3 (supra n. 14).

34. His Attic origin was worked out by J. Toepffer, *Attische Genealogie* (Berlin 1889) 165ff.; cf. Robert 1994ff. See now Morris 257ff. for an examination of how Daidalos the Cretan became an Athenian.

35. See Morris 12–15; for the manufacture of wings by Daidalos, ibidem 15–16 and ch. 6. The translation of *Iliad* 18.590–592 is taken from Morris 13.

36. Robert 1999ff.; scholarship in Beazley 222, nn. 2–3. Illustrations: Frontisi-Ducroux (supra n. 1), fig. 1; Morris, fig. 10d: "Daidalos or Ikaros?"

37. Beazley 222, fig. 1.

25

THE MURDER OF RHESOS ON A CHALCIDIAN NECK-AMPHORA BY THE INSCRIPTION PAINTER[1]

◆

MARION TRUE

Here are the Thracians, new come, separate, beyond all
    others
in place, and among them Rhesos their king, the son of
    Eioneus.
And his are the finest horses I ever saw, and the biggest;
they are whiter than snow, and their speed of foot is the
    wind's speed. . . .

                  Iliad 10.434–437[2]

Thus Dolon, the Trojan spy, described the recently arrived allies of Troy, the Thracians, when he was captured by Odysseus and Diomedes. After dispassionately beheading the wolf-skinned, marten-capped Dolon and making a hasty dedication of his animal disguise to their protectress Athena, the two Greek heroes set off to find the Thracian camp outside the walls of Ilion.

These two went ahead on their way through war gear and
    dark blood
and came suddenly to the Thracians for whom they were
    looking.
These were asleep, worn out with weariness, and their
    armour

lay in splendour and good order on the ground beside
    them
in three rows and beside each man stood his team of
    horses.
Rhesos slept in the center with his fast horses about
    him. . . .
As a lion advancing on the helpless herds unshepherded
of sheep or goats pounces upon them with wicked
    intention,
so the son of Tydeus attacked the Thracian people
until he had killed twelve. . . .

But when the son of Tydeus came to the king, and this was
the thirteenth man, he stripped the sweetness of life from
    him
as he lay heavily breathing. . . .

                  Iliad 10.469–496, passim[3]

In the surviving texts of the *Iliad*, the story of the murder of Rhesos and his sleeping troops is inextricably linked with the capture of Dolon. The Trojan spy, who was sent by Hektor to gather information on the movements of the Greek forces, supplied the information on

415

the Thracians' situation and fine horses to his Greek captors, who were themselves on a mission to spy on the Trojans. Yet, in spite of the popularity of the Doloneia as a subject for representation in the Late Archaic period,[4] the vivid description of the subsequent murder of the sleeping Rhesos and the theft of his superb horses apparently had little appeal for Greek artists of the sixth and fifth centuries, since it has not hitherto been confidently identified in any medium before the later fourth century. When the subject does finally appear, it is in the Greek colonies of South Italy on a group of Apulian vases. Until now, three complete vases and two fragments depicting this scene have been known (see below figs. 25.2–25.5).[5]

Given Emily Vermeule's fondness for both Homer and fine horses, this celebratory volume seems a most appropriate opportunity to introduce the first known Archaic representation of the murder of Rhesos. The subject decorates an exceptionally well preserved Chalcidian neck-amphora (figs. 25.1a–g, frontispiece).[6] Except for a clean break that separates the body from the glazed echinus foot, at the bottom of the red fillet that marks the juncture, the vase is intact, although there is a large chip missing from the fillet. The shape of the echinus mouth, glazed on its outer and upper surfaces and inside to the bottom of the neck, complements the foot, reflecting its profile in a modified, inverted version. The arched handles, joined at the shoulder of the vessel just above its point of greatest extent, and at the neck just beneath the rim, are oval in cross section, glazed outside and reserved within. Each side of the reserved neck is decorated with a palmette-lotus festoon (six alternating addorsed pairs per side) that is most similar in design to the characteristic florals on the necks of Tyrrhenian amphorae;[7] and a small raised fillet in added red separates the neck from the tongue pattern around the top of the shoulder of the body. The reserved body of the vessel is organized horizontally into five zones of decoration. Three bands of ornament—rays, steps, and lotus buds— fill the space between the foot and the primary figural frieze that surrounds the center of the body. This broad uninterrupted band, which occupies approximately one-third of the entire height of the vase, is separated by a pair of fine dilute glaze lines from the smaller secondary figural frieze on the shoulder.

On the obverse of the body, the main frieze presents

the critical moment just before the murder of King Rhesos himself (fig. 25.1d). The names of the two protagonists are inscribed[8] lest there be any confusion as to their identities: ▷ΙΟΜΕ▷Βϟ (retrograde) and Ϲ Ρ ΕϟΟϟ (retrograde). Dressed in a belted chitoniskos, with the baldric for his scabbard slung over his right shoulder, Diomedes clutches the now-awakened king by the throat with his left hand and prepares to plunge his drawn sword into Rhesos' neck with his right. Rhesos wears only a red himation pulled around his body below his naked breast.

On the reverse, the figure of Diomedes' accomplice Odysseus fills the center of the frieze (fig. 25.1e). He, too, is identified by inscription Ο▷ΥϟΕΥϟ, but his adversary is nameless. Dressed in a short chiton that is pleated in the front, Odysseus carries a quiver suspended by a strap over his left shoulder with the bow attached. His aggressive pose echoes that of Diomedes, but he has grasped the forehead of the Thracian at his feet and has already plunged his sword through the victim's throat, from which blood flows freely. The body of the man, whose eyes are now closed in death, is wrapped to the neck in shroudlike fashion in a red himation.

In addition to their victims, the ground around Diomedes' and Odysseus' feet is strewn with cushions and the figures of eleven other Thracians, all lying with their heads to the right. Three, possibly four, are beardless and all are covered with himatia of red or black, and in one case, red-dotted. Though all have their eyes closed, no wounds or indications of blood provide evidence that they are dead rather than asleep. According to the Homeric text, however, Rhesos was the last of thirteen Thracians to be killed. Since the total number of Thracians represented here agrees with this account, these may best be understood as the bodies of the soldiers whom the Greek heroes have already stabbed in their sleep.

As the passage from the *Iliad* recounts, the Thracians had gone to sleep outside the walls of Troy with their elaborate armor carefully arranged in the landscape around them. The artist has depicted it here in detail appropriate to its splendor. A frontal double-crested Corinthian helmet[9] and round shield (device: eagle flying to left; glazed rim with incised circles) hang together with a baldric and scabbard in the background behind Diomedes, and further to the left, a larger round shield

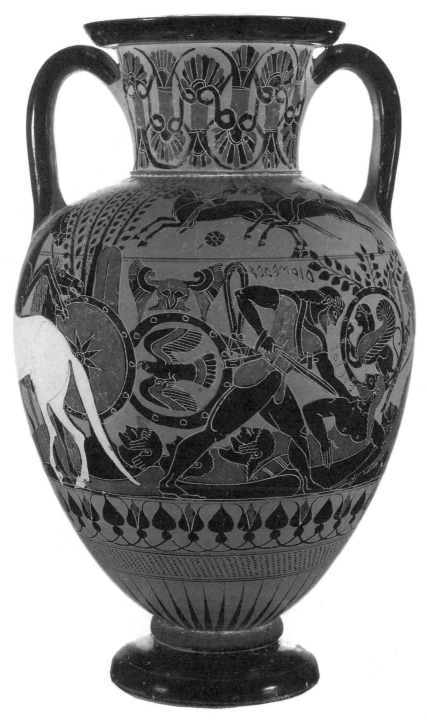

FIGURE 25.1a. Chalcidian amphora by the Inscription Painter, on loan to the J. Paul Getty Museum (L.88.AE.56). Side A: Diomedes prepares to kill the Thracian King, Rhesos. On the shoulder, two mounted youths gallop to the left. (Photographs courtesy of the J. Paul Getty Museum.)

(device: glazed star on added red ground; glazed rim with incised circles) is hung together with a red mantle from the branches of a tree. Another round shield (device: rampant sphinx to left; glazed rim with incised circles) is suspended beside a baldric and scabbard from the limbs of a tree behind the head of the unfortunate Rhesos, and a bit further to the right beneath the handle A/B, a crestless Corinthian helmet is suspended in profile from the background.

The figure of Odysseus is framed by two round shields: the one behind him (device: frontal bull's head;

glazed rim with white dots) appears to be hung on an upright post, and the one before his face (device: eagle flying to left; glazed rim with white dots) hangs from the branch of a tall tree. The thick trunk of the tree supports a third shield, this one oval in shape (device: pattern of zigzag lines alternately red and black;[10] glazed rim with red dots).

Though they were intended to separate the scenes of murder that occupy the front and back of the vessel, the images beneath the handles are hardly secondary in this composition. For here the artist has placed the objec-

FIGURE 25.1b. Side A/B of amphora (fig. 25.1a): pair of Thracian horses.

FIGURE 25.1c. Side B/A of amphora (fig. 25.1a): team of Thracian horses.

tives of all the carnage, the coveted horses of Rhesos, tethered to the trees and the post that support the armor. The Thracians slept with their teams beside them in the Homeric description. Like the chorus of a Greek tragedy, these animals provide the only emotional response to the violent activities taking place around them. Beneath handle A/B, two horses are tied to opposite directions; a large black mare with red mane rears up to the right on her hind legs, her mouth open to neigh in distress, while the red stallion behind stands facing left, pawing the ground. Under handle B/A is an entire quadriga team, two horses tied to the left and two to the right; in the foreground, a magnificent white stallion faces left, nervously stamping his feet as the three dark steeds behind him rear and whinny in agitated confusion. The white stallion's frightened state is particularly clearly shown: the white of his eye is visible around the glazed pupil.[11] The second horse facing left is black with a red mane and red belly. The nearer right-facing horse, like the mare under handle A/B, stands on its hind legs with its forelegs raised in the air. The farther one stands with head lifted and mouth open. Both are black with red manes.

The heads of the horses rearing beneath each handle and the branches of the trees to which the armor and horses are fastened break through the upper frame of the continuous main frieze, intruding into the shoulder zone that carries two smaller, secondary figural compositions. Between the handles, on side A, two youths, the foremost with his flesh in added red,[12] and the second armed with a spear, ride to the left on galloping horses, followed by a bird in flight (fig. 25.1f). On the shoulder of side B, a cavalcade of three youths rides to the right; the first two wear short chitons, while the third is nude, and the central youth looks back toward his follower (fig. 25.1g).

In all but one significant respect, the artist's rendering seems to follow the Homeric version of the story: here are the twelve Thracians who accompanied Rhesos, killed as they lay sleeping, surrounded by their fine horses and magnificent armor in the open landscape outside the walls of Troy. Rhesos, the last to die at the hands of Diomedes, is in the center. In the *Iliad*, however, Diomedes and Odysseus divided the tasks according to their skills: Diomedes opting to do the killing while Odysseus pulled the bodies of the dead to the side to clear a pas-

sageway through which he could lead out the horses. Here, the artist has made Odysseus an active participant in the killing. There can be no mistaking his role as he stabs the bleeding Thracian.

Until now, none of the preserved depictions of the murder of Rhesos, including that described in the Euripidean drama, has differed from the Homeric account. In all, Rhesos is slain while sleeping in the midst of his troops, and Diomedes and Odysseus divide the labors of killing and horse-stealing. The preserved scholiasts' comments to the *Iliad* text for Book 10 suggest, however, that at least two alternate versions of the Rhesos myth may have existed in the epic tradition before the Homeric poems were composed.[13] One variant was apparently reflected in the preserved contents of an oracle associated with the Thracian king and the other in a lost poem by Pindar. In the oracular version,[14] it has been foretold to Rhesos that should he sleep one night in Troy and taste its water and should his horses drink the water of the Skamandros and graze on Trojan fields, the city would not be able to be taken. For this reason, his death is essential for the success of the Greeks. According to the Pindaric version, as reconstructed from the preserved references,[15] Rhesos takes a brief but prominent role in the Trojan War, fighting on the side of Troy for one day, rendering great harm to the Greeks. His parents, mere mortals in the *Iliad*, are minor deities in this account: his father, the Thracian river Strymon, and his mother, the muse Euterpe. The Pindaric version as preserved in the **A** scholia also provides one other critical piece of information: in it, both Diomedes and Odysseus participate in the killing of the Thracians.

None of the information included in these two versions is part of the Rhesos story recounted in *Iliad* Book 10. Yet certain motifs and aspects of each fit well within the epic tradition[16] and they may document the existence of another non-Iliadic myth from the greater Trojan cycle in which Rhesos was a central figure. Given our artist's accuracy in the other details, it is unlikely that he simply took liberties with the Homeric text to balance the compositions on each side of the vase; more probably, he drew his imagery from a non-Homeric source, perhaps the so-called Pindaric version of the Rhesos story.[17] A non-Iliadic version may also be reflected in a later tragedy, the *Rhesus*,[18] as it, too, differs in some significant details from the *Iliad*.

FIGURE 25.1d. Detail of Diomedes and Rhesos, side A of amphora (fig. 25.1a).

FIGURE 25.1e. Detail of Odysseus and sleeping Thracian, side B of amphora (fig. 25.1a).

But while the source of his imagery may remain a matter of conjecture, the identity of this Late Archaic painter does not. For on the basis of both its shape and its highly original figural composition, the vase in the Getty Museum may be attributed to the Inscription Painter, the greatest master of the first generation of Chalcidian artists.[19] The proportions of the amphora and its taut, bulging contours place it comfortably among the earliest and strongest of the Chalcidian amphora shapes, the group of ten complete and fragmentary neck-amphorae that J. Keck called her first type.[20] With only one exception,[21] the known examples of this shape are by the Inscription Painter.

The works of the Inscription Painter are remarkable for the inventiveness of compositions sensitively adapted to the contours of the vessels, and for the skillful incorporation of broad planes of added colors—purplish red and white—that enhance the overall decorative impact by providing contrasts in both intensity and texture. These traits clearly distinguish this new neck-amphora as well. And while its individual features find many parallels among the Inscription Painter's best-known works, its unique composition surely places it among his most successful achievements.

In disposition and execution, the three ornamental patterns below the main frieze on the Rhesos amphora are much the same on all of the neck-amphorae of Keck's first type.[22] But though all the vases of this type are decorated with some type of floral ornament on the neck, these patterns vary significantly in their details. As Keck pointed out, the amphora in Basel[23] has a palmette-rosebud festoon. Würzburg 146[24] and Cabinet des Médailles 202 (figs. 25.6a–b)[25] have palmette-lotus festoons similar to the vase in Malibu, but the alternating fronds of the palmettes and petals of the lotus flowers are not picked out with added color. The festoon on the neck of the Rhesos amphora is closest in all its details to that on the neck of Leiden 1626,[26] which Rumpf placed among the artist's earliest efforts.

No exact parallels exist for the central figures of Diomedes and Odysseus. Diomedes' pose most closely resembles that of Theseus in combat with the Minotaur on the much-repainted hydria, Louvre F 18.[27] His red chitoniskos with its lower edge pulled up high over the outside of the right thigh and a rounded edge dipping between the legs to cover the genitals may be compared with that worn by Herakles in combat with Geryon on the belly-amphora, British Museum B 155.[28] This figure also shows very similar contours and incisions defining the musculature of the legs. A similarly drawn broad baldric appears on the figure of Memnon on the amphora fragment by our artist in Florence, no. 4210,[29] and on the figure of Ajax on the amphora once in the Pembroke-Hope collection, now lost.[30] His three fore-

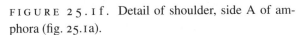

FIGURE 25.1f. Detail of shoulder, side A of amphora (fig. 25.1a).

FIGURE 25.1g. Detail of shoulder, side B of amphora (fig. 25.1a).

locks, incised from just the lower edge of the fillet and swept back toward the crown, reflect a style similar to those of the bearded Oineus on a fragment once in the d'Hancarville collection (preserved in a drawing);[31] the figure of a male (Paris?) at the left end of the Judgment of Paris scene on the hydria Bonn 464A;[32] the beardless Troilos on the dinos fragment, Reggio no. 1169;[33] the figure of Paris on the Würzburg krater no. 315;[34] and the youth on the fragment of a neck-amphora from the collection of Herbert Cahn, Basel (no. HC 1007), and now joined to Louvre CA 7305.[35]

The figure of Odysseus is closest in pose to the figure of Herakles on the British Museum amphora B 155,[36] though the pleated front of his short chiton is most similar to that worn by Memnon on the Florence fragment, no. 4210.[37] His hair is dressed in the same fashion as Diomedes', and the features of his face are very close as well. Diomedes, however, has an incised moustache that forms a continuous line with the upper contour of his beard, while Odysseus has just the indication of a short line above his upper lip, a detail that seems more typical of the Inscription Painter's bearded heads.[38]

Though hardly unique to this artist, round shields with glazed rims decorated with either painted dots or incised circles, and the device of an eagle seen from below flying to the left, found here on both sides of the vase, are numerous among the Inscription Painter's

works: the forward shields of the Geryon figures on both the British Museum amphora B 155[39] and Cabinet des Médailles 202[40] carry this device, as does the shield of Diomedes on the Pembroke-Hope amphora,[41] the mounted warrior Glaukos (?) riding to the left on Cabinet des Médailles 203,[42] and Hektor on Würzburg 315.[43] All show similar rendering of the bird with talons of one leg curled beneath the breast and a single band of added red on both wing coverts and at the root of the tail feathers. Free-flying birds on a number of vases also reflect the same model: for example, two flanking the frontal quadriga on side B of the amphora in the Cabinet des Médailles, no. 202,[44] one following the figure of Hektor's mounted groom on the side A of the Würzburg krater 315,[45] and one flying away from the figure of Glaukos beneath handle A/B on the amphora Cabinet des Médailles 203.[46] The frontal bull-head device on the shield behind Odysseus is without parallel in the artist's work, but the black inserts on either side of the head recall similar shapes set within the sides of an inner circle on two white shields on the hydria B 75 in the British Museum.[47] Though all of these shields are round hoplite shields, the decorative effect of the insets recalls the more complex contours of a Boiotian shield.[48]

The sphinx otherwise appears among the artist's known shield devices on side B of the psykter-amphora in Melbourne.[49] Held by the warrior Menestheus, the

FIGURE 25.2. Volute krater by the Rhesos Painter (name piece), Berlin, Staatliche Museen Preussischer Kulturbesitz, inv. V.I. 3157. Detail, side A: Odysseus leading away the horses of Rhesos. (Photograph courtesy Antikensammlung, Staatliche Museen, Berlin.) Photograph by Jutta Tietz-Glagou.

FIGURE 25.3. Volute krater by the Darius Painter, Berlin, Staatliche Museen Preussischer Kulturbesitz, inv. 1984.39. Detail, side A: Diomedes prepares to kill the sleeping Rhesos as Odysseus leads away the Thracian horses. (Photograph courtesy Antikensammlung, Staatliche Museen, Berlin.) Photograph by Johannes Laurentius.

shield bearing the sphinx is unfortunately partially covered by the shield of Glaukos, so the creature's face is obscured. The contours of her sickle-shaped wings, the incised line of her left haunch, and the S-curve of her tail are quite similar, however, though her forelegs are not raised. The profile of the sphinx on the Rhesos amphora is perhaps better compared to those of the women and youths on the Würzburg krater 315[50] and the amphora in the Cabinet des Médailles, no. 203.[51] Her single sickle-shaped wing is similar in its red covert and incised curled ends to the more extended pair on the figure of Geryon on the amphora in the Cabinet des Médailles, no. 202 (fig. 25.6a).[52]

The menacing image of the frontal Corinthian helmet suspended behind Diomedes can be compared in its out-

lines to the helmet worn by the forward-falling body of Geryon on the British Museum amphora B 155,[53] though the British Museum example is decorated with a single transverse crest rather than the double crests running front to back clearly but awkwardly shown in foreshortened perspective on the frontal head of Glaukos on the Pembroke-Hope amphora.[54] As Keck has pointed out, the frontal helmet is generally associated with figures of warriors who are dead or dying,[55] and its spectral appearance in the back of the Rhesos scene contributes an appropriately sinister tone. Among the figures lying on the ground on side B, a beardless youth to the right of the tree supporting the oval shield lies with his uncovered head frontally exposed, perhaps a subtle reference to the fate of the Thracians.

The continuous series of bodies that surrounds the Rhesos amphora is unique among known Chalcidian vases, but the Inscription Painter did create a sensitive

FIGURE 25.5. Unattributed fragment (HC 220) of closed vessel of unspecified shape. Basel, Collection of H. A. Cahn. (Photograph courtesy of H. A. Cahn.)

FIGURE 25.4. Fragment of a closed vessel of unspecified shape attributed to the Circle of the Birth of Athena Painter, Würzburg, Martin von Wagner-Museum, inv. H4705. Sleeping Thracian. (Photograph courtesy of the Martin von Wagner-Museum.)

portrait of death in the single figure of the fallen giant Eurytion on the amphora in the Cabinet des Médailles, no. 202 (he is partially visible in fig. 25.6a).[56] With his hand drawn up to his cheek, the giant has fallen forward on his face, with an arrow in his back. The treatment of the corpse's eye, in which both lids are still rendered as if slightly open, especially invites comparison with the eyes of all of Rhesos' companions. Five of the dead Thracians wear their hair dressed with long curls hanging before their ears; a similar treatment of the sidelocks appears on the head of Perseus on side B of British Museum amphora B 155.[57]

Horses clearly appealed to the Inscription Painter, as they appear in the principal friezes on seven of his neck-amphorae[58] and three kraters,[59] and dominate the cavalcades on the shoulders of five neck-amphorae[60] and one hydria.[61] In addition, two riders flanked a central palmette-lotus cross on the shoulder of the lost Pembroke-Hope neck-amphora,[62] and Bellerophon is mounted on the winged Pegasos on the fragmentary shoulder of the hydria in Bonn.[63]

In his grandeur and many details of his musculature,

the great white horse under handle B/A is closest to the two galloping stallions of the Dioskouroi on side B of the krater Würzburg 315.[64] The same strong diagonal incision that defines his shoulder, turning back on itself in a graceful arc at the top, is clear on the left horse of the Würzburg krater, as are the marked S-curve at the elbow and the distinctive folds of flesh beneath the elbow.[65] The Würzburg horses are also similar in their flowing manes, the clearly defined bony ridges above the eyes, the single long incisions running down the faces just beyond the tear ducts of the eyes, and the fishhook-shaped nostrils. The right stallion on the Würzburg krater shows a similar line for the curve of the jawbone as well.

Most of the same details are found among the other five horses on the Rhesos amphora, but they offer some different parallels with the Würzburg pair. The head of the red horse under handle A/B is very similar in its contours, especially with its forward-pointing ears, to the right horse on the Würzburg vase, while the forelegs of the black horse facing to the left behind the white stallion on B/A are raised in a pose very like that of the left horse on the krater; both it and the rearing black horse beneath handle A/B show finely incised lines around the edges of their open mouths similar to those on the right horse of Würzburg 315, indications of either teeth or the soft, wrinkled contours of the mouth broken to the bit.

The red manes of four of the horses of Rhesos hang in heavy, incised wavy strands on the neck, recalling those of the horses on side A of Würzburg 315; the neck-amphora in Würzburg, no. 146;[66] the neck-amphora in the Cabinet des Médailles, no. 203;[67] and on the British Museum krater B 15.[68] Among the horses on the last, the one facing to the left under handle B/A also has its tail drawn like those of all of the horses on the Rhesos amphora except the white one: with a pattern of short, incised parallel lines that run diagonally along the length of the tail, first to the left, then to the right, creating a hatched effect intended to suggest the texture of the coarse strands.[69]

Perhaps the most interesting aspect of this represen-

tation of the Thracian horses is the contradiction between their seemingly subsidiary roles within the composition, located as they are beneath the handles, and the artist's strategic placement of a single, massive white animal in the front of one confused team. The visual effect of this stallion is startling; in spite of the dramatic events on the primary sides of the vessel, the eye is continually drawn back to the frantic animals who were one of the primary motives for the killing. This effective use of white pigment as a compositional device is not unique among the Inscription Painter's vases.[70] In the lost fragment from the d'Hancarville collection,[71] for

FIGURE 25.6a. Chalcidian amphora by the Inscription Painter. Paris, Cabinet des Médailles 202. Side A: Herakles in combat with Geryon. (Photograph courtesy of the Cabinet des Médailles.)

FIGURE 25.6b. Side B/A of amphora (fig. 25.6a). Cattle of Geryon.

example, the outside trace horse of the profile quadriga team was white. But more directly relevant is the composition on the amphora in the Cabinet des Médailles, no. 202 (fig. 25.6b).[72] On this vase, the closest among the Inscription Painter's known works to the new amphora in both quality of execution and overall organization of the composition, Herakles is engaged in combat with the triple-bodied warrior Geryon. Like the horses of Rhesos, the giant's magnificent cattle are at stake in this combat, and the herd gathered beneath handle B/A shows an arrangement similar in both the placement of animals and the use of color. The five great bulls are in nervous disarray: three face right though one turns back to the left, and two face left, with their heads turned back to the right. At the front of the herd stands a splendid white bull with his head lowered as if prepared to charge. Added color is used effectively among the four cattle in the rear of the group as well: one has a red face, two have red necks, and one has red ears. And in a manner similar to the heads of the rearing horses and the trees to which they are tethered on the new amphora in Malibu, the horns of two break through the groundline of the shoulder frieze above, as do the crests of Geryon's helmets and the butt end of one of his spears.

Finally, the cavalcades on the shoulder of Cabinet des Médailles 202 (figs. 25.6a–b) are close in most details to the cavalcades on the amphora in Malibu: the poses of both figures on the shoulder of side A of the new vase, the front boy leaning back and the rear one holding his proper left arm stretched back behind him and a spear in his left hand, as well as the bird following at the end, are similar, as are the poses of the galloping horses with front legs raised and tails flying out behind. On the shoulder of side B, the central youth who turns to look back at his companion behind recalls the left figure on side B of the Würzburg krater 315.[73]

Unique among the preserved cavalcades of the Inscription Painter, the horsemen on the two sides ride in opposite directions toward the mass of leafy branches that interrupts the shoulder frieze around the lower root of handle B/A. The incorporation of landscape elements in the form of the leafy trees in the Rhesos scene recalls again the association between this episode and the capture of Dolon, for in both the Homeric account and among the Late Archaic representations of Dolon's cap-

ture, landscape elements play an important and consistent role.[74] After killing the spy and offering a brief prayer to Athena, Odysseus hung the skins with which Dolon had disguised himself on a tamarisk bush, to be reclaimed after the slaughter of the Thracians and dedicated with proper ceremony to his patron goddess.[75]

The weathered fragment of a dinos in Reggio depicting Troilos[76] also preserves the remains of two leafy branches growing around the lion-head waterspouts of the fountain house that forms the backdrop for the scene. Treated in a very graphic, simplified style, these closely resemble the branches of the trees that form the landscape setting in the camp of Rhesos. A second appearance of leafy branches as part of a composition by the Inscription Painter, though in this case not actually a landscape element, is found on another fragment in Reggio that was originally part of a lid, inv. no. 14777.[77] More schematically rendered and with touches of added white painted on the foliage, the branches are found with the remains of three centaurs, the foremost of whom presumably carried the branch as a weapon. Though the two Reggio fragments and the new Rhesos amphora offer the only examples of such foliage among the Inscription Painter's known works, they show an unusual interest in landscape setting that may also be reflected in the psykter-amphora, formerly in the Castellani collection and now Villa Giulia 50410, on which a fat, hairy satyr tries to hide himself behind a palm tree to spy on a dancing maenad.[78]

Rumpf included the Reggio dinos fragment and the Castellani psykter-amphora among the Inscription Painter's earliest works,[79] together with the fragment once in the d'Hancarville collection.[80] Transitional to his more fully developed, mature style is the neck-amphora in Leiden,[81] the vase that offers the closest parallel for the floral ornament on the neck of the new amphora. His maturity is best represented by the neck-amphora Cabinet des Médailles 202 (figs. 25.6a–b).[82] As this last vase is closest to the Rhesos amphora in numerous individual details of the figures, the overall organization of the figural composition on the surface of the vessel, and the effective use of large planes of added color, the amphora in Malibu should belong as well to the mature phase of the artist's career.

The Inscription Painter, who is generally credited as the originator of Chalcidian vase production,[83] most likely began working shortly before 570;[84] he was the leader of the first of the two generations that produced Chalcidian pottery until about 500 B.C., and himself was active probably until 530–525.[85] The Cabinet des Médailles amphora has been dated by L. Banti to the decade 550–540.[86] As an accomplished product of his fully developed style, the new amphora in Malibu may be placed comfortably in this same period, perhaps toward the later part of the decade.

With his portrayal of the murder of Rhesos and his comrades, the Inscription Painter achieved a successful balance between a well-resolved composition on each side of the vase and the extraordinary decorative detail that is characteristic of his best mature works. But in this dramatic scene he has added an element of emotional power that is otherwise lacking in his preserved compositions. Helplessly tethered in the midst of the Thracians, the distraught, proud horses reflect the horror of the murders taking place around them. Their instinctive response may provide a clue for the subject's apparent lack of appeal among the Greeks of the mainland in the sixth and fifth centuries B.C. For though the *Iliad* (10.460–464) clearly states that Odysseus and Diomedes were guided to the deed by their divine protectress Athena, and thus absolved of moral responsibility, they appear more stealthy than noble in killing the hapless Thracians as they sleep. Their behavior here is rather the antithesis of the true valor shown in well-matched combat (a favorite subject of the Greek artists of the Archaic and Classical periods), as the countless surviving descriptions and representations of armed combat in all media prove. The Inscription Painter has been described, somewhat unfairly, as more a decorator than a creative artist.[87] The Rhesos amphora proves anew that he belongs among the most original masters of the Late Archaic period.

NOTES

1. I am grateful to the owners of the vase for their generous permission to include it in this publication. I thank Erika Simon, Guntram Beckel, and Martina Edelmann of the Martin von Wagner-Museum, Würzburg; Herbert Cahn of Basel; Wolf-Dieter Heilmeyer of the Staatliche Museen Preussischer Kulturbesitz, Berlin and Luca Giuliani, formerly of the Staatliche Museen Preussischer Kulturbesitz, Berlin; and Hélène Nicolet-Pierre of the Bibliothèque Nationale, Paris, who provided photographs and permission for reproduction of objects in their collection. I am particularly indebted to Mario Iozzo, who generously provided a copy of his as-yet unpublished dissertation. Finally, I would like to express my appreciation to J. R. Guy, Karen Manchester, and Andrew Clark for their advice and assistance in the preparation of this article; any mistakes or omissions are the author's own.

The following abbreviations are used:

Fenik = B. Fenik, *"Iliad X" and the "Rhesus," The Myth*, CollLatomus 73 (Brussels 1964).

Iozzo = M. Iozzo, "Ceramica 'Calcidese': Nuovi documenti e problemi riproposti" (Ph.D. diss., Florence, 1990).

Keck = J. Keck, *Studien zur Rezeption fremder Einflüsse in der chalkidischen Keramik: Ein Beitrag zur Lokalisierungsfrage*, Archäologische Studien 8 (Frankfurt am Main 1988).

Moore = M. B. Moore, "Horses on Black-figured Greek Vases of the Archaic Period: Ca. 620–480 B.C." (Ph.D. diss., Institute of Fine Arts, N.Y.U., 1971).

Rumpf = A. Rumpf, *Chalkidische Vasen* (Berlin 1927).

2. *The Iliad of Homer*, trans. by Richmond Lattimore (Chicago 1961) 229.

3. Lattimore (supra n. 2) 231.

4. On Late Archaic representations of Dolon, see F. Brommer, *Odysseus: Die Taten und Leiden des Helden in antiker Kunst und Literatur* (Darmstadt 1983) 29–31, figs. 5–6; F. Lissarrague, "Iconographie de Dolon le Loup," *RA* 1980, 3–30, esp. 3–11, 14–26; and most recently, with extensive bibliography, D. Williams, *LIMC* III, "Dolon," 660–664, pls. 525–529. To the Late Archaic representations of Dolon's capture by Odysseus and Diomedes, add an Attic red-figured cup attributed to the Triptolemos Painter (J. R. Guy), in the J. Paul Getty Museum, 90.AE.35; I, the capture of Dolon; A, the dispute over the arms of Achilles; B, the balloting for the arms of Achilles.

5. The five previously known vases and fragments representing the murder of Rhesos: situla by the Lycurgus Painter, Naples 2910 (inv. 81863), *RVAp* I, 16/18; volute krater by the Rhesos Painter, Staatliche Museen, Berlin inv. v.I. 3157, *RVAp* I, 8/102a (here fig. 25.2); volute krater by the Darius Painter, Staatliche Museen, Berlin inv. 1984.39, L. Giuliani, *Bildervasen aus Apulien* (Berlin 1988) 10–13 (here fig. 25.3); fragment of a closed vase of unspecified shape from the Circle of the Birth of Athena Painter, Martin von-Wagner Museum,

Würzburg inv. H 4705, *RVAp* I, 2/34 and E. Simon, *Führer durch die Antikenabteilung des Martin-von-Wagner Museum der Universität Würzburg* (Mainz 1975), 203 (here fig. 25.4); fragment from a vase in the collection of Herbert Cahn, Basel, in F. Brommer (supra n. 4) 34, pl. 22b (here fig. 25.5).

6. The vase is on loan to the J. Paul Getty Museum, inv. no. L.88.AE.56. Height, 39.6 cm. Diameter of mouth, outside, 16.2 cm; inside, 11.5 cm. Diameter of body, 24.9 cm. Diameter of foot, 13.1 cm. Three thin rings in added red paint mark the glazed interior of the neck; the volume of the vase when filled to the rim with rice is 8.575 liters or approximately 2.6 Attic choes (1 chous=3.283 l.); 8.4 liters or 2.56 choes when filled to the upper painted ring; 8.225 liters or 2.5 choes when filled to the middle ring; 8.05 liters or 2.45 choes when filled to the lowest ring. To my knowledge, no volumetric study of Chalcidian pottery yet exists, but the capacity of this Chalcidian neck-amphora is very close to that of an early Attic black-figured ovoid neck-amphora in the J. Paul Getty Museum, 86.AE.72, by the Painter of Acropolis 606 (8.7 liters or 2.65 choes filled to rim); less close is the capacity of a Tyrrhenian amphora, 76.AE.87, by the Castellani Painter (9.5 liters or 2.89 choes filled to rim).

For Chalcidian pottery, the basic reference is still Rumpf; valuable also in spite of the erroneous premise is H. R. W. Smith, "The Origins of Chalcidian Ware," *CPCA* I.3 (1932) 85–146. A Ferrari, *I Vasi Calcidese, Problemi di pittura greca del VI secolo* A.C. (Torino 1978) offers a brief review of the issues raised by Chalcidian ceramics and a thoughtful stylistic analysis of the figural decoration on a selection of twenty-six vases. Much interesting new material is included in M. Iozzo, "Ceramica 'chalcidese' inedita da Reggio Calabria," *Xenia* 6 (1983) 3–24. Keck provides: a valuable overview of the scholarship since Rumpf; a new classification of the characteristic Chalcidian vase shapes and a discussion of chronological development within each shape; a detailed stylistic and iconographic analysis of Chalcidian vase painting with particular reference to the external sources of influence; and a catalogue of additions to and revisions in the corpus of known Chalcidian vases organized by shape (with inscribed vases and fragments listed separately). Iozzo offers the most comprehensive recent study which includes addenda to Rumpf; a review of all recent scholarship, including Keck; revisions of attribution and chronology; considerations of "Pseudo-Chalcidian" pottery and undecorated Chalcidian vases as well as the patterns of diffusion of Chalcidian fabric; and convincing conclusions on Rhegion as the place of manufacture. See also n. 8 infra.

7. Keck 33, n. 84; on the Tyrrhenian Group generally, see D. von Bothmer, "The Painters of 'Tyrrhenian' Vases," *AJA* 48 (1944) 161–170; "Six Hydriai," *AntK* 12 (1969) 26–29,

pls. 17–20; T. H. Carpenter, "On the Dating of the Tyrrhenian Group," *OJA* 3 (1984) 45–56. On particular vases, K. Schauenburg, "Zwei neue Tyrrhenische Amphoren," *AA* 1962, 58–70, and H. A. Shapiro, "Two Black-figure Neck-Amphorai," *Greek Vases in the Getty Museum* 4 (1989) 11–32.

8. The letter forms, particularly the vau [ꟼ] in the name of Rhesos, are in the characteristic script that was originally associated by A. Kirchoff specifically with Chalkis and her colonies in South Italy and Sicily, and that led to the identification of the fabric as Chalcidian. For the history of the study of the script and the conclusions on the origins of the vases, see the discussion in Rumpf 40–53 (with drawings of then-known inscriptions); more recently on the "Chalkidic" script and vases, L. Jeffrey, *The Local Scripts of Archaic Greece*, rev. ed. (Oxford 1990) 79–83, esp. 81, 244–245, esp. n. 3, and 454–456. Iozzo 215–217 discusses the important distinctions between the Archaic Euboean script and the letter forms found in the inscriptions on Chalcidian vases. In particular, the alpha, vau, and koppa are identified as significant indicators of the colonial origins of this fabric, most probably in Rhegion.

For the discussion of other evidence that supports the likely conclusion that these vases were not produced in Chalkis itself but in its colony, Rhegion, see: J. Boardman, "Pottery from Eretria," *BSA* 47 (1952) 44; G. Vallet, *Rhegion et Zancle* (Paris 1958) esp. 211–228; J. Boardman and F. Schweizer, "Clay Analysis of Archaic Greek Pottery," *BSA* 68 (1973) 267–283; A. Ferrari (supra n. 6) 13–24; F. Canciani, "Eine neue Amphora aus Vulci und das Problem der pseudo-chalkidischen Vasen," *JdI* 95 (1980) 142–162, esp. 147, n. 15; R. Lullies, "Bemerkungen zu den 'chalkidischen' Bauchamphoren," *RA* 1982, 53–56; R. E. Jones with John Boardman, "Provenance Studies of Greek Pottery of the Historic Period," *Greek and Cypriot Pottery. A Review of Scientific Studies* (Athens 1986) 686–688; Keck 11–13, and esp. 26–27; and, most recently, Iozzo 2–9, with additional bibliography, and 220–229.

9. On the distinctions between Corinthian and Chalcidian helmets, see A. M. Snodgrass, *Arms and Armour of the Greeks* (Ithaca 1967) 69–70, pl. 24; the apparently angular cheek pieces here indicate that the helmet is of the Corinthian type.

10. This unusual shield decoration is without any parallel known to the author. The pattern is often associated with the costumes of Scythian archers, however, and may be intended to suggest the barbaric nature of the Thracians. I thank Dr. Salvatore Settis for this observation.

11. On separately rendered pupils, see Moore 239–241; she notes there that while Attic painters generally preferred to indicate the pupils, Corinthian artists did not; they occur on Corinthian vases mostly on white horses, where they are ren-

dered in glaze, as they are in the example under discussion. Only one Chalcidian example is known to Moore: a winged horse on the shoulder of the hydria Orvieto 192, the name piece of the Group of the Orvieto Hydria (Rumpf, cat. no. 151).

12. This use of added red for the flesh of a complete male figure seems to be unparalleled among the works of the Inscription Painter, though in Rumpf's drawing for the hydria Bonn 464 A (Rumpf, cat. no. 150, pl. CXXXV), the face of Bellerophon appears to be in added red, and the thigh of the rider on side B of the neck amphora in Copenhagen, Thorvaldsens Museum 70 (Rumpf, cat. no. 55), seems to have an area of added red paint.

The significance of the use of added red for the flesh of some male figures in Greek vase painting has still never been satisfactorily explained, and there may be no one explanation. A. Seeberg, *Corinthian Komos Vases*, BICS Suppl. 27 (1972) 72, 76, n. 5, noted that red faces were common in Corinthian vase painting, the conventions of which surely influenced the use of added color in Chalcidian. For the most recent discussion and earlier bibliography on the subject, especially for Attic pottery, see *CVA* J. Paul Getty Museum 2 (1990) 62 under 86.AE.106 (A. Clark). Given the shoulder cavalcades' very subsidiary role on the Chalcidian vase under discussion, the artist's intention most likely was compositional interest.

13. Fenik, esp. 61–63. See also O. M. Davidson, "Dolon and Rhesos in the *Iliad*," *QUCC* I (1979) 61–66, esp. 61–63. I am grateful to Sarah Morris for bringing this article to my attention.

14. Fenik 6–7; Davidson (supra n. 13) 62.

15. Fenik 5–6; Davidson (supra n. 13) 61–62.

16. Fenik 37 (summary); Davidson (supra n. 13) 63.

17. As Iozzo 23 mentions, the battle compositions on both sides of a psykter-amphora by the same artist are also drawn from a non-Homeric version of the Trojan cycle. The vase, now in Melbourne in the National Gallery of Victoria, was originally published by A. D. Trendall, *The Felton Greek Vases in the National Gallery of Victoria* (Canberra 1958) 5ff., pls. 1–4; it is also in Keck, cat. no. IV1; Iozzo 12 provides the recent bibliography on the vase. Keck 170 also comments more generally on the iconographic originality of this artist, the Inscription Painter.

18. Fenik 16–40. For the *Rhesus*, see *Euripides*, vol. I, trans. by A. S. Way (Cambridge, Mass. 1978) 158–241. The *Rhesus*—associated with the great fifth-century playwright Euripides since the fourth century A.C., but never completely accepted as his work—has been discussed in detail by W. Ritchie, *The Authenticity of the Rhesus of Euripides* (Cambridge 1964), who attempts to prove its connection with Euripides. His conclusions are strongly and convincingly rebut-

ted by E. Fraenkel in his review of Ritchie's text in *Gnomon* 37 (1965) 228–241.

19. Rumpf 54–72; Keck 21–26; Iozzo 11–25.

20. Keck 29–30.

21. Vatican 225, Rumpf, cat. no. 24 (which belongs to his Group of the Belly Amphorae).

22. Keck 33.

23. Basel, Antikensammlung und Sammlung Ludwig, inv. no. Ka 416; Keck, cat. no. HA1; Iozzo 11, 14–15.

24. Rumpf, cat. no. 25.

25. Rumpf, cat. no. 3.

26. Rumpf, cat. no. 2.

27. Rumpf, cat. no. 12.

28. Rumpf, cat. no. 6.

29. Rumpf, cat. no. 1.

30. Rumpf, cat. no. 5; Moore, with thanks to Dietrich von Bothmer, supplies the citation for *Cat. Christie* 14–16, June 1849.

31. Rumpf, cat. no. 21.

32. Rumpf, supra n. 12.

33. Rumpf, cat. no. 18.

34. Rumpf, cat. no. 14.

35. Keck, cat. no. IV3, fragment c; Iozzo 11, 16.

36. Supra n. 28.

37. Supra n. 29.

38. See, for example, the walking man under handle B/A on Würzburg 315 (supra n. 34).

39. Supra n. 28.

40. Supra n. 25.

41. Supra n. 30.

42. Rumpf, cat. no. 4.

43. Supra n. 34.

44. Supra n. 25.

45. Supra n. 34.

46. Supra n. 42.

47. Rumpf, cat. no. 9.

48. Snodgrass (supra n. 9) 55.

49. Keck, cat. no. IV1; Iozzo 12, 22–23.

50. Supra n. 34.

51. Supra n. 42.

52. Supra n. 25.

53. Supra n. 28.

54. Supra n. 30.

55. Keck 137.

56. Supra n. 25.

57. Supra n. 28.

58. Cabinet des Médailles 202 (supra n. 25) and 203 (supra n. 42); Munich 594 (Rumpf, cat. no. 22); Würzburg 146 (supra n. 24); once d'Hancarville (supra n. 31); Thorvaldsens Museum 70 (supra n. 12); fragments from the collection of H.

Cahn, inv. no. HC 1007, joined to Louvre CA 7305 (supra n. 35); fragments in Ostermundigen (Moore 199, E34, pl. 92: 1; not accepted as Chalcidian by Keck 276, but included in Iozzo 11).

59. Würzburg 315 (supra n. 34); British Museum B 15 (Rumpf, cat. no. 113); Würzburg 147 (Rumpf, cat. no. 114).

60. Cabinet des Médailles 202 (supra n. 25) and 203 (supra n. 42); Würzburg 146 (supra n. 24); Antikensammlung und Sammlung Ludwig, Ka 417 (Keck, HA 1); Bologna 682, from Marzabotto (Keck, cat. no. HA 45; Iozzo, 11, 15).

61. Munich 596 (Rumpf, cat. no. 10).

62. Supra n. 30.

63. Supra n. 12. In addition, a frontal quadriga appears on the shoulder of a fragmentary hydria in a Swiss private collection (Keck, cat. no. IV9; Iozzo 12, 18).

64. Supra n. 34.

65. On wrinkles of flesh behind the elbows of horses on non-Attic vases, see Moore 311; she notes that in Chalcidian examples, such "lines are short," though this is not true for the extended fold lines that are executed in dilute glaze on the new vase in Malibu.

66. Supra n. 24.

67. Supra n. 42.

68. Supra n. 59.

69. Moore 344–345; she notes that the hatched pattern on the tail is a convention of Middle and Late Corinthian vase painters; among Chalcidian vases, she notes this pattern only in works by the Inscription Painter. In addition to the krater London B 15 (supra n. 59), she cites the fragment in Ostermundigen (supra n. 58).

70. The white of the horse is added over an undercoat of black glaze. Rumpf 56–57 and Keck 25 noted that among the earliest works by the Inscription Painter, the white pigment was applied directly on the clay ground of the vessel; among his more developed works, however, black glaze was used as an undercoat for the added white; this is especially clear on Cabinet des Médailles 202 (supra n. 25), where the added white of the great steer beneath handle B/A has worn away, revealing the black ground beneath.

71. Supra n. 31.

72. Supra n. 25.

73. Supra n. 34.

74. F. Lissarrague (supra n. 4) 20–21.

75. *Iliad* 10.460–469. Davidson (supra n. 13) discusses the significant associations between the use of the animal skin as clothing or disguise and the wearer's assumption of that creature's characteristics, with particular reference to the wolf-skin worn by Dolon to cover his body. As she points out, this use of the animal skin may well have its origins in early initiation rituals, such as those documented in Arcadian myth and the cult of Zeus Lykaios (64–66).

76. Supra n. 33.

77. Keck, cat. no IV6; Iozzo 13, 24.

78. Rumpf, cat. no. 111.

79. Rumpf 56.

80. Supra n. 31.

81. Supra n. 26.

82. Supra n. 25.

83. Rumpf 153; Keck 21; Iozzo 14.

84. Iozzo 21; Keck 21 would have the production of Chalcidian vases begin somewhat later, just before 550 B.C., and end around 510 B.C.

85. Rumpf 139–140; L. Banti, "Calcidesi, Vasi," *EAA* II, 263.

86. Banti (supra n. 85) 262.

87. Rumpf 70.

26

MENELAOS AND HELEN IN TROY

✦

MARTIN ROBERTSON

On the great skyphos in Boston[1] with the names of Hieron as potter and Makron as painter, the subject is Helen.[2] On one side of the vase she leaves Sparta with Paris, Aeneas walking ahead, Eros and Aphrodite decking her, Peitho behind; under the handle a boy follows the procession. On the other side (fig. 26.1) she flees to Aphrodite's protecting arms from Menelaos who, with helmet, shield, and greaves, advances on her drawing his sword. Behind Aphrodite stand a woman and an old man, named Kriseis and Kriseus; under the handle, behind Menelaos, Priam sits (fig. 26.2).

The scene of Menelaos attacking Helen with a sword, Aphrodite or Eros or occasionally Apollo intervening to protect her, recurs often in fifth-century art. Sometimes the scene is isolated, without context, but often it forms part of the Iliupersis, the final sack of Troy by the victorious Greeks. It is, I think, always assumed that such is the meaning of Makron's picture, but the figure of Priam makes it to my mind very difficult, indeed I would say almost impossible, for this to be right. The death of Priam is the climactic event of the Iliupersis, in many representations in the center round which other episodes are grouped. The treatment of the old king varies, but

within narrow limits. The Brygos Painter[3] has him, white-haired, white-bearded, reach out his hands for mercy to Neoptolemos, who strikes at him with the corpse of his grandson Astyanax. In the Kleophrades Painter's picture[4] he is stubbly and clasps his bloody head while, the dead child on his knees, he awaits the coup de grace from the Greek (see fig. 15.10 this volume). In both, however, he sits on the unavailing altar, a figure of terror and pity. Makron's Priam sits, quiet and spruce, on a richly covered stool, his right hand resting on his staff. He is at home; and only the gesture of his left hand shows disturbance at the untoward action he is witness to. Nor does he seem very old: balding and his hair behind gray, but his neat beard is black.

A case has been argued for Makron having muddled his mythology on a cup in Leningrad where he showed Theseus drawing a sword on a woman with the name of his mother Aithra where one might rather expect his stepmother Medea.[5] Even if this is right, however, it is a very different matter. Whatever the myth shown on the cup, it is not part of the common currency of the time as the Iliupersis is. I do not see how Makron *could* have drawn Priam in this way and meant him to be present at

FIGURE 26.1. Menelaos attacking Helen. Skyphos, Boston Museum of Fine Arts 13.186. Francis Bartlett Fund. (Photograph courtesy Museum of Fine Arts, Boston.)

the sack of his city; and in fact there is an alternative possibility which perfectly suits the way the artist here presents the king.

More than thirty years ago Beazley published a Corinthian krater,[6] painted, I suppose, some three-quarters of a century before Makron's vase, which shows three figures, Menelawos, Oliseus and Talthybios, sitting suppliant and approached by a large party, women on foot and men on horseback, led by Theano. Theano was the wife of Antenor, the wise old Trojan, Priam's contemporary, who consistently counseled peace with the Greeks. The subject, as Beazley showed, is an embassy to Troy to try to recover Helen by peaceful means. There are two references to such an embassy in the *Iliad*, Menelaos and Odysseus being named in both; Talthybios, as Agamemnon's herald, is a natural third. In one of these passages[7] Antenor says that he took the ambassa-

dors into his house and acted as their sponsor. From the other[8] it appears that a party among the Trojans wished to kill them. Proclus' summary of the *Cypria* refers without detail to such an embassy taking place after the first battle, in which Protesilaos was killed, when the Greeks had succeeded in landing but before the beginning of the siege.[9]

Suppose that in some account of this embassy, the *Cypria* or another, a story was told that Menelaos was seized with murderous rage when he set eyes again on the matchless beauty he had possessed and lost. Makron's rendering of Priam would perfectly fit the time and circumstance: ten years younger than at the sack and untouched by the terrible losses of those years, presiding at a discussion. Against this one could argue that the ambassadors would have gone as civilians, not as warriors. Certainly on the Corinthian krater Menelaos and Odysseus are bare-headed and robed (young Talthybios is dressed as a herald), but they carry spears and, more significantly, are girt with swords. If the writer of an account which lies somewhere behind the vase paintings envisaged them like this it would allow him to have Menelaos draw his sword. I can see the Attic vase painter

432

FIGURE 26.2. Priam (detail from fig. 26.1). Francis Bartlett Fund. (Photograph courtesy Museum of Fine Arts, Boston.)

proceeding from that action to imagine the hero fully armed more easily than I can see him imagining Priam at the sack in the way he shows him in this picture.

The figures behind Aphrodite, named Kriseis and Kriseus, do not help to fix the occasion. It is often supposed the vase painter had Chryseis and her father Chryses in mind. This is likely enough, but I suppose he rather took names with a Trojan association to give to two spectators than conceived these people as real participants. Chryses in the *Iliad* is priest of Apollo at Chryse, and it is there that his daughter is delivered to him after Agamemnon has reluctantly relinquished her at the beginning of the *Iliad*. They are not a likely couple to find in Troy at the sack, and though one might imagine a story which placed them there at the beginning of the war, none is recorded.

Clearly in one version of the legend the attack was set in the context of the Iliupersis; but the meeting of Menelaos and Helen then was not always envisaged like this. In Demodokos' song in the *Odyssey*,[10] Odysseus is said to have accompanied Menelaos to the house of Deiphobos; and Proclus in his summary of Arktinos' *Ilioupersis*[11] says that Menelaos, having found Helen there, killed Deiphobos and led her to the ships. This is how Menelaos and Helen are shown in many black-figure and early red-figure pictures, sometimes in pictures of the sack, often without context: a fully armed warrior leading a veiled woman. His sword is drawn but there is neither threat nor flight. Makron's picture is among the earlier in Attic vase painting to show the attack, though one painted by Oltos on a vase (to which we shall return) with the name of Pamphaios as potter must be considerably older. In the Peloponnese, Pausanias describes an attack-scene on the Chest of Kypselos,[12] but the bronze reliefs from shield-bands show only the hero leading his submissive wife away.[13] Euripides and Aristophanes refer to Helen disarming Menelaos by baring her breast, and a scholiast on the passage in Aristophanes' *Lysistrata* says that the story is in Ibykos, adding a reference to Leschas' *Little Iliad*.[14] It has been doubted whether this detail can actually have been in these early writers

433

(there is certainly no trace of it in Archaic art), but presumably they did describe the attack. The *Little Iliad* included an account of the sack, so that was presumably the setting of the act there, and other references to Iby-kos[15] rather suggest that he described it in the same context. Euripides certainly placed it there.

Hieron and Makron's vase has been known for more than a century. Twenty years ago another appeared which now has to be considered with it. That too (in Berlin)[16] is a big skyphos, of the same unusual design with sloping handles,[17] and with decoration similarly placed, but by a different though no less masterly hand: the Triptolemos Painter. One side has a warrior's departure; under each handle an altar; and on the other side a bearded warrior attacks a woman (fig. 26.3). The action in Makron's depiction moves from right to left, in the other form left to right, and there are other important differences; but to scholars familiar with Makron's picture on such a similar vase the immediately natural interpretation is Menelaos and Helen. Such I took it for; and as such Elfriede Knauer treated it in her admirable publication.[18] A year or two later, however, Roland Hampe[19] argued powerfully against this and in favor of a totally different story.

Four Doric columns mark the setting as an interior. Against the left-hand one leans a shield, and a spear slopes across the second from the right. In the center the warrior lunges forward, left arm out to seize the woman who flees, looking back and reaching her right hand out to him in supplication. In his right hand the warrior holds a naked sword and seems about to thrust. Beyond the woman a young man retreats, looking back. He wears a himation but no chiton and his hair is looped up under a diadem. His sword-belt is on, but not in the normal way (over the right shoulder and under the left arm, so that the scabbard hangs by the left thigh). Here it is slung round his neck, evidently snatched up and thrown on in a hurry; and as he flees he draws the sword. I suppose the spear and shield in the background are his, too, though they could belong to the attacker. Behind the warrior is Athena, in helmet and aegis, her spear held on her shoulder in her right hand. Her left arm is lost, but finger-ends show that the hand was raised, open.

If this represents Menelaos attacking Helen, is the scene laid at the embassy or at the sack? At the time of the sack Helen's Trojan husband was Deiphobos, at the time of the embassy Paris. The hair looped up under the decorated diadem would suit Paris well, but one cannot say that it is out of place for Deiphobos. There might be another reason for seeing this figure as Deiphobos, and we will return to that in a moment. The warrior's departure on the other side might be thought more relevant to the beginning of the war, but it need not be closely connected and is not out of place in any heroic context. If, however, Hampe's view is right, the question does not arise.

The objections to an identification as Menelaos and Helen are the absence of a deity intervening to protect the woman and, more importantly, the presence of one behind the warrior. Menelaos did not kill Helen, and no deity ever intended that he should. He drew his sword on her in a spasm of rage, but he did not use it. He is often shown either just pulling it from the sheath, as Makron has him, or letting it fall from his fingers under the renewed impact of his wife's beauty, a change of heart often underlined by the presence of Aphrodite or Eros. However, he does sometimes seem near dealing the death-blow, as here; notably in Oltos' picture,[20] where he holds the sword just as our warrior does and grips Helen's wrist (both figures are named). Oltos' pair is isolated, and there are many such representations where no helping deity is introduced. In a more fully realized setting like the Triptolemos Painter's the absence of such a figure is more surprising but need not be significant. Athena's presence behind the attacker raises a more serious problem, as Hampe saw.

The goddess can hardly be shown encouraging Menelaos in this self-defeating act which he did not in fact commit, but it is quite as hard to see this figure giving other than encouragement. True, at the beginning of the *Iliad*[21] Athena appears behind Achilles to restrain him from drawing his sword on Agamemnon; but she makes her intention very clear, seizing him by the hair before the weapon is unsheathed and telling him to stop. Athena in our picture does not touch the aggressor; and in Attic vase painting of this time a deity is constantly shown behind a hero and always as an encourager. On a hydria in Berlin by the Syleus Painter with a strange picture of Athena and Dionysos separating Theseus and Ariadne,[22] the goddess is in movement and gesture very like the one on the skyphos. On the hydria she is indeed directing the hero away from his will towards his des-

FIGURE 26.3. Menelaos attacking Helen? or Tydeus killing Ismene? Skyphos, Berlin Antikenmuseum 1970.9. (Photograph courtesy Antikenmuseum Berlin, Staatliche Museen Preussischer Kulturbesitz; photo by Ute Jung.)

tiny; but there Theseus, however unwillingly, is following her behest. I find it hard not to suppose that in the Triptolemos Painter's picture the goddess must be encouraging the hero in his action, and what with her encouragement he must carry it through.

Menelaos did indeed kill Deiphobos when he found Helen during the sack, and I suppose one might say that the warrior's attack in the picture is directed against the fleeing man. I find it hard, though, to read the picture that way. The warrior's left hand is lost, but it is hardly possible to restore it in any other way than as seizing the woman's shoulder. Given the conventions, as we perceive them, of representation in this period, I can hardly think that a contemporary could have read this picture otherwise than as "warrior kills woman."

Hampe pointed out that there is a story which meets

this requirement and was known to Attick vase painters of this time. The early lyric poet Mimnermus is reported as having written how Tydeus, at Athena's behest, killed Ismene because she slept with Theoklymenos.[23] A Corinthian neck-amphora in the Louvre,[24] of the same time and character as the embassy krater, shows Tydeus thrusting his sword at a bare-breasted Hysmena on a couch, while a naked man, Periklymenos, flees; clearly a version of the same tale. An Attic white-ground cup-tondo in the same collection,[25] which cannot be far in date from the two skyphoi, shows a naked woman on a couch put to the sword by a man; and the group is so like that on the Corinthian vase that Angelika Waiblinger is certainly right in identifying the subject as the same. The omission of Periklymenos or Theoklymenos is a function of the size and shape of the field to be decorated. The Triptolemos Painter has space both for him and for the vengeful goddess.

It has been suggested that, while the constancy of the iconographic structure between the group on the Corinthian neck-amphora and that on the Attic cup fully justifies the identification of the subject there, it is bad methodology to extend this identification to the quite

435

different iconography of the skyphos, where the woman is fully clad and trying to escape. This is a valuable caution, but I do not feel that it outweighs the arguments in favor of the identification. Clearly there is a connection between this new iconography for Tydeus and Ismene (if such it be) and Makron's iconography for Menelaos and Helen; but that in itself is unusual, and I do not think it unlikely that one artist's treatment of one story might influence another's treatment of a different story.

I have been arguing here, first, that Makron's picture shows Menelaos drawing his sword on Helen not at the sack but during the embassy ten years before; and, secondly, that Hampe was probably right to dissociate the Triptolemos Painter's picture from this story; but I am very far from certain of either conclusion. I could wish to have found a more satisfying end for my offering; but Emily Vermeule is a scholar who does not mind leaving a question open, and I hope there may be something in this for her to enjoy.

NOTES

1. Boston 13.186; *ARV²* 458.1; L. D. Caskey and J. D. Beazley, *Attic Vase Paintings in the Museum of Fine Arts, Boston* III (Oxford 1963) 32–37, no. 140, pls. 76–77.

2. On the iconography of Helen's story, see L. B. Ghali-Kahil, *Les enlèvements et le retour d'Hélène* (Paris 1955).

3. Cup, Louvre G 152; *ARV²* 369.1.

4. Hydria, Naples 2422; *ARV²* 189.74.

5. Leningrad 649; *ARV²* 460.13. C. Sourvinou-Inwood, *Theseus as Son and Stepson*, BICS Suppl. 40 (London 1979).

6. Astarita Collection (now Vatican); J. D. Beazley, "ΈΛΕΝΗΣ ΆΠΑΙΤΗΣΙΣ," *ProcBritAc* 43 (1957) 233–244.

7. *Iliad* 3.203–224.

8. *Iliad* 11.122–142, especially 123–125 and 138–142.

9. T. W. Allen, ed., *Homeri Opera* V (Oxford 1946) 104–105.

10. *Odyssey* 8.514–520.

11. *Homeri Opera* V (supra n. 9) 108 top.

12. Paus. 5.18.3.

13. E. Kunze, *Archaische Schildbänder*, OlForsch 2 (Berlin 1950) 163–167.

14. Eur. *Andr.* 627–631; Ar. *Lys.* 155; scholiast quoted, Roscher, s.v. Helene, 1945.

15. Ibykos frr. 15, 16; D. L. Page, *Poetae Melici Graeci* (Oxford 1962) nos. 296, 297.

16. Berlin 1970.9; not known to Beazley. See infra nn. 18, 19.

17. See M. Robertson, *The Art of Vase-Painting in Classical Athens* (Cambridge 1992) 104–105 and figs. 100–101; see also 114–115 and fig. 114.

18. E. R. Knauer, *Ein Skyphos des Triptolemosmalers*, BWPr 125 (Berlin 1973).

19. R. Hampe, "Tydeus und Ismene," *AntK* 18 (1975) 10–15.

20. Nicosthenic neck-amphora: Louvre G 3; *ARV²* 53.1; Ghali-Kahil (supra n. 2), pl. 49.2.

21. *Iliad* 1.188–222.

22. Berlin 2179; *ARV²* 252.52; K. A. Neugebauer, *Führer durch das Antiquarium* (Berlin 1932), pl. 45; Robertson (supra n. 17) 123, fig. 126.

23. Mimnermus fr. 21 in M. L. West, *Iambi et Elegi Graeci* II (Oxford 1972) 89.

24. Louvre E 640; H. Payne, *Necrocorinthia* (Oxford 1931) 327 no. 1437.

25. Louvre G 109; not listed by Beazley. A. Waiblinger, "Remarques sur une coupe à fond blanc du Musée du Louvre," *RA* 1972, 233–242.

27

STORIES FROM THE TROJAN CYCLE IN THE WORK OF DOURIS

◆

DIANA BUITRON-OLIVER

Douris represented stories from the Trojan cycle on vases throughout his career, but most of these belong to a period transitional between his earliest work and his more mature style, generally dated to the first decade of the fifth century B.C. At this time mythological subjects appear on over half his vases—they are never again so frequent in his work. Douris was then at the height of his creative powers. His drawing style had lost the stiff awkwardness of his earliest work; his figures are compact, and well proportioned, and move easily and gracefully. The mythological scenes are characterized by a richness of detail in the painting and a lavish use of dilute glaze to create textures and patterns.

Beyond an accomplished technical ability, Douris demonstrates that he is a painter of great subtlety, able to convey a number of ideas through the stories he chooses to represent; these ideas reflect a keen knowledge of oral and literary traditions and an unusual sensitivity to the society of his time. The two vases to be considered here illustrate the variety of his sources of inspiration. It is a pleasure to present these thoughts on Douris' approach to mythological subjects to Emily Vermeule, who has been a source of inspiration to so many students of antiquity.

IPHIGENEIA (FIGS. 27.1 - 27.4)

We begin with a story told in the *Kypria,* the lost poem which recounted the events that preceded the Trojan War. A fragmentary white lekythos in Palermo shows Iphigeneia, daughter of Agamemnon and Klytaimnestra, being led to sacrifice by the warrior Teukros. Two other warriors, now only partially preserved, follow Iphigeneia (the one directly behind her is preserved from the waist down, while only the right foot of the second remains). The vase was found at the sanctuary of Demeter Malophoros at Selinus, Sicily, in the 1920s and was published by E. Gabrici, who attributed it to Douris.[1]

Douris has taken care to tell us exactly what is happening by identifying the figures, ΙΦΙΛΕΝΕΙΑ,

FIGURE 27.1. Warrior taking Iphigeneia to sacrifice, detail, white lekythos, Palermo, Museo Archeologico NI 1886.

FIGURE 27.2. Iphigeneia led to sacrifice, detail, white lekythos, Palermo, Museo Archeologico NI 1886.

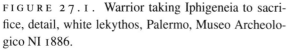; and, over the altar, we read Λ P, probably for ΑΡΤΕΜΙΔΟΣ, the altar of Artemis. There are no other inscriptions on the vase. Without the inscriptions the scene might be misidentified, for its composition is similar to representations of the recovery of Helen, and both are based on the motif of the bride led to her wedding.[2] In ordinary wedding scenes, the bride often lifts her veil, a traditional gesture indicating modesty. Here Iphigeneia may be lifting her veil to wipe away a tear.[3]

Iphigeneia is dressed in finery appropriate for a wedding. She wears a diaphanous and intricately pleated chiton, embroidered himation, sandals, diadem, earrings, necklace, bracelets, and veil. Teukros leads her forward; he grasps the edge of her himation and holds a sword poised over the sacrificial altar, which is situated near a palm tree. The altar and palm tree denote the sacred nature of the place and are often found in association with wedding preparations.[4] The altar is that of

Artemis, the goddess who demanded Iphigeneia's sacrifice, but who is also a goddess associated with the transition to womanhood through marriage.[5]

In choosing to show the sacrifice of Iphigeneia in a manner recalling the iconography of marriage scenes, Douris conveys a particular message which may be clarified by considering another of his white lekythoi painted during this period, one in Cleveland which shows not a Trojan subject, but one from heroic legend: Atalante racing along in all her finery pursued by two Erotes, one with a whip, the other with a garland[6] (figs. 27.5–27.7). John Boardman has suggested that Atalante, whose dislike of men is a constant theme in literature from Hesiod on, is fleeing from marriage. Her running pose probably alludes to the footrace in which she and her suitors engaged and which she always won, thereby allowing her to kill the suitor who had challenged her. The garland held by one Eros would be a symbol of the marriage Atalante flees, the whip held by

438

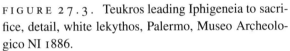

FIGURE 27.3. Teukros leading Iphigeneia to sacrifice, detail, white lekythos, Palermo, Museo Archeologico NI 1886.

FIGURE 27.4. Altar and palm tree, detail, white lekythos, Palermo, Museo Archeologico NI 1886.

the other suggests that such a reluctant bride would have to be beaten into submission.[7]

Atalante's rejection of men and her desire for chastity is linked with her dedication to Artemis. Iphigeneia too is dedicated to Artemis, but not from choice, since she was lured to Aulis under the pretext of marriage with Achilles, which makes the allusion to a wedding all the more poignant.[8] Ian Jenkins has suggested that the scene on the Palermo lekythos employs the iconography of the wedding in order to connect the change at marriage with the one that occurs at death.[9] It is beyond the scope of this paper to examine in detail the long tradition of correlating marriage with death. The marriage of Persephone, for example, was a paradigm for death, as well as the primary Greek myth of marriage.[10] Suffice it to say that the purpose of marriage was procreation, and since a high percentage of women died in childbirth, the equation of marriage and death would have had a vivid reality in antiquity.

The fate of Iphigeneia is in fact disputed. The earliest source is the *Kypria,* probably composed in the seventh century B.C.[11] The poem is known only through the summary by Photius of the *Chrestomathy* of Proclus, which told the entire story of Troy including the parts not embraced by the *Iliad* or the *Odyssey.* The story there ends not with her death, but with her translation to Tauris. This version seems to have been followed by Euripides in his play *Iphigeneia in Tauris,* where Iphigeneia is a priestess to Artemis.[12] In the Hesiodic *Catalogue of Women* a phantom is substituted for Iphigeneia, and Pausanias, referring to this work, says that Iphigeneia was changed into Hekate at the moment of sacrifice.[13] That she is sacrificed and dies is the premise of Aeschylus' *Agamemnon* and the theme of Euripides' later play, *Iphigeneia in Aulis.* In Euripides' earlier play Iphigeneia's duties as priestess required her to kill a number of young men; in this respect too she is comparable with Atalante. Cedric Boulter suggested that the two lekythoi

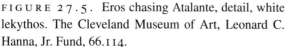

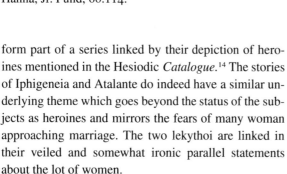

FIGURE 27.5. Eros chasing Atalante, detail, white lekythos. The Cleveland Museum of Art, Leonard C. Hanna, Jr. Fund, 66.114.

FIGURE 27.6. Atalante chased by Erotes, detail, white lekythos. The Cleveland Museum of Art, Leonard C. Hanna, Jr. Fund, 66.114.

form part of a series linked by their depiction of heroines mentioned in the Hesiodic *Catalogue*.[14] The stories of Iphigeneia and Atalante do indeed have a similar underlying theme which goes beyond the status of the subjects as heroines and mirrors the fears of many woman approaching marriage. The two lekythoi are linked in their veiled and somewhat ironic parallel statements about the lot of women.

The theme of marriage and death relates to the function of the vase as well. White lekythoi are decorated almost exclusively with funerary scenes only from the second quarter of the fifth century on, but even before then the shape had a funerary use alongside its household use.[15] The scenes on the two white lekythoi by Douris, in their correlation of marriage with death or sacrifice, would certainly have been appropriate as grave gifts. A cultic use is attested for the Iphigeneia

lekythos, as mentioned above, found in a sanctuary of Demeter; here the funerary connotations would have been particularly appropriate because of the association of marriage and death in the myth of Persephone.

THE ARMS OF ACHILLES (FIGS. 27.8 - 27.10)

We turn now to episodes that follow the events in the *Iliad*. A cup in Vienna has inspired more comment than almost any other vase by Douris because of its beauty and because of the detailed narrative featured in its three scenes: the story of the arms of Achilles. The cup was found in a tomb at Cerveteri in 1865 and was published in that same year.[16] It was signed by both painter and potter: ΛΟΡΙΣΕΛΡΑΦΣΕΝ appears in the

FIGURE 27.7. Eros chasing Atalante, white lekythos. The Cleveland Museum of Art, Leonard C. Hanna, Jr. Fund, 66.114. H: 31.7 cm.

FIGURE 27.8. Greek heroes quarreling over the arms of Achilles, side A, red figure kylix, Vienna, Kunsthistorisches Museum IV 3695.

tondo, and the name Python, unaccompanied by a verb, appears on the foot in this potter's customary manner of signing. Chairestratos is praised as *kalos* on side B, and an anonymous *pais* on side A. There are no other inscriptions beyond these, none of the identifying labels generally favored by Douris and often found on other vases of this period.

The story of the arms of Achilles is known from two poems summarized in the *Chrestomathy:* the *Aithiopis,* which ended with the quarrel of Ajax and Odysseus, and the *Little Iliad,* which began with the same story. Aeschylus wrote a trilogy on the subject, the three plays of which were entitled *The Award of the Arms, The Thracian Women,* and the *Women of Salamis;* but only frag-

ments of these are preserved. The date of the trilogy is not known but it is not inconceivable that it could have been produced as early as the 490s.[17]

The three scenes on the cup by Douris tell the story in sequence. Side A shows the quarrel that set off the tragedy leading to the suicide of Ajax (fig. 27.8). Ajax, on the left, has already drawn his sword and is lunging forward, his hotheadedness emphasized by his jutting chin and beard, and by the reddish hair he has been given through the use of dilute glaze—hair that contrasts with the black hair found on all other figures on the cup. Odysseus, on the right, has been slower to draw his sword; a restraining arm has kept him from pulling it all the way out of the scabbard. Agamemnon, in the center, sides with Odysseus: his pose, right elbow jutting out, profile head turned toward Ajax, repeats that of Odysseus and clashes with the advancing Ajax. The subject is made abundantly clear by the disputed armor in the center, while the composition, poses, and indi-

442

FIGURE 27.9. Greek heroes voting, side B, red-figure kylix, Vienna, Kunsthistorisches Museum IV 3695.

FIGURE 27.10. Odysseus giving the armor of Achilles to Neoptolemos, tondo, red figure kylix, Vienna, Kunsthistorisches Museum IV 3695. D tondo: 21.5 cm; D: 33.8 cm; H: 12.8 cm.

vidualized figures identify the opponents. This composition recalls a series of black-figure lekythoi of the end of the sixth century B.C. that show armed warriors parted by a man or by Athena. The figures are not named but they have sometimes been identified as Ajax and Odysseus quarrelling.[18]

Side B, which continues the story, presents the action with equal clarity: a vote is taking place, center stage held by Athena who stands before the block on which were placed the pebbles used to tally the votes (fig. 27.9). More votes have accumulated on the left side of the block, and it is in this direction that Athena faces, her right arm gesturing to Odysseus on the far left, who raises his hands in covetous glee. Ajax, on the far right, turns away from the disastrous vote and pulls his cloak over his head in the standard gesture of mourning.

The vote to determine to whom the arms of Achilles should be awarded first appeared on vases in the years between 500 and 480 B.C.[19] These vases also provide the earliest evidence we have for a vote as the method of making the judgment. In the earliest literary source, the *Odyssey,* Odysseus, regretting the anger displayed toward him by the ghost of Ajax in the Underworld, states that the award was judged by the "sons of the Trojans with Pallas Athene" (*Odyssey* 11.547). Various scholiasts' notes support similar methods of arriving at the decision, giving responsibility for the judgment to a group of Trojan prisoners who were asked to say whom they feared the most, or stating that the decision was based on a conversation overheard between two Trojan girls, one of whom was inspired by Athena to praise Odysseus above Ajax.[20] Fifth-century literary sources reflect more democratic methods of judging. One of the surviving fragments of Aeschylus' *Award of the Arms* seems to suggest that the decision was made after the rivals had made speeches. Both Pindar in *Nemean* 8, composed around 459 B.C., and Sophocles in the *Ajax,* written nearly twenty years later, imply that fraud took place in a secret vote: "The great prize is given to the supple liar. In their secret ballots the Danaans made much of Odysseus, and Aias lost the golden armor and died struggling in his own blood."[21]

Douris painted three other versions of this story and I have suggested elsewhere that he may have invented its iconography; the subject also appears in the work of his contemporaries.[22] These scenes, with their emphasis on the mechanics of a voting procedure, may reflect the new political atmosphere of the early fifth century resulting in particular from the legislative reforms of Kleisthenes which had taken place in 508/507 B.C. Kleisthenes' reorganization of the Assembly gave greater power to ordinary citizens and greater significance to their votes. Although most of the evidence for the actual voting procedure comes from fourth-century B.C. sources, it is generally believed to go back to the reorganization by Kleisthenes.[23]

Whether or not the voting scenes that appear on vases depicting the story of the arms of Achilles show an actual method of voting in early fifth-century Athens, the important point is that their appearance in the early fifth century may have been prompted by the enhanced importance of voting that resulted from the Kleisthenic reforms. George Huxley suggests that another example of the effect of the enhanced importance of voting can be seen in Athena's tie-breaking vote in Aeschylus' *Eumenides.* The story of Ajax was particularly appropriate because by the early fifth century, the Salaminian hero had been thoroughly Atticized. Ajax had a long-standing cult in Athens, and in 508 B.C. Kleisthenes, with Delphic assistance, named one of the ten new tribes for him; he thus became one of the eponymous heroes.[24] By focusing on this particular aspect of a tale about a newly important hero, the painter (or his patron) might have been commenting on the importance of the popular vote in his own time.

The tondo continues the narrative of the armor one stage further, but the action there has been variously interpreted (fig. 27.10). Some scholars see Odysseus receiving, not giving, the armor,[25] others, including Beazley, believe that it is Neoptolemos, Achilles' son, who receives the armor from Odysseus. Elements of the composition make the latter interpretation more likely. Odysseus extends the corslet toward Neoptolemos, leaving a space between it and himself; the direction of movement is from Odysseus to Neoptolemos. Neoptolemos is admiring the helmet, which faces him and not Odysseus. I suggest that the arrangement of the armor—helmet at head level, corslet at chest level, and greaves on the ground as if worn by an unseen figure—reminded viewers of the tradition that when Odysseus gave the armor to Neoptolemos, Neoptolemos saw the ghost of Achilles. A closer look at the helmet reveals how this subtle visual image is strengthened by the human appearance of this piece of armor. The black cheek pieces cover a shaded area that suggests the flesh that would once have been within. The tradition that the ghost of Achilles appeared to Neoptolemos when Odysseus gave him the armor is known today only in the *Chrestomathy,* but it is possible that one play of the lost trilogy by Aeschylus included a scene with the ghost of Achilles.

The picture in the tondo visually emphasizes the disputed armor which is the theme of both exterior scenes. It would be reasonable for Douris to depict armor that was current in the early fifth century, and the composite corslet, helmet, and greaves could certainly be contemporary with the artist.[26] The helmet is basically a Corinthian type, but with Chalcidian details—the opening for the ears, and the hinged cheek pieces.[27] It is elaborately ornamented; besides the black cheek pieces, it has relief dots suggesting hair along the forehead, and an intricate pattern at the base of the crest. The oval shield with arcs cut into its circumference has a device of a lion attacking a deer shown in black silhouette. It is a so-called Boiotian shield, which has been considered an imaginary type denoting heroic circumstances.[28] No such shape survives today, but the evidence for shields in general is scanty, probably because they were made mostly of perishable materials.[29] John Boardman argues a case for the existence of the Boiotian shield and suggests that their use might have been limited to specific functions: military, ceremonial, or votive. He points out that on vases it is most commonly worn by Ajax and Achilles.[30] The rest of the armor is also rendered in elaborate detail: the composite corslet with its shoulder pieces, scales, and pteryges; the greaves with their pattern of stylized bone and muscle; and the famous spear that only Achilles could wield.

This is Achilles' second set of armor, made by Hephaistos at Thetis' request after his first panoply had been lost to Hektor when Patroklos fell in battle (*Iliad* 17.130–131). Although Achilles regained the first set when he killed Hektor and stripped the body, that is the last we hear of it (22.321–322, 366–368). The presence of a single spear instead of the usual pair is consistent with this interpretation. Patroklos, when donning Achilles' first set of armor, takes a pair of spears rather than the spear of Achilles, the ash spear which Chiron had given to Peleus and which only Achilles knew how to wield. In his commentary on the *Chrestomathy,* Albert Severyns proposed that the ghost of Achilles appears in order to teach his son Neoptolemos the use of glorious arms, specifically how to use the tricky, double-pointed spear that Chiron gave to Peleus.[31]

The disputed armor appears in the quarrel scene on the exterior of this cup as well. The helmet and greaves are similar to those in the tondo, but not identical; the helmet has black cheek pieces but lacks the shaded area that suggests the ghost. The corslet and shield are different. The divine armor appears in the work of other painters of the period, in scenes of the quarrel and in scenes set in the forge of Hephaistos.[32] It is generally quite

elaborate. For example, the helmets may have scales (Makron), checkerboards (Brygos Painter), dilute hair on the forehead (Brygos Painter), or relief dots (Foundry Painter) as in the tondo by Douris.[33]

The description of Achilles' armor in Book 18 of the *Iliad* is fairly general, except for the shield. The salient characteristic of the armor is its brightness, and Douris may have hoped to convey some of the polished metal's brightness by frequent use of star ornaments on shield and corslet. This would certainly have been an appropriate motif, for in the *Iliad* the gleam of a warrior's armor is often compared with stars and other celestial bodies.[34] In this context, Beazley also thought of the *Iliad*. Four large stars appear in the tondo of the name piece of the Foundry Painter in Berlin, the same vase mentioned above which has a helmet similar to the one in the Douris tondo. In discussing this picture, Beazley suggested that the stars might make modest allusion to the long and detailed description of the shield (18.483–485):[35]

> He made the earth upon it, and the sky, and the sea's water, and the tireless sun, and the moon waxing into her fullness, and on it all the constellations that festoon the heavens. . . .

Finally, with regard to the shield, a vase painter familiar with the *Iliad* would find the lion emblem appropriate for the shield of a Homeric hero, for the simile of the lion is the most common one for describing fighting men.[36] Proposing that a vase painter had such a detailed knowledge of the *Iliad* or any specific literary source is fraught with risk. There are, however, other instances that suggest this possibility, as John Boardman has shown for the Kleophrades Painter.[37] In support of Douris' literacy is the fact that he is one of the most prolific writers of inscriptions on vases of the Late Archaic period, with inscriptions of all kinds, including fragments of known poems, appearing in his work.[38]

Douris' sources of inspiration were clearly not just literary. In his representation of the Iphigeneia story he may have been particularly influenced by cult tradition and marriage lore, and the voting scene in the Ajax story may well have been inspired by the political changes of the time. On a broader scale, Douris' inspiration for the

445

images he used might have come from another contemporary source, the theater. Many admirers of Greek pottery have considered the relationship between scenes on vases and theatrical performances.[39] This source of inspiration would have been particularly powerful in the first decade of the fifth century, when Douris represented more mythological stories than at any other time, because the importance of the theater in communal life was also increased by the advent of democracy.[40] In addition, it is possible that the foundation in Athens of the City Dionysia, the festival that included dramatic contests, occurred shortly before 500 B.C. W. R. Connor has suggested that the traditional date of 534 B.C. is too early, that it should be brought down to 501 B.C.[41] It would then come after the fall of the tyranny and shortly after the reforms of Kleisthenes and the beginning of the new democratic system. The record for prizes in tragedy thus might begin in 501 B.C. We know that a tradition existed that Aeschylus, who treated all the subjects discussed here, produced plays in competition with Pratinas and Chorilos in the 70th Olympiad, that is, 499–496 B.C.[42] Although we cannot with certainty link any of the subjects discussed here with specific performances, the dramatic staging of these powerful stories in Athens could well have had an impact on the subject matter of Athenian pottery.

NOTES

This paper has benefited from the help of several colleagues who have made suggestions for its improvement: Beth Cohen, George Huxley, Sarah Morris, Alan Shapiro, and Andrew Oliver.

1. Palermo NI 1886: *ARV*[2] 446.266; *Paralipomena* 375; *Beazley Addenda*[2] 241; E. Gabrici, *MonAnt* 32 (1927) 331–336. Fragments of the shoulder show that the ornament consisted of three palmettes enclosed in tendrils.

2. C. H. E. Haspels, "Deux fragments d'une coupe d'Euphronios," *BCH* 54 (1930) 437. See also I. Jenkins, "Is There Life After Marriage? A Study of the Abduction Motif in Vase Paintings of the Athenian Wedding Ceremony," *BICS* 30 (1983) 141–142; and A. J. N. W. Prag, *The Oresteia* (Warminster and Chicago 1985) 61. See also R. Seaford, "The Tragic Wedding," *JHS* 107 (1987) 106–130.

3. Cf. Prag (supra n. 2).

4. An explanation for the presence of Teukros is given by Gabrici (supra n. 1) 336. On the palm tree with altar motif see C. Sourvinou-Inwood, "Altars with Palm-Trees, Palm-Trees and Parthenoi," *BICS* 32 (1985) 125–146.

5. L. R. Farnell, *The Cults of the Greek States* vol. 2 (Oxford 1896) 444; Sourvinou-Inwood (supra n. 4) 125 and n. 2; and C. Sourvinou-Inwood, *Studies in Girls' Transitions* (Athens 1988) 132.

6. Cleveland 66.114: *Paralipomena* 376.266bis; *Beazley Addenda*[2] 241. Provenance unknown.

7. J. Boardman, "Atalanta," *The Art Institute of Chicago Centennial Lectures* (Chicago 1983) 3–19; and *LIMC* II.1, s.v. "Atalanta," 949. Cf. C. Bérard, "La Chasseresse Traquée," in M. Schmidt, ed., *Kanon. Festschrift Ernst Berger* (Basel 1988) 280–284.

8. In enticing Iphigeneia to Aulis on pretext of marriage with Achilles, Euripides follows Stesichorus; see D. L. Page, *Poetae Melici Graeci* (Oxford 1962) 116, Stesichorus 217. Iphigeneia is closely associated with Artemis in the cult at Brauron and elsewhere, see Farnell (supra n. 5) 440–444; and H. Lloyd-Jones, "Artemis and Iphigeneia," *JHS* 103 (1983) 87–102. It should be noted that Euripides makes Iphigeneia a willing and noble victim in *IA*.

9. Jenkins (supra n. 2) 141–142.

10. H. P. Foley, "Marriage and Sacrifice in Euripides' *Iphigeneia in Aulis*," *Arethusa* 15 (1982) 169.

11. G. L. Huxley, *Greek Epic Poetry* (Cambridge, Mass. 1969) 123, 144–145; J. Griffin, "The Epic Cycle and the uniqueness of Homer," *JHS* 97 (1977) 39–53; A. M. Snodgrass, "Poet and Painter in Eighth-century Greece," *PCPS* 205 (1979) 121. See also A. Severyns, *Le cycle épique dans l'école d'Aristarque* (Paris 1928) 324–342.

12. Huxley (supra n. 11) 127–128, 136; Eur. *IA* 6–30. The same happy ending was added by a later interpolator to Euripides' *IA*.

13. R. Merkelbach and M. L. West, *Fragmenta Hesiodea* (Oxford 1967) 13, 23a; 14, 23b; M. L. West, *The Hesiodic Catalogue of Women* (Oxford 1985) 134; Paus. 1.43.1; H. G. Evelyn-White, *Hesiod* (revised Loeb edition 1936) 205 fr. 71.

14. C. Boulter, *CVA* Cleveland 1 22. Boulter quotes a letter from J. D. Beazley which connects the two lekythoi stylistically.

15. J. D. Beazley, *Attic White Lekythoi* (Oxford 1938) 5–6; D. C. Kurtz, *Athenian White Lekythoi* (Oxford 1975) xix–xxi.

16. H. Brunn, *BdI* (1865) 217–218. The cup is Vienna 3695: *ARV*[2] 429.26; *Paralipomena* 374; *Beazley Addenda*[2] 236. It was found in the same tomb as another by Douris, Vienna 3694 (*ARV*[2] 427.3), painted five to ten years earlier.

17. H. J. Mette, *Die Fragmente der Tragödien des Aischy-*

los (Berlin 1959) 102–108; *Der Verlorene Aischylos* (Berlin 1963) 12–26; and D. Williams, "Ajax, Odysseus and the Arms of Achilles," *AntK* 23 (1980) 143.

18. For example see G. Hafner, *CVA* Karlsruhe 1 (Germany 7) 21, pl. 12. The subject also appears on other shapes (amphora: R. Lullies, *CVA* Munich 1 [Germany 3] 29, pl. 43; and band cup: *CVA* Laon 1 [France 20] pl. 21, 1, 6).

19. Williams (supra n. 17) 142.

20. *Odyssey* 11.547–548; on the scholiasts see Severyns (supra n. 11) 329–330.

21. Pind. *Nem.* 8. For the Aeschylus fragment see A. Nauck, *Tragicorum Graecorum Fragmenta* (1889) fr. 175; Mette 1959 (supra n. 17) fr. 286; H. Weir Smyth and H. Lloyd-Jones, *Aeschylus* (Loeb edition 1963) vol. 2, 438–439, fr. 90. See also the discussion by Williams (supra n. 17) 142–143; H. A. Shapiro, "Minutiae Archaeologicae. The Judgment of Arms on an Amphora in Kansas City," *BABesch* 56 (1981) 149–150; G. F. Pinney and R. Hamilton, "Secret Ballot," *AJA* 86 (1982) 581–584. Cf. M. Tiverios, *Mia "Krisis ton hoplon" tou zographou tou Sylea* (Athens 1985).

22. Cups by Douris: Paris, Cabinet des Médailles 675, 600, 597, 727 (part), 774, L224, and parts of 586, *ARV²* 428.14; Vatican, Astarita 133, *ARV²* 433.71; Vatican, Astarita 132, *ARV²* 433.72. See D. Buitron, *Douris* (Ph.D. diss., N.Y.U.) (Michigan, University Microfilms, 1976) 64. For the vases by other painters see Williams (supra n. 17) 138–143; also J. Boardman, "The Kleophrades Painter at Troy," *AntK* 19 (1976) 6–7, no. 14.

23. J. Ober, *Mass and Elite in Democratic Athens* (Princeton 1989) 68–70; on voting in fifth-century Athens see A. Boegehold, "Toward a Study of Athenian Voting Procedure," *Hesperia* 32 (1963) 366–374; E. S. Staveley, *Greek and Roman Voting and Elections* (London 1972) 84–86; M. H. Hansen, "How Did the Athenian *Ecclesia* Vote?" in *The Athenian Ecclesia* (Copenhagen 1983) 103–121.

24. See H. A. Shapiro, *Art and Cult under the Tyrants in Athens* (Mainz 1989) 154–157; cf. Williams (supra n. 17) 143–144.

25. F. Villard in *Archaic Greek Art* (New York 1971) 352–353; J. Boardman, *Athenian Red Figure Vases: The Archaic Period* (London 1975) caption to fig. 285.2; P. Ducrey, *Warfare in Ancient Greece* (New York 1985) 47, fig. 25.

26. On armor generally see A. M. Snodgrass, *Arms and Armour of the Greeks* (London 1967; reprint 1982). I have profited from discussions with Beth Cohen, who is writing a book on the iconography of armor and weapons in Greek art.

27. On helmets see H. Pflug in *Antike Helme Sammlung Lipperheide und andere Bestände des Antikenmuseums Berlin* (Mainz 1988).

28. Snodgrass (supra n. 26) 55; and A. M. Snodgrass, "Towards the Interpretation of the Geometric Figure-scenes," *AM* 95 (1980) 57.

29. Ducrey (supra n. 25) 50–52; P. C. Bol, *Argivische Schilde,* OlForsch 17 (Berlin 1989).

30. J. Boardman, "Symbol and Story in Geometric Art," in W. G. Moon, ed., *Ancient Greek Art and Iconography* (Madison 1983) 29–33.

31. Severyns (supra n. 11) 342. On the two sets of armor see D. von Bothmer, "The Arming of Achilles," *BMFA* 47 (1949) 84–90.

32. F. Brommer, *Vasenlisten zur griechischen Heldensage,* 3rd edition (Marburg 1973) 367–369.

33. Makron: Louvre C 11271, *ARV²* 460.12; Brygos Painter: London E69, *ARV²* 369.2, both illustrated in Williams (supra n. 17), pls. 34–35; Foundry Painter: Berlin 2294, *ARV²* 400.1, Boardman (supra n. 25), fig. 262.1.

34. For example, *Iliad* 5.5–8; 11.61–66; 19.381–382; and see B. Fenik, *Typical Battle Scenes in the Iliad* (Wiesbaden 1968) 11, 80.

35. J. D. Beazley, "A Greek Realist," in D. C. Kurtz, ed., *Greek Vases. Lectures by J. D. Beazley* (Oxford 1989) 78–79.

36. For example, *Iliad* 5.159–165, 297–310; 16.823; 18.579; and see Fenik (supra n. 34) 24, 33, 58.

37. Boardman (supra n. 22) 4.

38. H. Immerwahr, *Attic Script* (Oxford 1990) 85–87; J. R. Guy, "Dourian Literacy," in C. Bérard, C. Bron, and A. Pomari, eds., *Images et Société en Grèce ancienne* (Lausanne 1987) 223–225.

39. For example: L. Séchan, *Études sur la tragédie grecque dans ses rapports avec la céramique* (Paris 1926); E. Vermeule, "The Boston Oresteia Krater," *AJA* 70 (1966) 1–22; B. Döhle, "Beziehungen zwischen Drama und attischer Vasenmalerei in der 1. Hälfte des 5. Jahrhunderts v. Chr." *Wissenschaftliche Zeitschrift der Universität Rostock* 16 (1967) 431–435; Boardman (supra n. 22) 13–15; E. Simon, "Satyrplays on Vases in the time of Aeschylus," in D. Kurtz and B. Sparkes, eds., *The Eye of Greece* (Cambridge 1982) 123–148.

40. Cf. Boardman (supra n. 22) 13–15.

41. W. R. Connor, "City Dionysia and Athenian Democracy," *ClMed* 40 (1989) 7–32.

42. For testimonia see S. Radt, *Tragicorum Graecorum Fragmenta* vol. 3 (Göttingen 1985) 48.

28

PRIAM, KING OF TROY *

✦

MARGARET C. MILLER

The power of myth lies in its combined qualities of permanence and variability. Myth allows a constant adjustment of meaning as ideological perspectives shift; each passing generation may alter the surface structure of myth to express its own unique experience. The iconography of myth in Athens mirrors the transition from aristocratic to democratic ideology and in its wake the evolution of ethnic identity. Edith Hall in *Inventing the Barbarian* has recently discussed the "barbarization" of Greek myth in Attic drama and shown that by mid-fifth century the process was well under way. Iconographic evidence in general terms supports the evidence of tragedy, but even as there are more extant pots than plays, so we find that the patterns revealed in pots exhibit a wider variety in development. Like many another figure of myth, Priam, the king of Troy, starts his iconographic existence as a Greek hero and ends as an Oriental tyrant—but Priam orientalizes two generations after other "Oriental" kings. The change reflects the shifting response of democratic Athens to the *barbaros* and the aristocrat: Priam represents both the general trend and an individual variation within a complex succession of ideological appropriations.

On a monumental Apulian lekythos attributed to the Darius Painter, Priam stands an Oriental king (fig. 28.1).[1] His garb shows the curious mixture of elements that marks the generic Oriental dress of fourth-century Apulian red-figure. Even items of genuine (but ethnically heterogenous) Eastern origin are elaborated almost beyond recognition to create the effect of luxurious despotism: long-sleeved garment, richly decorated overgarment, jeweled cross straps, laced boots. An unusual level of "accuracy" appears in the close approximation of Priam's headgear with the Persian floppy *tiara*. As often, the addition of a good Greek himation over the ornate garments reduces the effect of Otherness. Priam, identified by inscription, wears a less extravagant dress on a contemporary Apulian volute-krater: the decorated, belted robe with cross straps and the high Thracian(?) boots suffice to signify the Oriental king.[2] Elsewhere, and more frequently, something like an elaborate spiky "Phrygian" hat completes the ensemble.[3]

Such fourth-century works vividly highlight the difference in the presentation of myth between the Archaic and Late Classical periods. The fact that the vases just mentioned are all Apulian rather than Attic is insignificant; in the few instances where Priam appears in later Attic red-figure, it is usually with the same kind of ethnic transformation. The difference between Archaic and Late Classical presentations reflects, rather, a radical difference in worldview. In Archaic Greek art, as in the works of Homer, all heroic figures appear as Greek. They wear Greek clothes, use Greek armor and implements, invoke Greek gods.[4] Ethnicity does not matter in the heroic world. One is either godlike or not; the foe must be heroic in order that combat be heroic. In the art of the sixth century, we see occasional experiments in suggesting foreign ethnicity, such as the exotic dress of the "Phrygians" on a Lakonian plate with the myth of Silenus and Midas, or Exekias' addition of a black to attend Ethiopian Memnon; and Boardman has recognized a subtle Lycian characterization of Glaukos at the hands of the Kleophrades Painter.[5] Such experiments do not catch on or fundamentally change the lack of ethnic distinction which remains unaltered well into the fifth century.

In Attic vase painting, the presentation of the Trojan War in general, and Priam in particular, abides by the same quality of ethnic indiscriminateness. Over the sixth and early fifth centuries Priam appears in depictions of a number of moments of his story; their compositional formats range across the spectrum of iconographic specificity. As the king of Troy, he receives Paris back from Mount Ida (?) and Helen at her arrival in Troy; both scenes are laden with ill omen.[6] More generic compositions portray his attendance as father at the arming and departure of his doomed sons into battle.[7] He is a tragic witness to the ambush and death of Troilos, and Achilles' victory over Hektor and its outcome.[8] He is iconographically most "specific" in the ransom of Hektor's body and in his own death.[9] These last two subjects numerically dominate the corpus of representations of Priam. For both, the pictorial traditions evolve independently of the canonical epic version toward the creation of the most visually telling and emotionally "true" depiction. It is on these—Ransom and Death, the heart of the Priam story—that I shall focus.

The first Oriental element to creep into the Ransom of Hektor is completely unexpected. Throughout the Attic tradition, the basic components of the scene are Achilles reclining on his *kline*, Hektor's body stretched out below or nearby, and Priam approaching from the left (see figs. 28.2–28.12). Of the three figures, only Achilles is essential; instances are known in which either Priam or Hektor is missing (see fig. 28.9). Alföldi, followed by Fehr, has described the artistic decision to present Achilles reclining in the Ransom scene as part of a widespread adoption of the Iranian aristocratic "Lebensideal" for heroic portrayal in Greek art; parallels are found in the sixth-century iconographic traditions for Dionysos and Herakles.[10] An early depiction of the Ransom of Hektor on a hydria in Zurich (figs. 28.2–28.3) suggests that Oriental luxury toreutic was also deemed appropriate to Greek heroic dignity: Achilles holds a lobed phiale.[11]

From the later sixth century, several painters elaborate the Ransom scene to include one or more gift-bearers to Achilles. Commentators note that the image bears striking similarity to Persian imperial iconography, in which depictions of processions of gift-bearers to the Great King play an important role.[12] It is even suggested that the very multiplication of numbers of attendants elevates Priam to the status of Great King.[13] In the earliest such elaboration, a black-figure amphora in Toledo, only one attendant bears gifts (fig. 28.4).[14] The inclusion of a tripod among his gifts fits well into the heroic and epic tradition, but the attendant also carries

FIGURE 28.1. Collection Musée d'art et d'histoire, Genève, HR 134: Apulian large lekythos (A), Darius Painter, c. 340–330. Detail of upper register. (Photograph courtesy Musée d'art et d'histoire.)

FIGURE 28.3. Archäologisches Institut der Universität Zürich, 4001: Attic hydria, Painter of London B76, c. 570–560. Detail. (Photograph by Silvia Hertig, Archäologische Sammlung der Universität Zürich.) (Photograph courtesy Archäologisches Institut der Universität.)

FIGURE 28.2. Archäologisches Institut der Universität Zürich, 4001: Attic hydria, Painter of London B76, c. 570–560. (Photograph (Nr. PF 548) by Silvia Hertig, Archäologische Sammlung der Universität Zürich.) (Photograph courtesy Archäologisches Institut der Universität.)

three Oriental lobed phialai. Does this mark the earliest attributive orientalization of Priam?[15] We might think so, were it not for the fact that on the same amphora Achilles himself again holds a lobed phiale, which he extends to Priam. If the image of gift-bearing has been appropriated by the painter from the Oriental sphere, it was still within the framework of the aristocratic "iranisches Lebensideal."

The procession to Achilles is elaborated most on a handful of Late Archaic red-figured vases (e.g., figs. 28.5–28.6, 28.7–28.8, 28.10–28.12). The group, which dates roughly 510–480, is sufficiently uniform for Kossatz-Deissmann and others to posit a common source.[16] Here we have a stronger suggestion of Oriental gift-bearers; on Oltos' cup in Munich, not only do the gifts include horses, metalware vessels and costly textiles, but one of the men with horses on side B wears

Oriental clothing and headgear (figs. 28.5–28.6).[17] Among the heroic gifts of armor and weapons, the Painter of the Fourteenth Brygos included Achaemenid lobed phialai (figs. 28.7–28.8). On the Brygos Painter's skyphos in Vienna, elaborate lobed phialai already stand on Achilles' table, similar to those in the hand of the first of the four gift-bearers (figs. 28.10–28.11, 28.12). Another (but very subtle) Eastern touch might be perceived in the shape of Priam's shoes, which resemble those on Achaemenid relief sculpture (see fig. 28.11).

Bulas viewed the addition of gift-bearers as a meaningless elaboration of the image, whose purpose was to illustrate the gifts in the cart mentioned in the *Iliad*; there was no need to read these vases, as others had done, as record of a lost epic treatment of the subject.[18] In his reluctance to reconstruct lost epics from vase paintings, Bulas was surely right; but this does not make the elaboration "meaningless." In glorifying the tribute paid to Achilles and the wealth of Priam, the Greek painters turned to the best model they could think of, Oriental royal iconography. That they could do so, and at the same time depict Achilles using the same goods, is very telling.

For most of the Archaic period we can say that foreign elements, when they appear, appear in visual sche-

FIGURE 28.4. Toledo, Ohio, The Toledo Museum of Art, 72.54: Attic amphora (detail, side A), Rycroft Painter (von Bothmer), c. 520–510. Gift of Edward Drummond Libbey. (Photograph courtesy The Toledo Museum of Art.)

mata (reclining royal hero; procession with gifts) or take attributive rather than vestimental forms. Their function is to emphasize the high status of both figures, Achilles as well as Priam. Two points arise: (1) foreign schemata and goods are indicative not of ethnic but of social standing; (2) for such visual appropriations to indicate status to occur, the model must be nonthreatening.

About 480 the Ransom of Hektor essentially drops out of the Attic repertoire for half a century; the significance of the disappearance is discussed below. There is one possible coda, in the Briseis Painter's cup in London. The tondo presents an unusual scene which Beazley hesitantly identified as Priam bypassing an oblivious guard at the entrance of Achilles' tent.[19] Here it may be possible to detect an attempt to suggest the old man's foreign identity by the treatment of a detail of clothing. From under "Priam's" enveloping himation peeps a handsomely bordered and fringed chiton; such elaboration of dress is not characteristic of the Briseis Painter's portraits of old men.

From the start, the pictorial and literary traditions make Priam a sympathetic character; good painters emphasize his frailty and venerability (see figs. 28.7 and

28.9; fig. 28.11). In the much more numerous depictions of Priam's death, a contrast between the armed Neoptolemos and the draped (or, occasionally, nude) Priam accentuates the opposition between vigorous youth and impotent old age.[20] Throughout the sixth century the composition with Neoptolemos attacking from the left, the traditional formula for victorious advance, reinforces the invincibility of the youthful hero.[21]

Red-figure painting of the late sixth and early fifth centuries develops a tendency to include the Death within episodic compositions of the *Ilioupersis*.[22] Here the earlier convention is abandoned in favor of a scheme in which Neoptolemos attacks from the right. Such a rupture with the iconographic tradition of victorious advance to the right signifies a change in attitude.[23] Of this series, the Vivenzio kalpis remains the most moving portrayal of sack and pillage in Greek art. Boardman, noting the full range of moods, from the horror and sacrilege of slaughter and rape, through grim courage, to hope and even liberty, has suggested that for the Kleophrades Painter, returning to an Athens looted and burned by Persians, the *Ilioupersis* provided the best mythological expression of his experience.[24] The viewer is expected to identify with the suffering of the Trojans and to abhor the brutality and desecration of a Neoptolemos and an Ajax. It is hardly surprising to find that the Trojans continue to wear Greek dress, and to use Greek attributes.

In the second quarter of the fifth century, a time of general decline of interest in the Troy theme in Attic ceramic, a distinctive *Ilioupersis* type appears in the works of the Altamura Painter and the Niobid Painter (fig. 28.13) and recurs in a late work of the Tyszkiewicz Painter (fig. 28.14).[25] Action centers around the almost hieratic image of Neoptolemos battering Priam with the body of Astyanax (or, once, attacking with sword in hand). Two factors distinguish the new treatment: the use of large figures densely clustered that characterizes the painters' work in general; and the return to the older schema with Neoptolemos advancing from the left. The general formal coherence of the group might seem to indicate a common model, but the wide variety in detail, such as the use of sword or child to kill Priam, suggests otherwise. The departure from the sympathetic treatments of the previous generation reflects a change in popular attitude but there is no corresponding change

FIGURE 28.5. Staatliche Antikensammlungen und Glyptothek München 2618: Attic cup (A), Oltos, c. 510. (Photograph courtesy Staatliche Antikensammlungen und Glyptothek.)

FIGURE 28.6. Staatliche Antikensammlungen und Glyptothek München 2618: Attic cup (B), Oltos, c. 510. (Photograph courtesy Staatliche Antikensammlungen und Glyptothek.)

in Priam's ethnicity. He is dressed in a dotted chiton and himation; the frequent appearance of decorated chitons on male figures in the corpus of the Altamura Painter, as well as on some of the works of the Niobid Painter, refutes any attempt to associate dotted chitons with foreign dress.[26] Nonetheless, we should note the Niobid Painter's inclusion of a fleeing girl who bears an Oriental lobed phiale with everted rim (e.g., fig. 28.13).[27] It is difficult to read the detail; it perhaps marks the beginning of a new trend, as an instance of attributive orientalization transferred to an attendant in allusion to the location. Yet the phiale may preserve a lingering vestige of the Archaic sensibility by which Oriental luxury provides an essential component of the *koine* of heroic aristocratic lifestyle.

Far more significant is the new formal composition given to the scene, with its visual echoes of the Tyrannicides' monument in the Agora. The Niobid Painter gave the sword-bearing Neoptolemos the familiar Aristogeiton-attitude on the krater in Ferrara (fig. 28.13); elsewhere Neoptolemos wields the body of Astyanax in a pose slightly reminiscent of Harmodios.[28] The Tyszkiewicz Painter went further, by giving a Harmodios-inspired Neoptolemos a companion in the Aristogeiton-pose (fig. 28.14). The close compositional parallel with Kritios and Nesiotes' sculptural group urges the comparison of tyrannicide with regicide.[29] Whether the

"Tyrannicide" stance necessarily connoted tyrannicide action in Attic art of this period has been much debated; in their sculptural composition Kritios and Nesiotes appear to have adopted preexisting artistic formulae for vigorous heroic action.[30] Given the prominence of the group in the Agora and in Athenian ideology, for Athenian viewers any subsequent use of the poses probably resonated against that image of youthful democratic heroism. Artists otherwise give the poses, or slight variations of them, to Greek heroes or youthful (heroic) gods doing battle against an enemy of civilization, which could with some stretching be argued as mythical parallels of blows for democracy: Apollo against the Giants, Orestes killing Aigisthos, Theseus dealing with various villains.[31] With the change of formal composition in depictions of the Death of Priam, the aged king became their paradigmatic equivalent (note on fig. 28.14 the garb of Neoptolemos' fellow-assassin: chiton, chlamys, and petasos, all evocative of Theseus).

For the sack of Troy Attic vase painters of the 460s refocused their interest on heroic action; Priam himself, still in Greek dress, was most frequently depicted as an ideal victim of heroic insuperability. With the end of this group of Early Classical kraters, the *Ilioupersis* almost disappears from Attic red-figure. The tension between form and content had come to a breaking point: since Priam was still a sympathetic subject, his paradigmatic

FIGURE 28.7. New York, the Shelby White and Leon Levy Collection. Photograph by Sheldon Collins. Attic cup (A), Painter of the Fourteenth Brygos, c. 490–480. (Photograph courtesy Shelby White and Leon Levy.)

relation to giants, villains, and (especially given his seated posture) tyrants was felt sufficiently awkward to kill his potential as a subject. Priam essentially drops out of Attic red-figure except for generic departure scenes (made specific only by the addition of inscriptions).[32]

An important aspect of the revolution in monumental painting of the 470s and 460s was the use of mythological parallels for contemporary military victories. The development is closely associated with the names of Polygnotos and Mikon. Both appear to have worked primarily in Athens and probably under the patronage of Kimon, son of the hero of Marathon and himself hero of Eion and the Eurymedon. References to the Herms erected by Kimon in the Agora after the victory at Eion, to his "Return" of Theseus to Athens in 476/5, and to

the programmes of painting of two buildings associated with him, the Theseion (470s) and the Stoa Poikile (460s), consistently present a complex of ideas linking past mythology with contemporary events.[33] A comparison between the Trojan War and the Persian Wars already appears in the epigrams on Kimon's Herms, which compare the battle against the "sons of the Medes" with Athenian participation under Menestheus in the Trojan War at the side of the Atreidai (Plut. *Kim.* 7.4–8.2; Aeschin. 3.183–185). It is important to note at this stage that the point of comparison was the pan-Hellenic nature of the force. The analogy only became possible after the start of the Greek offensive in 478.

The paintings of the Theseion focused more on the role of Theseus as leader against invaders, the first (and possibly determinative) manifestation in art of the major shift in Thesean iconography that reflects a shift in Athenian self-projection through myth (Plut. *Thes.* 36.1; *Kim.* 8.3–6).[34] It was not until the Stoa Poikile— associated with Kimon's brother-in-law, and probably built in the 460s after the Eurymedon—that explicit comparison between victory over Trojans and over Per-

FIGURE 28.8. New York, the Shelby White and Leon Levy Collection. Photograph by Sheldon Collins. Attic cup (B), Painter of the Fourteenth Brygos, c. 490/480. (Photograph courtesy Shelby White and Leon Levy.)

sians appears through the juxtaposition of a *Troy Taken* and the *Battle of Marathon.* Yet even here the comparison is ambiguous. Pausanias' description of the *Troy Taken* shows that Polygnotos' painting was not the depiction of a glorious victory, but a sober trial of Ajax for his rape of Cassandra (Paus. 1.15.1–3; see Plut. *Kim.* 4.6–7). It is a subject whose contemporary meaning is difficult to gauge; any political metaphor is more likely to bear upon the actions of the disgraced Spartan king Pausanias than upon anything else. Nothing indicates that the Trojans were depicted in Oriental dress, but a negative argument can hold no weight. Barron has found evidence for topical allusion in the ancient practice of inscribing names in painting, both in Athens and in the paintings of the Knidian Lesche at Delphi; they

FIGURE 28.9. New York, the Shelby White and Leon Levy Collection. Photograph by Sheldon Collins. Attic cup (I), Painter of the Fourteenth Brygos, c. 490/480. (Photograph courtesy Shelby White and Leon Levy.)

FIGURE 28.10. Kunsthistorisches Museum Wien, IV 3710: Attic skyphos (detail, side A), Brygos Painter, c. 485. (Photograph courtesy Kunsthistorisches Museum.)

FIGURE 28.11. Kunsthistorisches Museum Wien, IV 3710: Attic skyphos (detail, side A), Brygos Painter, c. 485. (Photograph courtesy Kunsthistorisches Museum.)

suggest a link between Kimon and Theseus, with allusions also to victory over the Persians.[35] In other words, there is evidence for verbal linkages but none yet for iconographic links. The Kimonian programme of propaganda may have paved the way for an equation of Trojan with Persian victory, but it is unclear whether the final step was taken. In this matter, we should follow Jeffery's reading of the system of decoration of the Stoa Poikile as the first expression of the *aretai* claimed by the Athenians, to be repeated by Herodotus (9.26–28).[36] The inclusion of Marathon was simply the addition of the most recent achievement to a long list of *aretai*; the long-term result of the collocation of the two themes was to suggest the use of the Trojan War as a mythical paradigm of Greek victory in the Persian Wars.

Can the paintings of the Knidian Lesche help? Schweitzer suggested that, in his description of the *Nekyia*, Pausanias' confusion about Paris' hand-clapping betrays his inability to recognize that Paris was depicted

as dancing the Oriental *oklasma* (Paus. 10.31.8); if Schweitzer is right, the painting reflects the start of an artistic tradition of presenting Paris as Oriental though it leaves open the question of his dress.[37] One is reminded of Aeschylus' use of a distinctive dance to characterize the "Phrygian" (Trojan) chorus in his *Phryges* or *Ransom of Hektor* of c. 490.[38] Elsewhere in the painting, Pausanias specifically notes that Orpheus is painted Greek, that neither his dress nor his headgear are Thracian (10.30.6). His surprise does more than foreground the contemporary Roman practice of presenting Orpheus in Oriental clothing. In imperial art Trojans similarly receive a "Phrygian" costume; but nowhere else in his description of the Lesche's paintings does Pausanias comment on dress. Might his silence mean that he saw nothing unusual about Polygnotos' Trojans, or, in other words, that Pausanias bears indirect witness to an early, Polygnotan, experiment in presenting mythological figures in contemporary ethnic dress?

456

FIGURE 28.12. Kunsthistorisches Museum Wien, IV 3710: Attic skyphos (A), Brygos Painter, c. 485. (Photograph courtesy Kunsthistorisches Museum.)

FIGURE 28.13. Fotografia del Museo Archeologico Nazionale di Ferrara, 2895 (T936 VT): Attic calyx-krater (A), Niobid Painter, c. 460. (Photograph courtesy Soprintendenza Archeologica dell'Emilia—Romagna—Bologna.)

One modern cliché about Classical Athenian iconography relates to the choice of themes for the decoration of the Parthenon: the compilation of Amazonomachy, Centauromachy, *Ilioupersis*, and Gigantomachy stresses victory over barbarism more powerfully than any previous employment of the individual themes. Yet on the Parthenon, the most important vehicle for state propaganda of Classical Athens, there is no indication that the Trojans were garbed as Orientals. One set of poorly preserved metopes, the West, shows Greeks fighting Orientals who have been called Persians, but are more commonly identified as Amazons.[39] The North metopes, with an *Ilioupersis*, are so badly battered that the death of Priam is not distinguishable; nonetheless on a couple of metopes the images are clear enough to ascertain that the Trojans wear Greek dress.[40] Yet the choice of Greek rather than Oriental dress for Trojans on the Parthenon may not be significant as a reflection of popular attitudes. Such vestimental differentiation for opponents of Greeks had a continuing iconographic utility in distinguishing Trojans from Amazons,[41] who had for some decades been customarily dressed as Orientals.

Our ceramic evidence fails about the mid-fifth century, though some scraps encourage hope of future discoveries. The fragmentary Polygnotan krater in Vienna, for example, apparently held an elaborated Ransom of Hektor, though unfortunately the figure of Priam is

FIGURE 28.14. Rome, Villa Giulia 3578: Attic column-krater (A), Tyszkiewicz Painter, 470–460. (Photograph courtesy Deutsches Archäologisches Institut, Rom, Neg. No. 80.225.)

FIGURE 28.15. Collection of the J. Paul Getty Museum, Malibu, California, 81.AE.183.2: Polygnotos, Attic red-figure vase of Italiote shape (B), c. 450–440. Terracotta. Detail of upper register. (Photograph courtesy J. Paul Getty Museum.)

lost.[42] The krater has the only known Attic depiction of the weighing of Hektor's body; scales also appear in works of non-Attic schools over the period 460–350 B.C.[43] Séchan, Döhle, and others have argued that the inclusion of a weighing scene in Aeschylus' notoriously innovative "staging" of the Ransom in his *Phryges* shaped subsequent artistic treatments.[44] How was Priam presented in Aeschylus' memorable drama? We are too ignorant of the conditions of dramatic production in the period of Marathon to answer with confidence and the representations of the scene cannot be reliably used as evidence for the production. All other concerns aside, the chronological and geographical gap between performance and supposed reflections is too great. In the case of the Vienna krater, the late date suggests reference to a revival rather than to the original.[45] Nonetheless it is worth noting that not until the fourth

century do any of the suspected Greek or Etruscan depictions of the play present an orientalized Priam.

A depiction of Priam does survive on a near-contemporary vase (fig. 28.15).[46] It is an unusually late rendering of Achilles' pursuit of Troilos with Polyxena. As elsewhere, Priam watches anxiously at the left; but here, uniquely, he is seated on the altar to which his children flee. More importantly, in contrast to the Greek dress of the children, the painter has introduced a distinctly odd, foreign-looking garment between Priam's chiton and himation, a garment doubtless intended to connote wealth or the East. It is sleeveless, and so *ependytes*-like, but open at the front, and so *kandys*-like: a real hybrid. The fact that the vessel seems to imitate a South Italian form suggests that it was intended for a foreign market or client. For a variety of reasons which cannot be discussed here, the scene can have nothing directly to do with drama; but perhaps the theater played a role in shaping the painter's perception of Priam?

From within the Trojan circle Paris and Troilos are the first to react to the new association of Phrygians/Orientals with Trojans in contemporary rhetoric and major art. Paris' stage persona well befits the pejorative stereotype articulated by Hall. On a fragmentary sky-

458

phos after the mid-fifth century in Syracuse, he is presented with the ultimate in un-Greek headgear, a forward-pointing "Phrygian" helmet; by the end of the century he dons a complete Oriental dress as notably in the name vase of the Painter of the Carlsruhe Paris.[47] By contrast, Troilos had started to wear elements of "Oriental" (actually Thracian) garb very early, but inconsistently. In the third quarter of the fifth century, roughly contemporary with the depiction of figure 28.15, he appears in a costume complete with *anaxyrides* and *kidaris* on a krater of the Painter of the Louvre Centauromachy.[48]

In vase painting, there is no good evidence for a universally admitted equation between Trojan and Oriental until the very end of the fifth century. Then representations of Priam show that in a radical shift of iconography he had moved in popular consciousness from the heroic exemplar of paternal bereavement, a figure deserving of pity, to a new primary role: the Oriental king. One bell-krater fragment from the Agora shows an *anaxyrides*-wearing figure seated on an altar and in close proximity two youthful Greek males; these should be Priam with Neoptolemos in an *Ilioupersis* (fig. 28.16).[49] The Agora fragment resolves the question of full vestimental orientalization of Priam in Attic art, which had been left open owing to the uncertainty of the school of the magnificent volute krater in Ferrara.[50] A contemporary Apulian krater with the Ransom of Hektor marks the introduction of the fully orientalized Priam into Apulian iconography.[51] On both kraters Priam wears a *kidaris* and a highly decorated sleeved garment; the Apulian krater breaks off at his legs, but on the Ferrara krater Priam wears *anaxyrides*. Moret points out that on both Priam is "Thracian" rather than Persian and that none of the other Trojans is orientalized.[52] What sparked the ultimate shift from social to ethnic meaning for Oriental clothing and goods in mythological scenes?

The question can be answered in a variety of ways. Hall has argued strongly that Attic tragedians, and specifically Aeschylus under the twin stimuli of democracy and victory over Persians, invented the "barbarian" (according to a Homeric scholiast, Aeschylus first turned the Trojans into Phrygians).[53] She views this as part of a much wider process of Athenian ethnic self-definition by negative definition of an alien "other," which was itself the first step of orientalism as defined by Said. Ori-

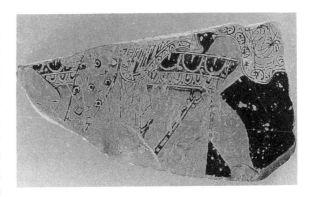

FIGURE 28.16 American School of Classical Studies at Athens, Agora Excavations P 18849: Attic bell-krater fr., Talos Painter (von Bothmer), c. 400. (Photograph courtesy American School of Classical Studies at Athens, Agora Excavations.)

entalism would seem to be well underway in Aeschylean drama by the time of the composition of the *Oresteia* (some time after the battle of the Eurymedon) in which Trojans and Priam provide a negative standard against which Agamemnon comes to be measured and to be found wanting (see *Ag.* 935–947).[54] We do not know whether Aeschylus let the parallel hang in verbal imagery alone, or whether in the productions of his plays it was underscored by costuming.[55]

It is generally agreed that by the end of the fifth century, a "tragic costume" which featured some components of Oriental dress was widely used in the Attic theater for foreign mythical kings as well as for Greek.[56] The evidence shows a prior development of tragic costume from dress that was standard in contemporary life. The Leningrad Painter's fragmentary hydria in Corinth of c. 470–460 provides the earliest known instance in which dress—in this case Persian—is certainly used to Orientalize a dramatic figure, and yet produced at a time when the available evidence suggests that most dramas retained Greek dress. Unfortunately the identity of the play remains unknown; Beazley made a number of suggestions and Page argued further for a tragedy on *Croesus*.[57] The latter possibility is particularly significant in this context. The sole argument for an identification as Croesus is the pyre, and the pyre provides a link with the amphora of Myson a generation earlier, on which

Croesus is Greek.[58] It is conceivable that Croesus was one of the first "mythical" kings to orientalize. As king of Lydia he was too closely associated with Sardis, the Sardis that every Athenian knew in its Achaemenid guise, for any presentation of him in Greek dress once conditions made it possible to think in ethnic terms.

The history of the depiction of Priam in Attic art reflects the major societal transitions of the Archaic and Classical periods, particularly the ideological shift from international aristocracy to regional democracy and the concomitant development of a sense of ethnicity, but it also shows the role of conditioned affection for the Epic Cycle. In Homer and in much of Archaic art, treatment of the Trojan War reveals empathy for the bravery and suffering of both sides. Heroic codes prevail over any consideration of race; a thoroughgoing internationalism characterizes the prevailing aristocratic ideology. When foreignness appears in art, it occurs in attributive rather than vestimental forms and is used in contexts where it is clear that it is meant to enhance the dignity of the hero. The heights of the *iranisches Lebensideal* form the prism through which myth is refracted in art of the period. The Orient is nonthreatening, and provides wealth appropriate for a hero.

During the first (defensive) phase of the Persian Wars, the Athenians seem to have identified more with the sufferings of the Trojans than with the heroism of the Greeks. The victories over the Persians when the Greeks moved from defensive to offensive action in the second quarter of the fifth century allowed a double shift of heroic paradigm from victory-under-attack, as offered by Theseus defending Attica from the Amazons, to victory-as-united-Greek-force, as when all the Hellenes fought at Troy. The next phase was the development of a Classical Athenian homology between Trojan and Persian/generic Oriental, but it would be wrong to consider the orientalization of Trojans as a precisely definable linear development from a specific moment or stimulus. To attempt to identify a *protos heuretes* of the orientalized Trojan would merely be to beg the question, for it would explain neither the invention nor its reception. The change in Priam is related to all other forms of orientalization as effects of a structural cause, ultimately a change in social ideology from an aristocratic to a democratic dominant. Once a concept of the Oriental

was developed, it was charged with negative values, to become the anti-Greek.

The first members of the Trojan circle to orientalize are Troilos and Paris, for whom there was perhaps less empathy. Priam long remained Greek iconographically, but after a short-lived compositional equation with *tyrannoi*, he was generally abandoned in art, even while Trojan themes dominated productions at the festival of Dionysos.[59] It is not simply a case of reduction of artistic interest in heroic as opposed to quotidian themes; over the same period, other myths gain in popularity. Furthermore, even while Priam continued to be depicted as an aged Greek, other mythic kings were being orientalized by attribute or schema: one thinks of Danaos fanned by a daughter and of Kepheus garbed in *kidaris* and sleeved chiton, both c. 460; and of Midas, questionably dressed as an Oriental, but surrounded by the accoutrements of an Oriental court, from c. 450.[60] The pattern of presentation of Priam in poetry and art thus provides at best only a partial paradigm of the Oriental kings as a group. Such variety of presentation reflects the inadequacy of a schematic vision of Athenian attitudes to the East. A multifaceted society will have a range of individual opinion, despite general trends over generations. Possibly a developing tension between sympathy for Priam's suffering and a sense that he is Oriental and therefore morally intractable proved too great: it could only be resolved by avoidance of Priam as a subject. Similarly Hektor, noble hero of epic, is largely ignored in the period of iconographic orientalization of myth from the mid-fifth century. When he does appear, as in the name vase of the Hector Painter, he continues to be a Greek hoplite; the uplifting patriotic equation between the departing warrior with the princes of old is maintained.[61]

Late in the fifth century Priam finally joins the ranks of "Orientals" in the popular Athenian worldview; in this guise he moves into the South Italian sphere.[62] What caused the final shift? There is a considerable time lag between Polygnotos' paintings, Aeschylus' plays, and the Agora bell-krater. Over the interval in Athens, orientalism blossomed to full scale, while in real terms an ambiguous relationship with the Persians had developed. The fact that Athenians had once defeated a Persian imperial army was not as significant as the fact that now the Athenians needed Persian wealth to help them to victory over Greeks. Over the last quarter of the fifth century their financial worries exposed the Athenians to manipulation by the Persians. The Persians were despised as "soft" precisely because they were in control; the slurs conform to a common pattern of cultural denigration of an entity feared.

In the context of the strain of need for Persian gold, the uncertain state of relations with the Persians, and the concomitant Athenian need to bolster self-respect by asserting cultural superiority, Priam finally underwent full orientalization. His status as king now dominated any other fact of his mythical personality; *anax* became morally cognate with *tyrannos* and *tyrannos* with *barbaros*. In the days of the so-called radical democracy any lingering vestiges of sympathy or respect for aristocracy had vanished.

NOTES

*This paper is offered in affectionate and respectful tribute to one who has thrown great light on heroic themes in Greek art.

Research was made possible by generous funding from the Dean of the Faculty of Arts and Science and the University of Toronto, and further assisted by the Social Sciences and Humanities Research Council of Canada. I warmly thank T. H. Carpenter and E. Csapo for their helpful comments on a version of the manuscript, M. B. Moore for permission to illustrate the Agora fragment and information about it, Shelby White and Leon Levy for permission to include their cup, M. Jentoft-Nilsen for her help with the vase illustrated in figure 28.15; and for general assistance the staff of the Ashmolean Museum Library and Beazley Archive at Oxford, and C. Johnson. I am grateful to the following for assistance with photographs: A. Bernhard-Walcher, Kunsthistorisches Museum, Vienna; F. Berti, Museo Archeologico Nazionale di Ferrara; J. Chamay, Musée d'art et d'histoire, Geneva; F. W. Hamdorf, Staatliche Antikensammlungen und Glyptothek, Munich; J. Jordan, Athenian Agora Excavations; H. Jung, Deutsches Archäologisches Institut, Rome; J. R. Mertens, The Metropolitan Museum of Art, New York; M. True, J. Paul Getty Museum; P. J. Whitesides, The Toledo Museum of Art; D. Wieland-Leibundgut, Archäologisches Institut der Universität, Zurich.

Throughout this paper, only the schools of non-Attic pots are stated.

1. Geneva, Musée d'art et d'histoire HR 134, c. 340–330: C. Aellen, A. Cambitoglou, and J. Chamay, *Le Peintre de Darius et son Milieu* (*Hellas et Roma* 4) (Geneva 1986) 136–149; *LIMC* IV, "Hekabe," no. 5; "Helene," no. 174, pl. 323.

2. Geneva, Musée d'art et d'histoire HR 44: Schulthess Ptr., c. 340–330, arrival of Helen at Troy (C. Aellen *et al.* [supra n. 1] 97–108: 100; *LIMC* IV, "Helene," no. 187, pl. 326).

3. St. Petersburg, Hermitage 1718: Apulian volute krater, Circle of Lycurgus Ptr./Ptr. of Boston 76.65, c. 350, Ransom of Hektor (*RVAp* 424.55; *LIMC* I, "Achilleus," no. 664, pl. 125). London BM F278: Apulian volute krater, late follower of the Baltimore Ptr./Lasimos Ptr., c. 320–310, Death of Priam (*RVAp* 931.118; *LIMC* IV, "Helene," no. 360; J.-M. Moret, *L'Ilioupersis dans la céramique italiote: Les mythes et leur expression figurée au IVe siècle* [Geneva 1975] pls. 20–21.

4. R. Zahn, *Die Darstellung der Barbaren in griechischer Literatur und Kunst der vorhellenistischen Zeit* (Heidelberg 1896) 9–42; a good discussion of the characterization in Homer, though now archaeological evidence disproves his suggestion that the lack of ethnic definition in Homer results from naiveté. See E. Hall, *Inventing the Barbarian: Greek Self-Definition through Tragedy* (Oxford 1989) 1–55, a consideration of the question from a literary perspective.

5. Rome, Villa Giulia 57231: Lakonian cup, Typhon Ptr. (C. M. Stibbe, *Lakonische Vasenmaler des sechsten Jahrhunderts v. Chr.* [Amsterdam 1972] no. 342). London BM B209: amphora, Exekias (*ABV* 144.8; M. Robertson, *Greek Painting* [Geneva 1959] 67). Polygnotos in his *Troy Taken* used the same approach for Memnon (Paus. 10.31.7); see also F. Lissarrague, *L'autre guerrier: Archers, peltastes, cavaliers dans l'imagerie attique* (Paris 1990) 21–29. Compare Pinney's discussion of Achilles' association with Scythians: "Achilles Lord of Scythia," in W. G. Moon, ed., *Ancient Greek Art and Iconography* (Madison 1983) 127–146. J. Boardman, "The Kleophrades Painter at Troy," *AntK* 19 (1976) 1–18, discusses (p. 18) New York MMA 08.258.58 (*ARV²* 185.36).

6. Paris: Tarquinia RC 6846: cup, Brygos Ptr., c. 485 (*ARV²* 369.4). Paris, Louvre G151: cup, Briseis Ptr., c. 470 (*ARV²* 406.8). Helen: Basel, Antikenmus. Kä 431: WhGr pyxis, Circle of the Penthesileia Ptr., c. 460–450 (*LIMC* IV, "Helene," no. 186, pl. 325).

7. Würzburg 247: neck-amphora, Group E, c. 540–530 (*ABV* 134.17). Munich 2307: amphora, Euthymides, c. 510

(ARV^2 26.1). In the more generic scene-types only the addition of inscriptions distinguishes Priam from any other father in a *Kriegers Abschied*.

8. Troilos: e.g., Florence MN 4209: volute-krater, François Vase, Kleitias and Ergotimos, c. 580 (*ABV* 76.1); Paris, Louvre Camp. 10651: BF hydria frr., unattributed, c. 550–525 (*CVA* Louvre 11, pl. 135.1–4). See Ch. Mota, "Sur les représentations figurées de la mort de Troilos et de la mort d'Astyanax," *RA* 50 (1957) 25–44. Achilles: Boston MFA 63.473: hydria, Leagros Group, c. 510 (*Paralipomena* 164 [362.31bis]). See E. T. Vermeule, "The Vengeance of Achilles. The Dragging of Hektor at Troy," *BMFA* 63 (1965) 34–52.

9. Ransom: see W. Basista, "Hektors Lösung," *Boreas* 2 (1979) 5–36, esp. 32–36. B. Fehr, *Orientalische und griechische Gelage* (Bonn 1971) 57–59. K. Bulas, *Les illustrations antiques de l'Iliade* (Lwow 1929) 27–28. Death: Boardman (supra n. 5) 7–8.

10. A. Alföldi, "Die Geschichte des Throntabernakels," *NouvClio* 1–2 (1949–1950) 537–566, esp. 557; Fehr (supra n. 9) 57–59, 79–81 (esp. 80). T. H. Carpenter is engaged in further study of the links between the Neo-Assyrian royal banquet and Archaic Greek iconography.

11. Zurich, Archäologisches Institut, 4001: hydria, Ptr. of London B76, c. 570–560 (*Paralipomena* 32 [85.1bis]; *LIMC* IV, "Hektor," no. 84, pl. 289). For the lobed phiale: H. Luschey, *Die Phiale* (Bleicherode and Munich 1939). M. Abka'i-Khavari, "Die achämenidischen Metallschalen," *AMIran* 21 (1988) 91–137.

12. See Fehr (supra n. 9) 80. M.-C. Villanueva-Puig, "Le Vase des Perses," *L'Or perse et l'histoire grecque* (*REA* 91, Bordeaux 1989) 277–298, esp. 292–293. The discovery of Achaemenid gift-bearing processions in relief sculpture at Meydancıkkale greatly improves the possibility that Attic painters were well familiar with this theme as an Achaemenid royal motif: E. Laroche and A. Davesne, "Les fouilles de Meydandjik, près de Gülnar (Turquie) et le trésor monétaire hellénistique," *CRAI* (1981) 356–370; A. Davesne et al., "Le site archéologique de Meydancıkkale (Turquie): Du royaume de Pirindu à la garnison ptolémaïque," *CRAI* (1987) 359–382.

13. L. Massei, "Problemi figurativi di episodi epici," *Studi Classici e Orientali* 18 (1969) 148–181, esp. 170.

14. Toledo, Museum of Art 72.54 (A): Rycroft Ptr., c. 520–510 (von Bothmer) (*LIMC* I, "Achilleus," no. 649, pl. 122.; *CVA* Toledo 1, pls. 4.1, 5.1). Compare: Edinburgh L 224.379: lekythos, Edinburgh Ptr., c. 500, (*ABL* 217.19 [*ABV* 476]; *LIMC* I, "Achilleus," no. 644, pl. 122; phialai with lobed rim [similar on Achilles' table?]).

15. The term "attributive orientalization" is used in contrast with "vestimental orientalization" owing to the interesting tendency of Attic painters to project character or status by means of attribute rather than dress until quite late in the history of red-figured painting.

16. A. Kossatz-Deissmann, *LIMC* I, "Achilleus," 159. The elaboration provided by Oltos and the youthful Kleophrades Ptr. makes untenable the suggestion that Aeschylus' *Phryges* inspired them; see B. Döhle, "Die 'Achilleis' des Aischylos in ihrer Auswirkung auf die attische Vasenmalerei des 5. Jahrhunderts," *Klio* 48–49 (1967) 63–143, esp. 137. Compare the extreme position that as vase painting can claim chronological priority here, Aeschylus was inspired by vase painters: Massei (supra n. 13) 165–177. Munich 2618: cup (A-B), Oltos, c. 510 (*ARV²* 61.74; *LIMC* I, "Achilleus," no. 656, pl. 123, with references) = figs. 28.5–6. Athens, Kerameikos Ker 1977 a-g + 4118 a-b: calyx-krater frr. (A-B), Kleophrades Ptr., c. 500 (*ARV²* 186.45; *LIMC* I, "Achilleus," no. 654, pl. 122). New York, Shelby White and Leon Levy Collection: cup (A-B, I), Ptr. of the Fourteenth Brygos, 490–480 (*ARV²* 399; *LIMC* I, "Achilleus," no. 661, pl. 125; D. von Bothmer, ed., *Glories of the Past. Ancient Art from the Shelby White and Leon Levy Collection* [New York 1990] no. 118) = figs. 28.7–9. Compare Side A of Vienna, Kunsthist. Mus. 3710: skyphos, Brygos Ptr., c. 485 (*ARV²* 380.171; *LIMC* I, "Achilleus," no. 659, pl. 124) = figs. 28.10–12. Kossatz-Deissmann suggests that other contemporary vases show excerpts from the full picture (Harvard 1972.40, hydria; Paris, Louvre G153, cup tondo).

17. Noted by Fehr (supra n. 9) 80, who also points to the evidence for Ionians working at Susa and Persepolis.

18. Bulas (supra n. 9) 28.

19. London BM E75: cup, Briseis Ptr., c. 480–470 (*ARV²* 406.2). The absence of Hermes and of any inscription makes certainty of identification impossible. Compare: Bryn Mawr P 198 (*ARV²* 407.17; *CVA* Bryn Mawr 1, pl. 13.3).

20. In the second half of the sixth century I count twenty-five Deaths out of a total of forty-two scenes involving Priam, as compared to five Ransoms and three Ambushes of Troilos; in the first half of the fifth century, its popularity, though reduced, continued (seventeen out of thirty-seven).

21. See O. Touchefeu, "Lecture des images mythologiques. Un example d'images sans texte, la morte d'Astyanax," in F. Lissarrague and F. Thelamon, eds., *Image et céramique grecque* (Rouen 1983) 21–27.

22. Malibu, J. Paul Getty Museum, 80.AE.154: cup (A-B), Oltos, c. 515–505 (*LIMC* IV, "Helene," no. 336bis, pl. 352; B. Wescoat, *Poets and Heroes. Scenes of the Trojan War* [Emory University Museum: Atlanta 1986] 59, 61, 71). Berlin 2281 + 2280: cup frr. (?A-B, I), near Euphronios, c. 500 (*ARV²* 19.1 + 19.2; see D. Williams, "The Ilioupersis cup in Berlin and Vatican," *JBerlMus* 18 [1976] 9–25, as Onesimos,

esp. 15–16, suggesting that this cup influenced subsequent treatment of the scene). Malibu, J. Paul Getty Museum 83.AE.362: cup frr. I, Onesimos, c. 500–490 (D. Williams, "Onesimos and the Getty Ilioupersis," *Greek Vases in the J. Paul Getty Museum* 5 [1991] 41–64, esp. 50–52, fig. 8e). Athens NM Acr. A 190: cup (A-B), unattributed, c. 500 (M. I. Wiencke, "An epic theme in Greek Art," *AJA* 58 [1954] 285–306, pl. 62, fig. 28; *LIMC* II, "Astyanax I," no. 17, pl. 684). Vienna, Univ. 53c23–53c24: cup frr. (A-B), ?I, Eleusis Ptr., c. 500 (*ARV*² 314.1; Wiencke, pl. 61.26). Paris, Louvre G152: cup (A-B), Brygos Ptr, c. 490 (*ARV*² 369.1). Naples 2422: kalpis, Kleophrades Ptr., c. 480 (*ARV*² 189.74). Athens, NM Acr. 355 (B78): cup frr. (A), Stieglitz Ptr., c. 480–470 (*ARV*² 828.29).

23. Touchefeu (supra n. 21) 25. It should be noted that some red-figure painters retain the traditional format, e.g., the contemporary vases: New York MMA 06.1021.99: amphora (A-B), Nikoxenos (*ARV*² 220.4); Berlin F2175: hydria, Ptr. of the Munich Amphora (*ARV*² 246.11; *LIMC* II, "Astyanax I," no. 20, pl. 684). Paris, CabMed. 571 plus: cup fr., Manner of the Brygos Ptr. (*ARV*² 386.a; *LIMC* IV, "Helene," no. 247, pl. 336). And in the following generation: Florence MN 73140: pelike (A), Earlier Mannerist (*ARV*² 586.51); St. Petersburg, Hermitage 658: cup (A), Telephus Ptr. (*ARV*² 817.3; *LIMC* IV, "Hekabe," no. 43); Boston MFA 03.869a-d: cup frr., Clinic Ptr. (*ARV*² 808.1). See once Liverpool 10704: Form VIII oinochoe (A), Follower of Douris (*ARV*² 805.76).

24. Boardman (supra n. 5) 14–15. E. D. Francis, *Image and Idea in Fifth-Century Greece* (London 1990) 39–40, suggests that a post-Marathon date is possible for the other examples (specifically the Brygos Ptr.'s cup in Paris).

25. Although at least seven *Iliouperseis* were painted by these painters c. 470–460, photographs of only four are published; the remaining three may not follow the same format. Altamura Ptr.: Boston MFA 59.178: calyx-krater (A-B) (*ARV*² 590.11); Ferrara MN T15C VP, oinochoe (*ARV*² 595.70; *non vidi*); Paris, Cab. Med., lid frr. (*ARV*² 595.73). Niobid Ptr.: Bologna MC 268: volute-krater (A) (*ARV*² 598.1); Ferrara MN 2895 (T936 VT): calyx-krater (A-B) (*ARV*² 601.18; *LIMC* IV, "Hekabe," no. 54, pl. 283) = fig. 13; Reggio: calyx-krater, 2 frr., Manner of Niobid Ptr. (*ARV*² 609.6bis; *non vidi*). Tyszkiewicz Ptr.: Rome, Villa Giulia 3578: column-krater (A-B) (*ARV*² 290.9) = fig. 14.

26. Altamura Ptr.: London BM E469 (*ARV*² 589.1); Ferrara MN 2737 (T381) (*ARV*² 589.3); Belfast Univ. Mus. L 58.13 (*ARV*² 591.19); Vienna, Kunsthist. Mus. 985 (*ARV*² 591.20); Thorvaldsen 96 + Erbach (*ARV*² 592.37); Ferrara MN 2738 (T311) (*ARV*² 593.41); Boston MFA 97.370 (*ARV*² 594.62); Berlin 1962.33 (*ARV*² 595.71bis, 1660); Oxford 1966.509 (*ARV*² 595.75). Niobid Ptr.: Boston MFA 33.56

(*ARV*² 600.12); Ferrara MN 2891 (T313) (*ARV*² 602.24); Bowdoin 08.3 (*ARV*² 606.68).

27. In two of his treatments: Bologna MC 268 and Ferrara MN 2895 (T936 VT).

28. Bologna MC 268 (Niobid Ptr.); Boston MFA 97.370 (Altamura Ptr.); Rome, Villa Giulia 3578 (Tyszkiewicz Ptr.).

29. A. J. N. W. Prag, *The Oresteia: Iconographic and Narrative Tradition* (Warminster 1985) 92, compares the composition with the Tyszkiewicz Ptr.'s deaths of Aigisthos, commenting on the lack of a sense that the scene is part of a sack of a city but rather like a domestic situation. See C. Dugas, "Tradition littéraire et tradition graphique dans l'antiquité grecque," *AntCl* 6 (1937) 5–26, esp. 18. The same is true of the oinochoe formerly in Liverpool (supra n. 23), where the replacement of the cuirass with a himation enhances the suggestion of regicide.

30. For reminder of which I am most grateful to T. H. Carpenter, as well as for the following. The pose is found in late-sixth-century vase painting: B. B. Shefton, "Some Iconographic Remarks on the Tyrannicides," *AJA* 64 (1960) 173–179, notes the presence of the "Harmodios blow" on Euphronios' krater in Arezzo (*ARV*² 15.16). Immediate antecedents of the tyrannicides' poses can be found in sixth-century Deaths of Priam. M. W. Taylor, in the course of his discussion of their use in Theseus' iconography c. 460–430, argued that throughout much of the fifth century in the arts the "Tyrannicide" poses signified to Athenians heroic acts for democracy: *The Tyrant Slayers: The Heroic Image in Fifth Century* B.C. *Athenian Art and Politics* (New York 1981) 78–134, esp. 124–126, 131–134, 193–194.

31. J. Barron, "New Light on Old Walls," *JHS* 92 (1972) 20–45 characterized the new Tyrannicide group as "at once . . . the favoured model for violent, warlike action" (p. 40). Gigantomachy: the "Harmodios blow" appears, e.g., Athens NM Acr. 211: cup fr., Euthymides (*ARV*² 29.20; *LIMC* IV, "Gigantes," no. 299, pl. 138); London BM E443: stamnos (A), Tyszkiewicz Ptr. (*ARV*² 292.29). Aigisthos: of the depictions included in *LIMC* I, "Aigisthos," nos. 6–13 (the Attic red-figured examples), the majority show the moment when Orestes plunges his sword into Aigisthos' breast, and do not offer true parallels. Three present Orestes with sword pulled back preparatory to a second thrust and in a stance closely approximating the "Aristogeiton stance": no. 10, Boston MFA 63.1246; no. 13, Boston MFA 91.227a + 91.226b; and Naples Astarita 530, stamnos frr., attributed to the Tyszkiewicz Ptr. (*ARV*² 291.20). Of these, the best parallel is the first, attributed to the Dokimasia Ptr. (*Paralipomena* 373.34quater). Theseus: see Taylor (supra n. 30) 78–134, and now S. P. Morris, *Daidalos and the Origins of Greek Art* (Princeton 1992) 349–350.

32. Philadelphia 30.44.4: neck-amphora, Group of Polygnotos, c. 450 (*ARV*[2] 1058.113; *LIMC* IV, "Hektor," no. 18). Rome, Vatican 16570: neck-amphora, Hector Ptr., c. 450–440 (*ARV*[2] 1036.1; *LIMC* IV, "Hektor," no. 19, pl. 284). Basel Market 1967: oinochoe Form 4, c. 430 (*LIMC* IV, "Hektor," no. 20, pl. 284). On the basis of these inscribed vases, others are linked, e.g., Munich 2415: stamnos, Kleophon Ptr., c. 440–430 (*ARV*[2] 1143.2; Touchefeu, *LIMC* IV, "Hektor," no. 27, includes as a possible scene). On the name vase of the Hector Ptr., Priam wears an *ependytes*, but even here it is not clear that the garment is meant to connote the East or simply wealthy dress: see M. C. Miller, "The *Ependytes* in Classical Athens," *Hesperia* 58 (1989) 313–329.

33. Much progress has been made over the past few decades regarding the whole question of the Polygnotan revolution in painting and its connections with Kimon. See now E. G. Pemberton, "The Beginning of Monumental Painting in Mainland Greece," in R. I. Curtis, ed., *Studia Pompeiana et Classica in Honour of Wilhelmina Jashemski* II (New York 1988) 181–197, with references; and the more controversial D. Castriota, *Myth, Ethos, and Actuality: Official Art in Fifth-Century Athens* (Madison 1992) 33–95.

34. E. Simon, "Polygnotan Painting and the Niobid Painter," *AJA* 67 (1963) 43–62; Barron (supra n. 31); S. Woodford, "More Light on Old Walls," *JHS* 94 (1974) 158–165.

35. J. Barron, "Bakchylides, Theseus and a Woolly Cloak," *BICS* 27 (1980) 1–8, esp. 3–4, some of which have been pointed out in earlier studies.

36. L. H. Jeffery, "The *Battle of Oinoe* in the Stoa Poikile," *BSA* 60 (1965) 41–57, esp. 51–52. See now Morris (supra n. 31) 307–317, esp. 313–316.

37. B. Schweitzer, "Der Paris des Polygnot," *Hermes* 71 (1936) 288–294, 294, esp. n. 2; he wonders whether the idea came to vase painting from the works of Polygnotos. M. Stansbury-O'Donnell is reluctant to accept Schweitzer's interpretation on the grounds that it would be too joyous: "Polygnotos's *Nekyia*: A Reconstruction and Analysis," *AJA* 94 (1990) 213–248 (see p. 228). If, however, read doubly as a further instance of Paris' antiheroic standing and as the first hint of developing orientalism in treatment of the Trojan prince, the stance is most apt.

38. Evidence discussed by Döhle (supra n. 16) 63, and Hall (supra n. 4) 132–133.

39. F. Brommer, *Die Metopen des Parthenon* (Mainz 1967) 191–195, gives the arguments for an identification as Persians, with previous scholarship, but remains agnostic. E. Berger, *Der Parthenon in Basel: Dokumentation zu den Metopen* (Mainz 1986) 99, returns to their identification as Amazons.

40. See Brommer (supra n. 39) pls. 118–122, for Metope N28, with Aeneas and Anchises; J. Dörig, "Les métopes nord du Parthénon," in E. Berger, ed., *Parthenon-Kongress Basel* (Mainz 1984) 202–205.

41. An observation for which I am grateful to T. H. Carpenter.

42. Vienna, Univ. 505: calyx-krater, Polygnotos, c. 430 (*ARV*[2] 1030.33; *LIMC* I, "Achilleus," no. 660).

43. Munich 3171 (J890): Etruscan RF amphora, Praxias Group, c. 460–450 (*EVP* 195.1; *LIMC* I, "Achle," no. 120; *LIMC* I, "Alkimos," no. 1, pl. 409; A. Kossatz-Deissmann, *Dramen des Aischylos auf westgriechischen Vasen* [Mainz 1978] pl. 3.1); Toronto, Royal Ontario Museum 926.32: Melian terracotta relief, c. 450–440 (*LIMC* I, "Achilleus," no. 662, pl. 125). Thereafter: Florence MN 70528: Etruscan RF stamnos, Settecamini Ptr., c. 350 (*EVP* 52.1, pl. 10.1–2; *LIMC* I, "Achle," no. 121); St. Petersburg, Hermitage 1718 (supra n. 3).

44. L. Séchan, *Études sur la tragédie grecque* (Paris 1926) 116–119. Döhle (supra n. 16) 93–95, 136–139.

45. Döhle (supra n.16) 141, for the possibility that Polygnotos responds to a revival of c. 440–430.

46. Malibu, J. Paul Getty Museum 81.AE.183.2: (B) Achilles and Troilos, Group of Polygnotos, c. 440 (M. Jentoft-Nilsen, "Two Vases of South Italian Shape by an Attic Painter," in J. P. Descoeudres, ed., *Greek Colonists and Native Populations: Proceedings of the First Australian Congress of Classical Archaeology held in Honour of Emeritus Professor A. D. Trendall July 9–14, 1985* [Oxford 1990] 243–249; "Two Attic Vases of Unique Shape," in J. Christiansen and T. Melander, eds., *Ancient Greek and Related Pottery* [Copenhagen 1988] 278–283). The subject appears only three times in this decade and to my knowledge does not recur thereafter in Attic painting.

47. Syracuse MN 2406: skyphos, Danae Ptr., c. 440–425 (*ARV*[2] 1076.16; *Syracuse, The Fairest Greek City* [Emory University Museum: Atlanta 1989] no. 10). Karlsruhe, Badisches Landesmuseum 259: kalpis, c. 410 (*ARV*[2] 1315.1; *LIMC* II, "Aphrodite," 1275, pl. 128; L. Burn, *The Meidias Painter* [Oxford 1987], pls. 39–40). See also: Cambridge, Harvard 1925.30.46: pelike, Ptr. of Louvre G 539, c. 410 (*ARV*[2] 1341.1; *LIMC* I, "Alexandros," no. 47, pl. 384). N.B. the intriguing possibility that the one young man dressed in Oriental costume in a scene tentatively identified as preparations for a "Ransom of Hektor" is Paris: Madrid 10920: hydria, Priam Ptr., c. 510–500 (*ABV* 332.17; *LIMC* I, "Alexandros," no. 71, pl.391).

48. The Antimenes Ptr., c. 520–510, likes to show Troilos with a highly decorated short cloak which may be reminiscent of Thracian dress, but also appears in quotidian scenes of ar-

istocratic Greek youths riding horses, e.g., Munich 1548: BF amphora (*ABV* 273.112; *LIMC* I, "Achilleus," no. 304, pl. 88); Munich 1722: BF hydria (*ABV* 269.33; *LIMC* I, "Achilleus," no. 303, pl. 88). See also: London BM E13: RF cup, Kachrylion (potter), c. 520–510 (*ARV²* 109; *LIMC* I, "Achilleus," no. 342, pl. 90). After the mid-fifth century Troilos starts to Thracize thoroughly: Heidelberg, Private: RF bell-krater, c. 450–440, Ptr. of the Louvre Centauromachy (*Paralipomena* 450 [1091.65bis]; *LIMC* I, "Achilleus," no. 339); Vatican 16557: stamnos, c. 440, Hector Ptr. (*ARV²* 1036.8; *LIMC* I, "Achilleus," no. 347).

49. Athens, Agora P 18849: bell-krater fr., Talos Ptr. (von Bothmer), c. 400 (R. Young, "An Industrial District of Ancient Athens," *Hesperia* 20 [1951] 135–288, esp. 255–256, no. 4, pl. 80.4). I am most grateful to M. B. Moore, now preparing the publication of the Attic red-figured pottery from the Agora, for her helpful comments.

50. Ferrara MN 1637 (T136 VP): Attic(?) volute-krater, unattributed, c. 400–390 (*LIMC* I, "Aias II," no. 91, pl. 268; "Astyanax," no. 4; P. E. Arias, "La tomba 136 di Valle Pega," *RivIstArch* 4 [1955] 95–178, distinguished three hands on the krater [p. 134]). See St. Petersburg, Hermitage II 1829.1: relief lekythos, c. 375–350 (E. A. Zervoudaki, "Attische polychrome Reliefkeramik des späten 5. und des 4. Jahrhunderts v. Chr.," *AM* 83 [1968] 1–88, esp. 24, pl. 16.1–2). Here Priam appears to be nude (i.e., Greek), but I have been unable to verify the matter by autopsy.

51. New York MMA 20.195: Apulian calyx-krater fr., Black Fury Ptr., c. 400–390 (*RVAp* 166.8; *LIMC* I, "Achilleus," 665, pl. 125). See also: St. Petersburg, Hermitage 1718 (supra n. 3). New York MMA 10.210.17A: Apulian calyx krater fr., c. 350, associated with the Konnakis Ptr. (*LIMC* I, "Achilleus," no. 666, pl. 126).

52. Moret (supra n. 3) 157.

53. Schol. *Iliad* 2.862 (ΣA) = fr. 446 Radt. See: Hall (supra n. 4) passim; E. Hall, "When did the Trojans turn into Phrygians? Alcaeus 42.15," *ZPE* 73 (1988) 15–18. The scholiast, however, may simply be working from the title of the play (*Phrygians* or *The Ransom of Hektor*) and concluding that Aeschylus made his chorus of Trojans Phrygians; precisely *how* or whether Aeschylus characterized those Phrygian Trojans, other than through dance, is uncertain.

54. See, e.g., Francis (supra n. 24) 33–35.

55. As assumed, e.g., by L. Séchan (supra n. 44) 116, for the *Phryges*, though the evidence refers only to distinctive dancing. Hall (supra n. 4) 84, reasonably supposes that the first production of the *Persae* involved ethnic costuming, but for this too there is no positive evidence. The lack of representations of a *kandys*, the aristocratic Iranian dress par excellence, until late in fifth-century art, may even be taken to provide evidence to the contrary: see A. S. F. Gow, "Notes on the *Persae* of Aeschylus," *JHS* 48 (1928) 133–158, esp. 142–152.

56. See J. Gould's and D. M. Lewis' revision of A. Pickard-Cambridge, *The Dramatic Festivals of Athens*² (Oxford 1968) 180–204, the utility of whose discussion of tragic costume remains unaltered by more recent discovery. N.B. Thoas on Ferrara MN T1145: calyx-krater, Iphigenia Ptr., c. 380 (*ARV²* 1440.1).

57. Corinth T1144 (*ARV²* 571.74; *TrGF* II: "Adespota" F 5e). J. D. Beazley, "Hydria-fragments in Corinth," *Hesperia* 24 (1955) 305–319. D. L. Page, "An early tragedy on the fall of Croesus?" *PCPS* 188 (1962) 47–49. Gould and Lewis (supra n. 56) 183.

58. Paris, Louvre G197 (*ARV²* 238.1).

59. Dugas (supra n. 29) suggests that the divorce between popularity of Trojan themes on the contemporary stage and lack of popularity in painting simply exemplifies the independent developments of the literary and artistic traditions.

60. Danaos: Munich 2429: hydria, Ptr. of the Louvre Centauromachy (*ARV²* 1094.102, 1682; *LIMC* III, "Danaos 1," pl. 254). Kepheus: Boston MFA 63.2663: pelike (B), Kensington Class (*Paralipomena* 448; as *ARV²* 1071). Midas: see M. C. Miller, "Midas as the Great King," *AntK* 31 (1988) 79–89. The scepter as royal emblem had had a long prior history in Greek art, see G. Siebert, "Σκηπτουχοι. Sur l'imagerie de la figure royale dans la peinture de vases grecques," *REA* 87 (1985) 263–279.

61. Vatican 16570: neck-amphora (*ARV²* 1036.1; Y. Korshak, "Der Peleusmaler und sein Gefährte, der Hektormaler," *AntK* 23 [1980] 124–136). It is later that Hektor is described as *megas anaktor*, or "Great King" (Eur. *Tro.* 1217; see Hall [supra n. 4] 119).

62. There is no point in trying to determine his precise iconographic "race" since by the end of the fifth century the generic Oriental iconographic type had developed, with elements drawn from several traditions.

29

NEON ILION AND ILIUM NOVUM: KINGS, SOLDIERS, CITIZENS, AND TOURISTS AT CLASSICAL TROY

◆

CORNELIUS C. VERMEULE III

Troy was haunted by the ghosts of the great and noble heroes, who had lived, fought and died there.[1]

The excavations at Troy over the last several years have revitalized my interest in the study of the coins, portraits, and inscriptions from the Greek and Roman cities of Ilion/Ilium. Visits to Troy in the spring and summer of 1986 and to the Athens National Museum's 1990 exhibition on the centenary of Schliemann's death brought these thoughts into focus. Thanks go to Emily Townsend Vermeule for sailing up the Dardanelles with me many times over the past thirty-five years, and for showing me Troy as she had known it on visits with Ekrem Akurgal, Nezih Firatli, Machteld Mellink, and others over the decades.

The present Ilians further tell us that the city was, in fact, not completely wiped out at its capture by the Achaeans and that it was never even deserted.[2]

As Neon Ilion, the town existed and survived as an historic place in a strategic landscape. Xerxes visited the town in 480 B.C., probably to honor King Priam for his celebrated resistance to a prolonged Greek assault. Alexander the Great made the cults of Ilion fashionable. After his death, the town was improved and fortified by his early successors, but in general terms Ilion's lot was hardly better than that of other such older Greek sanctuary-settlements in Asia Minor (Ephesus and Miletus, for instance) until the advent of the Romans.

For better or for worse, as Rome's fortunes rose in Asia so did those of Ilion, until it was ravaged by the Roman rogue-commander, Fimbria, in 86 B.C. Sulla promptly restored what he could, and shortly thereafter, the governor Gaius Claudius Nero acted to protect the city from the Cilician pirates. Julius Caesar, himself a victim of those pirates, made the city into Ilium Novum. Augustus furthered the rehabilitation and, through the reputed descent of the Julio-Claudians from the Trojan Aeneas, gave a dynastic reason for the process of pseudo-Romanization which became the trademark of tourism-promoting Ilians during the Roman Empire, until the catastrophes in the time of Gallienus (A.D. 260 or after, probably 267).

PART ONE: NEON ILION

The earliest, unwitting, tourists to Troy were perhaps the pairs of Locrian maidens, virgins from the noblest families, who were sent annually (a little after the fall of Troy?) for a year's service at the temple of Athena as "temple slaves."[3] The contract was supposed to last for a thousand years, a penalty imposed on the Locrians because Ajax the Lesser incurred Athena's wrath by dragging Cassandra away from the altar of the Palladion during the sack of Troy.[4] The custom endured until the second century B.C.

In 480 B.C., Xerxes visited the Pergamus (citadel) of Priam, but history tells us nothing concerning the condition of the city at that time. Stopping on his way from Sardis to the sack of Athens and his unforeseen defeat at Salamis, the Persian king sacrificed a thousand cattle in homage to Athena.[5] He may have used the beef to feed his advancing army.

About that same time, according to the date indicated by excavated finds, two tumuli were built north of and near Yenişehir-Sigeion. Early travelers thought them to be the tombs of Achilles and Patroclus, but recent speculation is that they were more likely raised for the exiled Athenian tyrant Hippias and his family.[6]

In the last quarter of the fifth century, the Greeks appear once again on the Trojan scene. In 427 B.C., the Athenians led by Paches may have taken the town, although evidence for this is not certain.[7] In 425–424 B.C., Ilion appears in the Athenian tribute list, where it is assessed for two talents.[8]

By 413 B.C., like the rest of the Troad, Ilion was under the control of Pharnabazus, the hereditary satrap of Phrygia, and his allies the Spartans, whom he was supporting in their war against Athens. The Spartan Mindarus, it has been recorded, performed a sacrifice there in 411 B.C.[9] Ilion was ruled by Zenis of Dardanus and then by Zenis' widow Mania, who put a garrison of Greek mercenaries in the place.

After Mania's death in 399 B.C., Ilion surrendered to the Spartan commander Dercylidas, who was now fighting against Pharnabazus as an ally of Tissaphernes in a power struggle between the two Persian generals.[10] Then, like all the Greek cities of Asia, Ilion fell to the Persians in 387 B.C. by the terms of the King's Peace.[11]

An Athenian commander named Charidemus seized Ilion in 360–359 B.C., trying to establish a private dominion in the Troad.[12] He did not prevail, however, and the passage of a decree of proxeny in favor of another Athenian, Menelaus, may have been connected with his overthrow.[13]

Alexander the Great visited Troy in 334 B.C. on his way to the conquest of the Achaemenid empire, before and also after his initial victory at the Granicus River. He found a little walled town, with a "small and cheap temple."[14] He first set up altars to Herakles and Athena in the plain of the Scamander.

As a lover of the Homeric sagas, Alexander raised Ilion to the rank of *polis*, declaring the city free and exempt from tribute.[15] He also greatly enriched the temple of Athena Ilias, where he offered sacrifices and where the Ilians showed Alexander arms used in the Trojan War, including a shield of Achilles. He left a set of his own armor as an offering in exchange for some of these weapons, which were later carried before him into battle. He made the required sacrifice to the spirit of King Priam, and was crowned with gold wreaths by Menoetius, his sailing-master, and Chares, an Athenian who arrived from Sigeion. Alexander then ran as an athlete to the tomb of Achilles, where he laid a wreath. His companion Hephaistion did likewise at the tomb of Patroclus.[16]

Plutarch reported that while Alexander was walking through Ilion and "examining its curiosities, some one asked him if he wished to see the lyre of Alexander (Paris); he answered that he desired to see the lyre of Achilles, to which he had chanted the glory and the deeds of great men."[17]

About 306 B.C., a league including the whole of the Troad was organized or revived by Antigonus Gonatas, and was centered around the worship of Athena Ilias. Although Ilion was only one member and the Synedrion governed, this focus on the sanctuary of Athena Ilias meant prosperity to the city. One Malusius of Gargara spent 5,000 gold staters on construction in the sanctuary and on building a theater.[18]

After Lysimachus overthrew Antigonus at Ipsus in 301 B.C., he turned his attention to improving Ilion. Strabo reported that he built a harbor and "surrounded the city with a wall about forty stadia in circuit."[19] He erected a splendid marble temple to Athena, honoring a promise made by Alexander the Great as he set off from

Ilion on his conquests and repeated in a letter after his victory over the Achaemenid kingdom.[20] To this period and in connection with these activities must belong the impressive relief of the cuirassed Alexander the Great on Bucephalus, which found its way to Madrid in the era of the early travelers.[21]

About 300 B.C., *dikastai* were sent by Rhodes, Cos, Delos, and Paros to Ilion, an early example of a practice so well documented in the stelai from Assos.[22]

In 278 B.C., Nicomedes, King of Bithynia, turned the Celtic Galatians under Lutarius loose in northwest Asia Minor. As a result the Gauls occupied Ilion temporarily, "but left it at once because of its lack of walls."[23]

Ilion prayed and sacrificed for Antiochus I in 275 B.C., in connection with the wars at the outset of his reign. The city did not have the material resources to furnish practical assistance. Later the city celebrated a festival in his honor, apparently even establishing a priest for his worship. The Ilians also voted to erect a golden, or more probably a gilded bronze, equestrian statue of the king as "Savior of the People." The freedom of Ilion was recognized, and the city, along with others in the Troad, became an ally of Antiochus.[24]

In 216 B.C., Ilion resisted a siege by the Aegosagae, the rebelling Celtic mercenaries of Attalus I, and was saved by the troops of Alexandria Troas. The Gauls were then exterminated by King Prusias I of Bithynia.[25]

Ilion, the legendary home of Aeneas, was the first Asiatic city to establish relations with Rome at the end of the third century B.C.[26] In the treaty of Phoenice concluded by the Senate of Rome with Philip V of Macedonia in 205 B.C., Ilion as an apparent ally of Pergamon obtained recognition as an independent state under the protection of the Romans.[27]

By about 200 B.C., the archaeology of Homeric Troy was a fully developed subject. Polemon of Ilion wrote a description of the city. As Schliemann recounted, "He noticed . . . the identical altar of Zeus Herkeios on which Priam had been slain, as well as the identical stone upon which Palamedes had taught the Greeks to play at dice."[28] When Antiochus III the Great threatened Smyrna and Lampsacus in 197 B.C., the city of Lampsacus, fearing capture and loss of freedom, sent envoys to Rome, and based a plea for Roman protection on their peoples' kinship through Ilion.[29] Heretofore, only Ilion had experienced dealings with Rome.[30]

On his way to invade Greece and to aid the Aetolians in 192 B.C., Antiochus III stopped in Ilion to offer sacrifice to Athena Ilias. Slightly earlier he had promised to "preserve their ancestral privileges." The Ilians may have sworn an oath of allegiance to the Seleucid king.[31]

About this time, the youthful Demetrios of Skepsis visited Ilion, and "he found the settlement so neglected that the buildings did not so much as have tiled roofs."[32] "Such a loss of prosperity is sufficiently explained by the incursions of the Gauls and the insecure state of the Troad during the latter part of the 3rd century."[33]

The first Roman to sacrifice to Athena Ilias was the praetor C. Livius Salinator, who landed near Ilion in 190 B.C. The Consul Lucius Scipio did likewise in the following year, camping under the walls with his army on the way to fight Antiochus III in the battle of Magnesia.[34]

At the conference leading to the Peace of Apamea in 188 B.C., following the defeat of Antiochus III at the hands of the Romans, Ilion was confirmed in her freedom and, furthermore, received some of the neighboring settlements (notably Rhoeteum and Gergithus), "less as a reward for recent services than in recognition of their descent."[35]

Ilion coined her first civic tetradrachms in 188 B.C., in the name not of the city but of Athena of Ilion (figs. 29.1a–b). Probably financed by the wealthy citizens whose names appear on them, these spectacular coins were traded to Seleucid territory to help meet the shortage of silver created by the huge indemnity to Rome as a consequence of the Apamea agreement, which so benefitted both Pergamon and little Ilion.[36]

Attalus II of Pergamon gave land (as well as cows and herdsmen) to the temple of Athena at Ilion before 138 B.C.[37] In 133 B.C., Asia was organized as a Roman province[38] and in 89 B.C., the Censor Lucius Julius Caesar denied the *publicani* the right to tax land belonging to the temple of Athena Ilias, as a result of an appeal made by advocates of the goddess.[39] This is the first instance of a Caesar helping the city of his legendary ancestors.[40]

Mithradates' offensive in 88–87 B.C. influenced the symbols on some coins of Ilion, which bore motifs connected with him, suggesting the king had partisans in high places in the city.[41]

In 86 B.C., C. Flavius Fimbria murdered the Roman

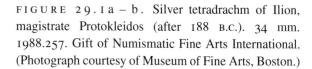

FIGURE 29.1a–b. Silver tetradrachm of Ilion, magistrate Protokleidos (after 188 B.C.). 34 mm. 1988.257. Gift of Numismatic Fine Arts International. (Photograph courtesy of Museum of Fine Arts, Boston.)

consul L. Valerius Flaccus, commander of the anti-Sullan Roman army in Asia. Seeking to enter Ilion, he and his troops were denied admission, and the citizens asked Sulla for aid. But after eleven days, the wily Fimbria persuaded the Ilians, as long-claimed kinsmen of Roma Aeterna, to admit him. Once inside the city, he ordered a general massacre, set fire to the city, and damaged but did not destroy the Macedonian temple of Athena Ilias, "the inviolability of which Rome had long acknowledged."[42] "When he boasted that he himself had overpowered on the eleventh day the city which Agamemnon had only with difficulty captured in the tenth year, although the latter had with him on his expedition the fleet of a thousand vessels and the whole of Greece, one of the Ilians said: 'Yes, for the city's champion was no Hector.' "[43]

Sulla set out to punish Fimbria, who moved southeast in the direction of Pergamon. In this territory Fimbria struck the rather crude and obviously hastily designed silver cistophoric tetradrachms in the Pergamene tradition, which hail him as Imperator. Two specimens survive, one in Oxford and a second in Boston (figs. 29.2a–b). Deserted by his troops as Sulla advanced, Fimbria committed suicide in 85 B.C., in the temple of Asklepios at Pergamon.

To compensate for the destruction Ilion had suffered, Sulla confirmed all the city's privileges. Motivated by Ilion's sentimental "kinship" with Rome, he restored as much as he could.[44]

In 80–79 B.C., Ilion honored the commander of militia from Poemanenum in northern Mysia, who, on orders from the governor (Gaius Claudius Nero), brought a company of soldiers to protect the "kinship" city from an attack by the well-equipped Cilician pirates.[45]

Impoverished in the aftermath of Mithradates, Fimbria, and the pirates, seven of the cities in the federation of the Troad borrowed money from the temple of Athena at Ilion for their common festival in 77 B.C. Even with low rates of interest, the cities defaulted and had to refinance their obligations.[46]

It was probably at the time of Pompey's victory over King Mithradates in 62 B.C.[47] that the city set up a statue of Pompey the Great, as Imperator for the third time and from the Demos.[48]

PART TWO: ILIUM NOVUM

The rebuilding of the Greco-Roman city began in 48 B.C., after Julius Caesar had visited the site. When he absentmindedly stepped in the long grass on the top of the so-called "Tomb of Hector," a farmer warned him not to tread on Hector's ghost.[49] For a brief time he even contemplated moving the capital there. According to Strabo, because Ascanius-Iulus was his ancestor "Caesar . . . allotted territory to them and also helped

FIGURE 29.2a–b. Silver cistophoric tetra-
drachm of C. Flavius Fimbria as Imperator. Struck near
Pergamon (about 86 B.C.). 24 mm. Acq. no. 1987.301.
Theodora Wilbour Fund in Memory of Zoë Wilbour.
(Photograph courtesy of Museum of Fine Arts, Boston.)

them to preserve their freedom and their immunity from
taxation; and to this day they remain in possession of
these favours."[50]

Roman engineers leveled the acropolis of Ilium and
filled in the terraces by constructing a series of vast
earthworks. They also seem to have renewed the early
Hellenistic Doric marble temple of Athena built by King
Lysimachus.

Julius Caesar emphasized his ancestral ties in 48 B.C.
by striking a denarius in the Latin West and also in the
Greek East (since specimens are found there) with a dia-
demed head of a Hellenistic Aphrodite-Venus on the obverse and with the "Flight of Aeneas" (Aeneas carrying
Anchises and a large Palladium) on the reverse. This silver coin, one of the most widely circulated of Caesar's
issues, was a worldwide affirmation of the Imperator's
divine, Trojan ancestry. The only inscription is CAE-
SAR, on the right side of the reverse.[51]

The temple of Athena was further restored and embellished by Augustus around 22 to 19 B.C., and a statue
was set up to him in 12 or 11 B.C.[52] Other statues were
also put up to Augustus,[53] to his friend P. Vedius Pollio,
and to his companion and son-in-law Marcus Agrippa.[54]
P. Vedius Pollio appears in an inscription found on the
Acropolis of Athens. He was not only a friend of Augustus but also was famous for his luxury, his debauch-
eries, and worse, since he threw slaves to his lampreys.[55]

The temple of Athena Ilias had a carved dedicatory
inscription to Augustus.[56] Like Julius Caesar, he had
confirmed the city's ancient privileges and given it new
territory. The marble head of Augustus from Ilium, now
in Berlin, is a Julio-Claudian transformation of the Pri-
maporta type and belonged to a statue set up just before
or after his death.[57]

A round base with a dedication to Antonia, daughter
of Octavia and Mark Antony, niece of Augustus, wife of
Nero Drusus, sister-in-law of the Emperor Tiberius
(A.D. 14 to 37), and mother of Germanicus Caesar, Claudius, and Livilla, shows how the Ilians could flatter their
powerful Julian "cousins." Antonia is styled "the goddess Aphrodite belonging to the race of Anchises."[58]

One night, Julia, the daughter of Augustus and wife
of Agrippa, arrived unannounced and unexpected at

Ilium and nearly drowned in a flash flood of the Scamander. Agrippa was furious at the citizens for not having prevented the near-disaster and fined the Ilians
100,000 denarii or drachmai. Remission of the fine and
forgiveness were secured through the mediation of Ni-
colaus of Damascus and King Herod the Great of
Judaea.[59]

P. Ovidius Naso (43 B.C. to A.D. 17) probably made
his visit to Troy early in his career when he was on the
Grand Tour, which included Athens. Although the *Fasti*,
where he wrote of seeing Ilium,[60] was not yet completed
in A.D. 8 when he was banished to Tomis on the northwest coast of the Black Sea, it seems doubtful Ovid
would have been permitted to go as a tourist to Troy on
the way to a harsh exile from which there never was a
reprieve.

Gaius Caesar, son of Julia and Agrippa and grandson
of Augustus, who adopted him, must have visited Ilium
during his proconsular progress into the East as governor of Asia in 1 B.C.–A.D. 1. The inscribed base of a
statue, found "on the acropolis," was dedicated to him
by the Boule and the Demos. He was hailed as kinsman
and patron-benefactor for his connection with Julius
Caesar and the legend of Troy, and probably for favors
he lavished on the city.[61]

In the fall of A.D. 17, Germanicus and Agrippina the
Elder visited Ilium because of their regard for its ancient
connection with Rome. The head and statue of Agrippina found at Troy (now divided between the University Museum, Philadelphia, and the Berlin Museums)
was doubtless dedicated in commemoration of this
occasion.[62]

One of these early Julio-Claudian progresses to Ilium
may have been the occasion when a statue of Priam was
set up. The base survives in the Louvre.[63] There is a metrical Greek inscription on two of its sides.[64] Priam appears in Greco-Roman reliefs, but there are no identified
statues.

Suetonius tells the anecdote of Tiberius' sarcastic reply in A.D. 23–24 to ambassadors from Ilium with tardy
condolences on the death of his son Drusus. He said, in
effect, "I too am grieved by your misfortune in losing
your eminent fellow-citizen, Hector."[65]

Two, possibly three, statues of Tiberius were erected
at Ilium. To the earliest statue belongs a youthful head
which, like the late portrait of Augustus with which it

was found, is now in Berlin.[66] The latest was set up in
A.D. 32–33.[67]

The Julio-Claudians felt more than a casual kinship
with Ilium, since the Dictator and the first Princeps had
made their descent from Aeneas and Iulus-Ascanius a
fashionable part of imperial iconography and, thanks to
Vergil, near-historical belief. Nero (A.D. 54–68) was the
last Julian to rule and thus the last Julian to speak out
publicly for the welfare of the latter-day Trojans, although his shining moment of oratory came while his
great-uncle Claudius (A.D. 41–54) still ruled.

In A.D. 53, while still a boy, Nero delivered an eloquent oration in Greek in the Forum Romanum on behalf of his ancestral city. The Emperor Claudius was so
moved that he exempted the Ilians from all taxes "after
[reading] aloud an old Greek letter of the Roman Senate
and People" offering a treaty of friendship and alliance
with Seleucus on condition that he would declare their
Ilian "kinsmen" exempt from tribute.[68] The council and
people of Ilium put up statues of young Nero as "kinsman of the city." Statues of Britannicus and Octavia
were included in a portico dedicated to the Emperor
Claudius and his wife Agrippina the Younger, daughter
of Germanicus. The head from a statue of Agrippina,
now also in Berlin with the Augustus and the young Tiberius,[69] must surely have been part of this monument.
Handsome fragments of the portico remain,[70] of which
the inscribed architrave is the most impressive. The
early imperial bouleuterion is the most complete Greco-
Roman building at Troy.

Pliny the Elder (A.D. 23–79), in the description of the
Troad in his *Natural History* (completed A.D. 77), called
Ilium a tourist attraction, "the scene of all the famous
story."[71] At this time a number of donors gave toward
the building of a temple to the Gens Flavia.[72] Presumably, in this connection there was a tripartite statue base
or bases to Vespasian, Titus, and Domitianus, the latter
being badly damaged, perhaps as a result of *damnatio*.[73]

A Roman versed in Homer, Vergil, and the topography of the Trojan plain could visit Ilium and bring home
an array of the city's imperial coins with the Homeric
tales, images, and symbols, like the Lupa Romana, unit-
ing Ilium and its great offspring, Rome.

The coins definitely show us that the citizens of Ilium
missed nothing that would promote their image as the
place for Romans of all classes to visit, from wandering

merchants through proconsular officials. Tours of the shrines around the plain and within the walls were designed to highlight the past.

The connection between the coin-types and monuments that actually existed at Ilium has been recognized since the turn of the century.[74] The coins explored most of the mythological, heroic, and historic possibilities of the Homeric city and its famous citizens or subjects. Hector was the leading hero, and Athena the foremost divinity, but Ganymede, Aphrodite, Anchises, Aeneas, Ascanius-Iulus, Priam, Hector's family, Dardanos with the maiden Bateia, and a cult-image of Zeus also figure in the repertory.

The historical series of coins of Ilium Novum began under the Flavians (A.D. 79–96) with the Flight of Aeneas on the reverse of a quasi-autonomous coin. An almost half-figure bust of Athena appears on the obverse. The reverse emphasizes the Roman connection, since Aeneas is leading Ascanius-Iulus as well as carrying Anchises. The controversial Palladium, which appeared on the denarii of Julius Caesar (above), has disappeared.[75]

In A.D. 124, Hadrian visited Ilium. The great coast road near the city seems to have been repaired in preparation for his arrival.[76] This road ran from Abydos through Ilium, Alexandria Troas, Assos, and Elaea, eventually reaching Cyme and Smyrna.[77] At Ilium, an altar was dedicated to Hadrian.[78]

Hadrian is said also to have rebuilt the tomb of the hero Ajax at Ilium, after the supposed original tomb had been washed away by the sea.[79] The upper part of a tall, slender stele surmounted by a richly carved anthemion was found near the "Tomb of Aias" and has been dated around 500 B.C. It seems likely that the traditionally minded, philhellene emperor Hadrian found this beautiful Ionian sculpture a perfect embellishment for his reconstructed tomb of Ajax.[80]

In the second and third centuries A.C., support for Ilium was a matter of public policy, and the city played up the ties of "kinship" with sets of touristic coins and diverse public monuments, including the costly water-supply system.

Philostratus, writing in the third century, relates that about A.D. 130, when Herodes Atticus was curator of the free cities of Asia, he asked Hadrian to give 12,000,000 sesterces to pay for an aqueduct to supply water to Ilium. When expenses had reached 28,000,000 sesterces, the procurators of Asia complained that the tribute of 500 cities was being wasted on a single spring. Herodes Atticus' father paid the cost overrun himself.[81]

Under Antoninus Pius (A.D. 138–161) "the favoured city of Ilium, repeatedly declared exempt from all payments of money to Rome and expressly absolved by Antoninus himself from the obligation of assuming the guardianship of any who were not natives of the city, was placed under the charge of a curator in A.D. 140. [This] citizen of Cyzicus . . . was praised for 'having by his curatorship and his advocacy corrected and accomplished many things of great importance, a man worthy of every honour because of his excellent character and his benevolence toward the city.' "[82]

It is surely at this time, stimulated by the nine-hundred-year anniversary of the founding of Rome (A.D. 147), that embellishments and, possibly, reconstructions were carried out in the theater at Ilium. To this period also belongs the marble *tondo* in Berlin, with the Lupa Romana.[83] The composition is free, sculptural, and illusionistic, with a background like that of Antonine medallions. The center foreground with the Wolf and Twins is like the Grimani or Palazzo Rondanini animal reliefs. Placed in the theater at Ilium, this addition was clearly designed to make tourists from Rome conscious of their Trojan roots.

The reign of Marcus Aurelius (A.D. 161–180) marks the first era of the sestertii or big medallic *aes* coins. The reverses tell much of Troy's mythological history. One shows Poseidon and Apollo building the walls of Troy for King Laomedon, Priam's father. (Unfortunately, Laomedon failed to pay Poseidon and Apollo for their work, bringing disasters upon Troy, at least one of which was illustrated on a rare sestertius of Septimius Severus [below].) Poseidon runs to the right, toward the center of the composition, a trident in his left hand. He holds out a mason's trowel to Apollo, who stands facing left in the pose of Lysippic statues of Hermes and Poseidon, a mortarboard on his extended right hand and two river-reeds (Scamander and Simois?) in his left hand. The walls of Troy appear across the background and there is an arched gate in the lower center of the structure, which has towers like any Roman frontier city of the second and third centuries A.C. (figs. 29.3a–b).[84] On other large bronze coins, Ganymede feeds the eagle,

FIGURE 29.3a–b. Poseidon and Apollo build the walls of Troy. Bronze sestertius of Ilium under Marcus Aurelius (A.D. 161–180). 36 mm. Chatswold Collection. (Photo courtesy of Museum of Fine Arts, Boston.)

while Athena Ilias stands on a column at the right;[85] Andromache with Astyanax bids farewell to Hector, shown in a helmet and holding a spear.[86] The composition of Ganymede dish-feeding the eagle, as if the bird were a family pet, became very popular all over the Roman Empire, on intaglio gems, in silver plate, and on the gold medallions struck when Severus Alexander (A.D. 222–235) attempted to revive the mystique of his Macedonian ancestors. The reverse of the Wolf and Twins, with the eagle on a rock (the Roman Capitol) behind, appears as a pure compliment from the old city (of the Twins' ancestors) to the foundation of Romulus.

Finally, the by-now canonical Roman composition of Aeneas carrying Anchises and leading Ascanius-Iulus from burning Troy appears in a format worthy of the medallions and sestertii of Antoninus Pius that were coined at the mint of Rome. It is reflected in the reverse of an Ilian sestertius of Marcus Aurelius' colleague and son-in-law, Lucius Verus (A.D. 161–169) (figs. 29.4a–b).[87]

As co-emperor (A.D. 177–180) with his father Marcus Aurelius, Commodus introduced a personal touch in the numismatic iconography of Ilium. On the reverse of a dupondius, the young emperor, crowned by Nike-Victoria, raises his hand to Athena Ilias. All three figures stand on garlanded or plain pedestals.[88] Commodus as Caesar (A.D. 174–177) also inaugurated the reverse of Hector setting fire to the Greek ships.[89]

During the reign of Commodus, the last Antonine (A.D. 180–192), a coin-reverse at Ilium bore a cult-image of an enthroned Zeus holding a small statue of Athena Ilias on his outstretched left hand.[90] The reverse is inscribed to the Ilian god of Mount Ida. This reverse brings to mind the colossal head of Zeus in Istanbul, which is discussed below under Tetrarchic commemorations at Troy. Commodus and his consort Crispina also are identified with reverses showing Priam enthroned wearing a Phrygian cap, holding a sceptre-staff vertically in his left hand, and labeled Priam of Ilion.[91] Evidence of a sculptural model for the reverse has survived in the base of the statue of Priam from Troy in the Louvre (see above) which could have been the Julio-Claudian (or Hadrianic?) inspiration for this strong numismatic type.

A collection of large bronze coins, all of the second century A.C., is mounted on a bronze "casserole" in the Museum of Fine Arts, Boston. This very Roman cere-

474

FIGURE 29.4a – b. The Flight of Aeneas. Bronze sestertius of Ilium under Lucius Verus (A.D. 161–169). 35 mm. Acq. no. 1983.7. Theodora Wilbour Fund in Memory of Zoë Wilbour. (Photograph courtesy of Museum of Fine Arts, Boston.)

monial utensil did not come from Asia Minor; but the coins, attached to its surface with their reverses outwards, certainly did. The owner, perhaps a tourist from the Latin West who visited Ilium and other cities in Mysia, Bithynia, Lydia, and Ionia (Smyrna), mounted his coins on the bowl the same way that Renaissance humanists had their Roman coins mounted on cabinets and bookcases. His souvenir from Ilium was a sestertius-sized bronze coin of Marcus Aurelius or Lucius Verus similar to the freestanding specimen illustrated here (figs. 29.4a–b). The vessel may have been a conversation piece at banquets, like the plate mentioned in the Historia Augusta around A.D. 260 to 280 (figs. 29.5a–b).[92] The anonymous tourist's fantasy may have centered on Hadrian's male companion Antinous, since he had two of the medallions that were dedicated at Smyrna in the hero's name by a member of the prominent Polemon family.[93]

The placement of the coins on the "casserole" suggests a traveler perhaps beginning his journey in Smyrna, lingering at Hierocaesarea in Lydia (two big bronzes), moving through Bithynia (a Hadrianic or early Antonine "medallion" of the Koinon Bithynion under Hadrian),[94] reaching the coast at Cyzicus in Mysia, and completing the itinerary at Ilium with the Flight of Aeneas medallic sestertius of Marcus Aurelius or Lucius Verus.[95] The route is roughly that of the geographic historian Strabo in reverse (unless the journey began at Ilium and ended at Smyrna). In either case, Ilium was a crucial commencement or conclusion to this geographical collection.

After Septimius Severus seized Rome in A.D. 193 and defeated Pescennius Niger in 194, "the big coins reappear at Ilium, as confident as ever."[96] The rarest is the splendid piece in the British Museum, a sestertius, on which Hector draws a spear from the nude body of Patroclus, upon which he rests his foot.[97] On other coins, Hector appears in his galloping biga and his standing quadriga. The very rare sestertius with Herakles and Hesione, the sea monster in the waves below, presents the myth involving the capture of the city by Herakles, a disaster that befell Ilium after King Laomedon had reneged on his promises to pay for services a second time.[98] This reverse type did not show Ilium-Troy in the best light and was soon withdrawn.

The Wolf and Twins with an eagle on a rock or pedestal behind appears again on a sestertius-sized coin of

475

FIGURE 29.5a – b. Ceremonial Utensil ("Casserole"). Bronze, with Greek imperial coins of Asia Minor in the second century A.C. mounted to suggest souvenirs of a journey between the Troad (Ilium) and Smyrna. H.: 0.165m. Diam. (max. incl. handle): 0.43m. Acq. no. 63.2644. Theodora Wilbour Fund in Memory of Zoë Wilbour. (Photograph courtesy of Museum of Fine Arts, Boston.)

Ilium in the name of Severus' son Caracalla as Caesar (A.D. 198–211).

Caracalla felt himself a descendent of Achilles through his royal Syrian mother, Julia Domna, and behaved in the grand manner on his passage to the East as the new Alexander the Great in A.D. 214. Like his Macedonian-Epirote ancestors, Caracalla was prepared to conquer the Parthians as the material successors to the Persians and even the Trojans.

In the late autumn of A.D. 214, Caracalla sacrificed at the tomb of Achilles, ran his troops in arms around it, and erected a bronze statue of Achilles.[99] The emperor also cremated his literary freedman and favorite, Festus, on a great pyre in imitation of the funeral rites of Patroclus and buried him in the largest tomb (Ucek Tepe) in the Troad.[100] He issued a coin bearing the figure of Athena Ilias to honor his mother, Julia Domna, who had

traveled with the troops. In her capacity as bringer of victory, Athena Ilias forms a coin-type (figs. 29.6a–b). In addition to his dynastic and sentimental posturing at Ilium, in A.D. 214 Caracalla had the coastal road renewed as Hadrian had done previously (above).[101] In A.D. 217–218, the usurper Macrinus produced a sestertius showing Hector struggling and fighting over the nude body of Patroclus. Alfred Bellinger[102] noted that what the complicated scene "loses in simplicity and skill of design it gains in the appearance of mortal combat."

The emperors Valerian and Gallienus, father and son, ruling jointly from A.D. 253 to 260, again struck the big Greek imperial sestertii like those of the Antonine and early Severan periods, showing the armed Hector in his quadriga as produced under Commodus.[103] The types focus on Hector, burning the Greek ships[104] and galloping forth, wearing full armor, in his two-horse chariot. In the latter composition, he is also hurling a stone with his raised right hand (figs. 29.7a–b).[105]

Toward the end of the sole reign of Gallienus (A.D. 260–267), the Goths unsuccessfully besieged the Temple of Apollo at Didyma. On their return voyage up the western coast of Asia Minor, the Goths plundered "the much-revered city of Ilium" but were beaten back by the Roman troops at Byzantium. The precise date is often given as A.D. 267.[106]

After the depredations of the Goths, the city entered the twilight zone. But, while Ilium could no longer strike coins with scenes from the battles and the fall of Troy, other Greek imperial cities could. A bronze coin of Samos under Gallienus has as its reverse a crude but forceful version of the Pergamene sculptural group of Achilles killing the Amazon queen Penthesilea.[107]

There were dedications and honors paid to Zeus (Jupiter) and Athena (Minerva) at Ilium in the names of the first *Seniores Augusti* (Tetrarchs), Diocletianus and Maximianus (A.D. 293–305).[108] In this connection, there is the colossal head of Zeus which was found on the Acropolis of Ilium in a well, amid the remains (architectural fragments and inscriptions) of the temple of Athena.[109] This Zeus is a Hellenistic masterpiece in the Pergamene style of 200 to 150 B.C. The statue could have been set up in the temple of Athena, or the smaller Doric temple nearby, at any time from the reign of Augustus to that of Diocletian.

Constantine the Great almost founded his Nova Roma at Sigeum near Ilium, or possibly at Ilium itself in A.D. 323–324, but his flirtation with a New Rome along the entrance to the Dardanelles was as brief as Julius Caesar's.[110] A major harbor was started, then abandoned. The grand circular pedestal of a statue of his son Constantinus II survives at Ilium from these activities.[111] The statue of Constantine that once stood on the porphyry column (the "Burnt Column" of Istanbul) was said to have originally been a statue of Apollo which stood in Ilium.[112]

Julian Caesar ("the Apostate") visited Ilium and the temple of Athena in A.D. 355.[113] He was amazed and gratified to find the altars still burning before the heroön of Hector and the hero's statue still being anointed. He also saw the grave of Achilles, still undamaged. In these years the Ilians did good business attracting tourists with their pseudo-Trojan monuments, memorials, and souvenirs.[114]

After a visit to Ilium by the empress Eudoxia, wife of Theodosius II in A.D. 421–444, she wrote in her *Ionia*: "Ilios between Ida and the sea, the city once so magnificent, merits that we shed tears over it, for it is so completely ruined that not even its foundations remain. *She who saw it bears witness to this*, to speak according to the gospel." Heinrich Schliemann speculated that she was speaking solely of the disappearance of the Homeric city, not of the Greek and Roman "historic Ilium."[115]

Ilium is hardly noticed in the days of the Byzantine empire, although the learned emperor Constantinus VII Porphyrogenitus (A.D. 945–959) wrote that there was a Bishop of Ilium (whose actual seat may have been elsewhere, however).[116]

Mehmed II, Ottoman conqueror of Constantinople in

FIGURE 29.6a – b. Athena Ilias, the Greek imperial cult-image. Bronze semis of Ilium in the name of Julia Domna (about A.D. 214). 26.5 mm. Acq. no. 64.1933. Theodora Wilbour Fund in Memory of Zoë Wilbour. (Photograph courtesy Museum of Fine Arts, Boston.)

May 1453, came to Troy ten years after the conquest and "gloried in the fact that he had defeated the descendants of those who had destroyed the city. They had, at last, he declared, paid the debt that they owed the people of Asia."[117] Mehmed, an exceptionally learned man, felt his ties to the Trojans were as good as those of the Romans, since Turks (=Turkos or Turkoi in Greek) were, according to his reasoning, also descendants of Teucer.[118]

Both the nostalgia for Troy and the strategic importance of the site persisted. In World War I, General Liman von Sanders felt the Allies would land on the Asiatic coast near the entrance to the Dardanelles, and thus in 1915 he sent two Ottoman divisions "to the region of the field of Troy."[119]

In 1922, after the fall of Smyrna, the British 3rd Hussars under Captain J. C. Petherick withdrew from Bithynia and Mysia to a series of positions around "the battlefield of Troy," and stood with their backs to the sea as Kemal Pasha's forces advanced toward the Dardanelles.[120]

EPILOGUE: HOMER'S IMAGE

At Amastris (modern Amasra) on the coast of the Pontus, a quasi-autonomous bronze coin of the period around A.D. 100 has as its obverse the letters OMH—POC around a draped bust of the bard based on the image of some fourth-century B.C. or Hellenistic man of letters.[121] The imagined iconographic images of the blind bard lost their noble fifth-century B.C. or their pseudo-naturalistic, heroic Alexandrine Hellenistic qualities in the art of the Greek imperial cities of northwest Asia Minor toward the end of the second century A.C.

The draped bust of Homer on the reverse of a bronze coin of Commodus Caesar (A.D. 175–177), struck at Nicaea in Bithynia, turned the poet into a battered old philosopher looking like one of the miracle men and magicians who wandered from city to city in Asia Minor and North Africa at the height of the Roman Empire, making overlong speeches (Apuleius in Tripolitania), providing cures (Apollonius of Tyana), or showing off exotic animals and reptiles (Alexander of Abunuteichus with his Glaukon).

FIGURE 29.7a-b. Hector charging into battle. Bronze sestertius of Ilium under Gallienus (A.D. 253–267). 37 mm. Acq. no. 61.193. Theodora Wilbour Fund in Memory of Zoë Wilbour. (Photograph courtesy Museum of Fine Arts, Boston.)

It was as if the songs and writings of Homer and his followers became mixed up with the world of festivals, sideshows, and tough professional athletics which by then was so much a part of urban life from the Thracian cities on the Danube to the Parthian frontiers of Syria.[122] The tourists to Troy and beyond must have had a confusing time in their searches for the true Homer in the lands about which he wrote.[123]

NOTES

*Members of the Department of Classical Art at the Museum of Fine Arts, Boston, have helped in the preparation of this paper. Amy Raymond and Florence Wolsky collaborated in putting this offering into its final form. Mary B. Comstock has helped bring order out of confusion, as she always has over thirty-five years with publications prepared on Huntington Avenue in Boston. At Harvard, David Gordon Mitten has been a constant companion in discussion of things Turkish, ancient and modern, numismatic and topographical. Sarah Morris deserves much thanks for making this paper more professional.

Quotations of, or references to, ancient authors are derived from volumes in the Loeb Classical Library.

Bellinger = A. R. Bellinger, *Troy, The Coins, Suppl. Monograph 2, University of Cincinnati* (Princeton 1961).

Boulter = C. Boulter, in the *Princeton Encyclopedia of Classical Sites* (Princeton 1976).

Cook = J. M. Cook, "The Topography of the Plain of Troy," in L. Foxhall and J. K. Davies, eds., *The Trojan War, Its Historicity and Context*, Papers of the First Greenbank Colloquium, Liverpool, 1981 (Bristol 1984) 163–172.

Einzelaufnahmen = P. Arndt and W. Amelung, *Photographische Einzelaufnahmen antiker Sculpturen*, ser. 6 (Munich 1912) col. 47, no. 1744.

Franke = P. R. Franke, *Kleinasien zur Römerzeit: griechisches Leben im Spiegel der Münzen* (Munich 1968).

Head-Jenkins = B. V. Head and G. K. Jenkins, *A Guide to the Principal Coins of the Greeks*, British Museum (London 1959).

IGRR = *Inscriptiones Graecae ad Res Romanas Pertinentes* (Paris 1901–).

Ilios = H. Schliemann, *Ilios: The City and Country of the Trojans* (New York 1881).

Inan-Rosenbaum = J. Inan and E. Rosenbaum, *Roman and Early Byzantine Portrait Sculpture in Asia Minor* (London 1966).

Jebb-Hogarth = R. C. Jebb and D. G. Hogarth, "Troy and Troad," in *Encyclopaedia Britannica*, 11th ed., (Cambridge, Eng. and New York 1911) vol. 27, pp. 314–318.

Kinross = Lord Kinross, *Ataturk, A biography of Mustafa Kemal, father of modern Turkey* (New York 1965).

Magie 1, 2 = D. Magie, *Roman Rule in Asia Minor, To the End of the Third Century after Christ*, vol. 1, Text, vol. 2, Notes (Princeton 1950).

McDonagh = B. McDonagh, *Blue Guide: Turkey, The Aegean and Mediterranean Coasts* (London and New York 1989).

Schmidt-Dounas = B. Schmidt-Dounas, "Metopen von Ilion," *IstMitt* 41 (1991) 363–415.

Sear = D. R. Sear, *Greek Imperial Coins and their Values, The Local Coinages of the Roman Empire* (London 1982).

Troja = H. Schliemann, *Troja, Results of the Latest Researches and Discoveries on the Site of Homer's Troy* (New York 1884).

Vermeule, *RIAGAM* = C. C. Vermeule, *Roman Imperial Art in Greece and Asia Minor* (Cambridge, Mass. 1968) Appendix C, "Works of Art and Inscriptions by Site," 457–458.

Vermeule, *Odysseus* = C. C. Vermeule III, "Perceptions of the Trojan Wars in the Fenway: the *Creeping Odysseus*," in *Fenway Court 1984, Isabella Stewart Gardner Museum*, 28–31.

Vermeule, *Survivals* = C. C. Vermeule, "From Tarentum to Troy and on to Tunisia: Homeric Survivals in the Hellenistic and Roman Worlds," in *Eumousia, Ceramic and Iconographic Studies in Honour of Alexander Cambitoglou*, MeditArch suppl. 1 (Sydney 1990) 253–256, pl. 51.

von Aulock 5, 16 = K. Kraft, H. von Aulock, et al., *Sylloge Nummorum Graecorum, Deutschland, Sammlung v. Aulock, Troas, Aeolis, Lesbos*, 5. Heft (Berlin 1959) "Ilion," nos. 1517–1543; also *Nachträge* II, *Troas*, 16. Heft (Berlin 1967) "Ilion," nos. 7603–7618.

Ziegler = K. Ziegler, *KlPauly*, vol. 5, "Troia," cols. 977–983. This is based on and has been expanded from E. Meyer, *RE*, Suppl. Bd. 14, "Troia," cols. 809–817, where all sources, ancient and modern, are given.

1. McDonagh 195.

2. Strabo 13.1.40. Quoted in a slightly different translation: Bellinger 1. According to M. Korfmann, Director of the Troy Excavation Project, and C. B. Rose, Head of the University of Cincinnati's Troy excavation team, the Homeric city appears to have been much larger than previously believed: *The Boston Globe* (February 23, 1993) 5.

3. Strabo 13.1.40.

4. W. Leaf, "The Lokrian Maidens," *BSA* 21 (1916) 148–154.

5. Herodotus 7.43.

6. Cook 167.

7. Bellinger 2, with sources and arguments.

8. B. D. Meritt, H. T. Wade-Gery, and M. F. McGregor, *The Athenian Tribute Lists* I (Cambridge, Mass. 1939) 120, col. III, line 132.

9. Xen., *Hell.* 1.1.4; Ziegler, col. 982.

10. Xen., *Hell.* 3.1.10–16; Diod. 14.38.3; Jebb-Hogarth 315.

11. Bellinger 2.

12. Dem. 23.152–154, "Against Aristocrates"; *Ilios* 170–171; Ziegler, col. 982.

13. Bellinger 2.

14. Strabo 13.1.26.

15. Magie 1, 82.

16. Arrian 1.11.7–8; Cook 163. McDonagh 198.

17. Plut. *Alex.* 15.2; *Ilios* 171–172.

18. Bellinger 3.

19. Strabo 13.1.26, but some scholars question Strabo's account, believing the city meant is not Ilion but Alexandria Troas, where a fortification wall enclosing the harbor has been found: W. Leaf, *Strabo on the Troad* (Cambridge 1923) 143; *The Princeton Encyclopedia of Classical Sites* (Princeton 1976) 39, "Alexandria Troas"; 407, "Ilion"; Schmidt-Dounas, 364–366.

20. Strabo 13.1.26. There are differing opinions on the dating of the temple of Athena: Schmidt-Dounas 363–415; B. M. Holden, *The Metopes of the Temple of Athena at Ilion* (Northampton 1964) 1–5.

21. *Einzelaufnahmen*, no. 1744; Vermeule, *RIAGAM* 457.

22. *CIG* 3598 = *SEG* IV, 662.

23. Strabo 13.1.27; Jebb-Hogarth 315; Magie 1, 311.

24. Magie 1, 95. The general model for a "golden" equestrian Antiochus could have been the gilded bronze statue of Demetrius Poliorcetes of 303 to 302 B.C. in the Agora of Athens; C. Houser, "Alexander's Influence on Greek Sculpture as Seen in a Portrait in Athens," in *Macedonia and Greece in Late Classical and Early Hellenistic Times*, National Gallery of Art, Studies in the History of Art, vol. 10 (Washington, D.C. 1982) 229–238.

25. Jebb-Hogarth 315.

26. Livy 29.12.14.

27. Livy 29.12.13–14; also, 29.11.2.

28. *Ilios* 168.

29. *IGRR* IV, 179 = *SIG* 2, 591.

30. Magie 1, 18.

31. Livy 35.43.3; *IGRR* IV, 192; also Magie 2, 948; Jebb-Hogarth 315.

32. Strabo 13.1.27.

33. Jebb-Hogarth 315.

34. Livy 37.33.4 and 37.37.2–5, also 37.9.7; Magie 1, 103.

35. Livy 38.39.10.

36. Bellinger 23–27.

37. Magie 1, 140.

38. Magie 1, 3.

39. Magie 1, 166; 2, 1056, n. 26 and extensive references.

40. *IGRR* IV, nos. 194–195. Bellinger 9 and n. 44.

41. Bellinger 34.

42. Magie 1, 228.

43. Strabo 13.1.27; Bellinger 9–10 and n. 47.

44. Strabo 13.1.27.

45. Bellinger 10.

46. Magie 1, 239.

47. Bellinger 11.

48. *IGRR* IV, no. 198.

49. Cook 163.

50. Strabo 13.1.27; Suet. *Caesar* 79.3.

51. E. A. Sydenham, *The Coinage of the Roman Republic* (London 1952) 168, no. 1013, pl. 27.

52. *IGRR* IV, no. 203.

53. *IGRR* IV, nos. 201–202.

54. *IGRR* IV, no. 204.

55. Tac. *Ann.* 1.10; *Troja* 229, the pedestal of the statue discovered at Hissarlik.

56. *IGRR* IV, no. 202.

57. Inan-Rosenbaum 57, no. 2; R. M. Gais, "A Portrait of Augustus in the Syracuse University Art Collection," *RM* 87 (1980) 341–344, pls. 119–120, the Troy Augustus.

58. *Troja* 232, no. 15.

59. Bellinger 12.

60. Ovid, *Fasti* 6.421; *Ilios* 178.

61. *IGRR* IV, no. 205. *Ilios* 178; Magie 2, 1343.

62. Vermeule, *RIAGAM* 192–193, fig. 122; 386, no. 3.

63. The base came from the Hertz collection, and before that it had belonged to the Duke of Buckingham, whose collection was sold in 1848.

64. E. Michon, Musée du Louvre, *Catalogue sommaire des marbres antiques* (Paris 1922) 159, no. 2614.

65. Suet. *Tib.*, 52.2.

66. Inan-Rosenbaum 62, no. 13.

67. Vermeule, *RIAGAM* 258.

68. *Ilios* 178; Suetonius, *Claud.*, 25.3; Tac., *Ann.*, 12.58.1. None of the above was affected by the modern consideration that the letter to *Seleucus Rex* (Seleucus II, Kallinikos) may have been a fabrication by the Ilians, rather than a genuine treaty of the third century B.C. (summation of arguments: Magie 2, 943, n. 40).

69. *Troy, Mycenae, Tiryns, Orchomenos, Heinrich Schliemann: The 100th Anniversary of his Death* (Athens 1990) 258, no. 199.

70. *IGRR* IV, nos. 208–209; Magie 2, 1400. Vermeule, *RIAGAM* 458.

71. Pliny *NH* 5.124.

72. *IGRR* IV, no. 210.

73. *IGRR* IV, no. 211.

74. B. V. Head, *Historia Nummorum, A Manual of Greek Numismatics* (Oxford 1911) 547.

75. Bellinger 47, no. T129. Franke, no. 283.

76. *CIL* III, no. 466.

77. Strabo 13.1.46–49, 63–65.

78. *IGRR* IV, no. 212. [Ed. note: a cuirassed statue of Hadrian was discovered at Troy in 1993: *Archaeology* Jan./Feb. 1994, p. 18.]

79. Philostratus, *Heroic* 2.3; Cook 163.

80. About 1892 the stele was photographed in the courtyard of Frank Calvert's Thymbra Farm. The little girl next to it (and to a second, slightly later anthemion stele) was the daughter of Emily Calvert Bacon and Francis Henry Bacon, later the architect of the Lincoln Memorial in Washington, D.C. The stele came to the Museum of Fine Arts, Boston, in 1903 through the Francis Bartlett Donation: L. D. Caskey, Museum of Fine Arts, Boston, *Catalogue of Greek and Roman Sculpture* (Cambridge, Mass. 1925) 25–26, no. 13. Mr. Caskey may have received the photo from one of the Calverts or the Bacons, since Francis Bacon and his cousin Francis Henry Bacon excavated and did the architectural reconstructions at Assos.

81. F. Millar, *The Emperor in the Roman World (31 B.C.–A.D. 337)* (Ithaca 1977) 199. Is Philostratus confusing similar tales told about Alexandria Troas or even Nicomedia or Nicaea in Bithynia?

82. Magie 1, 133

83. Vermeule, *RIAGAM* 458: Hadrianic or Antonine periods; *Troja* 212, fig. 122.

84. C. C. Vermeule III, *Divinities and Mythological Scenes in Greek Imperial Art: Art of Antiquity*, vol. 5, pt. 1, *Numismatic Studies* (London and Cambridge, Mass. 1983) 10–11, 29, pl. 16.

85. Bellinger 51, no. T149.

86. Bellinger 52, no. T150; Head-Jenkins 86, no. 11, pl. 47.

87. Vermeule, *Odysseus* 29, fig. 2.

88. Bellinger 56, no. T175.

89. Bellinger 56, no. T176.

90. von Aulock 16, no. 7015.

91. von Aulock 16, nos. 7616–7617.

92. M. Comstock and C. C. Vermeule III, *Greek, Etruscan and Roman Bronzes in the Museum of Fine Arts, Boston* (Greenwich 1971) 340–342, no. 479; additional bibliography in C. C. Vermeule III and M. B. Comstock, *Sculpture in Stone and Bronze* (Boston 1988) 125, no. 479. Having a cabinet of Greek imperial coins of the Troad and related cities of Asia Minor in a villa at Antium or Lanuvium was like the Earl Fitzwilliam or the Duke of Buckingham bringing home to their town houses and country seats in the British Isles souvenirs of their eighteenth- and early nineteenth-century visits to Italy.

93. Sear 123, no. 1331.

94. Sear 106, no. 1143; Franke 40, no. 4.

95. Bellinger no. T148.

96. Bellinger 63.

97. Sear 205, no. 2183.

98. Bellinger 64, no. T217. Why the Ilians of the age of Marcus Aurelius to Septimius Severus (A.D. 161–211) flirted with the Laomedon saga seemed puzzling, until Sarah Morris pointed out that Poseidon as well as Apollo (Ekatos) had sanctuaries, shrines, or temples in the region, and such large, medallic coins were good for the business of tourism at these sacred sites.

99. Dio 78.16.7.

100. *Ilios* 179–180. J. M. Cook notes that Caracalla could have added "the beautiful cone we now see" to the supposed Tomb of Achilles (Beşik Tepe) when he built the tumulus of his scribe Festus; Cook 168, 171, n. 2.

101. *CIL* III, no. 467.

102. Bellinger 72, no. T267.

103. Head-Jenkins 86, no. 12, pl. 47.

104. Bellinger 73, no. T291.

105. Vermeule, *RIAGAM* 154–155, fig. 87; *Romans and Barbarians*, Museum of Fine Arts (Boston 1976) 92, C72 (illus.); Vermeule, *Survivals* 255, pl. 51:4.

106. Ziegler, col. 982.

107. Vermeule, *Odysseus* 30, fig. 3; idem, *Survivals* 254, pl. 51, fig. 3.

108. *IGRR* IV, no. 214.

109. The head is now in the Istanbul Archaeological Museum: Inv. No. 85: Alpay Pasinli, *Istanbul Archaeological Museums* (Istanbul 1989) 1, fig. 1; G. Mendel, Musées Impériaux Ottomans, *Catalogue des sculptures* 2 (Constantinople 1912) 309–310, no. 580.

110. Boulter 407.

111. Inan-Rosenbaum 52, no. 1; Vermeule *RIAGAM* 458.

112. *Ilios* 180.

113. Boulter 407.

114. Jebb-Hogarth 315; *Ilios* 180–182. Bishop Pegasius, who gave Julian his tour of the area, later renounced Christianity and became a priest of the Emperor Julian's revived paganism: G. W. Bowersock, *Julian the Apostate* (Cambridge, Mass. 1978) 85.

115. *Troja* 225.

116. *Ilios* 183; Jebb-Hogarth 315.

117. McDonagh 199.

118. J. Raby, "Cyriacus of Ancona and the Ottoman Sultan Mehmed II," *JWarb* 43 (1980) 242–246; idem, "A Sultan of Paradox: Mehmed the Conqueror as a Patron of the Arts," *Oxford Art Journal* 5, no. 1 (1982) 3–8. With this belongs, in the contexts discussed here: idem, *DOP* 37 (1983) 21.

119. Kinross 88.

120. Kinross 380.

121. Franke, nos. 162, 167.

122. Vermeule, *Survivals* 254, pl. 51, fig. 2.

123. New work at Classical Troy was discussed in a lecture by Professor Stella Miller-Collett of the University of Cincinnati, "Troy Revisited: The Graeco-Roman Phases," in New York on Oct. 29, 1990, sponsored by the American Academy in Rome. A symposium, "Troy Revisited, Results of New Archaeological Excavations," was held in New York, on Feb. 25, 1993, cosponsored by Robert College, Istanbul, American Turkish Society, Inc., and the Univ. of Cincinnati's Classics Dept.

30

ALEXANDER AND ACHILLES—MACEDONIANS AND "MYCENAEANS" *

◆

ADA COHEN

Lionel Pearson expressed a commonly held view when he claimed, "It is likely enough that Alexander [the Great], with his tremendous enthusiasm for Homer, often thought of himself as reenacting incidents from the *Iliad*." [1] This probability, consistently publicized by the ancient writers who preserved and transmitted the story of Alexander, has constituted the single most fundamental insight into his character and his career, and raises interesting questions. These questions point to the larger issue of the complex relationship of the Macedonian world with a past that seems to have been remembered, at times pictorially conjured up, and even in some ways relived. They also invoke an even larger issue, that of the occasional appearance of a contingent past as subject matter in the respective present.[2] Whereas in our own present models are usually sought in the contemporary world, in antiquity they were conspicuously drawn from the distant past or could even have been more or less fictional, drawn from mythology and legend. Such was the case with Alexander's claim to Achillean heroism.

As Professor Vermeule tells her students, heroes must be dead, for only after death can their lives be seen complete and whole and their status judged for what it once was.[3] What makes Alexander interesting is the fact that he consciously pursued self-styled heroism while living. The private and the public components of this project are partially the topic of this paper. The inspiration that Alexander (and his companions) drew from Homer made him (and them) "true Mycenaeans," as Professor Vermeule would say. Alexander was not only a successful designer of a life lived as a project,[4] he was also a successful performer, engaging the cooperation of other performers in various media, not least artists and writers, articulate voices that could craft an associated representational image with clear public overtones.[5]

Stephen Greenblatt's words from a different context pertain to this one: "the power to impose a shape upon oneself is an aspect of the more general power to control identity—that of others at least as often as one's own." [6] This "autonomy" in self-fashioning is not to be taken for granted. It may have been pertinent to sixteenth-century England, Greenblatt's topic, and to the aristocracy in fourth-century Macedonia also; but this had not been the case with the Homeric heroes whom Alexander himself admired, heroes whose sense of self seems to have been explicitly directed by social codes of conduct and expectations, rather than being personally, purposely crafted.[7] Nevertheless, assuming that the social preconditions were fulfilled, the Homeric hero had *some* choice in self-presentation. In the *Iliad*, Achilles, intensely preoccupied with himself and the recognition of his status by the community, is the paradigm of an individual's pursuit of a heroic persona. Perhaps for that reason, he was also to become the hero closest to Alexander's ambitions.[8] Both Alexander and Achilles seem to have pursued personal greatness ($\dot{\alpha}\rho\epsilon\tau\dot{\eta}$)—with all the ambiguity the word involves—and fame. Fame has to do with immortality, with making one's mark on cultural memory, a situation manifested in ancient Greece by the appearance of hero-cults, which imply the recognition of an individual's achievements and honor.

In fourth-century Macedonia—and with Alexander in particular—publicly acknowledged and self-styled comparisons, especially with the Greek heroes of the past, became a mode of thinking and acquired special urgency. This urgency was not unrelated to the conscious pursuit of the Hellenic pedigree sought at least by the Macedonian royal family and aristocracy. Several individuals could be conjured up as models, depending on the situation. Specifically with Alexander, if anyone, for whatever reasons, could challenge the idea that he had been *born* a hero, he would make sure that no one could challenge the fact that he had *made* himself one. For a prince and then a king whose dynastic fortunes at times wavered, heroism was not a small investment.

In his study of the inspiration Julius Caesar drew from Alexander, Peter Green has tried to bring structure to the amorphous topic of an individual's patterning himself after models from the past. He has drawn distinctions among three different concepts, *aemulatio, imitatio,* and *comparatio,* distinctions that are relevant to the Greek no less than to the Roman world. As with Julius Caesar and Alexander, the relationship of the latter and Achilles is "something more often assumed than defined,"[9] and it deserves some clarification. It is not the same to compare oneself with a model (*imitatio*) and to be compared by others (*comparatio*), Green notes in reference to the concept of imitation, whereas emulation differs from imitation in that it contains an element of rivalry with the respective model and an attempt to surpass it. This categorization helps illuminate Caesar's case wonderfully. Alexander's case eludes equally precise distinctions, and all three concepts can be found to apply. Not only did Alexander construct a self in light of a past reality, but he also strove to correct Achilles' flaws as he occasionally perceived them (cf. Plut. *Moralia* 343b). Thus both paradigms (*imitatio* and *aemulatio*) must be kept in mind, nor was the parallel lost to contemporaries (*comparatio*). This last fact indicates that Alexander's self-fashioning into a hero had not only a personal but a cultural component. It suggests that the heroic (Bronze Age?) past was in that context a living and a relevant past, seen in terms of its sameness rather than its "otherness."

After Alexander the Great paid homage to Achilles' tomb at the beginning of his Asian expedition,[10] records of the event drew the inevitable conclusion: there was a parallel between the two personalities of which Alexander was well aware. The information has survived in Roman texts postdating the event by several centuries,[11] texts which could draw the comparison from the vantage point of subsequent historical developments and ideologies. Despite the specifically Roman readings that might apply to these, there is nothing un-Greek in their reports on Alexander's seizing on Achilles for a model.[12]

There is, for example, Arrian's story in his *Campaigns of Alexander,* dating to the second century A.C.: "One account says that Hephaestion laid a wreath on the tomb of Patroclus; another that Alexander laid one on the tomb of Achilles, calling him a lucky man, in that he had Homer to proclaim his deeds and preserve his memory" (Arrian 1.12.1, trans. A. de Sélincourt). The context is Alexander's visit to Troy in 334 B.C. As told, the story initially strikes one as an intensely personal affair, the realization of a personal romantic vision; but the public component of such a grand gesture cannot be overlooked. One is led to believe that this was more than the occasion of an ordinary, established hero-worship; it was a truly unique *event.* As such, it involved a single agent acting on his own behalf rather than the community's, but at the same time it conjured up a public tone, in that it was a self-dramatizing performance addressed to a military "audience." An otherwise conventional act of respect was conceived in terms of and came to acquire paradigmatic and allegorical value, if one considers that "in the simplest terms, allegory says one thing and means another."[13] Both the thing said, Alexander's pious conformity to traditional hero-worship, and the thing meant, Alexander's personal aspiration to heroism, must have been understood by that "audience." (Later in his life Alexander was to create a hero-cult in honor of the dead Hephaistion and organize funeral games patterned after and surpassing those offered to Patroklos by Achilles.[14])

Alexander had looked back to the Trojan War already before crossing the Hellespont, at Elaious where he had sacrificed on the tomb of Protesilaos, the first Achaian to disembark on Asia and die at the outset of that war.[15] That Alexander's own campaign was a new Trojan War was proclaimed by the donation of his armor to the temple of Athena at Troy, in exchange for weapons preserved from the earlier war.[16] There at Troy he stood picturing the heroic deeds which had once taken place: ἀνατυπούμενος τὰς ἡρωϊκὰς πράξεις (Plut. *Moralia* 331d).

Heroic deeds had been performed by many warriors in the *Iliad*, and many different characters had displayed heroic qualities of different sorts, so much so that the image of the hero conjured up in one's mind tends to be a composite, built not on theory but on paradigms: Achilles *and* Ajax, Diomedes *and* Odysseus, as well as Nestor, individuals with diverse claims to fame. It was such a composite that Alexander had in mind, and it must have operated on different levels, both internalized and externalized. But within this ambiguous formation Achilles' image stood out, especially in Alexander's early, more conspicuously idealistic days, prior to the Asian expedition, which ultimately became marked with signs of excess and abuse of power.

It is Alexander's early conception of heroism that especially concerns me here. Shaped by secular education rather than religious belief, it involved a special mixture of the Greek, the Macedonian, and the personal. I consider this early, not yet institutionalized heroism more interesting than Alexander's later claims to divinity[17] or the more prosaic genealogical associations he held with the other model hero Herakles, purportedly an ancestor from his father's side.[18] Even though the importance of Herakles can never be overestimated, there was a reflective side to Achilles' heroic persona, a human complexity, which eluded Herakles' usual representation in terms of naked physical power and which must have held an added appeal for Alexander's complex personality.

Diodorus, whose account is the earliest to have survived, makes the parallel between the two men clear in his report on the events of the years 326/5 B.C., the Greek encounter with the Indians. In the context of a riverine voyage, Alexander's army faced extremely dangerous currents which threatened, among others', Alexander's life. His narrow and brave escape from death was viewed, according to Diodorus, as another affinity with his heroic paradigm: "he sacrificed to the gods as having come through mortal danger, reflecting that he, like Achilles, had done battle with a river."[19]

Similarly anecdotal is Curtius' invocation of the parallel in the first century A.C.; a brutal, negative picture this time, connected with the siege of Gaza early in the Eastern expedition. Betis, the governor of the city, a man loyal to Darius the Persian king, was captured and brought to Alexander. According to Curtius' generally hostile report, "Alexander's anger turned to fury, his recent successes already suggesting to his mind foreign modes of behaviour. Thongs were passed through Betis' ankles while he still breathed, and he was tied to a chariot. Then Alexander's horses dragged him around the city while the king gloated at having followed the example of his ancestor Achilles in punishing his enemy."[20] Even for his treatment of women, according to Curtius, Alexander sought justification in the actions of his predecessor. His infatuation with the Bactrian Roxane, his future wife, is compared with Achilles' infatuation with Briseis (8.4.26).

It is not an accident that parallelisms were noticed also by Plutarch, antiquity's foremost biographer, who lived in the end of the first and the beginning of the second centuries A.C. For it is the genre of biography (which most of the other extant accounts partially resemble, especially Arrian's) that elaborates notions of self-consciousness and character. A pairing of Greek with Greek did not fit Plutarch's scheme of "parallel lives," and Alexander and Achilles do not constitute a pair in his account. But the story of the special attention paid by Alexander to Achilles' tomb is dutifully repeated (*Alex.* 15), as are the other points in light of which Alexander allegedly measured himself against his heroic model. The parallelism is for this writer positive throughout, honest and innocent.[21]

In the end one can find as many Alexanders as there have been historians, ancient but also modern.[22] In modern scholarship the question has often been raised (and variously been answered) whether Alexander's personal myth came to carry any kind of phenomenological reality for himself. Was he a romantic hero patterning himself on literary models or a disingenuous cynic unsentimentally crafting an identity for public consumption? Did he ever literally *believe* he was a second Achilles? There seems to have been both a personal and a political aspect to this mythical connection, and both seem to have been metaphorical rather than literal. The personal level comes out in strongest relief during his youthful days, prior to his assumption of the throne, when he had time and opportunity to reflect on educational ideals. Later in his career Alexander must have realized the need to control the way in which he was publicly seen at home and abroad, as well as the fact that his own once genuinely personal vision held public potential; it could become a kind of iconographic programme not least because in a circular way it had been shaped by shared communal ideals. Once articulated in these terms, such a programme may strike one as ridiculous and transparent, but this hardly affected the efficacy of the symbolism. From a certain point on, the personal and the political, reality and myth, blend inextricably, and there is no use in trying to sort them out neatly.

Alexander could believe in both the reality and the fiction associated with his legendary hero Achilles, and in turn make himself into both a real and a fictive character. Edmunds has articulated the point well: "In the life of Alexander myth becomes history only to become myth again, not only because his contemporary historians inevitably see him in terms of myth, but also because he saw himself in, and wanted to be seen in, those terms."[23] Similarly, the deeds of Achilles proved inspirational no less for being fictional than for being real to the "audiences" of Homer. Nevertheless, that they provided incentives for action pertains only to a few, notably Alexander, for whom idealism came to intersect with political formulations.

Ultimately Alexander realized the propagandistic value of controlled history, surrounding himself with writers who were to recast events in prose and in epic poetry. A distinct interest in biography emerged during his own lifetime;[24] that is, the history of his campaigns, which he commissioned his official historian Kallisthenes to write, was conceived of in unmistakably biographical (and Homeric) terms ('Αλεξάνδρου πρά-ξεις).[25] A writer, according to Kallisthenes, ought to "assign an individual words appropriate to his person": μὴ ἀστοχεῖν τοῦ προσώπου, ἀλλ᾽ οἰκείως αὐτῷ τε καὶ τοῖς πράγμασι τοὺς λόγους θεῖναι.[26] His uncle Aristotle was also interested in character, the *Nicomachean Ethics* being the case in point. Here, however, the thrust of the arguments is ultimately prescriptive rather than descriptive, concerned with *how* to build a good, virtuous character.[27] In Alexander's case this effort and its results were deemed important enough to warrant a whole work on how this individual was educated, Onesikritos' Πῶς 'Αλέξανδρος ἤχθη, written in Alexander's lifetime.[28]

This education seems to have stimulated Alexander's grand, initially romantic, Homeric connections. Both his early pedagogue Lysimachos and his later teacher Aristotle are reported to have encouraged these connections.[29] Aristotle manifested his own admiration for Homer's achievement in his *Poetics*, through his repeated references to the poet and to his works. Furthermore, Aristotle in the so-called *Hymn to Arete*, a poem in honor of a dead heroic friend (Hermeias), makes clear that notions of heroism, especially the Achillean kind, had retained currency in the fourth century.[30] The annotated version of the *Iliad* which Aristotle (or Kallisthenes) prepared for his pupil was allegedly kept under Alexander's pillow along with his dagger, an inspiration in times of war and peace and a source to be quoted at key moments.[31]

The three figures—Homer, Aristotle, and Alexander—have been visually brought together by Rembrandt's imagination in a picture conventionally titled "Aristotle Contemplating the Bust of Homer" and dated 1653 (fig. 30.1). Now in the Metropolitan Museum of Art, the painting shows an eccentrically dressed and jeweled Aristotle portrayed almost frontally. His head turns to look at the profile bust of the blind poet. This sculpture stands on a red table, and the philosopher rests his right hand on its head. Alexander's alleged presence is much more modest in scale, but quite plausible in this

FIGURE 30.1. Rembrandt, Aristotle with a Bust of Homer. The Metropolitan Museum of Art, Purchased with special funds and gifts of friends of the Museum, 1961 (61.198). (Photograph courtesy the Metropolitan Museum of Art. All rights reserved.)

context: a helmeted profile appears on the medal hanging from the splendid and flamboyant gold chain decorating Aristotle's chest, a probable likeness of Alexander.[32]

Rembrandt gives visual form to a relationship among exceptional personages, but Alexander was not the only one to reflect on the tales told by Homer. That Alexander took up the Homeric paradigm with unique force was a complex matter of choices and dispositions, but his individuality was historically constituted and cannot be understood apart from the collective culture and society that nurtured it. The crafting of an ideal character according to the prescriptions of poetry and education, hence according to social forms of expression and institutions, precludes complete freedom in the making of Alexander's self. His contemporaries, although less empowered and less destined for individualism and greatness than he was, must also have experienced an upbringing that stressed the heroic ideals of the *Iliad*.[33]

James Redfield has aptly referred to the *Iliad* as a

"kind of cultural institution, parallel to institutions of social interaction or of cult."[34] The epic formed the basis of education not only in southern Greece, but in northern Greece as well. It was the canonical textbook, one fulfilling the traditional preoccupation with exempla from the past, whose behavior could motivate and inspire to action. (Despite the gore and the strife of the *Iliad*, heroes manage to rise above the baseness of their immediate actions because these are subordinated to broader moral ideals of excellence and the glory displayed and won in that context.[35]) The specifics of formal education may not have been shared throughout Greece and certainly not by all classes, but a basic core of cultural knowledge can be taken for granted; this because Homeric poetry served both high and popular culture on different levels.[36]

A case for the continued relevance of the *Iliad* specifically to Macedonians of the Classical period can be made in a different way by conjuring up the political organization of the region. As has often been remarked, this structurally resembled Preclassical, rather than contemporary, southern Greek circumstances. Even at a time when democracy had become a hallmark of southern Greek poleis, Macedonia persisted with institutions long abandoned elsewhere but vividly portrayed in epic poetry.[37] The ideal of a rich, powerful, heroic king, leader in battle and in the assembly, had not been "deconstructed" in Macedonia. Homeric and Macedonian conceptions of a partly hereditary kingship coincided in this respect, both invoking broader Indo-European patterns whereby the army was a political assembly of sorts that occasionally expressed opinion and sentiment as to the king's decisions and actions. Furthermore, as their Homeric counterparts, the Hetairoi of the Macedonian king, elite companions who fought on horseback at his side and counseled him, seem to have been bound to their king with bonds of personal allegiance similar to those of Achilles' Hetairoi in the *Iliad*.[38]

This seemingly straightforward similarity is not without its problems, which stem from incomplete information as regards both the Homeric and Macedonian circumstances. On the one hand, the situation articulated in Homeric poetry is a highly controversial issue in that some critics believe it to reflect the complex political and social realities of the Mycenaean period, and others the simpler, poorer realities of the Early Iron Age, the eighth century also having been invoked.[39] On the other hand, with regard to the Macedonians, the exact role of the Hetairoi and the assembly in the decision-making process of the king is not known, the result being a continuing debate over the so-called constitutionalism of Macedonian monarchy.[40] Furthermore, the Homeric (and Mycenaean) picture involves early, loose versions of "city-states" and a number of local kings, each in charge of his own territory and people. In unsettled times such as those reflected in the *Iliad*, they all acknowledge the loosely conceived leadership of the most powerful king (Agamemnon in the epic). In that context there are degrees of kingly status; one can be kingly, but another can be kinglier ($\beta\alpha\sigma\iota\lambda\epsilon\acute{u}\tau\epsilon\rho\sigma$, as in *Iliad* 9.69 and 9.392).[41] By contrast, the Macedonian king's superiority is not measured against (or challenged by) other rulers, not in the same degree anyway, although rival royal houses of different origins must have been a reality in early Macedonian history.

The instability of both situations precludes point-to-point comparisons, and yet it does not truly challenge the reality of a broadly shared system of meanings. This sharing is often articulated in terms of survival, a kind of "living on" of earlier Homeric institutions and practices in the "retardataire" Macedonian lands. Whereas this position is hard to prove because there are too many shifting variables, it is not hard to understand how the Macedonians could easily (and no doubt impressionistically) recognize themselves in the epic and why this piece of literature attracted them so much. It is nevertheless appropriate at least to speculate as to whether any historical reasons were at play behind these connections and to try to articulate the various possibilities. As indicated above, the similarities between the Macedonian and Homeric sociopolitical systems have been repeatedly noted, but the question still begs to be asked: What might these mean?

One cannot begin to wrestle with this question without taking into account the "hard facts" of archaeology, which add a fascinating component to the issue of the relation of the Macedonians of Late Classical and early Hellenistic times to Bronze Age ideals and practices. On its own account the Macedonian material culture at large presents interesting affinities with the Mycenaean past, a past which is at least partially addressed in Homer: Macedonian tomb equipment and burial customs—

funeral pyres, funeral games, and sacrifices in honor of the dead, as reported in literary sources but also now glimpsed from the excavations at Vergina—recall both Mycenaean realities and Homeric interpretations.[42]

The love for and profusion of exquisite gold and silver vessels and jewelry in recently discovered burials, in association with the general impression of wealth and power afforded by other artifacts and tomb decoration, bring to mind the principles of glory exemplified by the much earlier Mycenaean Shaft Graves and then the tholos tombs with their princely ideals. In addition, the prominence of weaponry suggests shared forms of militarism. Even as specific a cultural artifact as the early Mycenaean gold-foil mask, molded and placed on the dead person's face, makes an eerie reappearance, if not in the Macedonian heartland, at least in its environs. The astonishing similarity of the funerary masks from the Shaft Graves to the much later Archaic masks from Illyrian Trebenishte (Upper Macedonia, near Lake Lychnitis), and Macedonian Sindos[43] is hard to dismiss—despite the wide chronological gap and despite the Thracian connections of the later examples—because these artifacts are simply too idiosyncratic and distinctive.

The following three questions can be isolated: Are shared forms

(a) fortuitous? Can this phenomenon be used to support an argument that similar political and social systems produce similar systems of thought and lifestyle and hence similar features in material culture?

(b) indicative of an intentional revival by the Macedonians (ultimately originating in the late sixth century B.C.) in order to exploit the symbolic power of the Bronze Age, a revival eventually internalized into a way of life? This would imply that the "Age of Heroes" was known to the Macedonians not only through literature but also through material culture; that they apprehended Homeric poetry as belonging to the Mycenaean past; and that they thought or knew that Bronze Age–looking "pots and pans" "fit" *with* the epic from which they derived so much inspiration; that they had access to actual Bronze Age remains and understood them as such. When modern scholarship still argues whether the individual or more probably the collective person called "Homer" fits more comfortably within a Mycenaean context or alternatively into the tenth, ninth, or eighth centuries, could it be that the Macedonians of the fourth century (and a bit earlier) saw no conflict, if some of them thought about the issue to begin with?

(c) indicative of a conservatism in the Macedonian cultural outlook? Did the Macedonians never leave the (Mycenaean?) Bronze Age, having been on the periphery of the Greek world for a long time? Could the argument be sustained that the Macedonians—unlike other Greeks—never gave up the signs of the Bronze Age not only in the realm of symbolism but also of everyday life?

Although it cannot be uniformly sustained, the impression derived from Macedonian pottery may favor this last interpretation. As Ch. Koukouli-Chrysanthaki and I. Vokotopoulou point out, an important local type of Late Bronze Age pottery (matt-painted) resembles Middle Bronze pottery from the Argolid, while this and some other types, including types with Mycenaean affinities, live on well into the Iron Age; metalwork typologies of the Iron Age exhibit the same kind of conservatism.[44] And even as late as the Hellenistic period, vases found at Pella could be stubbornly patterned after prehistoric models; in terms of detail they are updated enough so as not to create typological confusion, but in overall appearance Middle and Late Bronze Age echoes are unmistakable.[45] Of course the case for conservatism can be made without involving the Mycenaeans, for "Mycenaean" and "(Late) Bronze" are not synonymous, unless archaeology can show, as indeed it is beginning to do, that elements of Mycenaean culture existed in Bronze Age Macedon.

Could the Macedonians know anything about the Mycenaean past and, if so, how did they come to know it? This complex question is even harder to tackle in regard to Macedonia than its equivalent in regard to southern Greece.[46] The culturally mixed Late Bronze Age in northern Greece is insufficiently known, except perhaps for the area between the rivers Axios and Strymon (Central Macedonia) and the Chalkidike, where a series of settlements has been located and some excavated.[47] It is generally clear that in the Bronze Age Macedonia stood at the fringes of the Mycenaean world (Thessaly being the latter's northernmost limit),[48] but it did apparently receive significant Mycenaean influences.

Indications of contact with the Mycenaean world go back to the LH I period, the time of the Shaft Graves.[49] The mixed cultural influences on the artifacts found in those graves have been studied and elucidated. The nature of these influences is such as to preclude precise answers concerning the exact origins of the early Mycenaeans buried there, or, to put it differently, the origins of their astonishing wealth.[50] A theory of northern associations has been developed,[51] among others, and, if it could be proved, it would in turn add credibility to any case made for the *survival* of Mycenaean-type qualities in later Macedonia. From the early period the find of a gold "ring" at the site of Kastanas in central Macedonia, "the exact match" of a piece from a Shaft Grave at Mycenae, is worth singling out.[52] But as things presently stand in the literature, the Mycenaeans are supposed to have exercised an influence on the north mostly after their culture had been well established in the south; a later south-north route of contact, that is, can be traced less controversially than an early north-south route.

It is imported Mycenaean pottery mostly of the LH IIIA and B periods that points to a south-north contact, discovered primarily in coastal Macedonian sites, but also in others farther inland.[53] This pottery inspired local, simplified, wheel-made versions (late LH IIIB through LH IIIC), so it must have made an impact. These imitations continued to be produced into the Iron Age, well after their prototypes had disappeared from the rest of Greece.[54] It is presently difficult to make much out of imported Mycenaean pots, although there is nothing to preclude future finds in this direction as this area steadily enters the mainstream of archaeological investigation. There are, in fact, already tantalizing indications to this effect which await further research and publication, these mostly from tombs to the west and south in Macedonia.[55] If indeed a case for "Mycenaean" cemeteries can be sustained for some sites and for architecture in others, a more pervasive Mycenaean presence (return?) and hence "identity" could very well register in the future.[56]

To return to the question posed above, it is anyone's guess what the later Macedonians of the Classical period thought about such objects when they stumbled upon them—which they must have done at least by accident.[57] A "scientific," "archaeological" approach to past material culture could hardly have existed, but the possibility of historical consciousness (transmitted through tradition) of at least some members in ancient communities should not be underestimated. Ancient hero-worship associated with the discovery in the south of old tombs is a topic on which archaeology is shedding increasing light, especially as regards the treatment of Bronze Age tombs in the eighth and seventh centuries B.C.[58] Postburial offerings to a tomb of course raise some difficult issues; the objects may indicate respect rather than ritual and cult, and the means for distinguishing between them are not clear. What is clear is that a consciousness of the past associated with material finds existed at certain times in antiquity. Hero-worship in the Classical and Hellenistic periods has been a less popular subject, although such evidence does in fact exist. The issue is now being systematically tackled, unfortunately without the inclusion of Macedonia because of the present unavailability of data.[59] One has to return to the literary record, which, as indicated above, preserves indications of hero-worship practiced by Alexander when visiting the alleged tombs of Protesilaos, Achilles, Patroklos, Priam—instances, however, not necessarily indicative of established cult per se.

To engage the literary record again, early Greek historians such as Thucydides included accounts of the Trojan War in the context of their investigations of later periods, a "prehistory" of sorts, based partly on Homer but not entirely.[60] The importance of the poetic tradition in shaping early historical accounts cannot be emphasized enough, even though this interest did not encourage objective inquiry into archaeology or refined chronology regarding the events presented in the poems or the poems themselves.[61] Even the erudite Alexandrian scholars at a later date viewed epic poetry primarily as literature rather than history per se.[62] Nevertheless:

> With even partial possession of these bodies of old verse the Greeks had many more paths of access to the heroic world than we do. With that luxury of choice, they thought about it differently, not as chronologically remote . . . or hidden physically under veils of dirt and stone, but as an inherited world which could be activated by skill, *techne*.[63]

Thus in the fourth century B.C. Douris of Samos, merging tradition and *technē*, showed a general knowledge of when the Trojan War might have taken place *and* superimposed on the event a prejudice of his own, that a perfect one thousand years separated it from Alexander's expedition to Asia.[64] The date 1334 B.C. was conjured up through improvisation, but charges of deception would hardly pertain, and of course he may not even have been too far off the mark.

In this light, hypothesis (b) above, intentional revival, appears less farfetched than it does upon first consideration, and one should not be completely blind to its possibilities. It seems that this hypothesis and the third, cultural conservatism (hence survivals), are not mutually exclusive, and I suspect that future archaeological work will point to ways of interweaving the two with some nuance. The Macedonian case may have involved reconjuring up partially accessible earlier forms of symbolism, suggestive because they had never lost their relevance. In the south these forms were also accessible, more so given the fact that some Bronze Age remains were always partly visible; but their political relevance, that is, their association with kingship, was lost there. Archaeological investigation will undoubtedly provide aid in charting relationships, but it is presently fair to assume that the Macedonians' approach to the past was largely intuitive and dependent on the epic. They imagined their ancestors less on the basis of direct knowledge of archaeological remains such as boars'-tusk helmets, silver-studded swords, or body-shields, which the *Iliad* tells about (for example, 7.219–223, 10.261–265), and more on the basis of poetry.

One searches with only moderate success for the visual counterparts to Homeric poetry in its "contemporary" worlds, whether one considers its Mycenaean or its Iron Age strands. Indeed, had the Macedonians known a variety of works from either strand, they would not have found visual equivalents, at least not equivalent types of heroes. What they would have found is an interest in story-telling, scenes filled with small-scale participants involved in the unfolding of busy incident, but not much by way of dramatic images of the heroic, driven, self-sufficient persona. It is not legitimate a priori to assume that in a given culture or phase thereof different arts and different forms of literature develop along similar lines of expression or that one art form somehow *has* to "reflect" another contemporary one at a given moment. And it is not quite predictable under what circumstances consistently identifiable correlations might occur.

Perhaps the greatest visual claims to Homeric spirit are made by tiny early Mycenaean gems, items that are most likely to survive the centuries as heirlooms or surface finds.[65] Magnificent heraldic arrangements of human-animal duels on this type of object make such claims even more strongly than the excellent daggers of the Shaft Graves.[66] A fifteenth-century gem from Vapheio in particular with a man on foot confronting a wild boar with his spear seems a perfect illustration of a Mycenaean—and later Macedonian—sport, emblematic of aristocracy and manhood (fig. 30.2).[67] Nevertheless, it too lacks the *gravitas*, the exaggerated force one associates with the Homeric hero-hunter, emphasizing rather the ferociousness and size of the animal opponent and leaving the outcome open. The hunter has the weapon, but the boar has the force.

On the other hand, a number of explicitly heroic images have surfaced in Macedonian contexts of the fourth century, indicating an effort on the part of the Macedonians to appropriate Homeric ideals on their own account. These images were no doubt realized with the stylistic mediation of Classical art of the south, but the visual dependencies do not contradict firsthand reflections on and preoccupations with the epic on the part of the Macedonians who chose subject matter and compositional configurations. The naturalistic figural-style of the south seems to have presented itself as appropriate precisely because it could give clear form to Macedonian subjects and concerns.

To represent Homeric ideals, one first had to imagine them, and the Macedonian imagination led to representations which seem more Homeric than both the Geometric art of Homer's era and Mycenaean art, perhaps because of the intense effort invested in the process of claiming descent. In Macedonian works the hero is reconfigured and remade, only better. Images reveal most eloquently Alexander's and the Macedonians' repeated appropriation of the symbols of the "Age of Heroes" and indicate a kind of internalized preoccupation with self-constructing. Not unlike the literary sources regarding Alexander, these images make one wonder what it is that Macedonians *thought* about themselves when they

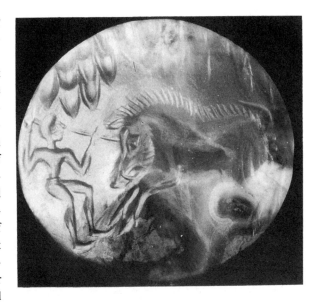

FIGURE 30.2. Sealstone from Vapheio with boar hunt. National Archaeological Museum, Athens (1772). (Photograph courtesy ICOM, Athens.)

chose to present themselves in Homeric behavioral patterns. Can we expect the two selves—the "real," interior one and the projected, external one—to have coincided in any way? It is not at all easy to distinguish social performance, itself not unproblematically encoded in the art, from inward reality. But, if images cannot be expected to reveal precise thoughts, they can be quite indicative of mentalities and cultural attitudes.

The principles of heroic behavior as codified in the *Iliad* have impressed themselves most explicitly on the famous hunt mosaics from Pella, as indicated by the air of conviction and the energized determination enveloping the unspecified lion or stag hunter, by his extroverted gesture and introverted expression, by the extraordinary self-control which he displays (figs. 30.3–30.4). The hunt mosaics constitute supreme examples of visualization of the heroic past in "modern" terms, and these, rather than the Achillean "quotations" in Alexander's surviving imagery, will be examined here, for they exemplify best the *spirit* of the enterprise addressed in this paper.

Just as the literary references to Alexander's self-

FIGURE 30.3. Pebble mosaic with lion hunt from Pella. Archaeological Museum, Pella. (Photograph courtesy I. M. Akamatis.)

fashioning as Achilles, these works speak not just to the strength of the Homeric tradition but also to its ability to accommodate ideals nurtured by diverse historical circumstances and diverse personal visions. The appearance and appropriation of the past in the literary and artistic discourse of a later, interpreting culture is not a simple affair. The contingent "present" (here fourth-century Macedon) can challenge the respective past at any moment and find it deficient. As long as this does not happen, the relevance and usefulness of the past must remain meaningful at least to some members of the culture.

The hunters from Pella, the second Macedonian capital, exude artifice. Some are swollen to heroic size, all display heroic nudity. Their motions and gestures are conceived of in terms of their symbolic pictorial impact, rather than in terms of the practical realities of the act they are about to perform. The initiative with which these figures are charged is symbolic, and the effect is one of arrested significance; the figures appear staged, almost ceremonial. The constructed ways in which individual naturalistic figures are put together in turn point to constructed meanings, and the latter to an extraordi-

nary degree of self-deliberation and self-manipulation.

Both the lion hunt and the stag hunt have been variously dated within the second half of the fourth century.[68] These pebble "four-color" mosaics were found along with several others in two big houses with peristyle courts, the lion hunt in "Building I," otherwise known as the "House of Dionysos," and the stag hunt in "Building II," or the "House of the Abduction of Helen."[69] The rooms which these mosaics decorated have been appropriately interpreted as *andrones*, men's dining halls.

The two figures in the stag hunt are over life-size, the lower bodies of both almost identically posed. They display confident use of subtle pebble gradation and shading, which renders the bodies muscular and athletic. They frame a beautiful and elegant stag, shown at the center being attacked by a hound. Its agony is vivid, its tongue protrudes from an open mouth. The movements of the hunters and their postures are bold but not untraditional. The hunter on the left wields a double axe. This weapon is also encountered in the late fourth-century painting of a hunt involving many different animals which decorates the façade of the famous Tomb II at Vergina, excavated in 1977 by M. Andronikos.[70] There the axe is held in an equally charged way. It is interesting that a series of bronze double axes, one or three blades coming out from the stem, have been found at Vergina in association with female Iron Age burials,

FIGURE 30.4. Gnosis, pebble mosaic with stag hunt from Pella. In situ. (Photograph courtesy I. M. Akamatis.)

dated to the early ninth century B.C. or even earlier.[71] Their origin and precise cultural and symbolic associations are unclear, and both the northern European Iron Age and the Bronze Age Mediterranean can be invoked. The latter case, suggesting continuity with Mycenaean or Minoan symbolism, would make a convenient argument in the present context; however, it cannot yet be sustained with an adequate degree of conviction.

The second hunter in the mosaic raises a sword. He is grabbing the stag by its antlers, a way of symbolizing mastery which goes all the way back to the Bronze Age:

a recent find of a Minoan sealing at Palaikastro shows a "Master of Animals" standing behind a horned animal with his hand on its horns, assisted by dogs (fig. 30.5).[72] Like the Minoan "predecessor," both Macedonians in the mosaic are nude, but with a mantle clasped at the neck and flowing behind their backs; both are blond, ξανθοί, in a Homeric (and Euripidean) fashion, whereby "heroic figures are automatically ξανθοί."[73] The composition is tight, less paratactic and more three-dimensional than that of the neighboring lion hunt mosaic.

The excellence of the mosaic indeed warrants the artist's signature, ΓΝΩΣΙΣ ΕΠΟΗΣΕΝ, proudly displayed in large characters above the figures. The effect of Gnosis' figures is so uniquely overpowering that a diversion is required in order to set this mosaic back

493

FIGURE 30.5. Drawing of Minoan sealing from Palaikastro with "Master of Animals." (Photograph courtesy Managing Committee of the British School at Athens; after *BSA* 84 [1989], fig. 17.)

within an artistic tradition of rendering bodies in space. The figures step on an undulating rocky ground, which, as a symbolic indication of depth, hides the foot of the hunter on the left. This is the same ground encountered in several late fifth/early fourth-century funerary stelai from Thebes, whose engraved images may have once been painted. The best preserved is the stele of Mnason (fig. 30.6),[74] which shows a warrior from the same tradition as the hunters from Pella and from Vergina.[75] Shown in a profile view, he lunges to the right towards an unseen enemy, protecting himself with his shield and attacking with his spear. He covers the whole field and even extends beyond its borders, in action only slightly less explosive than that of his Macedonian "descendants." His bare feet conform to the rise of the ground just as the feet of the stag hunters do. He is bearded and wears a light chlamys which leaves his right shoulder bare, and a conical Boiotian helmet on his head. Despite the clothes, one is made aware of his athletic corporeality.

In the stag hunt from Pella, individual figures such as this have been brought together in a kind of cooperation, whereby bodies interlock and overlap, even though each hunter has his own closure and self-sufficiency. This hunt is a joint undertaking by aristocratic men, united through common class interests, roles within the Macedonian court, and conception of the ideal self. The hat

FIGURE 30.6. Incised funerary stele of Mnason from Thebes. Archaeological Museum, Thebes (BE 54). (Photograph courtesy Archaeological Receipts Fund [T.A.P.], Greek Ministry of Culture.)

of the right-hand hunter, hovering emblematically above his head, is the only feature that particularizes these individuals. Headgear with a flair seems to have been the imaginative accessory of the Macedonian man, an emblem of his northern homeland.

The associations with the upper class are assured by the sumptuous contexts in which this mosaic and that with the lion hunt were found. But in terms of subject matter, it may not be immediately evident that hunting and its representation would actively participate in defining the ideals of the aristocratic life. Hunting in modern American culture, for example, lacks any such historical and ideological associations. However, in the context of Europe and the Near East the situation has been traditionally different. The European hunt—hunt as entertainment rather than subsistence—has in fact held a strangely persistent and diachronic class element, in modern times no less than in Greek antiquity.[76] In the Homeric world Odysseus' emblematic gold brooch clasping his woolen purple mantle makes clear that hunting and its representation were symbols of the aristocratic life. The face of this brooch carried a representation of a dappled fawn suffering the attack of a hound. Here is the way in which Odysseus himself, disguised as a beggar, describes it to Penelope: "My lord wore a thick purple cloak folded back on itself and displaying a golden brooch with a pair of sheaths for the pins. There was a device on the face of it: a hound holding down a dappled fawn in his forepaws and ripping it as it struggled. Everyone admired the workmanship, the hound ripping and throttling the fawn, the fawn lashing out at its feet in his efforts to escape—and the whole thing done in gold. . . . I tell you, all the women were fascinated by him" (Odyssey 19.225–235, trans. E. V. Rieu). In its conversion of such a scene into a proper hunt, the Pella mosaic carries the same concise symbolic references. Odysseus, who "wears" it in gold, and the Pella hunters, who enact the scene watched by male diners, are products of the same culture that privileged aristocracy and masculinity.

At this point one has to engage another aspect of the Macedonian tradition of the hunt, its role as a kind of male rite of passage. The tradition did not involve the deer or the lion but rather the boar, the animal second in the natural hierarchy after lions. Boars were also fierce, as the painting from Vergina shows in its middle foreground, with the added advantage of being easier to encounter in the Macedonian countryside. Athenaeus (1.18a) discusses the Macedonian custom according to which a man could not eat reclining before having killed a boar without nets or traps. At the age of thirty-five and despite his bravery, Kassander had to sit next to his father at meals, rather than recline, for he had not performed the deed.[77] The hunt operated as a symbolic step towards the attainment of full manhood. In Macedonia, Herakles Kynagidas was worshipped as the guardian of hunters by all men, young or old, while royal cults invoked him as a protector of the hunting king and his aristocratic entourage.[78] The young Macedonians in search of their first boar would have had plenty of adult

paradigms to emulate in their effort to achieve personal glory. They would also have known of mythological paradigms, such as Odysseus and Meleager (Odyssey 19.428–458, Iliad 9.537–546).

The answers to the question of the mosaics' exact date have not been uniform, proposals ranging between 340 and 300 B.C. D. Salzmann's authoritative corpus of Greek mosaics has dated them around 340/330–320/310 B.C. on the basis of stylistic comparisons of mosaic floral borders with similar motifs on better-dated South Italian vases and Greek architectural mouldings. On the basis of archaeological evidence, I. Touratsoglou has argued for a narrower range of dates in the last quarter of the fourth century.[79] The decades separating the two termini are crucial in this case for they encompass the career of Alexander. If early, the mosaics could provide glimpses into the historical forces and influences—otherwise known from the literary sources—which shaped him. Still, whether these mosaics prefigured Alexander's own persistent hunting iconography or whether they are echoes dating to the era of his immediate successors, the symbolic value of the theme for the Macedonians was wider. As Athenaeus' story as well as the iconography of some early Macedonian coins suggest,[80] the practice and symbolism of the hunt preceded Alexander and postdated him; they refer to the world in which he grew up and the world on which he, in turn, programmatically left his mark. Furthermore, the painting from Vergina Tomb II, if it belongs to the reign of Philip II, allows room for the possibility that this practice was given artistic consideration early on.

The figures in the Pella lion hunt are slightly smaller than life-size. The left hunter holds a lance in his right hand and a sheathed sword in the left. He is nude except for a white mantle bordered in brown, which covers his left arm and is held by a brooch at the neck. He wears a distinctive hat, one of the many types that have been called a καυσία.[81] The other hunter is bareheaded and blond, also nude, with a mantle flowing in strenuous activity behind his back. He swings a broad slightly curved sword, a μάχαιρα, which could not actually have been contained in the straight, thin scabbard from which he has just pulled it. As is typical, the lion is shown between the two hunters, turning its head towards one, its body towards the other.

Iliad 20.167–173 affords the opportunity for a masterful textual rendering of such a lion's situation, one without escape, such as witnessed in the mosaic and also in the painting from Vergina Tomb II, where the lion appears again with its attention divided. In the painting the lion has been hit already by a spear and is about to be hit again by a focal horseman toward whom it turns its head in fury; in the mosaic the lion is yet to be hit, but the outcome is predictable. In both cases the animal behaves like its Homeric counterpart:

> . . . when some one of the impetuous young men
>
> has hit him with the spear he whirls, jaws open, over his teeth foam
>
> breaks out, and in the depth of his chest the powerful heart groans;
>
> he lashes his own ribs with his tail and the flanks on both sides
>
> as he rouses himself to fury for the fight, eyes glaring,
>
> and hurls himself straight onward on the chance of killing some one
>
> of the men, or else being killed himself in the first onrush.
>
> (trans. R. Lattimore)

The pictorial animal versions, however, seem to have less room to move and less chance to resist.

The scene in the mosaic is not an exhibition of brutality, not an act of defense on the part of the humans, and it is more than a sport. It is rather a pictorial occasion for heroic grandstanding. As with the hunters in the stag mosaic (and the Vergina painting), there is a sense both of exhibitionism and of being watched, and at the same time a sense that all is unreal, that the "rehearsal" will end before the action is ever completed and before the lion (or the stag, despite its wounds) is killed; or alternatively that the "rehearsal" will never end, the stag hunter's weightless hat will never fall. Action is transformed to stasis, and stasis becomes a celebration of the male subjects. The hunters are both introverted and reflective, *and* aware of and performing for an unacknowledged audience a magnificent posed act. In this sense it does not matter that the sword in the lion hunt does not fit the scabbard or that the lance is broken a little beyond the tip and cannot produce results in the manner in which it is held. It does not matter that hunting a deer with an axe or hacking a lion with a sword are unlikely

ways of going about the task (even if works of art insist). One suspects that the animals are there not really to die but to afford the opportunity for display; weapons act as attributes in a demonstration of symbolism fraught with values rather than in the narration of a story. This pictorial state of affairs speaks of course more to ideology than to practice, ideology of the same type as that which led to the inclusion of leonine references in Alexander's portraiture.[82] Without being mythological, the hunting images aspire to the elevation enjoyed by mythological and Homeric heroes, who incarnate power and grandeur, who thrive in confrontation, and who are expected to impress by their very presence and the energy they exude.

Despite the intrinsic interest and broad suggestiveness of its theme, the value of the Pella lion mosaic has been weighed in light of its early identification as a reflection of *a* specific historical hunt undertaken in Syria and mentioned in Plutarch. In it Krateros, one of the most loyal of Alexander's officers and a close friend, reportedly saved Alexander's life.[83] This incident is more often discussed in connection with a round relief-base from Messene, now in the Louvre (fig. 30.7).[84] The left-hand figure on the stone base rushes on horseback against a lion whose body faces to the right but whose head turns towards the advancing horseman. The animal has been distracted from its attack on a hunting dog already grounded below its claws. The rider is dressed in short chiton and billowing mantle and wields a now-lost spear with his right hand. He is characterized as a Macedonian by his distinctive hat, again one of the many shapes that have been called a Macedonian καυσία. He seems small in comparison with his heroic companion on foot to the right, who is nude except for a lion hide wrapped around his left arm like a shield. Shown in a pose full of energy, this last hunter wields a double axe. Rider and horse on the one hand and man on foot on the other reach the same height. What the rider gains in being associated with the horse-owning aristocracy the other gains in superhuman size and connection with Herakles through his leonine attribute.

The base dates to the late fourth or early third century B.C. and has been connected with a sculptural monument dedicated by Krateros at Delphi in commemoration of the hunt mentioned above.[85] This bronze group, executed (at least partially) by Lysippos and Leochares,

FIGURE 30.7. Relief base from Messene with lion hunt, Louvre, Paris (MA 858). (© Photo Réunion des musées nationaux.)

supposedly showed Alexander fighting with the lion and Krateros rushing to help him, as well as the indispensable hounds. Accordingly, the rider in the base from Messene has been identified as Krateros and the footman as Alexander in the circumstances of that historical hunt,[86] even though the only one convincingly in danger is the dog. Not surprisingly, the reverse identification has also been proposed,[87] the differences having largely to do with individual scholars' understanding of what indicates danger in pictorial convention and what must have constituted glorification in antiquity: horsemanship, size, or nudity. It seems, however, that the emphasis in the picture is not on hierarchy between the hunters, but on different modes of male heroism and charged bodily display, on common endeavors of equals, who, however, act in relative isolation for personal honor.

As indicated previously, the lion hunt mosaic from Pella has also (albeit less persistently) been considered a reflection of the lost bronze dedication by Krateros at Delphi. All kinds of circuits have been constructed: relational circuits linking the one lost and two surviving monuments in ever-changing pairs, as well as narrative circuits concerning the sequence of events depicted in each and the presumed dangerous circumstances.[88] The left-hand hunter in the mosaic has been seen as Alexander, the overlapping between his foot and the lion's paw sometimes seen as a sign of danger. The reverse association can also be proposed, the right-hand hunter considered as Alexander.[89]

In the discussion of such proposals, the essentially non-narrative nature of both the Messene relief and the Pella mosaic is often overlooked. Both monuments seem to resist these and similar interpretations, varying in detail but not in attitude, and it seems best to consider the diverse literary and artistic evidence as complementary glimpses into values, mentalities, and attitudes, rather than as means of establishing dependencies of a very specific type. Viewed in this light, the lion hunt is no less and no more legitimate an historical monument than the stag hunt, which cannot be associated with *a* specific occasion. It will probably never be known whether the pebble lion hunt depicts a generic hunt of specific individuals, a specific hunt of specific individuals, or a generic hunt by generic hunters, devoid of incident. It is possible that in antiquity itself viewers could grasp it on different levels according to personal associations and knowledge. There is a lack of specificity and commitment in the picture, but this does not detract from its validity as an historical monument. It seems wrong to define history so narrowly, as a series of tiny incidents, rather than as the accumulated weight and substance of incidents.

The symbolic value in terms of behavior and self-definition which the hunt must have held for the Macedonian elite in the second half of the fourth century points to no less historical a fact than the pictorial recognition of *a* specific hunt of Alexander undertaken on *a* specific day. The same historical importance ought to be attached to the issue of Homeric self-fashioning to which the mosaics give visual form. Of course true Homeric fighters—and people like them—ought to be specifically named. But they can also be seen as exemplars of a community of fighters with shared ideals of individual glory. It is such ideals that the mosaics exemplify, and thus they reflect a wider cultural reality. Both mosaics and the Messene relief stem from the same historical milieu as the lost dedication of Krateros, and all three offer glimpses of the powerful effect the latter must have produced, even more powerful as it was all in the round. It is understandable that many conflicting views have been expressed as to how exactly to construct the association between the lost dedication and surviving works of art. Given the nature of the project, the problems are built-in. At the same time the surviving works cannot be given justice if viewed as "reflections" of an indeterminate kind and not as monuments on their own account, themselves having histories and meanings.

If one takes as a starting point the textual sources regarding Alexander and approaches the lion hunt mosaic with the hope of finding visual illustration to key stories, the search for identities cannot be resisted. But if one approaches the works in the reverse direction, examines art first and then goes to the texts that may illuminate it, the balance of analysis can be struck differently. An "innocent" first look at the mosaic would indicate no effort on the part of the artist to register a hierarchy of importance in reference to the two participants or a hierarchy of danger. The posed qualities of the picture, rather, refer back to the equally constructed historical gestures of Alexander in the effort to establish himself as a Homeric hero and to claim the Hellenic heritage coveted by him and his dynastic legacy. Those historical gestures, just as these pictorial ones, were meant to impress not by their specifics but by the weight of their accumulated significance. Of course Alexander copied Achilles *in specifics* when circumstances allowed it. But, most important, he copied Achilles *in spirit* as conjured up by his favorite epic. It is such an easily graspable abstraction and simulation of an aura that both Pella mosaics exemplify, and they do so whether one names the hunters Alexander or not.

The crafting of first a private then a public self, and the theatricalization of public life which Alexander's hero imitation entails, set a framework in which to place aspects of the iconography of the late fourth century. The ability to control oneself and intellectually scrutinize in an authorial sense one's own shape in life or art entails not only self-reflection and self-manipulation but also taking a distance from oneself. This kind of self-estrangement speaks to the fourth century and is not part of Homeric poetry, at least not with real urgency. The difference only proves the capacity of Homeric poetry to figure in a variety of productions and reproductions of meaning. In the fourth century the story of Alexander the Great, a king confident in his own originality but at the same time a product of his Macedonian aristocratic milieu, would have one believe that Homeric martial behavior was not only internalized but also at key moments resorted to with a heightened sense of self-consciousness. In the visual realm Homeric poetry seems to have supplied a system of references as well, as exemplified by the choreographed struggle enacted by the anonymous mosaic hunters discussed above. They represent the collective heroic values of the Macedonians, the Homeric identity, even the "Mycenaean" identity which archaeology is now, with difficulty, beginning to trace. The fact that these hunters conform to a visual "type"[90] only heightens this impression.

The discussion above has explored the possible connections among seemingly disparate manifestations of Macedonian culture in the later fourth century, those which individually evoke Homeric modes of expression and/or Homeric circumstance and which bear the potential for illuminating the Macedonians' view of and relation with the past. It has been maintained that this view, which gave vent to important self-presentations in life and art, was formulated foremost through direct reflections on epic poetry, but the attempt has also been made at least to consider how, if at all, several material connections with the Bronze Age as well as similarities in sociopolitical organization might have made it appropriate for the Macedonians to seize the epic with unique urgency. Because the Bronze Age in Macedonia is imperfectly known and the Mycenaean circumstances of southern Greece are only indirectly mediated in the epic, there are intractable difficulties in these issues. And yet the articulation of the problems and the coordination of disparate variables which point in the same direction speak tentatively in favor of a combined model of reminiscences of and analogies with Bronze Age realities.

NOTES

*The following abbreviations are used:

Ameling = W. Ameling, "Alexander und Achilleus. Eine Bestandsaufnahme," in W. Will, ed., *Zu Alexander d. Gr.* Festschrift G. Wirth (Amsterdam 1988) II.657–92.

Ancient Macedonia I = B. Laourdas and Ch. Makaronas, eds., *Ancient Macedonia*: Papers Read at the First International Symposium Held in Thessaloniki, 1968 (Thessaloniki 1970).

Ancient Macedonia III = *Ancient Macedonia III*: Papers Read at the Third International Symposium Held in Thessaloniki, 1977 (Thessaloniki 1983).

Ancient Macedonia IV = *Ancient Macedonia IV*: Papers Read at the Fourth International Symposium Held in Thessaloniki, 1983 (Thessaloniki 1986).

Bronze Age = E. Vermeule, *Greece in the Bronze Age* (Chicago and London 1972).

Edmunds = L. Edmunds, "The Religiosity of Alexander," *GRBS* 12 (1971) 363–391.

Harris = W. V. Harris, *Ancient Literacy* (Cambridge, Mass. 1989).

Image = E. Badian, ed., *Alexandre le Grand: image et réalité* (*Entretiens du Fondation Hardt* 22, Geneva 1976).

Macedonia-Australia = *Ancient Macedonia*: Exhibition Catalogue, Melbourne, Brisbane, Sydney, 1989 (Athens 1988).

Macedonia-Bologna = Η Μακεδονία από τα Μυκηναϊκά Χρόνια ως τον Μέγα Αλέξανδρο: Exhibition Catalogue, Museo Civico, Bologna (Thessaloniki 1988).

Macedonia and Greece = B. Barr-Sharrar and E. N. Borza, eds., *Macedonia and Greece in Late Classical and Early Hellenistic Times*, Studies in the History of Art 10 (Washington, D.C. 1982).

Momigliano = A. Momigliano, *The Development of Greek Biography* (Cambridge, Mass. 1971).

Pearson = L. Pearson, *The Lost Histories of Alexander the Great*, APA Monograph 20 (London and New York 1960).

1. Pearson 10. See also p. 46 for additional insights.

2. The imitation of glorious past exempla is not confined to antiquity: see Ch. L. Joost-Gauger, "The Early Beginnings of the Notion of 'Uomini Famosi' and the 'De Viris Illustribus' in Greco-Roman Literary Tradition," *Artibus et Historiae* 6 (1982) 97–115 and R. Starn, "Reinventing Heroes in Renaissance Italy," *Journal of Interdisciplinary History* 17 (1986) 67–84.

3. Cf. E. Vermeule, *Aspects of Death in Early Greek Art and Poetry* (Berkeley and Los Angeles 1979) 7.

4. This was so despite the concept "Fortune," in light of which the majority of ancient sources theorize his career.

5. On the artists, A. Stewart, *Faces of Power: Alexander's Image and Hellenistic Politics* (Berkeley and Los Angeles 1993); with different views and approaches, E. Schwarzenberg, "The Portraiture of Alexander," in *Image* 223–267 and "Der lysippische Alexander," *BonnJbb* 167 (1967) 58–118 (68–70 on Alexander and Achilles); see also T. Hölscher, *Ideal und Wirklichkeit in den Bildnissen Alexanders des Grossen* (Heidelberg 1971) and Ameling 686.

6. S. Greenblatt, *Renaissance Self-Fashioning: From More to Shakespeare* (Chicago and London 1980) 1.

7. A hero would be compared to a wild animal, but could not really be assumed to have imitated one! See *Iliad* 4.253, 11.323–325, 11.413–418, 17.281–283 with heroes as boars; *Iliad* 11.544–547 with a hero as an unidentified wild beast; *Iliad* 3.21–26, 5.135–143, 11.113–121, 11.548–556, 12.292–293, 12.298–301, 15.275–280, 15.630–636, 16.755–758, *Odyssey* 22.401–406 with lion imagery; *Iliad* 2.480–483 with bull imagery; *Iliad* 16.156–163, 16.352–357 with Greeks as wolves, etc. See H.-G. Buchholz, G. Jöhrens, and I. Maull, *Jagd und Fischfang*, ArchHom 2.J (Göttingen 1973) 10–14, and n. 59; C. Moulton, *Similes in the Homeric Poems*, Hypomnemata 49 (Göttingen 1977) 20–22, 46–49, 60–61, 89–90, 97–98, 139–141; W. C. Scott, *The Oral Nature of the Homeric Simile* (Leiden 1974) 58–62, 71.

8. Achilles provided inspiration to many others; see K. C. King, *Achilles: Paradigms of the War Hero from Homer to the Middle Ages* (Berkeley and Los Angeles 1987).

9. P. Green, "Caesar and Alexander: Aemulatio, Imitatio, Comparatio," *AJAH* 3 (1978) 1–26, quotation from 1. The evidence concerning Alexander's emulation of Achilles has been recently gathered by Ameling 657–692 and Stewart (supra n. 5) 78–86. See also L. Braudy, *The Frenzy of Renown: Fame and its History* (New York and Oxford 1986) 29–51 on the "longing of Alexander"; Hölscher (supra n. 5) 48–50; E. Mikrogiannakis, "Συγκρίσεις τοῦ Μεγ. Ἀλεξάνδρου," in *Ancient Macedonia III*, 177–179; P. Green, *Alexander of Macedon* (Harmondsworth 1974) 40–41, 532 n. 29, 541 n. 58.

10. Arrian 1.12.1; Plut., *Alex.* 15.7–9; Diodorus 17.17.3; see Ameling 676–677. For the localization of Achilles' alleged tomb, Strabo 13.1.32, 46; J. M. Cook, *The Troad* (Oxford 1973) 159–164, 184–187, and "The Topography of the Plain of Troy," in L. Foxhall and J. K. Davies, eds., *The Trojan War: Its Historicity and Context*, Papers of the First Greenbank Colloquium, Liverpool, 1981 (Bristol 1984) 163–172.

11. Almost none was earlier than the time of Augustus, except for a brief reference to the event at Troy in Cicero, *Pro Archia* 10.24; see also Cicero, *Epistolae ad Familiares* 5.12.7.

12. On Alexander's various lost histories and surviving fragments, see *FGrHist* IIB 618–828, nos. 117–153, translated by C. A. Robinson in *The History of Alexander* vol. I (Providence 1953). See also Pearson and P. Pédech, *Historiens compagnons d'Alexandre* (Paris 1984). For evaluations of Alexander's Roman historians, see P. A. Stadter, *Arrian of Nicomedia* (Chapel Hill 1980) esp. 60–88, 164–169; A. B. Bosworth, "Arrian and the Alexander Vulgate," in *Image* 1–33; Bosworth, *A Historical Commentary on Arrian's History of Alexander* I (Oxford 1980) esp. 16–38, and *From Arrian to Alexander* (Oxford 1988); N. G. L. Hammond, *Three Histories of Alexander the Great* (Cambridge 1983) and *Sources for Alexander the Great* (Cambridge 1993).

13. A. Fletcher, *Allegory: The Theory of a Symbolic Mode* (Ithaca and London 1964) 2.

14. Arrian 7.14; cf. Plut., *Alex.* 72.1–15; Diodorus 17.110.8, 17.114–115; Justin 12.12.11–12; Alexander's grief was intense, and the similarities to Achilles' were seen, not least by Alexander himself (cf. *Iliad* 18.22–116 and 23.6–225).

15. Arrian 1.11; cf. *Iliad* 2.700–702; Herodotus 9.116 describes the hero's tomb, looted and desecrated by Artayktes, local governor for the Persian king Xerxes. Herodotus' account links these fifth-century activities with the Trojan War, which makes culturally more understandable Alexander's claims to continue affairs initiated during the Trojan War and then the Persian Wars. On Herodotus and Protesilaos' tomb, see D. Boedeker, "Protesilaos and the End of Herodotus' *Histories*," *CA* 7 (1988) 30–48, a reference I owe to Professor Vermeule. On the significance of Alexander's gesture, H. U. Instinsky, *Alexander der Grosse am Hellespont* (Godesberg 1949) 12, 15, 17–28.

16. Arrian 1.11. See also 6.9.3 for the use of a special "sacred" shield by Alexander in battle.

17. On heroism see J. R. Hamilton, "Alexander's Early Life," *GaR* 12 (1965) 117–124, and Edmunds. In contrast to the present essay, Edmunds places the "heroic phase" of Alexander's career relatively late, after the most significant victories in the East. Edmunds understands Alexander's heroism as essentially religious, linked with (but not identical to) his later demand for divine honors. On deification, E. Badian, "The Deification of Alexander the Great," in H. J. Dell, ed., *Ancient Macedonian Studies in Honor of Charles F. Edson* (Thessaloniki 1981) 27–71; E. Fredricksmeyer, "Three Notes on Alexander's Deification," *AJAH* 4 (1979) 1–9; J. P. V. D. Balsdon, "The 'divinity' of Alexander," *Historia* 1 (1950) 363–388; P. A. Brunt, "The Aims of Alexander," *GaR* 12 (1965) 210–211.

18. Plut., *Alex.* 2.1; Diodorus 17.1.5. For Alexander's respect for and rivalry with Herakles, Arrian 3.3.2, 3.6.1, 4.28, 6.3.2. Alexander sacrificed to Herakles throughout his life, codified the presence of Herakles on his coinage, and was even portrayed on coins with a lion-scalp helmet, after his death but possibly even before; see A. R. Bellinger, *Essays on the Coinage of Alexander the Great* (New York 1963) 13–21; Hölscher (supra n. 5) 46–48, pl. 12.4; J. J. Pollitt, *Art in the Hellenistic Age* (Cambridge 1986) 25–26, fig. 13; O. Palagia, "Imitation of Herakles in Ruler Portraiture: A Survey, from Alexander to Maximinus Daza," *Boreas* 9 (1986) 139–142. See Edmunds 375 for comments on the suggestion that there was a change in Alexander's career from imitation of Achilles to imitation of Herakles, and U. Wilcken, *Alexander the Great*, trans. G. C. Richards, ed. E. N. Borza (New York 1967) 56.

19. Diodorus 17.97.3, trans. C. B. Wells. The reference is to *Iliad* 21.228–382.

20. Curtius 4.6.29. For Achilles' treatment of Hektor in this manner, see *Iliad* 22.395–404. See also Pearson 10.

21. See, for example, Plutarch's report on the lyre of Achilles, *Alex.* 15.8–9; *Mor.* 331d; cf. *Iliad* 9.186–191.

22. E. Badian, "Some Recent Interpretations of Alexander," in *Image* 279–303; G. Cary, *The Medieval Alexander* (Cambridge 1956).

23. Edmunds 390. For more general comments on the multiplicity of truths and histories, see P. Veyne, *Did the Greeks Believe in their Myths? An Essay on the Constitutive Imagination*, trans. P. Wissing (Chicago and London 1988) xii, 1; L. A. Montrose, "Professing the Renaissance: The Poetics and Politics of Culture," in H. A. Veeser, ed., *The New Historicism* (New York and London 1989) 20.

24. On the development and the literary forms that opened the way, see Momigliano. The first unmistakable evidence dates to the fourth century B.C. (pp. 43–64).

25. Pearson 33, 40–45; C. H. Fornara, *The Nature of History in Ancient Greece and Rome* (Berkeley and Los Angeles 1983) 34–35, 64.

26. *FGrHist* 124 F44; excellent comments in F. W. Walbank, "Speeches in Greek Historians," in *Selected Papers: Studies in Greek and Roman History and Historiography* (Cambridge 1985) 246–247 (essay originally published in 1965); but see the reservations of Fornara (supra n. 25) 145–146.

27. *Nicomachean Ethics* 1179a33-b4. On this topic see now N. Sherman, *The Fabric of Character: Aristotle's Theory of Virtue* (Oxford 1989), who emphasizes the rational pursuit of character and sees Aristotle's theories as practical in intent. Indeed, if there is one aspect that ancient and modern Greek educational systems share, this has to be it: the ultimate subordination of knowledge to the acquisition of moral character in light of distant or recent exempla, often literary.

28. *FGrHist* 134; Momigliano 82–83; Pearson 83–90, however, disassociates Onesikritos' title from education.

29. See Plut., *Alex.* 5.8, where Lysimachos is said to have called Alexander Achilles and himself Phoenix. On Aristotle see Plut., *Alex.* 7–8, 55, *Mor.* 327e-f, and E. Badian, "Greeks and Macedonians," in *Macedonia and Greece* 39. For a sceptical view on the relation between Alexander and Aristotle, see E. Voutiras, "Ἀριστοτέλης καὶ Ἀλέξανδρος," in Ἀμητός (Τιμητικὸς Τόμος για τον Καθηγητή Μανόλη Ἀνδρόνικο, Thessaloniki 1987) 179–185. For different views, see Edmunds 370 and J. W. Dye, "In Search of the Philosopher-King," *ArchNews* 11 (1982) 59–70.

30. See Edmunds 383–385; for the poem see J. M. Edmonds, *Lyra Graeca* vol. 3 (Cambridge, Mass. 1927) 410–412; C. M. Bowra, "Aristotle's Hymn to Virtue," *CQ* 32 (1938) 182–189; for the date of the poem and a persuasive

interpretation, see R. Renehan, "Aristotle as Lyric Poet: The Hermias Poem," *GRBS* 23 (1982) 251–274; references also by F. Schachermeyer in *Image* 50, n. 1. (Momigliano 82, Pearson 27, and A. B. Bosworth, *Conquest and Empire* [Cambridge 1988] 296 refer to the poem as Kallisthenes', probably based on Didymus, *De Demosthene Commenta* 5.64).

31. Plut., *Alex.* 8.2, 26.1; *Mor.* 327f–328a, 331d; Pliny, *H.N.* 7.29. According to Dio Chrysostom (*Or.* 4.39), Alexander had memorized the entire poem. On the "bookish" self- and worldview of Alexander, Braudy (supra n. 9) 39–40.

32. J. S. Held, *Rembrandt's "Aristotle" and other Rembrandt Studies* (Princeton 1969) 3–44; see also Ameling 669–670.

33. On the status of the recipients of formal education in the fourth century, see Harris 101–104 (cf. 108, n. 187).

34. J. M. Redfield, foreword to G. Nagy, *The Best of the Achaeans* (Baltimore and London 1929) xiii. On the pivotal role which the *Iliad* played in the education of Greece, H. I. Marrou, *A History of Education in Antiquity*, trans. G. Lamb (Madison and London 1982, originally published 1948) xiv, 9–13. See E. A. Havelock, *Preface to Plato* (Cambridge, Mass. 1963) 115–144 and "The Preliteracy of the Greeks," *New Literary History* 8 (1976–1977) 369–391 for summaries of this scholar's long-standing argument regarding the importance of the poetic tradition, especially when Greek culture was primarily oral. Harris 90–92 argues the relative unimportance of written next to orally communicated knowledge even in highly educated circles in the fifth and the fourth centuries; cf. p. 100. See also L. Pearson, *Popular Ethics in Ancient Greece* (Stanford 1962) 34–40.

35. See C. J. Rowe, "The Nature of Homeric Morality," in C. A. Rubino and C. W. Shelmerdine, eds., *Approaches to Homer* (Austin 1983) 248–275.

36. Harris 84 notes that between c. 450 and 322 B.C., the year of Aristotle's death, there was a significant increase in production and circulation of literary works (history and tragedy included). These nevertheless did not challenge the continued dominance of the Homeric poems; see Isokrates, *Panegyrikos* 159.

37. On Homeric kingship, see M. P. Nilsson, *Homer and Mycenae* (Philadelphia 1972; originally published 1933) 212–235; J. F. McGlew, "Royal Power and the Achaean Assembly at *Iliad* 2.84–393," *CA* 8 (1989) 283–295; P. Carlier, *La royauté en Grèce avant Alexandre* (Strasbourg 1984) 135–230. For linguistic survivals of Homeric elements in the Macedonian dialect, see I. K. Promponas, Ἡ συγγένεια μακεδονικῆς καὶ μυκηναϊκῆς διαλέκτου καὶ ἡ πρωτοελληνικὴ καταγωγὴ τῶν Μακεδόνων (Athens 1973). The very name Ἀλέξανδρος, Mycenaean and Homeric, seems to have been used exclusively by Macedonians in Classical

times, before becoming popular farther south in Greece, this after the precedence of Alexander the Great: A. B. Tataki, *Ancient Beroea: Prosopography and Society* (Μελετήματα 8, Athens 1988) 336–337; cf. J. Chadwick, *The Mycenaean World* (Cambridge 1976) 66–67.

38. See Sp. Marinatos, "Mycenaean Elements within the Royal Houses of Macedonia," in *Ancient Macedonia I* 45, 46 with n. 2, 48; in the same volume C. F. Edson, "Early Macedonia," 22–23, 30–32, and G. S. Stagakis, "Observations on the Ἑταῖροι of Alexander the Great," 86–102; N. G. L. Hammond and G. T. Griffith, *A History of Macedonia*, vol. II (550–336 B.C.) (Oxford 1979) 31; N. G. L. Hammond, *Alexander the Great: King, Commander and Statesman* (London 1981) 25; Wilcken (supra n. 18) 25; Ameling 659–660, 664.

39. For the Mycenaean period, see M. Nilsson (supra n. 37) 248–266; Nilsson, *The Mycenaean Origin of Greek Mythology* (Berkeley 1972; originally published 1932) 44, 238–251, and passim; D. L. Page, *History and the Homeric Iliad* (Berkeley and Los Angeles 1959) 118–154, 218–261; J. V. Luce, *Homer and the Heroic Age* (New York 1975); M. L. West, "The Rise of the Greek Epic," *JHS* 108 (1988) 151–172. For the view favoring a date early in the Iron Age, tenth or ninth centuries, M. I. Finley, *The World of Odysseus*, rev. ed. (New York 1965); idem, *Early Greece: The Bronze and Archaic Ages* (rev. ed. New York and London 1981) 80–86. I. Morris, "The Use and Abuse of Homer," *CA* 5 (1986) 81–129, argues for an *Iliad* reflective of the society of the eighth century. For these and other theories and a preference for the Archaic period, see Carlier (supra n. 37) 137–140 and 210–214. A. M. Snodgrass, "An Historical Homeric Society?," *JHS* 94 (1974) 114–115 emphasizes the composite nature of Homeric society.

40. E. N. Borza, *In the Shadow of Olympus* (Princeton 1990) 231–241, believes that the authority of the Macedonian king depended on nonconstitutional factors and revolved around his person rather than any group. R. M. Errington, *A History of Macedonia*, trans. C. Errington (Berkeley and Los Angeles 1990) 220, questions the evidence for an assembly but emphasizes the role of the aristocracy and the traditional respect shown by the king for (informal) public opinion; cf. also 221, 243–244.

41. See Carlier (supra n. 37) 144–145.

42. M. Andronikos, Βεργίνα. Οἱ Βασιλικοί Τάφοι καὶ οἱ Ἄλλες Ἀρχαιότητες (Athens 1984) 97; Ameling 660 and n. 19, 20.

43. See E. Vermeule's juxtaposition of plates XI.A (Shaft Graves) and XI.B (Trebenishte) in *Bronze Age* (also p. 95); for Trebenishte, N. G. L. Hammond in M. Sakellariou, ed., Μακεδονία. 4000 Χρόνια Ἑλληνικῆς Ἱστορίας καὶ Πολιτισμοῦ (Athens 1982) 66, 67, 68, fig. 34. For Sindos, *Macedonia*-

Australia No. 149, p. 208; *Sindos* (Thessaloniki 1985) cat. nos. 115, 239, 282, 322. On the close Greek connections of Sindos and the weaker connections of Trebenishte, see J. Bouzek and I. Ondrejová, "Sindos-Trebenishte-Duvanli. Interrelations between Thrace, Macedonia, and Greece in the 6th and 5th centuries BC," *Mediterranean Archaeology* 1 (1988) 84–94, esp. 87.

44. Ch. Koukouli-Chrysanthaki and I. Vokotopoulou, *Macedonia-Australia* 77, 79 (pottery), 81 (pottery and metalwork); also *Macedonia-Bologna* xx (Vokotopoulou) and xxvi (Souref); on the conservatism of pottery types, see also K. A. Wardle, "Excavations at Assiros, 1975–9: A Settlement Site in Central Macedonia and its Significance for the Prehistory of South-East Europe," *BSA* 75 (1980) 244, 252, 256, 262.

45. Ph. Petsas, *Pella: Alexander the Great's Capital* (Thessaloniki 1978) 50, and fig. 9.

46. For an excellent discussion and enumeration of possible ways of encountering the past through material remains as regards southern Greece, see E. D. T. Vermeule, " 'Priam's Castle Blazing': A Thousand Years of Trojan Memories," in M. J. Mellink, ed., *Troy and the Trojan War* (Bryn Mawr 1986) 77–92, esp. 82–84.

47. Late Bronze Age material excavated early in the century was studied by W. A. Heurtley, *Prehistoric Macedonia* (Cambridge 1939). A recent review has been presented by A. Cambitoglou and J. K. Papadopoulos, "The Earliest Mycenaeans in Macedonia," in E. French and C. Zerner, eds., *Wace and Blegen. Pottery as Evidence for Trade in the Aegean Bronze Age: 1939–1989*, Proceedings of the Conference sponsored by the American School of Classical Studies and the British School at Athens, December 2–3 1989 (Amsterdam 1993). I thank Dr. Papadopoulos for making this study available to me prior to its appearance in print. For a convenient summary of the finds from Assiros, K. A. Wardle, "Assiros: A Macedonian Settlement of the Late Bronze and Early Iron Age," in *Ancient Macedonia III*, 291–305.

48. B. Feuer, *The Northern Mycenaean Border in Thessaly,* BAR International Series 176 (Oxford 1983).

49. Cambitoglou and Papadopoulos (supra n. 47) present evidence for LH I and II material from the coastal site of Torone in the Chalkidike. They argue for the importance of such coastal sites as intermediaries between southern Greek and inland Macedonian sites. See Z. A. Stos-Gale and C. F. Macdonald, "Sources of Metals and Trade in the Bronze Age Aegean," in N. H. Gale, ed., *Bronze Age Trade in the Mediterranean*; SIMA 90 (Jonsered 1991) 270–281, for the possibility that some of the silver in the Shaft Graves may originate in the Chalkidike.

50. See E. Vermeule, *The Art of the Shaft Graves at Mycenae* (Norman, Okla. 1975).

51. Most recently argued by S. Diamant, "Mycenaean Origins: Infiltration from the North?" in E. B. French and K. A. Wardle, eds., *Problems in Greek Prehistory*: Papers Presented at the Centenary Conference of the British School of Archaeology at Athens, Manchester, 1986 (Bristol 1988) 153–159; but see the cautionary notes of A. F. Harding, *The Mycenaeans and Europe* (London 1984) 280–281, 287–288; see also the synthetic approach of Vermeule (supra n. 50) 22–26 on the important although "elusive" northern affinities.

52. B. Hänsel, "Mycenaean Greece and Europe," in the exhibition catalogue *The Mycenaean World: Five Centuries of Early Greek Culture 1600–1100 B.C.* (Athens 1988) 62; A. Hochstetter, "Spätbronzezeitliches und früheisenzeitliches Formengut in Makedonien und Balkanraum," in B. Hänsel, ed., *Südosteuropa zwischen 1600 und 1000 v. Chr.* (Berlin 1982) 100; A. Hochstetter, *Kastanas*, vol. 6 (*Die Kleinfunde*) (Berlin 1987) 15–16, 129, pl. 1.6 and pl. 25.9.

53. Heurtley (supra n. 47) 96, 111–112, 124; Ch. Koukouli-Chrysanthaki in *Macedonia-Australia* 19–21; D. W. Smit, "Mycenaean Penetration into Northern Greece," in J. G. P. West and N. M. W. De Vries, eds., *Thracians and Mycenaeans*: Proceedings of the Fourth International Congress of Thracology, Rotterdam, 1984 (Leiden 1989) 176–178; K. Souref in *Macedonia-Bologna* xxv–xxvii and in the same volume E. Poulaki-Pandermali (59–63). For Kastanas, see B. Hänsel, *JRGZM* 26 (1979) (Mainz 1982) 167–202, and in the same volume Chr. Podzweit 203–222; also Chr. Podzweit, "Der spätmykenische Einfluss in Makedonien," in *Ancient Macedonia IV* 467–484. On Assiros, see Wardle (supra n. 44) 250–252. For cautionary remarks on the Mycenaean material in northern Greece, see Borza (supra n. 40) 63–64 and Harding (supra n. 51) 235–239, 241–244.

54. *Macedonia-Australia* 77; Ch. Koukouli-Chrysanthaki, "Late Bronze Age in Eastern Macedonia," *Thracia Praehistorica*, Supplementum Pulpudeva 3 (1982) 233, 243–247, 249–256. See also M. Andronikos, Βεργίνα I. Τὸ Νεκροταφεῖον τῶν Τύμβων (Athens 1969) 167–168 on a few isolated, Mycenaean-style pots from the Iron Age cemetery of Vergina and its vicinity. The excavator dated two such pyxides to the tenth or eleventh century, a time when their shape was no longer encountered in the rest of the Greek world; see also M. Andronikos, "Χρονολογικὰ Προβλήματα τῆς Προϊστορικῆς Μακεδονίας," *Ancient Macedonia* II (Thessaloniki 1977) 3, where it is maintained that no example of a proper Bronze Age item was excavated in this cemetery.

55. For photographs of Mycenaean-type objects from the area of Kozani, see *Macedonia-Australia*, nos. 35–37, pp. 135–136; (here also included no. 47, p. 144 from Kastanas); from the area of Pieria, nos. 56–60, 62–63, pp. 149–

152, 153–154; (no. 75, p. 161 is a Thasian imitation of a Mycenaean alabastron). On a promising Mycenaean cemetery (c. 1300–1200 B.C.) in the area of Mt. Olympus (at Spathes), see E. Poulaki-Pandermali, "Ἀνασκαφή Ἀγ. Δημητρίου Ὀλύμπου," in Το Ἀρχαιολογικό Ἔργο στη Μακεδονία και Θράκη 1, 1987 (Thessaloniki 1988) 201–208; in the same volume, M. Tiverios, "Ὄστρακα από το Καραμπουρνάκι," 249–250, n. 19, and pl. 255. On the LH IIIB–C material from Olympus, see also E. Poulaki-Pandermali, "Ὄλυμπος -2. Μακεδονικόν ὄρος, μετεωρότατον," in Ἀμητός (supra n. 29) 697–717.

56. On cemeteries, E. Poulaki-Pandermali (supra n. 55); on Mycenaean-type architecture at Kastanas, B. Hänsel, "Siedlungskontinuität im spätbronzezeitlichen und früheisenzeitlichen Griechenland," in Thracia Praehistorica (supra n. 54) 279; W. A. Heurtley (supra n. 47) 126, 128, proposed early the presence of Mycenaean trading settlements in Macedonia, but the evidence he could then present in support of that argument does not seem sufficient. Nevertheless, the possibility of Mycenaean trading posts has not been discarded in more recent scholarship, for example Hänsel (above) 282.

57. Arthur Evans reported the astonishing case of an ivory ring allegedly from a Hellenistic tomb at Chania dated c. 300 B.C. On one side it almost exactly reproduces a warrior fight encountered on an engraved sardonyx from Shaft Grave III and on the other side a fight between a warrior and a lion, also encountered on a gold seal from the same Shaft Grave: "The Minoan and Mycenaean Element in Hellenic Life," JHS 32 (1912) 294–297 and PM III.125–127 with figs. 78, 79, 80a and b. See also Luce (supra n. 39) 105 and figs. 71, 72. One would very much like this artifact to be genuine, but there are rightful doubts: J. Boardman, The Cretan Collection in Oxford (Oxford 1961) 122 n. 1; G. S. Korres, "Μινωϊκαὶ Ἐπιβιώσεις καὶ Ἀναβιώσεις - Α," in Πεπραγμένα τοῦ Γ' Διεθνοῦς Κρητολογικοῦ Συνεδρίου (Athens 1973) 465.

58. The bibliography on hero-cults is enormous. The most exhaustive recent account is C. M. Antonaccio, "The Archaeology of Early Greek 'Hero Cult'" (Ph.D. diss., Princeton University, 1987) with a detailed review of scholarship (pp. 1–29). See also J. N. Coldstream, "Hero-cults in the Age of Homer," JHS 96 (1976) 8–17; see A. M. Snodgrass, "Les origines du culte des héros dans la Grèce antique," in G. Gnoli and J.-P. Vernant, eds., La mort, les morts dans les sociétés anciennes (Cambridge 1982) 107–119; J. Whitley, "Early States and Hero Cults: a Re-Appraisal," JHS 108 (1988) 173–182; Vermeule (supra n. 3) 206–207.

59. S. E. Alcock, "Tomb Cult and the Post-Classical Polis," AJA 95 (1991) 447–467.

60. Thuc. 1.9–11. See A. Raubitschek, "What the Greeks Thought of their Early History," AncW 20 (1989) 39–48.

61. M. I. Finley, "Myth, Memory and History," in The Use and Abuse of History (New York 1987) 11–33 (essay originally published 1965).

62. S. Foltiny, "The Ivory Horse Bits of Homer and the Bone Horse Bits of Reality," BonnJbb 167 (1967) 11.

63. E. Vermeule, "Baby Aigisthos and the Bronze Age," PCPS 213 (1987) 124. And there were individuals who tried to calculate the date of the Trojan War by means of generational reckoning; cf. Bronze Age 277; Vermeule 1986 (supra n. 46) 80; cf. also essay by Burkert in this volume.

64. On Douris' dating: J. Forsdyke, Greece Before Homer (London 1956) 62–63.

65. For example, Bronze Age, pl. XLIII; H. G. Buchholz et al. (supra n. 7), figs. 21 a–c, 22 b–c. See J. A. Sakellarakis, "Kretisch-mykenische Siegel in griechischen Heiligtümern," in U. Jantzen, ed., Neue Forschungen in griechischen Heiligtümern (Tübingen 1976) 283–308.

66. Bronze Age, pl. XII.

67. Bronze Age, pl. XIX D; CMS I, No. 227 (p. 260); The Mycenaean World (supra n. 52) no. 237 (p. 235).

68. The mosaics, widely discussed, are now officially published in a doctoral dissertation by E. Juri presented to the University of Athens and titled "Τα Ψηφιδωτά της Πέλλας" (Ph.D. diss., Thessaloniki 1985); see now also Ch. Makaronas and E. Juri, Οἱ Οἰκίες Ἁρπαγῆς τῆς Ἑλένης καί Διονύσου τῆς Πέλλας (Athens 1989) esp. 127–129, 142–143, 165–166, on the stag mosaic and 137–139, 144–145, 167–168 on the lion. See also P. Moreno, "La pittura greca dalle origini ad Apelle," Archeo 34 (1987) 5–8, 46, 50–51; P. Moreno, Pittura Greca (Rome 1987) 7, 134, 135, 139, 156, figs. 31, 175, 202. Earlier treatments include Petsas (supra n. 45) 95–97, 99–102, 107–111; Ch. Picard, "Le mosaïste grec Gnosis et les nouvelles chasses de Pella," RA 1963, 205–209; M. Andronikos, "Ancient Greek Painting and Mosaics in Macedonia," BalkSt 5 (1964) 287–302, especially 295–296, pl. VII, fig. 8; M. Robertson, "Greek Mosaics," JHS 85 (1965) 72–89, Greek Painting (Geneva 1959) 166, 169–170, and "Early Greek Mosaic," in Macedonia and Greece 241–249; Pollitt (supra n. 18) 40–42; D. Salzmann, Untersuchungen zu den antiken Kieselmosaiken von den Anfängen bis zum Beginn der Tesseratechnik, Archäologische Forschungen vol. 10 (Berlin 1982) 107–108, cat. no. 103, pl. 29, color pls. 101.2–6 and 102.1.2 for the stag hunt and 105–106, cat. no. 98, pls. 30.1.2 and 31.1–4, for the lion hunt; on the lion hunt, see also The Search for Alexander: Supplement II to the Catalogue (Museum of Fine Arts, Boston 1981) no. 15, p. 10.

69. Currently the interpretation of the buildings as private houses is preferred by the excavators. "Building I" is 3,160

m² in size, "Building II" 2,350 m²: Makaronas and Juri (supra n. 68) 18.

70. M. Andronikos, *The Royal Graves at Vergina* (Athens 1980) 18–20, and Andronikos (supra n. 42) 100–117, with figs. 57–70. A recent reconstruction of the painting created by G. Miltsakakis has been published in Αμητός (supra n. 29) XXIII, *ArchEph* 126 (1987), fig. 1, and *BCH* 112 (1988), fig. 83. On the painting see also P. H. von Blanckenhagen, "Painting in the Time of Alexander and Later," in *Macedonia and Greece* 257–258; P. Moreno, *Archeo* 34 (1987) 44–46, and *Pittura Greca* (supra n. 68) 115, 118, 120, 125, figs. 121, 150–153, 201, 203, 207–210; M. A. Elvira, "Anotaciones sobre la cacería pintada en la tumba de Filipo," *Archivo español de arqueologia* 58 (1985) 19–35, and "Reflexiones sobre el cuadro de cacería en la época de Alejandro," in J. M. Croisille, ed., *Neronia IV. Alejandro Magno, modelo de los emperadores romanos*, Collection Latomus vol. 209 (Brussels 1990) 113–131; M. Carroll-Spillecke, *Landscape Depictions in Greek Relief Sculpture: Development and Conventionalization*, European University Studies, Archaeology, series 38, vol. 11 (Frankfurt 1985) 151–155; A. Rouveret, *Histoire et imaginaire de la peinture ancienne*, BEFAR fasc. 274 (Rome 1989) 235–244; P. Briant, "Chasses royales macédoniennes et chasses royales perses: le theme de la chasse au lion sur la chasse de Vergina," *Dialogues d' histoire ancienne* 17.1 (1991) 211–255, a reference I owe to E. Carney; in the same volume, see A. M. Prestianni Giallombardo (257–304) and B. Tripodi (143–209).

71. Andronikos 1969 (supra n. 54) 249–251, 257, 276, 280, fig. 87; J. Bouzek, "Macedonia and Thrace in the Early Iron Age," in *Ancient Macedonia IV* 123.

72. L. H. Sackett and J. A. MacGillivray, "Boyhood of a God," *Archaeology* 42 (1989) 27–31, esp. 30; also J. A. MacGillivray et al., "Excavations at Palaikastro, 1988," *BSA* 84 (1989) 438–442, fig. 17, pl. 60(f).

73. C. Rowe, "Conceptions of Colour and Colour Symbolism in the Ancient World," *EranJb* 41 (1972) 349.

74. From Thebes, in the Thebes Archaeological Museum (BE 54), dated c. 420 B.C. On the stelai, K. Demakopoulou and D. Konsola, *Archaeological Museum of Thebes* (Athens 1986) 74–75; W. Schild-Xenidou, *Boiotische Grab- und Weihreliefs archaischer und klassischer Zeit* (Munich 1972) 41–44, cat. nos. 43–48; A. Kalogeropoulou, "Nuovo aspetto della stele di Saugenes," *AAA* 1 (1968) 92–96.

75. The cultural and visual interrelationships between war and hunt in art are explored in my doctoral dissertation, "Studies in Large-Scale Painting and Mosaic in the Late Classical and Early Hellenistic Periods: Battles, Hunts, Abductions" (Harvard University, 1990) (under revision for publication).

76. "What kind of man has been the least oppressed by work and the most easily able to engage in being happy? Obviously the aristocratic man. Certainly the aristocrats too had their jobs, frequently the hardest of all: war, responsibilities of government, care of their own wealth. . . . But the work of the aristocrat, which looks more like 'effort,' was of such a nature that it left him a great deal of free time. And this is what concerns us: what does a man do when, and in the extent that, he is free to do what he pleases?" (José Ortega y Gasset, *Meditations on Hunting*, trans. H. B. Wescott [New York 1985, originally written in Lisbon 1942] 27).

77. See P. Vidal-Naquet, *The Black Hunter: Forms of Thought and Forms of Society in the Greek World*, trans. A. Szegedy-Maszak (Baltimore and London 1986) 118; J. K. Anderson, *Hunting in the Ancient World* (Berkeley and Los Angeles 1985) 159, n. 3.

78. Hammond and Griffith (supra n. 38) 155 with n. 4, 156, 165.

79. Salzmann (supra n. 68); I. Touratsoglou, "Μεταλεξάνδρεια Πέλλα," *ArchDelt* 30 (1975) 165–184; see also Makaronas and Juri (supra n. 68) 6.

80. Hölscher (infra n. 84) 180–181; Stähler (infra n. 84) 259 and n. 7.

81. For various theories about the kausia, see B. M. Kingsley, "The Cap that Survived Alexander," *AJA* 85 (1981) 39–46 and "Alexander's Kausia and Macedonian Tradition," *Classical Antiquity* 10 (1991) 59–76; P. Dintsis, *Hellenistische Helme* (Rome 1986) 183–195, 304–312; Prestianni Giallombardo (supra n. 70); Ch. Saatsoglou-Paliadeli, "Aspects of Ancient Macedonian Costume," *JHS* 113 (1993) 122–147.

82. Plut., *Mor.* 335b; Schwarzenberg, *Image* 249–251.

83. Plut., *Alex.* 40.4–5; cf. Pliny, *H.N.* 34.64. On Krateros see Arrian 7.12; Diodorus 17.114.1–2; Plut. *Alex.* 47.9–10 and *Eumenes* 6.3; Curtius 6.8.2.

84. For the relief base (Louvre No. 858), see W. Fuchs, *Die Skulptur der Griechen* (Munich 1969) 363; M. Jacob-Felsch, *Die Entwicklung griechischer Statuenbasen und die Aufstellung der Statuen* (Waldsassen, Bayern 1969) 79, 176; T. Hölscher, *Griechische Historienbilder des 5. und 4. Jahrhunderts v. Chr.*, Beiträge zur Archäologie vol. 6 (Würzburg 1973) 181–185, with bibliography in n. 1103, p. 292; A. H. Borbein, "Die griechische Statue des 4. Jahrhunderts v. Chr.," *JdI* 88 (1973) 91–95; R. Vasić, "Das Weihgeschenk des Krateros in Delphi und die Löwenjagd in Pella," *AntK* 22 (1979) 106–109; D. Willers, "Zwei Löwenjagdgruppen des vierten Jahrhunderts v. Chr.," *Hefte des archäologischen Seminars der Universität Bern* 5 (1979) 21–26; *The Search for Alexander: Exhibition Catalogue* (Boston 1980) cat. no. 44, pp. 121–122 with additional references; Pollitt (supra n. 18) 38 and fig. 31; K. Stähler, "Krateros und Alexander. Zum Anathem des Krateros in Delphi," in *Migratio et Commutatio.*

Studien zur alten Geschichte und deren Nachleben, Festschrift T. Pekáry (St. Katharinen 1989) 258–264; Stewart (supra n. 5) 270–277, 281, 427.

85. The monument was set in place some time after his death in 320. The connection with this lost dedication has played a role in assigning a date to the base from Messene. Of the dedication itself nothing survives, except for some architectural remains of the rectangular building which had once housed it. For these remains, see F. Courby, *FdD* II.1 (Paris 1927) 237–240. The identification of the building was through an inscription, on which see Th. Homolle, "La chasse d' Alexandre," *BCH* 21 (1897) 598–600, P. Perdrizet, "Venatio Alexandri," *JHS* 19 (1899) 273–279, and R. Flacelière, *FdD* III, 4 (Paris 1954) 213–214. For comments on the reconstructions of the dedication, see Ch. Saatsoglou-Paliadeli, "Το ανάθημα του Κρατερού στους Δελφούς. Μεθοδολογικά Προβλήματα Αναπαράστασης," Εγνατία 1 (1989) 81–99.

86. G. Loeschcke, "Relief aus Messene," *JdI* 3 (1888) 189–193 and most scholars thereafter.

87. For example, P. Wolters and J. Sieveking, "Der Amazonenfries des Maussoleums," *JdI* 24 (1909) 190 n. 58.

88. Discussions in Hölscher (supra n. 84) 226–228, Vasić (supra n. 84) 106–109, Willers (supra n. 84) 21–26. Hölscher believes that the relief base from Messene is a fairly accurate reflection of the lost group but contests the association of the group with the Pella mosaic. Vasić, however, is receptive to a connection between the Pella mosaic and the lost dedication. Willers suggests that the models behind the mosaic would have been earlier than the dedication. All three authors agree that the Messene relief reflects the appearance of Krateros' sculptural commission. Robertson, *Macedonia and Greece* 246, considers both relief and mosaic unreliable. Saatsoglou-Paliadeli (supra n. 85) rejects the relief but believes that the mosaic may bear some relation to the iconography of the lost dedication.

89. See Vasić (supra n. 84) 108–109.

90. For example, the lion hunters' lower bodies are very similar to one another and have been shown to derive from the same "cartoon." See Salzmann (supra n. 68), pl. 99.4, 6.

31

AN ARRETINE BOWL AND
THE REVENGE OF ACHILLES

✦

JOHN J. HERRMANN, JR.

A fragmentary terra sigillata bowl on loan to the Museum of Fine Arts has undergone considerable damage, but nonetheless its iconography seems to be of more than usual interest (figs. 31.1a–e).[1] Its rim and much of its base have been systematically broken away, and a large section of its frieze of figures in low relief is missing.[2] The missing figures, moreover, were part of the focal grouping of the entire composition, but their subject can be easily recognized; a pair of wheels and four pairs of rear hooves must have belonged to a quadriga with its horses bounding forward in unison (fig. 31.1a). It is equally evident that this must have been the chariot of Achilles, since a nude male figure with arms extended behind his head is stretched out on the ground behind the quadriga; the lifeless body of Hector has been tied to Achilles' war-chariot to be abused (fig. 31.1b).

As has been pointed out elsewhere, the bowl is patently of Arretine origin and of Augustan date.[3] Annelies Kossatz-Deissmann has assembled a great number of representations of Achilles; according to her listing, this subject is not otherwise known from the pottery workshops of Arretium.[4] Many of the supporting figures on this bowl do not seem to appear in representations of the

scene in other media, and the identification of these figures is often far from clear.

One of the most enigmatic figures forms an integral part of the scene of dragging: a female in a state of agitation stands directly behind the body of Hector (fig. 31.1b). Arms outspread, she hefts a sword and dangles a stylized Corinthian helmet from its corkscrew-like crest attachment. The helmet is embellished with an unusual spiraling line, which recalls a ram's horn, curving forward from the back.[5] The woman's hair is pulled back tightly and spurts out in a short ponytail. She wears a long, sleeveless, high-belted tunic with a lengthy overfold. One shoulder-fastening has been undone, revealing her left breast. With drapery flowing, she rushes in the opposite direction from the movement of the corpse, turning her head back to view the (missing) chariot.

At first glance, this woman recalls the figures of Hecuba and Andromache that lament from the walls of Troy in most Roman treatments of the scene.[6] There is, however, no trace of the walls, and the woman is in no way separated, as an enemy should be, from the chariot. The female seems, in fact, to be exulting at Achilles' victory, and the helmet and sword she brandishes are

507

FIGURE 31.1a. Chariot of Achilles.

FIGURE 31.1b. Hector and Thetis.

presumably those stripped from Hector. A triumphant display of Hector's weapons over his dead body might be appropriate for Athena or Hera, the Greeks' vengeful divine supporters, but the immodest costume of this female excludes an identification as one of those chaste goddesses. She might, on the other hand, be Hellas, the personification of the Greeks; Hellas is attested with certainty only at much earlier dates—the fifth to the third centuries B.C.—but she, at any rate, is at times presented as relatively lightly clad and glamorous.[7] In connection with the dragging of Hector around the body or remains of Patroclus, Homer does mention one Olympian goddess for whom this costume would be somewhat more appropriate: Aphrodite, who kept dogs away from the body of Hector and anointed him with oil so that he would not be damaged by the dragging (*Iliad* 23.185–187). An exposed shoulder and, at times, an exposed breast are not uncommon identifying attributes of the goddess of love and beauty.

The dynamic action of the female, who moves away from rather than follows the body, is, however, difficult to reconcile with a benevolent, mortuary role. Paradoxically, in spite of her exultant mood, her costume probably does reflect mourning—and mourning of an intensity inappropriate for an Olympian divinity or even for a geographical personification. An unfastened shoulder strap and exposed breast are signs of extreme grief—as in the case of Hecuba and Andromache watching from walls of Troy.[8]

If she is a partisan of the Greeks (as seems almost certain to be the case) her mourning must be for Patroclus, not Hector. A female who has a strong identification with this role is Briseis, the favorite slave and (perhaps) wife of Achilles.[9] She had been in deep mourning for Patroclus, who had been kind to her at the moment of her capture (*Iliad* 19.282–301).[10] Her lamentations with disheveled hair and, at times, exposed breast at the deathbed of Patroclus or at the funerary monument were represented on several occasions in both Greek and Roman art.[11] Her presence at the center of a scene of action, however, sits uncomfortably with her otherwise domestic roles. As a captive, any connection with the weapons of war seems alien to her.

A preferable interpretation—particularly since it derives support from the text of Homer—is to see this ferocious mourner as Thetis. As Achilles returned to the Greek ships dragging the corpse of Hector, his divine mother incited the Myrmidons to lamentation (*Iliad* 23.13–14). The disheveled costume of a mourner would be appropriate for her in this role, and as the provider of Achilles' weapons, she most fittingly could carry the helmet and sword recovered from Hector. These were relics of Achilles' first suit of armor, which had been worn by Patroclus in his fatal encounter with Hector (*Iliad* 18.21, 82–85). The helmet and the sword, which were thereafter used by Hector, would be vivid reminders of Patroclus' death. Their display would be a suitable means for Thetis to stimulate the grief of the Greek onlookers. Since she had originally brought the weapons to Achilles, she would have been especially concerned

508

FIGURE 31.1c. A Myrmidon or Patroclus.

FIGURE 31.1d. Personification of Asia/Armenia.

with their recovery. The identification of Thetis, then, establishes the setting for this dragging of Hector as the Greek camp by the ships, far from the walls of Troy.[12]

The central action is flanked on each side by a standing figure, both of whom seem to function primarily as onlookers. They provide a bit of context for the main event—while relating rather awkwardly to the Homeric text. To the left is a nude warrior supporting an inverted spear and carrying a sword, which is partly covered by the cloak draped over his left shoulder (fig. 31.1c). In all probability, he is one of the Myrmidons mourning for Patroclus upon Achilles' arrival at the Greek camp. Since he is not wearing his armor nor is he evidently weeping, as specified by Homer (*Iliad* 23.15), another possible interpretation should, at least, be mentioned. It is conceivable that the figure is a statue of Patroclus; in an Apulian vase of the fourth century B.C., an aedicula in a scene of dragging contains a statue of Patroclus in just this pose, but with a shield in place of the sword and cloak.[13]

On the other side of the scene of dragging (in front of the horses), stands another "onlooker": a female figure in an elaborate and bizarre costume (fig. 31.1d). She wears a tall hat, whose form suggests a wedge or truncated pyramid, and a capelike mantle fastened centrally on her breast. With her left hand she holds out the edge of her mantle, an action that spreads the garment into a rich cascade of zigzagging folds. Her long-sleeved tunic

FIGURE 31.1e. Achilles sacrificing a Trojan prisoner.

FIGURES 31.1a – e. Arretine terra sigillata bowl, private collection, on loan to the Museum of Fine Arts, Boston. Photos: author.

FIGURE 31.2. Mould for an Arretine terra sigillata bowl by L. Avillius Sura: a Roman general and a personification of Armenia (repeated). Antikensammlung des Archäologischen Instituts, Tübingen. (Photo: Archäologisches Institut.)

is belted just below the breasts; the thickness of this blurred band suggests either a very thick belt or an overfold with a horizontal lower border. Two medallions or garterlike straps emerging from under the overfold raise the front lower edge of the tunic in places to create a garlandlike effect. At the left side, the tunic hangs lower and merges with the mantle. The female's legs seem to be clad in trousers rather than covered by a long undertunic, and she wears shoes.

The costume is clearly barbaric; the tall hat and the trousers alone make this evident. As a whole, it appears to be based on the ceremonial dress of eastern Anatolia.[14] Most of its features can be paralleled in the trappings of Antiochus I of Commagene (c. 69–31 B.C.) in the reliefs from Nemrud Dağ, Arsameia, and Sofraz Köy.[15] Numismatic evidence makes it clear that the same costume was used in neighboring Armenia, where this form of hat or *tiara* originated in the time of Tigranes the Great (95–56 B.C.).[16]

Armenian or Commagenian costume was taken up in Greco-Roman art for a limited number of purposes. A pair of large bronze statuettes of boys, probably representing geographic genii, wear costumes extremely similar to the female on the sigillata bowl; the bronzes were found in coastal Egypt and are now divided between the Metropolitan Museum of Art, New York, and the Walters Art Gallery in Baltimore.[17] Defeated Armenian soldiers seem to wear a very similar costume on Roman coinage from about 20 B.C. onward.[18] The same classicized version of Anatolian costume was also worn by female figures personifying Armenia.[19] In an Arretine mould in Tübingen, a figure identical to the one under discussion has long been interpreted as Armenia (fig. 31.2).[20] Armenia may also have been the subject of one of the statues of conquered nations by Coponius in the Theater of Pompey around 55 B.C.[21] If so, such a monument could well have been the source for images like the one seen here.

In any case, neither Armenia nor Commagene would have any significance in the Homeric context of this bowl. Since such exotically dressed females evidently had a primarily geographic meaning, it seems likely that here the woman represents Asia in a general sense. It must be admitted, however, that she does not correspond to any of the other, relatively scarce, images of Asia known thus far.[22] In any event, the gesture she makes by raising her right hand, palm upward, probably signifies pity for the fate of the dead Asian hero before her. Such an interpretation of the figure is, of course, non-Homeric, but an examination of the *Iliad* reveals no very suitable identity for the standing female. Conceivably, she could personify the Hellespont, which is mentioned by Homer when the Greeks return with Achilles to their ships (*Iliad* 23.2), but no other representations of this theme are known, and the noun *Hellespontos* is masculine rather than feminine. Hecuba could have been shown in Asiatic costume, but, as alluded to above, she normally laments from the walls of Troy in wild agitation and wears a conventional Greek chiton in a state of disarray.[23] Also as mentioned above, any allusion to the walls of Troy is missing on this sigillata bowl, and all the other figures seem to point to the Greek camp as the locus for the event. The few indications of physical surroundings reinforce this suggestion. Behind the figure of "Asia/Hellespontos" is a tree, evocative of a rustic encampment. A garland, tied to the tree and to the upper border of the figured zone with cloths, circles the entire vase; this embellishment evokes decorations for the funeral of Patroclus. Clearly, Hecuba cannot be present, and the Oriental costume must designate a geographic personification.

On the opposite side of the bowl is a group of figures that seems not to be directly connected with the dragging of Hector. A well-muscled nude spearman has seized a man in a short, single-strapped tunic (*exomis*) by the hair and yanks him backwards to deliver the coup de grace with a spear or javelin (fig. 31.1e). At first glance, this seems to be combat on the battlefield and therefore, Achilles killing Hector, but many features are incompatible with the Homeric account of a frontal conflict between heavily armed warriors (*Iliad* 22.304ff.). Here, the loser is unarmed and does not defend himself, and the action seems like a slaughter of the defenseless. It appears probable that this is Achilles murdering one of the twelve Trojan prisoners that he sacrificed on the funeral pyre of Patroclus (*Iliad* 23.22–23, 175–176). Achilles is in a state of "heroic nudity" while his victim is in a more mundane *exomis*. More importantly, Achilles holds him by the hair of his head; in other ancient representations, the sacrifice of the prisoners frequently is conducted in just this way.[24] It must be admitted, however, that even this interpretation does not fit the Homeric text perfectly. Achilles vowed to cut the throats of the Trojans (ἀποδειροτομέω) (*Iliad* 23.22)—although the means of execution he eventually used was not specified; the captives were simply "slain with bronze" (χαλκῷ δηϊόων) (*Iliad* 23.176). In most ancient repre-

sentations, moreover, the action is performed with a sword.[25] In several Etruscan treatments of the theme, Achilles/Achle is clearly cutting the throat of his victims.[26] Nonetheless, for all the awkwardness of the spear, the interpretation of the scene as the execution of the Trojan captives seems the preferable one.

In spite of its unprecedented and difficult features, the bowl presents its Homeric tales with considerable thematic consistency and continuity. This is clearly the second dragging of Hektor connected with the mourning for Patroclus at the return from Troy. The agitated Thetis gives the scene an emotional depth—rivaling that of the first dragging of Hector past the walls of the besieged city as Hector's family laments from the battlements. The introduction of a second episode—the sacrifice of the captives—is also focused on another of the many ceremonial honors for Patroclus. What links the two, however, is not so much the theme of mourning for Patroclus or the common locus and relatively continuous time span, but Achilles' very brutal actions. In both cases they are acts of personal revenge for the killing of Patroclus.

These two events are rarely juxtaposed; the only other instance listed by Kossatz-Deissmann is the famous Patroklos Krater created by the Darius Painter about 340–330 B.C. (see fig. 15.11 this volume).[27] There the presentation of Achilles' two principal acts of revenge is quite different, and a common prototype or even a common tradition seems unlikely. In the Darius Painter's version, the action has an even greater unity; the focus is on Achilles sacrificing the prisoners. His stationary chariot—with Hector's body attached—is by the pyre, and its team, whose reins are held by the charioteer Automedon, is being watered. If Thetis is present, she is scarcely recognizable among the dignified standing women.

In spite of its grand and unusual theme, the workmanship in the Homeric bowl is strikingly careless. High spots—in particular the heads—are blurred and without detail; they give the impression of having been smoothed by fingers after the bowl was removed—presumably without complete success—from its mould. The egg-and-dart moulding above Thetis was truncated when the rim was attached. The low foot is not well articulated. The mould itself may not have been in good condition when this cast was taken. The egg-and-tongue moulding (particularly above the figure of the Myrmidon) is blurred, as are the three tiers of veined leaves below the figures. The mould, in fact, appears to have had a major crack that started in the egg-and-dart in front of the Myrmidon, sliced down through the hanging drapery, and ended in Hector's arm. A large chip had broken away from the edge of the crack between the arm and the drapery. The general character of the piece suggests a grand composition that has moved into a rather dispirited final phase of production. The amount of wear is surprising, since no other bowls or fragments of bowls drawn from this mould could be identified.

There are many clear reference points for attributing and dating the sigillata bowl, even though there is no trace of a stamped signature. As has been previously pointed out, the unusual figure in eastern Anatolian costume—here identified as Asia or the Hellespont—appears only in the work of L. Avillius Sura of Arezzo. A fragmentary mould in Tübingen ascribed to Sura presents the figure twice (fig. 31.2).[28] Such moulds for decorated terra sigillata were, as is well known, produced by making a stamp with a figure or decorative element and impressing it into the mould, from which a vase would be cast. All these females in Eastern costume must have been made from the same series of stamps. Facing the female in the mould in Tübingen is a nude warrior with his cloak on his shoulder and his sword in his left hand; the figure duplicates the "Myrmidon/Patroclus" watching the dragging of Hector on the bowl under discussion (fig. 31.1c). In the case of the Tübingen mould, the figures are interpreted as a Roman general facing defeated Armenia. It should be noted that in a cast made from the mould the figures would face in the same direction they do in the sigillata bowl. The same warrior appeared on a vase stamped with the signature of L. Avillius Sura and his workman Hilario in Berlin (fig. 31.3).[29] In the case of the Berlin vase, the warrior faces a trophy and a different, less exotically dressed female personification, and the composition is interpreted as a Roman general and defeated Germany. In all probability, the damaged figure personifying another defeated region on the other side of the Berlin vase also represented Armenia in eastern Anatolian costume.[30]

The triumphal iconography in these works of L. Avillius Sura makes it possible to give a fairly precise date

FIGURE 31.3. Lost Arretine terra sigillata vase signed by L. Avillius Sura and Hilario: a Roman general and Germany flanking a trophy (Germany is out of sight at the right). Formerly Staatliche Museen Berlin. (Photo: Museum.)

for his activity. A putative Augustan monument celebrating the conquest of Artageira in Armenia in A.D. 3 and the successful campaign in Germany of M. Vinicius starting in A.D. 1 has been advanced by W. Kolbe and C. Watzinger as the model for these sigillata compositions. In that case, the mould in Tübingen and the vase in Berlin would date shortly after A.D. 3.[31] The use of the same figures on the Homeric bowl under discussion here must be essentially contemporary or slightly later—probably around A.D. 5–10.

The workshop of L. Avillius Sura is not, however, the only establishment at Arezzo that must be taken into consideration for an attribution of this Homeric bowl. The figure of Achilles sacrificing the Trojan prisoner turns up on vases produced by other workshops. A figure apparently made from the same stamp—or a variation on the same stamp—appears in isolation among acanthus vines on a footed bowl signed by L. Titius Thyrsus in the Metropolitan Museum of Art, New York

FIGURE 31.4a. A heroic youth (Theseus?) grappling with vines.

FIGURE 31.4b. Springing of vines.

FIGURES 31.4a, b. Arretine terra sigillata bowl signed by L. Titius Thyrsus. Metropolitan Museum of Art, New York. Rogers Fund, 1919. 19.192.41. (Photo: Museum.)

(fig. 31.4a).[32] The variations consist in removing his spear and his Trojan victim and placing vines in his hands instead. Another example of the same composition has appeared on a less well-preserved bowl recently at Sotheby's in New York (figs. 31.5a, c).[33] This bowl presumably was also produced by L. Titius Thyrsus. The energetic male figure returns with spear (and hence is identical to the Achilles on the present bowl) on two fragments of vases in Arezzo attributed to C. Cispius (figs. 31.6a, b).[34] The stamps were not physically the same, since the point of the spear is at slightly different distances away from Achilles' neck in each, but it is clear that all the stamps used to produce this figure were part of a very closely related group. A more modest decorative element in the Homeric bowl shows the same affiliations; the pleated, swallow-tailed drapery used to fasten the garland that runs behind the figures also turns up in the work of Cispius and Thyrsus, as on the back of the two bowls in New York (figs. 31.4b, 31.5b).[35] Sura omits the spherical weights used in the other two factories at the corners of the drapery, but this detail may have been added with a separate tool. The Sotheby's bowl moves even a step or two closer to the Homeric bowl. The figure of the energetic youth is also worn, much as the Achilles is. In addition, the moulding at the top of the frieze has become an ovolo underlined by a garland of wedgelike leaves, just as on the Homeric bowl (figs. 31.1a–e). The motif is extremely common in the Perennius workshop, but its appearance in this context strengthens the link between Sura and Thyrsus.

Arturo Stenico has discussed the relationships between the "javelin thrower" of C. Cispius and the "vine climber" of L. Titius Thyrsus and has noted many other overlappings or crossovers in the stamps they use. He has observed a similarly close relationship between the work of C. Cispius and L. Avillius Sura.[36] He concludes that several minor factories—including those of Thyrsus and Sura—worked in proximity to that of Cispius, who seems to have been by far the most productive in the realm of decorated ware. Thyrsus and Sura placed their names on many plain vases but on only one decorated piece each; their decorated production, therefore, may well have been tentative and soon-unsuccessful ventures, for which they borrowed stamps and perhaps workmen from Cispius and, it would now appear, from each other.[37]

FIGURE 31.5a, c. A heroic youth (Theseus?) grappling with vines.

FIGURE 31.5b. Springing of vines.

In the case of the Homeric vase under discussion here, it seems likely that the bowl was produced in the factory of L. Avillius Sura. The figures of the standing warrior and the woman in Anatolian costume are very distinctive and otherwise appear only in his work. The stamps that are held in common with other factories—the javelin thrower, the swallow-tailed drapery, and the ovolo moulding—can be explained as manifestations of the cooperation between Sura, Cispius, and Thyrsus.

It is difficult to establish a relative chronology for an Arretine pottery workshop that had a small oeuvre and lacked signatures of its multiple workmen. In the case of the factory of L. Avillius Sura, however, it seems possible to determine a sequence without this kind of evidence. It is reasonable to assume that the triumphal iconography preceded the Homeric since the stamps used in both categories of composition make more sense in the former than they do in the latter. The standing nude warrior and the Armenia figure seem well suited to face one another in tight, centralized, heraldic compositions as they do in the mould in Tübingen (fig. 31.2) and the vase in Berlin signed by Sura (fig. 31.3). The Armenian costume suits the meaning of the triumphal scene well,

FIGURE 31.5a – c. Arretine terra sigillata vase. Sotheby's, New York, June 1991. Photos © 1991 Sotheby's, Inc.

since Armenia was frequently at war with Rome in Late Republican and Augustan times. The nude warrior, who is a classicized version of Hellenistic figures like the portrait statue of Ofellius Ferus on Delos (late second century B.C.),[38] was a type often used for Roman honorary portrait statues;[39] the function that the warrior has on the mould in Tübingen and the vase in Berlin—that of honoring a victorious Roman general—is quite comparable. These same figures fit into the Homeric composition less well. A personification wearing the costume of Armenia or Commagene has to be conceptually distorted to relate it to the Trojan setting. The standing Myrmidon does not reflect the Homeric text for the second dragging of Hector, where, as noted above, the Myrmidons lament over Patroclus, and where they still wear their armor (*Iliad* 23.6–16). These figures, then, were transposed ready-made from the triumphal scenes to fill out the Homeric cast of characters.

It seems likely that at least one stamp used by Sura must have originated in the Cispius factory. The swallow-tailed drapery attached to the garland in the background suited Sura's composition so badly that only a part of it could be fitted in above the sacrificed Trojan; only the tips of the drapery were impressed (fig. 31.1e). The stamp makes much more sense in the works of Cispius—and for that matter, of L. Titius Thyrsus (figs. 31.4b, 31.5b)—where not only does it have the spherical weights pulling down the corners but it also falls from a substantial fastening and is a focal part of a composition with massive garlands, loops of drapery, or heavy vines.[40]

The situation is less clear in the case of the javelin-thrower/Achilles. The origin of this figure certainly cannot be found in the bowls in New York by Thyrsus (figs. 31.4a, 31.5a, c), where the athletic youth employs his energies to clamber through vines; the composition is clearly a decorative derivative in spite of the freshness and clarity of the stamp used. The tiny fragments with javelin-throwers by C. Cispius are too incomplete to permit judgement (figs. 31.6a, b); it is impossible to say to what kind of scene they belonged. They could have been part of an Amazonomachy or even a full Homeric sacrifice of captives, but nothing else in the work of Cispius suggests that he dealt with such themes. Ambitious, multifigured narrative compositions seem to be rare in his work, and the example of Thyrsus shows that such

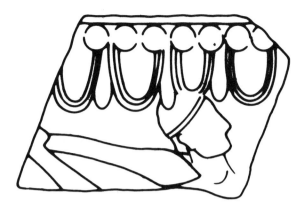

FIGURE 31.6a. Heroic spearman, probably Achilles, sacrificing a Trojan prisoner.

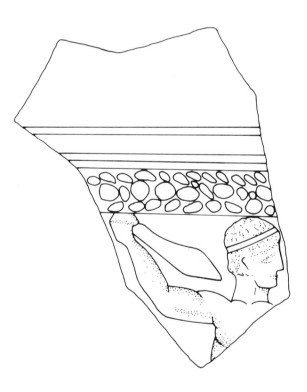

FIGURE 31.6a, b. Fragments of Arretine terra sigillata. Museo Archeologico, Arezzo. (Drawings by Yvonne Markowitz after A. Stenico, "Cispius" [see note 34].)

vigorous figures could be used as isolated vignettes.[41] Cispius could have employed the figure as a hunter confronting a lion; an overhand blow delivered from this stance is used by one of the hunters in the lion hunt mosaic from Pella[42] and by panther and stag hunters on the Alexander sarcophagus.[43] In spite of these parallels, however, no further evidence can be found in Cispius' work (or that of other Arretine potters) to support this hypothesis either.

The youths clambering through vines on the Metropolitan Museum and Sotheby's bowls (figs. 31.4 and 31.6), however, suggest another origin for the figure. Theseus is often shown holding onto a branch in his struggle with the bandit Sinis.[44] A cup by Aison in Madrid is particularly interesting in this context (fig. 31.7);[45] Theseus' pose is virtually identical to our athletic vine-climber/Achilles. The comparison goes farther with the sacrifice of the Trojan prisoner; Sinis and the prisoner are down on one knee and are being seized by the hair. Achilles' hand, moreover, passes across a branch of the tree behind him. The comparison with the Attic cup of around 410 B.C. strongly suggests that this scene of Achilles sacrificing a prisoner originated as Theseus punishing Sinis. The hero originally held onto the tree branch above and behind him. A spear was put into his hand to turn him into an Achilles. The victim's origin as Sinis explains his very unusual gesture of reaching away from his killer with his right hand; in countless scenes of combat, a loser reaches toward his assailant to ward him off, but Sinis reaches out for a tree to resist Theseus' pull. The tree is, of course, omitted in this changed context. The large size of this kneeling figure also agrees with an origin as Sinis, son of Poseidon famous for his strength. The origin of the vigorous youth as Theseus holding onto the fig tree helps to explain the decorative use of the figure clambering through the vines on the Sotheby's and Metropolitan cups. Thus all currently known applications of the figure are apparently derived from an Arretine representation of Theseus and Sinis, of which no fragments survive.

While many elements of the bowl's decoration clearly were created with stamps previously used, often with different meanings, in an allied group of Arretine workshops, one major group of figures—Thetis and the dragging the body of Hector—cannot be traced elsewhere in Arretine pottery. These figures may have made

FIGURE 31.7. Kylix by Aison with the deeds of Theseus, Madrid, Museo Arqueológico Nacional. (Drawing from *AntDenk* 2 [1908] pl. 1.)

their only Arretine appearance in this Homeric composition. The worn state of the figures tends to suggest that they too are reused or adapted, but it is hard to imagine that a figure like that of Hector (fig. 31.1b) could be conceived as anything other than what he is. Thetis (fig. 31.1b), on the other hand, could have been adapted from a figure of a frenzied maenad; maenads with outspread arms and with head turned down and back can be traced from the beginning of the fourth century onward, as on the fragmentary bronze krater in Berlin.[46] The Berlin maenad in this pose seems to have been virtually repeated on a fragmentary late Hellenistic silver pyxis in Athens.[47] A somewhat listless and more frontal version of the pose can be found in moulds from the Arretine factory of Rasinius.[48] A maenad on a Campana plaque in the British Museum[49] and another on a Claudian candelabrum base in Cassino[50] again show the pose, and their arms are spread to form a continuous straight line, as in Thetis on the Homeric bowl. In spite of these parallels, however, Thetis appears to represent a thorough reworking of preexisting conceptions, rather than a minor variation. A fundamental question thus remains unanswered; it cannot so far be determined when and by whom the "dragging group" on this bowl was conceived.

In assessing this Arretine bowl, it is worth stressing how unusual the iconography is in Roman terms. Kossatz-Deissmann has pointed out that the dragging of Hector is almost invariably situated in front of the walls of Troy in the visual arts of the Imperial period.[51] Placing the dragging of Hector in the Greek camp on the arrival from Troy is an original choice. The sacrifice of the Trojan prisoners seems to be unknown in the art of the Imperial period. The figure of Thetis inciting the Myrmidons to mourn is unusual by any standard, and these innovations mark a step in a Homeric direction. These secondary incidents in the Homeric *Iliad* are unlikely to have survived in any Latin summary or abridged translation; the mourning Thetis and the sacrifice of the Trojan captives are entirely omitted in the Neronian *Ilias latina*.[52] For all its deviations from the Homeric text, the bowl apparently reflects a fresh infusion of Homeric influence into the visual tradition.

It would be normal to assume that a cultivated patron commissioned a work incorporating such a generally neglected textual detail and that this work was executed in the realm of luxury crafts like marble sculpture, painting, or silverware. From there, the theme would have passed on to popular arts like terra sigillata. Indeed several cases have been identified where complex mythological designs on silverware were copied in Arretine terra sigillata.[53] Plaster casts of metalwork may have served as intermediate models.[54] Arretine pottery was not cast directly either from plaster casts or from silverware, but most such clay copies of metalwork follow their models quite closely. It has, however, become clear that this process did not take place in any simple or direct way in the case of this Arretine bowl. Four of its six surviving figures were created by reusing stamps available in the Arretine workshops of L. Avillius Sura and his associates Thyrsus and Cispius. These stamps, moreover, had previously been used to represent altogether different subjects. The Homeric bowl is a makeshift rendering of its grand theme, and its details were in large part devised within the potter's workshop.

There is, nonetheless, a specific reason to think that the overall composition of this Arretine bowl was inspired to some degree a work in another medium—presumably a silver vessel. A Megarian bowl in Mann-

FIGURE 31.8. "Megarian" bowl with the dragging of Hector. Reiss-Museum, Mannheim, inv. no. Cg 349. (Drawing by H. Gropengiesser.)

heim (fig. 31.8) has a number of striking compositional similarities with it.[55] The clay bowl, which probably is Thessalian of the second century B.C., shows the first dragging of Hector on one side and the duel of Hector and Achilles on the other. Both scenes take place before the walls of Troy, whose fortifications, surmounted by the grief-striken Hecuba, are shown above the lifeless body of Hector. In the duel, the two combatants are reinforced by Athena, who urges on Achilles, and by Athena in the guise of Deïphobos, who urges on Hector. In spite of the slightly different theme (the first rather than the second dragging of Hector), it is remarkable that, as far as can be determined, both the Megarian and the Arretine bowls had the same number and sexes of figures occuring in the same sequence. Hecuba above Hector is replaced by Thetis, and the dueling Hector and Achilles are replaced by Achilles sacrificing a captive. The figures flanking the duel have redirected their attention to the scene of dragging; Deïphobos becomes a Myrmidon, and Athena is replaced by Asia. Since the chariot of Achilles is largely missing on the Arretine bowl, it is impossible to verify whether Achilles was accompanied by Automedon, as on the piece in Mann-

FIGURE 31.9. Denarius of Mn. Cordius Rufus, 46 B.C.: obverse, crested Corinthian helmet surmounted by owl. Numismatic Fine Arts, *Auction Catalogue* 27 (Los Angeles and New York, 4–5 December 1991) no. 565. (Photography courtesy of Numismatic Fine Arts, Inc.)

heim, but given the other parallels, this seems likely. Hildegund Gropengiesser has conjectured that the Mannheim bowl was based on a silver bowl created in Macedonia in the second quarter of the third century B.C.[56] Since the composition of the Arretine bowl is so similar, it seems likely that it is somehow derived from the same source. The change of theme from the first to the second dragging of Hector and the reorientation of some of the figures may be due to a thorough Roman reworking of the composition, but it is also possible (and even probable) that the two draggings of Hector were conceived together as a pendants by the same early Hellenistic Greek silversmith.

It is highly probable for another reason that L. Avillius Sura was inspired by a piece of silverware rather than another ceramic work. Not only is the dragging of Hector apparently otherwise unknown in Arretine pottery, but it is also extremely rare in Hellenistic ceramics; in addition to the bowl in Mannheim, only one other ceramic treatment of the dragging is known: a Megarian bowl in Columbia, Missouri, in which Achilles' abuse of the body of Hector on one side is balanced only by an overturned chariot on the other.[57] In the absence of a continuous ceramic tradition, it is very probable that a silver vessel exercised its influence on the art of Augustan Italy.

While it thus seems clear that the Arretine bowl was inspired by a Hellenistic silver bowl, or a Roman copy or cast thereof, the fact remains that the Arretine translation has been made in terms of its own medium; as pointed out above, many of the stamps used to produce the bowl (Asia, Myrmidon/Patroclus, Achilles, the sacrificed Trojan, and the drapery) were borrowed from

other iconographic contexts. It seems virtually certain that the poses of the corresponding figures in the prototype would have been different. This seems most likely in the sacrifice of the captive and the standing Myrmidon. In the case of the personification of Asia, the silver prototype may have had an entirely different figure, perhaps Athena.

The dragging group cannot be traced back to earlier Arretine practice, and it might in theory have a better chance of reflecting the silver vessel that was the inspiration for the Arretine composition. One detail, however, strongly suggests that the dragging group was reworked in Roman terms. The helmet held by Thetis is a composite and stylized creation. It is essentially a conflation of the Attic and the Corinthian types. The spiral that curls forward from the back of the skull is Attic, as is the oblong neck guard. The cheek and nose guards, which have been elongated to form a horizontal beak projecting at a right angle from the neck guard, are those of the Corinthian. This conflation surely did not occur in early Hellenistic times and is hard to parallel in every detail at any time. It may be of chronological significance, however, that the silhouette of the helmet held by Thetis resembles that of a Corinthian helmet on a coin minted at Rome by Mn. Cordius Rufus, triumvir in 46 B.C. (fig. 31.9).[58] On the basis of this analogy, it seems likely that the immediate model for L. Avillius Sura's Arretine bowl was a piece of silverware dating from the time of Julius Caesar. This putative Republican creation would have been based on an (equally hypothetical) Hellenistic work.

Convenience, familiarity, and economy may have been the main reasons why L. Avillius Sura reused stamps current in his and associated workshops at Arretium. These borrowings, however, may also have added some distinct overtones of meaning for an audience in Augustan Italy. The figure of Asia, quite uncalled-for by the Homeric text, seems the most evident contemporary intrusion. Her eastern Anatolian costume evokes the enemies overcome by Rome in recent warfare and diplomacy in Armenia or, for that matter, Parthia. The recovery of the weapons of Patroclus—displayed so prominently by Thetis—could allude to the standards of Crassus recovered from the Parthians by Augustus and commemorated by a triumphal arch in 19 B.C.[59] Greek victory and revenge over a Trojan enemy can thus be seen as an emblem of Roman victory over a contemporary Asiatic enemy.

When seen in terms of contemporary political allegory, the message of Sura's bowl may seem unduly harsh; it is more in keeping with the early phase of Augustus' career than with the ever-more benevolent tone of imagery later in his reign.[60] The theme of revenge may, however, have been brought into prominence once again by the dedication, in 2 B.C.,[61] of the temple of Mars Ultor ("the avenger"), where the Parthian standards were kept, only a few years before the vase itself was moulded. Gaius Caesar's siege of Artageira in Armenia in A.D. 3 would have been an even more vivid stimulus for vengefulness. As has been pointed out above, this event had apparently been the occasion for the workshop of L. Avillius Sura to create the images of Armenia and the Roman general (fig. 31.2).[62] In the course of the siege, Gaius was wounded during negotiations, and in the following year he died from complications of his wounds.[63] The treachery of Addon, the perpetrator of the attack on Augustus' heir-apparent, undoubtedly explains Artageira's harsh fate; the city was sacked, and its walls were destroyed.[64] The composition on this vase seems to reflect the impact of the bitter victory on contemporary attitudes in distant Italy.

The reused stamp of the Oriental female (Armenia) then seems clearly intended to provide a contemporary resonance. By adding her, the siege of Troy is turned into a metaphor for that of Artageira. At any time after the imperial heir's death, the standing warrior could have been read as a statue of Patroclus in the Trojan context and a statue of Gaius Caesar in the contemporary setting. These reused stamps simultaneously reflect both the everyday routine of the Sura workshop and the interests of its public. In general, literary aspiration, practical expediency, and political awareness seem responsible for the alternately lax and close relationships to the Homeric text evoked by the bowl.

NOTES

1. T 587.1.1987: from an American private collection.
2. What remains is composed from nine connecting fragments. The bowl has a low foot and belongs to Dragendorff-

Watzinger type V: H. Dragendorff and C. Watzinger, *Arretinische Reliefkeramik* (Reutlingen 1948) 24, fig. 2.

3. The bowl has been partially published: J. Herrmann in A. Kozloff and D. Mitten, eds., *The Gods Delight: The Human Figure in Classical Bronze* (Cleveland 1988) 290, fig. 51c. The attribution and date will be discussed further infra.

4. A. Kossatz-Deissmann, *LIMC* I, "Achilleus," pp. 139–147, nos. 584–640, pls. 116–121.

5. A Corinthian helmet with this ram's horn spiral appears in images of Mars on Roman parade armor from Straubing in Raetia: J. Garbsch, *Römische Paraderüstungen. Münchener Beiträge zur Vor- und Frühgeschichte* 30 (1978) B 16, pl. 4, 2; G. Bauchhenss, *LIMC* II, "Ares/Mars," no. 478h, pl. 422.

6. Kossatz-Deissmann (supra. n. 4) pp. 145–147, especially nos. 578, 616, 617, 632, 639, pls. 116, 118, 121.

7. O. Palagia, *LIMC* IV, "Hellas," 4: a fragment of a vase by the Darius Painter, Copenhagen, Nat. Mus. 13320, where Hellas wears a transparent short-sleeved chiton and an elaborate necklace.

8. Kossatz-Deissmann (supra n. 4) nos. 632, 637, 639, pl. 121.

9. On Briseis as the wife of Achilles, see *Iliad* 9.336 (with note in Loeb edition) and note to 19.297–298.

10. A. Kossatz-Deissmann, *LIMC* III, "Briseis," pp. 157–158.

11. Kossatz-Deissmann (supra n. 10) nos. 18–23, pl. 136; Kossatz-Deissmann (supra n. 4) nos. 485–486a, pl. 108.

12. The dragging is not specifically described on arrival at the camp at the beginning of Book 23 of the *Iliad*, but the implication is unmistakable: Kossatz-Deissmann (supra n. 4) p. 138.

13. Museo Nazionale, Naples H 3228 (82921); Kossatz-Deissmann, (supra. n. 4) no. 604; Kossatz-Deissmann (supra n. 10) no. 19, pl. 136.

14. J. Herrmann (supra n. 3) 288–290, figs. 51 b-c. For an identical figure on an Arretine bowl presented in this perspective, see Dragendorff and Watzinger (supra n. 2) 160–161, pl. 33, no. 506.

15. On the Commagenian reliefs, see E. Akurgal, *Ancient Civilizations and Ruins of Turkey* (Istanbul 1970), pls. 109–110; M. Colledge, *Parthian Art* (Ithaca, N.Y. 1978) 99, pl. 32b; J. M. C. Toynbee, *Roman Historical Portraits* (Ithaca, N.Y. 1978) 134–135, illus. 261–262; E. Akurgal, *Griechische und römische Kunst in der Türkei* (Munich 1987) 118, pl. 192; J. Wagner, *Kommagene, Heimat der Götter* (Dortmund 1987) 76, 89, 95, 149, 167, 169–170, 173–174; R. R. R. Smith, *Hellenistic Royal Portraits* (Oxford 1988) 104, pl. 59.1–2.

16. Dragendorff and Watzinger (supra n. 2) 160–161, pl. 33, no. 506; J. Balty, *LIMC* II, "Armenia," pp. 610–613,

pl. 439; Smith (supra n. 16) 104, 120–121; J. Herrmann (supra n. 3) 288–290, figs. 51 b-c.

17. J. Herrmann (supra n. 3) cat. nos. 51–52. The relationship between these figures and eastern Anatolia was first discussed by A. H. Smith, "A Bronze Figure of a Youth in Oriental Costume," *JHS* 37 (1917) 136–139, figs. 1–2, pl. 2.

18. H. Ingholt, "The Prima Porta Statue of Augustus, 2," *Archaeology* 22 (1969) 315 (illus.).

19. Balty (supra n. 16) pp. 610–613, pl. 439.

20. Dragendorff and Watzinger (supra n. 2) 160–161, pl. 33, no. 506; Ingholt (supra n. 18) 316; Balty (supra n. 16) no. 8, pl. 439. Two more examples of the figure appear on fragments in Arezzo: A. Stenico, "Nuovi frammenti di L. Avillius Sura nel Museo Archeologico di Arezzo," *BullCom* 74 (1951–1952) 21–24, figs. 2–4.

21. F. Coarelli, "Architettura e arti figurative in Roma: 150–50 a.C.," in P. Zanker, *Hellenismus in Mittelitalien: Kolloquium in Göttingen vom 5. bis 9. Juni 1974* (Göttingen 1976) 28, fig. 25.

22. Balty, *LIMC* II, "Asia I, Asia II," pl. 387.

23. Kossatz-Deissmann (supra n. 4) nos. 586, 606, 608, 616–617, 628, 632, 637–639, pls. 116, 118, 121; A.-F. Laurens, *LIMC* IV, "Hekabe," nos. 23–28.

24. Kossatz-Deissmann (supra n. 4) nos. 487–488, pl. 108; G. Camporeale, *LIMC* I, "Achle," nos. 85, 90 a-b, pls. 150–151.

25. Kossatz-Deissmann (supra n. 4) no. 487 (vase by the Darius Painter).

26. Camporeale (supra n. 24) nos. 85, 90, pp. 205–206, 211.

27. Naples, Mus. Naz. H 3254; *FR* 2, pl. 89; A. Rocco, "Il 'pittore del vaso dei persiani,'" *ArchCl* 5 (1953) 176–180, pls. 84–86; Kossatz-Deissmann (supra n. 4) nos. 487, 603, pls. 108, 603 (with further bibliography); Kossatz-Deissmann (supra n. 10) no. 20, pl. 136.

28. Dragendorff and Watzinger (supra n. 2) 160–161, pl. 33, no. 506; Ingholt (supra n. 18) 316; Balty (supra n. 16) no. 9, pl. 439. Two fragments of bowls in Arezzo repeat the composition: Stenico (supra n. 20).

29. Formerly Antiquarium, Berlin, vas. inv. no. 4772: A. Oxé, *Arretinische Reliefgefässe vom Rhein* (Frankfurt 1933) 97–98, pl. 52, no. 220; Dragendorff and Watzinger (supra n. 2) 160; A. Oxé and H. Comfort, *Corpvs vasorvm arretinorvm. A Catalogue of the Signatures, Shapes and Chronology of Italian Sigillata* (Bonn 1968) 106–107, no. 265a. The vase was destroyed in World War II (letter from Ursula Kästner).

30. Dragendorff and Watzinger (supra n. 2) 160.

31. W. Kolbe, "Ein Doppelerfolg des Augustus in Kampf gegen Ost und Nord," *Germania* 23 (1939) 104–110; Dragendorff and Watzinger (supra n. 2) 161. Stenico questions the validity of seeing specific historical references in this or any Arretine vase: Stenico (supra n. 20).

32. C. Alexander, *CVA*, U.S.A. 9: *Metropolitan Museum of Art, New York*, fasc. 1: *Arretine Relief Ware* (Cambridge, Mass. 1943), pl. 33, acc. no. 19.192.41.

33. Sotheby's, *Antiquities and Islamic Art*, New York, June 18, 1991 (entry by Richard Keresey) no. 304: height 19.7 cm. The figure of the youth is repeated twice.

34. A. Stenico, "Sulla produzione di vasi con rilievi di C. Cispius," *Athenaeum* 33 (1955) no. 56–57, 195–196, 212, pl. 5.

35. Dragendorff and Watzinger (supra n. 2) 169, suppl. pl. 11, figs. 96, 98; Alexander (supra n. 33) pl. 33; Stenico (supra n. 34) nos. 2, 9, 13, 31, pls. 1–3.

36. Stenico (supra n. 34) 177–178, 181, 188 notes 2–3, 195–196, 201, 203, 211–212, 215–216.

37. Stenico (supra n. 34) 202–206, 216. For signatures of these factories, see also Oxé and Comfort (supra n. 29) 106–107, 143–146, 479–483.

38. M. Bieber, *The Sculpture of the Hellenistic Age* (New York 1961) 172, fig. 727.

39. C. Maderna, *Iuppiter, Diomedes und Merkur als Vorbilder für römische Bildnisstatuen* (Heidelberg 1988) Type UD, 78–80, 215–221, pls. 24–25. The earliest surviving statue of this type, which Maderna considers a variation on the Diomedes Cumae-Munich, dates from Flavian times.

40. Stenico (supra n. 34) nos. 2, 9, pls. 1–2.

41. Stenico conjectures that the javelin-throwers were set amidst foliate decoration: Stenico (supra n. 34) 212.

42. M. Robertson, *Greek Painting* (Geneva 1959) 166, 169–170; M. B. Hatzopoulos and L. D. Loukopoulos, eds., *Philip of Macedon* (Athens 1980) 156–157, fig. 83; C. Vermeule, in J. Herrmann, ed., *The Search for Alexander, Supplement II* (Boston 1981) no. 15; J. J. Pollitt, *Art in the Hellenistic Age* (New York 1986) fig. 34.

43. Pollitt (supra n. 42) figs. 32–33; B. S. Ridgway, *Hellenistic Sculpture I: The Styles of ca. 331–200 B.C.* (Madison 1990) pls. 10, 12.

44. K. Schefold and F. Jung, *Die Urkönige, Perseus, Bellerophon, Herakles und Theseus in der klassischen und hellenistischen Kunst* (Munich 1988) 236–237, 244, 250, figs. 287, 297, 301; M. Robertson, *The Art of Vase-painting in Classical Athens* (Cambridge 1992) 220, fig. 228.

45. Inv. 11265: *AntDenk* 2 (1908) 1, pl. 1; G. Leroux, *Vases grecs et italo-grecs du Musée Archéologique de Madrid* (Bordeaux and Paris 1912) 112, pl. 28, no. 196; *FR* 3, p. 48, fig. 21; E. Pfuhl, *Malerei und Zeichnung der Griechen* 2 (Mu-

nich 1923) 694, fig. 576; *ARV²* 1174; J. Boardman, *Athenian Red Figure Vases: The Classical Period* (London 1989) 147, fig. 292.4.

46. W. Züchner, *Der Berliner Mänadenkrater* (*BWPr* 98, 1938) 4, 12–14, fig. 1, pl. 4; Staatliche Museen Preussischer Kulturbesitz, *Antikenmuseum Berlin: Die ausgestellten Werke* (Berlin 1988) 136–137.

47. F. Matz, *Ein römisches Meisterwerk. Der Jahreszeiten-sarkophag Badminton-New York*, *JdI-EH* 19 (1958) 104–111, pl. 18b; K. Rhomiopoulou in *Treasures of Ancient Macedonia* (exhibition catalogue, Thessaloniki, n. d. [1978]) 35, no. 20, pl. 2.

48. A. Stenico, *La ceramica arretina*, I, *Rasinius* I (Varese-Milan 1960) 25, 57, nos. 7–8, stamp type 42.

49. G. M. A. Richter, "Was Roman Art of the First Centuries B.C. and A.D. Classicizing?" *JRS* 48 (1958) 14, pl. v, 17.

50. G. Carettoni, "Cassino—Esplorazione del teatro," *NSc* 1939, 116, fig. 11; H. -U. Cain, *Römische Marmorkandelaber* (Mainz am Rhein 1985) maenad type 5d, 129, 152–153, cat. no. 12, Beilage 12.

51. Kossatz-Deissmann (supra n. 4) 145–147.

52. On the date of the *Ilias latina*, see M. Scaffai, "Aspetti e problemi dell'Ilias latina'," *ANRW* 2.32.3 (1985) 1926–1941. For the small fragments of earlier Latin Iliads, see the listing of authors in Vollmer, *RE* 9 (1916) "Ilias latina," col. 1057.

53. E. Ettlinger, "Arretina und augusteisches Silber," *Gestalt und Geschichte. Festschrift Karl Schefold*, AntK-BH 4 (1967) 116–119.

54. G. Richter, "Ancient Plaster Casts of Greek Metalwork," *AJA* 62 (1958) 369ff.

55. H. Gropengiesser, "Ein Achilleus-Becher in Mannheim," in H. Cahn and E. Simon, eds., *Tainia. Festschrift Roland Hampe* (Mainz am Rhein 1980) 307–332, pls. 63–64.

56. Ibid., 331.

57. 61.26: G. Merker, "A New Homeric Illustration," *Muse* 1 (1967) 11–18; F. Brommer, *Vasenlisten zur griechischen Heldensage*, 3rd ed. (Marburg 1973) 346; D. Kemp-Lindemann, *Darstellungen des Achilleus in griechischer und römischer Kunst* (Bern and Frankfurt am Main 1975) 176; B. Wescoat, *Poets and Heroes: Scenes of the Trojan War* (Atlanta 1978) 44–45, no. 10; J. Biers in O. Overby, ed., *Illustrated Museum Handbook: A Guide to the Collections in the Museum of Art and Archaeology, University of Missouri-Columbia* (Columbia and London 1982) 27, no. 65; Gropengiesser (supra n. 55) 308, 314, figs. 3–4 (references provided by Dr. Jane C. Biers).

58. M. Crawford, *Roman Republican Coinage* (Cambridge 1974) 473, pl. 54, no. 463/2.

59. Nash 92.

60. See Paul Zanker's treatment of the Augustus/Neptune intaglio in Boston: P. Zanker, *The Power of Images in the Age of Augustus*, trans. A. Shapiro (Ann Arbor 1988) 97, fig. 82.

61. Ibid., 194.

62. Supra n. 31.

63. Dio Cassius 55.6–8; Velleius Paterculus 2.102.2–3.

64. Strabo 11.14.6.

NOTES ON CONTRIBUTORS

J. K. ANDERSON is professor emeritus of classical archaeology at the University of California, Berkeley. He took part in the excavations of the British School of Archaeology at Old Smyrna and Chios in 1950–1952 and in the Corinth excavations of the American School of Classical Studies at Athens in 1964. From 1952 to 1957 he was lecturer in classics at Otago in New Zealand and the rest of his career was at Berkeley. His chief interest is in applying the archaeological evidence to the interpretation of ancient texts and his latest book is *Hunting in the Ancient World* (1985), written when he was Visiting Fellow at the British School at Athens in 1982.

DAVID ASTON has worked on numerous excavations in Greece and Egypt and has contributed to various Egyptological journals. His research concerns primarily the Egyptian Third Intermediate Period and Egyptian pottery from the New Kingdom to the Ptolemaic Period. He is currently employed by the Austrian Archaeological Institute in Cairo, undertaking research into the pottery found at Tell el Dab'a.

J. L. BENSON is professor emeritus of ancient art at the University of Massachusetts at Amherst. He is the author of *Die Geschichte der korinthinischen Vases* (1953), *Horse, Bird and Man: The Origins of Greek Painting* (1970), *Corinth XIV:3.*

The Potters' Quarter. The Pottery (1984), and *Earlier Corinthian Workshops* (1989).

ANN L. T. BERGREN received her doctorate in classics from Harvard University and specializes in early Greek poetry. She is professor of classics at the University of California at Los Angeles and teaches architectural theory at the Southern California Institute of Architecture.

ANN BLAIR BROWNLEE is a graduate of Harvard University and currently assistant professor of ancient art at Rutgers University. She has excavated in Greece and Cyprus, and is a specialist in Attic vase painting; her dissertation on Attic black-figured dinoi is in preparation for the University of Michigan Press. She is finishing a study of the Attic black-figured pottery from the American excavations at Corinth.

DIANA BUITRON-OLIVER is a graduate of Smith College and the Institute of Fine Arts, New York University, and a specialist in Greek vase painting and Cypriot archaeology. She is the author of *Douris: A Master-Painter of Athenian Red-Figure Vases* (1995). A museum curator and consultant, she organized and edited *The Human Figure in Early Greek Art* (1988), *New Perspectives in Early Greek Art* (1991), and *The*

Greek Miracle: Classical Sculpture from the Dawn of Democracy (1992); she is also professorial lecturer at Georgetown University.

WALTER BURKERT is professor of classics at the University of Zürich and a specialist in ancient Greek religion and literature. He is the author of *Lore and Science in Ancient Pythagoreanism* (1972). In the United States he has delivered the Sather lectures at Berkeley (published as *Structure and History in Greek Mythology and Ritual* in 1979) and the Jackson lectures at Harvard (published as *Ancient Mystery Cults* in 1987), and has had several works translated and published here, including *Greek Religion* (1985) and *The Orientalizing Revolution* (1992).

JANE B. CARTER is a graduate of Harvard University and associate professor of classical studies at Tulane University. She has excavated at Knidos, Corinth, Kavousi, and Koukounaries (Paros) and is currently field director of the MARWP project at Pylos. Her dissertation was published as *Greek Ivory-Carving in the Orientalizing and Archaic Periods* (1985) and her forthcoming book is *The Beginning of Greek Sculpture*; her research involves Sparta, Crete, and the connections between Greece and the Near East.

HECTOR CATLING was director of the British School at Athens for eighteen years, after twelve years on the staff of the Ashmolean Museum, and five as a temporary officer in the Department of Antiquities, Cyprus. He has excavated in Cyprus and Greece, most recently at Knossos and Sparta, and was one of the first scholars to apply archaeometric analysis to Aegean pottery. He is the author of *Cypriot Bronzework in the Mycenaean World* (1964), edited "Archaeology in Greece" for *Archaeological Reports* from 1971 to 1989, and has contributed to the final publications of British School excavations at Lefkandi and Knossos, and of the American School excavations at Nichoria. He is currently preparing the results of his excavations at the Menelaion, Sparta, for publication.

ADA COHEN graduated from Brandeis University and Harvard University, with a dissertation on Hellenistic painting and mosaics; she was a Hirsch Fellow at the American School of Classical Studies at Athens. Currently she is assistant professor of art history at Dartmouth College and held a Getty Post-Doctoral Fellowship to complete a monograph on the Alexander Mosaic from Pompeii.

MARY B. COMSTOCK has been at the Museum of Fine Arts, Boston, since 1960, and is associate curator and keeper of coins in the Department of Classical Art. She has collaborated on a number of museum publications, including *Sculpture in Stone* (1976), *Greek, Etruscan and Roman Bronzes*, and, most recently, *Vase-Painting in Italy: Red-Figure and Related Works in the Museum of Fine Arts, Boston* (1993).

HANS GÜTERBOCK is professor emeritus of Hittitology at the Oriental Institute of the University of Chicago and a co-editor of the Chicago Hittite Dictionary. He has published widely in the field of Hittite literature and culture, from *Kumarbi* (1946) and *The Song of Ullikummi* (1952) to the recent (with Theo P. H. van den Hout) *The Hittite Instruction for the Royal Bodyguard* (1991). He has twice been honored with volumes of scholarly essays, on the occasions of his sixty-fifth and seventy-fifth birthdays. His publications on the Hittites and the Aegean world include contributions to *AJA* 87 (1983) and to *Troy and the Trojan War* (1986).

HENRY HANKEY, painter and draughtsman of pots, is author of *Archaeology: Artifacts and Artifiction* (Göteborg 1985)—its sequel has gone to press. VRONWY HANKEY read classics at Cambridge and is Honorary Research Fellow in Egyptology at University College, London. She has published Mycenaean pottery from Greece, Egypt, and the Levant and is coauthor (with Peter Warren) of *Aegean Bronze Age Chronology* (1989). Their children are also involved with archaeology, in particular Veronica Newman, a potter, who contributed to a recent study of Aegean stirrup jars (*BSA* 88 [1993] 105–124).

JOHN J. HERRMANN, Jr., is associate curator of classical art at the Museum of Fine Arts, Boston. He has conducted fieldwork in Italy and has written on architecture and architectural decoration in Late Antique Rome. Currently, his primary interest is in identifying and exploring the significance of the different marble sources exploited for sculpture in antiquity. He has also worked on numerous catalogues and exhibitions of ancient art at the Museum of Fine Arts, and on ancient minor arts. Most recently he contributed extensively to *Vase-Painting in Italy: Red-Figure and Related Works in the Museum of Fine Arts, Boston* (1993).

SINCLAIR HOOD was director of the British School at Athens from 1954 to 1962. He has directed excavations at Knossos between 1950 and 1987 and at Emporio on Chios (1950–1952). He is the author of *The Minoans* (1971), *The Arts in Prehistoric Greece* (1978), and *Excavations in Chios 1938–1955: Prehistoric Emporio and Ayio Gala* (1981).

SARA IMMERWAHR is professor emerita in the Department of Art at the University of North Carolina, Chapel Hill. A graduate of Mount Holyoke and Bryn Mawr, she is a specialist in the Aegean Bronze Age. Her publications include *The Athenian Agora XIII: The Neolithic and Bronze Ages* (1971) and *Aegean Painting in the Bronze Age* (1990).

VASSOS KARAGEORGHIS was director of the Department of Antiquities of the Republic of Cyprus from 1963 to 1989; he is now professor of archaeology at the University of Cyprus and director of the Archaeological Research Unit at the same university. He has excavated in Cyprus for over forty years and has published more than fifty books and 300 articles on the Bronze Age and the archaeology of Cyprus, including (with Emily Vermeule) *Mycenaean Pictorial Vase-Painting* (1982).

TIMOTHY KENDALL is associate curator of ancient Egyptian, Nubian, and Near Eastern art at the Museum of Fine Arts, Boston, where he has worked since 1974. He is a graduate of Oberlin College in classical archaeology, received an M.A. in Assyriology from the University of Chicago, and a Ph.D. in Mediterranean Studies at Brandeis University with a dissertation on warfare and military matters in the Nuzi tablets; he now directs excavations at Gebel Barkal in the Sudan.

ROBERT B. KOEHL is associate professor of classics and classical archaeology at Hunter College. A specialist in the Aegean Bronze Age who has excavated on Paros and Crete, he is the author of *Sarepta III. The Imported Bronze and Iron Age Wares* (1985) as well as articles on Aegean rhyta, frescoes, and pottery. He is currently completing a monograph on Aegean rhyta and pursuing research on the origins of the Cretan *andreion*.

MABEL L. LANG is professor emeritus of Greek at Bryn Mawr College. Her fieldwork includes Athens, Gordion, and Pylos, and her research involves archaeology, epigraphy, history, and literature from Mycenaean times to 400 B.C. Her publications include *The Palace of Nestor at Pylos*, II: *The Frescoes* (1969) and *Herodotean Narrative and Discourse* (1984); her latest book is *The Athenian Agora XXV: The Ostraka* (1990).

STEVEN H. LONSDALE is a graduate of Harvard College and the University of Cambridge, and currently associate professor of classics at Davidson College. He has recently published *Dance and Ritual Play in Greek Religion* (1993) and is currently researching a book on musical competitions and festivals in the Greco-Roman world.

EDDIE R. LOWRY, Jr., is a graduate of Harvard University and holds the Marie Zarwell Uihlein Chair in Classical Studies at Ripon College, where he is a professor of romance and clas-

sical languages and head of that department. His chief research interests are in early Greek poetry and Greek religion and mythology.

JODY MAXMIN attended Oberlin College and Oxford University; she is associate professor of art at Stanford University. She is a specialist in Attic vase painting, has published articles on ancient and European art, and writes poetry.

MACHTELD MELLINK is professor of Near Eastern archaeology, emerita, at Bryn Mawr College, where she held the Leslie Clark Professorship of Humanities in 1988. She is a specialist in the archaeology of Asia Minor and edited "Archaeology in Anatolia" for the *AJA* from 1955 to 1993. She has excavated for over four decades in Turkey, beginning with Tarsus in 1947–1949 and Gordion from 1950 to 1965; since 1963 she has been director of the Bryn Mawr College excavations at Elmalı in Lycia, Turkey. She was president of the Archaeological Institute of America from 1980 to 1984 and received the Gold Medal for Distinguished Archaeological Achievement in 1991.

MARGARET C. MILLER studied classics at the University of British Columbia, Oxford University, and Harvard University, with a doctoral thesis on the modes of contact between Athens and Persia and their reception in Athens. She has written many articles on this topic and has a book forthcoming on *Athens and Persia in the Fifth Century B.C. A Study in Cultural Receptivity*, and is working on another book on the orientalization of myth in Greek art. Currently she is assistant professor of fine art at the University of Toronto.

DAVID GORDON MITTEN is James Loeb Professor in the Department of the Classics at Harvard University, where he teaches archaeology and is curator of ancient art in the Arthur J. Sackler Museum. He is a specialist on small bronzes and numismatics and has organized and published many exhibitions of ancient bronzes, beginning with *Master Bronzes of the Classical World* (1967) with Suzanne Doeringer.

SARAH P. MORRIS is a graduate of Harvard University and professor in the Department of Classics and the Institute of Archaeology at the University of California, Los Angeles. She has participated in fieldwork in Israel, Turkey, and Greece, and studies prehistoric and Greek ceramics. She is the author of *Daidalos and the Origins of Greek Art* (1992), winner of the James R. Wiseman Book Award of the Archaeological Institute of America in 1993, and continues to explore the relationship between Greece and the Near East.

GREGORY NAGY is the Francis Jones Professor of Classical Greek Literature and chairman of the Department of the Classics at Harvard University, and a specialist in Archaic Greek poetry and oral poetics. He is the author of *The Best of the Achaeans: Concepts of the Hero in Archaic Greek Poetry* (1979), which won the Goodwin award of the American Philological Association, *Pindar's Homer: The Lyric Possession of an Epic Past* (1990), and other monographs and articles. He was elected president of the American Philological Association for 1990–1991, and is editor of the Myth and Poetics series for Cornell University Press.

J. MICHAEL PADGETT studied at the University of Minnesota and Harvard University, with a doctorate on Apulian vase painting; he was a curatorial assistant in the Department of Classical Art at the Boston Museum of Fine Arts and curator of classical art at the Tampa Museum of Art in Florida. He is now associate curator of classical art at The Art Museum, Princeton University. He is coauthor of *Vase-Painting in Italy: Red-Figure and Related Works in the Museum of Fine Arts, Boston* (1993).

AMY E. RAYMOND was curatorial assistant in the Department of Classical Art at the Museum of Fine Arts, Boston, where she assisted Emily Vermeule in cataloguing the Museum's Aegean Bronze Age collection. She is now a graduate student in the Department of the History of Art at the University of Toronto.

MARTIN ROBERTSON is Lincoln Professor of Classical Archaeology and Art, emeritus, at Oxford University and lives in Cambridge. He excavated at Perachora and published pottery from the British excavations at Al Mina and on Ithaca. He is the author of numerous publications on Greek art, including *Greek Painting* (1959), *A History of Greek Art* (1975), *The Parthenon Frieze* (1975), and *The Art of Vase-Painting in Classical Athens* (1992).

CYNTHIA W. SHELMERDINE attended Bryn Mawr College, the University of Cambridge, and Harvard University; she is associate professor of classics at the University of Texas at Austin. Her research involves archaeology and texts of the Aegean Bronze Age; she has published the Late Mycenaean pottery from Nichoria, a monograph on the perfumed oil industry at Pylos, and is codirector of the Pylos Regional Archaeological Project.

ERIKA SIMON began her career at Heidelberg with a dissertation published as *Opfernde Götter* (1953). Since 1964 she has been professor at Würzburg University and director of antiquities in the Martin von Wagner-Museum. In the United States she has been visiting professor at Bryn Mawr College and Princeton, and delivered lectures published as *Festivals of Athens* (1983). Among her many publications are *Die Portlandvase* (1957), *Pergamom und Hesiod* (1975), *Die konstantinische Deckengemälde in Trier* (1986), and monographs on Trajan's arch at Benevento, Augustus and the Ara Pacis, and the paintings from Boscoreale. She was recently honored with a volume of essays published as *Kotinos* (1993).

MARK D. STANSBURY-O'DONNELL is assistant professor and chairman of art history at the University of St. Thomas in St. Paul, Minnesota. He completed his doctoral work at Yale with a dissertation on medieval architecture; his recent research and publications have examined Greek narrative and painting, the subject of a book in progress.

FRANK STUBBINGS is a Fellow of Emmanuel College and was a lecturer in the Faculty of Classics at Cambridge until his retirement. His scholarship on the Aegean Bronze Age includes *Mycenaean Pottery in the Levant* (1951), several important chapters in the second edition of the *Cambridge Ancient History*, and (with Alan Wace) *A Companion to Homer* (1960).

MICHAEL TAYLOR studied classics and archaeology at the University of North Carolina at Chapel Hill and Harvard University. He attended the American School of Classical Studies at Athens and excavated in Greece and Cyprus. His thesis appeared as *The Tyrant Slayers. The Heroic Image in Fifth-Century B.C Athenian Art and Politics* (1981) and has just been republished (1991). He now practices law in Albemarle, North Carolina.

MARION TRUE attended New York University and Harvard University, and was curatorial assistant in the Department of Classical Art at the Museum of Fine Arts, Boston. Her publications include two CVA fascicules of Attic red- and black-figured pottery in the Boston Museum of Fine Arts. She is currently curator of antiquities at the J. Paul Getty Museum in Malibu, California.

CORNELIUS C. VERMEULE III is a graduate of Harvard University and curator of classical art at the Museum of Fine Arts, Boston. He is the author of numerous monographs and catalogues on Greek and Roman sculpture and numismatics, including *Greek Sculpture and Roman Taste* (1977) and *Greek and Roman Sculpture in America* (1981).

IRENE J. WINTER is professor and chair of the Department of Fine Arts at Harvard University. Her special field is the art of the ancient Near East, and she has published on Phoenician and North Syrian ivory and metalwork and on Assyrian and Sumerian sculpture. She is finishing a monograph on the history of Mesopotamian aesthetics in text and art.

FLORENCE Z. WOLSKY had the good fortune to be in one of the Emily Vermeule's classes at Boston University. She came to the Museum of Fine Arts in 1974 to assist Professor Vermeule with the preparation of her excavation publication, *Toumba tou Skourou* (1990), of which she became coauthor. She has remained at the Museum of Fine Arts in the Department of Classical Art where she is now a senior research associate.

INDEX OF HOMERIC PASSAGES

Iliad Book 1:
4–5: 209
8: 151
38: 237
54–171: 154
118–139: 127
188–222: 434
197–221: 154
201: 154
213: 162n9
260–274: 160
263–268: 160
601–604: 307n1, 398

Iliad Book 2:
papyrus fragment from Hawara (Egypt): 68
45: 27, 490
102–108: 189n11
111–115: 151
111–154: 151
171: 162n7
225–242: 151
246–332: 152
299–330: 161n4
319–325: 151

326–329: 151
350–353: 151, 161n4
459: 198
467–469: 198
480–483: 499n7
484–759: 2, 5, 29, 32, 152, 161, 181–189, 384–393, 501n37
498: 282n22
507: 189n5
520: 190n39
530: 176n17
546: 191n75
573: 189n3
621: 334n53
634: 191n62
638–643: 161
657–660: 145
699–709: 191n86
700–702: 500n15
719–728: 191n86
740–746: 160
798–801: 198
816–877: 32
862, scholiast: 459, 465n53
867: 33
876–877: 33

Iliad Book 3:
21–26: 499n7
98–100: 152
125–128: 152
141: 99
146–244: 152–153
156–157: 152
164–165: 152
184–190: 26
203–224: 432
230–232: 159
385: 99, 104
419: 99
439: 162n7

Iliad Book 4:
66: 153
75–84: 289
86–140: 157
101, 119: 33
110: 175n12
128–133: 162n7
164–168: 153
253: 499n7
293–309: 28, 31n35
319–321: 160
370–400: 154, 160, 200–201
371: 231
401: 196
406: 150
407–409: 201
411: 196
490: 162n7
512: 152

Iliad Book 5:
4–6: 203n25
5–8: 447n34
43: 160
49: 239
115–126: 154
123–143: 202n23
127–131: 203n25
129–132: 154
135–143: 499n7
136: 162n9
143: 196
151: 196
159–165: 447n36
166–296: 153

166–317: 154
175–176: 156
251: 196
256: 154
290–292: 153
297–310: 447n35
330–351: 203n25
406–409: 203n25
436–439: 155
439–444: 162n10
440–443: 199, 200, 203n25
590–606: 155
596–606: 203n25
627–663: 197, 198
632–659: 145
633–639: 198
676: 162n7
693: 240
722: 175n12
788: 152
799–859: 154
800–813: 160
808: 162n7
815: 154
846–864: 203n25
907: 203n25

Iliad Book 6:
78: 33
88: 239
97–101: 156
99: 152
119–136: 199–200
119–236: 5, 202n23
120: 195
121–127: 197
123: 200, 201
123–143: 202n23
125–126: 195
130: 196
132–137: 196
141: 196
145: 197
145–151: 193
145–211: 145
150–151: 202n17
150–211: 33, 34
153: 195, 200 (scholiast)
155–205: 26, 33, 217n27
168–169: 33, 34

179–180: 200
183: 201
187: 217n34
200: 200
206–210: 195
222–223: 200
224–225: 33
234: 195, 200
257: 239
276: 226, 239
281–283: 257
288–292: 247
290–292: 239, 252, 257
297–310: 239
305: 239
311: 239
326–331: 257
389: 200
402–403: 239, 245n50
414: 152
423: 152
433: 240
435: 162n9
483: 104

Iliad Book 7:
13–24: 195
44: 289
58–61: 287, 289
113: 152
132–156: 160
133–136: 189n10
154: 162n7
181–183: 154
219–223: 27, 258, 490
228: 152
241: 274
324: 217n34
355–362: 153
381–411: 154
436–441: 157

Iliad Book 8:
5–26: 157
69–74: 157
87–136: 155
92–98: 155
169: 162n9
170: 162n9
173: 33

221: 106n21
266–272: 328
300–302: 155
362–363: 162n7
378: 231
553: 231

Iliad Book 9:
32–49: 154
53–54: 156
69: 488
93: 217n34
186–191: 179n122, 500n21
287: 237
312–313: 217n25
314–426: 154
316: 202n13
336: 519n9
349–354: 157
380–384: 71
382: 70
392: 488
537–546: 495
594: 226
661: 99
696–709: 154

Iliad Book 10:
19: 206
261–271: 27, 31n29, 104, 127, 189n11, 258, 490
299–531: 8, 415–419, 419 (scholiasts), 425, 428n13
360–362: 356
366: 154
434–437: 415
460–469: 426, 429n75
485–488: 344, 358
507–512: 154
577: 106n34

Iliad Book 11:
19–28: 27
61–66: 447n34
113–121: 499n7
122–142: 432
160: 231
286: 33
323–325: 499n7
338–367: 155
347–348: 155
362–367: 155

363–390: 156
413–418: 499n7
462–463: 162n9
473–480: 340
480–488: 346, 361n23
544–547: 499n7
548–556: 354, 499n7
585–591: 346
598–847: 157
669–760: 160
683–684: 160
692–693: 160
708–709: 334n53
714: 162n7
717–719: 160
721: 162n7
749–751: 334n53
832: 160

Iliad Book 12:
12–33: 158
102: 195
292–293: 499n7
298–301: 499n7
310–314: 33
310–328: 195

Iliad Book 13:
20: 162n9
62: 289
150: 33
204: 226
471–473: 356

Iliad Book 14:
110–132: 154
170–171: 99
171–174: 106n34
286–291: 287
405: 27, 490
412–432: 361n21

Iliad Book 15:
69–71: 150, 158
71: 227
247: 199
275–280: 499n7
425: 33

458–465: 155
486: 33
582–590: 155
630–636: 499n7

Iliad Book 16:
90–93: 156
143: 160
156–163: 499n7
224: 99
352–357: 499n7
424–425: 156
457: 209
492–493: 195
514–515: 33
538–547: 195
542: 33
550–551: 33
593: 195, 274
617: 274
662–663: 195
675: 209
676–683: 33
702–711: 162n10
702–821: 157
707–709: 158
751–753: 354
755–758: 354, 499n7
759–764: 155
760: 162n11
784–787: 155
791–804: 153
823: 447n36

Iliad Book 17:
87–112: 155
125–138: 195
130–131: 445
142–168: 195
147: 202n13
171–173: 195
184: 33
216: 195
281–283: 499n7
389–393: 103, 106n32
477: 162n11
567–569: 162n7
605–607: 155
656–664: 354

Iliad Book 18:
21: 508
22–116: 500n14
25: 104
54–60: 177n49
82–85: 508
95–96: 157
155: 162n9
157: 162n9
177: 227
228: 162n9
229: 162n9
289: 257
349–351: 106n34
373–377: 297
468–617: 445
478–608: 7, 315–317, 330n2, 331nn5,8,9, 333n37
483–485: 445
491–496: 276, 320
497–508: 320, 321–323, 333n37
499–501: 321
509–510: 320
509–519: 328
516–519: 320
519: 240
520–540: 329
535–540: 321
541–589: 320
550–557: 320
569: 400
579: 447n36
583–587: 278
587–590: 283n34
590–592: 6, 7, 273, 291, 407, 411, 413n35
590–606: 273, 281n1, 320
593: 276, 277, 399
595–596: 101
596: 106n19
599: 278
601–602: 274, 278, 282n7
604–606: 309n33
606–607: 320
616: 353

Iliad Book 19:
38: 99, 106n34
95–133: 167, 177n48
199–208: 154
276–300: 119n15

282–301: 508
297–298: 519n9
349–354: 154
390: 160
408–410: 157
416–417: 156
595: 106n19

Iliad Book 20:
70–339: 154
87–98: 196, 197
156–258: 195
167–173: 495–496
176–177: 197
178–198: 197
188–194: 196
199–258: 194
200–214: 196, 197
213–214: 202n17
215–241: 196
244–257: 196–197
248–279: 241n*
302–308: 158
337–339: 157
419–454: 155
425–427: 155
427: 231
438–440: 154
445–448: 155
449–454: 155

Iliad Book 21:
20–21: 349
80: 162n9
139–202: 197
148–153: 197
151: 199
160–161: 197
176: 162n9
177: 162n9
183, 187: 197
228–382: 500n19
276–278: 157–158
304: 154
462–467: 194, 199, 200, 203n25

Iliad Book 22:
59–76: 226
71–76: 217n31

127–128: 277
131–365: 6
145–166: 277–278
165: 162n9, 283n30
208: 162n9
215–227: 154
224: 154
251: 162n9
260–354: 157
270–271: 154
276: 154
304–305: 200
304–329: 511
321–322: 445
358–359: 158
358–360: 162n5
359–360: 156
366–368: 445
395–404: 462n8, 500n20, 517
405–515: 119n15, 217n3
500: 239
506–507: 239

Iliad Book 23:
1–23: 9, 507, 517, 519n12
2: 511
6–16: 515
6–225: 500n14
13–14: 162n9, 278, 508
15: 509
21–23: 278, 511
30–34: 278
80–81: 158
108–257: 9, 127
174–176: 225, 511
185–187: 99, 106nn25,34, 508
257–897: 4, 363, 367, 372n37
340: 175n12
629: 160
638–642: 317, 324, 334n53
677–679: 161
712: 175n12
740–747: 248, 253, 353
817: 162n9

Iliad Book 24:
16: 162n9
29–30: 171
59–63: 363, 398

84–86: 158
131–132: 158
273: 162n9
322–691: 450, 451, 462n9
387: 199
540: 167
686: 162n9
732–735: 223

Odyssey Book 1:
126: 285
128: 285
144–155: 285
156–184: 253, 269n65
180–184: 3
319–320: 287, 288, 289, 307n10
325–338: 285

Odyssey Book 2:
10: 332n36
15: 70
85–88: 207
89–92: 208
93–103: 209
93–110: 6
108: 217n28
110: 208, 211, 212
113–114: 212
125–126: 207, 217n21
430: 256

Odyssey Book 3:
300: 70, 71
371–372: 287, 288, 307n10
466: 106n34

Odyssey Book 4:
15–19: 307n1
17–19: 277, 309n33, 399
83: 70
83–85: 128
111: 219n62
124: 99–101
124–130: 71
125–132: 4, 125, 128, 297
127: 70
220–234: 72
228: 70
272–278: 227

315–319: 70
351: 70
385: 70
477: 70
483: 70
499–510: 226
581: 70
614–619: 128, 248
678: 217n34
735: 217n28
739: 217n34

Odyssey Book 5:
44–46: 409
337–338: 288, 289
351–353: 288

Odyssey Book 6:
63–65: 277
100: 276
102–109: 277
106: 276
232–234: 256
273–275: 256

Odyssey Book 7:
22: 198
39: 256
44: 256
105–107: 101, 102, 105n17, 106n19, 198
107: 105nn4,9
108–111: 256
321–326: 262

Odyssey Book 8:
34: 256
40–45: 307n1
57–82: 307n1
61: 256
62–70: 400
73: 256
84: 106n21
104–108: 400
191: 256
251: 282n25
257: 404n37
262–265: 399
266–366: 219n62, 398
369: 256

370–380: 399
387–445: 248, 256
412: 256
445: 256
469–491: 307n1
474: 256
492–495: 227, 256
499–534: 398
514–520: 433

Odyssey Book 9:
51: 198
171: 332n36
408: 257
408–409: 257
422: 217n34

Odyssey Book 10:
229–295: 367
331: 256
332: 256

Odyssey Book 11:
189: 99
489–491: 257
547 and scholia: 444, 447n20
593–600: 200

Odyssey Book 13:
24–28: 307n1
73: 99
108: 106n21
118: 99
256–286: 248, 251, 399
292–293: 257
297–298: 257
299: 256
382: 256

Odyssey Book 14:
110: 256
124–130: 219n60
199–359: 399
229: 70
246: 70
246–304: 70
257: 70
258: 70
263: 70

275: 70
286: 70, 71
287–315: 248, 258
288–296: 248, 257
300: 251
462–506: 218n51

Odyssey Book 15:
118–119: 252
403–484: 249, 258
415–419: 249
425: 249
452–453: 249

Odyssey Book 16:
247–253: 285

Odyssey Book 17:
37: 211
381–385: 170, 175n12, 178n86, 238
421–444: 71
426: 70
426–444: 70
427: 70
432: 70
448: 70

Odyssey Book 18:
192–193: 99
251–255: 207

Odyssey Book 19:
54: 211
109–114: 219n59
124–128: 207
172–202: 399
203–212: 215
215–250: 219n57
225–235: 495
242: 102
318: 99
337: 99
386–475: 213
428–458: 495

Odyssey Book 20:
88: 219n58

Odyssey Book 21:
52: 104

Odyssey Book 22:
205–210: 288
239–240: 288
297–298: 288
345–349: 398–399
401–406: 499n7

Odyssey Book 23:
16–19: 212
26: 212
28: 212
35–38: 212
62: 212
73: 212
84–85: 213
88–90: 213
94–95: 213
107–109: 213
110: 212
111, 113–114: 213
115: 213
130–137: 277
130–151: 213
147: 282n25
153–165: 213
156–158: 218n52
159–163: 219n52
166–189: 213
178: 219n53
183–204: 6
190–201: 213–214
203: 219n62
205–206: 214, 219n62
225–230: 214
232: 215

Odyssey Book 24:
44–45: 106n34
65–84: 127
93–94: 200
191–202: 207, 217n19
445–449: 289

INDEX OF HOMERIC WORDS
(CITED IN GREEK SCRIPT)

αἰγυπιοῖσι: 287
Αἰνείας: 197
αἴνη, αἶνος: 197, 202n19
Αἴολος: 200
αἰόλος: 200
ἀκούοντες: 196
ἄκρη, ἀκροτάτῃ: 239
ἀλοιφή: 106n32
ἀνάσχειν: 239
ἀμβρόσιος (ἄμβροτος): 99, 101
ἀμβροσίῳ: 99
ἀναΐξασα: 289
ἀνένευε: 239
ἄνθεα: 198
ἀνοπαῖα: 307n10
ἄντην: 289
ἀπειλήσας: 195, 197
ἀπέλαμπεν: 100
ἀποδειροτομέω: 511
ἀργεννῇσι: 100
ἀργής: 100
ἀργύφεος (ἄργυφος): 100
ἀρετή: 484
ἄριστοι: 285

ἀστέρα: 289
Ἀστυάναξ: 239
ἀχλύν: 203n25

βαρβαρόφωνοι: 33
βασιλεύτερος: 488

γενεή: 201n1

δαίμων: 346, 361n23
δῃϊόων: 511
δημιοεργοί: 238, 244n47
δόμου ὑψηλοῖο: 285
δουροδόκη: 285

ἑανός: 100, 101, 102, 104
ἔθνεα πολλά: 198
εἰδομένος: 307n10
εἰκέλη: 289
εἷμα: 100, 101

537

εἵματα: 104
εἶναι: 196
εἰνοσίφυλλον: 198
ἐκγεγάμεν: 196
ἔλαιον: 99
ἐλαίῳ: 99, 101
ἔλεαιον: 106n32
ἐοικότες: 287
ἔπεα: 196
ἐπήπυον: 323
ἔσαν: 321
ἐσθής (ἔσθος): 100
ἔτλης: 197
εὔχομαι, εὔχεσθαι: 196, 202n18
εὐῶδες: 99
ἐῴκει: 289

θαρσαλέον: 195
θάρσει: 195, 197, 199
θεῖον: 99
θυήεις: 101
θυμῷ: 289
θυώδης: 101

ἴδες: 196
ἰόντε: 197
ἴρηξ: 289
ἶφι ἀνάσσει: 237

καλύπτρη: 100
καταθνητῶν ἀνθρώπων: 197, 199, 201
κέρδιστος: 195
κηώδης: 101
κόλπος: 101, 104
κρατερός: 196, 199
κρήδεμνον: 100, 101
κύανος: 317, 331n18

λαμπρός: 100
λαοὶ δέ: 323
λευκός: 102
λιπαρά: 100
λιπαρήν: 100
λιπαρό-: 100
λιπαρός: 101

λυγρά: 104
λυκηγενής: 33
Λύκιοι: 34

μαινόμενος: 200
μάχαιρα: 495
μήτηρ: 196
μυιάων ἁδινάων: 198
μυρίοι: 198

νεκτάρεος: 99, 101
νοήσας: 289

ξανθοί: 493

ὀθόναι: 101, 105n4
ὀθόνη: 100, 105n4
οἷον δ' ἀστέρα: 289
οἰωνοπόλος: 287
ὀπαί: 287
ὀρνίθων πετεηνῶν: 198
ὄρνις δ' ὣς ἀνοπαῖα διέπτατο: 307n10
ὄρνισιν ἐοικότες αἰγυπιοῖσι: 287
ὄψει: 196

Πανέλληνες: 176n17
πέπλος: 100, 101, 239
πέτεσθαι: 289
ποίκιλος: 102
πόλει ἄκρῃ, πόλει ἀκροτάτῃ: 239
πολέμοιο γέφυραι: 243n27
πόλιος: 102
πορφύρεος: 102
πότνι' Ἀθηναίη: 239

ῥήγεα: 99
ῥῆγος: 100
ῥοδόεντι: 99
ῥυσίπτολι: 239

σήματα: 104
σθαιρηδόν: 226

σίαλος: 101
σιγαλόεις: 100, 101
Σκαμάνδριον: 239
σπάργανον: 101
στίλβοντας: 101
στίλβων: 100
σύνθετο θυμῷ: 289

τάπης: 99, 100, 106n20
τεθνωμένος: 101
τερμιόεις: 102
τιθήνη, τιθήνας: 200, 203n27
τίς δὲ σύ ἐσσι, φέριστε . . . : 199
τίς πόθεν: 197
τρίς: 162n9

ὑψηλοῖο: 285

φαεινός (φαεινότερος): 100
φαίνετο: 289
φάναι: 202n18
φάρεα: 106n21

φᾶρος: 100, 102
φασί: 196
φήνῃ εἰδομένῃ: 307n10
φοινικόεις: 102
φρένες: 195, 201
φρεσὶν ᾗσι νοήσας: 289
φύει: 201n1
φύλλα, φύλοισιν: 198

χαλκῷ δηϊόων: 511
χάρις: 202n13
χεῖρας ἀνάσχειν: 239
χελιδόνι εἰκέλη ἄντην: 289
χιτών: 100, 101, 102

ψαμάθοισιν: 198

ὠκύπτερος: 289
ὠρώρει: 321
ὡς: 307n10
ὥς τ' ἴρηξ: 289

INDEX OF HOMERIC WORDS
(CITED AS TRANSLITERATION)

agnōsaske: 213

agora: 209

aidoia: 210

aidōs, aidō: 210, 217n31

Aiguptios: 70

ainos: 213, 218n51

aischron: 209

aischunōsi: 217n31

aitioi, aition: 207, 209, 210, 211

Aktorione: 334nn53,55

alēthea: 219n60

allēi eni chorēi: 213

allose: 213, 214

alphesiboiai: 274, 276, 278

amphiguēeis: 283n34

anagignōskō: 218n50

anagkē, anagkēs: 208, 211, 212

anagnousēi: 214, 219n57

anankē: 206

anax: 461

andri hekasōi: 208

anēr idris: 219n52

angeliai, angelias: 208

antipherizei: 215

aoidēn chariessan: 207, 217n19

aoidos, aoidoi: 170, 175n12, 398, 399, 400

apatēlia eidōs: 248, 257

Aphroditēi: 211

arariskein: 274

arēruīan prapidessi: 215

aretē, aretēs, aretēi: 207, 217n19, 400

ariphrades, ariphradea: 212, 214, 215

aristos hapantōn boulēi: 257

armenon: 274

Artemidi: 211

atalantos: 162n11

athurmata: 249, 253, 262

bētarmones: 274

biē, biēphin: 257

boulēi: 257

bouleusas: 248, 257

charienta de erga teleiei: 219n52

chariessan: 207

charin: 219n52

choros (khoros): 7, 273, 275, 276, 277, 280, 281n3, 282n22, 283n27, 291, 411
chruseēi: 211

daidallōn: 219n54
daimōn: 280
deiloio: 162n11
dēmiourgos: 170, 175n12, 178n86
dineo: 283n30
dokēse de hoi ēdē gignōskousa: 219n58
dolōi oude biēphin: 257
dolos: 205, 206, 209, 211, 212, 216n10, 217n34, 219n62, 257

echephōn: 219n62
echethumos: 219n62
eikelos: 212, 214
ēitheoi kai parthenoi: 277
ektheisai: 213
ektos: 213
elpei: 208
empedon, empeda: 214, 215, 219n62
epea pteroenta: 8
epistamenōs: 213
epoiei: 219n53
ērare: 175n12
eteon: 212, 213
etumon, etumoisin: 212, 215
euru-: 282n22

geras: 209
gignōskō: 218n50
gignōskousa, gignōskon: 219nn58,62
glaphura: 398
gnōsometh: 213
gunē: 278

harpaleōs: 256
hekasōi: 208
hērōs: 248
hēs: 207
hōi: 207
homoios, homoia: 212, 213, 215, 218n52, 219n52
hupischetai: 208

idris: 219n52
ikelē: 211
Iphianassa: 237

kairos: 205
kakon: 209
kala: 217n31
kalliston kai timēestaton: 248
kallos: 218n52
kednēn: 215
kerdos, kerdea: 205, 206, 207, 208, 209, 211, 212
khoros (choros): 7, 273, 275, 276, 277, 280, 281n3, 282n22, 283n27, 291, 411
kiōn: 205, 213, 214
kitharis: 397, 400n34
kitharizō: 400n34
klea: 179n122
kleos: 207, 219n59
kōmos: 279
krater: 248
krēdemnon: 288
kuklos, kukla: 175n12

logos: 214

mechanē: 209
medomai, mēdomai: 216n8
megalēi aretēi: 207
mega sēma: 213, 214
melainēi, melainan: 256
Menoitiades: 162n11
mēsato: 207, 216n8
mestor: 162n11
mētis, mētin: 6, 205–212, 215, 215n4, 216nn8,10,11, 217nn28,34, 257
metochlisseien: 213
metron: 206
Molione: 334nn53,55
monukhes: 278
morphē: 205, 219n62
mūthos etētumos: 212

nausiklutoi: 249, 256
nēi melainēi, nēa melainan: 256
nēmertes: 212

noeō: 218n50

noos, nous: 205, 208, 215n3

oikos: 207, 208, 209, 211, 212, 213, 214

paizō: 276
pan-a-ōrios: 167, 177n48
pan-Hellenes: 176n17
pantas: 208
parpepithōn hēisi phresin: 248
parthenoi ēitheoi t': 277
peira, peirata: 212, 213, 218n48, 219n57
peirazein emethen: 213
peirēmenē: 213
pelonto: 219n62
periklutos: 283n34
pesontos: 162n11
pharmakon: 214
pharos: 70
Phoinikes: 247
phorminx, phorminx glaphura: 397, 398, 404nn33–35
phormizō: 404n34
phresin: 248
phukta: 219n62
podessi: 278
poikille: 281n1
poludaidaloi: 248, 249
polukhalkos, polukhalkou: 249, 257, 261
polumētis: 249, 256
polupaipalos, polupaipaloi: 249, 256
polutropos: 256
posios peirēmenē: 213
prapidessi: 215

pseudea bouleusas: 248, 257
pseudea homoia etumoisin: 215
pseudont: 219n60
ptoliporthos: 257

sēma, sēmata: 205, 206, 210, 212, 213, 214, 215n3, 218n50, 219n62
sēmata ariphradea: 214, 215
sēmata empeda: 214, 215, 219nn57,62
Sidones: 247, 248
skeparnon: 408, 409
stikhas: 282n7
symballein: 219n57
syrinx: 398

tarsos: 156
technē: 205, 275
technēn pantoiēn: 219n52
teīchos/toīchos: 210, 218n42
tektēnaito: 206
tektōn: 175n12
telos: 212, 214
tetuktai en lechei askētōi: 213
thanontos: 162n11
themis: 219n60
theophi mestor atalantos: 162n11
thumarea: 215
timēestaton: 248
to egō kamon oude tis allos: 213
toīchos: 210
trekhō: 278
trōktēs, trōktai: 248, 249, 256
tropos: 206, 214